SCHAUM'S SOLVED PROBLEMS SERIES

3000 SOLVED PROBLEMS IN

ELECTRIC CIRCUITS

by

Syed A. Nasar

University of Kentucky

McGRAW-HILL

New York   St. Louis   San Francisco   Auckland   Bogotá   Caracas   Lisbon
London   Madrid   Mexico City   Milan   Montreal   New Delhi
San Juan   Singapore   Sydney   Tokyo   Toronto

Syed A. Nasar, Ph.D., *Professor of Electrical Engineering
at the University of Kentucky.*

Dr. Nasar has written many books, including two Schaum's Outlines, ELEC-
TRIC MACHINES AND ELECTROMECHANICS and BASIC ELECTRICAL
ENGINEERING; a power-systems text for Macmillan; and a textbook for
McGraw-Hill's College Division, INTRODUCTION TO ELECTRICAL EN-
GINEERING.

 This book is printed on recycled paper containing
10% postconsumer waste.

Project supervision by The Total Book.
Cover design by Wanda Siedlecka.
Index by Hugh C. Maddocks, Ph. D.

Library of Congress Cataloging-in-Publication Data

Nasar, S. A.
  Schaum's 3000 solved problems in electric circuits.
  1. Electric circuits—Problems, exercises, etc.
I. Title.   II. Title: Schaum's three thousand solved
problems in electric circuits.
TK454.N36   1988   621.319'2076   87-25974
ISBN 0-07-045936-3 (Formerly published under ISBN 0-07-045921-5.)

    6 7 8 9 10 11 12 13 14 15 16 17 18 19 20 PRS PRS 9 8 7 6

McGraw-Hill

A Division of The McGraw-Hill Companies

CONTENTS

To the Student

Think of it!—an expected score of 75% on any exam in Electric Circuits, *with no other preparation*! The reasoning is simple: There are only 4000 possible problems in the field (as you must know), and this book solves 3000 of them for you!

Speaking seriously, you have here the most careful and complete anthology of examination-type problems on the market today. In using the book, you should, of course, concentrate on the area of your maximum weakness—the Laplace transform or whatever. But do not neglect to work problems involving familiar material, too; you might well learn more efficient methods of handling them. The heuristic value of a clear circuit diagram need not be stressed: if a problem in this book should carry a diagram but doesn't, be sure to sketch out one before undertaking the solution. May your success be electric.

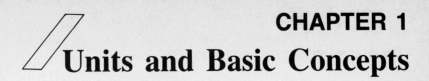

CHAPTER 1
Units and Basic Concepts

1.1 Powers of 10 appear frequently with units of measurements. These powers of 10 are written in abbreviated forms. If electric resistance is measured in ohms (Ω), express the following values in powers of 10 and write them in their abbreviated forms: 2000 Ω and 3,000,000 Ω.

> $2000\ \Omega = 2 \times 10^3\ \Omega = 2$ kiloohm $= 2$ kΩ $3,000,000\ \Omega = 3 \times 10^6\ \Omega = 3$ megohm $= 2$ MΩ

1.2 Electric capacitance is measured in farads (F). However, this is rather a large unit. Express the following values in powers of 10 and write them in their abbreviated forms: 0.000005 F, 0.0005 F, and 0.000000001 F.

> $0.000005\ \text{F} = 5 \times 10^{-6}\ \text{F} = 5$ microfarad $= 5\ \mu\text{F}$
>
> $0.0005\ \text{F} = 0.5 \times 10^{-3}\ \text{F} = 0.5$ millifarad $= 0.5$ mF $= 500\ \mu\text{F}$
>
> $0.000000001\ \text{F} = 1 \times 10^{-9}\ \text{F} = 1.0$ picofarad $= 1$ pF

1.3 The unit of electric inductance is henry (H). Express the following values in powers of 10 and write them in their abbreviated forms: 0.01 H and 0.003 H.

> $0.01\ \text{H} = 10 \times 10^{-3}\ \text{H} = 10$ millihenry $= 10$ mH $0.003\ \text{H} = 3 \times 10^{-3}\ \text{H} = 3$ millihenry $= 3$ mH

1.4 Electric frequency is measured in hertz (Hz). Express the following frequencies in powers of 10 and in their respective abbreviated forms: 1000 Hz, 5,000,000 Hz, and 100,000,000 Hz.

> $1000\ \text{Hz} = 1 \times 10^3\ \text{Hz} = 1$ kilohertz $= 1$ kHz $5,000,000\ \text{Hz} = 5 \times 10^6\ \text{Hz} = 5$ megahertz $= 5$ MHz
>
> $100,000,000\ \text{Hz} = 0.1 \times 10^9\ \text{Hz} = 0.1$ gigahertz $= 0.1$ GHz

1.5 Convert 2 minutes to milliseconds:

> $$2\ \text{min} = 2 \times 60\ \text{s} = 120\ \text{s} = \frac{120 \times 10^{-3}}{10^{-3}}\ \text{s} = 1.2 \times 10^5\ \text{ms}$$

1.6 Convert 5 kilometers to centimeters:

> $$5\ \text{km} = 5 \times 10^3\ \text{m} = 5 \times 10^3 \times 10^2\ \text{cm} = 5 \times 10^5\ \text{cm}$$

1.7 Convert 15 centimeters to millimeters:

> $$15\ \text{cm} = \frac{15}{10^2} \times 10^3 = 150\ \text{mm}$$

1.8 Electric current is measured in amperes (A). If an ampere is expressed as a flow of charge in coulombs per second (C/s), how many electrons pass a given point in 30 s in a conductor carrying 8-A current. The charge on an electron is approximately 1.6×10^{-19} C.

> Charge $= \text{A} \times \text{s} = 8 \times 30 = 240$ C 1.6×10^{-19} C correspond to 1 electron
>
> 240 C correspond to $(1 \times 240)/(1.6 \times 10^{-19}) = 15 \times 10^{20}$ electrons

1.9 Find the current in a conductor through which 2.5×10^{20} electrons pass in 8 s if the charge on an electron is approximately 1.6×10^{-19} C.

> $$I = \frac{(\text{no. of electrons})(\text{charge on electron, C})}{\text{time, s}} = \frac{2.5 \times 10^{20} \times 1.6 \times 10^{-19}}{8} = 5\ \text{A}$$

1.10 A charge of 360 C passes through a conductor in 20 s. What is the corresponding current in amperes?

> $$I = \frac{\text{C}}{\text{s}} = \frac{360}{20} = 18\ \text{A}$$

1.11 The current in an electric circuit rises exponentially as given by $i = 10(1 - e^{-2t})$ A. Calculate the charge flowing through the circuit in 250 ms.

$$q = \int i\, dt = \int_0^{0.250} 10(1 - e^{-2t})\, dt = 10\left(t + \frac{e^{-2t}}{2}\right)_0^{0.250} = 10(0.250 + \tfrac{1}{2}e^{-2\times 0.250} - 0 - \tfrac{1}{2}) = 0.5326\, \text{C}$$

1.12 A 75-W bulb draws a 680-mA current. How much time will be required to pass a 30-C charge through the bulb?

$$t = \frac{\text{charge, C}}{\text{current, A}} = \frac{30}{68 \times 10^{-3}} = 441.17\, \text{s} = 7.35\, \text{min}$$

1.13 A current of 6 A flows in a resistor. How many coulombs of charge pass through the resistor in 2 min?

$$q = (\text{current, A})(\text{time, s}) = 6 \times 2 \times 60 = 720\, \text{C}$$

1.14 The unit of force is the newton (N) and work is measured in netwon-meters (N · m), which is also the unit of energy. Alternatively, energy is expressed in joules (J), where $1\,\text{J} = 1\,\text{N} \cdot \text{m}$. Determine the work done in moving a 50-μC electric charge (Q) through a distance of 50 cm in the direction of a uniform electric field (E) of 50 kV/m, if the force F is given by $f = QE$.

$$\text{Force} = (\text{charge, C})(\text{electric field, V/m}) = 50 \times 10^{-6} \times 50 \times 10^{3} = 2.5\, \text{N}$$

$$\text{Work done} = \text{force} \times \text{distance} = 2.5 \times 50 \times 10^{-2} = 1.25\, \text{N} \cdot \text{m} = 1.25\, \text{J}$$

1.15 Power is defined as the rate of work done or the rate of energy conversion. Thus, the unit of power is the joule per second (J/s) which is equal to one watt (W). If the time taken to move the 50-μC charge of Prob. 1.14 through 50 cm is 10 ms, calculate the corresponding power.

$$\text{Power} = \frac{\text{work done}}{\text{time}} = \frac{1.25}{10 \times 10^{-3}} = 125\, \text{W}$$

1.16 We observed in Prob. 1.14 that an electric charge experiences a force in an electric field. Electric potential difference (between two points) is measured in volts (V), and is defined as the work done in moving a unit positive charge (from one point to the other). What is the potential difference between two points if it requires 220 μJ to move a 10-μC charge from one point to the other?

$$1\,\text{V} = 1\,\text{J/C} \quad \text{or} \quad V = \frac{220 \times 10^{-6}}{10 \times 10^{-6}} = 22\, \text{V}$$

1.17 From Prob. 1.16, $V = \text{J/C} = (\text{J/s})/(\text{C/s}) = \text{W/A}$. Calculate the potential difference across a resistor dissipating 30 W of power while taking 2.5 A of current. Also, calculate the ohmic value of the resistance.

$$V = \frac{W}{I} = \frac{30}{2.5} = 12\, \text{V} \qquad R = \frac{W}{I^2} = \frac{30}{(2.5)^2} = 4.8\, \Omega$$

1.18 An energy of 12 J is expended in moving a 2-C charge from infinity to a point A. Assuming infinity to be at zero potential, determine the potential difference between point A and infinity (i.e., the potential at A).

$$V_{A\infty} = \frac{\text{work or energy, J}}{\text{charge, C}} = \frac{12}{2} = 6\, \text{V}$$

1.19 If an additional energy of 3 J is required to move the 2-C charge of Prob. 1.18 from point A to another point B, calculate the potential difference between points A and B. Also determine the potential difference between point B and infinity.

$$V_{AB} = \frac{\text{work or energy, J}}{\text{charge, C}} = \frac{3}{2} = 1.5\, \text{V} \qquad V_{B\infty} = \frac{12 + 3}{2} = 7.5\, \text{V}$$

1.20 The potential difference between two conductors is 110 V. How much work is done in moving a 5-C charge from one conductor to the other?

$$\text{Work} = \text{energy} = 110 \times 5 = 550\, \text{J}$$

1.21 Determine the charge that requires 1-kJ energy to be moved from infinity to a point having a 12-V potential.

$$\text{Charge, C} = \frac{\text{energy, J}}{\text{potential, V}} = \frac{10^{3}}{12} = 83.33\, \text{C}$$

1.22   A car battery supplies 48 J of energy at 12 V over a certain period of time.   Determine the charge moved during this period.

$$q = \frac{48 \text{ J}}{12 \text{ V}} = 4 \text{ C}$$

1.23   Electric utilities employ as the unit of energy the kilowatt-hour (kWh).   The power consumed in a household over a 24-h period is as follows: 8 A.M. to 2 P.M.—1.5 kW; 2 P.M. to 6 P.M.—0.5 kW; 6 P.M. to 11 P.M.—2.6 kW; and 11 P.M. to 8 A.M.—1.0 kW.   What is the energy consumption in megajoules?

$$\text{Total kWh} = (\text{power, kW})(\text{time, h}) = 1.5 \times 6 + 0.5 \times 4 + 2.6 \times 5 + 1.0 \times 9 = 33 \text{ kWh}$$

$$= 33 \times 10^3 \times 60 \times 60 \text{ W} \cdot \text{s} = 118.8 \times 10^6 \text{ J} = 118.8 \text{ MJ}$$

1.24   An electric heater takes 1.2 kWh in 30 min at 120 V.   What is the current input to the heater?

$$I = \frac{U/t}{V} = \frac{1.2 \times 10^3 / 0.5}{120} = 20 \text{ A}$$

1.25   The heater of Prob. 1.24 has an efficiency of 99 percent.   The heat energy required to boil a certain amount of water is 99 kJ.   If the current taken by the heater is 20 A at 120 V, find the time required to boil the water.

$$\text{Efficiency} = \frac{\text{output}}{\text{input}} = \frac{99 \times 10^3}{\text{input}} = 0.99 \quad \text{or} \quad \text{input } U = \frac{99 \times 10^3}{0.99} = 100 \text{ kJ}$$

$$t = \frac{U}{P} = \frac{100 \times 10^3}{120 \times 20} = 41.67 \text{ s}$$

1.26   What is the ohmic value of the resistance of the heating element of the heater of Probs. 1.24 and 1.25?

$$R = \frac{V}{I} = \frac{120}{20} = 6 \, \Omega$$

1.27   A 110-V light bulb takes 0.9-A current and operates 12 h/day.   At the rate of 7 cents/kWh, determine the cost to operate the bulb for 30 days.

$$U = Pt = 110 \times 0.9 \times 10^{-3} \times 12 \times 30 = 35.64 \text{ kWh}$$

Cost of operation $= 35.64 \times \$0.07 = \$2.50$.

1.28   The voltage and current in a circuit element are respectively given by $v = 100\sqrt{2} \sin t$ V   and $i = 5\sqrt{2} \sin t$ A.   Calculate the instantaneous power and the average power delivered to the circuit.

$$\text{Instantaneous power} \quad p = vi = (100\sqrt{2} \sin t)(5\sqrt{2} \sin t) = 1000 \sin^2 t \text{ W} = 1000 \times \frac{1}{2}(1 - \cos 2t)$$

$$p = 500 - 500 \cos 2t \text{ W}$$

The cosine function averages to zero, so the average value of p, $P_{av} = 500$ W.

1.29   A resistor draws a current $i = 8 \sin \omega t$ A   at a voltage $v = 200 \sin \omega t$ V.   Calculate the energy consumed by the resistor per cycle (or over one period of the current wave).   Hence, determine the average power dissipated in the resistor.

$$\text{One period} = \frac{2\pi}{\omega} \text{ s}$$

$$\text{Energy } W = \int_0^{2\pi/\omega} vi \, dt = \int_0^{2\pi/\omega} (200 \sin \omega t)(8 \sin \omega t) \, dt = \frac{1600\pi}{\omega} \text{ J}$$

$$\text{Average power } P_{av} = \frac{W}{2\pi/\omega} = \frac{1600\pi}{\omega(2\pi/\omega)} = 800 \text{ W}$$

1.30   The energy capacity or rating of a battery is generally expressed in ampere-hour (Ah).   A battery is required to supply 0.5 A continuously for three days.   What must be the rating of the battery?

$$\text{Ah} = I \times \text{hr} = 0.5 \times 3 \times 24 = 36 \text{ Ah}$$

1.31   A battery is rated at 30 Ah.   For how many hours can it continuously supply a current of 2.5 A?

$$\text{Time} = \frac{\text{Ah}}{I} = \frac{30}{2.5} = 12 \text{ h}$$

1.32   The capacity of a car battery depends on the ambient temperature as shown in Fig. 1-1.   A certain battery is rated at 72 Ah at 25°C.   For how long can the battery supply a 16-A current at 0°C?

▮   From Fig. 1-1, at 0°C the rating of the battery reduces to $0.8 \times 72 = 57.6$ Ah.   Therefore,

$$\text{Time } t = \frac{\text{Ah}}{I} = \frac{57.6}{16} = 3.6 \text{ h} = 3 \text{ h } 36 \text{ min}$$

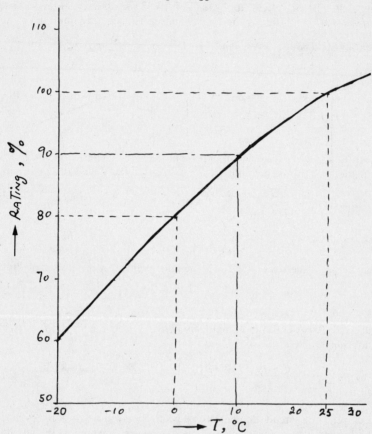

Fig. 1-1

1.33   The capacity of a car battery depends on the current drawn (or discharge) from the battery, as shown in Fig. 1-2. The battery is rated at 70 Ah at a discharge rate of 5 A as shown.   How long will the battery supply 20 A of current?

▮   From Fig. 1-2, at 20 A the rating of the battery becomes 58 Ah.   Hence,

$$\text{Time } t = \frac{\text{Ah}}{I} = \frac{58}{20} = 2.9 \text{ h} = 2 \text{ h } 54 \text{ min}$$

1.34   If the rating of the battery with a discharge characteristic shown in Fig. 1-2 is not allowed to go below 64 Ah, for how long can the battery supply the rated current?

▮   From Fig. 1-2 at 64 Ah, discharge rate = 12 A. Hence,

$$\text{Time } t = \frac{\text{Ah}}{I} = \frac{64}{12} = 5 \text{ h } 20 \text{ min}$$

1.35   Combine the characteristics of Figs. 1-1 and 1-2 to obtain the rating of the battery at 17 A and at 10°C if the battery is rated at 100 percent at 5 A and at 25°C.

▮   From Fig. 1-2, rating at   17 A = 60 Ah   which is considered as 100 percent at 25°C.   From Fig. 1-1, rating 10°C = $0.9 \times 60 = 54$ Ah.

1.36   The decay of charge in an electric circuit is given by $q = 50e^{-300t} \ \mu C$.   Determine the resulting current.

▮
$$i = \frac{dq}{dt} = -50 \times 300 \times 10^{-6} \ e^{-300t} = -15e^{-300t} \text{ mA}$$

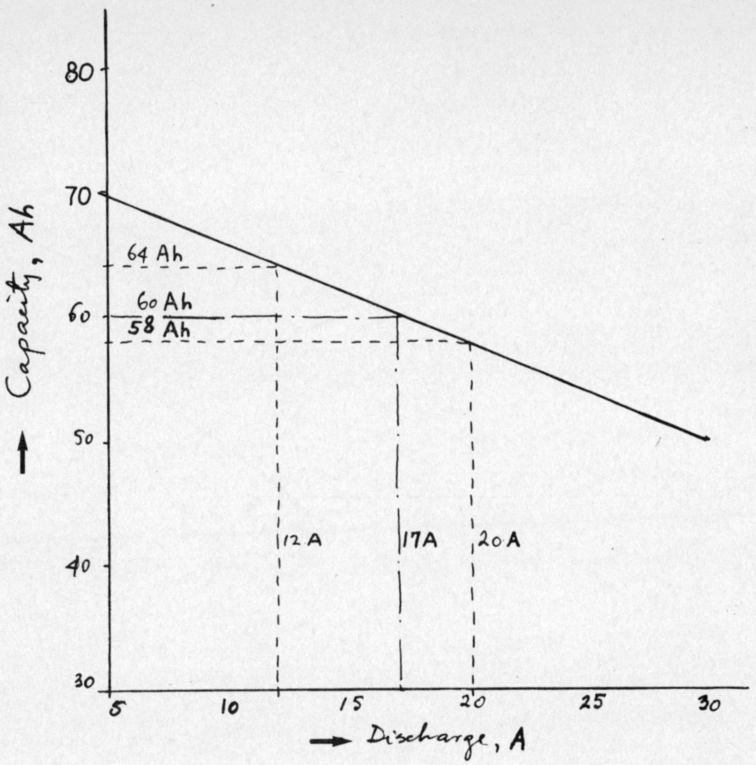

Fig. 1-2

1.37 Evaluate the current in Prob. 1.36 at the following instants: $t = 0$, $t = 10$ ms, and $t = \infty$.

▮   At $t = 0$: $i = -15e^0 = -15$ mA

$$t = 10^{-2} \text{ s}: \quad i = -15e^{-300 \times 10^{-2}} = -0.7468 \text{ mA}$$

$$t = \infty: \quad i = -15e^{-\infty} = 0$$

1.38 The voltage v and current i in an ac circuit are respectively given by $v = 34 \sin 377t$ V and $i = 2 \sin (377t - 60°)$ A. Determine the instantaneous and average powers delivered to the circuit.

▮ $p = vi = (34 \sin 377t)[2 \sin (377t - 60°)] = 68 \sin 377t \sin (377t - 60°)$

$\quad = 68 \times \frac{1}{2} [\cos (377t - 377t + 60°) - \cos (377t + 377t - 60°)] = 34 [\cos 60° - \cos (754t - 60°)]$ W

$$P_{av} = 34 \cos 60° = 17 \text{ W}$$

1.39 The voltage v and current i at the pair of terminals of an electric circuit are given by $v = 100 \sin t$ V and $i = -5 \sin t$ A. Evaluate the average power and state if the circuit absorbs or delivers power.

▮ $p = vi = (100 \sin t)(-5 \sin t) = -500 \sin^2 t$ W

$\quad\quad P_{av} = -500 \times \frac{1}{2}$ (since the average value of $\sin^2 t = \frac{1}{2}$) $= -250$ W

The negative sign indicates that negative power is absorbed by the circuit; i.e., the circuit delivers power.

1.40 The voltage v and current i in a circuit are given by $v = 10 \sin t$ V and $i = 2 \cos t$ A. Determine the instantaneous and average powers, and explain your result.

▮ $p = vi = (10 \sin t)(2 \cos t) = 20 \sin t \cos t = 10 \sin 2t$ W

The instantaneous power pulsates with twice the frequency of the voltage or current. $P_{av} = 0$ W, since the average value of $\sin 2t = 0$. Zero average power indicates that the circuit is nondissipative or conservative.

CHAPTER 2
Resistance and Ohm's Law

2.1 A copper conductor of circular cross section 5 mm in diameter is 5 m long. Calculate its resistance at 20°C if the resistivity of copper at 20°C is $1.72 \times 10^{-8} \, \Omega \cdot m$.

$$R = \frac{\rho l}{A} = \frac{(1.72 \times 10^{-8})5}{\pi(5 \times 10^{-3})^2/4} = 4.38 \, m\Omega$$

2.2 A 40-m metallic conductor of cross-sectional area 1 mm² has a resistance of 12 Ω. Calculate the conductivity of the metal.

$$\sigma = \frac{l}{RA} = \frac{40}{(12)(10^{-3})^2} = 3.33 \, MS/m$$

[Note that 1 siemens (S) = $1 \, \Omega^{-1}$.]

2.3 A cube of an alloy of resistivity $1.12 \, \mu\Omega \cdot m$ is 2 cm on a side. Determine the resistance between any two faces of the cube.

$$R = \frac{\rho l}{A} = \frac{(1.12 \times 10^{-6})(2 \times 10^{-2})}{(2 \times 10^{-2})^2} = 56 \, \mu\Omega$$

2.4 We have two cubes—one measuring l m on one side and the other $2l$ m. Find the ratio of conductivities of the materials of the cubes so that the resistance between any two faces of one cube is the same as that for the other cube.

$$R_1 = \frac{l}{\sigma_1 l^2} = \frac{1}{l\sigma_1} \quad \text{and} \quad R_2 = \frac{2l}{\sigma_2(2l)^2} = \frac{1}{2l\sigma_2}$$

$$\frac{1}{l\sigma_1} = \frac{1}{2l\sigma_2} \quad \text{or} \quad \frac{\sigma_1}{\sigma_2} = 2$$

2.5 Calculate the length of copper wire having a diameter of $\frac{1}{16}$ in and resistance of 2 Ω. Conductivity of copper is $5.8 \times 10^7 \, S/m$.

$$\tfrac{1}{16} \, in = \tfrac{1}{16} \times 2.54 \times 10^{-2} = 1.5875 \times 10^{-3} \, m$$

$$l = \sigma R A = 5.8 \times 10^7 \times 2 \times \frac{\pi}{4}(1.5875 \times 10^{-3})^2 = 229.6 \, m$$

2.6 A rectangular bus bar made of aluminum is 0.9 m long, 0.15 m wide, and 1.3 cm thick. If current in the bus bar flows along its length, and the conductivity of aluminum is $3.57 \times 10^8 \, S/m$, calculate the bus bar resistance.

$$R = \frac{l}{\sigma A} = \frac{0.9}{(3.57 \times 10^8)(0.15 \times 1.3 \times 10^{-2})} = 1.293 \, \mu\Omega$$

2.7 A transmission line cable consists of 19 strands of identical copper conductors, each 1.5 mm in diameter. The physical length of the cable is 2 km. But, because of the twist of each strand, the actual lengths of the conductors are increased by 5 percent. What is the resistance of the cable? Resistivity of copper is $1.72 \times 10^{-8} \, \Omega \cdot m$.

Allowing for twist, $l = (1.05)(2000) = 2100 \, m$. Area of cross section of 19 strands $= 19(\pi/4)(1.5 \times 10^{-3})^2 = 33.576 \times 10^{-6} \, m^2$.

$$R = \frac{\rho l}{A} = \frac{1.72 \times 10^{-8} \times 2100}{33.576 \times 10^{-6}} = 1.076 \, \Omega$$

2.8 Variation of resistance with temperature is expressed in terms of temperature coefficient α. Explicitly, the resistance R_T at a temperature T °C is related to the resistance at 0 °C by $R_T = R_0(1 + \alpha_0 T)$ as graphically depicted in Fig. 2-1, where α_0 is the temperature coefficient at 0 °C. The figure also shows the inferred absolute zero for copper. Using Fig. 2-1, find the resistance of a copper wire at −20 °C if its resistance at 0 °C is 20 Ω.

From Fig. 2-1 we have

$$\frac{234.5 + T_1}{R_1} = \frac{234.5 + T_2}{R_2}$$

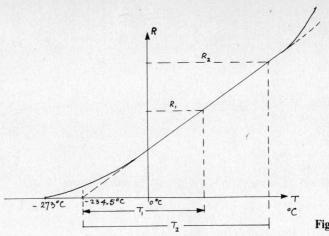

Fig. 2-1

From the data

$$R_2 = \frac{(234.5 - 20)20}{234.5 + 0} = 18.29 \ \Omega$$

2.9 Values of the temperature coefficient α for copper for different temperatures are plotted in Fig. 2-2, from which $\alpha_{20°C} = 0.00393°C^{-1}$. If the resistance of a given wire is 20 Ω at 20°C, what is its resistance at 60°C?

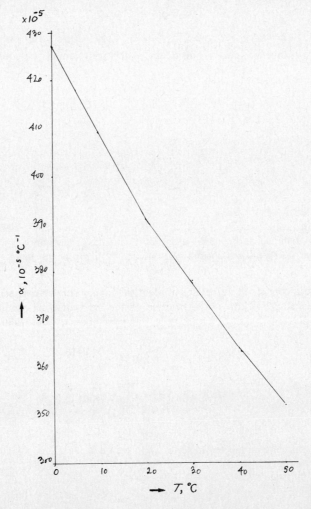

Fig. 2-2

$$R_2 = R_1[\ 1 + \alpha_1\ (T_2 - T_1)] = 20[1 + 0.00393(60 - 20)] = 23.144\Omega$$

2.10 A sample of copper wire has a resistance of 50 Ω at 10 °C. What is the maximum operating temperature if the resistance of the wire is to increase by at most 10 percent?

▎ $R_1 = 50\,\Omega$, $R_2 = 50 + 0.1 \times 50 = 55\,\Omega$. From Fig. 2-2, α at $10\,°C = 0.00409\,°C^{-1} = \alpha_1$. Since $R_2 = R_1[1 + \alpha_1(T_2 - T_1)]$, we obtain $55 = 50[1 + 0.00409(T_2 - 10)]$ or $T_2 = 34.45\,°C$.

2.11 A metallic conductor has a resistance of 7 Ω at 0 °C. At 20 °C the resistance becomes 7.8 Ω. Calculate the temperature coefficient of the metal at 20 °C.

▎
$$R_0 = R_1[1 + \alpha_1(0 - 20)] \qquad \text{or} \qquad 7 = 7.8[1 + \alpha_1(-20)]$$

Hence, $\alpha_1 = $ temperature coefficient at $20\,°C = 0.00513\,°C^{-1}$.

2.12 For the metal of the conductor of Prob. 2.11, determine the temperature coefficient at 0 °C.

▎
$$R_T = R_0(1 + \alpha_0 T) \qquad \text{or} \qquad 7.8 = 7(1 + \alpha_0 20) \qquad \text{or} \qquad \alpha_0 = 0.00571\,°C^{-1}$$

2.13 Obtain a general relationship between α_0 and α_T the respective temperature coefficients at 0 °C and at T °C.

▎
$$R_T = R_0(1 + \alpha_0 T) \tag{1}$$
$$R_0 = R_T(1 - \alpha_T T) \tag{2}$$

Solving for α_T from Eq. (2) yields

$$\alpha_T = \frac{R_T - R_0}{TR_T} \tag{3}$$

Substituting R_T from Eq. (1) into (3) gives

$$\alpha_T = \frac{R_0(1 + \alpha_0 T) - R_0}{TR_0(1 + \alpha_0 T)} = \frac{\alpha_0}{1 + \alpha_0 T} \tag{4}$$

2.14 Derive a general relationship between α_1 and α_2 the respective temperature coefficients at T_1 °C and at T_2 °C.

▎ From Eq. (4) of Prob. 2.13 we obtain

$$\frac{1}{\alpha_T} = \frac{1 + \alpha_0 T}{\alpha_0} = \frac{1}{\alpha_0} + T$$

Thus,
$$\frac{1}{\alpha_1} = \frac{1}{\alpha_0} + T_1 \qquad \text{and} \qquad \frac{1}{\alpha_2} = \frac{1}{\alpha_0} + T_2$$

By subtraction,

$$\frac{1}{\alpha_1} - \frac{1}{\alpha_2} = T_1 - T_2 \qquad \text{or} \qquad \alpha_2 = \frac{1}{1/\alpha_1 + (T_2 - T_1)}$$

2.15 The temperature coefficient of carbon at 0 °C is $-0.000515\,°C^{-1}$ and that of platinum is $0.00357\,°C^{-1}$ at 40 °C. A carbon coil has a resistance of 15 Ω and a platinum coil has a resistance of 12 Ω each at 20 °C. At what temperature will the two coils have the same resistance? Notice that the temperature coefficient for carbon is negative.

▎ From Eq. (4) of Prob. 2.13:

$$\alpha_0 = \frac{\alpha_T}{1 - T\alpha_T}$$

For platinum:
$$\alpha_0 = \frac{0.00357}{1 - 40 \times 0.00357} = 0.00416\,°C^{-1}$$

For the two resistances to be equal at a temperature T °C,

$$12(1 + 0.00416T) = 15(1 - 0.000515T)$$

or
$$1 + 0.00416T = 1.25 - 0.00064375T \qquad \text{or} \qquad T = 52\,°C$$

2.16 The two coils of Prob. 2.15 are connected in series and operate at 20 °C. Calculate the "effective" temperature coefficient α_e of the combination at 40 °C.

▎ From Eq. (4) of Prob. 2.13, at 20 C°:

For carbon:
$$\alpha = \frac{-0.000515}{1 - 0.000515 \times 20} = -0.000520\,°C^{-1}$$

From the data of Prob. 2.15:

$$R_{carbon} = 15[1 - 0.000520(40 - 20)] = 14.844\,\Omega$$

At 20 °C, we have (from Prob. 2.15):

For platinum:
$$\alpha = \frac{0.00416}{1 + 0.00416 \times 20} = 0.00384\,°C^{-1}$$

$$R_{platinum} = 12[1 + 0.00384(40 - 20)] = 12.9216\,\Omega$$

At 40 °C:
$$R_e = 14.844 + 12.9216 = 27.7656\,\Omega$$

At 20 °C:
$$R_e = 12.0 + 15.0 = 27.0\,\Omega$$

$$27.7656 = 27[1 + \alpha_e(40 - 20)] \quad \text{or} \quad \alpha_e = 0.001418\,°C^{-1}$$

2.17 The minimum current required for the operation of a relay coil is 500 mA at 120 V. If the current taken by the coil at 20 °C is 530 mA (at 120 V) and the temperature coefficient of the resistor material is 0.00427 °C^{-1} at 0° C, calculate the maximum temperature above which the relay will fail to operate.

❙ At 20 °C:
$$R_{20} = \frac{120}{530 \times 10^{-3}} = 226.41\,\Omega$$

At T °C (the maximum allowable temperature):

$$R_T = \frac{120}{500 \times 10^{-3}} = 240.0\,\Omega$$

Since $R_T = R_0(1 + \alpha_0 T)$ we have:

$$\frac{R_T}{R_{20}} = \frac{1 + \alpha_0 T}{1 + 20\alpha_0} \quad \text{or} \quad \frac{240}{226.41} = \frac{1 + 0.00427T}{1 + 0.00427 \times 20} \quad \text{or} \quad T = 35.26°C$$

2.18 The resistance of a 25-Ω resistor increases by 10 percent when its operating temperature increases from 15 to 50 °C. Calculate the mean temperature rise of the resistor from an ambient temperature of 20 °C when its resistance is 30 Ω and the temperature coefficient remains constant.

❙
$$R_{15} = 25 = R_0(1 + 15\alpha_0) \qquad R_{50} = 25 + 2.5 = R_0(1 + 50\alpha_0)$$

Solving for α_0 and R_0 yields:

$$\alpha_0 = 0.002985\,°C^{-1} \quad \text{and} \quad R_0 = 23.9286\,\Omega$$

At a temperature T °C we have:

$$30 = 23.92861(1 + 0.002985T) \quad \text{or} \quad T = 85\,°C$$

Temperature rise = $85 - 20 = 65$ °C.

2.19 "It has been experimentally found that the resistivity of conducting materials, such as copper and aluminum, varies linearly with temperature." Depict this statement graphically and mathematically.

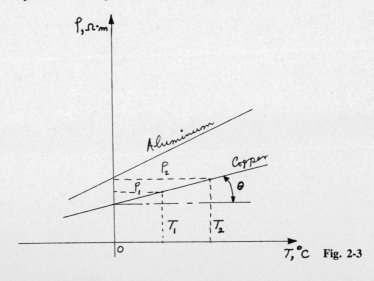

Fig. 2-3

❚ The statement is shown graphically in Fig. 2-3, from which we have:

$$\tan \theta = m = \frac{\rho_2 - \rho_1}{T_2 - T_1} \tag{1}$$

and

$$\rho_2 = \rho_1 + m(T_2 - T_1) = \rho_1\left[1 + \frac{m}{\rho_1}(T_2 - T_1)\right] \tag{2}$$

2.20 The resistance of a silver wire is $0.1\,\Omega$ at $20\,°C$. At what temperature will its resistance decrease by 25 percent if its temperature coefficient of resistance at $20\,°C$ is $0.0038\,°C^{-1}$.

❚ $R_2 = R_1[1 + \alpha_1(T_2 - T_1)]$ or $0.75 \times 0.1 = 0.1[1 + 0.0038(T_2 - 20)]$ or $T_2 = -45.8\,°C$

2.21 The resistivity of iron at 0 and $20\,°C$ is $8.68 \times 10^{-8}\,\Omega \cdot m$ and $9.75 \times 10^{-8}\,\Omega \cdot m$ respectively. Calculate its resistivity at $10\,°C$.

❚ From Eq. (1) of Prob. 2.19,

$$m = \frac{(9.75 - 8.68)10^{-8}}{20 - 0} = 0.0535 \times 10^{-8}$$

From Eq. (2) of Prob. 2.19,

$$\rho_{10} = \rho_{20} + m(10 - 20) = [9.75 + 0.0535(-10)] \times 10^{-8} = 9.215 \times 10^{-8}\,\Omega \cdot m$$

2.22 A piece of wire of uniform cross section has a resistance of $0.8\,\Omega$. If the length of the wire is doubled and its area of cross section is increased four times, what is its resistance? The temperature variation of resistance may be neglected.

❚ Original wire: $R_1 = \frac{\rho \ell_1}{A_1} = 0.8\,\Omega$

Wire with modified dimensions:

$$R_2 = \frac{\rho \ell_2}{A_2} = \frac{\rho 2\ell_1}{4A_1} = \frac{1}{2}\cdot\frac{\rho \ell_1}{A_1} = \frac{1}{2}0.8 = 0.4\,\Omega$$

2.23 An electromagnet is wound with a copper coil having 150 turns and a mean length of 20 cm per turn. The coil wire has a rectangular cross section 10×2 mm. Calculate the resistance of the coil at $55\,°C$ and determine the power dissipated in the coil at $55\,°C$ if the coil current is 6 A. The resistance of a 1-m long wire of 1 mm² cross section at $20\,°C$ is $0.00172\,\Omega$ and $\alpha_0 = (1/234.5)\,°C^{-1}$.

❚

$$\alpha_{20} = \frac{\alpha_0}{1 + 20\alpha_0} = \frac{1/234.5}{1 + 20/234.5} = \frac{1}{254.5}\,°C^{-1}$$

$$\rho_{20} = \frac{AR}{\ell} = \frac{1 \times 10^{-6} \times 0.0172}{1} = 1.72 \times 10^{-8}\,\Omega \cdot m$$

$$\rho_{55} = \rho_{20}[1 + \alpha_{20}(55 - 20)] = 1.72 \times 10^{-8}\left[1 + \frac{1}{254.5}(55 - 20)\right] = 1.96 \times 10^{-8}\,\Omega \cdot m$$

$$R_{55} = \rho_{55}\frac{\ell}{A} = \frac{1.96 \times 10^{-8} \times 150 \times 0.20}{10 \times 2 \times 10^{-6}} = 2.94 \times 10^{-2}\,\Omega$$

$$\text{Power} = I^2R = 6^2(2.94 \times 10^{-2}) = 1.0584\,W$$

2.24 The power taken by a resistive coil made of copper wire is 220 W at 110 V and $20\,°C$. Calculate the power consumed by the coil at 110 V and $120\,°C$. The temperature coefficient at $20\,°C$ is $0.00393\,°C^{-1}$.

❚

$$P_{20} = \frac{V^2}{R_{20}} \text{or} R_{20} = \frac{V^2}{P_{20}} = \frac{110^2}{220} = 55\,\Omega$$

$$R_{120} = R_{20}[1 + \alpha_{20}(120 - 20)] = 55[1 + 0.00393(100)] = 76.615\,\Omega$$

$$P_{120} = \frac{110^2}{76.615} = 157.93\,W$$

2.25 A flat aluminum ring 5 mm thick has a negligible air gap. If the inner and outer radii of the ring are 0.2 and 0.25 m respectively, determine the resistance of the ring at $20\,°C$. At this temperature the resistivity of aluminum is $2.78 \times 10^{-8}\,\Omega \cdot m$.

$$\text{Mean length } l = 2\pi r_{mean} \qquad r_{mean} = \tfrac{1}{2}(r_0 + r_i) = \tfrac{1}{2}(0.25 + 0.20) = 0.225 \text{ m}$$

$$l = 2\pi 0.225 = 1.4137 \text{ m}$$

$$\text{Area of cross section} = 5 \times 10^{-3}(0.25 - 0.20) = 2.5 \times 10^{-4} \text{ m}^2$$

$$\text{Resistance } R = \frac{\rho l}{A} = \frac{2.78 \times 10^{-8} \times 1.4137}{2.5 \times 10^{-4}} = 1.572 \times 10^{-4} \ \Omega$$

2.26 A resistor made of aluminum wire dissipates 25 W of power at 50 V at 20 °C. Calculate the current in a second resistor made of copper and having the same resistance as the first resistor and consuming four times the power of the first resistor.

$$R_1 = \frac{V^2}{P} = \frac{50^2}{25} = 100 \ \Omega = R_2 \qquad I_2^2 R_2 = 4 \times 25 = I_2^2(100) \qquad \text{or} \qquad I_2 = \sqrt{\frac{100}{100}} = 1.0 \text{ A}$$

2.27 A resistive coil draws 2.0 A at 110 V after operating for a long time. If the temperature rise is 55 °C above the ambient temperature of 20 °C, calculate the external resistance which must be initially connected in series with the coil to limit the current to 2.0 A. The temperature coefficient of the material of the coil is 0.0043 °C^{-1} at 20 °C.

$$\text{Hot temperature} = 20 + 55 = 75 \text{ °C}$$

$$R_{75} = \frac{110}{2} = 55 \ \Omega = R_{20}[1 + \alpha_{20}(75 - 20)] = R_{20}[1 + 0.0043(75 - 20)] \qquad \text{or} \qquad R_{20} = 44.48 \ \Omega$$

$$R_x + R_{20} = R_{75} \qquad \text{or} \qquad R_x = R_{75} - R_{20} = 55 - 44.48 = 10.52 \ \Omega$$

2.28 Conductor sizes (cross sections) in electric motors are chosen on the basis of current loadings expressed in A/m^2. In a particular machine, the allowable current rating is 3×10^6 A/m^2 in 0.5-m-long copper conductors. Calculate the conductor cross section if the loss in each conductor is not to exceed 1 W at 20 °C. The resistivity of copper at 20 °C is $1.72 \times 10^{-8} \ \Omega \cdot$ m.

$$\text{Power } P = I^2 R = (JA)^2 \frac{\rho \ell}{A} = J^2 A \rho \ell$$

where $J = I/A =$ current density or current loading, or

$$1 = (3 \times 10^6)^2 \times 1.72 \times 10^{-8} \times 0.5 A \qquad \text{or} \qquad A = 12.92 \text{ mm}^2$$

2.29 Wire of a certain material x and a given cross section has a resistance of 100 Ω/km and a temperature coefficient of 0.0025 °C^{-1}. Wire of another material y of a given cross section has a resistance of 50 Ω/km and a temperature coefficient of 0.00075 °C^{-1}. It is desired to make a coil having a 1000-Ω resistance and a temperature coefficient of 0.001 by using suitable lengths of the two wires in series. Calculate their respective lengths.

▮ Let R_x and R_y be the respective resistances at the given temperatures. Then at a temperature change ΔT, the total series resistance becomes

$$R_t = R_x(1 + 0.0025 \, \Delta T) + R_y(1 + 0.00075 \, \Delta T) \tag{1}$$

Since 0.001 is the temperature coefficient of the combination, we also have

$$R_t = (R_x + R_y)(1 + 0.001 \, \Delta T) \tag{2}$$

Combining Eqs. (1) and (2) yields:

$$R_x(1 + 0.0025 \, \Delta T) + R_y(1 + 0.00075 \, \Delta T) = (R_x + R_y)(1 + 0.001 \, \Delta T)$$

or

$$R_x(0.0015 \, \Delta T) = R_y(0.00025 \, \Delta T)$$

Thus, $R_x = \tfrac{25}{15} R_y = \tfrac{5}{3} R_y$, but $R_x + R_y = 1000 \ \Omega$. Consequently, $R_x = 625 \ \Omega$ and $R_y = 375 \ \Omega$. The respective lengths are:

$$\ell_x = \frac{1 \text{ km}}{100 \ \Omega} 625 \ \Omega = 6.25 \text{ km} \qquad \ell_y = \frac{1 \text{ km}}{50 \ \Omega} 375 \ \Omega = 7.5 \text{ km}$$

2.30 It is desired to maintain a 5-A constant current in a resistor made of copper wire through a temperature rise of 55 °C from 20 °C ambient temperature. The value of resistance at 20 °C is 40 Ω and the temperature coefficient is 0.00428 °C^{-1} at 0 °C. Determine the minimum and maximum voltage that must be available from the power supply to maintain the desired current.

$$V_{\min} \text{ (at } 20\,^{\circ}\text{C)} = R_{20}I = 40 \times 5 = 200 \text{ V}$$

$$\frac{R_{75}}{R_{20}} = \frac{1 + 75 \times 0.00428}{1 + 20 \times 0.00428} \qquad \text{or} \qquad R_{75} = 1.217 \times 40 = 48.67\ \Omega$$

$$V_{\max} \text{ (at } 75\,^{\circ}\text{C)} = R_{75}I = 48.67 \times 5 = 243.35 \text{ V}$$

2.31 Calculate the power dissipated in the resistor of Prob. 2.30 at 20 and at 75°C.

🞵 Since the current is 5 A at both temperatures,

$$P_{20} = I^2 R_{20} = 5^2 \times 40 = 1 \text{ kW} \qquad P_{75} = I^2 R_{75} = 5^2 \times 48.67 = 1.21675 \text{ kW}$$

2.32 Determine the current through and the voltage across the resistor of Prob. 2.30 if it is required that the power dissipated at 75 °C is the same as that at 20 °C and 200 V.

🞵

$$P_{75} = P_{20} = \frac{V_{20}^2}{R_{20}} = \frac{200^2}{40} = \frac{V_{75}^2}{R_{75}} = \frac{V_{75}^2}{48.67}$$

or

$$V_{75} = \sqrt{1000 \times 48.67} = 220.61 \text{ V} \qquad \text{and} \qquad I_{75} = \frac{220.61}{48.67} = 4.533 \text{ A}$$

2.33 Determine the ratio of powers dissipated in two resistors, each having the same length and each made of copper wire of circular cross section, but one having a diameter twice that of the other, and each being connected across the same voltage.

🞵

$$P_1 = \frac{V^2}{R_1} = \frac{V^2}{\rho\ell/A_1} = \frac{V^2 A_1}{\rho\ell} = \frac{\pi}{4}\frac{V^2 D_1^2}{\rho\ell}$$

Similarly,

$$P_2 = \frac{V^2}{R_2} = \frac{\pi}{4}\frac{V^2 D_2^2}{\rho\ell}$$

If $D_1 = 2D_2$, then

$$\frac{P_1}{P_2} = \frac{D_1^2}{D_2^2} = \frac{4D_2^2}{D_2^2} = 4$$

2.34 Find the ratio of powers in the two resistors of Prob. 2.33 when the resistors carry the same current.

🞵

$$P_1 = I^2 R_1 = I^2\,\frac{\rho\ell}{A_1} = \frac{4}{\pi}\frac{I^2\rho\ell}{D_1^2}$$

Similarly,

$$P_2 = I^2 R_2 = \frac{4}{\pi}\frac{I^2\rho\ell}{D_2^2}$$

If $D_1 = 2D_2$, then

$$\frac{P_1}{P_2} = \frac{1/D_1^2}{1/D_2^2} = \frac{D_2^2}{4D_2^2} = \frac{1}{4}$$

2.35 A 100-W 110-V light bulb has a filament made of an alloy having a temperature coefficient of 0.0055 °C^{-1} at 0 °C. The normal operating temperature of the bulb is 2000 °C. How much current will the bulb draw at the instant it is turned on when the room temperature is 20 °C? From your result verify that burnout of bulbs is more frequent at the instant they are turned on.

🞵 The ratio of resistances at the two temperatures is given by

$$\frac{R_{20}}{R_{2000}} = \frac{1 + 20\alpha_0}{1 + 2000\alpha_0} = \frac{1 + 20 \times 0.0055}{1 + 2000 + 0.0055} = 9.25 \times 10^{-2}$$

At 2000 °C:

$$R_{2000} = \frac{V^2}{P} = \frac{110^2}{100} = 121\ \Omega$$

At 20 °C:

$$R_{20} = 121 \times 9.25 \times 10^{-2} = 11.2\ \Omega \qquad \text{and} \qquad I_{20} = \frac{110}{11.2} = 9.82 \text{ A}$$

Compare with

$$I_{2000} = \tfrac{100}{110} = 0.91 \text{ A}$$

2.36 The current loading of the heating element of a 110-V 750-W electric heater is not to exceed 2600 A/in^2 (cf. Prob. 2.28). The resistivity of the wire material is $12 \times 10^{-8}\ \Omega\cdot$m. Calculate the length and the area of cross section of the heating element.

🞵

$$I = \frac{P}{V} = \frac{750}{110} = 6.818 \text{ A}$$

Since $$\frac{I}{A} = 2600 \text{ A/in}^2$$

$$\text{Area } A = \frac{6.818}{2600} \text{ in}^2 = 2.62 \times 10^{-3} \text{ in}^2 = 1.69 \text{ mm}^2$$

$$R = \frac{V^2}{P} = \frac{110^2}{750} = 16.13 \ \Omega = \frac{\rho\ell}{A} = \frac{12 \times 10^{-8}\ell}{1.69 \times 10^{-6}}$$

or $$\ell = \frac{16.13 \times 1.69 \times 10^{-6}}{12 \times 10^{-8}} = 227.16 \text{ m}$$

2.37 Heat energy is often measured in calories and 1 calorie (cal) = 4.184 joule (J). It is desired to design a heating element to boil a certain amount of water in 2 min requiring 40 kcal heat energy. If the heating element is to operate at 110 V, calculate its current and power ratings.

$\blacksquare$ $$1 \text{ kcal} = 4.184 \text{ kJ} = 4.184 \text{ kW} \cdot \text{s} = 4184 \text{ W} \cdot \text{s}$$

The heat energy required is

$$Q = 40 \text{ kcal} = 40 \times 4184 = 167,360 \text{ W} \cdot \text{s}$$

Let P be the power required. Then,

$$P = \frac{167,360 \text{ W} \cdot \text{s}}{120 \text{ s}} = 1395 \text{ W} \qquad I = \frac{P}{V} = \frac{1395}{110} = 12.7 \text{ A}$$

2.38 For the data of Prob. 2.37, determine the resistance of the heating element if the same amount of water is required to boil in 30 s.

$\blacksquare$ The same amount of energy must be delivered in one-fourth the time; so the power is now

$$P = 4(1395) = 5580 \text{ W} = VI \qquad \text{or} \qquad I = \frac{5580}{110} = 50.7 \text{ A} \qquad R = \frac{V}{I} = \frac{110}{50.7} = 2.17 \ \Omega$$

2.39 As the temperature of a heating element changes, its resistance also changes, and so does the temperature coefficient. In a certain case, the temperature varies linearly with time and is given by $T \ ^{\circ}\text{C} = (20 + 10t)$, where t is time in seconds. The temperature coefficient of the material is $0.0065 \ ^{\circ}\text{C}^{-1}$ at $0 \ ^{\circ}\text{C}$. If the initial resistance of the heating element is $2 \ \Omega$, find its resistance after 10 s.

$\blacksquare$ At $t = 0$: $\qquad\qquad T = 20 \ ^{\circ}\text{C} \qquad \text{and} \qquad R_{20} = 2 \ \Omega$

At $t = 10$ s: $\qquad\qquad T = 20 + 10 \times 10 = 120 \ ^{\circ}\text{C}$

$$R_{120} = R_{20}[1 + \alpha_{20}(120 - 20)]$$

From Eq. (4) of Prob. 2.13,

$$\alpha_{20} = \frac{\alpha_0}{1 + \alpha_0 20} = \frac{0.0065}{1 + 0.0065 \times 20} = 0.00575 \ ^{\circ}\text{C}^{-1}$$

$$R_{120} = 2[1 + 0.00575(120 - 20)] = 3.15 \ \Omega$$

2.40 For the heating element of Prob. 2.39, express the resistance as a function of time.

$\blacksquare$ Resistance at a temperature T is given by

$$R_T = R_0(1 + \alpha_0 T) = R(t)$$

From the data:

$$R_0 = R_1[1 + \alpha_{20}(0 - 20^{\circ})] = 2(1 - 20 \times 0.00575) = 1.77 \ \Omega \qquad T = 20 + 10t$$

Hence $\qquad\qquad R(t) = 1.77[1 + 0.0065(20 + 10t)] = (2 + 0.115t) \ \Omega$

2.41 If the heating element of Prob. 2.39 or 2.40 is connected across a 110-V source, calculate the initial and final powers.

$\blacksquare$ At $t = 0$: $\qquad\qquad R = 2 \ \Omega \qquad P_i = \frac{V^2}{R} = \frac{110^2}{2} = 6050 \text{ W}$

At $t = 10$ s: $\qquad\qquad R = 3.15 \ \Omega \qquad P_f = \frac{110^2}{3.15} = 3841 \text{ W}$

2.42 For Probs. 2.39 through 2.41 determine the energy dissipated in the heating element over the 10-s period.

▮
$$dU = \frac{V^2}{R(t)}\, dt = \frac{110^2}{2 + 0.115t}\, dt$$

or
$$U = 110^2 \int_0^{10} \frac{dt}{2 + 0.115t} = \frac{110^2}{0.115} \left[\ln (2 + 0.115t)\right]_0^{10} = 47.795 \text{ kJ} = 0.0133 \text{ kWh}$$

2.43 A block of iron is heated directly by dissipating power in the internal resistance of the block. Because of the temperature rise, the resistance increases exponentially with time and is given by $R(t) = 0.5e^{2t}\ \Omega$, where t is in seconds. The block is connected across a 110-V source and dissipates 1827 cal heat energy over a certain period of time. Calculate this period of time.

▮ Let t be the required time. Then energy dissipated is

$$U = \int_0^t \frac{V^2}{R(t)}\, dt = \int_0^t \frac{110^2}{0.5e^{2t}}\, dt = \frac{110^2}{0.5} \int_0^t e^{-2t}\, dt$$

$$= \frac{110^2}{-2 \times 0.5}\ (e^{-2t})_0^t = 110^2(1 - e^{-2t}) \text{ J}$$

Now
$$1827 \text{ cal} = 1827 \times 4.184 = 7644 \text{ J} = U$$

Thus
$$1 - e^{-2t} = \frac{7644}{110^2} = 0.632$$

or
$$e^{-2t} = 0.368 \quad \text{or} \quad -2t \ln e = \ln 0.368 \quad \text{or} \quad -2t = -1$$

Hence,
$$t = 0.5 \text{ s}$$

2.44 A light bulb, having a tungsten filament, draws 0.5 A at 110 V. The cold resistance of the filament is 20 Ω at 20 °C. At this temperature the temperature coefficient of resistance (for tungsten) is 0.005 °C^{-1}. Determine the operating temperature of the bulb.

▮ Resistance at the operating temperature T °C is

$$R_T = \frac{V}{I} = \frac{110}{0.5} = 220\ \Omega = R_{20}[1 + \alpha_{20}(T - 20)] = 20[1 + 0.005(T - 20)]$$

Solving for T yields $T = 2020$ °C.

2.45 The operating temperature of a tungsten-filament 110-V 40-W bulb is 2020 °C (cf. Prob. 2.44). The filament is made of a 0.01-mm-diameter wire having a resistivity of $5.55 \times 10^{-8}\ \Omega \cdot$m at 20 °C and a temperature coefficient of 0.005 °C^{-1}. Calculate the length of the filament wire.

▮ At 2020 °C:
$$R_{2020} = \frac{V^2}{P} = \frac{110^2}{40} = 302.5\ \Omega = R_{20}[1 + 0.005(2020 - 20)] = 11R_{20}$$

or
$$R_{20} = \frac{302.5}{11} = 27.5\ \Omega = \frac{\rho_{20}\ell}{A} = \frac{5.55 \times 10^{-8}\ell}{\pi/4[(0.01)^2 \times 10^{-6}]}$$

Hence
$$\ell = \frac{\pi \times 27.5 \times 10^{-2}}{4 \times 5.55} = 3.89 \text{ cm}$$

2.46 A 60-mm-thick electrode is cut from a solid 70-mm-radius hemisphere made of copper, as shown in Fig. 2-4. Calculate the current through the electrode if 6 V is applied across it. Resistivity of copper is $1.72 \times 10^{-8}\ \Omega \cdot$m.

▮ Let R be the resistance of the electrode. Then, for the infinitesimal disk shown in Fig. 2-4,

$$dR = \frac{\rho\, dx}{A} = \frac{\rho\, dx}{\pi r^2} = \frac{\rho\, dx}{\pi(b^2 - x^2)} \quad \text{or} \quad R = \frac{\rho}{\pi} \int_{x=0}^{x=a} \frac{dx}{(b^2 - x^2)} = \frac{\rho}{\pi} \left(\tanh^{-1} \frac{x}{b}\right)_0^a$$

$$= \frac{\rho}{\pi} \left(\tanh^{-1} \frac{a}{b} - \tanh^{-1} 0\right) = \frac{\rho}{\pi} \tanh^{-1} \frac{a}{b} = \frac{1.72 \times 10^{-8}}{\pi} \tanh^{-1} \frac{60}{70} = 0.702 \times 10^{-8}\ \Omega$$

$$I = \frac{V}{R} = \frac{6}{0.702 \times 10^{-8}} = 8.547 \times 10^8 \text{ A} = 854.7 \text{ MA}$$

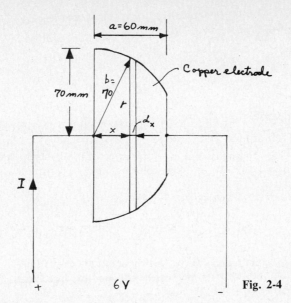

Fig. 2-4

2.47 A carbon resistor dissipates 60 W of power while drawing 0.5 A of current at 20 °C. How much power will be dissipated in the resistor at 100 °C if connected across a 120-V source? Temperature coefficient of carbon at 20 °C is $-0.0005 °C^{-1}$.

▮ At 20 °C: $$P_{20} = I^2 R_{20} \quad \text{or} \quad R_{20} = \frac{60}{0.5^2} = 240 \ \Omega$$

At 100 °C: $$R_{100} = R_{20}[1 - 0.0005(100 - 20)] = 240(1 - 0.04) = 230.4 \ \Omega$$

$$P_{200} = \frac{V^2}{R_{200}} = \frac{120^2}{230.4} = 62.5 \ W$$

2.48 We have two resistors wound with round copper wire. The length and the diameter of the first wire are ℓ and A respectively and those of the second wire are 0.25ℓ and $0.5A$. Determine the ratios of currents and powers for the two resistors if they are connected across the same voltage source.

▮ $$R_1 = \frac{\rho\ell}{A} \quad \text{and} \quad R_2 = \frac{\rho(0.25\ell)}{0.5A} = 0.5\frac{\rho\ell}{A} = 0.5R_1$$

$$\frac{I_1}{I_2} = \frac{V/R_1}{V/R_2} = \frac{R_2}{R_1} = \frac{0.5R_1}{R_1} = 0.5 \qquad \frac{P_1}{P_2} = \frac{V^2/R_1}{V^2/R_2} = \frac{R_2}{R_1} = 0.5$$

2.49 If the same current flows through the two resistors of Prob. 2.48, determine the ratios of voltages and powers.

▮ From Prob. 2.48, $R_2/R_1 = 0.5$,

$$\frac{V_1}{V_2} = \frac{IR_1}{IR_2} = \frac{R_1}{R_2} = \frac{1}{0.5} = 2 \qquad \frac{P_1}{P_2} = \frac{I^2R_1}{I^2R_2} = 2$$

2.50 Obtain the exact and approximate ratios of the resistances of a coil at two temperatures T_2 and T_1 assuming that the only other given quantity is the temperature coefficient α_0 at 0 °C.

▮ Let R_0 be the resistance at 0 °C. Then at the temperatures T_1 and T_2 we have

$$R_1 = R_0(1 + \alpha_0 T_1) \quad \text{and} \quad R_2 = R_0(1 + \alpha_0 T_2) \quad \text{or} \quad \frac{R_1}{R_2} = \frac{1 + \alpha_0 T_1}{1 + \alpha_0 T_2}$$

which is the exact ratio. Approximately,

$$\frac{R_1}{R_2} = (1 + \alpha_0 T_1)(1 + \alpha_0 T_2)^{-1} = (1 + \alpha_0 T_1)[1 - \alpha_0 T_2 + (\alpha_0 T_2)^2 - \cdots] \approx 1 + \alpha_0(T_1 - T_2)$$

CHAPTER 3
Series and Parallel Resistive Circuits

3.1 How much current will flow through a 2-Ω resistor connected in series with a 4-Ω resistor, and the combination connected across a 12-V source?   What is the voltage across each resistor?

$$R_s = R_1 + R_2 = 2 + 4 = 6\,\Omega \qquad I_1 = \frac{V}{R_s} = \frac{12}{6} = 2\,\text{A}$$

$$V_1 = I_1 R_1 = 2 \times 2 = 4\,\text{V} \qquad \text{and} \qquad V_2 = 2 \times 4 = 8\,\text{V}$$

3.2 A 2-Ω resistor is connected in parallel with a 4-Ω resistor and the combination across a 12-V source.   Find the current through each resistor and the total current supplied by the source.

$$I_{2\,\Omega} = \tfrac{12}{2} = 6\,\text{A} \qquad I_{4\,\Omega} = \tfrac{12}{4} = 3\,\text{A} \qquad I_{\text{total}} = 6 + 3 = 9\,\text{A}$$

3.3 What is the total resistance of the combination of a 2-Ω and a 4-Ω resistance in parallel?   Calculate the current supplied by a 12-V source connected across the combination.

$$\frac{1}{R_p} = \frac{1}{2} + \frac{1}{4} = \frac{3}{4} \qquad \text{or} \qquad R_p = \tfrac{4}{3}\,\Omega \qquad I = \frac{V}{R_p} = \frac{12}{4/3} = 9\,\text{A}$$

3.4 Two resistors of ohmic values R_1 and R_2 are connected in series, and the combination across a source of voltage V.   How is this voltage divided across the resistors?

$$R_s = R_1 + R_2 \qquad I = \frac{V}{R_s} = \frac{V}{R_1 + R_2}$$

$$V_1 = IR_1 = V\,\frac{R_1}{R_1 + R_2} \qquad V_2 = IR_2 = V\,\frac{R_2}{R_1 + R_2}$$

3.5 Two resistors of ohmic values R_1 and R_2 are connected in parallel, and the combination across a source of current I.   How is this current divided through the resistors?

$$\frac{1}{R_p} = \frac{1}{R_1} + \frac{1}{R_2} \qquad \text{or} \qquad R_p = \frac{R_1 R_2}{R_1 + R_2}\,\Omega$$

Let $V = $ voltage across the combination.   Then $V = IR_p = I_1 R_1 = I_2 R_2$.

Therefore,
$$I_1 = \frac{IR_p}{R_1} = I\,\frac{R_2}{R_1 + R_2} \qquad I_2 = \frac{IR_p}{R_2} = I\,\frac{R_1}{R_1 + R_2}$$

3.6 Use the results of Prob. 3.4 to solve Prob. 3.1.

$$V_1 = V\,\frac{R_1}{R_1 + R_2} = 12\,\frac{2}{2 + 4} = 4\,\text{V} \qquad V_2 = V\,\frac{R_2}{R_1 + R_2} = 12\,\frac{4}{2 + 4} = 8\,\text{V}$$

3.7 Use the results of Prob. 3.5 to solve Prob. 3.2.

$$I_1 = I\,\frac{R_2}{R_1 + R_2} = 9\,\frac{4}{2 + 4} = 6\,\text{A} \qquad I_2 = I\,\frac{R_1}{R_1 + R_2} = 9\,\frac{2}{2 + 4} = 3\,\text{A}$$

3.8 Calculate the power in each resistor of Prob. 3.1 and verify that the total power supplied by the source is the sum of the powers in the resistors.

$$P_1 = I_1^2 R_1 = 2^2 \times 2 = 8\,\text{W} \qquad P_2 = I_2^2 R_2 = 2^2 \times 4 = 16\,\text{W} \quad (\text{since} \quad I_1 = I_2 = 2\,\text{A})$$

$$P_1 + P_2 = 8 + 16 = 24\,\text{W} \qquad P_s = VI = 12 \times 2 = 24\,\text{W}$$

3.9 Determine the power in each resistor of Prob. 3.2. Verify that the total power supplied by the source is the sum of the powers in the resistors.

▌

$$P_1 = \frac{V^2}{R_1} = \frac{12^2}{2} = 72 \text{ W} \qquad P_2 = \frac{V^2}{R_2} = \frac{12^2}{4} = 36 \text{ W}$$

$$P_1 + P_2 = 72 + 36 = 108 \text{ W} \qquad P_s = VI = 12 \times 9 = 108 \text{ W}$$

3.10 A 3-Ω and a 6-Ω resistor are connected in parallel and the combination in series with an 8-Ω resistor. Calculate the total resistance.

▌

$$R_p = \frac{3 \times 6}{3 + 6} = 2 \text{ } \Omega \qquad R_{total} = R_p + R_s = 2 + 8 = 10 \text{ } \Omega$$

3.11 A 20-V source is connected across the resistor combination of Prob. 3.10. What is the voltage across the 8-Ω resistor?

▌

$$I = \frac{V}{R_{total}} = \frac{20}{10} = 2 \text{ A} \qquad V_{8\,\Omega} = 8 \times 2 = 16 \text{ V}$$

3.12 Determine the power absorbed by each resistor of Prob. 3.11.

▌

$$P_{8\,\Omega} = \frac{V_{8\,\Omega}^2}{8} = \frac{16^2}{8} = 32 \text{ W} \qquad V_{3\,\Omega} = V_{6\,\Omega} = V - V_{8\,\Omega} = 20 - 16 = 4 \text{ V}$$

$$P_{6\,\Omega} = \frac{4^2}{6} = \frac{8}{3} \text{ W} \qquad P_{3\,\Omega} = \frac{4^2}{3} = \frac{16}{3} \text{ W}$$

Check: Total power $= 32 + \frac{8}{3} + \frac{16}{3} = 40 \text{ W}$. Power from source $= VI = 20 \times 2 = 40 \text{ W}$.

3.13 For the circuit shown in Fig. 3-1, find the value of k so that the resistance of the combination is a minimum.

▌

$$R = \frac{ka}{2} + \frac{a}{k} \qquad R = \frac{k^2 a + 2a}{2k}$$

For R_{min}, $\partial R / \partial k = 0$, which implies that

$$2k(2ak) - 2(k^2 a + 2a) = 0 \qquad \text{or} \qquad 2k^2 - k^2 - 2 = 0 \qquad \text{or} \qquad k = \sqrt{2} = 1.414$$

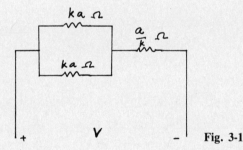

Fig. 3-1

3.14 If a voltage V is connected across the resistor combination of Prob. 3.13, find the condition for maximum power supplied from the source to the resistors.

▌ $P = V^2/R$ is a maximum when R is a minimum; $k = \sqrt{2}$.

3.15 What is the maximum power the resistors of Fig. 3-1 can absorb when connected across voltage V? Determine the input current at maximum power condition.

▌ From Probs. 3.13 and 3.14,

$$P = \frac{2V^2}{a} \frac{k}{k^2 + 2} = \frac{2V^2}{a} \frac{\sqrt{2}}{2 + 2} = \frac{V^2}{\sqrt{2}a} \text{ W} \qquad \text{and} \qquad I = \frac{P}{V} = \frac{V}{\sqrt{2}a} \text{ A}$$

3.16 Four resistors of ohmic values 5, 10, 15, and 20 Ω are connected in series and a 100-V source is applied across the combination. How is this voltage divided among the various resistors?

▮ Using the voltage division rule, we have

$$V_5 = \frac{5}{5 + 10 + 15 + 20} \, 100 \, V = 10 \, V$$

Similarly, $V_{10} = 20 \, V$, $V_{15} = 30 \, V$, $V_{20} = 40 \, V$.

3.17 Formulate the law of current division among three resistors R_1, R_2, and R_3 connected in parallel. The total input current is i.

▮ The common voltage across the resistors is $V = iR_{ep}$, where $1/R_{ep} = 1/R_1 + 1/R_2 + 1/R_3$. Hence,

$$i_1 = \frac{V}{R_1} = \frac{R_{ep}}{R_1} \, i \qquad i_2 = \frac{R_{ep}}{R_2} \, i \qquad i_3 = \frac{R_{ep}}{R_3} \, i$$

3.18 Determine the current through and the voltages across three resistors of ohmic values 5, 7, and 8 Ω, connected in series and across a 100-V source.

▮ Total resistance $= R_{es} = 5 + 7 + 8 = 20 \, \Omega$ Circuit current $= I = \dfrac{V}{R_{es}} = \dfrac{100}{20} = 5 \, A$

Voltage across the 5-Ω resistor $= 5I = 25 \, V$. Voltage across the 7-Ω resistor $= 7I = 35 \, V$. Voltage across the 8-Ω resistor $= 8I = 40 \, V$.

3.19 Determine the voltage across and the currents through three resistors of 5, 10, and 20 Ω, all connected in parallel and across a 100-V source. There is 100 V across each resistor.

▮ Current through the 5-Ω resistor $= \frac{100}{5} = 20 \, A$. Current through the 10-Ω resistor $= \frac{100}{10} = 10 \, A$. Current through the 20-Ω resistor $= \frac{100}{20} = 5 \, A$.

3.20 Determine the current and power drawn from the source in the circuit of Prob. 3.19.

▮ Total current from source $= 20 + 10 + 5 = 35 \, A$. Power supplied by source $= VI = 100 \times 35 = 3500 \, W$.

3.21 Reduce the circuit between the terminals a and b, Fig. 3-2, to a single resistor.

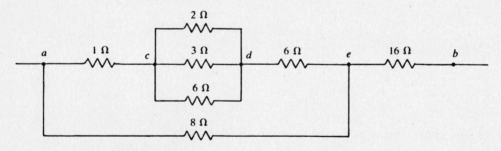

Fig. 3-2

▮ From the law of parallel resistances,

$$\frac{1}{R_{cd}} = \frac{1}{2} + \frac{1}{3} + \frac{1}{6} \qquad \text{or} \qquad R_{cd} = 1 \, \Omega$$

The series resistance between a and e is then $1 + 1 + 6 = 8 \, \Omega$, giving a net resistance

$$R_{ae} = \frac{(8)(8)}{8 + 8} = 4 \, \Omega \qquad R_{ab} = 4 + 16 = 20 \, \Omega$$

3.22 Calculate the resistances of 110-V light bulbs rated at 25, 60, 75, and 100 W.

▮ From $P = V^2/R$:

$$R_{25 \, W} = \frac{(110)^2}{25} = 484 \, \Omega \qquad R_{75 \, W} = \frac{(110)^2}{75} = 161.3 \, \Omega$$

$$R_{60 \, W} = \frac{(110)^2}{60} = 201.67 \, \Omega \qquad R_{100 \, W} = \frac{(110)^2}{100} = 121 \, \Omega$$

3.23 An electric heating pad rated at 110 V and 55 W is to be used at a 220-V source. It is proposed to connect the heating pad in series with a series-parallel combination of light bulbs, each rated at 110 V; bulbs are available having ratings of 25, 60, 75, and 100 W. Obtain a possible scheme of the pad-bulb combinations. At what rate will heat be produced by the pad with this modification?

▌ From Prob. 3.22 we know the resistances of the various light bulbs. The resistance of the heating pad is $R_p = (110)^2/55 = 220\,\Omega$. We must combine the bulbs to obtain a total resistance of 220 Ω; then, by voltage division, the pad voltage will be the required 110 V. One possibility is a 100-W bulb in series with a parallel combination of two 60-W bulbs: $R_b = R_{100} + \frac{1}{2}R_{60} = 121 + \frac{1}{2}(201.67) = 221.83\,\Omega$, which is on the safe side. Then

$$R_p + R_b = 220 + 221.83 = 441.83\,\Omega \qquad I_p = \frac{220}{441.83} = 0.498\,\text{A}$$

and so the heat output of the pad is $I_p^2 R_p = (0.498)^2(220) = 54.56\,\text{W}$.

3.24 Two resistors, made of different materials having temperature coefficients of resistance $\alpha_1 = 0.004\,°C^{-1}$ and $\alpha_2 = 0.005\,°C^{-1}$, are connected in parallel and consume equal power at 10 °C. What is the ratio of power consumed in resistance R_2 to that in R_1 at 60 °C?

▌ At 10 °C, $R_1 = R_2$, which implies

$$R_{01}(1 + 10\alpha_1) = R_{02}(1 + 10\alpha_2) \qquad \text{or} \qquad \frac{R_{01}}{R_{02}} = \frac{1 + 10\alpha_2}{1 + 10\alpha_1}$$

Consequently, the power ratio at 60 °C is

$$\frac{V^2/R_2}{V^2/R_1} = \frac{R_1}{R_2} = \frac{R_{01}(1 + 60\alpha_1)}{R_{02}(1 + 60\alpha_2)} = \frac{(1 + 10\alpha_2)(1 + 60\alpha_1)}{(1 + 10\alpha_1)(1 + 60\alpha_2)}$$

Substituting the numerical values of α_1 and α_2 yields the value 0.963.

3.25 A 200-V source is connected across the circuit shown in Fig. 3-2. Calculate the voltage across the 8-Ω resistor.

▌ From Prob. 3.21, $R_{ab} = 20\,\Omega$. Thus,

$$I = \frac{V}{R_{ab}} = \frac{200}{20} = 10\,\text{A} \qquad V_{eb} = R_{eb}I = 16 \times 10 = 160\,\text{V} \qquad V_{ae} = V_{8\,\Omega} = V - V_{eb} = 200 - 160 = 40\,\text{V}$$

3.26 In Prob. 3.25, determine the power dissipated in the 1-Ω and 8-Ω resistors.

▌ From Prob. 3.21,

$$V_{8\,\Omega} = 40\,\text{V} \qquad I_{8\,\Omega} = \tfrac{40}{8} = 5\,\text{A} \qquad P_{8\,\Omega} = (5)^2 8 = 200\,\text{W} \qquad I = 10\,\text{A}$$

From Prob. 3-25,

$$I_{1\,\Omega} = I - I_{8\,\Omega} = 10 - 5 = 5\,\text{A} \qquad P_{1\,\Omega} = (5)^2 1 = 25\,\text{W}$$

3.27 Find the ratio of the currents I_1/I_2 at 60 °C in the resistors of Prob. 3.24.

▌ From Prob. 3.24, $R_1/R_2 = 0.963 = P_2/P_1$. Since $P_2/P_1 = I_2^2 R_2/I_1^2 R_1$, we have

$$\frac{R_1}{R_2} = 0.963 = \frac{I_2^2}{I_1^2}\frac{R_2}{R_1} \qquad \text{or} \qquad \frac{I_1}{I_2} = \frac{R_2}{R_1} = \frac{1}{0.963} = 1.0384$$

Notice that this result also follows from $I_1 R_1 = I_2 R_2 = V$, since the two resistors are in parallel.

3.28 A battery has internal resistance R_i and terminal voltage V_t. Show that the power supplied to a resistive load cannot exceed $V_t^2/2R_i$.

▌ Let R_L be the load resistance. Then

$$I_L = \frac{V_t}{R_L + R_i}$$

and power taken by the load,

$$P_L = I_L^2 R_L = V_t^2 \frac{R_L}{(R_L + R_i)^2}$$

For maximum power, $\partial P_L/\partial R_L = 0$, which requires that

$$(R_L + R_i)^2 - R_L[2(R_L + R_i)] = 0 \qquad \text{or} \qquad R_L = R_i$$

Hence, $(P_L)_{\max} = V_t^2/2R_i$.

3.29 For the battery of Prob. 3.28, $V_t = 96\,\text{V}$ and $R_i = 50\,\text{m}\Omega$. Discrete loads of 150, 100, 50, 30, and 20 mΩ are connected, one at a time, across the battery. Plot the curve of power supplied versus the ohmic value of the load. Hence verify that the maximum power transfer occurs when $R_i = R_{\text{load}} = 50\,\text{m}\Omega$.

❚
$$P_L = V_t^2 \frac{R_L}{(R_L + R_i)^2}$$

Substituting the given numerical values yields:

$$P_{150} = 96^2 \frac{150}{(150+50)^2} = 34.56\,\text{kW} \qquad P_{30} = 96^2 \frac{30}{(30+50)^2} = 43.20\,\text{kW}$$

$$P_{100} = 96^2 \frac{100}{(100+50)^2} = 40.96\,\text{kW} \qquad P_{20} = 96^2 \frac{20}{(20+50)^2} = 37.62\,\text{kW}$$

$$P_{50} = 96^2 \frac{50}{(50+50)^2} = 46.08\,\text{kW}$$

which is plotted in Fig. 3-3 showing that $(P_L)_{\max}$ occurs at $R_L = 50\,\text{m}\Omega$.

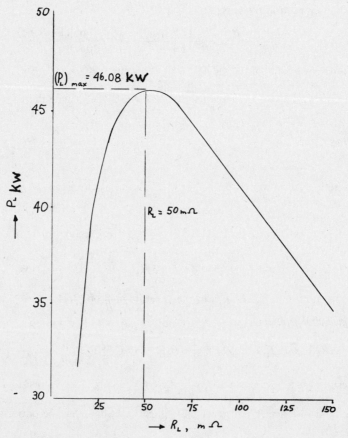

Fig. 3-3

3.30 A battery has an internal resistance of 0.5 Ω, and has an open-circuit voltage of 20 V. The battery supplies a 2-Ω load. Determine the power lost within the battery and the terminal voltage on load.

❚
$$I = \frac{20}{2+0.5} = 8\,\text{A} \qquad V_t = IR_L = 8 \times 2 = 16\,\text{V} \qquad P_{\text{lost}} = I^2 R_i = 8^2(0.5) = 32\,\text{W}$$

3.31 A resistor made of silver and another made of nickel, having temperature coefficients of resistance at 20 °C of 0.0038 °C^{-1} and 0.006 °C^{-1}, carry equal currents at 20 °C when connected across a voltage source. How will the total current be distributed if the temperature is raised to 150 °C?

❚ At 150°C,

$$R_{\text{silver}} = (R_{\text{silver}})_{20}[1 + 0.0038(150 - 20)] = 1.494(R_{\text{silver}})_{20}$$

$$R_{\text{nickel}} = (R_{\text{nickel}})_{20}[1 + 0.006(150 - 20)] = 1.78(R_{\text{nickel}})_{20}$$

Since the currents are equal at 20 °C, $(R_{\text{silver}})_{20} = (R_{\text{nickel}})_{20} = R$. Therefore, by current division (see Prob. 3.5) at 150 °C,

$$I_{\text{silver}} = \frac{1.78R}{1.78R + 1.494R} I = 0.5437I \quad \text{or} \quad 54.37\%$$

$$I_{\text{nickel}} = \frac{1.494R}{1.78R + 1.494R} I = 0.4563I \quad \text{or} \quad 45.63\%$$

3.32 Convert the delta-connected resistor bank of Fig. 3-4 into an equivalent wye-connected resistor bank.

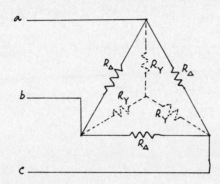

Fig. 3-4

❚ For equivalence, the resistance between any two terminals (say, *ab*) for both the wye and the delta connections must be the same. Thus, equating them we get

$$2R_Y = \frac{R_\Delta(R_\Delta + R_\Delta)}{R_\Delta + R_\Delta + R_\Delta} = \tfrac{2}{3}R_\Delta$$

Hence, $R_Y = \tfrac{1}{3}R_\Delta$.

3.33 Three unequal resistors are connected in wye as shown in Fig. 3-5. Obtain an equivalent delta-connected resistor bank.

❚ From Fig. 3-5 it follows that:

$$R_{ac} = R_1 + R_3 = \frac{R_A(R_B + R_C)}{R_A + R_B + R_C} \tag{1}$$

$$R_{ab} = R_1 + R_2 = \frac{R_C(R_A + R_B)}{R_A + R_B + R_C} \tag{2}$$

$$R_{bc} = R_2 + R_3 = \frac{R_B(R_A + R_C)}{R_A + R_B + R_C} \tag{3}$$

Solving R_A, R_B, and R_C yields:

$$R_A = \frac{1}{R_2}(R_1R_2 + R_2R_3 + R_3R_1) \qquad R_B = \frac{1}{R_1}(R_1R_2 + R_2R_3 + R_3R_1) \qquad R_C = \frac{1}{R_3}(R_1R_2 + R_2R_3 + R_3R_1)$$

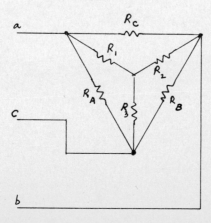

Fig. 3-5

3.34 Suppose three resistors R_A, R_B, and R_C are connected in delta as shown in Fig. 3-5. Obtain an equivalent wye-connected resistor bank.

▮ In this case also Eqs. (1), (2), and (3) of Prob. 3.33 are valid. Therefore, we solve for R_1, R_2, and R_3 to obtain

$$R_1 = \frac{R_A R_C}{R_A + R_B + R_C} \qquad R_2 = \frac{R_B R_C}{R_A + R_B + R_C} \qquad R_3 = \frac{R_A R_B}{R_A + R_B + R_C}$$

3.35 Convert the pi-connected resistors of Fig. 3-6a to an equivalent tee-connected set (Fig. 3-6b).

▮ Notice that pi- and tee-connections are, respectively, the same as delta- and wye-connections. Thus, using the results of Prob. 3.34, we obtain

$$R_1 = \frac{R_A R_C}{R_A + R_B + R_C} = \frac{9 \times 3}{9 + 6 + 3} = 1.5\,\Omega \qquad R_2 = \frac{R_B R_C}{R_A + R_B + R_C} = \frac{6 \times 3}{9 + 6 + 3} = 1.0\,\Omega$$

$$R_3 = \frac{R_A R_B}{R_A + R_B + R_C} = \frac{9 \times 6}{9 + 6 + 3} = 3.0\,\Omega$$

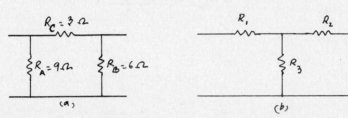

Fig. 3-6

3.36 Verify that the converse of Prob. 3.35 is true; that is, show that if $R_1 = 1.5\,\Omega$, $R_2 = 1.0\,\Omega$, and $R_3 = 3.0\,\Omega$ are connected in wye, its equivalent delta will have the values shown in Fig. 3-6a.

▮ Since $R_1 R_2 + R_2 R_3 + R_3 R_1 = 1.5 \times 1 + 1 \times 3 + 3 \times 1.5 = 9$, from the results of Prob. 3.33 we have:

$$R_A = \tfrac{9}{1} = 9\,\Omega \qquad R_B = \frac{9}{1.5} = 6\,\Omega \qquad R_C = \tfrac{9}{3} = 3\,\Omega$$

3.37 Determine the resistance across the terminals ab of the interconnected resistors of Fig. 3-7a.

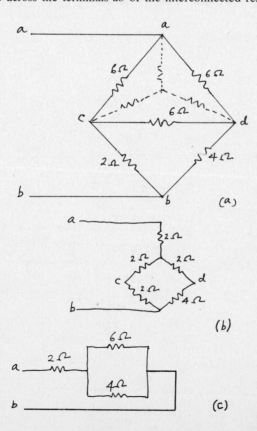

Fig. 3-7

| First, we convert the upper delta to a wye to obtain the interconnection shown in Fig. 3-7b which reduces to that given in Fig. 3-7c.   Finally, $R_{ab} = 2 + (6 \times 4)/(6 + 4) = 4.4 \ \Omega$.

3.38   What is the resistance across the terminals ab of the network shown in Fig. 3-8a?

| By converting the delta-connected resistors to an equivalent wye we obtain the interconnection shown in Fig. 3-8b.   Next combining the 3-Ω and 6-Ω resistors in parallel leads to the circuit shown in Fig. 3-8c.   Hence, $R_{ab} = 2 + 2 = 4 \ \Omega$.

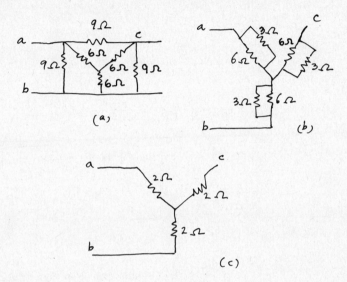

(a)

(b)

(c)   **Fig. 3-8**

3.39   For the network shown in Fig. 3-8a, calculate the voltage across the terminals ac if a 36-V battery is connected across the terminals ab.

| In this case, we convert the 6-Ω wye-connected resistors into an equivalent delta to obtain the circuit of Fig. 3-9a.   Combining the 9-Ω and 18-Ω resistors in parallel gives the circuit of Fig. 3-9b from which we obtain the currents as follows:

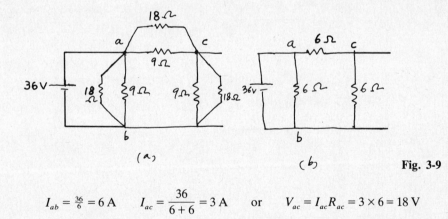

(a)   (b)   **Fig. 3-9**

$$I_{ab} = \tfrac{36}{6} = 6 \ \text{A} \qquad I_{ac} = \frac{36}{6 + 6} = 3 \ \text{A} \qquad \text{or} \qquad V_{ac} = I_{ac}R_{ac} = 3 \times 6 = 18 \ \text{V}$$

3.40   Calculate the power dissipated in the 9-Ω resistor connected across ab and in the 9-Ω resistor connected across bc of the network of Fig. 3-8a when a 36-V source is connected across ab.

| From Fig. 3-9a we have, $P_{9\Omega ab} = V_{ab}^2/R_{ab} = 36^2/9 = 144 \ \text{W}$.
From Problem 3.39, $V_{ac} = 18 \ \text{V}$.   Hence

$$V_{bc} = 36 - 18 = 18 \ \text{V} \qquad P_{9\Omega bc} = \frac{V_{bc}^2}{R_{bc}} = \frac{18^2}{9} = 36 \ \text{W}$$

3.41   For the circuit shown in Fig. 3-10a, determine R so that the power going into the terminals ab is maximum. Also calculate the maximum power.

The sequence of network reduction is shown in Figs. 3-10b–e.   From Fig. 3-10e the current drawn from the source is given by

$$I = \frac{12}{1 + 0.5R} \text{ A}$$

and power is

$$P = I^2(0.5R) = \frac{144(0.5R)}{(1 + 0.5R)^2}$$

For maximum power, $\partial P/\partial R = 0$ requires that $0.5(1 + 0.5R)^2 - 0.5R \times 2(1 + 0.5R)0.5 = 0$ or $R = 2\,\Omega$. Thus,

$$I = \frac{12}{1 + 0.5 \times 2} = 6\text{ A} \qquad \text{and} \qquad P_{max} = 6^2(0.5 \times 2) = 36\text{ W}$$

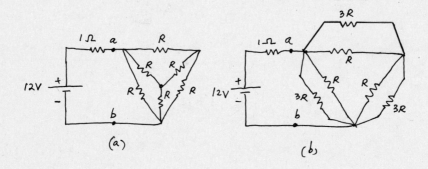

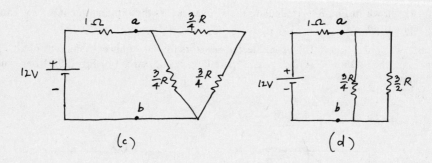

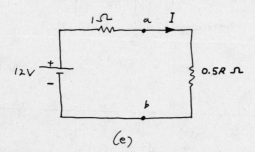

Fig. 3-10

3.42   For the circuit in Fig. 3-10a show by changing the delta-connected resistors to an equivalent wye that the maximum power entering the terminals ab is 36 W.

The network reduction is shown in Fig. 3-11a–c.   Notice that Fig. 3-11c is identical to Fig. 3-10e. Therefore, from the results of Prob. 3.41, we have

$$R = 2\,\Omega \qquad I = 6\text{ A} \qquad \text{and} \qquad P_{max} = 36\text{ W}$$

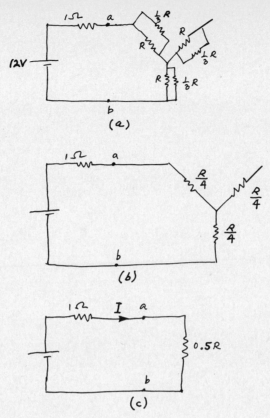

Fig. 3-11

3.43 Four 60-W 110-V bulbs are to be operated from a 230-V source. Determine the value of the resistance connected in series with the line so that the voltage across the bulbs does not exceed 110 V.

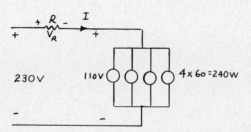

Fig. 3-12

▮ For the circuit shown in Fig. 3-12 we have total power drawn from the source,

$$P = 4 \times 60 = 240\,\text{W} \qquad \text{Input current } I = \frac{P}{V} = \frac{240}{110} = 2.1818\,\text{A}$$

Voltage across the series resistor,

$$V_R = 230 - 110 = 120\,\text{V} = IR \qquad \text{or} \qquad R = \frac{V_R}{I} = \frac{120}{2.1818} = 55\,\Omega$$

3.44 An alternate way of operating the bulbs of Prob. 3.43 is to connect them as shown in Fig. 3-13 with a series resistor. Calculate the value of the series resistance and state, giving reasons, which of the two methods is preferable.

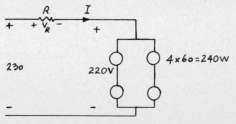

Fig. 3-13

▮ In this case,

$$I = \frac{P}{V_L} = \frac{240}{220} = 1.0909 \text{ A} \qquad V_R = 230 - 220 = 10 \text{ V} = RI$$

Thus
$$R = \frac{10}{1.0909} = 9.167 \, \Omega$$

I^2R loss in method of Prob. $3.43 = 120^2/55 = 261.82$ W. I^2R loss in method of the present problem = $10^2/9.167 = 10.9$ W.   Second method is more efficient but, if one bulb burns out, only two will function.

3.45   A 12-V battery is made of 36 cells each rated at 2 V and 1.5 A for a given duty cycle.   What is the line current and power that may be drawn from the battery?

▮ Since the battery is rated at 12 V and each cell at 2 V, cells connected in series = $\frac{12}{2} = 6$ cells.   Number of parallel paths = $\frac{36}{6} = 6$.   Rating for one parallel path = 1.5 A (given).

$$\text{Line current} = 6 \times 1.5 = 9 \text{ A} \qquad \text{Power} = VI = 12 \times 9 = 108 \text{ W}$$

(Otherwise,   power = $36 \times 2 \times 1.5 = 108$ W.)

3.46   For the circuit shown in Fig. 3-14, calculate R such that the power dissipated in the 3-Ω resistor is 300 W.

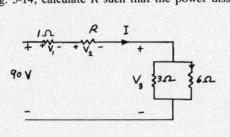

Fig. 3-14

▮
$$P_{3\,\Omega} = \frac{V_3^2}{3} = 300 \text{ W} \qquad \text{or} \qquad V_3 = 30 \text{ V}$$

$$I_{3\,\Omega} = \frac{V_3}{3} = \frac{30}{3} = 10 \text{ A} \qquad I_{6\,\Omega} = \frac{V_3}{6} = \frac{30}{6} = 5 \text{ A}$$

$$I = 10 + 5 = 15 \text{ A} = \frac{V}{1 + R + (6 \times 3)/(6+3)} = \frac{V}{3 + R} \quad \text{or} \quad V = 45 + 15R = 90 \text{ V} \quad \text{or} \quad R = \frac{90 - 45}{15} = 3 \, \Omega$$

3.47   For the value of R determined in Prob. 3.46, calculate the power absorbed by each resistor.   Verify that the total power thus obtained is the same as that supplied by the source.

▮ Total power absorbed = $15^2 \times 1 + 15^2 \times 3 + 30^2/3 + 30^2/6 = 1350$ W.   Power supplied by the source = $90 \times 15 = 1350$ W.

3.48   Calculate the voltage that must be connected across the terminals ab such that the voltage across the 2-Ω resistor is 10 V (Fig. 3-15).

▮ Input current to the circuit, $I = \frac{10}{2} = 5$ A.

$$R_{\text{parallel}} = \frac{6 \times 12}{6 + 12} = 4 \, \Omega \qquad R_{\text{total}} = 2 + 1 + 4 = 7 \, \Omega \qquad V = R_{\text{total}} I = 7 \times 5 = 35 \, V.$$

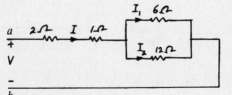

Fig. 3-15

3.49   Refer to Fig. 3-15.   Determine the voltage across the 6-Ω resistor.   Hence determine the currents I_1 and I_2 and verify that $I = I_1 + I_2$.

▮
$$V_{6\,\Omega} = V - V_{2\,\Omega} - V_{1\,\Omega} = 35 - 10 - 5 = 20 \text{ V}$$

$$I_1 = \frac{20}{6} = \frac{10}{3} \text{ A} \qquad I_2 = \frac{20}{12} = \frac{10}{6} \text{ A} \qquad I_1 + I_2 = \frac{10}{3} + \frac{10}{6} = \frac{20 + 10}{6} = 5 \text{ A} = I$$

3.50 Find the current in the 5-Ω resistor in the interconnection of resistors shown in Fig. 3-16a.

▌ By changing the delta-connected 3-Ω resistors into an equivalent wye we obtain the circuit of Fig. 3-16b, which is reduced to the circuit of Fig. 3-16c. Thus,

$$I = \frac{V}{R} = \frac{36}{2+1} = 12 \text{ A} \qquad V_{1\,\Omega} \text{ (Fig. 3-16b)} = RI = 1 \times 12 = 12 \text{ V}$$

$$V_{(1+5)\,\Omega} = V - V_{1\,\Omega} = 36 - 12 = 24 \text{ V}$$

Thus,

$$I_{5\,\Omega} = \frac{24}{1+5} = 4 \text{ A}$$

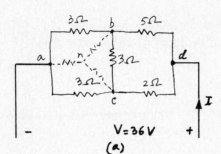

(a)

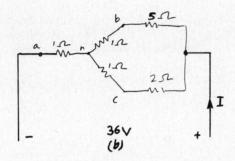

(b)

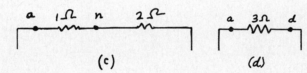

(c)   (d)   Fig. 3-16

3.51 By adding the powers absorbed by the resistors of Fig. 3-16c, verify that the sum is equal to the power supplied by the 36-V source.

▌ From the results of Prob. 3.50,

$$I_{5\,\Omega} = 4 \text{ A} \qquad \text{and} \qquad I_{2\,\Omega} = 8 \text{ A}$$

Thus,

$$V_{5\,\Omega} = 4 \times 5 = 20 \text{ V} \qquad \text{and} \qquad V_{2\,\Omega} = 8 \times 2 = 16 \text{ V}$$

Also the voltages across the top and bottom of the 3-Ω resistors become 16 and 20 V respectively as shown. The respective currents in these resistors are $\frac{16}{3}$ A and $\frac{20}{3}$ A. Hence the current I (Fig. 3-16a) in the vertically drawn 3-Ω resistor between bc becomes $I = \frac{16}{3} - 4 = \frac{4}{3}$ A.

Verification:

$$I_{2\,\Omega} = \frac{4}{3} + \frac{20}{3} = 8 \text{ A}$$

$$P_{\text{loss}} = \left(\frac{16}{3}\right)^2 \times 3 + (4)^2 \times 5 + \left(\frac{20}{3}\right)^2 \times 3 + (8)^2 \times 2 + \left(\frac{4}{3}\right)^2 \times 3 = 432 \text{ W} \qquad P_{\text{in}} = 36 \times 12 = 432 \text{ W}$$

3.52 Find the resistance between the terminals ad for the interconnected resistors shown in Fig. 3-16a.

▌ Using wye-delta transformations shown in Fig. 3-16b we obtain the circuit of Fig. 3-16d.

3.53 A *shunt* is used to extend the range of an ammeter by connecting it across the ammeter as shown in Fig. 3-17. The ammeter has a resistance of 0.1 Ω and gives a full-scale deflection of 2.5 A. Calculate the value of the shunt resistance to extend the range of the ammeter to 50 A.

▌ Refer to Fig. 3-17:

$$I_a = 2.5 \, \text{A} \qquad I = 50 \, \text{A} \qquad I_s = 50 - 2.5 = 47.5 \, \text{A}$$

$$I_a R_a = I_s R_s \qquad \text{or} \qquad 2.5 \times 0.1 = 47.5 R_s$$

Hence,

$$R_s = \frac{2.5 \times 0.1}{47.5} = 5.263 \, \text{m}\Omega$$

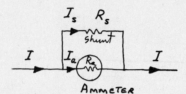

Fig. 3-17

3.54 The *multiplying power* of a shunt is defined as the ratio of the line current to the current through the ammeter. Obtain a general expression for the multiplying power.

▌ From Fig. 3-17 we have:

$$I_a R_a = (I - I_a) R_s \qquad \text{or} \qquad I_a(R_a + R_s) = I R_s \qquad \text{or} \qquad \text{Multiplying power} = \frac{I}{I_a} = 1 + \frac{R_a}{R_s}$$

3.55 The resistance of a coil is measured experimentally by the voltmeter-ammeter method. Two possible arrangements of the meters are shown in Fig. 3-18. The resistance of the voltmeter is 10 kΩ and that of the ammeter is 0.1 Ω. For the setup of Fig. 3-18a the voltmeter reads 5 V and the ammeter reading is 25 A. What is the value of the resistance?

▌ For Fig. 3-18a from Ohm's law:

$$5 = 25(0.1 + R) \qquad \text{or} \qquad R = \tfrac{5}{25} - 0.1 = 0.1 \, \Omega$$

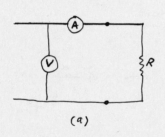

(a)

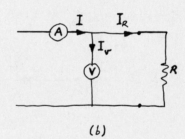

(b)

Fig. 3-18

3.56 If the ammeter reading in Fig. 3-18b is 25 A and the values of various resistances are the same as in Prob. 3.55, determine the voltmeter reading.

▌ By the rule of current division we have:

$$I_v = \frac{R}{R + R_v} I = \frac{0.1}{0.1 + 10,000} (25 \, \text{A})$$

$$\text{Voltmeter reading} = R_v I_v = (10,000) \frac{0.1}{0.1 + 10,000} (25) = 2.5 \, \text{V}$$

3.57 Based on the results of Probs. 3.55 and 3.56, if the resistance is measured as the ratio of the voltmeter-to-ammeter readings, state which of the two connections of Fig. 3-18 is preferred for the measurement of (a) a low resistance and (b) a high resistance.

▌ From Prob. 3.55:

$$R = \frac{V}{I} = \frac{5}{25} = 0.2 \, \Omega$$

From Prob. 3.56:

$$R = \frac{V}{I} = \frac{2.5}{25} = 0.1 \, \Omega$$

Clearly, Fig. 3-18b is suitable for the measurement of a low resistance and Fig. 3-18a is preferred for measuring a high resistance.

3.58 Calculate the value of the shunt resistance to be used with a galvanometer having a resistance of $10\,\Omega$ if the current through the galvanometer is not to exceed 5 percent of the total current.

▌ From Prob. 3.54 we have:

$$\frac{I}{I_a} = 1 + \frac{R_a}{R_s} \qquad \text{or} \qquad \frac{1}{0.05} = 1 + \frac{10}{R_s}$$

Hence, $\qquad\qquad\qquad\qquad\qquad\qquad R_s = \frac{10}{19} = 0.526\,\Omega$

3.59 An ammeter rated to read up to 5 A, having a resistance of $0.5\,\Omega$, is to be converted into a 150-V voltmeter by connecting a resistor in series with the ammeter. Calculate the value of this resistance.

▌ Let R be the value of the series resistance. Then by Ohm's law, $V = I(R + R_a)$, where R_a is the ammeter resistance. Substituting numerical values yields:

$$150 = 5(R + 0.5) \qquad \text{or} \qquad R = \frac{150}{5} - 0.5 = 29.5\,\Omega$$

3.60 A 300-V voltmeter draws 2 mA current for full-scale deflection. This voltmeter is used to measure the voltage across a 50-kΩ resistor connected in series with a 25-kΩ resistor, the combination of the resistors being connected across a 150-V source. What is the voltmeter reading?

▌ The voltmeter resistance $R_v = 300/(2 \times 10^{-3}) = 150\,\text{k}\Omega$. From the circuit of Fig. 3-19, the total resistance across the 150-V source is $R = 25 + (150 \times 50)/(150 + 50) = 62.5\,\text{k}\Omega$.

$$I = \frac{150}{62.5 \times 10^3} = 2.4\,\text{mA}$$

By current division rule,

$$I_v = \frac{50 \times 10^3 \times 2.4 \times 10^{-3}}{(150 + 50) \times 10^3} = 0.6\,\text{mA}$$

Thus the voltmeter reading is $\quad I_v R_v = 0.6 \times 10^{-3} \times 150 \times 10^3 = 90\,\text{V}.$

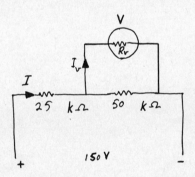

Fig. 3-19

3.61 If the voltmeter of Prob. 3.60 is now connected across the 25-kΩ resistor, what is the voltage across the 50-kΩ resistor?

▌ When the voltmeter is connected across the 25-kΩ resistor, the value of the combined parallel resistance becomes $R_p = (25 \times 150)/(25 + 150) = 21.428\,\text{k}\Omega$. Or the total circuit resistance is $50 + 21.428 = 71.428\,\text{k}\Omega$.

$$\text{Circuit current } I = \frac{150}{71.428} \times 10^{-3} = 2.1\,\text{mA}$$

$$\text{Voltage across } 50\,\text{k}\Omega = 50 \times 10^3 \times 2.1 \times 10^{-3} = 105\,\text{V}$$

3.62 A high-voltage dc transmission line supplies 900 MW of power over a distance of 800 km. This power is delivered at 600 kV. If the loop resistance of the line is $2\,\text{m}\Omega/\text{km}$, determine the sending-end voltage.

▌ The line is schematically represented in Fig. 3-20. Subscripts R and S are, respectively, used for receiving- and sending-end quantities. Then,

$$P_R = 900\,\text{MW (given)} \qquad I_R = I_S = I = \frac{900 \times 10^6}{600 \times 10^3} = 1.5\,\text{kA}$$

$$V_R = 600\,\text{kV (given)} \qquad R = 800 \times 2 \times 10^{-3} = 1.6\,\Omega$$

$$V_S = V_R + IR = 600 \times 10^3 + 1.5 \times 10^3 \times 1.6 = 602.4\,\text{kV}$$

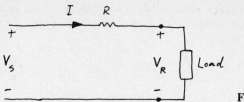

Fig. 3-20

3.63 Defining *efficiency of transmission* as the ratio of the power at the receiving end to the power at the sending end, calculate the efficiency of transmission of the line of Prob. 3.62. Verify that the same result is obtained by line-loss calculation.

❚ $P_R = 900\,\text{MW (given)}$ $P_S = V_s I_s = 602.4 \times 10^3 \times 1.5 \times 10^3 = 903.6\,\text{MW}$

Efficiency of transmission is $P_R/P_S = 900/903.6 = 99.6\%$. Line loss is $I^2 R = (1.5 \times 10^3)^2 \times 1.6 = 3.6\,\text{MW}$. $P_S = P_R + \text{line loss} = (900 + 3.6) \times 10^6 = 903.6\,\text{MW}$, which is the same as previously calculated.

3.64 A dc generator has an open-circuit voltage of 123 V. When connected across a 4-Ω resistor the generator delivers 3.6 kW of power. Calculate the internal power loss within the generator.

❚ $I^2 = \dfrac{3.6 \times 10^3}{4}$ or $I = 30\,\text{A} = \dfrac{123}{4 + R_g}$ or $R_g = \dfrac{123 - 120}{30} = 0.1\,\Omega$

Hence, $P_{\text{loss}} = I^2 R_g = 30^2 \times 0.1 = 90\,\text{W}$

3.65 A dc generator may be characterized by an ideal voltage source in series with a resistor. At the terminals of the generator, voltage and current measurements for two different operating conditions are $V_t = 115\,\text{V}$ at $I = 10\,\text{A}$ and $V_t = 105\,\text{A}$ at $I = 15\,\text{A}$. Model the generator by a voltage source in series with a resistor.

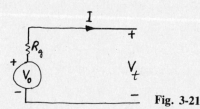

Fig. 3-21

❚ With the circuit model of the generator shown in Fig. 3-21, with the symbols defined, we have (for the two sets of data):

$$V_0 = V_t + IR_g \quad \text{or} \quad V_0 = 115 + 10R_g \quad \text{and} \quad V_0 = 105 + 15R_g$$

Solving for V_0 and R_g yields $V_0 = 135\,\text{V}$ and $R_g = 2.0\,\Omega$.

3.66 A dependent voltage source is shown in Fig. 3-22. For the data given determine the power supplied by the 12 V-source and that by the 3*I*-dependent voltage source.

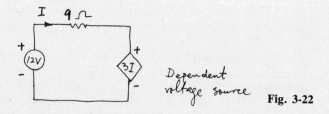

Dependent
voltage source   **Fig. 3-22**

❚ From Ohm's law, $12 - 9I + 3I$ or $I = 1.0\,\text{A}$.
Power delivered by the 12-V source is $12 \times 1 = 12\,\text{W}$.
Power delivered by the 3*I*-dependent voltage source is $-1.0 \times 3 \times 1.0 = -3\,\text{W}$.
Negative sign is used since the current is going into the source. Thus the dependent source is absorbing (rather than delivering) power.

3.67 A 500-Ω resistor is connected in parallel with a 250-Ω resistor and the combination is fed by a 25-A current source. Calculate the power absorbed by each resistor.

▌ The circuit is shown in Fig. 3-23. By current-division rule we have,

$$I_1 = \frac{500}{250 + 500} \, 25 = 16.67 \, \text{A} \qquad I_2 = \frac{250}{250 + 500} \, 25 = 8.33 \, \text{A}$$

Respective power losses are

$$I_1^2(250) = 69.472 \, \text{kW} \qquad \text{and} \qquad I_2^2(500) = 34.695 \, \text{kW}$$

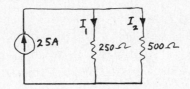

Fig. 3-23

3.68 Determine the voltage across the resistors of Fig. 3-23. Verify that the power supplied by the source is the same as the total power dissipated in the resistors.

▌ Voltage $V = I_1(250) = I_2(500) = 16.67 \times 250 = 4167.5 \, \text{V}$. Power $P = V(I_1 + I_2) = VI = 4167.5 \times 25 = 104.187 \, \text{kW}$. Power dissipated is $69.472 + 34.694 = 104.166 \, \text{kW}$.

3.69 Figure 3-24 shows a circuit containing a 25-A independent current source and a 5-V dependent current source. Calculate V and R.

▌ $I = 25 = 5 \, \text{V}$. Thus, $V = 5 \, \text{V}$. Also, $V = RI$, or $5 = R(25)$, or $R = 0.2 \, \Omega$.

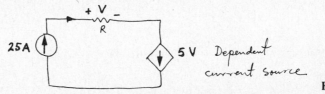

Fig. 3-24

3.70 For the circuit of Fig. 3-24, determine the power absorbed by R.

▌

$$P_R = \frac{V^2}{R} = \frac{5^2}{0.2} = 125 \, \text{W}$$

3.71 If the power supplied by the 25-A source of Fig. 3-24 is 150 W and the dependent source absorbs power, calculate the voltages across the 25-A source and 5-V dependent current source.

▌

$$V_{25\,\text{A}} = \frac{P_{25\,\text{A}}}{I_{25\,\text{A}}} = \frac{150}{25} = 6 \, \text{V} \qquad V_{5\,\text{V}} = \frac{P_{5\,\text{V}}}{I_{5\,\text{V}}} = \frac{150 - 125}{25} = 1 \, \text{V}$$

3.72 For the circuit in Fig. 3-25 the elements shown on the right are connected one at a time to the terminals ab. The control for the dependent sources is I_x. Determine the dependent parameter in each case.

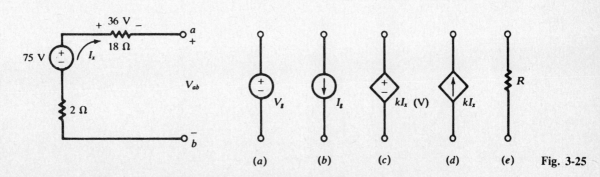

(a)   (b)   (c)   (d)   (e)   **Fig. 3-25**

❚ Since the voltage across the 18-Ω resistor is 36 V, the current I_x must be 2 A. Then $V_{ab} + (2)(2) - 75 + 36 = 0$ or $V_{ab} = 35$ V.

(a) $V_g = 35$ V   (d) $kI_x = -I_x$ $k = -1$

(b) $I_g = I_x = 2$ A   (e) $V_R = I_x R = 35$ V $R = 17.5\,\Omega$

(c) $kI_x = 35$ V $k = 17.5\,\Omega$

3.73 A generator generating a ramp voltage, $v = 6t$ V, is connected across a 25-Ω resistor. Determine the energy dissipated by the resistor during the interval $0 \leq t \leq 5$ s.

❚ Instantaneous power $p = v^2/R = 36t^2/25$ W. Energy is

$$W = \int_0^5 p\,dt = \int_0^5 \frac{36t^2}{25}\,dt = \frac{36}{25}\left(\frac{t^3}{3}\right)_0^5 = \frac{36}{25}\frac{5^3}{3} = 60 \text{ J}$$

3.74 A resistor supplied by a ramp generator producing a voltage $v = 10t$ V is used as a heating element to boil a certain amount of water. It takes 2 kcal of heat energy to boil the water in 30 s. Calculate the value of the resistance. (1 kcal = 4.184 kJ.)

❚ Proceeding as in Prob. 3.73,

$$W = 2 \text{ kcal} = 2 \times 4184 = 8368 \text{ J} = \int_0^{30} \frac{(10t)^2}{R}\,dt = \frac{100}{R}\left(\frac{t^3}{3}\right)_0^{30}$$

or

$$R = \frac{100 \times 30^3}{3 \times 8368} = 107.5\,\Omega$$

3.75 For the data of Prob. 3.74, if $v = 10$ V (constant), determine the value of the resistance.

❚ In this case,

$$W = 8368 \text{ J} = \int_0^{30} \frac{10^2}{R}\,dt = \frac{3000}{R} \qquad R = \frac{3000}{8368} = 0.3585\,\Omega$$

3.76 For the circuit shown in Fig. 3-26a determine the current drawn from the 15-V battery.

❚ First, we show the circuit reduction to a single equivalent resistor in Fig. 3-26b through d. Then, from Fig. 3-26d,

$$I = \frac{V}{R} = \frac{15}{5/2} = 6 \text{ A}$$

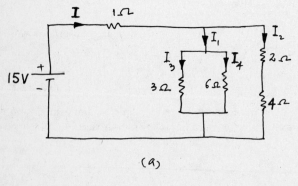

(a)

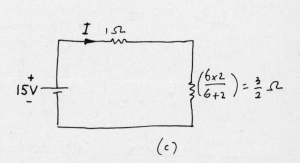

(c)

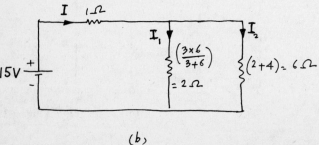

(b)

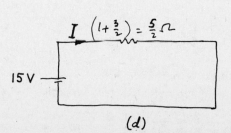

(d)

Fig. 3-26

3.77 Refer to Fig. 3-26a and calculate the power absorbed by the 2-Ω resistor.

❚ From Prob. 3.76, we have $I = 6$ A. Now, applying the current division rule to the circuit of Fig. 3-26b, we obtain $I_2 = [2/(2+6)]6 = 1.5$ A. Thus, $P_{2\,\Omega} = I_2^2(2) = (1.5)^2 2 = 4.5$ W.

3.78 What are the powers absorbed by the resistors of Fig. 3-26a? Verify that the sum of these powers equals the power drawn from the battery.

❚ From Fig. 3-26b and from Prob. 3.76 we have $I_1 = [6/(2+6)]6 = 4.5$ A, and from Fig. 3-26a we obtain

$$I_3 = \frac{6}{3+6} 4.5 = 3 \text{ A} \qquad I_4 = \frac{3}{3+6} 4.5 = 1.5 \text{ A}$$

From Prob. 3.77, $I_2 = 1.5$ A. Since $P = I^2 R$, we have

$$P_{1\,\Omega} = (6)^2 1 = 36 \text{ W} \qquad P_{2\,\Omega} = (1.5)^2 2 = 4.5 \text{ W} \qquad P_{3\,\Omega} = (3)^2 3 = 27 \text{ W}$$

$$P_{4\,\Omega} = (1.5)^2 4 = 9 \text{ W} \qquad P_{6\,\Omega} = (1.5)^2 6 = 13.5 \text{ W} \qquad P_{\text{total}} = 90 \text{ W}$$

Check: $P_{\text{battery}} = VI = 15 \times 6 = 90$ W.

3.79 If the 3-Ω resistor in the circuit of Fig. 3-26a is short-circuited, how much power will now be drawn from the battery? Also, determine the voltage across the 2-Ω resistor.

❚ From Fig. 3-26a it follows that short-circuiting the 3-Ω resistor short-circuits the 6-Ω resistor as well as the series combination of the 2-Ω and 4-Ω resistors. Hence, $V_{2\,\Omega} = 0$ V. The current is limited by the 1-Ω resistor, and we have $I = \frac{15}{1} = 15$ A. Power drawn from the battery is $VI = 15 \times 15 = 225$ W.

3.80 How much power is drawn from the battery if the 6-Ω resistor of the circuit of Fig. 3-26a is open-circuited?

❚ In this case the equivalent resistance

$$R = 1 + \frac{3(2+4)}{3+2+4} = 3 \ \Omega \qquad \text{thus} \qquad I = \frac{V}{R} = \frac{15}{3} = 5 \text{ A}$$

Power drawn from the battery is $15 \times 5 = 75$ W.

3.81 A resistive circuit is shown in Fig. 3-27a. Determine the equivalent resistance R.

❚ The circuit reductions are shown in Fig. 3-27b through d, from which $R = 1 + 2 = 3 \ \Omega$.

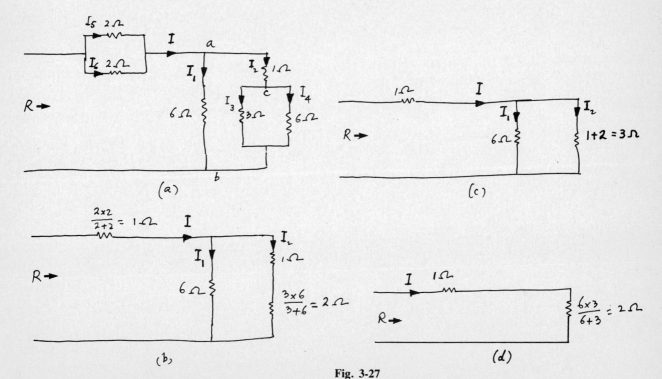

Fig. 3-27

3.82 Calculate the current through the 3-Ω resistor and the voltage across the 1-Ω resistor of the circuit of Fig. 3-27*a* when 120 V direct current is applied across the terminals of the circuit.

❚ From 3-27*d*:

$$I = \frac{V}{R} = \frac{120}{3} = 40 \text{ A}$$

From Fig. 3-27*c*:

$$I_2 = \frac{6}{6+3} \, 40 = 26.67 \text{ A}$$

Thus,

$$V_{1\,\Omega} = I_2(1) = 26.67 \times 1 = 26.67 \text{ V}$$

From Fig. 3-27*a*:

$$I_3 = \frac{6}{3+6} \, 26.67 = 17.77 \text{ A}$$

3.83 From the data of Prob. 3.82 verify that the voltage across the terminals *ab* is the sum of the voltages across the terminals *ac* and *cb*.

❚ From Prob. 3.82,

$$I_1 = 40 - 26.67 = 13.33 \text{ A} \qquad V_{ab} = I_1(6) = 13.33 \times 6 = 79.98 \text{ V}$$

$$I_2 = 26.67 \text{ A} \qquad V_{ac} = I_2(1) = 26.67 \times 1 = 26.67 \text{ V}$$

$$I_3 = 17.77 \text{ A} \qquad V_{cb} = I_3(3) = 17.77 \times 3 = 53.31 \text{ V}$$

Thus,

$$V_{ac} + V_{cb} = 26.67 + 53.31 = 79.98 \text{ V} = V_{ab}$$

3.84 For the circuit of Fig. 3-27*a* determine I_4. Thus calculate the power loss in each resistor. Verify that the sum of the power losses is the same as the power delivered by the source. (If the two results are not identical, determine the percent round-off error.)

❚

$$I_4 = \frac{3}{3+6} \, I_2 = \frac{3}{3+6} \, 26.67 = 8.89 \text{ A} \qquad I_5 = I_6 = \tfrac{1}{2} I = \tfrac{1}{2} \times 40 = 20 \text{ A}$$

$$\sum P_{\text{loss}} = (20)^2 2 + (20)^2 2 + (13.33)^2 6 + (26.67)^2 1 + (17.77)^2 3 + (8.89)^2 6 = 4798.93 \text{ W}$$

$$P_{\text{delivered}} = 120 \times 40 = 4800 \text{ W} \qquad \% \text{ error} = \frac{4800 - 4798.93}{4800} \times 100 = 0.022\%$$

3.85 Figure 3-28*a* shows a *ladder network*. From the data, determine the voltage V_x and the current I_x.

❚ The circuit reduction is shown in Fig. 3-28*b* through *e*.

From Fig. 3-28*e*:

$$I = \frac{12}{4+2} = 2 \text{ A}$$

From Fig. 3-28*d*:

$$I_1 = \frac{6}{6+3} \, 2 = 1.333 \text{ A}$$

From Fig. 3-28*b*:

$$I_x = \frac{3}{3+3} \, 1.333 = 0.667 \text{ A} = I_3$$

From Fig. 3-28*a*:

$$V_x = I_3(3) = 0.667 \times 3 = 2.0 \text{ V}$$

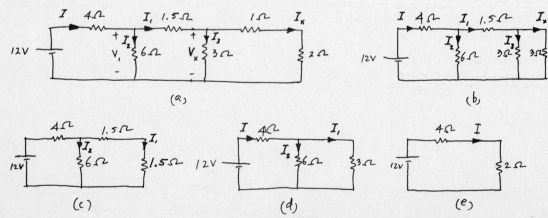

Fig. 3-28

3.86 Solve Prob. 3.85 without resorting to network reduction.

❚ From Fig. 3-28a we have:

$$I_x = \frac{V_x}{1+2} \quad \text{or} \quad V_x = 3I_x$$

$$I_3 = \frac{V_x}{3} = \frac{3I_x}{3} = I_x \qquad I_1 = I_3 + I_x = 2I_x$$

$$V_1 = I_1(1.5) + V_x = 2I_x(1.5) + 3I_x = 6I_x \qquad I_2 = \frac{V_1}{6} = \frac{6I_x}{6} = I_x$$

$$I = I_1 + I_2 = 2I_x + I_x = 3I_x \qquad 12 = I(4) + V_1 = 3I_x(4) + 6I_x = 18I_x$$

or, $$I_x = \tfrac{12}{18} = 0.667 \text{ A} = I_3 \quad \text{and} \quad V_x = I_x(3) = 3 \times 0.667 = 2.0 \text{ V}$$

3.87 Polarities of voltages across three resistors in series are shown in Fig. 3-29. Determine the potentials at the points a, b, c, and d.

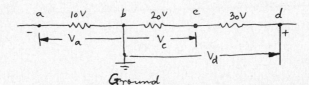

Fig. 3-29

❚ From Fig. 3-29,

$$V_a = -10 \text{ V} \qquad V_b = 0 \text{ V} \qquad V_c = +20 \text{ V} \qquad V_d = (30+20) = +50 \text{ V}$$

3.88 The conditions which determine the base bias of a transistor in an amplifier circuit are shown in Fig. 3-30. What are the potentials at points B, C, and E with respect to ground? What is the value of the base-to-emitter bias V_{BE}?

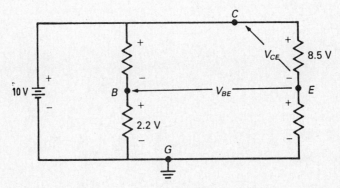

Fig. 3-30

❚ The potential at point B is $V_B = +2.2$ V. The potential at point C is $V_C = +10$ V. The potential at point E is $V_E = V_C - V_{CE} = +10$ V $- 8.5$ V $= +1.5$ V. The base-to-emitter voltage V_{BE} is $V_{BE} = V_{BG} + V_{GE} = 2.2$ V $- 1.5$ V $= +0.7$ V.

3.89 From the transistor amplifier circuit in Fig. 3-31 determine: (a) The voltage at the collector with respect to the emitter, V_{CE}; (b) the voltage at the base with respect to the emitter, V_{BE}; and (c) the voltage at the base with respect to the collector, V_{BC}.

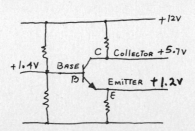

Fig. 3-31

▮ From Fig. 3-31,

$$V_{CE} = 5.7 - 1.2 = +4.5 \text{ V} \qquad V_{BE} = 1.4 - 1.2 = +0.2 \text{ V} \qquad V_{BC} = 1.4 - 5.7 = -4.3 \text{ V}$$

3.90 A three-wire power line feeding a house is shown in Fig. 3-32. The loads on the line are as follows: $P_1 = 1.2 \text{ kW}$, $P_2 = 3.6 \text{ kW}$, and $P_3 = 9.6 \text{ kW}$. Calculate the currents I_a, I_b, and I_n.

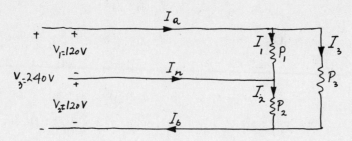

Fig. 3-32

▮ From the data:

$$I_1 = \frac{P_1}{V_1} = \frac{1.2 \times 10^3}{120} = 10 \text{ A} \qquad I_2 = \frac{P_2}{V_2} = \frac{3.6 \times 10^3}{120} = 30 \text{ A} \qquad I_3 = \frac{P_3}{V_3} = \frac{9.6 \times 10^3}{240} = 40 \text{ A}$$

$$I_a = I_1 + I_3 = 10 + 40 = 50 \text{ A} \qquad I_n = I_2 - I_1 = 30 - 10 = 20 \text{ A} \qquad I_b = I_2 + I_3 = 30 + 40 = 70 \text{ A}$$

3.91 A three-wire dc line supplying a resistive bank of loads is shown in Fig. 3-33. If the voltage between the terminals a and c is 240 V, determine the voltage between a and b.

▮ Combining the resistors across ac as an equivalent resistance, we have:

$$R_{ac} = 1.8 + \frac{(10 + 20)60}{10 + 20 + 60} + 2.2 = 24 \, \Omega$$

Thus

$$I_a = \frac{240}{24} = 10 \text{ A}$$

By current division:

$$I_1 = \frac{60}{30 + 60} \, 10 = 6.67 \text{ A}$$

Voltage drop across 1.8-Ω resistor is $1.8 \times 10 = 18$ V. Voltage drop across 10-Ω resistor is $10 \times 6.67 = 66.7$ V. Voltage across ab is $18 + 66.7 = 84.7$ V.

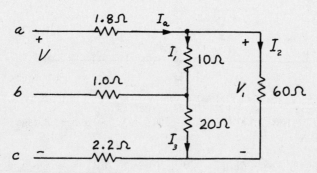

Fig. 3-33

3.92 Refer to the circuit of Fig. 3-33. If 240 V is now applied across the lines ab, what is the voltage across bc?

▮ In this case, the equivalent resistance R_{ab} becomes

$$R_{ab} = 1.8 + \frac{10(60 + 20)}{10 + 60 + 20} + 1.0 = 11.689 \, \Omega \qquad I_a = \frac{240}{11.689} = 20.53 \text{ A}$$

By current division:

$$I_2 = -I_3 = \frac{10}{10 + 80} \, 20.53 = 2.28 \text{ A}$$

Voltage across 20-Ω resistor is $2.28 \times 20 = 45.60$ V. Voltage across 1.0-Ω resistor is $20.53 \times 1 = 20.53$ V. Voltage across bc is $-(45.6 + 20.53) = -66.13$ V.

3.93 In the circuit of Fig. 3-33, with line *a* open, determine the resistance between the terminals *bc*.

$$R_{bc} = 1.0 + \frac{(10 + 60)20}{10 + 60 + 20} + 2.2 = 18.756\ \Omega$$

3.94 A 12-V battery is used to supply resistive loads at 12, 9, and 6 V, the respective currents being 4, 2, and 1 A. Design a suitable voltage divider.

▌ The voltage divider circuit is shown in Fig. 3-34. The total current supplied by the divider is $I_5 + I_6 = 2 + 1 = 3$ A. Let I_3 be 20 percent of the total divider current. Thus,

$$I_3 = 0.2 \times 3 = 0.6\ \text{A} \qquad I_2 = I_3 + I_6 = 0.6 + 1 = 1.6\ \text{A} \qquad I_1 = I_2 + I_5 = 1.6 + 2 = 3.6\ \text{A}$$

From Fig. 3-34,

$$I_3 R_3 = 6\ \text{V} \qquad \text{or} \qquad R_3 = \frac{6}{0.6} = 10\ \Omega$$

$$I_2 R_2 = 9 - 6 = 3\ \text{V} \qquad \text{or} \qquad R_2 = \frac{3}{1.6} = 1.875\ \Omega$$

$$I_1 R_1 = 12 - 9 = 3\ \text{V} \qquad \text{or} \qquad R_1 = \frac{3}{3.6} = 0.8333\ \Omega$$

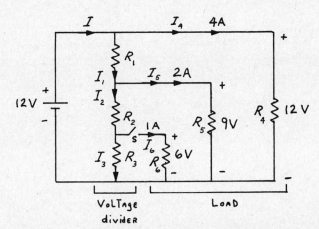

Voltage divider

Load

Fig. 3-34

3.95 Calculate the total power dissipated in the voltage divider when supplying the load shown in Fig. 3-34.

▌ From Prob. 3.94, $I = I_1 + I_4 = 3.6 + 4 = 7.6$ A. Power supplied from the battery is $P_{in} = VI = 12 \times 7.6 = 91.2$ W. Σ output power is $12I_4 + 9I_5 + 6I_6 = 12 \times 4 + 9 \times 2 + 6 \times 1 = 72$ W. P_{loss} is $91.2 - 72 = 19.2$ W.

3.96 Verify the result of Prob. 3.95 by adding the losses in the resistors R_1, R_2, and R_3 of the voltage divider of Fig. 3-34.

▌ From Prob. 3.94,

$$I_1^2 R_1 = (3.6)^2 0.8333 = 10.8\ \text{W} \qquad I_2^2 R_2 = (1.6)^2 1.875 = 4.8\ \text{W}$$

$$I_3^2 R_3 = (0.6)^2 10 = 3.6\ \text{W} \qquad \Sigma I^2 R = P_{loss} = 10.8 + 4.8 + 3.6 = 19.2\ \text{W}$$

which is the same as in Prob. 3.95.

3.97 For the voltage divider of Fig. 3-34, choose I_3 to be 60 percent of the total divider current and calculate the power loss in the voltage divider. Compare the result with that of Prob. 3.96.

▌ Proceeding as in Prob. 3.94,

$$I_3 = 0.6 \times 3 = 1.8\ \text{A} \qquad I_2 = I_3 + I_6 = 1.8 + 1 = 2.8\ \text{A} \qquad I_1 = I_2 + I_5 = 2.8 + 2 = 4.8\ \text{A}$$

$$R_3 = \frac{6}{1.8} = 3.333\ \Omega \qquad R_2 = \frac{3}{2.8} = 1.071\ \Omega \qquad R_1 = \frac{3}{4.8} = 0.625\ \Omega$$

$$P_{loss} = (4.8)^2 0.625 + (2.8)^2 1.071 + (1.8)^2 3.333 = 33.6\ \text{W}$$

which is much higher than the loss when I_3 was 20 percent of the divider current.

3.98 For the switch S open in Fig. 3-34, for the given values of R_4, R_5, and R_6 as in Prob. 3.94, and for the respective calculated values of R_1, R_2, and R_3, find the voltage across R_3.

▌ From the data of Prob. 3.94,

$$R_4 = \tfrac{12}{4} = 3\,\Omega \qquad R_5 = \tfrac{9}{2} = 4.5\,\Omega \qquad R_6 = \tfrac{6}{1} = 6\,\Omega$$

$$R_1 = 0.8333\,\Omega \qquad R_2 = 1.875\,\Omega \qquad \text{and} \qquad R_3 = 10\,\Omega$$

With S open, the total resistance across the battery becomes

$$R_T = \frac{R_4\{R_1 + [R_5(R_2 + R_3)]/(R_2 + R_3 + R_5)\}}{R_4 + R_1 + [R_5(R_2 + R_3)]/(R_2 + R_3 + R_5)}$$

$$= \frac{3\{0.8333 + [4.5(1.875 + 10)]/(10 + 1.875 + 4.5)\}}{3 + 0.8333 + [4.5(1.875 + 10)]/(10 + 1.875 + 4.5)} = 1.7326\,\Omega$$

$$I = \frac{12}{1.7326} = 6.926\,\text{A} \qquad I_1 = I - I_4 = 6.926 - 4 = 2.926\,\text{A}$$

By current division,

$$I_2 = I_3 = I_1 \frac{R_5}{R_2 + R_3 + R_5} = 2.926 \frac{4.5}{1.875 + 10 + 4.5} \doteq 0.804\,\text{A}$$

and
$$V_3 = I_3 R_3 = 0.804 \times 10 = 8.04\,\text{V}$$

3.99 With $R_4 = 3\,\Omega$, $R_5 = 4.5\,\Omega$, and $R_6 = 6\,\Omega$ in Fig. 3-34, find the voltage across R_3 with S open for the values of R_1, R_2, and R_3 calculated in Prob. 3.97.

▌ Proceeding as in Prob. 3.98, we have

$$R_T = \frac{3\{0.625 + [4.5(1.071 + 3.333)]/(4.5 + 1.071 + 3.333)\}}{3 + 0.625 + [4.5(1.071 + 3.333)]/(4.5 + 1.071 + 3.333)} = 1.461\,\Omega$$

$$I = \frac{12}{1.461} = 8.21\,\text{A} \qquad I_1 = I - I_4 = 8.21 - 4 = 4.21\,\text{A}$$

By current division,

$$I_2 = I_3 = 4.21 \frac{4.5}{4.5 + 1.071 + 3.333} = 2.127\,\text{A} \qquad V_3 = I_3 R_3 = 3.333 \times 2.127 = 7.09\,\text{V}$$

3.100 Define:

$$\text{Voltage regulation} \equiv \frac{(\text{no-load voltage}) - (\text{voltage on load})}{\text{voltage on load}}$$

Calculate the voltage regulation from the results of Probs. 3.98 and 3.99.

▌ From the results of Prob. 3.98:

$$\text{Voltage regulation} = \frac{8.04 - 6.0}{6.0} = 0.34 \text{ or } 34\%$$

From the results of Prob. 3.99:

$$\text{Voltage regulation} = \frac{7.09 - 6.0}{6.0} = 0.182 \text{ or } 18.2\%$$

3.101 Summarize the results of Probs. 3.94 through 3.100. What conclusions may be drawn from these results?

bleeder current I_b, %	loss, W	voltage regulation, %
20	19.2	34.0
60	33.6	18.2

Conclusion: Low bleeder current results in a low loss but a high voltage regulation whereas a high bleeder current results in a low voltage regulation but a high loss.

3.102 For the operation of a transistor amplifier, a power supply with a voltage divider shown in Fig. 3-35 is used. Calculate the values of R_1, R_2, and R_3.

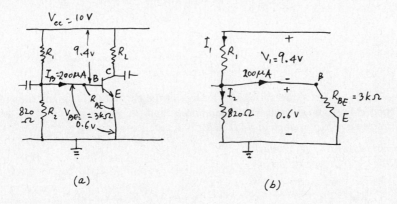

Fig. 3-35

▐ From Fig. 3-35,

$$V_2 = 25 \text{ V} \qquad V_3 = 25 \text{ V} \qquad \text{and} \qquad V_1 = 60 - (25 + 25) = 10 \text{ V}$$

Let I_3 be 10 percent of the maximum load current, which is 2 A. Therefore,

$$I_3 = 0.1 \times 2 = 0.2 \text{ A} \qquad I = I_3 + I_4 = 0.2 + 2 = 2.2 \text{ A} \qquad I_2 = I - I_1 = 2.2 - 1 = 1.2 \text{ A}$$

$$R_1 = \frac{V_1}{I} = \frac{10}{2.2} = 4.545 \ \Omega \qquad R_2 = \frac{V_2}{I_2} = \frac{25}{1.2} = 20.833 \ \Omega \qquad R_3 = \frac{V_3}{I_3} = \frac{25}{0.2} = 125.0 \Omega$$

3.103 A transistor base bias circuit and its equivalent are respectively shown in Fig. 3-36*a* and *b*. For the values shown in Fig. 3-36, determine R_1.

(a)   (b)   Fig. 3-36

▐ From Fig. 3-36*b*,

$$I_2 = \frac{V_{BE}}{R_2} = \frac{0.6}{820} = 731.7 \ \mu\text{A} \qquad I_1 = I_2 + I_B = 731.7 + 200 = 931.7 \ \mu\text{A}$$

$$V_1 = V_{cc} - V_{BE} = 10 - 0.6 = 9.4 \text{ V} \qquad R_1 = \frac{V_1}{I_1} = \frac{9.4}{931.7 \times 10^{-6}} = 10.09 \text{ k}\Omega$$

3.104 A dc generator having an internal resistance of 1 Ω supplies a resistive load shown in Fig. 3-37*a*. For what value of R_x will the load draw the maximum power from the generator?

▐ First we convert the delta-connected resistors to an equivalent wye, shown in Fig. 3-37*b*, which is finally reduced to the circuit of Fig. 3-37*c*. Therefore,

$$R_{\text{load}} = R_{ab} = \frac{10R_x}{10 + R_x} + \frac{10R_x}{10 + R_x} = \frac{20R_x}{10 + R_x}$$

For maximum power transfer (see Prob. 3-28),

$$R_g = R_{\text{load}} \qquad \text{or} \qquad 1 = \frac{20R_x}{10 + R_x}$$

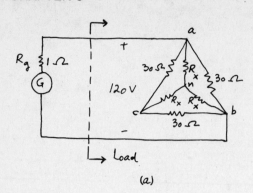

(a)

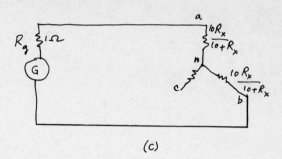

(c)

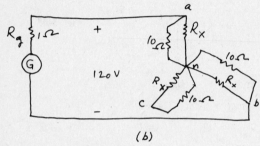

(b)

Fig. 3-37

Hence, $$R_x = \frac{10}{19}\ \Omega$$

3.105 For the three cases $R_x = 0$, $\frac{10}{19}\ \Omega$, and ∞, calculate the power absorbed by the load of Fig. 3-37a. The voltage across the load is 120 V.

▮ For $R_x = 0$, $R_\ell = 0$. Thus, in the absence of a load, $P_{\text{load}} = 0$.
For $R_x = \frac{10}{19}$, $R_\ell = R_g = [20(10/19)]/(10 + 10/19) = 1\ \Omega$. Thus, $P_{\text{load}} = 120^2/1 = 14.4$ kW.
For $R_x = \infty$, $R_\ell = 20\ \Omega$ and $P_{\text{load}} = 120^2/20 = 720$ W.

3.106 A wattmeter measures power by measuring the product of the current through and the voltage across a circuit. Two possible connections are shown in Fig. 3-38a and b; find the power measured in each case. The voltage coil of the wattmeter has a resistance of 9 kΩ and the resistance of the current coil is 6 Ω.

▮ For connection shown in Fig. 3-38a:

$$V = 150\text{ V} \qquad I = \frac{150}{6 + 150} = 0.9615\text{ A} \qquad P = VI = 144.23\text{ W}$$

For connection of Fig. 3-38b:

$$I - \frac{150}{6 + [9000(150)]/(9000 + 150)} = 0.9769\text{ A}$$

$$V = 150 - 0.9769 \times 6 = 144.14\text{ V} \qquad P = VI = 140.81\text{ W}$$

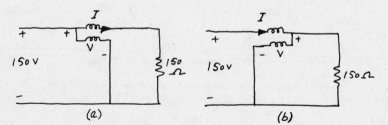

(a)   (b)   **Fig. 3-38**

3.107 What is the actual power dissipated in the 150-Ω resistor for the two connections shown in Fig. 3-38a and b?

▮ For Fig. 3-38a: $$P_{150\ \Omega} = I^2R = (0.9615)^2 150 = 138.68\text{ W}$$

For Fig. 3-38b: $$P_{150\ \Omega} = \frac{V^2}{R} = \frac{(144.14)^2}{150} = 138.51\text{ W}$$

3.108 How much power is absorbed by the wattmeter in the two connections of Fig. 3-38?

▋ For Fig. 3-38a:

$$P_c = I^2 R_c = (0.9615)^2 6 = 5.547 \text{ W} \qquad P_v = \frac{V^2}{R_v} = \frac{(150)^2}{9000} = 2.5 \text{ W} \qquad P_w = 5.547 + 2.5 = 8.047 \text{ W}$$

For Fig. 3-38b:

$$P_c = (0.9769)^2 6 = 5.726 \text{ W} \qquad P_v = \frac{(144.14)^2}{9000} = 2.308 \text{ W} \qquad P_w = 5.726 + 2.308 = 8.034 \text{ W}$$

3.109 For the interconnected resistors shown in Fig. 3-39a find the net resistance between the terminals 1 and 3.

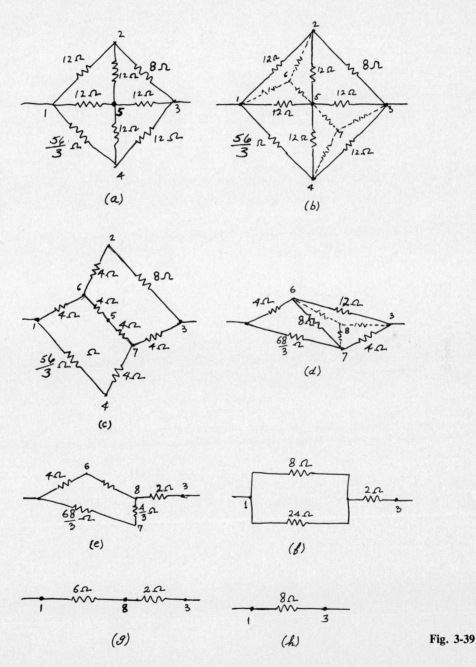

Fig. 3-39

▋ First, we convert the two delta-connected resistors to equivalent wyes, as shown in Fig. 3-39b. Subsequent reduction steps are shown in Fig. 3-39c through g. Finally, $R_{1-3} = 8 \, \Omega$.

3.110 Find the total resistance between points 1 and 2 shown in Fig. 3-40a.

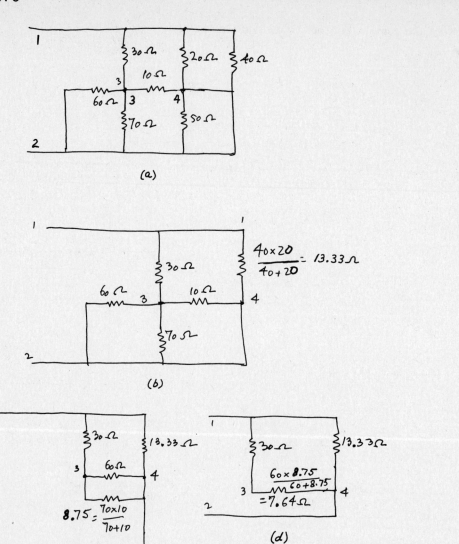

Fig. 3-40

▮ Notice that the 50-Ω resistor is short-circuited and the 20-Ω and 40-Ω resistors are in parallel so the network reduces to that of Fig. 3-40b.   Subsequent reduction steps are shown in Fig. 3-40c and a from which

$$R_{1-2} = \frac{13.33 \times 37.64}{13.33 + 37.64} = 9.844 \ \Omega$$

CHAPTER 4

Kirchhoff's Laws

4.1 Kirchhoff's voltage law (KVL) states that the algebraic sum of the voltages around any loop of a circuit is zero. Apply this law to the circuit shown in Fig. 4-1.

❚ The direction of current I is arbitrarily chosen as indicated in Fig. 4-1. The voltage across each resistor is assigned a polarity; it is understood that Ohm's law yields $V = IR$ if I enters the positive terminal of a resistor, and $V = -IR$ otherwise. Application of KVL to Fig. 4-1 leads to $V_1 + V_2 + V_3 - V = 0$, where $V_1 = IR_1$, $V_2 = IR_2$, and $V_3 = IR_3$.

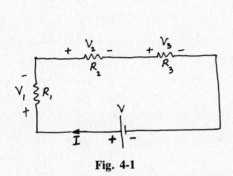

Fig. 4-1

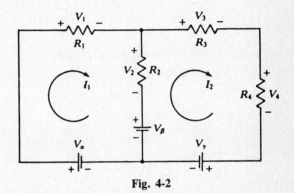

Fig. 4-2

4.2 Write the Kirchhoff's voltage equations for the two indicated loops of the network of Fig. 4-2. Assume polarities as marked. Also, express V_2 in terms of I_1, I_2, and R_2.

❚ Loop 1: $\quad -V_\alpha + V_1 + V_2 + V_\beta = 0$

Loop 2: $\quad -V_\beta - V_2 + V_3 + V_4 + V_\gamma = 0$

Voltage across R_2: $\quad V_2 = (I_1 - I_2)R_2$

4.3 Kirchhoff's current law (KCL) states that the algebraic sum of all currents leaving or of all currents entering any node of a circuit is zero. A node of a network is shown in Fig. 4-3, with currents flowing in the directions shown. Apply KCL to find the magnitude and direction of I.

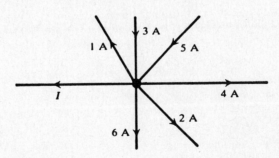

Fig. 4-3

❚ Assume the indicated direction for I: $\quad -I - 1 + 3 + 5 - 4 - 2 - 6 = 0$. Hence, $I = -5$ A; i.e., 5 A into the node.

4.4 Apply KVL to obtain an expression for the equivalent resistance formed by n resistances $R_1, R_2, \ldots, R_n$ connected in series.

❚ Let V be the voltage across the series circuit combination, I the current through it, and R_{es} the equivalent resistance. Then, from Ohm's law,

$$V = I(R_1 + R_2 + \cdots + R_n) = IR_{es} \quad \text{whence} \quad R_{es} = \sum_{k=1}^{n} R_k$$

4.5 Resistances $R_1, R_2, \ldots, R_n$ are connected in parallel. Obtain an expression for the equivalent resistance by using KCL.

❚ Let I be the total current into the parallel combination, V the voltage across it, and R_{ep} the equivalent resistance. Then, from KCL,

$$I = V\left(\frac{1}{R_1} + \frac{1}{R_2} + \cdots + \frac{1}{R_n}\right) = \frac{V}{R_{ep}} \qquad \text{or} \qquad \frac{1}{R_{ep}} = \sum_{k=1}^{n} \frac{1}{R_k}$$

4.6 If the voltages, currents, and resistances in a series circuit can be respectively transformed to currents, voltages, and conductances of a parallel circuit, such that the KVL equations of the series circuit go over into the KCL equations of the parallel circuit, then the circuits are said to be *duals* of each other. Construct the dual network for three resistors, R_1, R_2, and R_3, connected in series with a voltage source V.

❚ The network is shown in Fig. 4-4a. We draw the dual network, Fig. 4-4b, by replacing the series elements by parallel elements. The equations for the two networks are:

(a) $\quad V = IR_1 + IR_2 + IR_3$ $\qquad$ (b) $\quad I = \dfrac{V}{R_1} + \dfrac{V}{R_2} + \dfrac{V}{R_3} = VG_1 + VG_2 + VG_3$

where conductances G_1, G_2, and G_3 are the reciprocals of the respective resistances.

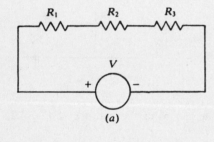

(a)

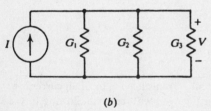

(b) $\qquad$ **Fig. 4-4**

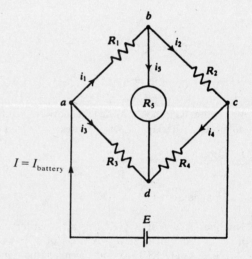

Fig. 4-5

4.7 A bridge circuit is shown in Fig. 4-5. With the currents as marked, write (a) Kirchhoff's current law at the four nodes and (b) Kirchhoff's voltage law around the loops *abda*, *bcdb*, and *adca*.

❚ (a) $\qquad$ Node a: $\quad I = i_1 + i_3$ $\qquad$ Node c: $\quad i_2 = I + i_4$

$\qquad\qquad$ Node b: $\quad i_1 = i_2 + i_5$ $\qquad$ Node d: $\quad 0 = i_3 + i_4 + i_5$

(b) $\qquad$ Loop *abda*: $\quad i_1 R_1 + i_5 R_5 = i_3 R_3$ $\qquad$ Loop *adca*: $\quad i_3 R_3 - i_4 R_4 = E$

$\qquad\qquad$ Loop *bcdb*: $\quad i_5 R_5 = i_2 R_2 + i_4 R_4$

4.8 For the circuit of Prob. 4.5, consider the special case of the balanced bridge $(i_5 = 0)$. (a) If $R_1 = 10\,\Omega$, $R_2 = 20\,\Omega$, and $R_3 = 30\,\Omega$, determine R_4. (b) If $E = 45\,\text{V}$, calculate the current supplied by the battery.

❚ (a) Since $i_5 = 0$, we have $i_1 = i_2$ and $i_3 = -i_4$. Also, nodes b and d are at the same potential. Thus,

$$i_1 R_1 = i_3 R_3 \qquad i_2 R_2 = i_1 R_2 = -i_4 R_4 = i_3 R_4$$

From the above we obtain

$$\frac{R_1}{R_2} = \frac{R_3}{R_4} \qquad \text{or} \qquad R_4 = \frac{R_2 R_3}{R_1} = \frac{(20)(30)}{10} = 60\,\Omega$$

(*b*) The effective resistance R_e across the battery becomes

$$R_e = \frac{(10+20)(30+60)}{10+20+30+60} = 22.5\,\Omega \quad \text{and} \quad I_{\text{battery}} = \frac{E}{R_e} = \frac{45}{22.5} = 2.0\,\text{A}$$

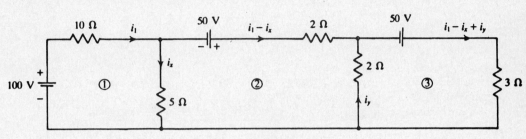

Fig. 4-6

4.9   Determine the currents i_x and i_y in the network shown in Fig. 4-6.

▐   On the basis of KCL, the currents in the remaining branches are also marked in Fig. 4-6.   By KVL for meshes 1, 2, and 3,

$$100 = 10i_1 + 5i_x \qquad 50 = 2(i_1 - i_x) - 2i_y - 5i_x \qquad 50 = 3(i_1 - i_x + i_y) + 2i_y$$

Solving these simultaneous equations yields $i_x = -3.87\,\text{A}$, $i_y = 0.51\,\text{A}$.   The negative sign on i_x implies that the actual current flows in the direction opposite to that given in Fig. 4.6.

4.10   This problem relates to the concept of *source transformation*.   Replace the voltage source v and its internal (series) resistance R_v in Fig. 4-7*a* by a current source i with internal (shunt) resistance R_i in Fig. 4-7*b*, such that the current through R remains unchanged.

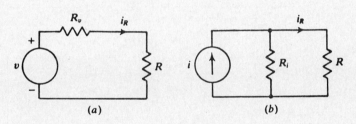

(*a*)   (*b*)   **Fig. 4-7**

▐   From Fig. 4-7*a*: $$i_R = \frac{v}{R_v + R}$$

From Fig. 4-7*b*: $$i_R = \frac{iR_i}{R_i + R}$$

Then, for equivalence: $$\frac{v}{R_v + R} = \frac{iR_i}{R_i + R}$$

which will hold if we take $i = v/R_v$ and $R_i = R_v$.

4.11   Find the current in, and the voltage across, the 2-Ω resistor in Fig. 4-8*a*.

▐   Using the results of Prob. 4.10, we transform the 5-A current source to a voltage source; the circuit then becomes as shown in Fig. 4-8*b*.   For the two loops, KVL gives

$$25 - 15I_1 - 10 + 3I_2 - 3I_1 = 0 \qquad 20 - 3I_2 + 3I_1 - 2I_2 = 0$$

which when solved yield $I_2 = 5\,\text{A}$ and $V_{ab} = (5)(2) = 10\,\text{V}$.

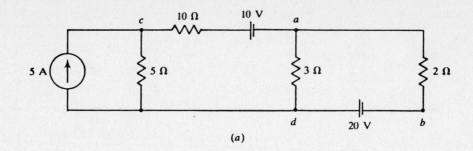

(a)

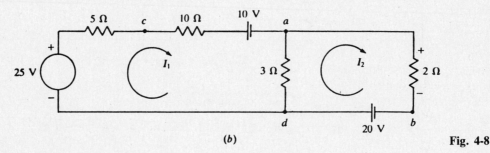

(b)

Fig. 4-8

4.12 Determine I of Fig. 4-9 by mesh analysis.

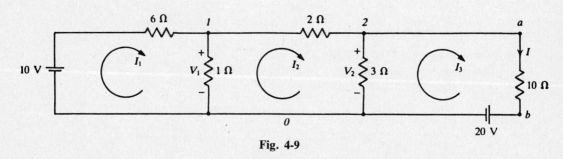

Fig. 4-9

▌ In terms of the three mesh currents I_1, I_2, and I_3 ($=I$) indicated in Fig. 4-9, we have

$$7I_1 - I_2 = 10 \qquad -I_1 + 6I_2 - 3I_3 = 0 \qquad -3I_2 + 13I_3 = -20$$

Solving for I_3 yields $\quad I_3 = I = -1.68\,\text{A}$.

4.13 Evaluate I of Fig. 4-9 by nodal analysis.

▌ Figure 4-9 can be redrawn so that the two principal nodes labeled 0 coincide. Choosing this single node 0 as the reference, we have the nodal equations

$$\frac{10 - V_1}{6} - \frac{V_1}{1} - \frac{V_1 - V_2}{2} = 0 \qquad \frac{V_1 - V_2}{2} - \frac{V_2}{3} - \frac{V_2 - 20}{10} = 0$$

from which $V_2 = 3.2\,\text{V}$. Hence,

$$I = \frac{V_2 - 20}{10} = -1.68\,\text{A}$$

4.14 A resistive network with voltage and current sources is shown in Fig. 4-10a. Determine the currents I_1 and I_2 by mesh analysis.

▌ To apply mesh analysis, we first transform the 10-A current source in parallel with the 5-Ω resistor to a $10 \times 5 = 50\,\text{V}$ voltage source in series with a 5-Ω resistor. Thus, we obtain the network of Fig. 4-10b, for which mesh equations are

$$35I_1 - 20I_2 = 50 \qquad -20I_1 + 50I_2 = -100$$

Solving, $\quad I_1 = 0.37\,\text{A} \quad$ and $\quad I_2 = -1.85\,\text{A}$.

4.15 Solve for I_1 and I_2 of the network of Fig. 4-10a by nodal analysis.

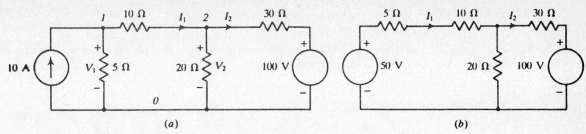

Fig. 4-10

▮ For nodal analysis, define the node voltages V_1 and V_2 as shown in Fig. 4-10a. At nodes 1 and 2, respectively, KCL gives

$$\frac{V_1}{5} + \frac{V_1 - V_2}{10} = 10 \qquad \frac{V_2}{20} + \frac{V_2 - 100}{30} = \frac{V_1 - V_2}{10}$$

which have the solution

$$V_1 = \tfrac{1300}{27} \text{ V} \qquad V_2 = \tfrac{400}{9} \text{ V}$$

Thus, $$I_1 = \frac{V_1 - V_2}{10} = \frac{10}{27} = 0.37 \text{ A} \qquad I_2 = \frac{V_2 - 100}{30} = \frac{-50}{27} = -1.85 \text{ A}$$

4.16 For the network of Fig. 4-10a, calculate the power supplied by the current source and by the voltage source. Verify that the sum of the powers from the two sources is the total power dissipated in all the resistances.

▮
$$\text{Power supplied by the 10-A source} = 10 \times V_1 = \frac{10(1300)}{27} = 481.48 \text{ W}$$

$$\text{Power supplied by the 100-V source} = 100(-I_2) = (100)(1.85) = 185 \text{ W}$$

$$\text{Total power supplied by the two sources} = 481.48 + 185 = 666.48 \text{ W}$$

$$\text{Power dissipated in the 5-}\Omega \text{ resistance} = \frac{V_1^2}{5} = \frac{1}{5}\left(\frac{1300}{27}\right)^2 = 463.65 \text{ W}$$

$$\text{Power dissipated in the 10-}\Omega \text{ resistance} = I_1^2 \times 10 = (0.37)^2(10) = 1.37 \text{ W}$$

$$\text{Power dissipated in the 20-}\Omega \text{ resistance} = \frac{V_2^2}{20} = \frac{1}{20}\left(\frac{400}{9}\right)^2 = 98.76 \text{ W}$$

$$\text{Power dissipated in the 30-}\Omega \text{ resistance} = I_2^2 \times 30 = (1.85)^2(30) = 102.67 \text{ W}$$

$$\text{Total power dissipated} = 463.65 + 1.37 + 98.76 + 102.67 = 666.45 \text{ W}$$

4.17 Determine the current I shown in Fig. 4-11.

▮ Without the values of the resistors, it is not possible to calculate the branch currents. However, the network within the shaded area may be viewed as a single node, at which KCL gives

$$2 - 3 - I - 4 = 0 \qquad \text{or} \qquad I = -5 \text{ A}$$

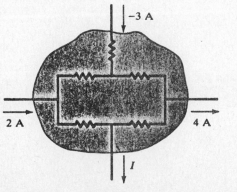

Fig. 4-11

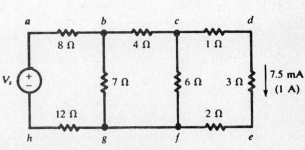

Fig. 4-12

4.18 For the ladder network shown in Fig. 4-12, find the source voltage V_s which results in a current of 7.5 mA in the 3-Ω resistor.

   I A current of 1 A will be assumed. The voltage necessary to produce 1 A is in the same ratio to 1 A as V_s is to 7.5 mA because of the linearity of the network.

$$V_{cf} = 1(1 + 3 + 2) = 6 \text{ V} \qquad I_{cf} = \tfrac{6}{6} = 1 \text{ A}$$

Then, by KCL,

$$I_{bc} = 1 + 1 = 2 \text{ A} \qquad v_{bg} = 2(4) + 6 = 14 \text{ V} \qquad I_{bg} = \tfrac{14}{7} = 2 \text{ A}$$

Again from KCL,

$$I_{ab} = 2 + 2 = 4 \text{ A} \qquad \text{and} \qquad V_{ah} = 4(8) + 14 + 4(12) = 94 \text{ V}$$

Now, scaling down,

$$\frac{V_{ah}}{1 \text{ A}} = \frac{V_s}{7.5 \text{ mA}} \qquad \text{whence} \qquad V_s = 0.705 \text{ V}$$

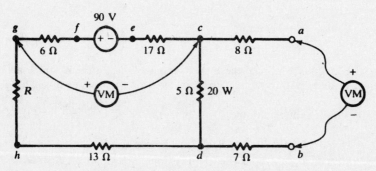

Fig. 4-13

4.19 Determine the readings of an ideal voltmeter connected in Fig. 4-13 to (*a*) terminals *a* and *b* and (*b*) terminals *c* and *g*. The average power in the 5-Ω resistor is 20 W.

   I
$$P = I^2(5) \qquad I = \sqrt{\frac{20}{5}} = \pm 2 \text{ A}$$

The direction of I through the 5-Ω resistor is determined by noting that the polarity of the 90-V source requires that the current pass from *d* to *c*. Thus *d* is positive with respect to *c* and $V_{dc} = (2)(5) = 10$ V.

(*a*) An *ideal* voltmeter indicates the voltage without drawing any current. It may be considered as having an infinite resistance. KVL applied to the closed-loop *acdba* results in

$$V_{ac} + V_{cd} + V_{db} + V_{ba} = 0 \qquad 0 - 10 + 0 - VM = 0 \qquad VM = -10 \text{ V}$$

   If the meter is of the digital type, it will indicate -10 V. A moving-coil galvanometer will try to go downscale, with the pointer stopping at the pin. If the leads are reversed, it will indicate 10 V. (And with its + lead at point *b*, it is known that *b* is 10 V positive with respect to *a*.)

(*b*) KVL applied to the path *cefgc* gives

$$V_{ce} + V_{ef} + V_{fg} + V_{gc} = 0 \qquad 2(17) - 90 + 2(6) + VM = 0 \qquad VM = 44 \text{ V}$$

   In this connection, the meter reads positive 44 V, indicating that point *g* is 44 V above point *c*.

4.20 Determine the current supplied by the 100-V battery in the circuit of Fig. 4-14.

   I With the currents marked in Fig. 4-14, the required current is $I_1 + I_2$. Writing the loop currents, for the loop 1241 we have

$$50 - 10I_1 - 10I_3 + 10I_2 = 0 \tag{1}$$

For the loop 2342 we have:

$$-10(I_1 - I_3) + 50 + 10(I_2 + I_3) + 10I_3 = 0 \tag{2}$$

For the loop 1431 (containing the 100-V battery) we get:

$$-10I_2 - 10(I_2 + I_3) + 100 - 10(I_1 + I_2) = 0 \qquad (3)$$

Solving for I_1 and I_2 in Eq. (3) yields

$$I_1 = \tfrac{25}{4}\,\text{A} \qquad \text{and} \qquad I_2 = \tfrac{5}{4}\,\text{A}$$

Hence,

$$I_1 + I_2 = \tfrac{25}{4} + \tfrac{5}{4} = 7.5\,\text{A}$$

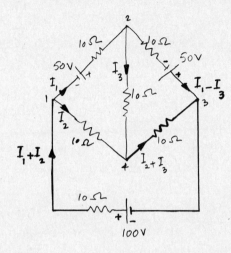

Fig. 4-14

4.21 How much power is consumed in the 10-Ω resistor across the terminals 2 and 4 in Fig. 4-14?

▮ Power = $I_3^2(10)$ W. From Eqs. (1) and (2) of Prob. 4.20 we have:

$$I_1 - I_2 + I_3 = 5 \qquad \text{and} \qquad I_1 - I_2 - 3I_3 = 5$$

Thus, $I_3 = 0$ and power $= 0$.

4.22 Determine the current I supplied by the battery to the resistive network shown in Fig. 4-15.

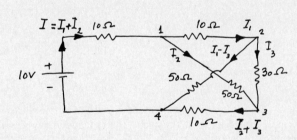

Fig. 4-15

▮ We apply KVL to the following loops:

Loop 1231: $\quad -10I_1 - 30I_3 + 50I_2 = 0$

Loop 2342: $\quad -30I_3 - 10(I_2 + I_3) + 50(I_1 - I_3) = 0$

Loop 1241: $\quad -10I_1 - 50(I_1 - I_3) + 10 - 10(I_1 + I_2) = 0$

Rewriting the above equations yields

$$-I_1 + 5I_2 - 3I_3 = 0 \qquad 5I_1 - I_2 - 9I_3 = 0 \qquad -7I_1 - I_2 + 5I_3 = -1$$

Solving for the currents we obtain

$$I_1 = \tfrac{1}{5}\,\text{A} \qquad I_2 = \tfrac{1}{10}\,\text{A} \qquad \text{and} \qquad I_3 = \tfrac{1}{10}\,\text{A}$$

Hence,

$$I = I_1 + I_2 = \frac{1}{5} + \frac{1}{10} = \frac{3}{10} = 0.3\,\text{A}$$

4.23 For the network shown in Fig. 4-16, calculate the power supplied (or absorbed) by each voltage source.

▮ Applying KVL to the loops, for the assumed directions of current flow we obtain

$$5I_1 - 100 + 50 - I_2 = 0 \qquad -200 + 10(I_1 + I_2) + 5I_1 - 100 = 0$$

or

$$5I_1 - I_2 = 50 \qquad 15I_1 + 10I_2 = 300$$

Thus

$$I_1 = 12.3077 \text{ A} \qquad I_2 = 11.538 \text{ A} \qquad I_1 + I_2 = 23.8457 \text{ A}$$

$$P_{100 \text{ V}} = I_1(100) = 12.3077 \times 100 = 1230.77 \text{ W (supplied)}$$

$$P_{50 \text{ V}} = I_2(50) = 11.538 \times 50 = 576.9 \text{ W (supplied)}$$

$$P_{200 \text{ V}} = (I_1 + I_2)200 = 23.8457 \times 200 = 4769.14 \text{ W (supplied)}$$

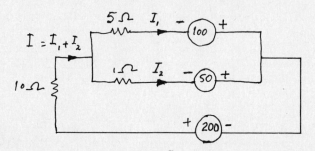

Fig. 4-16

4.24 Determine the power absorbed by each resistor of the network of Fig. 4-16. Verify that the sum of the powers absorbed by the resistors is equal to the total power supplied by the sources.

▮

$$P_{10 \, \Omega} = (I_1 + I_2)^2 10 = 23.8457^2 \times 10 = 5686.17 \text{ W}$$

$$P_{5 \, \Omega} = I_1^2(5) = 12.3077^2 \times 5 = 757.40 \text{ W}$$

$$P_{1 \, \Omega} = I_2^2(1) = 11.538^2 \times 1 = 133.12 \text{ W}$$

$$\sum P_{\text{absorbed}} = 6576.70 \text{ W}$$

From Prob. 4.23, $\sum P_{\text{supplied}} = 6576.81$ W.

4.25 Solve for the current in the 2-Ω resistor of the network of Fig. 4-17 by mesh analysis.

▮ There are three meshes, and we define I_k as the current flowing in mesh k ($k = 1, 2, 3$). Then, KVL gives

$$6I_1 + 4(I_1 - I_2) = 20 \qquad 5I_2 + 3(I_2 - I_3) + 4(I_2 - I_1) = 0 \qquad 2I_3 + 3(I_3 - I_2) = 10$$

Solving for I_3, the current in the 2-Ω resistor, we get $I_3 = 2.98$ A.

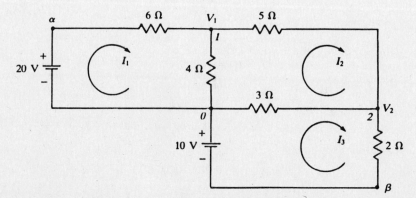

Fig. 4-17

4.26 By nodal analysis, obtain the current in the 2-Ω resistor of the network of Fig. 4-17.

❚ In Fig. 4-17 we identify the principal nodes 0, 1, and 2, and choose node 0 as the reference node. Next, we define the voltages of nodes 1 and 2 with respect to node 0: $V_{10} = V_1$, $V_{20} = V_2$. We now apply KCL at nodes 1 and 2 to obtain

$$\frac{20 - V_1}{6} + \frac{V_2 - V_1}{5} - \frac{V_1}{4} = 0 \qquad \frac{V_1 - V_2}{5} - \frac{V_2 + 10}{2} - \frac{V_2}{3} = 0$$

Solving for V_2, we get $V_2 = -4.046$ V. Hence, the current in the 2-Ω resistor is

$$I_3 = \frac{V_2 + 10}{2} = \frac{-4.046 + 10}{2} = 2.98 \text{ A}$$

and is directed from node 2 to node β. This result is in agreement with that of Prob. 4.25.

4.27 Using mesh analysis, find the currents I_1 and I_2 in the network of Fig. 4-18a.

❚ Transforming the current sources to voltage sources yields the circuit of Fig. 4-18b, for which the mesh equations become

$$100 - 4I_1 - 10I_1 - 2(I_1 - I_2) - 40 = 0 \qquad 40 - 2(I_2 - I_1) - I_2 - 10(I_2 - I_3) = 0 \qquad -20 - 10(I_3 - I_2) = 0$$

These equations simplify to

$$16I_1 - 2I_2 = 60 \qquad -2I_1 + 13I_2 - 10I_3 = 40 \qquad -10I_2 + 10I_3 = -20$$

Solving for I_1 and I_2 yields $I_1 = 5$ A and $I_2 = 10$ A.

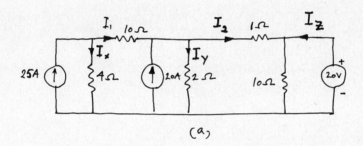

(a)

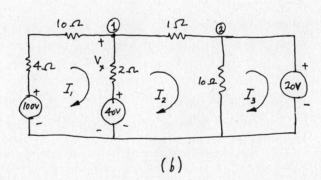

(b)

Fig. 4-18

4.28 Apply nodal analysis to the network of Fig. 4-18b and solve for the currents I_1 and I_2.

❚ Let V_x be the voltage shown at node 1. At this node, we have

$$\frac{V_x - 100}{14} + \frac{V_x - 40}{2} + \frac{V_x - 20}{1} = 0$$

Thus,
$$22V_x = 660 \qquad \text{or} \qquad V_x = 30 \text{ V}$$

$$I_1 = \frac{100 - V_x}{14} = \frac{100 - 30}{14} = 5 \text{ A} \qquad I_2 = \frac{V_x - 20}{1} = \frac{30 - 20}{1} = 10 \text{ A}$$

4.29 Calculate the power supplied by each source to the entire network of Fig. 4-18a. Determine if all sources supply power.

Since $I_1 = 5\,\text{A}$ (from Prob. 4.27), from Fig. 4-18a,

$$25 = I_1 + I_x = 5 + I_x \qquad \text{or} \qquad I_x = 20\,\text{A}$$

$$V_{4\,\Omega} = 20 \times 4 = 80\,\text{V} \qquad P_{25\,\text{A}} = 25 \times 80 = 2000\,\text{W}$$

Similarly,

$$20 = I_y - I_1 + I_2 = I_y - 5 + 10 \qquad \text{or} \qquad I_y = 15\,\text{A}$$

$$V_{2\,\Omega} = 15 \times 2 = 30\,\text{V} \qquad P_{20\,\text{A}} = 30 \times 20 = 600\,\text{W}$$

and

$$I_z + I_2 - \tfrac{20}{10} = 0 \qquad \text{or} \qquad I_z + 10 - 2 = 0$$

or

$$I_z = -8\,\text{A} \qquad P_{20\,\text{V}} = -8 \times 20 = -160\,\text{W}$$

So the 20-V source absorbs power and the other sources supply power.

4.30 Calculate the power absorbed by each resistor of the network of Fig. 4-18a and determine the total power absorbed by all the resistors.

▮ From the results of Probs. 4.28 and 4.29,

$$P_{4\,\Omega} = (I_x)^2 4 = (20)^2 4 = 1600\,\text{W}$$
$$P_{10\,\Omega} = (I_1)^2 10 = (5)^2 10 = 250\,\text{W}$$
$$P_{2\,\Omega} = (I_y)^2 2 = (15)^2 2 = 450\,\text{W}$$
$$P_{1\,\Omega} = (I_2)^2 1 = (10)^2 1 = 100\,\text{W}$$
$$P_{10\,\Omega} = \frac{(20)^2}{10} = 40\,\text{W}$$
$$\overline{\qquad\qquad\qquad\qquad} $$
$$\sum P = 2440\,\text{W}$$

4.31 Using the result of Prob. 4.29, verify the result of Prob. 4.30.

▮ $\sum P_{\text{supplied}} = \sum P_{\text{absorbed}} = \sum P$ or $P_{25\text{A}} + P_{20\text{A}} + P_{20\text{V}} = \sum P$ or $2000 + 600 - 160 = 2440 = \sum P$ which is the same as in Prob. 4.30.

4.32 Solve for the current in the 5-Ω resistor of the circuit shown in Fig. 4-19a.

▮ Writing the mesh equations, we have

$$90 - 8I_1 - 8(I_1 - I_2) = 0 \qquad 4I_2 + 8(I_2 - I_1) + 8(I_2 - I_3) = 0 \qquad 6I_3 + 5I_3 + 8(I_3 - I_2) = 0$$

These equations simplify to

$$8I_1 - 4I_2 = 45 \qquad -2I_1 + 5I_2 - 2I_3 = 0 \qquad -8I_2 + 19I_3 = 0$$

Solving for I_3 yields $I_3 = 1.5\,\text{A}$.

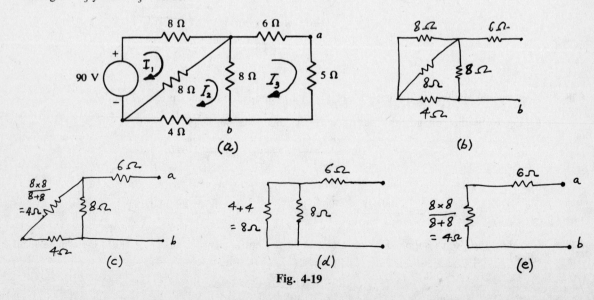

Fig. 4-19

4.33 In the circuit of Fig. 4-19a find the voltage across *ab* if the 5-Ω resistor is removed and the terminals *ab* are open-circuited.

▎ Writing the mesh equations we obtain

$$90 - 8I_1 - 8(I_1 - I_2) = 0 \quad \text{and} \quad 8I_2 + 4I_2 + 8(I_2 - I_1) = 0$$

or

$$16I_1 - 8I_2 = 90 \qquad -8I_1 + 20I_2 = 0$$

Thus,

$$I_2 = 2.8125 \text{ A} \quad \text{and} \quad V_{ab} = I_2(8) = 2.8125 \times 8 = 22.5 \text{ V}$$

4.34 With the 5-Ω resistor removed from the circuit of Fig. 4-19a, the 90-V source is short-circuited. Determine the resistance that will be measured across *ab*.

▎ With the voltage source short-circuited, the network reduction is shown in Fig. 4-19b through *e*. Hence, $R_{ab} = 10 \, \Omega$.

4.35 Refer to the results of Probs. 4.33 and 4.34. Using the open-circuit voltage V_{ab} of Prob. 4.33 in series with the short-circuit resistance R_{ab} of Prob. 4.34, connect the 5-Ω resistor across *ab* as shown in Fig. 4-20. Find the current in the 5-Ω resistor. Verify that the result agrees with that of Prob. 4.32.

▎ From Fig. 4-21

$$I = \frac{22.5}{10 + 5} = 1.5 \text{ A}$$

which is the same as in Prob. 4.32.

The network to the left of *ab* is known as the *Thévenin equivalent circuit* (see Chap. 5).

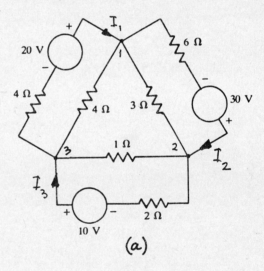

(a)

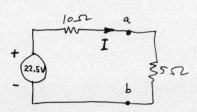

Fig. 4-20

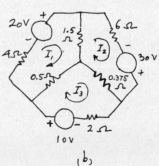

(b)

Fig. 4-21

4.36 Calculate the current in the 2-Ω resistor of the network shown in Fig. 4-21a.

▎ First we transform the delta-connected resistors to an equivalent wye to obtain the network of Fig. 4-21b. Writing the mesh equations, we get

$$6I_1 - 1.5I_2 - 0.5I_3 = 20 \qquad -1.5I_1 + 7.875I_2 - 0.375I_3 = 30 \qquad -0.5I_1 - 0.375I_2 + 2.875I_3 = 10$$

Solving for I_3, which is the current in the 2-Ω resistor, yields $I_3 = 5 \text{ A}$.

4.37 Determine the power delivered by the 30-V source in the network of Fig. 4-21a.

∎
$$P_{30\,V} = 30I_2 \text{ W}$$

Solving for I_2 from the mesh equations of Prob. 4.36, we obtain $I_2 = 5$ A. Thus, $P_{30\,V} = 30 \times 5 = 150$ W.

4.38 How much current flows through the 1-Ω resistor of the network of Fig. 4-21a?

∎ From Fig. 4-21a,
$$V_{1\Omega} + V_{2\Omega} = 10 \quad \text{or} \quad V_{1\Omega} = 10 - V_{2\Omega} = 10 - 5 \times 2 = 0 \quad \text{or} \quad I_{1\Omega} = 0 \text{ A}$$

4.39 Find the value of R in Fig. 4-22 such that the power supplied by the 100-V source to the network is the same as the power supplied by the 5-A source.

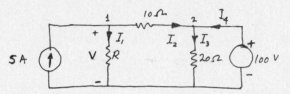

Fig. 4-22

∎ At node 1:
$$5 = \frac{V}{R} + \frac{V - 100}{10} \tag{1}$$

At node 2:
$$\frac{V - 100}{10} + I_4 = \frac{100}{20} = 5 \tag{2}$$

For equal power:
$$100I_4 = 5V \tag{3}$$

From Eqs. (1) and (2) we obtain:
$$\frac{V}{R} + \frac{V}{10} = 15 \tag{4}$$

$$I_4 + \frac{V}{10} = 15 \tag{5}$$

Thus,
$$I_4 = \frac{V}{R} \tag{6}$$

Finally, Eqs. (3) and (6) yield
$$\frac{100\,V}{R} = 5V \quad \text{or} \quad R = 20 \ \Omega$$

4.40 Find the current in the 10-Ω resistor of the circuit shown in Fig. 4-23a.

∎ By source transformation we obtain the circuit of Fig. 4-23b for which we have
$$50 = 30I_1 - 30I_2 \qquad -100 = -30I_1 + 80I_2 \qquad \text{or} \qquad -50 = 50I_2$$

Hence, $I_2 = I_{10\,\Omega} = -1$ A.

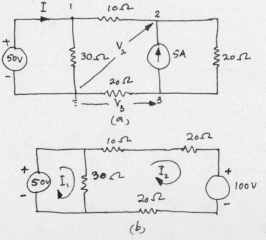

(a)

(b)

Fig. 4-23

4.41 Solve Prob. 4.40 by using nodal analysis only.

❚ With the voltages V_2 and V_3 and the current I defined in Fig. 4-23a, for node 1 we have

$$I = \frac{50}{30} + \frac{50 - V_2}{10} \qquad \text{or} \qquad 30I + 3V_2 = 200 \tag{1}$$

For node 2 we have

$$\frac{50 - V_2}{10} + 5 = \frac{V_2 - V_3}{20} \qquad \text{or} \qquad 3V_2 - V_3 = 200 \tag{2}$$

Finally, for node 3 we obtain

$$\frac{V_2 - V_3}{20} = 5 + \frac{V_3}{20} \qquad \text{or} \qquad V_2 - 2V_3 = 100 \tag{3}$$

Solving for V_2 from Eqs. (2) and (3) yields $V_2 = 60$ V.

Hence, $$I_{10\,\Omega} = \frac{50 - V_2}{10} = \frac{50 - 60}{10} = -1 \text{ A}$$

4.42 In the circuit of Fig. 4-23a calculate the current through the 50-V voltage source and the voltage across the 5-A current source.

❚ From Eq. (1) of Prob. 4.41, we have $I = \frac{1}{30}(200 - 3V_2) = \frac{1}{30}(200 - 3 \times 60) = \frac{2}{3}$ A = current through the 50-V voltage source.
From Eq. (3) $2V_3 = V_2 - 100 = 60 - 100 = -40$ or $V_3 = -20$ V.
Voltage across the 5-A source $= V_2 - V_3 = 60 - (-20) = 80$ V.

4.43 For the circuit of Fig. 4-23a verify that the total power dissipated in the resistors equals the total power supplied by the two sources.

❚ $$P_{\text{supplied}} = P_{50\,\text{V}} + P_{5\,\text{A}} = 50 \times \tfrac{2}{3} + 5 \times 80 = 433.33 \text{ W}$$

$$P_{\text{dissipated}} = \frac{(50)^2}{30} + (1)^2 10 + \frac{(20)^2}{20} + \frac{(80)^2}{20} = 433.33 \text{ W} = P_{\text{supplied}}$$

4.44 Find the power dissipated in the 20-Ω resistor of the circuit of Fig. 4-24a by using nodal analysis.

❚ To use nodal analysis we convert to the 10-V voltage source to an equivalent current source to obtain the circuit of Fig. 4-24b. Defining the node voltages V_1 and V_2 as shown, we obtain:

For node 1, $$1 = \frac{V_1}{10} + \frac{V_1}{4} + \frac{V_1 - V_2}{20}$$

For node 2, $$\frac{V_1 - V_2}{20} = \frac{V_2}{8} + 2$$

Solving for V_1 and V_2 yields $V_1 = 1.11$ V and $V_2 = -11.11$ V.

Thus, $$I_{20\,\Omega} = \frac{V_1 - V_2}{20} = \frac{1.11 - (-11.11)}{20} = 0.611 \text{ A} \qquad \text{and} \qquad P_{20\,\Omega} = (0.611)^2 20 = 7.466 \text{ W}$$

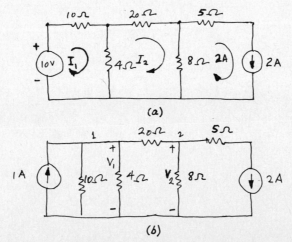

(a)

(b)

Fig. 4-24

4.45 By applying only mesh equations to the circuit of Fig. 4-24a find the power dissipated in the 20-Ω resistor.

▌ Writing the mesh equations for the currents I_1 and I_2 in Fig. 4-24a, we obtain

$$10 = 14I_1 - 4I_2 \qquad 0 = -4I_1 + 32I_2 - 2(8)$$

Solving for I_2 yields

$$I_2 = \tfrac{33}{54} \text{ A} \qquad \text{or} \qquad P_{20\,\Omega} = \left(\frac{33}{54}\right)^2 20 = 7.469 \text{ W}$$

4.46 Solve for the power supplied by the 12-V source shown in Fig. 4-25a by network reduction, source transformation, and finally using KVL and KCL.

▌ The network reduction is shown in Fig. 4-25b and c and the source transformation in Fig. 4-25d.
From KVL, for the mesh current I we have

$$12 - I(1) + 2 - I(0.8) - I(1.6) - 1(0.8) = 0 \qquad \text{or} \qquad I = \frac{13.2}{3.4} = 3.88 \text{ A}$$

and
$$P_{12\,\text{V}} = 12I = 12 \times 3.88 = 46.56 \text{ W}$$

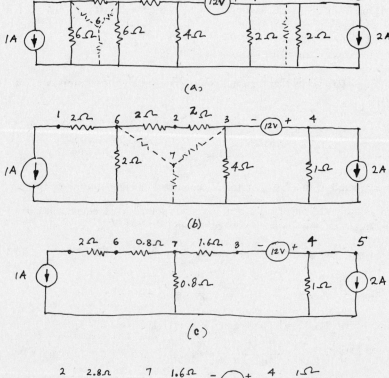

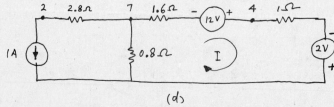

Fig. 4-25

4.47 Solve for the power supplied by the 12-V source of Fig. 4-25a using the following steps: First convert the two current sources to voltage sources. Then use network reduction and, finally, obtain the power by applying KVL and KCL. Verify that the result is the same as in Prob. 4.46.

▌ The source transformations and the network reduction are shown in Fig. 4-26a. Thus we obtain the circuit shown in Fig. 4-26b. The mesh equations become

$$-6 = 15I_1 - 2I_2 \qquad 12 = 4.67I_2 - 2I_1 - 2I_3 \qquad 4 = 4I_3 - 2I_2$$

Solving for I_2 gives $\quad I_2 = \tfrac{198}{51} = 3.88 \text{ A} \quad$ or $\quad P_{12\,\text{V}} = 12 \times 3.88 = 46.56 \text{ W}$.

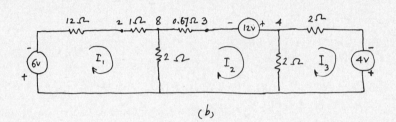

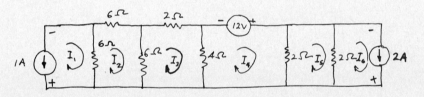

(b)

Fig. 4-26

4.48   Without using network reduction and source transformation, solve Prob. 4-46 by using only mesh equations.

▮ First, we redraw the circuit (Fig. 4-27), identify the mesh currents, and write the corresponding equations. Notice from Fig. 4-27 that $I_1 = -1\,\text{A}$ and $I_6 = 2\,\text{A}$. For the remaining currents, we have

$$-6(-1) + 18I_2 - 6I_3 = 0 \qquad \text{or} \qquad 3I_2 - I_3 = -1 \tag{1}$$

$$-6I_2 + 12I_3 - 4I_4 = 0 \qquad \text{or} \qquad -3I_2 + 6I_3 - 2I_4 = 0 \tag{2}$$

$$-4I_3 + 6I_4 - 2I_5 = 12 \qquad \text{or} \qquad -2I_3 + 3I_4 - I_5 = 6 \tag{3}$$

$$-2I_4 + 4I_5 = 2(2) \qquad \text{or} \qquad -I_4 + 2I_5 = 2 \tag{4}$$

Solving for I_4 yields $I_4 = \frac{198}{51} = 3.882\,\text{A}$ and $P_{12\,\text{V}} = 12 \times 3.882 = 46.59\,\text{W}$.

Fig. 4-27

4.49   Find the power delivered (or absorbed) by each source shown in Fig. 4-27.

▮ Solving for I_2 and I_5 from Eqs. (1) through (4) of Prob. 4-48, we obtain $I_2 = 0.117\,\text{A}$ and $I_5 = 2.94\,\text{A}$. Voltage across the 1-A source $= (1 + 0.117)6 = 6.702\,\text{V}$. $P_{1\,\text{A}} = 1 \times 6.702 = 6.702\,\text{W} = P_{\text{supplied}}$. Voltage across the 2-A source $= (2 - 2.94)2 = -1.88\,\text{V}$. $P_{2\,\text{A}} = 2(-1.88) = -3.76\,\text{W} = P_{\text{absorbed}}$; $P_{12\,\text{V}} = 45.59\,\text{W} = P_{\text{supplied}}$ (calculated earlier).

4.50   For the circuit of Fig. 4-27, verify that the net power supplied from the sources equals the total power dissipated in the resistors.

$$P_{\text{dissipated}} = (I_2 - I_1)^2 6 + I_2^2(6) + (I_3 - I_2)^2 6 + I_3^2(2) + (I_4 - I_3)^2 4 + (I_5 - I_4)^2 2 + (I_5 - I_6)^2 2$$

$$= (0.117 + 1)^2 6 + 6(0.117)^2 + (1.35 - 0.117)^2 6 + (1.35)^2 2 + (3.88 - 1.35)^2 4 + (2.94 - 3.88)^2 2$$

$$+ (2.94 - 2)^2 2 = 49.47\,\text{W}$$

$P_{\text{supplied}} = 45.59 + 6.702 - 3.76 = 48.53\,\text{W}$;   error $= 0.94\,\text{W}$ due to roundoff.

4.51   A network excited only by current sources is shown in Fig. 4-28. Determine the current through the 2-Ω resistor.

▮ Defining the node voltages V_1 and V_2 as shown, we have:

For node 1:

$$10 = \frac{V_1}{4} + 5 + \frac{V_1 - V_2}{2}$$

or

$$3V_1 - 2V_2 = 20 \tag{1}$$

For node 2:
$$5 + \frac{V_1 - V_2}{2} = \frac{V_2}{8} + \frac{V_2}{16}$$

or
$$-8V_1 + 11V_2 = 80 \qquad (2)$$

Solving for V_1 and V_2 yields

$$V_1 = 22.353 \text{ V} \qquad V_2 = 23.529 \text{ V}$$

$$I_{2\,\Omega} = I = \frac{V_1 - V_2}{2} = \frac{22.353 - 23.529}{2} = -0.588 \text{ A} .$$

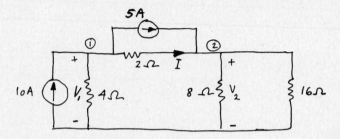

Fig. 4-28

4.52 Verify the power balance for the network of Fig. 4-28.

❚ Power balance implies that

$$P_\text{supplied from sources} = P_\text{absorbed by resistors}$$

$$P_{10\,A} = 10V_1 = 10 \times 22.353 = 223.53 \text{ W}$$

$$V_{5\,A} = V_2 - V_1 = 23.529 - 22.353 = 1.176 \text{ V}$$

$$P_{5\,A} = 5V_{5\,A} = 5 \times 1.176 = 5.88 \text{ W}$$

$$\sum P_\text{supplied} = 223.53 + 5.88 = 229.41 \text{ W}$$

$$P_{4\,\Omega} = \frac{V_1^2}{4} = \frac{(22.353)^2}{4} = 124.9141 \text{ W}$$

$$P_{2\,\Omega} = I^2(2) = (0.588)^2 2 = 0.6915 \text{ W}$$

$$P_{8\,\Omega} = \frac{V_2^2}{8} = \frac{(23.529)^2}{8} = 69.2017 \text{ W}$$

$$P_{16\,\Omega} = \frac{V_2^2}{16} = \frac{(23.529)^2}{16} = 34.60 \text{ W}$$

$$\sum P_\text{absorbed} = 229.41 \text{ W} = \sum P_\text{supplied}$$

4.53 For the network shown in Fig. 4-29, write a set of mesh equations to solve for the currents I_1, I_2, and I_3.

❚ The mesh equations are:
$$V_1 = (R_1 + R_4 + R_5)I_1 - R_5 I_2 - R_4 I_3 \qquad V_2 = -R_5 I_1 + (R_2 + R_5 + R_6)I_2 - R_6 I_3$$
$$V_3 = -R_4 I_1 - R_6 I_2 + (R_3 + R_4 + R_6)I_3$$

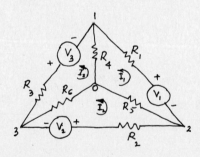

Fig. 4-29

4.54 In Fig. 4-29 if all the voltages are equal, each being 10 V, and if all the resistances are also equal, each being 5 Ω, find the currents I_1, I_2, and I_3.

❚ From symmetry we have $I_1 = I_2 = I_3 = I$.
  Thus, we may use only one of the three mesh equations of Prob. 4.53. Hence, $V = 3RI - RI - RI = RI$, or $10 = 5I$, or $I = \frac{10}{5} = 2 \text{ A}$.

4.55 In Fig. 4-29, let the resistors R_4 and R_5 be short-circuited, $R_2 = R_3 = 5\,\Omega$, $R_6 = 10\,\Omega$, and $V_2 = 2V_3 = 10$ V. What is the current in R_6?

▮ Since R_4 and R_5 are short-circuited, the circuit reduces to that shown in Fig. 4-30. So, we use only the last two of the mesh equations of Prob. 4.53. With the given numerical values we obtain

$$10 = (5 + 10)I_2 - 10I_3 = 15I_2 - 10I_3 \quad 5 = -10I_2 + (5 + 10)I_3 = -10I_2 + 15I_3 \quad \text{or} \quad I_2 = \tfrac{8}{5}\,\text{A} \quad \text{and} \quad I_3 = \tfrac{7}{5}\,\text{A}$$

Current in $R_6 = I = I_3 - I_2 = \tfrac{7}{5} - \tfrac{8}{5} = -0.2$ A.

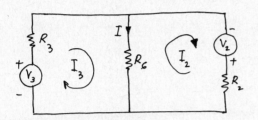

Fig. 4-30

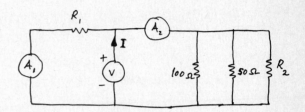

Fig. 4-31

4.56 The two ideal ammeters in the circuit of Fig. 4-31 read a current of 8 A each. The power absorbed by the resistors is 3200 W. Determine V, R_1, and R_2.

▮ Writing the nodal equation gives

$$\frac{V}{100} + \frac{V}{50} + \frac{V}{R_2} = 8 \quad \text{or} \quad I = 8 + 8 = 16 \text{ A}$$

Now, since $P = VI = \Sigma\, I^2R$, we have

$$3200 = V(8 + 8) \quad \text{or} \quad V = 200 \text{ V} \qquad \frac{V}{R_1} = 8 \text{ A} \quad \text{or} \quad R_1 = \frac{V}{8} = \frac{200}{8} = 25\,\Omega$$

Finally,

$$\frac{V}{R_2} = 8 - \frac{V}{100} - \frac{V}{50} \quad \text{or} \quad \frac{200}{R_2} = 8 - \tfrac{200}{100} - \tfrac{200}{50} = 2 \text{ A} \quad \text{or} \quad R_2 = \tfrac{200}{2} = 100\,\Omega$$

4.57 Find the ratio I_2/I_s for the circuit shown in Fig. 4-32.

▮ Writing the nodal and mesh equations, we obtain, respectively,

$$I_s = \frac{V}{R_1} + I_2 \qquad V + \mu V = I_2R_2 = V(1 + \mu) \tag{1}$$

or

$$V = \frac{I_2R_2}{1 + \mu} \tag{2}$$

Substituting Eq. (2) into Eq. (1) yields

$$I_s = I_2\left[\frac{R_2}{R_1(1 + \mu)} + 1\right] \quad \text{or} \quad \frac{I_2}{I_s} = \frac{(1 + \mu)R_1}{R_2 + (1 + \mu)R_1}$$

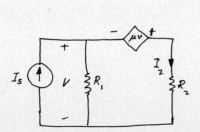

Fig. 4-32

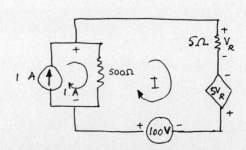

Fig. 4-33

4.58 Determine the total power dissipated in the two resistors of the circuit of Fig. 4-33.

▌ Since the voltage across the 5-Ω resistor is V_R,

$$I = \frac{V_R}{5} \tag{1}$$

Now writing the mesh equation we have

$$100 = 500(I - 1) + V_R - 5V_R \tag{2}$$

Substituting Eq. (1) into Eq. (2) yields

$$500 + 100 = 500\,\frac{V_R}{5} + V_R - 5V_R \quad \text{or} \quad V_R = \tfrac{600}{96} = 6.25 \text{ V} \quad \text{and} \quad I = \frac{6.25}{5} = 1.25 \text{ A}$$

$$P_{500\,\Omega} = (I - 1)^2 500 = (1.25 - 1)^2 500 = 31.25 \text{ W} \qquad P_{5\,\Omega} = \frac{(V_R)^2}{5} = \frac{(6.25)^2}{5} = 7.8125 \text{ W}$$

Total power dissipated = 39.0625 W.

4.59 Verify that the power calculated in Prob. 4.58 is the same as the total power supplied by the two sources.

▌ $\qquad V_{1\,A} = (-I + 1)500 = (-1.25 + 1)500 = -125 \text{ V} \qquad P_{5V_R} = 5V_R(I) = 5 \times 6.25 \times 1.25 = 39.0625 \text{ W}$

$\qquad P_{1\,A} = V_{1\,A}(1) = (-125)1 = -125 \text{ W} \qquad\qquad P_{100\,V} = 100(I) = 100 \times 1.25 = 125 \text{ W}$

$\Sigma\,P_{\text{supplied}} = -125 + 39.0625 + 125 = 39.0625$ W, which is the same as in Problem 4.58. Notice that the 1-A current source absorbs power.

4.60 If the power dissipated in the 12-Ω resistor of Fig. 4-34 is 147 W, what is the value of the source voltage V_s?

▌ Since $\quad P_{12\,\Omega} = 147 \text{ W} = I^2(12), \quad I = \sqrt{\frac{147}{12}} = 3.5 \text{ A}.$
Combining the 16-Ω and 4-Ω resistors in parallel and solving for I_1 yields

$$V_s = \left(8.8 + \frac{16 \times 4}{16 + 4}\right)I_1 \quad \text{or} \quad I_1 = \frac{V_s}{12} \quad \text{and} \quad V_x = 8.8I_1 = \frac{8.8V_s}{12} \text{ V}$$

With $\quad I = 3.5 \text{ A}\quad$ (calculated above), we apply nodal analysis to node 1 to obtain

$$\frac{V_x}{7.3} = 3.5 + \frac{V}{14} = \frac{1}{7.3}\frac{8.8V_s}{12} = 0.1V_s$$

Finally, for the mesh containing the 12-Ω resistor, we have

$$I(8.2 + 12 + 5.8 + 14) - \frac{V_x}{7.3}14 = 0 \quad \text{or} \quad 3.5(40) = \frac{14V_x}{7.3} = 14(0.1V_s) \quad \text{or} \quad V_s = 100 \text{ V}$$

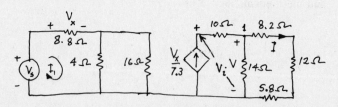

Fig. 4-34

4.61 In the circuit of Fig. 4-34, calculate the current through the voltage source and the voltage across the controlled-current source.

▌ As determined in Prob. 4.60, the current through the voltage source is

$$I_1 = \frac{V_s}{12} = \frac{100}{12} = 8.33 \text{ A}$$

The voltage across the controlled-current source is

$$V_i = V_{10\,\Omega} + V_{14\,\Omega} = 10\,\frac{V_x}{7.3} + 14\left(\frac{V_x}{7.3} - I\right) = 10(0.1V_s) + 14(0.1V_s - I) = 10 \times 0.1 \times 100 + 14(0.1 \times 100 - 3.5) = 191 \text{ V}$$

4.62 Verify that the total power supplied by the two sources in Fig. 4-34 equals the total power absorbed by the resistors.

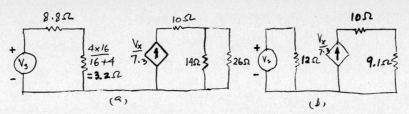

Fig. 4-35

▮ From the results of Prob. 4.60 and 4.61,

$$P_{\text{supplied}} = V_s I_1 + V_i \frac{V_x}{7.3} = 100 \times 8.33 + 191 \times 0.1 \times 100 = 2743 \text{ W}$$

To determine the power absorbed by the resistors we reduce the network shown in Fig. 4-35a and b. Since $V_s = 100$ V and $V_x/7.3 = 0.1 V_s = 10$ A,

$$P_{\text{absorbed}} = \frac{(100)^2}{12} + (10)^2(10 + 9.1) = 2743 \text{ W}$$

which is the same as the power supplied.

4.63 Determine the power supplied (or absorbed) by the controlled-voltage source in the network of Fig. 4-36.

▮ Defining the node voltage V_1 (Fig. 4-36), the nodal equation becomes:

$$2 + \frac{V_1 - 4}{2} + \frac{V_1 - 3V_R}{5} = 0 \quad \text{and} \quad V_R = V_1 - 4$$

Solving for V_1 yields $V_1 = -24$ V. Now,

$$I = \frac{3V_R - V_1}{5} = \frac{3(V_1 - 4) - V_1}{5} = \frac{3(-24 - 4) - (-24)}{5} = -12 \text{ A}$$

$$V_R = -24 - 4 = -28 \text{ V} \qquad P_{3V_R} = 3V_R I = 3(V_1 - 4)I = 3(-24 - 4)(-12) = 1008 \text{ W}$$

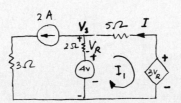

Fig. 4-36

4.64 Solve Prob. 4.63 by using mesh analysis.

▮ Let the mesh current be I_1. Then, the corresponding mesh equation becomes

$$4 + V_R - 5I_1 - 3V_R = 0 \quad \text{or} \quad 5I_1 = 4 - 2V_R \quad \text{but} \quad V_R = -2(I_1 + 2)$$

Thus, $$5I_1 = 4 + 4(I_1 + 2) \quad \text{or} \quad I_1 = 12 = -I$$

Hence, $$I = -12 \text{ A} \qquad V_R = -2(12 + 2) = -28 \text{ V} \quad \text{and} \quad P_{3V_R} = 3(-28)(-12) = 1008 \text{ W}$$

4.65 Determine the open-circuit voltage (across the terminals ab) with the polarities as marked in the circuit of Fig. 4-37.

▮ For the mesh we have $I = 3$ A, $V_{4\Omega} = 4I = 12$ V, and $V_{ab} = 20 - V_{4\Omega} = 20 - 12 = 8$ V.

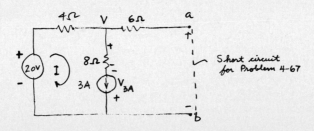

Fig. 4-37

4.66 What is the voltage across the 3-A current source in Fig. 4-37?

❚ $$-V_{3\,A} = V_{ab} - V_{8\,\Omega} = 8 - 3 \times 8 = -16 \quad \text{or} \quad V_{3\,A} = 16 \text{ V}$$

4.67 In the circuit of Fig. 4-37 if the terminals ab are short-circuited, determine the current through the short circuit.

❚ With the short circuit, we write the nodal equation as

$$\frac{20 - V}{4} = 3 + \frac{V}{6} \quad \text{or} \quad V = \tfrac{24}{5} \text{ V} \quad \text{and} \quad I_{\text{short-circuit}} = \frac{V}{6} = \frac{24}{5 \times 6} = 0.8 \text{ A}$$

4.68 Solve for the current I_1 shown in the network of Fig. 4-38a.

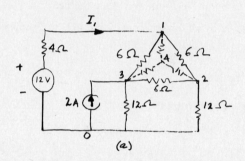

(a)

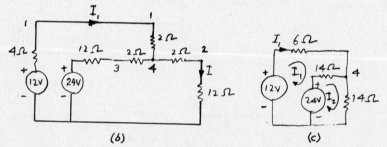

(b)   (c)   **Fig. 4-38**

❚ First, we change the current source to a voltage source and transform the 6-Ω delta-connected resistors to an equivalent wye, shown in Fig. 4-38b, which is then reduced to the network of Fig. 4-38c. For this network, the mesh equations become

$$12 - 6I_1 - 14I_1 + 14I_2 - 24 = 0 \quad \text{or} \quad -12 = 20I_1 - 14I_2 \tag{1}$$

and $$24 - 14I_2 - 14I_2 + 14I_1 = 0 \quad \text{or} \quad 24 = -14I_1 + 28I_2 \tag{2}$$

From Eqs. (1) and (2), $I_1 = 0$ A

4.69 The circuit of Fig. 4-38a is redrawn in Fig. 4-39. Using only nodal equations, find the current I_2.

❚ At node 1:

$$\frac{12 - V_1}{4} = \frac{V_1 - V_3}{6} + \frac{V_1 - V_2}{6} \quad \text{or} \quad 7V_1 - 2V_2 - 2V_3 = 36 \tag{1}$$

At node 2: $$\frac{V_1 - V_2}{6} = \frac{V_2}{12} + \frac{V_2 - V_3}{6} \quad \text{or} \quad 2V_1 - 5V_2 + 2V_3 = 0 \tag{2}$$

At node 3: $$\frac{V_1 - V_3}{6} + 2 + \frac{V_2 - V_3}{6} = \frac{V_3}{12} \quad \text{or} \quad -2V_1 - 2V_2 + 5V_3 = 24 \tag{3}$$

Solving for V_2 from Eqs. (1), (2), and (3) yields $V_2 = \tfrac{72}{7}$ V. Hence,

$$I_2 = \frac{V_2}{12} = \frac{72}{12 \times 7} = \frac{6}{7} \text{ A}$$

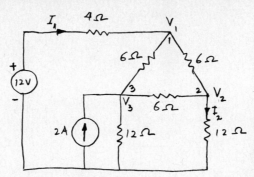

Fig. 4-39

4.70 Determine the total power dissipated by all the resistors of Fig. 4-39 and show that the entire power is supplied by the 2-A current source.

▌ From Eqs. (1), (2), and (3) of Prob. 4.69 we have

$$V_1 = 12 \text{ V} \qquad V_2 = \tfrac{72}{7} \text{ V} \qquad \text{and} \qquad V_3 = \tfrac{96}{7} \text{ V}$$

Since $V_1 = 12 \text{ V}$, $I_1 = 0 \text{ A}$, $P_{4\,\Omega} = 0$.

Power in the remaining seven resistors becomes:

$$\sum P_{\text{dissipated}} = \tfrac{1}{6}[(V_1 - V_3)^2 + (V_1 - V_2)^2 + (V_2 - V_3)^2] + \frac{(V_2)^2}{12} + \frac{(V_3)^2}{12}$$

$$= \tfrac{1}{6}[(12 - \tfrac{96}{7})^2 + (12 - \tfrac{72}{7})^2 + (\tfrac{72}{7} - \tfrac{96}{7})^2] + \tfrac{1}{12}(\tfrac{72}{7})^2 + \tfrac{1}{12}(\tfrac{96}{7})^2 = 27.428 \text{ W}$$

Voltage across the 2-A source,

$$V_3 = \tfrac{96}{7} \text{ V} \qquad P_{2\text{ A}} = \tfrac{96}{7} \times 2 = 27.428 \text{ W}$$

which is the same as the total dissipated power. Since $I_1 = 0$, $P_{12\text{ V}} = 12 \times I_1 = 0$.

4.71 Since I_1 in Fig. 4-39 is zero, the 12-V source may be disconnected (by open-circuiting). Verify by network reduction that $I_2 = \tfrac{6}{7}$ A.

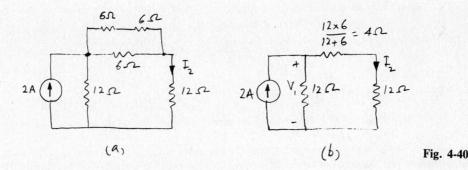

(a)   (b)   **Fig. 4-40**

▌ Network reduction is shown in Fig. 4-40a and b. With the node voltage defined in Fig. 4-40b, we have

$$2 = \frac{V_1}{12} + \frac{V_1}{12 + 4} = \frac{7}{48} V_1 \qquad \text{or} \qquad V_1 = \tfrac{96}{7} \text{ V}$$

Hence,

$$I_2 = \frac{V_1}{4 + 12} = \frac{96}{7 \times 16} = \frac{6}{7} \text{ A}$$

4.72 Using nodal analysis, find the voltage across the 10-A current source in the circuit of Fig. 4-41.

▌ Let the node voltages be V_1, V_2, and V_3, as shown in Fig. 4-41. At the three respective nodes we have:

$$\frac{10 - V_1}{5} = \frac{V_1 - V_3}{10} + \frac{V_1 - V_2}{10} \qquad \text{or} \qquad 4V_1 - V_2 - V_3 = 20 \qquad\qquad (1)$$

$$\frac{V_1 - V_2}{10} = \frac{V_2}{10} + \frac{V_2 - V_3}{10} \quad \text{or} \quad V_1 - 3V_2 + V_3 = 0 \tag{2}$$

$$\frac{V_1 - V_3}{10} + \frac{V_2 - V_3}{10} = \frac{V_3}{5} + 10 \quad \text{or} \quad V_1 + V_2 - 4V_3 = 100 \tag{3}$$

Solving for V_3 from Eqs. (1), (2), and (3) gives $V_3 = -\frac{204}{7}$ V, which is the required voltage.

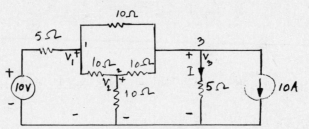

Fig. 4-41

4.73 In the circuit of Fig. 4-41, transform the 10-V source to a current source and the wye-connected 10-Ω resistors to an equivalent delta. Thus calculate the voltage across the 10-A source.

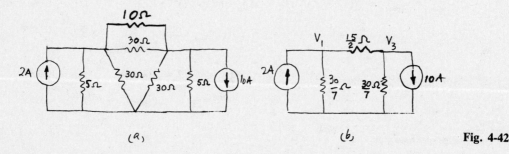

Fig. 4-42

▮ The source transformation and the equivalent circuits are shown in Fig. 4-42a and b. From Fig. 4-42b we obtain:

For node 1: $\qquad 2 = \dfrac{V_1}{30/7} + \dfrac{V_1 - V_3}{15/2} \quad \text{or} \quad 60 = 11V_1 - 4V_3$

For node 2: $\qquad \dfrac{V_1 - V_3}{15/2} = \dfrac{V_3}{30/7} + 10 \quad \text{or} \quad -300 = -4V_1 + 11V_3$

Solving for V_3 yields $V_3 = -\frac{204}{7}$ V, which is consistent with the result obtained earlier.

4.74 For the circuit of Fig. 4-41, verify that the total power absorbed by all the resistors is the same as the net power supplied by the two sources.

▮ From the results of Prob. 4.72, we have

$$V_1 = -\tfrac{36}{7} \text{ V} \qquad V_2 = -\tfrac{80}{7} \text{ V} \qquad V_3 = -\tfrac{204}{7} \text{ V}$$

$$\sum P_{\text{absorbed by resistors}} = \frac{[10 - (-36/7)]^2}{5} + \frac{[-36/7 - (-204/7)]^2}{10}$$

$$+ \frac{[-36/7 - (-80/7)]^2}{10} + \frac{(-80/7)^2}{10} + \frac{[-80/7 - (-204/7)]^2}{10} + \frac{(-204/7)^2}{5} = 321.71 \text{ W}$$

$$\sum P_{\text{supplied by sources}} = P_{10\,\text{A}} + P_{10\,\text{V}} = 10 \times \frac{204}{7} + \frac{10[10 - (-36/7)]}{5} = 321.71 \text{ W}$$

4.75 Find the current in each of the resistors of the circuit shown in Fig. 4-43.

▮ For node 1: $\qquad 9 = \dfrac{V_1 - V_2}{4} + \dfrac{V_1}{5} + \dfrac{V_1 - V_2 - 32}{2} \quad \text{or} \quad 19V_1 - 15V_2 = 500$

For node 2:
$$4 + \frac{V_1 - V_2}{4} + \frac{V_1 - V_2 - 32}{2} = \frac{V_2}{10} \quad \text{or} \quad 15V_1 - 17V_2 = 240$$

Solving for V_1 and V_2 yields $V_1 = 50$ V, $V_2 = 30$ V. Hence,

$$I_1 = \frac{V_1}{5} = \frac{50}{5} = 10 \text{ A} \qquad I_2 = \frac{V_1 - V_2 - 32}{2} = \frac{50 - 30 - 32}{2} = -6 \text{ A}$$

$$I_3 = \frac{V_1 - V_2}{4} = \frac{50 - 30}{4} = 5 \text{ A} \quad \text{and} \quad I_4 = \frac{V_2}{10} = \frac{30}{10} = 3 \text{ A}$$

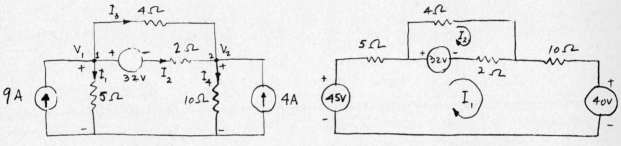

Fig. 4-43   Fig. 4-44

4.76 Transform the two current sources in the circuit of Fig. 4-43 to voltage sources and find the current in the 4-Ω resistor.

▌ The transformed circuit is shown in Fig. 4-44, for which we have:

$$45 - 32 - 40 = 17I_1 - 2I_2 \quad \text{or} \quad -27 = 17I_1 - 2I_2 \quad \text{and} \quad 32 = -2I_1 + 6I_2$$

Solving for I_2 yields $I_2 = 5$ A.

4.77 In the circuit of Fig. 4-45, determine the node voltages V_1, V_2, and V_3.

▌ The node equations yield

$$9 + \frac{V_1 - V_2}{1} + \frac{V_1}{50} = 0 \qquad \frac{V_1 - V_2}{1} = \frac{V_2}{15} + \frac{V_2}{20} + \frac{V_2 - V_3}{2} \qquad \frac{V_2 - V_3}{2} = \frac{V_3}{47} + \frac{V_3 - 170}{4}$$

Solving for the node voltages V_1, V_2, and V_3 yields

$$V_1 = 50 \text{ V} \qquad V_2 = 60 \text{ V} \qquad V_3 = 94 \text{ V}$$

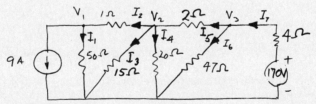

Fig. 4-45

4.78 Solve for the power balance in the network of Fig. 4-45.

▌ With the currents marked in Fig. 4-45 and using the results of Prob. 4-77, we have:

$$I_1 = \frac{V_1}{50} = \frac{50}{50} = 1 \text{ A} \qquad I_2 = \frac{V_2 - V_1}{1} = \frac{60 - 50}{1} = 10 \text{ A} \qquad I_3 = \frac{V_2}{15} = \frac{60}{15} = 4 \text{ A} \qquad I_4 = \frac{V_2}{20} = \frac{60}{20} = 3 \text{ A}$$

$$I_5 = \frac{V_3 - V_2}{2} = \frac{94 - 60}{2} = 17 \text{ A} \qquad I_6 = \frac{V_3}{47} = \frac{94}{47} = 2 \text{ A} \qquad I_7 = \frac{170 - V_3}{4} = \frac{170 - 94}{4} = 19 \text{ A}$$

$$\sum P_{\text{resistors}} = 50(I_1)^2 + 1(I_2)^2 + 15(I_3)^2 + 20(I_4)^2 + 2(I_5)^2 + 47(I_6)^2 + 4(I_7)^2$$

$$= 50(1)^2 + 1(10)^2 + 15(4)^2 + 20(3)^2 + 2(17)^2 + 47(2)^2 + 4(19)^2 = 2780 \text{ W}$$

$$\sum P_{\text{sources}} = 170(I_7) + 9(-V_1) = 170 \times 19 - 9 \times 50 = 2780 \text{ W}$$

Notice that the 9-A current source absorbs power.

4.79 Calculate the current in each resistor of the network of Fig. 4-46.

$$I_{10\,\Omega} = I_1 = \tfrac{20}{10} = 2\,\text{A} \qquad I_{1\,\Omega} = I_2 = \frac{20-10-9}{1} = 1\,\text{A}$$

$$I_{20\,\Omega} = I_3 = \frac{20-50-10}{20} = -2\,\text{A} \qquad I_{5\,\Omega} = I_4 = \tfrac{10}{5} = 2\,\text{A} \qquad I_{2\,\Omega} = I_5 = \tfrac{10}{2} = 5\,\text{A}$$

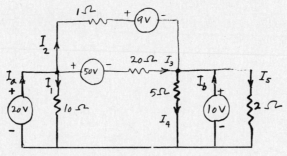

Fig. 4-46

4.80 Determine the currents through each voltage source of the circuit of Fig. 4-46.

$$I_{20\,\text{v}} = I_a = I_1 + I_2 + I_3 = 2 + 1 - 2 = 1\,\text{A}$$

$$I_{50\,\text{v}} = I_3 = -2\,\text{A} \qquad I_{9\,\text{v}} = I_2 = 1\,\text{A}$$

$$I_{10\,\text{v}} = I_b = -I_3 + I_4 + I_5 - I_2 = 2 + 2 + 5 - 1 = 8\,\text{A}$$

4.81 Which of the sources supply power and which absorb power in the circuit of Fig. 4-46? Determine the total power absorbed by the resistors.

$$P_{20\,\text{v}} = 20(I_a) = 20(1) = 20\,\text{W (supplied)} \qquad P_{50\,\text{v}} = 50(-I_3) = 50(2) = 100\,\text{W (supplied)}$$

$$P_{9\text{v}} = 9(-I_2) = 9(-1) = -9\,\text{W (absorbed)} \qquad P_{10\,\text{v}} = 10(I_b) = 10(8) = 80\,\text{W (supplied)}$$

Total power absorbed by the resistors $= 20 + 100 - 9 + 80 = 191\,\text{W}$.

4.82 An operational amplifier is schematically represented in Fig. 4-47a, and Fig. 4-47b shows the corresponding equivalent circuit. For the ideal model assume $I_+ = I_- = 0$ and $V_+ = V_-$. Draw the equivalent circuit of the inverting operational amplifier shown in Fig. 4-47c.

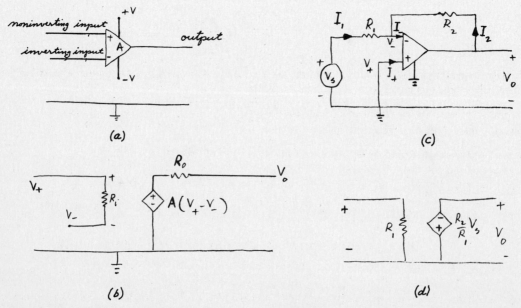

Fig. 4-47

❙ For the circuit of Fig. 4-47c we have

$$I_1 + I_2 = I_- = 0 \quad \text{or} \quad \frac{V_s - V_-}{R_1} + \frac{V_0 - V_-}{R_2} = 0 \tag{1}$$

Now $V_- = V_+ = 0$ (since V_+ is grounded). Thus Eq. (1) becomes:

$$\frac{V_s}{R_1} + \frac{V_0}{R_2} = 0 \quad \text{or} \quad V_0 = -\frac{R_2}{R_1}V_s$$

Hence, we obtain the equivalent circuit of Fig. 4-47d.

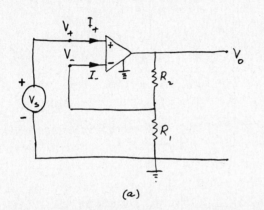
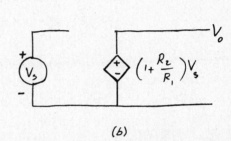

(a) (b) **Fig. 4-48**

4.83 Draw the equivalent circuit of the ideal noninverting operational amplifier shown in Fig. 4-48a.

❙ Since $V_- = V_+ = V_s$ and $I_- = 0,$ we have

$$\frac{V_s}{R_1} + \frac{V_s - V_0}{R_2} = 0$$

Solving for V_0 yields $V_0 = (1 + R_2/R_1)V_s.$ Hence, we obtain the equivalent circuit of Fig. 4-48b.

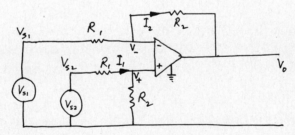

Fig. 4-49

4.84 The circuit shown in Fig. 4-49 responds to the difference of two input signals. Find an expression for V_0 and, hence, show that this circuit is a differential amplifier.

❙ Since the operational amplifier is ideal, we have

$$V_- = V_{s1} - I_2 R_1 = V_{s1} - R_1 \frac{V_{s1} - V_0}{R_1 + R_2}$$

and, by voltage division,

$$V_+ = \frac{R_2}{R_1 + R_2} V_{s2} \quad \text{but} \quad V_- = V_+$$

Thus,

$$V_{s1} - R_1 \frac{V_{s1} - V_0}{R_1 + R_2} = \frac{R_2}{R_1 + R_2} V_{s2}$$

Solving for V_0 yields $V_0 = (R_2/R_1)(V_{s2} - V_{s1}).$

4.85 For the operational amplifier circuit of Fig. 4-50 determine V_0. All voltages shown are with respect to ground.

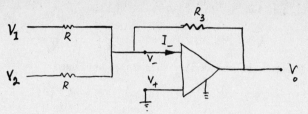

Fig. 4-50

▐ Since $I_- = 0$ and $V_- = V_+ = 0$, the nodal equation becomes

$$\frac{V_1}{R} + \frac{V_2}{R} + \frac{V_0}{R_3} = 0 \quad \text{or} \quad V_0 = -\left(\frac{R_3}{R} V_1 + \frac{R_3}{R} V_2\right) = -\frac{R_3}{R}(V_1 + V_2)$$

4.86 The equivalent circuit of an operational amplifier circuit is shown in Fig. 4-51. Determine its input resistance.

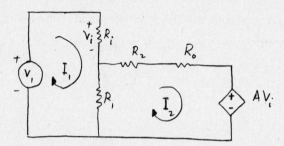

Fig. 4-51

▐ Writing the loop equations we have:

$$V_1 = V_i + R_1(I_1 - I_2) = (R_i + R_1)I_1 - R_1 I_2 \tag{1}$$

or $$-AV_i = -AR_i I_1 = -R_1 I_1 + (R_1 + R_2 + R_0)I_2 \qquad I_2 = \frac{R_1 - AR_i}{R_1 + R_2 + R_0} I_1 \tag{2}$$

Substituting Eq. (2) into Eq. (1) yields

$$V_1 = \left(R_i + R_1 - R_1 \frac{R_1 - AR_i}{R_1 + R_2 + R_0}\right)I_1$$

or the input resistance is

$$\frac{V_1}{I_1} = R_i + R_1\left(1 - \frac{R_1 - AR_i}{R_1 + R_2 + R_0}\right) = R_i + \frac{(R_2 + R_0 + AR_i)R_1}{R_1 + R_2 + R_0}$$

4.87 In the circuit of Fig. 4-52, find the currents through each resistor.

▐ Let the required currents be I_1, I_2, and I_3 as shown. The nodal equations may then be written as:

$$4 = 6I_1 + I_1 + I_2 = 6\frac{V_1}{2} + \frac{V_1}{2} + \frac{V_1 - 20}{3} \quad \text{or} \quad V_1 = \frac{64}{23} \text{ V}$$

Hence,

$$I_1 = \frac{V_1}{2} = \frac{64}{23 \times 2} = \frac{32}{23} \text{ A}$$

$$I_2 = \frac{V_1 - 20}{3} = \frac{(64/23) - 20}{3} = -\frac{132}{23} \text{ A}$$

$$I_3 = \frac{20}{4} = 5 \text{ A}$$

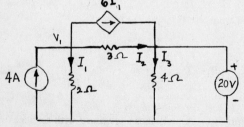

Fig. 4-52

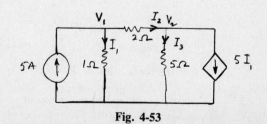

Fig. 4-53

4.88 Evaluate the currents through the resistors of the circuit shown in Fig. 4-53.

▌ Writing the nodal equations we obtain

$$5 = I_1 + I_2 = \frac{V_1}{1} + \frac{V_1 - V_2}{2} \qquad \frac{V_1 - V_2}{2} = I_2 = I_3 + 5I_1 = \frac{V_2}{5} + 5\frac{V_1}{1}$$

which, respectively, simplify to

$$3V_1 - V_2 = 10 \qquad 45V_1 = -7V_2$$

Thus,
$$V_1 = 1.06 \text{ V} \qquad V_2 = -6.82 \text{ V}$$

and
$$I_1 = \frac{V_1}{1} = \frac{1.06}{1} = 1.06 \text{ A} \qquad I_2 = \frac{V_1 - V_2}{2} = \frac{1.06 - (-6.82)}{2} = 3.94 \text{ A}$$

$$I_3 = \frac{V_2}{5} = \frac{-6.82}{5} = -1.364 \text{ A}$$

4.89 Find k in the circuit of Fig. 4-54 such that the power dissipated in the 2-Ω resistor does not exceed 50 W.

▌ Since $P_{2\,\Omega} = 2(I_1)^2 \leq 50 \text{ W}$, we have $I_1 \leq \sqrt{\frac{50}{2}} = 5 \text{ A}$ and $V_1 = 2I_1 \leq 10 \text{ V}$. With the critical values, the nodal equations are:

$$6 + I_2 = I_1 = 5 \quad \text{or} \quad I_2 = -1 \text{ A} = \frac{16 - kI_1 - V_1}{4} = \frac{16 - 5k - 10}{4} \quad \text{or} \quad -4 = 6 - 5k \quad k = 2$$

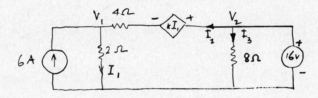

Fig. 4-54

4.90 For the value of k determined in Prob. 4.89, determine the power supplied by each source of the circuit of Fig. 4-54.

▌
$$P_{6\,\text{A}} = 6(V_1) = 6 \times 10 = 60 \text{ W} \qquad P_{kI_1} = kI_1(-I_2) = 2 \times 5 \times 1 = 10 \text{ W}$$

$$P_{16\,\text{V}} = 16(I_2 + I_3) = 16(-1 + \tfrac{16}{8}) = 16 \text{ W}$$

4.91 Calculate the power dissipated in the resistors of the circuit of Fig. 4-54 and verify the power balance in the circuit.

▌
$$P_{2\,\Omega} = (I_1)^2 2 = (5)^2 2 = 50 \text{ W} \qquad P_{4\,\Omega} = (I_2)^2 4 = (1)^2 4 = 4 \text{ W}$$

$$P_{8\,\Omega} = (I_3)^2 8 = (2)^2 8 = 32 \text{ W} \qquad \sum P_{\text{dissipated}} = 86 \text{ W}$$

From Prob. 4.90, $\sum P_{\text{supplied}} = 60 + 10 + 16 = 86 \text{ W}$.

4.92 Determine the node voltages V_1, V_2, V_3, and V_4 shown in the circuit of Fig. 4-55.

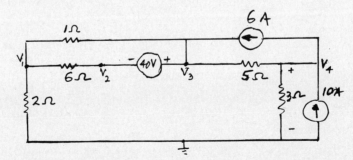

Fig. 4-55

▌ Writing the nodal equations we have

$$\frac{V_1}{2} + \frac{V_1 - V_3}{1} + \frac{V_1 + 40 - V_3}{6} = 0 \quad \text{or} \quad 10V_1 - 7V_3 = -40 \tag{1}$$

$$\frac{V_1 - V_3}{1} + \frac{V_1 + 40 - V_3}{6} + 6 = \frac{V_3 - V_4}{5} \qquad \text{or} \qquad 35V_1 - 41V_3 + 6V_4 = -380 \tag{2}$$

and

$$6 + \frac{V_4}{3} = 10 + \frac{V_3 - V_4}{5} \qquad \text{or} \qquad 3V_3 - 8V_4 = -60 \tag{3}$$

Solving for V_1, V_3, and V_4 from Eqs. (1), (2), and (3) yields

$$V_1 = 10 \text{ V} \qquad V_3 = 20 \text{ V} \qquad V_4 = 15 \text{ V}$$

Finally, $V_2 + 40 = 20$ or $V_2 = -20$ V.

4.93 Calculate the currents in the resistors of the circuit of Fig. 4-55.

I $\qquad I_{2\,\Omega} = \dfrac{V_1}{2} = \dfrac{10}{2} = 5 \text{ A} \qquad I_{1\,\Omega} = \dfrac{V_1 - V_3}{1} = \dfrac{10 - 20}{1} = -10 \text{ A} \qquad I_{6\,\Omega} + I_{1\,\Omega} + I_{2\,\Omega} = 0$

or $\qquad I_{6\,\Omega} = -5 + 10 = 5 \text{ A} \qquad I_{5\,\Omega} = \dfrac{V_3 - V_4}{5} = \dfrac{20 - 15}{5} = 1 \text{ A} \qquad I_{3\,\Omega} = \dfrac{V_4}{3} = \dfrac{15}{3} = 5 \text{ A}$

4.94 Verify the power balance for the circuit of Fig. 4-55.

I $\qquad \sum P_{\text{dissipated}} = (5)^2 2 + (10)^2 1 + (5)^2 6 + (1)^2 5 + (5)^2 3 = 380 \text{ W}$

$\qquad \sum P_{\text{supplied}} = 40(5) + 6(V_3 - V_4) + 10V_4 = 200 + 6 \times 5 + 10 \times 15 = 380 \text{ W}$

4.95 Solve for I in the circuit of Fig. 4-56. Also determine the current in the 3-Ω resistor.

I Writing the nodal equation yields

$$\frac{12 - V}{4} + 5 = \frac{V}{3} + 4I \qquad I = \frac{12 - V}{4}$$

Solving for I yields

$$I = 0.6 \text{ A} \qquad I_{3\,\Omega} = \frac{V}{3} = \frac{12 - 4I}{3} = \frac{12 - 4(0.6)}{3} = 3.2 \text{ A}$$

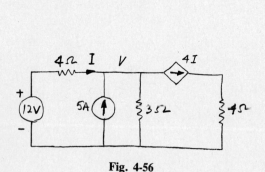

Fig. 4-56

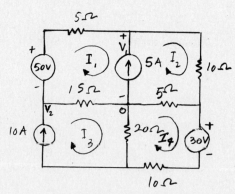

Fig. 4-57

4.96 Solve for the four mesh currents shown in the network of Fig. 4-57.

I Let the voltage across the 5-A source be V_1. Then $50 = 20I_1 + V_1 - 15I_3 = 20I_1 + V_1 - 150$, since $I_3 = 10 \text{ A}$. $I_2 - I_1 = 5$. $-30 = 35I_4 - 5I_2 - 20I_3 = 35I_4 - 5I_2 - 200$, since $I_3 = 10 \text{ A}$. $V_1 = 15I_2 - 5I_4$. The above equations simplify to

$$20I_1 + V_1 = 200 \qquad I_2 - I_1 = 5$$
$$35I_4 - 5I_2 = 170 \qquad V_1 + 5I_4 - 15I_2 = 0$$

Solving these yields

$$I_1 = 4.46 \text{ A} \qquad I_2 = 9.46 \text{ A} \qquad I_4 = 6.22 \text{ A} \qquad V_1 = 110.8 \text{ V}$$

4.97 Verify that Kirchhoff's current law is satisfied at the node 0 of the circuit of Fig. 4-57.

❚ KCL at node 0 reads

$$5 + (I_4 - I_2) + (I_3 - I_4) + I_1 - I_3 = 0 \quad \text{or} \quad 5 - I_2 + I_1 = 5 - 9.46 + 4.46 = 0$$

4.98 How much power is supplied by each source in the circuit of Fig. 4-57?

❚

$$P_{50\,v} = 50I_1 = 50 \times 4.46 = 223\text{ W} \qquad P_{5\,A} = 5V_1 = 5 \times 110.8 = 554\text{ W}$$

$$P_{30\,v} = 30(-I_4) = 30(-6.22) = -186.6\text{ W (absorbed)}$$

$$P_{10\,A} = 10V_2 = [15(I_3 - I_1) + 20(I_3 - I_4)]10 = 10[15(10 - 4.46) + 20(10 - 6.22)] = 1587\text{ W}$$

$$\text{Net power delivered} = 223 + 554 - 186.6 + 1587 = 2178\text{ W}$$

4.99 Verify the power balance in the network of Fig. 4-57.

❚

$$P_{5\,\Omega} = 5(I_1)^2 = 5(4.46)^2 = 99.458\text{ W} \qquad P_{10\,\Omega} = 10(I_2)^2 = 10(9.46)^2 = 894.916\text{ W}$$

$$P_{10\,\Omega} = 10(I_4)^2 = 10(6.22)^2 = 386.884\text{ W} \qquad P_{15\,\Omega} = 15(I_1 - I_3)^2 = 15(4.46 - 10)^2 = 460.374\text{ W}$$

$$P_{5\,\Omega} = 5(I_2 - I_4)^2 = 5(9.46 - 6.22)^2 = 52.488\text{ W} \qquad P_{20\,\Omega} = 20(I_4 - I_3)^2 = 20(6.22 - 10)^2 = 285.768\text{ W}$$

$\Sigma = 2179.9\text{ W}$, which is approximately the same as the power calculated in Prob. 4.98. A difference of 1.9 W is due to roundoff error.

4.100 For the circuit of Fig. 4-58, find the value of R such that it absorbs 5 W of power.

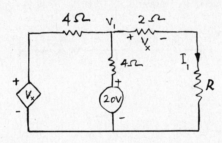

Fig. 4-58

❚ From Fig. 4-58:

$$I_1 = \frac{V_1}{2 + R}$$

$$P_R = I_1^2 R = \left(\frac{V_1}{2 + R}\right)^2 R = 5 \tag{1}$$

The nodal equation may be written as

$$\frac{V_x - V_1}{4} + \frac{20 - V_1}{4} = I_1 = \frac{V_1}{2 + R} \qquad V_x = 2I_1 = \frac{2V_1}{2 + R}$$

Combining these two equations yields

$$\frac{V_x}{4} - \frac{V_1}{4} + 5 - \frac{V_1}{4} = \frac{V_1}{2 + R} = \frac{V_1}{2(2 + R)} - \frac{V_1}{2} + 5$$

or $\qquad V_1\left(\frac{1}{2} + \frac{1}{2(2 + R)}\right) = 5 \qquad \text{or} \qquad V_1 = \frac{10(2 + R)}{3 + R}$ $\tag{2}$

From Eqs. (1) and (2) we obtain

$$\left[\frac{10^2 R}{(3 + R)^2}\right]^2 = 5$$

Solving for R yields $\quad R = 13.325\ \Omega \quad \text{or} \quad 0.675\ \Omega$

CHAPTER 5
Network Theorems

5.1 Thévenin's theorem may be stated as follows: At the terminals 12 in Fig. 5-1a, the arbitrary linear network A, containing resistances and energy sources, can be replaced by an equivalent circuit consisting of a voltage source V_{Th} in series with a resistance R_{Th}. The voltage V_{Th} is the open-circuit voltage across 12, and R_{Th} is the ratio of

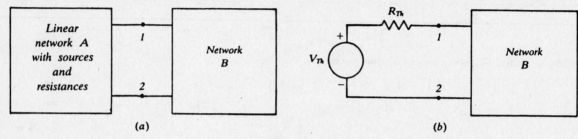

(a)   (b)

Fig. 5-1

the open-circuit voltage to the short-circuit current. Alternatively, R_{Th} is the equivalent resistance at the terminals 12 when all independent sources are suppressed. Figure 5-1a shows the arbitrary network, and its Thévenin equivalent is pictured in Fig. 5-1b. Replace the network of Fig. 5-2a to the left of terminals ab by its Thévenin equivalent circuit. Hence, determine I.

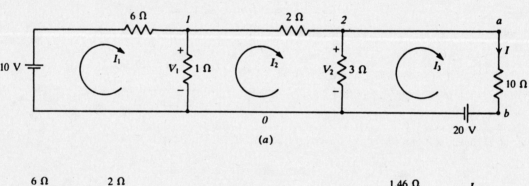

(a)

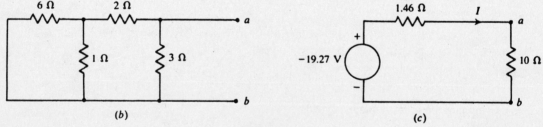

(b)   (c)

Fig. 5-2

To determine R_{Th}, short-circuit the voltage sources to obtain the network of Fig. 5-2b. The 6 Ω and 1 Ω in parallel are equivalent to

$$\frac{(6)(1)}{6+1} = \frac{6}{7}\ \Omega$$

which, in series with the 2 Ω, is equivalent to

$$\tfrac{6}{7} + 2 = \tfrac{20}{7}\ \Omega$$

Then, the parallel combination of $(20/7)$ Ω and 3 Ω gives

$$R_{\mathrm{Th}} = R_{ab} = \frac{(20/7)(3)}{(20/7)+3} = \frac{60}{41} = 1.46\ \Omega$$

To find V_{Th}, open-circuit the terminals ab. The 10-V battery then sees a resistance

$$6 + \frac{(1)(2+3)}{1+2+3} = \frac{41}{6} \, \Omega$$

and so a current of

$$\frac{10}{41/6} = \frac{60}{41} = 1.46 \, A$$

is drawn from it, of which

$$\frac{1}{1+2+3} (1.46) = 0.243 \, A$$

passes through the 3-Ω resistor. Then,

$$V_{Th} = (0.243)(3) - 20 = -19.27 \, V$$

Thévenin's equivalent circuit becomes as shown in Fig. 5-2c, whence

$$I = \frac{-19.27}{1.46 + 10} = -1.68 \, A$$

The negative sign indicates that the current actually flows in the $10 \, \Omega$ from b to a.

5.2 Calculate the Thévenin voltage and resistance at the terminals ab of the circuit of Fig. 5-3a.

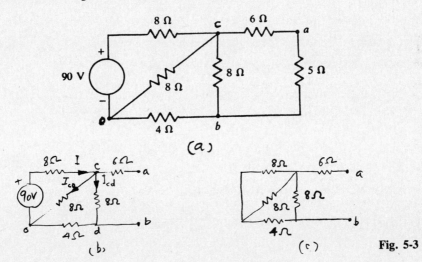

Fig. 5-3

❙ The Thévenin voltage is the open-circuit voltage appearing across the terminals ab, which is the same as the voltage across cd. For this open-circuited network we need not consider the 6-Ω resistor. The equivalent resistance seen by the 90 V is given by

$$R_e = 8 + \frac{8(8+4)}{8+8+4} = 12.8 \, \Omega$$

The current I, shown in Fig. 5-3b, becomes

$$I = \frac{90}{12.8} = 7.03 \, A$$

Thus, the voltage

$$V_{co} = 90 - 8I = 90 - 7.03(8) = 33.75 \, V$$

Current

$$I_{co} = \frac{33.75}{8} = 4.22 \, A \qquad \text{and} \qquad I_{cd} = 7.03 - 4.22 = 2.81 \, A$$

Hence,
$$V_{cd} = V_{Th} = 2.81 \times 8 = 22.48 \, V$$

To find the Thévenin resistance, we refer to Fig. 5.3c from which we obtain

$$R_{Th} = R_{ab} = 6 + \frac{(4+4)8}{4+4+8} = 10 \, \Omega$$

5.3 Reduce the delta-connected resistors of Fig. 5-3*a* to an equivalent wye. Find the Thévenin voltage and resistance for the modified circuit. Verify that the results agree with those of Prob. 5.2.

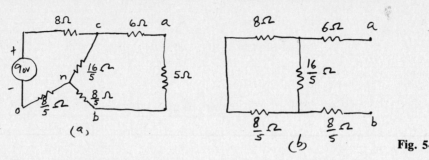

Fig. 5-4

▮ The network reduction is shown in Fig. 5-4*a*. The Thévenin voltage is across *cn*, which is the voltage across the 16/5 Ω resistor and is given by

$$V_{Th} = V_{cn} = \frac{90}{8 + 16/5 + 8/5} \frac{16}{5} = \frac{90}{4} = 22.5 \text{ V}$$

The circuit for the Thévenin resistance is shown in Fig. 5-4*b* from which

$$R_{Th} = \frac{(8 + 8/5)16/5}{8 + 8/5 + 16/5} + \frac{8}{5} + 6 = 10 \ \Omega$$

5.4 Determine the current i_x in the 5-Ω resistor of the circuit shown in Fig. 4-6, by using Thévenin's theorem.

▮ The circuit to determine the Thévenin voltage is shown in Fig. 5-5*a*, from which we have (for the two meshes)

$$100 + 50 = 14I_1 - 2I_2 \qquad 50 = -2I_1 + 5I_2$$

Solving for I_1 yields

$$I_1 = 12.88 \text{ A}$$

Thus, $$V_{Th} = 100 - I(10) = 100 - 12.88(10) = -28.8 \text{ V}$$

Figure 5-5*b* shows the circuit to determine the Thévenin resistance. Therefore,

$$R_{Th} = \frac{10(2 + 1.2)}{10 + 2 + 1.2} = 2.42 \ \Omega$$

Hence, $$I_x = \frac{V_{Th}}{R_{Th} + 5} = \frac{-28.8}{2.42 + 5} = -3.87 \text{ A}$$

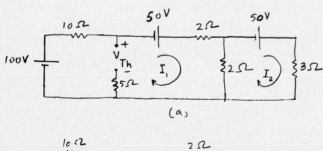

(a)

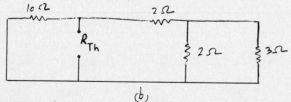

(b)

Fig. 5-5

Fig. 5-6

5.5 For the circuit shown in Fig. 4-5, we have $R_1 = 10 \ \Omega$, $R_2 = 20 \ \Omega$, $R_3 = 30 \ \Omega$, and $R_4 = 60 \ \Omega$. Using the Thévenin equivalent circuit show that the current in R_5 is zero and is independent of the values of the battery voltage E and R_5.

❚ The circuit, shown in Fig. 5-6, is drawn to determine the Thévenin voltage. Thus, we obtain

$$I_1 = \frac{E}{10 + 20} = \frac{E}{30} \text{ A}$$

And $\quad I_2 = \dfrac{E}{30 + 60} = \dfrac{E}{90}$ A $\quad -V_{Th} = V_{10\,\Omega} - V_{30\,\Omega} = I_1(10) - I_2(30) = \dfrac{E}{30}(10) - \dfrac{E}{90}(30) = 0$ V

Hence the current in $\quad R_5 = 0$ A.

5.6   Using Thévenin's theorem, determine the current in the 2-Ω resistor of the network shown in Fig. 4-8a.

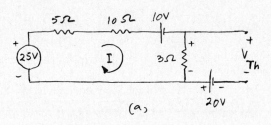

(a)

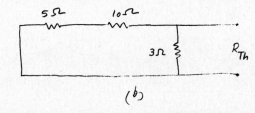

(b)   **Fig. 5-7**

❚ First, we change the 5-A current source to an equivalent voltage source. Consequently, we have the Thévenin equivalent circuit to determine V_{Th} as shown in Fig. 5-7a. Writing the mesh equation yields

$$25 - 10 = (5 + 10 + 3)I \quad \text{or} \quad I = \frac{15}{18} = \frac{5}{6} \text{ A}$$

Hence, $\qquad\qquad 20 = -3\left(\dfrac{5}{6}\right) + V_{Th} \quad \text{or} \quad V_{Th} = 20 + 2.5 = 22.5$ V

The circuit to determine R_{Th} is shown in Fig. 5-7b from which

$$R_{Th} = \frac{(10 + 5)3}{10 + 5 + 3} = 2.5 \ \Omega$$

Thus, $\qquad\qquad\qquad I_{2\,\Omega} = \dfrac{V_{Th}}{R_{Th} + 2} = \dfrac{22.5}{2.5 + 2} = 5 \text{ A}$

5.7   Find the current I in the 10-Ω resistor of the circuit of Fig. 4-9. Use Thévenin's theorem.

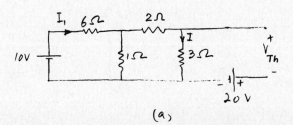

(a)

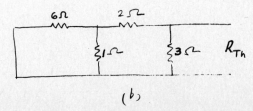

(b)   **Fig. 5-8**

▮ The circuit to determine the Thévenin voltage is shown in Fig. 5-8a, from which

$$I_1 = \frac{10}{6 + (5 \times 1)/(5 + 1)} = 1.46 \text{ A}$$

By current division,

$$I = (1.46) \frac{1}{1 + 5} = 0.244 \text{ A}$$

Thus, $\qquad V_{3\,\Omega} = 3(0.244) = 0.732 \text{ V} \qquad$ and $\qquad V_{\text{Th}} = -20 + 0.732 = -19.268 \text{ V}$

From Fig. 5-8b,

$$R_{\text{Th}} = \frac{(2 + 6/7)3}{2 + 6/7 + 3} = 1.463 \,\Omega$$

Finally, $\qquad I = \frac{V_{\text{Th}}}{R_{\text{Th}} + 10} = \frac{-19.268}{1.463 + 10} = -1.68 \text{ A}$

5.8 By applying Thévenin's theorem to the circuit of Fig. 4-10a determine the current I_1 in the 10-Ω resistor.

▮ After converting the current source to a voltage source, the Thévenin equivalent circuits to determine V_{Th} and R_{Th} are shown in Fig. 5-9a and b, respectively.

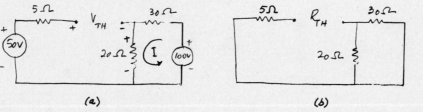

(a) $\qquad\qquad\qquad$ (b) $\qquad\qquad\qquad$ **Fig. 5-9**

From Fig. 5-9a we obtain

$$I = \frac{100}{30 + 20} = 2 \text{ A} \qquad \text{and} \qquad V_{20\,\Omega} = 2(20) = 40 \text{ V}$$

Also, $\qquad\qquad 50 = V_{\text{Th}} + V_{20} = V_{\text{Th}} + 40 \qquad \text{or} \qquad V_{\text{Th}} = 50 - 40 = 10 \text{ V}$

From Fig. 5-9b we have

$$R_{\text{Th}} = 5 + \frac{30 \times 20}{30 + 20} = 17 \,\Omega$$

Hence, $\qquad\qquad I_1 = \frac{V_{\text{Th}}}{R_{\text{Th}} + 10} = \frac{10}{17 + 10} = 0.37 \text{ A}$

5.9 Find the current in the 30-Ω resistor of the circuit of Fig. 4-10a by Thévenin's theorem.

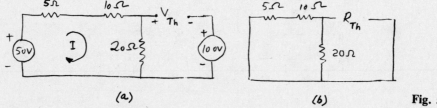

(a) $\qquad\qquad\qquad$ (b) $\qquad\qquad\qquad$ **Fig. 5-10**

▮ From the circuit of the Fig. 5-10a we have

$$I = \frac{50}{35} = 1.43 \text{ A}$$

$$100 + V_{\text{Th}} = 20(1.43)$$

or $\qquad\qquad V_{\text{Th}} = -71.43 \text{ V}$

From Fig. 5-10*b*,

$$R_{Th} = \frac{20(5+10)}{20+5+10} = 8.57\ \Omega$$

Hence,

$$I_{30\ \Omega} = \frac{V_{Th}}{30 + R_{Th}} = \frac{-71.43}{30 + 8.57} = -1.85\ A$$

5.10 Determine the current supplied by the 100-V source to the circuit of Fig. 4-14 by applying Thévenin's theorem.

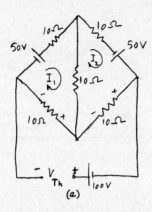 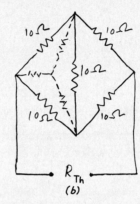

Fig. 5-11

❚ The Thévenin equivalent circuits are drawn in Fig. 5-11*a* and *b*.
From Fig. 5-11*a*, for the two meshes we obtain

$$50 = 30I_1 - 10I_2 \qquad \text{and} \qquad 50 = -10I_1 + 30I_2$$

Hence,

$$I_1 = I_2 = 2.5\ A$$

For the mesh containing V_{Th} we have

$$100 - V_{Th} + 10(I_1) + 10(I_2) = 0 \qquad \text{or} \qquad V_{Th} = 100 + 10(2.5) + 10(2.5) = 150\ V$$

From Fig. 5-11*b* we get

$$R_{Th} = \frac{10}{3} + \frac{1}{2}\left(10 + \frac{10}{3}\right) = 10\ \Omega$$

Therefore the required current is

$$I_{100\ V} = \frac{V_{Th}}{R_{Th} + 10} = \frac{150}{20} = 7.5\ A$$

5.11 By applying Thévenin's theorem, determine the current supplied by the battery of the circuit of Fig. 4-15.

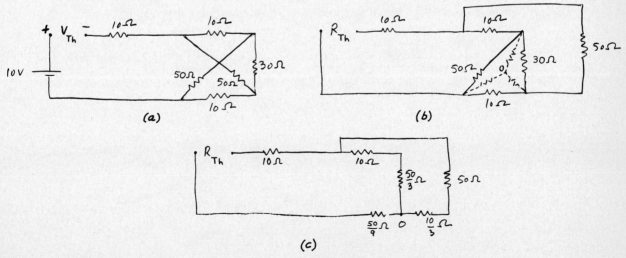

Fig. 5-12

❚ The Thévenin equivalent circuits are drawn in Fig. 5-12a and b.
From Fig. 5-12a it is clear that no current flows through the resistors. Therefore,

$$V_{Th} = 10 \text{ V}$$

To obtain R_{Th} we reduce the circuit of Fig. 5-12b to that shown in Fig. 5-12c from which

$$R_{Th} = \frac{50}{9} + \frac{(10 + 50/3)(50 + 10/3)}{10 + 50/3 + 50 + 10/3} + 10 = \frac{100}{3} \ \Omega$$

Hence,

$$I = \frac{V_{Th}}{R_{Th}} = \frac{10}{100/3} = 0.3 \text{ A}$$

5.12 Using Thévenin's theorem find the current in the 1-Ω resistor of the circuit of Fig. 4-16.

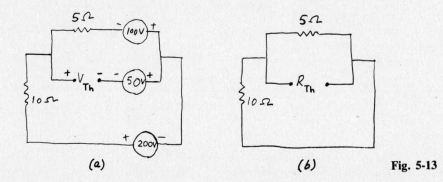

Fig. 5-13

❚ From the corresponding Thévenin equivalent circuits drawn in Fig. 5-13a and b we have

$$V_{Th} = 50 \text{ V} \qquad \text{and} \qquad R_{Th} = \frac{10 \times 5}{10 + 5} = \frac{10}{3} \ \Omega$$

Hence,

$$I_{1 \Omega} = \frac{V_{Th}}{R_{Th} + 1} = \frac{50}{10/3 + 1} = \frac{150}{13} = 11.538 \text{ A}$$

5.13 Solve for the current in the 2-Ω resistor of the network of Fig. 4-17, by Thévenin's theorem.

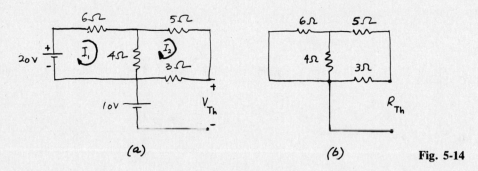

Fig. 5-14

❚ The Thévenin's equivalent circuits are shown in Fig. 5-14a and b. Thus, we obtain

$$20 = 10I_1 - 4I_2$$

$$0 = -4I_1 + 12I_2$$

Or,

$$I_2 = \frac{10}{13} \text{ A} \qquad V_{3 \Omega} = 3\left(\frac{10}{13}\right) = \frac{30}{13} \text{ V}$$

$$V_{Th} = 10 + \frac{30}{13} = 12.31 \text{ V} \qquad R_{Th} = \frac{\{[6 \times 4)/(6 + 4)] + 5\}3}{3 + 5 + [(6 \times 4)/(6 + 4)]} = 2.134 \ \Omega$$

$$I_{2 \Omega} = \frac{V_{Th}}{R_{Th} + 2} = \frac{12.31}{2.134 + 2} = 2.98 \text{ A}$$

5.14 Find the current in the 1-Ω resistor of the circuit of Fig. 4-18a by Thévenin's theorem.

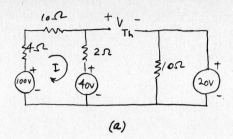
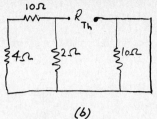

(a)   (b)   **Fig. 5-15**

▌ First, we transform the current sources to voltage sources as shown in Fig. 4-18b. Then, we define V_{Th} and R_{Th} shown in Fig. 5-15a and b, respectively.

From Fig. 5-15a,

$$I = \frac{100-40}{10+4+2} = \frac{15}{4}\ \text{A} \qquad V_{Th} = 100 - I(10+4) - 20 = 100 - \frac{15}{4}(14) - 20 = \frac{55}{2}\ \text{V}$$

From Fig. 5-15b,

$$R_{Th} = \frac{(10+4)2}{10+4+2} = \frac{7}{4}\ \Omega$$

Hence,

$$I_{1\,\Omega} = \frac{V_{Th}}{1+R_{Th}} = \frac{55/2}{1+7/4} = 10\ \text{A}$$

5.15 By Thévenin's theorem, determine the current in the 4-Ω resistor of the circuit shown in Fig. 4-18b.

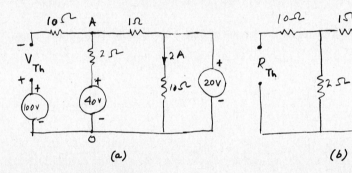

(a)   (b)   **Fig. 5-16**

▌ By nodal analysis, from Fig. 5-16a, we have

$$I_{OA} = \frac{40-20}{2+1} = \frac{20}{3}\ \text{A} \qquad V_{AO} = 40 - 2\left(\frac{20}{3}\right) = \frac{80}{3}\ \text{V} \qquad V_{Th} = 100 - \frac{80}{3} = \frac{220}{3}\ \text{V}$$

From Fig. 5-16b,

$$R_{Th} = 10 + \frac{2(1)}{2+1} = \frac{32}{3}\ \Omega$$

Hence

$$I_{4\,\Omega} = \frac{V_{Th}}{4+R_{Th}} = \frac{220/3}{4+32/3} = 5\ \text{A}$$

5.16 In Fig. 4-22, given $R = 5\ \Omega$, find the current in the 20-Ω resistor by Thévenin's theorem.

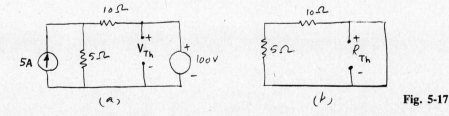

(a)   (b)   **Fig. 5-17**

▌ From Fig. 5-17a and b we have

$$V_{Th} = 100\ \text{V} \qquad \text{and} \qquad R_{Th} = 0\ \Omega$$

Hence,

$$I_{20\,\Omega} = \frac{V_{\text{Th}}}{20 + R_{\text{Th}}} = \frac{100}{20 + 0} = 5\,\text{A}$$

5.17 Calculate the current in the 10-Ω resistor of the circuit shown in Fig. 4-23a by Thévenin's theorem.

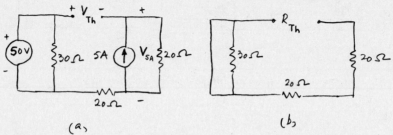

(a)   (b)   Fig. 5-18

▌ From Fig. 5-18a,

$$V_{5\,\text{A}} = 5 \times 20 = 100\,\text{V} \qquad 50 - V_{\text{Th}} - 100 = 0$$

Or

$$V_{\text{Th}} = -50\,\text{V}$$

From Fig. 5-18b,

$$R_{\text{Th}} = 20 + 20 = 40\,\Omega$$

Hence

$$I_{10\,\Omega} = \frac{V_{\text{Th}}}{10 + R_{\text{Th}}} = \frac{-50}{10 + 40} = -1\,\text{A}$$

5.18 Find the current in the 20-Ω resistor of the circuit of Fig. 4-24a by Thévenin's theorem.

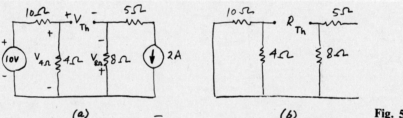

(a)   —   (b)   Fig. 5-19

▌ From Fig. 5-19a

$$V_{8\,\Omega} = 2 \times 8 = 16\,\text{V} \qquad \text{(with polarities as shown)}$$

$$V_{4\,\Omega} = \frac{10}{10 + 4}\,(4) = \frac{20}{7}\,\text{V} \qquad \text{and} \qquad V_{4\,\Omega} - V_{\text{Th}} + V_{8\,\Omega} = 0$$

Thus,

$$V_{\text{Th}} = \frac{20}{7} + 16 = \frac{132}{7}\,\text{V}$$

From Fig. 5-19b,

$$R_{\text{Th}} = \frac{10 \times 4}{10 + 4} + 8 = \frac{76}{7}\,\Omega$$

Hence,

$$I_{20\,\Omega} = \frac{V_{\text{Th}}}{20 + R_{\text{Th}}} = \frac{132/7}{20 + 76/7} = \frac{132}{216} = 0.611\,\text{A}$$

5.19 Find the current in the 20-Ω resistor of the circuit of Fig. 4-24b by Thévenin's theorem.

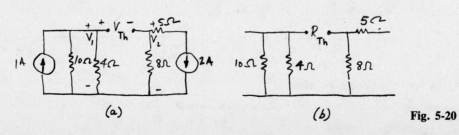

(a)   (b)   Fig. 5-20

❚ From Fig. 5-20a solving for V_1 and V_2 yields

$$\frac{V_1}{10} + \frac{V_1}{4} = 1 \quad \text{or} \quad V_1 = \frac{20}{7} \text{ V} \quad \text{and} \quad V_2 = -16 \text{ V}$$

Thus, $\qquad V_1 - V_{Th} - V_2 = 0 \quad \text{or} \quad \frac{20}{7} - V_{Th} + 16 = 0 \quad \text{or} \quad V_{Th} = \frac{132}{7} \text{ V}$

From Fig. 5-20b

$$R_{Th} = \frac{10 \times 4}{10 + 4} + 8 = \frac{76}{7} \ \Omega$$

Hence, $\qquad I_{20\,\Omega} = \frac{V_{Th}}{20 + R_{Th}} = \frac{132/7}{20 + 76/7} = \frac{132}{216} = 0.611 \text{ A}$

5.20 Determine the current through the 12-V source of Fig. 4-25a by applying Thévenin's theorem and nodal analysis.

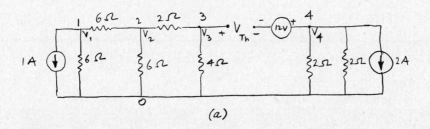

(a)

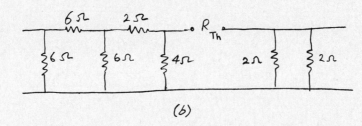

(b) $\qquad\qquad\qquad\qquad\qquad$ **Fig. 5-21**

❚ From Fig. 5-21a we have

$$1 + \frac{V_1}{6} + \frac{V_1 - V_2}{6} = 0 \quad \text{or} \quad 6 = -2V_1 + V_2$$

$$\frac{V_1 - V_2}{6} = \frac{V_2}{6} + \frac{V_2}{2 + 4} \quad \text{or} \quad 3V_2 = V_1$$

Thus $\qquad V_2 = -\frac{6}{5} \text{ V} \quad V_3 = \left(\frac{V_2}{2+4}\right)4 = \frac{-6/5}{6}(4) = -\frac{4}{5} \text{ V} \quad V_4 = -\frac{1}{2}(2)(2) = -2 \text{ V}$

and $\qquad V_{Th} - 12 + V_4 - V_3 = 0 \quad \text{or} \quad V_{Th} = 12 - V_4 + V_3 = 12 + 2 - \frac{4}{5} = \frac{66}{5} \text{ V}$

From Fig. 5-21b,

$$R_{Th} = 1 + \frac{4 \times 6}{4 + 6} = \frac{17}{5} \ \Omega$$

$$I_{12\,V} = \frac{V_{Th}}{R_{Th}} = \frac{66/5}{17/5} = 3.88 \text{ A}$$

5.21 Repeat Prob. 5.20 using the circuit of Fig. 4-25d.

❚ In this case, by inspection, we have

$$V_{Th} = 12 + 2 - 1(0.8) = 13.2 \text{ V} \qquad R_{Th} = 1 + 0.8 + 1.6 = 3.4 \ \Omega$$

Hence $\qquad I_{12\,V} = \frac{V_{Th}}{R_{Th}} = \frac{13.2}{3.4} = 3.88 \text{ A}$

5.22 Find the current in the 2-Ω resistor of the circuit of Fig. 4-28 by Thévenin's theorem.

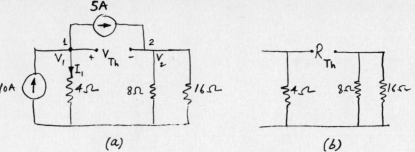

(a)   (b)   **Fig. 5-22**

▌ From Fig. 5-22a we obtain

$$I_1 = 10 - 5 = 5\,\text{A} \qquad V_1 = 4(5) = 20\,\text{V} \qquad V_2 = \frac{5(16)(8)}{16 + 8} = \frac{80}{3}\,\text{V}$$

Thus,

$$V_{\text{Th}} = V_1 - V_2 = -\frac{20}{3}$$

From Fig. 5-22b,

$$R_{\text{Th}} = 4 + \frac{16 \times 8}{16 + 8} = \frac{28}{3}\,\Omega \qquad I_{2\,\Omega} = \frac{V_{\text{Th}}}{2 + R_{\text{Th}}} = \frac{-20/3}{22 + 28/3} = -0.588\,\text{A}$$

5.23 In Fig. 4-30, given $R_2 = R_3 = 5\,\Omega$, $R_6 = 10\,\Omega$, and $V_2 = 2V_3 = 10\,\text{V}$, find the current in R_6 by Thévenin' theorem.

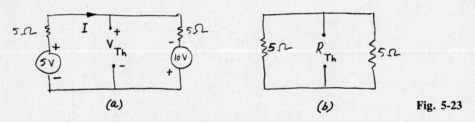

(a)   (b)   **Fig. 5-23**

▌ From Fig. 5-23a and b we obtain

$$5 + 10 = I(5 + 5) \qquad \text{or} \qquad I = \frac{15}{10} = 1.5\,\text{A}$$

Thus,

$$V_{\text{Th}} = 5 - 5(1.5) = -2.5\,\text{V} \qquad \text{and} \qquad R_{\text{Th}} = \frac{5 \times 5}{5 + 5} = 2.5\,\Omega$$

Hence

$$I_{R6} = \frac{V_{\text{Th}}}{10 + R_{\text{Th}}} = \frac{-2.5}{10 + 2.5} = -0.2\,\text{A}$$

5.24 Determine the current in the 5-Ω resistor of the circuit of Fig. 4-33, by Thévenin's theorem.

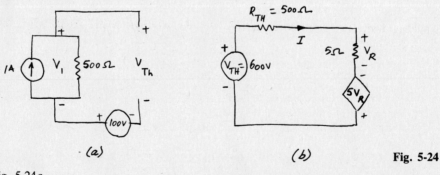

(a)   (b)   **Fig. 5-24**

▌ From Fig. 5-24a,

$$V_1 = 1(500) = 500\,\text{V} \qquad \text{and} \qquad 100 + 500 - V_{\text{Th}} = 0 \qquad \text{or} \qquad V_{\text{Th}} = 600\,\text{V}$$

Also,

$$R_{\text{Th}} = 500\,\Omega$$

From Fig. 5-24b,

$$I = \frac{V_R}{5}$$

Thus, $\qquad 600 = 500\left(\frac{V_R}{5}\right) + V_R - 5V_R \qquad$ or $\qquad V_R = 6.25 \text{ V} \qquad$ and $\qquad I = \frac{6.25}{5} = 1.25 \text{ A}$

5.25 Determine the current through the short-circuited terminals ab in the circuit of Fig. 4-37 by Thévenin's theorem.

▌ By open-circuiting ab in Fig. 4-37, we obtain

$$V_{\text{Th}} = 20 - 4(3) = 8 \text{ V}$$

Also from Fig. 4-37,

$$R_{\text{Th}} = 6 + 4 = 10 \text{ }\Omega$$

Thus, $$I_{ab} = \frac{V_{\text{Th}}}{R_{\text{Th}}} = \frac{8}{10} = 0.8 \text{ A}$$

5.26 Find the current in the 4-Ω resistor of the circuit shown in Fig. 4-38a without any network reduction. Use Thévenin's theorem.

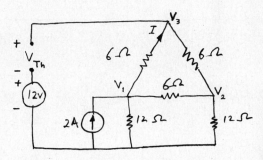

Fig. 5-25

▌ To determine V_{Th} we redraw the circuit as shown in Fig. 5-25 from which we obtain

$$\frac{V_1}{12} + \frac{V_1 - V_2}{6} + \frac{V_1 - V_2}{6+6} = 2 \qquad \text{or} \qquad 4V_1 - 3V_2 = 24 \qquad \text{and} \qquad \frac{V_1 - V_2}{6} + \frac{V_1 - V_2}{6+6} = \frac{V_2}{12}$$

Or $$3V_1 - 4V_2 = 0$$

Thus, $$V_1 = \frac{96}{7} \text{ V} \qquad V_2 = \frac{72}{7} \text{ V}$$

and $\qquad V_1 - V_2 = \frac{24}{7} \text{ V} \qquad I = \frac{V_1 - V_2}{6+6} = \frac{24}{7(12)} = \frac{2}{7} \text{ A} \qquad V_3 = V_1 - I(6) = \frac{96}{7} - \frac{2}{7}(6) = 12 \text{ V}$

Hence, $\qquad -V_{\text{Th}} = 12 - V_3 = 0 \text{ V} \qquad$ and $\qquad I_{4\,\Omega} = 0 \text{ A}$

5.27 By applying Thévenin's theorem to the circuit of Fig. 4-38b determine the current I in the 12-Ω resistor connected to node 2.

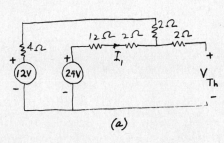

(a)

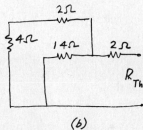

(b)　　　　**Fig. 5-26**

▌ From Fig. 5-26a we have

$$I_1 = \frac{24 - 12}{12 + 2 + 2 + 4} = \frac{3}{5} \text{ A}$$

Thus,

$$V_{\text{Th}} = 24 - I_1(12 + 2) = 24 - \frac{3}{5}(14) = \frac{78}{5} \text{ V}$$

From Fig. 5-26b,

$$R_{\text{Th}} = 2 + \frac{14(6)}{14 + 6} = \frac{31}{5} \ \Omega$$

Hence

$$I = I_{12\,\Omega} = \frac{V_{\text{Th}}}{12 + R_{\text{Th}}} = \frac{78/5}{12 + 31/5} = \frac{6}{7} \text{ A}$$

5.28 Find the current I in the 5-Ω resistor of the circuit of Fig. 4-41 by Thévenin's theorem.

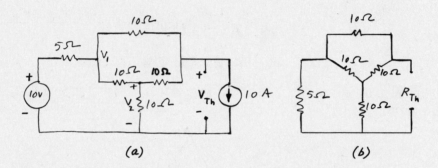

(a)   (b)

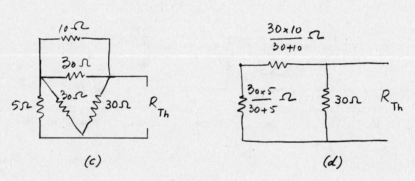

(c)   (d)   **Fig. 5-27**

| From Fig. 5-27a we have

$$\frac{10 - V_1}{5} = \frac{V_1 - V_{\text{Th}}}{10} + \frac{V_1 - V_2}{10}$$

or

$$4V_1 - V_2 - V_{\text{Th}} = 20 \qquad \frac{V_1 - V_2}{10} = \frac{V_2}{10} + \frac{V_2 - V_{\text{Th}}}{10}$$

or

$$-V_1 + 3V_2 - V_{\text{Th}} = 0 \qquad \frac{V_1 - T_{\text{Th}}}{10} + \frac{V_2 - V_{\text{Th}}}{10} = 10$$

or

$$V_1 + V_2 - 2V_{\text{Th}} = 100$$

Solving for V_{Th} yields

$$V_{\text{Th}} = -\frac{1020}{13} \text{ V}$$

Now, referring to Fig. 5-27b, we transform it to an equivalent delta shown in Fig. 5-27c, which may be reduced to that shown in Fig. 5-27c. Therefore, from Fig. 5-27d we obtain

$$R_{\text{Th}} = \frac{(165/14)30}{165/14 + 30} = \frac{110}{13} \ \Omega$$

Hence,

$$I_{5\,\Omega} = \frac{V_{\text{Th}}}{5 + R_{\text{Th}}} = \frac{-(1020/13)}{5 + (110/13)} = -\frac{204}{35} \text{ A}$$

5.29 Find the current in the 5-Ω resistor of the circuit of Fig. 4-43 by Thévenin's theorem.

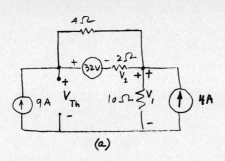 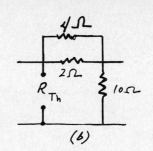

Fig. 5-28

I From Fig. 5-28a we obtain

$$9 = \frac{V_{Th} - 32 - V_1}{2} + \frac{V_{Th} - V_1}{4} \qquad \frac{V_1}{10} = 4 + \frac{V_{Th} - V_1}{4} + \frac{V_{Th} - 32 - V_1}{2}$$

or

$$3V_{Th} - 3V_1 = 100 \qquad \text{and} \qquad 15V_{Th} - 17V_1 = 240$$

Hence,

$$V_{Th} = \frac{490}{3} \text{ V}$$

From Fig. 5-28b,

$$R_{Th} = 10 + \frac{(4)(2)}{4+2} = \frac{34}{3} \ \Omega$$

Thus,

$$I_{5\,\Omega} = \frac{V_{Th}}{5 + R_{Th}} = \frac{490/3}{5 + 34/3} = 10 \text{ A}$$

5.30 Determine the current in the 2-Ω resistor of the circuit of Fig. 4-43, by Thévenin's theorem.

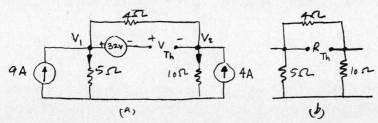

Fig. 5-29

I The Thévenin equivalent circuits are shown in Fig. 5-29a and b from which we obtain

$$9 = \frac{V_1}{5} + \frac{V_1 - V_2}{4} \qquad \text{or} \qquad 9V_1 - 5V_2 = 180$$

$$\frac{V_2}{10} = 4 + \frac{V_1 - V_2}{4} \qquad \text{and} \qquad 5V_1 - 7V_2 = -80$$

Thus,

$$V_1 = \frac{830}{19} \text{ V} \qquad V_2 = \frac{810}{19} \text{ V}$$

Since,

$$V_2 + V_{Th} + 32 = V_1 \qquad V_{Th} = \frac{830}{19} - \frac{810}{19} - 32 = -\frac{588}{19} \text{ V}$$

$$R_{Th} = \frac{(10+5)4}{10+5+4} = \frac{60}{19} \ \Omega \qquad I_{2\,\Omega} = \frac{V_{Th}}{2 + R_{Th}} = \frac{-588/19}{2 + 60/19} = -6 \text{ A}$$

5.31 Evaluate the current in the 50-Ω resistor of the circuit of Fig. 4-45 by Thévenin's theorem.

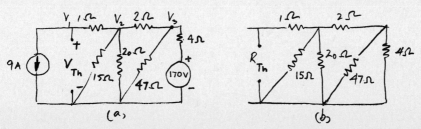

Fig. 5-30

❙ From Fig. 5-30a we have

$$V_1 = V_{\text{Th}}$$

$$\frac{V_2 - V_1}{1} = 9 \qquad \text{or} \qquad V_2 - V_1 = 9$$

$$\frac{V_3 - V_2}{2} = 9 + \frac{V_2}{20} + \frac{V_2}{15} \qquad \text{or} \qquad -37V_2 + 30V_3 = 540$$

$$\frac{170 - V_3}{4} = \frac{V_3}{47} + \frac{V_3 - V_2}{2} \qquad \text{or} \qquad -94V_2 + 145V_3 = 7990$$

Solving for V_2 yields

$$V_2 = 63.42 \text{ V}$$

Hence, $$V_{\text{Th}} = V_1 = V_2 - 9 = 63.42 - 9 = 54.42 \text{ V}$$

From Fig. 5-30b we obtain

$$R_{\text{Th}} = 4.42 \ \Omega$$

Thus, $$I_{50\ \Omega} = \frac{V_{\text{Th}}}{50 + R_{\text{Th}}} = \frac{54.42}{50 + 4.42} = 1.0 \text{ A}$$

5.32 Calculate the current I_3 in the circuit of Fig. 4-46 by Thévenin's theorem.

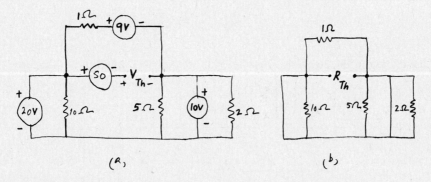

Fig. 5-31

❙ From the Thévenin equivalent circuits of Fig. 5-31a and b we have

$$V_{\text{Th}} + 50 - 20 + 10 = 0$$

or $$V_{\text{Th}} = -40 \text{ V} \qquad R_{\text{Th}} = 0 \ \Omega$$

Hence, $$I_3 = \frac{V_{\text{Th}}}{20 + R_{\text{Th}}} = -\frac{40}{20 + 0} = -2 \text{ A}$$

5.33 Find the current I_2 in Fig. 4-46 by Thévenin's theorem.

❙ By inspection,

$$20 - V_{\text{Th}} - 9 - 10 = 0$$

or $$V_{\text{Th}} = 1 \text{ V} \qquad R_{\text{Th}} = 0 \ \Omega$$

Hence $$I_2 = \frac{V_{\text{Th}}}{1 + R_{\text{Th}}} = \frac{1}{1 + 0} = 1 \text{ A}$$

5.34 Find the current in the 3-Ω resistor of the circuit of Fig. 4-55 by Thévenin's theorem.

❙ The Thévenin equivalent circuits are shown in Fig. 5-32a and b. From Fig. 5-32a,

$$I_{2\ \Omega} = 10 \text{ A}$$

or $$V_1 = 10 \times 2 = 20 \text{ V}$$

Also, $$\frac{V_2 - V_1}{1} + \frac{V_2 - 20 - 40}{6} = 10 \qquad \text{or} \qquad V_2 = \frac{240}{7} \text{ V}$$

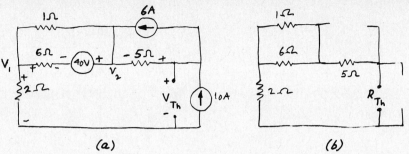

Fig. 5-32

Finally,
$$\frac{V_{Th} - V_2}{5} = 4 \quad \text{or} \quad V_{Th} = 20 + V_2 = 20 + \frac{240}{7} = \frac{380}{7} \text{ V}$$

From Fig. 5-32*b*,
$$R_{Th} = 5 + \tfrac{6}{7} + 2 = \tfrac{55}{7} \ \Omega$$

Hence,
$$I_{3\,\Omega} = \frac{V_{Th}}{3 + R_{Th}} = \frac{380/7}{3 + 55/7} = 5 \text{ A}$$

5.35 By Thévenin's theorem, calculate the current through the galvanometer, having a resistance of $20\,\Omega$, in the Wheatstone bridge shown in Fig. 5-33*a*.

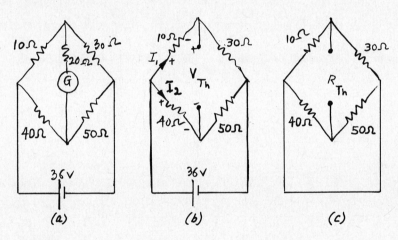

Fig. 5-33

▌ From Fig. 5-33*b* we have
$$I_1 = \frac{36}{10 + 30} = 0.9 \text{ A} \qquad I_2 = \frac{36}{40 + 50} = 0.4 \text{ A}$$
$$V_{10\,\Omega} = I_1(10) = 0.9 \times 10 = 9 \text{ V} \qquad V_{40\,\Omega} = I_2(40) = 0.4 \times 40 = 16 \text{ V}$$

Also,
$$V_{10\,\Omega} + V_{Th} - V_{40\,\Omega} = 0 \quad \text{or} \quad V_{Th} = V_{40\,\Omega} - V_{10\,\Omega} = 16 - 9 = 7 \text{ V}$$

From Fig. 5-33*c*,
$$R_{Th} = \frac{10 \times 30}{10 + 30} + \frac{40 \times 50}{40 + 50} = 29.72 \ \Omega$$

Hence,
$$I_G = \frac{V_{Th}}{20 + R_{Th}} = \frac{7}{20 + 29.72} = 0.14 \text{ A}$$

5.36 Determine the current in the 10-Ω resistor of the circuit of Fig. 5-34*a*.

▌ From Fig. 5-34*a*,
$$I_1 = \frac{36}{40 + [50(30 + 20)]/(50 + 30 + 20)} = \frac{36}{65} \text{ A}$$
$$I_2 = \frac{1}{2} I_1 = \frac{18}{65} \text{ A}$$

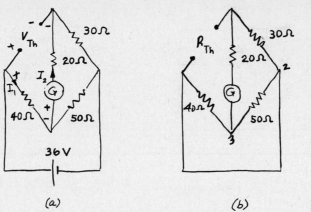

Fig. 5-34

And
$$V_{Th} - (V_{20\,\Omega} + V_{40\,\Omega}) = 0$$

Or
$$V_{Th} = V_{20\,\Omega} + V_{40\,\Omega} = I_2(20) + I_1(40) = \frac{18}{65} \times 20 + \frac{36}{65}(40) = \frac{360}{13} \text{ V}$$

From Fig. 5-34b,

$$R_{Th} = \frac{228}{13}\ \Omega$$

Hence
$$I_{10\,\Omega} = \frac{V_{Th}}{10 + R_{Th}} = \frac{360/13}{10 + 228/13} = \frac{360}{358} = 1.0 \text{ A}$$

5.37 Find the current in the 3-Ω resistor of the circuit of Fig. 5-35a by Thévenin's theorem.

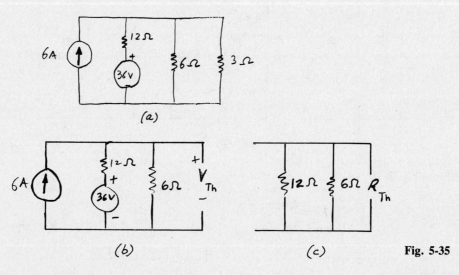

Fig. 5-35

▌ From Fig. 5-35b we have

$$6 = \frac{V_{Th} - 36}{12} + \frac{V_{Th}}{6} \quad \text{or} \quad V_{Th} = 36 \text{ V}$$

From Fig. 5-35c we obtain

$$R_{Th} = \frac{12 \times 6}{12 + 6} = 4\ \Omega$$

Hence,

$$I_{3\,\Omega} = \frac{V_{Th}}{3 + R_{Th}} = \frac{36}{3 + 4} = \frac{36}{7} = 5.143 \text{ A}$$

5.38 By Thévenin's theorem, find the current in the 19.2-Ω resistor of the circuit shown in Fig. 5-36a.

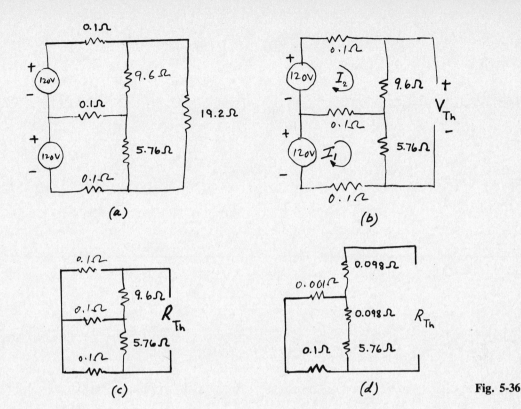

Fig. 5-36

▌ From Fig. 5-36b,

$$5.96I_1 - 0.1I_2 = 120 \qquad -0.1I_1 + 9.8I_2 = 120$$

Or $$I_1 = 20.34 \text{ A} \qquad \text{and} \qquad I_2 = 12.45 \text{ A}$$

Hence, $$V_{\text{Th}} = 9.6I_2 + 5.76I_1 = 9.6 \times 12.45 + 5.76 \times 20.34 = 236.7 \text{ V}$$

From Fig. 5-36c and d

$$R_{\text{Th}} = 0.098 + \frac{(0.098 + 5.76)(0.001 + 0.1)}{0.098 + 5.76 + 0.001 + 0.1} = 0.197 \ \Omega \qquad I_{19.2\,\Omega} = \frac{236.7}{19.2 + 0.197} = 12.2 \text{ A}$$

5.39 Find the current in the 9-Ω resistor of the circuit of Fig. 5-37a by Thévenin's theorem.

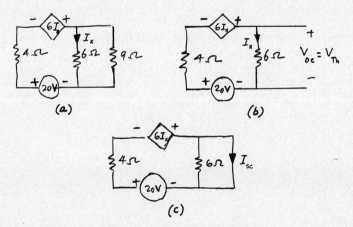

Fig. 5-37

▌ Since the circuit contains a dependent voltage source, we obtain $R_{\text{Th}} = V_{\text{OC}}/I_{\text{SC}}$, where V_{OC} and I_{SC} are, respectively, defined in Fig. 5-37b and c.
From Fig. 5-37b,

$$20 + 6I_x = 4I_x + 6I_x \qquad \text{or} \qquad I_x = 5 \text{ A} \qquad \text{and} \qquad V_{\text{OC}} = V_{\text{Th}} = 5 \times 6 = 30 \text{ V}$$

From Fig. 5-37c,

$$20 = 4I_{SC} \quad \text{or} \quad I_{SC} = 5\,\text{A}$$

Hence,

$$R_{Th} = \frac{V_{OC}}{I_{SC}} = \frac{30}{5} = 6\,\Omega \quad \text{and} \quad I_{9\,\Omega} = \frac{V_{Th}}{9 + R_{Th}} = \frac{30}{9 + 6} = 2\,\text{A}$$

5.40 Find the current in the 10-Ω resistor of the circuit of Fig. 5-38a.

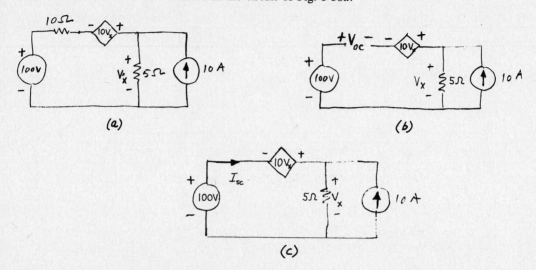

Fig. 5-38

▮ Proceeding as in Prob. 5.39, from Fig. 5-38b we have

$$100 - V_{OC} + 10V_x - V_x = 0 \quad \text{and} \quad V_x = 10 \times 5 = 50\,\text{V} \quad \text{or} \quad V_{OC} = V_{Th} = 550\,\text{V}$$

From Fig. 5-38c we obtain

$$100 + 10V_x - V_x = 0 \quad \text{or} \quad V_x = -\frac{100}{9}\,\text{V}$$

Also,

$$I_{SC} + 10 = -\frac{100/9}{5} \quad \text{or} \quad I_{SC} = -\frac{550}{45}\,\text{A}$$

Thus,

$$R_{Th} = \frac{V_{OC}}{I_{SC}} = \frac{550}{-550/45} = -45\,\Omega$$

Hence,

$$I_{10\,\Omega} = \frac{550}{10 - 45} = -15.7\text{A}$$

5.41 Calculate the current in the 6-Ω resistor of the circuit of Fig. 5-39a by Thévenin's theorem.

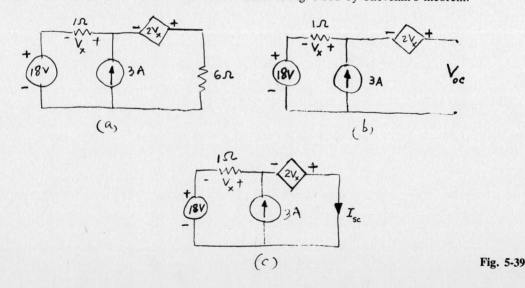

Fig. 5-39

▮ First, we calculate V_{OC} from Fig. 5-39b. Thus,

$$18 + V_x + 2V_x - V_{OC} = 0$$

But
$$V_x = 3 \times 1 = 3 \text{ V} \quad \text{or} \quad V_{OC} = V_{Th} = 27 \text{ V}$$

From Fig. 5-39c,

$$18 + V_x + 2V_x = 0 \quad \text{or} \quad 18 + 3V_x = 0$$

But
$$\frac{V_x}{1} = 3 - I_{SC} \quad \text{or} \quad I_{SC} = 9 \text{ A}$$

Thus,
$$R_{Th} = \frac{V_{OC}}{I_{SC}} = \frac{27}{9} = 3 \ \Omega$$

Hence
$$I_{6\Omega} = \frac{27}{3 + 6} = 3 \text{ A}$$

5.42 Determine the current in the 2-Ω resistor of the circuit of Fig. 4-55 by Thévenin's theorem.

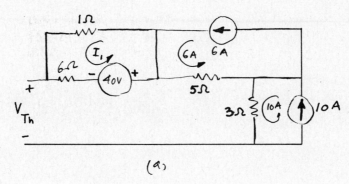

(a)

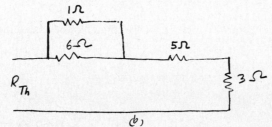

(b)

Fig. 5-40

▮ From Fig. 5-40a,

$$-40 + I_1 + 6I_1 = 0 \quad \text{or} \quad I_1 = \frac{40}{7} \text{ A} \qquad V_{6\,\Omega} = 6\left(\frac{40}{7}\right) = \frac{240}{7} \text{ V}$$

$$V_{5\,\Omega} = 6 \times 5 = 30 \text{ V} \qquad V_{3\,\Omega} = 10 \times 3 = 30 \text{ V} \qquad V_{Th} = \frac{240}{7} - 40 + 30 + 30 = \frac{380}{7} \text{ V}$$

From Fig. 5-40b,

$$R_{Th} = 5 + 3 + \frac{6 \times 1}{6 + 1} = \frac{62}{7} \ \Omega \qquad I_{2\,\Omega} = \frac{V_{Th}}{2 + R_{Th}} = \frac{380/7}{2 + 62/7} = 5 \text{ A}$$

5.43 Find the current in the 24-Ω resistor of the circuit of Fig. 5-41a by Thévenin's theorem.

▮ To determine V_{Th}, we remove the 24-Ω resistor. Then,

$$V_{Th} = V_{ab} = -10I_x(12) = -120I_x = V_x$$

But
$$I_x = \frac{48 - 3V_x}{1000} = \frac{48 - 3V_{Th}}{1000}$$

Thus,
$$V_{Th} = -120 \frac{(48 - 3V_{Th})}{1000} \quad \text{or} \quad V_{Th} = -9V = V_{OC}$$

To determine R_{Th} we short-circuit the terminals ab. The circuit reduces to that shown in Fig. 5-41b, since

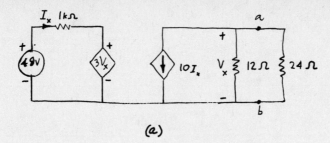

(a)

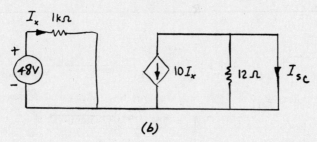

(b)

Fig. 5-41

$V_x = 0$. Thus,

$$I_{SC} = -10I_x \quad \text{and} \quad I_x = \frac{48}{1000} \quad \text{or} \quad I_{SC} = -0.48$$

Hence,

$$R_{Th} = \frac{V_{OC}}{I_{SC}} = \frac{9}{0.48} = 18.75 \ \Omega$$

Finally,

$$I_{24\ \Omega} = \frac{9}{24 + 18.75} = 0.21 \ A$$

5.44 Find the current in the 14-Ω resistor of the circuit of Fig. 5-42 by Thévenin's theorem.

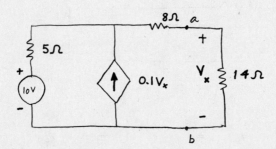

Fig. 5-42

▋ To find $V_{Th} = V_{OC}$, we open-circuit ab. Thus,

$$V_{OC} = V_{Th} = 10 - (-0.1V_x)5 = 10 + 0.5V_{OC}$$

Or

$$V_{OC} = 20V = V_{Th}$$

Next we short-circuit ab resulting in $V_x = 0$ and $0.1V_x = 0$. Thus,

$$I_{SC} = \frac{10}{5+8} = \frac{10}{13} \ A \quad \text{or} \quad R_{Th} = \frac{V_{OC}}{I_{SC}} = \frac{20}{10/13} = 26 \ \Omega \quad \text{and} \quad I_{14\ \Omega} = \frac{20}{14+26} = 0.5 \ A$$

5.45 Determine the current in the 16-Ω resistor of the circuit of Fig. 5-43 by Thévenin's theorem.

▋ Open-circuiting ab in Fig. 5-43 yields

$$V_{OC} = V_{Th} = 40 \ V \quad \text{since} \quad I_x = 0$$

Short-circuiting ab implies that $I_{SC} = I_x$. And

$$I_{SC} + 0.8I_{SC} = \frac{40 - V_1}{10}$$

But $$V_1 = 6I_{SC}$$

Therefore, $$I_{SC} = \frac{40}{24}\text{ A} \quad \text{and} \quad R_{Th} = \frac{V_{OC}}{I_{SC}} = \frac{40}{40/24} = 24\ \Omega$$

Hence, $$I_{16\ \Omega} = \frac{40}{16 + 24} = 1.0\text{ A}$$

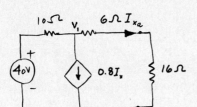

Fig. 5-43

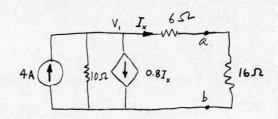

Fig. 5-44

5.46 Repeat Prob. 5.45 by converting the 40-V voltage source to an equivalent current source.

▌ The new circuit is shown in Fig. 5-44 from which the open-circuit voltage is

$$V_{OC} = 10 \times 4 = 40\text{V} = V_{Th}$$

To find I_{SC}, we short-circuit ab and use the nodal equation to obtain

$$4 = \frac{V_1}{10} + 0.8I_x + I_x \quad \text{and} \quad I_x = \frac{V_1}{6} = I_{SC}$$

Hence, $$I_{SC} = \frac{40}{24}\text{ A}$$

which is identical to the result of Prob. 5.45.

5.47 Determine the current in the 8-Ω resistor of the circuit of Fig. 4-54, for $k = 2$, by Thévenin's theorem.

▌ By inspection, with the 8-Ω resistor removed,

$$V_{OC} = V_{Th} = 16\text{ V}$$

When the 8-Ω resistor is short-circuited,

$$I_{SC} = \infty \quad \text{and}$$

Thus, $$R_{Th} = \frac{16}{\infty} = 0\Omega \quad I_{8\Omega} = \frac{16}{0 + 8} = 2.0\text{A}$$

5.48 Find the current I in the circuit of Fig. 4-56 by Thévenin's theorem.

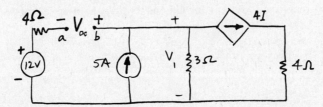

Fig. 5-45

▌ First, we remove the 4-Ω resistor to obtain the circuit shown in Fig. 5-45 to determine V_{OC}. Thus, $I = 0$ and

$$V_1 = 5 \times 3 = 15\text{ V} \quad \text{and} \quad 12 + V_{OC} - V_1 = 0 \quad \text{or} \quad V_{OC} = 15 - 12 = 3\text{ V}$$

To find I_{SC} we short-circuit ab through which $I_{SC} = I$ flows. Then,

$$\frac{12 - V_1}{4} + 5 = \frac{V_1}{3} + \frac{4(12 - V_1)}{4}$$

or, $$V_1 = 9.6\text{V}$$

and $$I_{SC} = \frac{12 - V_1}{4} = 0.6\text{A}$$

$$R_{Th_1} = \frac{3}{0.6} = 5\Omega$$

5.49 Obtain the Thévenin equivalent circuit at the terminals *ab* of the circuit shown in Fig. 5.46*a*.

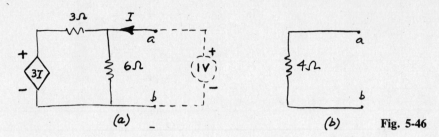

(a) (b) **Fig. 5-46**

❚ Note that this circuit does not contain any independent sources. To obtain the Thévenin equivalent we apply a voltage source of 1 V at *ab*. Therefore,

$$I = \frac{1}{6} + \frac{1 - 3I}{3} \quad \text{or} \quad I = \frac{1}{4} \text{ A} \quad \text{and} \quad R_{\text{Th}} = \frac{1}{1/4} = 4 \text{ } \Omega$$

The Thévenin equivalent circuit is shown in Fig. 5-46*b*.

5.50 The equivalent circuit of an operational amplifier is shown in Fig. 5-47. Find the Thévenin equivalent resistance at the output terminals. Assume $R_1 \ll R_i$.

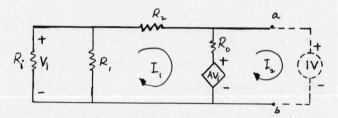

Fig. 5-47

❚ As in Prob. 5.49, we apply a voltage source of 1 V across *ab*. We further observe that the parallel combination of R_1 and R_i is approximately R_1, since $R_1 \ll R_i$. Then, for the resulting circuit we have

$$I_1(R_1 + R_2 + R_0) - I_2 R_0 + AV_i = 0 \qquad AV_i - 1 + I_1 R_0 - I_2 R_0 = 0 \qquad V_i = I_1 R_1$$

Solving for I_2 yields

$$I_2 = \frac{-(R_1 + AR_1 + R_2 + R_0)}{R_0(R_1 + R_2)}$$

Hence,

$$R_{\text{Th}} = \frac{1}{-I_2} = \frac{R_0(R_1 + R_2)}{R_1(1 + A) + R_2 + R_0}$$

5.51 Apply Thévenin's theorem to the circuit to the left and to the right of node 1 of the network shown in Fig. 5-2*a*. Hence, determine the current in the 1-Ω resistor.

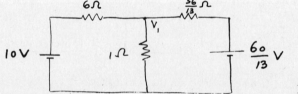

Fig. 5-48

❚ To the left of node 1, the Thévenin equivalent is simply the 10-V source in series with the 6-Ω resistor. To the right of node 1, we have

$$V_{\text{Th}} = V_{3\,\Omega} = \frac{20}{13} \times 3 = \frac{60}{13} \text{ V} \quad \text{and} \quad R_{\text{Th}} = 2 + \frac{10 \times 3}{13} = \frac{56}{13} \text{ } \Omega$$

Finally, we obtain the circuit of Fig. 5-48, from which

$$\frac{10 - V_1}{6} + \frac{(60/13) - V_1}{(56/13)} - \frac{V_1}{1} = 0 \quad \text{or} \quad V_1 = 1.96 \text{ V} \quad \text{and} \quad I_{1\Omega} = \frac{V_1}{1} = 1.96 \text{ A}$$

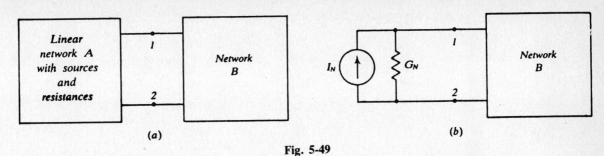

Fig. 5-49

5.52 Norton's equivalent circuit is the dual of Thévenin's equivalent circuit and may be obtained from the latter by source transformation. Explicitly, *Norton's theorem* may be stated as follows: At the terminals 12 in Fig. 5-49a, the arbitrary linear network A, containing resistances and energy sources, can be replaced by an equivalent circuit consisting of a current source I_N in parallel with a conductance G_N, shown in Fig. 5-49b.

The current I_N is the short-circuit current (through 12, when these terminals are short-circuited) and G_N is the ratio of the short-circuit current to the open-circuit voltage. Note that $G_N = 1/R_{Th}$, where R_{Th} is the Thévenin equivalent resistance.

Find the current in the 10-Ω resistor of the circuit of Fig. 5-2a by Norton's theorem.

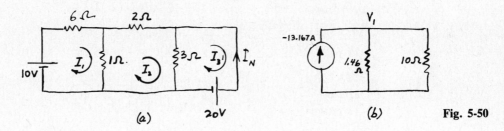

Fig. 5-50

▮ From Prob. 5.1, $R_{Th} = 1.46 \, \Omega$, or

$$G_N = \frac{1}{R_{Th}} = \frac{1}{1.46} = 0.685 \, \text{S}$$

To determine I_N we refer to the circuit of Fig. 5-50a from which

$$10 = 7I_1 - I_2 \qquad 0 = -I_1 + 6I_2 - 3I_3 \qquad -20 = -3I_2 + 3I_3$$

Solving for I_3 yields

$$I_3 = -I_N = 13.167 \, \text{A}$$

Therefore, from Fig. 5-50b,

$$-13.167 = \frac{V_1}{1.46} + \frac{V_1}{10} \qquad \text{or} \qquad V_1 = -16.8 \, \text{V}$$

Hence,

$$I_{10 \, \Omega} = -\frac{16.8}{10} = -1.68 \, \text{A}$$

5.53 In Prob. 5.52 we have shown the details of calculating I_N. However, from Figs. 5-1 and 5-49 it follows that

$$G_N = \frac{1}{R_{Th}} \tag{1}$$

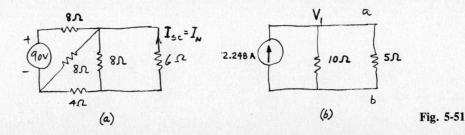

Fig. 5-51

and

$$I_N = \frac{V_{\text{Th}}}{R_{\text{Th}}}$$

(2)

Apply these results to the circuit of Fig. 5-3 to obtain directly the current through the 5-Ω resistor.

I From Prob. 5.2,

$$R_{\text{Th}} = \frac{1}{G_N} = 10 \, \Omega \quad \text{and} \quad V_{\text{Th}} = 22.48 \, \text{V}$$

Thus,

$$I_N = \frac{22.48}{10} = 2.248 \, \text{A}$$

Hence we obtain the circuit of Fig. 5-51b from which we have

$$2.248 = \frac{V_1}{10} + \frac{V_1}{5} = 0.03V_1 \quad \text{or} \quad V_1 = 7.5 \, \text{V} \quad \text{and} \quad I_{5\,\Omega} = \frac{7.5}{5} = 1.5 \, \text{A}$$

5.54 Obtain a Norton equivalent circuit to determine the current in the 5-Ω resistor of the circuit of Fig. 4-6.

I From Prob. 5.4 we have

$$R_{\text{Th}} = 2.42 \, \Omega \quad \text{and} \quad V_{\text{Th}} = -28.8 \, \text{V}$$

Hence,

$$I_N = \frac{V_{\text{Th}}}{R_{\text{Th}}} = -\frac{28.8}{2.42} = -11.9 \, \text{A} \qquad G_N = \frac{1}{R_{\text{Th}}} = \frac{1}{2.42} = 0.413 \, \text{S}$$

Thus, we obtain the desired circuit shown in Fig. 5-52.

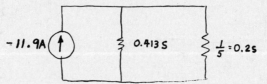

Fig. 5-52

5.55 Determine the current in the 10-Ω resistor of the circuit of Fig. 5-53a by Norton's theorem.

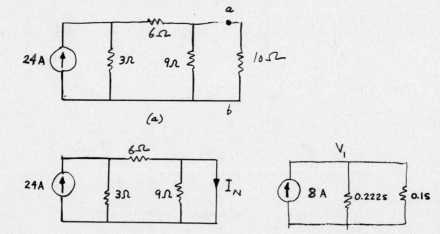

Fig. 5-53

I To determine I_N we short-circuit ab to obtain the circuit of Fig. 5-53b from which, by current division,

$$I_N = 8 \, \text{A}$$

With the source and short-circuit removed from Fig. 5-53b we obtain

$$R_N = \frac{1}{G_N} = \frac{9(6+3)}{9+6+3} = 4.5 \, \Omega \quad \text{or} \quad G_N = \frac{1}{4.5} = 0.222 \, \text{S}$$

Hence we obtain the Norton equivalent circuit of Fig. 5-53c which yields

$$V_1(0.222 + 0.1) = 8 \quad \text{or} \quad V_1 = 24.84 \, \text{V} \qquad I_{10\,\Omega} = I_{0.1\,\text{S}} = 2.484 \, \text{A}$$

5.56 Obtain the Norton equivalent circuit for the network of Fig. 5-54a to determine the current in the 50-Ω resistor.

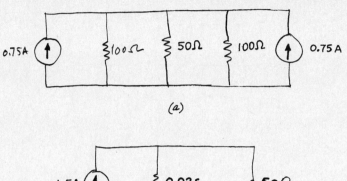

(a)

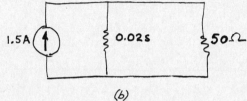

(b)   **Fig. 5-54**

▌ With the 50-Ω resistor short-circuited, the total current will flow through the short circuit. Thus,

$$I_N = 0.75 + 0.75 = 1.5 \text{ A}$$

Next, with the sources and the 50-Ω resistor removed, the two 100-Ω resistors become in parallel resulting in a net resistance of 50 Ω. Therefore,

$$G_N = \frac{1}{50} = 0.02 \text{ S}$$

Consequently, the Norton circuit of Fig. 5-55b follows, from which

$$I_{50\,\Omega} = 0.75 \text{ A}$$

5.57 The network shown in Fig. 5-55a is an equivalent circuit of a transistor switching circuit. If the base-to-emitter resistance is 125 Ω, calculate the current through it by Norton's theorem.

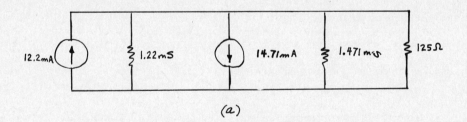

(a)

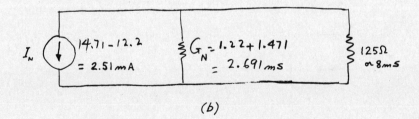

(b)   **Fig. 5-55**

▌ The Norton equivalent of the circuit of Fig. 5-55a is shown in Fig. 5-55b from which

$$I_B = I_N \frac{G_{BE}}{G_{BE} + G_N} = 2.51 \times 10^{-3} \left[\frac{8 \times 10^{-3}}{(8 + 2.691)10^{-3}} \right] = 1.878 \times 10^{-3} = 1.878 \text{ mA}$$

5.58 Find the Norton equivalent at the terminals ab of the circuit of Fig. 5-56a.

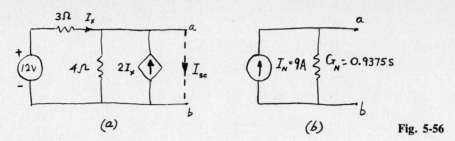

Fig. 5-56

▮ First, we short-circuit ab. Then

$$I_{sc} = I_x + 2I_x = 3I_x$$

But

$$I_x = \frac{12}{4} = 3 \text{ A} \qquad I_{SC} = 3 \times 3 = 9 \text{ A}$$

Next, we determine the open-circuit voltage V_{OC} at ab. From Fig. 5-56a with ab open-circuited,

$$I_x = \frac{12 - V_{OC}}{3} \quad \text{and} \quad I_x + 2I_x = \frac{V_{OC}}{4} \quad \text{or} \quad I_x = \frac{V_{OC}}{12} \quad \text{or} \quad \frac{V_{OC}}{12} = \frac{12 - V_{OC}}{3} \quad \text{or} \quad V_{OC} = \frac{48}{5} \text{ V}$$

Hence,

$$G_N = \frac{I_{SC}}{V_{OC}} = \frac{9}{48/5} = \frac{45}{48} \quad \text{and} \quad I_N = I_{SC} = 9 \text{ A}$$

Thus, we obtain the circuit shown in Fig. 5-56b.

5.59 The circuit in Fig. 5-57 contains two types of independent sources. Obtain the Norton equivalent circuit at ab.

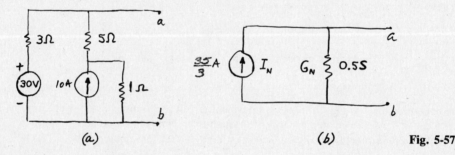

Fig. 5-57

▮ By short-circuiting ab we observe that

$$I_{SC} = I_N = \frac{35}{3} \text{ A}$$

Removing the sources and the short-circuit yields

$$R_N = \frac{3(5 + 1)}{3 + 5 + 1} = 2 \ \Omega$$

Hence we obtain the Norton circuit of Fig. 5-57b.

5.60 Converting the current source of the circuit of Fig. 4-10a results in the circuit of Fig. 4-10b. Find the current in the 10-Ω resistor by applying Norton's theorem.

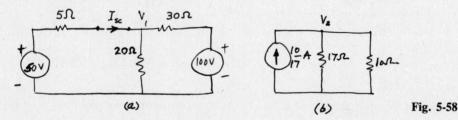

Fig. 5-58

▮ Short-circuiting the 10-Ω resistor results in the circuit of Fig. 5-58a, from which

$$\frac{50 - V_1}{5} + \frac{100 - V_1}{30} = \frac{V_1}{20} \quad \text{or} \quad V_1 = = \frac{800}{17} \text{ V}$$

And
$$I_{SC} = \frac{50 - V_1}{5} = \frac{50 - (800/17)}{5} = \frac{10}{17} \text{ A}$$

Removing the short-circuit and the sources yields
$$R_N = 5 + \frac{30 \times 20}{30 + 20} = 17 \, \Omega$$

Thus we obtain the Norton circuit of Fig. 5-58b which yields
$$\frac{10}{17} = \frac{V_2}{17} + \frac{V_2}{10} \quad \text{or} \quad V_2 = \frac{100}{27} \text{ V} \quad \text{and} \quad I_{10\,\Omega} = \frac{V_2}{10} = \frac{100}{10 \times 27} = 0.37 \text{ A}$$

5.61 Obtain the Norton equivalent of the circuit shown in Fig. 5-59a.

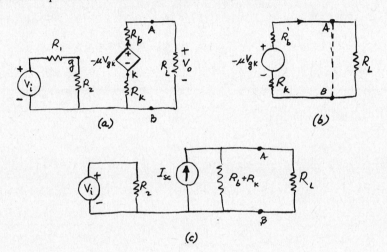

Fig. 5-59

▮ We short-circuit AB (Fig. 5-59b) to obtain
$$I_{SC} = \frac{-\mu V_{gk}}{R_b + R_k}$$

where
$$V_{gk} = -I_{SC}R_k - V_i$$

The Norton equivalent becomes as shown in Fig. 5-59c.

5.62 The circuit of Fig. 5-60a contains only a dependent source. Obtain its Norton equivalent.

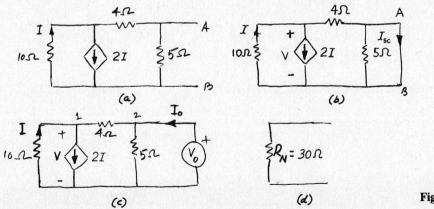

Fig. 5-60

▮ First we short-circuit AB as shown in Fig. 5-60b, from which
$$\frac{V}{10} + 2I + \frac{V}{4} = 0 \quad \text{or} \quad \frac{V}{10} + 2\left(-\frac{V}{10}\right) + \frac{V}{4} = 0 \quad \text{or} \quad V = 0 \quad \text{and} \quad I_{SC} = 0$$

To find R_N we refer to Fig. 5-60c where
$$R_N = \frac{V_0}{I_0}$$

And at node 1,

$$\frac{V}{10} + 2\left(-\frac{V}{10}\right) + \frac{V - V_0}{4} = 0 \quad \text{or} \quad V = \frac{5}{3} V_0$$

At node 2,

$$I_0 = \frac{V_0}{5} + \frac{V_0 - V}{4} = \frac{V_0}{5} + \frac{V_0}{4} - \frac{5V_0}{12} = \frac{2V_0}{60} \quad \text{or} \quad R_N = \frac{V_0}{I_0} = 30\,\Omega$$

Hence we obtain the Norton circuit of Fig. 5-60d.

5.63 Find the current in the 5-Ω resistor of the circuit of Fig. 5-61 by Norton's theorem.

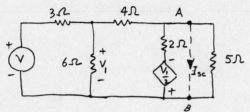

Fig. 5-61

▮ At node A, after short-circuiting the 5-Ω resistor, we obtain

$$\frac{V_1}{4} - \frac{V_1/2}{2} - I_{\text{sc}} = 0 \quad \text{or} \quad I_{\text{sc}} = 0$$

Hence no current will flow through the 5-Ω resistor, $I_{5\,\Omega} = 0$.

5.64 Determine the Norton equivalent of the circuit of Fig. 5-61.

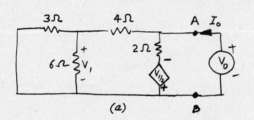
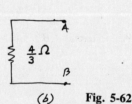

(a)   (b)   Fig. 5-62

▮ From Prob. 5.63,

$$I_{\text{sc}} = I_N = 0$$

To find R_N we use the circuit of Fig. 5-62a from which

$$I_0 = \frac{V_0 - V_1}{4} + \frac{V_0 + V_1/2}{2} = \frac{3}{4} V_0 \quad \text{or} \quad \frac{V_0}{I_0} = R_N = \frac{4}{3}\,\Omega$$

Thus we obtain the Norton circuit of Fig. 5-62b.

5.65 Find the current in the 1-Ω resistor of the circuit of Fig. 5-63a by Norton's theorem.

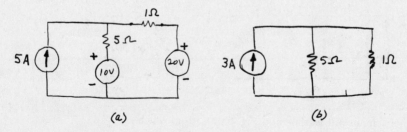

(a)   (b)   Fig. 5-63

▮ Short-circuiting the 1-Ω resistor yields

$$5 + I_{\text{sc}} - \frac{20 - 10}{5} = 0 \quad \text{or} \quad I_{\text{sc}} = -3A = I_N$$

By inspection,

$$R_N = 5\,\Omega$$

Hence we obtain the Norton circuit of Fig. 5-63b from which

$$\frac{V}{1}+\frac{V}{5}=3 \quad \text{or} \quad V=\frac{15}{6}=2.5\,\text{V} \quad \text{and} \quad I_{1\,\Omega}=\frac{V}{1}=2.5\,\text{A}$$

5.66 Two networks are shown in Fig. 5-64; the ammeters in both circuits have negligible resistances. Calculate the ammeter readings in the two networks and comment on the results. Note that in the two networks the positions of the ammeter and the voltage source are interchanged.

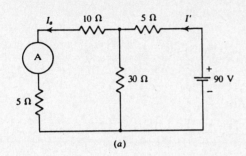 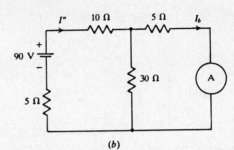

(a)   (b)   **Fig. 5-64**

▌ In Fig. 5-64a, the resistance seen by the voltage source is

$$R'_e = 5 + \frac{(10+5)(30)}{10+5+30} = 15\,\Omega$$

so that

$$I' = \frac{90}{15} = 6\,\text{A}$$

Hence, by current division,

$$\text{Ammeter reading} = I_a = \frac{30}{45}(6) = 4\,\text{A}$$

Similarly, for Fig. 5-64b,

$$R''_e = 15 + \frac{(30)(5)}{30+5} = \frac{135}{7}\,\Omega \quad \text{and} \quad I'' = \frac{90}{135/7} = \frac{14}{3}\,\text{A}$$

By current division,

$$\text{Ammeter reading} = I_b = \frac{30}{35}\left(\frac{14}{3}\right) = 4\,\text{A}$$

The equality of the ammeter readings constitutes a special case of the *reciprocity theorem*: In a linear bilateral network, if a voltage V in some branch produces a current I in some other branch, then the same voltage V in the second branch will produce the same current I in the first branch.

5.67 Solve for the current I of Fig. 5-65a by applying the superposition theorem.

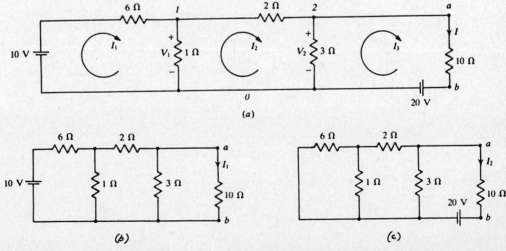

Fig. 5-65

▌ According to the superposition theorem, we determine the current due to each source (in the absence of all other sources). The net current is the sum of all these currents. So let us eliminate the 20-V source by replacing it by a short circuit. The network of Fig. 5-65a then becomes as shown in Fig. 5-65b. Combining resistances as in Prob. 5.2, we find $I_1 = 0.0636$ A. Next, we eliminate the 10-V source to obtain the circuit of Fig. 5-65c. Proceeding as before, we determine $I_2 = -1.744$ A. Consequently,

$$I = I_1 + I_2 = 0.0636 - 1.744 = -1.68 \text{ A}$$

5.68 Determine the current I_1 in the circuit of Fig. 4-10a by superposition.

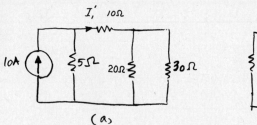 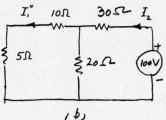

(a)   (b)   **Fig. 5-66**

▌ For superposition, we first excite the circuit by the current source only as shown in Fig. 5-66a from which we observe that the 10-A current from the source is divided into a 5-Ω resistor and a $10 + [(20 \times 30)/(20 + 30)] = 22$-Ω resistor. Hence, by current division,

$$I'_1 = 10\left(\frac{5}{5 + 22}\right) = 1.852 \text{ A}$$

Next, removing the current source and keeping only the voltage source, from Fig. 5-66b we obtain

$$I_2 = \frac{100}{30 + \{[20(10 + 5)]/(20 + 10 + 5)\}} = 2.593 \text{ A}$$

By current division,

$$I''_1 = 2.593 \frac{20}{20 + 10 + 5} = 1.481 \text{ A}$$

Hence, $$I_1 = I'_1 - I''_1 = 1.852 - 1.481 = 0.37 \text{ A}$$

5.69 Calculate the current I in the circuit of Fig. 4-16 by superposition.

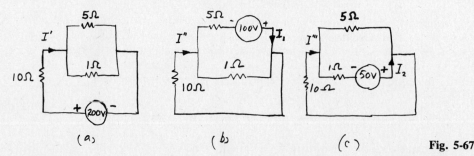

(a)   (b)   (c)   **Fig. 5-67**

▌ We use one source at a time as shown in the circuits of Fig. 5-67a to c. From Figure 5-67a we have

$$I' = \frac{200}{10 + [(5 \times 1)/(5 + 1)]} = 18.46 \text{ A}$$

Fig. 5-67b yields

$$I_1 = \frac{100}{5 + [(10 \times 1)/(10 + 1)]} = 16.92 \text{ A} \quad \text{and} \quad I'' = 16.92 \frac{1}{10 + 1} = 1.54 \text{ A}$$

Similarly, from Fig. 5-67c we obtain

$$I_2 = \frac{50}{1 + [(5 \times 10)/(5 + 10)]} = 11.54 \text{ A} \quad \text{and} \quad I''' = 11.54 \frac{5}{5 + 10} = 3.85 \text{ A}$$

Hence, $$I = I' + I'' + I''' = 18.46 + 1.54 + 3.85 = 23.85 \text{ A}$$

5.70 Find the current in the 2-Ω resistor of the circuit of Fig. 4-17 by superposition.

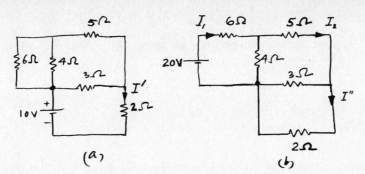

Fig. 5-68

▮ From Fig. 5-68a, with the 20-V source removed, we obtain

$$I' = \frac{10}{2 + (3\{5 + [(6 \times 4)/(6+4)]\})/\{3 + 5 + [(6 \times 4)/(6+4)]\}} = 2.42 \text{ A}$$

From Fig. 5-68b we have

$$I_1 = \frac{20}{6 + \{4(5 + [(3 \times 2)/(3+2)])\}/\{4 + 5 + [(3 \times 2)/(3+2)]\}} = 2.37 \text{ A}$$

$$I_2 = 2.37 \frac{4}{\{4 + 5 + [(3 \times 2)/(3+2)]\}} = 0.93 \text{ A}$$

$$I'' = 0.93 \frac{3}{3+2} = 0.56 \text{ A}$$

$$I_{2\,\Omega} = I' + I'' = 2.42 + 0.56 = 2.98 \text{ A}$$

5.71 Find an expression for the output (v_0) of the amplifier circuit of Fig. 5-69. Assume an ideal basic op amp. What mathematical operation does the circuit perform?

▮ The principle of superposition is applicable to this linear circuit. With $v_{S2} = 0$ (shorted), the voltage appearing at the noninverting terminal is found by voltage division to be

$$v_2 = \frac{R}{R + R} v_{S1} = \frac{v_{S1}}{2}$$

Let v_{o1} be the value of v_o with $v_{S2} = 0$. Now,

$$v_{o1} = \left(1 + \frac{R_2}{R_1}\right) v_2 = \left(1 + \frac{R_2}{R_1}\right) \frac{v_{S1}}{2}$$

Similarly, with $v_{S1} = 0$,

$$v_{o2} = \left(1 + \frac{R_2}{R_1}\right) \frac{v_{S2}}{2}$$

By superposition, the total output is

$$v_o = v_{o1} + v_{o2} = \frac{1}{2}\left(1 + \frac{R_2}{R_1}\right)(v_{S1} + v_{S2})$$

The circuit is seen to be a noninverting adder.

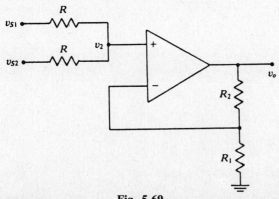

Fig. 5-69

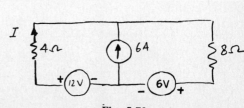

Fig. 5-70

5.72 Calculate the current in the 4-Ω resistor of the circuit of Fig. 5-70 by superposition.

Assuming that all currents in the 4-Ω resistor are in clockwise direction, with the 6-A and 6-V sources removed, due to the 12-V source we get

$$I' = \frac{12}{4+8} = 1.0 \text{ A}$$

With the 6-A and 12-V sources removed, for the 6-V source we have

$$I'' = -\frac{6}{4+8} = -0.5 \text{ A}$$

Finally, with the two voltage sources, we obtain for the 6-A source, by current division:

$$I''' = -6\left(\frac{8}{4+8}\right) = -4.0 \text{ A}$$

Hence,

$$I_{4\,\Omega} = I' + I'' + I''' = 1.0 - 0.5 - 4.0 = -3.5 \text{ A}$$

5.73 Calculate the current in the 4-Ω resistor of the circuit of Fig. 5-71a by superposition.

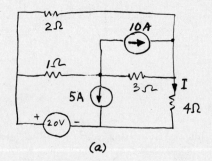

(a)

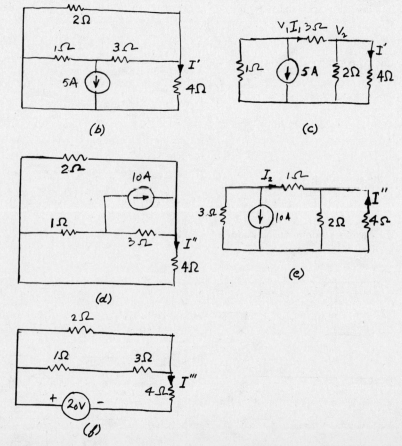

(b)

(c)

(d)

(e)

(f)

Fig. 5-71

▮ Considering one source at a time, from Fig. 5-71b we note that the 2-Ω and the 4-Ω resistors are in parallel, so that the circuit may be redrawn in Fig. 5-71c. By current division we have

$$I_1 = -5 \frac{1}{1 + 3 + [(2 \times 4)/(2 + 4)]} = -0.9375 \text{ A} \qquad \text{and} \qquad I' = -0.9375 \frac{2}{2 + 4} = -0.3125 \text{ A}$$

Similarly, we redraw the circuit of Fig. 5-71d as that in Fig. 5-71e, from which

$$I_2 = -10 \frac{3}{3 + 1 + [(2 \times 4)/(2 + 4)]} = -5.625 \text{ A} \qquad \text{and} \qquad -I'' = -5.625 \frac{2}{2 + 4} = -1.875 \text{ A} \qquad \text{or} \qquad I'' = 1.875 \text{ A}$$

Finally, from Fig. 5-71f we obtain

$$I''' = \frac{20}{4 + \{[2(1 + 3)]/(2 + 1 + 3)\}} = 3.75 \text{ A}$$

Hence,
$$I = I' + I'' + I''' = -0.3125 + 1.875 + 3.75 = 5.3125 \text{ A}$$

5.74 Determine the indicated voltage V_{12} in the circuit of Fig. 5-72 by superposition.

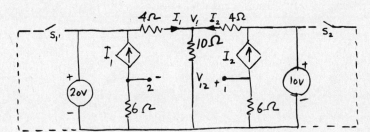

Fig. 5-72

▮ Instead of redrawing the circuit, we remove the voltage sources by closing S_2 or S_1. Let S_1 be open and S_2 closed. Then,

$$\frac{20 - V_1}{4} = \frac{V_1}{10} + \frac{V_1}{4}$$

Or, $$V_1 = \frac{25}{3} \text{ V} \qquad I_1 = \frac{20 - V_1}{4} = \frac{20 - 25/3}{4} = \frac{35}{12} \text{ A} \qquad I_2 = -\frac{V_1}{4} = -\frac{25/3}{4} = -\frac{25}{12} \text{ A}$$

$$V'_{12} = 6(I_1 - I_2) = \frac{6}{12}(35 + 25) = 30 \text{ V}$$

Next, let S_2 be open and S_2 closed. Then,

$$\frac{10 - V_1}{4} = \frac{V_1}{10} + \frac{V_1}{4}$$

or $$V_1 = \frac{25}{6} \text{ V} \qquad I_1 = -\frac{V_1}{4} = -\frac{25}{24} \text{ A}$$

$$I_2 = \frac{10 - V_1}{4} = \frac{10 - 25/6}{4} = \frac{35}{24} \text{ A} \qquad V''_{12} = 6(I_1 - I_2) = -\frac{6}{24}(25 + 35) = -15 \text{ V}$$

or $$V_{12} = V'_{12} + V''_{12} = 30 - 15 = 15 \text{ V}$$

5.75 Find the current through the dependent voltage source, $2V_1$, of the circuit shown in Fig. 5-73 by superposition.

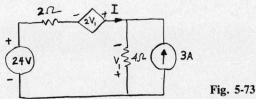

Fig. 5-73

▮ First we remove the 3-A current source. Then,

$$24 - 2I' + 2V_1 + 4V_1 = 0 \qquad \text{and} \qquad V_1 = -4I'$$

Thus,
$$I' = \frac{24}{14} \text{ A}$$

Next, we remove the 24-V voltage source. Then, from nodal analysis,
$$I'' = -\frac{36}{14} \text{ A}$$

Hence,
$$I = I' + I'' = -\left(\frac{36-24}{14}\right) = -0.857 \text{ A}$$

5.76 For the operational amplifier circuit of Fig. 5-74, find V_0 by superposition. Note that $V_+ = 0$.

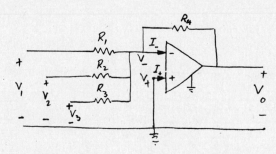

Fig. 5-74

❙ Removing the voltages V_2 and V_3 by short-circuiting them we have
$$V'_0 = -\frac{R_4}{R_1} V_1$$

Similarly,
$$V''_0 = -\frac{R_4}{R_2} V_2 \quad \text{and} \quad V'''_0 = -\frac{R_4}{R_3} V_3$$

Hence,
$$V_0 = V'_0 + V''_0 + V'''_0 = -\left(\frac{R_4}{R_1} V_1 + \frac{R_4}{R_2} V_2 + \frac{R_4}{R_3} V_3\right)$$

5.77 Find V_0 for the operational amplifier circuit shown in Fig. 5-75 by superposition. Given $I_+ = I_- = 0$ and $V_+ = V_-$.

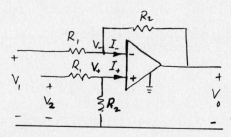

Fig. 5-75

❙ Removing V_2 and applying V_1 we have
$$V'_0 = -\frac{R_2}{R_1} V_1$$

Removing V_1 and applying V_2 yields (with $I_+ = I_- = 0$ and $V_+ = V_-$)
$$V''_0 = \frac{R_2}{R_1} V_2$$

Hence,
$$V_0 = V'_0 + V''_0 = \frac{R_2}{R_1} (V_2 - V_1)$$

5.78 By superposition, calculate the current I in the circuit shown in Fig. 5-76a.

❙ First, we remove the 70-V source to obtain the circuit of Fig. 5-76b. We combine the 2-Ω and 20-Ω resistors in parallel and then write the mesh equations as
$$\left(\frac{20}{11}+4\right)I'_1 + 2I'_1 - \frac{20}{11} I' = 0 \qquad \left(\frac{20}{11}+10\right)I' - \frac{20}{11} I'_1 = 50 + 2I'_1$$

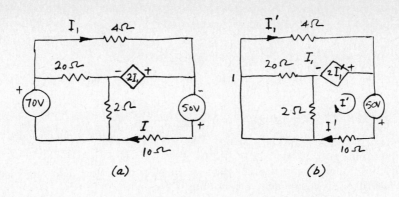

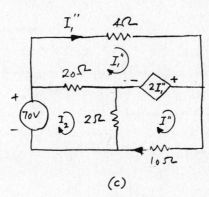

Fig. 5-76

Solving for I' yields

$$I' = 4.575 \text{ A}$$

Next, with the 50-V source removed, the mesh equations for the circuit of Fig. 5-76c become

$$22I_2 - 2I'' - 20I_1'' = 70 \qquad 12I'' - 2I_2 = 2I_1'' \qquad 24I_1'' - 20I_2 = -2I_1''$$

Solving for I'' gives

$$I'' = 3.425 \text{ A}$$

Hence,

$$I = I' + I'' = 4.575 + 3.425 = 8.0 \text{ A}$$

5.79 Determine the Thévenin voltage at the terminals ab of the network shown in Fig. 5-77a by superposition.

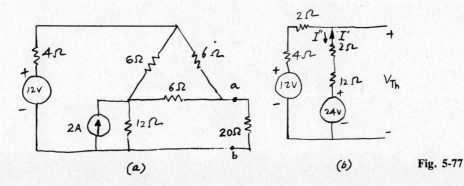

Fig. 5-77

▌ To obtain the Thévenin voltage V_{Th}, we open-circuit ab, convert the delta-connected resistors to an equivalent wye, and transform the 2-A current source to a voltage source. Hence we obtain the circuit shown in Fig. 5-26a, which is redrawn in Fig. 5-77b.

Now, with the 12-V source removed, we have

$$I' = \frac{24}{12 + 2 + 2 + 4} = 1.2 \text{ A}$$

Similarly, with the 24-V source removed, we obtain

$$I'' = \frac{12}{12 + 2 + 2 + 4} = 0.6 \text{ A}$$

Hence,

$$I = I' - I'' = 1.2 - 0.6 = 0.6 \text{ A} \qquad \text{and} \qquad V_{\text{Th}} = 24 - 0.6(12 + 2) = 15.6 \text{ V}$$

Verification:

$$I = I' - I'' = \frac{24 - 12}{12 + 2 + 2 + 4} = 0.6 \text{ A}$$

5.80   Find the Thévenin voltage V_{Th} shown in the circuit of Fig. 5-27*a* by superposition.
Removing the 10-V source, converting the 10-Ω wye-connected resistors, and combining the series-parallel resistors yields the circuit of Fig. 5-78*a*.   See also Fig. 5-27*c* and *d*.

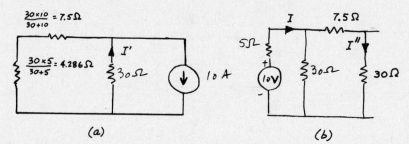

(a)   (b)   **Fig. 5-78**

❚ From Fig. 5-78*a* we obtain

$$I' = 10\left(\frac{7.5 + 4.286}{30 + 7.5 + 4.286}\right) = 2.82 \text{ A}$$

Next, we remove the 10-A source and insert the 10-V source in series with the 5-Ω resistor to obtain the circuit of Fig. 5-78*b*.   Then,

$$I = \frac{10}{5 + \{[30(7.5 + 30)]/[30 + 7.5 + 30]\}} = 0.4615 \text{ A}$$

And

$$I'' = I\left(\frac{30}{30 + 7.5 + 30}\right) = 0.205 \qquad I_{30\,\Omega} = I'' - I' = 0.205 - 2.82 = -2.615 \text{ A}$$

$$V_{\text{Th}} = V_{30\,\Omega} = -2.615 \times 30 = -78.45 \text{ V}$$

5.81   Determine the Thévenin voltage shown in the circuit of Fig. 5-28*a* by superposition.

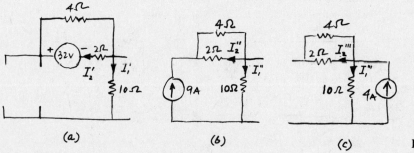

(a)   (b)   (c)   **Fig. 5-79**

❚ With the notation of Fig. 5-28*a*, we have

$$V_{\text{Th}} - 32 + V_2 - V_1 = 0$$

Therefore, to find V_{Th} we must determine V_1 and V_2 which requires the calculation of the currents in the 2-Ω and 10-Ω resistors.
We apply one source at a time as shown in Fig. 5-79*a* to *c*.   From Fig. 5-79*a*,

$$I_1' = 0 \text{ A} \qquad I_2' = \tfrac{32}{6} = \tfrac{16}{3} \text{ A}$$

From Fig. 5-79*b*,

$$I_1'' = 9 \text{ A} \qquad I_2'' = -9\left(\frac{4}{2 + 4}\right) = -6 \text{ A}$$

From Fig. 5-79c,

$$I_1''' = 4 \text{ A} \qquad I_2''' = 0 \text{ A}$$

Thus,
$$I_1 = I_1' + I_1'' + I_1''' = 0 + 9 + 4 = 13 \text{ A} \qquad I_2 = I_2' + I_2'' + I_2''' = \tfrac{16}{3} - 6 + 0 = -\tfrac{2}{3} \text{ A}$$

$$V_1 = I_1(10) = 13(10) = 130 \text{ V} \qquad V_2 = I_2(2) = -\tfrac{2}{3}(2) = -\tfrac{4}{3} \text{ V}$$

Hence,
$$V_{\text{Th}} = 32 + V_1 - V_2 = 32 + 130 + \tfrac{4}{3} = 163.33 \text{ V}$$

5.82 Obtain the Thévenin voltage shown in the circuit of Fig. 5-29a by superposition.

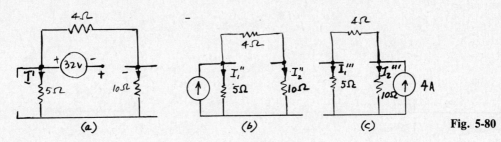

Fig. 5-80

❚ From Fig. 5-29a,

$$32 + V_{\text{Th}} + V_2 - V_1 = 0$$

where
$$V_1 = I_{5\,\Omega}(5) \qquad \text{and} \qquad V_2 = I_{10\,\Omega}(10)$$

From Fig. 5-80a,

$$I_1' = 0 \qquad I_2' = 0$$

From Fig. 5-80b,

$$I_1'' = 9\left(\frac{10+4}{10+4+5}\right) = 6.63 \text{ A} \qquad I_2'' = 9\left(\frac{5}{10+4+5}\right) = 2.37 \text{ A}$$

From Fig. 5-80c,

$$I_1''' = 4\left(\frac{10}{10+5+4}\right) = 2.11 \text{ A} \qquad I_2''' = 4\left(\frac{5+4}{10+5+4}\right) = 1.89 \text{ A} \qquad I_{5\,\Omega} = 0 + 6.63 + 2.11 = 8.74 \text{ A}$$

Or
$$V_1 = 8.74 \times 5 = 43.7 \text{ V} \qquad I_{10\,\Omega} = 0 + 2.37 + 1.89 = 4.26 \text{ A}$$

or
$$V_2 = 4.26 \times 10 = 42.6 \text{ V}$$

Finally,
$$V_{\text{Th}} = V_1 - V_2 - 32 = 43.7 - 42.6 - 32 = -30.9 \text{ V}$$

5-83 Determine the V_{Th} of the circuit of Fig. 5-32a by superposition.

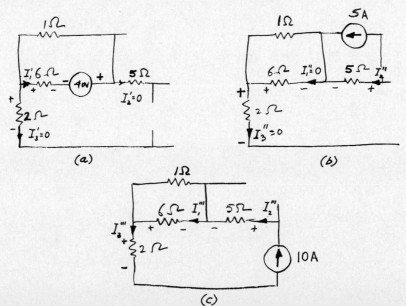

Fig. 5-81

▮ From Fig. 5-32a,

$$V_{\text{Th}} - V_{5\,\Omega} - 40 + V_{6\,\Omega} - V_{2\,\Omega} = 0$$

To find the voltages across various resistors we must determine the currents through them. For superposition we draw the circuits of Figs. 5-81a to c each having one source, others being removed.

From Fig. 5-81a, $\qquad\qquad\qquad I_1' = \dfrac{40}{7}$ A

From Fig. 5-81b, $\qquad\qquad\qquad I_1'' = 0$

From Fig. 5-81c,

$$I_1''' = 10\left(\frac{1}{1+6}\right) = \frac{10}{7}\,\text{A} \qquad I_{6\,\Omega} = I_1' - I_1''' = \frac{40}{7} - \frac{10}{7} = \frac{30}{7}\,\text{A} \qquad I_{6\,\Omega} = I_{6\,\Omega}(6) = \frac{30}{7} \times 6 = \frac{180}{7}\,\text{V}$$

From Fig. 5-81a, $\qquad\qquad\qquad I_2' = 0\,\text{A}$

From Fig. 5-81b, $\qquad\qquad\qquad I_2'' = -5\,\text{A}$

From Fig. 5-81c, $\quad I_2'' = 10\,\text{A} \qquad I_{5\,\Omega} = I_2'' + I_2''' = -5 + 10 = 5\,\text{A} \qquad V_{5\,\Omega} = I_{5\,\Omega}(5) = 5 \times 5 = 25\,\text{V}$

From Fig. 5-81a and b,

$$I_3' = I_3'' = 0$$

From Fig. 5-81c,

$$I_{2\,\Omega} = I_3''' = 10\,\text{A} \qquad V_{2\,\Omega} = I_{2\,\Omega}(2) = 10 \times 2 = 20\,\text{V}$$

Hence, $\qquad\qquad V_{\text{Th}} - 25 - 40 + \dfrac{180}{7} - 20 = 0 \qquad\text{or}\qquad V_{\text{Th}} = 59.28\,\text{V}$

5.84 Determine the current through the 10-Ω resistor of the circuit of Fig. 5-38a by superposition.

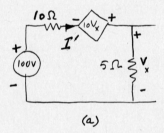

(a)

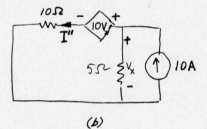

(b)

Fig. 5-82

▮ We remove the current source to obtain the circuit of Fig. 5-82a. Thus,

$$100 = 10I' - 10V_x + 5I' \qquad V_x = 5I'$$

Thus, $\qquad\qquad 100 = 10I' - 50I' + 5I' \qquad\text{or}\qquad I' = -\dfrac{100}{35}\,\text{A}$

Next, from Fig. 5-82b, where we have removed the voltage source, we obtain

$$10 = \frac{V_x}{5} + I'' \qquad V_x - 10V_x - 10I'' = 0$$

or $\qquad I'' = \dfrac{450}{35}\,\text{A} \qquad\text{or}\qquad I = I'' - I' = \dfrac{450}{35} + \dfrac{100}{35} = 15.71\,\text{A} \qquad$ (from right to left)

5.85 Find the current in the 6-Ω resistor of the circuit of Fig. 5-39a by superposition.

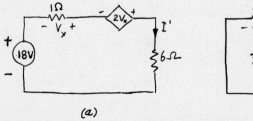

(a)

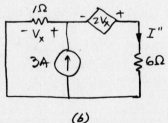

(b)

Fig. 5-83

❚ Retaining one source at a time we obtain the circuits of Fig. 5-83a and b. From Fig. 5-83a,

$$18 + V_x + 2V_x = 6I' \qquad V_x = -(1) I'$$

or

$$I' = 2A$$

From Fig. 5-83b,

$$3 = \frac{V_x}{1} + \frac{V_x + 2V_x}{6}$$

Or

$$V_x = 2 \qquad I'' = \frac{V_x + 2V_x}{6} = \frac{2+4}{6} = 1 \text{ A}$$

Hence,

$$I_{6\,\Omega} = I' + I'' = 2 + 1 = 3 \text{ A}$$

5.86 Find the current in the 4-Ω resistor of the circuit of Fig. 5-84a by superposition.

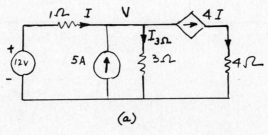

(a)

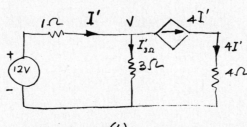

(b)

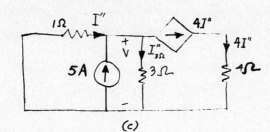

(c)   **Fig. 5-84**

❚ From Fig. 5-84b we have

$$\frac{12-V}{1} = \frac{V}{3} + 4\left(\frac{12-V}{1}\right) \qquad \text{or} \qquad V = 13.5 \text{ V}$$

And

$$I' = \frac{12-13.5}{1} = -\frac{3}{2} \text{ A} \qquad 5 + I'' = 4I'' + \frac{V}{3} \qquad I'' = -\frac{V}{1}$$

Or

$$I'' = \frac{15}{8} \text{ A} \qquad I_{4\,\Omega} = 4(I' + I'') = 4\left(-\frac{3}{2} + \frac{15}{8}\right) = 1.5 \text{ A}$$

5.87 Verify, by nodal analysis, that the current I is one-fourth the current in the 4-Ω resistor of the circuit of Fig. 5-84a.

❚ From Fig. 5-84a,

$$I = \frac{12-V}{1} \qquad \text{or} \qquad V = 12 - I$$

and $I + 5 = \dfrac{V}{3} + 4I$ or $I + 5 = \dfrac{12 - I}{3} + 4I$ or $3I + 15 = 12 - I + 12I$ or $I = \dfrac{3}{8} \text{ A} = \dfrac{1}{4} I_{4\,\Omega}$

5.88   Find the current in the 3-Ω resistor of Fig. 5-84a, by superposition.

∥ From Fig. 5-84b,

$$I'_{3\,\Omega} = I' - 4I' = -3I' = -3\left(-\dfrac{3}{2}\right) = \dfrac{9}{2} \text{ A} \qquad \text{(from Prob. 5.86)}$$

From Fig. 5-84b,

$$I''_{3\,\Omega} = I'' + 5 - 4I'' = 5 - 3I'' = 5 - 3(\tfrac{15}{8}) = -\tfrac{5}{8} \text{ A} \qquad \text{(from Prob. 5.86)}$$

$$I_{3\,\Omega} = I'_{3\,\Omega} + I''_{3\,\Omega} = \tfrac{9}{2} - \tfrac{5}{8} = \tfrac{31}{8} = 3.875 \text{ A}$$

5.89   Apply superposition to the network of Fig. 5-85a to find the current in the 1-Ω resistor.

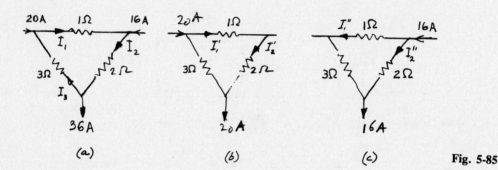

Fig. 5-85

∥ From Fig. 5-85b, $I'_1 = 20\left(\dfrac{3}{3 + 1 + 2}\right) = 10 \text{ A}$

From Fig. 5-85c, $I''_1 = 16\left(\dfrac{2}{3 + 1 + 2}\right) = 16/3 \text{ A}$

Hence, $I_1 = I_{1\,\Omega} = I'_1 - I''_1 = 10 - 16/3 = \dfrac{14}{3} \text{ A}$

5.90   Find the voltage across the 2-Ω resistor of the circuit of Fig. 5-85a by superposition.

∥ From Fig. 5-85b,

$$I'_2 = I'_1 = 10 \text{ A} \qquad \text{(from Prob. 5.89)}$$

From Fig. 5-85c $I''_2 = 16\left(\dfrac{1 + 3}{1 + 3 + 2}\right) = \dfrac{32}{3} \text{ A}$

or $I_2 = I'_2 + I''_2 = 10 + \dfrac{32}{3} = \dfrac{62}{3} \text{ A}$ $V_{2\,\Omega} = I_2(2) = \dfrac{62}{3}(2) = \dfrac{124}{3} = 41.33 \text{ V}$

5.91   In a linear resistive circuit, whereas superposition of currents is valid, show that superposition of powers is not valid.

∥ Let currents I' and I'' flow through a resistance R due to one source at a time in the network (with all other sources removed).   Then the total current $I = I' + I''$ (assuming two sources only for simplicity).   Power dissipated in R is

$$P_R = I^2 R = (I' + I'')^2 R = (I')^2 R + (I'')^2 R + 2(I')(I'')R \neq (I')^2 R + (I'')^2 R$$

5.92   Refer to the circuit of Fig. 4-5. Given $R_1 = 2\,\Omega$, $R_2 = 3\,\Omega$, $R_3 = 2\,\Omega$, $R_4 = 6\,\Omega$, and $R_5 = 1\,\Omega$. If $E = 1$V, calculate the current I_5. Then, apply superposition and reciprocity to calculate the current through E if a 2-V source is connected in series with R_5, with the negative polarity connected to b.

∥ To calculate I_5 we redraw the circuit in Fig. 5-86a.   For the three mesh currents we have

$$5I_1 - I_2 - 2I_3 = 0 \qquad -I_1 + 10I_2 - 6I_3 = 0 \qquad -2I_1 - 6I_2 + 8I_3 = 1$$

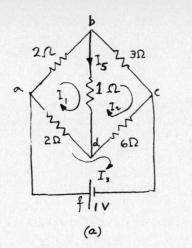

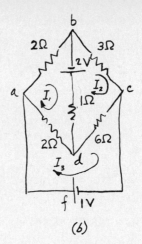

(a)　　　　　(b)　　　　　**Fig. 5-86**

Solving for I_1, I_2, and I_3 yields

$$I_1 = 0.1757 \text{ A} \qquad I_2 = 0.2162 \text{ A}$$

$$I_5 = I_1 - I_2 = -0.0405 \quad \text{and} \quad I_3 = 0.331 = \text{current through } E$$

Now, by reciprocity, if the 1-V source is transferred to the branch bd as shown in Fig. 5-86b, then the current $I_5 = -0.0405$ A will flow through cfa. By superposition, a 2-V source will produce $-2 \times 0.0405 = -0.081$-A current through cfa.

Hence, the new current through cfa with a 2-V source in the network is

$$I_{bd} = 0.331 - 0.081 = 0.25 \text{ A}$$

5.93 Refer to Fig. 5-86b. By mesh analysis verify the result of Prob. 5.92.

❚ For the three mesh currents we obtain

$$5I_1 - I_2 - 2I_3 = 2 \qquad -I_1 + 10I_2 - 6I_3 = -2 \qquad -2I_1 - 6I_2 + 8I_3 = 1$$

Solving for the three currents yields

$$I_1 = 0.5 \text{ A} \qquad I_2 = 0 \text{ A} \qquad I_3 = 0.25 \text{ A}$$

5.94 For the circuit of Fig. 5-86b show by superposition that no current flows through the 3-Ω resistor.

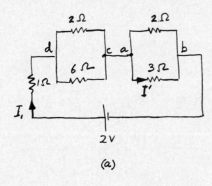

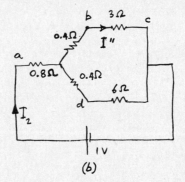

(a)　　　　　(b)　　　　　**Fig. 5-87**

❚ The circuits to which we apply superposition are shown in Fig. 5-87a and b. From Fig. 5-87a,

$$I_1 = \frac{2}{1 + [(2 \times 6)/(2 + 6)] + [(2 \times 3)/(2 + 3)]} = \frac{2}{3.7} \text{ A} \qquad I' = \frac{2}{3.7}\left(\frac{2}{2 + 3}\right) = 0.2162 \text{ A}$$

In Fig. 5-87b we show the abd delta-connected resistors (with the voltage source removed) transformed to an equivalent wye. Then

$$I_2 = \frac{1}{0.8 + \{[(3 + 0.4)(6 + 0.4)]/[3 + 0.4 + 6 + 0.4]\}} = 0.331 \text{ A} \qquad I'' = 0.3311 \frac{6 + 0.4}{3 + 0.4 + 6 + 0.4} = 0.2162 \text{ A}$$

Hence, $$I_{3\,\Omega} = I' - I'' = 0.2162 - 0.2162 = 0$$

5.95 By superposition, find the current in the 1-Ω resistor of the current-excited bridge circuit shown in Fig. 5-88.

❚ With the 5-A current source removed,

$$I_1 = 10\,\text{A} \quad\text{and}\quad I_1' = 10\left(\frac{6}{6+1+3}\right) = 6\,\text{A}$$

With the 10-A current source removed,

$$I_1'' = 5\,\frac{6+3}{6+3+1} = 4.5\,\text{A} \qquad I = I_1'' - I_1' = 4.5 - 6 = -1.5\,\text{A}$$

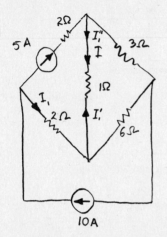

Fig. 5-88

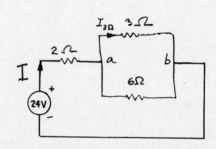

Fig. 5-89

5.96 Calculate the current in the 3-Ω resistor of the circuit of Fig. 5-89. From this result, by reciprocity theorem, determine the current in the 2-Ω resistor if the 24-V source is removed and a 6-V source is connected in series with the 3-Ω resistor, with the positive polarity connected to a.

❚ From Fig. 5-89,

$$I = \frac{24}{2 + [(3 \times 6)/(3 + 6)]} = 6\,\text{A} \qquad I_{3\,\Omega} = 6\,\frac{6}{3+6} = 4\,\text{A}$$

Thus, a 24-V source in series with the 2-Ω resistor produces a 4-A current in the 3-Ω resistor. By reciprocity, a 24-V source in series with the 3-Ω resistor will produce a 4-A current in the 2-Ω resistor. By linearity, a 6-V source will produce 1-A current in the 2-Ω resistor. Because of the specified polarity, the current will flow from right to left.

5.97 Calculate the current I_1 in the circuit of Fig. 4-21a by superposition.

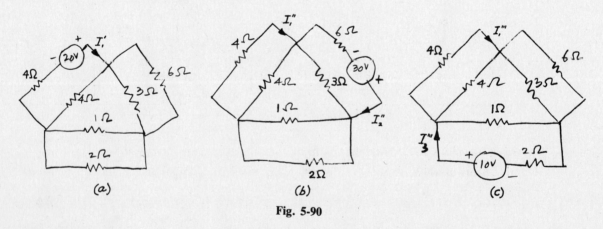

Fig. 5-90

❚ From Fig. 5-90a,

$$I_1' = \frac{20}{4 + \dfrac{4[(6 \times 3)/(6+3) + (2 \times 1)/(2+1)]}{4 + [(6 \times 3)/(6+3)] + [(2 \times 1)/(2+1)]}} = \frac{25}{7} = 3.571\,\text{A}$$

From Fig. 5-90*b*,

$$I_2'' = \frac{30}{6 + [(8/3 \times 3)/(8/3 + 3)]} = \frac{255}{63} = 4.0476 \text{ A}$$

$$I_1'' = \frac{1}{2}\left(4.0476 \frac{3}{3 + 8/3}\right) = 1.071 \text{ A}$$

Finally from Fig. 5-90*c*,

$$I_3''' = \frac{10}{2 + \{[1(2+2)]/(1+2+2)\}} = \frac{50}{14} = 3.571 \text{ A} \qquad I_1''' = \frac{1}{2}\left[3.571\left(\frac{1}{1+2+2}\right)\right] = 0.357 \text{ A}$$

Hence,

$$I_1 = I_1' + I_1'' + I_1''' = 3.571 + 1.071 + 0.357 = 5.0 \text{ A}$$

5.98 Find the Thévenin voltage V_{Th} shown in the circuit of Fig. 5-91 by superposition.

❚ From Fig. 5-91,

$$V_{\text{Th}} = V_{1\,\Omega} = I_1(2) \text{ V}$$

With the 6-A source removed,

$$I_1' = 10\left(\frac{1}{3+2+1}\right) = 1.67 \text{ A}$$

With the 10-A source removed,

$$I_1'' = 6\left(\frac{3}{1+2+3}\right) = 3 \text{ A} \qquad \text{or} \qquad I_1 = I_1'' - I_1' = 3 - 1.67 = 1.33 \text{ A} \qquad \text{or} \qquad V_{\text{Th}} = 1.33(2) = 2.67 \text{ V}$$

5.99 Verify the result of Prob. 5.98 by nodal analysis.

❚ For node 1,

$$6 + 10 = \frac{V_1}{3} + \frac{V_1 - V_{\text{Th}}}{1} \qquad \text{or} \qquad 48 = 4V_1 - 3V_{\text{Th}}$$

For node 2,

$$10 + \frac{V_{\text{Th}}}{2} = \frac{V_1 - V_{\text{Th}}}{1} \qquad \text{or} \qquad 20 = 2V_1 - 3V_{\text{Th}}$$

Solving for V_{Th} yields

$$V_{\text{Th}} = 2.67 \text{ V}$$

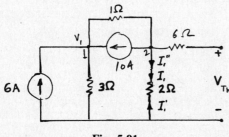

Fig. 5-91

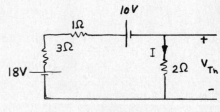

Fig. 5-92

5.100 Transform the current sources of the circuit of Fig. 5-91 to equivalent voltage sources, and hence obtain the voltage V_{Th}.

❚ The new circuit is shown in Fig. 5-92 from which

$$I = \frac{18 - 10}{3 + 1 + 2} = \frac{8}{6} \text{ A} \qquad V_{\text{Th}} = I(2) = \frac{8}{6} \times 2 = \frac{8}{3} = 2.67 \text{ V}$$

CHAPTER 6
Capacitors

6.1 The circuit element C, measured in farads (F) and shown in Fig. 6-1, is called the capacitor for which the voltage-current relationships are

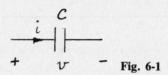

Fig. 6-1

$$v = \frac{1}{C} \int i \, dt + k \qquad i = C \frac{dv}{dt}$$

If the voltage across a 50-μF capacitor is $v = 100 \sin 200t$ V, what is the current through the capacitor?

▮ $\quad i = C \dfrac{dv}{dt} = 50 \times 10^{-6}(100 \times 200 \cos 200t) = \cos 200 \, t \quad$ A

6.2 Since current is defined as the rate of change of charge, we may write $i = dq/dt$, where q is the charge in coulombs (C). From the data of Prob. 6.1, find an expression for the charge on the capacitor.

▮ Since $\qquad\qquad\qquad\qquad\qquad i = \dfrac{dq}{dt} \qquad q = \displaystyle\int_0^t i \, dt$

and $\qquad\qquad\qquad v = \dfrac{q}{C} \quad$ or $\quad q = Cv = 50 \times 10^{-6} \times 100 \sin 200t = 5000 \sin 200t \qquad \mu$C

6.3 A current $i = 10 \cos 377t$ A is switched through a 100-μF capacitor at $t = 0$. Determine the rms voltage across the capacitor.

▮ $\quad v = \dfrac{1}{C}\displaystyle\int_0^t i \, dt = \dfrac{1}{100 \times 10^{-6}} \int_0^t 10 \cos 377t \, dt = \dfrac{10 \sin 377t}{100 \times 377 \times 10^{-6}} = 265.25 \sin 377t$ V $\quad V = \dfrac{265.25}{\sqrt{2}} = 187.6$ V

6.4 Find the charge associated with the capacitor and the current of Prob. 6.3.

▮ $\qquad\qquad q = \displaystyle\int_0^t i \, dt = 10 \int_0^t \cos 377t \, dt = \dfrac{10}{377} \sin 377 \, t = 26.525 \sin 377t \qquad$ mC

6.5 Determine the instantaneous and average powers in the capacitor of Prob. 6.3.

▮ $\qquad p = vi = (265.25 \sin 377t)(10 \cos 377t) = \dfrac{2652.5}{2} \sin 2 \times 377t = 1326.25 \sin 754t$ W

With $\quad T = (1/60)$ s the period of the current wave,

$$p_{av} = \frac{1}{T} \int_0^T p \, dt = 0$$

6.6 Obtain an expression for the energy stored in a capacitor C (F) charged to voltage V (V).

▮ In a time dt, energy dW is given by

$$dW = p \, dt = vi \, dt = vC \frac{dv}{dt} \, dt \qquad \text{or} \qquad W = C \int_0^v v \, dv = \frac{1}{2} CV^2 \qquad \text{J}$$

6.7 Determine the energy stored in the capacitor of Prob. 6.1.

▮ Since $W = \frac{1}{2}CV^2$, we have, from Prob. 6.1,

$$w(t) = \tfrac{1}{2} C[v(t)]^2 = \tfrac{1}{2} \times 50 \times 10^{-6}(100 \sin 200t)^2 = \tfrac{1}{2} \times 50 \times 10^{-6}(100)^2 \sin^2 200t$$

$$= 25 \times 10^{-2} \times \tfrac{1}{2}(1 - \cos 2 \times 200t) = 125(1 - \cos 400t) \qquad \text{mJ}$$

6.8 What are the time-average and peak values of the energy stored in the capacitor of Probs. 6.1 and 6.7?

116

▮ From Prob. 6.7,

$$w(t) = 125 - 125 \cos 400t \qquad \text{mJ}$$

The time-average value of the second term is zero. Hence

$$w(t)_{\text{av}} = 125 \text{ mJ}$$

The peak energy occurs at $400t = \pi$. Or, at $t = (\pi/400)$ s, we obtain

$$w(t)|_{\text{max}} = 125 + 125 = 250 \text{ mJ}$$

6.9 A voltage pulse given by

$$v(t) = \begin{cases} 0 & t \leq 0 \\ 2t \text{ V} & 0 \leq t \leq 2 \\ 4e^{-(t-2)} \text{ V} & 2 \leq t \end{cases}$$

is applied across a 10-μF capacitor. Sketch the voltage across and the current through the capacitor.

▮
$$i = C \frac{dv}{dt} = 0 \qquad t < 0$$

$$= 10 \times 10^{-6}(2) = 20 \ \mu\text{A} \qquad 0 < t < 2$$

$$= 10 \times 10^{-6}[-4e^{-(t-2)}] = -40 \, e^{-(t-2)} \qquad \mu\text{A} \qquad 2 < t$$

Hence the sketches shown in Fig. 6-2.

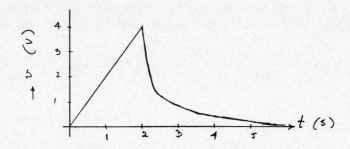

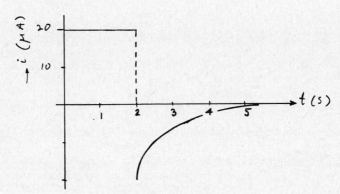

Fig. 6-2

6.10 Sketch the power and energy curves from the data of Prob. 6.9.

▮
$$p = vi$$
$$= 0 \qquad t \leq 0$$
$$= 2t(20) = 40t \qquad \mu\text{W} \qquad 0 \leq t < 2$$
$$= 4e^{-(t-2)}[-40e^{-(t-2)}] = -160e^{-2(t-2)} \qquad \mu\text{W} \qquad 2 < t$$

$$w = \tfrac{1}{2} C v^2$$
$$= \tfrac{1}{2} \times 10 \times 10^{-6} \times 0 = 0 \qquad t \leq 0$$
$$= \tfrac{1}{2} \times 10 \times 10^{-6}(2t)^2 = 20t^2 \qquad \mu\text{J} \qquad 0 \leq t \leq 2$$
$$= \tfrac{1}{2} \times 10 \times 10^{-6}[4e^{-(t-2)}]^2 = 80e^{-2(t-2)} \qquad \mu\text{J} \qquad 2 \leq t$$

See Fig. 6-3.

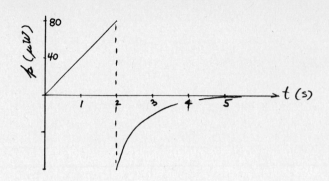

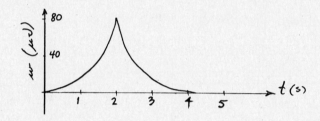

Fig. 6-3

6.11 Obtain the equivalent capacitance for two capacitances C_1 and C_2 connected (a) in series and (b) in parallel. Generalize a and b to the case of n capacitances.

▮ (a)
$$v = \frac{1}{C_{es}} \int i \, dt = v_1 + v_2 = \frac{1}{C_1} \int i \, dt + \frac{1}{C_2} \int i \, dt \quad \text{whence} \quad \frac{1}{C_{es}} = \frac{1}{C_1} + \frac{1}{C_2}$$

n capacitances in series:
$$\frac{1}{C_{es}} = \sum_{k=1}^{n} \frac{1}{C_k}$$

(b)
$$i = C_{ep} \frac{dv}{dt} = i_1 + i_2 = C_1 \frac{dv}{dt} + C_2 \frac{dv}{dt} \quad \text{whence} \quad C_{ep} = C_1 + C_2$$

n capacitances in parallel:
$$C_{ep} = \sum_{k=1}^{n} C_k$$

6.12 A 40-μF capacitor is charged to store 0.2 J of energy. An uncharged 60-μF capacitor is then connected in parallel with the first one through perfectly conducting leads. What is the final energy of the system?

▮ The initial charge on the 40-μF capacitor is obtained from $W = Q^2/2C$ (Prob. 6.21); thus,

$$0.2 = \frac{Q^2}{2(40 \times 10^{-6})} \quad \text{or} \quad Q = 4 \times 10^{-3} \text{C}$$

When the capacitors are connected in parallel, the common voltage V is given by

$$V = \frac{\text{total } Q}{\text{total } C} = \frac{4 \times 10^{-3}}{(40 + 60)10^{-6}} = 40 \text{ V}$$

Then

Final energy in 40-μF capacitor $= \frac{1}{2}(40 \times 10^{-6})(40)^2 = 0.032 \text{ J}$

Final energy in 60-μF capacitor $= \frac{1}{2}(60 \times 10^{-6})(40)^2 = 0.048 \text{ J}$

Final total energy $= 0.032 + 0.048 = 0.08 \text{ J}$. The energy lost, $0.2 - 0.08 = 0.12 \text{ J}$, represents work done by the charges on one another in spreading out over the two capacitors.

6.13 What is the equivalent capacitance between the terminals ab of the capacitive system shown in Fig. 6-4a?

▮ Using the results of Prob. 6.11, we obtain Fig. 6-4b to d from which

$$C_{eq} = 14 \text{ C}$$

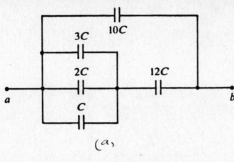

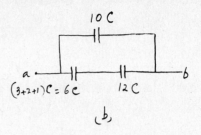

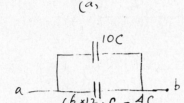

Fig. 6-4

6.14 A 40-μF capacitor is connected in parallel with a 60-μF capacitor and across a time-varying voltage source. At a certain instant, the total current supplied by the source is 10 A. Determine the instantaneous currents through the individual capacitors.

❚ Since the capacitors are in parallel, the voltage v across them is related to the currents i_1 and i_2 by

$$i_1 = C_1 \frac{dv}{dt} \qquad i_2 = C_2 \frac{dv}{dt}$$

or

$$\frac{i_1}{i_2} = \frac{C_1}{C_2} = \frac{40}{60}$$

But

$$i_1 + i_2 = 10 \text{ A}$$

Hence,

$$i_{40\,\mu F} = 4 \text{ A} \qquad i_{60\,\mu F} = 6 \text{ A}$$

6.15 A 50-μF capacitor is charged to 300 μC. An uncharged 100-μF capacitor is then connected in parallel with the first capacitor. Evaluate the charge transferred to the 100-μF capacitor.

❚ For two capacitors C_1 and C_2, connected in parallel and charged to a voltage V, we have

$$C_1 V = Q_1 \qquad C_2 V = Q_2$$

or

$$\frac{C_1}{C_2} = \frac{Q_1}{Q_2}$$

From the data,

$$\frac{50}{100} = \frac{Q_1}{Q_2} \quad \text{and} \quad Q_1 + Q_2 = 300 \ \mu C$$

Hence, $Q_1 = 100 \ \mu C$ and $Q_2 = 200 \ \mu C$ (transferred to the 100-μF capacitor)

6.16 A combination of four capacitors is shown in Fig. 6-5. Find the value of C to obtain an equivalent capacitance of 0.5 μF.

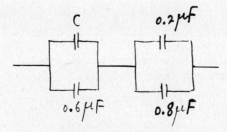

Fig. 6-5

▮ Applying the rules for series-parallel capacitors to Fig. 6-5 we obtain

$$C_{eq} = \frac{(C + 0.6)(0.2 + 0.8)}{C + 0.6 + 0.2 + 0.8} = 0.5 \qquad \text{or} \qquad \frac{C + 0.6}{C + 1.6} = 0.5$$

Hence
$$C = 0.4 \ \mu F$$

6.17 Find the equivalent capacitance of the combination of capacitors shown in Fig. 6-6a.

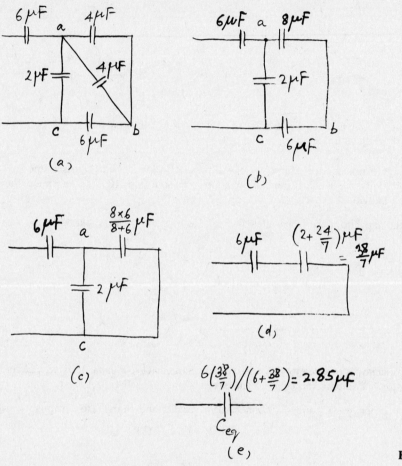

Fig. 6-6

▮ The network reduction procedure is shown in Fig. 6-6b to e from which

$$C_{eq} = 2.85 \ \mu F$$

6.18 A series combination of two capacitors $C_1 = 20 \ \mu F$ and $C_2 = 40 \ \mu F$ is connected across a dc source of 100 V. How is this voltage divided across the capacitors?

▮
$$V_1 + V_2 = 100$$

Since the capacitors are in series

$$C_1 V_1 = C_2 V_2 \qquad \text{or} \qquad 20 V_1 = 40 V_2$$

Hence,
$$V_1 = 66.67 \ V \qquad V_2 = 33.33 \ V$$

6.19 Express the two series-connected capacitors of Prob. 6.18 as an equivalent capacitor. What is the charge in the equivalent capacitor? Also, find the charges on C_1 and C_2.

▮
$$C_{eq} = \frac{C_1 C_2}{C_1 + C_2} = \frac{20 \times 40}{20 + 40} = 13.33 \ \mu F \qquad\qquad Q = CV = 13.33 \times 100 \times 10^{-6} = 1333 \ \mu C$$

$$Q_1 = C_1 V_1 = 20 \times 66.67 \times 10^{-6} = 1333 \ \mu C \qquad\qquad Q_2 = C_2 V_2 = 40 \times 33.33 \times 10^{-6} = 1333 \ \mu C$$

6.20 What is the energy stored in each capacitor of Prob. 6.18? Verify that the total energy stored in the two capacitors equals the energy stored in the equivalent capacitor of Prob. 6.19.

$$W_1 = \tfrac{1}{2}C_1V_1^2 = \tfrac{1}{2} \times 20 \times 10^{-6}(66.67)^2 = 44.446 \text{ mJ}$$

$$W_2 = \tfrac{1}{2} \times 40 \times 10^{-6}(33.33)^2 = 22.22 \text{ mJ}$$

$$W_1 + W_2 = 44.44 + 22.22 = 66.66 \text{ mJ} \qquad W_e = \tfrac{1}{2} \times 13.33(100)^2 \times 10^{-6} = 66.66 \text{ mJ}$$

6.21 Obtain an expression for the energy stored in a capacitor C in terms of the charge Q on it.

From Prob. 6.6,
$$W = \tfrac{1}{2}CV^2$$

But
$$Q = CV \quad \text{or} \quad V = \frac{Q}{C}$$

Hence,
$$W = \frac{1}{2}\,C\!\left(\frac{Q}{C}\right)^2 = \frac{Q^2}{2C}$$

6.22 An uncharged 50-μF capacitor is connected to a 40-mA constant current source. Determine the voltage across the capacitor after (a) 5 μs and (b) 10 ms.

Since
$$Q = \int i\, dt \quad \text{and} \quad i = I \text{ (a constant)} \qquad Q = It = CV$$

or
$$V = \frac{I}{C}\,t$$

(a)
$$V = \frac{40 \times 10^{-3}}{50 \times 10^{-6}} \times 5 \times 10^{-6} = 4 \text{ mV}$$

(b)
$$V = \frac{40 \times 10^{-3}}{50 \times 10^{-6}} \times 10 \times 10^{-3} = 8 \text{ V}$$

6.23 The voltage across a 50-μF capacitor rises at a constant rate of 10 V/ms. Calculate the current through the capacitor. What is the increase in the charge at the capacitor plates as the voltage increases by 60 V?

$$i = C\,\frac{dv}{dt} = 50 \times 10^{-6} \times \frac{10}{10^{-3}} = 500 \text{ mA} \qquad \Delta Q = C\,\Delta V = 50 \times 10^{-6} \times 60 = 3000 \ \mu\text{C}$$

6.24 A 200-μF capacitor is charged to store 90-mJ energy by a constant current of 0.1 A. What is the voltage across the capacitor?

Since
$$W = \frac{1}{2}\,CV^2 \qquad V = \sqrt{\frac{2W}{C}} = \left(\frac{2 \times 90 \times 10^{-3}}{200 \times 10^{-6}}\right)^{1/2} = 30 \text{ V}$$

6.25 How long does it take to charge the capacitor of Prob. 6.24, and what is the value of the charge on the capacitor?

$$Q = \sqrt{2CW} = \sqrt{2(200 \times 10^{-6})(90 \times 10^{-3})} = 6 \text{ mC} \qquad \text{and} \qquad t = \frac{Q}{I} = \frac{6 \times 10^{-3}}{0.1} = 60 \text{ ms}$$

6.26 A 30-μF capacitor is charged by a voltage source having a sawtooth waveform shown in Fig. 6-7. Determine the charging current.

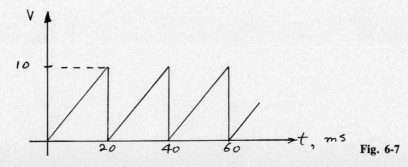

Fig. 6-7

❙ From Fig. 6-7,
$$\frac{dv}{dt} = \frac{10}{20 \times 10^{-3}} = 0.5 \times 10^3 \text{ V/s}$$

Thus,
$$i = C\frac{dv}{dt} = 30 \times 0.5 \times 10^{-6} \times 10^3 = 15 \text{ mA}$$

which remains constant.

6.27 Refer to the data of Prob. 6.18. After the series-connected capacitors are fully charged, the dc source is removed and the capacitors are then connected in parallel. Calculate the final charge on each capacitor.

❙ From Prob. 6.19, $Q = 1333 \ \mu\text{C}$. When connected in parallel, $C = C_1 + C_2 = (20 + 40) \times 10^{-6} = 60 \ \mu\text{F}$.

Thus
$$V = \frac{Q}{C} = \frac{1333}{60} = 22.217 \text{ V}$$

Hence, $Q_1 = C_1 V = 20 \times 22.217 \times 10^{-6} = 444.33 \ \mu\text{C}$ $\qquad Q_2 = C_2 V = 40 \times 22.217 \times 10^{-6} = 888.66 \ \mu\text{C}$

6.28 The voltages across two capacitors C_1 and C_2 connected in series are 4 V and 2 V, respectively, when the combination is connected across a 6-V source. A 2-μF capacitor is now connected across C_1 and the voltage now measured across C_2 is 3 V. Evaluate C_1 and C_2.

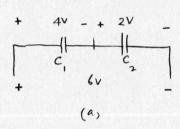 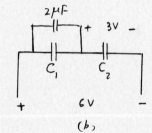

Fig. 6-8

❙ From Fig. 6-8a,
$$4C_1 = 2C_2$$

From Fig. 6-8b,
$$(C_1 + 2)3 = 3C_2$$

Solving for C_1 and C_2 yields

$$C_1 = 2 \ \mu\text{F} \qquad C_2 = 4 \ \mu\text{F}$$

6.29 A 100-μF capacitor is charged to 100 V. It is then connected to a 400-μF uncharged capacitor. How much energy is dissipated in the connecting leads?

❙ Initially energy
$$W_i = \tfrac{1}{2}C_1 V^2 = \tfrac{1}{2} \times 100 \times 10^{-6}(100)^2 = 0.5 \text{ J}$$

When connected in parallel, the initial charge $Q_i = C_1 V = 100 \times 10^{-6} \times 100 = 10 \text{ mC}$ is redistributed to the parallel combination $C = C_1 + C_2 = (100 + 400) \ \mu\text{F}$ capacitor.

The common voltage then becomes

$$V = \frac{Q}{C} = \frac{10 \times 10^{-3}}{500 \times 10^{-6}} = 20 \text{ V} \qquad W_1 = \tfrac{1}{2}C_1 V^2 = \tfrac{1}{2} \times 100 \times 10^{-6}(20)^2 = 0.02 \text{ J}$$

$$W_2 = \tfrac{1}{2}C_2 V^2 = \tfrac{1}{2} \times 400 \times 10^{-6}(20)^2 = 0.08 \text{ J}$$

Final energy:
$$W_f = W_1 + W_2 = 0.02 + 0.08 = 0.1 \text{ J}$$

Energy dissipated:
$$W_i - W_f = 0.5 - 0.1 = 0.4 \text{ J}$$

6.30 A 20-μF capacitor is connected in parallel with a 30-μF capacitor. At $t = 0$ the combination is connected across a voltage source. At a certain instant the voltage begins to increase and the current drawn from the source is 5 mA. Determine the current division between the capacitors. Also calculate the rate of change of voltage across the capacitors.

❙
$$i_1 = C_1\frac{dv}{dt} = 20 \times 10^{-6}\frac{dv}{dt} \qquad i_2 = C_2\frac{dv}{dt} = 30 \times 10^{-6}\frac{dv}{dt}$$

$$\frac{i_1}{i_2} = \frac{2}{3} \qquad i_1 + i_2 = 5 \text{ mA}$$

Hence $\qquad i_1 = 2\,\text{mA} \qquad i_2 = 3\,\text{mA} \qquad$ and $\qquad \dfrac{dv}{dt} = \dfrac{2 \times 10^{-3}}{20 \times 10^{-6}} = \dfrac{3 \times 10^{-3}}{30 \times 10^{-6}} = 100\,\text{V/s}$

6.31 A 30-μF capacitor is sequentially charged by a 12-V battery and then discharged through a resistor R by switching between positions 1 and 2 (Fig. 6-9) at a rate of 100 operations per second. Determine the average current through the resistor.

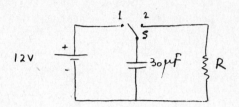

Fig. 6-9

With the switch at position 1,

$$Q = CV = 30 \times 10^{-6} \times 12 = 360\,\mu\text{C}$$

Provided R is small enough, essentially all this charge passes through the resistor during discharge. Thus, Q through R in 100 operations $= 360 \times 10^{-6} \times 100 = 36\,\text{mC}$, which takes 1 s. Hence the average current $= 36\,\text{mC}/1\,\text{s} = 36\,\text{mA}$.

6.32 How large can R be in Prob. 6.31 and still allow a 99% discharge of the capacitor in the time available (10^{-2} s)?

▌ By KVL, the discharge process is governed by $-R\,dq/dt = q/C$, which integrates to $q = Q\,e^{-t/RC}$. Thus, the critical value of R satisfies

$$0.01 = e^{-0.01/R(30 \times 10^{-6})} \qquad \text{or} \qquad 100 = e^{333/R} \qquad \text{or} \qquad R = \frac{333}{\ln 100} \approx 72\,\Omega$$

6.33 For the circuit shown in Fig. 6-10, determine the voltages v_1 and v_2, with S open.

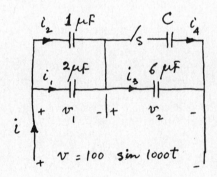

Fig. 6-10

▌ With S open,

$$C_{\text{eq}} = \frac{(1+2)6}{1+2+6} = 2\,\mu\text{F} \qquad i = i_3 = C_{\text{eq}}\frac{dv}{dt} = (2 \times 10^{-6})(100)(1000 \cos 1000t) = 0.2 \cos 1000t \qquad \text{A}$$

$$v_2 = \frac{1}{6 \times 10^{-6}} \int i_3\,dt = \frac{1}{6 \times 10^{-6}} \int 0.2 \cos 1000t\,dt = 33.33 \sin 1000t \qquad \text{V}$$

$$v_1 = v - v_2 = (\sin 1000t)(100 - 33.33) = 66.67 \sin 1000t \qquad \text{V}$$

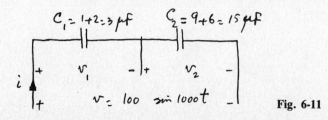

Fig. 6-11

6.34 For the circuit of Prob. 6.33, with S closed, find C such that the current from the source has a peak value of 0.25 A.

■ From Fig. 6-10, with S closed,

$$C_{eq} = \frac{(1+2)(6+C)}{1+2+6+C} = \frac{18+3C}{9+C}$$

$$i = C_{eq} \frac{dv}{dt} = \frac{18+3C}{9+C} (100 \times 1000 \cos 1000t) \times 10^{-6} = 0.25 \cos 1000t \quad \text{A} \quad \text{or} \quad C = 9\,\mu\text{F}$$

6.35 For the value of C determined in Prob. 6.34, with S closed, find v_1 and v_2 from Fig. 6-10.

■ The capacitors may be combined as shown in Fig. 6-11. Since $i = 0.25 \cos 1000t$ A from Prob. 6.34,

$$v_1 = \frac{1}{C_1} \int i\,dt = \frac{1}{3 \times 10^{-6}} \int 0.25 \cos 1000t\,dt = 83.33 \sin 1000t \quad \text{V}$$

$$v_2 = \frac{1}{C_2} \int i\,dt = \frac{1}{15 \times 10^{-6}} \int 0.25 \cos 1000t\,dt = 16.67 \sin 1000t \quad \text{V}$$

Note that $v_1 + v_2 = v = 100 \sin 1000t$ V.

6.36 With $C = 9\,\mu\text{F}$ and S closed, determine the current through each capacitor of the circuit of Fig. 6-10.

■ With the currents shown in Fig. 6-10 and the values v_1 and v_2 calculated in Prob. 6.35, we have

$$i_1 = 2 \times 10^{-6} \frac{d}{dt} (83.33 \sin 1000t) = 166.66 \cos 1000t \quad \text{mA}$$

$$i_2 = 1 \times 10^{-6} \frac{d}{dt} (83.33 \sin 1000t) = 83.33 \cos 1000t \quad \text{mA}$$

$$i_3 = 6 \times 10^{-6} \frac{d}{dt} (16.67 \sin 1000t) = 100 \cos 1000t \quad \text{mA}$$

$$i_4 = 9 \times 10^{-6} \frac{d}{dt} (16.67 \sin 1000t) = 150 \cos 1000t \quad \text{mA}$$

6.37 Find the capacitance at the terminals of the wye-connected circuit shown in Fig. 6-12, taking any two terminals at a time.

■
$$C_{ab} = \frac{C_1 C_2}{C_1 + C_2} \qquad C_{bc} = \frac{C_2 C_3}{C_2 + C_3} \qquad C_{ca} = \frac{C_3 C_1}{C_3 + C_1}$$

6.38 The capacitors of Prob. 6.37 are reconnected in delta as shown in Fig. 6-13. Determine the capacitance at the terminals taking any two terminals at a time.

■
$$C_{ab} = C_2 + \frac{C_1 C_3}{C_1 + C_3} \qquad C_{bc} = C_3 + \frac{C_2 C_1}{C_2 + C_1} \qquad C_{ca} = C_1 + \frac{C_2 C_3}{C_2 + C_3}$$

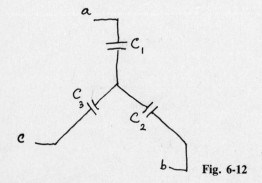

Fig. 6-12

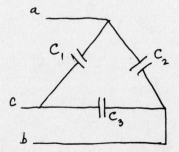

Fig. 6-13

6.39 Let three capacitors, each having a capacitance C_y, be connected in wye (Fig. 6-12). If three capacitors, each having a capacitance C_d, are connected in delta (Fig. 6-13), determine the equivalent relationships between the two connections.

❚ From Prob. 6-37,
$$C_{ab} = C_{bc} = C_{ca} = \frac{(C_y)^2}{C_y + C_y} = \frac{1}{2} C_y$$

From Prob. 6.38,
$$C_{ab} = C_{bc} = C_{ca} = C_d + \frac{(C_d)^2}{C_d + C_d} = \frac{3}{2} C_d$$

For the two to be equivalent we must have
$$\tfrac{1}{2} C_y = \tfrac{3}{2} C_d \quad \text{or} \quad C_y = 3 C_d \quad \text{and} \quad C_d = \tfrac{1}{3} C_y$$

6.40 Conductor-to-conductor and conductor-to-sheath capacitances of a three-core cable are shown in Fig. 6-14a. Determine the per-phase capacitance (defined as the *net* capacitance between a conductor and sheath and ground).

❚ Figure 6-14b shows all the capacitances and their interconnections. The delta-connected capacitances C_c are then converted to an equivalent wye, shown in Fig. 6-14c, using the results of Prob. 6.39. Hence
$$C_n = C_s + 3 C_c$$

shown in Fig. 6-14d.

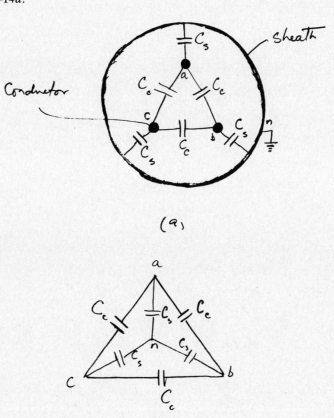

(a)

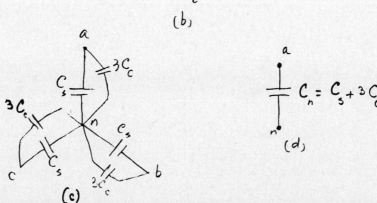

Fig. 6-14

6.41 In a test on a three-conductor cable, the three conductors are bunched together and the capacitance measured between the bunched conductors and sheath is C_1. In a second test, two conductors are bunched with the sheath, and the capacitance measured between these and the third conductor is C_2. Determine C_s and C_c, shown in Fig. 6-14*a*.

▋ From the first test we obtain
$$C_1 = 3C_s$$

From the second test we get
$$C_2 = C_s + 2C_c$$

Hence,
$$C_c = \tfrac{1}{2}(C_2 - \tfrac{1}{3}C_1) \qquad C_s = \tfrac{1}{3}C_1$$

6.42 In a certain test, the capacitance C_3 is measured between two conductors, with the third conductor connected to the sheath. Determine C_n shown in Fig. 6-14*d*.

▋ For the connection indicated we have
$$C_3 = C_c + \tfrac{1}{2}C_c + \tfrac{1}{2}C_s = \tfrac{1}{2}(3C_c + C_s) = \tfrac{1}{2}C_n \qquad \text{from Prob. 6.40}$$

Hence,
$$C_n = 2C_3$$

6.43 Find the capacitance between the terminals *ab* of the circuit shown in Fig. 6-14*b*.

▋ First the delta-connected capacitors are transformed to an equivalent wye, as shown in Fig. 6-14*c*, from which
$$C_{ab} = \frac{C_{an}C_{bn}}{C_{an} + C_{bn}} = \frac{1}{2}C_{an} \qquad \text{by symmetry}$$

Hence,
$$C_{ab} = \tfrac{1}{2}(3C_c + C_s)$$

6.44 Convert the wye-connected capacitors in Fig. 6-14*b* to an equivalent delta and verify the result of Prob. 6.43.

▋ From wye-delta equivalence we have
$$C_d = \tfrac{1}{3}C_s$$

and the circuit becomes that shown in Fig. 6-15 from which
$$C_{ab} = C_c + \tfrac{1}{3}C_s + \tfrac{1}{2}(C_c + \tfrac{1}{3}C_s) = \tfrac{1}{2}(C_c + 2C_c + \tfrac{1}{3}C_s + \tfrac{2}{3}C_s) = \tfrac{1}{2}(3C_c + C_s)$$

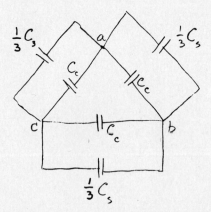

Fig. 6-15

6.45 The capacitances per kilometer of a three-wire cable are 0.90 μF between the three wires bunched and the sheath and 0.40 μF between one wire and the other two connected to the sheath. Determine the line-to-ground capacitance for a 20-km-long cable.

▋ From Prob. 6.41
$$C_1 = 0.9\ \mu\text{F} = 3C_s \qquad \text{or} \qquad C_s = 0.3\ \mu\text{F/km}$$

and
$$C_2 = 0.4 = C_s + 2C_c = 0.3 + 2C_c \qquad C_c = \tfrac{1}{2}(0.4 - 0.3) = 0.05\ \mu\text{F/km}$$

From Prob. 6.40
$$C_n = C_s + 3C_c = 0.3 + 3 \times 0.05 = 0.45\ \mu\text{F/km} \qquad (C_n)_{20\text{ km}} = 20 \times 0.45 = 9.0\ \mu\text{F}$$

6.46 The capacitance between any two conductors of a three-core cable, with the third conductor grounded, is 0.6 μF/km. Calculate the line-to-ground capacitance for a 25-km-long cable.

▌ From Prob. 6.42,

$$C_n = 2 \times 0.6 = 1.2 \ \mu\text{F/km} \qquad \text{or} \qquad (C_n)_{25 \ \text{km}} = 1.2 \times 25 = 30 \ \mu\text{F}$$

6.47 Find the capacitance between any two conductors of the cable of Prob. 6.45.

▌ From Prob. 6.43,

$$C_{ab} = \tfrac{1}{2}(3C_c + C_s) = \tfrac{1}{2}(3 \times 0.05 + 0.3) \times 20 = 4.5 \ \mu\text{F}$$

6.48 In a three-conductor cable a short circuit occurs between the conductor a and the sheath. What is the capacitance between the conductors a and b, if $C_s = C_c = C$? Compare the result with that of an unfaulted cable.

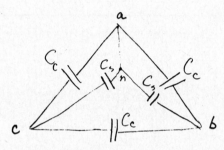

Fig. 6-16

▌ The circuit of Fig. 6-14b changes to that of Fig. 6-16 from which

$$C_{ab} = C_c + C_s + \frac{C_c(C_c + C_s)}{C_c + C_c + C_s} = C + C + \frac{C(C + C)}{C + C + C} = \frac{8}{3} C$$

For the unfaulted cable, from Prob. 6.43,

$$C_{ab} = \tfrac{1}{2}(3C_c + C_s) = \tfrac{1}{2}(3C + C) = 2C$$

6.49 Find the capacitance at the terminals ab of the circuit shown in Fig. 6-17a.

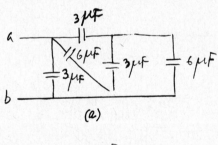

(a)

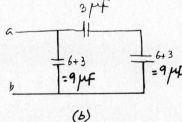

(b) **Fig. 6-17**

▌ By series-parallel combination we obtain the circuit of Fig. 6-17b from which

$$C_{ab} = 9 + \frac{3 \times 9}{3 + 9} = 11.25 \ \mu\text{F}$$

6.50 What is the equivalent capacitance at the terminals *ab* of the circuit shown in Fig. 6-18*a*?

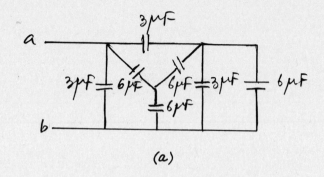

(a)

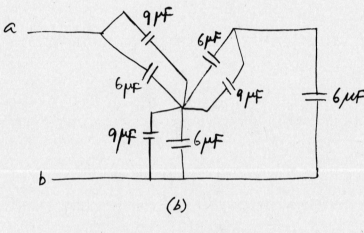

(b)

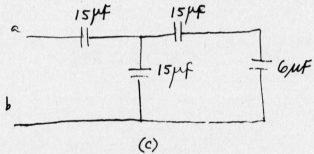

(c)

Fig. 6-18

▌ The circuit reduction steps are shown in Fig. 6-18*b* and *c*, from which

$$C_{ab} = \frac{15[(15 \times 6)/(15 + 6) + 15]}{15 + [(15 \times 6)/(15 + 6) + 15]} = 8.44 \ \mu F$$

CHAPTER 7
Inductors

7.1 The circuit element shown in Fig. 7-1 is known as an inductor, and has the voltage-current relationship

$$v = L \frac{di}{dt} \quad \text{or} \quad i = \frac{1}{L} \int v \, dt + k$$

where L is the inductance in henries (H). A 50-mH inductor carries a 5-A current which reverses in 25 ms. What is the average induced voltage across the inductor?

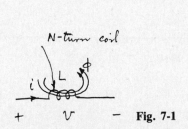

+ v −   **Fig. 7-1**

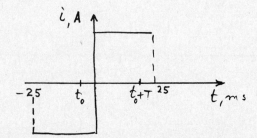

Fig. 7-2

▌ The induced voltage v is zero except at the instant of current reversal, when it is infinite. However, over an interval $T = 25$ ms (Fig. 7-2) we have

$$i(t_0 + T) - i(t_0) = \frac{1}{L} \int_{t_0}^{t_0 + T} v \, dt = \frac{T}{L} v_{av} \quad \text{or} \quad v_{av} = L \frac{i(t_0 + T) - i(t_0)}{T} = 50 \times 10^{-3} \frac{5 - (-5)}{25 \times 10^{-3}} = 20 \text{ V}$$

7.2 Plot the voltage across an inductor L if the current through it is as shown in Fig. 7-3a.

▌ Since $v = L \, di/dt$, we obtain the voltage as shown in Fig. 7-3b.

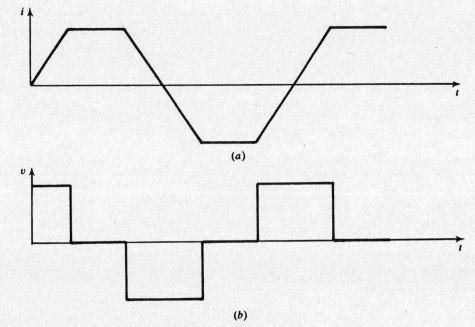

(a)

(b)

Fig. 7-3

7.3 Determine the equivalent inductance of n inductors $L_1, L_2, \ldots,$ in series.

▌ With common current i, we have

$$v = L_{es} \frac{di}{dt} = L_1 \frac{di}{dt} + L_2 \frac{di}{dt} + \cdots = (L_1 + L_2 + \cdots) \frac{di}{dt}$$

Hence
$$L_{es} = \sum_{k=1}^{n} L_k$$

7.4 What is the equivalent inductance of n inductors $L_1, L_2, \ldots,$ in parallel?

❚ With common voltage v we have
$$i = \frac{1}{L_{ep}} \int v \, dt = \frac{1}{L_1} \int v \, dt + \frac{1}{L_2} \int v \, dt + \cdots = \left(\frac{1}{L_1} + \frac{1}{L_2} + \cdots \right) \int v \, dt$$

Hence,
$$\frac{1}{L_{ep}} = \sum_{k=1}^{n} \frac{1}{L_k}$$

7.5 Two inductors, $L_1 = 30$ mH and $L_2 = 60$ mH, are connected in parallel. What is the equivalent inductance?

$$\frac{1}{L_{ep}} = \frac{1}{L_1} + \frac{1}{L_2}$$

or
$$L_{ep} = \frac{L_1 L_2}{L_1 + L_2} = \frac{(30)(60)}{30 + 60} = 20 \text{ mH}$$

7.6 The combination of inductors of Prob. 7.5 is connected in series with a 10-mH inductor. Determine the equivalent inductance.

❚
$$L_{es} = L_1 + L_2 = 20 + 10 = 30 \text{ mH}$$

7.7 The current through a 60-mH inductor is given by $i = 15 \sin 377t$ A. Determine the associated power.

❚
$$v = L \frac{di}{dt} = 60 \times 10^{-3} \times 15 \times 377 \cos 377t = 339.3 \cos 377t \qquad \text{V}$$
$$p = vi = (339.3 \cos 377t)(15 \sin 377t) = 2544.75 \sin 754t \qquad \text{W}$$

7.8 Determine the energy stored in an inductor L having a current I.

$$\text{Voltage} = v = L \frac{di}{dt} \qquad \text{Power} = p = vi = Li \frac{di}{dt} \qquad \text{Energy} = W = \int_0^t p \, dt = L \int_0^I i \, di = \frac{1}{2} LI^2$$

7.9 Find the energy stored in the inductor of Prob. 7.7.

❚
$$w(t) = \frac{1}{2} Li^2 = \frac{1}{2} \times 60 \times 10^{-3} (15)^2 \sin^2 377t = \frac{1}{2} \times 60 \times 10^{-3} \times 225 \times \frac{1}{2} (1 - \cos 2 \times 377t)$$
$$= 3.375(1 - \cos 754t) \qquad \text{J}$$

7.10 What are the time-average and peak values of the energy stored in the inductor of Prob. 7.7?

❚ From Prob. 7.9, $\qquad w(t) = 3.375(1 - \cos 754t) \qquad$ J

The time-average value of the second term is zero. Hence,
$$w(t)|_{av} = 3.375 \text{ J}$$

The peak energy occurs at $754t = \pi$. Or, $t = \pi/754$ s,
$$w(t)|_{max} = 3.375 + 3.375 = 6.75 \text{ J}$$

7.11 Flux linkage λ is defined by $\lambda = N\phi = Li$, where L is inductance, i is the current through the inductor, N is the number of turns making the inductor, and ϕ is the flux "linking" the N turns (see Fig. 7-1). Determine the flux linking a 100-turn coil having a $50 \cos 377t$ voltage connected across it.

❚ Since
$$\lambda = Li = N\phi \qquad \text{and} \qquad v = L \frac{di}{dt}$$

then
$$v = \frac{d\lambda}{dt} = N \frac{d\phi}{dt} = (50 \cos 377t)$$

Thus,
$$\phi = \frac{1}{N} \int v \, dt = \frac{1}{100} \int_0^t 50 \cos 377t \, dt = \frac{50}{100} \frac{\sin 377t}{377} = 1.326 \sin 377t \qquad \text{mWb}$$

Note: The unit of flux is the weber (Wb).

7.12 The voltage across a 50-mH inductor is given by

$$v(t) = 0 \qquad t \leqq 0 \qquad v(t) = 10te^{-t} \text{ V} \qquad t \geqq 0$$

Sketch the voltage across and the current through the inductor.

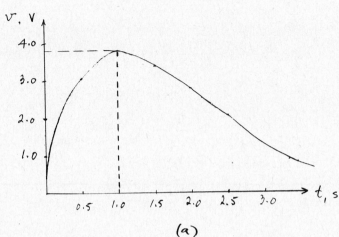

(a)

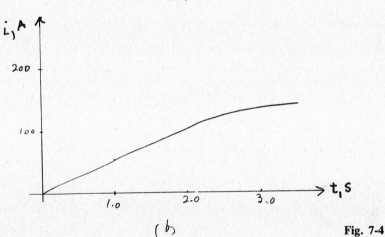

(b)

Fig. 7-4

$\blacksquare$ The plot of $v(t)$ is shown in Fig. 7-4a.

$$i = \frac{1}{L} \int v \, dt = \frac{1}{50 \times 10^{-3}} \int 10te^{-t} \, dt = \frac{10^3 \times 10}{50} [-e^{-t}(t+1)]_0^t = \frac{10 \times 10^3}{50} [-e^{-t}(t+1)+1]$$

$$= 200(1 - e^{-t} - te^{-t}) \qquad \text{A}$$

which is sketched in Fig. 7-4b.

7.13 The current through a 200-mH inductor is given by

$$i = 2e^{-t} - 2e^{-2t} \qquad \text{A}$$

What is the energy stored after 1 s? Also determine the voltage across the inductor after 1 s.

$\blacksquare$ $\qquad v = L \frac{di}{dt} = 200 \times 10^{-3} \frac{d}{dt} (2e^{-t} - 2e^{-2t}) = 200 \times 10^{-3} \times 2(-e^{-t} + 2e^{-2t})$

At $t = 1$ s, $\qquad v = 200 \times 10^{-3} \times 2(-e^{-1} + 2e^{-2}) = -38.87 \text{ mV}$

Energy, $\qquad W = \frac{1}{2} Li^2 = \frac{1}{2} \times 200 \times 10^{-3}(2e^{-t} - 2e^{-2t})^2 = \frac{1}{2} \times 200 \times 10^{-3} \times 4(e^{-2t} + e^{-4t} - 2e^{-3t})$

At $t = 1$ s, $\qquad W = \frac{1}{2} \times 200 \times 10^{-3} \times 4(e^{-2} + e^{-4} - 2e^{-3}) = 21.63 \text{ mJ}$

7.14 Three inductors are connected as shown in Fig. 7-5. Given $L_1 = 2L_2$, find L_1 and L_2 such that the equivalent inductance is 0.7 H.

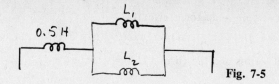

Fig. 7-5

▌ From Fig. 7-5,

$$L_{eq} = 0.5 + \frac{L_1 L_2}{L_1 + L_2} = 0.7 \qquad \text{or} \qquad \frac{2L_2(L_2)}{2L_2 + L_2} = 0.7 - 0.5$$

Hence
$$L_2 = 0.3\,\text{H} \qquad L_1 = 0.6\,\text{H}$$

7.15 Three inductances, 0.6 mH, 0.12 mH, and L mH, are connected in parallel. Find L for the equivalent inductance to be maximum. What is the maximum value of the equivalent inductance?

▌ The 0.6-mH and 0.12-mH inductances in parallel yield

$$L_p = \frac{0.6 \times 0.12}{0.6 + 0.12} = 0.1\,\text{mH}$$

Thus,
$$L_{eq} = \frac{LL_p}{L + L_p} = \frac{0.1L}{L + 0.1} = \frac{0.1}{1 + (0.1/L)}\,\text{mH}$$

which is maximum as $L \to \infty$. and the maximum $L_{eq} = 0.1\,\text{mH}$.

7.16 A current of the waveform shown in Fig. 7-6a passes through a 2-H inductor. Sketch the corresponding voltage waveform.

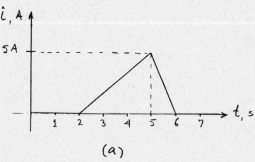

(a)

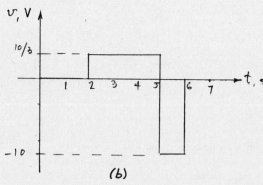

(b)

Fig. 7-6

▌

$$i = 0 \qquad v = L\frac{di}{dt} = 0 \qquad 0 \leqq t < 2\,\text{s}$$

$$i = \tfrac{5}{3}t - \tfrac{10}{3} \qquad v = 2 \times \tfrac{5}{3} = \tfrac{10}{3}\,\text{V} \qquad 2 < t < 5\,\text{s}$$

$$i = -5t + 30 \qquad v = 2(-5) = -10\,\text{V} \qquad 5 < t < 6\,\text{s}$$

Hence the sketch shown in Fig. 7-6b.

7.17 How much power is associated with the inductor of Prob. 7.16?

$$p = vi$$
$$= 0 \qquad 0 \leqq t \leqq 2\,\text{s}$$
$$= \tfrac{10}{3}\left(\tfrac{5}{3}t - \tfrac{10}{3}\right) = \left(\tfrac{50}{9}t - \tfrac{100}{9}\right) \qquad \text{W} \qquad 2 \leqq t < 5\,\text{s}$$
$$= -10(-5t + 30) = (50t - 300) \qquad \text{W} \qquad 5 < t < 6\,\text{s}$$

7.18   A 40-mH inductor is connected in parallel with a 60-mH inductor and across a time-varying voltage. At a certain instant, the total current supplied by a source is 10 A. Determine the instantaneous currents through the individual inductors.

❙ Since the inductors are in parallel, for the common voltage v we have

$$v = L_1 \frac{di_1}{dt} = L_2 \frac{di_2}{dt}$$

Thus,
$$i_1 = \frac{1}{L_1} \int v\,dt \qquad i_2 = \frac{1}{L_2} \int v\,dt$$

And
$$\frac{i_1}{i_2} = \frac{L_2}{L_1} = \frac{60}{40}$$

Also
$$i_1 + i_2 = 10$$

Hence,
$$i_{40\,\text{mH}} = 6\,\text{A} \qquad i_{60\,\text{mH}} = 4\,\text{A}$$

7.19   Find the currents i_1, i_2, and i_3 shown in the circuit of Fig. 7-7 with the switch S open.

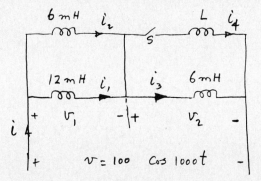

Fig. 7-7

❙
$$i = i_3 = \frac{1}{L_{eq}} \int v\,dt$$

where
$$L_{eq} = 6 + \frac{6 \times 12}{6 + 12} = 10\,\text{mH} \qquad v = 100 \cos 1000t$$

Then,
$$i = i_3 = \frac{1}{10 \times 10^{-3}} \int 100 \cos 1000t\,dt = \frac{10^3 \times 100 \sin 1000t}{10 \times 1000} = 10 \sin 1000t \qquad \text{A}$$

From Fig. 7-7,
$$i_1 = \frac{1}{L_1} \int v_1\,dt \qquad i_2 = \frac{1}{L_2} \int v_1\,dt$$

Or
$$\frac{i_1}{i_2} = \frac{L_2}{L_1} = \frac{6}{12} = 0.5 \qquad i_1 + i_2 = i_3 = 10 \sin 1000t$$

$$i_1 = 3.33 \sin 1000t \qquad \text{A} \qquad i_2 = 6.67 \sin 1000t \qquad \text{A}$$

7.20   Determine the voltages v_1 and v_2 shown in Fig. 7-7, with S open.

❙
$$v_1 = L_1 \frac{di_1}{dt} = 12 \times 10^{-3} \frac{d}{dt}(3.33 \sin 1000t) = 40 \cos 1000t \qquad \text{V}$$

$$v_2 = v - v_1 = \cos 1000t(100 - 40) = 60 \cos 1000t \qquad \text{V}$$

Note that $v_2 = 6 \times 10^{-3}\,di_3/dt$.

7.21 For the circuit of Fig. 7-7, with S closed, find L such that the current from the source has a peak value of 12.5 A.

▮ From Fig. 7-7 with S closed, we have

$$L_{eq} = \left(\frac{6 \times 12}{6 + 12} + \frac{6L}{6 + L} \right) mH = \frac{24 + 10L}{6 + L} mH$$

$$i = \frac{1}{L_{eq}} \int v \, dt = \frac{(6 + L)10^3}{24 + 10L} \int 100 \cos 1000t \, dt = \left(\frac{6 + L}{24 + 10L} \right) 100 \sin 1000t$$

or $\qquad\qquad 12.5 = \frac{(6 + L)100}{24 + 10L} \qquad$ from which $\qquad L = 12 \, mH$

7.22 For the value of L determined in Prob. 7.21, with S closed, find i_1, i_2, i_3, and i_4 from Fig. 7-7.

▮ Since $\quad i = 12.5 \sin 1000t$ A

and $\qquad\qquad\qquad\qquad \dfrac{i_1}{i_2} = \dfrac{L_2}{L_1} = 0.5 \qquad i_1 + i_2 = 12.5$

$$i_4 = i_1 = 4.167 \sin 1000t \quad A \qquad i_3 = i_2 = 8.333 \sin 1000t \quad A$$

7.23 Find v_1 and v_2, with S closed, with L obtained in Prob. 7.21.

▮ $\qquad\qquad v_1 = 12 \times 10^{-3} \dfrac{d}{dt} (4.167 \sin 1000t) = 50 \cos 1000t \text{ V} = v_2$

7.24 Find the inductance at the terminals of the wye-connected circuit shown in Fig. 7-8, taking any two terminals at a time.

▮ From Fig. 7-8,

$$L_{ab} = L_1 + L_2 \qquad L_{bc} = L_2 + L_3 \qquad L_{ca} = L_3 + L_1$$

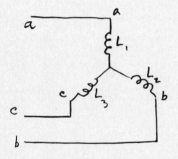

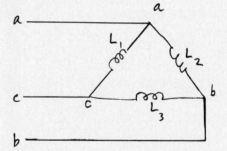

Fig. 7-8   Fig. 7-9

7.25 The inductors of Prob. 7.24 are reconnected in delta as shown in Fig. 7-9. Determine the inductance at the terminals, taking any two terminals at a time.

▮ From Fig. 7-9,

$$L_{ab} = \frac{L_2(L_1 + L_3)}{L_1 + L_2 + L_3} \qquad L_{bc} = \frac{L_3(L_2 + L_1)}{L_1 + L_2 + L_3} \qquad L_{ca} = \frac{L_1(L_3 + L_2)}{L_1 + L_2 + L_3}$$

7.26 Let the three inductors, each having an inductance L_y, be connected in wye (Fig. 7-8). If three inductors, each having an inductance L_d, are connected in delta determine the equivalent relationship between the two connections.

From Prob. 7.24, $\qquad\qquad\qquad L_{ab} = L_{bc} = L_{ca} = L_y + L_y = 2L_y$

From Prob. 7.25, $\qquad\qquad L_{ab} = L_{bc} = L_{ca} = \dfrac{L_d(L_d + L_d)}{L_d + L_d + L_d} = \dfrac{2}{3} L_d$

From equivalence we must have,

$$2L_y = \tfrac{2}{3}L_d \qquad \text{or} \qquad L_y = \tfrac{1}{3}L_d \qquad \text{and} \qquad L_d = 3L_y$$

7.27 Find the equivalent inductance at the terminals *ab* for the circuit shown in Fig. 7-10*a* by converting the 1-H wye-connected inductors to an equivalent delta.

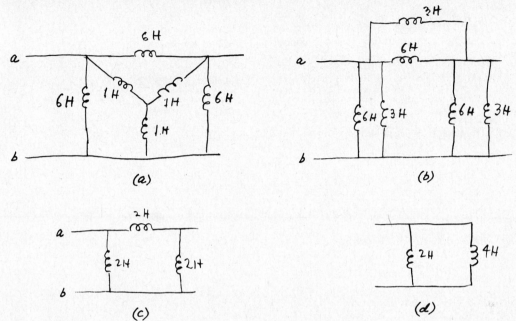

Fig. 7-10

I The steps in circuit reduction are shown in Fig. 7-10*b* to *d* from which

$$L_{ab} = \frac{2 \times 4}{2 + 4} = 1.33 \, \text{H}$$

7.28 Verify that the result of Prob. 7.27 is correct by transforming the delta-connected inductors to an equivalent wye.

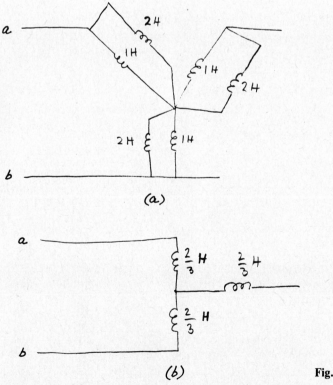

Fig. 7-11

❚ In this case, the steps in circuit reduction are shown in Fig. 7-11a and b from which

$$L_{ab} = (\tfrac{2}{3} + \tfrac{2}{3}) = 1.33 \text{ H}$$

7.29 A 40-mH inductor is charged to store 2 J of energy. An uncharged 60-mH inductor is then connected in parallel to the first one through perfectly conducting leads. How much energy is transferred to the second inductor?

❚ In terms of the flux linkage λ (which is conserved), we have $W = \lambda^2/2L$. Thus,

$$2 = \frac{\lambda^2}{2 \times 40 \times 10^{-3}} \quad \text{or} \quad \lambda = 0.4 \text{ Wb}$$

Since the voltage, or the flux linkage λ, remains unchanged, we have

$$i(L_1 + L_2) = \lambda \quad \text{or} \quad i = \frac{\lambda}{L_1 + L_2} = \frac{0.4}{(40 + 60) \times 10^{-3}} = 4 \text{ A}$$

Hence,

$$W_2 = \tfrac{1}{2} L_2 i^2 = \tfrac{1}{2} \times 60 \times 10^{-3}(4)^2 = 0.48 \text{ J}$$

7.30 How is a 300-mWb flux divided between a 50-mH and a 100-mH inductor connected in series?

❚ Let the series current be i. Then

$$\lambda_1 = L_1 i \qquad \lambda_2 = L_2 i$$

or

$$\frac{\lambda_1}{\lambda_2} = \frac{L_1}{L_2} = \frac{50}{100} = \frac{1}{2}$$

But

$$\lambda = \lambda_1 + \lambda_2 = 300 \times 10^{-3}$$

Hence

$$\lambda_1 = 100 \text{ mWb} \qquad \lambda_2 = 200 \text{ mWb}$$

CHAPTER 8
AC Sources, Waveforms, and Circuit Relationships

8.1   A time-varying voltage is given by $v = V_m \sin \omega t$.   Sketch this waveform.   Identify the instantaneous and maximum values, the frequency, and the period of the voltage.

▮ The instantaneous and maximum values are denoted by v and V_m, respectively, in Fig. 8-1.   The period T is defined by the condition $v(t + T) = v(t)$ for all t; thus,

$$\text{period } T = \frac{2\pi}{\omega} \text{ s} \qquad \text{frequency } f = \frac{1}{T} = \frac{\omega}{2\pi} \text{ Hz}$$

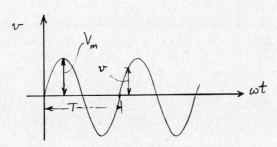

Fig. 8-1

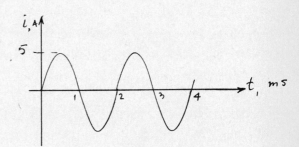

Fig. 8-2

8.2   What is the period of a 60-Hz voltage wave?

▮
$$T = \frac{1}{f} = \frac{1}{60} = 16.7 \text{ ms}$$

8.3   Find the frequency of the waveform shown in Fig. 8-2.

▮ From Fig. 8-2, $\qquad\qquad\qquad\qquad T = 2 \text{ ms} = 2 \times 10^{-3} \text{ s}$

Thus, $\qquad\qquad\qquad\qquad\qquad f = \frac{1}{T} = \frac{1}{2 \times 10^{-3}} = 500 \text{ Hz}$

8.4   What is the angular frequency of a waveform having a period of 2 ms?

▮
$$T = \frac{2\pi}{\omega} \qquad \text{or} \qquad \omega = \frac{2\pi}{T} = \frac{2\pi}{2 \times 10^{-3}} = 3141.6 \text{ rad/s}$$

8.5   What is   (*a*) the maximum value and   (*b*) the period of a waveform given by $v = 100 \sin 377t$ V?

▮ $\qquad\qquad\qquad$ (*a*) $V_m = 100$ V $\qquad$ (*b*) $T = \frac{2\pi}{\omega} = \frac{2\pi}{377} = 16.7 \text{ ms}$

8.6   A voltage wave and two current waves, shown in Fig. 8-3, have respective maximum values V_m, I_{m1}, and I_{m2}. The waveforms are sinusoidal.   Write mathematical expressions for these waves.

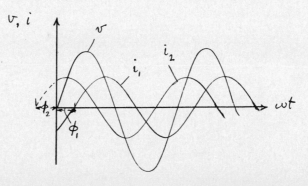

Fig. 8-3

$$v(t) = V_m \sin \omega t \qquad i_1(t) = I_{m1} \sin (\omega t - \phi_1) \qquad i_2(t) = I_{m2} \sin (\omega t + \phi_2)$$

Note that i_1 lags behind v by ϕ_1 and i_2 leads v by ϕ_2. These angles—ϕ_1 and ϕ_2—are known as phase angles.

8.7 Find the period, frequency, and the amplitude of the current waveform shown in Fig. 8-4.

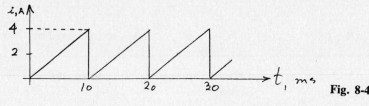

Fig. 8-4

$$T = 10 \text{ ms} \qquad f = \frac{1}{T} = \frac{1}{10 \times 10^{-3}} = 100 \text{ Hz} \qquad I_m = 4 \text{ A}$$

8.8 What is the period of a sinusoidal waveform having a 100-MHz frequency?

$$T = \frac{1}{f} = \frac{1}{100 \times 10^6} = 10^{-8} \text{ s} \qquad \text{or} \quad 10 \text{ ns}$$

8.9 Find the frequency in hertz and the angular frequency in rad/s of a waveform whose period is 5 ms.

$$f = \frac{1}{T} = \frac{1}{5 \times 10^{-3}} = 200 \text{ Hz} \qquad \omega = 2\pi f = 2\pi(200) = 1256.64 \text{ rad/s}$$

8.10 What are the amplitude, frequency, and period of a voltage wave $v = 200 \sin 377t$ V?

$$V_m = 200 \text{ V}$$

Since

$$\omega = 2\pi f = 377 \text{ rad/s} \qquad f = \frac{377}{2\pi} = 60 \text{ Hz} \qquad T = \frac{1}{f} = \frac{1}{60} = 16.67 \text{ ms}$$

8.11 A voltage wave is given by $v = 100 \sin 314t$. How long does it take this waveform to complete one-fourth cycle?

$T = 2\pi/\omega = 2\pi/314 = 20 \text{ ms}$, which is the time for 1 cycle. Thus, the time for one-quarter cycle $= \frac{1}{4} \times 20 = 5$ ms.

8.12 What are the phase relationships between the following waveforms?

(a) $\qquad\qquad\qquad v = 100 \sin (\omega t + 30°) \qquad i = 10 \sin (\omega t + 60°)$

(b) $\qquad\qquad\qquad v = 100 \sin (\omega t + 30°) \qquad i = 10 \sin (\omega t - 30°)$

(c) $\qquad\qquad\qquad v = 100 \sin (\omega t - 60°) \qquad i = 10 \sin (\omega t - 90°)$

(a) i leads v by $(60° - 30°) = 30°$.
(b) i lags v by $[30° - (-30°)] = 60°$.
(c) i lags v by $[-60° - (-90°)] = 30°$.

8.13 Sketch the waveforms of the voltages and currents of Prob. 8.12 and verify the results obtained in Prob. 8.7.

The waveforms are shown in Fig. 8-5a to c.

8.14 Determine the average value of the current waveform $i = I_m \sin \omega t$ over (a) a period and (b) a half-period.

(a) Since $\omega = 2\pi/T$,

$$I_{avg} = \frac{1}{T} \int_{t_0}^{t_0+T} I_m \sin \frac{2\pi}{T} t \, dt = -\frac{I_m}{2\pi} \cos \frac{2\pi}{T} t \Big]_{t_0}^{t_0+T} = 0$$

(b) $\quad I_{avg} = \frac{2}{T} \int_{t_0}^{t_0+T/2} I_m \sin \frac{2\pi}{T} t \, dt = -\frac{I_m}{\pi} \cos \frac{2\pi}{T} t \Big]_{t_0}^{t_0+T/2} = -\frac{I_m}{\pi} \left(-\cos \frac{2\pi t_0}{T} - \cos \frac{2\pi t_0}{T} \right) = \frac{2I_m}{\pi} \cos \omega t_0$

Thus, the average value depends on the initial point t_0. For $t_0 = 0$, $I_{avg} = 2I_m/\pi \approx 0.6366 I_m$.

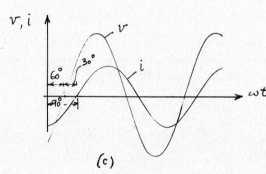

Fig. 8-5

8.15 Determine the instantaneous and average powers dissipated in a resistor R connected across an ac voltage $v = V_m \sin \omega t$.

$$p = \frac{v^2}{R} = \frac{V_m^2}{R} \sin^2 \omega t = \frac{V_m^2}{2R} (1 - \cos 2\omega t) \qquad p_{\text{av}} = \frac{V_m^2}{2R}$$

8.16 Determine the dc voltage that must be connected across a resistor R such that the power dissipated is the same as the average power determined in Prob. 8.15.

$$P_{\text{dc}} = \frac{V_{\text{dc}}^2}{R} = \frac{V_m^2}{2R} \qquad \text{from Prob. 8.15}$$

Or

$$V_{\text{dc}} = \frac{V_m}{\sqrt{2}}$$

This value is known as the *effective*, or *root-mean-square*, value.

8.17 By rms we imply "the square root of the mean value of the square." Determine the rms value of the current waveform shown in Fig. 8.6.

$$I_{\text{rms}} = \sqrt{\frac{10^2 \cdot 2 + (-4)^2 \cdot 2 + 2^2 \cdot 2 + 0^2 \cdot 2}{8}} = 5.477 \text{ A}$$

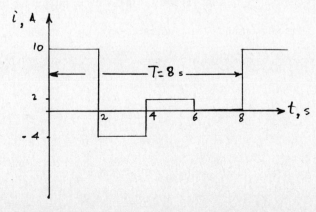

Fig. 8-6

8.18 Find the ratio rms value/average value of an ac sinusoidal voltage, where the average is taken over the first half-cycle.

▌ From Prob. 8.16, $$V_{\text{rms}} = \frac{V_m}{\sqrt{2}}$$

From Prob. 8.14,

$$V_{\text{avg}} = \frac{2V_m}{\pi} \qquad \frac{V_{\text{rms}}}{V_{\text{avg}}} = \frac{V_m/\sqrt{2}}{2V_m/\pi} = 1.11$$

This ratio is known as the *form factor* of the waveform.

8.19 Determine the rms value, average value, and form factor of the current waveform shown in Fig. 8-4.

▌ From Fig. 8-4, $$i = 400t \text{ A} \qquad (0 < t < 10 \text{ ms})$$

$$\text{rms} = \sqrt{\frac{1}{T} \int_0^T i^2 \, dt} = \sqrt{\frac{1}{10 \times 10^{-3}} \int_0^{10 \times 10^{-3}} (400t)^2 \, dt} = \sqrt{\frac{(400)^2}{10 \times 10^{-3}} \left[\frac{t^3}{3} \right]_0^{10 \times 10^{-3}}} = 2.31 \text{ A}$$

$$\text{average} = 2 \text{ A} \quad \text{(linear function)} \quad \text{form factor} = \frac{2.31}{2} = 1.155$$

8.20 Determine the rms value, average value, and form factor of the current waveform shown in Fig. 8-7.

▌ The wave has period $T = 3$ s.

$$I_{\text{rms}} = \sqrt{\frac{10^2 \cdot 2 + 0^2 \cdot 1}{3}} = 8.16 \text{ A} \qquad I_{\text{avg}} = \frac{10 \cdot 2 + 0 \cdot 1}{3} = 6.67 \text{ A}$$

$$\text{form factor} = \frac{\text{rms value}}{\text{average value}} = \frac{8.16}{6.67} = 1.22$$

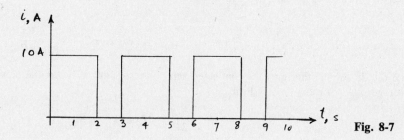

Fig. 8-7

8.21 Obtain the voltage-current relationship for a resistor R connected across an ac voltage $v = V_m \sin \omega t$.

▌ Since $$v = Ri \quad \text{and} \quad v = V_m \sin \omega t \qquad (1)$$

Or $$V_m \sin \omega t = Ri$$

Or $$i = \frac{V_m}{R} \sin \omega t = I_m \sin \omega t \qquad (2)$$

and $$V_m = RI_m \qquad V = RI$$

where V and I are rms values. Note from (1) and (2) that the current and the voltage are in the same phase.

8.22 Obtain the voltage-current relationships for an inductor L carrying a current $i = I_m \sin \omega t$.

▌ Since $$v = L \frac{di}{dt}$$

and $$i = I_m \sin \omega t \qquad (1)$$

we obtain $$v = L \frac{d}{dt} (I_m \sin \omega t) = \omega L I_m \cos \omega t = V_m \cos \omega t = V_m \sin (\omega t + 90°) \qquad (2)$$

Or $$V_m = \omega L I_m \quad \text{and} \quad V = \omega L I \equiv X_L I$$

where $X_L = \omega L$ is defined as the *inductive reactance*, and is measured in ohms.

Note from (1) and (2) that the current through the inductor lags the voltage across the inductor by 90°.

8.23 What are the various forms of voltage-current relationships for a capacitor C connected across a voltage source, $v = V_m \sin \omega t$?

▮ Since
$$i = C \, dv/dt \quad \text{and} \quad v = V_m \sin \omega t \qquad\qquad (1)$$

we obtain
$$i = \omega C V_m \cos \omega t = I_m \cos \omega t = I_m \sin(\omega t + 90°) \qquad\qquad (2)$$

Or
$$I_m = \omega C V_m \quad \text{and} \quad V = \frac{I}{\omega C} \equiv X_c I$$

where $X_c = 1/\omega C$ is defined as the *capacitive reactance* in ohms.

From (1) and (2) it follows that the current through the capacitor leads the voltage across it by 90°.

8.24 An inductor draws 5 A of current at 110 V 60 Hz. Express the instantaneous voltage and current mathematically.

▮ First, we note that (unless stated otherwise) the values are all rms. Thus,
$$I_m = \sqrt{2}(5) = 7.07 \text{ A} \qquad \omega = 2\pi f = 2\pi(60) = 377 \text{ rad/s}$$

And
$$i = 7.07 \sin 377t \text{ A} \qquad V_m = \sqrt{2}(110) = 155.56 \text{ V}$$

Since the current lags the voltage by 90° in an inductive circuit (see Prob. 8.22), we have
$$v = 155.56 \sin(\omega t + 90°) = 155.56 \cos \omega t \text{ V}$$

8.25 Determine the inductive reactance and the inductance from the data of Prob. 8.24.

▮
$$X_L = \frac{V}{I} = \frac{110}{5} = 22 \, \Omega$$

Now
$$X_L = \omega L = 337 L$$

Hence,
$$L = \frac{22}{377} = 58.36 \text{ mH}$$

8.26 A capacitor draws 2 A of current at 120 V 50 Hz. Express the instantaneous voltage and current mathematically.

▮ Proceeding as in Prob. 8.24,
$$I_m = \sqrt{2}(2) = 2.828 \text{ A} \qquad \omega = 2\pi(50) = 314 \text{ rad/s}$$
$$i = 2.828 \sin 314t \text{ A} \qquad V_m = \sqrt{2}(120) = 169.7 \text{ V}$$

Since the current leads the voltage by 90° in a capacitive circuit (see Prob. 8.23), we have
$$v = 169.7 \sin(\omega t - 90°) = -169.7 \cos \omega t \text{ V}$$

8.27 Determine the capacitive reactance and the capacitance from the data of Prob. 8.26.

▮
$$X_c = \frac{V}{I} = \frac{120}{2} = 60 \, \Omega$$

Now,
$$X_c = \frac{1}{\omega C} = \frac{1}{314 C}$$

Hence,
$$C = \frac{1}{314 \times 60} = 53.0 \, \mu\text{F}$$

8.28 The voltage across a 0.5-H inductor is $v = 200 \sin 100t$ V. What is the instantaneous current?

▮
$$X_L = \omega L = 100 \times 0.5 = 50 \, \Omega \qquad I_m = \frac{V_m}{X_L} = \frac{200}{50} = 4 \text{ A}$$

Since i lags v by 90°, we finally have
$$i = I_m \sin(\omega t - 90°) = 4 \sin(100t - 90°) \qquad \text{A}$$

8.29 The current through a 50-μF capacitor is $i = 2 \sin 1000t$ A. What is the instantaneous voltage?

$$X_c = \frac{1}{\omega C} = \frac{1}{1000 \times 50 \times 10^{-6}} = 20\,\Omega \qquad V_m = I_m X_c = 2 \times 20 = 40\,\text{V}$$

Since the voltage lags the current by 90°, we have

$$v = V_m \sin(\omega t - 90°) = 40 \sin (1000t - 90°)\,\text{V}$$

8.30 The voltage and current through a circuit element are $v = 100 \sin (377t + 20°)\,\text{V}$ and $i = 4 \sin (377t - 70°)\,\text{A}$. Identify the element and find its value.

▮ The voltage leads the current by $20 - (-70) = 90°$. Hence, the element is an inductor.

Now,
$$X_L = \frac{V_m}{I_m} = \frac{100}{4} = 25\,\Omega = \omega L = 377L \qquad \text{or} \qquad L = 66.3\,\text{mH}$$

8.31 The voltage and current for a circuit element are

$$v = 200 \sin (314t - 10°) \quad \text{V} \qquad i = 20 \sin (314t - 10°) \quad \text{A}$$

Identify the element and find its value.

▮ Since the voltage and the current are in the same phase, the element is a resistor, the ohmic value of which is given by

$$R = \frac{V_m}{I_m} = \frac{200}{20} = 10\,\Omega$$

8.32 The voltage and current for a circuit element are

$$v = 6 \cos (1000t - 80°) \quad \text{V} \qquad i = 3 \cos (1000t + 10°) \quad \text{A}$$

Identify the element and find its value.

▮ Since the current is ahead of the voltage by $10 - (-80) = 90°$, the element is capacitive and

$$X_c = \frac{V_m}{I_m} = \frac{6}{3} = 2\,\Omega \qquad = \frac{1}{\omega C} = \frac{1}{1000C} \qquad \text{or} \qquad C = \frac{1}{2 \times 1000} = 500\,\mu\text{F}$$

8.33 The voltage across and the current through an ac circuit are given by

$$v = V_m \sin \omega t \qquad i = I_m \sin (\omega t - \phi)$$

Find the instantaneous power.

▮ The instantaneous power is given by

$$p = vi = V_m \sin \omega t I_m \sin (\omega t - \phi) = V_m I_m \tfrac{1}{2} \cos [(\omega t - \omega t + \phi) - \cos (\omega t + \omega t - \phi)]$$
$$= \tfrac{1}{2} V_m I_m [\cos \phi - \cos (2\omega t - \phi)]$$

8.34 Determine the average power for the circuit of Prob. 8.33, in terms of rms values of voltage and current.

▮ Since the time-average value of $\cos (2\omega t - \phi)$ is zero, from the result of Prob. 8.33 we have

$$p_{\text{av}} \equiv P = \tfrac{1}{2} V_m I_m \cos \phi$$

Now $V = V_m / \sqrt{2}$ and $I = I_m / \sqrt{2}$. Hence, $P = VI \cos \phi$, where $\cos \phi$ is known as the *power factor*.

8.35 An ac circuit is purely resistive, having an equivalent resistance of $15\,\Omega$ at the terminals. A 110-V 60-Hz ac source is connected across the terminals. Determine the input current, power, and power factor.

▮
$$I = \frac{V}{R} = \frac{110}{15} = 7.33\,\text{A} \qquad P = I^2 R = (7.33)^2 15 = 806.67\,W = VI \cos \phi$$

Hence,
$$\cos \phi = \frac{806.67}{110 \times 7.33} = 1.0$$

Otherwise, since the current through and the voltage across a resistor are in phase, its power factor is $\cos 0° = 1.0$.

8.36 How much power is dissipated in the circuit element of Prob. 8.32 and what is its power factor?

▮ Power factor, $\cos\phi = \cos 90° = 0$ (leading, since the current leads the voltage. This is a convention.)

$$\text{Power} = VI\cos 90° = 0\,\text{W}$$

8.37 Repeat Prob. 8.36 for the data of Prob. 8.30.

▮ Power factor, $\cos\phi = \cos 90° = 0$ (lagging since the current lags the voltage):

$$\text{Power} = VI\cos 90° = 0\,\text{W}$$

8.38 An ac circuit draws 5-A current at 220 V and consumes 1000 W power. What is its power factor?

▮ Since $P = VI\cos\phi$, where P is the power in watts, we have

$$\cos\phi = \frac{P}{VI} = \frac{1000}{5 \times 220} = 0.91$$

8.39 The voltage and the current in an ac circuit are

$$v = 200\sin(377t + 30°) \qquad i = 10\sin(377t + 60°)$$

Determine the average power.

▮ From the data, $V = 200/\sqrt{2}\,\text{V}$, $I = 10/\sqrt{2}\,\text{A}$, and $\phi = 60° - 30° = 30°$. Hence,

$$\text{Average power} = \left(\frac{200}{\sqrt{2}}\right)\left(\frac{10}{\sqrt{2}}\right)\cos 30° = 866\,\text{W}$$

8.40 The voltage and current in ac circuit are

$$v = 100\sin(377t - 30°) \quad \text{V} \qquad i = 6\sin(377t + 30°) \quad \text{A}$$

What is the power factor? Is it leading or lagging?

▮ $$\phi = 30 - (-30) = 60° \qquad \cos\phi = \cos 60° = 0.5\ \text{leading}$$

8.41 A circuit draws 3 A current at 50 V and consumes 150 W power. Determine the power factor and the nature of the circuit.

▮ $$\cos\phi = \frac{P}{VI} = \frac{150}{(50)(3)} = 1$$

The circuit is resistive.

8.42 A 5-Ω resistor, a 100-μF capacitor, and a 100-mH inductor are connected in parallel across a 100-V 60-Hz source. Determine the average power drawn by the circuit.

▮ Since the capacitor and the inductor do not draw any power (Probs 8.36 and 8.37), the power is dissipated only in the resistor. Hence,

$$P = \frac{V^2}{R} = \frac{(100)^2}{5} = 2\,\text{kW}$$

8.43 What is the reactance of 50-mH inductor at (*a*) dc and (*b*) 60 Hz ac?

▮ (*a*) At dc, $X_L = \omega L = (0)(50 \times 10^{-3}) = 0\,\Omega$. Thus, an inductor acts as short circuit across dc.
(*b*) At 60 Hz,

$$\omega = 2\pi f = 2\pi \times 60 = 377\,\text{rad/s} \qquad X_L = \omega L = 377 \times 50 \times 10^{-3} = 18.85\,\Omega$$

8.44 Determine the inductance of a coil having a 50-Ω reactance at 60 Hz.

▮ $$L = \frac{X_L}{\omega} = \frac{X_L}{2\pi f} = \frac{50}{2\pi(60)} = 132.63\,\text{mH}$$

8.45 Determine the frequency at which a 50-mH inductor has a 50-Ω reactance.

▮ $$\omega = \frac{X_L}{L} = \frac{50}{50 \times 10^{-3}} = 1000\,\text{rad/s} = 2\pi f$$

Thus,
$$f = \frac{1000}{2\pi} = 159.15 \text{ Hz}$$

8.46 What is the reactance of a 500-μF capacitor at (*a*) dc and (*b*) 100 Hz?

▌ (*a*) At dc:
$$X_c = \frac{1}{\omega C} = \frac{1}{(0)(500 \times 10^{-6})} = \infty \, \Omega$$

Thus, a capacitor acts as an open circuit across dc.

(*b*) At 100 Hz:
$$X_c = \frac{1}{2\pi \times 100 \times 500 \times 10^{-6}} = 3.18 \, \Omega$$

8.47 Determine the capacitance of a capacitor having a 50-Ω reactance at 60 Hz.

▌
$$C = \frac{1}{\omega X_c} = \frac{1}{2\pi f X_c} = \frac{1}{2\pi \times 60 \times 50} = 53.05 \, \mu\text{F}$$

8.48 At what frequency will a 100-μF capacitor have a 100-Ω reactance?

▌
$$\omega = \frac{1}{C X_c} = \frac{1}{100 \times 10^{-6} \times 100} = 100 \text{ rad/s} = 2\pi f$$

Thus,
$$f = \frac{100}{2\pi} = 15.9 \text{ Hz}$$

8.49 The power factor of a circuit is 0.866 lagging. If the input power is 600 W at a voltage $v = \sqrt{2} \times 110 \sin(377t + 10°) \, V$, what is the instantaneous current?

▌ Given:
$$\cos \phi = 0.866 \text{ lagging} \quad \text{or} \quad \phi = \cos^{-1}(0.866) = 30° \text{ lagging}$$
$$P = VI \cos \phi \quad \text{or} \quad 600 = (110)I(0.866)$$

or
$$I = \frac{600}{110(0.866)} = 6.3 \text{ A} \quad \text{and} \quad I_m = 6.3\sqrt{2} = 8.9 \text{ A}$$

Now $\phi = 30°$ lagging implies that i lags v by 30°. Hence $i = 8.9 \sin(377t - 20°) \, A$.

8.50 Determine the power factor and the input power for a circuit with $v = 50 \sin(t + 10°) \, V$ and $i = 2 \sin(t + 20°) \, A$.

▌ Power factor angle, $\phi = 20 - 10 = 10°$ $\cos \phi = \cos 10° = 0.9848$ leading

$$\text{Power} = \left(\frac{50}{\sqrt{2}}\right)\left(\frac{2}{\sqrt{2}}\right) \cos 10° = 49.24 \text{ W}$$

CHAPTER 9

Complex Numbers and Phasors

9.1 A complex number represents a point on a plane with reference to two perpendicular axes. The horizontal axis is called the *real axis* and the vertical axis the *imaginary axis*. The symbol j is used to denote the unit along the imaginary axis. Locate the following complex numbers in a complex plane:

$$\mathbf{A} = 3 + j4 \qquad \mathbf{B} = -j5 \qquad \mathbf{C} = -6 - j6 \qquad \mathbf{D} = 4 - j5$$

▌ The locations of these points are shown in Fig. 9-1. If we join these points to the origin, with arrowheads directed toward the points, we obtain directed line segments such as $\overrightarrow{OA}$, $\overrightarrow{OB}$, etc., which are called *phasors*.

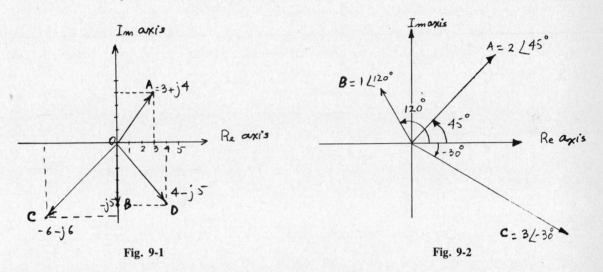

Fig. 9-1   **Fig. 9-2**

9.2 With the definition of a phasor just given, locate the following phasors:

$$\mathbf{A} = 2 \,\underline{/45°} \qquad \mathbf{B} = 1 \,\underline{/120°} \qquad \mathbf{C} = 3 \,\underline{/-30°}$$

▌ The locations of the phasors are shown in Fig. 9-2. This form of representation is known as *polar form*, in contrast to the form shown in Fig. 9-1, which is known as the *rectangular form*.

9.3 Diagrams such as those of Figs. 9-1 and 9-2 are known as phasor diagrams. By means of a general phasor diagram obtain the relationships to convert polar forms to rectangular forms, and vice versa.

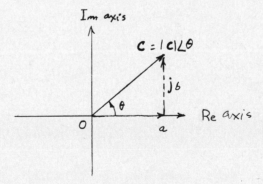

Fig. 9-3

▌ Consider the phasor $\overrightarrow{OC}$ (or $\mathbf{C}$) shown in Fig. 9-3. In rectangular form we may write

$$\mathbf{C} = a + jb$$

Or

$$|\mathbf{C}| = \sqrt{a^2 + b^2} \tag{1}$$

Also
$$\theta = \tan^{-1} \frac{b}{a} \qquad (2)$$

Equations (1) and (2) give the conversion from rectangular to polar fom.   Polar to rectangular form conversion is given by

$$a = |\mathbf{C}| \cos \theta \qquad (3)$$
$$b = |\mathbf{C}| \sin \theta \qquad (4)$$

9.4   Given: $\mathbf{A} = 2 + j2$.   Express $\mathbf{A}$ in its polar form.

❚ $|\mathbf{A}| = \sqrt{2^2 + 2^2} = \sqrt{8}$ $\tan \theta = \frac{2}{2} = 1$, or $\theta = 45°$

Hence, $\mathbf{A} = \sqrt{8} \, \underline{/45°}$

9.5   Given $\mathbf{A} = -3 + j4$,   what is the corresponding polar form?

$$|\mathbf{A}| = \sqrt{(-3)^2 + 4^2} = 5$$

❚   Referring to Fig. 9-4, we have

$$\alpha = \tan^{-1} \tfrac{4}{3} = 53.13° \quad \text{or} \quad \theta = 180° - \alpha = 126.87°$$

Hence, $\mathbf{A} = 5 \, \underline{/126.87°}$

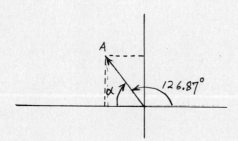

Fig. 9-4

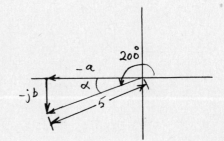

Fig. 9-5

9.6   Convert $\mathbf{A} = 4 \, \underline{/-30°}$ to its rectangular form.

❚   Let $\mathbf{A} = a + jb$.   Then,
$$a = 4 \cos (-30°) \quad \text{and} \quad b = 4 \sin (-30°)$$

Hence $\mathbf{A} = 3.464 - j2.0$

9.7   Convert $\mathbf{A} = 5 \, \underline{/200°}$ to its rectangular form.

❚   Let $\mathbf{A} = -a - jb$ (see Fig. 9.5).   From Fig. 9-5, $\alpha = 200 - 180 = 20°$.   Then,
$$-a = -5 \cos 20° = -4.7 \qquad -b = -5 \sin 20° = -1.71$$

Hence $\mathbf{A} = -4.7 - j1.71$

9.8   The imaginary quantity j is defined by $j = \sqrt{-1}$.   Locate j^2, j^3, and j^4 on a phasor diagram.   What conclusion may be drawn from this diagram?

❚   Since $j = \sqrt{-1}$,   we have
$$j^2 = -1 \qquad j^3 = (j^2)j = -j \qquad j^4 = (j^3)j = -j^2 = 1$$

These are shown as phasors in Fig. 9-6.   We may conclude that j may be treated as an operator which when applied to a phasor rotates it by 90° in the counterclockwise direction.

9.9   Find the reciprocals of the following phasors: (*a*) j;   (*b*) $3 + j4$;   (*c*) $6 \, \underline{/30°}$.   In each case separate the real and imaginary parts.   For *b* plot the phasor and its complex conjugate.

❚   (*a*)   Reciprocal of
$$j = \frac{1}{j} = \frac{j}{(j)(j)} = -j$$

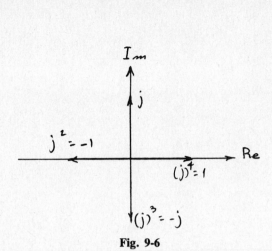

Fig. 9-6

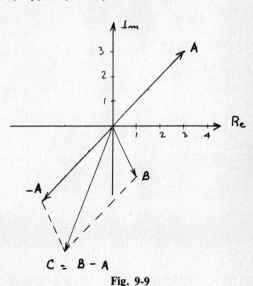

Fig. 9-7

(*b*) Reciprocal of $$3 + j4 = \frac{1}{3 + j4}$$

Multiplying the numerator and the denominator by $3 - j4$ (the *complex conjugate* of $3 + j4$), we obtain

$$\frac{1}{3 + j4} = \frac{3 - j4}{(3 + j4)(3 - j4)} = \frac{3 - j4}{9 + 16} = \frac{1}{25} (3 - j4)$$

The phasor $(3 + j4)$ and its complex conjugate are shown in Fig. 9-7.

(*c*) From Fig. 9-7 we infer that the phasors $|A| \underline{/\theta}$ and $|A| \underline{/-\theta}$ are complex conjugates, with product $|A|^2$. Thus,

$$\frac{1}{6 \underline{/30°}} = \frac{6 \underline{/-30°}}{(6 \underline{/30°})(6 \underline{/-30°})} = \frac{1}{6} \underline{/-30°} = \frac{1}{6} (\cos 30° - j \sin 30°) = 0.144 - j0.083$$

9.10 To add (or subtract) two or more phasors we add (or subtract) the respective real and imaginary parts. According to this rule obtain $\mathbf{C} = \mathbf{A} + \mathbf{B}$, where $\mathbf{A} = 4 + j2$ and $\mathbf{B} = 2 + j4$. Show $\mathbf{A}$, $\mathbf{B}$, and $\mathbf{C}$ graphically.

$$\mathbf{C} = \mathbf{A} + \mathbf{B} = (4 + j2) + (2 + j4) = (4 + 2) + j(2 + 4) = 6 + j6$$

The phasors are plotted in Fig. 9-8.

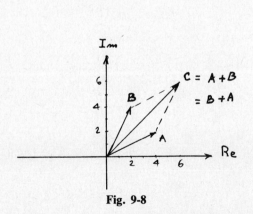

Fig. 9-8

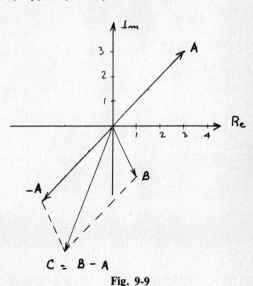

Fig. 9-9

9.11 Subtract $\mathbf{A} = 3 + j3$ from $\mathbf{B} = 1 - j2$. Show the operation graphically.

$$\mathbf{C} = \mathbf{B} - \mathbf{A} = (1 - j2) - (3 + j3) = (1 - 3) - j(2 + 3) = -2 - j5$$

which is shown in Fig. 9-9.

9.12 Multiply two phasors $\mathbf{A} = 2 + j3$ and $\mathbf{B} = 1 + j2$. Separate real and imaginary parts. Express the results in rectangular and polar forms.

$$\mathbf{A} \cdot \mathbf{B} = (2 + j3)(1 + j2) = 2 + j4 + j3 - 6 = -4 + j7 = 8.06 \,\underline{/119.74°}$$

9.13 Express $\mathbf{A}$ and $\mathbf{B}$ of Prob. 9.12 first in polar form. Verify that $\mathbf{A} \cdot \mathbf{B}$ in polar form may be obtained by multiplying the magnitudes and adding the angles.

$$\mathbf{A} = 3.605 \,\underline{/56.31°} \qquad \mathbf{B} = 2.236 \,\underline{/63.43°}$$

$$\mathbf{A} \cdot \mathbf{B} = (3.605)(2.236) \,\underline{/(56.31 + 63.43)} = 8.06 \,\underline{/119.74°}$$

which agrees with the result of Prob. 9.12.

9.14 The procedure for Prob. 9.13 can be extended to division where we divide the magnitudes and subtract the angles. Hence evaluate $\mathbf{A}/\mathbf{B}$, where $\mathbf{A}$ and $\mathbf{B}$ are the same as in Prob. 9.12.

From Prob. 9.13,

$$\mathbf{A} = 3.605 \,\underline{/56.31°} \qquad \mathbf{B} = 2.236 \,\underline{/63.43°}$$

Hence,
$$\frac{\mathbf{A}}{\mathbf{B}} = \frac{3.605}{2.236} \,\underline{/(56.31 - 63.43)} = 1.612 \,\underline{/-7.12°}$$

9.15 Verify the result of Prob. 9.14 in rectangular form.

$$\frac{\mathbf{A}}{\mathbf{B}} = \frac{2 + j3}{1 + j2} = \frac{(2 + j3)(1 - j2)}{(1 + j2)(1 - j2)} = \frac{(2 - j4 + j3 + 6)}{5} = \frac{1}{5}(8 - j1) = 1.6 - j0.2 = 1.612 \,\underline{/-7.12°}$$

which agrees with result of Prob. 9.14.

9.16 Calculate (**a**) $10 \,\underline{/45°} + 10 \,\underline{/-45°}$; (**b**) $(6.8 + j3.2) + (5 - j1.2)$; (**c**) $2 \,\underline{/60°} + 3 \,\underline{/-30°} - 4 \,\underline{/45°}$; and (**d**) $2 \,\underline{/60°} + (5 - j1.232)$.

(**a**) $\quad 10 \,\underline{/45°} = 10(\cos 45° + j \sin 45°) \qquad 10 \,\underline{/-45°} = 10(\cos 45° - j \sin 45°) \;\; \Sigma = 10(\cos 45° + \cos 45°) = 14.14$

(**b**) $\qquad\qquad\qquad (6.8 + j3.2) + (5 - j1.2) = (6.8 + 5) + j(3.2 - 1.2) = 11.8 + j2$

(**c**) $\qquad 2 \,\underline{/60°} = 2(\cos 60 + j \sin 60) = 1 + j1.732 \qquad 3 \,\underline{/-30°} = 3(\cos 30 - j \sin 30) = 2.598 - j1.5$

$$-4 \,\underline{/45°} = -4(\cos 45 + j \sin 45) = -2.828 - j2.828 \;\; \Sigma = 0.77 - j2.596$$

(**d**) $\qquad\qquad 2 \,\underline{/60°} = 2(\cos 60 + j \sin 60) = 1 + j1.732 \qquad \Sigma = 6 + j0.5$

9.17 Perform the following calculations in polar form: (**a**) $(3 + j3)(5 + j8)$; (**b**) $(5 \,\underline{/45°})(4 \,\underline{/20°})$; (**c**) $(5 \,\underline{/45°})(4 \,\underline{/-20°})$; and (**d**) $(5 \,\underline{/45°})(4 \,\underline{/20°})(3 \,\underline{/-75°})$.

(**a**) $\qquad\qquad\qquad\qquad\qquad 3 + j3 = 4.243 \,\underline{/45°} \qquad 5 + j8 = 9.434 \,\underline{/58°}$

$$(3 + j3)(5 + j8) = (4.243)(9.434) \;\; (45° + 58°) = 40 \,\underline{/103°}$$

(**b**) $\qquad\qquad\qquad\qquad (5 \,\underline{/45°})(4 \,\underline{/20°}) = (5)(4) \,\underline{/(45° + 20°)} = 20 \,\underline{/65°}$

(**c**) $\qquad\qquad\qquad\qquad (5 \,\underline{/45°})(4 \,\underline{/-20°}) = (5)(4) \,\underline{/(45° - 20°)} = 20 \,\underline{/25°}$

(**d**) $\qquad\qquad (5 \,\underline{/45°})(4 \,\underline{/20°})(3 \,\underline{/-75°}) = (5)(4)(3) \,\underline{/(45° + 20° - 75°)} = 60 \,\underline{/-10°}$

9.18 Perform the following calculations in polar form: (**a**) $(3 + j3)/(5 + j8)$; (**b**) $(5 \,\underline{/45°})/(4 \,\underline{/20°})$; (**c**) $(5 \,\underline{/45°})/(4 \,\underline{/-20°})$; (**d**) $(5 \,\underline{/45°})(4 \,\underline{/-20°})/(3 \,\underline{/75°})$.

(**a**) $\qquad 3 + j3 = 4.243 \,\underline{/45°} \qquad 5 + j8 = 9.434 \,\underline{/58°} \qquad \dfrac{3 + j3}{5 + j8} = \dfrac{4.243}{9.434} \,\underline{/(45 - 58)} = 0.45 \,\underline{/-13°}$

(**b**) $\qquad\qquad\qquad\qquad\qquad \dfrac{5 \,\underline{/45°}}{4 \,\underline{/20°}} = \dfrac{5}{4} \,\underline{/(45 - 20)} = 1.25 \,\underline{/25°}$

(c)
$$\frac{5\;\underline{/45°}}{4\;\underline{/-20°}} = \frac{5}{4}\;\underline{/(45 + 20)} = 1.25\;\underline{/65°}$$

(d)
$$\frac{(5\;\underline{/45°})(4\;\underline{/-20°})}{3\;\underline{/75°}} = \frac{(5)(4)}{3}\;\underline{/(45 - 20 - 75)} = 6.67\;\underline{/-50°}$$

9.19 Phasors are used to denote sinusoidal alternating quantities. For instance, $v = V_m \sin(\omega t - \phi)$ is written as $\mathbf{V} = V\;\underline{/-\phi}$, where $V = V_m/\sqrt{2}$ is the rms value. Similarly, $i = I_m \sin(\omega t + \theta)$ is written as $\mathbf{I} = I\;\underline{/\theta}$. Express the following currents as phasors: (a) $141.4 \sin \omega t$, (b) $10 \sin(\omega t + 60°)$, and (c) $2 \cos \omega t$.

❙ (a)
$$I_m = 141.4 \quad \text{or} \quad I = \frac{141.4}{\sqrt{2}} = 100$$

Thus $\mathbf{I} = 100\;\underline{/0°}$.

(b)
$$\mathbf{I} = \frac{10}{\sqrt{2}}\;\underline{/60°} = 7.07\;\underline{/60°}$$

(c)
$$\mathbf{I} = \frac{2}{\sqrt{2}}\;\underline{/90°} = 1.414\;\underline{/90°}$$

9.20 Express the following current phasors as instantaneous currents, all at a frequency ω: (a) $10\;\underline{/0°}$; (b) $25\;\underline{/-30°}$; and (c) $6\;\underline{/-90°}$.

❙ (a)
$$i = \sqrt{2}(10) \sin \omega t = 14.14 \sin \omega t$$

(b)
$$i = \sqrt{2}(25) \sin(\omega t - 30°) = 35.35 \sin(\omega t - 30°)$$

(c)
$$i = \sqrt{2}(6) \sin(\omega t - 90°) = -8.484 \cos \omega t$$

9.21 The instantaneous voltage and current for an ac circuit are

$$v = 155.6 \sin 377t \quad \text{V} \qquad i = 7.07 \sin(377t - 30°) \quad \text{A}$$

Represent these as complex exponentials.

❙
$$v = 155.6 e^{j377t} \quad \text{V} \quad \text{and} \quad i = 7.07\, e^{j377t - (\pi/6)} \quad \text{A}$$

Note that radian measure must be used in the argument of a complex exponential.

9.22 For the voltage and current given in Prob. 9.21, determine (a) the frequency (in hertz), (b) the period (in seconds).

❙ (a)
$$\omega = 377 = 2\pi f \quad \text{or} \quad f = \frac{377}{2\pi} = 60 \text{ Hz}$$

(b)
$$T = \frac{1}{f} = \frac{1}{60} = 0.0167 \text{ s}$$

9.23 The voltages across two series-connected circuit elements are $v_1 = 50 \sin \omega t$ V and $v_2 = 30 \sin(\omega t - 30°)$ V. What is the rms value of the applied voltage? Also determine the phase angle of this voltage with respect to v_1.

❙ In phasor notation,

$$\mathbf{V}_1 = \frac{50}{\sqrt{2}}\;\underline{/0°} = 35.36 + j0 \qquad \mathbf{V}_2 = \frac{30}{\sqrt{2}}\;\underline{/-30°} = 18.37 - j10.6$$

$$\mathbf{V} = \mathbf{V}_1 + \mathbf{V}_2 = (35.36 + 18.37) - j10.6 = 53.73 - j10.6 = 54.75\;\underline{/-11.16°} \quad \text{V}$$

Hence
$$|\mathbf{V}| = 54.75 \text{ V} \qquad \phi = -11.16°$$

9.24 Two circuit elements are connected in parallel. The current through one of them is $i_1 = 3 \sin(\omega t - 60°)$ A and the total line current drawn by the circuit is $i = 10 \sin(\omega t + 90°)$. Determine the rms value of the current through the second element.

❙ In phasor notation,

$$\mathbf{I}_1 = \frac{3}{\sqrt{2}}(\cos 60° - j \sin 60°) = 1.06 - j1.832 \qquad \mathbf{I} = \frac{10}{\sqrt{2}}(\cos 90° + j \sin 90°) = 0 + j7.072$$

Since $\mathbf{I} = \mathbf{I}_1 + \mathbf{I}_2$, we have

$$\mathbf{I}_2 = \mathbf{I} - \mathbf{I}_1 = j7.072 - 1.06 + j1.832 = -1.06 + j8.904 \quad \text{and} \quad |\mathbf{I}_2| = 8.967 \text{ A}$$

9.25 What is the instantaneous current i_2 in Prob. 9.24?

▮ From Prob. 9.23, $\qquad\qquad I_{2m} = \sqrt{2}(8.967) = 12.68 \text{ A}$

and $\qquad\qquad \phi = \tan^{-1}\left(\dfrac{8.904}{-1.06}\right) = 180 - 82.73 = 97.27° \qquad i_2 = 12.68 \sin(\omega t + 97.27°) \qquad \text{A}$

9.26 In a parallel circuit consisting of two elements, we have $\mathbf{I}_1 = 40 \underline{/20°} \text{ A}$, $\mathbf{I}_2 = 30 \underline{/-65°} \text{ A}$, and $\mathbf{V} = 100 \underline{/0°} \text{ V}$. Determine the rms line current and the power factor.

▮ $\qquad\qquad \mathbf{I} = \mathbf{I}_1 + \mathbf{I}_2 = 40 \underline{/20°} + 30 \underline{/-65°} = 40(\cos 20 + j \sin 20) + 30(\cos 65 - j \sin 65)$

$$= 37.588 + j13.681 + 12.678 - j27.189 = 50.266 - j13.508$$

And $\qquad |\mathbf{I}| = 52.05 \text{ A} \qquad \tan \phi = -\dfrac{13.508}{50.266} \qquad \text{or} \qquad \phi = -15°$

And power factor $\cos \phi = 0.966$ lagging.

9.27 Determine the input power to the circuit of Prob. 9.26.

▮ $\qquad\qquad\qquad P = VI \cos \phi = (100)(52.05) \cos 15° = 5027.6 \text{ W}$

9.28 Determine the input power to each circuit element of Prob. 9.26. Verify that the total input power calculated in Prob. 9.27 is the sum of the powers for the two elements.

▮ $\qquad\qquad\qquad P_1 = VI_1 \cos \phi_1 = (100)(40) \cos 20° = 3758.8 \text{ W}$

$$P_2 = VI_2 \cos \phi_2 = (100)(30) \cos 65° = 1267.8 \text{ W} \qquad P_1 + P_2 = 5026.6 \text{ W}$$

which is approximately equal to the power calculated in Prob. 9.27.

9.29 If the current through the circuit of Prob. 9.23 is $\mathbf{I} = 5 \underline{/0°} \text{ A}$, calculate the input power.

▮ $\qquad\qquad\qquad\qquad P = VI \cos \phi$

From Prob. 9.21, $\qquad\qquad P = (54.76)(5) \cos(-11.16°) = 268.62 \text{ W}$

9.30 Find the power dissipated in each element of the circuit of Prob. 9.23 for $\mathbf{I} = 5 \underline{/0°}$ (as in Prob. 9.29). Verify that the sum of the powers is the same as the total power calculated in Prob. 9.29.

▮ From Prob. 9.23,

$$P_1 = V_1 I \cos \phi_1 = (35.36)(5) \cos(0°) = 176.80 \text{ W} \qquad P_2 = V_2 I \cos \phi_2 = \left(\frac{30}{\sqrt{2}}\right)(5) \cos(-30°) = 91.87 \text{ W}$$

$$P_1 + P_2 = 268.67 \text{ W}$$

which is the same as calculated in Prob. 9.29.

9.31 For the circuit shown in Fig. 9-10, we have $\mathbf{I}_1 = 6 \underline{/30°}$, $\mathbf{I}_2 = 2 \underline{/20°}$. Find i_3 at 60 Hz.

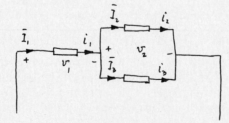

Fig. 9.10

▮ $\qquad\qquad\qquad\qquad \mathbf{I}_1 = \mathbf{I}_2 + \mathbf{I}_3$

Or, $\mathbf{I}_3 = \mathbf{I}_1 - \mathbf{I}_2 = 6 \underline{/30°} - 2 \underline{/20°} = 6(\cos 30° + j \sin 30°) - 2(\cos 20° + j \sin 20°) = 5.196 + j3 - 1.879 - j0.684$

$$= 3.317 + j2.316 = 4.045 \underline{/34.9°}$$

Thus $\qquad I_{3m} = \sqrt{2}(4.045) = 5.72$ A $\qquad \phi = 34.9°$ $\qquad \omega = 2\pi f = 2\pi(60) = 377$

Hence, $\qquad\qquad\qquad\qquad\qquad i_3 = 5.72 \sin(377t + 34.9°)$

9.32 In ac circuits the product of rms voltage and rms current is defined as *apparent power*, measured in voltamperes (VA). If $v = 150 \sin(\omega t + 30°)$ V and $i = 2 \sin(\omega t - 30°)$ A, what is the apparent power?

▮ $\qquad\qquad\qquad\qquad\qquad V = \dfrac{150}{\sqrt{2}}$ V $\qquad$ and $\qquad I = \dfrac{2}{\sqrt{2}}$ A

Hence, $\qquad\qquad\qquad$ Apparent power $= \dfrac{150}{\sqrt{2}} \dfrac{2}{\sqrt{2}} = 150$ VA.

9.33 Just as $P = VI \cos\phi$ denotes the *true*, or *active*, *power* in an ac circuit, the quantity $VI \sin\phi$ is defined as the *reactive power*; it is measured in voltamperes reactive (var). Find the reactive power for the circuit of Prob. 9.32.

▮ In this case $\phi = 30° - (-30°) = 60°$.

$$V = \frac{150}{\sqrt{2}} \text{ V} \qquad \text{and} \qquad I = \frac{2}{\sqrt{2}} \text{ A}$$

Hence, $\qquad\qquad$ Reactive power $= VI \sin\phi = \left(\dfrac{150}{\sqrt{2}}\right)\left(\dfrac{2}{\sqrt{2}}\right) \sin 60° = 129.9$ var

9.34 Given $v = 200 \sin 377t$ V and $i = 8 \sin(377t - 30°)$ A for an ac circuit, determine (*a*) the power factor, (*b*) true power, (*c*) apparent power, and (*d*) reactive power.

▮ (*a*) The current lags the voltage by $\theta = 30°$.
(*b*) From the data, $V = (200/\sqrt{2})$ V and $I = (8/\sqrt{2})$ A. Therefore,

$$\text{True power} = VI \cos\theta = \frac{200}{\sqrt{2}} \frac{8}{\sqrt{2}} (0.866) = 692.8 \text{ W}$$

(*c*) $\qquad\qquad\qquad$ Apparent power $= VI = \dfrac{200}{\sqrt{2}} \dfrac{8}{\sqrt{2}} = 800$ VA

(*d*) $\qquad\qquad\qquad$ Reactive power $= VI \sin\theta = \dfrac{200}{\sqrt{2}} \dfrac{8}{\sqrt{2}} (0.5) = 400$ var

CHAPTER 10
AC Circuits Under Steady State

10.1 From Chap. 9 we know that the voltage across, and the current through, a resistor R are in the same phase. Express this as a phasor relationship.

❚ $$|\mathbf{I}_R|\,\mathbf{V}_R = |\mathbf{V}_R|\,\mathbf{I}_R \quad \text{or} \quad \mathbf{V}_R = R\mathbf{I}_R$$

10.2 Draw a phasor diagram for a resistor showing the **VI** relationship. Also show the *vi* relationship between the waveforms in the time domain.

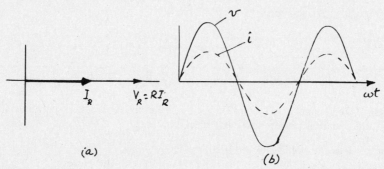

Fig. 10-1

❚ The phasor diagram is shown in Fig. 10-1*a* assuming the common phase angle to be 0°. The *vi* relationship in the time domain is given in Fig. 10-1*b*.

10.3 Repeat Prob. 10.1 for an inductor L operating at angular frequency ω.

❚ In an inductor the current lags the voltage by 90°. Also $|\mathbf{I}_L| = |\mathbf{V}_L|/\omega L$ (see Chap. 9). Thus, if $\mathbf{V}_L = V_L\,\underline{/0°}$, then $\mathbf{I}_L = I_L\,\underline{/-90°} = V_L/\omega L(\underline{/-90°}) = \mathbf{V}_L/j\omega L$, since $1/j$ corresponds to a rotation by 90° in the clockwise direction (see Fig. 9-6).

10.4 Repeat Prob. 10.2 for the inductor of Prob. 10.3.

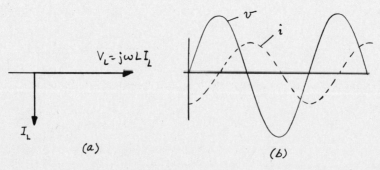

Fig. 10-2

❚ The phasor diagram and the *vi* relationship are shown in Fig. 10-2*a* and *b*.

10.5 Repeat Prob. 10.1 for a capacitor C operating at angular frequency ω.

❚ In a capacitor the current leads the voltage by 90° and $|\mathbf{I}_C| = |\mathbf{V}_C|/(1/\omega C)$ (see Chap. 9). So, if $\mathbf{V}_C = V_C\,\underline{/0°}$, then $\mathbf{I}_C = I_C\,\underline{/90°} = [V_C/(1/\omega C)](\underline{/90°}) = j\omega C\mathbf{V}_C$, since j corresponds to a rotation by 90° in the counterclockwise direction (see Fig. 9-6).

10.6 Repeat Prob. 10.2 for the capacitor of Prob. 10.5.

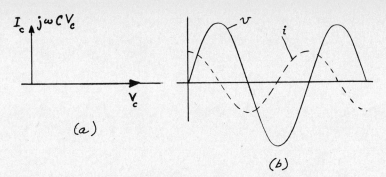

(a)

(b)   **Fig. 10-3**

❚ The phasor diagram and the *vi* relationship are shown in Fig. 10-3*a* and *b*.

10.7 From Probs. 10.1, 10.3, and 10.5, express resistance, and inductive and capacitive reactances, as complex numbers in rectangular and polar forms.

❚ $$R = R + j0 = R \underline{/0°} \qquad X_L = 0 + j\omega L = \omega L \underline{/90°} \qquad X_c = 0 - \frac{j}{\omega C} = \frac{1}{\omega C} \underline{/-90°}$$

10.8 *Impedance* **Z** of a circuit is defined as the ratio of the voltage **V** across the circuit to the current **I** through the circuit. Find the impedance of a circuit having a resistance R in series with an inductance L operating at angular frequency ω.

❚ The circuit is drawn in Fig. 10-4, from which

$$\mathbf{V}_R = R\mathbf{I} \qquad \mathbf{V}_L = j\omega L\mathbf{I} \qquad \mathbf{V} = \mathbf{V}_R + \mathbf{V}_L = R\mathbf{I} + j\omega L\mathbf{I} = (R + j\omega L)\mathbf{I}$$

Thus

$$\mathbf{Z} = \frac{\mathbf{V}}{\mathbf{I}} = R + j\omega L = R + jX_L$$

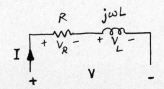

Fig. 10-4

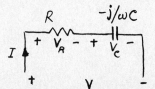

Fig. 10-5

10.9 Find the impedance of the *RC* series circuit shown in Fig. 10-5, at angular frequency ω.

❚ Proceeding as in Prob. 10.8,

$$\mathbf{V}_R = R\mathbf{I} \qquad \mathbf{V}_C = \left(-\frac{j}{\omega C}\right)\mathbf{I} \qquad \mathbf{V} = \mathbf{V}_R + \mathbf{V}_C = \left(R - \frac{j}{\omega C}\right)\mathbf{I}$$

Hence,

$$\mathbf{Z} = \frac{\mathbf{V}}{\mathbf{I}} = R - \frac{j}{\omega C} = R - jX_C$$

10.10 What is the impedance of an *LC* series circuit? At what frequencies will the impedance be zero or infinite?

❚ $$\mathbf{V}_L = j\omega L\mathbf{I} \qquad \mathbf{V}_C = \frac{-j}{\omega C}\mathbf{I} \qquad \mathbf{V} = j\left(\omega L - \frac{1}{\omega C}\right)\mathbf{I}$$

or

$$\mathbf{Z} = \frac{\mathbf{V}}{\mathbf{I}} = j\left(\omega L - \frac{1}{\omega C}\right) = j(X_L - X_C)$$

For $\mathbf{Z} = 0$, we must have $\omega L = 1/\omega C$, or $\omega = 1/\sqrt{LC}$ and $\mathbf{Z} = \infty$ at $\omega = 0$.

10.11 Determine the impedance of an *RLC* series circuit (Fig. 10-6*a*).

❚ In this case, for the circuit current **I**, the terminal voltage **V** may be written as

$$\mathbf{V} = \left[R + j\left(\omega L - \frac{1}{\omega C}\right)\right]\mathbf{I} \tag{1}$$

or

$$\mathbf{Z} = \frac{\mathbf{V}}{\mathbf{I}} = R + j\left(\omega L - \frac{1}{\omega C}\right) = R + j(X_L - X_C) \tag{2}$$

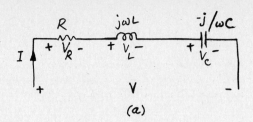

(a)

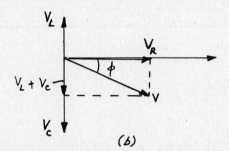

(b)   Fig. 10-6

10.12 At what frequency will the input current and the terminal votage of an *RLC* series circuit be in phase with each other?

▌ For **V** and **I** to be in phase, the circuit must act like a purely resistive circuit. Thus, the imaginary part of the impedance must be zero. Hence, from Eq. (1) or (2) of Prob. 10.11, we must have $\omega L = 1/\omega C$ or $\omega = 1/\sqrt{LC}$.

10.13 Draw a phasor diagram for the *RLC* series circuit of Fig. 10-6a.

▌ The phasor diagram is shown in Fig. 10-6b, where

$$\mathbf{V} = \mathbf{V}_R + \mathbf{V}_L + \mathbf{V}_C \qquad \mathbf{V}_R = R\mathbf{I} \qquad \mathbf{V}_L = j\omega L\mathbf{I} \qquad \mathbf{V}_C = -\frac{j}{\omega C}\mathbf{I}$$

and ϕ is power factor angle.

10.14 *Admittance* **Y** is defined as the reciprocal of impedance **Z**; that is, $\mathbf{Y} = 1/\mathbf{Z}$. Using this definition, find the admittance of a parallel *RL* circuit, shown in Fig. 10-7, under sinusoidal steady state.

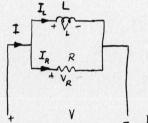

Fig. 10-7

▌ From Fig. 10-7,

$$\mathbf{V}_R = \mathbf{V}_L = \mathbf{V} \qquad \text{and} \qquad \mathbf{I} = \mathbf{I}_R + \mathbf{I}_L = \frac{\mathbf{V}}{R} + \frac{\mathbf{V}}{j\omega L} = (G - jB_L)\mathbf{V} = \mathbf{YV}$$

where $\mathbf{Y} = G - jB = $ admittance, $G = 1/R = $ conductance, and $B_L = 1/\omega L = 1/X_L = $ inductive susceptance.

10.15 Find the admittance of an *RC* parallel circuit.

▌ Proceeding as in Prob. 10.14,

$$\mathbf{V} = \mathbf{V}_R = \mathbf{V}_C \qquad \text{and} \qquad \mathbf{I} = \mathbf{I}_R + \mathbf{I}_C = \frac{\mathbf{V}}{R} + j\omega C\mathbf{V} = (G + jB_c)\mathbf{V} = \mathbf{YV}$$

where $\mathbf{Y} = G + jB_C = $ admittance and $B_C = \omega C = 1/X_C = $ capacitive susceptance.

10.16 Repeat Prob. 10.15 for the general *RLC* parallel circuit shown in Fig. 10-8.

▮ In this case we have

$$\mathbf{V} = \mathbf{V}_L = \mathbf{V}_C = \mathbf{V}_R \quad \text{and} \quad \mathbf{I} = \mathbf{I}_L + \mathbf{I}_C + \mathbf{I}_R$$

Hence,

$$\mathbf{Y} = \frac{\mathbf{I}}{\mathbf{V}} = G + j(B_C - B_L)$$

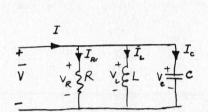

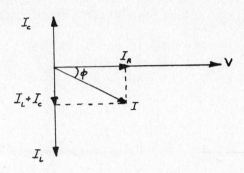

Fig. 10-8   Fig. 10-9

10.17 Draw a phasor diagram for the circuit of Fig. 10-8.

▮ The phasor diagram is shown in Fig. 10-9 where ϕ is the power factor angle.

10.18 A 4-Ω resistor in series with a 7.96-mH inductor is connected across a 110-V 60-Hz source. Determine **(a)** the impedance, **(b)** input current, and **(c)** the voltages across the resistor and the inductor. **(d)** Draw a phasor diagram showing the current and the voltages.

▮

$$X_L = \omega L = 2\pi f L = 2\pi(60)(7.96 \times 10^{-3}) = 3 \; \Omega$$

(a) $\mathbf{Z} = R + jX_L = 4 + j3 = 5 \; \underline{/36.87°} \; \Omega$ **(b)** $\mathbf{I} = \dfrac{\mathbf{V}}{\mathbf{Z}} = \dfrac{110\underline{/0°}}{5\underline{/36.87°}} = 22\underline{/-36.87°} \; \text{A}$

(c) $\mathbf{V}_R = R\mathbf{I} = 4(22)\underline{/-36.87°} = 88 \; \underline{/-36.87°} \; \text{V}$

$\mathbf{V}_L = jX_L\mathbf{I} = j3(22) \; \underline{/-36.87°} = 66 \; \underline{/90° - 36.87°} = 66 \; \underline{/53.13°} \; \text{V}$

(d) See Fig. 10-10.

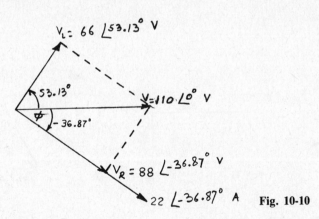

Fig. 10-10

10-19 Find the power factor and the power input to the circuit of Prob. 10.18. Verify that the total input power is dissipated in the resistor.

▮ From Fig. 10-10, $\phi = -36.87°$. Thus,

$$\text{Power factor} = \cos(-36.87°) = 0.8 \text{ lagging}$$

$$\text{Input power } P_{\text{in}} = VI \cos \phi = (110)(22)(0.8) = 1936 \text{ W}$$

$$\text{Power dissipated in } R = I^2 R = (22)^2 4 = 1936 \text{ W}$$

10.20 Given $v = 200 \sin 377t$ V and $i = 8 \sin (377t - 30°)$ A for an ac circuit. Determine (*a*) the power factor, (*b*) true power, (*c*) apparent power, and (*d*) reactive power.

▌ (*a*) The current lags the voltage by $\theta = 30°$. Power factor $= \cos 30° = 0.866$ lagging.

   (*b*) From the data, $V = (200/\sqrt{2})$ V and $I = (8/\sqrt{2})$ A. Therefore, true power $= VI \cos \theta = (200/\sqrt{2})(8/\sqrt{2})(0.866) = 692.8$ W.

   (*c*) Apparent power $= VI = (200/\sqrt{2})(8/\sqrt{2}) = 800$ VA.

   (*d*) Reactive power $= VI \sin \theta = (200/\sqrt{2})(8/\sqrt{2})(0.5) = 400$ var.

10.21 A coil has a resistance of $10\,\Omega$ and draws a current of 5 A when connected across a 100-V 60-Hz source. Determine (*a*) the inductance of the coil, (*b*) the power factor of the circuit, and (*c*) the reactive power.

▌ (*a*)
$$Z = \frac{100}{5} = \sqrt{R^2 + (\omega L)^2} = \sqrt{10^2 + (377L)^2} \quad \text{or} \quad L = 45.94 \text{ mH}$$

   (*b*)
$$\cos \theta = \frac{R}{Z} = \frac{1}{2} \quad \text{or} \quad \theta = 60°$$

   (*c*)
$$\text{Reactive power} = VI \sin \theta = (100)(5)(\sin 60°) = 433 \text{ var}$$

10.22 A series *RLC* circuit is excited by a 100-V 79.6-Hz source and has the following data: $R = 100\,\Omega$, $L = 1$ H, $C = 5\,\mu$F. Calculate (*a*) the input current and (*b*) the voltages across the elements.

▌ (*a*)
$$\omega = 2\pi f = 2\pi(79.6) = 500 \text{ rad/s} \qquad X_L = \omega L = (500)(1) = 500\,\Omega$$

$$X_C = \frac{1}{\omega C} = \frac{10^6}{(500)(5)} = 400\,\Omega$$

$$\mathbf{Z} = R + j(X_L - X_C) = 100 + j(500 - 400) = 100 + j100 = 141.4\,\underline{/45°}\,\Omega$$

$$\mathbf{I} = \frac{\mathbf{V}}{\mathbf{Z}} = \frac{100\,\underline{/0°}}{141.4\,\underline{/45°}} = 0.707\,\underline{/-45°}\text{ A}$$

   (*b*)
$$\mathbf{V}_R = R\mathbf{I} = (100)(0.707\,\underline{/-45°}) = 70.7\,\underline{/-45°}\text{ V}$$

$$\mathbf{V}_L = jX_L\mathbf{I} = (500\,\underline{/90°})(0.707\,\underline{/-45°}) = 353.5\,\underline{/45°}\text{ V}$$

$$\mathbf{V}_C = -jX_C\mathbf{I} = (400\,\underline{/-90°})(0.707\,\underline{/-45°}) = 282.8\,\underline{/-135°}\text{ V}$$

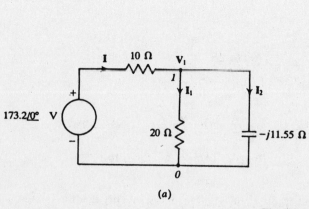

(*a*)

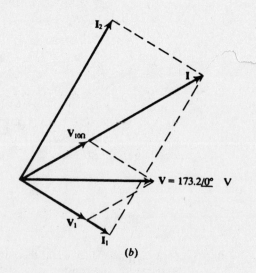

(*b*)

Fig. 10-11

10.23 For the circuit shown in Fig. 10-11*a*, evaluate the current through, and the voltage across, each element. Then draw a phasor diagram showing all the voltages and currents.

▌ Applying nodal analysis at node 1, with $\mathbf{V}_1 = \mathbf{V}_{10}$,

$$\frac{\mathbf{V}_1 - 173.2}{10} + \frac{\mathbf{V}_1}{20} + \frac{\mathbf{V}_1}{-j11.55} = 0 \quad \text{whence} \quad \mathbf{V}_1 = 100\,\underline{/-30°}\text{ V}$$

From this, $\quad \mathbf{V}_{10\,\Omega} = 173.2\,\underline{/0°} - \mathbf{V}_1 = 100\,\underline{/30°}\,\text{V}\qquad \mathbf{I} = \dfrac{\mathbf{V}_{10\,\Omega}}{10} = \dfrac{100\,\underline{/30°}}{10} = 10\,\underline{/30°}\,\text{A}$

$$\mathbf{I}_1 = \dfrac{\mathbf{V}_1}{20} = \dfrac{100\,\underline{/-30°}}{20} = 5\,\underline{/-30°}\,\text{A}\qquad \mathbf{I}_2 = \dfrac{\mathbf{V}_1}{j11.55} = \dfrac{100\,\underline{/-30°}}{11.55\,\underline{/-90°}} = 8.66\,\underline{/60°}\,\text{A}$$

It can be readily verified that $\mathbf{I} = \mathbf{I}_1 + \mathbf{I}_2$. The phasor diagram of Fig. 10-11b shows all voltages and currents.

10.24 For the circuit shown in Fig. 10-12, calculate the current supplied by the voltage source and the voltage across the current source.

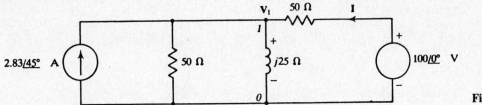

Fig. 10-12

▮ At node 1 we have, with $\mathbf{V}_1 = \mathbf{V}_{10}$ = voltage across current source,

$$\text{Current in} = \text{current out}\qquad 2.83\,\underline{/45°} - \dfrac{\mathbf{V}_1}{50} = \dfrac{\mathbf{V}_1}{j25} + \dfrac{\mathbf{V}_1 - 100}{50}$$

from which $\mathbf{V}_1 = 25 + j75\,\text{V}$. Then the current from the voltage source is $\mathbf{I} = (100 - \mathbf{V}_1)/50 = 1.5 - j1.5\,\text{A}$.

10.25 For the circuit of Fig. 10-12, by using the relationship $P = \text{Re}\,(\mathbf{VI}^*)$, determine the power delivered by (*a*) the voltage source and (*b*) the current source. (*c*) Verify that the sum of these two powers is the power dissipated in the two resistances.

▮ (*a*) Since, from Prob. 10.24, $\mathbf{I} = 1.5 - j1.5\,\text{A}$, $\quad P_V = \text{Re}\,[(100 + j0)(1.5 + j1.5)] = 150\,\text{W}$.

(*b*) Again, from Prob. 10.24, $\mathbf{V}_1 = 25 + j75\,\text{V}$ and $2.83\,\underline{/45°} = 2 + j2\,\text{A}$. Thus,

$$P_I = \text{Re}\,[(25 + j75)(2 - j2)] = 50 + 150 = 200\,\text{W}$$

(*c*) Power dissipated in the two resistances,

$$I^2(50) + \dfrac{V_1^2}{50} = [(1.5)^2 + (1.5)^2]50 + \dfrac{(25)^2 + (75)^2}{50} = 225 + 125 = 350\,\text{W} = P_V + P_I$$

10.26 A voltage source $V\,\underline{/0°}$ having an internal impedance $\mathbf{Z}_s = R_s + jX_s$ supplies a load having impedance $\mathbf{Z}_L = R_L + jX_L$. If R_L and X_L are individually variable, show that maximum power is transferred to the load when $R_L = R_s$ and $X_L = -X_s$; that is, when $\mathbf{Z}_L = \mathbf{Z}_s^*$. (This is known as the *maximum power transfer condition*.) What is the power transferred to the load under this condition?

▮ Because $\mathbf{Z}_s$ and $\mathbf{Z}_L$ are in series, we have the load current

$$I_L = \dfrac{V}{\sqrt{(R_s + R_L)^2 + (X_s + X_L)^2}}$$

Power transferred to the load is

$$P = I_L^2 R_L = \dfrac{V^2 R_L}{(R_s + R_L)^2 + (X_s + X_L)^2} \leq \dfrac{V^2 R_L}{(R_s + R_L)^2} = \dfrac{V^2}{4R_s}\left[1 - \left(\dfrac{R_s - R_L}{R_s + R_L}\right)^2\right] \leq \dfrac{V^2}{4R_s}$$

Equality in the first line is attained for $X_L = -X_s$; in the second, for $R_L = R_s$. Hence, P attains its absolute maximum, $V^2/4R_s$, for $\mathbf{Z}_L = \mathbf{Z}_s^*$.

10.27 A 20-Ω resistance is connected in series with a parallel combination of a capacitance C and a 15-mH pure inductance. At angular frequency $\omega = 1000\,\text{rad/s}$, find C such that the line current is 45° out of phase with the line voltage.

▮ For $\mathbf{V}$ and $\mathbf{I}$ to be 45° out of phase, the net reactance of the parallel LC combination must be $\pm20\,\Omega$, since $R = 20\,\Omega$. Hence,

$$\dfrac{1}{\pm j20} = \dfrac{1}{j(1000)(0.015)} + j1000\,C \qquad\text{or}\qquad C = \tfrac{1}{1000}(\tfrac{1}{15} \mp \tfrac{1}{20}) = 16.67\,\mu\text{F},\ 116.7\,\mu\text{F}$$

For the smaller (larger) capacitance, $\mathbf{I}$ lags (leads) $\mathbf{V}$ by 45°.

10.28 A 46-mH inductive coil has a resistance of 10 Ω. (a) How much current will it draw if connected across a 100-V 60-Hz source? (b) What is the power factor of the coil?

▌ (a) $\omega L = (2\pi \times 60)(46 \times 10^{-3}) = 17.34\ \Omega$ and $\mathbf{Z}_L = 10 + j17.34 = 20.0\ \underline{/60°}$. Then,

$$\mathbf{I}_L = \frac{(100\ \underline{/0°})}{(20.0\ \underline{/60°})} = 5.0\ \underline{/-60°}\ \text{A}$$

(b) Power factor = $\cos 60° = 0.5$ lagging.

10.29 A capacitor is connected across the coil of Prob. 10.28 to make the power factor of the overall circuit unity. Determine the value of the capacitance.

▌ The admittance of the parallel combination will be $1/\mathbf{Z}_L + j\omega C = 1/(10 + j17.34) + j377C = \frac{1}{40} + j(377C - 0.0434)$.

For unity power factor, the imaginary part must vanish, yielding $C = 0.0434/377 = 115\ \mu\text{F}$.

10.30 A 20-Ω resistor is connected in parallel to a 26.52-mH inductor. The circuit operates at 60 Hz. What is (a) the input impedance and (b) the input admittance of the circuit?

▌ $$\mathbf{Z}_R = 20\ \underline{/0°}\ \Omega \qquad \mathbf{Z}_L = 2\pi(60)(26.52 \times 10^{-3})\ \underline{/90°} = 10\ \underline{/90°}\ \Omega$$

(a) $$\mathbf{Z} = \frac{\mathbf{Z}_R \mathbf{Z}_L}{\mathbf{Z}_R + \mathbf{Z}_L} = \frac{(20\ \underline{/0°})(10\ \underline{/90°})}{20 + j10} = 8.95\ \underline{/63.4°}\ \Omega$$

(b) $$\mathbf{Y} = \frac{1}{\mathbf{Z}} = \frac{1}{8.95\ \underline{/63.4°}} = 0.1117\ \underline{/-63.4°}\ \text{S}$$

10.31 Three circuit elements $R = 2.5\ \Omega$, $X_L = 4\ \Omega$, and $X_C = 10\ \Omega$ are connected in parallel, the reactances being at 60 Hz. Determine the admittance of each element and, hence, obtain the input admittance.

▌ $$\mathbf{Y}_R = G = \frac{1}{R} = 0.4 + j0 \qquad \mathbf{Y}_L = -jB_L = -j\frac{1}{X_L} = 0 - j0.25 \qquad \mathbf{Y}_C = jB_C = j\frac{1}{X_C} = 0 + j0.10$$

Hence, $$\mathbf{Y} = \mathbf{Y}_R + \mathbf{Y}_L + \mathbf{Y}_C = 0.4 - j0.15\ \text{S}$$

10.32 If the circuit of Prob. 10.31 is connected across a 10-V 60-Hz ac source, determine (a) the currents through each branch and (b) the input current.

▌ (a) $\mathbf{I}_R = \mathbf{V}\mathbf{Y}_R = (10\ \underline{/0°})(0.4\ \underline{/0°}) = 4\ \underline{/0°}\ \text{A}$ $\mathbf{I}_L = \mathbf{V}\mathbf{Y}_L = (10\ \underline{/0°})(0.25\ \underline{/-90°}) = 2.5\ \underline{/-90°}\ \text{A}$

$$\mathbf{I}_C = \mathbf{V}\mathbf{Y}_C = (10\ \underline{/0°})(0.10\ \underline{/90°}) = 1.0\ \underline{/90°}\ \text{A}$$

(b) $\mathbf{I} = \mathbf{V}\mathbf{Y} = (10\ \underline{/0°})(0.4 - j0.15) = (10\ \underline{/0°})(0.4272\ \underline{/-20.56°}) = 4.272\ \underline{/-20.56°}\ \text{A}$

10.33 Verify that the power input to the circuit of Prob. 10.32 is all dissipated in the resistor.

▌ $$P_{\text{in}} = VI\cos\phi = (10)(4.272)(\cos 20.56) = 40\ \text{W} \qquad P_R = \frac{V^2}{R} = \frac{100}{2.5} = 40\ \text{W}$$

10.34 At what frequency would the circuit of Prob. 10.31 be in resonance?

▌ The condition $\omega = 1/\sqrt{LC}$ (Prob. 10.12) holds also for parallel resonance. Thus, from the given reactances at 60 Hz,

$$\omega = \frac{1}{\sqrt{(4/377)(1/377 \times 10)}} = \frac{377\sqrt{10}}{2}\ \text{rad/s} \qquad \text{or about 95 Hz}$$

10.35 A 6-Ω resistor is connected in parallel with a 300-μF capacitor, and the circuit is supplied by a 10-A 60-Hz current source. Find the instantaneous currents through the resistor and the capacitor.

▌ $$X_C = \frac{1}{\omega C} = \frac{1}{2\pi(60)(300 \times 10^{-6})} = 8.84\ \Omega \qquad \mathbf{Z} = \frac{R(-jX_C)}{R - jX_C} = \frac{(6)(8.84)\ \underline{/-90°}}{6 - j8.84} = 4.965\ \underline{/-34.17°}\ \Omega$$

Voltage across the circuit,

$$\mathbf{V} = \mathbf{Z}\mathbf{I} = (4.965 \underline{/-34.17°})(10 \underline{/0°}) = 49.65 \underline{/-34.17°} \text{ V}$$

$$\mathbf{I}_R = \frac{\mathbf{V}}{R} = \frac{49.65}{6} \underline{/-34.17°} = 8.275 \underline{/-34.17°} \text{ A} \qquad \mathbf{I}_C = \frac{\mathbf{V}}{-jX_C} = \frac{49.65 \underline{/-34.17°}}{8.84 \underline{/-90°}} = 5.617 \underline{/55.83°} \text{ A}$$

$$i_R = I_{Rm} \sin(\omega t + \phi_R) = \sqrt{2}(8.275) \sin(377t - 34.17°) = 11.7 \sin(377t - 34.17°) \text{ A}$$

Similarly, $\qquad\qquad i_C = \sqrt{2}(5.617) \sin(377t + 55.83°) = 9.42 \sin(377t + 55.83°)$ A

10.36 For Prob. 10.35 verify that the input current $\mathbf{I}$ is the phasor sum of $\mathbf{I}_R$ and $\mathbf{I}_C$.

$\blacksquare$ From Prob. 10.35,

$$\mathbf{I}_R = 8.275 \underline{/-34.17°} = 6.846 - j4.648 \qquad \mathbf{I}_C = 5.617 \underline{/55.83°} = 3.154 + j4.647$$

Hence, $\qquad\qquad\qquad\qquad \mathbf{I}_R + \mathbf{I}_C = 10 + j0 = 10 \underline{/0°} = \mathbf{I}$

10.37 An inductive coil consumes 500 W of power at 10 A and 110 V and 60 Hz. Determine the resistance and the inductance of the coil.

$\blacksquare$ Since $I^2 R = 500$ W at $I = 10$ A, $R = 500/(10)^2 = 5 \ \Omega$. Now,

$$Z = \frac{V}{I} = \frac{110}{10} = 11 \ \Omega = \sqrt{R^2 + (\omega L)^2} \qquad \text{or} \qquad (\omega L)^2 = (11)^2 - (5)^2 = 96$$

or $377L = \sqrt{96}$ since $\omega = 2\pi f = 2\pi(60) = 377$. Hence, $L = \sqrt{96}/377 = 25.99$ mH.

10.38 A lossy capacitor dissipates 11 W of power while taking 0.3 A of current at 110 V and 60 Hz. Represent this capacitor by a circuit having an ideal capacitor in parallel with a resistor and find the numerical values of the circuit elements.

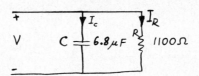

Fig. 10-13

$\blacksquare$ The circuit is shown in Fig. 10-13, for which we have to evaluate R and C. From the data, since $P = V^2/R$,

$$R = \frac{V^2}{P} = \frac{(110)^2}{11} = 1100 \ \Omega \qquad I_R = \frac{V}{R} = \frac{110}{1100} = 0.1 \text{ A}$$

$$I = 0.3 = \sqrt{I_R^2 + I_C^2} \qquad I_C = \sqrt{(0.3)^2 - (0.1)^2} = 0.2828 \text{ A} = \omega CV$$

Hence, $\qquad\qquad\qquad\qquad C = \frac{I_C}{\omega V} = \frac{0.2828}{(377)(110)} = 6.82 \ \mu\text{F}$

10.39 An RL parallel circuit is shown in Fig. 10-14a. Obtain its series equivalent such that the series circuit draws the same current and power at a given voltage.

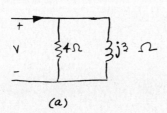

(a)

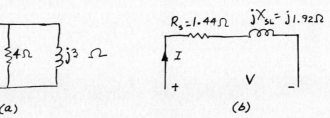

(b) $\qquad\qquad$ **Fig. 10-14**

$\blacksquare$ The equivalent series circuit is shown in Fig. 10-14b. From Fig. 10-14a,

$$\mathbf{Z} = \frac{R(jX_L)}{R + jX_L} = \frac{(4 \underline{/0°})(3 \underline{/90°})}{4 + j3} = \frac{12 \underline{/90°}}{5 \underline{/36.87°}} = 2.4 \underline{/53.13°} = 1.44 + j1.92 = R_s + jX_{Ls}$$

10.40 Generalize the result of Prob. 10.39 to the circuit of Fig. 10-15a.

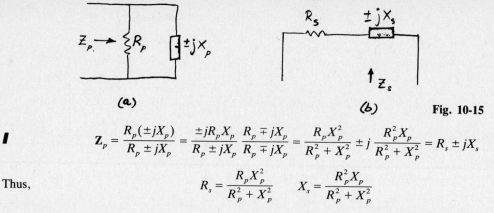

(a)   (b)   **Fig. 10-15**

$$\mathbf{Z}_p = \frac{R_p(\pm jX_p)}{R_p \pm jX_p} = \frac{\pm jR_pX_p}{R_p \pm jX_p}\frac{R_p \mp jX_p}{R_p \mp jX_p} = \frac{R_pX_p^2}{R_p^2 + X_p^2} \pm j\frac{R_p^2X_p}{R_p^2 + X_p^2} = R_s \pm jX_s$$

Thus,
$$R_s = \frac{R_pX_p^2}{R_p^2 + X_p^2} \qquad X_s = \frac{R_p^2X_p}{R_p^2 + X_p^2}$$

10.41 Solve Prob. 10.39 in reverse; that is, obtain the circuit of Fig. 10-14a as the parallel equivalent of the circuit of Fig. 10-14b.

$$\mathbf{Z}_s = 1.44 + j1.92$$

or
$$\mathbf{Y}_s = \frac{1}{\mathbf{Z}_s} = G_p - jB_p = \frac{1}{1.44 + j1.92} = \frac{1.44 - j1.92}{(1.44 + j1.92)(1.44 - j1.92)} = \frac{1.44 - j1.92}{5.76} = 0.25 - j0.333$$

Thus,
$$R_p = \frac{1}{G_p} = \frac{1}{0.25} = 4\ \Omega \qquad X_p = \frac{1}{B_p} = \frac{1}{0.333} = 3\ \Omega$$

10.42 Generalize the result of Prob. 10.41; that is, given an R_sX_s series circuit, find its equivalent parallel circuit.

Since $\mathbf{Z}_s = R_s \pm jX_s$,

$$\mathbf{Y}_s = \frac{1}{\mathbf{Z}_s} = \frac{1}{R_s \pm jX_s} = \frac{R_s \mp jX_s}{(R_s \pm jX_s)(R_s \mp jX_s)} = \frac{R_s}{R_s^2 + X_s^2} \mp j\frac{X_s}{R_s^2 + X_s^2} = G_p \mp jB_p$$

Thus,
$$R_p = \frac{1}{G_p} = \frac{R_s^2 + X_s^2}{R_s} \qquad X_p = \frac{1}{B_p} = \frac{R_s^2 + X_s^2}{X_s}$$

10.43 Obtain the series equivalent of the circuit shown in Fig. 10-16a.

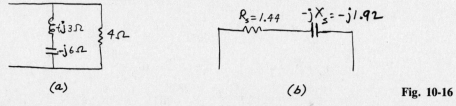

(a)   (b)   **Fig. 10-16**

From Fig. 10-16a, $R_p = 4\ \Omega$, $jX_p = j3 - j6 = -j3$. From the results of Prob. 10.40,

$$R_s = \frac{R_pX_p^2}{R_p^2 + X_p^2} = \frac{4(3)^2}{(4)^2 + (3)^2} = \frac{36}{25} = 1.44\ \Omega \qquad X_s = \frac{R_p^2X_p}{R_p^2 + X_p^2} = \frac{(4)^23}{(4)^2 + (3)^2} = \frac{48}{25} = 1.92\ \Omega \text{ (capacitive)}$$

Hence $\mathbf{Z}_s = 1.44 - j1.92$ shown in Fig. 10-16b.

10.44 The equivalent circuit of a transformer is shown in Fig. 10-17. Given: $\mathbf{V}_\ell = 2400\ \underline{/0°}$ and $\mathbf{I}_\ell = 62.5\ \underline{/-36.8°}$. Calculate $\mathbf{V}_1$ and $\mathbf{I}_1$.

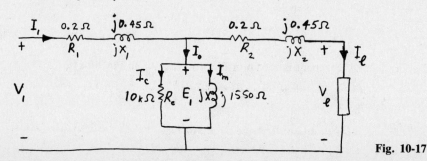

Fig. 10-17

❚ With the numerical values and the symbols shown in Fig. 10-17 we obtain:

$$I_\ell = 62.5 \underline{/-36.8°} = 50 - j37.5 \text{ A}$$

$$E_1 = (2400 + j0) + (50 - j37.5)(0.2 + j0.45) = 2427 + j15 = 2427 \underline{/0.35°} \text{ V}$$

$$I_m = \frac{2427 \underline{/0.35°}}{1550 \underline{/90°}} = 1.56 \underline{/-89.65°} = 0.0095 - j1.56 \text{ A}$$

$$I_c = \frac{2427 + j15}{10 \times 10^3} \approx 0.2427 + j0 \text{ A}$$

Therefore, $\quad I_0 = I_c + I_m = 0.25 - j1.56 \text{ A} \quad\quad I_1 = I_0 + I_\ell = 50.25 - j39.06 = 63.65 \underline{/-37.85°} \text{ A}$

$$V_1 = (2427 + j15) + (50.25 - j39.06)(0.2 + j0.45) = 2455 + j30 = 2455 \underline{/0.7°}$$

10.45 Calculate the power dissipated in the circuit of Fig. 10-17 for the data of Prob. 10.44; also determine the input power.

❚ $\qquad\qquad$ Power dissipated $= (I_1)^2 R_1 + (I_c)^2 R_c + (I_\ell)^2 R_2$

$$= (63.65)^2(0.2) + (0.2427)^2(10\,000) + (62.5)^2(0.2) = 2.18 \text{ kW}$$

Input power = output power + dissipated power $= (V_\ell I_\ell \cos \phi)10^{-3} + 2.18 \text{ kW}$

$$= (2400)(62.5)(\cos 36.8)10^{-3} + 2.18 \text{ kW} = 120.1 + 2.18 = 122.28 \text{ kW}$$

10.46 Repeat Prob. 10.44 for the modified circuit shown in Fig. 10-18.

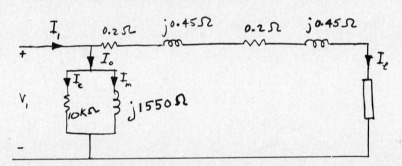

Fig. 10-18

❚ From Fig. 10-18,

$$R = 0.2 + 0.2 = 0.4 \text{ Ω} \qquad jX = j(0.45 + 0.45) = j0.9 \text{ Ω}$$

From Prob. 10.44, $\qquad\qquad I_\ell = 62.5 \underline{/-36.8°} \quad$ and $\quad V_\ell = 2400 \underline{/0°}$

Hence, $\qquad\quad V_1 = (2400 + j0) + (50 - j37.5)(0.4 + j0.9) = 2453 + j30 = 2453 \underline{/0.7°} \text{ V}$

$$I_c = \frac{2453 \underline{/0.7°}}{10 \times 10^3} = 0.2453 \underline{/0.7°} \text{ A} \qquad I_m = \frac{2453 \underline{/0.7°}}{1550 \underline{/90°}} = 1.58 \underline{/-89.3°} \text{ A}$$

$$I_0 = 0.2453 - j1.58 \text{ A} \qquad I_1 = 50.25 - j39.08 = 63.66 \underline{/-37.9°} \text{ A}$$

10.47 For the circuit shown in Fig. 10-19, $R = 8 \text{ Ω}$, $X_L = 12 \text{ Ω}$, and $X_C = 6 \text{ Ω}$. If $I = 10 \underline{/0°}$, find V_R, V_L, V_C, and V in rectangular and polar forms.

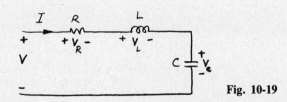

Fig. 10-19

❚ $\quad V_R = IR = (10 \underline{/0°})8 = 80 \underline{/0°} = 80 + j0° \text{ V} \qquad V_L = I(jX_L) = (10 \underline{/0°})(12 \underline{/90°}) = 120 \underline{/90°} = 0 + j120 \text{ V}$

$V_C = I(-jX_c) = (10 \underline{/0°})(6 \underline{/-90°}) = 60 \underline{/-90°} = 0 - j60 \text{ V} \qquad V = V_R + V_L + V_C = 80 + j60 = 100 \underline{/36.87°} \text{ V}$

10.48 In the bridge circuit shown in Fig. 10-20, calculate the current through the inductor, the capacitor, and the three resistors.

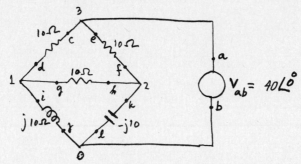

Fig. 10-20

▮ Choosing 0 as the reference node, writing the node equations for nodes 1 and 2 (after multiplying through by 10), we obtain:

$$(2 - j)\mathbf{V}_1 - \mathbf{V}_2 = 40 \underline{/0°} \qquad -\mathbf{V}_1 + (2 + j)\mathbf{V}_2 = 40 \underline{/0°}$$

Thus

$$\mathbf{V}_1 = \mathbf{V}_{ij} = 10(3 + j1) \qquad \mathbf{V}_2 = \mathbf{V}_{kl} = 10(3 - j1) \qquad \mathbf{V}_{gh} = \mathbf{V}_1 - \mathbf{V}_2 = j20$$

$$\mathbf{V}_{cd} = \mathbf{V}_{ab} - \mathbf{V}_1 = 10 - j10 \qquad \mathbf{V}_{ef} = \mathbf{V}_{ab} - \mathbf{V}_2 = 10 + j10$$

$$\mathbf{I}_{ij} = \frac{\mathbf{V}_j}{j10} = 1 - j3 \text{ A} \qquad \mathbf{I}_{kl} = 1 + j3 \text{ A} \qquad \mathbf{I}_{gh} = j2 \text{ A}$$

$$\mathbf{I}_{cd} = 1 - j1 \text{ A} \qquad \mathbf{I}_{ef} = 1 + j1 \text{ A}$$

10.49 Draw a phasor diagram showing all the voltages of the circuit of Fig. 10-20.

▮ Choosing $\mathbf{V}_{ab}$ as the reference phasor, the phasor diagram is shown in Fig. 10-21.

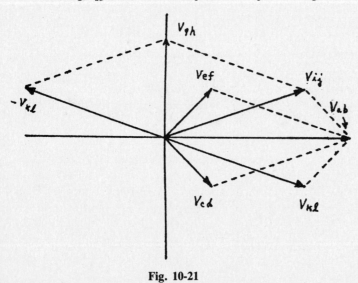

Fig. 10-21

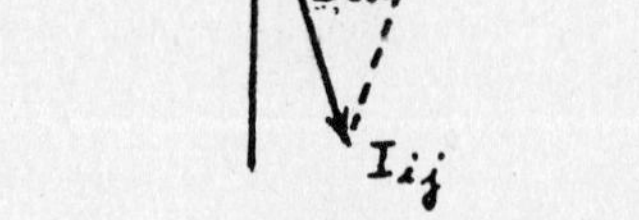

Fig. 10-22

10.50 Draw a phasor diagram showing all the currents in the circuit of Fig. 10-20.

▮ The phasor diagram is shown in Fig. 10-22.

10.51 How much power is supplied by the voltage source to the circuit of Fig. 10-20? Verify that this power is dissipated entirely in the resistors.

▮ Since $\mathbf{I}_{ba} = \mathbf{I}_{cd} + \mathbf{I}_{ef}$ we have, from the results of Prob. 10.48, $\mathbf{I}_{ba} = (1 - j1) + (1 + j1) = 2 \underline{/0°} \text{ A}$. Input power $= V_{ab}I_{ab} \cos \phi = (40)(2) \cos 0° = 80 \text{ W}$. Power dissipated in the resistors $= 10(|1 - j|^2 + |1 + j1|^2 + |j2|^2) = 10(2 + 2 + 4) = 80 \text{ W}$ (verified).

10.52 For the circuit shown in Fig. 10-23, we have $v_{ab} = 141.4 \sin 4000t \text{ V}$ and $i_{ji} = 4 \sin (4000t + 45°) \text{ A}$. Determine the currents through and the voltages across each element.

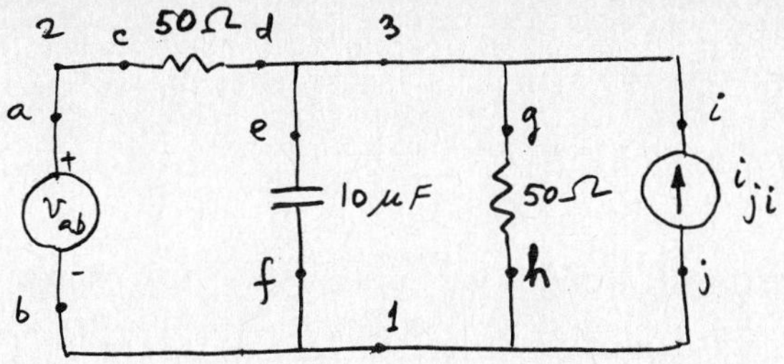

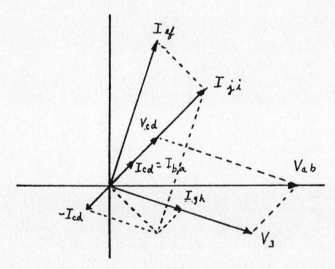

Fig. 10-23

❙ Choosing node 1 as the reference node, we have:

$$\mathbf{V}_3\left(\frac{1}{50} + \frac{1}{50} + \frac{j}{25}\right) = \frac{100}{50} + (2 + j2) \qquad \text{or} \qquad \mathbf{V}_3 = \mathbf{V}_{ef} = \mathbf{V}_{gh} = \mathbf{V}_{ij} = 25(3 - j1) = 79 \underline{/-18.4°} \text{ V}$$

$$\mathbf{I}_{gh} = 1.5 - j0.5 = 1.58 \underline{/-18.4°} \text{ A} \qquad \mathbf{I}_{ef} = 1 + j3 = 3.16 \underline{/71.6°} \text{ A}$$

$$\mathbf{V}_{cd} = \mathbf{V}_{ab} - \mathbf{V}_3 = 25(1 + j1) = 35.3 \underline{/45°} \text{ V} \qquad \mathbf{I}_{cd} = 0.5 + j0.5 = 0.71 \underline{/45°} \text{ A}$$

10-53 Draw a phasor diagram showing all voltages and currents in the circuit of Fig. 10-23.

❙ The phasor diagram is shown in Fig. 10-24.

Fig. 10-24

10.54 Determine the powers supplied by the voltage source and the current source in the circuit of Fig. 10-23.

❙ Power supplied by the voltage source:

$$|V_{ab}|\,|I_{ba}|\cos\phi_v = |V_{ab}|\,|I_{cd}|\cos\phi_v = \frac{141.4}{\sqrt{2}}(0.71)\cos 45° = 50 \text{ W}$$

Power supplied by the current source:

$$|V_{ij}|\,|I_{ji}|\cos\phi_i = |V_3|\,|I_{ji}|\cos\phi_i = 79\frac{4}{\sqrt{2}}\cos(45 + 18.4) = 100 \text{ W}$$

10.55 Calculate the total power absorbed by the two resistors of the circuit of Fig. 10-23. Verify that this power equals the sum of the powers supplied by the two sources.

❙ Power absorbed by the resistors:

$$(I_{cd})^2 50 + (I_{gh})^2 50 = (0.707)^2 50 + (1.58)^2 50 = 25 + 125 = 150 \text{ W}$$

Sum of the powers from the two sources (from Prob. 10.54) is $50 + 100 = 150$ W (verified).

10.56 For the circuit shown in Fig. 10-25, find the power delivered by the source.

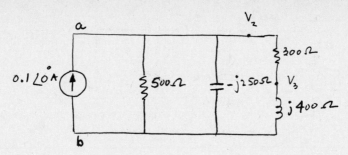

Fig. 10-25

┃ By using nodal analysis (after multiplying through by 1500), we obtain

$$(8 + j6)\mathbf{V}_2 - 5\mathbf{V}_3 = 150 \qquad -5\mathbf{V}_2 + (5 - j3.75)\ \mathbf{V}_3 = 0$$

Solving for $\mathbf{V}_2$ yields $\quad \mathbf{V}_2 = \mathbf{V}_{ab} = 25\ \underline{/-36.87°}$ V. Hence, power supplied is

$$V_{ab}I_{ba}\cos\phi = (25)(0.1)\cos 36.87° = 2\ \text{W}$$

10.57 How much power is dissipated in the 300-Ω resistor of the circuit of Fig. 10-25?

┃

$$P_{500\,\Omega} = \frac{V_2^2}{500} = \frac{(25)^2}{500} = 1.25\ \text{W}$$

From Prob. 10.56, $\quad P_{\text{in}} = 2\ \text{W}$. Hence, $\quad P_{300\,\Omega} = 2 - 1.25 = 0.75\ \text{W}$. Otherwise,

$$\mathbf{I}_{300\,\Omega} = \frac{\mathbf{V}_3}{j400} = \frac{20\ \underline{/0°}}{400\ \underline{/90°}} = \frac{1}{20}\ \underline{/-90°}\ \text{A}$$

where $\mathbf{V}_3$ is obtained from Prob. 10.56. Hence, $\quad P_{300\,\Omega} = (1/20)^2 300 = 0.75\ \text{W}$.

10.58 Calculate the total power delivered to the circuit of Fig. 10-26.

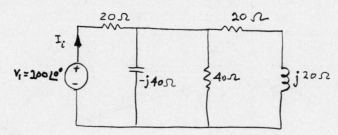

Fig. 10-26

┃ The input impedance is

$$\mathbf{Z}_i = 20 + \frac{1}{1/(-j40) + 1/40 + 1/(20 + j20)} = 40\ \Omega$$

Thus, $\qquad \mathbf{I}_i = \frac{\mathbf{V}_i}{\mathbf{Z}_i} = \frac{200\ \underline{/0°}}{40\ \underline{/0°}} = 5\ \underline{/0°}\ \text{A} \qquad$ and $\qquad P_i = V_i I_i \cos\phi = (200)(5)(\cos 0°) = 1\ \text{kW}$

10.59 A $(15 + j20)$-Ω impedance is supplied by a 125-V 60-Hz source. How much energy is delivered to the impedance during one cycle of the applied voltage?

┃ Let $\quad \mathbf{V} = 125\ \underline{/0°}$. Then

$$\mathbf{I} = \frac{125\ \underline{/0°}}{15 + j20} = 5\ \underline{/-53.1°} \qquad P = (125)(5)\cos(53.1°) = 375\ \text{W}$$

$$\text{Energy} = \text{power} \times \text{time} = (375\ \text{J/s})(\tfrac{1}{60}\ \text{s}) = 6.25\ \text{J}$$

10.60 The terminal voltage and current for a series circuit are $\quad v = 141.4\sin 2000t$ V $\quad$ and $\quad i = 7.07\sin(2000t + 36.87°)$ A. Obtain the simplest two-element circuit which would have the above vi relationship.

┃ In terms of phasors,

$$V = \frac{141.4}{\sqrt{2}} \underline{/0°} = 100 \underline{/0°} \text{ V} \qquad I = \frac{7.07}{\sqrt{2}} \underline{/36.87°} = 5 \underline{/36.87°} \text{ A} \qquad Z = R + jX = \frac{100 \underline{/0°}}{5 \underline{/36.87°}} = 20 \underline{/-36.87°} = 16 - j12$$

Thus, $\qquad\qquad\qquad\qquad R = 16 \,\Omega \qquad C = \dfrac{1}{\omega X_C} = \dfrac{1}{(2000)(12)} = 41.67 \,\mu\text{F}$

10.61 A two-element series circuit draws 600 W of power and 10 A of current at 100 V and $500/\pi$ Hz. Specify the values of these circuit elements.

❚ Since $V = 100$ V and $I = 10$ A,

$$|\mathbf{Z}| = \tfrac{100}{10} = 10 \,\Omega \qquad \cos\theta = \frac{P}{VI} = \frac{600}{(100)(10)} = 0.6 \qquad \text{or} \qquad \theta = \pm53.1°$$

Hence, $\mathbf{Z} = 10(\cos 53.1° \pm j \sin 53.1°) = (6 \pm j8) \,\Omega$ and $R = 6\,\Omega$, $X = \pm j8 \,\Omega$, which requires either an 8-mH inductor or a 125-μF capacitor.

10.62 An inductive coil having a 30-Ω resistance and unknown inductance is connected in parallel with a 100-Ω resistor. The combination is connected across a 100-V $50/\pi$-Hz source. If the power delivered by the source is 400 W, find the value of the inductance.

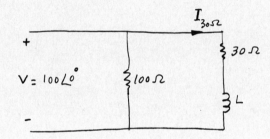

Fig. 10-27

❚ From Fig. 10-27,

$$P_{100\,\Omega} = \frac{(100)^2}{100} = 100 \text{ W} \qquad P_{30\,\Omega} = 400 - 100 = 300 \text{ W} = (I_{30\,\Omega})^2 30$$

or $\qquad\qquad\qquad\qquad I_{30\,\Omega} = \sqrt{\dfrac{300}{30}} = 3.162 \text{ A} \qquad (V)^2 = (V_{30\,\Omega})^2 + (V_L)^2$

or $\quad (100)^2 = (3.162 \times 30)^2 + (V_L)^2 \quad$ or $\quad V_L = 31.62 \mathbf{V}_{\text{volt}} = I_{30\,\Omega} X_L \quad$ or $\quad X_L = \dfrac{31.62}{3.162} = 10 \,\Omega$

Hence, $\qquad\qquad\qquad\qquad\qquad L = \dfrac{10}{2\pi(50/\pi)} = 100 \text{ mH}$

10.63 The resistance R and the inductance L of a coil are to be determined experimentally. The available equipment are a voltmeter and an 8-Ω resistor. The 8-Ω resistor is connected in series with the coil and the combination across a 120-V 60-Hz source. If the voltmeter reads 32 V across the resistor and 104 V across the coil, determine R and L.

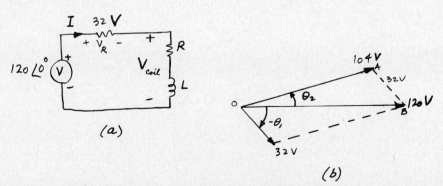

(a)

(b)

Fig. 10-28

❚ The circuit and the phasor diagram for the experiment are shown in Fig. 10-28a and b respectively, from which $32\,\underline{/-\theta_1} + 104\,\underline{/\theta_2} = 120\,\underline{/0^\circ}$. The law of cosines gives

$$\cos\theta_2 = \frac{(104)^2 + (120)^2 - (32)^2}{2(104)(120)} = 0.9692 \quad \text{or} \quad \theta_2 = 14.25^\circ$$

Similarly,
$$\theta_1 = -53.1^\circ \quad \text{or} \quad V_R = 32\,\underline{/-53.1^\circ}\,\text{V}$$

$$\mathbf{I}_{\text{coil}} = \mathbf{I} = \frac{V_R}{R} = \frac{32}{8}\,\underline{/-53.1^\circ} = 4\,\underline{/-53.1^\circ}\,\text{A} \qquad \mathbf{Z}_{\text{coil}} = \frac{V_{\text{coil}}}{\mathbf{I}_{\text{coil}}} = \frac{104\,\underline{/14.25^\circ}}{4\,\underline{/-53.1^\circ}} = 10 + j24$$

Hence $R = 10\,\Omega$, $L = 24/377 = 63.66\,\text{mH}$.

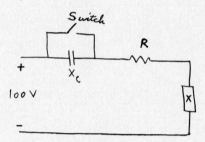

Fig. 10-29

10.64 In the circuit shown in Fig. 10-29, X is purely reactive. With the switch closed, the circuit draws 1 A of current at 100 V and consumes 80 W of power. With the switch open, the current remains unchanged at 1 A. Determine X and X_C.

❚
$$R = \frac{P}{I^2} = \frac{80}{(1)^2} = 80\,\Omega$$

With the switch closed:
$$Z = \frac{V}{I} = \frac{100}{1} = \sqrt{(80)^2 + X^2} \quad \text{or} \quad X = \pm 60\,\Omega$$

With the switch open:
$$Z = 100 = \sqrt{(80)^2 + (X - X_C)^2} \quad \text{or} \quad |X - X_C| = |X| = 60$$

The unique solution with positive X_C is $X_C = 120\,\Omega$ and $X = +60\,\Omega$.

10.65 A circuit draws 2 A at 120 V and 60 Hz and consumes 120 W of power. A capacitor of unknown value is connected in series with the given circuit and the combination put across the same voltage source. It is found that the magnitude of the input current is increased. Determine the values of the original circuit elements.

❚ Let $\mathbf{Z} = Z\,\underline{/\phi}\,\Omega$. Now, since the current increases when a capacitor is connected in series, the original circuit is inductive and ϕ is positive. Or,

$$\phi = \cos^{-1}\frac{P}{VI} = \frac{120}{\cos^{-1}(120)(2)} = 60^\circ \qquad |\mathbf{Z}| = \frac{V}{I} = \frac{120}{2} = 60\,\Omega$$

Thus
$$\mathbf{Z} = 60\,\underline{/60^\circ} = 30 + j51.96 \qquad R = 30\,\Omega$$

$$\omega L = 51.96\,\Omega \quad \text{or} \quad L = \frac{51.96}{377} = 137.83\,\text{mH}$$

10.66 For the circuit shown in Fig. 10-30, calculate C such that the input current is 45° out of phase with the input voltage at a frequency $\omega = 2000\,\text{rad/s}$.

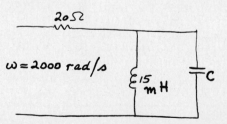

Fig. 10-30

▮ For the input current to be 45° out of phase with the input voltage, the net reactance of the parallel portion of the circuit must be $\pm 20\,\Omega$. Therefore, $\pm j/20 = -j/\omega L + j\omega C$, or

$$C = \frac{1}{\omega}\left(\frac{1}{\omega L} \pm \frac{1}{20}\right) = \frac{1}{2000}\left(\frac{1}{2000 \times 15 \times 10^{-3}} \pm \frac{1}{20}\right) = \frac{10^{-3}}{120}(2 \pm 3) = 41.66\,\mu F$$

10.67 An inductive load takes 480 W of power at 0.8 lagging power factor while operating at 120 V and 60 Hz. It is desired to make the power factor of the input current (with respect to the input voltage) unity by connecting a capacitor in parallel with the load. What is the value of the capacitance?

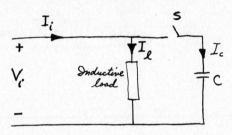

Fig. 10-31

▮ The circuit configuration is shown in Fig. 10-31. Then

$$I_L = \frac{480}{(120)(0.8)} = 5\,A \qquad \text{and} \qquad \phi = \cos^{-1} 0.8 = -36.87°$$

Thus, $\mathbf{I}_L = 5\,\underline{/-36.87°} = 4 - j3$. Let $\mathbf{I}_C = jb$. Then $\mathbf{I}_i = \mathbf{I}_L + \mathbf{I}_C = 4 + j(b - 3)$ or $\mathbf{I}_C = j3 = j\omega CV$.

Hence,

$$C = \frac{3}{(377)(120)} = 66.3\,\mu F$$

10.68 A variable capacitor C is connected in parallel with an inductive coil of inductance 0.2 H and resistance $10\,\Omega$. The combination is connected across a 10-V 50-Hz voltage source. Find the value of C which will result in a minimum current from the source.

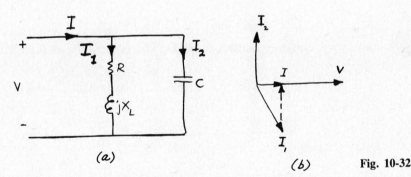

(a) (b) **Fig. 10-32**

▮ The circuit and the phasor diagram are shown in Fig. 10-32a and b, where $R = 10\,\Omega$, $jX_L = j314(0.2) = j62.8\,\Omega$. The current $\mathbf{I}$ will be minimum when the circuit operates at unity power factor. For this condition $X_L = X_C = 62.8 = 1/\omega C$. Hence,

$$C = \frac{1}{(314)(62.8)} = 50.7\,\mu F$$

10.69 The circuit of Fig. 10-33a shows an ac generator with internal impedance $R_g + jX_g$ delivering power to a load. (a) Obtain an expression for the magnitude of the current in terms of the voltage source and the elements of the circuit. (b) Use the expression for current to obtain an expression for the power dissipated in R_x. (c) Show that, if R_x and X_x are considered as the variables (with P as a parameter), the relationship of part (b) can be written in the form of the equation of a circle the center of which is at the point $(V^2/2P - R_g, -X_g)$ and the radius of which is $(V^2/2P)(1 - 4R_g P/V^2)^{1/2}$. (d) Let $V = 100$ V and R_g and X_g be 10 and $20\,\Omega$, respectively. Draw the circles for various convenient values of P between zero and the value at which the radius of the circle is zero. Label each circle with the value of power to which it corresponds.

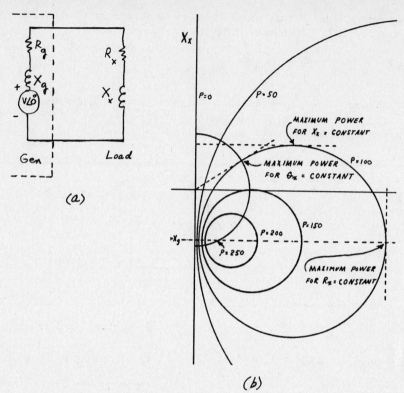

(a)

(b)   Fig. 10-33

▮   (a) $I = \dfrac{V}{\sqrt{(R_x + R_g)^2 + (X_x + X_g)^2}}$ (b) $P = I^2 R_x = \dfrac{V^2 R_x}{(R_x + R_g)^2 + (X_x + X_g)^2}$

(c) The relationship of part (b) may be rewritten as:

$$\left[R_x + \left(R_g - \frac{V^2}{2P} \right) \right]^2 + (X_x + X_g)^2 = \frac{V^4}{4P^2} \left(1 - \frac{4R_g P}{V^2} \right)$$

which is the equation of a circle as described.   (d) The circles are shown in Fig. 10-33b.

10.70   An ac bridge circuit is shown in Fig. 10-34.   Obtain the condition for balance when no current flows through the detector D.

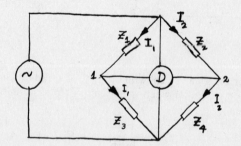

Fig. 10-34

▮   Since the current through D is zero, nodes 1 and 2 are at the same potential.   Thus, $\mathbf{I}_1$ flows through $\mathbf{Z}_1$ and $\mathbf{Z}_3$ whereas $\mathbf{I}_2$ flows through $\mathbf{Z}_2$ and $\mathbf{Z}_4$.   Under balance condition we have $\mathbf{I}_1 \mathbf{Z}_1 = \mathbf{I}_2 \mathbf{Z}_2$ and $\mathbf{I}_1 \mathbf{Z}_3 = \mathbf{I}_2 \mathbf{Z}_4$. Hence, the required condition is $\mathbf{Z}_1 / \mathbf{Z}_3 = \mathbf{Z}_2 / \mathbf{Z}_4$.

10.71   As a special case for the bridge of Fig. 10-34, we have $\mathbf{Z}_1 = R_1$, $\mathbf{Z}_2 = R_x + j\omega L_x$, $\mathbf{Z}_3 = 1/j\omega C_3$,   and $\mathbf{Z}_4 = R_4 + 1/j\omega C_4$.   The bridge is balanced.   Solve for the unknowns R_x and L_x.

▮   From Prob. 10.70 we have

$$Z_1 Z_4 = Z_2 Z_3 \quad \text{or} \quad R_1\left(R_4 + \frac{1}{j\omega C_4}\right) = \frac{1}{j\omega C_3}(R_x + j\omega L_x) \quad \text{or} \quad R_1 R_4 - j\frac{R_1}{\omega C_4} = \frac{L_x}{C_3} - j\frac{R_x}{\omega C_3}$$

Equating the real parts and solving for L_x yields

$$L_x = R_1 R_4 C_3 \tag{1}$$

Equating the imaginary parts and solving for R_x gives

$$R_x = R_1 \frac{C_3}{C_4} \tag{2}$$

10.72 Verify that (*a*) the operation of the bridge of Prob. 10.71 is independent of frequency and (*b*) the bridge can be balanced by adjusting resistances only.

❚ (*a*) Since the frequency ω does not enter in the balance conditions (1) and (2) of Prob. 10.71, the operation is independent of frequency. (*b*) Condition (2) of Prob. 10.71 can be satisfied by adjusting R_1 only (for a given C_3/C_4. Then condition (1) can be satisfied by adjusting R_4 only.

10.73 For the circuit shown in Fig. 10-35 determine the condition such that the input impedance is purely resistive at all frequencies.

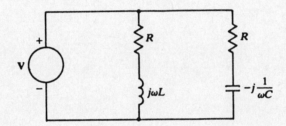

Fig. 10-35

❚ The voltage source "sees" the impedances $R + j\omega L$ and $R - j(1/\omega C)$ in parallel; hence, the *input impedance* is

$$Z_{\text{in}} = \frac{(R + j\omega L)[R - j(1/\omega C)]}{2R + j[\omega L - (1/\omega C)]} = \frac{R^2 + L/C + jRX}{2R + jX} \tag{1}$$

where $X = \omega L - 1/\omega C$. Subtracting R from both sides of Eq. (1),

$$Z_{\text{in}} - R = \frac{L/C - R^2}{2R + jX} \tag{2}$$

and Eq. (2) shows that $Z_{\text{in}} = R$ for all ω if $L/C = R^2$.

10.74 For the circuit of Fig. 10-35 we have $L = 100\,\text{mH}$, $C = 10\,\mu\text{F}$, $R = 100\,\Omega$, and $V = 100\,\text{V}$. Calculate the input power.

❚ From the data we may verify that

$$\frac{L}{C} = \frac{100 \times 10^{-3}}{10 \times 10^{-6}} = 10^4 = (100)^2 = R^2$$

Thus, according to Prob. 10.73, the input impedance is purely resistive, or

$$Z_{\text{in}} = R = 100\,\Omega \quad I = \frac{V}{R} = \frac{100}{100} = 1\,\text{A} \quad \text{Power} = VI \cos\phi = (100)(1)(1) = 100\,W$$

10.75 The bridge of Fig. 10-34 is used to measure the resistance and inductance of a coil. The arms of the bridge are: $Z_1 = R_1/(1 + j\omega C R_1)$, $Z_2 = R_2$, $Z_3 = R_3$, and $Z_4 = R_x + j\omega L_x$. For balanced conditions we have $R_1 = 10\,\text{k}\Omega$, $C = 0.5\,\mu\text{F}$, $R_2 = 400\,\Omega$, and $R_3 = 600\,\Omega$. (*a*) Derive the general conditions for balance. (*b*) Determine R_x and L_x.

❚ (*a*) For balance we must have

$$Z_1 Z_4 = Z_2 Z_3 \quad \text{or} \quad \frac{R_1(R_x + j\omega L_x)}{1 + j\omega C R_1} = R_2 R_3 \quad \text{or} \quad R_1 R_x + j\omega L_x R_1 = R_2 R_3 + j\omega C R_1 R_2 R_3$$

Equating the real and imaginary parts, the conditions for balance are

$$R_1 R_x = R_2 R_3 \tag{1}$$
$$L_x = C R_2 R_3 \tag{2}$$

(b) For the given numerical values, from Eqs. (1) and (2) we obtain

$$R_x = \frac{(400)(600)}{10,000} = 24\ \Omega \qquad L_x = (0.5)10^{-6}(400)(600) = 120\ \text{mH}$$

10.76 Two impedances $\mathbf{Z}_1 = 10\ \underline{/-53.13^\circ}\ \Omega$ and $\mathbf{Z}_2 = 20\ \underline{/36.87^\circ}\ \Omega$ are connected in parallel. The combination draws $2 + j1\ \text{A}$ current from a voltage source. Determine the complex power for each branch.

▮ Total admittance is

$$\mathbf{Y} = \mathbf{Y}_1 + \mathbf{Y}_2 = \frac{1}{\mathbf{Z}_1} + \frac{1}{\mathbf{Z}_2} = \tfrac{1}{10}\ \underline{/53.14^\circ} + \tfrac{1}{20}\ \underline{/-36.87^\circ}$$

$$= (0.06 + j0.08) + (0.04 - j0.03) = 0.1 + j0.05 = 0.1118\ \underline{/26.5^\circ}\ \text{S}$$

$$\mathbf{I} = 2 + j1 = 2.236\ \underline{/26.5^\circ}\ \text{A} \qquad \mathbf{V} = \frac{\mathbf{I}}{\mathbf{Y}} = \frac{2.236\ \underline{/26.5^\circ}}{0.1118\ \underline{/26.5^\circ}} = 20\ \underline{/0^\circ}\ \text{V}$$

$$\mathbf{I}_1 = \mathbf{V}\mathbf{Y}_1 = (20\ \underline{/0^\circ})(\tfrac{1}{10}\ \underline{/53.13^\circ}) = 2\ \underline{/53.13^\circ}\ \text{A} \qquad \mathbf{I}_2 = \mathbf{V}\mathbf{Y}_2 = (20\ \underline{/0^\circ})(\tfrac{1}{20}\ \underline{/-36.87^\circ}) = 1\ \underline{/-36.87^\circ}\ \text{A}$$

$$\mathbf{S}_1 = \mathbf{V}\mathbf{I}_1^* = (20\ \underline{/0^\circ})(2\ \underline{/-53.13^\circ}) = 40\ \underline{/-53.13^\circ} = 24 - j32\ \text{VA}$$

$$\mathbf{S}_2 = \mathbf{V}\mathbf{I}_2^* = (20\ \underline{/0^\circ})(1\ \underline{/36.87^\circ}) = 20\ \underline{/36.87^\circ} = 16 + j12\ \text{VA}$$

10.77 For the circuit of Prob. 10.76 verify that the total complex power is the sum of the two complex powers obtained in Prob. 10.76.

▮ From Prob. 10.76,

$$\mathbf{S}_1 = 24 - j32 \qquad \mathbf{S}_2 = 16 + j12$$

Thus, $\mathbf{S} = \mathbf{S}_1 + \mathbf{S}_2 = 40 - j20\ \text{VA}$. Otherwise,

$$\mathbf{S} = \mathbf{V}\mathbf{I}^* = (20\ \underline{/0^\circ})(2.236\ \underline{/-26.5^\circ}) = 44.72\ \underline{/-26.5^\circ} = 40 - j19.95\ \text{VA}$$

The slight error is due to roundoff.

10.78 A parallel circuit consisting of two impedances is shown in Fig. 10-36. Replace it by an equivalent series circuit and, hence, calculate the input current $\mathbf{I}$.

▮
$$\mathbf{Z} = \frac{\mathbf{Z}_1 \mathbf{Z}_2}{\mathbf{Z}_1 + \mathbf{Z}_2} = \frac{(8 + j6)(10 + j5)}{8 + j6 + 10 + j5} = \frac{50 + j100}{18 + j11} = 5.3\ \underline{/32^\circ}\ \Omega$$

Since $\mathbf{V} = 200\ \underline{/0^\circ}\ \text{V}$,

$$\mathbf{I} = \frac{\mathbf{V}}{\mathbf{Z}} = \frac{200\ \underline{/0^\circ}}{5.3\ \underline{/32^\circ}} = 37.74\ \underline{/-32^\circ}\ \text{A}$$

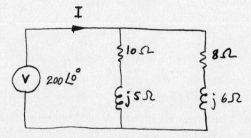

Fig. 10-36

10.79 Determine the power factor of the circuit of Fig. 10-36 by calculating the power dissipated in the equivalent resistor. Verify that the result is consistent with that of Prob. 10.78.

▮ From Prob. 10.78, $\mathbf{Z} = 5.3\ \underline{/32^\circ} = (4.495 + j2.808)\ \Omega$. Thus, $R = 4.495\ \Omega$.

$$P = I^2 R = (37.74)^2(4.495) = 6.402\ \text{kW} \qquad \cos\phi = \frac{P}{VI} = \frac{6402}{(200)(37.74)} = 0.848\ \text{lagging}$$

From Prob. 10.78, $\cos\phi = \cos(-32^\circ) = 0.848$ lagging.

10.80 A series-parallel circuit is shown in Fig. 10-37. Determine the currents $\mathbf{I}$, $\mathbf{I}_1$, and $\mathbf{I}_2$.

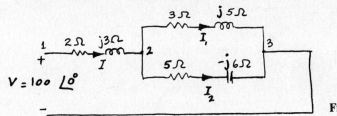

Fig. 10-37

▮ The input impedance $\mathbf{Z}_i$ is given by

$$\mathbf{Z}_i = 2 + j3 + \frac{(3 + j5)(5 - j6)}{3 + j5 + 5 - j6} = 2 + j3 + \frac{(5.82\,\underline{/59°})(7.81\,\underline{/-50.2°})}{8.06\,\underline{/-7.12°}}$$

$$= 2 + j3 + 5.65\,\underline{/15.92°} = 7.43 + j4.55 = 8.71\,\underline{/31.48°}\ \Omega$$

$$\mathbf{I} = \frac{\mathbf{V}}{\mathbf{Z}_i} = \frac{100\,\underline{/0°}}{8.71\,\underline{/31.48°}} = 11.48\,\underline{/-31.48°}\ \text{A}$$

The voltage across the parallel branch is

$$\mathbf{V}_{23} = \mathbf{I}\mathbf{Z}_{23} = (11.48\,\underline{/-31.48°})(5.65\,\underline{/15.92°}) = 64.86\,\underline{/-15.56°}\ \text{V}$$

$$\mathbf{I}_1 = \frac{\mathbf{V}_{23}}{\mathbf{Z}_1} = \frac{64.86\,\underline{/-15.56°}}{5.83\,\underline{/59°}} = 11.12\,\underline{/-74.56°}\ \text{A} \qquad \mathbf{I}_2 = \frac{\mathbf{V}_{23}}{\mathbf{Z}_2} = \frac{64.86\,\underline{/-15.56°}}{7.81\,\underline{/-50.19°}} = 8.3\,\underline{/34.63°}\ \text{A}$$

10.81 Draw a phasor diagram for the circuit of Fig. 10-37 showing $\mathbf{V}_{12}$, $\mathbf{V}_{23}$, $\mathbf{V}$, $\mathbf{I}$, $\mathbf{I}_1$, and $\mathbf{I}_2$.

▮ From Prob. 10.80,

$$\mathbf{V}_{12} = \mathbf{I}(2 + j3) = (11.48\,\underline{/-31.48°})(3.6\,\underline{/53.3°}) = 41.39\,\underline{/24.83°}\ \text{V} \qquad \mathbf{V}_{23} = 64.86\,\underline{/-15.56°}\ \text{V}$$

$$\mathbf{V} = 100\,\underline{/0°}\ \text{V} \qquad \mathbf{I} = 11.48\,\underline{/-31.48°}\ \text{A} \qquad \mathbf{I}_1 = 11.12\,\underline{/-74.56°}\ \text{A} \qquad \mathbf{I}_2 = 8.3\,\underline{/34.63°}\ \text{A}$$

Hence we draw the phasor diagram of Fig. 10-38.

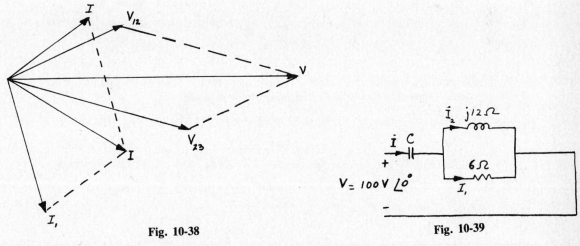

Fig. 10-38   **Fig. 10-39**

10.82 The circuit of Fig. 10-39 operates at a frequency of 50 Hz. Determine the value of C in order that the input voltage $\mathbf{V}$ and the input current $\mathbf{I}$ are in the same phase.

▮ Input impedance:

$$\mathbf{Z} = -\frac{j}{\omega C} + \frac{(6)(j12)}{6 + j12} = -\frac{j}{\omega C} + \frac{(j72)(6 - j12)}{36 + 144} = -\frac{j}{\omega C} + j2.4 + 4.8$$

For $\mathbf{V}$ and $\mathbf{I}$ to be in the same place, the imaginary part of $\mathbf{Z}$ must be zero. Thus, $1/\omega C = 2.4$. At 50 Hz, $\omega = 2\pi(50) = 314$. Hence,

$$C = \frac{1}{(2.4)(314)} = 1326.9\ \mu\text{F}$$

10.83 For the C obtained in Prob. 10.82 calculate the power input to the circuit of Fig. 10-39 by: (*a*) $VI \cos \phi$; (*b*) I^2R, where R is the resistive portion of $\mathbf{Z}$ (obtained in Prob. 10.82); and (*c*) $(I_1)^2 6$, where I_1 is the current through the 6-Ω resistor. Verify that the results are identical.

▮ (*a*) Since $\mathbf{Z} = 4.8\,\Omega$, $\mathbf{I} = (100/4.8)\ \underline{/0°} = 20.83\ \underline{/0°}$ A. Hence, $VI \cos \phi = (100)(20.83)(\cos 0°) = 2083$ W
(*b*) $I^2R = (20.83)^2(4.8) = 2083$ W. (*c*) By current division rule,

$$\mathbf{I}_1 = \mathbf{I}\frac{\mathbf{Z}_2}{\mathbf{Z}_1 + \mathbf{Z}_2} = (20.83\ \underline{/0°})\frac{j12}{6 + j12} = \frac{(20.83\ \underline{/0°})(12\ \underline{/90°})}{13.42\ \underline{/63.4°}} = 18.63\ \underline{/26.56°}\ \text{A}$$

$$I_1^2 R = (18.63)^2(6) = 2083\ \text{W}$$

10.84 For the circuit shown in Fig. 10-40, we have $\mathbf{V}_1 = 10\ \underline{/0°}$ V. Find $\mathbf{I}_1$, $\mathbf{I}_2$, and $\mathbf{I}_3$.

▮
$$\mathbf{I}_1 = \frac{10 + j0}{3 + j2} = \frac{10\ \underline{/0°}}{3.60\ \underline{/33.69°}} = 2.77\ \underline{/-33.69°}\ \text{A}$$

$$\mathbf{I}_2 = \mathbf{I}_1\frac{\mathbf{Z}_3}{\mathbf{Z}_2 + \mathbf{Z}_3} = (2.77\ \underline{/-33.7°})\frac{9 - j6}{19 + j2} = \frac{(2.77\ \underline{/-33.7°})(10.82\ \underline{/-33.7°})}{19.1\ \underline{/6°}} = 1.57\ \underline{/-73.4°}\ \text{A}$$

$$\mathbf{I}_3 = \mathbf{I}_1\frac{\mathbf{Z}_2}{\mathbf{Z}_2 + \mathbf{Z}_3} = (2.77\ \underline{/-33.7°})\frac{10 + j8}{19 + j2} = \frac{(2.77\ \underline{/-33.7°})(12.8\ \underline{/38.7°})}{19.1\ \underline{/6°}} = 1.86\ \underline{/-1°}\ \text{A}$$

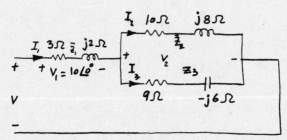

Fig. 10-40

10.85 Determine the terminal voltage $\mathbf{V}$ for the circuit of Fig. 10-40.

▮ $\mathbf{V} = \mathbf{V}_1 + \mathbf{V}_2$. Since $\mathbf{V}_1 = 10\ \underline{/0°} = 10 + j0$ V (given) and, from Prob. 10.84,

$$\mathbf{V}_2 = \mathbf{I}_3\mathbf{Z}_3 = (1.86\ \underline{/-1°})(10.82\ \underline{/-33.7°}) = 20.13\ \underline{/-34.7°} = 16.55 - j11.46\ \text{V}$$

we obtain $\qquad \mathbf{V} = (10 + j0) + (16.55 - j11.46) = 26.55 - j11.46 = 28.9\ \underline{/-23.3°}\ \text{V}$

10.86 Obtain the complex power in each of the three impedances of the circuit of Fig. 10-40. Verify that the sum of the three complex powers is the same as the input complex power.

▮
$$\mathbf{S}_1 = \mathbf{V}_1\mathbf{I}_1^* = (10\ \underline{/0°})(2.77\ \underline{/33.7°}) = 27.7\ \underline{/33.7°} = 23.05 + j15.37\ \text{VA}$$

$$\mathbf{S}_2 = \mathbf{V}_2\mathbf{I}_2^* = (20.13\ \underline{/-34.7°})(1.57\ \underline{/73.4°}) = 31.6\ \underline{/38.7°} = 24.66 + j19.76\ \text{VA}$$

$$\mathbf{S}_3 = \mathbf{V}_3\mathbf{I}_3^* = (20.13\ \underline{/-34.7°})(1.86\ \underline{/1°}) = 37.44\ \underline{/-33.7°} = 31.15 - j20.77\ \text{VA}$$

$$\mathbf{S} = \mathbf{S}_1 + \mathbf{S}_2 + \mathbf{S}_3 = 78.86 + j14.36\ \text{VA} = \mathbf{VI}_1^* = (28.9\ \underline{/-23.3°})(2.77\ \underline{/33.7°}) = 80\ \underline{/10.4°} = 78.68 + j14.44\ \text{VA}$$

which are approximately equal.

10.87 Repeat Prob. 10.86 for the circuit of Fig. 10-37.

▮ From Prob. 10.81,
$$\mathbf{S}_1 = \mathbf{V}_{12}\mathbf{I}^* = (41.39\ \underline{/24.83°})(11.48\ \underline{/31.48°}) = 475.16\ \underline{/56.31°} = 263.57 + j395.36\ \text{VA}$$

$$\mathbf{S}_2 = \mathbf{V}_{23}\mathbf{I}_1^* = (64.86\ \underline{/-15.56°})(11.12\ \underline{/74.56°}) = 721.24\ \underline{/59°} = 371.46 + j618.22\ \text{VA}$$

$$\mathbf{S}_3 = \mathbf{V}_{23}\mathbf{I}_2^* = (64.86\ \underline{/-15.56°})(8.3\ \underline{/-34.63°}) = 538.34\ \underline{/-50.19°} = 344.67 - j413.54\ \text{VA}$$

$$\mathbf{S} = \mathbf{S}_1 + \mathbf{S}_2 + \mathbf{S}_3 = 979.7 + j600 = \mathbf{VI}^* = (100\ \underline{/0°})(11.48\ \underline{/31.48°}) = 1148\ \underline{/31.48°} = 979.04 + j599.49\ \text{VA}$$

Hence $\qquad\qquad\qquad\qquad \mathbf{S} = \mathbf{S}_1 + \mathbf{S}_2 + \mathbf{S}_3 = \mathbf{VI}^*$

10.88 Three circuit elements $R = 10\,\Omega$, $L = 0.1\,\text{H}$, and $C = 600\,\mu\text{F}$ are connected in parallel and the combination is placed across a 110-V 60-Hz source. Determine the input current and input power. Also calculate the power factor angle.

▌ $$\mathbf{Y}_1 = \frac{1}{R} = \frac{1}{10} + j0 = 0.1 + j0 \qquad \mathbf{Y}_2 = \frac{1}{j\omega L} = 0 - \frac{j}{(377)(0.1)} = 0 - j0.0265$$

$$\mathbf{Y}_3 = \frac{1}{-j/\omega C} = j\omega C = j377(600 \times 10^{-6}) = 0 + j0.2262$$

Thus, $\mathbf{Y} = \mathbf{Y}_1 + \mathbf{Y}_2 + \mathbf{Y}_3 = 0.1 + j0.1997 = 0.223\,\underline{/63.4°}\,\text{S}$. Let $\mathbf{V} = 110\,\underline{/0°}$. Input current $\mathbf{I} = \mathbf{VY} = (110\,\underline{/0°})(0.223\,\underline{/63.4°}) = 24.57\,\underline{/63.4°}\,\text{A} = 11 + j21.97\,\text{A}$. Input power $= VI\cos\phi = (110)(24.57)\cos 63.4° = 1210\,\text{W}$. Power factor angle $\phi = 63.4°$.

10.89 Determine the power dissipated in the 10-Ω resistor of the circuit of Prob. 10.88. If the power factor angle is found to be 63.4°, calculate the input current for the circuit.

▌ $P_R = V^2/R = (110)^2/10 = 1210\,\text{W}$. Hence $I = 1210/(110\cos 63.4°) = 24.57\,\text{A}$ as determined in Prob. 10.88.

10.90 We have two circuits: Circuit 1 draws no direct current whereas circuit 2 takes 5 A at 50 V dc. When connected across 50-V 60-Hz ac, circuit 1 takes a 2-A current and circuit 2 draws 3 A. Identify the circuit elements and obtain their numerical values.

▌ Since circuit 1 is an open circuit to dc, it is a capacitor. When connected across a 50-V 60-Hz source, it takes a 2-A current. Thus,

$$V_C = 50 = I/wC = 2/377\,C \qquad \text{or} \qquad C = 106\,\mu\text{F}$$

Now, at 50-V dc, circuit 2 takes a 5-A current. Hence, the circuit is inductive and its resistive component is $R = \frac{50}{5} = 10\,\Omega$. At 50-V 60-Hz ac,

$$I = \frac{V}{Z} = \frac{50}{Z} = 3 \qquad \text{or} \qquad Z = \frac{50}{3} = 16.67\,\Omega$$

Hence $$\omega L = \sqrt{(16.67)^2 - (10)^2} = 13.33\,\Omega \qquad \text{or} \qquad L = \frac{13.33}{377} = 35.37\,\text{mH}$$

10.91 A 110-V 60-Hz inductive load draws $(500 - j500)$-VA complex power. A capacitor C is connected across the load to bring the overall power factor to 0.866 lagging. Determine the value of C, and new value of complex power of the load/capacitor combination.

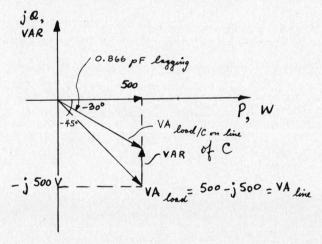

Fig. 10-41

▌ First, we show the complex power for the load in Fig. 10-41, which shows a lagging power factor angle of 45°. From Fig. 10-41, it follows that to change the power factor to 0.866, we have: Reactive power supplied by C is $500\tan 30° = 211.3\,\text{var}$ or $I_C = 211.3/110 = 1.921\,\text{A} = \omega CV = (377)C(110)$. Hence, $C = 46.325\,\mu\text{F}$.

New $\text{VA} = \sqrt{(500)^2 + (211.3)^2} = 542.8\,\text{VA}$ and the corresponding complex power $\mathbf{S} = P + jQ = 500 - j211.3\,\text{VA}$.

10.92 Determine the reading of a voltmeter connected between points 1 and 2 of the circuit of Fig. 10-42.

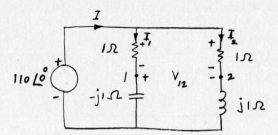

Fig. 10-42

▮ The impedances are:

$$\mathbf{Z}_1 = 1 - j1 = 1.414\ \underline{/-45°}\ \Omega \qquad \mathbf{Z}_2 = 1 + j1 = 1.414\ \underline{/45°}\ \Omega$$

$$\mathbf{Z} = \frac{\mathbf{Z}_1\mathbf{Z}_2}{\mathbf{Z}_1 + \mathbf{Z}_2} = \frac{(1.414\ \underline{/-45°})(1.414\ \underline{/45°})}{(1 - j1) + (1 + j1)} = \frac{2\ \underline{/0°}}{2\ \underline{/0°}} = 1\ \underline{/0°}\ \Omega$$

Thus
$$\mathbf{I} = \frac{\mathbf{V}}{\mathbf{Z}} = \frac{110\ \underline{/0°}}{1\ \underline{/0°}} = 110\ \underline{/0°}\ \text{A}$$

By current division,

$$\mathbf{I}_1 = \mathbf{I}\frac{\mathbf{Z}_2}{\mathbf{Z}_1 + \mathbf{Z}_2} = \frac{(110\ \underline{/0°})(1.414\ \underline{/45°})}{2\ \underline{/0°}} = 77.77\ \underline{/45°}\ \text{A}$$

Similarly
$$\mathbf{I}_2 = \frac{(110\ \underline{/0°})(1.414\ \underline{/-45°})}{2\ \underline{/0°}} = 77.77\ \underline{/-45°}\ \text{A}$$

The voltmeter reading V_{12} is given by

$$\mathbf{V}_{1\,\Omega} + \mathbf{V}_{12} - \mathbf{V}_{1\,\Omega} = 0 \qquad \text{or} \qquad (77.77\ \underline{/45°})(1) + \mathbf{V}_{12} - (77.77\ \underline{/-45°})(1) = 0$$

or
$$55 + j55 + \mathbf{V}_{12} - 55 + j55 = 0 \qquad \text{or} \qquad -\mathbf{V}_{12} = j55 + j55 = j110\ \text{V}$$

Hence the voltmeter reading is 110 V.

10.93 Obtain the active and reactive powers of the circuit of Fig. 10-42.

▮ Taking the current from Prob. 10.92, $\mathbf{S} = \mathbf{VI}^* = (110\ \underline{/0°})(110\ \underline{/0°}) = 12100 + j0$. Hence $P = 12100$ W, $Q = 0$ var.

10.94 Check Prob. 10.93 by adding the complex powers in the two branches.

▮ For $\mathbf{Z}_1$ we have $\mathbf{S}_1 = \mathbf{VI}_1^* = (110\ \underline{/0°})(77.77\ \underline{/-45°}) = 6050 - j6050$ VA. For $\mathbf{Z}_2$ we obtain $\mathbf{S}_2 = \mathbf{VI}_2^* = (110\ \underline{/0°})(77.77\ \underline{/+45°}) = 6050 + j6050$ VA. Hence $\mathbf{S}_1 + \mathbf{S}_2 = 12100 + j0 = \mathbf{S}$.

10.95 Find the current through the capacitor of the circuit of Fig. 10-43.

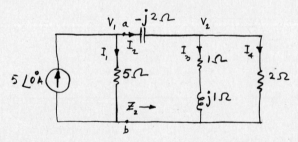

Fig. 10-43

▮ Impedance presented between ab:

$$\mathbf{Z}_2 = -j2 + \frac{2(1 + j1)}{2 + 1 + j1} = -j2 + \frac{2.828\ \underline{/45°}}{3.162\ \underline{/18.43°}} = -j2 + 0.894\ \underline{/26.56°}$$

$$= -j2 + 0.8 + j0.4 = 0.8 - j1.6 = 1.79\ \underline{/-63.4°}\ \Omega$$

$$\mathbf{I}_2 = \text{current through capacitor} = 5\ \underline{/0°}\ \frac{5\ \underline{/0°}}{5 + 0.8 - j1.6} = 4.16\ \underline{/15.4°}\ \text{A}$$

10.96 Calculate the current in the 15-Ω resistor of the circuit shown in Fig. 10-44.

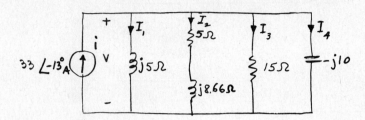

Fig. 10-44

❚ First we determine the input admittance:

$$\mathbf{Y} = \mathbf{Y}_1 + \mathbf{Y}_2 + \mathbf{Y}_3 + \mathbf{Y}_4 = \frac{1}{j5} + \frac{1}{5 + j8.66} + \frac{1}{15} + \frac{1}{-j10} = 0.117 - j0.187 = 0.221 \underline{/-58^\circ} \text{ S}$$

or

$$\mathbf{Z} = \frac{1}{\mathbf{Y}} = \frac{1}{0.221 \underline{/-58^\circ}} = 4.53 \underline{/58^\circ} \ \Omega \qquad \mathbf{V} = \mathbf{ZI} = (4.53 \underline{/58^\circ})(33 \underline{/-13^\circ}) = 149.5 \underline{/45^\circ} \text{ V}$$

$$\mathbf{I}_3 = \mathbf{Y}_3 \mathbf{V} = (\tfrac{1}{15} \underline{/0^\circ})(149.5 \underline{/45^\circ}) = 9.97 \underline{/45^\circ} \text{ A}$$

10.97 Determine the complex power drawn from the current source of the circuit of Fig. 10-44.

❚ From Prob. 10.96, $\mathbf{Z} = 4.53 \underline{/58^\circ}$. So the circuit is inductive.

$$\mathbf{S} = P + jQ = \mathbf{VI}^* = (149.5)(33) \underline{/(45 + 13)} = 4933.5 \underline{/58^\circ} = 2614 + j4184 \text{ VA}$$

10.98 Calculate the input active and reactive powers in the circuit elements of Fig. 10-44. Hence determine the complex power. Verify that the result agrees with that of Prob. 10.97.

❚
$$P_1 = 0 \text{ W} \qquad Q_1 = \frac{V^2}{X_1} = \frac{(149.5)^2}{5} = 4470 \text{ var} \qquad S_1 = P_1 + jQ_1 = 0 + j4470$$

Now,
$$\mathbf{I}_2 = \mathbf{Y}_2 \mathbf{V} = \frac{1}{5 + j8.66} (149.5 \underline{/45^\circ}) \qquad |\mathbf{I}_2| = 14.95 \text{ A} \qquad \text{and} \qquad P_2 = (I_2)^2 5 = (14.95)^2 5 = 1117.5 \text{ W}$$

$$Q_2 = (I_2)^2 X_2 = (14.95)^2 8.66 = 1935.5 \text{ var} \qquad S_2 = P_2 + jQ_2 = 1117.5 + j1935.5 \text{ VA}$$

$$P_3 = (I_3)^2 15 = (9.97)^2 \ 15 = 1490 \text{ W} \qquad Q_3 = 0 \qquad S_3 = 1490 + j0 \text{ VA}$$

$$P_4 = 0 \qquad Q_4 = \frac{V^2}{X_4} = \frac{(149.5)^2}{10} = 2235 \text{ var} \qquad S_4 = 0 - j2235 \text{ VA}$$

$$\mathbf{S} = \mathbf{S}_1 + \mathbf{S}_2 + \mathbf{S}_3 + \mathbf{S}_4 = j4470 + 1117.5 + j1935.5 + 1490 - j2235 = 2607.5 + j4170.5 \text{ VA}$$

which is approximately the same as obtained in Prob. 10.97. The error of about 0.3 percent is due to roundoff.

10.99 Determine L in the circuit shown in Fig. 10-45.

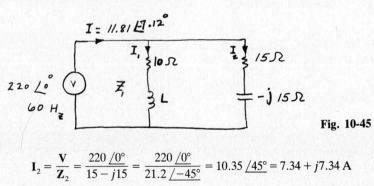

Fig. 10-45

❚
$$\mathbf{I}_2 = \frac{\mathbf{V}}{\mathbf{Z}_2} = \frac{220 \underline{/0^\circ}}{15 - j15} = \frac{220 \underline{/0^\circ}}{21.2 \underline{/-45^\circ}} = 10.35 \underline{/45^\circ} = 7.34 + j7.34 \text{ A}$$

$$\mathbf{I}_1 = \mathbf{I} - \mathbf{I}_2 = 11.81 \underline{/-7.12} - (7.34 + j7.34) = 4.38 - j8.8 = 9.83 \underline{/-63.6^\circ} \text{ A} = \frac{\mathbf{V}}{\mathbf{Z}_1} = \frac{220 \underline{/0^\circ}}{10 + jX_L}$$

from which
$$X_L = 20 \ \Omega = \omega L = 377L \qquad \text{or} \qquad L = 53.05 \text{ mH}$$

10.100 Determine $\mathbf{Z}_x$ in the circuit shown in Fig. 10-46.

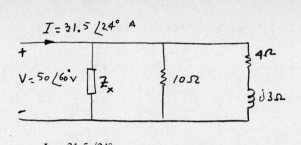

Fig. 10-46

▮ $$\mathbf{Y} = \frac{\mathbf{I}}{\mathbf{V}} = \frac{31.5\ \underline{/24^\circ}}{50\ \underline{/60^\circ}} = 0.63\ \underline{/-36^\circ} = 0.51 - j0.37 = \mathbf{Y}_x + \frac{1}{10} + \frac{1}{4 + j3}$$

Thus, $$\mathbf{Y}_x = 0.354\ \underline{/-45^\circ}\ \text{S} \quad \text{or} \quad \mathbf{Z}_x = 2 + j2\ \Omega$$

10.101 Find the voltage $\mathbf{V}_{AB}$ in the circuit of Fig. 10-47.

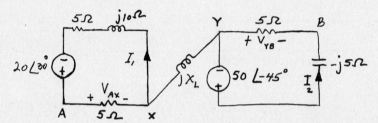

Fig. 10-47

▮ Notice that the inductor jX_L is irrelevant because no current flows through it. Thus, $\mathbf{V}_{XY} = 0$.

Now, $$\mathbf{I}_1 = \frac{20\ \underline{/30^\circ}}{10 + j10} = 1.414\ \underline{/-15^\circ}\ \text{A} \qquad \mathbf{I}_2 = \frac{50\ \underline{/-45^\circ}}{5 - j5} = 7.07\ \underline{/0^\circ}\ \text{A}$$

$$\mathbf{V}_{AX} = \mathbf{I}_1(5) = (1.414\ \underline{/-15^\circ})5 = 7.07\ \underline{/-15^\circ}\ \text{V} \qquad \mathbf{V}_{YB} = -\mathbf{I}_2(5) = -(7.07\ \underline{/0^\circ})5 = -35.35\ \underline{/0^\circ}\ \text{V}$$

Hence $$\mathbf{V}_{AB} = \mathbf{V}_{AX} + \mathbf{V}_{XY} + \mathbf{V}_{YB} = 7.07\ \underline{/-15^\circ} + 0 - 35.35\ \underline{/0^\circ} = -28.6 - j1.83 = 28.7\ \underline{/183.7^\circ}\ \text{V}$$

10.102 Determine $\mathbf{V}_{AB}$ in the circuit of Fig. 10-48.

▮ By current division we obtain

$$\mathbf{I}_1 = \mathbf{I}\frac{\mathbf{Z}_2}{\mathbf{Z}_1 + \mathbf{Z}_2} = 18\ \underline{/45^\circ}\ \frac{j8}{30 + j8} = 4.64\ \underline{/120.1^\circ}\ \text{A} \qquad \mathbf{I}_2 = \mathbf{I}\frac{\mathbf{Z}_1}{\mathbf{Z}_1 + \mathbf{Z}_2} = 18\ \underline{/45^\circ}\ \frac{30}{30 + j8} = 17.40\ \underline{/30.1^\circ}\ \text{A}$$

For the path AB we have

$$\mathbf{V}_{AB} = \mathbf{V}_{AX} + \mathbf{V}_{XB} = \mathbf{I}_1(20) - \mathbf{I}_2(j6) = (4.64\ \underline{/120.1^\circ})20 - (17.40\ \underline{/30.1^\circ})j6$$

$$= 92.8\ \underline{/120.1^\circ}\ \text{I}\ 104.4\ \underline{/-59.9^\circ} = 11.6\ \underline{/-59.9^\circ}\ \text{V}$$

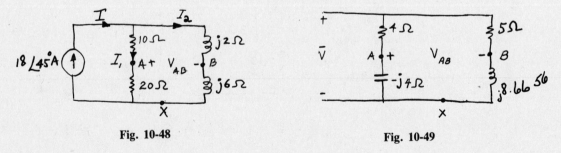

Fig. 10-48   Fig. 10-49

10.103 In the circuit of Fig. 10-49, we have $\mathbf{V}_{AB} = 48.3\ \underline{/30^\circ}$. Evaluate $\mathbf{V}$.

▮ By voltage division,

$$\mathbf{V}_{AX} = \frac{-j4}{4 - j4}\mathbf{V} = \frac{1}{1 + j}\mathbf{V} \qquad \mathbf{V}_{BX} = \frac{j8.66}{5 + j8.66}\mathbf{V}$$

and
$$V_{AB} = V_{AX} - V_{BX} = \left(\frac{1}{1+j} - \frac{j8.66}{5+j8.66}\right)V = \frac{V}{-0.268 + j1}$$

Hence,
$$V = (-0.268 + j1)V_{AB} = (1.035 \underline{/105°})(48.3 \underline{/30°}) = 50 \underline{/135°}\ V$$

10.104 Determine Z_x in the circuit of Fig. 10-50.

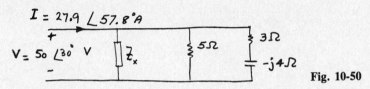

Fig. 10-50

▮ $$Y = \frac{I}{V} = \frac{27.9 \underline{/57.8°}}{50 \underline{/30°}} = 0.558 \underline{/27.8°}\ S = 0.494 + j0.26 = Y_x + \frac{1}{5} + \frac{1}{3-j4} = Y_x + 0.2 + 0.12 + j0.16$$

Thus
$$Y_x = 0.174 + j0.1 = 0.2 \underline{/29.9°}\ S \quad \text{or} \quad Z_x = 5 \underline{/-29.9°}\ \Omega$$

10.105 Calculate the current I in the circuit of Fig. 10-51.

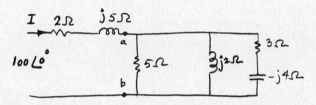

Fig. 10-51

▮ First, we determine Y_{ab}:
$$Y_{ab} = \frac{1}{5} + \frac{1}{j2} + \frac{1}{3-j4} = 0.2 - j0.5 + 0.12 + j0.16 = 0.32 - j0.34 = 0.467 \underline{/-46.7°}\ S$$

or
$$Z_{ab} = \frac{1}{0.467} \underline{/46.7°} = 2.14 \underline{/46.7°} = 1.47 + j1.56$$

$$Z = 2 + j5 + 1.47 + j1.56 = 3.47 + j6.56 = 7.42 \underline{/62°}$$

Thus
$$I = \frac{100}{7.42 \underline{/62°}} = 13.48 \underline{/-62°}\ A$$

10.106 How much reactive power is taken by the circuit of Fig. 10-51?

▮ From Prob. 10.105 the complex power is given by $S = VI^* = (100 \underline{/0°})(13.48 \underline{/62°}) = 1348 \underline{/62°} = 633 + j1190$. Thus, reactive power is 1190 var.

10.107 Several impedances are connected in series. Given: $Z_1 = 15 \underline{/30°}\ \Omega$ and $Z_5 = 10 \underline{/0°}\ \Omega$. If the voltage across Z_1 is $V_1 = 60 \underline{/15°}\ V$, find V_5, the voltage across Z_5.

▮ $$I_1 = I_2 = \cdots = I_5 = \frac{V_1}{Z_1} = \frac{60 \underline{/15°}}{15 \underline{/30°}} = 4 \underline{/-15°}\ A \qquad V_5 = I_5 Z_5 = (4 \underline{/-15°})(10 \underline{/0°}) = 40 \underline{/-15°}\ V$$

10.108 Several impedances are connected in parallel. Given: $Y_1 = 0.015 \underline{/0°}\ S$ and $Y_5 = 0.05 \underline{/30°}\ S$. If the current through Y_1 is $I_1 = 2.24 \underline{/31.16°}$, determine I_5, the current through Y_5.

▮ $$V_1 = V_2 = \cdots = V_5 = \frac{I_1}{Y_1} = \frac{2.24 \underline{/31.16°}}{0.015 \underline{/0°}} = 149.3 \underline{/31.16°}\ V$$

$$I_5 = V_5 Y_5 = (149.3 \underline{/31.16°})(0.05 \underline{/30°}) = 7.465 \underline{/60.16°}\ A$$

10.109 A 5-Ω resistor is connected in series with a 3-Ω capacitive reactance, and the combination across a 4-Ω resistor. If the total input current is $40 \underline{/0°}\ A$, determine the power factor of the circuit. Is the power factor dependent on the input current (or voltage)?

▮ From the data,

$$\mathbf{Z} = \frac{(5-j3)4}{5-j3+4} = \frac{20-j12}{9-j3} = 2.4 - j0.53 = 2.46\ \underline{/-12.45°}\ \Omega$$

Power factor $= \cos(-12.45°) = 0.976$ leading, which is independent of the input.

10.110 Determine the complex power for the circuit of Prob. 10.109.

▮ From Prob. 10.109, $R = 2.4\ \Omega$ and $X = 0.53\ \Omega$. $P = I^2R = (40)^2 2.4 = 3840$ W, $Q = I^2X = (40)^2 0.53 = 848$ var. Hence, $\mathbf{S} = P - jQ = 3840 - j848$ VA.

10.111 An impedance, $(3+j4)\ \Omega$, is connected in parallel with a 10-Ω resistor. If the input power to this circuit is 1100 W, what is the power in each resistor?

▮ Let $\mathbf{Z}_1 = 3 + j4$, $\mathbf{Z}_2 = 10 + j0$. Then $\mathbf{I}_1\mathbf{Z}_1 = \mathbf{I}_2\mathbf{Z}_2$, or

$$\frac{|\mathbf{I}_1|}{|\mathbf{I}_2|} = \frac{|\mathbf{Z}_2|}{|\mathbf{Z}_1|} = \frac{10}{\sqrt{3^2+4^2}} = 2$$

Also,

$$\frac{P_1}{P_2} = \frac{|I_1|^2R_1}{|I_2|^2R_2} = (2)^2\tfrac{3}{10} = 1.2 \quad \text{and} \quad P_1 + P_2 = 1100\ \text{W}$$

Hence,

$$P_1 = 600\ \text{W} \quad \text{and} \quad P_2 = 500\ \text{W}$$

10.112 Two impedances, $\mathbf{Z}_1 = 2 + j4$ and $\mathbf{Z}_2 = R + j0$, are connected in parallel. Determine R so that the power factor of the circuit is 0.9 lagging.

▮ Equivalent admittance is given by $\mathbf{Y}_e = 1/(2+j4) + 1/R = (1/10 + 1/R) - j/5$ S. For 0.9 lagging power factor, the angle of the admittance must be $\cos^{-1} 0.9 = -25.84°$. Thus,

$$\frac{1/5}{1/10 + 1/R} = \tan 25.84° = 0.484 \quad \text{or} \quad R = 3.2\ \Omega$$

10.113 A 250-VA 0.5-lagging-power-factor load is connected in parallel to a 180-W 0.8-leading-power-factor load, and the combination to 300-VA 100-var inductive load. Determine the complex power for the combination of the three loads.

▮
$$\mathbf{S}_1 = 250\ \underline{/\cos^{-1} 0.5} = 250\ \underline{/60°} = 250(\cos 60 + j\sin 60) = 125 + j216.5\ \text{VA}$$

$$\mathbf{S}_2 = 180 - j180\tan(\cos^{-1}0.8) = 180 - j135.0\ \text{VA} \quad \mathbf{S}_3 = \sqrt{(300)^2 - (100)^2} + j100 = 282.8 + j100\ \text{VA}$$

Thus,
$$\mathbf{S} = \mathbf{S}_1 + \mathbf{S}_2 + \mathbf{S}_3 = 587.8 + j181.5\ \text{VA}$$

10.114 Two impedances, $\mathbf{Z}_1 = (2+j3)\ \Omega$ and $\mathbf{Z}_2 = (3+j6)\ \Omega$, are connected in parallel. The apparent power for the second branch is 1490 VA. Determine the total complex power.

▮ Since $|\mathbf{S}_2| = (I_2)^2|\mathbf{Z}_2|$, we obtain

$$(I_2)^2 = \frac{1490}{\sqrt{3^2+6^2}} = 222\ \text{A}^2$$

By current division,

$$\frac{\mathbf{I}_1}{\mathbf{I}_2} = \frac{3+j6}{2+j3} \quad \text{or} \quad \mathbf{S}_1 = (I_1)^2\mathbf{Z}_1 = 768(2+j3) = 1536 + j2304$$

$$\mathbf{S}_2 = (I_2)^2\mathbf{Z}_2 = 222(3+j6) = 666 + j1332 \quad \text{and} \quad \mathbf{S} = \mathbf{S}_1 + \mathbf{S}_2 = 2202 + j3636$$

10.115 An impedance $\mathbf{Z}_1 = (4+j4)\ \Omega$ is connected in parallel with an impedance $\mathbf{Z}_2 = (12+j6)\ \Omega$. If the input reactive power is 2500 var (lagging), what is the total active power?

▮
$$\mathbf{Y}_3 = \mathbf{Y}_1 + \mathbf{Y}_2 = \frac{1}{4+j4} + \frac{1}{12+j6} = 0.2488\ \underline{/-39.57°}\ \text{S}$$

Then $P = 2500\cot 39.57° = 3025$ W.

10.116 Find the power consumed in each branch of the circuit of Prob. 10.115.

▮ From Prob. 10.115,

$$\mathbf{Y}_1 = \frac{1}{4 + j4} = 0.177 \underline{/-45^\circ} \qquad \mathbf{Y}_2 = \frac{1}{12 + j6} = 0.0745 \underline{/-26.6^\circ}$$

$$\frac{I_1}{I_2} = \frac{Y_1}{Y_2} = \frac{0.177}{0.0745} \qquad \frac{P_1}{P_2} = \frac{(I_1)^2 4}{(I_2)^2 12} = \left(\frac{0.177}{0.0745}\right)^2 \frac{4}{12} = 1.88$$

But $P_1 + P_2 = 3025$ W; hence, $P_1 = 1975$ W and $P_2 = 1050$ W.

10.117 A general two-loop network is shown in Fig. 10-52. Write the mesh equation in complex (or phasor) form and formally solve for the mesh currents.

❙ By KVL we have, in general, $\mathbf{Z}_{11}\mathbf{I}_1 + \mathbf{Z}_{12}\mathbf{I}_2 = \mathbf{V}_1$ and $\mathbf{Z}_{21}\mathbf{I}_1 + \mathbf{Z}_{22}\mathbf{I}_2 = \mathbf{V}_2$, which may be written in matrix form as

$$\begin{bmatrix} \mathbf{Z}_{11} & \mathbf{Z}_{12} \\ \mathbf{Z}_{21} & \mathbf{Z}_{22} \end{bmatrix} \begin{bmatrix} \mathbf{I}_1 \\ \mathbf{I}_2 \end{bmatrix} = \begin{bmatrix} \mathbf{V}_1 \\ 0 \end{bmatrix}$$

where $\mathbf{Z}_{11} = \mathbf{Z}_A + \mathbf{Z}_B =$ self-impedance of mesh 1 through which $\mathbf{I}_1$ flows; $\mathbf{Z}_{22} = \mathbf{Z}_B + \mathbf{Z}_C$ is the self-impedance of mesh 2 through which $\mathbf{I}_2$ flows; and $\mathbf{Z}_{12} = \mathbf{Z}_{21} = \mathbf{Z}_B$ which is common to $\mathbf{I}_1$ and $\mathbf{I}_2$.

Using Cramer's rule, the formal solutions are:

$$\mathbf{I}_1 = \frac{\begin{vmatrix} \mathbf{V}_1 & \mathbf{Z}_{12} \\ 0 & \mathbf{Z}_{22} \end{vmatrix}}{\Delta} \qquad \text{and} \qquad \mathbf{I}_2 = \frac{\begin{vmatrix} \mathbf{Z}_{11} & \mathbf{V}_1 \\ \mathbf{Z}_{21} & 0 \end{vmatrix}}{\Delta}$$

where $\Delta =$ determinant of the $\mathbf{Z}$ matrix.

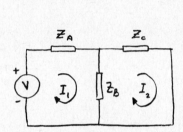

Fig. 10-52

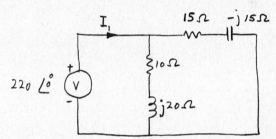

Fig. 10-53

10.118 Using the procedure described in Prob. 10.117, solve for the current $\mathbf{I}_1$ in the circuit of Fig. 10-53.

❙ Identifying the various impedances we have $\mathbf{Z}_{11} = 10 + j20$, $\mathbf{Z}_{12} = \mathbf{Z}_{21} = -(10 + j20)$, and $\mathbf{Z}_{22} = (15 - j15) + (10 + j20)$. Hence,

$$\Delta = \begin{vmatrix} 10 + j20 & -(10 + j20) \\ -(10 + j20) & 25 + j5 \end{vmatrix} = 450 + j150 = 474.3 \underline{/18.4^\circ}$$

Now, since $\mathbf{V} = 220 \underline{/0^\circ}$ V, we obtain

$$\mathbf{I}_1 = \frac{\begin{vmatrix} 220 + j0 & -(10 + j20) \\ 0 & 25 + j5 \end{vmatrix}}{474.3 \underline{/18.4^\circ}} = \frac{220(25.5 \underline{/11.3^\circ})}{474.3 \underline{/18.4^\circ}} = 11.82 \underline{/-7.1^\circ}$$

10.119 Extend the result of Prob. 10.117 to a three-mesh circuit. In particular, solve for $\mathbf{I}_3$ shown in the circuit of Fig. 10-54.

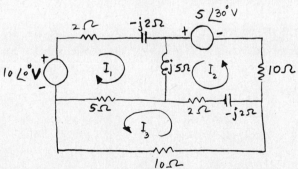

Fig. 10-54

▮ For the mesh currents shown, in matrix form the **VI** relationship is:

$$\begin{bmatrix} 7+j3 & j5 & 5 \\ j5 & 12+j3 & -(2-j2) \\ 5 & -(2-j2) & 17-j2 \end{bmatrix}\begin{bmatrix} \mathbf{I_1} \\ \mathbf{I_2} \\ \mathbf{I_3} \end{bmatrix} = \begin{bmatrix} 10\,\underline{/0^\circ} \\ 5\,\underline{/30^\circ} \\ 0 \end{bmatrix}$$

$$\Delta = \begin{vmatrix} 7+j3 & j5 & 5 \\ j5 & 12+j3 & -(2-j2) \\ 5 & -(2-j2) & 17-j2 \end{vmatrix} = 1534.5\,\underline{/25^\circ}$$

Thus,

$$\mathbf{I_3} = \frac{\begin{vmatrix} 7+j3 & j5 & 10\,\underline{/0^\circ} \\ j5 & 12+j3 & 5\,\underline{/30^\circ} \\ 5 & -2+j2 & 0 \end{vmatrix}}{\Delta} = \frac{667.96\,\underline{/-169^\circ}}{1534.5\,\underline{/25^\circ}} = 0.435\,\underline{/-194^\circ}\ \text{A}$$

10.120 For the network shown in Fig. 10-55, what **V** makes $\mathbf{I_2} = 0$?

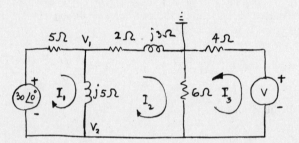

Fig. 10-55

▮ Proceeding as in Prob. 10.119,

$$\mathbf{I_2} = \frac{\begin{vmatrix} 5+j5 & 30\,\underline{/0^\circ} & 0 \\ -j5 & 0 & 6 \\ 0 & \mathbf{V} & 10 \end{vmatrix}}{\Delta} = 0 \qquad \text{or} \qquad (5+j5)(-6)\mathbf{V} + 30\,\underline{/0^\circ}(j5)10 = 0$$

Solving for **V** yields $\mathbf{V} = 35.4\,\underline{/45^\circ}\ \text{V}$.

10.121 Express the result of a nodal analysis of a general network in matrix form.

▮ For an admittance **Y** across which we have a voltage **V**, the current **I** is given by $\mathbf{YV} = \mathbf{I}$.   For a system of currents and voltages, this result is generalized to $[\mathbf{Y}][\mathbf{V}] = [\mathbf{I}]$,   where the $[\mathbf{Y}]$ is the admittance matrix and is given by

$$[\mathbf{Y}] = \begin{bmatrix} \mathbf{Y_{11}} & \mathbf{Y_{12}} & \mathbf{Y_{13}} & \cdots \\ \mathbf{Y_{21}} & \mathbf{Y_{22}} & \mathbf{Y_{23}} & \cdots \\ \cdot & \cdot & \cdot & \cdots \\ \cdot & \cdot & \cdot & \cdots \\ \cdot & \cdot & \cdot & \cdots \end{bmatrix} \qquad [\mathbf{V}] = \begin{bmatrix} \mathbf{V_1} \\ \mathbf{V_2} \\ \cdot \\ \cdot \\ \cdot \end{bmatrix} \quad \text{and} \quad [\mathbf{I}] = \begin{bmatrix} \mathbf{I_1} \\ \mathbf{I_2} \\ \cdot \\ \cdot \\ \cdot \end{bmatrix}$$

In the symmetric $[\mathbf{Y}]$ matrix $\mathbf{Y}_{ii}$ is the self-admittance of node i (the sum of all the admittances connected to node i) and $\mathbf{Y}_{ij}$ is the coupling admittance between nodes i and j.

10.122 Use Prob. 10.121 to solve Prob. 10.120.

▮ Defining the node voltages as $\mathbf{V_1}$ and $\mathbf{V_2}$ (Fig. 10-55), the matrix equation becomes

$$\begin{bmatrix} \dfrac{1}{5} + \dfrac{1}{j5} + \dfrac{1}{2+j3} & -\left(\dfrac{1}{5} + \dfrac{1}{j5}\right) \\[2mm] -\left(\dfrac{1}{5} + \dfrac{1}{j5}\right) & \dfrac{1}{5} + \dfrac{1}{j5} + \dfrac{1}{4} + \dfrac{1}{6} \end{bmatrix}\begin{bmatrix} \mathbf{V_1} \\ \mathbf{V_2} \end{bmatrix} = \begin{bmatrix} \dfrac{30}{5}\,\underline{/0^\circ} \\[2mm] \dfrac{-30\,\underline{/0^\circ}}{5} - \dfrac{\mathbf{V}}{4} \end{bmatrix}$$

For $\mathbf{I_2} = 0$,   we must have $\mathbf{V_1} = 0$,   or

$$\begin{vmatrix} 30\,\dfrac{\angle 0°}{5} & -0.2+j0.2 \\[2mm] -30\,\dfrac{\angle 0°}{5}-\dfrac{\mathbf V}{4} & 0.617-j0.2 \end{vmatrix}=0$$

which yields $\mathbf{V}=35.4\ \underline{/45°}\ \mathrm{V}$.

10.123   Find the current $\mathbf{I}$ in the circuit of Fig. 10-56 by nodal analysis.

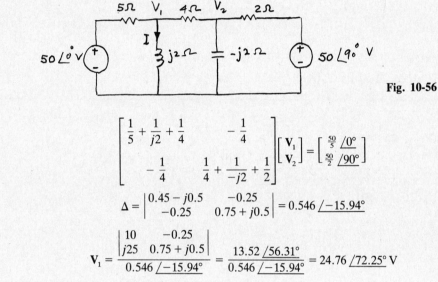

Fig. 10-56

$$\begin{bmatrix} \dfrac{1}{5}+\dfrac{1}{j2}+\dfrac{1}{4} & -\dfrac{1}{4} \\[3mm] -\dfrac{1}{4} & \dfrac{1}{4}+\dfrac{1}{-j2}+\dfrac{1}{2} \end{bmatrix}\begin{bmatrix} \mathbf V_1 \\[2mm] \mathbf V_2 \end{bmatrix}=\begin{bmatrix} \frac{50}{5}\ \underline{/0°} \\[2mm] \frac{50}{2}\ \underline{/90°} \end{bmatrix}$$

$$\Delta=\begin{vmatrix} 0.45-j0.5 & -0.25 \\ -0.25 & 0.75+j0.5 \end{vmatrix}=0.546\ \underline{/-15.94°}$$

$$\mathbf V_1=\dfrac{\begin{vmatrix} 10 & -0.25 \\ j25 & 0.75+j0.5 \end{vmatrix}}{0.546\ \underline{/-15.94°}}=\dfrac{13.52\ \underline{/56.31°}}{0.546\ \underline{/-15.94°}}=24.76\ \underline{/72.25°}\ \mathrm V$$

Hence, $\mathbf I=(24.76\ \underline{/72.25°})/(2\ \underline{/90°})=12.38\ \underline{/-17.75°}\ \mathrm A$.

10.124   Determine the input impedance $\mathbf Z_{i1}=\mathbf V/\mathbf I_1$ for the network shown in Fig. 10-57.

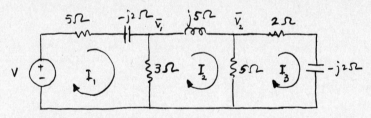

Fig. 10-57

▐   The input impedance is given by $\mathbf Z_{i1}=\Delta/\Delta_{11}$,   where Δ is the determinant of the impedance matrix and Δ_{11} is the cofactor of $\mathbf Z_{i1}$.   Hence,

$$\mathbf Z_{i1}=\dfrac{\begin{vmatrix} 8-j2 & -3 & 0 \\ -3 & 8+j5 & -5 \\ 0 & -5 & 7-j2 \end{vmatrix}}{\begin{vmatrix} 8+j5 & -5 \\ -5 & 7-j2 \end{vmatrix}}=\dfrac{315.5\ \underline{/16.2°}}{45.2\ \underline{/24.9°}}=6.98\ \underline{/-8.7°}\ \Omega$$

10.125   For the circuit of Fig. 10-57, determine $\mathbf V_2$ which results in a voltage $5\ \underline{/0°}\ \mathrm V$ across the 5-Ω resistor.

▐   Notice that the voltage across the 5-Ω resistor is the same as the node voltage $\mathbf V_2$.   Thus, by nodal analysis we obtain:

$$\mathbf{V}_2 = 5\,\underline{/0^\circ} = \cfrac{\begin{vmatrix} \dfrac{1}{5-j2} + \dfrac{1}{3} + \dfrac{1}{j5} & \dfrac{\mathbf{V}}{5-j2} \\[2mm] \dfrac{-1}{j5} & 0 \end{vmatrix}}{\begin{vmatrix} \dfrac{1}{5-j2} + \dfrac{1}{3} + \dfrac{1}{j5} & \dfrac{-1}{j5} \\[2mm] \dfrac{-1}{j5} & \dfrac{1}{j5} + \dfrac{1}{5} + \dfrac{1}{2-j2} \end{vmatrix}} = \mathbf{V}(0.134\,\underline{/-61^\circ})$$

Thus,

$$\mathbf{V} = \frac{5\,\underline{/0^\circ}}{0.134\,\underline{/-61^\circ}} = 37.3\,\underline{/61^\circ}\ \text{V}$$

10.126 Determine $\mathbf{I}_1$ in the circuit of Fig. 10-58 by mesh analysis.

❚ The mesh equations in matrix form may be written as

$$\begin{bmatrix} 4+j2 & -4 \\ -4 & 4-j1 \end{bmatrix}\begin{bmatrix} \mathbf{I}_1 \\ \mathbf{I}_2 \end{bmatrix} = \begin{bmatrix} 2\,\underline{/0^\circ} \\ -6\,\underline{/0^\circ} \end{bmatrix}$$

Solving for $\mathbf{I}_1$, we obtain

$$\mathbf{I}_1 = \frac{\begin{vmatrix} 2+j0 & -4 \\ -6+j0 & 4-j1 \end{vmatrix}}{\begin{vmatrix} 4+j2 & -4 \\ -4 & 4-j1 \end{vmatrix}} = \frac{-16-j2}{2+j4} = 3.6\,\underline{/123.7^\circ}\ \text{A}$$

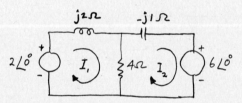

Fig. 10-58

10.127 Find the power supplied (or absorbed) by each source of the circuit of Fig. 10-58.

❚ To find the power we must know $\mathbf{I}_1$ and $\mathbf{I}_2$. From Prob. 10.126, $\mathbf{I}_1 = 3.6\,\underline{/123.7^\circ}$ A and

$$\mathbf{I}_2 = \frac{\begin{vmatrix} 4+j2 & 2 \\ -4 & -6 \end{vmatrix}}{\begin{vmatrix} 4+j2 & -4 \\ -4 & 4-j1 \end{vmatrix}} = -\frac{16+j12}{2+j4} = \frac{20\,\underline{/-143.13^\circ}}{4.47\,\underline{/63.4^\circ}} = 4.47\,\underline{/-206.53^\circ} = 4.47\,\underline{/153.47^\circ}\ \text{A}$$

Thus $P_1 = V_1 I_1 \cos\phi_1 = (2)(3.6)\cos 123.7 = -4\,\text{W}$ (absorbed) and

$$P_2 = V_2 I_2 \cos\phi_2 = (6)(4.47)\cos(180-153.47) = 24\,\text{W}\ \text{(supplied)}$$

10.128 Determine the power dissipated in the 4-Ω resistor of the circuit of Prob. 10.127. Verify the power balance.

❚
$$P_{4\,\Omega} = (|\mathbf{I}_1 - \mathbf{I}_2|)^2 4 = |\,(3.6\,\underline{/123.7^\circ} - 4.47\,\underline{/153.47^\circ})\,|^2 4 = |\,(2+j1)\,|^2\,4 = 20\,\text{W}$$

From Prob. 10.127 $\Sigma P_{\text{source}} = -4 + 24 = 20\,\text{W},$ which is the power absorbed by the resistor.

10.129 Write a set of nodal equations in matrix form for the circuit of Fig. 10-59. Then evaluate $\mathbf{V}_1$ from the following data: $\mathbf{Y}_1 = 0.25\,\underline{/0^\circ}$ S, $\mathbf{Y}_2 = 0.2\,\underline{/-90^\circ}$ S, $\mathbf{Y}_3 = 0.5\,\underline{/90^\circ}$ S, $\mathbf{I}_1 = 6\,\underline{/0^\circ}$ A, and $\mathbf{I}_2 = 4\,\underline{/0^\circ}$ A.

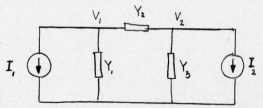

Fig. 10-59

▮ The general nodal equations may be written as

$$\begin{bmatrix} Y_1 + Y_2 & -Y_2 \\ -Y_2 & Y_2 + Y_3 \end{bmatrix} \begin{bmatrix} V_1 \\ V_2 \end{bmatrix} = \begin{bmatrix} -I_1 \\ -I_2 \end{bmatrix}$$

Substituting the numerical values and solving for V_1 yields:

$$V_1 = \frac{\begin{vmatrix} -6 & -j0.2 \\ -4 & j0.3 \end{vmatrix}}{\begin{vmatrix} 0.25 - j0.2 & j0.2 \\ j0.2 & j0.3 \end{vmatrix}} = \frac{-j1.8 + j0.8}{j0.075 + 0.06 + 0.04} = \frac{-j1.0}{0.1 + j0.075} = \frac{1.0 \underline{/-90°}}{0.125 \underline{/36.87°}} = 8.0 \underline{/-126.87°} \text{ V}$$

10.130 Convert the current source of the circuit of Fig. 10-60a to a voltage source and find the current through the capacitor by mesh analysis.

▮ If the current through the capacitor is I_2, the mesh equations may be written as

$$\begin{bmatrix} 8 + j4 & -(3 + j4) \\ -(3 + j4) & 8 - j1 \end{bmatrix} \begin{bmatrix} I_1 \\ I_2 \end{bmatrix} = \begin{bmatrix} 100 \underline{/0°} \\ -50 \underline{/30°} \end{bmatrix}$$

Solving for I_2 yields

$$I_2 = \frac{\begin{vmatrix} 8 + j4 & 100 \\ -3 - j4 & -43.3 - j25 \end{vmatrix}}{\begin{vmatrix} 8 + j4 & -3 - j4 \\ -3 - j4 & 8 - j1 \end{vmatrix}} = \frac{53.6 + j26.8}{75 + j0} = \frac{59.92 \underline{/26.56°}}{75 \underline{/0°}} = 0.80 \underline{/26.56°} \text{ A}$$

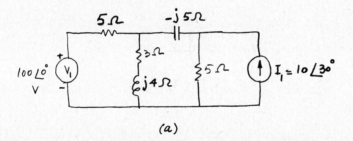

(a)

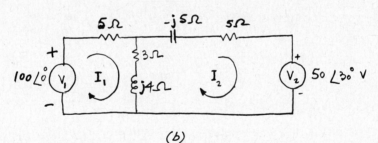

(b)

Fig. 10-60

10.131 Convert the voltage source of the circuit of Fig. 10-60a to a current source and find the current through the capacitor by nodal analysis.

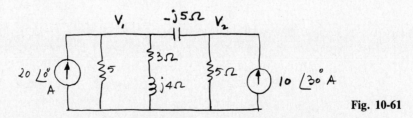

Fig. 10-61

▮ The circuit is shown in Fig. 10-61. The current through the capacitor is $(1/-j5)(V_1 - V_2)$. The node equations may be written as

$$\begin{bmatrix} 0.32 + j0.04 & -j0.2 \\ -j0.2 & 0.2 + j0.2 \end{bmatrix} \begin{bmatrix} V_1 \\ V_2 \end{bmatrix} = \begin{bmatrix} 20 \\ 8.66 + j5 \end{bmatrix}$$

Solving for V_1 and V_2 yields:

$$V_1 = \frac{\begin{vmatrix} 20 & -j0.2 \\ 8.66 + j5 & 0.2 + j0.2 \end{vmatrix}}{\Delta} \qquad V_2 = \frac{\begin{vmatrix} 0.32 + j0.04 & 20 \\ -j0.2 & 8.66 + j5 \end{vmatrix}}{\Delta}$$

where

$$\Delta = \begin{vmatrix} 0.32 + j0.04 & -j0.2 \\ -j0.2 & 0.2 + j0.2 \end{vmatrix} = 0.096 + j0.072 = 0.12 \,\underline{/36.87°}$$

Thus,

$$V_1 = \frac{3.0 + j5.732}{0.12 \,\underline{/36.87°}} = \frac{6.47 \,\underline{/62.37°}}{0.12 \,\underline{/36.87°}} = 48.66 + j23.2 \text{ V}$$

and

$$V_2 = \frac{2.57 + j5.9464}{0.12 \,\underline{/36.87°}} = \frac{6.478 \,\underline{/66.63°}}{0.12 \,\underline{/36.87°}} = 46.86 + j26.8 \text{ V}$$

or

$$V_1 - V_2 = 1.8 - j3.6 = 4.02 \,\underline{/-63.43°} \text{ V}$$

Capacitor current is $(4.02 \,\underline{/-63.43°})/(5 \,\underline{/-90°}) = 0.8 \,\underline{/26.57°}$ A, which agrees with the result of Prob. 10.130.

10.132 Solve for the current I_2 in the network of Fig. 10-62.

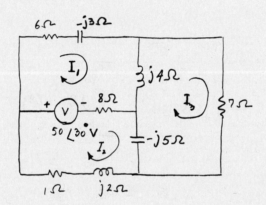

Fig. 10-62

▮ The mesh equations may be written as

$$\begin{bmatrix} 14 + j1 & -8 & -j4 \\ -8 & 9 - j3 & j5 \\ -j4 & j5 & 7 - j1 \end{bmatrix} \begin{bmatrix} I_1 \\ I_2 \\ I_3 \end{bmatrix} = \begin{bmatrix} 50 \,\underline{/30°} \\ -50 \,\underline{/30°} \\ 0 \end{bmatrix}$$

Solving by Cramer's rule,

$$\Delta = \begin{vmatrix} 14 + j1 & -8 & -j4 \\ -8 & 9 - j3 & j5 \\ -j4 & j5 & 7 - j1 \end{vmatrix} = 676 \,\underline{/-28.16°}$$

and

$$I_2 = \frac{\begin{vmatrix} 14 + j1 & 50 \,\underline{/30°} & -j4 \\ -8 & 50 \,\underline{/-30°} & j5 \\ -j4 & 0 & 7 - j1 \end{vmatrix}}{\Delta} = \frac{1950 \,\underline{/-148.53°}}{676 \,\underline{/-28.16°}} = 2.88 \,\underline{/-120.37°} \text{ A}$$

10.133 Determine the complex power drawn by the $(1 + j2)$-Ω impedance of the circuit of Fig. 10-62.

▮ From Prob. 10.132, $I_2 = 2.88$ A. Then,

$$S = VI_2^* = ZI_2 I_2^* = I_2^2 Z = (2.88)^2 (1 + j2) = 8.29 + j16.58 \text{ VA}$$

10.134 Find the current in the 2-Ω resistor of the circuit of Fig. 10-63.

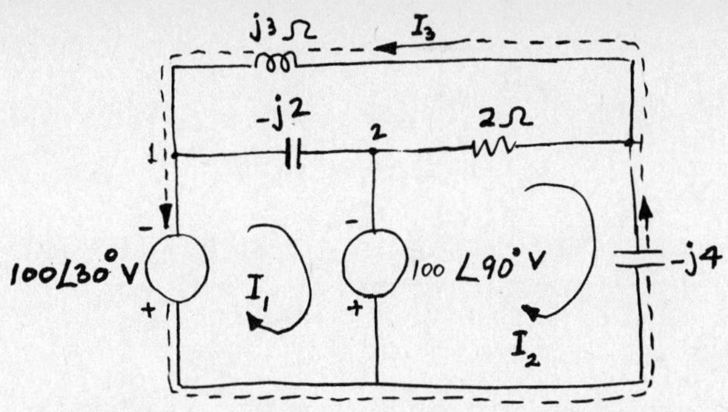

Fig. 10-63

▌ In Fig. 10-63 the loops are chosen such that the 2-Ω resistor lies on only one of them.

$$
\begin{bmatrix} -j2 & 0 & 0 \\ 0 & 2-j4 & j4 \\ 0 & j4 & -j1 \end{bmatrix}
\begin{bmatrix} I_1 \\ I_2 \\ I_3 \end{bmatrix} =
\begin{bmatrix} 100\ \underline{/90^\circ} - 100\ \underline{/30^\circ} \\ -100\ \underline{/90^\circ} \\ 100\ \underline{/30^\circ} \end{bmatrix}
$$

$$
I_2 = \frac{\begin{vmatrix} -j2 & (100\ \underline{/90^\circ} - 100\ \underline{/30^\circ}) & 0 \\ 0 & -100\ \underline{/90^\circ} & j4 \\ 0 & 100\ \underline{/30^\circ} & -j1 \end{vmatrix}}{\begin{vmatrix} -j2 & 0 & 0 \\ 0 & 2-j4 & j4 \\ 0 & j4 & -j1 \end{vmatrix}} = \frac{721.1\ \underline{/-163.9^\circ}}{24.3\ \underline{/-99.5}} = 29.7\ \underline{/-64.4^\circ}\ \text{A}
$$

10.135 Convert the voltage sources of the circuit of Fig. 10-64a to current sources and write a set of nodal equations in matrix form for the new circuit.

▌ The circuit with current sources is shown in Fig. 10-64b for which

$$
I_1 = \frac{50\ \underline{/30^\circ}}{-j2} = \frac{50\ \underline{/30^\circ}}{2\ \underline{/-90^\circ}} = 25\ \underline{/120^\circ}\ \text{A} \qquad
I_2 = \frac{75\ \underline{/20^\circ}}{j4} = \frac{75\ \underline{/20^\circ}}{4\ \underline{/90^\circ}} = 18.75\ \underline{/-70^\circ}\ \text{A}
$$

Choosing node 5 as the reference node for nodes 1 through 4, we have

$$
\frac{V_1}{3} + \frac{V_1 - V_2}{-j2} + \frac{V_1 - V_4}{-j5} = -25\ \underline{/120^\circ} \qquad
\frac{V_2}{2} + \frac{V_2 - V_1}{-j2} + \frac{V_2 - V_3}{j3} = 25\ \underline{/120^\circ}
$$

$$
\frac{V_3}{5} + \frac{V_3 - V_4}{j4} + \frac{V_3 - V_2}{j3} = -18.75\ \underline{/-70^\circ} \qquad
\frac{V_4}{4} + \frac{V_4 - V_3}{j4} + \frac{V_4 - V_1}{-j5} = 18.75\ \underline{/-70^\circ}
$$

which may be written as

$$
\begin{bmatrix}
-\dfrac{1}{j2} + \dfrac{1}{3} - \dfrac{1}{j5} & \dfrac{1}{j2} & 0 & \dfrac{1}{j5} \\[2mm]
\dfrac{1}{j2} & \dfrac{1}{2} - \dfrac{1}{j2} + \dfrac{1}{j3} & -\dfrac{1}{j3} & 0 \\[2mm]
0 & -\dfrac{1}{j3} & \dfrac{1}{5} + \dfrac{1}{j4} + \dfrac{1}{j3} & -\dfrac{1}{j4} \\[2mm]
\dfrac{1}{j5} & 0 & -\dfrac{1}{j4} & \dfrac{1}{4} + \dfrac{1}{j4} - \dfrac{1}{j5}
\end{bmatrix}
\begin{bmatrix} V_1 \\ V_2 \\ V_3 \\ V_4 \end{bmatrix} =
\begin{bmatrix} -25\ \underline{/120^\circ} \\ 25\ \underline{/120^\circ} \\ -18.75\ \underline{/-70^\circ} \\ 18.75\ \underline{/-70^\circ} \end{bmatrix}
$$

10.136 Find the active power supplied by the current source to the circuit of Fig. 10-65.

▌ First we determine the input admittance:

$$
Y_1 = \frac{I}{V_1} = \frac{\begin{vmatrix} \dfrac{1}{10} + \dfrac{1}{j5} + \dfrac{1}{2} & -\dfrac{1}{2} \\[2mm] -\dfrac{1}{2} & \dfrac{1}{2} + \dfrac{1}{3+j4} - \dfrac{1}{j10} \end{vmatrix}}{\dfrac{1}{2} + \dfrac{1}{3+j4} + \dfrac{1}{-j10}} = 0.31\ \underline{/-50^\circ}\ \text{S}
$$

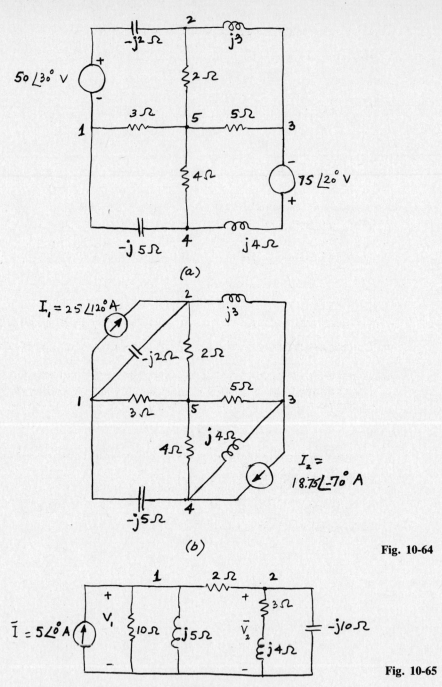

(a)

(b)

Fig. 10-64

Fig. 10-65

Thus, $$V_1 = \frac{I}{Y_i} = \frac{5\underline{/0°}}{0.31\underline{/-50°}} = 16.13\underline{/50°}\,V$$

or Input power $P = VI\cos\phi = (16.13)(5)\cos 50° = 51.84\,W$

10.137 Without solving for V_2 in the circuit of Fig. 10-65, determine the current through the 2-Ω resistor.

▌ Since $V_1 = 16.13\underline{/50°}$ (from Prob. 10.136),

$$I_{10\,\Omega} = \frac{16.13\underline{/50°}}{10\underline{/0°}} = 1.613\underline{/50°} = 1.037 + j1.236\,A \qquad I_{j5\,\Omega} = \frac{16.13\underline{/50°}}{5\underline{/90°}} = 3.226\underline{/-40°} = 2.471 - j2.074\,A$$

and $$I = 5\underline{/0°} = 5 + j0\,A \text{ (given)}$$

Thus, $$I_{2\,\Omega} = I - (I_{10\,\Omega} + I_{j5\,\Omega}) = 1.492 + j0.838 = 1.71\underline{/29.3°}\,A$$

10.138 Evaluate the voltage $\mathbf{V}_2$ in the circuit of Fig. 10-65.

❚ From Prob. 10.136, $\mathbf{V}_1 = 16.13 \underline{/50°}$ V. From Prob. 10.137, $\mathbf{I}_{2\,\Omega} = 1.71 \underline{/29.3°}$ A. Hence,

$$\mathbf{V}_2 = \mathbf{V}_1 - \mathbf{I}_{2\,\Omega}2 = 16.13 \underline{/50°} - (1.71 \underline{/29.3°})2 = 10.37 + j12.36 - 2.984 - j1.676 = 7.386 + j10.684$$
$$= 12.98 \underline{/55.34°} \text{ V}$$

10.139 Calculate the total power dissipated in the resistors of the circuit of Fig. 10-65. Verify that this power is the same as the input power obtained in Prob. 10.136.

❚ From Prob. 10.138, $\mathbf{V}_2 = 12.98 \underline{/55.34°}$ V. Thus,

$$\mathbf{I}_{3\,\Omega} = \frac{12.98 \underline{/55.34°}}{3 + j4} = 2.596 \underline{/2.2°} \text{ A} \qquad \mathbf{I}_{2\,\Omega} = 1.71 \underline{/29.3°} \text{ A (from Prob. 10.137)}$$

$$\mathbf{I}_{10\,\Omega} = 1.613 \underline{/50°} \text{ A (from Prob. 10.137)}$$

$\Sigma P_{\text{dissipated}} = (2.596)^2 3 + (1.71)^2 2 + (1.613)^2 10 = 52 \text{ W}$, which agrees with the power (51.84 W) calculated in Prob. 10.136.

10.140 Determine the reactive power for each element of the circuit of Fig. 10-65. Sum these reactive powers and obtain the complex power by using the result of Prob. 10.139. Verify that the complex power thus obtained is the same as the power obtained from the relationship $\mathbf{S} = \mathbf{VI}^*$.

❚ To find the reactive powers, we determine the currents through the reactive elements.

From Prob. 10.137, $\mathbf{I}_{j5\,\Omega} = 3.226 \underline{/-40°}$ A. From Prob. 10.139, $\mathbf{I}_{j4\,\Omega} = 2.596 \underline{/2.2°}$ A, and

$$\mathbf{I}_{-j10\,\Omega} = \frac{\mathbf{V}_2}{-j10} = \frac{12.98 \underline{/55.34°}}{10 \underline{/-90°}} = 1.298 \underline{/145.34°} \text{ A}$$

$$\Sigma Q_{\text{reactive}} = (3.226)^2 5 + (2.596)^2 4 - (1.298)^2 10 = 62.14 \text{ var}$$

From Prob. 10.139, $P = 52$ W. Thus, $\mathbf{S} = 52 + j62.14$ VA. Now, to verify:

$$\mathbf{S} = \mathbf{V}_1\mathbf{I}^* = (16.13 \underline{/50°})(5 \underline{/0°}) = 51.85 + j61.78 \text{ VA}$$

(The two are approximately equal.)

10.141 Obtain the Thévenin equivalent at the terminals ab of the circuit shown in Fig. 10-66.

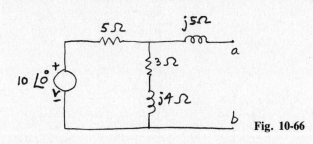

Fig. 10-66

❚ $$\mathbf{Z}_{\text{Th}} = j5 + \frac{5(3 + j4)}{5 + 3 + j4} = 2.5 + j6.25 \,\Omega \qquad \mathbf{V}_{\text{Th}} = \frac{10 \underline{/0°}}{8 + j4}(3 + j4) = 5.59 \underline{/26.56°} \text{ V}$$

10.142 Determine the current through the 1-Ω resistor of the circuit of Fig. 10-67 by Thévenin's theorem.

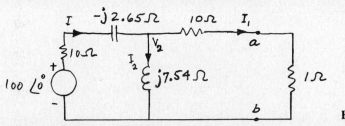

Fig. 10-67

❙ From Fig. 10-67,

$$\mathbf{Z}_{\text{Th}} = 10 + \frac{(10 - j2.65)j7.65}{10 - j2.65 + j7.54} = 14.59 + j5.3 = 15.52 \, \underline{/19.56°} \, \Omega$$

$$\mathbf{V}_{\text{Th}} = \frac{100 \, \underline{/0°}}{10 - j2.65 + j7.54} \, j7.54 = 67.74 \, \underline{/64°} \, \text{V}$$

Thus,

$$\mathbf{I}_{1 \, \Omega} = \frac{\mathbf{V}_{\text{Th}}}{\mathbf{Z}_{\text{Th}} + (1 \, \Omega)} = \frac{67.74 \, \underline{/64°}}{14.59 + j5.3 + 1} = 4.11 \, \underline{/45°} \, \text{A}$$

10.143 Knowing the current in the 1-Ω resistor, without writing mesh equations, find the output complex power from the voltage source of the circuit of Fig. 10-67.

❙ Since $\quad I_{1 \, \Omega} = 4.11 \, \underline{/45°} = 2.905 + j2.905 \, \text{A}$

$$\mathbf{V}_2 = \mathbf{I}_{1 \, \Omega}(10 + 1) = 45.21 \, \underline{/45°} \, \text{V} \qquad \mathbf{I}_2 = \frac{\mathbf{V}_2}{j7.54} = \frac{45.21 \, \underline{/45°}}{7.54 \, \underline{/90°}} = 6 \, \underline{/-45°} = 4.242 - j4.242 \, \text{A}$$

$$\mathbf{I} = \mathbf{I}_1 + \mathbf{I}_2 = (2.905 + j2.905) + (4.242 - j4.242) \, \text{A} = 7.147 - j1.337 = 7.27 \, \underline{/-10.6°} \, \text{A}$$

$$\mathbf{S} = \mathbf{VI}^* = (100 \, \underline{/0°})(7.27 \, \underline{/10.6°}) = 727 \, \underline{/10.6°} = 714.6 + j133.7 \, \text{VA}$$

10.144 By calculating the sum of the powers dissipated in the resistors of the circuit of Fig. 10-67, verify that the result is consistent with that obtained from Re $\mathbf{S}$ in Prob. 10.143.

❙ $$\sum P_{\text{resistors}} = (I)^2 10 + (I_1)^2 (10 + 1) = (7.27)^2 (10) + (4.11)^2 (11) = 714.34 \, \text{W} \approx 714.6 \, \text{W}$$

10.145 Obtain the Norton equivalent (phasor version) of the circuit of Fig. 10-66.

❙ To find $\mathbf{I}_N$ we short-circuit the terminals ab. Thus, by current division,

$$\mathbf{I}_N = \frac{10 \, \underline{/0°}}{5 + [j5(3 + j4)]/(3 + j9)} \frac{3 + j4}{3 + j9} = 0.83 \, \underline{/-41.63°} \, \text{A} \qquad \mathbf{Y}_N = \frac{1}{\mathbf{Z}_{\text{Th}}} = \frac{1}{2.5 + j6.25} = 0.148 \, \underline{/-68.2°} \, \text{S}$$

10.146 Obtain the Thévenin equivalent (phasor version) at the terminals ab of the network shown in Fig. 10-68.

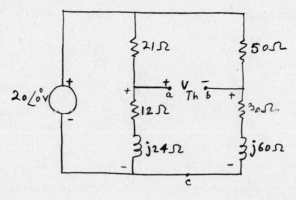

Fig. 10-68

❙ By voltage division,

$$\mathbf{V}_{ac} = \frac{12 + j24}{33 + j24} 20 \, \underline{/0°} \qquad \mathbf{V}_{bc} = \frac{30 + j60}{80 + j60} 20 \, \underline{/0°}$$

$$\mathbf{V}_{\text{Th}} = \mathbf{V}_{ab} = \mathbf{V}_{ac} - \mathbf{V}_{bc} = \left(\frac{12 + j24}{33 + j24} - \frac{30 + j60}{80 + j60} \right) 20 \, \underline{/0°} = 0.326 \, \underline{/169.4°}$$

$$\mathbf{Z}_{\text{Th}} = \frac{21(12 + j24)}{33 + j24} + \frac{50(30 + j60)}{80 + j60} = 47.35 \, \underline{/26.8°} \, \Omega$$

10.147 Replace the network of Fig. 10-69 at the terminals ab by its Thévenin equivalent.

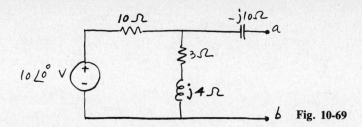

Fig. 10-69

▌ By voltage division,

$$\mathbf{V}_{\text{Th}} = \frac{(3+j4)(10\,/0°)}{13+j4} = 3.68\,/36.03°\text{ V} \qquad \mathbf{Z}_{\text{Th}} = -j10 + \frac{10(3+j4)}{10+3+j4} = 8.38\,/-69.23°\text{ Ω}$$

10.148 Obtain the Norton equivalent of the network of Fig. 10-69 at the terminals. Verify that $\mathbf{I}_N = \mathbf{V}_{\text{Th}}/\mathbf{Z}_{\text{Th}}$.

▌ By current division,

$$\mathbf{I}_N = \frac{10\,/0°}{10+[(-j10)(3+j4)]/(3-j6)} \frac{3+j4}{3-j6} = 0.44\,/105.26°\text{ A}$$

$$\mathbf{Y}_N = \frac{1}{\mathbf{Z}_{\text{Th}}} = \frac{1}{8.38\,/-69.23°} = 0.119\,/69.23°\text{ S}$$

Verification: From Prob. 10.147,

$$\frac{\mathbf{V}_{\text{Th}}}{\mathbf{Z}_{\text{Th}}} = \frac{3.68\,/36.03°}{8.38\,/-69.23°} = 0.44\,/105.26°\text{ A}$$

which agrees with $\mathbf{I}_N$ calculated otherwise.

10.149 Three impedances, $\mathbf{Z}_1$, $\mathbf{Z}_2$, and $\mathbf{Z}_3$, are connected in wye, whereas three other impedances, $\mathbf{Z}_A$, $\mathbf{Z}_B$, and $\mathbf{Z}_C$, are connected in delta, as shown in Fig. 10-70a and b, respectively. Obtain the conditions for their equivalence.

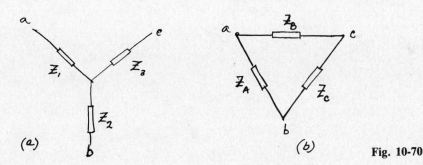

Fig. 10-70

▌ For equivalence we must have the same impedance at a given pair of terminals in both connections. Therefore,

$$\mathbf{Z}_1 + \mathbf{Z}_3 = \frac{\mathbf{Z}_B(\mathbf{Z}_A + \mathbf{Z}_C)}{\mathbf{Z}_A + \mathbf{Z}_B + \mathbf{Z}_C} \qquad \mathbf{Z}_2 + \mathbf{Z}_3 = \frac{\mathbf{Z}_C(\mathbf{Z}_A + \mathbf{Z}_B)}{\mathbf{Z}_A + \mathbf{Z}_B + \mathbf{Z}_C} \qquad \text{and} \qquad \mathbf{Z}_2 + \mathbf{Z}_1 = \frac{\mathbf{Z}_A(\mathbf{Z}_B + \mathbf{Z}_C)}{\mathbf{Z}_A + \mathbf{Z}_B + \mathbf{Z}_C}$$

Solving these yields the wye-to-delta transformation $(\mathbf{N} \equiv \mathbf{Z}_1\mathbf{Z}_2 + \mathbf{Z}_2\mathbf{Z}_3 + \mathbf{Z}_3\mathbf{Z}_1)$:

$$\mathbf{Z}_A = \frac{\mathbf{N}}{\mathbf{Z}_3} \qquad \mathbf{Z}_B = \frac{\mathbf{N}}{\mathbf{Z}_2} \qquad \mathbf{Z}_C = \frac{\mathbf{N}}{\mathbf{Z}_1}$$

Similarly, the delta-to-wye transformation is $(\mathbf{D} \equiv \mathbf{Z}_A + \mathbf{Z}_B + \mathbf{Z}_C)$:

$$\mathbf{Z}_1 = \frac{\mathbf{Z}_A\mathbf{Z}_B}{\mathbf{D}} \qquad \mathbf{Z}_2 = \frac{\mathbf{Z}_A\mathbf{Z}_C}{\mathbf{D}} \qquad \mathbf{Z}_3 = \frac{\mathbf{Z}_B\mathbf{Z}_C}{\mathbf{D}}$$

10.150 If the three impedances in a delta connection are equal to one another, obtain the ratio $\mathbf{Z}_\Delta/\mathbf{Z}_Y$.

▌ Let $\mathbf{Z}_A = \mathbf{Z}_B = \mathbf{Z}_C = \mathbf{Z}_\Delta$. Then $\mathbf{Z}_1 = \mathbf{Z}_2 = \mathbf{Z}_3 = (\mathbf{Z}_\Delta)^2/3\mathbf{Z}_\Delta = \mathbf{Z}_Y$. Thus, $\mathbf{Z}_\Delta/\mathbf{Z}_Y = 3$.

10.151 *Given*: $\mathbf{Z}_1 = 5\,\Omega$, $\mathbf{Z}_2 = j10\,\Omega$, and $\mathbf{Z}_3 = 10\,\Omega$ connected in wye, as shown in Fig. 10-70*a*. Find the equivalent delta impedances.

$$\mathbf{Z}_A = \frac{\mathbf{Z}_1\mathbf{Z}_2 + \mathbf{Z}_2\mathbf{Z}_3 + \mathbf{Z}_3\mathbf{Z}_1}{\mathbf{Z}_3} = \frac{5(j10) + 5(10) + (j10)10}{10} = 5 + j15\,\Omega$$

Similarly, $\qquad\qquad\qquad\qquad \mathbf{Z}_B = 15 - j5\,\Omega \qquad \mathbf{Z}_C = 10 + j30\,\Omega$

10.152 *Given*: $\mathbf{Z}_A = (3 - j2)\,\Omega$, $\mathbf{Z}_B = (2 + j3)\,\Omega$, and $\mathbf{Z}_C = (2 + j16)\,\Omega$ in Fig. 10-70*b*. Find the equivalent wye impedances.

$$\mathbf{Z}_1 = \frac{\mathbf{Z}_A\mathbf{Z}_B}{\mathbf{Z}_A + \mathbf{Z}_B + \mathbf{Z}_C} = \frac{(3 - j2)(2 + j3)}{7 + j17} = 0.5 - j0.5\,\Omega$$

Similarly, $\qquad\qquad\qquad\qquad \mathbf{Z}_2 = 3 - j1\,\Omega \qquad \text{and} \qquad \mathbf{Z}_3 = 1 + j3\,\Omega$

10.153 Find the input impedance of the network of Fig. 10-71.

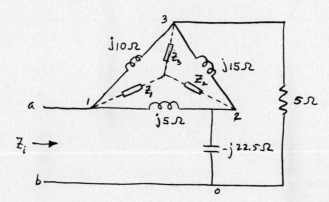

Fig. 10-71

First convert the delta-connected reactances to an equivalent wye as shown by dashed lines in Fig. 10-71. Thus,

$$\mathbf{Z}_1 = \frac{(j5)(j10)}{j30} = j1.67\,\Omega \qquad \mathbf{Z}_2 = \frac{(j5)(j15)}{j30} = j2.5\,\Omega \qquad \mathbf{Z}_3 = \frac{(j10)(j15)}{j30} = j5\,\Omega$$

Notice that $\mathbf{Z}_3$ and the 5-Ω resistor are in series. Similarly, $\mathbf{Z}_2$ and the capacitor are in series, and the two series combinations are in parallel. Therefore,

$$\mathbf{Z}_2 - j22.5 = j2.5 - j22.5 = -j20 \qquad \mathbf{Z}_3 + 5 = 5 + j5$$

Finally, $\qquad\qquad \mathbf{Z}_i = \mathbf{Z}_1 + \frac{(5 + j5)(-j20)}{5 + j5 - j20} = j1.67 + 8 + j4 = 8 + j5.67 = 9.8\,\underline{/35.2°}\,\Omega$

10.154 In the circuit of Fig. 10-71, if $100\,\underline{/0°}$ V is applied at *ab*, what is the input power? Verify that this power is the same as that absorbed by the 5-Ω resistor.

Since $\mathbf{Z}_i = 9.8\,\underline{/35.2°}\,\Omega$, from Prob. 10.153,

$$\mathbf{I} = \frac{\mathbf{V}}{\mathbf{Z}_i} = \frac{100\,\underline{/0°}}{9.8\,\underline{/35.2°}} = 10.2\,\underline{/-35.2°}\,\text{A}$$

Input power $P = VI \cos\,\phi = (100)(10.2) \cos\,(-35.2°) = 833.8\,\text{W}$. Now, $P_{5\,\Omega} = (I_{5\,\Omega})^2 5$. By current division,

$$I_{5\,\Omega} = (10.2\,\underline{/-35.2°})\,\frac{j2.5 - j22.5}{5 + j5 + j2.5 - j22.5} = (10.2\,\underline{/-35.2°})(1.256\,\underline{/18.43°}) = 12.91\,\underline{/-16.77°}\,\text{A}$$

or $\qquad\qquad\qquad\qquad\qquad P_{5\,\Omega} = (12.91)^2 5 = 833.3\,\text{W}$

10.155 Find the input impedance at the terminals *ab* of the network shown in Fig. 10-72.

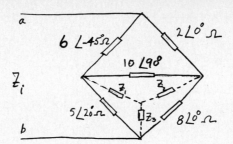

Fig. 10-72

▮ Converting the lower delta-connected impedances into an equivalent wye, as shown by dashed lines, we obtain

$$\mathbf{Z}_1 = \frac{(5\ /20°)(10\ /90°)}{5\ /20° + 10\ /90° + 8\ /0°} = 2.9\ /67.32°\ \Omega \qquad \mathbf{Z}_2 = \frac{(10\ /90°)(8\ /0°)}{17.27\ /42.68°} = 4.63\ /47.32°\ \Omega$$

$$\mathbf{Z}_3 = \frac{(8\ /0°)(5\ /20°)}{17.27\ /42.68°} = 2.32\ /-22.68°\ \Omega$$

$$\mathbf{Z}_1 + 6\ /-45° = (1.12 - j2.67) + (4.24 - j4.24) = 5.59\underline{/-16.34°}\ \Omega$$

$$\mathbf{Z}_2 + 2\ /0° = 5.14 + j3.4 = 6.16\ /33.48°\ \Omega$$

Hence, $$\mathbf{Z}_i = 2.14 - j0.89 + \frac{(5.59\ /-16.34°)(6.16\ /33.48°)}{(5.59\ /-16.34°) + (6.16\ /33.48°)} = 2.14 - j0.89 + 3.2 + j0.41$$

$$= 5.34 - j0.48 = 5.36\ /-5.14°\ \Omega$$

10.156 By converting the wye-connected impedances of the circuit of Fig. 10-73 to an equivalent delta (shown by dashed lines) obtain the input impedance at the terminals *ab*.

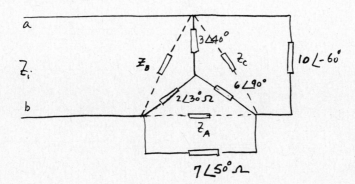

Fig. 10-73

▮ $$\mathbf{Z}_A = \frac{(2\ /30°)(3\ /40°) + (3\ /40°)(6\ /90°) + (6\ /90°)(2\ /30°)}{3\ /40°} = \frac{33.62\ /117.49°}{3\ /40°} = 11.21\ /77.49°\ \Omega$$

$$\mathbf{Z}_B = \frac{33.62\ /117.49°}{6\ /90°} = 5.6\ /27.49°\ \Omega \qquad \mathbf{Z}_C = \frac{33.62\ /117.49°}{2\ /30°} = 16.81\ /87.49°\ \Omega$$

Now the parallel combinations ($\mathbf{Z}_C$ and $10\ /-60°\ \Omega$) and ($\mathbf{Z}_A$ and $7\ /50°\ \Omega$) are in series. Let this impedance be $\mathbf{Z}_{se}$. Then

$$\mathbf{Z}_{se} = \frac{(16.81\ /87.49°)(10\ /-60°)}{(16.81\ /87.49°) + (10\ /-60°)} + \frac{(11.21\ /77.49°)(7\ /50°)}{(11.21\ /77.49°) + (7\ /50°)} = 16.89\ /-27.32° + 4.43\ /60.51°$$

$$= 17.19 - j3.9 = 17.62\ /-12.77°\ \Omega$$

Finally, $$\mathbf{Z}_i = \frac{\mathbf{Z}_B \mathbf{Z}_{se}}{\mathbf{Z}_B + \mathbf{Z}_{se}} = \frac{(5.6\ /27.49°)(17.62\ /-12.77°)}{(5.6\ /27.49°) + (17.62\ /-12.77°)} = 4.45\ /18.1°\ \Omega$$

10.157 Determine the voltage $\mathbf{V}_x$ in the circuit of Fig. 10-74a. Then transpose the current source, as shown in Fig. 10-72b, and determine $\mathbf{V}_x$. Hence verify the reciprocity theorem.

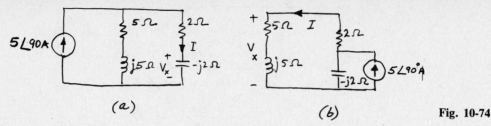

(a)   (b)   **Fig. 10-74**

▌ From Fig. 10-74a,

$$I = \frac{5 + j5}{7 + j3} \, 5 \, \underline{/90°}$$

Thus,

$$V_x = \frac{5 + j5}{7 + j3} \, (5 \, \underline{/90°})(-j2) = 9.53 \, \underline{/21.8°} \, V$$

From Fig. 10-74b,

$$V_x = (5 + j5)I = (5 + j5) \frac{(-j2)5 \, \underline{/90°}}{7 + j3} = 9.53 \, \underline{/21.8°} \, V$$

10.158 Verify the reciprocity theorem by determining I_x in the circuit of Fig. 10-75a. Then insert the voltage source in the branch where I_x flowed and find the current in the branch which formerly contained the source (see Fig. 10-75b)

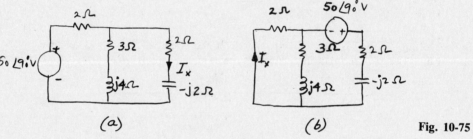

(a)   (b)   **Fig. 10-75**

▌ From Fig. 10-75a,

$$Z_i = 2 + \frac{(3 + j4)(2 - j2)}{5 + j2} = \frac{24 + j6}{5 + j2} \, \Omega$$

Thus,

$$I_x = \frac{50 \, \underline{/90°}}{Z_i} \frac{3 + j4}{5 + j2} = \frac{50 \, \underline{/90°}(3 + j4)}{24 + j6} \, A$$

From Fig. 10-75b,

$$Z_i = (2 - j2) + \frac{2(3 + j4)}{5 + j4} = \frac{24 + j6}{5 + j4} \, \Omega$$

Thus,

$$I_x = \frac{50 \, \underline{/90°}}{Z_i} \frac{3 + j4}{5 + j4} = \frac{50 \, \underline{/90°}(3 + j4)}{24 + j6} \, A$$

10.159 A $(6 + j10)$-Ω coil is supplied by a $(30 \sin 10t)$-V ac source connected in series with a 12-V battery, as shown in Fig. 10-76. The internal impedance of the generator is $(0.1 + j2)$ Ω and that of the battery is negligible. Determine the current i by superposition.

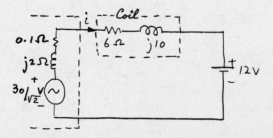

Fig. 10-76

With the battery replaced by its internal impedance,

$$\mathbf{I} = \frac{\mathbf{V}}{\mathbf{Z}_T} = \frac{(30/\sqrt{2})\underline{/0°}}{(0.1 + j2) + (6 + j10)} = 1.58\,\underline{/-63°}\,\text{A}$$

or $\qquad i_{ac} = 1.58\,\sqrt{2}\,\sin(10t - 63°) = 2.23\sin(10t - 63°)\,\text{A}$

With the generator now replaced by its internal impedance,

$$I_{dc} = \frac{12}{R_T} = \frac{12}{6 + 0.1} = 1.97\,\text{A}$$

Hence, $\qquad i = i_{ac} + I_{dc} = 2.23\sin(10t - 63°) + 1.97\,\text{A}$

10.160 Determine the current in the 4-Ω inductor of the circuit of Fig. 10-77 by superposition.

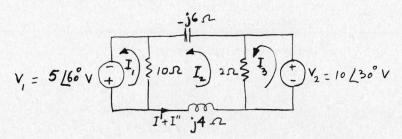

Fig. 10-77

First remove $\mathbf{V}_2$ and replace it by a short circuit. Then, owing to $\mathbf{V}_1$ alone,

$$\mathbf{I}' = \frac{5\,\underline{/60°}}{j4 - j6} = 2.5\,\underline{/150°}\,\text{A}$$

Next, remove $\mathbf{V}_1$ and replace it by a short circuit. Then, owing to $\mathbf{V}_2$ alone,

$$\mathbf{I}'' = \frac{10\,\underline{/30°}}{j4 - j6} = 5\,\underline{/120°}\,\text{A}$$

Thus, $\qquad \mathbf{I}_{j4\,\Omega} = \mathbf{I}' + \mathbf{I}'' = 2.5\,\underline{/150°} + 5\,\underline{/120°} = 7.27\,\underline{/130°}\,\text{A}$

10.161 Repeat Prob. 10.160 by solving mesh equations.

We define the mesh currents as shown in Fig. 10-77. Then

$$\begin{bmatrix} 10 & -10 & 0 \\ -10 & 12 - j2 & -2 \\ 0 & -2 & 2 \end{bmatrix}\begin{bmatrix} \mathbf{I}_1 \\ \mathbf{I}_2 \\ \mathbf{I}_3 \end{bmatrix} = \begin{bmatrix} 5\,\underline{/60°} \\ 0 \\ 10\,\underline{/30°} \end{bmatrix}$$

Solving for $\mathbf{I}_2$ yields

$$\mathbf{I}_2 = \frac{\begin{vmatrix} 10 & 5\,\underline{/60°} & 0 \\ -10 & 0 & -2 \\ 0 & 10\,\underline{/30°} & 2 \end{vmatrix}}{\begin{vmatrix} 10 & -10 & 0 \\ -10 & 12 - j2 & -2 \\ 0 & -2 & 2 \end{vmatrix}} = \frac{290.9\,\underline{/40°}}{40\,\underline{/-90°}} = 7.27\,\underline{/130°}\,\text{A}$$

which agrees with the previous result.

10.162 In the circuit of Fig. 10-78 we have $\quad \mathbf{I}_1 = 20\,\underline{/60°}\,\text{A}, \quad \mathbf{I}_2 = 50\,\underline{/30°}\,\text{A}, \quad \mathbf{I}_3 = 10\,\underline{/210°}\,\text{A}, \quad \mathbf{I}_4 = 70\,\underline{/100°}\,\text{A},$
$\mathbf{Z}_5 = 6\,\underline{/25°}\,\Omega, \quad$ and $\quad \mathbf{Z}_6 = 15\,\underline{/40°}\,\Omega.$ Determine $\quad$ (a) the current through $\mathbf{Z}_3$ and $\quad$ (b) the voltage across $\mathbf{Z}_5$.

(a) $\qquad \mathbf{I}_3 - \mathbf{I}_2 = 10\,\underline{/210°} - 50\,\underline{/30°} = (-8.66 - j5) - (43.3 + j25) = -51.96 - j30 = 60\,\underline{/210°}\,\text{A}$

(b) $\qquad \mathbf{I}_2\mathbf{Z}_5 = (50\,\underline{/30°})(6\,\underline{/25°}) = 300\,\underline{/55°}\,\text{V}$

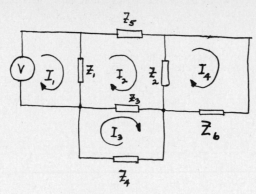

Fig. 10-78

10.163 Calculate the apparent power, true power, and reactive power taken by Z_5 of Prob. 10.162.

$$S_{Z_5} = V_{Z_5} I_2^* = (300\ \underline{/55°})(50\ \underline{/-30°}) = 15{,}000\ \underline{/25°} = 13{,}594 + j6339$$

Thus, $S = 15.000\ \text{kVA}$ $P = 13.594\ \text{kW}$ $Q = 6.339\ \text{kvar}$

10.164 Solve for the currents I_1 and I_2 in the circuit of Fig. 10-79a.

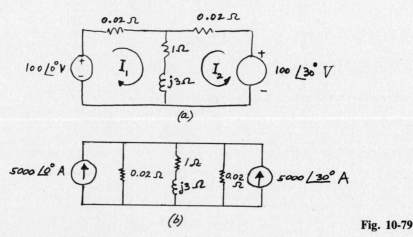

(a)

(b)

Fig. 10-79

The mesh equations may be written as

$$\begin{bmatrix} 1.02 + j3 & 1 + j3 \\ 1 + j3 & 1.02 + j3 \end{bmatrix}\begin{bmatrix} I_1 \\ I_2 \end{bmatrix} = \begin{bmatrix} 100\ \underline{/0°} \\ 100\ \underline{/30°} \end{bmatrix}$$

$$\Delta = \begin{vmatrix} 1.02 + j3 & 1 + j3 \\ 1 + j3 & 1.02 + j3 \end{vmatrix} = 0.127\ \underline{/71.4°}$$

Thus
$$I_1 = \frac{\begin{vmatrix} 100\ \underline{/0°} & 1 + j3 \\ 100\ \underline{/30°} & 1.02 + j3 \end{vmatrix}}{0.127\ \underline{/71.4°}} = \frac{165.7\ \underline{/-3.4°}}{0.127\ \underline{/71.4°}} = 1308.8\ \underline{/-74.8°}\ \text{A}$$

$$I_2 = \frac{\begin{vmatrix} 1.02 + j3 & 100\ \underline{/0°} \\ 1 + j3 & 100\ \underline{/30°} \end{vmatrix}}{0.127\ \underline{/71.4°}} = \frac{162.0\ \underline{/176.2°}}{0.127\ \underline{/71.4°}} = 1279.9\ \underline{/104.8°}\ \text{A}$$

10.165 Determine the true power supplied by each source of the circuit of Fig. 10-79a. Verify that the sum of the powers supplied equals the sum of the powers dissipated in the resistors.

Owing to $100\ \underline{/0°}$-V source we have $P_1 = 100(1308.8)\cos 74.8° = 34.315\ \text{kW}$. Owing to $100\ \underline{/30°}$ source we have $P_2 = 100(1279.9)\cos(104.8 - 30°) = 33.558\ \text{kW}$, or

$$P_1 + P_2 = 67.873\ \text{kW}$$

$$\sum P_{\text{dissipated}} = (1308.8)^2(0.02) + (1279.9)^2(0.02) + |(1308.8\ \underline{/-74.8°} + 1279.9\ \underline{/104.8°})|^2\ 1$$

$$= (34.26 + 32.76 + 0.916) = 67.93\ \text{kW}$$

10.166 In the circuit of Fig. 10-80, determine the complex power supplied by the $40 \underline{/0°}$-V source.

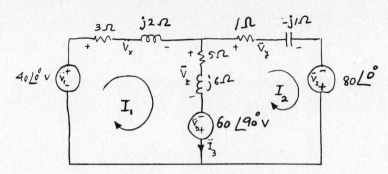

Fig. 10-80

▐ The mesh equations may be written as

$$40 \underline{/0°} + 60 \underline{/90°} = 40 + j60 = (8 + j8)\mathbf{I}_2 + (-5 - j6)\mathbf{I}_2 \qquad 80 \underline{/0°} - 60 \underline{/90°} = 80 - j60 = (-5 - j6)\mathbf{I}_1 + (6 + j5)\mathbf{I}_2$$

$$\Delta = \begin{vmatrix} 8 + j8 & -5 - j6 \\ -5 - j6 & 6 + j5 \end{vmatrix} = 33.84 \underline{/55.84°}$$

Thus

$$\mathbf{I}_1 = \frac{\begin{vmatrix} 40 + j60 & -5 - j6 \\ 80 - j60 & 6 + j5 \end{vmatrix}}{33.84 \underline{/55.84°}} = \frac{1018.63 \underline{/46.6°}}{33.84 \underline{/55.84°}} = 30.1 \underline{/-9.24°} \text{ A}$$

and $\mathbf{S}_1 = \mathbf{VI}_1^* = (40 \underline{/0°})(30.1 \underline{/9.24°}) = 1204 \underline{/9.24°} = 1188.38 + j193.33$ VA

10.167 What is the voltage aross the capacitor of the circuit of Fig. 10-80?

▐ The voltage across the capacitor is $\mathbf{V}_C = (-j1)\mathbf{I}_2$. $\mathbf{I}_2$ is found from the mesh equations of Prob. 10.166:

$$\mathbf{I}_2 = \frac{\begin{vmatrix} 8 + j8 & 40 + j60 \\ -5 - j6 & 80 - j60 \end{vmatrix}}{\Delta} = \frac{1188.1 \underline{/36.1°}}{33.84 \underline{/55.84°}} = 35.1 \underline{/-19.74°} \text{ A}$$

Hence $\mathbf{V}_C = (1 \underline{/-90°})(35.1 \underline{/-19.74°}) = 35.1 \underline{/-109.74°}$ V

10.168 Determine the sum of the complex powers supplied by the three sources of the circuit of Fig. 10-80.

▐ From Probs. 10.166 and 10.167 we have

$$\mathbf{S}_1 = 1188.38 + j193.33 \text{ VA} \qquad \mathbf{I}_1 = 30.1 \underline{/-9.24°} = 29.71 - j4.83 \text{ A} \qquad \mathbf{I}_2 = 35.1 \underline{/-19.74°} = 33.04 - j11.85 \text{ A}$$

Thus

$$\mathbf{I}_3 = \mathbf{I}_1 - \mathbf{I}_2 = -3.33 + j7.02 = 7.77 \underline{/115.44°} \text{ A}$$

$$\mathbf{S}_2 = \mathbf{V}_2 \mathbf{I}_2^* = (80 \underline{/0°})(35.1 \underline{/19.74°}) = 2808 \underline{/19.74°} = 2643 + j948.4 \text{ VA}$$

and

$$\mathbf{S}_3 = \mathbf{V}_3 \mathbf{I}_3^* = (60 \underline{/90°})(7.77 \underline{/-115.44°}) = 466.2 \underline{/-25.44°} = 421 - j200.3 \text{ VA}$$

Hence, $\sum \mathbf{S} = \mathbf{S}_1 + \mathbf{S}_2 + \mathbf{S}_3 = (1188.38 + j193.33) + (2643 + j948.4) + (421 - j200.3) = 4252.38 + j941.43$ VA

10.169 Find the sum of the complex powers drawn by all the passive elements of the circuit of Fig. 10-80. Verify that the result is the same as that obtained in Prob. 10.168.

▐ For the nomenclature of Fig. 10-80 and by using the results of the preceding problems, we obtain

$$\mathbf{V}_x = (3 + j2)\mathbf{I}_1 = (3.6 \underline{/33.7°})(30.1 \underline{/-9.24°}) = 108.36 \underline{/24.46°} \text{ V}$$

Thus, $\mathbf{S}_x = \mathbf{V}_x \mathbf{I}_1^* = (108.36 \underline{/24.46°})(30.1 \underline{/9.24°}) = 3261.64 \underline{/33.7°} = 2713.5 + j1809.7$ VA

Similarly, $\mathbf{V}_y = (1 - j1)\mathbf{I}_2 = (1.414 \underline{/-45°})(35.1 \underline{/-19.74°}) = 49.63 \underline{/-64.74°}$ V

$$\mathbf{S}_y = \mathbf{V}_y \mathbf{I}_2^* = (49.63 \underline{/-64.74°})(35.1 \underline{/19.74°}) = 1742 \underline{/-45°} = 1231.78 - j1231.78 \text{ VA}$$

and $\mathbf{V}_z = (5 + j6)\mathbf{I}_3 = (7.81 \underline{/50.2°})(7.77 \underline{/115.44°}) = 60.69 \underline{/165.63°}$ V

$$\mathbf{S}_z = \mathbf{V}_z \mathbf{I}_3^* = (60.69 \underline{/165.63°})(7.77 \underline{/-115.44°}) = 471.56 \underline{/50.19°} = 301.91 + j362.24 \text{ VA}$$

$$\sum \mathbf{S} = \mathbf{S}_x + \mathbf{S}_y + \mathbf{S}_z = (2713.53 + j1809.7) + (1231.78 - j1231.78) + (301.91 + j362.24) = 4247.22 + j940.16 \text{ VA}$$

which is very close to the result of Prob. 10.169.

10.170 A circuit having a voltage source and a current source is shown in Fig. 10-81*a*. Combine the current source with a 10-Ω inductor, convert it to a voltage source, and draw the resulting circuit.

❚ $\mathbf{V}_2 = (100 \underline{/0°})(j10) = 1000 \underline{/90°}$ V. Hence the circuit of Fig. 10-81*b*.

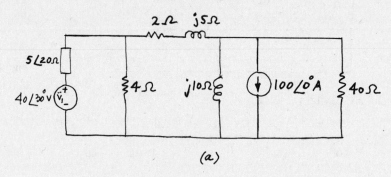

(a)

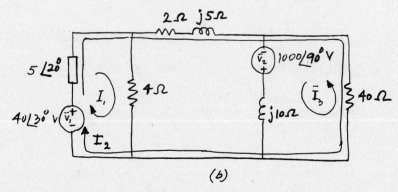

(b)

Fig. 10-81

10.171 In the circuit of Fig. 10-81*b* calculate the current in the 4-Ω resistor.

❚ To determine the desired current we choose the mesh currents $\mathbf{I}_1, \mathbf{I}_2,$ and $\mathbf{I}_3$ as shown, so that we have to solve for $\mathbf{I}_1$ only.

The mesh equations may be written as

$$\begin{bmatrix} 8.7 + j1.71 & 4.7 + j1.71 & 0 \\ 4.7 + j1.71 & 46.7 + j6.71 & -40 \\ 0 & -40 & 40 + j10 \end{bmatrix} \begin{bmatrix} \mathbf{I}_1 \\ \mathbf{I}_2 \\ \mathbf{I}_3 \end{bmatrix} = \begin{bmatrix} 40 \underline{/30°} \\ 40 \underline{/30°} \\ 1000 \underline{/90°} \end{bmatrix}$$

$$\Delta = \begin{vmatrix} 8.7 + j1.71 & 4.7 + j1.71 & 0 \\ 4.7 + j1.71 & 46.7 + j6.71 & -40 \\ 0 & -40 & 40 + j10 \end{vmatrix} = 5908 \underline{/91.1°}$$

Thus, $\mathbf{I}_1 = \mathbf{I}_{4\,\Omega} = \dfrac{\begin{vmatrix} 40 \underline{/30°} & 4.7 + j1.71 & 0 \\ 40 \underline{/30°} & 46.7 + j6.71 & -40 \\ 1000 \underline{/90°} & -40 & 40 + j10 \end{vmatrix}}{\Delta} = \dfrac{175,453 \underline{/-71°}}{5908 \underline{/91.1°}} = 29.7 \underline{/-162.1°}$ A

10.172 Determine $\mathbf{I}_1$ in the circuit of Fig. 10-82.

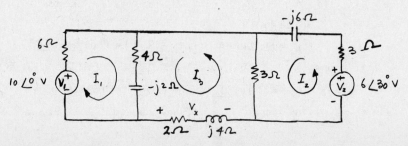

Fig. 10-82

▮ The mesh equations may be written as

$$\begin{bmatrix} 10-j2 & 0 & 4-j2 \\ 0 & 6-j6 & -3 \\ 4-j2 & -3 & 9+j2 \end{bmatrix}\begin{bmatrix} I_1 \\ I_2 \\ I_3 \end{bmatrix} = \begin{bmatrix} 10\,\underline{/0°} \\ 6\,\underline{/30°} \\ 0 \end{bmatrix} = \begin{bmatrix} 10+j0 \\ 5.2+j3 \\ 0 \end{bmatrix}$$

Thus,

$$\Delta = \begin{vmatrix} 10-j2 & 0 & 4-j2 \\ 0 & 6-j6 & -3 \\ 4-j2 & -3 & 9+j2 \end{vmatrix} = 627.7\,\underline{/-35.67°}$$

and

$$I_1 = \frac{\begin{vmatrix} 10+j0 & 0 & 4-j2 \\ 5.2+j3 & 6-j6 & -3 \\ 0 & -3 & 9+j2 \end{vmatrix}}{\Delta} = \frac{648.2\,\underline{/-40.95°}}{627.7\,\underline{/-35.67°}} = 1.03\,\underline{/-5.27°}\ \text{A}$$

10.173 How much complex power is supplied by each voltage source of the circuit of Fig. 10-82?

▮ $$S_1 = V_1 I_1^* = (10\,\underline{/0°})(1.03\,\underline{/5.27°}) = 10.3\,\underline{/5.27°}\ \text{VA}$$

To determine S_2 we must know I_2, which is obtained from Prob. 10.172 as

$$I_2 = \frac{\begin{vmatrix} 10-j2 & 10 & 4-j2 \\ 0 & 5.2+j3 & -3 \\ 4-j2 & 0 & 9+j2 \end{vmatrix}}{\Delta} = \frac{472.6\,\underline{/57.73°}}{627.7\,\underline{/-35.67°}} = 0.75\,\underline{/93.4°}\ \text{A}$$

Thus, $$S_2 = V_2 I_2^* = (6\,\underline{/30°})(0.75\,\underline{/-93.4°}) = 4.5\,\underline{/-63.4°}\ \text{VA}.$$

10.174 Evaluate the voltage V_x in the circuit of Fig. 10-82.

▮ $V_x = (2+j4)I_3$,   where

$$I_3 = \frac{\begin{vmatrix} 10-j2 & 0 & 10 \\ 0 & 6-j6 & 5.2+j3 \\ 4-j2 & -3 & 0 \end{vmatrix}}{\Delta} = \frac{422.3\,\underline{/82.66°}}{627.7\,\underline{/-35.67°}} = 0.67\,\underline{/188.33°}\ \text{A}$$

Hence, $$V_x = (2+j4)(0.67\,\underline{/118.33°}) = (4.472\,\underline{/63.43°})(0.67\,\underline{/118.33°}) = 3\,\underline{/181.76°}\ \text{V}$$

10.175 How much total power is dissipated in the resistors of the circuit of Fig. 10-82?   Verify that the result is the same as the sum of true powers supplied by the two sources.

▮ $$\sum P_{\text{dissipated}} = (|I_1|)^2 6 + |I_1 + I_3|^2 4 + |I_2 - I_3|^2 3 + (|I_2|)^2 3$$

$$= (1.03)^2 6 + |0.363 - j0.192|^2\ 4 + |0.619 + j0.846|^2 3 + (0.75)^2 3 = 12.02\ \text{W}$$

From Prob. 10.173,

$$\sum P_{\text{supplied}} = 4.5\cos 63.4° + 10.3\cos 5.27° = 12.27\ \text{W}$$

The results are close and the error of $(12.27 - 12.02)/12.27 = 2.0$ percent is due to roundoff.

10.176 Determine the current I_1 in the circuit of Fig. 10-83.

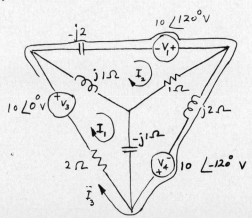

Fig. 10-83

▮ As shown in Fig. 10-83, we choose the mesh currents so that we have to solve for only one current. Thus, the mesh equations become

$$\begin{bmatrix} 2 & -j1 & 2 \\ -j1 & 1-j1 & -j2 \\ 2 & -j2 & 2 \end{bmatrix} \begin{bmatrix} I_1 \\ I_2 \\ I_3 \end{bmatrix} = \begin{bmatrix} 10 \\ 10\,\underline{/120°} \\ 0 \end{bmatrix}$$

$$I_1 = \frac{\begin{vmatrix} 10 & -j1 & 2 \\ 10\,\underline{/120°} & 1-j1 & -j2 \\ 0 & -j2 & 2 \end{vmatrix}}{\begin{vmatrix} 2 & -j1 & 2 \\ -j1 & 1-j1 & -j2 \\ 2 & -j2 & 2 \end{vmatrix}} = \frac{77.96\,\underline{/-7.37°}}{2\,\underline{/0°}} = 38.98\,\underline{/-7.37°}\text{ A}$$

10.177 Calculate the power drawn by the 12-Ω resistor of the circuit of Fig. 10-84.

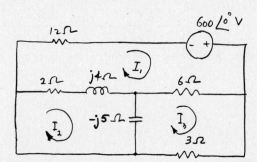

Fig. 10-84

▮ For the meshes shown we have

$$\begin{bmatrix} 20+j4 & -2-j4 & -6 \\ -2-j4 & 2-j1 & j5 \\ -6 & j5 & 9-j5 \end{bmatrix} \begin{bmatrix} I_1 \\ I_2 \\ I_3 \end{bmatrix} = \begin{bmatrix} 60\,\underline{/0°} \\ 0 \\ 0 \end{bmatrix}$$

Solving for I_1 yields:

$$I_1 = \frac{\begin{vmatrix} 60 & -2-j4 & -6 \\ 0 & 2-j1 & j5 \\ 0 & j5 & 9-j5 \end{vmatrix}}{\begin{vmatrix} 20+j4 & -2-j4 & -6 \\ -2-j4 & 2-j1 & j5 \\ -6 & j5 & 9-j5 \end{vmatrix}} = \frac{2549.1\,\underline{/-26.57°}}{617.2\,\underline{/-26.57°}} = 4.13\,\underline{/0°}\text{ A}$$

Hence, $P_{12\,\Omega} = (4.13)^2 12 = 204.7$ W.

10.178 What is the voltage across the 2-Ω resistor of the circuit of Fig. 10-85?

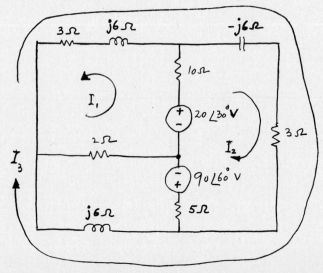

Fig. 10-85

❙ We choose the mesh currents so that we have to solve for $\mathbf{I}_1$ only. Thus, the mesh equations are:

$$\begin{bmatrix} 15+j6 & 10 & -3-j6 \\ 10 & 18-j6 & 3-j6 \\ -3-j6 & 3-j6 & 6+j6 \end{bmatrix}\begin{bmatrix} \mathbf{I}_1 \\ \mathbf{I}_2 \\ \mathbf{I}_3 \end{bmatrix} = \begin{bmatrix} 20\,\underline{/30°} \\ 20\,\underline{/30°} - 90\,\underline{/60°} \\ 0 \end{bmatrix} = \begin{bmatrix} 17.32+j10 \\ -27.68-j67.94 \\ 0 \end{bmatrix}$$

$$\mathbf{I}_1 = \frac{\begin{vmatrix} 17.32+j10 & 10 & -3-j6 \\ -27.68-j67.94 & 18-j6 & 3-j6 \\ 0 & 3-j6 & 6+j6 \end{vmatrix}}{\begin{vmatrix} 15+j6 & 10 & -3-j6 \\ 10 & 18-j6 & 3-j6 \\ -3-j6 & 3-j6 & 6+j6 \end{vmatrix}} = \frac{12{,}395\,\underline{/86.7°}}{1414\,\underline{/60.9°}} = 8.77\,\underline{/25.8°}\ \text{A}$$

and
$$\mathbf{V}_{2\,\Omega} = 2(8.77\,\underline{/25.8°}) = 17.54\,\underline{/25.8°}\ \text{V}.$$

10.179 The detector of the bridge circuit of Fig. 10-86 has 5-Ω resistance. Determine the current through it for the conditions shown.

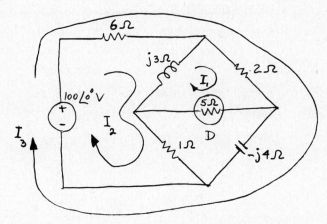

Fig. 10-86

❙ Again, we choose the mesh currents so that we have to solve for $\mathbf{I}_1$ only. The mesh equations become

$$\begin{bmatrix} 7+j3 & -j3 & 2 \\ -j3 & 7+j3 & 6 \\ 2 & 6 & 8-j4 \end{bmatrix}\begin{bmatrix} \mathbf{I}_1 \\ \mathbf{I}_2 \\ \mathbf{I}_3 \end{bmatrix} = \begin{bmatrix} 0 \\ 100 \\ 100 \end{bmatrix}$$

Hence
$$\mathbf{I}_1 = \frac{\begin{vmatrix} 0 & -j3 & 2 \\ 100 & 7+j3 & 6 \\ 100 & 6 & 8-j4 \end{vmatrix}}{\begin{vmatrix} 7+j3 & -j3 & 2 \\ -j3 & 7+j3 & 6 \\ 2 & 6 & 8-j4 \end{vmatrix}} = \frac{1000\,\underline{/0°}}{284.78\,\underline{/-10.5°}} = 3.51\,\underline{/10.5°}\ \text{A}$$

10.180 What is the current in the 3-Ω resistor of the circuit of Fig. 10-87?

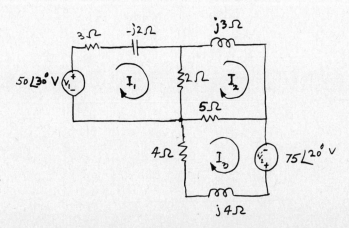

Fig. 10-87

▮ With the mesh currents shown, we have

$$\begin{bmatrix} 5-j2 & -2 & 0 \\ -2 & 7+j3 & -5 \\ 0 & -5 & 9+j4 \end{bmatrix} \begin{bmatrix} I_1 \\ I_2 \\ I_3 \end{bmatrix} = \begin{bmatrix} 43.3+j25 \\ 0 \\ 70.48+j25.65 \end{bmatrix}$$

$$I_1 = \frac{\begin{vmatrix} 43.3+j25 & -2 & 0 \\ 0 & 7+j3 & -5 \\ 70.48+j25.65 & -5 & 9+j4 \end{vmatrix}}{\begin{vmatrix} 5-j2 & -2 & 0 \\ -2 & 7+j3 & -5 \\ 0 & -5 & 9+j4 \end{vmatrix}} = \frac{3319.4\,\underline{/82.1°}}{290.6\,\underline{/45.4°}} = 11.42\,\underline{/36.7°}\ \text{A}$$

10.181 Determine the complex power supplied by each source of the circuit of Fig. 10-87.

▮ Since $I_1 = 11.42\underline{/36.7°}$ A, from Prob. 10.180,

$$S_1 = V_1 I_1^* = (50\underline{/30°})(11.42\ \underline{/-36.7°}) = 571\ \underline{/-6.7°}\ \text{VA}$$

To determine S_2 we must solve the mesh equations of Prob. 10.180 for I_3:

$$I_3 = \frac{\begin{vmatrix} 5-j2 & -2 & 43.3+j25 \\ -2 & 7+j3 & 0 \\ 0 & -5 & 70.48+j25.65 \end{vmatrix}}{290.6\,\underline{/45.4°}} = \frac{3271.5\,\underline{/22.8°}}{290.6\,\underline{/45.4°}} = 11.26\,\underline{/-22.6°}\ \text{A}$$

Hence,

$$S_2 = V_2 I_3^* = (75\ \underline{/20°})(11.26\ \underline{/22.6°}) = 844.5\ \underline{/42.6°}\ \text{VA}$$

10.182 Determine the sum of active and reactive powers absorbed by the passive circuit elements of the circuit of Fig. 10-87. Check the sum against $S_1 + S_2$ of Prob. 10.181.

▮ First, we obtain I_2 from Prob. 10.180:

$$I_2 = \frac{\begin{vmatrix} 5-j2 & 43.3+j25 & 0 \\ -2 & 0 & -5 \\ 0 & 70.48+j25.65 & 9+j4 \end{vmatrix}}{290.6\,\underline{/45.4°}} = \frac{2700\,\underline{/15.8°}}{290.6\,\underline{/45.4°}} = 9.29\,\underline{/-29.6°}\ \text{A}$$

$$I_{2\Omega} = I_2 - I_1 = 9.29\ \underline{/-29.6°} - 11.2\ \underline{/36.7°} = -1.08 - j11.41$$

or $\quad I_{2\Omega} = 11.46$ A $\quad I_{5\Omega} = I_2 - I_3 = (8.07 - j4.6) - (10.39 - j4.32)$ $\quad$ or $\quad I_{5\Omega} = 2.34$ A

Thus, $\quad P = (I_1)^2 3 + (I_{2\Omega})^2 2 + (I_{5\Omega})^2 5 + (I_3)^2 4 = (11.42)^2 3 + (11.46)^2 2 + (2.34)^2 5 + (11.26)^2 4 = 1188.44$ W

$$Q = (I_1)^2(-2) + (I_2)^2 3 + (I_3)^2 4 = (11.42)^2(-2) + (9.29)^2 3 + (11.26)^2 4 = 505.23\ \text{var}$$

and $\quad S = P + jQ = 1188.44 + j505.23$ VA. From Prob. 10.181,

$$S_1 = 571\ \underline{/-6.7°} = 567.1 - j66.62 \qquad S_2 = 844\ \underline{/42.6°} = 621.3 + j571.28$$

Thus, $\quad S_1 + S_2 = 1188.40 + j504.66$ VA, in agreement with S above.

10.183 By nodal analysis, determine the voltage V_2 of the circuit of Fig. 10-88.

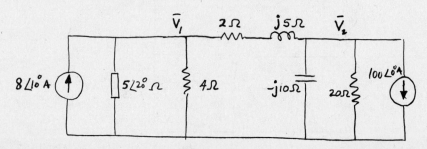

Fig. 10-88

| For node 1:

$$8\,\underline{/10°} = \left(\frac{1}{5\,\underline{/20°}} + \frac{1}{4} + \frac{1}{2+j5}\right)\mathbf{V}_1 - \frac{1}{2+j5}\,\mathbf{V}_2$$

For node 2:

$$-100\,\underline{/0°} = -\frac{1}{2+j5}\,\mathbf{V}_1 + \left(\frac{1}{2+j5} + \frac{1}{-j10} + \frac{1}{20}\right)\mathbf{V}_2$$

or

$$7.88 + j1.39 = (0.5069 - j0.2408)\mathbf{V}_1 - (0.0690 - j0.1724)\mathbf{V}_2$$

$$-100 + j0 = (0.0690 - j0.1724)\mathbf{V}_1 + (0.1190 - j0.0724)\mathbf{V}_2$$

Solving by determinants, we find

$$\mathbf{V}_2 = \frac{54.88\,\underline{/155.42°}}{0.0796\,\underline{/-31.49°}} = 689.5\,\underline{/186.91°}\,\text{V}$$

10.184 By nodal analysis, determine the current through the 1-Ω resistor of the circuit of Fig. 10-79a.

| First, we convert the voltage sources to current sources and obtain the circuit of Fig. 10-79b, from which we obtain:

$$5000\,\underline{/0°} + 5000\,\underline{/30°} = \left(\frac{1}{0.02} + \frac{1}{1+j3} + \frac{1}{0.02}\right)\mathbf{V} \quad\text{or}\quad \mathbf{V} = 96.5\,\underline{/15.17°}\,\text{V}$$

$$\mathbf{I}_{1\,\Omega} = \frac{\mathbf{V}}{1+j3} = \frac{96.5\,\underline{/15.17°}}{3.16\,\underline{/71.57°}} = 30.52\,\underline{/-56.4°}\,\text{A}$$

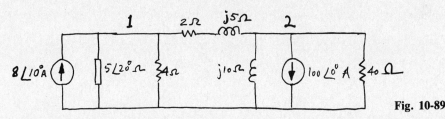

Fig. 10-89

10.185 Convert the voltage source of the circuit of Fig. 10-81a to a current source, write a set of node equations, and determine the voltage across the 4-Ω resistor.

| From the equivalent circuit, Fig. 10-89, we have:

For node 1: $\quad 8\,\underline{/10°} = \left(\dfrac{1}{5\,\underline{/20°}} + \dfrac{1}{4} + \dfrac{1}{2+j5}\right)\mathbf{V}_1 - \dfrac{1}{2+j5}\,\mathbf{V}_2$

For node 2: $\quad -100\,\underline{/0°} = -\dfrac{1}{2+j5}\,\mathbf{V}_1 + \left(\dfrac{1}{2+j5} + \dfrac{1}{j10} + \dfrac{1}{40}\right)\mathbf{V}_2$

or $\quad 7.88 + j1.39 = (0.5069 - j0.2408)\mathbf{V}_1 + (-0.0690 + j0.1724)\mathbf{V}_2$

$$-100 + j0 = (-0.0690 + j0.1724)\mathbf{V}_1 + (0.0940 - j0.2724)\mathbf{V}_2$$

Solving by determinants,

$$\mathbf{V}_1 = \frac{16.285\,\underline{/110.79°}}{0.1371\,\underline{/-87.07°}} = 118.78\,\underline{/197.86°}\,\text{V}$$

10.186 For the circuit of Fig. 10-89, determine the current through the $(2+j5)$-Ω impedance.

| From the node equations of Prob. 10.185,

$$\mathbf{V}_2 = \frac{54.875\,\underline{/155.43°}}{0.1371\,\underline{/-87.07°}} = 400.26\,\underline{/242.50°}\,\text{V}$$

The voltage across the $(2+j5)$-Ω impedance is

$$\mathbf{V} = \mathbf{V}_1 - \mathbf{V}_2 = 118.2\,\underline{/197.86} - 400.26\,\underline{/242.50} = (-113.05 - j36.43) - (-184.83 - j355.02) = 326.85\,\underline{/77.28°}\,\text{V}$$

and $\qquad \mathbf{I} = \dfrac{\mathbf{V}}{\mathbf{Z}} = \dfrac{326.85\,\underline{/77.28°}}{2+j5} = 60.69\,\underline{/9.08°}\,\text{A}$

10.187 Convert the voltage sources of the circuit of Fig. 10-82 to current sources and determine the current through the 4-Ω resistor by nodal analysis.

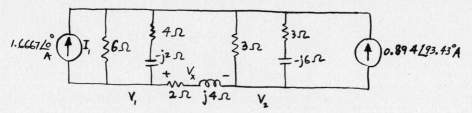

Fig. 10-90

▮ The new circuit is shown in Fig. 10-90 for which the nodal equations become

$$-1.6667\,\underline{/0^\circ} = \left(\frac{1}{6} + \frac{1}{4 - j2} + \frac{1}{2 + j4}\right)\mathbf{V}_1 - \frac{1}{2 + j4}\,\mathbf{V}_2$$

$$-0.894\,\underline{/93.43^\circ} = -\frac{1}{2 + j4}\,\mathbf{V}_1 + \left(\frac{1}{2 + j4} + \frac{1}{3} + \frac{1}{3 - j6}\right)\mathbf{V}_2$$

or

$$-1.6667 + j0 = (0.4667 - j0.1000)\mathbf{V}_1 + (-0.1000 + j0.2000)\mathbf{V}_2$$

$$0.0535 - j0.8924 = (-0.1000 + j0.2000)\mathbf{V}_1 + (0.5000 - j0.0667)\mathbf{V}_2$$

Solving by determinants,

$$\mathbf{V}_1 = \frac{1.0067\,\underline{/179.36^\circ}}{0.260\,\underline{/-9.104^\circ}} = 3.87\,\underline{/188.46^\circ}\text{ V} \qquad \text{whence} \qquad \mathbf{I}_{4\,\Omega} = \frac{\mathbf{V}_1}{4 - j2} = \frac{3.87\,\underline{/188.46^\circ}}{4.47\,\underline{/-26.56^\circ}} = 0.865\,\underline{/215.02^\circ}\text{ A}$$

10.188 Determine the voltage $\mathbf{V}_x$ shown in Fig. 10-90.

▮ From the node equations of Prob. 10.187,

$$\mathbf{V}_2 = \frac{0.2473\,\underline{/-159.05^\circ}}{0.260\,\underline{/-9.104^\circ}} = 0.95\,\underline{/-149.95^\circ}\text{ V}$$

and

$$\mathbf{V}_x = \mathbf{V}_1 - \mathbf{V}_2 = (-3.83 - j0.57) - (-0.82 - j0.48) = 3.01\,\underline{/-178.22^\circ}\text{ V}$$

10.189 How much complex power is supplied by each of the two current sources of the circuit of Fig. 10-90?

$$\mathbf{S}_1 = \mathbf{V}_1\mathbf{I}_1^* = (3.87\,\underline{/188.46^\circ})(1.667\,\underline{/0^\circ}) = 6.45\,\underline{/188.46^\circ}\text{ VA}$$

$$\mathbf{S}_2 = \mathbf{V}_2\mathbf{I}_2^* = (0.95\,\underline{/-149.95^\circ})(0.894\,\underline{/-93.43^\circ}) = 0.8493\,\underline{/-243.38^\circ}\text{ VA}$$

10.190 By using nodal analysis, find the voltage across the 1-Ω resistor of the circuit of Fig. 10-83.

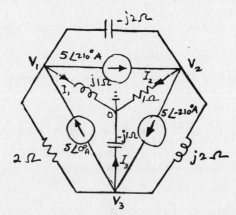

Fig. 10-91

▮ First we convert the voltage sources to current sources to obtain the circuit of Fig. 10-91. The nodal equations may then be written as:

For node 1:

$$5\,\underline{/0^\circ} - 5\,\underline{/210^\circ} = \left(\frac{1}{2} + \frac{1}{j1} + \frac{1}{-j2}\right)\mathbf{V}_1 - \left(\frac{1}{-j2}\right)\mathbf{V}_2 - \frac{1}{2}\,\mathbf{V}_3$$

For node 2:

$$5\,\underline{/210^\circ} - 5\,\underline{/-210^\circ} = -\frac{1}{-j2}\,\mathbf{V}_1 + \left(\frac{1}{-j2} + \frac{1}{1} + \frac{1}{j2}\right)\mathbf{V}_2 - \frac{1}{j2}\,\mathbf{V}_3$$

For node 3: $5 \underline{/-210°} - 5 \underline{/0°} = -\frac{1}{2} \mathbf{V}_1 - \frac{1}{j2} \mathbf{V}_2 + \left(\frac{1}{2} + \frac{1}{-j1} + \frac{1}{j2} \right) \mathbf{V}_3$

$$9.33 + j2.5 = (0.5 - j0.5)\mathbf{V}_1 + (0 - j0.5)\mathbf{V}_2 + (-0.5 + j0)\mathbf{V}_3$$

$$0 - j5 = (0 - j0.5)\mathbf{V}_1 + (1 + j0)\mathbf{V}_2 + (0 + j0.5)\mathbf{V}_3$$

$$-9.33 + j2.5 = (-0.5 + j0)\mathbf{V}_1 + (0 + j0.5)\mathbf{V}_2 + (0.5 + j0.5)\mathbf{V}_3$$

Solving by determinants,

$$\mathbf{V}_2 = \frac{2.5 \underline{/-90°}}{0.25 \underline{/0°}} = 10.0 \underline{/-90°} \text{ V} \qquad \text{and} \qquad \mathbf{I}_{1\,\Omega} = \frac{\mathbf{V}_2}{1 \underline{/0°}} = \mathbf{V}_2 = 10.0 \underline{/-90°} \text{ A}$$

10.191 Determine the currents through the 1-Ω inductive reactance and the 1-Ω capacitive reactance of the wye-connected impedances in Fig. 10-91. Verify that the sum of the currents reaching node 0 is zero.

❙ From the node equations of Prob. 10.190 we obtain

$$\mathbf{V}_1 = \frac{\begin{vmatrix} 9.33 + j2.5 & -j0.5 & -0.5 \\ -j5 & 1 & j0.5 \\ -9.33 + j2.5 & j0.5 & 0.5 + j0.5 \end{vmatrix}}{0.25 \underline{/0°}} = \frac{9.745 \underline{/97.36°}}{0.25 \underline{/0°}} = 39 \underline{/97.36°} \text{ V}$$

$$\mathbf{V}_3 = \frac{\begin{vmatrix} 0.5 - j0.5 & -j0.5 & 9.33 + j2.5 \\ -j0.5 & 1 & -j5 \\ -0.5 & j0.5 & -9.33 + j2.5 \end{vmatrix}}{0.25 \underline{/0°}} = \frac{9.745 \underline{/82.64°}}{0.25 \underline{/0°}} = 39 \underline{/82.64°} \text{ V}$$

The three currents are

$$\mathbf{I}_1 = \frac{\mathbf{V}_1}{1 \underline{/90°}} = \frac{39 \underline{/97.36°}}{1 \underline{/90°}} = 39 \underline{/7.36°} = 38.68 + j5 \qquad \mathbf{I}_2 = 10 \underline{/-90°} = -j10 \text{ A (from Prob. 10.190)}$$

$$\mathbf{I}_3 = \frac{\mathbf{V}_3}{1 \underline{/-90°}} = \frac{39 \underline{/82.64°}}{1 \underline{/-90°}} = 39 \underline{/172.64°} = -38.68 + j5 \text{ A}$$

Thus, $\mathbf{I}_1 + \mathbf{I}_2 + \mathbf{I}_3 = (38.68 + j5) - j10 + (-38.68 + j5) = 0$ (verified)

10.192 Calculate the current through the 6-Ω resistor of the circuit of Fig. 10-84 by nodal analysis.

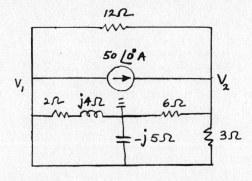

Fig. 10-92

❙ First, we convert the voltage source to a current source to obtain the circuit of Fig. 10-92 for which the node equations are:

Node 1: $-50 \underline{/0°} = \left(\frac{1}{12} + \frac{1}{2 + j4} + \frac{1}{-j5} + \frac{1}{3} \right) \mathbf{V}_1 - \left(\frac{1}{12} + \frac{1}{3} \right) \mathbf{V}_2$

Node 2: $50 \underline{/0°} = -\left(\frac{1}{12} + \frac{1}{3} \right) \mathbf{V}_1 + \left(\frac{1}{12} + \frac{1}{6} + \frac{1}{3} \right) \mathbf{V}_2$

or (currents and admittances being real here)

$$-50 = 0.5166 \mathbf{V}_1 - 0.4166 \mathbf{V}_2 \qquad 50 = -0.4166 \mathbf{V}_1 + 0.5833 \mathbf{V}_2$$

Solving, $\mathbf{V}_2 = 39.13 = 39.13 \underline{/0°} \text{ V}$, and $\mathbf{I} = \mathbf{V}_2/R = 39.13 \underline{/0°}/6 \underline{/0°} = 6.52 \underline{/0°} \text{ A}$.

10.193 The circuit of Fig. 10-93 has a voltage source and a dependent current source. Determine the current through the 25-Ω resistor.

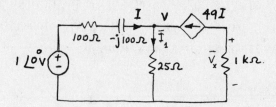

Fig. 10-93

▮ By KCL,

$$\mathbf{I}_1 = 50\mathbf{I} = 50\,\frac{1\,\underline{/0°} - \mathbf{V}}{100 - j100} = \frac{1 - 25\mathbf{I}_1}{2 - j2}$$

Solving, $\mathbf{I}_1 = 1/(27 - j2) = 36.94\,\underline{/4.2°}$ mA.

10.194 What is the voltage across the 1-kΩ resistor of the circuit of Fig. 10-93?

▮ By using the results of Prob. 10.193, we have

$$\mathbf{V}_x = (-49\mathbf{I})(1000) = \left(-\frac{49}{50}\,\mathbf{I}_1\right)(1000) = -980\mathbf{I}_1 = (980\,\underline{/180°})(0.03694\,\underline{/4.2°}) = 36.2\,\underline{/184.2°}\ \text{V}$$

10.195 How much complex power is delivered by the 5 /30°-A current source to the circuit of Fig. 10-94?

▮ $\mathbf{S}_1 = \mathbf{V}_1(5\,\underline{/-30°})$ VA. To solve for $\mathbf{V}_1$, we use nodal analysis:

$$\frac{\mathbf{V}_1}{j2} + \frac{\mathbf{V}_1 - \mathbf{V}_2}{-j1} = 5\,\underline{/30°} \qquad \frac{\mathbf{V}_2}{2} = 2\mathbf{V}_1 + \frac{\mathbf{V}_1 - \mathbf{V}_2}{-j1}$$

which may be written as

$$\frac{j}{2}\,\mathbf{V}_1 - j\mathbf{V}_2 = 5\,\underline{/30°} \qquad -(2 + j1)\mathbf{V}_1 + (\tfrac{1}{2} + j1)\mathbf{V}_2 = 0$$

From these, $\mathbf{V}_1 = 3.07\,\underline{/167.48°}$ V and $\mathbf{S}_1 = (3.07\,\underline{/167.48°})(5\,\underline{/-30°}) = 15.35\,\underline{/137.48°}$ VA.

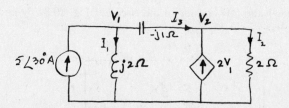

Fig. 10-94

10.196 Determine the complex power supplied by the dependent current source of the circuit of Fig. 10-94.

▮ In this case, $\mathbf{S}_2 = \mathbf{V}_2 2\mathbf{V}_1^*$. From Prob. 10.195, $\mathbf{V}_1^* = 3.07\,\underline{/-167.48°}$ V, and the node equations give

$$\mathbf{V}_2 = \frac{11.82\,\underline{/56.57°}}{1.82\,\underline{/-74.05°}} = 6.15\,\underline{/130.62°}\ \text{V}$$

Hence, $\mathbf{S}_2 = (6.15\,\underline{/130.62°})2(3.07\,\underline{/-167.48°}) = 37.78\,\underline{/-36.86°}$ VA.

10.197 From the results of Probs. 10.195 and 10.196, verify the complex-power balance for the circuit of Fig. 10-94.

▮ Complex power supplied by the two sources:

$$\mathbf{S}_1 + \mathbf{S}_2 = 15.35\,\underline{/137.48°} + 37.78\,\underline{/-36.86°} = 18.91 - j12.29\ \text{VA}$$

Complex power absorbed:

$$P = P_{2\,\Omega} = \frac{(V_2)^2}{2} = \frac{(6.15)^2}{2} = 18.91\ \text{W} \qquad Q = Q_{j2\,\Omega} - Q_{-j1\,\Omega} = \frac{(V_1)^2}{2} - \frac{(|V_1 - V_2|)^2}{1} = \frac{(3.07)^2}{2} - \frac{17}{1} = -12.29\ \text{var}$$

Thus, $\mathbf{S} = P + jQ = 18.91 - j12.29$ VA, which is the same as the total power supplied.

10.198 The circuit of Fig. 10-95 contains an independent voltage source and a dependent voltage source. How much power is delivered by the dependent source?

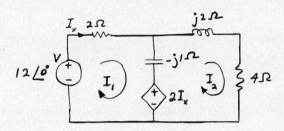

Fig. 10-95

▮ Since $\mathbf{I}_x = \mathbf{I}_1$, the mesh equations become

$$\begin{bmatrix} 4 - j1 & j1 \\ -2 + j1 & 4 + j \end{bmatrix} \begin{bmatrix} \mathbf{I}_1 \\ \mathbf{I}_2 \end{bmatrix} = \begin{bmatrix} 12 \\ 0 \end{bmatrix}$$

Hence, $\mathbf{I}_1 = \dfrac{\begin{vmatrix} 12 & j1 \\ 0 & 4 + j \end{vmatrix}}{\begin{vmatrix} 4 - j1 & j1 \\ -2 + j1 & 4 + j \end{vmatrix}} = \dfrac{48 + j12}{18 + j2} = \dfrac{49.48 \underline{/14°}}{18.11 \underline{/6.34°}} = 2.73 \underline{/7.66°} \text{ A} = \mathbf{I}_x$

$\mathbf{V}_x = 2\mathbf{I}_x = 5.46 \underline{/7.66°} \text{ V}$ $\mathbf{I}_2 - \mathbf{I}_1 = 1.48 \underline{/-32.9°} - 2.73 \underline{/7.66°} = -1.463 - j1.168 = 1.872 \underline{/-141.4°} \text{ A}$

or $\text{Re } \mathbf{S}_x = \text{Re } [\mathbf{V}_x (\mathbf{I}_2 - \mathbf{I}_1)^*] = \text{Re } [(5.46 \underline{/7.66°})(1.872 \underline{/141.4°})] = -8.77 \text{ W (absorbed)}$

10.199 Verify the active-power balance in the circuit of Fig. 10-95.

▮ From the mesh equations of Prob. 10.198, $\mathbf{I}_2 = 1.48 \underline{/-32.9°} \text{ A}$.

$$P_{\text{absorbed}} = 4(I_2)^2 + 2(I_1)^2 + 8.77 \text{ (from Prob. 10.198)} = 4(1.48)^2 + 2(2.73)^2 + 8.77 = 32.44 \text{ W}$$

$$P_{\text{supplied}} = \text{Re } [(12 \underline{/0°})\mathbf{I}_1^*] = \text{Re } [(12 \underline{/0°})(2.73 \underline{/-7.66°})] = 32.46 \text{ W (verified)}$$

10.200 Obtain the Thévenin equivalent of the circuit of Fig. 10-96 at the terminals ab.

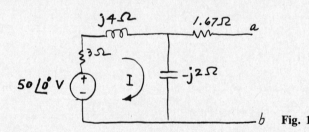

Fig. 10-96

▮ $\mathbf{V}_{\text{Th}} = (-j2)\mathbf{I} = (2 \underline{/-90°}) \dfrac{50 \underline{/0°}}{3 + j4 - j2} = (2 \underline{/-90°})(13.85 \underline{/-33.69°}) = 27.7 \underline{/-123.69°} \text{ V}$

$\mathbf{Z}_{\text{Th}} = 1.67 + \dfrac{(-j2)(3 + j4)}{-j2 + 3 + j4} = 1.67 + 0.92 - j2.61 = 2.59 - j2.61 = 3.68 \underline{/-45.2°} \text{ } \Omega$

10.201 Represent the circuit of Fig. 10-97 at the terminals ab by its Thévenin equivalent.

▮ $\mathbf{Z}_p = \dfrac{j5(-j4)}{j5 - j4} = -j20 \text{ } \Omega$ $\mathbf{I} = \dfrac{100 \underline{/0°}}{10 + j20 - j20 + 10} = 5 \underline{/0°}$

Thus, $\mathbf{V}_{\text{Th}} = \mathbf{I}(10) = 50 \underline{/0°} \text{ V}$ $\mathbf{Z}_{\text{Th}} = 7 + \dfrac{10(10 + j20 - j20)}{10 + 10 + j20 - j20} = 12 \text{ } \Omega$

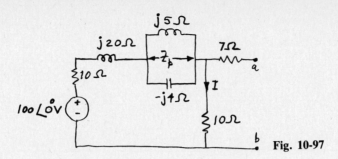

Fig. 10-97

10.202 If the terminals *ab* of the circuit of Fig. 10-97 are short-circuited, determine the current through the capacitor.

▌ By the Thévenin equivalent circuit developed in Prob. 10.201, the current delivered by the generator is

$$I_g = \frac{V_{Th}}{Z_{Th}} = \frac{50 \angle 0°}{12 \angle 0°} = 4.167 \angle 0° \text{ A}$$

This current is divided in *LC*-parallel circuit. Hence, by current division,

$$I_C = I_g \frac{j5}{j5 - j4} = 4.167 \angle 0° \frac{j5}{j1} = 20.83 \angle 0° \text{ A}$$

10.203 Determine the load impedance Z_L across *ab* of the circuit of Fig. 10-97 which will draw maximum power from the source. Also calculate the maximum power.

▌ For maximum power, using the Thévenin equivalent, we must have

$$Z_L = Z_{Th} = 12 \angle 0° \qquad I_L = \frac{V_{Th}}{Z_{Th} + Z_L} = \frac{50}{12 + 12} = 2.08 \text{ A} \qquad \text{and} \qquad P_{max} = (I_L)^2 12 = (2.08)^2 12 = 51.92 \text{ W}$$

10.204 Obtain the Thévenin equivalent at the terminals *ab* of the circuit shown in Fig. 10-98.

▌ $$Y_{parallel} = \frac{1}{3} + \frac{1}{5} + \frac{1}{j4} = 0.589 \angle -25.1° \text{ S} \qquad \text{or} \qquad Z_{parallel} = \frac{1}{0.589 \angle -25.1°} = 1.698 \angle 25.1° \text{ Ω}$$

Thus, $$Z_{Th} = 1.698 \angle 25.1° + (-j3) = 2.75 \angle -56° \text{ Ω}$$

To determine V_{Th} we combine the 3-Ω and 5-Ω resistors in parallel to obtain $R_p = [(5)(3)]/(5+3) = 1.875 \text{ Ω}$. Hence,

$$V_{Th} = 50 \angle 30° \left(\frac{1.875}{1.875 + j4} \right) = 21.22 \angle -34.9° \text{ V}$$

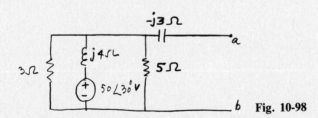

b **Fig. 10-98**

10.205 If a $(6 + j9)$ Ω load is connected at *ab* of the circuit of Fig. 10-98, determine the complex power drawn by the load.

▌ Using the Thévenin equivalent developed in Prob. 10.204, we determine the load current, I_L, as given by

$$I_L = \frac{21.22 \angle -34.9°}{2.75 \angle -56° + (6 + j9)} = 2.1 \angle -76.6° \text{ A} \qquad V_L = I_L(6 + j9) = 22.7 \angle -20.3° \text{ V}$$

Hence, $$S_L = V_L I_L^* = (22.7 \angle -20.3°)(2.1 \angle 76.6°) = 47.67 \angle 56.3° \text{ VA}$$

10.206 Determine by Thévenin's theorem the load that must be connected across the terminals *ab* of the circuit of Fig. 10-99 to draw the maximum power from the source. Also find the maximum power.

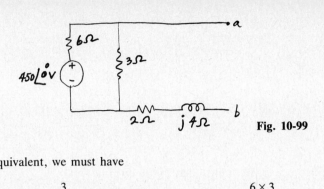

Fig. 10-99

▮ For the Thévenin equivalent, we must have

$$\mathbf{V}_{Th} = 450\ \underline{/0°}\ \frac{3}{3+6} = 150\ \underline{/0°}\ V \qquad \mathbf{Z}_{Th} = (2+j4) + \frac{6\times3}{6+3} = 5.66\ \underline{/45°}\ \Omega$$

For maximum power transfer, $\mathbf{Z}_L = \mathbf{Z}_{Th}^* = 5.66\ \underline{/-45°} = 4 - j4$. Thus

$$\mathbf{I}_L = \frac{\mathbf{V}_{Th}}{\mathbf{Z}_L + \mathbf{Z}_{Th}} = \frac{150\ \underline{/0°}}{8} = 18.75\ \underline{/0°}\ A$$

and maximum power is $P_{max} = (I_L)^2 R_L = (18.75)^2\,(4) = 1406\ W$.

10.207 Obtain the Thévenin equivalent of the circuit to the left of the terminals *ab* in Fig. 10-100. Determine the currents through the 14-Ω resistor and the $j10\,\Omega$ reactor.

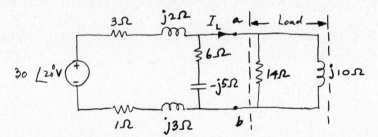

Fig. 10-100

▮ From Fig. 10-100, with *ab* open,

$$\mathbf{V}_{Th} = 30\ \underline{/20°}\ \frac{6-j5}{(1+j3)+(3+j2)+(6-j5)} = 23.43\ \underline{/-19.81°}\ V$$

$$\mathbf{Z}_{Th} = \frac{[(3+j2)+(1+j3)](6-j5)}{3+j2+1+j3+6-j5} = 5\ \underline{/11.55°} = 4.9 + j1\ \Omega$$

$$\mathbf{Z}_L = \frac{14(j10)}{14+j10} = 4.73 + j6.62 = 8.14\ \underline{/54.5°}\ \Omega$$

$$\mathbf{I}_L = \frac{\mathbf{V}_{Th}}{\mathbf{Z}_{Th}+\mathbf{Z}_L} = \frac{23.43\ \underline{/-19.81°}}{(4.9+j1)+(4.73+j6.62)} = 1.91\ \underline{/-58.17°}\ A$$

$$\mathbf{V}_L = \mathbf{I}_L \mathbf{Z}_L = (1.91\ \underline{/-58.17°})(8.14\ \underline{/54.5°}) = 15.55\ \underline{/-3.67°}\ V$$

Hence, $\qquad \mathbf{I}_{14\,\Omega} = \dfrac{15.55\ \underline{/-3.67°}}{14} = 1.11\ \underline{/-3.67°}\ A \qquad \mathbf{I}_{j10\,\Omega} = \dfrac{15.55\ \underline{/-3.69°}}{10\ \underline{/90°}} = 1.55\ \underline{/-93.69°}\ A$

10.208 The Thévenin equivalent values of a section of a circuit are $\mathbf{Z}_{Th} = 5\ \underline{/20°}\ \Omega$ and $\mathbf{V}_{Th} = 100\ \underline{/60°}\ V$. Determine the parameters of the Norton equivalent circuit.

▮ $$\mathbf{I}_N = \frac{\mathbf{V}_{Th}}{\mathbf{Z}_{Th}} = \frac{100\ \underline{/60°}}{5\ \underline{/20°}} = 20\ \underline{/40°}\ A \qquad \mathbf{Y}_N = \frac{1}{\mathbf{Z}_{Th}} = \frac{1}{5\ \underline{/20°}} = 0.2\ \underline{/-20°}\ S$$

10.209 By Thévenin's theorem, determine the current through the 4-Ω resistor of the circuit of Fig. 10-95.

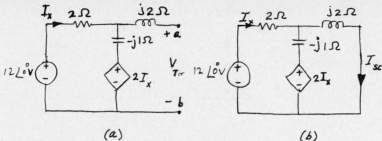

$$(a) \qquad\qquad (b) \qquad\qquad \textbf{Fig. 10-101}$$

▮ First, we determine $\mathbf{V}_{\text{Th}}$ from Fig. 10-101a from which

$$2\mathbf{I}_x + (-j1)\mathbf{I}_x + 2\mathbf{I}_x = 12 \underline{/0°} \qquad \text{or} \qquad \mathbf{I}_x = \frac{12\underline{/0°}}{4-j1} = 2.91 \underline{/14°}\ \text{A}$$

and $\qquad \mathbf{V}_{\text{Th}} = \mathbf{I}_x(-j1) + 2\mathbf{I}_x = \mathbf{I}_x(2-j1) = (2.91\underline{/14°})(2.24\underline{/-26.56°}) = 6.51\underline{/-12.56°}\ \text{V}$

From Fig. 10-101b,

$$-2\mathbf{I}_x + 12\underline{/0°} = (2-j1)\mathbf{I}_x - \mathbf{I}_{sc}(-j1) \qquad 2\mathbf{I}_x = -\mathbf{I}_x(-j1) + \mathbf{I}_{sc}(j2-j1)$$

which may also be written as

$$(4-j1)\mathbf{I}_x + (j1)\mathbf{I}_{sc} = 12\underline{/0°} \qquad (-2+j1)\mathbf{I}_x + (j1)\mathbf{I}_{sc} = 0 \qquad \text{or} \qquad \mathbf{I}_{sc} = 4.24\underline{/-98.13°}$$

and $\qquad \mathbf{Z}_{\text{Th}} = \dfrac{\mathbf{V}_{\text{Th}}}{\mathbf{I}_{sc}} = \dfrac{6.51\underline{/-12.56°}}{4.24\underline{/-98.13°}} = 1.53\underline{/85.57°}\ \Omega = 0.118 + j1.52\ \Omega$

Hence, $\qquad \mathbf{I}_{4\,\Omega} = \dfrac{\mathbf{V}_{\text{Th}}}{\mathbf{Z}_{\text{Th}} + 4} = \dfrac{6.51\underline{/-12.56°}}{4.39\underline{/20.26°}} = 1.48\underline{/-32.82°}\ \text{A}$

10.210 What is the voltage across the 3-Ω resistor of the circuit of Fig. 10-102?

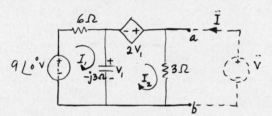

$$\textbf{Fig. 10-102}$$

▮ By mesh analysis we obtain

$$6\mathbf{I}_1 - j3(\mathbf{I}_1 - \mathbf{I}_2) = 9\underline{/0°} \qquad -\mathbf{V}_1 - 2\mathbf{V}_1 + 3\mathbf{I}_2 = 0 \qquad \text{and} \qquad \mathbf{V}_1 = -j3(\mathbf{I}_1 - \mathbf{I}_2)$$

The above equations may be combined to yield

$$(2-j)\mathbf{I}_1 + j\mathbf{I}_2 = 3\underline{/0°} \qquad j3\mathbf{I}_1 + (1-j3)\mathbf{I}_2 = 0 \qquad \text{or} \qquad \mathbf{I}_2 = \frac{-j9}{2-j7}$$

Hence, $\qquad \mathbf{V}_{3\,\Omega} = \mathbf{I}_2 3 = \dfrac{(-j9)3}{2-j7} = 2.78\underline{/-16°}\ \text{V}$

10.211 An impedance $\mathbf{Z}_L = 2.47\underline{/16°}$ is connected at the terminals ab of the circuit of Fig. 10-102. Determine the current through $\mathbf{Z}_L$ by Thévenin's theorem.

▮ Notice that we have already determined $\mathbf{V}_{\text{Th}}$ in Prob. 10.210. Thus, $\mathbf{V}_{\text{Th}} = \mathbf{V}_{3\,\Omega} = 2.78\underline{/-16°}$ V. To determine $\mathbf{Z}_{\text{Th}}$, we short-circuit the $9\underline{/0°}$-V voltage source and apply a voltage $\mathbf{V}$ at ab such that a current $\mathbf{I}$ flows, as shown by dashed lines in Fig. 10-102. Then, $\mathbf{Z}_{\text{Th}} = \mathbf{V}/\mathbf{I}$: Now, from Fig. 10-202 (as modified by the dashed lines), we have

$$\mathbf{V}_1 = -2\mathbf{V}_1 + \mathbf{V} \qquad \text{or} \qquad \mathbf{V}_1 = \frac{\mathbf{V}}{3} \qquad \text{and} \qquad \mathbf{I} = \frac{\mathbf{V}}{3} + \frac{\mathbf{V}_1}{6} + \frac{\mathbf{V}_1}{-j3} = \mathbf{V}\frac{7+j2}{18}$$

Hence $\qquad \mathbf{Z}_{\text{Th}} = \dfrac{\mathbf{V}}{\mathbf{I}} = \dfrac{18}{7+j2} = 2.47\underline{/-16°}\ \Omega = 2.377 - j0.679\ \Omega$

Thus, $\qquad \mathbf{I}_L = \dfrac{\mathbf{V}_{\text{Th}}}{\mathbf{Z}_{\text{Th}} + \mathbf{Z}_L} = \dfrac{2.78\underline{/-16°}}{2.47\underline{/-16°} + 2.47\underline{/16°}} = \dfrac{2.78\underline{/-16°}}{2.377 + 2.377} = 0.584 \underline{/-16°}\ \text{A}$

10.212 Find the Norton equivalent at the terminals *ab* of the circuit of Fig. 10-103*a*.

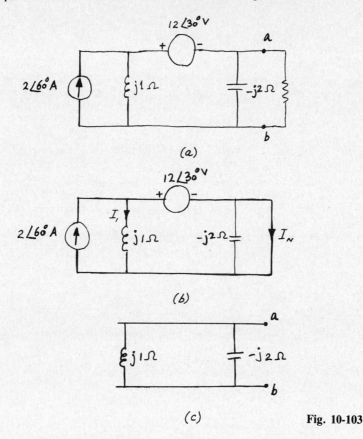

Fig. 10-103

▌ First, we find $\mathbf{I}_N$ from Fig. 10-103*b*. Thus,

$$\mathbf{I}_N = 2\,\underline{/60°} - \mathbf{I}_1 = 2\,\underline{/60°} - \frac{12\,\underline{/30°}}{j1} = 13.1\,\underline{/112.4°}\ \text{A}$$

Next, we obtain $\mathbf{Z}_{Th}$ from Fig. 10-103*c*, from which

$$\mathbf{Z}_{Th} = \frac{(j1)(-j2)}{j1 - j2} = j2\ \Omega \quad \text{or} \quad \mathbf{Y}_N = \frac{1}{\mathbf{Z}_{Th}} = \frac{1}{j2} = 0.5\,\underline{/-90°}\ \text{S}$$

10.213 Calculate the current in the 5-Ω resistor of the circuit of Fig. 10-104*a*.

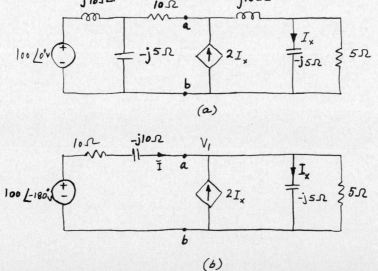

Fig. 10-104

▌ First, we replace the circuit to the left of *ab* by its Thévenin equivalent to obtain the circuit of Fig. 10-104*b*, for which

$$\mathbf{V}_{\text{Th}} = 100 \underline{/0°}\, \frac{-j5}{j10 - j5} = 100 \underline{/-180°}\, \text{V} \qquad \mathbf{Z}_{\text{Th}} = \frac{(-j5)(j10)}{-j5 + j10} + 10 = 10 - j10$$

By using nodal analysis at node *a*, we obtain:

$$\frac{-100 - \mathbf{V}_1}{10 - j10} + 2\mathbf{I}_x = \mathbf{I}_x + \frac{\mathbf{V}_1}{5} \quad \text{and} \quad \mathbf{I}_x = \frac{\mathbf{V}_1}{-j5} \quad \text{or} \quad \frac{-100 - \mathbf{V}_1}{10 - j10} - \frac{2\mathbf{V}_1}{j5} = -\frac{\mathbf{V}_1}{j5} + \frac{\mathbf{V}_1}{5}$$

Solving for $\mathbf{V}_1$ yields $\mathbf{V}_1 = 24.27 \underline{/-104.04°}\, \text{V}$.

Hence,
$$\mathbf{I}_{5\,\Omega} = \frac{\mathbf{V}_1}{5} = \frac{24.27}{5} \underline{/-104.04°} = 4.85 \underline{/-104.04°}\, \text{A}$$

10.214 Determine the true power supplied by each source of the circuit of Fig. 10-104*b*.

▌ To find the power P_v supplied by the voltage source, we must know $\mathbf{I}$. Thus,

$$\mathbf{I} = \frac{-100 - \mathbf{V}_1}{10 - j10} = \frac{-100 - 24.27 \underline{/-104.04°}}{10 - j10} = 6.86 \underline{/210.95°}\, \text{A}$$

$$P_v = \text{Re}\,\mathbf{VI}^* = \text{Re}\,[(100 \underline{/-180°})(6.86 \underline{/-210.95°})] = 588.28\, \text{W}$$

Similarly,
$$P_I = \text{Re}\,\mathbf{V}_1 2\mathbf{I}_x^* = 2\,\text{Re}\left[(24.27 \underline{/-104.04°})\left(\frac{24.27}{5} \underline{/14.04°}\right)\right] = 0\, \text{W}$$

10.215 Verify that in the circuit of Fig. 10-104, the power dissipated in the resistors is entirely supplied by the voltage source.

▌
$$P_{\text{dissipated}} = I^2 10 + \frac{(V_1)^2}{5} = (6.86)^2 10 + \frac{(24.27)^2}{5} = 588.4\, \text{W}$$

which is the true power supplied by the voltage source, the power supplied from the current source being zero (from Prob. 10.214).

10.216 Verify the reactive-power balance for the circuit of Fig. 10-104.

▌ Total reactive power absorbed $= -(10)(I)^2 - (5)(I_x)^2 = -[(6.86)^2 10 + (4.85)^2 5] = -588.2\, \text{var}$

From Prob. 10.214,
$$Q_v = \text{Im}\,(\mathbf{VI}^*) = \text{Im}\,[(100 \underline{/-180°})(6.86 \underline{/210.95°})] = -352.8\, \text{var}$$

and $Q_I = \text{Im}\,\mathbf{V}_1 2\mathbf{I}_x^* = 2\,\text{Im}\left[(24.27 \underline{/-104.04°})\left(\frac{24.27}{j5} \underline{/104.04°}\right)\right] = -235.6\, \text{var} \qquad Q_v + Q_I = -588.4\, \text{var}$

10.217 Solve for the current $\mathbf{I}$ in the circuit of Fig. 10-105*a* by superposition.

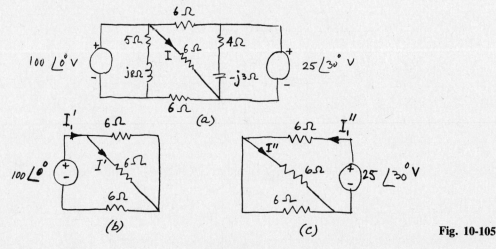

Fig. 10-105

▌ Since the impedances $(5 + j8)\,\Omega$ and $(4 - j3)\,\Omega$ have no effect on $\mathbf{I}$, we use only the circuits of Fig. 10-105*b* and *c*. Hence,

$$I_1' = \frac{100\ \underline{/0°}}{6+3} = 11.11\ \underline{/0°}\ A \quad \text{and} \quad I' = \frac{11.11\ \underline{/0°}}{2} = 5.56\ \underline{/0°}\ A$$

Similarly, $\qquad I_1'' = \dfrac{25\ \underline{/30°}}{6+3} = 2.78\ \underline{/30°}\ A \quad$ and $\quad I'' = \dfrac{2.78\ \underline{/30°}}{2} = 1.39\ \underline{/30°}\ A$

Hence, $\qquad\qquad\qquad\qquad I = I' + I'' = 5.56\ \underline{/0°} + 1.39\ \underline{/30°} = 6.8\ \underline{/5.87°}\ A$

10.218 By superposition, find the current in the capacitor of the circuit of Fig. 10-106a.

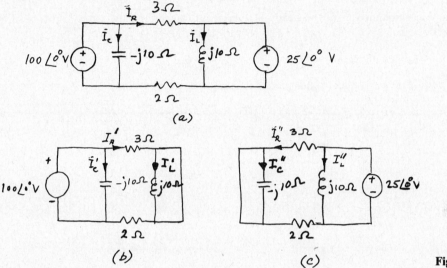

Fig. 10-106

❚ The circuits with one source at a time are shown in Fig. 10-106b and c. From Fig. 10-106b it follows that $I_C' = 100\ \underline{/0°}/-j10 = 10\ \underline{/90°}\ A$. From Fig. 10-106c it is clear that $I_C'' = 0\ A$. Hence, $I_C = I_C' + I_C'' = 10\ \underline{/90°}\ A$.

10.219 Determine the current in the inductor of the circuit of Fig. 10-106a by superposition.

❚ Again, from Fig. 10-106b we have $I_L' = 0\ A$, and from Fig. 10-106c we obtain $I_L'' = 25\ \underline{/0°}/j10 = 2.5\ \underline{/-90°}\ A$. Hence, $I_L = I_L' + I_L'' = 2.5\ \underline{/-90°}\ A$.

10.220 By superposition determine the current in the 3-Ω resistor of the circuit of Fig. 10-106a.

❚ Figure 10-106b yields $I_R' = 100\ \underline{/0°}/(3+2) = 20\ \underline{/0°}\ A$. Figure 10-106c gives $I_R'' = 25\ \underline{/0°}/(3+2) = 5\ \underline{/0°}\ A$. Hence, $I_R = I_R' - I_R'' = 20\ \underline{/0°} - 5\ \underline{/0°} = 15\ \underline{/0°}\ A$.

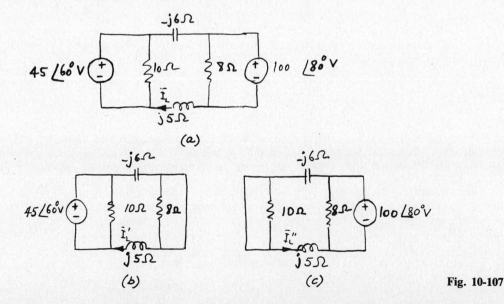

Fig. 10-107

10.221 Find the current in the inductor of the circuit of Fig. 10-107a by superposition.

❚ The component circuits, Fig. 10-107b and c, give

$$I_L' = \frac{45\,\underline{/60°}}{-j6+j5} = 45\,\underline{/150°}\,\text{A} \quad\text{and}\quad I_L'' = \frac{100\,\underline{/80°}}{-j6+j5} = 100\,\underline{/170°}\,\text{A}$$

Thus, $I_L = I_L' - I_L'' = 45\,\underline{/150°} - 100\,\underline{/170°} = 59.73\,\underline{/4.93°}\,\text{A}.$

10.222 Using superposition, determine the steady-state current through the 12-V battery of the circuit of Fig. 10-108a in the time domain.

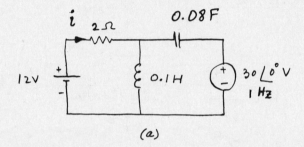

(a)

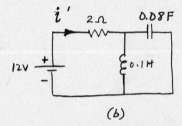

(b)

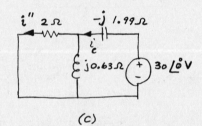

(c) **Fig. 10-108**

❚ For superposition, we use the circuits of Fig. 10-108b and c. In Fig. 10-108b the capacitor acts as an open circuit and the inductor as a short circuit under steady state. Hence, $i' = \frac{12}{2} = 6\,\text{A}.$

In Fig. 10-108c we have shown the ohmic values of inductance and capacitance at 1 Hz, since $X_L = 2\pi(1)(0.1) = 0.63\,\Omega$ and $X_C = \frac{1}{2}\pi\sqrt{(1)(0.08)} = 1.99\,\Omega$. Thus,

$$I_C = \frac{30\,\underline{/0°}}{-j1.99 + [2(j0.63)(2+j0.63)]} = 20.96\,\underline{/82.78°}\,\text{A}$$

and, by current division,

$$I'' = (20.96\,\underline{/82.78°})\,\frac{j0.63}{2+j0.63} = 6.3\,\underline{/155.29°}\,\text{A}$$

which, in the time domain, becomes $i'' = \sqrt{2}(6.3)\sin(2\pi t + 155.29°)$. Thus $i = i' - i'' = 6 - 8.91\sin(6.28t + 155.29°)\,\text{A}.$

10.223 A 6-V dc generator has a 0.5-V 7200-Hz ripple in the generated voltage. A load having a 2-mH inductance and a 100-Ω resistance is connected across the generator terminals. If the internal resistance and inductance of the generator are 3 Ω and 1 mH respectively, determine the steady-state time-domain current.

❚ The generator may be represented by two voltage sources in series and the circuit for the generator and load becomes as shown in Fig. 10-109a. We may then apply superposition by using the circuits of Fig. 10-109b and c. From Fig. 10-109b, under steady state, $i' = 6/103 = 58.3\,\text{mA}.$ From Fig. 10-109c we obtain

$$I'' = \frac{0.5\,\underline{/0°}}{103 + j135.65} = 2.9\,\underline{/-52.8°}\,\text{mA}$$

Hence, $i = 58.3 + \sqrt{2}(2.9)\sin(2\pi 7200t - 52.8°) = 58.3 + 4.1\sin(45,239t - 52.8°)\,\text{mA}.$

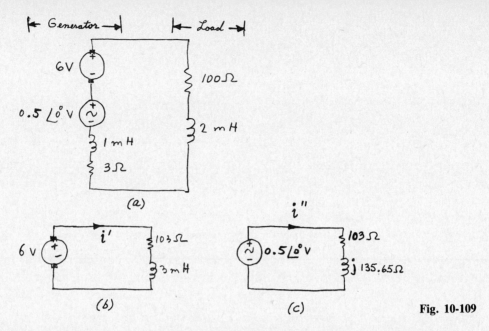

Fig. 10-109

10.224 Using superposition determine the current through the 4-Ω resistor of the circuit of Fig. 10-110a.

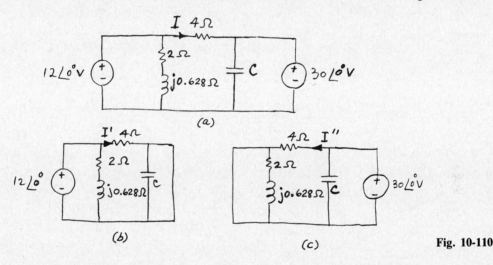

Fig. 10-110

▮ In applying superposition, using Fig. 10-110b and c, it is clear that the inductive and capacitive branches have no effect on I' and I''. Hence, from Fig. 10-110b, $I' = 12 \underline{/0°}/4 = 3 \underline{/0°}$ A, and from Fig. 10-110c, $I'' = 30 \underline{/0°}/4 = 7.5 \underline{/0°}$ A. Thus, $I = I' - I'' = 3 \underline{/0°} - 7.5 \underline{/0°} = 4.5 \underline{/180°}$ A.

10.225 What complex power is absorbed by the inductive branch of the circuit of Fig. 10-110a?

▮
$$I_L = \frac{12 \underline{/0°}}{2 + j0.628} = 5.72 \underline{/-17.44°} \text{ A} \qquad V_L = 12 \underline{/0°} \text{ (given)}$$

Thus, $\qquad S_L = V_L I_L^* = (12 \underline{/0°})(5.72 \underline{/17.44°}) = 68.69 \underline{/17.44°} = 65.53 + j20.59$ VA

10.226 Determine the value of C in the circuit of Fig. 10-110a if C takes 5 var. The operating frequency of the circuit is 60 Hz.

▮
$$Q_C = \frac{(V_C)^2}{X_C} = \frac{(30)^2}{X_C} = 5 \qquad \text{or} \qquad X_C = \frac{1}{\omega C} = \frac{1}{377C} = \frac{(30)^2}{5}$$

Hence, $\quad C = 14.74 \ \mu$F.

10.227 What are the total active and reactive powers supplied by the two sources of the circuit of Fig. 10-110a? The value of C is that found in Prob. 10.226.

From Probs. 10.225 and 10.226, the active power supplied by the sources is the same as the powers absorbed by the resistors:

$$P = (4.5)^2 4 + 65.53 = 146.53 \text{ W} \qquad Q = 20.59 - 5.0 = 15.59 \text{ var}$$

10.228 Determine the ammeter reading in the circuit of Fig. 10-111.

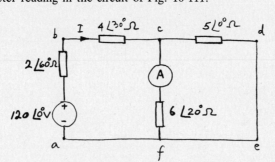

Fig. 10-111

$$\mathbf{Z}_{\text{in}} = 2\,\underline{/60°} + 4\,\underline{/30°} + \frac{(5\,\underline{/0°})(6\,\underline{/20°})}{5\,\underline{/0°} + 6\,\underline{/20°}} = 8.32\,\underline{/30°}\,\Omega \qquad \mathbf{I} = \frac{120\,\underline{/0°}}{8.32\,\underline{/30°}} = 14.42\,\underline{/-30°}\,\text{A}$$

By current division,

$$\mathbf{I}_{cf} = (14.42\,\underline{/-30°}) \frac{5\,\underline{/0°}}{5\,\underline{/0°} + 6\,\underline{/20°}} = 6.67\,\underline{/-41°}\,\text{A}$$

Ammeter reading is 6.67 A.

10.229 Find the transfer impedance between branch *abc* and branch *cf* of the circuit of Fig. 10-111.

$$\mathbf{Z}_{\text{transfer}} = \frac{\mathbf{V}_{\text{in}}}{\mathbf{I}_{\text{out}}} = \frac{\mathbf{V}_{abc}}{\mathbf{I}_{cf}} = \frac{120\,\underline{/0°}}{6.67\,\underline{/-41°}} = 17.9\,\underline{/41°}\,\Omega$$

10.230 Calculate the current in branch *abc* (Fig. 10-111) if the generator is replaced with an ammeter and the ammeter in branch *cf* is replaced with an $80\,\underline{/20°}$-V generator, as shown in Fig. 10-112.

$$\mathbf{Z}_{\text{transfer}} = \frac{\mathbf{V}_{\text{in}}}{\mathbf{I}_{\text{out}}} = \frac{\mathbf{V}_{cf}}{\mathbf{I}_{abc}} = 17.9\,\underline{/41°} \text{ (from Prob. 10.229)} \quad \text{or} \quad \mathbf{I}_{abc} = \frac{80\,\underline{/20°}}{17.9\,\underline{/41}} = 4.47\,\underline{/-21°}\,\text{A}$$

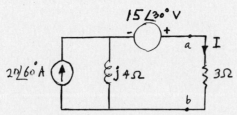

Fig. 10-112

10.231 Solve for **I** in the circuit of Fig. 10-112 by superposition.

Owing to the current source only (by current division),

$$\mathbf{I}' = (20\,\underline{/60°}) \frac{j4}{3 + j4} = 16\,\underline{/96.87°}\,\text{A} = -1.91 + j15.88 \text{ A}$$

Owing to the voltage source only,

$$\mathbf{I}'' = \frac{15\,\underline{/30°}}{3 + j4} = 3\,\underline{/-23.13°}\,\text{A} = 2.76 - j1.18 \text{ A}$$

Thus, $\mathbf{I} = \mathbf{I}' + \mathbf{I}'' = 0.85 + j14.7 = 14.72\,\underline{/86.7°}\,\text{A}$.

10.232 Convert the current source to a voltage source in the circuit of Fig. 10-112 and solve for **I**.

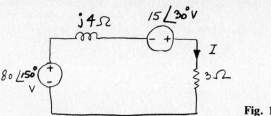

Fig. 10-113

▌ The modified circuit becomes as shown in Fig. 10-113, from which

$$I = \frac{80\ \underline{/150°} + 15\ \underline{/30°}}{3 + j4} = \frac{-56.29 + j47.5}{3 + j4} = 14.73\ \underline{/86.7°}\ A$$

10.233 The circuit of Fig. 10-114a is excited by sources of different frequencies. Determine the current $i(t)$.

▌ We solve the problem by superposition. Thus, from Fig. 10-114b, *in terms of maximum values*,

$$I' = \frac{2\ \underline{/30°}}{4 + j6 + 1 - j1} = 0.28\ \underline{/-15°}\ A \quad \text{or} \quad i'(t) = 0.28 \sin{(3t - 15°)}\ A$$

and from Fig. 10-114c,

$$I'' = -(3\ \underline{/10°})\,\frac{4 + j10}{4 + j10 + 1 - j3/5} = -3.03\ \underline{/16.21°}\ A \quad \text{or} \quad i''(t) = -3.03 \cos{(5t + 16.21°)}\ A$$

Hence, $i(t) = i'(t) + i''(t) = 0.28 \sin{(3t - 15°)} - 3.03 \cos{(5t + 16.21°)}\ A$.

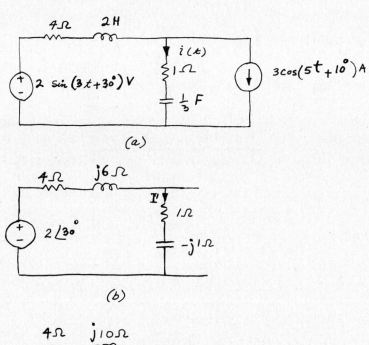

(a)

(b)

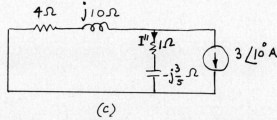

(c)

Fig. 10-114

10.234 Determine the average power delivered to the 1-Ω resistor of the circuit of Fig. 10-114a.

▌ From the results of Prob. 10.233, the power due to the voltage source is $P' = \frac{1}{2}(0.28)^2 1 = 39.3\ \text{mW}$. The power due to the current source is $P'' = \frac{1}{2}(3.03)^2 1 = 4.59\ \text{W}$. Thus, $P_{1\,\Omega} = P' + P'' = 0.0393 + 4.59 = 4.63\ \text{W}$.

10.235 In the circuit of Fig. 10-114a, if the current source has the same frequency ($\omega = 3$ rad/s) as the voltage source, show that we cannot use superposition of average power.

▌ From Prob. 10.233, $\mathbf{I'} = 0.28\ \underline{/-15°}$ A. Owing to the current source,

$$\mathbf{I''} = -3\ \underline{/10°}\ \frac{4+j6}{4+j6+1-j1} = -3.06\ \underline{/21.31°}\ \text{A}$$

Thus, $$i'(t) = 0.28\sin(3t - 15°)\ \text{A}$$

$$i''(t) = -3.06\cos(3t + 21.31°) = -3.06\sin(3t + 90° + 21.31°) = -3.06\sin(3t + 111.31°)\ \text{A}$$

Now we have both currents due to sinusoidal excitations, and

$$\mathbf{I} = \mathbf{I'} + \mathbf{I''}(1\ \underline{/90°}) = 0.28\ \underline{/-15°} - 3.06\ \underline{/111.31°} = 3.23\ \underline{/-64.69°}\ \text{A}$$

Thus, $$P_{1\,\Omega} = \tfrac{1}{2}(3.23)^2 1 = 5.23\ \text{W}$$

By superposition,

$$P = P' + P'' = 0.0393 + \tfrac{1}{2}(3.06)^2 1 = 4.72\ \text{W} \neq P_{1\,\Omega}$$

10.236 If a current through a resistor R is composed by superposition of two parts owing to sinusoidal sources of different frequencies such that $i(t) = I_{1m}\sin\omega_1 t + I_{2m}\sin\omega_2 t$, find its rms value and show that the rms value is *not* the sum of the rms values of the two components.

▌ Average power dissipated in R is

$$P = \tfrac{1}{2}I_{1m}^2 R + \tfrac{1}{2}I_{2m}^2 R = (I_1^2 + I_2^2)R \tag{1}$$

where I_1 and I_2 are rms values of the two components. If I is the rms value of $i(t)$ then

$$P = I^2 R \tag{2}$$

Comparing Eq. (1) with Eq. (2), we observe that $I = \sqrt{I_1^2 + I_2^2}$, which is obviously *not* the sum of rms values.

10.237 Solve for $i(t)$ for the circuit of Fig. 10-115a by applying Thévenin's theorem. Base phasors on maximum values.

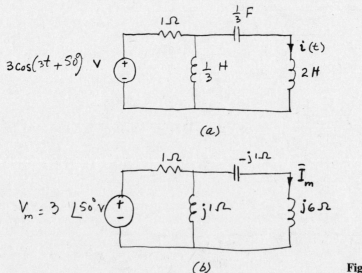

(a)

(b)   Fig. 10-115

▌ At $\omega = 3$ rad/s, for the given voltage, the circuit of Fig. 10-115a is redrawn as that of Fig. 10-115b from which

$$\mathbf{V}_{Th} = \frac{j1}{1+j1}\,3\ \underline{/50°} = 2.12\ \underline{/95°}\ \text{V} \qquad \mathbf{Z}_{Th} = 0.71\ \underline{/45°} - j1 = 0.5 - j0.5\ \Omega$$

$$\mathbf{I} = \frac{2.12\ \underline{/95°}}{0.5 - j0.5 + j6} = 0.38\ \underline{/10.19°}\ \text{A}$$

Thus, $i(t) = 0.38\cos(3t + 10.19°)$ A.

10.238 Determine $i(t)$ in the circuit of Fig. 10-116a. Notice that the sources are of different frequencies.

▌ In terms of maximum values from Fig. 10-116b and 10-116c, we obtain, by superposition,

$$\mathbf{I}' = \frac{3\ \underline{/50°}}{1+j2} = 1.34\ \underline{/-13.43°}\ \text{A} \quad \mathbf{I}'' = \frac{1}{1+j1}\ 2\ \underline{/100°} = 1.41\ \underline{/55°}\ \text{A}$$

$$i' = 1.34\sin(2t - 13.43°)\ \text{A} \qquad i'' = 1.41\cos(t + 55°)\ \text{A}$$

$$i = i' + i'' = 1.34\sin(2t - 13.43°) + 1.41\cos(t + 55°)\ \text{A}$$

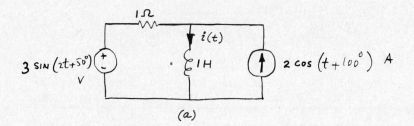

(a)

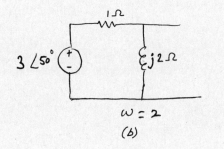 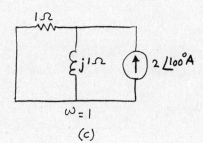

(b)   (c)   **Fig. 10-116**

10.239 Change the frequency of the voltage source in Fig. 10-116a from 2 rad/s to 1 rad/s and repeat Prob. 10.238. Obtain your solution (a) by using superposition, and (b) with both sources acting simultaneously. (c) Would method (b) be valid for the original circuit of Fig. 10-116a?

▌ (a) In terms of maximum values,

$$\mathbf{I}' = \frac{3\ \underline{/50°}}{1+j1} = 2.12\ \underline{/5°}\ \text{A} \qquad i'(t) = 2.12\sin(t + 5°)\ \text{A} \qquad i'' = 1.41\cos(t + 55°)\ \text{A}$$

Thus, $i(t) = 2.12\sin(t + 5°) + 1.41\cos(t + 55°) = 2.12(\sin t \cos 5° + \cos t \sin 5°)$

$$+ 1.41(\cos t \cos 55° - \sin t \sin 55°) = 0.95\sin t + 0.99\cos t\ \text{A}$$

(b) $$\mathbf{I} = \frac{3\ \underline{/50°}}{1+j1} + \frac{1}{1+j1}(-2\ \underline{/10°}) = 2.12\ \underline{/5°} - 1.41\ \underline{/-35°} = 0.95 + j0.99$$

which, together with $\omega = 1$ rad/s, implies that $i(t) = 0.95\sin t + 0.99\cos t$.

(c) No, because the sources are of different frequencies.

10.240 In the circuit of Fig. 10-117 determine the power delivered by the sources. Verify that this is the average power dissipated in the resistor.

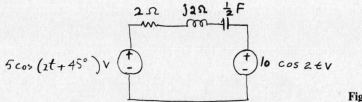

Fig. 10-117

▌ $$\mathbf{I} = \frac{10\ \underline{/0°} - 5\ \underline{/45°}}{2 + j2 - j} = \frac{7.37\ \underline{/-28.68°}}{2.24\ \underline{/26.57°}} = 3.30\ \underline{/-55.24°}\ \text{A}$$

where 3.30 A represents a maximum value.

$$P_{5\,\mathrm{V}} = -\tfrac{1}{2}\,\mathrm{Re}\,[(5\,\underline{/45°})(3.3\,\underline{/55.24°})] = 1.47\,\mathrm{W} \qquad P_{10\,\mathrm{V}} = \tfrac{1}{2}\,\mathrm{Re}\,[(10\,\underline{/0°})(3.3\,\underline{/55.24°})] = 9.41\,\mathrm{W}$$

$$P_{2\,\Omega} = \tfrac{1}{2} \times 2\,|\mathbf{I}|^2 = 10.88\,\mathrm{W}$$

Thus, $1.47\,\mathrm{W} + 9.41\,\mathrm{W} = 10.88\,\mathrm{W}$.

10.241 In the circuit of Fig. 10-118, determine the average power and complex power delivered by the source at $\omega = 1\,\mathrm{rad/s}$.

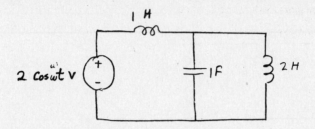

Fig. 10-118

$$\mathbf{I} = \frac{2\,\underline{/0°}}{j1 + [(j2)(-j1)]/(j2 - j1)} = \frac{2\,\underline{/0°}}{-j1} = 2\,\underline{/90°}\,\mathrm{A} \qquad \mathbf{S} = \tfrac{1}{2}[(2\,\underline{/0°})(2\,\underline{/-90°})] = 2\,\underline{/-90°}\,\mathrm{VA} \qquad P = \mathrm{Re}\,\mathbf{S} = 0$$

10.242 (*a*) Determine the power factor of the circuit shown in Fig. 10-119 at $\omega = 2\,\mathrm{rad/s}$. (*b*) Could this circuit be replaced by a resistor in series with an inductor? If so, give the values of these elements.

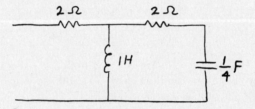

Fig. 10-119

(*a*) $$\mathbf{Z}_{\mathrm{eq}} = 2 + \frac{(j2)(2 - j2)}{2} = 4 + j2 = 4.41\,\underline{/26.57°}\,\Omega$$

Power factor $= \cos 26.57° = 0.89$ lagging.

(*b*) Yes; from (*a*), $\mathbf{Z}_{\mathrm{eq}} = R + j\omega L$, with $R = 4\,\Omega$, $\omega L = 2\,\Omega$ or $L = 1\,\mathrm{H}$.

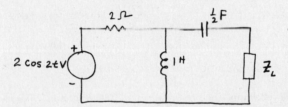

Fig. 10-120

10.243 In the circuit of Fig. 10-120, find $\mathbf{Z}_L$ such that maximum average power is delivered to it. Calculate this average power.

Basing phasors on maximum values, we have

$$\mathbf{V}_{\mathrm{Th}} = \frac{j2}{2 + j2}\,2 = 1.41\,\underline{/45°}\,\mathrm{V} \qquad \mathbf{Z}_{\mathrm{Th}} = -j1 + \frac{j4}{2 + j2} = = 1 + j0\,\Omega$$

$$\mathbf{Z}_L = \mathbf{Z}_{\mathrm{Th}}^* = 1 + j0\,\Omega \qquad \mathbf{I}_L = \frac{1.41\,\underline{/45°}}{2} = 0.705\,\underline{/45°}\,\mathrm{A} \qquad P = \tfrac{1}{2}(I_L)^2 1 = 0.25\,\mathrm{W}$$

10.244 Determine the voltage $v(t)$ in the circuit of Fig. 10-121.

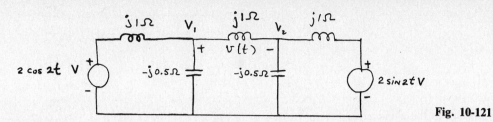

Fig. 10-121

❚ From Fig. 10-121, $\mathbf{V} = \mathbf{V}_1 - \mathbf{V}_2$. To solve by nodal analysis we replace the $2\cos 2t$ voltage source by $j2$ and the $2\sin 2t$ source by 2. Hence, for the two nodes we have

$$-j\mathbf{V}_2 = -2 \qquad -j\mathbf{V}_1 = j2$$

and
$$\mathbf{V} = 2.83\ \underline{/135°} \quad \text{or} \quad v(t) = 2.83 \sin(2t + 135°)\ \text{V}$$

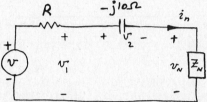

Fig. 10-122

10.245 For the circuit of Fig. 10-122 we have $v_1 = 10 \sin(1000t + 60°)$ V and $v_2 = 5 \sin(1000t - 45°)$ V. Find $\mathbf{Z}_n$.

❚ In the frequency domain we have

$$\mathbf{V}_1 = 10\ \underline{/60°}\ \text{V} \qquad \mathbf{V}_2 = 5\ \underline{/-45°}\ \text{V} \qquad \mathbf{V}_n = \mathbf{V}_1 - \mathbf{V}_2 \qquad \mathbf{I}_n = \frac{\mathbf{V}_2}{-j10} = \frac{5\ \underline{/-45°}}{10\ \underline{/-90°}} = 0.5\ \underline{/45°}\ \text{A}$$

Thus,
$$\mathbf{Z}_n = \frac{\mathbf{V}_n}{\mathbf{I}_n} = \frac{10\ \underline{/60°} - 5\ \underline{/-45°}}{0.5\ \underline{/45°}} = 24.5\ \underline{/38.2°}\ \Omega$$

10.246 The circuit of Fig. 10-123a operates at 1 MHz. Solve for $v(t)$.

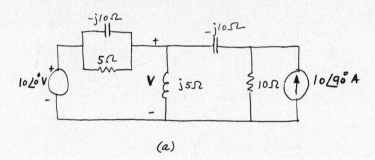

(a)

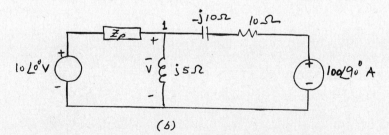

(b)

Fig. 10-123

❚ First, we convert the current source to a voltage source to obtain the circuit of Fig. 10-123b in which $\mathbf{Z}_p = [5(-j10)]/(5 - j10)$. Then writing the node equation for node 1 we have

$$\frac{(10-\mathbf{V})(5-j10)}{-j50} = \frac{\mathbf{V}}{j5} + \frac{\mathbf{V}-j100}{10-j10}$$

Solving for **V** yields

$$\mathbf{V} = \frac{-5+j4.8}{0.25-j0.05} = \frac{6.93\ \underline{/136.2°}}{0.255\ \underline{/-11.3°}} = 27.2\ \underline{/147.5°}\ \text{V} \quad \text{or} \quad v(t) = 27.2\sin(2\pi \times 10^6 t + 147.5°)\ \text{V}$$

10.247 Determine the ammeter reading in the circuit of Fig. 10-124. The meter reads rms values.

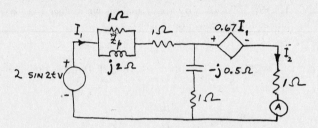

Fig. 10-124

▮ In terms of its maximum value $\mathbf{V} = 2\ \underline{/0°}\ \text{V}$ and $\mathbf{Z}_p = j2/(1+j2) = 0.8 + j0.4\ \Omega$. The mesh equations become

$$(2.8 - j0.1)\mathbf{I}_1 - (1 - j0.5)\mathbf{I}_2 = 2\ \underline{/0°} \qquad -(1 - 0.67 - j0.5)\mathbf{I}_1 + (2 - j0.5)\mathbf{I}_2 = 0$$

Solving for $\mathbf{I}_2$ yields

$$\mathbf{I}_2 = \frac{0.66 - j1.0}{5.47 - j0.935} = 0.216\ \underline{/-46.9°}\ \text{A} \quad \text{or} \quad \text{Ammeter reading} = \frac{0.216}{\sqrt{2}} = 152.8\ \text{mA}$$

10.248 Draw a phasor diagram showing the voltages and currents indicated in Fig. 10-125a.

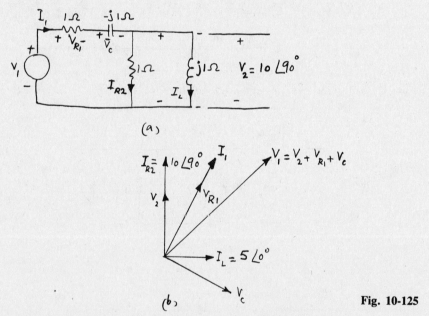

Fig. 10-125

▮
$$\mathbf{V}_2 = 10\ \underline{/90°} \qquad \mathbf{I}_{R2} = 10\ \underline{/90°}\ \text{A} \qquad \mathbf{I}_L = \frac{10\ \underline{/90°}}{2\ \underline{/90°}} = 5\ \underline{/0°}\ \text{A}$$

$$\mathbf{I}_1 = \mathbf{I}_L + \mathbf{I}_{R2} = 5 + j10\ \text{A} \qquad \mathbf{V}_{R1} = 1(5 + j10) = 11.18\ \underline{/63.4°}\ \text{V}$$

$$\mathbf{V}_C = (-j1)(5 + j10) = 10 - j5 = 11.18\ \underline{/-26.6°}\ \text{V}$$

$$\mathbf{V}_1 = \mathbf{V}_2 + \mathbf{V}_{R1} + \mathbf{V}_C = j10 + 5 + j10 + 10 - j5 = 15 + j15 = 21.2\ \underline{/45°}$$

Hence the phasor diagram of Fig. 10-125b.

10.249 Find $v_1(t)$ in the circuit of Fig. 10-126 if $v_2 = \sin 0.5t\ \text{V}$.

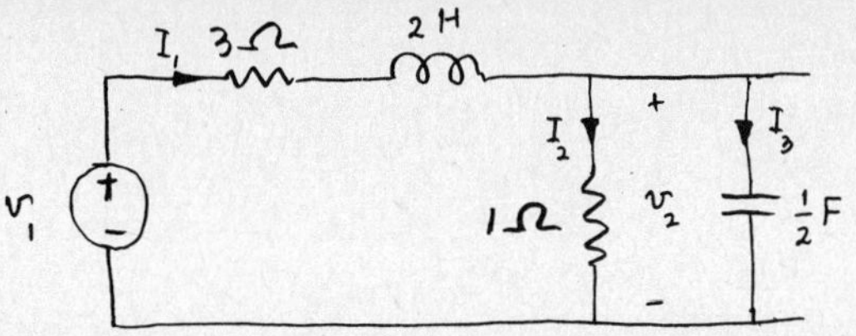

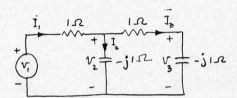

Fig. 10-126

▌ In terms of maximum value, $V_2 = 1 \underline{/0°}$ V. The admittance of the RC-parallel branch is $Y_2 = 1 + j0.5\frac{1}{2} = 1 + j0.25$ S. The series impedance is $Z_1 = 3 + j0.5(2) = 3 + j1.0 \ \Omega$.

$$I_2 = \frac{1 \underline{/0°}}{1} = 1 + j0 \qquad I_3 = (1 \underline{/0°})(j0.25) = 0 + j0.25 \qquad I_1 = I_2 + I_3 = 1 + j0.25$$

$$V_1 = V_2 + I_1(3 + j1.0) = (1 + j0) + (1 + j0.25)(3 + j1.0) = 3.75 + j1.75 = 4.14 \underline{/25°} \text{ V}$$

or $$v_1(t) = 4.14 \sin(0.5t + 25°) \text{ V}$$

10.250 For the circuit of Fig. 10-127, $v_2 = 2 \sin 2t$ V. Find $v_1(t)$ and $v_3(t)$.

Fig. 10-127

▌ In terms of maximum values,

$$V_2 = 2 \underline{/0°} \qquad V_3 = \frac{V_2}{1 - j1}(-j1) = \frac{-j2}{1 - j1} = 1.414 \underline{/-45°} \text{ V} \qquad \text{or} \qquad v_3(t) = 1.414 \sin(2t - 45°) \text{ V}$$

$$I_1 = I_2 + I_3 = \frac{V_2}{-j1} + \frac{V_2}{1 - j1} = \frac{2 \underline{/0°}}{-j} + \frac{2 \underline{/0°}}{1 - j1} = j2 + 1 + j1 = 1 + j3 \text{ A}$$

$$V_1 = 1(1 + j3) + V_2 = 1 + j3 + 2 = 3 + j3 = 4.24 \underline{/45°} \text{ V} \qquad \text{or} \qquad v_1(t) = 4.24 \sin(2t + 45°) \text{ V}$$

10.251 In the bridge circuit of Fig. 10-128, $R_1C_1 = R_2C_2 \equiv T$, $V_1 = V_1 \underline{/0°}$ V, and $V_2 = V_2 \underline{/\phi}$. Show that $V_1 = V_2$.

▌ By current and voltage division we obtain

$$V_2 = V_1 \left(\frac{1/j\omega C_2}{R_2 + 1/j\omega C_2} - \frac{R_1}{R_1 + 1/j\omega C_1} \right) = V_1 \left(\frac{1}{1 + j\omega R_2 C_2} - \frac{j\omega R_1 C_1}{1 + j\omega R_1 C_1} \right)$$

$$= V_1 \left(\frac{1}{1 + j\omega T} - \frac{j\omega T}{1 + j\omega T} \right) = V_1 \frac{1 - j\omega T}{1 + j\omega T}$$

Thus $$V_1(1 - j\omega T) = V_2(1 + j\omega T) \qquad \text{or} \qquad \frac{V_1}{V_2} = \frac{|V_1|}{|V_2|} = \frac{|1 + j\omega T|}{|1 - j\omega T|} = 1$$

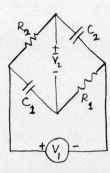

Fig. 10-128

10.252 Determine the phase angle ϕ for the circuit of Prob. 10.251.

▮ From Prob. 10.251 we have $(V_1 \underline{/0^\circ})(1 - j\omega T) = (V_2 \underline{/\phi})(1 + j\omega T)$. Hence, $\tan^{-1}(-\omega T) = \phi + \tan^{-1}(\omega T)$ or $-\tan^{-1}(\omega T) = \phi + \tan^{-1}(\omega T)$. Hence $\phi = -2\tan^{-1}(\omega T)$.

10.253 In the circuit of Fig. 10-129, $R_1 = R_2 = \sqrt{L/C}$. Show that $\mathbf{V}_L = \mathbf{V}_{R2}$ at all frequencies.

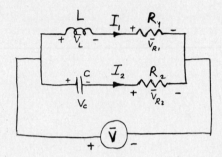

Fig. 10-129

▮
$$\mathbf{V}_L = \frac{\mathbf{V}}{R_1 + j\omega L} j\omega L = \frac{\mathbf{V}}{1 + (1/j\omega\sqrt{LC})}$$

since $R_1 = \sqrt{L/C}$. Similarly,

$$\mathbf{V}_{R2} = \frac{\mathbf{V}}{R_2 + 1/j\omega C} R_2 = \frac{\mathbf{V}}{1 + 1/j\omega\sqrt{LC}}$$

Thus, $\mathbf{V}_L = \mathbf{V}_{R2}$ at all frequencies.

10.254 For the data of Prob. 10.253, determine $\mathbf{I}_1$ and $\mathbf{I}_2$.

▮ From Fig. 10-129 and Prob. 10.253,
$$\mathbf{V}_{R1} = \mathbf{V} - \mathbf{V}_L = \mathbf{V}\left(1 - \frac{1}{1 + 1/j\omega\sqrt{LC}}\right) = \frac{\mathbf{V}}{1 + j\omega\sqrt{LC}}$$

Consequently,
$$\mathbf{I}_1 = \frac{\mathbf{V}_{R1}}{R_1} = \sqrt{\frac{C}{L}}\,\mathbf{V}_{R1} = \frac{\sqrt{C/L}}{1 + j\omega\sqrt{LC}}\,\mathbf{V}$$

Similarly,
$$\mathbf{I}_2 = \frac{\mathbf{V}_{R2}}{R_2} = \sqrt{\frac{C}{L}}\,\mathbf{V}_{R2} = \frac{\sqrt{C/L}}{1 - j(1/\omega\sqrt{LC})}\,\mathbf{V}$$

10.255 Ammeters are connected in the two branches of the circuit of Fig. 10-129. For $R_1 = R_2 = \sqrt{L/C}$, determine the frequency at which the ammeters will show equal readings.

▮ For the ammeters to show equal readings we must have $|\mathbf{I}_1| = |\mathbf{I}_2|$, which holds if and only if

$$|1 + j\omega\sqrt{LC}| = \left|1 - j\frac{1}{\omega\sqrt{LC}}\right| \quad \text{or} \quad \omega\sqrt{LC} = \frac{1}{\omega\sqrt{LC}} \quad \text{or} \quad \omega = \frac{1}{\sqrt{LC}}$$

10.256 Find the total power dissipated in the resistors of the circuit of Fig. 10-130.

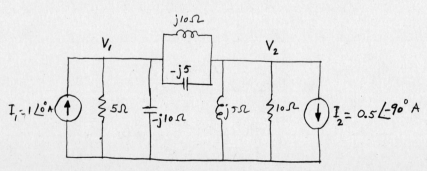

Fig. 10-130

▮ By nodal analysis we obtain:

$$\frac{V_1}{5} + \frac{V_1}{-j10} + \frac{V_1 - V_2}{-j5} + \frac{V_1 - V_2}{j10} = 1 \qquad \frac{V_2 - V_1}{-j5} + \frac{V_2 - V_1}{j10} + \frac{V_2}{j5} + \frac{V_2}{10} = -(-j0.5)$$

which simplify to

$$(0.2 + j0.2)V_1 - j0.1V_2 = 1 \qquad -j0.1V_1 + (0.1 - j0.1)V_2 = j0.5$$

Using Cramer's rule and solving for V_1 and V_2 yields

$$V_1 = \frac{0.1 - j0.1 - 0.05}{0.02 - j0.02 + j0.02 + 0.02 + 0.01} = 1 - j2 = 2.24 \underline{/-63.4°} \text{ V}$$

$$V_2 = \frac{-0.1 + j0.1 + j0.1}{0.02 - j0.02 + j0.02 + 0.02 + 0.01} = -2 + j4 = 4.47 \underline{/116.6°} \text{ V}$$

$$P_{5\,\Omega} = \frac{(V_1)^2}{5} = \frac{(2.24)^2}{5} = 1.0 \text{ W} \qquad P_{10\,\Omega} = \frac{(V_2)^2}{10} = \frac{(4.47)^2}{10} = 2.0 \text{ W} \qquad \text{Total power loss} = 3.0 \text{ W}$$

10.257 How much active power is supplied by each of the two sources of the circuit of Fig. 10-130?

▮
$$P_{1\,A} = VI_1 \cos \phi_1 = (2.24)(1) \cos(-63.4°) = 1 \text{ W}$$
$$P_{0.5\,A} = V_2 I_2 \cos \phi_2 = (4.47)(-0.5) \cos(116.6° + 90°) = 2 \text{ W}$$

10.258 What is the total reactive power absorbed by all the elements of the circuit of Fig. 10-130?

▮ Total reactive power absorbed equals total reactive power supplied. Complex power supplied,

$$S = S_1 + S_2 = V_1 I_1^* + V_2 I_2^* = (2.24 \underline{/-63.4°})(1 \underline{/0°}) + (4.47 \underline{/116.6°})(-0.5 \underline{/90°})$$

$$= (2.24 \underline{/-63.4°}) - (2.235 \underline{/206.6°}) = 3 - j1$$

or, reactive power absorbed = 1 var.

10.259 In the circuit of Fig. 10-131, calculate the complex power supplied by each source.

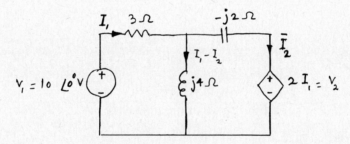

Fig. 10-131

▮ To solve for the power, we must know the currents I_1 and I_2. Writing the mesh equations yields

$$3I_1 + j4(I_1 - I_2) = 10 \underline{/0°} \qquad \text{or} \qquad (3 + j4)I_1 - j4I_2 = 10$$

and

$$j4(I_2 - I_1) - j2I_2 + 2I_1 = 0 \qquad \text{or} \qquad (2 - j4)I_1 + j2I_2 = 0$$

Hence,

$$I_1 = \frac{14 + j8}{13} = 1.24 \underline{/29.7°} \text{ A} \qquad I_2 = \frac{20 + j30}{13} = 2.77 \underline{/56.3°} \text{ A}$$

Thus,

$$S_1 = V_1 I_1^* = (10 \underline{/0°})(1.24 \underline{/-29.7°}) = 12.4 \underline{/-29.7°} = 10.77 - j6.14 \text{ VA}$$

$$S_2 = -V_2 I_2^* = -2I_1 I_2^* = -(2)(1.24 \underline{/29.5})(2.77 \underline{/-56.3°}) = -6.87 \underline{/-26.6°} = -6.14 + j3.08 \text{ VA}$$

10.260 Calculate the total complex power absorbed by the elements of the circuit of Fig. 10-131. Hence verify that the result of Prob. 10.259 is correct.

▮
$$P_{3\,\Omega} = (I_1)^2 3 = (1.24)^2 3 = 4.61 \text{ W}$$

$$Q_{j4\Omega} = j|(I_1 - I_2)|^2 4 = j|(1.24 \underline{/29.7°}) - (2.77 \underline{/56.3°})|^2 4 = j(1.75)^2 4 = j12.27 \text{ var}$$

$$Q_{-j2\,\Omega} = -j(I_2)^2 2 = -j(2.77)^2 2 = -j15.35 \text{ var} \qquad \text{or} \qquad S = 4.61 + j12.27 - j15.35 = 4.61 - j3.08 \text{ VA}$$

From Prob. 10.259, $S = S_1 + S_2 = 10.77 - j6.14 - 6.14 + j3.08 = 4.63 - j3.06$ VA, which agrees with the above result.

10.261 Determine V_1 of the circuit of Fig. 10-130 by using superposition.

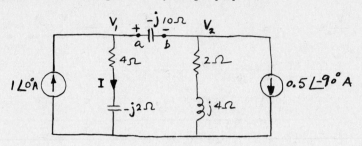

Fig. 10-132

∎ First we reduce the circuit of Fig. 10-130 to that shown in Fig. 10-132 (by combining all the parallel elements), from which:

Due to I_1:

$$V_1' = 1 \underline{/0°} \frac{(4 - j2)(-j10 + 2 + j4)}{4 - j2 - j10 + 2 + j4} = 2 - j2 \text{ V}$$

Due to I_2:

$$V_1'' = (-0.5 \underline{/-90°}) \frac{(2 + j4)(4 - j2)}{4 - j2 - j10 + 2 + j4} = -1 \text{ V}$$

Hence

$$V = V_1' + V_1'' = 2 - j2 - 1 = 1 - j2 \text{ V}$$

10.262 Rework Prob. 10.261 by using Thévenin's theorem.

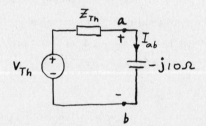

Fig. 10-133

∎ For this problem also we use the reduced circuit of Fig. 10-132 and obtain the Thévenin equivalent at ab, shown in Fig. 10-133. Thus,

$$V_{Th} = (1 \underline{/0°})(4 - j2) + (0.5 \underline{/-90°})(2 + j4) = 6 - j3 \text{ V} \qquad Z_{Th} = 4 - j2 + j4 + 2 = 6 + j2 \text{ Ω}$$

and

$$I_{ab} = \frac{V_{Th}}{Z_{Th} - j10} = \frac{6 - j3}{6 + j2 - j10} = 0.6 + j0.3$$

Hence,

$$I = 1 \underline{/0°} - I_{ab} = 1 - 0.6 - j0.3 = 0.4 - j0.3 \text{ A}$$

Finally,

$$V_1 = I(4 - j2) = (0.4 - j0.3)(4 - j2) = 1 - j2 \text{ V}$$

10.263 Draw a phasor diagram for the currents shown in the circuit of Fig. 10-134a.

∎ The phasor diagram is shown in Fig. 10-134b.

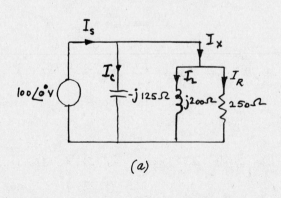

(a)

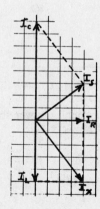

(b) 　　　Fig. 10-134

10.264 If $\mathbf{I}_3 = 2 \underline{/0°}$ A in the circuit of Fig. 10-135a, find all other currents and voltages and draw a phasor diagram.

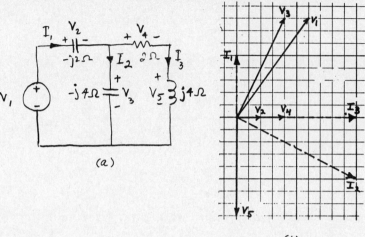

(a)

(b)   Fig. 10-135

I $\mathbf{I}_1 = j1$ A $\quad \mathbf{I}_2 = -2 + j1 \quad \mathbf{I}_3 = 2$ A

$\mathbf{V}_1 = 6 + j8$ V $\quad \mathbf{V}_2 = 2$ V $\quad \mathbf{V}_3 = 4 + j8$ V $\quad \mathbf{V}_4 = 4$ V $\quad \mathbf{V}_5 = j8$ V

The phasor diagram is shown in Fig. 10-135b.

10.265 In Fig. 10-136a $\mathbf{V} = 1 \underline{/0°}$ V. Draw a phasor diagram showing all currents.

I The phasor diagram is shown in Fig. 10-136b.

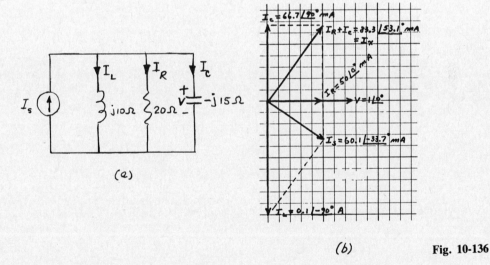

(a)

(b)   Fig. 10-136

10.266 Two impedances $\mathbf{Z}_1 = 9.8 \underline{/-78°}$ Ω and $\mathbf{Z}_2 = 18.5 \underline{/21.8°}$ Ω are connected in parallel and the combination in series with an impedance $\mathbf{Z}_3 = 5 \underline{/53.1°}$ Ω. If this circuit is connected across a 100-V source, how much true power will be supplied by the source?

I $\quad \mathbf{Y}_p = \mathbf{Y}_1 + \mathbf{Y}_2 = \dfrac{1}{9.8 \underline{/-78°}} + \dfrac{1}{18.5 \underline{/21.8°}} = 0.107 \underline{/48.14°}$ S $\quad$ or $\quad \mathbf{Z}_p = \dfrac{1}{\mathbf{Y}_p} = 6.236 - j6.961$ Ω

$$\mathbf{Z}_{in} = 5 \underline{/53.1°} + \mathbf{Z}_p = (3 + j4) + (6.236 - j6.961) = 9.7 \underline{/-17.78°} \text{ Ω}$$

$$\mathbf{I} = \frac{100 \underline{/0°}}{9.7 \underline{/-17.78°}} = 10.3 \underline{/17.78°} \text{ A} \qquad P = VI \cos \theta = (100)(10.3)(\cos 17.78°) = 980 \text{ W}$$

10.267 The circuit of Prob. 10.266 operates at 60 Hz. Determine the value of inductance which must be connected in series with the circuit so that the power factor becomes unity.

▌ From Prob. 10.266, $\mathbf{Z}_{in} = 9.236 - j2.961$. With the inductor in series we have $\mathbf{Z}'_{in} = 9.236 - j2.961 + jX_L$. For the unity power factor, $X_L = \omega L = 2.961$ or $L = 2.961/2\pi60 = 7.85$ mH.

10.268 Find the current $\mathbf{I}_1$ through the $6\ \underline{/40°}$-Ω impedance of the circuit of Fig. 10-137.

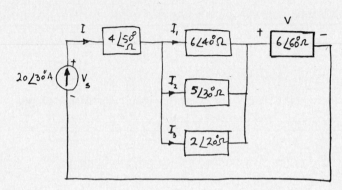

Fig. 10-137

▌ For the parallel branch we have

$$\mathbf{Y}_p = \frac{1}{6\ \underline{/40°}} + \frac{1}{5\ \underline{/30°}} + \frac{1}{2\ \underline{/20°}} = 0.8585\ \underline{/-26.14°}\ \text{S}$$

By current division, the required current is

$$\mathbf{I}_1 = \mathbf{I}\frac{\mathbf{Y}_1}{\mathbf{Y}_p} = 20\ \underline{/30°}\ \frac{1}{(6\ \underline{/40°})(0.8585\ \underline{/-26.14°})} = 3.88\ \underline{/16.14°}\ \text{A}$$

10.269 How much complex power is absorbed by the $6\ \underline{/60°}$-Ω impedance of the circuit of Fig. 10-137?

▌ The voltage across the given impedance is $\mathbf{V} = \mathbf{ZI} = (6\ \underline{/60°})(20\ \underline{/30°}) = 120\ \underline{/90°}$ V. Thus $\mathbf{S} = \mathbf{VI}^* = (120\ \underline{/90°})(20\ \underline{/-30°}) = 2400\ \underline{/60°}$ VA.

10.270 If the circuit of Fig. 10-137 operates at 60 Hz, find the current $\mathbf{I}_2$ in the time domain.

▌ As in Prob. 10.268,

$$\mathbf{I}_2 = \mathbf{I}\frac{\mathbf{Y}_2}{\mathbf{Y}_p} = 20\ \underline{/30°}\ \frac{1}{(5\ \underline{/30°})(0.8585\ \underline{/-26.14°})} = 4.66\ \underline{/26.14°}\ \text{A}$$

Hence $\qquad i_2 = \sqrt{2}(4.66)\sin(2\pi60t + 26.14°) = 6.59\sin(377t + 26.14°)$ A

10.271 From the results of Probs. 10.268 and 10.270, solve for the current $\mathbf{I}_3$ shown in the circuit of Fig. 10.137.

▌ By KCL, $\mathbf{I}_3 = \mathbf{I} - (\mathbf{I}_1 + \mathbf{I}_2)$. Now,

$$\mathbf{I} = 20\ \underline{/30°} = 17.32 + j10\ \text{(given)} \qquad \mathbf{I}_1 = 3.88\ \underline{/16.14°} = 3.73 + j1.08\ \text{(from Prob. 10.268)}$$

$$\mathbf{I}_2 = 4.66\ \underline{/26.14°} = 4.18 + j2.05\ \text{(from Prob. 10.270)}$$

Thus, $\qquad \mathbf{I}_3 = 9.41 + j6.87 = 11.65\ \underline{/36.13°}$ A

10.272 Determine the voltage $\mathbf{V}_s$ across the current source of the circuit of Fig. 10-137.

▌ $\qquad \mathbf{V}_s = \mathbf{I}(4\ \underline{/50°} + 6\ \underline{/60°}) + \mathbf{I}_1(6\ \underline{/40°}) = (20\ \underline{/30°})(9.96\ \underline{/56°}) + 23.3\ \underline{/56.14°} = 218.52\ \underline{/83°}$ V

10.273 How much total power is absorbed by all the resistive components of the impedances of the circuit of Fig. 10-137?

▌ $\qquad P_R = \text{Re } \mathbf{V}_s\mathbf{I}^* = \text{Re } [(218.52\ \underline{/83°})(20\ \underline{/-30°})] = \text{Re } (4370.4\ \underline{/53°}) = 2630$ W

10.274 A certain series-parallel circuit contains an impedance $\mathbf{Z}_1 = 1 - j1\ \Omega$ in series with a parallel combination of $\mathbf{Z}_2 = 1 + j1\ \Omega$ and $\mathbf{Z}_3 = 1 - j1\ \Omega$. The sinusoidal driving voltage is $240\ \underline{/30°}$ V. Sketch the circuit and determine (a) the driving-point impedance and (b) the driving-point admittance.

❙ The circuit is shown in Fig. 10-138, from which

$$\mathbf{Z}_P = \frac{(1 + j1)(1 - j1)}{(1 + j1) + (1 - j1)} = 1.0\ \Omega$$

(a) $$\mathbf{Z}_{in} = \mathbf{Z}_1 + \mathbf{Z}_P = (1 - j1) + 1.0 = 2 - j1 = 2.2359\ \underline{/-26.57°}\ \Omega$$

(b) $$\mathbf{Y}_{in} = \frac{1}{\mathbf{Z}_{in}} = \frac{1}{2.236\ \underline{/-26.57°}} = 0.4472\ \underline{/26.57°}\ \text{S}$$

10.275 Find the voltage across $\mathbf{Z}_1$ in the circuit of Fig. 10-138.

❙ $$\mathbf{I} = \mathbf{VY} = (240\ \underline{/30°})(0.4472\ \underline{/26.57°}) = 107.34\ \underline{/56.57°}\ \text{A}$$

$$\mathbf{V}_{Z1} = \mathbf{IZ}_1 = (107.34\ \underline{/56.57°})(1 - j1) = 151.78\ \underline{/11.57°}\ \text{A}$$

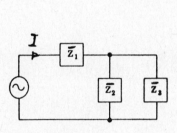

Fig. 10-138

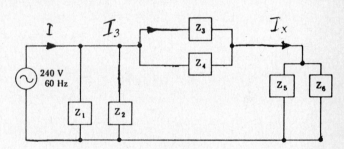

Fig. 10-139

10.276 Determine the current supplied by the voltage source of the circuit of Fig. 10-139, where

$\mathbf{Z}_1 = (3 + j2) = 3.606\ \underline{/33.69°}\ \Omega$ $\quad \mathbf{Z}_2 = (4 + j1) = 4.123\ \underline{/14.036°}\ \Omega$ $\quad \mathbf{Z}_3 = (2 - j5) = 5.385\ \underline{/-68.199°}\ \Omega$

$\mathbf{Z}_4 = (3 + j6) = 6.708\ \underline{/63.435°}\ \Omega$ $\quad \mathbf{Z}_5 = (4 + j7) = 8.062\ \underline{/60.255°}\ \Omega$ $\quad \mathbf{Z}_6 = (2 + j3) = 3.606\ \underline{/56.310°}\ \Omega$

❙ $\mathbf{Z}_{P(1,2)} = 1.952\ \underline{/24.53°}\ \Omega$ $\quad \mathbf{Z}_{P(3,4)} = 7.0827\ \underline{/-16.06°}\ \Omega$ $\quad \mathbf{Z}_{P(5,6)} = 2.4932\ \underline{/57.53°}\ \Omega$

$$\mathbf{Z}_{P(3,4)} + \mathbf{Z}_{P(5,6)} = \mathbf{Z}_A = 7.0827\ \underline{/-16.06°} + 2.4932\ \underline{/57.53°} = (8.1448 + j0.1441) = 8.1460\ \underline{/1.0133°}\ \Omega$$

$$\mathbf{Z}_{in} = \frac{(1.952\ \underline{/24.53°})(8.1460\ \underline{/1.0133°})}{(1.7758 + j0.81041) + (8.1448 + j0.1441)} = 1.5957\ \underline{/20.04°}\ \Omega$$

$$\mathbf{I} = \frac{\mathbf{V}}{\mathbf{Z}_{in}} = \frac{240\ \underline{/0°}}{1.5957\ \underline{/20.04°}} = 150.41\ \underline{/-20.04°}\ \text{A}$$

10.277 Find the current through $\mathbf{Z}_3$ of the circuit of Fig. 10-139.

❙ The current $\mathbf{I}_3$ is determined by the division of the current $\mathbf{I}_x$.

$$\mathbf{I}_x = \frac{\mathbf{V}}{\mathbf{Z}_{P(3,4)} + \mathbf{Z}_{P(5,6)}} = \frac{240\ \underline{/0°}}{8.146\ \underline{/1.01°}} = 29.46\ \underline{/-1.01°}\ \text{A}$$

Hence, $$\mathbf{I}_3 = 29.46\ \underline{/-1.01°}\ \frac{0.1857\ \underline{/68.2°}}{0.1412\ \underline{/16.06°}} = 38.74\ \underline{/51.13°}\ \text{A}$$

10.278 How much total reactive power is absorbed by the impedances of the circuit of Fig. 10-139.

$$Q = \text{Im}\,\mathbf{S} = \text{Im}\,\mathbf{VI}^* = \text{Im}\,[(240\ \underline{/0°})(150.41\ \underline{/20.04°})] = \text{Im}\,(36{,}098.4\ \underline{/20.04°}) = 12.37\ \text{kvar}$$

10.279 The voltage across a certain parallel section of a series-parallel circuit is $120\ \underline{/60°}$ V. The parallel section consists of a $(2.0 + j3.0)$-Ω branch in parallel with a $(4.0 - j8.0)$-Ω branch. Determine (a) the current in each branch and (b) the total current to the parallel section.

❚   Let the branches be labeled A and B. Then $\mathbf{Z}_A = 2 + j3 = 3.61 \,\underline{/56.31°}\ \Omega$, $\mathbf{Z}_B = 4 - j8 = 8.94 \,\underline{/-63.43°}\ \Omega$.

(a) $\mathbf{I}_A = \dfrac{120 \,\underline{/60°}}{3.61 \,\underline{/56.31°}} = 33.24 \,\underline{/3.69°}\ \text{A}$ $\mathbf{I}_B = \dfrac{120 \,\underline{/60°}}{8.94 \,\underline{/-63.43°}} = 13.42 \,\underline{/123.43°}\ \text{A}$

(b) $\mathbf{I} = \mathbf{I}_A + \mathbf{I}_B = (33.17 + j2.14) + (-7.39 + j11.2) = 29.02 \,\underline{/27.36°}\ \text{A}$

10.280   For the circuit shown in Fig. 10-140, determine   (a) the input impedance and   (b) the input current.

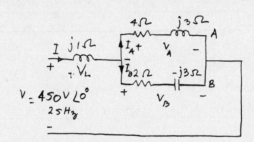

Fig. 10-140

❚ $\mathbf{Z}_A = 4 + j3 = 5 \,\underline{/36.87°}\ \Omega$ $\mathbf{Z}_B = 2 - j3 = 3.61 \,\underline{/-56.31°}\ \Omega$

(a) $\mathbf{Z}_P = \dfrac{\mathbf{Z}_A \mathbf{Z}_B}{\mathbf{Z}_A + \mathbf{Z}_B} = 3.00 \,\underline{/-19.44°}$ $\mathbf{Z}_{\text{in}} = (2.83 - j1.00) + j1.0 = 2.83 \,\underline{/0°}\ \Omega$

(b) $\mathbf{I} = \dfrac{\mathbf{V}}{\mathbf{Z}_{\text{in}}} = \dfrac{450 \,\underline{/0°}}{2.83 \,\underline{/0°}} = 159.01\ \text{A}$

10.281   Solve for $\mathbf{I}_B$ and $\mathbf{V}_A$ in the circuit of Fig. 10-140.

❚ $\mathbf{I}_B = \mathbf{I}\,\dfrac{\mathbf{Y}_B}{\mathbf{Y}_P} = 159.01\,\dfrac{0.277 \,\underline{/56.31°}}{0.333 \,\underline{/19.44°}} = 132.5 \,\underline{/36.87°}\ \text{A}$

               $\mathbf{V}_A = \mathbf{I}\mathbf{Z}_P = (159.01)(3.00 \,\underline{/-19.44°}) = 477 \,\underline{/-19.44°}\ \text{V}$

10.282   Determine the current $\mathbf{I}_A$ in the circuit of Fig. 10-140 in the time domain.

❚ $\mathbf{I}_A = \mathbf{I}\,\dfrac{\mathbf{Y}_A}{\mathbf{Y}_P} = 159.01\,\dfrac{0.20 \,\underline{/-36.87°}}{0.333 \,\underline{/19.44°}} = 95.53 \,\underline{/-56.31°}\ \text{A}$

               $i_A = 95.53 \sqrt{2} \sin (50\pi t - 56.31°)\ \text{A}$

10.283   Draw the phasor diagram showing all the voltages and currents of the circuit of Fig. 10-140.

❚   See Fig. 10-141.

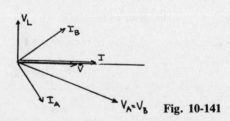

Fig. 10-141

10.284   If 450-V dc is applied across the circuit of Fig. 10-140, determine I, I_A, and I_B under steady state.

     Since C acts as an open circuit and L as a short circuit to dc (under steady state), we have $I_B = 0$ and $I = I_A = \frac{450}{4} = 112.5\ \text{A}$.

10.285   What is the voltage across the 10-Ω resistor of the circuit of Fig. 10-142?

❚   Since $\mathbf{I} = 5 \,\underline{/20°}\ \text{A}$, $\mathbf{V}_1 = R\mathbf{I} = 10(5 \,\underline{/20°}) = 50 \,\underline{/20°}\ \text{V}$.

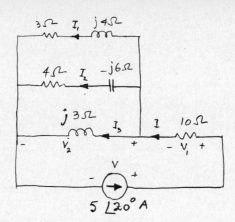

Fig. 10-142

10.286 Solve for the current I_2 in the circuit of Fig. 10-142.

▮ The admittance of the parallel branch is

$$Y_P = \frac{1}{3+j4} + \frac{1}{4-j6} + \frac{1}{j3} = 0.4262 \underline{/-62.48°} \text{ S}$$

By current division,

$$I_2 = I\frac{Y_2}{Y_P} = 5\underline{/20°}\,\frac{1/(4-j6)}{0.4262\underline{/-62.48°}} = 1.63\underline{/138.8°} \text{ A}$$

10.287 Determine V_2, the voltage across the parallel branch, in the circuit of Fig. 10-142.

▮ $\qquad V_2 = I_2Z_2 = (1.63\underline{/138.8°})(4-j6) = 11.75\underline{/82.5°} \text{ V}$

10.288 Find V, the voltage across the source in Fig. 10-142, from the results of Probs. 10.285 and 10.287.

▮ $\qquad V = V_1 + V_2 = 50\underline{/20°} + 11.75\underline{/82.5°} = 48.52 + j28.75 = 56.4\underline{/30.65°} \text{ V}$

10.289 What is the input impedance of the circuit of Fig. 10-142?

▮ $\qquad Z_{in} = 10 + Z_P = 10 + \dfrac{1}{0.4262\underline{/-62.48°}} = 11.08 + j2.08 = 11.27\underline{/10.64°}\,\Omega$

10.290 Recalculate V (Prob. 10.288) from the result of Prob. 10.289.

▮ $V = Z_{in}I = (11.27\underline{/10.64°})(5\underline{/20°}) = 56.35\underline{/30.64°} \text{ V}$,   which agrees with the result of Prob. 10.288.

10.291 How much complex power is delivered by the source of the circuit of Fig. 10-142?

▮ $\qquad S = VI^* = (56.4\underline{/30.64°})(5\underline{/-20°}) = 282\underline{/10.64°} \text{ VA}$

10.292 Solve for the currents I_1 and I_3 in the circuit of Fig. 10-142.

▮ $\qquad I_1 = 5\underline{/20°}\,\dfrac{1}{(3+j4)(0.4262\underline{/-62.48°})} = 2.35\underline{/29.35°} \text{ A}$

$$I_3 = 5\underline{/20°}\,\frac{1}{(j3)(0.4262\underline{/-62.48°})} = 3.91\underline{/-7.52°} \text{ V}$$

10.293 Find the voltages across the various elements of the circuit of Fig. 10-142.

▮ $\qquad V_{j3\,\Omega} = V_2 = 11.75\underline{/82.5°} \text{ V} \qquad V_{-j6\,\Omega} = (1.63\underline{/138.8°})(6\underline{/-90°}) = 9.78\underline{/48.8°} \text{ V}$

$$V_{j4\,\Omega} = (2.35\underline{/29.35°})(4\underline{/90°}) = 9.4\underline{/119.35°} \text{ V} \qquad V_{3\,\Omega} = 3(2.35\underline{/29.35°}) = 7.05\underline{/29.35°} \text{ V}$$

$$V_{4\,\Omega} = (1.63\underline{/138.8°})4 = 6.52\underline{/138.8°} \text{ V} \qquad V_{10\,\Omega} = V_1 = 50\underline{/20°} \text{ V}$$

10.294 Draw a phasor diagram showing all the currents and voltages in the circuit of Fig. 10-142.

▮ See Fig. 10-143.

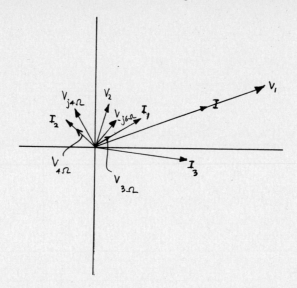

Fig. 10-143

10.295 Verify that the true power supplied by the source of the circuit of Fig. 10-142 is the same as the sum of the powers dissipated in the resistors.

$$P_{\text{source}} = \text{Re } \mathbf{S} = \text{Re } (282 \, \underline{/10.64°}) = 277.15 \text{ W}$$

$$P_{\text{dissipated}} = 3(I_1)^2 + 4(I_2)^2 + 10(I)^2 = 3(2.35)^2 + 4(1.63)^2 + 10(5)^2 = 277.19 \text{ W}$$

CHAPTER 11

Magnetically Coupled Circuits

11.1 Figure 11-1 illustrates magnetic coupling of two circuits, which is measured by the *mutual inductance M*. Like L, M carries the units H. Including coupling, write the equation of either circuit in terms of instantaneous values and in terms of sinusoidal steady-state values (phasors).

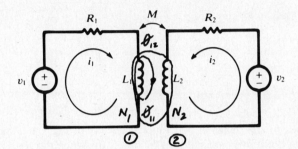

Fig. 11-1

▌ The required equations are:

$$R_1 i_1 + L_1 \frac{di_1}{dt} \pm M \frac{di_2}{dt} = v_1 \qquad \text{or} \qquad (R_1 + j\omega L_1)\mathbf{I}_1 \pm j\omega M \mathbf{I}_2 = \mathbf{V}_1 \tag{1}$$

$$R_2 i_2 + L_2 \frac{di_2}{dt} \pm M \frac{di_1}{dt} = v_2 \qquad \text{or} \qquad (R_2 + j\omega L_2)\mathbf{I}_2 \pm j\omega M \mathbf{I}_1 = \mathbf{V}_2 \tag{2}$$

11.2 The mutual coupling between the circuits of Fig. 11-1 is shown in more detail in Fig. 11-2, where the two coils are shown on a common core which channels the magnetic flux ϕ. To determine the proper signs on the voltages of mutual inductance, apply the right-hand rule to each coil: If the fingers wrap around in the direction of the assumed current, the thumb points in the direction of the flux. Resulting positive directions for ϕ_1 and ϕ_2 are shown on the figure. If fluxes ϕ_1 and ϕ_2 aid one another, then the signs on the voltages of mutual inductance are the same as the signs on the voltages of self-inductance. Apply this rule to find the sign for M in Eqs. (1) of Prob. 11.1.

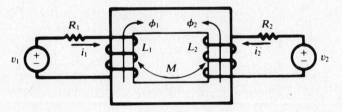

Fig. 11-2

▌ In Fig. 11-2, ϕ_1 and ϕ_2 oppose each other; consequently, Eqs. (1) would be written with the minus sign.

11.3 The circuit of Fig. 11-3(a) represents a transformer in which source v_1 drives a current i_1, with a corresponding flux ϕ_1 as shown. Now, *Lenz's law* implies that the polarity of the induced voltage in the second circuit is such that, if the circuit is completed, a current will pass through the second coil in such a direction as to create a flux opposing the main flux established by i_1. The right-hand rule, with the thumb pointing in the direction of ϕ_2, provides the direction of the *natural current* i_2. The induced voltage is the driving voltage for the second circuit, as suggested in Fig. 11-3b. This voltage is present whether or not the circuit is closed. When the switch is closed, current i_2 is established, with a positive direction as shown. Suppose the switch in the passive loop is closed at $t = 0$ when $i_1 = 0$. Write the KVL equations for the two loops.

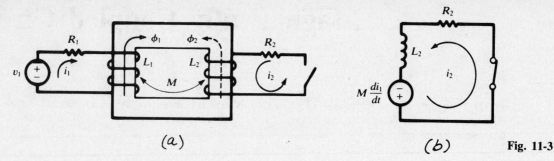

(a)   (b)   Fig. 11-3

▮ The equation of the passive loop is

$$R_2 i_2 + L_2 \frac{di_2}{dt} - M \frac{di_1}{dt} = 0$$

whereas that of the active loop is

$$R_1 i_1 + L_1 \frac{di_1}{dt} - M \frac{di_2}{dt} = v_1$$

11.4   Write the KVL equations for the magnetically coupled circuits of Fig. 11-4 operating under steady-state ac. The circuit also shows the dot convention stated as follows: (*a*) When the assumed currents both enter or both leave a pair of coupled coils by the dotted terminals, the signs on the *M* terms will be the same as the signs on the *L* terms;   but (*b*) if one current enters by a dotted terminal while the other leaves by a dotted terminal, the signs on the *M* terms will be opposite to the signs on the *L* terms.

▮ The KVL equations in matrix form may be written as

$$\begin{bmatrix} R_1 + j\omega L_1 & -j\omega M \\ -j\omega M & R_2 + j\omega L_2 \end{bmatrix} \begin{bmatrix} \mathbf{I}_1 \\ \mathbf{I}_2 \end{bmatrix} = \begin{bmatrix} \mathbf{V}_1 \\ 0 \end{bmatrix}$$

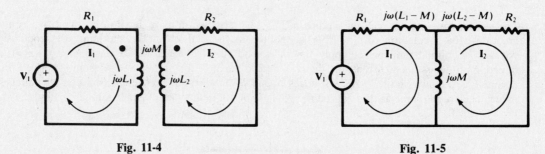

Fig. 11-4   Fig. 11-5

11.5   Represent the circuit of Fig. 11-4 by a conductively coupled circuit.

▮ Let the desired circuit be as shown in Fig. 11-5, where an inductive reactance $X_M = \omega M$, carries the two mesh currents in opposite directions, whence $\mathbf{Z}_{12} = \mathbf{Z}_{21} = -j\omega M$ in the **Z** matrix. If now an inductance $L_1 - M$ be placed in the first loop, the mesh current equation for this loop will be $(R_1 + j\omega L_1)\mathbf{I}_1 - j\omega M \mathbf{I}_2 = \mathbf{V}_1$. Similarly, $L_2 - M$ in the second loop results in the same mesh current equation as for the coupled-coil circuit. Thus, the circuit of Fig. 11-5 is equivalent to that of Fig. 11-4.

11.6   In Fig. 11-1, we have shown two fluxes—ϕ_{11} linking with coil 1, and ϕ_{12} linking with coils 1 and 2 both. This latter flux gives rise to the mutual coupling between the two coils and is known as the *mutual flux*. The flux ϕ_{11} is known as the *leakage flux*. With the use of the definition of inductance as flux linkage per ampere (see Prob. 7.11) and defining *coupling coefficient* $k = \phi_{12}/\phi_1 = \phi_{21}/\phi_2$, obtain an expression for *k* in terms of self- and mutual inductances. Coils 1 and 2 in Fig. 11-1 have N_1 and N_2 turns, respectively.

▮ From Prob. 7.11, since $\lambda = N\phi = Li$, we have

$$L \frac{di}{dt} = N \frac{d\phi}{dt} = e \text{ (induced voltage)}$$

From Fig. 11-1, induced voltage e_2 in coil 2 is given by

$$e_2 = M \frac{di_1}{dt} = N_2 \frac{d}{dt} \phi_{12}$$

or
$$M = N_2 \frac{d\phi_{12}}{di_1} \tag{1}$$

Similarly, e_1 in coil 1 is given by

$$e_1 = M \frac{di_2}{dt} = N_1 \frac{d}{dt} \phi_{21}$$

or
$$M = N_1 \frac{d\phi_{21}}{di_2} \tag{2}$$

Multiplying Eqs. (1) and (2) yields

$$M^2 = \left(N_2 \frac{d\phi_{12}}{di_1} \right)\left(N_1 \frac{d\phi_{21}}{di_2} \right) \tag{3}$$

Now
$$k = \frac{\phi_{12}}{\phi_1} - \frac{\phi_{21}}{\phi_2} \tag{4}$$

$$L_1 = \frac{N_1 \phi_1}{i_1} \tag{5}$$

and
$$L_2 = \frac{N_2 \phi_2}{i_2} \tag{6}$$

Substituting Eqs. (4) through (6) into (3) gives

$$M^2 = k^2 \left(N_1 \frac{d\phi_1}{di_1} \right)\left(N_2 \frac{d\phi_2}{di_2} \right) = k^2 L_1 L_2$$

Hence,
$$k = \frac{M}{\sqrt{L_1 L_2}}$$

11.7 The device shown in Fig. 11-6 is a transformer. Represent this by an equivalent circuit. Identify all the circuit parameters.

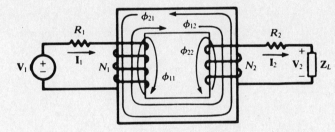

Fig. 11-6

❚ Referring to Fig. 11-6, the *primary winding* of N_1 turns is connected to the source voltage $\mathbf{V}_1$ and the *secondary winding* of N_2 turns is connected to the load impedance $\mathbf{Z}_L$. The coil resistances are shown by lumped parameters R_1 and R_2. Current $\mathbf{I}_2$ produces flux $\phi_2 = \phi_{21} + \phi_{22}$ and $\mathbf{I}_1$ produces $\phi_1 = \phi_{12} + \phi_{11}$. In terms of the coupling coefficient k,

$$\phi_{11} = (1-k)\phi_1 \qquad \phi_{22} = (1-k)\phi_2$$

From these flux relationships, *leakage inductances* L_{11} and L_{22} can be related to the self-inductances L_1 and L_2 by

$$L_{11} = (1-k)L_1 \qquad L_{22} = (1-k)L_2$$

The corresponding *leakage reactances* are

$$X_{11} = (1-k)X_1 \qquad X_{22} = (1-k)X_2$$

The flux common to both windings in Fig. 11-6 is the *mutual flux* $\phi_m = \phi_{12} - \phi_{21}$. This flux induces the coil emfs by Faraday's law.

$$e_1 = N_1 \frac{d\phi_m}{dt} \qquad e_2 = N_2 \frac{d\phi_m}{dt}$$

Defining the turns ratio, $a = N_1/N_2$, we obtain from these the basic equation of the transformer, $e_1/e_2 = a$. In terms of rms values, $E_1/E_2 = a$.

The relationship between the mutual inductance can be developed by analysis of the secondary induced emf, as follows:

$$e_2 = N_2 \frac{d\phi_m}{dt} = N_2 \frac{d\phi_{12}}{dt} - N_2 \frac{d\phi_{21}}{dt} = N_2 \frac{d\phi_{12}}{dt} - N_2 \frac{d(k\phi_2)}{dt}$$

Using the results of Prob. 11.6, we have

$$e_2 = M \frac{di_1}{dt} - kL_2 \frac{di_2}{dt} = M \frac{di_1}{dt} - \frac{M}{a} \frac{di_2}{dt}$$

Now, defining the *magnetizing current* i_ϕ by the equation

$$i_1 = \frac{i_2}{a} + i_\phi \qquad \text{or} \qquad I_1 = \frac{I_2}{a} + I_\phi$$

we have

$$e_2 = M \frac{di_\phi}{dt} \qquad \text{or} \qquad E_2 = jX_M I_\phi$$

Hence, in terms of the coil emfs and various reactances and resistances, we obtain the equivalent circuits of Fig. 11-7*a* and *b*.

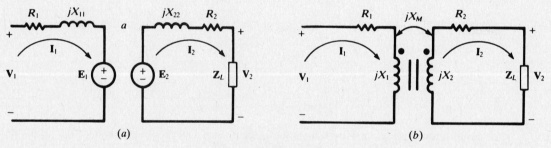

(a)   (b)

Fig. 11-7

11.8 From the circuit of Fig. 11-7*b* determine the input impedance of the transformer.

▮ The governing equations are

$$V_1 = (R_1 + jX_1)I_1 + jX_M I_2 \qquad 0 = jX_M I_1 + (R_2 + jX_2 + Z_L)I_2$$

Eliminating I_2 gives

$$V_1 = (R_1 + jX_1)I_1 + jX_M \frac{-jX_M}{R_2 + jX_2 + Z_L} I_1 \qquad \text{or} \qquad Z_{in} = \frac{V_1}{I_1} = (R_1 + jX_1) + \frac{X_M^2}{R_2 + jX_2 + Z_L}$$

11.9 An ideal transformer is represented by Fig. 11-8. It is characterized by the fact that it is lossless $(R_1 = R_2 = 0)$, has no leakages $(X_{11} = X_{22} = 0)$, and has an infinitely permeable core $(X_M = \infty)$. Under these conditions determine its input impedance for a load Z_L.

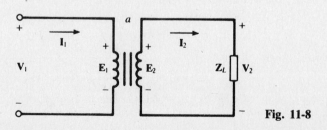

Fig. 11-8

❚ From Fig. 11-8, $\mathbf{V}_1 = \mathbf{E}_1 = a\mathbf{E}_2 = a\mathbf{V}_2$. Since the transformer is lossless,

$$\mathbf{V}_1\mathbf{I}_1 = \mathbf{V}_2\mathbf{I}_2 \qquad \text{or} \qquad \frac{\mathbf{V}_1}{\mathbf{V}_2} = \frac{\mathbf{I}_2}{\mathbf{I}_1} = a$$

Hence,
$$\mathbf{Z}_{in} = \frac{\mathbf{V}_1}{\mathbf{I}_1} = \frac{a\mathbf{V}_2}{\mathbf{I}_2/a} = a^2\frac{\mathbf{V}_2}{\mathbf{I}_2} = a^2\mathbf{Z}_L$$

11.10 For an ideal transformer the *ampere-turn dot rule* states that the algebraic sum of the ampere turns for a transformer is zero. Now refer to the three-winding transformer shown in Fig. 11-9. It has turns $N_1 = 20$, $N_2 = N_3 = 10$. Find $\mathbf{I}_1$ given that $\mathbf{I}_2 = 10.0\,\underline{/-53.13°}\,\text{A}$, $\mathbf{I}_3 = 10.0\,\underline{/-45°}\,\text{A}$.

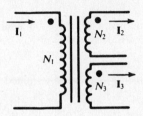

Fig. 11-9

❚ With the dots and current directions as shown, $N_1\mathbf{I}_1 - N_2\mathbf{I}_2 - N_3\mathbf{I}_3 = 0$, from which $20\mathbf{I}_1 = 10(10.0\,\underline{/-53.13°}) + 10(10.0\,\underline{/-45°})$ or $\mathbf{I}_1 = 6.54 - j7.54 = 9.98\,\underline{/-49.06°}\,\text{A}$.

11.11 When one coil of a magnetically coupled pair has a current 5.0 A, the resulting fluxes ϕ_{11} and ϕ_{12} are 0.2 and 0.4 mWb, respectively. If the turns are $N_1 = 500$ and $N_2 = 1500$, find L_1, L_2, M, and the coefficient of coupling k.

❚ $\phi_1 = \phi_{11} + \phi_{12} = 0.6\,\text{mWb}$. From Prob. 11.6,

$$L_1 = \frac{N_1\phi_1}{I_1} = \frac{500(0.6)}{5.0} = 60\,\text{mH} \qquad M = \frac{N_2\phi_{12}}{I_1} = \frac{1500(0.4)}{5.0} = 120\,\text{mH} \qquad k = \frac{\phi_{12}}{\phi_1} = 0.667$$

Then, from $M = k\sqrt{L_1 L_2}$, $L_2 = 540\,\text{mH}$.

11.12 Two coupled coils have self-inductances $L_1 = 50\,\text{mH}$ and $L_2 = 200\,\text{mH}$, and a coefficient of coupling $k = 0.50$. If coil 2 has 1000 turns, and $i_1 = 5.0\sin 400t\,\text{A}$, find the voltage at coil 2 and the flux ϕ_1.

❚ $M = k\sqrt{L_1 L_2} = 0.50\sqrt{(50)(200)} = 50\,\text{mH}$ $\qquad v_2 = M\frac{di_1}{dt} = 0.05\frac{d}{dt}(5.0\sin 400t) = 100\cos 400t$

Assuming a linear magnetic circuit,

$$M = \frac{N_2\phi_{12}}{i_1} = \frac{N_2(k\phi_1)}{i_1} \qquad \text{or} \qquad \phi_1 = \frac{M}{N_2 k}i_1 = 5.0 \times 10^{-4}\sin 400t\,\text{Wb}$$

11.13 Write the mesh equations in terms of instantaneous values for the circuit of Fig. 11-10.

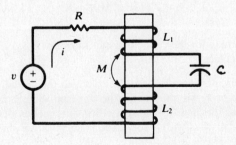

Fig. 11-10

❚ Examination of the winding sense shows that the signs on the M terms are opposite to the signs on the L terms.

$$Ri + L_1\frac{di}{dt} - M\frac{di}{dt} + \frac{1}{C}\int i\,dt + L_2\frac{di}{dt} - M\frac{di}{dt} = v \qquad (1)$$

or

$$Ri + L' \frac{di}{dt} + \frac{1}{C} \int i\, dt = v \qquad (2)$$

where $L' = L_1 + L_2 - 2M$. Because $M \le \sqrt{L_1 L_2} \le (L_1 + L_2)/2$, L' is nonnegative.

11.14 Rewrite the mesh equations of the circuit of Fig. 11-10 for sinusoidal steady condition.

❚ These equations follow directly from Eqs. (1) and (2) of Prob. 11.13. Thus,

$$\left(R + j\omega L_1 - j\omega M + \frac{1}{j\omega C} + j\omega L_2 - j\omega M\right)\mathbf{I} = \mathbf{V} \qquad \text{or} \qquad \left(R + j\omega L' + \frac{1}{j\omega C}\right)\mathbf{I} = \mathbf{V}$$

where $L' = L_1 + L_2 - 2M$.

11.15 In a series *aiding connection*, two coupled coils have an equivalent inductance L_A; in a series *opposing* connection, L_B. Obtain an expression for M in terms of L_A and L_B.

❚ As in Prob. 11.13, $L_1 + L_2 + 2M = L_A$ and $L_1 + L_2 - 2M = L_B$, which give $M = \frac{1}{4}(L_A - L_B)$. This problem suggests a method by which M can be determined experimentally.

11.16 Write the mesh current equations for the coupled coils with currents i_1 and i_2 shown in Fig. 11-11.

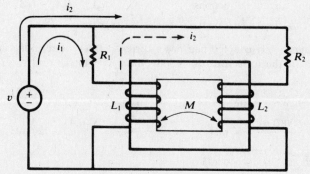

Fig. 11-11

❚ The winding sense and selected current directions result in signs on the M terms as follows:

$$R_1 i_1 + L_1 \frac{di_1}{dt} + M \frac{di_2}{dt} = v \qquad R_2 i_2 + L_2 \frac{di_2}{dt} + M \frac{di_1}{dt} = v$$

11.17 Repeat Prob. 11.16 if i_2 is given by the dashed line in Fig. 11-11.

❚

$$R_1(i_1 - i_2) + L_1 \frac{d}{dt}(i_1 - i_2) + M \frac{di_2}{dt} = v$$

$$R_1(i_2 - i_1) + R_2 i_2 + L_2 \frac{di_2}{dt} - M \frac{d}{dt}(i_2 - i_1) + L_1 \frac{d}{dt}(i_2 - i_1) - M \frac{di_2}{dt} = 0$$

11.18 Obtain the dotted equivalent circuit for the coupled circuit shown in Fig. 11-12a, and use it to find the voltage $\mathbf{V}$ across the 10-Ω capacitive reactance.

❚ To place the dots on the circuit, consider only the coils and their winding sense. Drive a current into the top of the left coil and place a dot at this terminal. The corresponding flux is upward. By Lenz's law, the flux at the right coil must be upward-directed to oppose the first flux. Then the natural current leaves this winding by the upper terminal, which is marked with a dot. See Fig. 11-12b for the complete dotted equivalent circuit, with currents $\mathbf{I}_1$ and $\mathbf{I}_2$ chosen for calculation of $\mathbf{V}$.

$$\begin{bmatrix} 5 - j5 & 5 + j3 \\ 5 + j3 & 10 + j6 \end{bmatrix}\begin{bmatrix} \mathbf{I}_1 \\ \mathbf{I}_2 \end{bmatrix} = \begin{bmatrix} 10\,\underline{/0°} \\ 10 - j10 \end{bmatrix} \qquad \mathbf{I}_1 = \frac{\begin{vmatrix} 10 & 5 + j3 \\ 10 - j10 & 10 + j6 \end{vmatrix}}{\Delta_z} = 1.015\,\underline{/113.96°}\ \text{A}$$

and $\mathbf{V} = \mathbf{I}_1(-j10) = 10.15\,\underline{/23.96°}\ \text{V}$

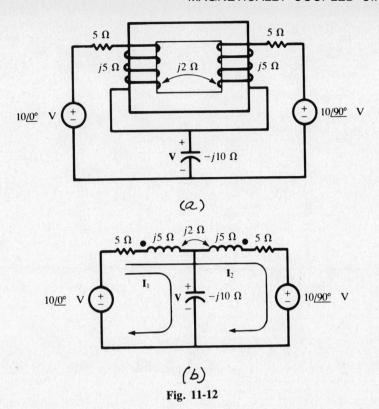

(a)

(b)

Fig. 11-12

11.19 Obtain the dotted equivalent for the circuit shown in Fig. 11-13a and use the equivalent to find the equivalent inductive reactance.

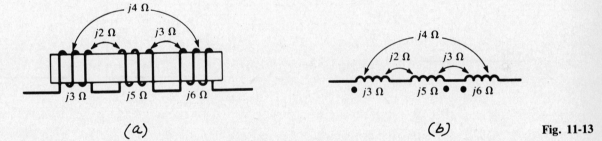

(a)   (b)   **Fig. 11-13**

▌ Drive a current into the first coil and place a dot where this current enters. The natural current in both of the other windings establishes an opposing flux to that set up by the driven current. Place dots where the natural current leaves the windings. (Some confusion is eliminated if the series connections are ignored while determining the locations of the dots.) The result is shown in Fig. 11-13b.

$$\mathbf{Z} = j3 + j5 + j6 - 2(j2) + 2(j4) - 2(j3) = j12\ \Omega$$

i.e., an inductive reactance of $12\ \Omega$.

11.20 Compute the voltage $\mathbf{V}$ for the coupled circuit shown in Fig. 11-14.

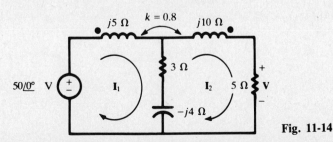

Fig. 11-14

$X_M = (0.8\sqrt{5(10)}) = 5.66\ \Omega$, and so the **Z** matrix is

$$\begin{bmatrix} 3+j1 & -3-j1.66 \\ -3-j1.66 & 8+j6 \end{bmatrix}$$

Then

$$I_2 = \frac{\begin{vmatrix} 3+j1 & 50 \\ -3-j1.66 & 0 \end{vmatrix}}{\Delta_z} = 8.62\ \underline{/-24.79°}\ A$$

and

$$V = I_2(5) = (8.62\ \underline{/-24.79°})(5) = 43.1\ \underline{/-24.79°}\ V$$

11.21 Repeat Prob. 11.20 with the polarity of one coil reversed.

▮ In this case, the **Z** matrix is as follows:

$$\mathbf{Z} = \begin{bmatrix} 3+j1 & -3+j9.66 \\ -3+j9.66 & 8+j6 \end{bmatrix} \qquad I_2 = \frac{\begin{vmatrix} 3+j1 & 50 \\ -3+j9.66 & 0 \end{vmatrix}}{\Delta_z} = 3.82\ \underline{/-112.12°}\ A$$

and $V = I_2(5) = 19.1\ \underline{/-112.12°}\ V.$

11.22 Obtain the equivalent inductance of the parallel-connected, coupled coils shown in Fig. 11-15.

▮ Currents I_1 and I_2 are selected as shown; then $Z_{in} = V_1/I_1$.

$$\mathbf{Z} = \begin{bmatrix} j\omega0.3 & j\omega0.043 \\ j\omega0.043 & j\omega0.414 \end{bmatrix} \quad \text{and} \quad Z_{in} = \frac{\Delta_z}{\Delta_{11}} = \frac{(j\omega0.3)(j\omega0.414) - (j\omega0.043)^2}{j\omega0.414} = j\omega0.296$$

or $L_{eq} = 0.296\ H.$

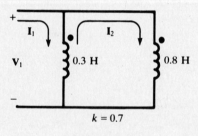

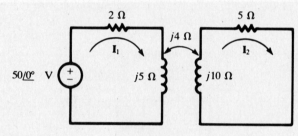

Fig. 11-15   Fig. 11-16

11.23 For the coupled circuit shown in Fig. 11-16, show that dots are not needed so long as the second loop is passive.

▮ Currents I_1 and I_2 are selected as shown.

$$I_1 = \frac{\begin{vmatrix} 50 & \pm j4 \\ 0 & 5+j10 \end{vmatrix}}{\begin{vmatrix} 2+j5 & \pm j4 \\ \pm j4 & 5+j10 \end{vmatrix}} = \frac{250+j500}{-24+j45} = 10.96\ \underline{/-54.64°}\ A \qquad I_2 = \frac{\begin{vmatrix} 2+j5 & 50 \\ \pm j4 & 0 \end{vmatrix}}{\Delta_z} = 3.92\ \underline{/-118.07 \mp 90°}\ A$$

The value of Δ_z is unaffected by the sign on M. Since the numerator determinant for I_1 does not involve the coupling impedance, I_1 is also unaffected. The expression for I_2 shows that a change in the coupling polarity results in a 180° phase shift. With no other phasor voltage present in the second loop, this change in phase is of no consequence.

11.24 For the coupled circuit shown in Fig. 11-17, find the ratio V_2/V_1 which results in zero current I_1.

▮

$$I_1 = 0 = \frac{\begin{vmatrix} V_1 & j2 \\ V_2 & 2+j2 \end{vmatrix}}{\Delta_z}$$

Then $V_1(2+j2) - V_2(j2) = 0,$ from which $V_2/V_1 = 1 - j1.$

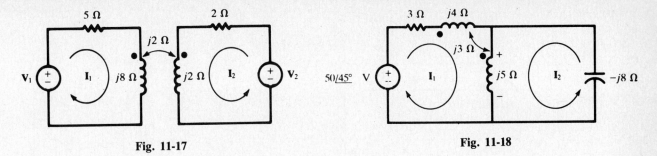

Fig. 11-17   Fig. 11-18

11.25 In the circuit of Fig. 11-18, find the voltage across the 5-Ω reactance with the polarity shown.

▌ For the indicated choice of mesh currents,

$$\mathbf{I}_1 = \frac{\begin{vmatrix} 50\underline{/45°} & j8 \\ 0 & -j3 \end{vmatrix}}{\begin{vmatrix} 3+j15 & j8 \\ j8 & -j3 \end{vmatrix}} = \frac{150\underline{/-45°}}{109-j9} = 1.37\underline{/-40.28°}\,\text{A}$$

Similarly, $\mathbf{I}_2 = 3.66\underline{/-40.28°}\,\text{A}$.

The voltage across the $j5$ is partly conductive, from the currents $\mathbf{I}_1$ and $\mathbf{I}_2$, and partly mutual, from current $\mathbf{I}_1$ in the 4-Ω reactance: $\mathbf{V} = (\mathbf{I}_1 + \mathbf{I}_2)j5 + \mathbf{I}_1(j3) = 29.97\underline{/49.72°}\,\text{V}$. Of course, the same voltage must exist across the capacitor: $\mathbf{V} = -\mathbf{I}_2(-j8) = 29.27\underline{/49.72°}\,\text{V}$.

11.26 Obtain Thévenin and Norton equivalent circuits at terminals *ab* for the coupled circuit shown in Fig. 11-19*a*.

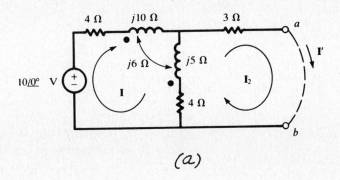

(a)

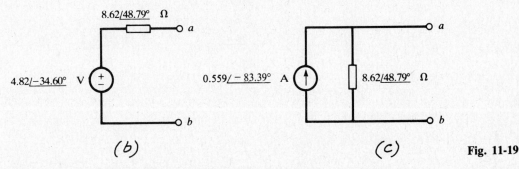

(b)   (c)   Fig. 11-19

▌ In open circuit, a single clockwise loop current $\mathbf{I}$ is driven by the voltage source: $\mathbf{I} = (10\underline{/0°})/(8+j3) = 1.17\underline{/-20.56°}\,\text{A}$. Then $\mathbf{V}_{\text{Th}} = \mathbf{I}(j5+4) - \mathbf{I}(j6) = 4.82\underline{/-34.60°}\,\text{V}$.

To find the short-circuit current I', two clockwise mesh currents are assumed, with $\mathbf{I}_2 = \mathbf{I}'$.

$$I' = \frac{\begin{vmatrix} 8+j3 & 10 \\ -4+j1 & 0 \end{vmatrix}}{\begin{vmatrix} 8+j3 & -4+j1 \\ -4+j1 & 7+j5 \end{vmatrix}} = 0.559\underline{/-83.39°}\,\text{A} \quad\text{and}\quad \mathbf{Z}_{\text{Th}} = \frac{\mathbf{V}_{\text{Th}}}{I'} = \frac{4.82\underline{/-34.60°}}{0.559\underline{/-83.39°}} = 8.62\underline{/48.79°}\,\Omega$$

The equivalent circuits are shown in Fig. 11-19*b* and *c*.

11.27 Obtain a conductively coupled equivalent circuit for the magnetically coupled circuit shown in Fig. 11-20a.

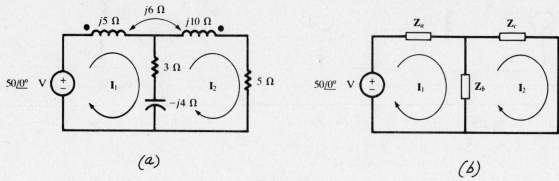

Fig. 11-20

▮ Select mesh currents I_1 and I_2 as shown, and write the KVL equations in matrix form.

$$\begin{bmatrix} 3+j1 & -3-j2 \\ -3-j2 & 8+j6 \end{bmatrix}\begin{bmatrix} I_1 \\ I_2 \end{bmatrix} = \begin{bmatrix} 50\,\underline{/0°} \\ 0 \end{bmatrix}$$

The impedances in Fig. 11-20b are chosen to give the identical Z matrix. Thus, since I_1 and I_2 pass through the common impedance Z_b in opposite directions, Z_{12} in the matrix is $-Z_b$. Then, $Z_b = 3+j2\ \Omega$. Since Z_{11} is to include all impedances through which I_1 passes, $3+j1 = Z_a + (3+j2)$, from which $Z_a = -j1\ \Omega$. Similarly, $Z_{22} = 8+j6 = Z_b + Z_c$ and $Z_c = 5+j4\ \Omega$.

11.28 For the transformer circuit of Fig. 11-7b, $k = 0.96$, $R_1 = 1.2\ \Omega$, $R_2 = 0.3\ \Omega$, $X_1 = 20\ \Omega$, $X_2 = 5\ \Omega$, $Z_L = 5.0\,\underline{/36.87°}\ \Omega$, and $V_2 = 100\,\underline{/0°}$ V. Obtain the coil emfs E_1 and E_2, and the magnetizing current I_ϕ.

▮
$$X_{11} = (1-k)X_1 = (1-0.96)(20) = 0.8\ \Omega \qquad X_{22} = (1-k)X_2 = 0.2\ \Omega$$

$$a = \sqrt{\frac{X_1}{X_2}} = 2 \qquad X_M = k\sqrt{X_1 X_2} = 9.6\ \Omega$$

Now a circuit of the form Fig. 11-7a can be constructed, starting from the phasor voltage-current relationship at the load and working back through E_2 to E_1.

$$I_2 = \frac{V_2}{Z_L} = \frac{100\,\underline{/0°}}{5.0\,\underline{/36.87°}} = 20\,\underline{/-36.87°}\ A$$

$$E_2 = I_2(R_2 + jX_{22}) + V_2 = (20\,\underline{/-36.87°})(0.3 + j0.2) + 100\,\underline{/0°} = 107.2 - j0.4\ V$$

$$E_1 = aE_2 = 214.4 - j0.8\ V \qquad I_\phi = \frac{E_2}{jX_M} = -0.042 - j11.17\ A$$

11.29 For the linear transformer of Prob. 11.28, calculate the input impedance at the terminals where V_1 is applied.

▮ Completing the construction begun in Prob. 11.28,

$$I_1 = I_\phi + \frac{1}{a}I_2 = (-0.042 - j11.17) + 10\,\underline{/-36.87°} = 18.93\,\underline{/-65.13°}\ A$$

$$V_1 = I_1(R_1 + jX_{11}) + E_1 = (18.93\,\underline{/-65.13°})(1.2 + j0.8) + (214.4 - j0.8) = 238.2\,\underline{/-3.62°}\ V$$

Therefore,
$$Z_{in} = \frac{V_1}{I_1} = \frac{238.2\,\underline{/-3.62°}}{18.93\,\underline{/-65.13°}} = 12.58\,\underline{/61.51°}\ \Omega$$

11.30 In Fig. 11-21 three identical transformers are primary wye-connected and secondary delta-connected. A single load impedance carries current $I_L = 30\,\underline{/0°}$ A. Given $I_{b2} = 20\,\underline{/0°}$ A and $I_{a2} = I_{c2} = 10\,\underline{/0°}$ A, with $N_1 = 10N_2 = 100$, find the primary currents I_{a1}, I_{b1}, I_{c1}.

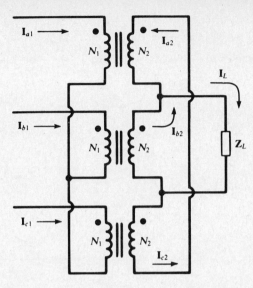

Fig. 11-21

▮ The ampere-turn dot rule is applied to each transformer.

$$N_1 I_{a1} + N_2 I_{a2} = 0 \quad \text{or} \quad I_{a1} = -\tfrac{10}{100}(10\,\underline{/0^\circ}) = -1\,\underline{/0^\circ}\ \text{A}$$

$$N_1 I_{b1} - N_2 I_{b2} = 0 \quad \text{or} \quad I_{b1} = \tfrac{10}{100}(20\,\underline{/0^\circ}) = 2\,\underline{/0^\circ}\ \text{A}$$

$$N_1 I_{c1} + N_2 I_{c2} = 0 \quad \text{or} \quad I_{c1} = -\tfrac{10}{100}(10\,\underline{/0^\circ}) = -1\,\underline{/0^\circ}) = -1\,\underline{/0^\circ}\ \text{A}$$

The sum of the primary currents provides a check: $I_{a1} + I_{b1} + I_{c1} = 0$.

11.31 A pair of coupled coils is shown in Fig. 11-22a. Redraw the figure by eliminating the geometrical information and replacing it by the dot notation. If the coil resistances are negligible, write the voltage equations for the circuit.

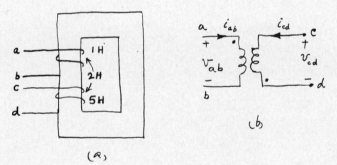

(a)

Fig. 11-22

▮ The required circuit is shown in Fig. 11-22b for which

$$v_{ab} = 1\frac{di_{ab}}{dt} - 2\frac{di_{cd}}{dt} \tag{1}$$

$$v_{cd} = -2\frac{di_{ab}}{dt} + 5\frac{di_{cd}}{dt} \tag{2}$$

11.32 In the circuit of Fig. 11-22b $v_{ab} = 100 \sin 1000t$ V and $i_{ab} = 5 \sin(1000t + 30^\circ)$ A. Determine v_{cd}.

▮ From Eq. (1) of Prob. 11.31,

$$\frac{di_{cd}}{dt} = \frac{1}{2}\left(\frac{di_{ab}}{dt} - v_{ab}\right)$$

Thus

$$v_{cd} = -2\frac{di_{ab}}{dt} + \frac{5}{2}\left(\frac{di_{ab}}{dt} - v_{ab}\right)$$

Substituting the given expressions for v_{ab} and i_{ab} yields $v_{cd} = 2385 \sin(1000t + 114.8^\circ)$ V.

11.33 Terminals b and c of the coils of Fig. 11-22a are connected and a voltage $v_{ad} = 400 \cos 1000t$ V is applied across a and d. Determine v_{ab} and v_{cd}.

▌ The circuit becomes as shown in Fig. 11-23, which gives

$$v_{ab} = 1\frac{di_{ad}}{dt} - 2\frac{di_{ad}}{dt} = -1\frac{di_{ad}}{dt} \qquad v_{cd} = 5\frac{di_{ad}}{dt} - 2\frac{di_{ad}}{dt} = 3\frac{di_{ad}}{dt} \qquad v_{ad} = 400 \cos 1000t = v_{ab} + v_{cd} = 2\frac{di_{ad}}{dt}$$

Hence, $di_{ad}/dt = 200 \cos 1000t$ A/s, giving $v_{ab} = -200 \cos 1000t$ V and $v_{cd} = 600 \cos 1000t$ V.

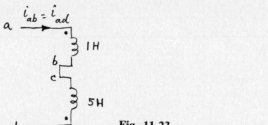

Fig. 11-23

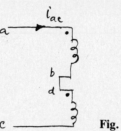

Fig. 11-24

11.34 Repeat Prob. 11.33, assuming that b and d are now connected and $v_{ac} = 400 \cos 1000t$ V.

▌ The circuit becomes as shown in Fig. 11-24, from which

$$i_{ac} = i_{ab} = -i_{cd} \qquad v_{ab} = 1\frac{di_{ac}}{dt} + 2\frac{di_{ac}}{dt} \qquad v_{dc} = 5\frac{di_{ac}}{dt} + 2\frac{di_{ac}}{dt}$$

$$v_{ac} = v_{ab} + v_{dc} = 10\frac{di_{ac}}{dt} = 400 \cos 1000t \text{ V}$$

Thus, $\dfrac{di_{ac}}{dt} = 40 \cos 1000t$ A/s so that $v_{ab} = 120 \cos 1000t$ V and $v_{cd} = -280 \cos 1000t$ V

11.35 Obtain expressions for currents i_{ab} and i_{cd} in Prob. 11.31.

▌ Solving Eqs. (1) and (2) and integrating yields

$$i_{ab} = \int (5v_{ab} + 2v_{cd})\,dt \qquad i_{cd} = \int (v_{cd} + 2v_{ab})\,dt$$

11.36 Three coupled coils are wound on a core as shown in Fig. 11-25a. Redraw it by using the dot notation. Use circles to relate coil 1 to the other coils and squares to relate coils 2 and 3. Neglecting coil resistances write the voltage equations.

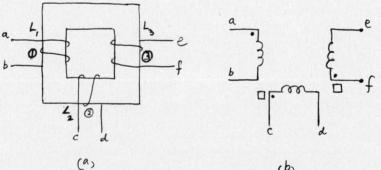

(a)

(b)

Fig. 11-25

▌ The required circuit is shown in Fig. 11-25b. The voltage equations are

$$v_{ab} = L_1\frac{di_{ab}}{dt} + M_{12}\frac{di_{cd}}{dt} - M_{13}\frac{di_{ef}}{dt} \qquad v_{cd} = M_{12}\frac{di_{ab}}{dt} + L_2\frac{di_{cd}}{dt} - M_{23}\frac{di_{ef}}{dt}$$

$$v_{ef} = -M_{13}\frac{di_{ab}}{dt} - M_{23}\frac{di_{cd}}{dt} + L_3\frac{di_{ef}}{dt}$$

11.37 For the coupled coils shown in Fig. 11-26, L_1, L_2, and M are equal to 9, 16, and 12 mH, respectively. The currents i_{ab} and i_{cd} are identical and equal to $3 \sin 1000t$ A. Find the voltages v_{ab} and v_{cd}.

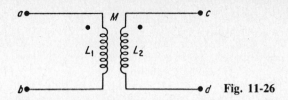

Fig. 11-26

$$v_{ab} = L_1 \frac{di_{ab}}{dt} + M \frac{di_{cd}}{dt} = 63 \cos 1000t \text{ V} \qquad v_{cd} = M \frac{di_{ab}}{dt} + L_2 \frac{di_{cd}}{dt} = 84 \cos 1000t \text{ V}$$

11.38 Find the total instantaneous power absorbed by the magnetic field of the coils of Fig. 11-26 (Prob. 11.37). What is the maximum energy stored in the magnetic field?

$$p = v_{ab}i_{ab} + v_{cd}i_{cd} = 220.5 \sin 2000t \text{ W}$$

At $t = 0$, stored energy w is zero because both i_{ab} and i_{cd} are zero. Thus,

$$w = \int_0^t p \, d\tau = 220.5 \int_0^t \sin 2000\tau \, d\tau = 0.11(1 - \cos 2000t) \text{ J} \qquad w_{\max} = 0.22 \text{ J}$$

11.39 The current i_{ab} in the coupled coils of Prob. 11.31 is held constant at 1 A. The current i_{cd} has the form shown in Fig. 11-27. Plot the voltages v_{ab} and v_{cd} for one period (8 time units).

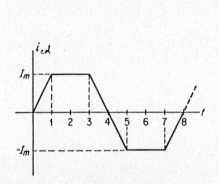

Fig. 11-27

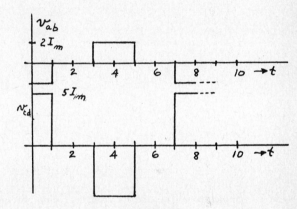

Fig. 11-28

$$v_{ab} = 1\frac{di_{ab}}{dt} - 2\frac{di_{cd}}{dt} = -2\frac{di_{cd}}{dt}$$

Thus, $\qquad v_{ab,\max} = V_{m1} = 2I_m \qquad v_{cd} = -2\frac{di_{ab}}{dt} + 5\frac{di_{cd}}{dt} = 5\frac{di_{cd}}{dt} \qquad$ and $\qquad v_{cd,\max} = V_{m2} = 5I_m$

The plots are shown in Fig. 11-28.

11.40 Sketch the power absorbed by each winding over $0 \le t \le 8$, using the data of Prob. 11.39.

$p_1 = v_{ab}i_{ab} = 1v_{ab}$ (see Fig. 11-28) and $p_2 = v_{cd}i_{cd}$ (see Figs. 11-28 and 11-27). The plots are shown in Fig. 11-29.

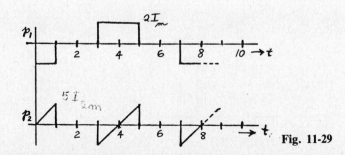

Fig. 11-29

11.41 Sketch the total energy absorbed in the magnetic field of the coils of Prob. 11.39, over $0 \le t \le 8$.

▮ $w = \frac{1}{2}L_1 i_{ab}^2 + \frac{1}{2}L_2 i_{cd}^2 - M i_{ab} i_{cd}$. Inserting the known numerical values gives $w = \frac{1}{2} + \frac{5}{2}i_{cd}^2 - 2i_{cd} = \frac{1}{10} + \frac{5}{2}(i_{cd} - \frac{2}{5})^2$ J. Referring to Fig. 11-27, we see that the w curve will be flat between $t = 1$ and $t = 3$, and between $t = 5$ and $t = 7$; it will be parabolic over the rest of the cycle. We shall always have $w \ge 0.1$ J, with equality at certain times only if $I_m \ge 0.4$ A. Figure 11-30 graphs w in the representative cases $I_m = 0.2$, 0.4, and 0.8 A.

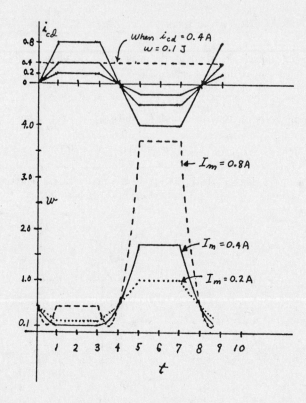

Fig. 11.30

11.42 An electronic amplifier is modeled by the circuit shown in Fig. 11-31. Determine the turns ratio of the ideal coupling transformer for maximum power transfer to the load resistor R.

▮ Power absorbed by R is

$$P_R = R(I_2)^2 \qquad N_2 I_2 = N_1 I_1 \qquad V_{65} = I_2 R = \frac{N_2}{N_1}V_{43} \qquad \mu V_{ab} = V_{43} + I_1 r_p$$

Combining the above four equations,

$$P_R = \frac{\mu^2 V_{ab}^2 (N_1/N_2)^2 R}{[r_p + (N_1/N_2)^2 R]^2}$$

The expression above is a maximum when $N_1/N_2 = \sqrt{r_p/R}$.

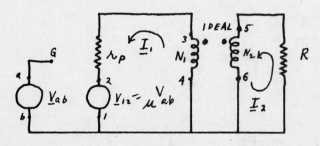

Fig. 11-31

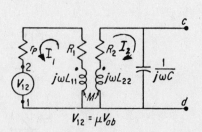

Fig. 11-32

11.43 Figure 11-32 shows the equivalent circuit of an amplifier. Obtain an expression for the voltage gain $G = V_{cd}/V_{ab}$.

▮ Establishing mesh currents counterclockwise and clockwise in the left and right meshes respectively,

$$[(r_p + R_1) + j\omega L_{11}]\mathbf{I}_1 + \qquad\qquad j\omega M \mathbf{I}_2 = \mu V_{ab}$$

$$j\omega M \mathbf{I}_1 + \left[R_2 + j\left(\omega L_{22} - \frac{1}{\omega C}\right)\right]\mathbf{I}_2 = 0$$

Solve for $\mathbf{I}_2$ and then obtain

$$G = \frac{\mathbf{I}_2/j\omega C}{V_{ab}} = \frac{-\mu M/C}{[(r_p + R_1) + j\omega L_{11}]\left[R_2 + j\left(\omega L_{22} - \frac{1}{\omega C}\right)\right] + \omega^2 M^2}$$

11.44 In the amplifier of Prob. 11.43, if $r_p \gg \sqrt{(R_1)^2 + (\omega L_{11})^2}$, obtain a simplified expression for the gain of the amplifier.

▮ We may write

$$(r_p + R_1) + j\omega L_{11} = r_p\left(1 + \frac{R_1 + j\omega L_{11}}{r_p}\right) = r_p\left(1 + \frac{(R_1^2 + \omega^2 L_{11}^2)^{1/2}\,\underline{/\theta}}{r_p}\right) \approx r_p$$

for the given condition. Therefore

$$G \approx \frac{-\mu M/C}{r_p[R_2 + j(\omega L_{22} - 1/\omega C)] + \omega^2 M^2}$$

11.45 An equivalent circuit of a transformer-coupled amplifier is shown in Fig. 11-33. Determine the voltage gain $G = V_{cd}/V_{ab}$, assuming that $r_p \gg 1/\omega C_1$.

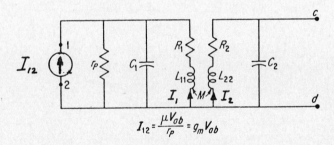

$$I_{12} = \frac{\mu V_{ab}}{r_p} = g_m V_{ab}$$

Fig. 11-33

▮ Choosing mesh currents upward through both of the inductances,

$$\left[R_1 + j\left(\omega L_{11} - \frac{1}{\omega C_1}\right)\right]\mathbf{I}_1 + \qquad\qquad j\omega M \mathbf{I}_2 = \left(-j\frac{1}{\omega C_1}\right)g_m V_{ab}$$

$$j\omega M \mathbf{I}_1 + \left[R_2 + j\left(\omega L_{22} - \frac{1}{\omega C_2}\right)\right]\mathbf{I}_2 = 0$$

$$\mathbf{I}_2 = j\omega C_2 V_{cd}$$

Elimination of $\mathbf{I}_1$ and $\mathbf{I}_2$ between the three equations yields

$$G = \frac{V_{cd}}{V_{ab}} = \frac{-jg_m(M/\omega C_1 C_2)}{[R_1 + j(\omega L_{11} - 1/\omega C_1)][R_2 + j(\omega L_{22} - 1/\omega C_2)] + \omega^2 M^2}$$

11.46 In a two-winding unloaded transformer, the flux linking the primary and the mutual flux are 10 mWb and 8 mWb, respectively. What is (*a*) the primary leakage flux, and (*b*) the coefficient of coupling?

▮ (*a*) Leakage flux $= 10 - 8 = 2$ mWb. (*b*) Coefficient of coupling, $k = \frac{8}{10} = 0.8$.

11.47 If the fluxes in the transformer of Prob. 11.46 are produced by a 2.4-A primary current, and $N_1 = 100$ turns and $N_2 = 160$ turns, determine the self- and mutual inductances of the two windings.

$$L_1 = N_1 \frac{\phi_1}{I_1} = 100 \frac{0.01}{2.4} = 0.417 \text{ H} \qquad M = N_2 \frac{\phi_{12}}{I_1} = 160 \frac{0.008}{2.4} = 0.533 \text{ H} = k\sqrt{L_1 L_2} = 0.8\sqrt{0.417 L_2}$$

Hence, $L_2 = 1.064$ H.

11.48 For a certain two-winding transformer, $N_1 = 250$, $N_2 = 300$, $k = 0.82$. The reluctance seen by the two windings is 420 ampere-turns per weber. What is the mutual inductance between the two windings?

$$M = k \frac{N_1 N_2}{\mathscr{R}} = 0.82 \frac{(250)(300)}{420} = 146 \text{ H}$$

11.49 A transformer has a coefficient of coupling of 0.7 and primary and secondary turns of 270 and 540, respectively. The primary has a resistance of 10 Ω and draws 2 A at 120 V 60 Hz. What is the no-load secondary voltage?

Representing the transformer by the circuit of Fig. 11-7b (with $Z_L = \infty$), we have

$$\mathbf{V}_1 = (R_1 + jX_1)\mathbf{I}_1 \qquad \text{or} \qquad (V_1)^2 = (I_1 R_1)^2 + (I_1 X_1)^2$$

$$I_1 R_1 = 2(10) = 20 \text{ V} \qquad V_1 = 120 \text{ V (given)}$$

Thus, $\qquad I_1 X_1 = \sqrt{(120)^2 - (20)^2} = 118.32 \text{ V} = E_1 \qquad \dfrac{E_2}{E_1} = k \dfrac{N_2}{N_1}$

Thus, $\qquad E_2 = 0.7 \frac{540}{270} 118.32 = 165.65 \text{ V}$

11.50 A 60-Hz 240-V generator connected to the primary of a transformer causes $20\ \underline{/10°}$ A in a load connected to the secondary. The coefficient of coupling is 0.75, and the parameters of the transformer (measured at 60 Hz) are $R_1 = 2.3\ \Omega$, $X_1 = 80\ \Omega$, $R_2 = 4.8\ \Omega$, $X_2 = 100\ \Omega$. Determine (*a*) the magnitude and phase angle of the primary current and (*b*) the primary current if the load is removed.

Magnetizing reactance is $X_m = k\sqrt{X_1 X_2} = 0.75\sqrt{(80)(100)} = 67.1\ \Omega$.

(*a*) $\qquad \mathbf{I}_1 = \dfrac{\mathbf{E}_{\text{gen}} + jX_m \mathbf{I}_2}{R_1 + jX_1} = \dfrac{240\ \underline{/0°} + j67.1(20\ \underline{/10°})}{2.3 + j80} = 16.5\ \underline{/1.3°}\ \text{A}$

(*b*) With $\mathbf{I}_2 = 0$, $\mathbf{I}_1 = (240\ \underline{/0°})/(2.3 + j80) = 3\ \underline{/-88.4°}$ A.

11.51 The equivalent resistance and equivalent reactance (referred to the high-voltage side) for a certain 25-kVA 2400/600-V 60-Hz transformer are 2.8 and 6.0 Ω, respectively. If a load impedance of $10\ \underline{/20°}$ Ω is connected to the low side, determine (*a*) the equivalent input impedance of the combined transformer and load; (*b*) the primary current if 2400 V is applied to the high-voltage side.

(*a*) Using the procedure of Prob. 11.9,

$$\mathbf{Z}_{\text{in}} = (R_{e,\text{HS}} + jX_{e,\text{HS}}) + \mathbf{Z}_{\text{load,HS}} = (2.8 + j6.0) + 10\ \underline{/20°}\left(\frac{2400}{600}\right)^2$$

$$= (2.8 + j6.0) + (150.35 + j54.72)$$

$$= (153.15 + j60.72) = 164.75\ \underline{/21.63°}\ \Omega$$

(*b*) From Ohm's law,

$$\mathbf{I}_{p,\text{HS}} = \frac{\mathbf{V}_{\text{HS}}}{\mathbf{Z}_{\text{in,HS}}} = \frac{2400\ \underline{/0°}}{164.75\ \underline{/21.63°}} = 14.57\ \underline{/-21.63°}\ \text{A}$$

11.52 A 50-kVA 4160/600-V 60-Hz transformer has an equivalent impedance referred to the high side of $9.5\ \underline{/50°}$ Ω. Determine the input impedance of the combined transformer and load if the secondary is supplying rated kVA at 600 V to an 0.80-pf lagging load.

▮ The power factor angle is $\theta = \cos^{-1} 0.80 = 36.86°$ lagging. The phasor power supplied by the secondary is

$$\mathbf{S}_2 = 50{,}000\ \underline{/36.86°}\ \text{VA} \qquad \mathbf{S}_2 = \mathbf{V}_2\mathbf{I}_2^*$$

$$50{,}000\ \underline{/36.86} = (600\ \underline{/0°})\mathbf{I}_2^* \qquad \mathbf{I}_2^* = 83.33\ \underline{/36.86°} \qquad \mathbf{I}_2 = 83.33\ \underline{/-36.86°}\ \text{A}$$

From Ohm's law,

$$\mathbf{Z}_{\text{load}} = \frac{\mathbf{V}_2}{\mathbf{I}_2} = \frac{600\ \underline{/0°}}{83.33\ \underline{/-36.86°}} = 7.20\ \underline{/36.86°}\ \Omega \qquad \mathbf{Z}_{\text{load,HS}} = 7.20\ \underline{/36.86°}(\tfrac{4160}{600})^2 = 346.11\ \underline{/36.86°}\ \Omega$$

$$\mathbf{Z}_{\text{in,HS}} = R_{e,\text{HS}} + jX_{e,\text{HS}} + \mathbf{Z}_{\text{load,HS}} = 9.50\ \underline{/50°} + 346.11\ \underline{/36.86°} \qquad \mathbf{Z}_{\text{in,HS}} = 355.37\ \underline{/37.21°}\ \Omega$$

11.53 Determine the required turns ratio for an impedance-matching transformer that will provide maximum power transfer to a 6-Ω loudspeaker from an amplifier with an output impedance of 50 kΩ resistive. The circuit is shown in Fig. 11-34a.

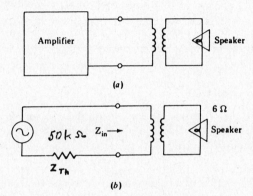

(a)

(b)

Fig. 11-34

▮ The output impedance of an amplifier is its Thévenin impedance. Thus the amplifier acts as a generator whose Thévenin impedance (resistance, in this case) is 50 kΩ, as shown in Fig. 11-34b. For maximum power transfer, the amplifier must "see" a load the resistance of which is equal to its own resistance. Placing a transformer between the load and the amplifier causes the amplifier to "see" a resistance equal to $Z_{\text{in}} = (N_1/N_2)^2 Z_{\text{load}}$. Thus, for maximum power transfer, Z_{in} must equal 50 000 Ω.

$$50\,000 = \left(\frac{N_1}{N_2}\right)^2 6 \qquad \frac{N_1}{N_2} = 91.3$$

11.54 An impedance-matching transformer is used to couple a 20-Ω resistive load to an amplifier whose Thévenin equivalent is given in Fig. 11-35a. Determine (**a**) the turns ratio required for maximum power transfer; (**b**) the primary current; (**c**) the secondary current; and (**d**) the secondary voltage.

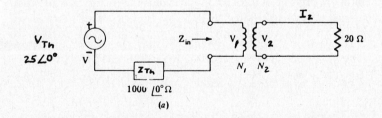

(a)

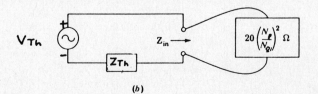

(b)

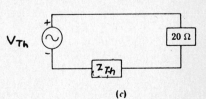

(c)

Fig. 11-35

▮ (a) For a perfect match the $\mathbf{Z}_{in}$ of the combined transformer and load must equal $\mathbf{Z}_{Th}^*$. Thus,

$$\mathbf{Z}_{Th}^* = \mathbf{Z}_{in} = \left(\frac{N_1}{N_2}\right)^2 \mathbf{Z}_{load} \qquad 1000 \underline{/0°} = \left(\frac{N_1}{N_2}\right)^2 (20 \underline{/0°}) \qquad \frac{N_1}{N_2} = 7.07$$

(b) The equivalent circuit for perfect matching is shown in Fig. 11-35b. Applying Ohm's law,

$$\mathbf{I}_1 = \frac{\mathbf{V}_{Th}}{\mathbf{Z}_{Th} + \mathbf{Z}_{in}} = \frac{25 \underline{/0°}}{1000 + 1000} = 0.0125 \underline{/0°} \text{ A}$$

(c)
$$\frac{\mathbf{I}_2}{\mathbf{I}_1} = \frac{N_1}{N_2} \qquad \frac{\mathbf{I}_2}{0.0125 \underline{/0°}} = \frac{7.07}{1} \qquad \mathbf{I}_2 = 0.0884 \underline{/0°} \text{ A}$$

(d) Referring to Fig. 11-35a,

$$\mathbf{V}_2 = \mathbf{I}_2 \mathbf{Z}_{load} \qquad \mathbf{V}_2 = 20\mathbf{I}_2 = 20(0.0884) \underline{/0°} = 1.768 \text{ V}$$

11.55 For the circuit and data of Prob. 11.54, calculate (a) the power delivered to the load if the transformer is not used and (b) the percent increase in delivered power when the transformer is used.

▮ (a) The circuit becomes as shown in Fig. 11-35c.

$$\mathbf{I} = \frac{\mathbf{V}_{Th}}{\mathbf{Z}_{Th} + 20} = \frac{25 \underline{/0°}}{1000 + 20} = 0.0245 \text{ A} \qquad P = I_{load}^2 R_{load} = (0.0245)^2 (20) = 12 \text{ mW}$$

(b) From Prob. 11.54, $P = (0.0884)^2 (20) = 156.3$ mW (with the transformer). Percent increase is $[(0.1563 - 0.0120)/0.0120](100\%) = 1202.5\%$. The addition of an impedance-matching transformer resulted in a twelve-fold increase in power delivered to the load.

11.56 Two coupled coils, having a coefficient of coupling 0.9, have a 10-H mutual inductance. Other data are $N_1 = 100$ and $N_2 = 300$. Determine the primary current to produce 0.8-Wb flux to link with the secondary coil.

▮
$$M = N_2 \frac{\phi_{12}}{I_1} \qquad \text{or} \qquad 300 = 100 \frac{0.8}{I_1}$$

Thus, $I_1 = 24$ A.

11.57 From the data of Prob. 11.56, find the self-inductances of the coils.

▮
$$\phi_{12} = k\phi_1 \qquad \text{or} \qquad 0.8 = 0.9\phi_1 \qquad \text{or} \qquad \phi_1 = 0.89 \text{ Wb}$$

$$L_1 = N_1 \frac{\phi_1}{I_1} = 100 \frac{0.89}{24} = 3.7 \text{ H} \qquad M = k\sqrt{L_1 L_2} \qquad \text{or} \qquad 10 = 0.9\sqrt{3.7 L_2}$$

Thus $L_2 = 33.37$ H.

11.58 A 30-A current in the primary of a transformer results in a primary flux of 0.5 Wb. Given: $N_1 = 2N_2 = 200$ and $k = 0.9$. Find L_1, L_2, and M.

▮
$$M = N_2 \frac{\phi_{12}}{I_1} = N_2 \frac{k\phi_1}{I_1} = 100 \frac{0.9 \times 0.5}{30} = 1.5 \text{ H}$$

$$L_1 = N_1 \frac{\phi_1}{I_1} = 200 \frac{0.5}{30} = 3.33 \text{ H} \qquad M = k\sqrt{L_1 L_2} \qquad \text{or} \qquad 1.5 = 0.9\sqrt{3.33 L_2}$$

Thus, $L_2 = 0.83$ H.

11.59 A 120-V primary voltage produces a $15 \underline{/-60°}$ A secondary current in a transformer. Other data are: $k = 0.86$, $R_1 = 1.8 \, \Omega$, $R_2 = 4.6 \, \Omega$, $X_1 = 57 \, \Omega$, and $X_2 = 150 \, \Omega$. Calculate the primary current.

▮ Proceeding as in Prob. 11.50, we have

$$X_m = k\sqrt{X_1 X_2} = 0.86\sqrt{(57)(150)} = 79.5 \, \Omega$$

Thus,
$$\mathbf{I}_1 = \frac{120 \underline{/0°} + (15 \underline{/-60°})(79.5 \underline{/90°})}{1.8 + j57} = 22.8 \underline{/-60.8°} \text{ A}$$

11.60 Repeat Prob. 11.59 for (a) $\mathbf{I}_2 = 0$ and (b) $\mathbf{I}_2 = 15 \underline{/60°}$ A.

> (a) $\mathbf{I}_1 = \dfrac{120 \underline{/0°}}{1.8 + j57} = 2.1 \underline{/-88.7°}$ A   (b) $\mathbf{I}_1 = \dfrac{120 \underline{/0°} + (15 \underline{/60°})(79.5 \underline{/90°})}{1.8 + j57} = 19.1 \underline{/58.7°}$ A

11.61 A transformer draws a $4 \underline{/25°}$-A primary current of 60 V. Other data are: $R_1 = 3.9\,\Omega$, $X_1 = 65\,\Omega$, $X_M = 48\,\Omega$. Determine the secondary current.

> In this case, we have

$$4 \underline{/25°} = \frac{60 \underline{/0°} + \mathbf{I}_2(j48)}{3.9 + j65} = \frac{60 \underline{/0°} + \mathbf{I}_2(j48)}{65.11 \underline{/86.6°}} \quad \text{or} \quad 260.46 \underline{/111.6°} - 60 \underline{/0°} = \mathbf{I}_2(48 \underline{/90°})$$

Hence, $\mathbf{I}_2 = 6 \underline{/32.7°}$ A.

11.62 A 4160/208-V transformer has a load impedance of $0.01 \underline{/30°}\,\Omega$ connected to the low-voltage side. The equivalent impedance referred to the high-voltage side is $2 \underline{/70°}\,\Omega$. What is the input impedance of the transformer and the load?

> Referred to the high-voltage side,

$$\mathbf{Z}_{\text{load}} = \left(\frac{4160}{208}\right)^2 (0.01 \underline{/30°}) = 4 \underline{/30°} = 3.46 + j2\,\Omega$$

Thus, $\quad \mathbf{Z}_{\text{in}} = 4 \underline{/30°} + 2 \underline{/70°} = 3.46 + j2 + 0.68 + j1.88 = 4.14 + j3.88 = 5.68 \underline{/43.1°}\,\Omega$

11.63 A 2300/120-V transformer is connected to a $0.04 \underline{/10°}$-Ω load on the low-voltage side. If the equivalent impedance referred to the high-voltage side is $4 \underline{/70°}\,\Omega$, calculate the primary current.

> Referred to the high-voltage side

$$\mathbf{Z}_{\text{load}} = \left(\frac{2300}{120}\right)^2 (0.04 \underline{/10°}) = 14.69 \underline{/10°}\,\Omega \qquad \mathbf{Z}_{\text{in}} = 14.69 \underline{/10°} + 4 \underline{/70°} = 17.02 \underline{/21.76°}\,\Omega$$

Thus, $$\mathbf{I}_1 = \frac{2300}{17.02 \underline{/21.76°}} = 135.14 \underline{/-21.76°}\,\text{A}$$

11.64 The primary and secondary impedances of a 2.2-kV/600 − V transformer are $\mathbf{Z}_1 = (1.4 + j3.2)\,\Omega$ and $\mathbf{Z}_2 = (0.11 + j0.25)\,\Omega$. If the secondary current is $41.67 \underline{/-36.87°}$ A at $600 \underline{/0°}$ V, determine the magnitude of the primary input voltage.

> $$\mathbf{Z}_{\text{load}} = \frac{600 \underline{/0°}}{41.67 \underline{/-36.87°}} = 14.4 \underline{/36.87°} = 11.52 + j8.64\,\Omega$$

$$\mathbf{Z}_2 + \mathbf{Z}_{\text{load}} = (0.11 + j0.25) + (11.52 + j8.64) = 14.64 \underline{/37.39°}\,\Omega \text{ (referred to low-voltage side)}$$

$$= \left(\frac{2200}{600}\right)^2 (14.64 \underline{/37.39°}) = 196.81 \underline{/37.39°}\,\Omega \text{ (referred to high-voltage side)}$$

$$\mathbf{Z}_{\text{in}} = (1.4 + j3.2) + 196.81 \underline{/37.39°} = 199.87 \underline{/37.88°}\,\Omega$$

$$\frac{I_1}{I_2} = \frac{N_2}{N_1} \quad \text{or} \quad I_1 = \frac{600}{2200}\,41.67 = 11.36\,\text{A}$$

Hence, $V_1 = I_1(Z_{\text{in}}) = (11.36)(199.87) = 2271.4$ V.

11.65 Find the input current to the two magnetically coupled coils of Fig. 11-36.

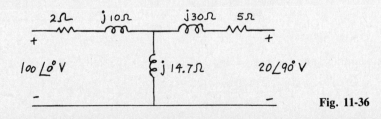

Fig. 11-36

▮ The circuit equations may be written as:

$$(2 + j10 + j14.7)\mathbf{I}_1 + j14.7\mathbf{I}_2 = 100 \,\underline{/0^\circ}$$

$$j14.7\mathbf{I}_1 + (5 + j30 + j14.7)\mathbf{I}_2 = 20 \,\underline{/90^\circ}$$

Solving for $\mathbf{I}_1$ yields $\mathbf{I}_1 = 5.03 \,\underline{/-86.44^\circ}$ A

11.66 For the coupled circuit of Fig. 11-37, we have $R_1 = 70\,\Omega$, $X_1 = 62.83\,\Omega$, $R_2 = 80\,\Omega$, $X_2 = 251.33\,\Omega$, and $|X_M| = 94.25\,\Omega$. Determine $\mathbf{I}$ if $\mathbf{V}_T = 120 \,\underline{/0^\circ}$ V.

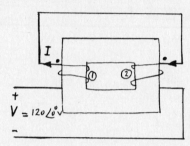

Fig. 11-37

▮ The dots show that X_M is negative (see Prob. 11.4).

$$\mathbf{V}_T = \mathbf{I}[(R_1 + R_2) + j(X_1 + X_2 - 2|X_M|)]$$

$$120 \,\underline{/0^\circ} = \mathbf{I}\{(70 + 80) + j[62.83 + 251.33 - 2(94.25)]\}$$

$$\mathbf{I} = \frac{120 \,\underline{/0^\circ}}{195.68 \,\underline{/39.95^\circ}} = 0.61 \,\underline{/-39.95^\circ} \text{ A}$$

11.67 Repeat Prob. 11.66 if the connections to coil 2 are interchanged.

▮ Now X_M is positive.

$$\mathbf{V}_T = \mathbf{I}[(R_1 + R_2) + j(X_1 + X_2 + 2|X_M|)]$$

$$120 \,\underline{/0^\circ} = \mathbf{I}\{(70 + 80) + j[62.83 + 251.33 + 2(94.25)]\} = \mathbf{I}(524.56 \,\underline{/73.38^\circ})$$

$$\mathbf{I} = 0.23 \,\underline{/-73.38^\circ} \text{ A}$$

11.68 For each sketch in Fig. 11-38, determine the equivalent inductance of the series-connected coupled coils, if L_1 and L_2 are 2 and 8 H, respectively, and $k = 1$.

▮ $|M| = k\sqrt{L_1 L_2} = 1\sqrt{(2)(8)} = 4$ H. For Fig. 11-38a and c an assumed direction of current through the series connection will show current entering one dot and leaving the other dot. Hence M is negative, and $L_{eq} = L_1 + L_2 - 2|M| = 2 + 8 - 2(4) = 2$ H. For Fig. 11-38b and d an assumed direction of current through the series connection will show the current entering both dots or leaving both dots. Hence M is positive, and $L_{eq} = L_1 + L_2 + 2|M| = 2 + 8 + 2(4) = 18$ H.

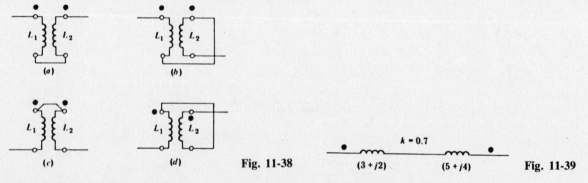

(a)   (b)   (c)   (d)   Fig. 11-38 $k = 0.7$ $(3 + j2)$ $(5 + j4)$ Fig. 11-39

11.69 For the coupled coils shown in Fig. 11-39, determine (a) $|X_M|$; (b) R_{eq}; (c) X_{eq}; (d) Z_{eq}.

▮ (a) $|X_M| = k\sqrt{X_1 X_2} = 0.7\sqrt{(2)(4)} = 1.98\,\Omega$ (b) $R_{eq} = 3 + 5 = 8\,\Omega$
(c) From Fig. 11-39 we see that X_M is negative. Thus, $X_{eq} = X_1 + X_2 - 2|X_M| = 2 + 4 - 2(1.98) = 2.04\,\Omega$.
(d) $\mathbf{Z}_{eq} = R_{eq} + jX_{eq} = 8 + j2.04 = 8.26 \,\underline{/14.31^\circ}\,\Omega$

11.70   In the coupled circuit of Fig. 11-40 determine the ammeter reading.

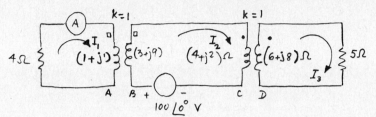

Fig. 11-40

▮ The ammeter reads $|\mathbf{I}_1|$, to solve for which we use mesh analysis. First, however, the mutual reactances between the coils AB and CD must be determined:

$$X_{MAB} = k\sqrt{X_A X_B} = 1\sqrt{(1)(9)} = 3 \ \Omega \qquad X_{MCD} = k\sqrt{X_C X_D} = 1\sqrt{(2)(8)} = 4 \ \Omega$$

Now the mesh equations become

$$(5 + j1)\mathbf{I}_1 - j3\mathbf{I}_2 \qquad\qquad\qquad = 0$$
$$-j3\mathbf{I}_1 + (7 + j11)\mathbf{I}_2 - j4\mathbf{I}_3 \qquad = 100 \ \underline{/0^\circ}$$
$$-j4\mathbf{I}_2 \qquad\qquad + (11 + j8)\mathbf{I}_3 = 0$$

Solving for $\mathbf{I}_1$ yields $\mathbf{I}_1 = 4.23 \ \underline{/32.87^\circ}$ A. Ammeter reads 4.23 A.

11.71   Three coils (A, B, and C), with $k = 1$,   are wound on a common core so that they are mutually coupled and may be represented by the circuit of Fig. 11-41. Determine $\mathbf{I}_1$.

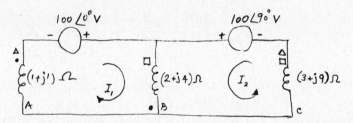

Fig. 11-41

▮ The mutual reactances are

$$X_{MAB} = 1\sqrt{(1)(4)} = 2 \ \Omega \qquad X_{MBC} = 1\sqrt{(4)(9)} = 6 \ \Omega \qquad X_{MCA} = 1\sqrt{(9)(1)} = 3 \ \Omega$$

The mesh equations may now be written as

$$[(1 + j1) + (2 + j4) + 2(j2)]\mathbf{I}_1 + [(2 + j4) + j2 + j3 - j6]\mathbf{I}_2 \quad = 100 \ \underline{/0^\circ}$$
$$[(2 + j4) + j2 + j3 - j6]\mathbf{I}_1 + [(2 + j4) + (3 + j9) - 2(j6)]\mathbf{I}_2 = 100 \ \underline{/90^\circ}$$

or

$$(3 + j9)\mathbf{I}_1 + (2 + j3)\mathbf{I}_2 \qquad\qquad = 100 \ \underline{/0^\circ}$$
$$(2 + j3)\mathbf{I}_1 + (5 + j1)\mathbf{I}_2 \qquad\qquad = 100 \ \underline{/90^\circ}$$

Solving for $\mathbf{I}_1$ yields $\mathbf{I}_1 = 21.42 \ \underline{/-80.16}$ A.

11.72   Repeat Prob. 11.71 assuming that coils are wound on separate cores.

▮ In this case all X_M's $= 0$,   and the mesh equations become

$$[(1 + j1) + (2 + j4)]\mathbf{I}_1 + (2 + j4)\mathbf{I}_2 \qquad\qquad = 100 \ \underline{/0^\circ}$$
$$(2 + j4)\mathbf{I}_1 + [(2 + j4) + (3 + j9)]\mathbf{I}_2 = 100 \ \underline{/90^\circ}$$

Solving for $\mathbf{I}_1$ yields $\mathbf{I}_1 = 23.22 \ \underline{/-77.65^\circ}$ A.

11.73   Determine the complex power supplied by each generator of the circuit of Prob. 11.72.

▮ Solving for $\mathbf{I}_2$ in Prob. 11.72 yields $\mathbf{I}_2 = 11.55 \ \underline{/-300.25^\circ}$ A. Thus,

$$\mathbf{S}_1 = \mathbf{V}_1 \mathbf{I}_1^* = (100 \ \underline{/0^\circ})(23.22 \ \underline{/77.65^\circ}) = 496.6 + j2268.3 \text{ VA}$$

$$\mathbf{S}_2 = \mathbf{V}_2 \mathbf{I}_2^* = (100 \ \underline{/90^\circ})(11.55 \ \underline{/300.25^\circ}) = 997.7 + j581.9 \text{ VA}$$

11.74 The coupled circuit of Fig. 11-42a is to be represented by an equivalent T circuit shown in Fig. 11-42b. Determine the parameters of the T circuit.

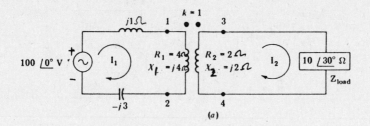

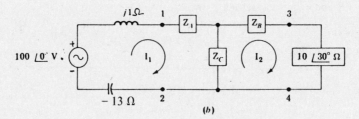

Fig. 11-42

$$X_M = k\sqrt{X_1 X_2} = 1\sqrt{(4)(2)} = 2.83 \ \Omega$$

For the magnetically coupled circuit, the mesh equations are

$$100 \underline{/0^\circ} = (j1 + 4 + j4 - j3 + 0)\mathbf{I}_1 + \qquad (0 - j2.83)\mathbf{I}_2$$
$$0 = \qquad (0 - j2.83)\mathbf{I}_1 + (2 + j2 + 10 \underline{/30^\circ} + 0)\mathbf{I}_2$$

or

$$100 = (4 + j2)\mathbf{I}_1 + (-j2.83)\mathbf{I}_2$$
$$0 = (-j2.83)\mathbf{I}_1 + (2 + j2 + 10 \underline{/30^\circ})\mathbf{I}_2$$

For the conductively coupled circuit, the mesh equations are

$$100 \underline{/0^\circ} = (j1 + \mathbf{Z}_A + \mathbf{Z}_C - j3)\mathbf{I}_1 + (-\mathbf{Z}_C)\mathbf{I}_2$$
$$0 = (-\mathbf{Z}_C)\mathbf{I}_1 + (\mathbf{Z}_C + \mathbf{Z}_B + 10 \underline{/30^\circ})\mathbf{I}_2$$

For the two circuits to be equivalent, we must have

$$4 + j2 = \mathbf{Z}_A + \mathbf{Z}_C - j2 \qquad -j2.83 = -\mathbf{Z}_C \qquad 2 + j2 + 10 \underline{/30^\circ} = \mathbf{Z}_C + \mathbf{Z}_B + 10 \underline{/30^\circ}$$

Solving the three simultaneous equations yields

$$\mathbf{Z}_A = 4 + j1.17 \ \Omega \qquad \mathbf{Z}_B = 2 - j0.83 \ \Omega \qquad \mathbf{Z}_C = j2.83 \ \Omega$$

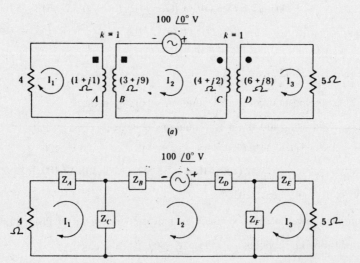

Fig. 11-43

11.75 Replace the transformers in Fig. 11-43a by equivalent T sections.

▎ Figure 11-43b represents the circuit with the equivalent T sections whose parameters are to be determined. The mesh equations for the magnetically coupled circuit of Fig. 11-43a were obtained in Prob. 11.70 as

$$0 = (5 + j1)\mathbf{I}_1 + (-j3)\mathbf{I}_2 \qquad\quad + (0)\mathbf{I}_3$$

$$100 = (-j3)\mathbf{I}_1 \quad + (7 + j11)\mathbf{I}_2 + (-j4)\mathbf{I}_3$$

$$0 = (0)\mathbf{I}_1 \qquad + (-j4)\mathbf{I}_2 \qquad + (11 + j8)\mathbf{I}_3$$

The mesh equations for the conductively coupled equivalent circuit in Fig. 11-43b are

$$0 = (4 + \mathbf{Z}_A + \mathbf{Z}_C)\mathbf{I}_1 + (-\mathbf{Z}_C)\mathbf{I}_2$$

$$100 = (-\mathbf{Z}_C)\mathbf{I}_1 + (\mathbf{Z}_B + \mathbf{Z}_C + \mathbf{Z}_D + \mathbf{Z}_F) = \mathbf{I}_2 + (-\mathbf{Z}_F)\mathbf{I}_3$$

$$0 = (-\mathbf{Z}_F)\mathbf{I}_2 + (\mathbf{Z}_F + \mathbf{Z}_E + 5)\,\mathbf{I}_3$$

Equating the respective coefficients,

$$5 + j1 = 4 + \mathbf{Z}_A + \mathbf{Z}_C \qquad -j3 = -\mathbf{Z}_C$$

$$7 + j11 = \mathbf{Z}_C + \mathbf{Z}_B + \mathbf{Z}_D + \mathbf{Z}_F \qquad -j4 = -\mathbf{Z}_F \qquad 11 + j8 = \mathbf{Z}_F + \mathbf{Z}_E + 5$$

Solving the five simultaneous equations yields

$$\mathbf{Z}_A = 1 - j2\ \Omega \qquad \mathbf{Z}_E = 6 + j4\ \Omega \qquad \mathbf{Z}_C = j3\ \Omega \qquad \mathbf{Z}_F = j4\ \Omega \qquad \mathbf{Z}_B + \mathbf{Z}_D = 7 + j4\ \Omega$$

Referring to Fig. 11-34b, $\mathbf{Z}_B$ is in series with $\mathbf{Z}_D$ and is, therefore, represented as one impedance $(\mathbf{Z}_B + \mathbf{Z}_D)$.

11.76 Assign polarity markings to the coils of Fig. 11-44a.

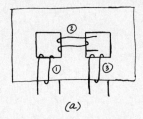

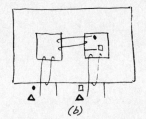

(a)   (b)   **Fig. 11-44**

▎ The markings are shown in Fig. 11-44b where the dots are for coils 1 and 2, triangles for coils 1 and 3, and squares for coils 2 and 3.

11.77 Determine the input impedance for the circuit in Fig. 11-45. The impedances of the respective coils are $\mathbf{Z}_1 = (5 + j9)\ \Omega$ and $\mathbf{Z}_2 = (3 + j4)\ \Omega$.

▎ $\mathbf{Z}_{in} = 3 + j4 + 3 + j4 = 6 + j8 = 10\ \underline{/53.13°}\ \Omega$.

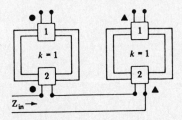

Fig. 11-45

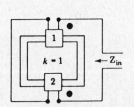

Fig. 11-46

11.78 Determine the input impedance for the circuit shown in Fig. 11-46. The impedances of the respective coils are $\mathbf{Z}_1 = (5 + j9)\ \Omega$ and $\mathbf{Z}_2 = (3 + j4)\ \Omega$.

▎ $X_M = 1\sqrt{(9)(4)} = 6\ \Omega \qquad \mathbf{Z}_{in} = 5 + j9 + 3 + j4 - 2(j6) = 8 + j1 = 8.06\ \underline{/7.13°}\ \Omega$

11.79 For each connection shown in Fig. 11-47, determine the overall inductance of the coupled coils in series if $L_1 = 3\ \text{H}$, $L_2 = 5\ \text{H}$, $k = 0.60$.

▎ $M = 0.6\sqrt{(3)(5)} = 2.32\ \text{H}$.
(a) $L = 3 + 5 - 2(2.32) = 3.36\ \text{H}$ (b) $L = 3 + 5 - 2(2.32) = 3.36\ \text{H}$
(c) $L = 3 + 5 + 2(2.32) = 12.64\ \text{H}$ (d) $L = 3 + 5 + 2(2.32) = 12.64\ \text{H}$

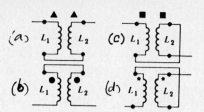

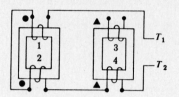

Fig. 11-47   Fig. 11-48

11.80   The coil impedances in Fig. 11-48 are $Z_1 = (3 + j8) \Omega$, $Z_2 = (1 + j2)$ **V**, $Z_3 = (5 + j1) \Omega$, $Z_4 = (6 + j3) \Omega$. If $k = 1.0$, determine the impedance measured at terminals $T_1 T_2$.

▌ $M_{12} = 1\sqrt{(8)(2)} = 4 \Omega$ $Z = (3 + j8) + (1 + j2) - 2(j4) + (6 + j3) = (10 + j5) \Omega$

11.81   For the circuit of Fig. 11-49 calculate the mutual reactance and mutual inductance.

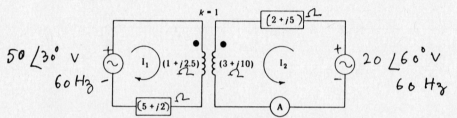

Fig. 11-49

▌ $X_M = k\sqrt{X_1 X_2} = 1\sqrt{(2.5)(10)} = 5 \Omega$ $X_M = 2\pi f M$

Thus, $M = 5/2\pi(60) = 13.26 \, \text{mH}$.

11.82   In the circuit of Fig. 11-49 determine the ammeter reading.

▌   The mesh equations become

$$[(1 + j2.5) + (5 + j2)]\mathbf{I}_1 + (j5)\mathbf{I}_2 \qquad\qquad = 50 \underline{/30°}$$
$$(j5)\mathbf{I}_1 + [(2 + j5) + (3 + j10)]\mathbf{I}_2 = 20 \underline{/60°}$$

Solving for $\mathbf{I}_2$ yields $\mathbf{I}_2 = 1.12 \underline{/-128.61°} \, \text{A}$.   Ammeter reads 1.12 A.

11.83   Determine the ammeter readings in the circuit of Fig. 11-50.

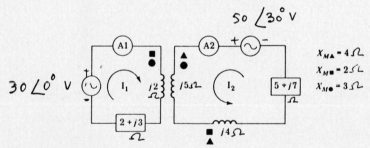

Fig. 11-50

▌   The mesh equations are

$$[(2 + j3) + j2]\mathbf{I}_1 + (j2 + j3)\mathbf{I}_2 \qquad\qquad = 30 \underline{/0°}$$
$$(j2 + j3)\mathbf{I}_1 + [j4 + j5 + (5 + j7) + 2(j4)]\mathbf{I}_2 = 50 \underline{/30°}$$

Solving these equations yields $\mathbf{I}_1 = 5.12 \underline{/-78.04°} \, \text{A}$ and $\mathbf{I}_2 = 1.09 \underline{/-31.16°} \, \text{A}$.   Thus, A1 reads 5.12 A and A2 reads 1.09 A.

11.84   Determine the complex power drawn by the $(5 + j7)$-Ω impedance of the circuit of Fig. 11-50.

▌ $S = \mathbf{VI}^*$.   From Prob. 11.83,

$$\mathbf{I}^* = \mathbf{I}_2^* = 1.09 \underline{/31.16°} \, \text{A} \qquad \text{and} \qquad \mathbf{V} = (5 + j7)(1.09 \underline{/-31.16°}) = 9.37 \underline{/23.36°} \, \text{V}$$

Hence, $S = (9.37 \underline{/23.36°})(1.09 \underline{/31.16°}) = 5.94 + j8.31 \, \text{VA}$.

11.85 Determine the ammeter readings in the coupled circuit of Fig. 11-51.

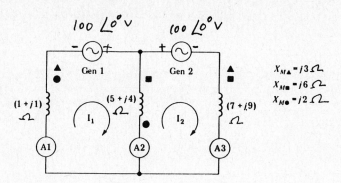

Fig. 11-51

▮ The mesh equations may be written as:

$$[1 + j1 + 5 + j4 + 2(j2)]\mathbf{I}_1 + [-(5 + j4) + (j6 - j3 - j2)]\mathbf{I}_2 = 100\ \underline{/0°}$$

$$[-(5 + j4) + (j6 - j3 - j2)]\mathbf{I}_1 + [5 + j4 + 7 + j9 - 2(j6)]\mathbf{I}_2 = -100\ \underline{/0°}$$

Hence, $\mathbf{I}_1 = 7.56\ \underline{/-76.72°}$ A and $\mathbf{I}_2 = 6.32\ \underline{/-160.23°}$ A. A1 reads 7.56 A; A3 reads 6.32 A; A2 reads $|7.56\ \underline{/-76.72°} - 6.32\ \underline{/-160.23°}|$, or 9.29 A.

11.86 Determine the complex power supplied by each source of the circuit of Fig. 11-51.

▮
$$\mathbf{S}_1 = \mathbf{V}_1\mathbf{I}_1^* = (100\ \underline{/0°})(7.56\ \underline{/76.72°}) = 173.7 + j735.8\ \text{VA}$$

$$\mathbf{S}_2 = -\mathbf{V}_2\mathbf{I}_2^* = (-100\ \underline{/0°})(6.32\ \underline{/160.23°}) = 594.8 - j213.77\ \text{VA}$$

11.87 What is the ammeter reading in the circuit of Fig. 11-52?

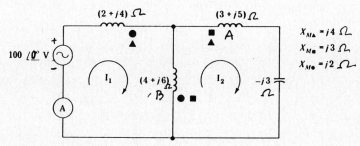

Fig. 11-52

▮ The mesh equations are

$$[(2 + j4) + (4 + j6) + 2(j2)]\mathbf{I}_1 + [-(4 + j6) - j2 - j4 - j3]\mathbf{I}_2 = 100\ \underline{/0°}$$

$$[-(4 + j6) - j2 - j4 - j3]\mathbf{I}_1 + [(4 + j6) + (3 + j5) - j3 + 2(j3)]\mathbf{I}_2 = 0$$

Hence $\mathbf{I}_1 = 18.89\ \underline{/15.01°}$ A. The ammeter reading is 18.89 A.

11.88 Calculate the coefficient of coupling between coils A and B of the circuit of Fig. 11-52.

▮ $X_A = 5\ \Omega$ and $X_B = 6\ \Omega$. Also $X_M = 3\ \Omega$ (given). Hence, $k = X_M/\sqrt{X_A X_B} = 3/\sqrt{(5)(6)} = 0.548$.

11.89 Determine the number of turns of coil B of the circuit of Fig. 11-52 if coil A has 300 turns.

▮
$$\frac{L_A}{L_B} = \frac{X_A}{X_B} = \left(\frac{N_A}{N_B}\right)^2 \quad \text{or} \quad \frac{5}{6} = \left(\frac{300}{N_B}\right)^2$$

Thus, $N_B \approx 329$ turns.

11.90 Find the ammeter reading in the circuit of Fig. 11-53.

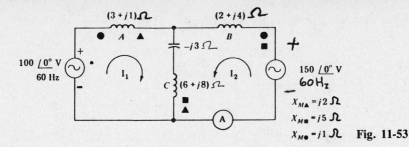

Fig. 11-53

▮ The mesh equations are

$$[-j3 + (3 + j1) + (6 + j8) + 2(j2)]\mathbf{I}_1 + [-j3 + (6 + j8) + j2 - j5 + j1]\mathbf{I}_2 = 100\ \underline{/0°}$$

$$[-j3 + (6 + j8) + j2 - j5 + j1]\mathbf{I}_1 + [-j3 + (6 + j8) + (2 + j4) - 2(j5)]\mathbf{I}_2 = 150\ \underline{/0°}$$

Solving for $\mathbf{I}_2$ we obtain $\mathbf{I}_2 = 21.71\ \underline{/25.53°}$ A, and the ammeter reads 21.71 A.

11.91 Determine the voltage across the capacitance of the circuit of Fig. 11-53.

▮ $\mathbf{V}_C = -jX_C(\mathbf{I}_1 + \mathbf{I}_2)$ $X_C = 3\ \Omega$ (from Fig. 11-53) $\mathbf{I}_2 = 21.71\ \underline{/25.53°}$ A (from Prob. 11.90)

The mesh equations of Prob. 11.90 may be solved to yield $\mathbf{I}_1 = 8.57\ \underline{/-132.77°}$ A. Hence,

$$\mathbf{V}_C = -j3(8.57\ \underline{/-132.77°} + 21.71\ \underline{/25.53°}) = (3\ \underline{/-90°})(14.11\ \underline{/12.53°}) = 42.33\ \underline{/-77.47°}\ \text{V}$$

11.92 What is the inductance of coil B of the circuit of Fig. 11-53?

▮ $$X_B = 4\ \Omega = 2\pi f L_B \quad \text{or} \quad L_B = \frac{4}{2\pi(60)} = 10.61\ \text{mH}$$

11.93 Determine the ammeter reading in the circuit of Fig. 11-54.

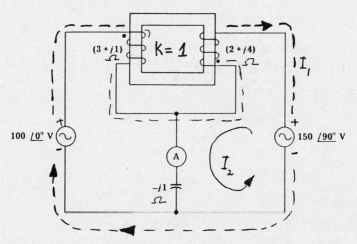

Fig. 11-54

▮ We choose the mesh currents as shown in Fig. 11-54. Then we have to solve for $\mathbf{I}_2$ only.

$$[(3 + j1) + (2 + j4) + 2(j2)]\mathbf{I}_1 + [-(2 + j4) + (-j2)]\mathbf{I}_2 = 100\ \underline{/0°} - 150\ \underline{/90°}$$

$$[-(2 + j4) + (-j2)]\mathbf{I}_1 + [(2 + j4) - j1]\mathbf{I}_2 = 150\ \underline{/90°}$$

which give $\mathbf{I}_2 = 61.7\ \underline{/74.42°}$ A. Thus, the ammeter reads 61.7 A.

11.94 Determine the polarity markings for the coupled coils of Fig. 11-55a and draw the corresponding circuit.

▮ See Fig. 11-55b.

11.95 For the polarities determined in Prob. 11.94, find the mutual reactances between the coils if $k = 1$.

▮ Referring to Fig. 11-55b,

$$X_{M\bullet} = 1\sqrt{(1)(4)} = 2\ \Omega \quad X_{M\square} = 1\sqrt{(4)(9)} = 6\ \Omega \quad X_{M\triangle} = 1\sqrt{(9)(1)} = 3\ \Omega$$

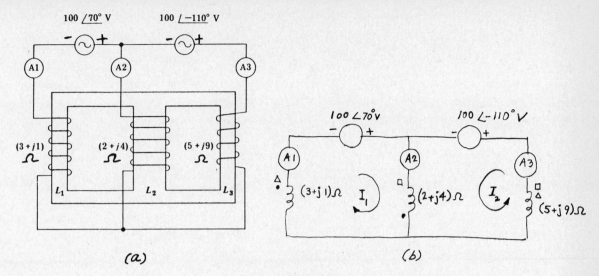

Fig. 11-55

11.96 Determine the reading of the ammeter A3 in the circuit of Fig. 11-55a.

▌ The mesh equations are

$$[(2 + j4) + (3 + j1) + 2(j2)]\mathbf{I}_1 + [(2 + j4) + j2 - j6 + j3]\mathbf{I}_2 \quad = 100 \underline{/70°}$$

$$[(2 + j4) + j2 - j6 + j3]\mathbf{I}_1 + [(2 + j4) + (5 + j9) - 2(j6)]\mathbf{I}_2 = -100 \underline{/-110°}$$

Solving for $\mathbf{I}_2$ yields $\mathbf{I}_2 = 10.48 \underline{/72.4°}$ A. Hence, A3 reads 10.48 A.

11.97 How much power is dissipated in the resistor of the coil L_2 of the circuit of Fig. 11-55a?

▌ Power dissipated, $P = |\mathbf{I}_1 + \mathbf{I}_2|^2(2)$ W. From the mesh equations of Prob. 11.96, we obtain $\mathbf{I}_1 = 8.41 \underline{/-12.83°}$ A. Thus,

$$\mathbf{I}_1 + \mathbf{I}_2 = 8.41 \underline{/-12.83} + 10.48 \underline{/72.4°} = 8.2 - j1.87 + 3.17 + j9.99 = 13.98 \underline{/35.37°} \text{ A}$$

Hence, $P = (13.98)^2(2) = 390.88$ W.

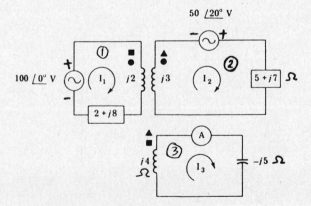

Fig. 11-56

11.98 Find the ammeter reading in the circuit of Fig. 11-56, assuming $k = 1$.

▌ First, we determine the mutual reactances:

$$X_{M\bullet} = 1\sqrt{(2)(3)} = 2.45 \; \Omega \qquad X_{M\blacksquare} = 1\sqrt{(2)(4)} = 2.83 \; \Omega \qquad X_{M\blacktriangle} = 1\sqrt{(3)(4)} = 3.46 \; \Omega$$

The mesh equations may now be written as

$$[j2 + (2 + j8)]\mathbf{I}_1 \quad + (-j2.45)\mathbf{I}_2 + (-j2.83)\mathbf{I}_3 = 100 \underline{/0°}$$

$$-j2.45\mathbf{I}_1 + [j3 + (5 + j7)]\mathbf{I}_2 \quad + j3.46\mathbf{I}_3 = 50 \underline{/20°}$$

$$-j2.83\mathbf{I}_1 \quad + j3.46\mathbf{I}_2 + (j4 - j5)\mathbf{I}_3 = 0$$

Solving for $\mathbf{I}_3$ yields $\mathbf{I}_3 = 6.13 \underline{/49.44°}$ A.   Hence the ammeter reads 6.13 A.

11.99 How much reactive power is taken by loop 3 of the circuit of Fig. 11-56?

▮ $$Q = I_3^2(X_L - X_C) = (6.13)^2(4 - 5) = -37.58 \text{ var}$$

11.100 Calculate the complex power supplied by the voltage source in the circuit of Fig. 11-57, given $k = 1$.

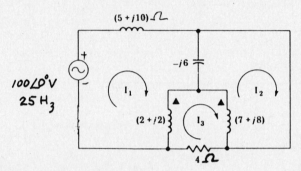

Fig. 11-57

▮ $X_M = 1\sqrt{(2)(8)} = 4\,\Omega$.   The mesh equations are

$$[(5 + j10) - j6 + (2 + j2)]\mathbf{I}_1 + [-(-j6) - j4]\mathbf{I}_2 \quad + [-(2 + j2) + j4]\mathbf{I}_3 \quad = 100 \underline{/0°}$$

$$[-(-j6) - j4]\mathbf{I}_1 + [-j6 + (7 + j8)]\mathbf{I}_2 + [-(7 + j8) + j4]\mathbf{I}_3 \quad = 0$$

$$[-(2 + j2) + j4]\mathbf{I}_1 + [-(7 + j8) + j4]\mathbf{I}_2 + [(2 + j2) + (7 + j8) + 4 - 2(j4)]\mathbf{I}_3 = 0$$

Solving for $\mathbf{I}_1$ yields $\mathbf{I}_1 = 8.71 \underline{/-50.79°}$ A.   Hence,

$$\mathbf{S} = \mathbf{VI}_1^* = (100 \underline{/0°})(8.71 \underline{/50.79°}) = 871 \underline{/50.79°} = 550.73 + j674.78 \text{ VA}$$

11.101 If the 100-V ac source in the circuit of Fig. 11-57 is replaced by a 100-V battery, what will the ammeter read?

▮ The steady-state circuit for dc source is as shown in Fig. 11-58.

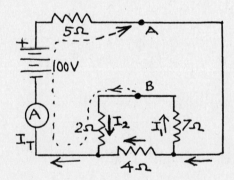

Fig. 11-58

$$Z_p = \frac{4(2 + 7)}{4 + (2 + 7)} = 2.77\,\Omega \qquad Z_{\text{in}} = 5 + 2.77 = 7.77\,\Omega \qquad I_T = \frac{100}{7.77} = 12.87 \text{ A}$$

11.102 Find the voltage across the capacitor and the energy stored in the capacitor, from the data of Prob. 11.101.

▮ The voltage across the capacitor may be obtained by describing the path shown with the dotted line in Fig. 11-58:

$$V_{AB} = \sum \text{ driving volts} - \sum \text{ volt drops} = 100 - [2I_2 + 5(12.87)]$$

$$I_k = I_T \frac{Y_k}{Y_T} \qquad Y_T = \frac{1}{Z_p} = \frac{1}{2.77} = 0.3611 \text{ S}$$

$$I_K = 12.87 \frac{0.1111}{0.3611} = 3.96 \text{ A} = I_2 \qquad Y_K = \frac{1}{7+2} = 0.1111 \text{ S}$$

$$V_{AB} = 100 - [2(3.96) + 5(12.87)] = 27.73 \text{ V}$$

Now $$X_C = \frac{1}{2\pi f C} \qquad \text{or} \qquad 6 = \frac{1}{2\pi(25C)}$$

Thus $$C = 1061 \ \mu\text{F} \qquad W = (1/2)CV^2 = (1/2)(1061 \times 10^{-6})(27.73)^2 = 408 \text{ mJ}$$

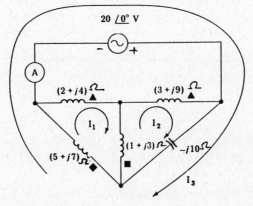

Fig. 11-59

11.103 What is the ammeter reading in the circuit of Fig. 11-59?

▌ Using the outer loop for $\mathbf{I}_3$ reduces the number of impedance terms. The mutual reactances are

$$X_{M\blacktriangle} = 1\sqrt{(4)(9)} = 6 \ \Omega \qquad X_{M\blacksquare} = 1\sqrt{(7)(3)} = 4.58 \ \Omega$$

$$0 = [(1 + j3) + (5 + j7) + (2 + j4) - 2j4.58]\mathbf{I}_1 + [-(1 + j3) + j4.58 + j6]\mathbf{I}_2 \quad + [(5 + j7) - j4.58]\mathbf{I}_3$$

$$0 = [-(1 + j3) + j4.58 + j6]\mathbf{I}_1 \qquad\qquad + [(1 + j3) + (3 + j9) - j10]\mathbf{I}_2 + (-j10 + j4.58)\mathbf{I}_3$$

$$20 \underline{/0^\circ} = [(5 + j7) - j4.58]\mathbf{I}_1 \qquad\qquad + (-j10 + j4.58)\mathbf{I}_2 \qquad\qquad + [-j10 + (5 + j7)]\mathbf{I}_3$$

Solving for $\mathbf{I}_3$ yields $\mathbf{I}_3 = 1.6 \underline{/19^\circ}$ A. Hence the ammeter reads 1.6 A.

11.104 How much total complex power is drawn by all the passive circuit elements of the circuit of Fig. 11-59?

▌ The complex power drawn by the passive element equals complex power supplied by the source:

$$\mathbf{S} = \mathbf{VI}^* = (20 \underline{/0^\circ})(1.6 \underline{/-19^\circ}) = 32 \underline{/-19^\circ} = 30.26 - j10.42 \text{ VA}$$

11.105 Determine the parameters of the equivalent T section that can be used to replace the transformer in Fig. 11-60a.

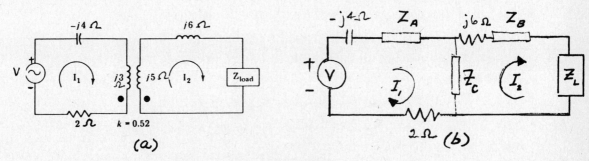

Fig. 11-60

▮ The T equivalent is shown in Fig. 11-60b. For Fig. 11-60a we have

$$X_M = 0.52\sqrt{3 \times 5} = 2.01\ \Omega \qquad \mathbf{V} = (-j4 + j3 + 2)\mathbf{I}_1 + (-j2.01)\mathbf{I}_2 \qquad 0 = (-j2.01)\mathbf{I}_1 + (j5 + j6 + \mathbf{Z}_{\text{load}})\mathbf{I}_2$$

For the T section of Fig. 11-60b the mesh equations are

$$\mathbf{V} = (-j4 + \mathbf{Z}_A + \mathbf{Z}_C + 2)\mathbf{I}_1 + (-\mathbf{Z}_C)\mathbf{I}_2$$

$$0 = (-\mathbf{Z}_C)\mathbf{I}_1 + (\mathbf{Z}_B + \mathbf{Z}_C + j6 + \mathbf{Z}_{\text{load}})\mathbf{I}_2$$

Equating coefficients of $\mathbf{I}_1$ and $\mathbf{I}_2$,

$$\mathbf{Z}_A + \mathbf{Z}_C + 2 - j4 = 2 - j1 \qquad \mathbf{Z}_C = j2.01 \qquad \mathbf{Z}_C + \mathbf{Z}_B + j6 + \mathbf{Z}_{\text{load}} = j11 + \mathbf{Z}_{\text{load}}$$

Solving, $\qquad\qquad\qquad\qquad\qquad \mathbf{Z}_A = j0.99\ \Omega \qquad \mathbf{Z}_B = j2.99\ \Omega \qquad \mathbf{Z}_C = j2.01\ \Omega$

11.106 Determine the parameters of an equivalent T section that can be used to replace the transformer in Fig. 11-61.

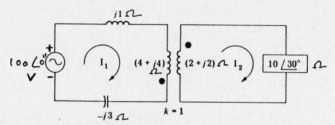

Fig. 11-61

▮ Mutual reactance is $X_M = 1\sqrt{(4)(2)} = 2.83\ \Omega$.
Mesh equations for the circuit of Fig. 11-61 are

$$100\ \underline{/0^\circ} = [j1 - j3 + (4 + 4j)]\mathbf{I}_1 + j2.83\mathbf{I}_2$$

$$0 = j2.83\mathbf{I}_1 + [(2 + j2) + 10\ \underline{/30^\circ}]\mathbf{I}_2$$

Mesh equations for the T section are:

$$100\ \underline{/0^\circ} = (j1 - j3 + \mathbf{Z}_A + \mathbf{Z}_C)\mathbf{I}_1 + (-\mathbf{Z}_C)\mathbf{I}_2$$

$$0 = -\mathbf{Z}_C\mathbf{I}_1 + (\mathbf{Z}_C + \mathbf{Z}_B + 10\ \underline{/30^\circ})\mathbf{I}_2$$

Thus, $\qquad 4 + j2 = j1 - j3 + \mathbf{Z}_A + \mathbf{Z}_C \qquad -\mathbf{Z}_C = j2.83 \qquad 2 + j2 + 10\ \underline{/30^\circ} = \mathbf{Z}_C + \mathbf{Z}_B + 10\ \underline{/30^\circ}$

Solving for the impedances,

$$\mathbf{Z}_A = (4 + j6.83)\ \Omega \qquad \mathbf{Z}_B = (2 + j4.83)\ \Omega \qquad \mathbf{Z}_C = -j2.83\ \Omega$$

11.107 Obtain the T equivalent for the coupled circuit shown in Fig. 11-62.

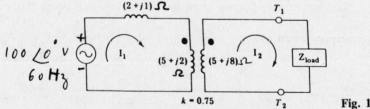

Fig. 11-62

▮ The mutual reactance is $X_M = 0.75\sqrt{2 \times 8} = 3.0\ \Omega$. For the coupled circuit,

$$100\ \underline{/0^\circ} = (2 + j1 + 5 + j2)\mathbf{I}_1 + (-j3)\mathbf{I}_2$$

$$0 = (-j3)\mathbf{I}_1 + (5 + j8 + \mathbf{Z}_{\text{load}})\mathbf{I}_2$$

For the T equivalent,

$$100\ \underline{/0^\circ} = (2 + j1 + \mathbf{Z}_A + \mathbf{Z}_C)\mathbf{I}_1 + (-\mathbf{Z}_C)\mathbf{I}_2$$

$$0 = -\mathbf{Z}_C\mathbf{I}_1 + (\mathbf{Z}_B + \mathbf{Z}_C + \mathbf{Z}_{\text{load}})\mathbf{I}_2$$

Solving for the impedances,

$$\mathbf{Z}_A = (5 - j1)\ \Omega \qquad \mathbf{Z}_B = (5 + j5)\ \Omega \qquad \mathbf{Z}_C = j3\ \Omega$$

11.108 Determine the Thévenin equivalent to the left of the terminals T_1 and T_2 in Fig. 11-62.

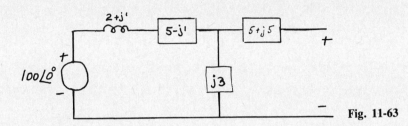

Fig. 11-63

▮ To determine the Thévenin equivalent we use the T equivalent obtained in Prob. 11.107 and shown in Fig. 11-63. Thus,

$$\mathbf{V}_{Th} = 100\ \underline{/0°}\ \frac{j3}{(2+j1)+(5-j1)+j3} = 39.39\ \underline{/66.8°}\ \text{V}$$

Now,

$$\mathbf{Z}_P = \frac{(2+j1+5-j1)(j3)}{(2+j1+5-j1)+(j3)} = 2.76\ \underline{/66.8°} = (1.086 + j2.535)\ \Omega$$

$$\mathbf{Z}_{Th} = (1.086 + j2.535) + (5 + j5) = (6.086 + j7.535) = 9.69\ \underline{/\ 51.07°}\ \Omega$$

11.109 Determine the $\mathbf{Z}_{load}$ in Fig. 11-62 for maximum power transfer and calculate the corresponding active and reactive powers.

▮ For this problem, we may use the Thévenin equivalent of Prob. 11.108. Thus, for maximum power transfer, $\mathbf{Z}_{load} = \mathbf{Z}_{Th}^* = 9.69\ \underline{/-51.07°}\ \Omega$. Now,

$$\mathbf{I} = \frac{\mathbf{V}_{Th}}{\mathbf{Z}_{Th} + \mathbf{Z}_{load}} = \frac{39.39\ \underline{/66.8°}}{9.69\ \underline{/-51.07°} + 9.69\ \underline{/51.07°}} = 3.24\ \underline{/66.8°}\ \text{A}$$

Thus, $P = I^2R = (3.24)^2(6.086) = 63.89\ \text{W}$ $Q = I^2X_C = (3.24)^2(7.535) = 79.10\ \text{var leading}$

11.110 Repeat Prob. 11.107 for the circuit of Fig. 11-64a.

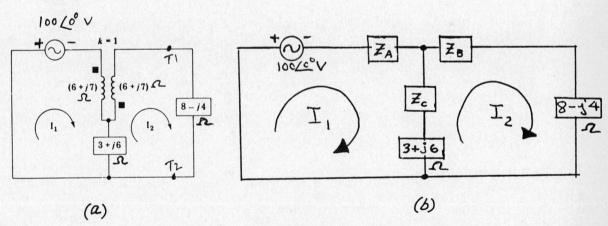

(a)   **(b)**

Fig. 11-64

▮ For Fig. 11-64a we have $X_M = 1\sqrt{(7)(7)} = 7\ \Omega$.

$$-100\ \underline{/0°} = [(6+j7)+(3+j6)]\mathbf{I}_1 + [-(3+j6)+j7]\mathbf{I}_2$$
$$0 = [-(3+j6)+j7]\mathbf{I}_1 \quad + [(6+j7)+(8-j4)+(3+j6)]\mathbf{I}_2$$

For the T equivalent of Fig. 11-64b the mesh equations are

$$-100\ \underline{/0°} = [\mathbf{Z}_A + \mathbf{Z}_C + (3+j6)]\mathbf{I}_1 + [-\mathbf{Z}_C - (3+j6)]\mathbf{I}_2$$
$$0 = [-\mathbf{Z}_C - (3+j6)]\mathbf{I}_1 \quad + [\mathbf{Z}_B + \mathbf{Z}_C + (3+j6) + (8-j4)]\mathbf{I}_2$$

Comparing coefficients yields:

$$\mathbf{Z}_A + \mathbf{Z}_C + (3+j6) = (6+j7) + (3+j6) \qquad -\mathbf{Z}_C - (3+j6) = -(3+j6) + j7$$

$$\mathbf{Z}_B + \mathbf{Z}_C + (3+j6) + (8-j4) = (6+j7) + (8-j4) + (3+j6)$$

Hence, $\qquad \mathbf{Z}_A = (6+j14)\,\Omega \qquad \mathbf{Z}_B = (6+j14)\,\Omega \qquad \mathbf{Z}_C = -j7\,\Omega$

11.111 Repeat Prob. 11.108 for the circuit of Fig. 11-64a.

▯ Proceeding as before we have

$$\mathbf{V}_{\text{Th}} = 100\,\frac{3-j1}{(6+j14)+(3-j1)} = 19.99\,\underline{/-73.73^\circ}\ \text{V}$$

and $$\mathbf{Z}_P = \frac{(6+j14)(3-j1)}{(6+j14)+(3-j1)} = (3.03-j.37)\,\Omega$$

$$\mathbf{Z}_{\text{Th}} = (3.03-j.37) + (6+j14) = (9.03+j13.63)\,\Omega$$

11.112 Find the current in the $(8-j4)$-Ω impedance of the circuit of Fig. 11-64a.

▯ By using the Thévenin equivalent obtained in Prob. 11.111, we obtain

$$\mathbf{I} = \frac{19.99\,\underline{/-73.73^\circ}}{(9.03+j13.63) + (8-j4)} = 1.02\,\underline{/-103.36^\circ}\ \text{A}$$

11.113 Repeat Prob. 11.107 for the circuit of Fig. 11-65a.

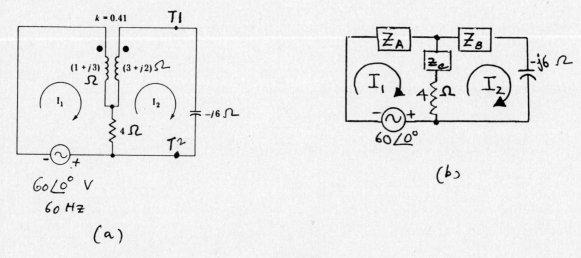

Fig. 11-65

▯ For Fig. 11-65a we have $\quad X_M = 0.41\sqrt{(3)(2)} = 1.0\,\Omega$.

$$-60\,\underline{/0^\circ} = [(1+j3)+4]\mathbf{I}_1 + (-4-j1)\mathbf{I}_2$$

$$0 = (-4-j1)\mathbf{I}_1 + (3+j2-j6+4)\mathbf{I}_2$$

For the T network shown in Fig. 11-65b we have:

$$-60\,\underline{/0^\circ} = (\mathbf{Z}_A + \mathbf{Z}_C + 4)\mathbf{I}_1 + (-\mathbf{Z}_C - 4)\mathbf{I}_2$$

$$0 = (-\mathbf{Z}_C - 4)\mathbf{I}_1 + (\mathbf{Z}_B + \mathbf{Z}_C - j6 + 4)\mathbf{I}_2$$

Hence $\quad \mathbf{Z}_A + \mathbf{Z}_C + 4 = (1+j3)+4 \qquad -\mathbf{Z}_C - 4 = -4 - j1 \qquad \mathbf{Z}_B + \mathbf{Z}_C - j6 + 4 = (3+j2) - j6 + 4$

and $$\mathbf{Z}_A = (1+j2)\,\Omega \qquad \mathbf{Z}_B = (3+j1)\,\Omega \qquad \mathbf{Z}_C = j1\,\Omega$$

11.114 Repeat Prob. 11.108 for the circuit of Fig. 11-65a.

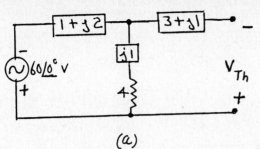

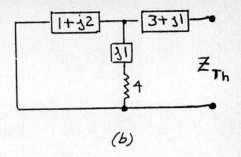

(a)   (b)

Fig. 11-66

▮ From Fig. 11-66a we obtain

$$\mathbf{V}_{Th} = 60\ \underline{/0°}\ \frac{4+j1}{(1+j2)+(4+j1)} = 42.39\ \underline{/-16.92°}\ \text{V}$$

and from Fig. 11-66b we get

$$\mathbf{Z}_P = \frac{(1+j2)(4+j1)}{(1+j2)+(4+j1)} = (1.09 + j1.15)\ \Omega$$

$$\mathbf{Z}_{Th} = (1.09 + j1.15) + (3 + j1) = 4.62\ \underline{/27.73°}\ \Omega$$

11.115 Determine the current through and the voltage across the capacitor of the circuit of Fig. 11-65a.

▮ Using the Thévenin equivalent of Prob. 11.114, we have

$$\mathbf{I}_2 = \mathbf{I}_C = \frac{42.39\ \underline{/-16.92°}}{(4.09 + j2.15) - j6} = 7.55\ \underline{/26.35°}\ \text{A}$$

$$\mathbf{V}_C = \mathbf{I}_C(-jX_C) = (7.55\ \underline{/26.35°})(6\ \underline{/-90°}) = 45.3\ \underline{/-63.65°}\ \text{V}$$

11.116 What is the maximum energy stored in the capacitor of the circuit of Fig. 11-65a?

▮ $\quad W_{max} = \frac{1}{2}C(V_{max})^2 \qquad C = \frac{1}{2\pi f X_C} = \frac{1}{2\pi(60)(6)} = 442.1\ \mu\text{F} \qquad V_C = 45.3\ \text{V (from Prob. 11.115)}$

or $\qquad\qquad\qquad\qquad\qquad\qquad V_{max} = \sqrt{2}V_C = \sqrt{2}(45.3) = 64.06\ \text{V}$

Hence, $\quad W_{max} = \frac{1}{2}(442.1 \times 10^{-6})(64.06)^2 = 907\ \text{mJ}.$

11.117 Find the voltage $v_c(t)$ across the capacitor of the circuit shown in Fig. 11-67.

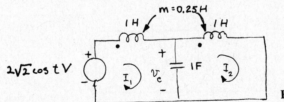

Fig. 11-67

▮ $\mathbf{V} = 2\ \underline{/0°}$, and since $\omega = 1\ \text{rad/s}$, we have

$$X_1 = X_2 = 1\ \Omega \qquad X_M = 0.25\ \Omega \qquad \text{and} \qquad X_c = 1\ \Omega$$

The mesh equations become

$$j1.25\mathbf{I}_2 = 2 \qquad j1.25\mathbf{I}_1 = 0$$

Thus, $\qquad\qquad\qquad\qquad \mathbf{I}_1 = 0 \qquad \text{and} \qquad \mathbf{I}_2 = -j1.6\ \text{A}$

$$\mathbf{V}_c = -\mathbf{I}_2(-jX_c) = -(-j1.6)(-j1) = 1.6\ \text{V} \qquad \text{or} \qquad (V_c)_{max} = 1.6(\sqrt{2}) \qquad \text{and} \qquad v_c(t) = 2.26\cos t\ \text{V}$$

11.118 The mutually coupled circuit shown in Fig. 11-68 is that of an *autotransformer*. For an ideal autotransformer the ratio of the voltages $V_1/V_2 = (N_1 + N_2)/N_2 = a + 1$, where $a = N_1/N_2$ (as may be inferred from Fig. 11-68). Determine the current transformation ratio I_L/I_{ab}.

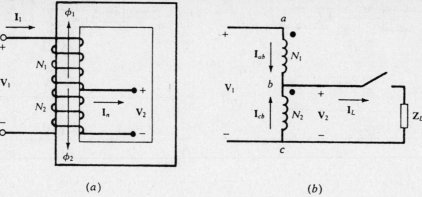

(a)   (b)   **Fig. 11-68**

▌ From Fig. 11-68a and b the apparent-power balance is expressed by

$$V_1 I_1 = V_1 I_{ab} = V_2 I_L \quad \text{or} \quad \frac{I_L}{I_{ab}} = \frac{V_1}{V_2} = a + 1$$

11.119 Obtain an expression for the output complex power of an ideal autotransformer (Fig. 11-68) in terms of the current through the winding having N_1 turns.

▌
$$\mathbf{S}_2 = \mathbf{V}_2 \mathbf{I}_L^* = \mathbf{V}_2 (\mathbf{I}_{ab}^* + \mathbf{I}_{cb}^*) = \mathbf{V}_2 \mathbf{I}_{ab}^* + \mathbf{V}_2 \mathbf{I}_{cb}^* \tag{1}$$

But
$$\frac{I_{cb}}{I_{ab}} = \frac{N_1}{N_2} = a$$

or
$$\mathbf{I}_{cb}^* = a \mathbf{I}_{ab}^* \tag{2}$$

From Eqs. (1) and (2), $\mathbf{S}_2 = \mathbf{V}_2 \mathbf{I}_{ab}^* + a(\mathbf{V}_2 \mathbf{I}_{ab}^*) = \mathbf{S}_c + \mathbf{S}_i$, where the first term corresponds to power transferred by conduction and the second term represents that by induction or by transformer action.

11.120 For the ideal autotransformer shown in Fig. 11-69, find $\mathbf{V}_2$, $\mathbf{I}_{cb}$, and the input current $\mathbf{I}_1$.

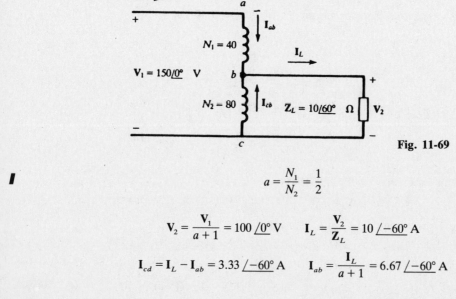

Fig. 11-69

▌
$$a = \frac{N_1}{N_2} = \frac{1}{2}$$

$$\mathbf{V}_2 = \frac{\mathbf{V}_1}{a + 1} = 100 \underline{/0°}\text{ V} \qquad \mathbf{I}_L = \frac{\mathbf{V}_2}{\mathbf{Z}_L} = 10 \underline{/-60°}\text{ A}$$

$$\mathbf{I}_{cd} = \mathbf{I}_L - \mathbf{I}_{ab} = 3.33 \underline{/-60°}\text{ A} \qquad \mathbf{I}_{ab} = \frac{\mathbf{I}_L}{a + 1} = 6.67 \underline{/-60°}\text{ A}$$

11.121 In Prob. 11.120, find the apparent power delivered to the load by transformer action and that supplied by conduction.

▌
$$\mathbf{S}_{cond} = \mathbf{V}_2 \mathbf{I}_{ab}^* = (100 \underline{/0°})(6.67 \underline{/60°}) = 667 \underline{/60°}\text{ VA} \qquad \mathbf{S}_{trans} = a\mathbf{S}_{cond} = 333 \underline{/60°}\text{ VA}$$

11.122 A 10-kVA 440/110-V two-winding transformer is reconnected as a stepdown 550/440-V autotransformer. Compare the voltampere rating of the autotransformer with that of the original two-winding transformer and calculate S_i and S_c.

▮ Refer to Fig. 11-68b. The rated current in the 110-V winding (or in ab) is

$$I_1 = \frac{10,000}{110} = 90.91 \text{ A}$$

Current in the 440-V winding (or in bc) is

$$I_{cb} = I_L - I_1 = \frac{10,000}{440} = 22.73 \text{ A}$$

which is the rated current of the winding bc. The load current is

$$I_L = I_1 + I_{cb} = 90.91 + 22.73 = 113.64 \text{ A}$$

Check: For the autotransformer $a = \frac{550}{440} = 1.25$ and

$$I_L = aI_1 = 1.25 \frac{10,000}{110} = 113.64 \text{ A}$$

which agrees with I_L calculated above. Hence the rating of the autotransformer is

$$S_{\text{auto}} = V_1 I_1 = 550 \frac{10,000}{110} = 50 \text{ kVA}$$

Inductively supplied apparent power is

$$S_i = V_2(I_L - I_1) = \frac{a-1}{a} S = \frac{1.25-1}{1.25} 50 = 10 \text{ kVA}$$

which is the voltampere rating of the two-winding transformer. The conductively supplied power is

$$S_c = \frac{S}{a} = \frac{50}{1.25} = 40 \text{ kVA}$$

11.123 Repeat Prob. 11.122 for a 440/550-V step-up connection.

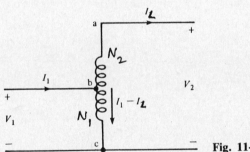

Fig. 11-70

▮ The step-up connection is shown in Fig. 11-70. The rating of winding ab is 110 V and the load current I_L flows through ab. Hence

$$I_L = \frac{10,000}{110} = 90.91 \text{ A}$$

The output voltage is $V_2 = 550$ V. Thus the voltampere rating of the autotransformer is $V_2 I_L = 550(10,000/110) = 50$ kVA, which is the same as in Prob. 11.122. Power transferred inductively $= 50 - 40 = 10$ kVA. Consequently, a two-winding transformer connected as an autotransformer will have a voltampere rating $a/(a-1)$ times its rating as a two-winding transformer.

11.124 A 10-kVA 4160/450-V 25-Hz ideal autotransformer is used for step-down operation and is delivering rated kVA at rated voltage and 0.85 pf lagging. Determine (*a*) the current to the load and (*b*) the current supplied by the generator.

▮ Refer to Fig. 11-68b.

(*a*) $\theta = \cos^{-1} 0.85 = 31.79°$ $S_2 = 10,000 \underline{/31.79°}$ VA $S_2 = V_2 I_L^*$

$10,000 \underline{/31.79°} = (450 \underline{/0°})I_L^*$ $I_L^* = 22.22 \underline{/31.79°}$ $I_L = 22.22 \underline{/-31.79°}$ A (**b**) $\mathbf{I}_L/\mathbf{I}_1 = N_1/N_2$ where $N_1/N_2 = 4160/450 = a$.

$$\frac{22.22\ \underline{/-31.79°}}{\mathbf{I}_1} = \frac{4160}{450} \qquad \mathbf{I}_1 = 2.4\ \underline{/-31.79°}\ \text{A}$$

11.125 In an ideal step-up autotransformer (Fig. 11-70) $N_1 = 200$ and $N_2 = 400$. If 100 V is applied across the primary, what is the voltage across the load?

❚ $$N_1 + N_2 = 200 + 400 = 600 \qquad \frac{V_2}{V_1} = \frac{N_1 + N_2}{N_1} = \frac{600}{200} = \frac{V_2}{100}$$

Thus, $V_2 = 300$ V.

11.126 For the autotransformer of Prob. 11.125, determine the input current if a 30-Ω resistor is connected as a load on the secondary.

❚ $$I_L = \frac{V_2}{Z_2} = \frac{300}{30} = 10\ \text{A} \qquad V_1 I_1 = V_2 I_L$$

Thus, $I_1 = \frac{300}{100}(10) = 30$ A.

11.127 A 280-turn ideal autotransformer has a secondary tapped at 14 turns. If the input voltage is 240 V and the secondary load is a 6-mΩ resistor, find the current in the section of the winding supplying the load.

❚ Since $V_2/V_1 = N_2/N_1$,

$$V_2 = \frac{14}{280}\,240 = 12\ \text{V} \qquad I_L = \frac{12}{0.006} = 2000\ \text{A} \qquad V_1 I_1 = V_2 I_L$$

or $I_1 = \frac{12}{240}(2000) = 100$ A.
From Fig. 11-68b, $I_{cb} = I_L - I_1 = 2000 - 100 = 1900$ A.

11.128 The input apparent power to an ideal step-down autotransformer is 20 kVA at 400 V. If the current I_{cb} (Fig. 11-68) = 30 A, determine the load voltage.

❚ $I_1 = 20,000/400 = 50$ A. From Fig. 11-68a, $I_L = 50 + 30 = 80$ A,

$$S_1 = 20,000 = S_2 = V_2 I_L = 80 V_2$$

Thus, $$V_2 = \frac{20,000}{80} = 250\ \text{V}$$

11.129 In the autotransformer of Prob. 11.128, how much power is transferred to the load by (**a**) conduction and (**b**) induction?

❚ (**a**) $P_c = V_2 I_1 = (250)(50) = 12.5$ kVA   (**b**) $P_i = V_2 I_{cb} = (250)(30) = 7.5$ kVA

11.130 An ideal transformer is used to couple a 50-Ω resistor load to a generator whose internal impedance is $400\ \underline{/0°}\ \Omega$. If the coil connected to the generator has 100 turns, determine the required number of secondary turns so that maximum power will be transferred to the load.

❚ $\mathbf{Z}_{\text{gen}} = 400\ \underline{/0°}\ \Omega$. For maximum power transfer, the generator must "see" a $400\ \underline{/0°}$-Ω load. Thus, $\mathbf{Z}_{\text{in}} = 400\ \underline{/0°}\ \Omega$,

$$\mathbf{Z}_{\text{in}} = \left(\frac{N_1}{N_2}\right)^2 \mathbf{Z}_{\text{load}} \qquad 400 = \left(\frac{100}{N_2}\right)^2 50 \qquad N_2 = 35.4\ \text{turns}$$

11.131 The primary and secondary turns of an impedance-matching transformer are 200 and 600, respectively. Determine (**a**) the input impedance at the primary terminals if a $20\ \underline{/30°}$-Ω load is connected to the 600-turn secondary, and (**b**) the rms primary current if the source voltage is $50 \sin 300t$ V.

❚ (**a**) $$\mathbf{Z}_{\text{in}} = \left(\frac{N_1}{N_2}\right)^2 \mathbf{Z}_{\text{load}} \qquad \mathbf{Z}_{\text{in}} = \left(\frac{200}{600}\right)^2 (20\ \underline{/30°}) = 2.22\ \underline{/30°}\ \Omega$$

(**b**) $$V_1 = \frac{50}{\sqrt{2}} = 35.36\ \text{V} \qquad \mathbf{I}_1 = \frac{35.36\ \underline{/0°}}{2.22\ \underline{/30°}} = 15.93\ \underline{/-30°}\ \text{A}$$

11.132 For the operating condition stated in Prob. 11.131, calculate (*a*) the secondary current (rms), (*b*) the secondary voltage (rms), and (*c*) the active power drawn by the load.

▮ (*a*) $N_1 I_1 = N_2 I_2$ $200(15.93) = 600 I_2$ or $I_2 = 5.31$ A

(*b*) $\dfrac{V_1}{V_2} = \dfrac{N_1}{N_2}$ $\dfrac{35.36}{V_2} = \dfrac{200}{600}$

Thus $V_2 = 106.08$ V.

(*c*) For an ideal transformer, the active power drawn by the load is equal to the power input to the transformer. Thus,

$$\mathbf{S}_1 = \mathbf{V}_1 \mathbf{I}_1^* = (35.36\,\underline{/0^\circ})(15.93\,\underline{/30^\circ}) = 563.28\,\underline{/30^\circ} = 487.81 + j281.64 \text{ VA}$$

$$P_1 = 487.81 \text{ W}$$

11.133 A 100-Hz generator supplies a 2.0-Ω resistor through an ideal transformer whose primary to secondary turns ratio is 200/600. The rms voltage across the load is 120 V. Determine (*a*) the primary current and (*b*) the input impedance of the circuit.

▮ (*a*) $I_2 = \dfrac{V_2}{Z_2} = \dfrac{120}{2} = 60$ A $\dfrac{V_1}{V_2} = \dfrac{N_1}{N_2}$ $\dfrac{V_1}{120} = \dfrac{200}{600}$

$V_1 = 40$ V $V_1 I_1 = V_2 I_2$ $40 I_1 = 120(60)$ $I_1 = 180$ A

(*b*) $\mathbf{Z}_{\text{in}} = \left(\dfrac{N_1}{N_2}\right)^2 \mathbf{Z}_{\text{load}} = \left(\dfrac{200}{600}\right)^2 (2) = 0.22 \ \Omega$

11.134 Find the input impedance of the circuit shown in Fig. 11-71.

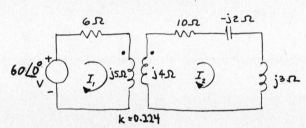

Fig. 11-71

▮ Writing the mesh equations we have

$$(6 + j5)\mathbf{I}_1 - j\mathbf{I}_2 = 60\,\underline{/0^\circ}$$

$$-j\mathbf{I}_1 + (10 - j2 + j3 + j4)\mathbf{I}_2 = 0$$

Hence, $\mathbf{Z}_i = \dfrac{60\,\underline{/0^\circ}}{\mathbf{I}_1} = 6 + j5 + \dfrac{1^2}{10 - j2 + j3 + j4} = 6 + j5 + \dfrac{1}{10 + j5} = 6.1 + j5 \ \Omega$

11.135 A 200-μF capacitor is connected in series with the primary winding of a 60-Hz ideal transformer. The primary winding impedance is $(2 + j10) \ \Omega$ and the secondary circuit impedance is $(0.4 + j0.2) \ \Omega$. If the turns ratio is 2, determine the input impedance.

▮

$$X_C = \frac{1}{\omega C} = \frac{1}{(377)(200)10^{-6}} = 13.26 \ \Omega$$

$$\mathbf{Z}_{\text{secondary ref. to primary}} = 2^2 (0.4 + j0.2) = 1.6 + j0.8 \ \Omega$$

$\mathbf{Z}_{\text{primary}} = 2 + j10 - j13.26 = 2 - j3.26 \ \Omega$ $\mathbf{Z}_i = 1.6 + j0.8 + 2 - j3.26 = 3.6 - j2.46 \ \Omega$

CHAPTER 12
Resonance

12.1   *Resonance* is the condition that exists in ac circuits under steady state when the input current is in phase with the input voltage. Using this definition, find the frequency at which a series *RLC* circuit will be in resonance.

▮ For resonance, we must have

$$\mathbf{Z} = R + j(X_L - X_C) = R + j0 \quad \text{or} \quad X_L = X_C \quad \text{or} \quad \omega_r L = \frac{1}{\omega_r C}$$

Hence

$$\omega_r = \frac{1}{\sqrt{LC}} \quad \text{or} \quad f_r = \frac{1}{2\pi\sqrt{LC}} = \text{resonance frequency (Hz)}$$

12.2   Draw a phasor diagram showing the current and all the voltages in a series resonant circuit.

▮ The circuit and the phasor diagram are shown in Fig. 12-1. Notice that $\mathbf{V}_L + \mathbf{V}_C = 0$ and $\mathbf{V} = \mathbf{V}_R = R\mathbf{I}$.

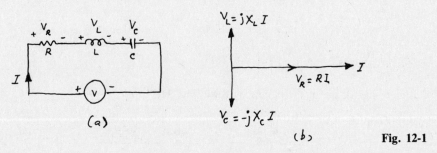

Fig. 12-1

12.3   Plot X_L, X_C, and R as functions of frequency f. Thus show how the resonance frequency can be obtained graphically.

▮ See Fig. 12-2, which shows that, at $f = f_r$, $X_L = X_C$.

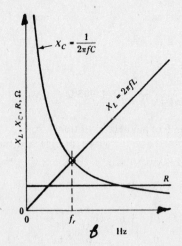

Fig. 12-2

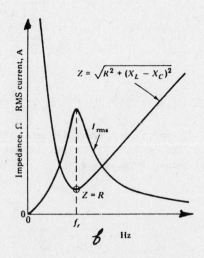

Fig. 12-3

12.4   For a series *RLC* circuit, plot impedance and current as functions of frequency. Hence obtain the resonance frequency.

▮ See Fig. 12-3, from which $Z = R$ and $I = I_m$ at $f = f_r$.

12.5   Show graphically how the power-factor angle of a series *RLC* circuit varies with frequency. Hence determine the resonance frequency.

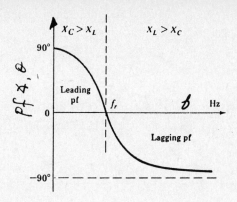

Fig. 12-4

▌ See Fig. 12-4, which shows that at f_r, $\theta = 0$.

12.6 A coil with inductance and resistance of 1.0 mH and 2.0 Ω, respectively, is connected in series with a capacitor and a 120-V 5-kHz supply. Determine the value of capacitance that will cause the system to be in resonance.

▌ The circuit is similar to that shown in Fig. 12-1a, for which

$$f_r = \frac{1}{2\pi\sqrt{LC}} \qquad \text{or} \qquad 5000 = \frac{1}{2\pi\sqrt{0.001\,C}}$$

Solving, $C = 1.01 \times 10^{-6}\,\text{F} = 1.01\,\mu\text{F}$.

12.7 From the data of Prob. 12.6 determine (a) the current at the resonance frequency and (b) the maximum instantaneous energy stored in the magnetic field of the inductance at the resonance frequency.

▌ (a) At series resonance, $\mathbf{Z}_{\text{in}} = R$.

$$\mathbf{I} = \frac{\mathbf{V}}{R} = \frac{120\,\underline{/0^\circ}}{2} = 60\,\underline{/0^\circ}\,\text{A}$$

(b) $W_{\text{max}} = \frac{1}{2}LI_{\text{max}}^2 = LI_{\text{rms}}^2 = (1.0 \times 10^{-3})(60)^2 = 3.6\,\text{J}$

12.8 The *quality factor* Q of an ac circuit is defined by

$$Q = \frac{2\pi\,(\text{maximum energy stored per cycle})}{\text{energy dissipated per cycle}} \qquad (1)$$

Using this definition, obtain Q in various forms for a resonant series *RLC* circuit.

▌ From Eq. (1), $\qquad\qquad Q_s = \frac{2\pi\,[\frac{1}{2}\,L(I_m)^2]}{(I)^2 R T_r} \qquad (2)$

where $I = $ rms current at resonance and $T_r = $ period at resonance frequency. Substituting $I_m = \sqrt{2}I$ and $T_r = 1/f_r = 2\pi/\omega_r$ in Eq. (2) yields

$$Q_s = \frac{\omega_r L}{R} \qquad (3)$$

Since $\omega_r = 1/\sqrt{LC}$, Eq. (3) may also be written as

$$Q_s = \frac{1}{\omega_r RC} = \frac{1}{R}\sqrt{\frac{L}{C}} \qquad (4)$$

12.9 A series *RLC* circuit has a variable resistance. If the frequency of the input voltage is varied, sketch the currents as functions of frequency for two arbitrary values of the resistance.

▌ See Fig. 12-5.

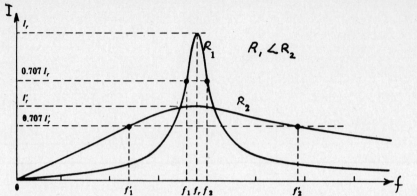

Fig. 12-5

12.10 In the circuit of Fig. 12-1a, $R = 2.42\,\Omega$, $L = 25.4$ mH,   and $C = 52\,\mu$F.   Evaluate Q_s as given by (3) and (4) of Prob. 12.8.

❚ $f_r = \dfrac{1}{2\pi\sqrt{LC}} = \dfrac{1}{2\pi\sqrt{0.0254(52 \times 10^{-6})}} = 138.6$ Hz $Q_s = \dfrac{\omega_r L}{R} = \dfrac{2\pi(138.6)(0.0254)}{2.42} = 9.13$

$Q_s = \dfrac{1}{\omega_r RC} = \dfrac{1}{2\pi(138.6)(2.42)(52 \times 10^{-6})} = 9.13$ $Q_s = \dfrac{1}{R}\sqrt{\dfrac{L}{C}} = \dfrac{1}{2.42}\sqrt{\dfrac{0.0254}{52 \times 10^{-6}}} = 9.13$

12.11 For the circuit shown in Fig. 12-6, R_1, R_2, and R_3 are 0.51, 1.3, and 0.24 Ω, respectively; C_1 and C_2 are 25 and 62 μF, respectively; L_1 and L_2 are 32 and 15 mH, respectively.   Determine the resonance frequency.

❚   Before the resonance frequency formula may be used, the circuit must be reduced to the form shown in Fig. 12-1a.

$$R_{eq} = R_1 + R_2 + R_3 = 0.51 + 1.3 + 0.24 = 2.05\ \Omega$$

$$L_{eq} = L_1 + L_2 = 0.032 + 0.015 = 0.047\ \text{H} \qquad \frac{1}{C_{eq}} = \frac{1}{C_1} + \frac{1}{C_2} = \frac{1}{62 \times 10^{-6}} + \frac{1}{25 \times 10^{-6}}$$

$$C_{eq} = 17.8 \times 10^{-6}\ \text{F} \qquad f_r = \frac{1}{2\pi\sqrt{L_{eq}C_{eq}}} = \frac{1}{2\pi\sqrt{0.047 \times 17.8 \times 10^{-6}}} = 174\ \text{Hz}$$

12.12 For the resonant circuit of Prob. 12.11 find   (**a**) Q_s,   (**b**) $Q_{\text{coil 1}}$, and   (**c**) $Q_{\text{coil 2}}$.

❚   (**a**) $Q_s = \dfrac{1}{R_{eq}}\sqrt{\dfrac{L_{eq}}{C_{eq}}} = \dfrac{1}{2.05}\sqrt{\dfrac{0.047}{17.8 \times 10^{-6}}} = 25$ (**b**) $Q_{\text{coil 1}} = \dfrac{\omega_r L_1}{R_1} = \dfrac{2\pi(174)(0.032)}{0.51} = 68.6$

(**c**) $Q_{\text{coil 2}} = \dfrac{\omega_r L_2}{R_2} = \dfrac{2\pi(174)(0.015)}{1.3} = 12.6$

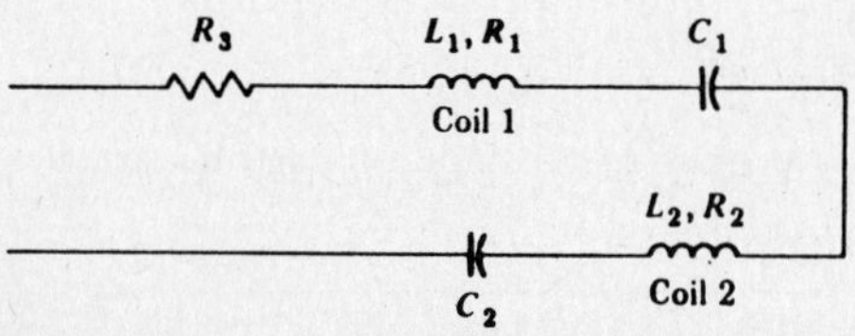

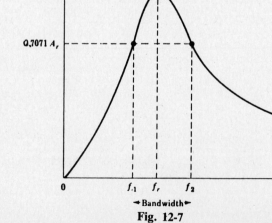

Fig. 12-6

Fig. 12-7

12.13 Fig. 12.7 shows a general form of resonance curve. The range of frequencies within which the variable does not drop below $1/\sqrt{2}$ times its maximum value is called the passband or *bandwidth*. Thus, the bandwidth is

$$\text{BW} = f_2 - f_1 \tag{1}$$

Determine the powers dissipated at the frequencies f_1 and f_2 in a series RLC circuit and compare the results with the power dissipated at resonance frequency.

▮ At $f = f_1$, $\qquad\qquad\qquad\qquad P_1 = I_1^2 R = \left(\dfrac{1}{\sqrt{2}} I_r\right)^2 R = \tfrac{1}{2} I_r^2 R$

At $f = f_2$, $\qquad\qquad\qquad\qquad P_2 = I_2^2 R = \left(\dfrac{1}{\sqrt{2}} I_r\right)^2 R = \tfrac{1}{2} I_r^2 R$

At $f = f_r$, $\qquad\qquad\qquad\qquad P_r = I_r^2 R$

Because $P_1 = P_2 = \tfrac{1}{2} P_r$, the frequencies f_1 and f_2 are known as *half-power frequencies*.

12.14 Obtain a relationship between the resonance frequency f_r and the half-power frequencies f_1 and f_2 for a series RLC circuit.

▮ From Fig. 12-7, the current at f_1 and f_2 drops to $1/\sqrt{2}$ of its <u>resonant value</u>. Thus the impedance must be equal to $\sqrt{2}$ times the resonant value, which is R; i.e., $\sqrt{R^2 + (X_L - X_C)^2} = \sqrt{2}R$, which implies that $X_L - X_C = \pm R$, or

$$\omega L - \frac{1}{\omega C} = \pm R \tag{1}$$

For $X_L < X_C$ which corresponds to f_1 or ω_1, Eq. (1) yields

$$\omega_1 = -\frac{R}{2L} + \frac{1}{2}\sqrt{\left(\frac{R}{L}\right)^2 + \frac{4}{LC}} \tag{2}$$

Similarly, for $X_L > X_C$ corresponding to f_2 or ω_2, Eq. (1) gives

$$\omega_2 = \frac{R}{2L} + \frac{1}{2}\sqrt{\left(\frac{R}{L}\right)^2 + \frac{4}{LC}} \tag{3}$$

Multiplying Eqs. (2) and (3) yields

$$\omega_1 \omega_2 = \frac{1}{4}\left[\left(\frac{R}{L}\right)^2 + \frac{4}{LC}\right] - \frac{1}{4}\left(\frac{R}{L}\right)^2 = \frac{1}{LC} = (\omega_r)^2 \qquad \text{or} \qquad \omega_r = \sqrt{\omega_1 \omega_2}$$

Hence, $\qquad\qquad\qquad\qquad\qquad\qquad\qquad\qquad f_r = \sqrt{f_1 f_2} \tag{4}$

12.15 Find the bandwidth BW of a series RLC circuit in terms of its parameters.

▮ From Eqs. (2) and (3) of Prob. 12.14, we have

$$\text{BW} = f_2 - f_1 = \left[\frac{R}{4\pi L} + \frac{1}{4\pi}\sqrt{\left(\frac{R}{L}\right)^2 + \frac{4}{LC}}\right] - \left[\frac{-R}{4\pi L} + \frac{1}{4\pi}\sqrt{\left(\frac{R}{L}\right)^2 + \frac{4}{LC}}\right] = \frac{R}{2\pi L} \tag{1}$$

12.16 Express the bandwdith of a series RLC circuit in terms of Q_s and f_r.

▮ From Eq. (3) of Prob. 12.8 we have $R/L = \omega_r/Q_s$ and $1/2\pi = f_r/\omega_r$. Substituting these into Eq. (1) of Prob. 12.15 yields

$$\text{BW} = \frac{R}{2\pi L} = \frac{f_r}{\omega_r}\frac{\omega_r}{Q_s} = \frac{f_r}{Q_s}$$

12.17 With reference to Figs. 12-5 and 12-7, comment on the relationship among f_1, f_2, f_r, and BW.

▮ As indicated in the figures, the resonance frequency is *not* centrally located with respect to the two half-power frequencies, especially when BW is large (Q_s is small). Indeed, as the geometric mean of f_1 and f_2 (Prob. 12.14), f_r must always be *below* their arithmetic mean. However, if $Q \cong 10$, the resonance frequency is sufficiently centered with respect to the half-power frequencies to allow us to write

$$f_2 \approx f_r + \frac{\text{BW}}{2} \qquad\qquad f_1 \approx f_r - \frac{\text{BW}}{2} \tag{1}$$

12.18 A series circuit has a resonance frequency of 150 kHz and a bandwidth of 75 kHz. Determine the half-power frequencies.

▌ Since $Q_s = 150/75 = 2 < 10$ approximations (1) of Prob. 12.17 cannot be used. The exact relations are $\text{BW} = f_2 - f_1$ and $f_r = \sqrt{f_1 f_2}$, and we may work in kilohertz. Thus, we eliminate f_2 between $75 = f_2 - f_1$ and $150 = \sqrt{f_1 f_2}$ to obtain $f_1^2 + 75f_1 - 22{,}500 = 0$. Solving, $f_1 = 117.1$ kHz and $f_2 = 75 + f_1 = 192.1$ kHz.

12.19 Determine the parameters of a series RLC circuit that will resonate at 10 kHz, have a bandwidth of 1 kHz, and draw 15.3 W from a 200-V generator operating at the resonance frequency of the circuit.

▌ For a series circuit operating at resonance,

$$V_R = V = 200 \text{ V} \qquad P_R = \frac{V_R^2}{R} \qquad 15.3 = \frac{(200)^2}{R} \qquad R = 2.61 \text{ k}\Omega$$

$$Q_s = \frac{f_r}{\text{BW}} = \frac{10}{1} = 10 \qquad Q_s = \frac{2\pi f_r L}{R} \qquad 10 = \frac{2\pi(10{,}000)L}{2610} \qquad L = 416 \text{ mH}$$

$$f_r = \frac{1}{2\pi\sqrt{LC}} \qquad 10{,}000 = \frac{1}{2\pi\sqrt{0.416C}} \qquad C = 610 \text{ pF}$$

12.20 A series RLC circuit has a Q_s of 5.1 at its resonance frequency of 100 kHz. Assuming the power dissipation of the circuit is 100 W when drawing a current of 0.80 A, determine the circuit parameters.

▌

$$P_R = I^2 R \qquad 100 = (0.8)^2 R \qquad R = 156\,\Omega \qquad Q_s = \frac{2\pi f_r L}{R}$$

$$5.1 = \frac{2\pi(100{,}000)L}{156} \qquad L = 1.26 \text{ mH} \qquad f_r = \frac{1}{2\pi\sqrt{LC}}$$

$$100{,}000 = \frac{1}{2\pi\sqrt{(1.26 \times 10^{-3})C}} \qquad C = 2.01 \text{ nF}$$

12.21 What is the bandwidth of the circuit of Prob. 12.20?

▌

$$Q_s = \frac{f_r}{\text{BW}} \qquad 5.1 = \frac{100 \text{ kHz}}{\text{BW}} \qquad \text{BW} = 19.6 \text{ kHz}$$

12.22 Determine the half-power frequencies of the circuit of Prob. 12.20.

▌ Proceed as in Prob. 12.18.

$$(100)^2 = f_1 f_2 \qquad 19.6 = f_2 - f_1$$

Substituting,

$$10^4 = f_1(19.6 + f_1) \qquad f_1^2 + 19.6f_1 - 10^4 = 0 \qquad f_1 = \frac{-19.6 + \sqrt{(19.6)^2 + 4(10^4)}}{2} = 90.7 \text{ kHz}$$

and $f_2 = 19.6 + f_1 = 110.3$ kHz.

12.23 A 125-V ac source supplies a series circuit consisting of a 20.5-μF capacitor and a coil whose resistance and inductance are 1.06 Ω and 25.4 mH, respectively. The generator frequency is the resonance frequency of the circuit. Determine (a) the resonance frequency and (b) the current.

▌ (a) $f_r = \dfrac{1}{2\pi\sqrt{LC}} = \dfrac{1}{2\pi\sqrt{0.0254(20.5 \times 10^{-6})}} = 220.6$ Hz

(b) At resonance, $\mathbf{Z}_r = R$; hence

$$\mathbf{I} = \frac{\mathbf{V}}{\mathbf{Z}_r} = \frac{125\,\underline{/0°}}{1.06} = 117.9\,\underline{/0°}\text{ A}$$

12.24 From the data of Prob. 12.23, calculate the voltage across (*a*) the capacitor and (*b*) the coil.

   (*a*) $X_C = X_L = 2\pi f_r L = 2\pi(220.6)(0.0254) = 35.21\,\Omega$

       $V_C = IX_C = (117.9)(35.21) = 4151\,V$

   (*b*) $\mathbf{V}_{coil} = IR + IjX_L = 117.9\,\underline{/0°}(1.06 + j35.21)$

          $= (117.9\,\underline{/0°})(35.23\,\underline{/88.3°}) = 4154\,\underline{/88.3°}\,V$ or $V_{coil} = 4154\,V$

12.25 For Prob. 12.23, determine the resistance that must be connected in series with the circuit to limit the capacitor voltage to 300 V.

$$V_C = IX_C \qquad 300 = I(35.21) \qquad I = 8.520\,A$$
$$I = \frac{V}{R} = 8.52 = \frac{125}{R} \qquad R = 14.67\,\Omega$$

Hence the required additional series resistance is

$$14.67 = 1.06 + R_x \qquad R_x = 13.61\,\Omega$$

12.26 In a series *RLC* circuit under resonance, express the voltages across the capacitor and the inductor in terms of Q_s and the applied voltage.

$$V_C = V_L = IX_L = \frac{V}{R}\,\omega_r L = VQ_s$$

12.27 A coil with resistance and inductance of 40 Ω and 50 mH, respectively, is connected in series with a 450-pF capacitor and a generator. Determine (*a*) the resonance frequency and (*b*) the circuit impedance at the resonance frequency.

   (*a*) $f_r = \dfrac{1}{2\pi\sqrt{LC}} = \dfrac{1}{2\pi\sqrt{(0.050)(450\times10^{-12})}} = 33{,}553\,Hz = 33.553\,kHz$

   (*b*) $Z_r = R = 40\,\Omega$

12.28 A 60-V source having an internal resistance of 10 Ω is connected to the circuit of Prob. 12.27. Determine (*a*) the circuit current and (*b*) the voltage across the capacitor.

   (*a*) $\mathbf{I} = \dfrac{V}{R} = \dfrac{60\,\underline{/0°}}{40+10} = 1.2\,\underline{/0°}\,A \qquad X_C = \dfrac{1}{2\pi fC} = \dfrac{1}{2\pi(33{,}553)(450\times10^{-12})} = 10.54\,k\Omega$

   (*b*) $V = IX_C = (1.2\,A)(10.54\,k\Omega) = 12.65\,kV$

12.29 A 25-μF capacitor is connected in series with a coil whose inductance is 5.0 mH. Determine (*a*) the resonance frequency; (*b*) the resistance of the coil if a 40-V source operating at the resonance frequency causes a circuit current of 3.6 mA; and (*c*) the *Q* of the coil.

   (*a*) $f_r = \dfrac{1}{2\pi\sqrt{LC}} = \dfrac{1}{2\pi\sqrt{(0.005)(25\times10^{-6})}} \qquad f_r = 450.2\,Hz$

   (*b*) $I = \dfrac{V}{R} \qquad 0.0036 = \dfrac{40}{R} \qquad R = 11.1\,k\Omega$

   (*c*) $Q_{coil} = \dfrac{\omega_r L}{R} = \dfrac{2\pi(450.2)(0.005)}{11.1\times10^3} = 1.28\times10^{-3}$

12.30 A coil with inductance and resistance of 3.0 mH and 20 Ω, respectively, is connected in series with a capacitor and a 12-V 5.0-kHz source. Determine (*a*) the value of capacitance that will cause the system to be in resonance and (*b*) the circuit current at the resonance frequency.

   (*a*) $f_r = \dfrac{1}{2\pi\sqrt{LC}} \qquad 5000 = \dfrac{1}{2\pi\sqrt{0.003C}} \qquad C = 338\,nF$

   (*b*) $Z_r = 20\,\Omega$ or $I_r = \dfrac{V}{Z_r} = \dfrac{12}{20} = 0.6\,A$

12.31   What is the maximum stored energy in the capacitor of Prob. 12.30?

$$V_C = IX_C = 0.6 \frac{1}{2\pi(5000)(338 \times 10^{-9})} = 56.5 \text{ V} \qquad V_{C(\max)} = 56.5\sqrt{2} = 79.9 \text{ V}$$

$$W_{\max} = \tfrac{1}{2}CV_C^2 = \tfrac{1}{2}(338 \times 10^{-9})(79.9)^2 = 1.08 \text{ mJ}$$

12.32   A coil having a 2-Ω resistance is connected in series with a 50-μF capacitor. The circuit resonates at 100 Hz. What is the inductance of the coil?

At resonance, $X_L = X_C$ or $2\pi(100)L = 1/2\pi(100)50(10^{-6})$.   Thus, $L = 50.66 \text{ mH}$.

12.33   If the circuit of Prob. 12.32 is connected across a 100-V 100-Hz ac source, determine the power dissipated in the coil.

At resonance, $I = V/R = \frac{100}{2} = 50 \text{ A}$ and $P_{\text{coil}} = I^2R = (50)^2 2 = 5 \text{ kW}$.

12.34   Calculate the voltages across the capacitor and the coil of Prob. 12.33.

$$V_C = IX_C = 50 \frac{1}{2\pi(100)(50)(10^{-6})} = 1591.5 \text{ V}$$

$$X_L = \omega L = 2\pi(100)(50.66 \times 10^{-3}) = 31.83 \,\Omega \qquad V_{\text{coil}} = 50\sqrt{(2)^2 + (31.83)^2} = 1594.6 \text{ V}$$

12.35   A 120-V 20-Hz source supplies a series circuit consisting of a 5.0-Ω capacitive reactance, a 1.6-Ω resistor, and a coil with resistance and inductive reactance of 3.0 and 1.2 Ω, respectively. Determine (*a*) the input impedance and (*b*) the circuit current.

(*a*) $\mathbf{Z}_{\text{in}} = (3 + j1.2) + 1.6 - j5 = 5.97 \underline{/-39.56°} \,\Omega$

(*b*). $\mathbf{I} = \dfrac{\mathbf{V}}{\mathbf{Z}_{\text{in}}} = \dfrac{120 \underline{/0°}}{5.97 \underline{/-39.56°}}$ $\mathbf{I} = 20.11 \underline{/39.56°} \text{ A}$

12.36   Calculate (*a*) the voltage across the coil and (*b*) the resonance frequency in the circuit of Prob. 12.35.

(*a*) $\mathbf{V}_{\text{coil}} = \mathbf{I}_{\text{coil}}\mathbf{Z}_{\text{coil}} = (20.11 \underline{/39.56°})(3 + j1.2) = 64.98 \underline{/61.36°} \text{ V}$

$$X_L = 2\pi fL \qquad X_C = \frac{1}{2\pi fC} \qquad 1.2 = 2\pi(20)L \qquad 5 = \frac{1}{2\pi(20)C}$$

$$L = 9.5 \text{ mH} \qquad C = 1592 \,\mu\text{F}$$

(*b*) $f_r = \dfrac{1}{2\pi\sqrt{LC}} = \dfrac{1}{2\pi\sqrt{(9.5 \times 10^{-3})(1592 \times 10^{-6})}} = 40.93 \text{ Hz}$

12.37   Determine the Q of a coil whose resistance and inductance are 10 Ω and 0.04 H, respectively, if the coil is at resonance at 2 kHz.

$$Q_{\text{coil}} = \frac{\omega_r L}{R} = \frac{2\pi(2000)(0.04)}{10} = 50.27$$

12.38   A coil whose resistance and inductance are 5.0 Ω and 32 mH, respectively, is connected in series with a 796-pF capacitor. Determine (*a*) the resonance frequency of the circuit; (*b*) the quality factor; and (*c*) the bandwidth.

(*a*) $f_r = \dfrac{1}{2\pi\sqrt{(32 \times 10^{-3})(796 \times 10^{-12})}}$ $f_r = 31.53 \text{ kHz}$

(*b*) $Q_s = \dfrac{\omega_r L}{R} = \dfrac{2\pi(31.53 \times 10^3)(32 \times 10^{-3})}{5} = 1268$ (*c*) $Q_s = \dfrac{f_r}{\text{BW}}$ or $1268 = \dfrac{31{,}530}{\text{BW}}$

Thus, $\text{BW} = 24.9 \text{ Hz}$.

12.39 The circuit of Prob. 12.38 is connected to a 120-V source and operates at resonance frequency. Calculate **(a)** the input current and **(b)** the voltage across the capacitor.

❚ (a) $I = \dfrac{V_T}{Z_r} = \dfrac{120}{5} = 24\,\text{A}$

(b) $X_C = \dfrac{1}{2\pi f C} = \dfrac{1}{2\pi(31.53 \times 10^3)(796 \times 10^{-12})} = 6341\,\Omega$ $V_C = I_r X_C = 24(6341) = 152\,\text{kV}$

12.40 A 400-V 200-Hz ac source is connected in series with a capacitor and a coil whose resistance and inductance are $20\,\text{m}\Omega$ and $6\,\text{mH}$, respectively. If the circuit is in resonance at 200 Hz, determine **(a)** the capacitance of the capacitor and **(b)** the circuit current.

❚ (a) $f_r = \dfrac{1}{2\pi\sqrt{LC}}$ $200 = \dfrac{1}{2\pi\sqrt{0.006C}}$ $C = 105.54\,\mu\text{F}$ **(b)** $I_r = \dfrac{V}{Z_r} = \dfrac{400}{0.020} = 20\,\text{kA}$

12.41 In the circuit of Prob. 12.40, determine **(a)** the voltage across the capacitor and **(b)** the maximum instantaneous energy stored in the coil.

❚ (a) $V_C = IX_C = (20 \times 10^3)\dfrac{1}{2\pi(200)(105.54 \times 10^{-6})} = 151\,\text{kV}$

(b) $W_{max} = \frac{1}{2}LI^2_{max} = \frac{1}{2}(0.006)(20{,}000\sqrt{2})^2 = 2.4\,\text{MJ}$

12.42 Calculate the half-power frequencies for the circuit of Prob. 12.40.

❚ $Q = \dfrac{\omega_r L}{R} = \dfrac{2\pi(200)(0.006)}{0.020} = 377$ and $\text{BW} = \dfrac{f_r}{Q} = \dfrac{200}{377} = 0.53\,\text{Hz}$

Since $Q > 10$, Prob. 12.17 gives

$$f_2 \approx f_r + \frac{\text{BW}}{2} = 200 + 0.265 = 200.265\,\text{Hz} \qquad f_1 \approx f_r - \frac{\text{BW}}{2} = 200 - 0.265 = 199.74\,\text{Hz}$$

12.43 A series resonant circuit has a resistance of $1\,\text{k}\Omega$ and half-power frequencies of 20 and 100 kHz. Determine **(a)** the bandwidth and **(b)** the resonance frequency.

❚ (a) $\text{BW} = f_2 - f_1 = 100 - 20 = 80\,\text{kHz}$ **(b)** $f_r = \sqrt{f_2 f_1} = \sqrt{(100)(20)} = 44.72\,\text{kHz}$

12.44 Calculate the inductance and the capacitance of the circuit of Prob. 12.43.

❚
$$Q = \frac{f_r}{\text{BW}} = \frac{44.72}{80} = 0.56 \qquad Q = \frac{\omega_r L}{R} \qquad 0.56 = \frac{2\pi(44{,}720)(L)}{1000}$$

$$L = 2.0\,\text{mH} \qquad \omega_r L = \frac{1}{\omega_r C} \qquad 2\pi(44{,}720)(0.002) = \frac{1}{2\pi(44{,}720)C} \qquad C = 6.3\,\text{nF}$$

12.45 For the circuit of Fig. 12-1a sketch the current and the various voltages as functions of frequency.

❚ See Fig. 12-8.

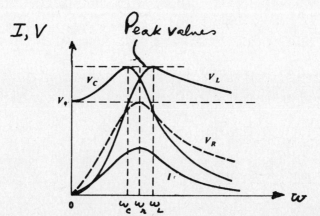

Fig. 12-8

12.46 Evaluate the frequencies ω_C and ω_L of Fig. 12-8.

❚ From Fig. 12-1a,

$$Z = \sqrt{R^2 + (X_L - X_C)^2} \quad \text{and} \quad I = \frac{V}{Z} \quad V_C = IX_C = \frac{VX_C}{Z} \quad V_L = IX_L = \frac{VX_L}{Z}$$

Squaring both sides, $V_C^2 = V^2 X_C^2 / Z^2$ and $V_L^2 = V^2 X_L^2 / Z^2$. Expressing X_C, X_L, and Z in terms of ω,

$$V_C^2 = \frac{V^2}{(\omega C)^2 [R^2 + (\omega L - 1/\omega C)^2]} \qquad V_L^2 = \frac{V^2}{[R^2 + (\omega L - 1/\omega C)^2]/(\omega L)^2}$$

To find the frequency ω_C for which V_C is largest, we minimize the denominator of the expression for V_C^2. Thus, differentiating with respect to ω, equating the result to zero, and solving, we find

$$\omega_C = \sqrt{\frac{1}{LC} - \frac{R^2}{2L^2}} = \omega_r \sqrt{1 - \frac{1}{2Q_s^2}}$$

By a similar procedure,

$$\omega_L = \sqrt{\frac{2}{2LC - R^2C^2}} = \frac{\omega_r}{\sqrt{1 - 1/2Q_s^2}}$$

Observe the interesting relation $\omega_C \omega_L = \omega_r^2 = \omega_1 \omega_2$ (cf. Prob. 12.14).

12.47 From Fig. 12-9, determine (a) the resonance frequency, (b) the cutoff half-power frequencies, (c) bandwidth, and (d) the quality factor.

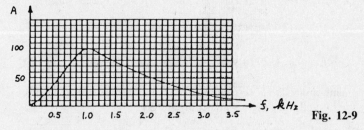

Fig. 12-9

❚ (a) $f_r = 1.0 \text{ kHz}$. (b) At $A = 100/\sqrt{2} \approx 71$, $f_1 = 0.7 \text{ kHz}$ and $f_2 = 1.6 \text{ kHz}$. (c) $\text{BW} = f_2 - f_1 = 0.9 \text{ kHz}$. (d) $Q = f_r/\text{BW} = 1.0/0.9 = 1.1$.

12.48 A resonant series RLC circuit having $R = 5\,\Omega$ operates from a 20-V source. Determine the power at half-power frequency.

❚
$$I = \frac{V}{R} = \frac{20}{5} = 4 \text{ A} \qquad P_{\text{half-power}} = \tfrac{1}{2}P_{\max} = \tfrac{1}{2}(I_m)^2 R = I^2 R = (4)^2(5) = 80 \text{ W}$$

12.49 The bandwidth of a series resonance circuit is 100 Hz and the resonance frequency is 1000 Hz. If the circuit resistance is $10\,\Omega$, determine L and C.

❚
$$Q_s = \frac{f_r}{\text{BW}} = \frac{1000}{100} = 10 = \frac{\omega_r L}{R} = \frac{2\pi(1000)L}{10}$$

Thus, $L = 15.91 \text{ mH}$; and, from $Q_s = 1/\omega_r RC$, $C = 1/2\pi(1000)(10)(10) = 1.59 \,\mu\text{F}$.

12.50 Find the half-power frequencies of a series RLC circuit having $Q_s = 60$ and $f_r = 12 \text{ kHz}$.

❚ Since $Q_s > 10$, we have (Prob. 12.17),

$$f_1 \approx f_r - \frac{\text{BW}}{2} = f_r - \frac{f_r}{2Q_s} = 12,000 - \frac{12,000}{2(60)} = 11,900 \text{ Hz} \qquad f_2 \approx 12,000 + 1000 = 12,100 \text{ Hz}$$

12.51 If we define $\omega/\omega_r \equiv a$ (a dimensionless relative frequency), obtain an expression for the admittance of a series RLC circuit in terms of R, Q_s, and a.

❚
$$Y = \frac{1}{R + j(\omega L - 1/\omega C)} = \frac{1/R}{1 + j(a\omega_r L/R - 1/a\omega_r CR)} = \frac{1}{R[1 + jQ_s(a - 1/a)]}$$

12.52 Express the half-power frequencies in terms of $a \equiv \omega/\omega_r$ and Q_s, and show that, for $Q_s > 10$, the two values of a at half-power points are approximately given by $a = 1 \pm 1/(2Q_s)$.

❚ From Prob. 12.14, half-power frequencies are given by

$$\omega = \sqrt{(\omega_r)^2 + (R/2L)^2} \pm \frac{R}{2L} \quad \text{or} \quad \frac{\omega}{\omega_r} = a = \sqrt{1 + \left(\frac{R}{2\omega_r L}\right)^2} \pm \frac{R}{2\omega_r L} = \sqrt{1 + (1/2\,Q_s)^2} \pm \frac{1}{2Q_s}$$

For $Q_s = 10$, the radical becomes $\sqrt{1.0025} \approx 1$.

12.53 In a series RLC circuit, $L = 100\,\text{mH}$ and $C = 10\,\mu\text{F}$. Plot the magnitude of the admittance of the circuit as a function of $a \equiv \omega/\omega_r$ for $R = 10, 25,$ and $100\,\Omega$. Also indicate the corresponding values of Q.

❚ See Fig. 12-10.

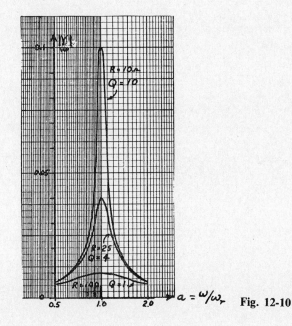

Fig. 12-10

12.54 From the graph of Fig. 12-10 find the bandwidths.

❚
$$\text{BW} = \frac{\omega_r}{2\pi Q} = \frac{1/\sqrt{LC}}{2\pi Q} = \frac{1000\,\text{Hz}}{2\pi Q}$$

$$= 15.9\,\text{Hz} \quad \text{for} \quad R = 10\,\Omega$$

$$= 39.7\,\text{Hz} \quad \text{for} \quad R = 25\,\Omega$$

$$= 159\,\text{Hz} \quad \text{for} \quad R = 100\,\Omega$$

12.55 Show that the condition for resonance in a parallel RLC circuit (Fig. 12-11) is the same as that in a series RLC circuit.

❚ For resonance, the circuit impedance (or admittance) must be purely resistive. For Fig. 12-11 we have

$$\mathbf{Y} = \frac{1}{R} + j\left(\omega C - \frac{1}{\omega L}\right)$$

Resonance occurs when

$$\omega C - \frac{1}{\omega L} = 0 \quad \text{or} \quad \omega = \frac{1}{\sqrt{LC}} \quad \text{or} \quad f = \frac{1}{2\pi\sqrt{LC}}$$

which is the same as that of Prob. 12.1.

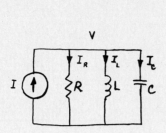

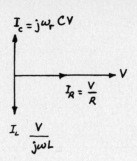

Fig. 12-11   Fig. 12-12

12.56 Draw a phasor diagram showing the voltage and all the currents in a parallel resonant circuit.

❚ See Fig. 12-12.   Notice that $I_L + I_C = 0$ and $I = I_R = V/R$.

12.57 Using the definition of Q given by Eq. (1) of Prob. 12.8, obtain an expression for Q_p for a parallel resonant circuit.

❚ From Eq. (1) of Prob. 12.8,

$$Q_p = \frac{2\pi(w_L + w_C)_{max}}{P_R T_r} \tag{1}$$

We let $i = I_m \cos \omega_r t$.   Then $v = Ri = RI_m \cos \omega_r t$.   Thus,

$$w_L = \tfrac{1}{2} L i_L^2 = \frac{1}{2} \left(\int_0^t \frac{1}{L} v\, dt \right)^2 = \tfrac{1}{2} I_m^2 R^2 C \sin^2 \omega_r t \tag{2}$$

where we have used $\omega_r^2 = 1/LC$.   Furthermore,

$$w_C = \tfrac{1}{2} C v^2 = \tfrac{1}{2} I_m^2 R^2 C \cos^2 \omega_r t \tag{3}$$

From Eqs. (2) and (3),

$$w_L + w_C = (w_L + w_C)_{max} = \tfrac{1}{2} I_m^2 R^2 C \qquad \text{(conservation of energy)} \tag{4}$$

$$T_r = \frac{1}{f_r} \tag{5}$$

and

$$P_R = \tfrac{1}{2} I_m^2 R \tag{6}$$

Substituting Eqs. (4) through (6) into Eq. (1) yields

$$Q_p = 2\pi f_r RC = R \sqrt{\frac{C}{L}} = \frac{R}{\omega_r L} = \omega_r RC \tag{7}$$

12.58 A coil having resistance R_{coil} and inductance L_{coil} is connected in parallel with a capacitor C and across a voltage source $\mathbf{V}$ (Fig. 12-13).   Determine the equivalent conductance and susceptance of the circuit at angular frequency ω.

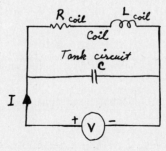

Fig. 12-13

❚ The input admittance for the circuit in Fig. 12-13 is

$$\mathbf{Y} = \frac{1}{R_{coil} + jX_{L\,coil}} + \frac{1}{-jX_C} = \frac{1}{R_{coil} + j\omega L_{coil}} + \frac{1}{-j(1/\omega C)}$$

Rationalizing the respective denominators, and then separating the real and imaginary terms,

$$\mathbf{Y} = \frac{R_{coil} - j\omega L_{coil}}{R_{coil}^2 + \omega^2 L_{coil}^2} + j\omega C = \frac{R_{coil}}{R_{coil}^2 + \omega^2 L_{coil}^2} - \frac{j\omega L_{coil}}{R_{coil}^2 + \omega^2 L_{coil}^2} + j\omega C$$

$$= \underbrace{\frac{R_{coil}}{R_{coil}^2 + \omega^2 L_{coil}^2}}_{\uparrow \atop G} + j\underbrace{\left(\frac{-\omega L_{coil}}{R_{coil}^2 + \omega^2 L_{coil}^2} + \omega C \right)}_{\uparrow \atop B}$$

12.59 Find the resonance frequency for the circuit of Prob. 12.58.

▮ The condition for resonance is $B = 0$ (and $\omega \neq 0$); this gives

$$\omega_r = 2\pi f_r = \sqrt{\frac{1}{L_{coil} C} - \frac{R_{coil}^2}{L_{coil}^2}} \tag{1}$$

12.60 When is resonance impossible in the circuit of Prob. 12.58?

▮ If $R_{coil}^2 > L_{coil}/C$, ω_r as given by Eq. (1) of Prob. 12.59 is imaginary, and so resonance cannot occur.

12.61 For the circuit of Prob. 12.58 if $R_{coil} = 0$, show that the circuit will draw no current at resonance.

▮ If $R_{coil} = 0$, then

$$\mathbf{Y} = \frac{1}{jX_{L\,coil}} + \frac{1}{-jX_C} = \frac{1}{j}\left(\frac{1}{X_{L\,coil}} - \frac{1}{X_C} \right)$$

but, at resonance, $X_{L\,coil} = X_C$; so $\mathbf{Y} = 0$ and no current is drawn.

12.62 In the circuit of Prob. 12.58 (Fig. 12-13), $L_{coil} = 2\,\text{mH}$, $C = 7.75\,\mu\text{F}$, and R_{coil} is variable. Show, graphically, the variation in the resonance frequency.

▮ See Fig. 12-14.

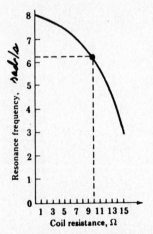

Fig. 12-14

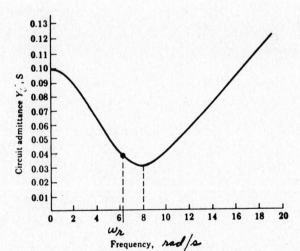

Fig. 12-15

12.63 If $R_{coil} = 10\,\Omega$, $L_{coil} = 2\,\text{mH}$, and $C = 7.75\,\mu\text{F}$ in the circuit of Prob. 12.58, plot the admittance magnitude as a function of frequency.

▮ See Fig. 12-15. Note that the frequency at which resonance occurs and the frequency at which Y is a minimum are not the same; coincidence can occur only for the ideal condition $R_{coil} = 0$ (by Prob. 12.61). The equation relating admittance magnitude to radian frequency is

$$Y = \sqrt{\left(\frac{R_{coil}}{R_{coil}^2 + \omega^2 L_{coil}^2} \right)^2 + \left(\frac{-\omega L_{coil}}{R_{coil}^2 + \omega^2 L_{coil}^2} + \omega C \right)^2}$$

12.64 For the data of Prob. 12.63 plot the input impedance and the input current as functions of frequency.

▌ See Fig. 12-16.

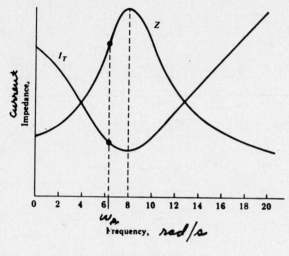

Fig. 12-16

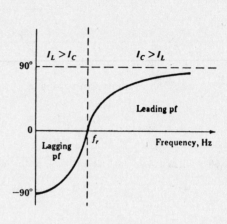

Fig. 12-17

12.65 Sketch the phase angle of the circuit of Prob. 12.63 as a function of frequency.

▌ See Fig. 12-17.

12.66 A 60-V source supplies a parallel circuit consisting of a 2.5-μF capacitor and a coil whose resistance and inductance are 260 mH and 15 Ω, respectively. Determine the resonance frequency.

▌ By Prob. 12.59,

$$f_r = \frac{1}{2\pi} \sqrt{\frac{1}{L_{coil}C} - \frac{R_{coil}^2}{L_{coil}^2}} = \frac{1}{2\pi} \sqrt{\frac{1}{(0.260)(2.5 \times 10^{-6})} - \frac{(15)^2}{(0.260)^2}} = 197 \, \text{Hz}$$

12.67 The circuit of Fig. 12-13 is modified to that shown in Fig. 12-18. Show that the resonance frequency is independent of R and is still given by Eq. (1) of Prob. 12.59.

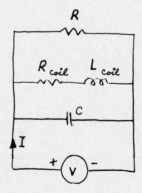

Fig. 12-18

▌ From Fig. 12-18, we have

$$\mathbf{Y} = \frac{1}{R} + j\omega C + \frac{1}{R_{coil} + j\omega L_{coil}} = \frac{1}{R} + \frac{R}{R_{coil}^2 + \omega^2 L_{coil}^2} + j\omega \left(C - \frac{L_{coil}}{R_{coil}^2 + \omega^2 L_{coil}^2} \right)$$

Setting Im $(\mathbf{Y}) = 0$ and solving for ω_r again gives Eq. (1) of Prob. 12.59.

12.68 Find the Q_p at resonance for the circuit shown in Fig. 12-18.

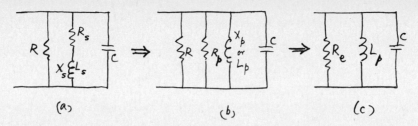

Fig. 12-19

▌ The given circuit is reduced to that of Fig. 12-19c by the steps indicated in Fig. 12-19. Combining the coil and the resistor R, shown in Fig. 12-19b, we have:

$$R_p = \frac{R_s^2 + X_s^2}{R_s} = R_s + \frac{X_s^2}{R_s}\frac{R_s}{R_s} = R_s(1 + Q_s^2)$$

Similarly,

$$X_p = \frac{R_s^2 + X_s^2}{X_s} = \frac{R_s^2}{X_s}\frac{X_s}{X_s} + X_s = X_s\left(1 + \frac{1}{Q_s^2}\right)$$

Now, we combine R_p and R of Fig. 12-19b to obtain R_e of Fig. 12-19c such that $R_e = R_p R/(R_p + R)$. Hence,

$$Q_p = \omega_r C R_e = \frac{R_e}{\omega_r L_p} = R_e \sqrt{\frac{C}{L_p}} \tag{1}$$

$$= \frac{f_r}{\text{BW}} \tag{2}$$

as in Prob. 12.16.

12.69 Simplify the results of Prob. 12.59 when $Q_{\text{coil}} \gtrsim 10$.

▌ From Eq. (1) of Prob. 12.59,

$$\omega_r^2 = \frac{1}{L_{\text{coil}}C} - \frac{R_{\text{coil}}^2}{L_{\text{coil}}^2}$$

Rearranging terms,

$$\omega_r^2 + \frac{R_{\text{coil}}^2}{L_{\text{coil}}^2} = \frac{1}{L_{\text{coil}}C} \tag{1}$$

but

$$Q_{\text{coil}} = \frac{\omega_r L_{\text{coil}}}{R_{\text{coil}}} \tag{2}$$

Solving Eq. (2) for R_{coil}, substituting into Eq. (1), and solving for ω_r yields

$$\omega_r^2 + \frac{\omega_r^2 L_{\text{coil}}^2}{L_{\text{coil}}^2 Q_{\text{coil}}^2} = \frac{1}{L_{\text{coil}}C} \quad \text{or} \quad \omega_r^2\left(1 + \frac{1}{Q_{\text{coil}}^2}\right) = \frac{1}{L_{\text{coil}}C} \quad \text{or} \quad \omega_r = \sqrt{\frac{1}{L_{\text{coil}}C}\frac{Q_{\text{coil}}^2}{1 + Q_{\text{coil}}^2}}$$

If $Q \gtrsim 10$,

$$\frac{Q_{\text{coil}}^2}{1 + Q_{\text{coil}}^2} \approx 1 \quad \text{and} \quad \omega_r \approx \frac{1}{\sqrt{L_{\text{coil}}C}}$$

12.70 A parallel circuit consisting of a 65-pF capacitor and a coil whose inductance and resistance are 56 μH and 60 Ω, respectively, is connected to the output of a transistor, as shown in Fig. 12-20a. The transistor acting as a current source has a source resistance of 37 kΩ. Determine (a) the resonance frequency and (b) Q_{coil} at the resonance frequency.

▌ (a) By Prob. 12.59,

$$f_r = \frac{1}{2\pi}\sqrt{\frac{1}{L_{\text{coil}}C} - \frac{R_{\text{coil}}^2}{L_{\text{coil}}^2}} = \frac{1}{2\pi}\sqrt{\frac{1}{(56 \times 10^{-6})(65 \times 10^{-12})} - \frac{(60)^2}{(56 \times 10^{-6})^2}} = 2.63\ \text{MHz}$$

(b) $Q_{\text{coil}} = \dfrac{\omega_r L_{\text{coil}}}{R_{\text{coil}}} = \dfrac{2\pi(2.63 \times 10^6)(56 \times 10^{-6})}{60} = 15.4$

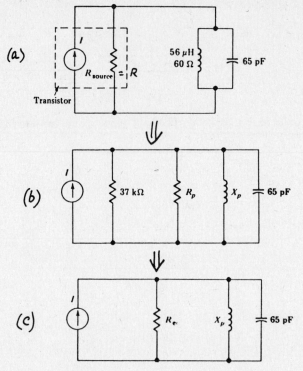

Fig. 12-20

12.71 What is the Q_p of the circuit of Fig. 12-20a at resonance?

▌ Reduce the given circuit to that of Fig. 12-20c; thus, as in Prob. 12.68,

$$R_p = R_{coil}(1 + Q^2_{coil}) = 60[1 + (15.4)^2] = 14.3 \text{ k}\Omega \qquad R_e = \frac{RR_p}{R + R_p} = \frac{37,000 \times 14,300}{37,000 + 14,300} = 10.3 \text{ k}\Omega$$

$$Q_p = \omega_r C R_e = 2\pi(2.63 \times 10^6)(65 \times 10^{-12})(10.3 \times 10^3) = 11$$

12.72 Determine the bandwidth of the circuit of Fig. 12-20a.

▌ From Prob. 12.71 we have

$$Q_p = \frac{f_r}{BW} \qquad 11 = \frac{2.63 \times 10^6}{BW} \qquad BW = 239 \text{ kHz}$$

12.73 Determine the capacitance of the circuit of Fig. 12-21a so that it will resonate at 22.3 kHz and have a bandwidth of 4.05 kHz, when including a coil whose resistance and inductance are 56 Ω and 3.2 mH respectively; assume the circuit is supplied by a current source whose source resistance is 8081 Ω.

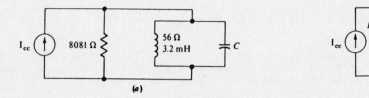

Fig. 12-21

▌ From Fig. 12-21,

$$Q_{coil} = \frac{\omega_r L_{coil}}{R_{coil}} = \frac{2\pi(22.3 \times 10^3)(0.0032)}{56} = 8$$

$Q_{coil} < 10$; hence high-Q formulas cannot be used. Instead, as in Prob. 12.68,

$$R_p = R_{\text{coil}}(1 + Q^2_{\text{coil}}) = 56[1 + (8)^2] = 3640 \, \Omega$$

$$R_e = \frac{R_{\text{source}}R_p}{R_{\text{source}} + R_p} = \frac{8081 \times 3640}{8081 + 3640} = 2509.58 \, \Omega \qquad Q_p = \frac{f_r}{\text{BW}} = \frac{22.3 \times 10^3}{4.05 \times 10^3} = 5.51$$

Also $Q_p = \omega_r C R_e$ (Prob. 12.68). Thus, $5.51 = 2\pi(22.3 \times 10^3)(C)2509.58$ and $C = 15.7 \, \text{nF}$.

12.74 How much additional parallel resistance is required to change the bandwdith of the circuit of Fig. 12-21a to 6 kHz?

❚ From Fig. 12-21b,

$$Q_p = \frac{f_r}{\text{BW}} = \frac{22.3 \times 10^3}{6 \times 10^3} = 3.72 = \omega_r C R_e \qquad 3.72 = 2\pi(22.3 \times 10^3)(15.7 \times 10^{-9})R_e$$

$$R_e = 1691 \, \Omega \qquad \frac{1}{R_e} = \frac{1}{R_{\text{source}}} + \frac{1}{R_p} + \frac{1}{R_x}$$

$$\frac{1}{1691} = \frac{1}{8081} + \frac{1}{3640} + \frac{1}{R_x} \qquad R_x = 5184 \, \Omega$$

12.75 A circuit consisting of a capacitor in parallel with a coil whose inductance and resistance are 1.05 mH and 100 Ω, respectively, is driven at its resonance frequency of 600 kHz from a constant-current source. The source consists of a 2.30-mA 600-kHz constant-current generator in parallel with a 60-kΩ source resistance. Determine (a) Q_{coil} and (b) capacitance.

❚ The circuit is similar to that shown in Fig. 12-20a.

(a) $\quad Q_{\text{coil}} = \dfrac{\omega_r L_{\text{coil}}}{R_{\text{coil}}} = \dfrac{2\pi(600 \times 10^3)(0.00105)}{100} = 39.58$

(b) Since $Q_{\text{coil}} > 10$,

$$f_r = \frac{1}{2\pi\sqrt{LC}} \qquad 600 \times 10^3 = \frac{1}{2\pi\sqrt{0.00105\,C}} \qquad C = 67 \, \text{pF}$$

12.76 Determine (a) Q_p and (b) the bandwidth of the circuit of Prob.12.75.

❚ (a) $\quad R_p = R_{\text{coil}}(1 + Q^2_{\text{coil}}) = 100[1 + (39.58)^2] = 156.8 \, \text{k}\Omega$

$$R_e = \frac{R_p R_{\text{source}}}{R_p + R_{\text{source}}} = \frac{(156.8)(60)}{156.8 + 60} = 43.39 \, \text{k}\Omega$$

$$Q_p = \omega_r C R_e = 2\pi(600 \times 10^3)(67 \times 10^{-12})(43,390) = 11.0$$

(b) $\quad Q_p = \dfrac{f_r}{\text{BW}} \qquad 11.0 = \dfrac{600 \times 10^3}{\text{BW}} \qquad \text{BW} = 54.5 \, \text{kHz}$

12.77 What is the maximum energy stored in the capacitor of the circuit of Prob. 12.75? Also determine the power dissipated in the resistor.

❚ The voltage across the capacitor is the voltage across the parallel circuit. Referring to Fig. 12-20c, at resonance, $Z_{\text{in}} = R_e$. Therefore,

$$V = IR_e = 0.0023(43,390) = 99.8 \, \text{V} \qquad W_{C\,\text{max}} = \tfrac{1}{2}(67 \times 10^{-12})(99.8\sqrt{2})^2 = 667 \, \text{nJ}$$

$$P = I^2 R_e = (0.0023)^2(43,390) = 230 \, \text{mW}$$

12.78 Determine all currents in the circuit shown in Fig. 12-22.

❚ Since $X_L = X_C$, the circuit is in resonance. Thus,

$$\mathbf{I}_R = \frac{120\,\underline{/0°}}{10} = 12\,\underline{/0°}\,\text{A} \qquad \mathbf{I}_L = \frac{120\,\underline{/0°}}{4\,\underline{/90°}} = 30\,\underline{/-90°}\,\text{A} \qquad \mathbf{I}_C = \frac{120\,\underline{/0°}}{4\,\underline{/-90°}} = 30\,\underline{/90°}\,\text{A}$$

$$\mathbf{I}_1 = \mathbf{I}_L + \mathbf{I}_C = 30\,\underline{/-90°} + 30\,\underline{/90°} = 0\,\text{A} \qquad \mathbf{I} = \mathbf{I}_R = 12\,\underline{/0°}\,\text{A}$$

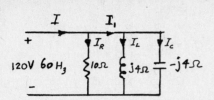

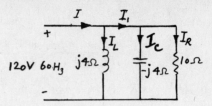

Fig. 12-22

Fig. 12-23

12.79   Determine $\mathbf{I}$ and $\mathbf{I}_1$ in the circuit of Fig. 12-23.

    ❙ Notice that the circuit is in resonance.   Hence,

$$\mathbf{I} = \frac{120\ \underline{/0°}}{10} = 12\ \underline{/0°}\ \text{A} \qquad \mathbf{I}_1 = \mathbf{I}_C + \mathbf{I}_R = 30\ \underline{/90°} + 12\ \underline{/0°} = 32.31\ \underline{/68.2°}\ \text{A}$$

12.80   A parallel RLC circuit has $R = 0.5\ \Omega$, $L = 10\ \text{mH}$, and $C = 2.5\ \text{mF}$.   Determine the resonance frequency and the corresponding input currents at 24 V.

    ❙

$$f_r = \frac{1}{2\pi\sqrt{LC}} = \frac{1}{2\pi\sqrt{(0.01)(2.5 \times 10^{-3})}} = 31.83\ \text{Hz}$$

At resonance, $I = V/R = 24/0.5 = 48\ \text{A}$.

12.81   A 0.5-μF capacitor is connected in parallel with a coil whose resistance and inductance are $1.0\ \Omega$ and $2.0\ \text{H}$, respectively.   The parallel circuit is supplied by a 100-V sinusoidal generator that is operating at the resonance frequency of the circuit.   Determine (*a*) the resonance frequency; (*b*) the input impedance; and (*c*) the current.

    ❙ (*a*)   By Prob. 12.59,

$$f_r = \frac{1}{2\pi}\sqrt{\frac{1}{L_{\text{coil}}C} - \frac{R_{\text{coil}}^2}{L_{\text{coil}}^2}} = \frac{1}{2\pi}\sqrt{\frac{1}{2(0.5 \times 10^{-6})} - \left(\frac{1}{2}\right)^2} = 159.15\ \text{Hz}$$

      (*b*)   At the resonance frequency, $\mathbf{Y}_{\text{in}} = G + j0$,   where

$$G = \frac{R_{\text{coil}}}{R_{\text{coil}}^2 + \omega_r^2 L_{\text{coil}}^2} = \frac{1}{1 + (2\pi \times 159.15)^2(2)^2} = 0.25\ \mu\text{S} \qquad Z_{\text{in}} = \frac{1}{G} = \frac{1}{0.25 \times 10^{-6}} = 4\ \text{M}\Omega$$

      (*c*) $I = \dfrac{V}{Z_{\text{in}}} = \dfrac{100}{4 \times 10^6} = 25\ \mu\text{A}$

12.82   A parallel section consisting of a 5.4-μF capacitor in parallel with a coil whose resistance and inductance are $18.8\ \Omega$ and $8.0\ \text{mH}$, respectively, is driven at its resonance frequency by a 240-V sinusoidal generator. Determine the resonance frequency.

    ❙

$$f_r = \frac{1}{2\pi}\sqrt{\frac{1}{L_{\text{coil}}C} - \frac{R_{\text{coil}}^2}{L_{\text{coil}}^2}} = \frac{1}{2\pi}\sqrt{\frac{10^6}{(0.008)(5.4)} - \left(\frac{18.8}{0.008}\right)^2} = 668\ \text{Hz}$$

12.83   A 480-V 60-Hz source supplies energy to a parallel circuit consisting of a $25\ \underline{/30°}$-Ω branch and a $12\ \underline{/-40°}$-Ω branch (Fig. 12-24).   Determine the impedance of a circuit element that, if connected in series with the source, will cause the system to be in resonance.

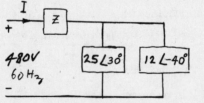

Fig. 12-24

    ❙ $\mathbf{Z}_p = \dfrac{(25\ \underline{/30°})(12\ \underline{/-40°})}{25\ \underline{/30°} + 12\ \underline{/-40°}} = 9.61\ \underline{/-18.82°}\ \Omega \qquad \mathbf{Z}_{\text{in}} = \mathbf{Z}_p + \mathbf{Z} = (9.10 - j3.1) + \mathbf{Z}$

For the system to be in resonance, $\mathbf{Z}_{\text{in}}$ must have no imaginary term.   Hence $\mathbf{Z} = +j3.1 = jX_L$.   Since $X_L = 2\pi f L$, $3.1 = 120\pi L$ or $L = 8.23\ \text{mH}$.

12.84 Find the input current and input power for the circuit of Prob. 12.83.

▮ From Prob.12.83, at resonance,

$$Z_{\text{in}} = 9.10\,\Omega \qquad I = \frac{480}{9.10} = 52.75\text{ A} \qquad P = (480)(52.75) = 25.32\text{ kW}$$

12.85 A series-parallel circuit consisting of a $(5 - j3)$-Ω impedance in series with a parallel section consisting of $(4 + j2)$-Ω and $(2 + j3)$-Ω impedances is supplied by a 490-V 30-Hz generator. Sketch the circuit and determine (a) the input impedance and (b) the input current.

▮ The circuit is shown in Fig. 12-25.

(a) $\quad \mathbf{Z}_p = \dfrac{(4 + j2)(2 + j3)}{4 + j2 + 2 + j3} = 2.06\,\underline{/43.07°}\;\Omega$

$\quad \mathbf{Z}_{\text{in}} = \mathbf{Z}_p + (5 - j3) = (1.51 + j1.41) + (5 - j3) = 6.70\,\underline{/-13.73°}\;\Omega$

(b) $\quad \mathbf{I} = \dfrac{\mathbf{V}}{\mathbf{Z}_{\text{in}}} = \dfrac{490\,\underline{/0°}}{6.70\,\underline{/-13.73°}} = 73.12\,\underline{/13.73°}\text{ A}$

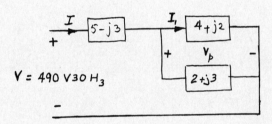

Fig. 12-25

12.86 (a) For the circuit of Prob. 12.85 determine the current in the $(4 + j2)$-Ω impedance. (b) Is the series-parallel circuit operating at its resonance frequency? Explain.

▮ (a) The voltage across the parallel branch is

$$\mathbf{V}_p = \mathbf{I}\mathbf{Z}_p = (73.12\,\underline{/13.73°})(2.06\,\underline{/43.07°}) = 150.63\,\underline{/56.80°}\text{ V}$$

$$\mathbf{I}_1 = \frac{\mathbf{V}_p}{\mathbf{Z}_1} = \frac{150.63\,\underline{/56.8°}}{4 + j2} = 33.7\,\underline{/30.23°}\text{ A}$$

(b) No: If the circuit were at resonance the phase angle between $\mathbf{V}$ and $\mathbf{I}$ would be zero.

12.87 A tank circuit is supplied by a current source whose source resistance is 56 kΩ. The tank circuit is composed of a 56-nF capacitor in parallel with a coil whose inductance and resistance are 35 mH and 80 Ω, respectively. Determine (a) f_r and (b) Q_{coil}.

▮ (a) By Prob. 12.59,

$$f_r = \frac{1}{2\pi}\sqrt{\frac{1}{L_{\text{coil}}C} - \frac{R_{\text{coil}}^2}{L_{\text{coil}}^2}} = \frac{1}{2\pi}\sqrt{\frac{1}{(0.035)(56 \times 10^{-9})} - \left(\frac{80}{0.035}\right)^2} = 3578\text{ Hz}$$

(b) $\quad Q_{\text{coil}} = \dfrac{\omega_r L_{\text{coil}}}{R_{\text{coil}}} = \dfrac{2\pi(3578)(0.035)}{80} = 9.83$

12.88 Determine (a) $\mathbf{Z}_{\text{in}}$ and (b) Q_p of the circuit of Prob. 12.87.

▮ (a) $\quad R_p = R_{\text{coil}}(1 + Q_{\text{coil}}^2) = 80[1 + (9.83)^2] = 7.81\text{ k}\Omega$

$$Z_{\text{in}} = R_e = \frac{R_p R_s}{R_p + R_s} = \frac{(7.81)(56)}{7.81 + 56} = 6.854\text{ k}\Omega$$

(b) $\quad Q_p = \omega_r C R_e = 2\pi(3578)(56 \times 10^{-9})(6.854 \times 10^3) = 8.62$

12.89 Find (a) the bandwidth and (b) the half-power frequencies of the circuit of Prob. 12.87.

$\blacksquare$ (a) $$Q_p = \frac{f_r}{\text{BW}} \quad \text{or} \quad 8.62 = \frac{3578}{\text{BW}} \quad \text{or} \quad \text{BW} = 415$$

(b) From Prob. 12.87(b), $Q_{\text{coil}} < 10$.

$$f_r = \sqrt{f_2 f_1} \qquad \text{BW} = f_2 - f_1 \qquad 3578 = \sqrt{f_2 f_1} \qquad 415 = f_2 - f_1$$

$$f_2 = 415 + f_1 \qquad 12.80 \times 10^6 = f_2 f_1 \qquad 12.80 \times 10^6 = (415 + f_1)f_1$$

$$f_1^2 + 415 f_1 - 12.8 \times 10^6 = 0. \quad \text{Hence} \quad f_1 = 3376 \text{ Hz}, \quad f_2 = 3791 \text{ Hz}.$$

12.90 Determine the capacitance required for a tank circuit that uses a 35-μH 60-Ω coil and resonates at 1.65 MHz. The tank circuit is to be fed from a 1.65-MHz 2.0-mA constant-current generator whose source resistance is 60 kΩ.

$\blacksquare$ The circuit is shown in Fig. 12-26.

$$Q_{\text{coil}} = \frac{\omega_r L}{R} = \frac{2\pi(1.65 \times 10^6)(35 \times 10^{-6})}{60} = 6 < 10$$

so we use Eq. (1) of Prob. 12.59:

$$1.65 \times 10^6 = \frac{1}{2\pi} \sqrt{\frac{1}{35 \times 10^{-6} C} - \left(\frac{60}{35 \times 10^{-6}}\right)^2} \qquad C = 259 \text{ pF}$$

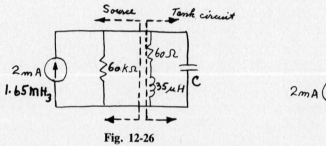

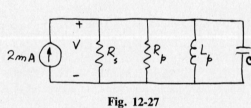

Fig. 12-26   Fig. 12-27

12.91 Calculate the current through the capacitor of the circuit of Prob. 12.90.

$\blacksquare$ The circuit of Fig. 12-26 is modified to that shown in Fig. 12-27 from which (cf. Prob. 12.68)

$$R_p = R_{\text{coil}}(1 + Q_{\text{coil}}^2) = 60[1 + (6)^2] = 2.22 \text{ k}\Omega$$

$$R_e = R_{\text{in}} = \frac{R_s R_p}{R_s + R_p} = \frac{(60)(2.22)}{60 + 2.22} = 2.141 \text{ k}\Omega \qquad V = IR_{\text{in}} = (0.002)(2141) = 4.28 \text{ V}$$

$$X_C = \frac{1}{2\pi f C} = \frac{1}{2\pi(1.65 \times 10^6)(259 \times 10^{-12})} = 373 \text{ }\Omega \qquad I_C = \frac{V}{X_C} = \frac{4.28}{373} = 11.5 \text{ mA}$$

12.92 Repeat Prob. 12.90 if the coil is replaced by one having $R_{\text{coil}} = 40 \text{ }\Omega$ and $L_{\text{coil}} = 350 \text{ }\mu$H.

$\blacksquare$ $$Q_{\text{coil}} = \frac{\omega_r L}{R} = \frac{2\pi(1.65 \times 10^6)(350 \times 10^{-6})}{40} = 90.7$$

Since $Q_{\text{coil}} > 10$, we may write

$$f_r = \frac{1}{2\pi} \sqrt{\frac{1}{L_{\text{coil}} C}} \qquad 1.65 \times 10^6 = \frac{1}{2\pi\sqrt{350 \times 10^{-6} C}} \qquad C = 26.6 \text{ pF}$$

12.93 Repeat Prob. 12.91 for the data of Prob. 12.92.

$\blacksquare$ $$R_p = R_{\text{coil}}(1 + Q_{\text{coil}}^2) = 40[1 + (90.7)^2] = 329.1 \text{ k}\Omega$$

$$R_e = R_{\text{in}} = \frac{R_s R_p}{R_s + R_p} = \frac{(60)(329.1)}{60 + 329.1} = 50.75 \text{ k}\Omega \qquad V = IR_{\text{in}} = (0.002)(50,750) = 101.5 \text{ V}$$

$$X_C = \frac{1}{2\pi(1.65 \times 10^6)(26.6 \times 10^{-12})} \qquad X_C = 3626 \text{ }\Omega \qquad I_C = \frac{V}{X_C} = \frac{101.5}{3626} = 28 \text{ mA}$$

12.94 A tank circuit consisting of a coil whose resistance and inductance are $40.6\,\Omega$ and $21.5\,\text{mH}$, respectively, is connected in parallel with a capacitor and supplied by a 1000-Hz 125-V generator of negligible impedance. Assuming the circuit is at resonance, determine its bandwidth.

$$Q_{\text{coil}} = \frac{\omega_r L_{\text{coil}}}{R_{\text{coil}}} = \frac{2\pi(1000)(0.0215)}{40.6} = 3.33 < 10$$

$$R_e = R_p = R_{\text{coil}}(1 + Q_{\text{coil}}^2) = 40.6[1 + (3.33)^2] = 490.8\,\Omega$$

Then, from Prob. 12.68,

$$\text{BW} = \frac{2\pi f_i^2 L_{\text{coil}}}{R_e} = \frac{2\pi(10^6)(0.0215)}{490.8} = 275\,\text{Hz}$$

12.95 A current source consisting of a sinusoidal 2.6-mA constant-current generator in parallel with a 60-kΩ resistor supplies a tank circuit whose parameters are $C = 105\,\text{nF}$, $L_{\text{coil}} = 10.5\,\text{mH}$, and $R_{\text{coil}} = 106\,\Omega$. Determine (a) f_r and (b) Q_{coil} at the resonance frequency.

(a) $\quad f_r = \frac{1}{2\pi}\sqrt{\frac{1}{CL_{\text{coil}}} - \frac{R_{\text{coil}}^2}{L_{\text{coil}}^2}} = \frac{1}{2\pi}\sqrt{\frac{1}{(105 \times 10^{-9})(0.0105)} - \left(\frac{106}{0.0105}\right)^2} = 4518\,\text{Hz}$

(b) $\quad Q_{\text{coil}} = \frac{\omega_r L_{\text{coil}}}{R_{\text{coil}}} = \frac{2\pi(4518)(0.0105)}{106} = 2.81$

12.96 What is the bandwidth of the circuit of Prob. 12.95?

Using a circuit similar to that of Fig. 12-27,

$$R_p = R_{\text{coil}}(1 + Q_{\text{coil}}^2) = 106[1 + (2.81)^2] = 943\,\Omega \qquad R_e = \frac{R_s R_p}{R_s + R_p} = \frac{(60,000)(943)}{60,000 + 943} = 928.4\,\Omega$$

$$Q_p = \omega_r C R_e = 2\pi(4518)(105 \times 10^{-9})(928.4) = 2.77 = \frac{f_r}{\text{BW}}$$

$$2.77 = \frac{4518}{\text{BW}} \qquad \text{BW} = 1631\,\text{Hz}$$

12.97 Under resonance, determine the voltage across the capacitor and the current through the coil of the circuit of Prob. 12.95.

$$\mathbf{V} = \mathbf{I}Z_{\text{in}} = (0.0026\,\underline{/0°})(928.4\,\underline{/0°}) = 2.41\,\underline{/0°}\,\text{V}$$

$$X_{\text{coil}} = 2\pi f_r L_{\text{coil}} = 2\pi(4518)(0.0105) = 298\,\Omega$$

$$\mathbf{Z}_{\text{coil}} = R + jX_L = (106 + j298) = 316.29\,\underline{/70.42°}\,\Omega$$

$$\mathbf{I}_{\text{coil}} = \frac{\mathbf{V}}{\mathbf{Z}_{\text{coil}}} = \frac{2.41\,\underline{/0°}}{316.29\,\underline{/70.42°}} = 7.63\,\underline{/-70.42°}\,\text{mA}$$

12.98 For the amplifier represented by the circuit of Fig. 11-32, find the gain at the resonance frequency of the secondary.

Substituting $\omega = \omega_r = 1/\sqrt{L_{22}C}$ in the result of Prob. 11.43, we obtain

$$G = \frac{-\mu M/C}{r_p R_2 + (\omega_r M)^2}$$

12.99 In the amplifier circuit of Fig. 11-33, if the primary and the secondary have the same resonance frequency, obtain an expression for the gain in terms of Q, $a \equiv \omega/\omega_r$ and the coefficient of coupling k.

From Prob. 11.45, we have

$$\mathbf{G} = \frac{-jg_m(M/\omega C_1 C_2)}{[R_1 + j(\omega L_{11} - 1/\omega C_1)][R_2 + j(\omega L_{22} - 1/\omega C_2)] + \omega^2 M^2}$$

Letting $M = k\sqrt{L_{11}L_{22}}$ and $\omega_r = 1/\sqrt{L_{11}C_1} = 1/\sqrt{L_{22}C_2}$, and dividing numerator and denominator by $\omega_r^2 L_{11}L_{22}$,

$$G = \frac{-jg_m k\sqrt{L_{11}L_{22}}/\omega C_1 C_2 (\omega_r^2 L_{11}L_{22})}{[R_1/\omega_r L_{11} + j(\omega/\omega_r - \omega_r/\omega)][R_2/\omega_r L_{22} + j(\omega/\omega_r - \omega_r/\omega)] + k^2 \omega^2 L_{11}L_{22}/\omega_r^2 L_{11}L_{22}}$$

Letting $Q = \omega_r L/R = 1/\omega_r RC$ and $a = \omega/\omega_r$,

$$G = \frac{-j(g_m/\omega_r \sqrt{C_1 C_2})(k/a)}{[1/Q_1 + j(a - 1/a)][1/Q_2 + j(a - 1/a)] + k^2 a^2}$$

$$= \frac{-j(g_m/\omega_r \sqrt{C_1 C_2})(k/a)}{[1/Q_1 Q_2 + k^2 a^2 - (a - 1/a)^2] + j(a - 1/a)(1/Q_1 + 1/Q_2)} \tag{1}$$

12.100 Define $\delta = a - 1$ (with $a \approx 1$). If $Q_1 = Q_2 = Q$ in the amplifier of Prob. 12.99, express the gain in terms of δ.

❚ Substitute $a \approx 1$ and

$$a - \frac{1}{a} = \frac{a^2 - 1}{a} = \frac{a + 1}{a}(a - 1) \approx 2\delta$$

in Eq. (1) of Prob. 12.99 (with $Q_1 = Q_2 = Q$):

$$G = \frac{-j(g_m/\omega_r \sqrt{C_1 C_2})(k/1)}{(1/Q^2 + k^2 - 4\delta^2) + j2\delta(2/Q)} = \frac{-j(g_m/\omega_r \sqrt{C_1 C_2})kQ^2}{[1 + (kQ)^2 - (2Q\delta)^2] + j(4Q\delta)}$$

12.101 For the amplifier of Prob. 12.99, we have $\omega_r = 10^6$ rad/s, $g_m = 1500$ μS, $C_1 = C_2 = 1$ nF, and $Q_1 = Q_2 = 40$. Plot $|G|$ (obtained in Prob. 12.100) as a function of $Q\delta$, with $-2 < Q\delta < 2$, for $k = 2/Q$, $1/Q$, and $1/2Q$.

❚ For the given values we have

$$G = \frac{1.5kQ^2}{[1 + (kQ)^2 - (2Q\delta)^2] + j(4Q\delta)}$$

Letting $y = Q\delta$,

$$G = \begin{cases} \dfrac{80}{(5 - 4y^2) + j4y} & \text{for } k = 2/Q \\[3mm] \dfrac{40}{(2 - 4y^2) + j4y} & \text{for } k = \dfrac{1}{Q} \\[3mm] \dfrac{20}{[1.25 - 4y^2] + j4y} & \text{for } k = \dfrac{1}{2Q} \end{cases}$$

the magnitudes of which are plotted in Fig. 12-28.

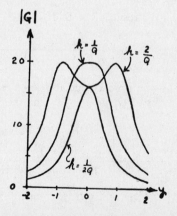

Fig. 12-28

12.102 For a series RLC circuit, obtain an expression for $\mathbf{V}_C/\mathbf{V}$ in terms of $Q = \omega L/R$ and $a = \omega/\omega_r$.

$$\mathbf{V} = \left[R + j\left(\omega L - \frac{1}{\omega C}\right)\right]\mathbf{I} \qquad \mathbf{V}_C = -\frac{j\mathbf{I}}{\omega C}$$

Thus
$$\frac{\mathbf{V}_C}{\mathbf{V}} = \frac{\mathbf{Y}}{\mathbf{Y}_C} = \frac{1/R[1 + jQ(a - 1/a)]}{j\omega C} = \frac{1}{j(a/Q)[1 + jQ(a - 1/a)]} = \frac{1}{-(a^2 - 1) + j(a/Q)}$$

12.103 Plot $|\mathbf{V}_C/\mathbf{V}|$, as obtained in Prob. 12.102, as a function of a for $Q = 1, 4,$ and 10.

See Fig. 12-29.

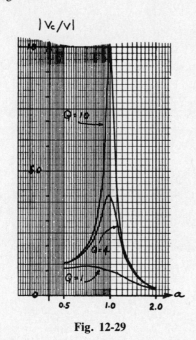

Fig. 12-29

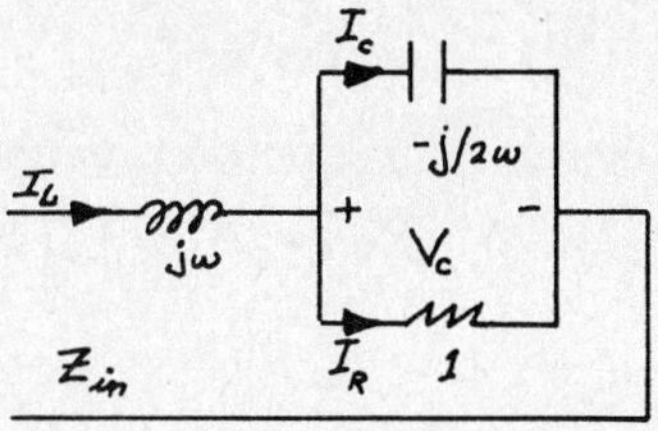

Fig. 12-30

12.104 Determine the frequency at which the circuit of Fig. 12-30 will be in resonance.

For resonance, we must have $\mathrm{Im}\,(\mathbf{Z}_{\mathrm{in}}) = 0$. Now,

$$\mathbf{Z}_{\mathrm{in}} = j\omega + \frac{-j/2\omega}{1 - j/2\omega} = j\omega - \frac{j}{2\omega - j} = j\omega - \frac{j(2\omega + j)}{1 + 4\omega^2}$$

$$\mathrm{Im}\,(\mathbf{Z}_{\mathrm{in}}) = \omega - \frac{2\omega}{1 + 4\omega^2} = 0 \qquad \text{or} \qquad \omega = 0.5\,\text{rad/s}$$

12.105 If the capacitor and the inductor of the circuit of Fig. 12-30 are interchanged, what is the resonance frequency?

Proceeding as in Prob. 12.104,

$$\mathbf{Z}_{\mathrm{in}} = \frac{-j}{2\omega} + \frac{j\omega}{1 + j\omega} = -\frac{j}{2\omega} + \frac{j\omega(1 - j\omega)}{1 + \omega^2} = \frac{-j}{2\omega} + \frac{j\omega}{1 + \omega^2} + \frac{\omega^2}{1 + \omega^2}$$

$$\mathrm{Im}\,(\mathbf{Z}_{\mathrm{in}}) = -\frac{1}{2\omega} + \frac{\omega}{1 + \omega^2} = 0 \qquad \text{or} \qquad \omega = 1\,\text{rad/s}$$

12.106 The voltage across the capacitor of the circuit of Fig. 12-30 is $V_C = 20\sqrt{2}\sin 0.5t$ V. Find the instantaneous current through the inductor.

Solving the problem in the frequency domain we have (since $\omega = \omega_r = 0.5\,\text{rad/s}$ and $\mathbf{V}_C = 20\,\underline{/0°}$ V),

$$\mathbf{I}_C = \frac{20\,\underline{/0°}}{-j1} = 20\,\underline{/90°}\,\text{A} \qquad \mathbf{I}_R = \frac{20\,\underline{/0°}}{1\,\underline{/0°}} = 20\,\underline{/0°}\,\text{A}$$

$$\mathbf{I}_L = 20\,\underline{/90°} + 20\,\underline{/0°} = 20\sqrt{2}\,\underline{/45°}\,\text{A} \qquad \text{or} \qquad i_L = 40\sin(0.5t + 45°)\,\text{A}$$

12.107 What are the instantaneous energies stored in the capacitor and inductor of the circuit of Fig. 12-30 for the data of Prob. 12.106?

❚ Since $\omega = 0.5 \, \text{rad/s}$, we have $L = 1.0 \, \text{H}$ and $C = 2 \, \text{F}$. Thus,

$$w_L = \tfrac{1}{2}L(i_L)^2 = \tfrac{1}{2}(1)[40 \sin(0.5t + 45°)]^2 = 800 \sin^2(0.5t + 45°) \, \text{J}$$

$$w_C = \tfrac{1}{2}C(v_C)^2 = \tfrac{1}{2}(2)(20\sqrt{2} \sin 0.5t)^2 = 800 \sin^2 0.5t \, \text{J}$$

12.108 Determine the Q of the circuit of Fig. 12-30.

❚ From Eq. (1) of Prob. 12.57,

$$Q = \frac{\omega_r(w_L + w_C)_{\text{max}}}{P_R}$$

From Prob. 12.107 and standard trigonometrical identities,

$$w_L + w_C = 800\left(1 + \frac{\sin 1.0t - \cos 1.0t}{2}\right) \, \text{J}$$

Maximizing by calculus, we find

$$(w_L + w_C)_{\text{max}} = 800\left(1 + \frac{\sqrt{2}}{2}\right) \, \text{J} \qquad P_R = I^2R = (20)^2 1 = 400 \, \text{W} \qquad \omega_r = 0.5 \, \text{rad/s}$$

Hence
$$Q = \frac{(0.5)(800)(1 + \sqrt{2}/2)}{400} = 1 + \frac{\sqrt{2}}{2} \approx 1.707$$

12.109 If the resistor and the inductor of the circuit are interchanged, what is the resonance frequency?

❚ The resistor has no effect on the frequency. Since $L = 1.0 \, \text{H}$ and $C = 2 \, \text{F}$,

$$f_r = \frac{1}{2\pi\sqrt{LC}} = \frac{1}{2\pi\sqrt{(1)(2)}} = 0.1125 \, \text{Hz}$$

CHAPTER 13
Frequency Response and Filters

13.1 For the RC circuit of Fig. 13-1a, sketch V_{out} as a function of frequency and show the cutoff frequency f_c.

▌ By KVL we have

$$V_{\text{out}} = V_{\text{in}} \frac{X_C}{\sqrt{R^2 + X_C^2}} \qquad (1)$$

which is qualitatively plotted in Fig. 13-1b, where $V_{\text{out}} = 0.707\, V_{\text{in}}$ at $f = f_c$.

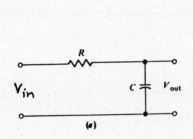

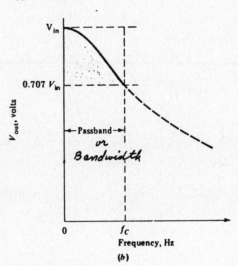

Fig. 13-1

13.2 Relate R, C and f_c for the circuit of Fig. 13-1a.

▌ At $f = f_c$, $V_{\text{out}} = 0.707 V_{\text{in}}$. Substituting in Eq. (1) of Prob. 13.1 yields

$$(0.707)^2 = \frac{X_C^2}{R^2 + X_C^2} \qquad \text{or} \qquad R = X_C = \frac{1}{2\pi f_c C}$$

13.3 The circuit of Fig. 13-1a is a *low-pass filter*. Design one having a cutoff frequency of 500 Hz.

▌ Let $R = 500\,\Omega$. Then $C = 1/2\pi f_c R = 1/2\pi(500)(500) = 636.7$ nF.

13.4 A low-pass RC filter has a 800-Hz cutoff frequency. If $R = 2\,\text{k}\Omega$, what is the value of C?

▌ $$f_c = \frac{1}{2\pi RC} \qquad 800 = \frac{1}{2\pi(2000)C} \qquad C = 99.5\,\text{nF}$$

13.5 In a low-pass RC filter, having a cutoff frequency of 2 kHz, $C = 80$ nF. Determine R.

▌ $$2000 = \frac{1}{2\pi R(80 \times 10^{-9})} \qquad R = 995\,\Omega$$

13.6 The RL circuit of Fig. 13-2 is also a low-pass filter. Determine its cutoff frequency f_c.

▌ $$V_{\text{out}} = V_{\text{in}} \frac{R}{\sqrt{R^2 + X_L^2}}$$

At $f = f_c$, $V_{\text{out}} = 0.707 V_{\text{in}}$. Thus,

$$(0.707)^2 = \frac{R^2}{R^2 + X_L^2} \qquad \text{or} \qquad R = X_L = 2\pi f_c L$$

Hence, $f_c = R/2\pi L$ Hz.

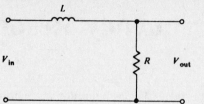

Fig. 13-2

13.7 Repeat Prob. 13.3 for an RL circuit.

▮ Let $R = 500\,\Omega$. Then

$$L = \frac{R}{2\pi f_c} = \frac{500}{2\pi(500)} = 159.15\,\text{mH}$$

13.8 For the circuit of Prob. 13.7, determine V_{out} at 0 Hz, 100 Hz, 500 Hz, 1 kHz, and 100 kHz for a 100-V input.

▮

$$V_{\text{out}} = 100 \frac{500}{\sqrt{(500)^2 + (2\pi f \times 159.15 \times 10^{-3})^2}}$$

The following table gives the desired result.

f, Hz	V_{out}, V
0	100.0
100	98.0
500	70.7
1000	44.7
100,000	0.5

13.9 Find L in a low-pass RL filter having $R = 1.5\,\text{k}\Omega$ and a cutoff frequency of 1600 Hz.

▮ $$f_c = \frac{R}{2\pi L} \qquad 1600 = \frac{1500}{2\pi L} \qquad L = 149\,\text{mH}$$

13.10 A low-pass RL filter has $L = 25\,\text{mH}$ and a cutoff frequency of 4 kHz. Determine R.

▮ $$4000 = \frac{R}{2\pi(0.025)} \qquad R = 628\,\Omega$$

13.11 The circuit of Fig. 13-3a acts as a high-pass filter. Plot V_{out} as a function of frequency and determine the cutoff frequency.

▮ From KVL,

$$V_{\text{out}} = V_{\text{in}} \frac{R}{\sqrt{R^2 + X_C^2}}$$

at cutoff $V_{\text{out}} = 0.707V_{\text{in}}$. Thus,

$$(0.707)^2 = \frac{R^2}{R^2 + X_C^2} \qquad \text{or} \qquad R = X_C = \frac{1}{2\pi f_c C}$$

Hence, $f_c = 1/2\pi RC$ Hz.

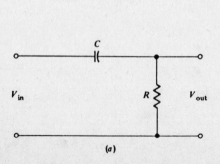

(a)

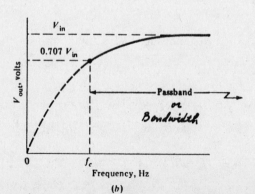

(b)

Fig. 13-3

13.12 The RL circuit of Fig. 13-4 also acts as a high-pass filter.   Determine its cutoff frequency.

$\blacksquare$

$$V_{out} = V_{in} \frac{X_L}{\sqrt{R^2 + X_L^2}}$$

At cutoff, $V_{out} = 0.707 V_{in}$ or

$$(0.707)^2 = \frac{(2\pi f_c L)^2}{R^2 + (2\pi f_c L)^2}$$

Thus, $f_c = R/2\pi L$ Hz.

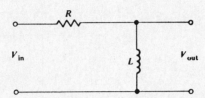

Fig. 13-4

13.13 Design an RL high-pass filter having a cutoff frequency of 2 kHz.

$\blacksquare$ Let $R = 2\,k\Omega$.   Then,

$$L = \frac{R}{2\pi f_c} = \frac{2 \times 10^3}{2\pi(2 \times 10^3)} = 159.15\,mH$$

13.14 For the circuit of Prob. 13.13, determine V_{out} at 0 Hz, 100 Hz, 500 Hz, 2 kHz, and 100 kHz for a 100-V input.

$\blacksquare$

$$V_{out} = 100 \frac{2\pi f(159.15 \times 10^{-3})}{\sqrt{(2000)^2 + (2\pi f 159.15 \times 10^{-3})^2}}$$

The desired result is given below:

f, Hz	V_{out}, V
0	0.00
100	5.00
500	24.25
2000	70.70
100,000	99.98

13.15 A high-pass RC filter has $R = 1250\,\Omega$ and a cutoff frequency of 1600 Hz.   Determine C.

$\blacksquare$

$$f_c = \frac{1}{2\pi RC} \qquad 1600 = \frac{1}{2\pi(1.25 \times 10^3)C} \qquad C = 79.6\,nF$$

13.16 A high-pass RC filter has $C = 0.65\,nF$ and a cutoff frequency of 9 kHz.   Determine R.

$\blacksquare$

$$9000 = \frac{1}{2\pi R(650 \times 10^{-12})} \qquad R = 27.2\,k\Omega$$

13.17 An RL high-pass filter has $R = 1.6\,k\Omega$ and a cutoff frequency of 10 kHz.   Find L.

$\blacksquare$

$$f_c = \frac{R}{2\pi L} \qquad 10,000 = \frac{1600}{2\pi L} \qquad L = 25.5\,mH$$

13.18 The circuit of Fig. 13-5a may be used as a bandpass filter.   Obtain an expression for its output voltage, and show its frequency response.

$\blacksquare$ The circuit of Fig. 13-5a shows the load on the filter.   Combining the load resistance with the filter resistance, we obtain the circuit of Fig. 13-5b from which

$$V_{out} = V_{in} \frac{R_T}{\sqrt{R_T^2 + (X_L - X_C)^2}} = V_{in} \frac{R_T}{\sqrt{R_T^2 + [2\pi fL - 1/(2\pi fC)]^2}}$$

where $R_T = R_{out}R_L/(R_{out} + R_L)$.   A typical frequency response plot is shown in Fig. 13-5c.

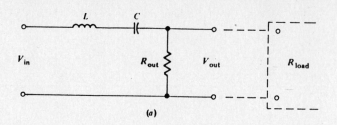

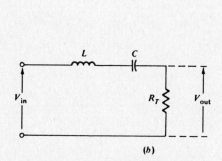

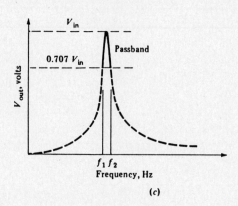

Fig. 13-5

13.19 State quantitatively the criteria which may be used to characterize a bandpass filter.

∎ The criteria are $f_r = 1/2\pi\sqrt{LC}$; selectivity $Q_s = \omega_r L/R$; bandwidth $\text{BW} = f_r/Q_s$.

13.20 A parallel circuit yielding a bandpass characteristic similar to that of Fig. 13-5c is shown in Fig. 13-6. Assuming that the load draws negligible current, obtain an expression for $\mathbf{V}_{\text{out}}$.

∎
$$\mathbf{V}_{\text{out}} = \mathbf{V}_{\text{in}} \frac{\mathbf{Z}_{ab}}{R_1 + \mathbf{Z}_{ab}} \quad \text{where} \quad \mathbf{Z}_{ab} = \frac{(R_{\text{coil}} + jX_{\text{coil}})(-jX_C)}{(R_{\text{coil}} + jX_{\text{coil}}) + (-jX_C)}$$

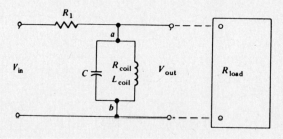

Fig. 13-6

13.21 Assuming the circuit parameters in Fig. 13-5a are $L_{\text{coil}} = 50\,\text{mH}$, $C = 127\,\text{nF}$, $R_{\text{out}} = 63\,\Omega$, $R_{\text{load}} = 600\,\Omega$, determine (a) the resonance frequency and (b) the bandwidth.

∎ (a) $f_r = \dfrac{1}{2\pi\sqrt{LC}} = \dfrac{1}{2\pi\sqrt{(0.05)(127\times10^{-9})}} = 2\,\text{kHz}$

(b) $R_T = \dfrac{R_{\text{out}}R_{\text{load}}}{R_{\text{out}} + R_{\text{load}}} = \dfrac{63(600)}{63+600} = 57\,\Omega$

$Q_s = \dfrac{\omega_r L}{R_T} = \dfrac{2\pi(2000)(0.05)}{57} = 11 \qquad Q_s = \dfrac{f_r}{\text{BW}} \qquad 11 = \dfrac{2000}{\text{BW}} \qquad \text{BW} = 182$

13.22 For the circuit of Prob. 13.21 determine the cutoff frequencies.

∎ Since $Q_s > 10$,

$$f_2 = f_r + \frac{\text{BW}}{2} = 2000 + \frac{182}{2} = 2091\,\text{Hz} \qquad f_1 = f_r - \frac{\text{BW}}{2} = 2000 - \frac{182}{2} = 1909\,\text{Hz}$$

13.23   If the input voltage to the circuit of Prob. 13.21 is 30 V, calculate the output voltage at f_r, f_1, f_2, and $10f_r$.

I
$$V_{out} = V_{in} \frac{R_T}{\sqrt{R_T^2 + (X_L - X_C)^2}}$$

At the resonance frequency $X_L = X_C$. Hence,

$$V_{out} = V_{in} \frac{R_T}{R_T} = 30 \frac{57}{57} = 30 \text{ V}$$

At $f_1 = 1909$ Hz,

$$X_L = 2\pi f L = 2\pi(1909)(0.05) = 600 \text{ }\Omega$$

$$X_C = \frac{1}{2\pi f C} = \frac{1}{2\pi(1909)(127 \times 10^{-9})} = 656 \text{ }\Omega$$

$$V_{out} = 30 \frac{57}{\sqrt{(57)^2 + (600 - 656)^2}} = 21.4 \text{ V}$$

At $f_2 = 2091$ Hz,

$$X_L = 656 \text{ }\Omega, \quad X_C = 600 \text{ }\Omega \quad V_{out} = 30 \frac{57}{\sqrt{(57)^2 + (656 - 600)^2}} = 21.4 \text{ V}$$

At $f = 10f_r = 10(2000) = 20,000$,

$$X_L = 2\pi(20,000)(0.05) = 6.28 \times 10^3 \text{ }\Omega$$

$$X_C = \frac{1}{2\pi(20,000)(127 \times 10^{-9})} = 62.7 \text{ }\Omega$$

$$V_{out} = 30 \frac{57}{\sqrt{(57)^2 + (6280 - 62.7)^2}} = 0.28 \text{ V}$$

13.24   For the filter circuit of Fig. 13-5a we have $R_L = 50$ kΩ, $L_{coil} = 45$ mH, and $R_{coil} \simeq 0$. Design a bandpass filter having cutoff frequencies of 25 and 23 kHz.

I $$\text{BW} = f_2 - f_1 = 25,000 - 23,000 = 2 \text{ kHz} \qquad f_2 = f_r + \frac{\text{BW}}{2} \qquad 25,000 = f_r + \frac{2000}{2}$$

or $$f_r = 24,000 \text{ Hz} = \frac{1}{2\pi\sqrt{LC}} = \frac{1}{2\pi\sqrt{0.045C}}$$

$$C = 978 \text{ pF} \qquad Q_s = \frac{f_r}{\text{BW}} = \frac{24,000}{2000} = 12 = \frac{\omega_r L}{R_T}$$

$$12 = \frac{2\pi(24,000)(0.045)}{R_T} \qquad R_T = 565 \text{ }\Omega \qquad \frac{1}{R_T} = \frac{1}{R_{out}} + \frac{1}{R_{load}}$$

$$\frac{1}{565} = \frac{1}{R_{out}} + \frac{1}{50,000} \qquad R_{out} = 571 \text{ }\Omega$$

13.25   Design a series-resonance-type bandpass filter that has cutoff frequencies of 15 and 35 kHz. The load resistance is 60 kΩ, and the coil has an inductance of 50 mH and negligible resistance.

I $$\text{BW} = (35 - 15)10^3 = 20 \text{ kHz} \qquad f_2 = f_r + \frac{\text{BW}}{2}$$

$$35 \times 10^3 = f_r + \frac{20 \times 10^3}{2} \qquad \text{or} \qquad f_r = 25 \text{ kHz}$$

$$f_r = \frac{1}{2\pi\sqrt{LC}} \qquad \text{or} \qquad 25000 = \frac{1}{2\pi\sqrt{0.050C}}$$

Hence $C = 811$ pF.

13.26   Assume the circuit parameters for the series-resonance bandpass filter in Fig. 13-5a are $C = 1.8$ pF, $L_{coil} = 25$ mH, $R_{out} = 52 \text{ }\Omega$, and $R_{load} = 9000 \text{ }\Omega$. Determine (a) the resonance frequency and (b) the bandwidth.

❙ (a) $f_r = \dfrac{1}{2\pi\sqrt{LC}} = \dfrac{1}{2\pi\sqrt{(0.025)(1.8 \times 10^{-12})}} = 750{,}644 \text{ Hz}$

(b) $R_T = \dfrac{R_{\text{out}}R_{\text{load}}}{R_{\text{out}} + R_{\text{load}}} = \dfrac{52(9000)}{52 + 9000} = 51.7\ \Omega$

$Q_S = \dfrac{\omega_r L}{R_T} = \dfrac{2\pi(750{,}644)(0.025)}{51.67} = 2280 = \dfrac{f_r}{\text{BW}}$ or $2280 = \dfrac{750{,}644}{\text{BW}}$

Thus, BW = 329 Hz.

13.27 For the filter of Prob. 13.26, determine the cutoff frequencies.

❙ $f_2 = f_r + \dfrac{\text{BW}}{2} = 750{,}644 + \dfrac{329}{2} = 750{,}809 \text{ Hz}$ $f_1 = f_r - \dfrac{\text{BW}}{2} = 750{,}644 - \dfrac{329}{2} = 750{,}480 \text{ Hz}$

13.28 Obtain an expression for the output voltage as a function of frequency from the circuit of Prob. 13.26, for a 60-V input voltage.

❙ $V_{\text{out}} = V_{\text{in}} \dfrac{R_T}{\sqrt{R_T^2 + (X_L - X_C)^2}} = 60\,\dfrac{51.7}{\sqrt{(51.7)^2 + [6.28f(0.025) - 1/(6.28f\,1.8 \times 10^{-12})]}}\ \text{V}$

13.29 From the result of Prob. 13.28, determine the output voltage at resonance frequency, cutoff frequencies, and at $10f_r$.

❙ The result is tabulated below:

f	V_{out}
750,644	60.00
750,834	39.31
750,495	44.47
750,440	0.00266

13.30 The circuit of Fig. 13-7 acts as a *bandstop* filter. Its resonance frequency and bandwidth are shown in Fig. 13-8. Obtain a relationship between the input and output voltages.

❙ $V_{\text{out}} = V_{\text{in}} \dfrac{Z_{ab}}{Z_{\text{circ}}}$ $\mathbf{Z}_{ab} = R_{\text{coil}} + j(X_L - X_C)$ $\mathbf{Z}_{\text{circ}} = R_1 + R_{\text{coil}} + j(X_L - X_C)$

Hence $V_{\text{out}} = V_{\text{in}} \dfrac{\sqrt{R_{\text{coil}}^2 + (X_L - X_C)^2}}{\sqrt{(R_{\text{coil}} + R_1)^2 + (X_L - X_C)^2}}$

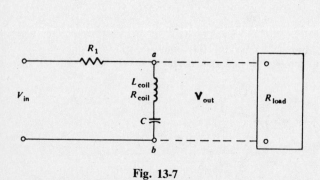

Fig. 13-7

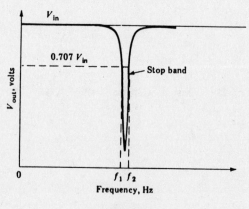

Fig. 13-8

13.31 Sketch the frequency of the circuit of Fig. 13-7.

❙ See Fig. 13-8.

13.32 The parallel circuit of Fig. 13-9 also acts as a bandstop filter. Relate its output voltage to the input voltage.

$$\mathbf{V}_{out} = \mathbf{V}_{in} \frac{R_{out}}{R_{out} + \mathbf{Z}_{ab}}$$

where

$$\mathbf{Z}_{ab} = \frac{(R_{coil} + jX_{L\ coil})(-jX_C)}{(R_{coil} + jX_{L\ coil}) + (-jX_C)}$$

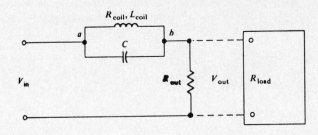

Fig. 13-9

13.33 In the circuit of Fig. 13-7, $R_1 = 1000\ \Omega$, $L_{coil} = 160\ mH$, $R_{coil} = 2\ \Omega$, and $C = 396\ pF$. Determine its bandwidth.

$$f_r = \frac{1}{2\pi\sqrt{LC}} = \frac{1}{2\pi\sqrt{0.160(396 \times 10^{-12})}} = 20\ kHz$$

$$Q_s = \frac{\omega_r L}{R_s} = \frac{2\pi(20,000)(0.160)}{2 + 1000} = 20 = \frac{f_r}{BW} \qquad \text{or} \qquad 20 = \frac{20,000}{BW}$$

Thus, BW = 1000 Hz.

13.34 What are the cutoff frequencies of the circuit of Prob. 13.33?

Since $Q > 10$,

$$f_2 = f_r + \frac{BW}{2} = 20,000 + \frac{1000}{2} = 20,500\ Hz \qquad f_1 = f_r - \frac{BW}{2} = 20,000 - \frac{1000}{2} = 19,500\ Hz$$

13.35 Find the output voltage of the circuit of Prob. 13.33 as a fraction of the input voltage at resonance frequency and at cutoff frequencies.

At resonance, $X_L = X_C$; hence,

$$V_{out} = V_{in} \frac{\sqrt{(R_{coil})^2}}{\sqrt{(R_{coil} + R_1)^2}} = V_{in} \frac{2}{1002} = 0.002 V_{in}$$

At $f_1 = 19,500\ Hz$,

$$X_L = 2\pi(19,500)(0.160) = 19.6\ k\Omega \qquad X_C = \frac{1}{2\pi(19,500)(396 \times 10^{-12})} = 20.6\ k\Omega$$

$$X_L - X_C = -1000\ \Omega \qquad V_{out} = V_{in} \frac{\sqrt{(2)^2 + (-1000)^2}}{\sqrt{(2 + 1000)^2 + (-1000)^2}} = 0.706 V_{in}$$

$$f_2 = 20,500\ Hz \qquad X_L = 2\pi(20,500)(0.160) = 20.6\ k\Omega$$

$$X_C = \frac{1}{2\pi(20,500)(396 \times 10^{-12})} = 19.6\ k\Omega \qquad X_L - X_C = 1000\ \Omega$$

$$V_{out} = V_{in} \frac{\sqrt{(2)^2 + (1000)^2}}{\sqrt{(1000)^2 + (1000)^2}} = 0.706 V_{in}$$

13.36 Determine the capacitance required for a series resonance bandstop filter that will block 85 kHz. The inductance and resistance of the coil are 60 mH and 15 Ω, respectively, $R_1 = 2000\ \Omega$, and $R_{load} = 1.4\ M\Omega$.

Referring to Fig. 13-7,

$$f_r = \frac{1}{2\pi\sqrt{LC}} \qquad 85,000 = \frac{1}{2\pi\sqrt{0.06C}} \qquad C = 58\ pF$$

13.37 What is the bandwidth of the circuit of Prob. 13.36?

$$Q_s = \frac{\omega_r L}{R} = \frac{2\pi(85,000)(0.06)}{15 + 2000} = 15.9 = \frac{f_r}{\text{BW}} \quad \text{or} \quad 15.9 = \frac{85,000}{\text{BW}}$$

Thus, $\text{BW} = 5.34\,\text{kHz}$.

13.38 The circuit of Fig. 13-10 is a *double-resonant* filter. The two resonance frequencies are for the tank (parallel) circuit and for the series circuit. If $C_1 = 3.5\,\text{nF}$, determine the remaining parameters required in order that the filter will reject a 100-kHz signal but accept 50 kHz.

▌ The resonance frequency of the stopband is determined by the tank circuit. Assuming $Q_{\text{coil}} \geqq 10$,

$$f_r = \frac{1}{2\pi\sqrt{LC}} \qquad 100,000 = \frac{1}{2\pi\sqrt{L_1(3.5 \times 10^{-9})}} \qquad L_1 = 724\,\mu\text{H}$$

The impedance of the tank circuit at 50 kHz is

$$X_{L1} = 2\pi(50,000)(724 \times 10^{-6}) = 227\,\Omega \qquad X_{C1} = \frac{1}{2\pi(50,000)(3.5 \times 10^{-9})} = 910\,\Omega$$

$$\mathbf{Z}_{\text{tank}} = \frac{X_{L1}X_{C1}}{j(X_{L1} - X_{C1})} = \frac{(227)(910)}{j(227 - 910)} = j302\,\Omega$$

Thus, at 50 kHz the tank circuit behaves as a pure inductive reactance of $302\,\Omega$. To cause series resonance at 50 kHz, capacitor C_2 must have a capacitive reactance of $302\,\Omega$.

$$X_c = \frac{1}{2\pi fC} \quad \text{or} \quad 302 = \frac{1}{2\pi(50,000)C}$$

Thus, $C = 10.5\,\text{nF}$.

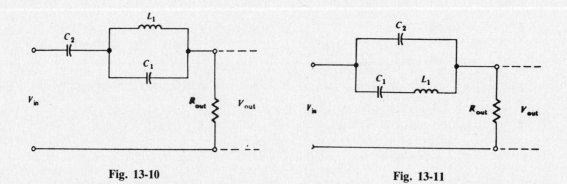

Fig. 13-10   Fig. 13-11

13.39 The circuit of Fig. 13-11 is also a double-resonant filter. If $L_1 = 2.5\,\text{mH}$, determine the remaining parameters to reject 150 kHz and accept 200 kHz.

▌ The resonance frequency of the passband is determined by L_1 and C_1:

$$f_r = \frac{1}{2\pi\sqrt{L_1 C_1}} \qquad 200,000 = \frac{1}{2\pi\sqrt{0.025 C_1}} \qquad C_1 = 25\,\text{pF}$$

At 150 kHz, the impedance of the series LC branch is

$$\mathbf{Z}_{\text{ser}} = jX_{L1} - jX_{C1} \qquad X_{L1} = 2\pi(150,000)(0.025) = 23.6\,\text{k}\Omega$$

$$X_{C1} = \frac{1}{2\pi(150,000)(25 \times 10^{-12})} = 42.5\,\text{k}\Omega \qquad \mathbf{Z}_{\text{ser}} = j23,600 - j42,500 = -j18,900\,\Omega$$

Thus the series branch is in effect a capacitive reactance of $18,900\,\Omega$ at 150 kHz. For tank resonance to occur the parallel branch must have an inductive reactance of $18,900\,\Omega$.

$$X_{L2} = 2\pi fL_2 \qquad 18,900 = 2\pi(150,000)L_2 \qquad L_2 = 20\,\text{mH}$$

13.40 Assume the circuit parameters for the bandstop filter shown in Fig. 13-7 are $R_1 = 1500\,\Omega$, $L_{\text{coil}} = 140\,\text{mH}$, $R_{\text{coil}} = 1.5\,\Omega$, and $C = 300\,\text{pF}$. Determine (a) f_r and (b) the bandwidth.

▮ *(a)* $f_r = \dfrac{1}{2\pi\sqrt{LC}} = \dfrac{1}{2\pi\sqrt{(0.14)(300\times10^{-12})}} = 24{,}558$ Hz

    (b) Assuming the load draws insignificant current,

$$Q_s = \frac{\omega_r L}{R} = \frac{2\pi(24{,}558)(0.140)}{1500+1.5} = 14.39 \qquad Q_s = \frac{f_r}{\text{BW}} \qquad \text{or} \qquad 14.39 = \frac{24{,}558}{\text{BW}}$$

Hence, BW = 1707 Hz.

13.41 For the circuit of Prob. 13.40, find the cutoff frequencies.

▮ $\qquad\qquad f_1 = 24{,}558 - \dfrac{1707}{2} = 23{,}705$ Hz $\qquad f_2 = 24{,}558 + \dfrac{1707}{2} = 25{,}412$ Hz

13.42 For the circuit of Prob. 13.40, determine the input impedance as a function of frequency.

▮ $\qquad\qquad \mathbf{Z}_{\text{in}} = \sqrt{(1501.5)^2 + [2\pi f(0.14) - \dfrac{1}{2\pi f}\ (300\times10^{-12})]^2}$

13.43 What is the output voltage for a 30-V input at resonance frequency in the circuit of Prob. 13.40?

▮ $\qquad V_{\text{out}} = 30\,\dfrac{|\mathbf{Z}_{ab}|}{|\mathbf{Z}_{\text{in}}|} \qquad$ where $\qquad \mathbf{Z}_{ab} = \sqrt{(1.5)^2 + \left[2\pi f(0.14) - \dfrac{1}{2\pi f(300\times10^{-12})}\right]^2}\ \Omega$

and $\mathbf{Z}_{\text{in}}$ is found in Prob. 13.42. Hence, at $f_r = 24.558$ kHz, $V_{\text{out}} = 0.444$ V.

13.44 Determine the required capacitance for a series resonance bandstop filter that will block 65 kHz. The load resistance is 50 kΩ, R_1 is 3000 Ω, and the coil inductance and resistance are 55 mH and 10 Ω, respectively.

▮ $\qquad\qquad f_r = \dfrac{1}{2\pi\sqrt{LC}} \qquad$ or $\qquad 65{,}000 = \dfrac{1}{2\pi\sqrt{0.055C}}$

Hence, $C = 109$ pF.

13.45 What is the voltage across the load in Prob. 13.44 at resonance frequency? Given: $V_{\text{in}} = 80$ V.

▮ At resonance $\mathbf{Z}_{ab} = 10\,\Omega$ resistive,

$$R_T = \frac{10\times50{,}000}{10+50{,}000} \cong 10\,\Omega \qquad V_{\text{out}} = 80\,\frac{10}{10+3000} = 0.27\text{ V}$$

13.46 Assume capacitance C_1 for the double-resonant filter shown in Fig. 13-11 is 2.1 nF. Determine the remaining parameters that will block 90 kHz and accept 100 kHz.

▮ $\qquad\qquad f_r = \dfrac{1}{2\pi\sqrt{L_1 C_1}} \qquad$ or $\qquad 100{,}000 = \dfrac{1}{2\pi\sqrt{L_1(2.1\times10^{-9})}}$

Thus, $L_1 = 1.207$ mH.
  At 90 kHz,

$$X_{L1} = 2\pi(90{,}000)(1.207\times10^{-3}) = 682.2\,\Omega \qquad X_{C1} = \frac{1}{2\pi 90{,}000(2.1\times10^{-9})} = 842.52\,\Omega$$

$$\mathbf{Z}_{\text{ser}} = jX_{L1} - jX_{C1} = j(682.2 - 842.52) = -j160.32\,\Omega$$

For parallel resonance to occur at 90 kHz,

$$jX_{L2} = +j160.32 \qquad 2\pi(90{,}000)L_2 = 160.32$$

Hence, $L_2 = 284\ \mu$H.

13.47 Assume capacitor C_1 in Fig. 13-10 has a capacitance of 6.5 nF. Determine the remaining parameters that will block 75 kHz and accept 20 kHz.

▮ For stopband,

$$f_r = \frac{1}{2\pi\sqrt{L_1 C_1}} \qquad 75{,}000 = \frac{1}{2\pi\sqrt{L_1(6.5\times10^{-9})}} \qquad L_1 = 693\ \mu\text{H}$$

At 20 kHz,

$$X_{L1} = 2\pi(20,000)(693 \times 10^{-6}) = 87.0\ \Omega \qquad X_{C1} = \frac{1}{2\pi(20,000)(6.5 \times 10^{-9})} = 1224.9\ \Omega$$

The impedance of the parallel section at 20 kHz is

$$\mathbf{Z}_p = \frac{87\ \underline{/90°} \times 1224.9\ \underline{/-90°}}{j87 - j1224.9} = j93.65\ \Omega$$

For series resonance to occur at 20 kHz,

$$X_{C2} = 93.65 \qquad \text{or} \qquad \frac{1}{2\pi(20,000)C_2} = 93.65$$

Hence $C_2 = 85$ nF

13.48 For the circuit shown in Fig. 13-12, determine the ratio $\mathbf{V}_2/\mathbf{V}_1$.

▮ By mesh analysis we have

$$141.4\mathbf{I}_1 + j100\mathbf{I}_2 = 100\ \underline{/0°} \qquad j100\mathbf{I}_1 + 141.4\mathbf{I}_2 = 0$$

Thus,
$$\mathbf{I}_1 = 0.471\ \underline{/0°}\ \text{A} \qquad \mathbf{I}_2 = 0.333\ \underline{/-90°}\ \text{A}$$

$$\mathbf{V}_1 = 100 - (0.471)(141.4) = 33.4\ \underline{/0°}\ \text{V} \qquad \mathbf{V}_2 = (0.333\ \underline{/-90°})(141.4) = 47.10\ \underline{/-90°}\ \text{V}$$

$$\frac{\mathbf{V}_2}{\mathbf{V}_1} = \frac{47.10\ \underline{/-90°}}{33.4\ \underline{/0°}} = -j1.41$$

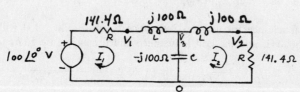

Fig. 13-12

13.49 In the circuit of Fig. 13-12 let $L = 100$ mH and $C = 10\ \mu$F. Define $a = \omega/\omega_r$, (ω_r being the resonance frequency) and plot $|\mathbf{V}_2/\mathbf{V}_1|$ as a function of a.

▮ Using nodal analysis, after some manipulation it may be shown that

$$\left|\frac{\mathbf{V}_2}{\mathbf{V}_1}\right| = \frac{1}{\sqrt{1 - 4a^2 + 4a^6}} \tag{1}$$

where $a = \omega/\omega_r$, and $\omega_r = \sqrt{2/LC} = 10^3\sqrt{2}$. Hence Eq. (1) is plotted as shown in Fig. 13-13.

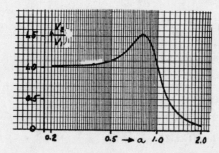

Fig. 13-13

13.50 A filter circuit using an operational amplifier is shown in Fig. 13-14a. It may be represented by its equivalent circuit shown in Fig. 13-14b. If $\mathbf{Z}_1 = R_1$ and $\mathbf{Z}_2$ corresponds to an RC parallel circuit with elements R_2 and C, obtain the ratio $\mathbf{V}_o/\mathbf{V}_i$.

▮ From Fig. 13-14b we have $\mathbf{V}_o/\mathbf{V}_i = -\mathbf{Z}_2/\mathbf{Z}_1$. Now, $\mathbf{Z}_1 = R_1$ and

$$\mathbf{Z}_2 = \frac{R_2(1/j\omega C)}{R_2 + 1/j\omega C} = \frac{R_2}{1 + j\omega CR_2}$$

Thus,
$$\frac{\mathbf{V}_o}{\mathbf{V}_i} = \frac{-R_2/R_1}{1 + j\omega CR_2} \tag{1}$$

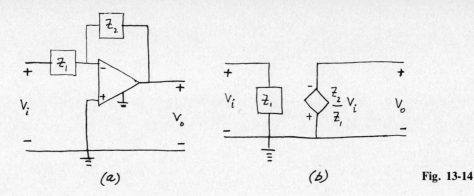

Fig. 13-14

13.51 Obtain the filter characteristic of the circuit of Prob. 13.50.

▌ We may substitute $R = -R_2/R_1$ and $CR_2 = L$ in Eq. (1) of Prob. 13.50 to obtain

$$\frac{V_o}{V_i} = \frac{R}{1 + j\omega L} \qquad \text{or} \qquad V_o = V_i \frac{R}{\sqrt{R^2 + X_L^2}}$$

which is identical to the result of Prob. 13.6. Hence the circuit acts as a low-pass filter.

13.52 What is the cutoff frequency of the filter of Prob. 13.50?

▌ From Prob. 13.6, $f_c = R/2\pi L$. From Prob. 13.51, $R = R_2/R_1$ and $L = R_2 C$. Hence

$$f_c = \frac{R_2/R_1}{2\pi R_2 C} = \frac{1}{2\pi R_1 C}$$

13.53 The operational amplifier circuit of Fig. 13-15a may be represented by its equivalent circuit shown in Fig. 13-15b. If $\mathbf{Z}_1 = 1/j\omega C_1$ and $\mathbf{Z}_2$ consists of an RC parallel circuit, with elements R and C_2, determine $\mathbf{V}_o/\mathbf{V}_i$.

▌ $$\frac{V_o}{V_i} = 1 + \frac{\mathbf{Z}_2}{\mathbf{Z}_1} \qquad \mathbf{Z}_1 = \frac{1}{j\omega C_1} \qquad \text{and} \qquad \mathbf{Z}_2 = \frac{R(1/j\omega C_2)}{R + 1/j\omega C_2} = \frac{R}{1 + j\omega C_2 R}$$

Hence, $$\frac{V_o}{V_i} = 1 + \frac{R/(1 + j\omega C_2 R)}{1/j\omega C_1} = \frac{j\omega(RC_1 + RC_2) + 1}{j\omega RC_2 + 1} \tag{1}$$

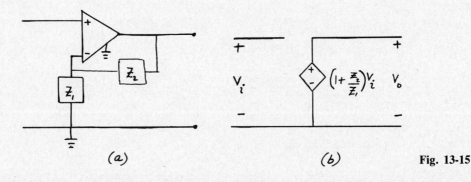

(a)   (b)   Fig. 13-15

13.54 Approximate, by straight lines, the frequency response of the circuit of Fig. 13-15a.

▌ From Eq. (1) of Prob. 13.53,

$$\frac{V_o}{V_i} = \frac{j\omega(RC_1 + RC_2) + 1}{j\omega RC_2 + 1} = \frac{j\omega T_1 + 1}{j\omega T_2 + 1} \qquad \text{or} \qquad \frac{|V_o|}{|V_i|} = \frac{\sqrt{(\omega T_1)^2 + 1}}{\sqrt{(\omega T_2)^2 + 1}}$$

where $T_1 = R(C_1 + C_2)$ and $T_2 = RC_2$. Notice that $T_2 < T_1$ and the approximate frequency response is shown in Fig. 13-16.

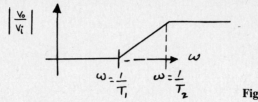

Fig. 13-16

13.55 Show that the circuit of Fig. 13-17 acts as a low-pass filter.

▮ By nodal analysis we have

$$\frac{V_1 - V_C}{6} = \frac{V_C}{1/j\omega} + \frac{V_2}{6} \qquad \text{or} \qquad V_1 - V_2 = (1 + j\omega 6)V_C$$

$$5V_C = V_2 - V_C \qquad \text{or} \qquad 6V_C = V_2$$

Consequently, $\qquad\qquad V_1 - V_2 = (1 + j\omega 6)\dfrac{V_2}{6} \qquad$ or $\qquad \dfrac{V_2}{V_1} = \dfrac{6}{7 + j6\omega}$

which is similar to the result of Prob. 13.6. Hence, the circuit is a low-pass filter.

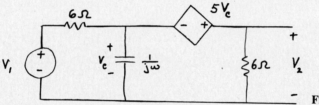

Fig. 13-17

13.56 What is the cutoff frequency of the filter of the circuit of Fig. 13-17?

▮ From Prob. 13.55 we have

$$V_2 = V_1 \frac{6}{\sqrt{49 + (6\omega)^2}}$$

At cutoff $V_2 = 0.707 V_1$ or

$$(0.707)^2 = \frac{(6)^2}{49 + (6\omega_C)^2} \qquad \text{or} \qquad \omega_C = 2\pi f_C = 0.8$$

Thus, $\qquad\qquad\qquad\qquad\qquad f_c = 0.13 \text{ Hz}$

13.57 Obtain a relationship between V_o and V_i shown in the circuit of Fig. 13-18.

▮ $$I = \frac{V_i - V_o}{1000} = \frac{V_o}{1000/j\omega} + \frac{V_o}{1 + j\omega} = V_o\left(\frac{j\omega}{1000} + \frac{1}{1 + j\omega}\right)$$

Hence, $\qquad\qquad\qquad\qquad \dfrac{V_o}{V_i} = \dfrac{1 + j\omega}{(1 + j\omega)^2 + 1000}$

13.58 What is the input impedance of the circuit of Fig. 13-18 at resonance?

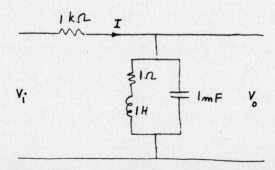

Fig. 13-18

$$\omega_r = \frac{1}{\sqrt{LC}} = \frac{1}{\sqrt{(1)(10^{-3})}} = 31.6 \text{ rad/s} \qquad Q_s = \frac{(31.6)(1)}{1} = 31.6 > 10$$

Thus, $\mathbf{Z}_{\text{parallel}} = (Q_s)^2 R = (31.6)^2 1 = 1000 \ \Omega.$ Hence, $\mathbf{Z}_{\text{in}} = 1000 + 1000 = 2 \text{ k}\Omega.$

13.59 Determine the cutoff frequencies of the circuit of Fig. 13-18.

From Prob. 13.58,

$$f_r = \frac{\omega_r}{2\pi} = \frac{31.6}{2\pi} = 5.03 \text{ Hz} \qquad BW = \frac{f_r}{Q} = \frac{5.03}{31.6} = 0.16 \text{ Hz}$$

Thus,

$$f_1 = 5.03 - \frac{0.16}{2} = 4.95 \text{ Hz} \qquad f_2 = 5.03 + \frac{0.16}{2} = 5.11 \text{ Hz}$$

13.60 The circuit of Fig. 13-19 is a double-tuned filter. If $C = 100 \text{ pF}$, find L_1 and L_2 if a frequency of 400 kHz is to be rejected and a frequency of 800 kHz accepted.

For series resonance,

$$f_s = \frac{1}{2\pi\sqrt{L_1 C}} = 800 \times 10^3 \qquad \text{or} \qquad L_1 = \frac{1}{(2\pi 800 \times 10^3)^2 (100 \times 10^{-12})} = 0.396 \text{ mH}$$

At 400 kHz,

$$X_L = \omega L_1 = 2\pi f L_1 = (2\pi)(400 \times 10^3)(0.396 \times 10^{-3}) = 995 \ \Omega$$

$$X_C = \frac{1}{\omega C} = \frac{1}{2\pi(400 \times 10^3)(100 \times 10^{-12})} = 3979 \ \Omega$$

$$j(X_L - X_C) = j(995 - 3979) = -j2984$$

At resonance at 400 kHz, $X_L = X_C$ or

$$L_2 = \frac{X_C}{\omega} = \frac{2984}{2\pi(400 \times 10^3)} = 1.19 \text{ mH}$$

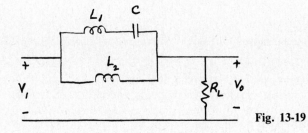

Fig. 13-19

CHAPTER 14
Three-Phase Circuits

14.1 Three voltage waveforms are shown in Fig. 14-1. Write mathematical expressions for these voltages.

❚ We may mathematically express this system of voltages as

$$v_{a'a} = V_m \sin \omega t \qquad v_{b'b} = V_m \sin (\omega t - 120°) \qquad v_{c'c} = V_m \sin (\omega t - 240°)$$

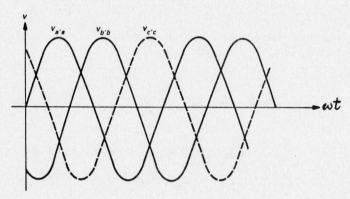

Fig. 14-1

14.2 Express the voltages of Prob. 14.1 as phasors.

❚ These voltages may be written in phasor notation as

$$\mathbf{V}_{a'a} = V \underline{/0°} = V(1 + j0) \qquad \mathbf{V}_{b'b} = V \underline{/-120°} = V(-0.5 - j0.866)$$

$$\mathbf{V}_{c'c} = V \underline{/-240°} = V(-0.5 + j0.866) \qquad \text{where} \qquad V = \frac{V_m}{\sqrt{2}}$$

14.3 Draw a phasor diagram showing the three voltages of Prob. 14.2. Show three voltage sources corresponding to these three voltages.

❚ Figure 14-2a shows the phasor diagram, whereas Fig. 14-2b shows the three voltage sources corresponding to the three equations. Consequently, we may define a three-phase (voltage) source having three equal voltages which are 120° out of phase with one another. In particular, we call this system a *three-phase balanced system*—in contrast to an unbalanced system, in which the magnitudes may be unequal and/or the phase displacements may not be 120°.

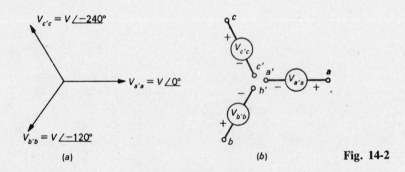

(a)   (b)   **Fig. 14-2**

14.4 What is the phasor sum of the three voltages in a balanced three-phase system?

❚ From Prob. 14.2, we have:

$$\sum \mathbf{V} = \mathbf{V}_{a'a} + \mathbf{V}_{b'b} + \mathbf{V}_{c'c} = V + (-0.5 - j0.866)V + (-0.5 + j0.866)V = 0$$

14.5   The order in which the three voltages of Fig. 14-1 attain their maxima is known as the *phase sequence*.   By this definition, determine the phase sequence of the voltages of Fig. 14-1.

▌ We abbreviate $v_{a'a}$, $v_{b'b}$, and $v_{c'c}$ as v_a, v_b, and v_c respectively.   Now referring to Figs. 14-1 and 14-2a, we observe that the voltages attain their maximum values in the order v_a, v_b, and v_c.   This order is known as the *phase sequence abc*.   A reverse phase sequence will be *acb*, in which case the voltages v_c and v_b lag v_a by 120 and 240°, respectively.

14.6   A way to interconnect the voltage sources of Fig. 14-2b is shown in Fig. 14-3, and is known as the *wye connection*.   Obtain a relationship between the *line voltages* and the *phase voltages*.

▌ The line voltages are related to the phase voltages such that $\mathbf{V}_{oa} + \mathbf{V}_{ab} = \mathbf{V}_{ob}$ or

$$\mathbf{V}_{ab} = \mathbf{V}_{ob} - \mathbf{V}_{oa} \tag{1}$$

Similarly, $\mathbf{V}_{bc} = \mathbf{V}_{oc} - \mathbf{V}_{ob}$ and $\mathbf{V}_{ca} = \mathbf{V}_{oa} - \mathbf{V}_{oc}$.   From Eq. (1) and Fig. 14-2 we may write $\mathbf{V}_{ab} = V(-0.5 - j0.866) - V(1 + j0) = V(-1.5 - j0.866)$.   In polar form,

$$\mathbf{V}_{ab} = \sqrt{3}V \,\underline{/-120°} \tag{2}$$

Similar relationships are valid for the phasors V_{bc} and V_{ca}.   Because V_{ab} is the voltage across the lines *a* and *b* and V is the magnitude of the voltage across the phase, we may generalize Eq. (2) to $V_l = \sqrt{3}V_p$ where V_l is the voltage across any two lines and V_p is the phase voltage.

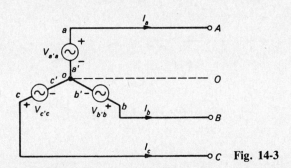

Fig. 14-3

14.7   Draw a phasor diagram showing the phase and line voltage relationships of Prob. 14.6.

▌ See Fig. 14-4.

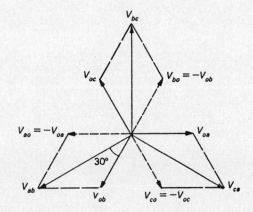

Fig. 14-4

14.8   What is the relationship between the phase and line currents of a wye-connected system?   Draw the corresponding phasor diagram.

▌ For the wye connection it is clear from Fig. 14-3 that the line currents $\mathbf{I}_l$ and phase currents $\mathbf{I}_p$ are the same.   Thus, we may write $\mathbf{I}_l = \mathbf{I}_p$.   The mutual phase relationships of the currents are given in Fig. 14-5.

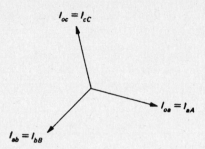

Fig. 14-5

14.9 Repeat Prob. 14.6 for the connection shown in Fig. 14-6, which is known as the *delta connection*. Draw the corresponding phasor diagram.

❙ From Fig. 14-6 it follows that $V_l = V_p$. See Fig. 14-7 for the phasor diagram.

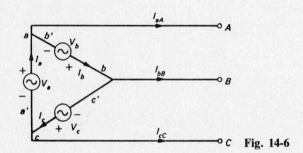

Fig. 14-6

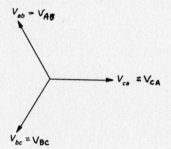

Fig. 14-7

14.10 Repeat Prob. 14.8 for the delta connection.

❙ We show in Fig. 14-6 the phase currents and line currents for the delta-connected system. The phase currents and line currents are related to each other by

$$\mathbf{I}_{aA} = \mathbf{I}_{ca} - \mathbf{I}_{ab} = \sqrt{3}\,\mathbf{I}_{ca}\,\underline{/30°} \qquad \mathbf{I}_{bB} = \sqrt{3}\,\mathbf{I}_{ab}\,\underline{/30°} \qquad \text{and} \qquad \mathbf{I}_{cC} = \sqrt{3}\mathbf{I}_{bc}\,\underline{/30°}$$

These relationships may be generalized to $I_l = \sqrt{3}I_p$, where I_l is the line current and I_p is the phase current.

14.11 Draw a phasor diagram showing the currents of Prob. 14.10.

❙ See Fig. 14-8.

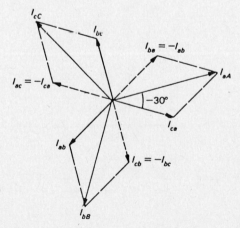

Fig. 14-8

14.12 The circuit of Fig. 14-9a is supplied by a 240-V three-phase source. Determine $\mathbf{I}_c$.

❙ From Fig. 14-9b, the voltage $\mathbf{V}_{ca}$ is applied to the $3\,\underline{/0°}$-Ω load. So, for the given direction of $\mathbf{I}_a$, we have

$$I_a = \frac{-\mathbf{V}_{ca}}{3\,\underline{/0°}} = \frac{-240\,\underline{/120°}}{3\,\underline{/0°}} = -80\,\underline{/120°}\ \text{A}$$

Similarly,
$$\mathbf{I}_b = \frac{240\,\underline{/-120°}}{4\,\underline{/60°}} = 60\,\underline{/-180°}\ \text{A}$$

Now, since $\mathbf{I}_a + \mathbf{I}_b + \mathbf{I}_c = 0$, we have
$$\mathbf{I}_c = -(\mathbf{I}_a + \mathbf{I}_b) = -(-80\,\underline{/120°} + 60\,\underline{/-180°}) = -72.11\,\underline{/-106.1°}\ \text{A}$$

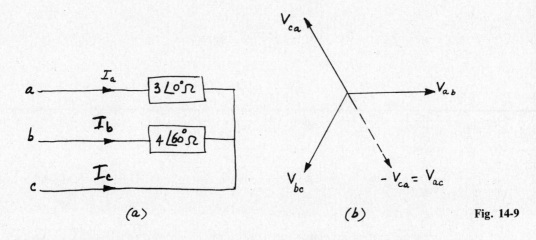

(a)   (b)   Fig. 14-9

14.13   If the circuit of Fig. 14-9a operates at 60 Hz, write the phase currents in the time domain.

❚   Since $\omega = 2\pi f = 2\pi(60) = 377\ \text{rad/s}$,

$i_a = -80\sqrt{2}\sin(377t + 120°)\ \text{A}$ $i_b = 60\sqrt{2}\sin(377t - 180°)\ \text{A}$ $i_c = -72.11\sqrt{2}\sin(377t - 106.1°)\ \text{A}$

14.14   The circuit of Fig. 14-10a has $\mathbf{Z}_1 = 5\,\underline{/10°}\ \Omega$, $\mathbf{Z}_2 = 9\,\underline{/30°}\ \Omega$, and $\mathbf{Z}_3 = 10\,\underline{/80°}\ \Omega$, and is supplied by a three-phase 450-V source.   Solve for $\mathbf{I}_a$.

❚   From Fig. 14-10a and b,

$$\mathbf{I}_a = \frac{\mathbf{V}_{ab}}{\mathbf{Z}_1} + \frac{\mathbf{V}_{ac}}{\mathbf{Z}_2} = \frac{450\,\underline{/0°}}{5\,\underline{/10°}} + \frac{-450\,\underline{/120°}}{9\,\underline{/30°}} = 110.29\,\underline{/-36.52°}\ \text{A}$$

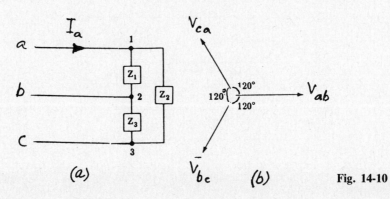

(a)   (b)   Fig. 14-10

14.15   The circuit of Fig. 14-11 is supplied by a 240-V three-phase four-wire system.   Determine the three line currents.

❚   Referring to Fig. 14-4 and choosing $\mathbf{V}_{ab}$ as the reference, we have

$$\mathbf{V}_{ab} = 240\,\underline{/0°}\ \text{V} \qquad \mathbf{V}_{ao} = \frac{240}{\sqrt{3}}\,\underline{/-30°} = 138.56\,\underline{/-30°}\ \text{V}$$

Similarly,
$$\mathbf{V}_{bo} = 138.56\,\underline{/-150°}\ \text{V} \qquad \text{and} \qquad \mathbf{V}_{co} = 138.56\,\underline{/90°}\ \text{V}$$

Hence, $$\mathbf{I}_a = \frac{\mathbf{V}_{ao}}{3\,\underline{/0°}} = \frac{138.56\,\underline{/-30°}}{3\,\underline{/0°}} = 46.19\,\underline{/-30°}\,\text{A}$$

Similarly, $$\mathbf{I}_b = \frac{\mathbf{V}_{bo}}{4\,\underline{/60°}} = 34.64\,\underline{/-210°}\,\text{A} \qquad \mathbf{I}_c = \frac{\mathbf{V}_{co}}{5\,\underline{/90°}} = 27.71\,\underline{/0°}\,\text{A}$$

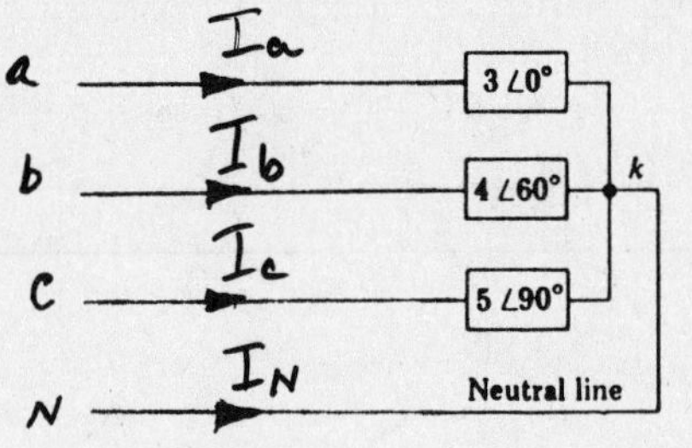

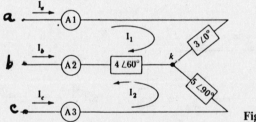

Fig. 14-11

14.16 What is the current $\mathbf{I}_N$ in the circuit of Fig. 14-11?

❙ By KCL, $\mathbf{I}_a + \mathbf{I}_b + \mathbf{I}_c + \mathbf{I}_N = 0$. Using the results of Prob. 14.15, we have $(40.00 - j23.10) + (-30 + j17.32) + (27.71 + j0) + \mathbf{I}_N = 0$. Thus $\mathbf{I}_N = -38.15\,\underline{/-8.71°}\,\text{A}$.

14.17 Determine the three ammeter readings for the circuit shown in Fig. 14-12. The circuit is supplied by a three-phase 240-V 60-Hz source.

❙ The two mesh equations may be written as

$$\mathbf{V}_{ab} = (3\,\underline{/0°} + 4\,\underline{/60°})\mathbf{I}_1 + (4\,\underline{/60°})\mathbf{I}_2 \qquad \mathbf{V}_{cb} = (4\,\underline{/60°})\mathbf{I}_1 + (5\,\underline{/90°} + 4\,\underline{/60°})\mathbf{I}_2$$

or $$240\,\underline{/0°} = 6.08\,\underline{/34.72°}\mathbf{I}_1 + 4\,\underline{/60°}\mathbf{I}_2 \qquad -240\,\underline{/-120°} = 4\,\underline{/60°}\mathbf{I}_1 + 8.70\,\underline{/76.71°}\mathbf{I}_2$$

Solving for $\mathbf{I}_1$ and $\mathbf{I}_2$ yields

$$\mathbf{I}_1 = 41.39\,\underline{/-56.39°}\,\text{A} \qquad \mathbf{I}_2 = 23.29\,\underline{/26.18°}\,\text{A}$$

Referring to Fig. 14-12, we have

$$\mathbf{I}_a = \mathbf{I}_1 = 41.4\,\underline{/-56.4°}\,\text{A} \qquad \mathbf{I}_c = \mathbf{I}_2 = 23.3\,\underline{/26.2°}\,\text{A}$$

$$\mathbf{I}_b = -(\mathbf{I}_1 + \mathbf{I}_2) = -(41.4\,\underline{/-56.4°} + 23.3\,\underline{/26.2°}) = -50\,\underline{/-28.91°}\,\text{A}$$

Therefore, ammeter A_1 reads 41.4 A; ammeter A_2 reads 50.0 A; and ammeter A_3 reads 23.3 A.

Fig. 14-12

14.18 Solve Prob. 14.17 by converting the wye-connected impedances to an equivalent delta.

❙ The equivalent delta-connected impedances are shown in Fig. 14-13, for which we have, by wye-delta transformation,

$$\mathbf{Z}_A = \frac{(3\,\underline{/0°})(5\,\underline{/90°}) + (5\,\underline{/90°})(4\,\underline{/60°}) + (4\,\underline{/60°})(3\,\underline{/0°})}{5\,\underline{/90°}} = \frac{37.16\,\underline{/107.74°}}{5\,\underline{/90°}} = 7.43\,\underline{/17.74°}\,\Omega$$

Similarly, $$\mathbf{Z}_B = 9.29\,\underline{/47.74°}\,\Omega \quad \text{and} \quad \mathbf{Z}_C = 12.39\,\underline{/107.74°}\,\Omega$$

The three line currents to the equivalent delta are:

$$\mathbf{I}_a = \frac{\mathbf{V}_{ab}}{\mathbf{Z}_A} + \frac{\mathbf{V}_{ac}}{\mathbf{Z}_B} = \frac{240\,\underline{/0°}}{7.43\,\underline{/17.74°}} + \frac{-(240\,\underline{/120°})}{9.29\,\underline{/47.74°}} = 41.4\,\underline{/-56.4°}\,\text{A}$$

Similarly, $\quad \mathbf{I}_b = \dfrac{-(240\ \underline{/0°})}{7.43\ \underline{/17.74°}} + \dfrac{240\ \underline{/-120°}}{12.39\ \underline{/107.74°}} = 50.0\ \underline{/151.1°} = -50\ \underline{/-28.91°}\ \text{A}$

and $\quad\quad \mathbf{I}_c = \dfrac{240\ \underline{/120°}}{9.29\ \underline{/47.74°}} + \dfrac{-(240\ \underline{/-120°})}{12.39\ \underline{/107.74°}} = 23.3\ \underline{/26.2°}\ \text{A}$

As expected, the three line currents obtained through the application of the wye-delta transformation are identical to those obtained by using loop analysis.

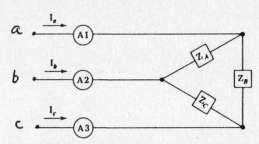

Fig. 14-13

14.19 An unbalanced three-phase load supplied by a three-phase four-wire system is shown in Fig. 14-14. The currents in phases A and B are 10 and 8 A, respectively, and phase C is open. The load power factor angle for phase A is 30° and for phase B is 60°, lagging in both cases. Determine the current in the neutral.

▮ With $\mathbf{V}_A$ as the reference phasor:

$$\mathbf{I}_A = 10\ \underline{/-30°} = 8.66 - j5\ \text{A} \qquad \mathbf{I}_B = 8\ \underline{/-180°} = -8.0 + j0\ \text{A}$$

Hence, $\quad\quad\quad \mathbf{I}_N = \mathbf{I}_A + \mathbf{I}_B = 0.66 - j5 = 5.04\ \underline{/-82.5°}\ \text{A}$

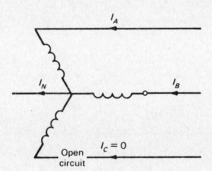

Fig. 14-14

14.20 Draw a phasor diagram for the circuit of Prob. 14.19.

▮ See Fig. 14-15.

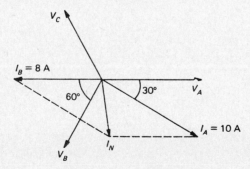

Fig. 14-15

14.21 A balanced three-phase load is wye-connected, and has an impedance $\mathbf{Z}_p = (4 - j3)\ \Omega$ in each phase. Find the line current if this load is connected across a 220-V three-phase source.

▮ $$V_p = \dfrac{220}{\sqrt{3}} = 127\ \text{V} \qquad \mathbf{Z}_p = 4 - j3 = 5\ \underline{/-36.87°}\ \Omega$$

$$I_l = I_p = \dfrac{127}{5\ \underline{/-36.87°}} = 25.4\ \underline{/36.87°}\ \text{A}$$

14.22 Draw a phasor diagram for the currents and voltages of the circuit of Prob. 14.21.

▮ See Fig. 14-16, which also shows the circuit diagram.

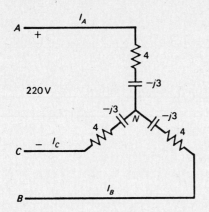

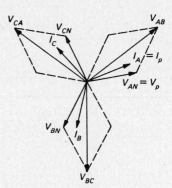

Fig. 14-16

14.23 Calculate the phase currents for the delta-connected load shown in Fig. 14-17a.

▮ We show the voltages in the phasor diagram of Fig. 14-17b. Thus,

$$\mathbf{I}_{1\text{-}2} = \frac{\mathbf{V}_{ab}}{10\,\underline{/60^\circ}} = \frac{450\,\underline{/0^\circ}}{10\,\underline{/60^\circ}} = 45\,\underline{/-60^\circ}\,\text{A}$$

Since the load is balanced, we may write $\mathbf{I}_{2\text{-}3} = 45\,\underline{/-180^\circ}\,\text{A}$ and $\mathbf{I}_{3\text{-}1} = 45\,\underline{/60^\circ}\,\text{A}$, which are shown in Fig. 14-17c.

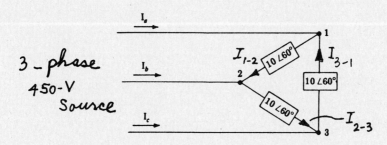

(a)

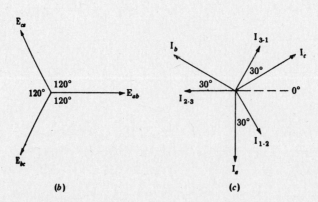

(b)   (c)   Fig. 14-17

14.24 Determine the line currents in the circuit of Prob. 14.23.

▮ From Fig. 14-17,

$$\mathbf{I}_a = \mathbf{I}_{1\text{-}2} - \mathbf{I}_{3\text{-}1} = 45\,\underline{/-60^\circ} - 45\,\underline{/60^\circ} = 77.9\,\underline{/-90^\circ}\,\text{A}$$

Similarly, $\mathbf{I}_b = 77.9\,\underline{/150^\circ}\,\text{A}$ and $\mathbf{I}_c = 77.9\,\underline{/30^\circ}\,\text{A}$

14.25 A wye-connected load has a $5\,\underline{/20°}$-Ω impedance per phase and is connected across a 120-V three-phase source. Calculate the line current and the phase current.

▮ $\mathbf{V}_{an} = 120/\sqrt{3}\,\underline{/-30°} = 69.28\,\underline{/-30°}$ V, where $\mathbf{V}_{ab} = 120\,\underline{/0°}$. Thus, $\mathbf{V}_{bn} = 69.28\,\underline{/-150°}$ V and $\mathbf{V}_{cn}$
$= 69.28\,\underline{/90°}$ V.

Hence, $$\mathbf{I}_a = \frac{\mathbf{V}_{an}}{5\,\underline{/20°}} = \frac{69.28\,\underline{/-30°}}{5\,\underline{/20°}} = 13.86\,\underline{/-50°}\ \text{A}$$

Similarly, $\mathbf{I}_b = 13.86\,\underline{/-170°}$ A and $\mathbf{I}_c = 13.86\,\underline{/70°}$ A. The line currents are the same as the phase currents.

14.26 If the neutral of the load of Prob. 14.25 is connected to the neutral of the source, determine the neutral current.

▮ $\mathbf{I}_N = -(\mathbf{I}_a + \mathbf{I}_b + \mathbf{I}_c) = 13.86\,\underline{/-50°} + 13.86\,\underline{/-170°} + 13.86\,\underline{/70°}$ (from Prob. 14.25)
$= (8.91 - j10.62) + (-13.65 - j2.41) + (4.74 + j13.02) = 0$ A

14.27 A three-phase delta-connected load having a $(3 + j4)$-Ω impedance per phase is connected across a 220-V three-phase source. Calculate the magnitude of the line current.

▮ $$V_{\text{line}} = V_{\text{phase}} = 220\ \text{V} \qquad Z_{\text{phase}} = 3 + j4 = 5\,\underline{/53.2°}\ \Omega$$
$$I_{\text{phase}} = \tfrac{220}{5} = 44\ \text{A} \qquad I_{\text{line}} = \sqrt{3} \times 44 = 76.21\ \text{A}$$

14.28 A 220-V three-phase source supplies a three-phase wye-connected load having an impedance of $(3 + j4)$ Ω per phase. Calculate the phase voltage across each phase of the load.

▮ $$V_{\text{phase}} = \frac{220}{\sqrt{3}} = 127\ \text{V} \qquad Z_{\text{phase}} = 3 + j4 = 5\,\underline{/53.2°}\ \Omega \qquad I_{\text{phase}} = \tfrac{127}{5} = 25.4\ \text{A} = I_{\text{line}}$$

14.29 Calculate the line current $\mathbf{I}_A$ in the delta-connected system shown in Fig. 14-18.

▮ $$\mathbf{I}_A = \mathbf{I}_{AB} - \mathbf{I}_{CA} = \frac{240\,\underline{/0°}}{3\,\underline{/20°}} - \frac{240\,\underline{/120°}}{4\,\underline{/10°}} = 127.16\,\underline{/-41.19°}\ \text{A}$$

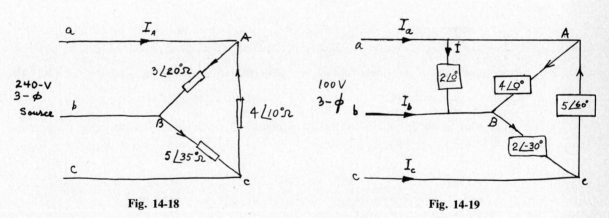

Fig. 14-18   **Fig. 14-19**

14.30 Determine the current $\mathbf{I}_a$ for the three-phase system shown in Fig. 14-19.

▮ $$\mathbf{I}_a = \mathbf{I} + \mathbf{I}_{AB} - \mathbf{I}_{CA} = \frac{100\,\underline{/0°}}{2\,\underline{/0°}} + \frac{100\,\underline{/0°}}{4\,\underline{/0°}} - \frac{100\,\underline{/120°}}{5\,\underline{/60°}} = 67.27\,\underline{/-14.92°}\ \text{A}$$

14.31 In the circuit of Fig. 14-19, verify that $\mathbf{I}_C$ is unaffected by the $2\,\underline{/0°}$-Ω impedance. Also calculate $\mathbf{I}_c$.

▮ $$\mathbf{I}_c = \mathbf{I}_{CA} - \mathbf{I}_{BC} = \frac{100\,\underline{/120°}}{5\,\underline{/60°}} - \frac{100\,\underline{/-120°}}{2\,\underline{/-30°}} = 68.05\,\underline{/81.55°}\ \text{A}$$

14.32 In a three-phase four-wire system the currents in two phases are $10\,\underline{/-36.87°}$ A and $6\,\underline{/-53.13°}$ A and the third phase is open-circuited. Determine the current through the neutral.

▮ $$\mathbf{I}_N = -(10\,\underline{/-36.87°} + 6\,\underline{/-53.13°}) = -[(8 - j6) + (3.6 - j4.8)] = -15.85\,\underline{/-42.95°}\ \text{A}$$

14.33 If $v = V_m \sin \omega t$ is the voltage across and $i = I_m \sin \omega t$ is the current through a resistor, determine the instantaneous and average powers, and show that the instantaneous power pulsates at a frequency 2ω.

$$p = (V_m \sin \omega t)(I_m \sin \omega t) = V_m I_m \sin^2 \omega t = \tfrac{1}{2} V_m I_m (1 - \cos 2\omega t)$$

$$P = \tfrac{1}{2} V_m I_m = \frac{V_m}{\sqrt{2}} \frac{I_m}{\sqrt{2}} = VI$$

where V and I are rms values.

14.34 Extend the result of Prob. 14.33 to a three-phase balanced system. Verify that the instantaneous power has no pulsating component. Obtain an expression for the total average power.

$$p = v_a i_a + v_b i_b + v_c i_c = (V_m \sin \omega t)(I_m \sin \omega t) + [V_m \sin (\omega t - 120°)][I_m \sin (\omega t - 120°)]$$

$$+ [V_m \sin (\omega t + 120°)][I_m \sin (\omega t + 120°)] = V_m I_m (\sin^2 \omega t + \tfrac{1}{4} \sin^2 \omega t + \tfrac{3}{4} \cos^2 \omega t$$

$$+ \tfrac{1}{4} \sin^2 \omega t + \tfrac{3}{4} \cos^2 \omega t)$$

$$= \tfrac{3}{2} V_m I_m (\sin^2 \omega t + \cos^2 \omega t) = \tfrac{3}{2} V_m I_m = 3 \frac{V_m}{\sqrt{2}} \frac{I_m}{\sqrt{2}} = 3 V_p I_p$$

where V_p and I_p are rms values of phase voltage and current. Since the instantaneous power is constant, the average power is the same as the total instantaneous power; that is, $P_T = 3 V_p I_p$.

14.35 What is the total power in a three-phase circuit having a balanced load with a phase power factor angle θ_p?

$$\text{Power per phase} = V_p I_p \cos \theta_p$$

$$\text{Total power} \quad P_T = 3 V_p I_p \cos \theta_p \tag{1}$$

14.36 Express Eq. (1) of Prob. 14.35 in terms of line values. Verify that the results for wye and delta connections are the same.

For wye connection, $I_p = I_l$, $V_p = V_l / \sqrt{3}$, so that Eq. (1) of Prob. 14.35 becomes $P_T = \sqrt{3} V_l I_l \cos \theta_p$. For delta connection, $I_p = I_l / \sqrt{3}$, $V_p = I_l$, and Eq. (1) of Prob. 14.35 yields $P_T = \sqrt{3} V_l I_l \cos \theta_p$.

14.37 Depict graphically the instantaneous and average powers in a three-phase balanced system.

A graphical representation of the instantaneous power in a three-phase system is given in Fig. 14-20. It is seen that the total instantaneous power is constant and is equal to three times the average power. This feature is of great value in the operation of three-phase motors where the constant instantaneous power implies an absence of torque pulsations and consequent vibrations.

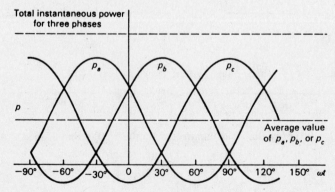

Fig. 14-20

14.38 Find the power delivered to the load of Prob. 14.27.

Since $\mathbf{Z}_p = 3 + j4 = 5 \underline{/53.2°} \, \Omega$, $\theta_p = 53.2°$. Thus, $P_T = \sqrt{3}(220)(76.21) \cos 53.2° = 17.4 \text{ kW}$.

14.39 Determine the power consumed by the load of Prob. 14.28.

▌ From Prob. 14.28, we have

$$V_l = 220 \text{ V} \qquad I_l = 25.4 \text{ A} \qquad \text{and} \qquad \theta_p = 53.2°$$

Hence, $P_T = \sqrt{3}(220)(25.4) \cos 53.2° = 5.8 \text{ kW}$.

14.40 Three impedances, $\mathbf{Z}_1 = 6 \underline{/20°} \ \Omega$, $\mathbf{Z}_2 = 8 \underline{/40°} \ \Omega$, and $\mathbf{Z}_3 = 10 \underline{/0°} \ \Omega$, are connected in wye and are supplied by a 480-V three-phase source. Solve for the line currents.

▌ The currents are:

$$\mathbf{I}_a = \frac{(480/\sqrt{3}) \underline{/-30°}}{6 \underline{/20°}} = 46.19 \underline{/-50°} \text{ A} \qquad \mathbf{I}_b = 34.64 \underline{/-190°} \text{ A} \qquad \mathbf{I}_c = 27.71 \underline{/90°} \text{ A}$$

14.41 Determine the power drawn by each impedance of the circuit of Prob. 14.40.

▌ $\quad \mathbf{I}_a = 46.19 \underline{/-50°} \text{ A} \qquad \mathbf{V}_{an} = \frac{480}{\sqrt{3}} \underline{/-30°} = 277.13 \underline{/-30°} \text{ V} \qquad \theta_a = -30° - (-50°) = 20°$

Hence, $P_a = P_{Z1} = (277.13)(46.19) \cos 20° = 12.03 \text{ kW}$. Similarly,

$$P_b = P_{Z2} = (277.13)(34.64) \cos 40° = 7.35 \text{ kW} \qquad \text{and} \qquad P_c = P_{Z3} = (277.13)(27.71) \cos 0° = 7.68 \text{ kW}$$

14.42 Find the reactive power of the circuit of Prob. 14.40.

▌
$$Q_a = Q_{Z1} = (277.13)(46.19) \sin 20° = 4.38 \text{ kvar}$$
$$Q_b = Q_{Z2} = (277.13)(34.64) \sin 40° = 6.17 \text{ kvar}$$
$$Q_c = Q_{Z3} = (277.13)(27.71) \sin 0° = 0 \qquad Q = Q_a + Q_b + Q_c = 10.55 \text{ kvar}$$

14.43 What is the overall power factor of the circuit of Prob. 14.40?

▌ From Prob. 14.41 we have $P = P_a + P_b + P_c = 27.06 \text{ kW}$ and from Prob. 14.42, $Q = 10.55 \text{ kvar}$. Thus,

$$\mathbf{S} = P + jQ = 27.06 + j10.55 \text{ kVA} = 29.05 \text{ kVA}$$

$$\text{Power factor } \cos \theta = \frac{P}{S} = \frac{27.06}{29.05} = 0.93 \text{ lagging}$$

14.44 For the load shown in Fig. 14-16, calculate the power consumed by the load.

▌
$$V_p = \frac{220}{\sqrt{3}} = 127 \text{ V} \qquad Z_p = 4 - j3 = 5 \underline{/-36.87°} \ \Omega$$

$$I_l = I_p = \frac{127}{5 \underline{/-36.87}} = 25.4 \underline{/36.87°} \text{ A}$$

Hence, $P = \sqrt{3} \times 220 \times 25.4 \cos 36.87 = 7.74 \text{ kW}$.

14.45 A three-phase balanced load has a 10-Ω resistance in each of its phases. The load is supplied by a 220-V three-phase source. Calculate the power absorbed by the load if it is connected in wye; calculate the same if it is connected in delta.

▌ In the wye connection,

$$V_p = \frac{220}{\sqrt{3}} = 127 \text{ V} \qquad I_p = \frac{127}{10} = 12.7 \text{ A} = I_l \qquad \cos \theta_p = 1 \quad \text{(load being purely resistive)}$$

Hence, $P = \sqrt{3} V_l I_l \cos \theta_p = \sqrt{3} \times 220 \times 12.7 \times 1 = 4.84 \text{ kW}$.
  In the delta connection,

$$V_l = 220 \text{ V} \qquad I_p = \tfrac{220}{10} = 22 \text{ A} \qquad I_l = \sqrt{3} \times 22 = 38.1 \text{ A}$$

Hence, $P = \sqrt{3}V_lI_l \cos\theta_p = \sqrt{3} \times 220 \times 38.1 \times 1 = 14.52$ kW.

Notice that the power consumed in the delta connection is three times that of the wye connection.

14.46 A three-phase 450-V 25-Hz source supplies power to a balanced three-phase resistive load. If the line current is 100 A and, determine the active and reactive powers drawn by the load.

▌ The power factor of a resistor load is 1.0.

$$P = \sqrt{3}V_{\text{line}}I_{\text{line}} \cos 0° \qquad P = \sqrt{3}(450)(100)(1) = 77.94 \text{ kW} \qquad Q = \sqrt{3}(450)(100)\sin 0° = 0$$

14.47 A three-phase 600-V 25-Hz source supplies power to a balanced three-phase motor load. If the line current is 40 A and the power factor of the motor is 0.80, determine the active and reactive powers drawn by the motor.

▌ $$P = \sqrt{3}V_{\text{line}}I_{\text{line}} \cos\theta_p \qquad P = \sqrt{3}(600)(40)(0.8) = 33.26 \text{ kW}$$

Since $\cos\theta_p = 0.8$, $\sin\theta_p = 0.6$; hence, $Q = \sqrt{3}(600)(40)(0.6) = 24.945$ kvar.

14.48 A 25-hp induction motor is operating at rated load from a three-phase 450-V 60-Hz system. The efficiency and power factor of the motor are 87 and 90 percent, respectively. Determine (*a*) the active power in kW and (*b*) the apparent power in kVA.

▌ A three-phase motor is a balanced load, and the phase angle for the given motor load is $\theta = \cos^{-1} 0.90 = 25.84°$.

(*a*) $P = \dfrac{\text{hp}(746)}{\text{eff.}} = \dfrac{25(746)}{0.87} = 21,436.78 \text{ W} \qquad P = 21.44 \text{ kW}$

(*b*) $\text{pf} = \dfrac{P}{S} \qquad 0.9 = \dfrac{21.44}{S} \qquad S = 23.82 \text{ kVA}$

14.49 Determine the reactive power and the line current for the motor of Prob. 14.48.

▌ $$Q = S(\sin\theta_p) \qquad \theta_p = \cos^{-1}(0.9) = 25.84° \qquad S = 23.82 \text{ kVA} \quad \text{(from Prob. 14.47)}$$

$$Q = 23.82\,(\sin 25.84°) = 10.38 \text{ kvar} \qquad P = \sqrt{3}V_lI_l \cos\theta_p \qquad \text{or} \qquad I_l = \frac{21,436.8}{\sqrt{3}(450)0.9} = 30.56 \text{ A}$$

14.50 The load on a three-phase wye-connected 220-V system consists of three 6-Ω resistances connected in wye and in parallel with three 9-Ω resistances connected in delta. Calculate the magnitude of the line current.

▌ Converting the delta load to a wye, $R_w = \frac{1}{3} \times 9 = 3\,\Omega$. This resistance combined with the wye-connected load of 6 Ω per phase gives a per-phase resistance R_p as $R_p = (6 \times 3)/(6 + 3) = 2\,\Omega$. The phase voltage is $220/\sqrt{3} = 127$ V. Hence, $I_p = I_l = \frac{127}{2} = 63.5$ A.

14.51 A wye-connected load has a $(5 + j10)$ Ω impedance/phase. Also, a $(2 + j6)$ Ω impedance is connected between lines a and b. Determine the current $\mathbf{I}_a$.

▌ $$\mathbf{V}_{ab} = 240 \underline{/0°} \text{ V} \qquad \mathbf{V}_{an} = \frac{240}{\sqrt{3}} \underline{/-30°} = 138.56 \underline{/-30°} \text{ V}$$

Thus, $$\mathbf{I}_a = \frac{240 \underline{/0°}}{2 + j6} + \frac{138.56 \underline{/-30°}}{5 + j10} = 49.68 \underline{/-76.9°} \text{ A}$$

14.52 Solve for $\mathbf{I}_c$ in the circuit of Prob. 14.51, and verify that it is independent of the $(2 + j6)$-Ω impedance.

▌ $$\mathbf{V}_{cn} = \frac{240}{\sqrt{3}} \underline{/90°} = 138.56 \underline{/90°} \qquad \mathbf{I}_c = \frac{138.56 \underline{/90°}}{5 + j10} = 12.39 \underline{/26.57°} \text{ A}$$

14.53 If the neutral of the circuit of Prob. 14.51 is connected to the neutral of the source, determine the neutral current.

▌ $$\mathbf{I}_N = -(\mathbf{I}_a + \mathbf{I}_b + \mathbf{I}_c) \qquad \mathbf{I}_a = 49.68 \underline{/-76.9°} \text{ A} \quad \text{(from Prob. 14.51)}$$

$$\mathbf{I}_c = 12.39 \underline{/26.57°} \text{ A} \quad \text{(from Prob. 14.52)}$$

$$\mathbf{I}_b = \frac{138.56 \underline{/-150°}}{5 + j10} - \frac{240 \underline{/0°}}{2 + j6} = 40.32 \underline{/117.54°} \text{ A}$$

Hence, $\mathbf{I}_N = -(49.68 \underline{/-76.9°} + 48.32 \underline{/117.54°} + 12.39 \underline{/26.57°}) = 0$ A.

14.54 The power factor of each phase of a balanced wye-connected 5-Ω impedance is 0.6 lagging. This impedance is connected to a source having a 100-V phase voltage. Determine the apparent power drawn by the circuit.

$$V_p = 100 \text{ V (given)} \qquad I_p = \frac{100}{5} = 20 \text{ A} \qquad \theta_p = \cos^{-1} 0.6 = 53.13°$$

$$P = 3(100)(20)(0.6) = 3.6 \text{ kW} \qquad Q = 3(100)(20) \sin 53.13° = 4.8 \text{ kvar}$$

Thus, $\mathbf{S} = P + jQ = 3.6 + j4.8 \text{ kVA}$.

14.55 A balanced delta-connected load draws 10 A of line current and 3 kW at 220 V. Determine the values of resistance and reactance of each phase of the load.

$$V_l = V_p = 220 \text{ V} \qquad I_p = \frac{I_l}{\sqrt{3}} = \frac{10}{\sqrt{3}} = 5.77 \text{ A}$$

Thus, $$Z_p = \frac{220}{5.77} = 38.1 \ \Omega \qquad P = \sqrt{3} V_l I_l \cos \theta_p$$

or $$3000 = \sqrt{3}(220)(10) \cos \theta_p \qquad \text{or} \qquad \cos \theta_p = 0.7873$$

$$R_p = Z_p \cos \theta_p = (38.1)(0.7873) = 30.0 \ \Omega \qquad X_p = \sqrt{(Z_p)^2 - (R_p)^2} = \sqrt{(38.1)^2 - (30)^2} = 23.5 \ \Omega$$

14.56 The connection shown in Fig. 14-21 is known as an open-delta connection. Calculate the power absorbed by the resistors (with the values as shown). The load is connected to a 220-V three-phase source.

❚ The magnitudes of the currents in the resistors are $I_A = I_c = \dfrac{220}{5} = 44 \text{ A}$. Thus, $P = (44)^2 5 + (44)^2 5 = 19.36 \text{ kW}$.

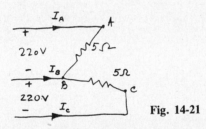

Fig. 14-21

14.57 In wye-connected resistive load, shown in Fig. 14-22, the resistor of phase B burns out. For the values shown, determine the power absorbed by the resistors.

❚ In this case, the circuit no longer acts as a three-phase circuit, and $I_A = I_C = 220/(5 + 5) = 22 \text{ A}$. Thus, $P = (22)^2(5 + 5) = 4.84 \text{ kW}$.

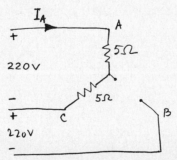

Fig. 14-22

14.58 The apparent power input to a balanced wye-connected load is 30 kVA, and the corresponding true power is 15 kW at 50 A. Calculate the phase and line voltages.

$$\cos \theta_p = \frac{\text{kW}}{\text{kVA}} = \frac{15}{30} = 0.5 \qquad I_l = 50 \text{ A} \quad \text{(given)}$$

$$P = 15,000 = \sqrt{3} V_l I_l \cos \theta = \sqrt{3} V_l(50)(0.5) \qquad \text{or} \qquad V_l = 346.42 \text{ V} = \sqrt{3} V_p$$

Hence, $V_p = 346.42/\sqrt{3} = 200 \text{ V}$.

14.59 Determine the kvar drawn by the load of Prob. 14.58.

▮ $$\mathbf{S} = P + jQ \quad \text{or} \quad Q = \sqrt{(S)^2 - (P)^2} = \sqrt{(30)^2 - (15)^2} = 25.98 \text{ kvar}$$

14.60 Calculate the input power to a three-phase load formed by a delta-connection of the load of Prob. 14.58, at the value of the line voltage determined in Prob. 14.58.

▮ From Prob. 14.58,

$$Z_p = \tfrac{200}{50} = 4\ \Omega \qquad I_p = \frac{V_p}{Z_p} = \frac{346.42}{4} = 86.6 \text{ A}$$

$$I_l = \sqrt{3} I_p = \sqrt{3}(86.6) = 150 \text{ A} \qquad P = \sqrt{3} V_l I_l \cos \theta_p = \sqrt{3}(346.42)(150)(0.5) = 45 \text{ kW}$$

14.61 Find the ohmic values of the resistance and the reactance of the load in Prob. 14.60.

▮ From Prob. 14.60,

$$Z_p = 4\ \Omega \qquad R_p = Z_p \cos \theta_p = 4(0.5) = 2\ \Omega \qquad X_p = Z_p \sin \theta_p = 4(0.866) = 3.46\ \Omega$$

14.62 For the three-phase four-wire system shown in Fig. 14-23, we have the loads as shown. Determine the line currents.

▮ $$\mathbf{V}_p = \frac{230}{\sqrt{3}}\ \underline{/0^\circ} = 132.8\ \underline{/0^\circ} \text{ V} \qquad \mathbf{I}'_A = \frac{30,000\ \underline{/-30^\circ}}{\sqrt{3}(230)(0.866)} = 86.96\ \underline{/-30^\circ} \text{ A}$$

$$\mathbf{I}'_B = 86.96\ \underline{/-150^\circ} \text{ A} \qquad \mathbf{I}'_C = 86.96\ \underline{/90^\circ} \text{ A}$$

$$\mathbf{I}''_A = \frac{10,000}{132.8}\ \underline{/0^\circ} = 75.3\ \underline{/0^\circ} \text{ A} \qquad \mathbf{I}''_B = \frac{15,000}{132.8}\ \underline{/-120^\circ} = 112.95\ \underline{/-120^\circ} \text{ A} \qquad \mathbf{I}''_C = \frac{20,000}{132.8}\ \underline{/120^\circ} = 150.6\ \underline{/120^\circ} \text{ A}$$

$$\mathbf{I}_A = \mathbf{I}'_A + \mathbf{I}''_A = 86.96\ \underline{/-30^\circ} + 75.3\ \underline{/0^\circ} = 156.75\ \underline{/-16.1^\circ} \text{ A}$$

$$\mathbf{I}_B = 86.96\ \underline{/-150^\circ} + 112.9\ \underline{/-120^\circ} = 164.04\ \underline{/-126.58^\circ} \text{ A}$$

$$\mathbf{I}_C = 86.96\ \underline{/90^\circ} + 150.6\ \underline{/120^\circ} = 229.46\ \underline{/109^\circ} \text{ A}$$

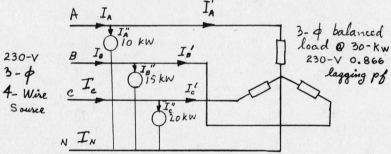

Fig. 14-23

14.63 Draw a phasor diagram showing the line currents determined in Prob. 14.62 and, hence, determine the current $\mathbf{I}_N$ through the neutral.

▮ See Fig. 14-24, from which $\mathbf{I}_N \simeq 47\ \underline{/117^\circ} \text{ A}$.

14.64 Verify analytically the result of Prob. 14.63.

▮ From Prob. 14.62,

$$\mathbf{I}_A = 150.6 - j43.47 \qquad \mathbf{I}_B = -97.75 - j131.73 \qquad \mathbf{I}_C = -74.70 + j216.96$$

$$\mathbf{I}_N = \mathbf{I}_A + \mathbf{I}_B + \mathbf{I}_C = -21.86 + j41.76 = 47.14\ \underline{/117.63^\circ} \text{ A}$$

which agrees with the result obtained graphically.

14.65 A 460-V three-phase 60-Hz source supplies energy to the following three-phase balanced loads: a 200-hp induction-motor load operating at 94 percent efficiency and 0.88 pf lagging, a 50-kW resistance-heating load, and a combination of miscellaneous loads totaling 40 kW at a 0.70 lagging power factor. Determine (*a*) the total kW supplied; (*b*) the total kvar supplied; (*c*) the total apparent power.

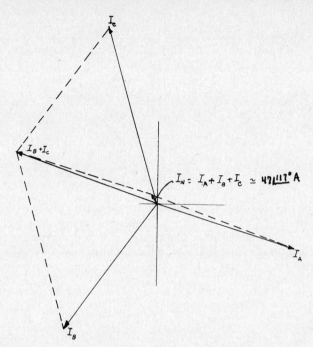

$$I_N = I_A + I_B + I_C \simeq 47 \underline{/117°} \, A$$

Fig. 14-24

** (*a*)   Active power:**
For motor,

$$P_M = \frac{\text{hp}(746)}{\text{eff.}} = \frac{200(746)}{0.94(1000)} = 158.72 \, \text{kW}$$

For heating load, $P_H = 50 \, \text{kW}$.
For miscellaneous load, $P_{\text{misc}} = 40 \, \text{kW}$.
Total kW $= P_T = 158.72 + 50 + 40 = 248.72 \, \text{kW}$.

(*b*)   Reactive power:
For motor,

$$\theta_M = \cos^{-1} 0.88 = 28.36° \qquad \tan \theta = \frac{Q_M}{P_M} \qquad \tan 28.36° = \frac{Q_M}{158.72}$$

$$Q_M = 85.68 \, \text{kvar}$$

For heating load,

$$\theta_H = 0° \qquad Q_H = 0 \, \text{kvar}$$

For miscellaneous load,
$$\theta_{\text{misc}} = \cos^{-1} 0.70 = 45.57° \qquad \tan \theta = \frac{Q_{\text{misc}}}{P_{\text{misc}}} \qquad \tan 45.57° = \frac{Q_{\text{misc}}}{40}$$

$$Q_{\text{misc}} = 40.81 \, \text{kvar}$$

Total kvar $= Q_T = Q_M + Q_H + Q_{\text{misc}} \qquad Q_T = 85.68 + 0 + 40.81 = 126.49 \, \text{kvar}$

(*c*)   Apparent power,
$$\mathbf{S}_{3\phi,\text{bal}} = P_{3\phi,\text{bal}} + jQ_{3\phi,\text{bal}} = 248.72 + j126.49 = 279 \, \underline{/27.0°} \, \text{kVA}$$

14.66   Calculate the total line current for the circuit of Prob. 14.65.

■ $$S = \sqrt{3} V_l I_l \qquad \text{or} \qquad 279,000 = \sqrt{3}(460) I_l$$

Thus, $I_l = 279,000 / \sqrt{3}(460) = 350 \, \text{A}$.

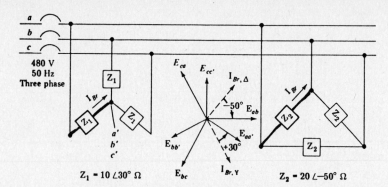

$$Z_1 = 10 \,\angle 30° \,\Omega \qquad\qquad Z_2 = 20 \,\angle{-50°} \,\Omega \qquad\qquad \textbf{Fig. 14-25}$$

14.67 A balanced wye-connected load and a balanced delta-connected load are supplied by a three-phase 480-V 50-Hz generator, as shown in Fig. 14-25. The branch impedances of the wye and delta loads are $10 \,\underline{/30°}\,\Omega$ and $20\,\underline{/-50°}\,\Omega$, respectively. Determine the active and reactive powers drawn by each three-phase load. Determine the phasor voltage and phasor current for *any* one branch of each three-phase load, and then substitute into the power equation for balanced three-phase loads.

    ❚ The branches selected for this example are drawn with heavy lines in Fig. 14-25. The branch currents are determined by using the standardized phasor diagram and Ohm's law. Thus, for the selected branch of the wye bank,

$$\mathbf{I}_{\text{br},Y} = \frac{\mathbf{E}_{aa'}}{\mathbf{Z}_1} = \frac{480/\sqrt{3}\,\underline{/-30°}}{10\,\underline{/30°}} \qquad \mathbf{I}_{\text{br},Y} = 27.71\,\underline{/-60°}\,\text{A} \qquad \mathbf{V}_{\text{br},Y} = \mathbf{E}_{aa'} = 277.13\,\underline{/-30°}\,\text{V}$$

For the selected branch of the delta band,

$$\mathbf{I}_{\text{br},\Delta} = \frac{\mathbf{E}_{ab}}{\mathbf{Z}_2} = \frac{480\,\underline{/0°}}{20\,\underline{/-50°}} \qquad \mathbf{I}_{\text{br},\Delta} = 24\,\underline{/50°}\,\text{A} \qquad \mathbf{V}_{\text{br},\Delta} = \mathbf{E}_{ab} = 480\,\underline{/0°}\,\text{V}$$

Thus,
$$P_{3\phi,\text{bal}} = 3 V_{\text{br}} I_{\text{br}} \cos\!\!\diagup\!\!\substack{V_{\text{br}} \\ I_{\text{br}}}$$

Using the phasor diagram, measure the angle *from* the branch-current phasor *to* the respective branch-voltage phasor. The direction is shown with heavy arrows in the phasor diagram. For the selected branch of the wye bank,

$$P_{Y,\text{bal}} = 3(277.13)(27.71)\cos(+30°) = 19{,}951.2\,\text{W} \qquad Q_{Y,\text{bal}} = 3(277.13)(27.71)\sin(+30°) = 11{,}518.9\,\text{var}$$

For the selected branch of the delta bank,

$$P_{\Delta,\text{bal}} = 3(480)(24)\cos(-50°) = 22{,}214.7\,\text{W} \qquad Q_{\Delta,\text{cal}} = 3(480)(24)\sin(-50°) = -26{,}474.5\,\text{var}$$

Thus
$$Q_{3\phi,\text{bal}} = 3 V_{\text{br}} I_{\text{br}} \sin\!\!\diagup\!\!\substack{V_{\text{br}} \\ I_{\text{br}}}$$

14.68 Determine the total apparent power and the overall power factor of the circuit of Prob. 14.67.

    ❚
$$P_T = P_Y + P_\Delta = 19.95 + 22.21 = 42.16\,\text{kW} \qquad Q_T = Q_Y + Q_\Delta = 11.52 + (-26.47) = -14.95\,\text{kvar}$$
$$\mathbf{S}_T = P_T + jQ_T = 42.16 - j14.95 = 44.74\,\underline{/-19.5°}\,\text{kVA}$$

Power factor is $\cos(-19.5°) = 0.94$ leading.

14.69 In the circuit of Fig. 14-26, determine the line current $\mathbf{I}_A$ for the impedance values shown.

    ❚ From Fig. 14-26,

$$\mathbf{V}_{ab} = 450\,\underline{/0°}\,\text{V} \qquad \mathbf{V}_{bc} = 450\,\underline{/-120°}\,\text{V} \qquad \mathbf{V}_{ca} = 450\,\underline{/120°}\,\text{V}$$

$$\mathbf{V}_{aa'} = \frac{450}{\sqrt{3}}\,\underline{/-30°} = 259.8\,\underline{/-30°}\,\text{V}$$

Thus, $\quad \mathbf{I}_A = \dfrac{\mathbf{V}_{a'}}{\mathbf{Z}_1} + \dfrac{\mathbf{V}_{ab}}{\mathbf{Z}_2} + \dfrac{\mathbf{V}_{ac}}{\mathbf{Z}_3} = \dfrac{259.8\,\underline{/-30}}{13\,\underline{/20°}} + \dfrac{450\,\underline{/0°}}{15\,\underline{/45°}} + \dfrac{-450\,\underline{/120°}}{3\,\underline{/30°}} = 189.6\,\underline{/-79.65°}\,\text{A}$

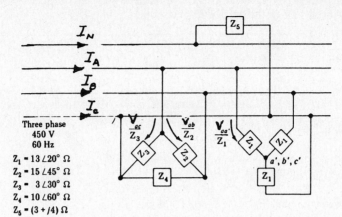

Three phase
450 V
60 Hz

$Z_1 = 13 \angle 20° \ \Omega$
$Z_2 = 15 \angle 45° \ \Omega$
$Z_3 = 3 \angle 30° \ \Omega$
$Z_4 = 10 \angle 60° \ \Omega$
$Z_5 = (3 + j4) \ \Omega$

Fig. 14-26

14.70 What is the current, $\mathbf{I}_N$, in the neutral of the three-phase four-wire system shown in Fig. 14-26?

$$\mathbf{I}_N = \frac{\mathbf{V}_{cc'}}{\mathbf{Z}_5} \quad \text{but} \quad \mathbf{V}_{cc'} = \frac{450}{\sqrt{3}} \ \underline{/90°} = 259.8 \ \underline{/90°} \text{ V}$$

Thus,

$$\mathbf{I}_N = \frac{259.8 \ \underline{/90°}}{3 + j4} = -51.96 \ \underline{/36.87°} \text{ A}$$

14.71 A four-wire three-phase 450-V 60-Hz system supplies power to the following loads: three impedances ($13 \ \underline{/20°}$ each) connected in wye; an unbalanced delta load consisting of $15\underline{/45°} \ \Omega$ between lines a and b, $3 \ \underline{/30°} \ \Omega$ between lines a and c, and $10 \ \underline{/60°} \ \Omega$ between lines b and c; a single-phase load of $(3 + j4) \ \Omega$ between line c and the neutral line. Draw the corresponding circuit and calculate the current in line a.

The circuit is shown in Fig. 14-27, from which $\mathbf{Z}_1 = 13 \ \underline{/20°} \ \Omega$, $\mathbf{Z}_2 = 15 \ \underline{/45°} \ \Omega$, $\mathbf{Z}_3 = 3 \ \underline{/30°} \ \Omega$, $\mathbf{Z}_4 = 10 \ \underline{/60°} \ \Omega$, and $\mathbf{Z}_5 = 3 + j4 = 5 \ \underline{/53.13°} \ \Omega$.

$$\mathbf{I}_a = \frac{\mathbf{V}_{aa'}}{\mathbf{Z}_1} + \frac{\mathbf{V}_{ab}}{\mathbf{Z}_2} + \frac{\mathbf{V}_{ac}}{\mathbf{Z}_3} \qquad \mathbf{V}_{aa'} = \frac{450 \ \underline{/-30°}}{\sqrt{3}} = 259.8 \ \underline{/-30°} \text{ V}$$

$$= \frac{259.8 \ \underline{/-30°}}{13 \ \underline{/20°}} + \frac{450 \ \underline{/0°}}{15 \ \underline{/45°}} + \frac{-450 \ \underline{/120°}}{3 \ \underline{/30°}} = 189.6 \ \underline{/-79.65°} \text{ A}$$

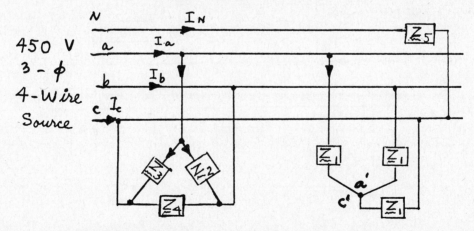

450 V
3 - φ
4 - Wire
Source

Fig. 14-27

14.72 Determine the current $\mathbf{I}_N$ in the circuit of Fig. 14-27.

$$\mathbf{I}_N = \frac{\mathbf{V}_{cc'}}{\mathbf{Z}_5} = \frac{259.8 \ \underline{/-90°}}{5 \ \underline{/53.13°}} = 51.96 \ \underline{/-143.13°} \text{ A}$$

14.73 Calculate the line current $\mathbf{I}_c$ in the circuit of Fig. 14-27.

$$\mathbf{I}_c = \frac{\mathbf{V}_{ca}}{\mathbf{Z}_3} + \frac{\mathbf{V}_{cb}}{\mathbf{Z}_4} + \frac{\mathbf{V}_{cc'}}{\mathbf{Z}_1} + \frac{\mathbf{V}_{cc'}}{\mathbf{Z}_5} = \frac{450 \ \underline{/120°}}{3 \ \underline{/30°}} + \frac{-450 \ \underline{/-120°}}{10 \ \underline{/60°}} + \frac{259.8 \ \underline{/90°}}{13 \ \underline{/20°}} + \frac{259.8 \ \underline{/90°}}{5 \ \underline{/53.13°}} = 220.7 \ \underline{/64.96°} \text{ A}$$

14.74 From the results of Probs. 14.71 through 14.73 determine $\mathbf{I}_b$.

▮ Since $\mathbf{I}_a + \mathbf{I}_b + \mathbf{I}_c + \mathbf{I}_N = 0$,

$$\mathbf{I}_b = -(\mathbf{I}_a + \mathbf{I}_c + \mathbf{I}_N) = -(189.6\,\underline{/-79.65°} + 220.7\,\underline{/64.96°} + 51.96\,\underline{/-143.13°}) = 87.7\,\underline{/168.3°}\text{ A}$$

14.75 A wye-connected load and a delta-connected load are supplied by a four-wire 400-V three-phase 50-Hz system. The connections for the wye load are $2\,\underline{/20°}\,\Omega$ to line a, $30\,\underline{/50°}\,\Omega$ to line c, and $6\,\underline{/75°}\,\Omega$ to line b. The connections for the delta load are $50\,\underline{/30°}\,\Omega$ between lines a and b, $25\,\underline{/-60°}\,\Omega$ between lines b and c, and $17.3\,\underline{/90°}\,\Omega$ between lines a and c. Sketch the circuit and calculate the current $\mathbf{I}_b$.

▮ The circuit is shown in Fig. 14-28 from which $\mathbf{Z}_1 = 50\,\underline{/30°}\,\Omega$, $\mathbf{Z}_2 = 25\,\underline{/-60°}\,\Omega$, $\mathbf{Z}_3 = 17.3\,\underline{/90°}\,\Omega$, $\mathbf{Z}_4 = 2\,\underline{/20°}\,\Omega$, $\mathbf{Z}_5 = 6\,\underline{/75°}\,\Omega$, and $\mathbf{Z}_6 = 30\,\underline{/50°}\,\Omega$.

$$\mathbf{V}_{bb'} = \frac{400}{\sqrt{3}}\,\underline{/-150°} = 230.94\,\underline{/-150°}\text{ V}$$

$$\mathbf{I}_b = \frac{\mathbf{V}_{bb'}}{\mathbf{Z}_5} + \frac{\mathbf{V}_{bc}}{\mathbf{Z}_2} + \frac{\mathbf{V}_{bc}}{\mathbf{Z}_2} = \frac{230.94\,\underline{/-150°}}{6\,\underline{/75°}} + \frac{-400\,\underline{/0°}}{50\,\underline{/30°}} + \frac{400\,\underline{/-120°}}{25\,\underline{/-60°}} = 31.38\,\underline{/146.4°}\text{ A}$$

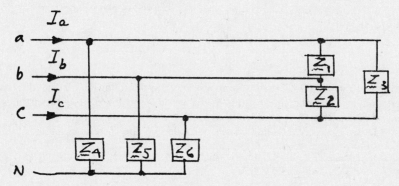

Fig. 14-28

14.76 In the circuit of Fig. 14-29 find the current $\mathbf{I}_1$.

▮ $$\mathbf{I}_1 = \frac{450\,\underline{/0°}}{38\,\underline{/0°}} = 11.84\,\underline{/0°}\text{ A}$$

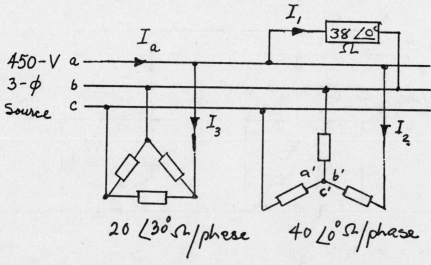

Fig. 14-29

14.77 Determine the current $\mathbf{I}_2$ in the circuit of Fig. 14-29.

▮ $$\mathbf{V}_{aa'} = \frac{450}{\sqrt{3}}\,\underline{/-30°} = 259.8\,\underline{/-30°}\text{ V} \qquad \mathbf{I}_2 = \frac{\mathbf{V}_{aa'}}{40\,\underline{/0°}} = \frac{259.8\,\underline{/-30°}}{40\,\underline{/0°}} = 6.5\,\underline{/-30°}\text{ A}$$

14.78 What is the current $\mathbf{I}_3$ in the circuit of Fig. 14-29?

▮ $$\mathbf{I}_3 = \frac{\mathbf{V}_{ab}}{20\,\underline{/30°}} + \frac{\mathbf{V}_{ac}}{20\,\underline{/30°}} = \frac{450\,\underline{/0°}}{20\,\underline{/30°}} + \frac{-450\,\underline{/120°}}{20\,\underline{/30°}} = 38.97\,\underline{/-60°}\text{ A}$$

14.79 From the results of the preceding three problems obtain $\mathbf{I}_a$.

$$\mathbf{I}_a = \mathbf{I}_1 + \mathbf{I}_2 + \mathbf{I}_3 = 11.84 \,\underline{/0°} + 6.5 \,\underline{/-30°} + 38.97 \,\underline{/-60°} = 52.3 \,\underline{/-45°} \text{ A}$$

14.80 Determine the current $\mathbf{I}_a$ in the circuit shown in Fig. 14-30. The delta consisting of $\mathbf{Z}_2$'s is closed.

$$\mathbf{I}_a = \frac{\mathbf{V}_{aa'}}{\mathbf{Z}_1} + \frac{\mathbf{V}_{ab}}{\mathbf{Z}_2} + \frac{\mathbf{V}_{ac}}{\mathbf{Z}_2} \qquad \mathbf{V}_{aa'} = \frac{208}{\sqrt{3}} \,\underline{/-30°} = 120 \,\underline{/-30°} \text{ V}$$

$$\mathbf{V}_{ab} = 208 \,\underline{/0°} \text{ V} \qquad \text{and} \qquad \mathbf{V}_{ac} = -208 \,\underline{/120°} \text{ V}$$

Thus,

$$\mathbf{I}_a = \frac{120 \,\underline{/-30°}}{6 \,\underline{/50°}} + \frac{208 \,\underline{/0°}}{4 \,\underline{/25°}} + \frac{-208 \,\underline{/120°}}{4 \,\underline{/25°}} = 108.52 \,\underline{/-59.5°} \text{ A}$$

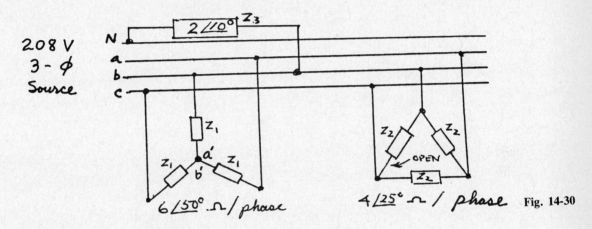

Fig. 14-30

14.81 With the delta closed determine $\mathbf{I}_N$ in the circuit of Fig. 14-30.

Notice that delta-connected $\mathbf{Z}_2$'s have no effect on $\mathbf{I}_N$. Thus

$$\mathbf{I}_N = \frac{\mathbf{V}_{b'b}}{\mathbf{Z}_3} = \frac{-120 \,\underline{/-150°}}{2 \,\underline{/10°}} = -60 \,\underline{/-160°} \text{ A}$$

14.82 If the $\mathbf{Z}_2$ connected between the lines b and c in the circuit of Fig. 14-30 is opened, find $\mathbf{I}_c$.

$$\mathbf{I}_c = \frac{\mathbf{V}_{cc'}}{\mathbf{Z}_1} + \frac{\mathbf{V}_{ca}}{\mathbf{Z}_2} = \frac{120 \,\underline{/90°}}{6 \,\underline{/50°}} + \frac{208 \,\underline{/120°}}{4 \,\underline{/25°}} = 65.54 \,\underline{/80.53°} \text{ A}$$

14.83 Repeat Prob. 14.82 for $\mathbf{I}_b$.

$$\mathbf{I}_b = \frac{\mathbf{V}_{bb'}}{\mathbf{Z}_1} + \frac{\mathbf{V}_{bb'}}{\mathbf{Z}_3} + \frac{\mathbf{V}_{ba}}{\mathbf{Z}_2} = \frac{120 \,\underline{/-150°}}{2 \,\underline{/10°}} + \frac{120 \,\underline{/-150°}}{6 \,\underline{/50°}} + \frac{-208 \,\underline{/0°}}{4 \,\underline{/25°}} = 122.58 \,\underline{/176.12°} \text{ A}$$

14.84 In the circuit of Fig. 14-31, $\mathbf{Z}_1 = 10 \,\underline{/20°} \,\Omega$, $\mathbf{Z}_2 = 10 \,\underline{/50°} \,\Omega$, $\mathbf{Z}_3 = 10 \,\underline{/80°} \,\Omega$, $\mathbf{Z}_4 = 10 \,\underline{/-10°} \,\Omega$, and $\mathbf{Z}_5 = 10 \,\underline{/-40°} \,\Omega$. The circuit is supplied by a 450-V three-phase four-wire source. Determine $\mathbf{I}_N$.

$$\mathbf{I}_N = -\frac{\mathbf{V}_{cc'}}{\mathbf{Z}_1} = -\frac{(450/\sqrt{3}) \,\underline{/90°}}{10 \,\underline{/20°}} = -25.98 \,\underline{/70°} \text{ A}$$

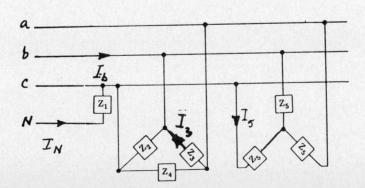

Fig. 14-31

14.85 Determine the currents $\mathbf{I}_3$ and $\mathbf{I}_5$ shown in the circuit of Fig. 14-31:

$$\mathbf{I}_3 = \frac{\mathbf{V}_{ab}}{\mathbf{Z}_3} = \frac{450\,\underline{/0°}}{10\,\underline{/80°}} = 45\,\underline{/-80°}\ \text{A} \qquad \mathbf{I}_5 = \frac{\mathbf{V}_{cc'}}{\mathbf{Z}_5} = \frac{(450/\sqrt{3})\,\underline{/90°}}{10\,\underline{/-40°}} = 25.98\,\underline{/130°}\ \text{A}$$

14.86 Solve for the current $\mathbf{I}_b$ in the circuit of Fig. 14-31.

$$\mathbf{I}_b = \frac{\mathbf{V}_{ba}}{\mathbf{Z}_3} + \frac{\mathbf{V}_{bc}}{\mathbf{Z}_2} + \frac{\mathbf{V}_{bb'}}{\mathbf{Z}_5} = \frac{-450\,\underline{/0°}}{10\,\underline{/80°}} + \frac{450\,\underline{/-120°}}{10\,\underline{/50°}} + \frac{259.8\,\underline{/-150°}}{10\,\underline{/-40°}} = 62.2\,\underline{/168.8°}\ \text{A}$$

14.87 The circuit of Fig. 14-32 is energized by a 450-V three-phase 60-Hz source. Determine $\mathbf{I}_a$.

At 60 Hz

$$X_{L1} = \omega L_1 = (377)(7.96 \times 10^{-3}) = 3\ \Omega \qquad X_{C1} = \frac{1}{\omega C_1} = \frac{1}{(377)(530.5 \times 10^{-6})} = 5\ \Omega$$

$$X_{L2} = \omega L_2 = (377)(15.92 \times 10^{-3}) = 6\ \Omega \qquad X_{C2} = \frac{1}{\omega C_2} = \frac{1}{(377)(331.6 \times 10^{-6})} = 8\ \Omega$$

Thus,

$$\mathbf{I}_a = \frac{\mathbf{V}_{ab}}{24\,\underline{/0°}} + \frac{\mathbf{V}_{aa'}}{5\,\underline{/-90°}} + \frac{\mathbf{V}_{ab}}{6\,\underline{/90°}} + \frac{\mathbf{V}_{ac}}{8\,\underline{/-90°}}$$

$$= \frac{450\,\underline{/0°}}{24\,\underline{/0°}} + \frac{259.8\,\underline{/-30°}}{5\,\underline{/-90°}} + \frac{450\,\underline{/0°}}{6\,\underline{/90°}} + \frac{-450\,\underline{/120°}}{8\,\underline{/-90°}} = 93.46\,\underline{/-1.15°}\ \text{A}$$

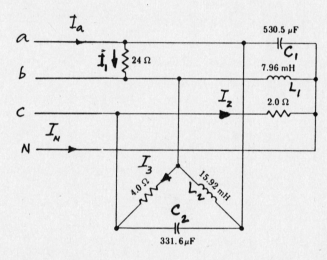

Fig. 14-32

14.88 Solve for $\mathbf{I}_N$ in the circuit of Fig. 14-32.

$$\mathbf{I}_N = \frac{\mathbf{V}_{c'c}}{2\,\underline{/0°}} + \frac{\mathbf{V}_{b'b}}{3\,\underline{/90°}} + \frac{\mathbf{V}_{a'a}}{5\,\underline{/-90°}} = \frac{-259.8\,\underline{/90°}}{2\,\underline{/0°}} + \frac{-259.8\,\underline{/-150°}}{3\,\underline{/90°}} + \frac{-259.8\,\underline{/-30°}}{5\,\underline{/-90°}} = 250.5\,\underline{/-86°}\ \text{A}$$

14.89 How much active power is supplied by the source to the circuit of Fig. 14-32?

$$P_{\text{supplied}} = \sum P_{\text{absorbed}} = (I_1)^2 24 + (I_2)^2 2 + (I_3)^2 4 = \left(\frac{450}{24}\right)^2 24 + \left(\frac{259.8}{2}\right)^2 2 + \left(\frac{450}{4}\right)^2 4 = 92.81\ \text{kW}$$

14.90 In the three-phase system shown in Fig. 14-33a phase b gets open-circuited owing to a fault. Convert the remaining wye-connected load to an equivalent delta.

$$\mathbf{Z}_A = \frac{j3(5.82\,\underline{/75.96°}) + (5.82\,\underline{/75.96°})4 + 4(j3)}{5.82\,\underline{/75.96°}} = \frac{40.43\,\underline{/106.22°}}{5.82\,\underline{/75.96°}} = 6.95\,\underline{/30.26°}\ \Omega$$

Similarly, $\qquad \mathbf{Z}_B = \dfrac{40.43\,\underline{/106.22°}}{4\,\underline{/0°}} = 10.11\,\underline{/106.22°}\ \Omega \qquad \mathbf{Z}_C = \dfrac{40.43\,\underline{/106.22°}}{j3} = 13.48\,\underline{/16.22°}\ \Omega$

where $\mathbf{Z}_A$, $\mathbf{Z}_B$, and $\mathbf{Z}_C$ are shown in Fig. 14-33b.

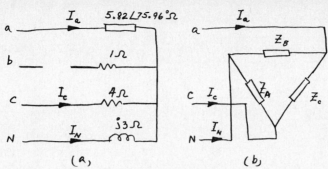

Fig. 14-33

14.91 If the circuit of Fig. 14-33a is connected across a 450-V three-phase source, calculate the current I_N.

▮ We use the circuit of Fig. 14-33b to solve for the currents in the various impedances, the voltages across which are

$$\mathbf{V}_{ac} = -\mathbf{V}_{ca} = -450 \underline{/120°} \text{ V} \qquad \mathbf{V}_{aN} = \frac{450}{\sqrt{3}} \underline{/-30°} = 259.8 \underline{/-30°} \text{ V} \qquad \text{and} \qquad \mathbf{V}_{cN} = 259.8 \underline{/90°} \text{ V}$$

Thus,

$$\mathbf{I}_a = \frac{259.8 \underline{/-30°}}{10.11 \underline{/106°}} + \frac{-450 \underline{/120°}}{13.48 \underline{/16.2°}} = -10.54 - j50.27 \text{ A}$$

$$\mathbf{I}_c = \frac{450 \underline{/120°}}{13.48 \underline{/16.2°}} + \frac{259.8 \underline{/90°}}{6.45 \underline{/30.26°}} = 10.89 + j64.71 \text{ A} \qquad \mathbf{I}_a + \mathbf{I}_c + \mathbf{I}_N = 0$$

Hence, $\mathbf{I}_N = -(\mathbf{I}_a + \mathbf{I}_c) = 10.54 + j50.27 - 10.89 - j64.71 = -0.35 - j14.44 = 14.44 \underline{/-91.4°} \text{ A}$.

14.92 In the circuit of Fig. 14-34 phase b gets open-circuited while the circuit is connected to a 450-V three-phase source. Determine I_N.

▮ Proceeding as in Prob. 14.91,

$$\mathbf{I}_a = \frac{-450 \underline{/120°}}{8 \underline{/-90°}} + \frac{259.8 \underline{/-30°}}{5 \underline{/-90°}} = 74.69 + j73.13 \text{ A}$$

$$\mathbf{I}_c = \frac{450 \underline{/120°}}{8 \underline{/-90°}} + \frac{259.8 \underline{/90°}}{2 \underline{/0°}} = -48.71 + j101.79 \text{ A}$$

$$\mathbf{I}_N = -(\mathbf{I}_a + \mathbf{I}_c) = -74.69 - j73.13 + 48.71 - j101.79 = -25.98 - j174.92 = 176.84 \underline{/-98.45°} \text{ A}$$

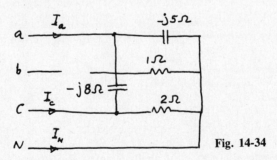

Fig. 14-34

14.93 Calculate the power dissipated in the 6-Ω resistor of the circuit of Fig. 14-35.

▮ Power dissipated $= (I_N)^2 6$, where

$$\mathbf{I}_N = \frac{\mathbf{V}_{bN}}{6} \qquad \text{and} \qquad \mathbf{V}_{bN} = \frac{480 \underline{/-150°}}{\sqrt{3}} = 277 \underline{/-150°} \text{ V}$$

Thus, $\mathbf{I}_N = \dfrac{277 \underline{/-150°}}{6 \underline{/0°}} = 46.17 \underline{/-150°} \text{ A}$ and Power dissipated $= (46.17)^2 6 = 12.79 \text{ kW}$

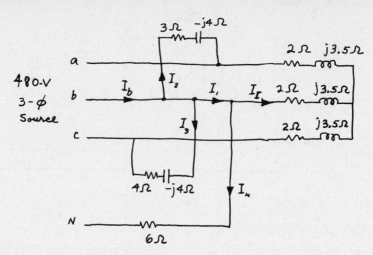

Fig. 14-35

14.94 Determine the apparent power taken by the $(2 + j3.5)\,\Omega$ impedance in phase b of the circuit shown in Fig. 14-35.

$$\mathbf{Z}_b = 2 + j3.5 = 4.03\ \underline{/60.26°}\ \Omega \qquad \mathbf{I} = \frac{\mathbf{V}_{bN}}{\mathbf{Z}_b} = \frac{277\ \underline{/-150°}}{4.03\ \underline{/60.26}} = 68.73\ \underline{/-210.26°}\ \text{A}$$

$$\mathbf{S} = (I)^2(\mathbf{Z}_b) = (68.73)^2(2 + j3.5) = 9.45 + j16.53\ \text{kVA}$$

14.95 Verify that the result of Prob. 14.94 can also be obtained from $\mathbf{S} = \mathbf{VI}^*$.

From Prob. 14.94,

$$\mathbf{V} = \mathbf{V}_{bn} = 277\ \underline{/-150°}\ \text{V} \qquad \mathbf{I}^* = 68.73\ \underline{/210.26°}\ \text{A}$$

Thus, $\mathbf{S} = \mathbf{VI}^* = (277\ \underline{/-150°})(68.73\ \underline{/210.26°}) = 9.44 + j16.53\ \text{kVA}$, which is the same as in Prob. 14.94.

14.96 Determine the current $\mathbf{I}_1$ in the circuit of Fig. 14-35.

$$\mathbf{I}_1 = \frac{\mathbf{V}_{bn}}{6} + \frac{\mathbf{V}_{bn}}{2 + j3.5} = \frac{277\ \underline{/-150°}}{6} + \frac{277\ \underline{/-150°}}{4.03\ \underline{/60.26°}} = 46.17\ \underline{/-150°} + 68.73\ \underline{/-210.26°} = 100\ \underline{/-173.37°}\ \text{A}$$

14.97 How much power is supplied to phase b of the circuit of Fig. 14-35?

$$P_b = V_{bn}I_b \cos\theta_p \qquad \mathbf{V}_{bn} = 277\ \underline{/-150°}\ \text{V}$$

$$\mathbf{I}_b = \mathbf{I}_1 + \mathbf{I}_2 + \mathbf{I}_3 = 100\ \underline{/-173.37°} + \frac{-480\ \underline{/0°}}{3 - j4} + \frac{480\ \underline{/-120°}}{4 - j4}$$

$$= 100\ \underline{/-173.37°} - 96\ \underline{/53.13°} + 84.8\ \underline{/-75°} = -135 - j147.2 = 199.74\ \underline{/-133°}\ \text{A}$$

$$\theta_p = -150 - (-133) = -17°$$

Thus, $P_b = (277)(199.74) \cos(-17°) = 52.91\ \text{kW}$.

14.98 Three impedances, $\mathbf{Z}_{ab} = 8\ \underline{/20°}\ \Omega$, $\mathbf{Z}_{bc} = 15\ \underline{/65°}\ \Omega$, and $\mathbf{Z}_{ca} = 10\ \underline{/0°}\ \Omega$, are connected in delta and across a 300-V three-phase source. Find the line current $\mathbf{I}_a$.

$$\mathbf{I}_a = \frac{\mathbf{V}_{ab}}{\mathbf{Z}_{ab}} + \frac{\mathbf{V}_{ac}}{\mathbf{Z}_{ac}} = \frac{300}{8\ \underline{/20°}} + \frac{-300\ \underline{/120°}}{10\ \underline{/0°}} = 63.48\ \underline{/-37.68°}\ \text{A}$$

14.99 Repeat Prob. 14.98 if the phase sequence of the source is reversed.

With reversed phase sequence we have

$$\mathbf{I}_a = \frac{\mathbf{V}_{ac}}{\mathbf{Z}_{ac}} + \frac{\mathbf{V}_{ab}}{\mathbf{Z}_{ab}} = \frac{-300\ \underline{/120°}}{16\ \underline{/65°}} + \frac{300\ \underline{/0°}}{8\ \underline{/20°}} = 37.66\ \underline{/-50.87°}\ \text{A}$$

14.100 Determine the three ammeter readings in the circuit of Fig. 14-36, where $\mathbf{Z}_1 = 10\ \underline{/25°}\ \Omega$, $\mathbf{Z}_2 = 20\ \underline{/60°}\ \Omega$, $\mathbf{Z}_3 = 15\ \underline{/0°}\ \Omega$, and the three-phase applied voltage is 300 V.

$$\mathbf{I}_a = \frac{\mathbf{V}_{ab}}{\mathbf{Z}_1} + \frac{\mathbf{V}_{ac}}{\mathbf{Z}_3} = \frac{300\ \underline{/0°}}{10\ \underline{/25°}} + \frac{-300\ \underline{/120°}}{15\ \underline{/0°}} = 47.78\ \underline{/-38.89°}\ A$$

So A1 reads 47.8 A.

$$\mathbf{I}_b = \frac{\mathbf{V}_{ba}}{\mathbf{Z}_1} + \frac{\mathbf{V}_{bc}}{\mathbf{Z}_2} = \frac{-300\ \underline{/0°}}{10\ \underline{/25°}} + \frac{300\ \underline{/-120°}}{20\ \underline{/60°}} = 44.05\ \underline{/163.27°}\ A$$

Ammeter A2 reads 44.1 A.

$$\mathbf{I}_c = \frac{\mathbf{V}_{ca}}{\mathbf{Z}_3} + \frac{\mathbf{V}_{cb}}{\mathbf{Z}_2} = \frac{300\ \underline{/120°}}{15\ \underline{/0°}} + \frac{-300\ \underline{/-120°}}{20\ \underline{/60°}} = 18.03\ \underline{/73.90°}\ A$$

Thus, A3 reads 18.0 A.

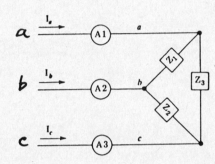

Fig. 14-36

14.101 Repeat Prob. 14.100 for a reversed phase sequence and compare the results.

In this case we obtain the circuit of Fig. 14-37, from which

$$\mathbf{I}_a = \frac{\mathbf{V}_{ab}}{\mathbf{Z}_1} + \frac{\mathbf{V}_{ac}}{\mathbf{Z}_2} = \frac{300\ \underline{/0°}}{10\ \underline{/25°}} + \frac{-300\ \underline{/120°}}{20\ \underline{/60°}} = 32.35\ \underline{/-52.51°}\ A$$

A1 reads 32.4 A.

$$\mathbf{I}_b = \frac{\mathbf{V}_{ba}}{\mathbf{Z}_1} + \frac{\mathbf{V}_{bc}}{\mathbf{Z}_3} = \frac{-300\ \underline{/0°}}{10\ \underline{/25°}} + \frac{300\ \underline{/-120°}}{15\ \underline{/0°}} = 37.48\ \underline{/-172.89°}\ A$$

A2 reads 37.5 A.

$$\mathbf{I}_c = \frac{\mathbf{V}_{cb}}{\mathbf{Z}_3} + \frac{\mathbf{V}_{ca}}{\mathbf{Z}_2} = \frac{-300\ \underline{/-120°}}{15\ \underline{/0°}} + \frac{300\ \underline{/120°}}{20\ \underline{/60°}} = 35.0\ \underline{/60°}\ A$$

A3 reads 35.0 A. The following tabulation emphasizes the effect of phase sequence on the line currents to an unbalanced three-phase load.

| Line | Amperes | |
	Sequence *abc*	Sequence *cba*
a	47.8	32.4
b	44.1	37.5
c	18.0	35.0

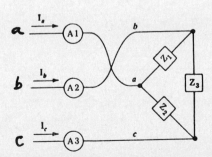

Fig. 14-37

14.102 Power is measured in a three-phase circuit by two wattmeters, as shown in Fig. 14-38a. Draw a phasor diagram showing the voltages across and the currents through the two wattmeters.

▮ The phasor diagram is shown in Fig. 14-38b.

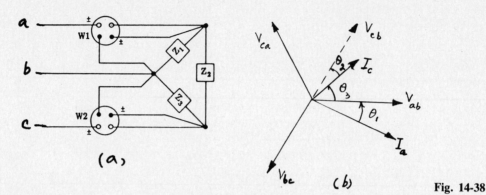

Fig. 14-38

14.103 Determine the angles θ_1, θ_2, and θ_3 shown in Fig. 14-38b. Also calculate the currents $\mathbf{I}_a$ and $\mathbf{I}_c$ if $\mathbf{Z}_1 = 10\ \underline{/20°}\ \Omega$, $\mathbf{Z}_2 = 30\ \underline{/10°}\ \Omega$, and $\mathbf{Z}_3 = 5\ \underline{/30°}\ \Omega$, and the circuit is connected to a 450-V three-phase source.

▮
$$\mathbf{I}_a = \frac{\mathbf{V}_{ab}}{\mathbf{Z}_1} + \frac{\mathbf{V}_{ac}}{\mathbf{Z}_2} = \frac{450\ \underline{/0°}}{10\ \underline{/20°}} + \frac{-450\ \underline{/120°}}{30\ \underline{/10°}} = 55.84\ \underline{/-31.88°}\ \text{A}$$

$$\mathbf{I}_c = \frac{\mathbf{V}_{ca}}{\mathbf{Z}_2} + \frac{\mathbf{V}_{cb}}{\mathbf{Z}_3} = \frac{450\ \underline{/120°}}{30\ \underline{/10°}} + \frac{-450\ \underline{/-120°}}{5\ \underline{/30°}} = 93.78\ \underline{/39.06°}\ \text{A}$$

Thus, $\theta_1 = 31.88°$, $\theta_3 = 39.06°$, and $\theta_2 = 120° - \theta_3 - 60° = 120° - 39.06° - 60° = 20.94°$.

14.104 From the results of Probs. 14.102 and 14.103 determine the wattmeter readings in the circuit of Fig. 14-38a.

▮
$$W1 = V_{ab}I_a \cos \theta_1 = (450)(55.84) \cos 31.88° = 21.3\ \text{kW}$$

$$W2 = V_{cb}I_c \cos \theta_2 = (450)(93.78) \cos 20.94 = 39.4\ \text{kW}$$

14.105 Show that the sum of the two wattmeter readings gives the total instantaneous power input to the circuit of Fig. 14-39.

▮ Current through $W1 = i_a$; voltage across $W1 = v_{ac} = v_a - v_c$; instantaneous power read by $W1 = (v_a - v_c)i_a$. Current through $W2 = i_b$; voltage across $W2 = v_{bc} = v_b - v_c$; instantaneous power read by $W2 = (v_b - v_c)i_b$. Total instantaneous power read by $W1$ and $W2$,

$$v_a i_a + v_b i_b - v_c(i_a + i_b) = p \tag{1}$$

but $i_a + i_a + i_c = 0$ so that Eq. (1) becomes $p = v_a i_a + v_b i_b + v_c i_c$, which is the total instantaneous three-phase power.

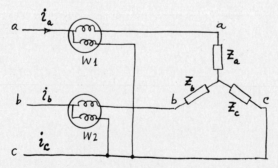

Fig. 14-39

14.106 If the impedances in the circuit of Fig. 14-39 are identical, that is, $\mathbf{Z}_a = \mathbf{Z}_b = \mathbf{Z}_c = \mathbf{Z}$, and the power factor angle is θ (lagging), draw a phasor diagram showing all voltages and current.

▮ See Fig. 14-40, where $\mathbf{V}_a = \mathbf{V}_{an}$, $\mathbf{V}_b = \mathbf{V}_{bn}$, and $\mathbf{V}_c = \mathbf{V}_{cn}$.

14.107 With a balanced load, using the phasor diagram of Fig. 14-40, show that the sum of the two wattmeter readings equals the power consumed by the circuit of Fig. 14-39.

▌ Current through $W1 = I_a$; voltage across $W1 = V_{ac} = V_a - V_c$. From Fig. 14-40, $\mathbf{V}_{ac}$ is behind $\mathbf{I}_a$ by $30° - \theta$, so that reading of $W1 = V_{ac}I_a \cos(30° - \theta)$. Similarly, from Figs. 14-39 and 14-40, it follows that the reading of $W2 = V_{bc}I_b \cos(30° + \theta)$. Now, in terms of line quantities, we have $I_a = I_b = I_l$ and $V_{ac} = V_{bc} = V_l$. Thus,

$$W1 + W2 = V_lI_l \cos(\theta - 30°) + V_lI_l \cos(\theta + 30°) = V_lI_l(2 \cos 30° \cos \theta)$$

$$= \sqrt{3}V_lI_l \cos \theta = \text{total three-phase power}$$

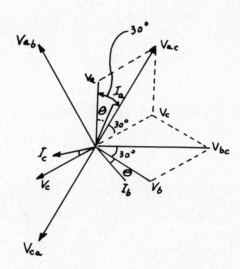

Fig. 14-40

14.108 A 220-V three-phase motor takes 21,437 W at 0.71 lagging power factor. What is the line current?

▌ $$P = \sqrt{3}V_lI_l \cos \theta \qquad \text{or} \qquad 21,437 = \sqrt{3}(220)I_l(0.71)$$

Hence, $I_l = 79.2$ A.

14.109 Let the motor of Prob. 14.108 be wye-connected and balanced. If wattmeters are connected in lines a and c to measure the input power to this motor, determine the individual wattmeter readings.

▌ $$\cos \theta = 0.71 \qquad \text{or} \qquad \theta = \cos^{-1} 0.71 = 44.77°$$

$$W1 = V_{ab}I_a \cos(44.77° + 30°) = (220)(79.24) \cos 74.77° = 4580 \text{ W}$$

$$W2 = V_{cb}I_c \cos(90° - 44.77° - 60°) = (220)(79.24) \cos 14.77 = 16,857 \text{ W}$$

14.110 Use the approach of Prob. 14.107 to find the wattmeter readings of Prob. 14.109.

▌ $$W1 = V_lI_l \cos(\theta + 30°) = (220)(79.24) \cos(44.77 + 30°) = 4580 \text{ W}$$

$$W2 = (220)(79.24) \cos(44.77 - 30°) = 16,857 \text{ W}$$

14.111 The line current to a lightly loaded three-phase motor, operating from a 450-V three-phase system, is 24 A. The power factor of the motor is 0.47 lagging. If the two-wattmeter method is used to measure the three-phase power supplied to the motor, what would each wattmeter read?

▌ $\theta = \cos^{-1} 0.47 = 61.966°$ $W1 = V_lI_l \cos(\theta° + 30°) = (450)(24) \cos(61.966° + 30°) = -371$

$$W2 = V_lI_l \cos(\theta° - 30°) = (450)(24) \cos(61.966° - 30°) = 9162$$

14.112 Obtain an expression for the power factor angle θ in terms of the wattmeter readings of Prob. 14.107.

▌ From Prob. 14-107,

$$W1 + W2 = \sqrt{3}V_lI_l \cos \theta \tag{1}$$

But $$W1 - W2 = V_lI_l[\cos(\theta + 30°) - \cos(\theta - 30°)] = -V_lI_l \sin\theta \qquad (2)$$

Thus, Eqs. (1) and (2) yield

$$\tan\theta = \sqrt{3}\,\frac{W2 - W1}{W2 + W1}$$

14.113 Two wattmeters, connected to measure three-phase power, read 60 and 40 kW (for $W1$ and $W2$ respectively). Determine the total power and the power factor.

▮ $P = W1 + W2 = 60 + 40 = 100$ kW $\quad \tan\theta = \sqrt{3}\,\dfrac{W2 - W1}{W2 + W1} = \sqrt{3}\,\dfrac{40 - 60}{40 + 60} = -0.3464 \quad$ or $\quad \theta = -19.1°$

and the power factor is $\cos(-19.1) = 0.945$ lagging.

14.114 Calculate the total apparent power from the data of Prob. 14.113.

▮ $\qquad\qquad S\cos\theta = W1 + W2 \quad$ or $\quad S = \dfrac{60 + 40}{0.945} = 105.8$ kVA

14.115 What is the per-phase reactive power in the circuit of Prob. 14.113?

▮ $\qquad\qquad$ Total $\quad Q = \sqrt{S^2 - P^2} = \sqrt{(105.8)^2 - (100)^2} = 34.6$ kvar

or per-phase reactive power $= \frac{1}{3}Q = \frac{1}{3}(34.6) = 11.53$ kvar.

14.116 A balanced wye-connected load draws a line current of 60 A from a 450-V 60-Hz three-phase system. The power factor of the load is 0.70 lagging. Determine the active power, apparent power, and reactive power drawn by the load.

▮ $$P = \sqrt{3}V_lI_l \cos\theta = \sqrt{3}(450)(60)(0.7) = 32.736 \text{ kW}$$
$$S = \sqrt{3}V_lI_l = \sqrt{3}(450)(60) = 46.765 \text{ kVA}$$
$$Q = \sqrt{S^2 - P^2} = \sqrt{(46.765)^2 - (32.736)^2} = 33.396 \text{ kvar}$$

14.117 A three-phase motor draws a line current of 30 A when supplied from a 450-V three-phase 25-Hz source. The motor efficiency and power factor are 90 and 75 percent, respectively. Determine the active power drawn by the motor.

▮ $$P = \sqrt{3}V_lI_l \cos\theta = \sqrt{3}(450)(30)(0.75) = 17.537 \text{ kW}$$

14.118 Calculate the motor output and the total input reactive power for the motor of Prob. 14.117.

▮ $$P_{out} = (\text{efficiency})(P_{in}) = (0.9)(17.537) = 15.783 \text{ kW} \quad \text{or} \quad 21.16 \text{ hp}$$
$$Q = P\tan\theta = (17.537)\tan(\cos^{-1}0.75) = (17.537)(\tan 41.41°) = 15.47 \text{ kvar}$$

14.119 A four-wire 208-V three-phase 60-Hz system is used to supply power to a three-phase 5-hp induction motor and a single-phase 6-kW heater connected between line c and the neutral line. The operating efficiency and power factor of the motor are 81 and 71 percent, respectively. Draw the corresponding circuit diagram and calculate the current in line c.

▮ The circuit is shown in Fig. 14-41. For motor load,

$$P = \frac{5 \times 746}{0.81} = 4604.94 \text{ W} = \sqrt{3}V_lI_l \cos\theta = \sqrt{3}(208)I_l(0.71) \qquad \text{or} \qquad I_l = 18 \text{ A} = I_{cc'}$$

Power factor $= 0.71 = \cos\theta \quad$ or $\quad \theta = 47.77°$ lagging. Thus, $\mathbf{I}_{cc'} = 18\,\underline{/-47.77°}$ A. Thus, $\mathbf{I}_c = \mathbf{I}_{cc'} + \mathbf{V}_{cc'}/R_{heater}$ where $R_{heater} = 6000/(208/\sqrt{3})^2 = 0.416\,\Omega$. Hence

$$\mathbf{I}_c = 18\,\underline{/-47.77°} + \frac{(208/\sqrt{3})\,\underline{/90°}}{0.416} = 275.62\,\underline{/87.6°} \text{ A}$$

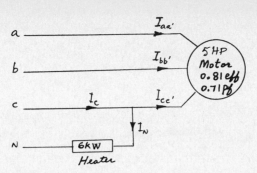

Fig. 14-41

14.120 Draw a phasor diagram showing all the currents and voltages of the circuit of Prob. 14.119.

▮ To draw the phasor diagram we must know $I_a = I_{aa'}$ and $I_b = I_{bb'}$. These are obtained from the results of Prob. 14.119. Hence $I_a = I_{aa'} = 18 \underline{/-77.77°}$ A and $I_b = I_{bb'} = 18 \underline{/-197.77°}$ A, and the phasor diagram becomes as shown in Fig. 14-42.

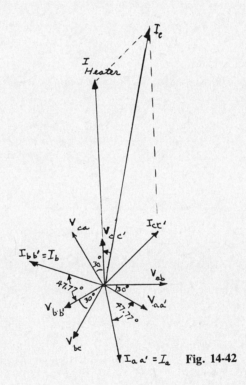

Fig. 14-42

14.121 A 450-V three-phase three-wire 60-Hz feeder supplies power to a 25-hp induction motor and a 30-hp induction motor. The 25-hp motor is operating at full load, is 87 percent efficient, and has a power factor of 90 percent. The 30-hp motor is operating at one-half of its rated horsepower; at this load, it is 88 percent efficient and has a power factor of 74 percent. Sketch a one-line diagram for the system and determine the feeder active power.

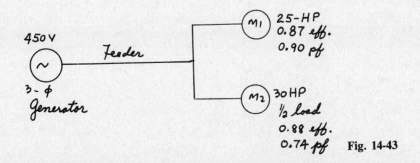

Fig. 14-43

❚ The one-line diagram is shown in Fig. 14-43. For the two motors we have:

$$P_{M1} = \frac{25 \times 746}{0.87} = 21{,}436.78 \text{ W} \qquad P_{M2} = \frac{\frac{1}{2}(30)(746)}{0.88} = 12{,}715.91 \text{ W} \qquad P = P_{M1} + P_{M2} = 34{,}152.69 \text{ W}$$

14.122 Calculate the total reactive power supplied by the feeder of Prob. 14.121.

❚ The power factor angles are:

$$\theta_1 = \cos^{-1}(0.9) = 25.84° \qquad \theta_2 = \cos^{-1}(0.74) = 42.27°$$
$$Q_{M1} = P_1 \tan \theta_1 = (21{,}436.78) \tan 25.84° = 10{,}381.41 \text{ var}$$
$$Q_{M2} = P_2 \tan \theta_2 = (12{,}715.91) \tan 42.27° = 11{,}558.42 \text{ var}$$
$$Q = Q_{M1} + Q_{M2} = 10{,}381.41 + 11{,}558.42 = 21{,}939.83 \text{ var}$$

14.123 What is the overall power factor of the system of motors of Prob. 14.122?

❚ From Prob. 14.121, $P = 34{,}152.69 \text{ W}$. From Prob. 14.21,

$$Q = 21{,}939.83 \text{ var} \qquad \tan \theta = \frac{Q}{P} = \frac{21{,}939.83}{34{,}152.69} = 0.642 \qquad \text{or} \qquad \theta = 31.72°$$

and the power factor is $\cos \theta = \cos 32.72° = 0.84$ lagging.

14.124 Calculate the line current through any of the feeders of Prob. 14.121.

❚ Apparent power,

$$\mathbf{S} = P + jQ = 34{,}152.69 + j21{,}939.83 = 40{,}592.64 \underline{/32.72°} \text{ VA} \quad \text{or} \quad S = \sqrt{3}V_l I_l = 40{,}592.64$$

Hence, $I_l = 40{,}592.64 / \sqrt{3}(450) = 52.08 \text{ A}$.

14.125 A 440-V three-phase source supplies a 10-kVA 0.8-pf-lagging load, which is connected in wye, and a delta-connected 10-kVA unity power factor load. Calculate the total apparent power input to the two loads.

❚
$$P = P_Y + P_\Delta = (10)(0.8) + (10)(1) = 18 \text{ kW} \qquad Q = Q_Y + Q_\Delta = (10)(0.6) + 0 = 6 \text{ kvar}$$
$$\mathbf{S} = P + jQ = 18 + j6 = 18.97 \underline{/18.43°} \text{ kVA}$$

14.126 What is the overall power factor of the two leads of Prob. 14.125? Verify that the same result is obtained from true power calculations.

❚
$$\cos \theta = \cos 18.43° = 0.95 \qquad I_l = \frac{S}{\sqrt{3}V_l} = \frac{18.97 \times 10^3}{\sqrt{3}(440)} = 24.89 \text{ A}$$
$$P = \sqrt{3}V_l I_l \cos \theta \qquad \text{or} \qquad \cos \theta = \frac{18{,}000}{\sqrt{3}(440)(24.89)} = 0.949 \approx 0.95$$

14.127 Calculate the line currents to each of the loads of Prob. 14.125.

❚
$$S_Y = \sqrt{3}V_l I_Y \quad \text{or} \quad I_Y = \frac{10{,}000}{\sqrt{3}(440)} = 13.12 \text{ A} \qquad S_\Delta = \sqrt{3}V_l I_\Delta \quad \text{or} \quad I_\Delta = \frac{10{,}000}{\sqrt{3}(440)} = 13.12 \text{ A}$$

14.128 A three-phase three-wire 500-V 60-Hz source supplies a three-phase induction motor, a wye-connected capacitor bank that draws 2 kvar per phase, and a balanced three-phase heater that draws a total of 10 kW. The induction motor is operating at its rated 75-hp load and has an efficiency and power factor of 90.5 and 89.5 percent, respectively. Sketch a one-line diagram of the system and determine (*a*) the system kW; (*b*) the system kvars; (*c*) the system kVA.

❚ A one-line diagram is shown in Fig. 14-44. From the data given:

(*a*) $\quad P_M = \dfrac{75 \times 746}{0.905} = 61.82 \text{ kW} \qquad P_C = 0 \qquad P_H = 10 \text{ kW}$

or $\quad P = P_M + P_c + P_H = 71.82 \text{ kW} \qquad \theta_M = \cos^{-1} 0.895 = 26.49°$

(b) $Q_M = P_M \tan \theta_M = (61.82) \tan 26.49° = 30.81$ kvar (lagging)

$Q_c = -(2 + 2 + 2) = -6$ kvar (leading) $Q_H = 0$

Thus, $Q = Q_M + Q_C + Q_H = 30.81 - 6.0 = 24.81$ var.

(c) Finally, $S = P + jQ = 71.82 + j24.81 = 75.98 \underline{/19.06°}$ kVA

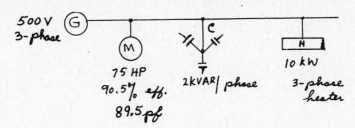

Fig. 14-44

14.129 What is (a) the line current and (b) the overall power factor of the system of load of Prob. 14.128?

▮ (a) $S = \sqrt{3}V_l I_l = 75,980$ or $I_l = \dfrac{75,980}{\sqrt{3}(500)} = 87.73$ A

(b) Power factor $= \cos \theta = \cos 19.06° = 0.95$ lagging.

14.130 Determine the line currents drawn by each load of the system of Prob. 14.128.

▮ $P_M = \sqrt{3}V_l I_M \cos \theta_M$. Thus,

$$I_M = \frac{61,820}{\sqrt{3}(500)(0.895)} = 79.76 \text{ A} \qquad S_C = \sqrt{3}V_l I_C$$

or $I_C = \dfrac{6000}{\sqrt{3}(500)} = 6.93$ A $P_H = \sqrt{3}V_l I_H(1)$ or $I_H = \dfrac{10,000}{\sqrt{3}(500)} = 11.55$ A

14.131 A balanced delta-connected load whose impedance is $45 \underline{/70°}$ Ω per branch, a three-phase motor that draws a total of 10 kVA at 0.65 pf lagging, and a wye-connected load whose impedance is 10 Ω (resistance) per branch are supplied from a three-phase three-wire 208-V 60-Hz source. Sketch the circuit and determine the line current to each three-phase load.

▮ The circuit is drawn in Fig. 14-45. For the Y load,

$$\mathbf{I}_{aY} = \frac{120 \underline{/-30°}}{10 \underline{/0°}} = 12 \underline{/-30°} \text{ A}$$

For the Δ load,

$$\mathbf{I}_{a\Delta} = \frac{\mathbf{V}_{ab}}{45 \underline{/70°}} + \frac{\mathbf{V}_{ac}}{45 \underline{/70°}} = \frac{208 \underline{/0°}}{45 \underline{/70°}} + \frac{-208 \underline{/120°}}{45 \underline{/70°}} = 8 \underline{/-100°} \text{ A}$$

For the motor,

$$S_M = \sqrt{3}V_l I_{aM} \qquad 10,000 = \sqrt{3}(208)I_{aM} \qquad \text{or} \qquad I_{aM} = 27.76 \text{ A}$$

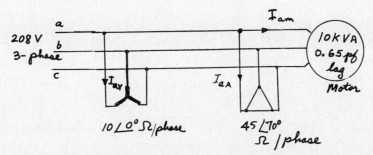

Fig. 14-45

14.132 Determine the active and reactive powers taken by each load of the circuit of Prob. 14.131.

▮ For the Y load,

$$P_Y = \sqrt{3}V_l I_l \cos\theta_{pY} = \sqrt{3}(208)(12)\cos 0° = 4320 \text{ W} \qquad Q_Y = \sqrt{3}V_l I_l \sin\theta_{pY} = 0$$

For the Δ load,

$$P_\Delta = \sqrt{3}V_l I_l \cos\theta_{p\Delta} = \sqrt{3}(208)(8)\cos 70° = 986 \text{ W} \qquad Q_\Delta = \sqrt{3}(208)(8)\sin 70° = 2709 \text{ var}$$

For the motor,

$$P_M = S_M \cos\theta_M = (10{,}000)(0.65) = 6500 \text{ W}$$

Now, $\cos\theta_M = 0.65$. Thus,

$$\theta_M = \cos^{-1} 0.65 = 49.46° \qquad Q_M = P_M \tan\theta_M = 6500 \tan 49.46° = 7600 \text{ var}$$

14.133 What is the overall power factor of the system of Prob. 14.131?

$$\mathbf{S} = P + jQ = (4320 + 986 + 6500) + j(0 + 2709 + 7600) = 11{,}806 + j10{,}309$$

$$\tan\theta = 0.873 \qquad \theta = 41.13° \qquad \text{Power factor} = \cos\theta = 0.753 \text{ lagging}$$

14.134 For the circuit shown in Fig. 14-46, determine the currents $\mathbf{I}_a$ and $\mathbf{I}_c$. Given: $\mathbf{Z}_1 = 20\,\underline{/0°}\,\Omega$, $\mathbf{Z}_2 = 14\,\underline{/45°}\,\Omega$, and $\mathbf{Z}_3 = 14\,\underline{/-45°}\,\Omega$, and a 208-V three-phase applied voltage.

▮
$$\mathbf{I}_a = \frac{\mathbf{V}_{ab}}{\mathbf{Z}_1} + \frac{\mathbf{V}_{ac}}{\mathbf{Z}_2} = \frac{208\,\underline{/0°}}{20\,\underline{/0°}} + \frac{-208\,\underline{/120°}}{14\,\underline{/45°}} = 15.78\,\underline{/-65.46°}\text{ A}$$

$$\mathbf{I}_c = \frac{\mathbf{V}_{ca}}{\mathbf{Z}_2} + \frac{\mathbf{V}_{cb}}{\mathbf{Z}_3} = \frac{208\,\underline{/120°}}{14\,\underline{/45°}} + \frac{-208\,\underline{/-120°}}{14\,\underline{/-45°}} = 28.70\,\underline{/90°}\text{ A}$$

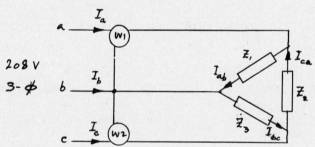

Fig. 14-46

14.135 Find the wattmeter readings in the circuit of Fig. 14-46.

$$W1 = V_{ab} I_a \cos\measuredangle{\overset{\mathbf{V}_{ab}}{\underset{\mathbf{I}_a}{}}} = (208)(15.78)\cos 65.46° = 1363.21 \text{ W}$$

$$W2 = V_{cb} I_c \cos\measuredangle{\overset{\mathbf{V}_{cb}}{\underset{\mathbf{I}_c}{}}} = (208)(28.7)\cos(-30°) = 5169.83 \text{ W}$$

14.136 Calculate $\mathbf{I}_b$ in the circuit of Fig. 14-46. Determine the phasor sum of the three currents in the three phases. Explain the significance of your result.

▮
$$\mathbf{I}_b = \frac{\mathbf{V}_{ba}}{\mathbf{Z}_1} + \frac{\mathbf{V}_{bc}}{\mathbf{Z}_3} = \frac{-208\,\underline{/0°}}{20\,\underline{/0°}} + \frac{208\,\underline{/-120°}}{14\,\underline{/-45°}} = 15.78\,\underline{/-114.54°}\text{ A}$$

$$\mathbf{I}_{ab} = \frac{\mathbf{V}_{ab}}{\mathbf{Z}_1} = \frac{208\,\underline{/0°}}{20\,\underline{/0°}} = 10.4\,\underline{/0°}\text{ A} \qquad \mathbf{I}_{bc} = \frac{\mathbf{V}_{bc}}{\mathbf{Z}_3} = \frac{208\,\underline{/-120°}}{14\,\underline{/-45°}} = 14.86\,\underline{/-75°}\text{ A}$$

$$\mathbf{I}_{ca} = \frac{\mathbf{V}_{ca}}{\mathbf{Z}_2} = \frac{208\,\underline{/120°}}{14\,\underline{/45°}} = 14.86\,\underline{/75°}\text{ A}$$

$$\mathbf{I}_0 = \mathbf{I}_{ab} + \mathbf{I}_{bc} + \mathbf{I}_{ca} = 10.4\,\underline{/0°} + 14.86\,\underline{/-75°} + 14.86\,\underline{/75°} = 18.09 + j0 \text{ A} = 18.09\,\underline{/0°}\text{ A} \neq 0$$

The current $\mathbf{I}_0$ is a circulating current in the closed delta.

14.137 Verify that the sum of the line currents in a delta-connected load is always zero.

    ▮ Referring to Fig. 14-46, we have

$$\mathbf{I}_a = \mathbf{I}_{bc} - \mathbf{I}_{ab} \qquad \mathbf{I}_b = \mathbf{I}_{ab} - \mathbf{I}_{ca} \qquad \mathbf{I}_c = \mathbf{I}_{ca} - \mathbf{I}_{bc}$$

or $\mathbf{I}_a + \mathbf{I}_b + \mathbf{I}_c = 0$ (verified).

14.138 Use the result of Prob. 14.137 to find $\mathbf{I}_b$ and verify that the result is consistent with that obtained in Prob. 14.136.

    ▮ From Prob. 14.137,

$$\mathbf{I}_b = -\mathbf{I}_a - \mathbf{I}_c = -15.78 \,\underline{/-65.46°} - 28.7 \,\underline{/90°} \quad \text{(from Prob. 14.134)}$$
$$= -6.55 + j14.35 - j28.7 = -6.55 - j14.35 = 15.77 \,\underline{/-115.6° \text{ A}}$$

which is close to the result of Prob. 14.136.

14.139 Draw a phasor diagram showing the voltages and currents which affect the readings of the wattmeters $W1$ and $W2$ in the circuit of Fig. 14-46.

    ▮ See Fig. 14-47.

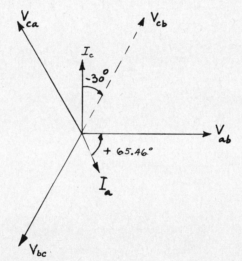

Fig. 14-47

14.140 The two-wattmeter method is used to measure the power drawn by a balanced delta-connected load. Each branch of the load draws 2.5 kW at a power factor of 0.80 lagging. The supply voltage is 120 V, three phase, 25 Hz. Sketch the circuit showing wattmeters in lines a and c, and determine the respective wattmeter readings.

    ▮ The circuit is similar to that shown in Fig. 14-46, except that in the present problem the load is balanced. For the load we have a rating of 2.5 kW/phase with 0.8 pf lagging. Thus, $\theta = \cos^{-1} 0.8 = 36.87°$. Three-phase power $= 3(2.5) = 7.5 \text{ kW} = \sqrt{3} V_l I_l \cos \theta$. Thus, $I_l = 7500/\sqrt{3}(120)(0.8) = 45.11 \text{ A}$ and

$$W1 = V_l I_l \cos (\theta + 30°) = (120)(45.11) \cos (36.87° + 30°) = 2126 \text{ W}$$
$$W2 = V_l I_l \cos (\theta - 30°) = (120)(45.11) \cos (36.87 - 30°) = 5734 \text{ W}$$

14.141 Three parallel-connected three-phase loads are supplied by a three-phase 240-V 60-Hz source. The loads are three-phase, 10 kVA, 0.80 power factor lagging; three-phase, 10 kVA, unity power factor; three-phase, 10 kVA, 0.80 power factor leading. Sketch the circuit showing wattmeters in lines a and c, and determine **(a)** the system active power; **(b)** the system reactive power; **(c)** the system apparent power.

    ▮ The system is represented by the circuit of Fig. 14-48 where the loads are:
    Load A—10 kVA, 0.8 pf lagging; load B—10 kVA, unity pf; load C—10 kVA, 0.8 pf leading.

(a) $P = P_A + P_B + P_C = 10(0.8) + 10 + 10(0.8) = 26 \text{ kW}$
(b) $Q = Q_A + Q_B + Q_C = 8 \tan 36.87 + 0 - 8 \tan 36.87 = 0 \text{ kvar}$
(c) $S = P + jQ = 26 + j0 = 26 \text{ kVA}$

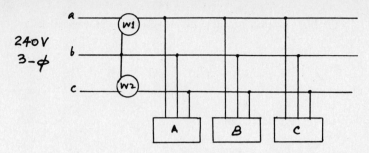

Fig. 14-48

14.142 Determine the overall power factor of the loads of Prob. 14-141 and calculate the line current.

$$\text{Power factor} = \frac{P}{S} = \frac{26}{26} = 1 \qquad I_l = \frac{S}{\sqrt{3}V_l} = \frac{26{,}000}{\sqrt{3}(240)} = 62.55 \text{ A}$$

14.143 What are the readings of the wattmeters of Prob. 14.141?

Since $\cos\theta = 1$ and $\theta = 0°$,

$$W1 = V_l I_l \cos(\theta + 30°) = 240(62.55)\cos 30° = 13{,}000 \text{ W}$$

$$W2 = V_l I_l \cos(\theta - 30°) = 240(62.55)\cos(-30°) = 13{,}000 \text{ W}$$

14.144 A 100-kVA balanced three-phase load operates at 0.65 pf lagging at 450 V. Determine the active and reactive powers of the load.

$$S\cos\theta = P \qquad \text{or} \qquad P = 100(0.65) = 65 \text{ kW}$$

$$\theta = \cos^{-1} 0.65 = 49.46° \qquad Q = S(\sin\theta) = 100(\sin 49.46°) = 75.99 \text{ kvar}$$

14.145 If the load of Prob. 14.144 is connected in delta, what is the phase impedance?

$$I_l = \frac{S}{\sqrt{3}V_l} = \frac{100{,}000}{\sqrt{3}(450)} = 128.3 \text{ A} \qquad \mathbf{I}_p = \frac{128.3}{\sqrt{3}} = 74.08 \,\underline{/-49.46°}\, \text{A}$$

$$\mathbf{Z}_p = \frac{450 \,\underline{/0°}}{74.08 \,\underline{/-49.46°}} = 6.07 \,\underline{/49.46°}\, \Omega$$

14.146 Determine the power dissipated in the resistive components of the load of Prob. 14.144. Hence determine the total power and verify the result of Prob. 14.144.

$$R_p = \mathbf{Z}_p \cos\theta = 6.07\cos 49.46° = 3.95 \,\Omega \qquad P_p = (I_p)^2 R_p = (74.08)^2(3.95) = 21.676 \text{ kW}$$

$$P = 3P_p = 3(21.676) = 65 \text{ kW}$$

14.147 Repeat Prob. 14.146 for reactive power.

$$X_p = \mathbf{Z}_p \sin\theta = 6.07\sin 49.46° = 4.61 \,\Omega \qquad Q_p = (I_p)^2 X_p = (74.08)^2(4.61) = 25.31 \text{ kvar}$$

$$Q = 3Q_p = 3(25.31) = 75.93 \text{ kvar}$$

14.148 If power is measured by two wattmeters in the circuit of Prob. 14.144, determine the wattmeter readings.

$$W1 = V_l I_l \cos(\theta + 30°) = 450(128.3)\cos(49.46° + 30°) = 10{,}561 \text{ W}$$

$$W2 = V_l I_l \cos(\theta - 30°) = 450(128.3)\cos(49.46 - 30°) = 54{,}437 \text{ W}$$

14.149 What equivalent load connected in wye will produce results identical to those of Probs. 14-144 through 14-148?

By wye-delta transformation,

$$\text{Per phase} \quad \mathbf{Z}_Y = \tfrac{1}{3}\mathbf{Z}_\Delta = \tfrac{1}{3}(6.07\,\underline{/49.46°}) = 2.023\,\underline{/49.46°}\,\Omega$$

14.150 Determine the kVA rating of a bank of delta-connected capacitors required to improve the power factor of the system of Prob. 14.144 to 0.9 lagging.

    ❚   Since $\cos \theta_f = 0.9$, $\theta_f = \cos^{-1} 0.9 = 25.84°$,
Reactive kVA of the load and capacitor, $Q_f = P \tan \theta_f = 65 \tan 25.84° = 31.48$ kvar.
Reactive kVA of the load without capacitor, $Q_i = P \tan \theta_i = 75.99$ kvar, from Prob. 14.144.
Reactive kVA of capacitor bank, $Q_c = Q_i - Q_f = 75.99 - 31.48 = 44.51$ kvar, which is also the kVA rating since the capacitors are considered lossless.

14.151 If the system of Prob. 14.150 operates at 60 Hz, determine the capacitance of each capacitor in the bank.

$$\text{kvar/capacitor} = \frac{44.51}{3} = 14.84 \text{ kvar} = \frac{V_C^2}{X_C} = \frac{(450)^2}{X_C}$$

Thus,
$$X_C = \frac{(450)^2}{14{,}840} = 13.65 \ \Omega = \frac{1}{2\pi f C} = \frac{1}{2\pi (60) C}$$

Hence, $C = 1/2\pi(60)(13.65) = 194.32 \ \mu\text{F}$.

14.152 A 240-V 25-Hz three-phase system supplies a 100-kW 0.6-pf-lagging balanced load. Determine the capacitance in each phase of a wye-connected capacitor bank to adjust the power factor to 0.95 lagging.

    ❚   Initial power factor angle $\theta_i = \cos^{-1} 0.6 = 53.13°$ Final power factor angle $\theta_f = \cos^{-1} 0.95 = 18.19°$

       Initial reactive kVA $= 100 \tan 53.13° = 133.33$ kvar   Final reactive kVA $= 100 \tan 18.19° = 32.86$ kvar

$$\text{kvar of capacitor band} = 133.33 - 32.86 = 100.47 \text{ kvar} = \frac{3(V_C)^2}{X_C} = \frac{3(240/\sqrt{3})^2}{X_C}$$

Thus, $X_C = \dfrac{1}{2\pi f C} = 0.57 \ \Omega$ or $\dfrac{1}{2\pi(25)C} = 0.57$ and $C = 11.12 \text{ mF/phase}$

14.153 Repeat Prob. 14.152 for a delta-connected capacity bank.

    ❚   Proceeding as in Prob. 14.152, we have:

$$\frac{100{,}470}{3} = \frac{(240)^2}{X_C} \quad \text{or} \quad X_C = 1.72 = \frac{1}{2\pi(25)C}$$

Hence, $C = 3.70 \text{ mF}$.

14.154 For the instrumentation shown in Fig. 14-49 we have the following readings: $W1 = 2000$ W, $A1 = 18$ A, and $V1 = 440$ V; $W2 = 8000$ W, $A2 = 18$ A, and $V2 = 440$ V. Find the power factor of the system.

    ❚ $S = \sqrt{3} V_l I_l = \sqrt{3}(440)(18) = 13717.4 \text{ VA}$ $P = W1 + W2 = 2000 + 8000 = 10{,}000 \text{ W}$

$$\text{Power factor} = \frac{P}{S} = \frac{10{,}000}{13717.4} = 0.729$$

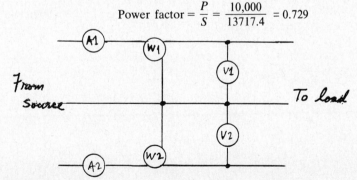

Fig. 14-49

14.155 Determine the kVA rating of a delta-connected capacity bank needed to improve the power factor of the system of Prob. 14.154 to 0.8 lagging.

    ❚ $\theta_i = \cos^{-1} 0.729 = 43.2°$ $Q_i = P_i \tan \theta_i = 10{,}000 \tan 43.2° = 9390.6 \text{ var}$

       $\cos \theta_f = 0.8$ or $\theta_f = \cos^{-1} 0.8 = 36.87°$ $Q_f = 10{,}000 \tan 36.87° = 7500 \text{ var}$

$$Q_{\text{capacitor}} = Q_i - Q_f = 9390.6 - 7500 = 1890.6 \text{ var} = 1.89 \text{ kvar}$$

which is also the kVA rating.

14.156 Repeat Prob. 14.155 to determine the capacitance of a wye-connected bank to adjust the power factor to 0.8 lagging. The system operates at 60 Hz.

▌ From Prob. 14.155,

$$Q_c = 1890.6 \text{ var} \quad \text{or} \quad \text{Per phase} \quad Q_C = \tfrac{1}{3}(1890.6) = \frac{(V_C)^2}{X_C} \quad \text{or} \quad 630.2 = \frac{(440/\sqrt{3})^2}{X_C}$$

Thus, $\qquad X_c = 102.4 \ \Omega = \dfrac{1}{2\pi(60)C} \quad \text{and} \quad C = 25.90 \ \mu\text{F}$

14.157 A three-phase 230-V 100-kVA load operates at 0.8 lagging power factor. The power factor is to be improved to 0.8 leading by a capacitor bank. However, the capacitors are lossy and take 50-kW power when connected to a 230-V three-phase source. Determine the kVA rating of the capacitor bank.

▌ $\qquad$ Initial kvar = 100(0.6) = 60 kvar $\qquad$ Final kvar = 100(−0.6) = −60 kvar

$$\text{kvar of capacitor bank} = 60 - (-60) = 120 \text{ kvar}$$

$$\text{kVA rating of the capacitor bank} = \sqrt{P^2 + Q^2} = \sqrt{(50)^2 + (120)^2} = 130 \text{ kVA}$$

14.158 Calculate the three line currents in the circuit of Fig. 14-50.

▌
$$\mathbf{I}_a = \frac{\mathbf{V}_{ab}}{\mathbf{Z}_1} + \frac{\mathbf{V}_{ac}}{\mathbf{Z}_3} = \frac{2400 \ \underline{/0^\circ}}{100 \ \underline{/20^\circ}} + \frac{-2400 \ \underline{/120^\circ}}{80 \ \underline{/30^\circ}} = 44.37 \ \underline{/-59.45^\circ} \text{ A}$$

$$\mathbf{I}_b = \frac{\mathbf{V}_{ba}}{\mathbf{Z}_1} + \frac{\mathbf{V}_{bc}}{\mathbf{Z}_2} = \frac{-2400 \ \underline{/0^\circ}}{100 \ \underline{/20^\circ}} + \frac{2400 \ \underline{/-120^\circ}}{80 \ \underline{/30^\circ}} = 49.01 \ \underline{/-172.03^\circ} \text{ A}$$

$$\mathbf{I}_c = \frac{\mathbf{V}_{ca}}{\mathbf{Z}_3} + \frac{\mathbf{V}_{cb}}{\mathbf{Z}_2} = \frac{2400 \ \underline{/120^\circ}}{80 \ \underline{/30^\circ}} + \frac{-2400 \ \underline{/-120^\circ}}{80 \ \underline{/30^\circ}} = 51.96 \ \underline{/60^\circ} \text{ A}$$

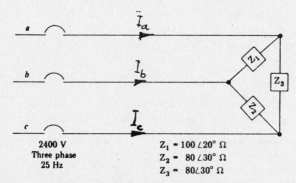

$$\begin{aligned}
&\text{2400 V} && Z_1 = 100 \ \underline{/20^\circ} \ \Omega \\
&\text{Three phase} && Z_2 = 80 \ \underline{/30^\circ} \ \Omega \\
&\text{25 Hz} && Z_3 = 80 \ \underline{/30^\circ} \ \Omega
\end{aligned}$$

Fig. 14-50

14.159 Determine the total active power drawn by the load of Prob. 14.158.

▌ Using the two-wattmeter method,

$$P = V_{ab}I_a \cos \overset{\mathbf{V}_{ab}}{\underset{\mathbf{I}_a}{\Big\langle}} + V_{cb}I_c \cos \overset{\mathbf{V}_{cb}}{\underset{\mathbf{I}_c}{\Big\langle}} = 2400(44.37) \cos 59.45^\circ + 2400(51.96) \cos 0^\circ = 178.3 \text{ kW}$$

(From Prob. 14.158 it follows that $\mathbf{V}_{cb}$ and $\mathbf{I}_c$ are in the same phase.)

14.160 What is the total reactive power taken by the load of Prob. 14.158?

▌ $\qquad\qquad\qquad Q = 2400(44.37) \sin 59.45^\circ + 0 = 91.7 \text{ kvar}$

14.161 Find the overall power factor of the load of the circuit shown in Fig. 14-50.

▌ From Prob. 14.159, $P = 178.3$ kW; from Prob. 14.160, $Q = 91.7$ kvar.

$$\tan \theta = \frac{Q}{P} = \frac{91.7}{178.3} = 0.5143 \quad \text{or} \quad \theta = \tan^{-1}(0.5143) = 27.22^\circ \quad \text{and} \quad \cos \theta = 0.889$$

14.162 How much apparent power is supplied to the load of the circuit of Fig. 14-50? Verify the result of Prob. 14.161 from apparent power calculation.

$$S = \sqrt{P^2 + Q^2} = \sqrt{(178.3)^2 + (91.7)^2} = 200.5 \text{ kVA} \qquad \cos\theta = \frac{P}{S} = \frac{178.3}{200.5} = 0.889$$

14.163 Determine the active power, reactive power, and the power factor of each load of the circuit shown in Fig. 14-51.

$$\mathbf{I}_1 = \frac{\mathbf{V}_{aN}}{\mathbf{Z}_1} = \frac{(600/\sqrt{3})\;\underline{/-30^\circ}}{50\;\underline{/10^\circ}} = 6.93\;\underline{/-40^\circ}\text{ A} \qquad \mathbf{I}_2 = \frac{\mathbf{V}_{bN}}{\mathbf{Z}_2} = \frac{(600/\sqrt{3})\;\underline{/-150^\circ}}{40\;\underline{/5^\circ}} = 8.66\;\underline{/-155^\circ}\text{ A}$$

$$\mathbf{I}_3 = \frac{\mathbf{V}_{cN}}{\mathbf{Z}_3} = \frac{(600/\sqrt{3})\;\underline{/90^\circ}}{15\;\underline{/-30^\circ}} = 23.09\;\underline{/120^\circ}\text{ A}$$

$$\mathbf{S}_1 = \mathbf{V}_{aN}\mathbf{I}_1^* = (346.41\;\underline{/-30^\circ})(6.93\;\underline{/40^\circ}) = 2400.62\;\underline{/10^\circ} = 2364.15 + j416.86\text{ VA}$$

$$\mathbf{S}_2 = \mathbf{V}_{bN}\mathbf{I}_2^* = (346.41\;\underline{/-150^\circ})(8.66\;\underline{/155^\circ}) = 2999.91\;\underline{/5^\circ} = 2988.49 + j261.46\text{ VA}$$

$$\mathbf{S}_3 = \mathbf{V}_{cN}\mathbf{I}_3^* = (346.41\;\underline{/90^\circ})(23.09\;\underline{/-120^\circ}) = 7998.61\;\underline{/-30^\circ} = 6927 - j3999.30\text{ VA}$$

$$P_1 = 2364.15\text{ W} \qquad Q_1 = 416.86\text{ var} \qquad \cos\theta_1 = \cos 10^\circ = 0.980$$

$$P_2 = 2988.49\text{ W} \qquad Q_2 = 261.46\text{ var} \qquad \cos\theta_2 = \cos 5^\circ = 0.996$$

$$P_3 = 6927\text{ W} \qquad Q_3 = -3999.30\text{ var} \qquad \cos\theta_3 = \cos 30^\circ = 0.866$$

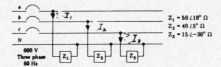

Fig. 14-51

14.164 Obtain the system's active and reactive powers for the circuit of Fig. 14-51.

$$\mathbf{S} = \mathbf{S}_1 + \mathbf{S}_2 + \mathbf{S}_3 = 2400.62\;\underline{/10^\circ} + 2999.91\;\underline{/5^\circ} + 7998.61\;\underline{/-30^\circ} = 12{,}279.64 - j3320.98$$

$$P = 12.28\text{ kW} \qquad Q = -3.32\text{ kvar}$$

14.165 What is the overall power factor of the system of loads shown in Fig. 14-51?

From Prob. 14.164,

$$\tan\theta = \frac{Q}{P} = \frac{-3.32}{12.28} = -0.27 \qquad \text{or} \qquad \theta = -15.13^\circ \qquad \text{and} \qquad \cos\theta = 0.965$$

14.166 Determine the parameters of equivalent series-connected circuit elements to represent each impedance of the circuit of Fig. 14-51.

$$\mathbf{Z}_1 = R_1 + j\omega L_1 = 50\;\underline{/10^\circ} = 49.24 + j8.68\;\Omega$$

$$R_1 = 49.24\;\Omega \qquad \omega = 2\pi(60) = 377 \qquad L_1 = \frac{8.68}{377} = 23\text{ mH}$$

Similarly, $\mathbf{Z}_2 = 40\;\underline{/5^\circ} = 39.85 + j3.49\;\Omega$ yields $R_2 = 39.85\;\Omega \qquad L_2 = 9.25\text{ mH}$

and $\mathbf{Z}_3 = 15\;\underline{/-30^\circ} = 12.99 - j7.5\;\Omega$ gives $R_3 = 12.99\;\Omega \qquad C_3 = 353.67\;\mu\text{F}.$

14.167 Determine the parameters of equivalent parallel-connected circuit elements to represent the impedances of the circuit of Fig. 14-51.

$$\mathbf{Y}_1 = \frac{1}{\mathbf{Z}_1} = \frac{1}{50\;\underline{/10^\circ}} = 0.02\;\underline{/-10^\circ} = 0.0197 - j0.0035\text{ S}$$

$$R_1 = \frac{1}{0.0197} = 50.77\;\Omega \qquad jX_1 = \frac{1}{0.0035\;\underline{/-90^\circ}} = 287.94\;\underline{/90^\circ} = j2\pi(60)L_1$$

Thus, $L_1 = 0.764\text{ H}$. Similarly, for the other impedances we have

$$R_2 = 40.15\;\Omega \qquad L_2 = 1.22\text{ H} \qquad R_3 = 17.32\;\Omega \qquad \text{and} \qquad C_3 = 88.42\;\mu\text{F}$$

Notice that the components of the equivalent parallel circuit are relatively larger compared to the equivalent series circuit parameters obtained in Prob. 14.165.

14.168 For the circuit shown in Fig. 14-52a use a delta-to-wye transformation to obtain the impedance between the terminals 3 and 4.

❚ The steps are indicated in Fig. 14-52b and c, from which $\mathbf{Z}_{34} = 20 + j0 = 20\ \underline{/0°}\ \Omega$.

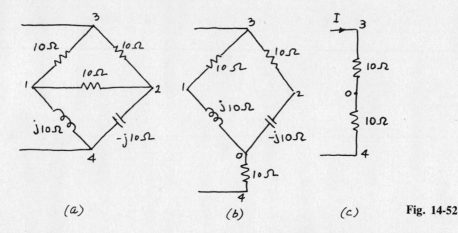

(a)   (b)   (c)   **Fig. 14-52**

14.169 If a $40\ \underline{/0°}$-V source is connected across the circuit of Fig. 14-52a, determine the voltage $\mathbf{V}_{31}$.

❚ From Fig. 14-52c,

$$\mathbf{I}_{34} = \frac{40\ \underline{/0°}}{20\ \underline{/0°}} = 2\ \underline{/0°}\ \text{A} \qquad \mathbf{V}_{34} = 10\mathbf{I}_{34} = 20\ \underline{/0°}\ \text{V}$$

$$\mathbf{I}_{31} = \frac{\mathbf{V}_{34}}{10 + j10} = \frac{20\ \underline{/0°}}{10 + j10} = \sqrt{2}\ \underline{/-45°}\ \text{A} \qquad \mathbf{V}_{31} = 10\mathbf{I}_{31} = 14.14\ \underline{/-45°}\ \text{V}$$

14.170 Obtain an expression for the reactive power in a three-phase system in terms of two wattmeter readings if power in the system is measured by two wattmeters (which read $W1$ and $W2$).

❚ From Prob. 14.107,

$$W1 = V_l I_l \cos{(\theta + 30°)} \qquad W2 = V_l I_l \cos{(\theta - 30°)}$$

or $\qquad\qquad W1 - W2 = V_l I_l [\cos{(\theta + 30°)} - \cos{(\theta - 30°)}] = V_l I_l \sin{\theta}$

But $\quad Q = \sqrt{3}V_l I_l \sin{\theta}$. Hence, the total reactive power is given by $\quad Q = \sqrt{3}(W1 - W2)$ var.

14.171 The current coil of a wattmeter is connected in phase a and the voltage coil is connected between phases b and c of a wye-connected three-phase load, as shown in Fig. 14-53a. Draw a phasor diagram showing the wattmeter current and voltage with respect to the phase voltages.

❚ The wattmeter current is $\mathbf{I}_a$ and the voltage is $\mathbf{V}_{bc}$, as shown in the phasor diagram of Fig. 14-53b.

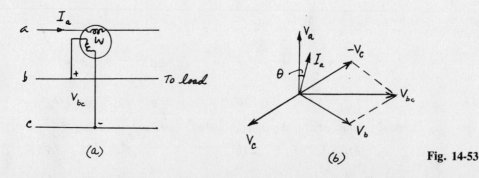

(a)   (b)   **Fig. 14-53**

14.172 From Fig. 14-53a and b show that the single wattmeter may be used to measure reactive power in a balanced three-phase circuit.

▮ From Fig. 14-53a the wattmeter reading is

$$W = V_{bc} I_a \cos \measuredangle$$

From Fig. 14-53b the angle between $\mathbf{V}_{bc}$ and $\mathbf{I}_a$ is $90° - \theta$. Hence

$$W = V_{bc} I_a \cos(90° - \theta) = V_l I_l \sin \theta \quad \text{or} \quad Q = \sqrt{3} V_l I_l \sin \theta = \sqrt{3} W$$

14.173 A three-phase load operates at 440 V, 0.6 pf lagging. Two wattmeters used to measure the input power read a total of 20 kW. Find the individual readings of the wattmeters.

▮ $$\cos \theta = 0.6 \quad \text{or} \quad \theta = 53.13°$$

$$\tan \theta = \frac{\sqrt{3}(W1 - W2)}{W1 + W2} = \tan 53.13° = 1.33 \quad \text{or} \quad W1 - W2 = \frac{1.33}{\sqrt{3}}(W1 + W2) = \frac{(1.33)(20)}{\sqrt{3}}$$

Thus, $W1 - W2 = 15.4$ and $W1 + W2 = 20$. Hence, $W1 = 17.7$ kW and $W2 = 2.3$ kW.

14.174 The total input power in a three-phase circuit, as measured by two wattmeters, is 50 W. At what power factor will the wattmeter readings be equal? Determine this reading.

▮ If the wattmeters readings are equal, then each reads $\frac{1}{2}50 = 25$ W. Also, $\tan \theta = 0$ or $\theta = 0$. Hence, the power factor is $\cos \theta = 1$.

14.175 At what power factor will one of the wattmeter readings be zero in a three-phase system.

▮ Let $W2 = 0$. Then

$$\tan \theta = \sqrt{3} \frac{W1 - 0}{W1 + 0} = \sqrt{3} \quad \text{or} \quad \theta = \tan^{-1} \sqrt{3} = 60° \quad \text{and} \quad \cos \theta = \cos 60° = 0.5$$

14.176 The input power to a three-phase load, measured by two wattmeters, is 100 kW, the wattmeter readings being equal. If the power factor of the load is changed to 0.866 leading and the load still draws 100 kW, determine the readings of the wattmeters.

▮ $$\cos \theta = 0.866 \quad \text{or} \quad \theta = 30° \quad \tan \theta = \frac{\sqrt{3}(W1 - W2)}{W1 + W2}$$

or $W1 - W2 = 33.33$ and $W1 + W2 = 100.00$. Hence, $W1 = 66.67$ kW and $W2 = 33.33$ kW.

14.177 The three phases of a delta-connected load consist of $10\,\underline{/45°}\,\Omega$ impedances. The load is connected across a 200-V three-phase source. How much power is consumed by the load?

▮ $$I_p = \frac{V_p}{Z_p} = \frac{200\,\underline{/0°}}{10\,\underline{/45°}} = 20\,\underline{/-45°} \quad P_p = (I_p)^2 R_p \quad Z_p = R_p + jX_p = 7.07 + j7.07$$

Hence, $P = 3P_p = 3(20)^2 7.07 = 8484$ W.

14.178 If power input to the load of Prob. 14.177 is measured by two wattmeters, find the reading of each wattmeter.

▮ From Prob. 14.177:

$$W1 + W2 = 8484 \quad \tan \theta = \tan 45° = 1 = \sqrt{3} \frac{W1 - W2}{W1 + W2} \quad \text{or} \quad W1 - W2 = 4898.38$$

Hence, $$W2 = 1792.8 \quad \text{and} \quad W1 = 6691.2 \text{ W}.$$

14.179 A three-phase wye-connected load is balanced and has a $(4 + j3)$-Ω impedance per phase. The load is connected to a 220-V three-phase source. If power input to the load is measured by two wattmeters, determine the wattmeter readings.

$$V_p = \frac{220}{\sqrt{3}} = 127 \text{ V} \qquad I_l = I_p = \frac{V_p}{Z_p} = \frac{127 \, \underline{/0°}}{4 + j3} = 25.4 \, \underline{/-36.87°} \qquad \cos \theta_p = \cos 36.87° = 0.8$$

$$P = \sqrt{3} V_l I_l \cos \theta_p = \sqrt{3}(220)25.4(0.8) = 7742.7 = W1 + W2$$

$$\tan \theta = 0.75 = \sqrt{3} \frac{W1 - W2}{W1 + W2} \qquad \text{or} \qquad W1 - W2 = 3352.8 \text{ W}$$

Thus, $W1 = 5547.75 \text{ W}$ and $W2 = 2194.95 \text{ W}$.

14.180   Repeat Prob. 14.179 if the impedances are connected in delta.

$$I_p = \frac{220}{5} = 44 \text{ A} \qquad I_l = \sqrt{3} I_p = \sqrt{3}(44) = 76.208 \text{ A}$$

$$P = \sqrt{3}(220)(76.208)(0.8) = 23,230.6 = W1 + W2$$

$$\tan \theta = 0.75 = \sqrt{3} \frac{W1 - W2}{W1 + W2} \qquad \text{or} \qquad 10,059.4 = W1 - W2$$

Hence $W1 = 16,645 \text{ W}$ and $W2 = 6585 \text{ W}$.

14.181   A three-phase balanced load is connected across a 220-V three-phase source.   A wattmeter reads 600 W when its current coil is connected in line a and its voltage coil across lines a and b.   Next, the voltage coil is connected between lines b and c, but the current coil remains in line a.   The wattmeter again reads 600 W.   Calculate the load power factor.

$$W1 = V_l I_l \cos(30° + \theta) \qquad W2 = V_{bc} I_a \cos \angle$$

As seen from Fig. 14-53b, the angle between V_{bc} and I_a is $90° - \theta$.   Since $W1 = W2$,   we finally have
$$V_l I_l \cos(30° + \theta) = V_l I_l \cos(90° - \theta) \qquad \text{or} \qquad 30° + \theta = 90° - \theta$$

Thus, $2\theta = 60°$ and $\theta = 30°$.   Hence, the power factor is $\cos \theta = \cos 30° = 0.866$.

14.182   Determine the line current in the load of Prob. 14.181.

$$P = W1 = 600 = (220)(I_l) \cos(30° + 30°). \qquad \text{Hence,} \quad I_l = 5.45 \text{ A}.$$

14.183   The ratio of the wattmeter readings in a three-phase inductive system is 2:1, when power is measured by the two-wattmeter method.   Determine the power factor of the load.

Let $W2 = x$ and $W1 = 2x$.   Then,

$$\tan \theta = \sqrt{3} \frac{W1 - W2}{W1 + W2} = \sqrt{3} \frac{2x - x}{2x + x} = \frac{1}{\sqrt{3}}$$

or $\theta = 30°$ and $\cos \theta = \cos 30° = 0.866$.

14.184   How much active and reactive powers are supplied by the source shown in the circuit of Fig. 14-54?

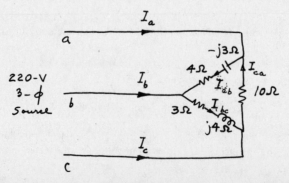

Fig. 14-54

I

$$\mathbf{I}_{ab} = \frac{\mathbf{V}_{ab}}{4 - j3} \qquad \text{or} \qquad I_{ab} = \frac{220}{5} = 44 \text{ A}$$

$$\mathbf{I}_{bc} = \frac{\mathbf{V}_{bc}}{3 + j4} \qquad \text{or} \qquad I_{bc} = \frac{220}{5} = 44 \text{ A}$$

$$\mathbf{I}_{ca} = \frac{\mathbf{V}_{ca}}{10} \qquad \text{or} \qquad I_{ca} = \frac{220}{10} = 22 \text{ A}$$

$$P = (I_{ab})^2 4 + (I_{bc})^2 3 + (I_{ca})^2 10 = (44)^2 4 + (44)^2 3 + (22)^2 10 = 18,392 \text{ W}$$

$$Q = (I_{ab})^2(-3) + (I_{bc})^2 4 + 0 = (44)^2(-3) + (44)^2 4 = 1936 \text{ var}$$

14.185 Determine the apparent power and the overall power factor of the load of Prob. 14.184.

I $\quad \mathbf{S} = P + jQ = 18,392 + j1936 = 18,494 \underline{/6.0^\circ}$. Power factor is $\cos 6.0^\circ = 0.995$.

14.186 Determine the line currents $\mathbf{I}_a$, $\mathbf{I}_b$, and $\mathbf{I}_c$ in the circuit of Fig. 14-54.

I $\quad \mathbf{I}_{ab} = \dfrac{220 \underline{/0^\circ}}{5 \underline{/-36.87^\circ}} = 44 \underline{/36.87^\circ} \text{ A} \qquad \mathbf{I}_{bc} = \dfrac{220 \underline{/-120^\circ}}{5 \underline{/53.13^\circ}} = 44 \underline{/-173.13^\circ} \text{ A} \qquad \mathbf{I}_{ca} = \dfrac{220 \underline{/120^\circ}}{10 \underline{/0^\circ}} = 22 \underline{/120^\circ}$

$$\mathbf{I}_a = \mathbf{I}_{ab} - \mathbf{I}_{ca} = 44 \underline{/36.87^\circ} - 22 \underline{/120^\circ} = 46.78 \underline{/9^\circ} \text{ A}$$

$$\mathbf{I}_b = \mathbf{I}_{bc} - \mathbf{I}_{ab} = 44 \underline{/-173.13^\circ} - 44 \underline{/36.87^\circ} = 85 \underline{/-158^\circ} \text{ A}$$

$$\mathbf{I}_c = \mathbf{I}_{ca} - \mathbf{I}_{bc} = 22 \underline{/120^\circ} - 44 \underline{/-173.13^\circ} = 40.73 \underline{/36.6^\circ} \text{ A}$$

14.187 In the circuit of Fig. 14-54, verify that the phasor sum of the line currents is zero.

I From Prob. 14.186,

$$\mathbf{I}_a = 46.78 \underline{/9^\circ} = 46.2 + j7.35 \text{ A} \qquad \mathbf{I}_b = 85 \underline{/-158^\circ} = -78.88 - j31.66 \text{ A}$$

$$\mathbf{I}_c = 40.73 \underline{/36.6^\circ} = 32.68 + j24.31 \text{ A} \qquad \sum = 0 + j0$$

14.188 Draw a phasor diagram showing the line currents and voltages pertaining to the circuit of Fig. 14-54.

I See Fig. 14-55.

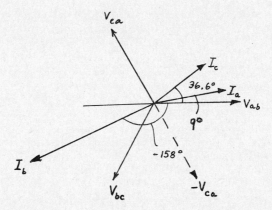

Fig. 14-55

14.189 The current coil of a wattmeter is connected in line a and the voltage coil across the lines a and c of the circuit of Fig. 14-54. Determine the wattmeter reading.

I
$$W = V_{ac} I_a \cos \theta$$

From Fig. 14-54 and Prob. 14.187 the angle between $\mathbf{V}_{ac}$ and $\mathbf{I}_a$ is $(60 + 9) = 69^\circ$. Hence, $W = (220)(46.78) \cos 69^\circ = 3688.18$ W.

14.190 Find the circulating current in the delta-connected load shown in Fig. 14-54.

I $\quad \mathbf{I}_{\text{circ}} = \mathbf{I}_{ab} + \mathbf{I}_{bc} + \mathbf{I}_{ca} = 44 \underline{/36.87^\circ} + 44 \underline{/-173.13^\circ} + 22 \underline{/120^\circ} = 44.66 \underline{/115.86^\circ} \text{ A}$

14.191 Replace the delta-connected load of Fig. 14-54 by an equivalent wye-connected load.

▌ The wye-connected load is shown in Fig. 14-56, for which we have

$$\mathbf{Z}_a = \frac{10(4-j3)}{10+4-j3+3+j4} = 2.936\,\underline{/-40.24°}\;\Omega \qquad \mathbf{Z}_b = \frac{(4-j3)(3+j4)}{10+4-j3+3+j4} = 1.468\,\underline{/12.9°}\;\Omega$$

$$\mathbf{Z}_c = \frac{10(3+j4)}{10+4-j3+3+j4} = 2.936\,\underline{/49.8°}\;\Omega$$

Whereas we have obtained an equivalent wye, it may be readily seen that by using this circuit it is more difficult to obtain the results of Probs. 14.184 through 14.189. The reason for this difficulty is that we do not know the voltages $\mathbf{V}_{an}$, $\mathbf{V}_{bn}$, and $\mathbf{V}_{cn}$.

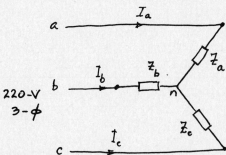

Fig. 14-56

14.192 The above-mentioned difficulty may be circumvented by using *Millman's theorem* which enables us to determine $\mathbf{V}_{an}$, $\mathbf{V}_{bn}$, etc. According to Millman's theorem, the voltage of the load neutral point n with respect to the neutral of the source n' is given by

$$\mathbf{V}_{nn'} = \frac{\mathbf{V}_{an'}\mathbf{Y}_a + \mathbf{V}_{bn'}\mathbf{Y}_b + \mathbf{V}_{cn'}\mathbf{Y}_c}{\mathbf{Y}_a + \mathbf{Y}_b + \mathbf{Y}_c} \qquad (1)$$

Apply Millman's theorem to obtain the voltages $\mathbf{V}_{an}$, $\mathbf{V}_{bn}$, and $\mathbf{V}_{cn}$ of the circuit of Fig. 14-56.

▌ From Prob. 14.191,

$$\mathbf{Y}_a = \frac{1}{2.936\,\underline{/-40.24°}} = = 0.34\,\underline{/40.24°} = 0.26 + j0.22\;\text{S}$$

$$\mathbf{Y}_b = \frac{1}{1.468\,\underline{/12.9°}} = 0.68\,\underline{/-12.9°} = 0.664 - j0.152\;\text{S}$$

$$\mathbf{Y}_c = \frac{1}{2.936\,\underline{/49.8°}} = 0.34\,\underline{/-49.8°} = 0.22 - j0.26\;\text{S}$$

$$\sum \mathbf{Y} = 1.144 - j0.192 = 1.16\,\underline{/-9.52°}\;\text{S}$$

Now, $\mathbf{V}_{an'} = 127\,\underline{/0°}$ V, $\mathbf{V}_{bn'} = 127\,\underline{/-120°}$ V, and $\mathbf{V}_{cn'} = 127\,\underline{/120°}$ V. Thus from Eq. (1) above,

$$\mathbf{V}_{nn'} = \frac{1}{1.16\,\underline{/-9.52°}}[(127\,\underline{/0°})(0.34\,\underline{/40.24°}) + (127\,\underline{/-120°})(0.68\,\underline{/-12.9°}) + (127\,\underline{/120°})(0.34\,\underline{/-49.8°})]$$

$$= 10.86\,\underline{/164.9°}\;\text{V}$$

$$\mathbf{V}_{an} = \mathbf{V}_{an'} - \mathbf{V}_{nn'} = 127\,\underline{/0°} - 10.86\,\underline{/164.9°} = 137.5\,\underline{/-1.18°}\;\text{V}$$

$$\mathbf{V}_{bn} = \mathbf{V}_{bn'} - \mathbf{V}_{nn'} = 127\,\underline{/-120°} - 10.86\,\underline{/164.9°} = 124.65\,\underline{/-115.17°}\;\text{V}$$

$$\mathbf{V}_{cn} = \mathbf{V}_{cn'} - \mathbf{V}_{nn'} = 127\,\underline{/120°} - 10.86\,\underline{/164.9°} = 119.55\,\underline{/116.32°}\;\text{V}$$

14.193 Repeat Prob. 14.186 for the circuit of Fig. 14-56.

▌

$$\mathbf{I}_a = \frac{\mathbf{V}_{an}}{\mathbf{Z}_a} = \frac{137.5\,\underline{/-1.18°}}{2.936\,\underline{/-40.24°}} = 46.8\,\underline{/39.06°}\;\text{A}$$

$$\mathbf{I}_b = \frac{\mathbf{V}_{bn}}{\mathbf{Z}_b} = \frac{124.65\,\underline{/-115.17°}}{1.468\,\underline{/12.9°}} = 84.9\,\underline{/-128.07°}\;\text{A}$$

$$\mathbf{I}_c = \frac{\mathbf{V}_{cn}}{\mathbf{Z}_c} = \frac{119.55\,\underline{/116.32°}}{2.936\,\underline{/49.8°}} = 40.72\,\underline{/66.52°}\;\text{A}$$

As expected, the results are in close agreement.

14.194 Repeat Prob. 14.184 for the circuit of Fig. 14-56.

$$\mathbf{Z}_a = 2.936 \underline{/-40.24°} = 2.24 - j1.89 \ \Omega \qquad \mathbf{Z}_b = 1.468 \underline{/12.9°} = 1.43 + j0.33 \ \Omega$$
$$\mathbf{Z}_c = 2.936 \underline{/49.8°} = 1.89 + j2.24 \ \Omega$$
$$P = (I_a)^2 2.24 + (I_b)^2 1.43 + (I_c)^2 1.89 = (46.8)^2(2.24) + (84.9)^2(1.43) + (40.72)^2(1.89) = 18{,}347 \ \text{W}$$
$$Q = (46.8)^2(-1.89) + (84.9)^2(0.33) + (40.72)^2(2.24) = 1953 \ \text{var}$$

Considering roundoff errors the results are in good agreement.

14.195 Repeat Prob. 14.185 for the circuit of Fig. 14-56.

$$\mathbf{S} = P + jQ = 18{,}347 + j1953 = 18{,}450 \underline{/6.11°} \qquad \cos 6.11° = 0.994$$

14.196 Draw a phasor diagram showing all the voltages and currents pertaining to the circuit of Fig. 14-56 and compare the result with the phasor diagram of Fig. 14-55.

See Fig. 14-57.

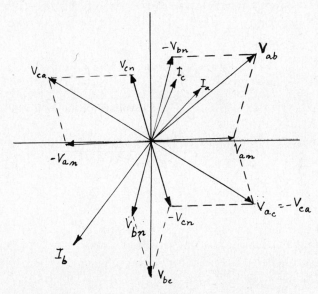

Fig. 14-57

14.197 Calculate the line current, in the wye-connected purely resistive circuit of Fig. 14-58a, if the line voltage is 220-V three-phase balanced.

Since a direct solution is cumbersome, we convert the wye-connected load to a delta-connected load shown in Fig. 14-58b, for which we have obtained the values of the results from

$$R_{ab} = \frac{R_a R_b + R_b R_c + R_c R_a}{R_c} = \frac{18 + 54 + 27}{9} = 11 \ \Omega, \ \text{etc.}$$

Now,
$$\mathbf{I}_a = \mathbf{I}_{ab} - \mathbf{I}_{ca} = \frac{\mathbf{V}_{ab}}{11} - \frac{\mathbf{V}_{ca}}{16.5} = \frac{220 \underline{/0°}}{11} - \frac{220 \underline{/120°}}{16.5} = 29.06 \underline{/-23.42°} \ \text{A}$$

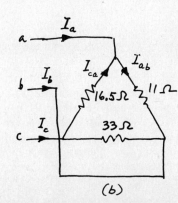

(a)   (b)   **Fig. 14-58**

14.198 Because of certain incorrect connections, such as incorrect polarities, a three-phase circuit takes the form shown in Fig. 14-59. Solve for I_a and I_b with the polarities as shown.

❚ The mesh equations become

$$11.5I_a - I_b - 10I = 127 \underline{/0°} \qquad -I_a + 21.5I_b - 20I = 127 \underline{/0°} \qquad -10I_a - 20I_b + (60 + j30)I = 0$$

Solving for I_a and I_b yields

$$I_a = \frac{(127 \underline{/0°})(1150 + j675)}{7625 + j7387} = 15.95 \underline{/-13.7°} \text{ A}$$

$$I_b = \frac{(127 \underline{/0°})(850 + j375)}{7625 + j7387} = 11.11 \underline{/-20.3°} \text{ A}$$

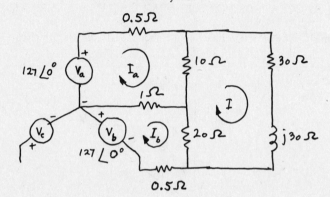

Fig. 14-59

14.199 How much apparent power is supplied by each source to the circuit of Prob. 14.198?

❚ $$S_a = V_a I_a^* = (127 \underline{/0°})(15.95 \underline{/13.7°}) = 2025.65 \underline{/13.7°} = 1968 + j479.75 \text{ VA}$$

$$S_b = V_b I_b^* = (127 \underline{/0°})(11.11 \underline{/20.3°}) = 1410.97 \underline{/20.3°} = 1323.23 + j489.52 \text{ VA}$$

14.200 Determine the power dissipated in the 30-Ω resistor of the circuit of Fig. 14-59.

❚ Solving for I from the kVL equations of Prob. 14.198 we obtain

$$I = \frac{127 \underline{/0°}(475)}{7625 + j7387} = 5.69 \underline{/-44.1°} \text{ A} \qquad P_{30\,\Omega} = (I)^2 30 = (5.69)^2 30 = 970 \text{ W}$$

14.201 Calculate the currents in the 1-Ω, 10-Ω, and 20-Ω resistors of the circuit of Fig. 14-59.

❚ $$I_{10\,\Omega} = I_a - I = 15.95 \underline{/-13.7°} - 5.69 \underline{/-44.1°} = 11.41 + j0.18 = 11.41 \underline{/0.9°} \text{ A}$$

$$I_{20\,\Omega} = I_b - I = 11.11 \underline{/-20.3°} - 5.69 \underline{/-44.1°} = 6.33 \underline{/0.9°} \text{ A}$$

$$I_{1\,\Omega} = I_b - I_a = 11.11 \underline{/-20.3°} - 15.95 \underline{/-13.7°} = -5.07 - j0.08 = 5.077 \underline{/-179.01°} \text{ A}$$

14.202 Verify the active power balance in the circuit of Fig. 14-59.

❚ $$P_{\text{supplied}} = P_a + P_b = 1323.23 + 1968.0 = 3291.23 \text{ W}$$

$$P_{\text{dissipated}} = (15.95)^2(0.5) + (11.11)^2(0.5) + (11.41)^2(10) + (6.33)^2(20) + (5.077)^2(1) + 970 = 3287.95 \text{ W}$$

14.203 Verify the reactive power balance in the circuit of Fig. 14-59.

❚ $$Q_{\text{supplied}} = Q_a + Q_b = 479.75 + 489.52 = 969.27 \text{ var} \qquad Q_{\text{absorbed}} = Q_L = (I)^2 X_L = (5.69)^2 30 = 970.0 \text{ var}$$

14.204 A method of solving a three-phase unbalanced circuit is the method of *symmetrical components*. According to this method, a set of three-phase unbalanced phasors (voltages or currents) can be resolved into three sets of symmetrical components, which are termed the *positive-sequence*, *negative-sequence*, and *zero-sequence* components. The phasors of a set of positive-sequence components have a counterclockwise phase rotation (or phase sequence), *abc*; the negative-sequence components have the reverse phase sequence, *acb*; and the zero-sequence components are all in phase with each other. These sequence components are represented geometrically in Fig. 14-60a through c. Graphically combine these components to obtain an unbalanced system.

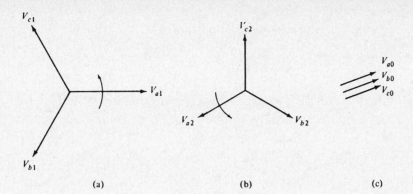

(a)   (b)   (c)

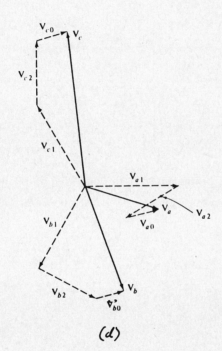

(*d*)   Fig. 14-60

❚ The phasors of Fig. 14-60*a* through *c* are combined to obtain the phasor diagram of Fig. 14-60*d*. Conversely, we may say that the voltages V_a, V_b, and V_c can be resolved into their symmetrical components of Figs. 14-60*a* through *c*.

14.205 Express, mathematically, the voltages V_a, V_b, and V_c as phasor sums of V_{a0}, V_{a1}, and V_{a2}, the symmetrical components of V_a. From Fig. 14-60 notice that the positive-sequence component is designated with a subscript 1. The subscripts 2 and 0 are used for the negative- and zero-sequence components, respectively.

❚ According to the method of symmetrical components, as illustrated in Fig. 14-60, we have

$$\mathbf{V}_a = \mathbf{V}_{a0} + \mathbf{V}_{a1} + \mathbf{V}_{a2} \tag{1}$$

$$\mathbf{V}_b = \mathbf{V}_{b0} + \mathbf{V}_{b1} + \mathbf{V}_{b2} \tag{2}$$

$$\mathbf{V}_c = \mathbf{V}_{c0} + \mathbf{V}_{c1} + \mathbf{V}_{c2} \tag{3}$$

We now introduce an operator **a** such that it causes a rotation of 120° in the counterclockwise direction (just as the *j* operator produces a 90° rotation), such that

$$\mathbf{a} = 1\underline{/120°} = 1 \times e^{j120} = -0.5 + j0.866 \qquad \mathbf{a}^2 = 1\ \underline{/240°} = -0.5 - j0.866 = \mathbf{a}^*$$

$$\mathbf{a}^3 = 1\ \underline{/360°} = 1\ \underline{/0°} \qquad 1 + \mathbf{a} + \mathbf{a}^2 = 0$$

Using the above-mentioned properties of the **a** operator, we may write the components of a given sequence in terms of any chosen component. Expressed mathematically, we have, from Fig. 14-60,

$$\mathbf{V}_{b1} = \mathbf{a}^2\mathbf{V}_{a1} \qquad \mathbf{V}_{c1} = \mathbf{a}\mathbf{V}_{a1} \qquad \mathbf{V}_{b2} = \mathbf{a}\mathbf{V}_{a2}$$

$$\mathbf{V}_{c2} = \mathbf{a}^2\mathbf{V}_{a2} \qquad \mathbf{V}_{a0} = \mathbf{V}_{b0} = \mathbf{V}_{c0}$$

Consequently, Eqs. (1) through (3) become (in terms of components of phase a),

$$\mathbf{V}_a = \mathbf{V}_{a0} + \mathbf{V}_{a1} + \mathbf{V}_{a2} \tag{4}$$

$$\mathbf{V}_b = \mathbf{V}_{a0} + \mathbf{a}^2\mathbf{V}_{a1} + \mathbf{a}\mathbf{V}_{a2} \tag{5}$$

$$\mathbf{V}_c = \mathbf{V}_{a0} + \mathbf{a}\mathbf{V}_{a1} + \mathbf{a}^2\mathbf{V}_{a2} \tag{6}$$

14.206 Express mathematically the symmetrical components of $\mathbf{V}_a$ in terms of $\mathbf{V}_a$, $\mathbf{V}_b$, and $\mathbf{V}_c$.

❚ Solving for the sequence components from Eqs. (4) through (6) of Prob. 14.205:

$$\mathbf{V}_{a0} = \tfrac{1}{3}(\mathbf{V}_a + \mathbf{V}_b + \mathbf{V}_c) \tag{1}$$

$$\mathbf{V}_{a1} = \tfrac{1}{3}(\mathbf{V}_a + \mathbf{a}\mathbf{V}_b + \mathbf{a}^2\mathbf{V}_c) \tag{2}$$

$$\mathbf{V}_{a2} = \tfrac{1}{3}(\mathbf{V}_a + \mathbf{a}^2\mathbf{V}_b + \mathbf{a}\mathbf{V}_c) \tag{3}$$

In deriving Eqs. (1) through (3), properties of $\mathbf{a}$ such as those given in Prob. 14.205 have been used. Relationships similar to those of Eqs. (1) through (3) are valid for phase and sequence currents also; that is, for current relationships, we simply replace the $\mathbf{V}$'s in Eqs. (1) through (3) by $\mathbf{I}$'s.

14.207 A three-phase wye-connected load is connected across a three-phase balanced supply system. Obtain a set of equations giving the relationships between the symmetrical components of line and phase voltages.

❚ The symmetrical system, the assumed directions of voltages, and the nomenclature are shown in Fig. 14-61, from which we have

$$\mathbf{V}_{ab} = \mathbf{V}_a - \mathbf{V}_b \qquad \mathbf{V}_{bc} = \mathbf{V}_b - \mathbf{V}_c \qquad \mathbf{V}_{ca} = \mathbf{V}_c - \mathbf{V}_a$$

Because $\mathbf{V}_{ab} + \mathbf{V}_{bc} + \mathbf{V}_{ca} = 0$, we get $\mathbf{V}_{ab0} = \mathbf{V}_{bc0} = \mathbf{V}_{ca0} = 0$. We choose $\mathbf{V}_{ab}$ as the reference phasor. For the positive-sequence component, we have

$$\mathbf{V}_{ab1} = \tfrac{1}{3}(\mathbf{V}_{ab} + \mathbf{a}\mathbf{V}_{bc} + \mathbf{a}^2\mathbf{V}_{ca}) = [(\mathbf{V}_a - \mathbf{V}_b) + \mathbf{a}(\mathbf{V}_b - \mathbf{V}_c) + \mathbf{a}^2(\mathbf{V}_c - \mathbf{V}_a)]$$

$$= \tfrac{1}{3}[(\mathbf{V}_a + \mathbf{a}\mathbf{V}_b + \mathbf{a}^2\mathbf{V}_c) - (\mathbf{a}^2\mathbf{V}_a + \mathbf{V}_b + \mathbf{a}\mathbf{V}_c)] = \tfrac{1}{3}[(\mathbf{V}_a + \mathbf{a}\mathbf{V}_b + \mathbf{a}^2\mathbf{V}_c) - \mathbf{a}^2(\mathbf{V}_a + \mathbf{a}\mathbf{V}_b + \mathbf{a}^2\mathbf{V}_c)]$$

$$= \tfrac{1}{3}[(1 - \mathbf{a}^2)(\mathbf{V}_a + \mathbf{a}\mathbf{V}_b + \mathbf{a}^2\mathbf{V}_c)] = (1 - \mathbf{a}^2)\mathbf{V}_{a1} = \sqrt{3}V_{a1}e^{j30°} \tag{1}$$

Similarly, for the negative-sequence component, we obtain

$$\mathbf{V}_{ab2} = \tfrac{1}{3}(\mathbf{V}_{ab} + \mathbf{a}^2\mathbf{V}_{bc} + \mathbf{a}\mathbf{V}_{ca}) = \tfrac{1}{3}[(\mathbf{V}_a - \mathbf{V}_b) + \mathbf{a}^2(\mathbf{V}_b - \mathbf{V}_c) + \mathbf{a}(\mathbf{V}_c - \mathbf{V}_a)]$$

$$= \tfrac{1}{3}[(\mathbf{V}_a + \mathbf{a}^2\mathbf{V}_b + \mathbf{a}\mathbf{V}_c) - (\mathbf{a}\mathbf{V}_a + \mathbf{V}_b + \mathbf{a}^2\mathbf{V}_c)] = \tfrac{1}{3}[(\mathbf{V}_a + \mathbf{a}^2\mathbf{V}_b + \mathbf{a}\mathbf{V}_c) - \mathbf{a}(\mathbf{V}_a + \mathbf{a}^2\mathbf{V}_b + \mathbf{a}\mathbf{V}_c)]$$

$$= \tfrac{1}{3}(1 - \mathbf{a})(\mathbf{V}_a + \mathbf{a}^2\mathbf{V}_b + \mathbf{a}\mathbf{V}_c) = (1 - \mathbf{a})\mathbf{V}_{a2} = \sqrt{3}V_{a2}e^{-j30°} \tag{2}$$

In Eqs. (1) and (2) above, $\mathbf{V}_{a1}$ and $\mathbf{V}_{a2}$ are, respectively, the positive- and negative-sequence components of the phase voltage $\mathbf{V}_a$.

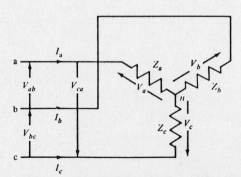

Fig. 14-61

14.208 The line voltages across a three-phase wye-connected load, consisting of a 10-Ω resistance in each phase, are unbalanced such that $\mathbf{V}_{ab} = 220 \,\underline{/131.7°}$ V, $\mathbf{V}_{bc} = 252 \,\underline{/0°}$ V, and $\mathbf{V}_{ca} = 195 \,\underline{/-122.6°}$ V. Determine the sequence phase voltages.

▌ Since line voltages are given, we determine the sequence components of line voltages. Thus, from Eqs. (2) and (3) of Prob. 14.206,

$$\mathbf{V}_{bc1} = \tfrac{1}{3}(\mathbf{V}_{bc} + a\mathbf{V}_{ca} + a^2\mathbf{V}_{ab})$$

$$= \tfrac{1}{3}(252 \,\underline{/0°} + 1 \,\underline{/120°} \times 195 \,\underline{/-122.6°} + 1 \,\underline{/-120°} \times 220 \,\underline{/131.7°}) = 221 + j12 \text{ V}$$

$$\mathbf{V}_{bc2} = \tfrac{1}{3}(\mathbf{V}_{bc} + a^2\mathbf{V}_{ca} + a\mathbf{V}_{ab})$$

$$= \tfrac{1}{3}(252 \,\underline{/0°} + 1 \,\underline{/-120°} \times 195 \,\underline{/-122.6°} + 1 \,\underline{/120°} \times 220 \,\underline{/131.7°}) = 31 - j11.9$$

From Eq. (1) of Prob. 14.206,

$$\mathbf{V}_{bc0} = \tfrac{1}{3}(\mathbf{V}_{bc} + \mathbf{V}_{ca} + \mathbf{V}_{ab}) = \tfrac{1}{3}(252 \,\underline{/0°} + 195 \,\underline{/-122.6°} + 220 \,\underline{/131.7°}) = 0 \text{ V}$$

Sequence components of phase voltages are $\mathbf{V}_{a0} = 0$. Since $\mathbf{V}_{bc1} = -j\sqrt{3}V_{a1}$ and $\mathbf{V}_{bc2} = j\sqrt{3}V_{a2}$,

$$\mathbf{V}_{a1} = \frac{\mathbf{V}_{bc1}}{\sqrt{3}(-j)} = \frac{221 + j12}{\sqrt{3}(-j)} = -6.9 + j127.5 \text{ V}$$

$$\mathbf{V}_{a2} = \frac{\mathbf{V}_{bc2}}{\sqrt{3}(j)} = \frac{31 - j11.9}{\sqrt{3}(j)} = -6.9 - j17.9 \text{ V}$$

14.209 Determine the voltages across the 10-Ω resistances and the currents through them.

▌ From Eqs. (4) through (6) of Prob. 14.205 we obtain

$$\mathbf{V}_a = -6.9 + j127.5 - 6.9 - j17.9 = -13.8 + j109.6 \text{ V}$$

$$\mathbf{V}_b = a^2\mathbf{V}_{a1} + a\mathbf{V}_{a2} = 132.8 - j54.8 \text{ V}$$

(upon substitution and simplification). The line currents are given by

$$\mathbf{I}_a = \frac{\mathbf{V}_a}{R} = \tfrac{1}{10}(-13.8 + j109.6) = -1.38 + j10.96 = 11.05 \text{ A} \,\underline{/97.2°}$$

$$\mathbf{I}_b = \frac{\mathbf{V}_b}{R} = \tfrac{1}{10}(132.8 - j54.8) = 13.28 - j5.48 = 14.37 \text{ A} \,\underline{/-22.4°}$$

Since $\mathbf{I}_a + \mathbf{I}_b + \mathbf{I}_c = 0$, we finally get $\mathbf{I}_c = -\mathbf{I}_a - \mathbf{I}_b = -(-1.38 + j10.96 + 13.28 - j5.48) = -11.9 - j5.48 = 13.1 \,\underline{/-155.3°}$ A.

14.210 Corresponding to sequence currents, we may define sequence impedances. Thus the *positive-sequence impedance* corresponds to an impedance through which only positive-sequence currents flow. Similarly, when only negative-sequence currents flow, the impedance is known as the *negative-sequence impedance*, and when zero-sequence currents alone are present, the impedance is called the *zero-sequence impedance*. A three-phase synchronous generator, grounded through an impedance $\mathbf{Z}_n$, is shown in Fig. 14-62. The generator is not supplying any load, but because of a fault at the generator terminals, currents $\mathbf{I}_a$, $\mathbf{I}_b$, and $\mathbf{I}_c$ flow through the phases a, b, and c, respectively. Obtain sequence networks (or equivalent circuits) for the positive-, negative-, and zero-sequence currents.

▌ Let the generator-induced voltages be $\mathbf{E}_a$, $\mathbf{E}_b$, and $\mathbf{E}_c$ in the three phases (Fig. 14-62a). The induced voltages in the generator are balanced. Therefore, these voltages are of positive sequence only. For the positive-sequence (phase) voltage, we have

$$\mathbf{V}_{a1} = \mathbf{E}_a - \mathbf{I}_{a1}\mathbf{Z}_1 \tag{1}$$

where $\mathbf{I}_{a1}\mathbf{Z}_1$ is the positive-sequence voltage drop in the positive-sequence impedance (of the generator) $\mathbf{Z}_1$. If $\mathbf{Z}_2$ is the negative-sequence impedance of the generator, the negative-sequence voltage at the terminal of a phase is simply

$$\mathbf{V}_{a2} = -\mathbf{I}_{a2}\mathbf{Z}_2 \tag{2}$$

since there is no negative-sequence generated voltage. The generator zero-sequence currents flow through $\mathbf{Z}_n$ as well as through $\mathbf{Z}_{g0}$, the generator zero-sequence impedance. The total zero-sequence current through $\mathbf{Z}_n$ is

$I_{a0} + I_{b0} + I_{c0} = 3I_{a0}$, but the current through Z_{g0} is I_{a0}. Hence, $V_{a0} = -I_{a0}Z_{g0} - 3I_{a0}Z_n$, which is also written as

$$V_{a0} = -I_{a0}Z_0 \qquad (3)$$

where $Z_0 = Z_{g0} + 3Z_n$. Sequence networks corresponding to Eqs. (1) through (3) are shown in Fig. 14-62b through d.

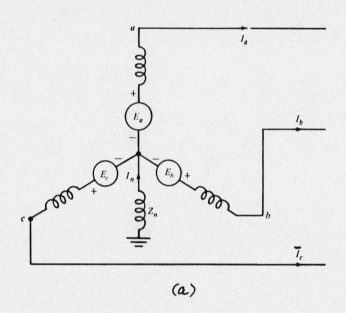

(a)

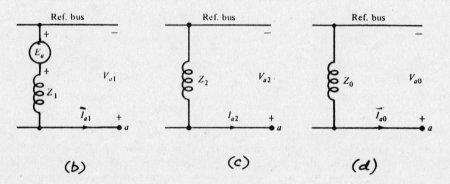

(b)   (c)   (d)   **Fig. 14-62**

14.211 A line-to-ground fault occurs on phase a of the generator of Fig. 14-62a. Derive a sequence network representation of this condition and determine the current in phase a.

▮ The constraints corresponding to the fault are $I_b = I_c = 0$ (lines being open-circuited) and $V_a = 0$ (line-to-ground short-circuit). Consequently, the symmetrical components of the current in phase a are given by

$$I_{a0} = \tfrac{1}{3}(I_a + I_b + I_c) = \tfrac{1}{3}I_a \qquad I_{a1} = \tfrac{1}{3}(I_a + aI_b + a^2I_c) = \tfrac{1}{3}I_a \qquad I_{a2} = \tfrac{1}{3}(I_a + a^2I_b + aI_c) = \tfrac{1}{3}I_a$$

Hence $I_{a0} = I_{a1} = I_{a2} = \tfrac{1}{3}I_a$. Consequently, the sequence networks must be connected in series, as shown in Fig. 14-63. The sequence voltages appear across the respective sequence networks.

To determine the current, we have from Fig. 14-63, $V_{a0} + V_{a1} + V_{a2} = E_a - I_{a1}Z_1 - I_{a1}Z_2 - I_{a1}Z_0$. But $V_a = V_{a0} + V_{a1} + V_{a2} = 0$. Consequently,

$$I_{a1} = \frac{E_a}{Z_1 + Z_2 + Z_0} = \frac{1}{3}I_a \qquad \text{and} \qquad I_a = \frac{3E_a}{Z_1 + Z_2 + Z_0}$$

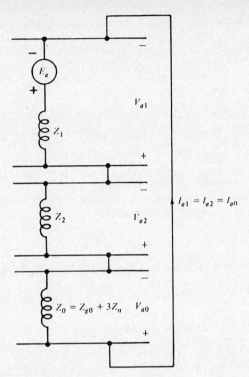

Fig. 14-63

14.212 The line currents in a three-phase four-wire system are $\mathbf{I}_a = (300 + j400)$ A, $\mathbf{I}_b = (200 + j200)$ A, and $\mathbf{I}_c = (-400 - j200)$ A. Determine the positive-, negative-, and zero-sequence components.

$\blacksquare$ $\quad \mathbf{I}_{a1} = \frac{1}{3}(\mathbf{I}_a + a\mathbf{I}_b + a^2\mathbf{I}_c) = \frac{1}{3}(300 + j400 + 73.2 - j273.2 + 372.9 - j246.2) = 249 - j119.4 = 276 \underline{/25.6°}$ A

$\mathbf{I}_{a2} = \frac{1}{3}(\mathbf{I}_a + a^2\mathbf{I}_b + a\mathbf{I}_c) = \frac{1}{3}[(300 + j400) + 1 \underline{/-120°}(200 + j200) + 1 \underline{/120°}(-400 - j200)]$

$\quad = \frac{1}{3}(300 + j400 + 282.8 \underline{/-75°} + 447.2 \underline{/+33.4°}) = \frac{1}{3}(300 + j400 + 73.2 - j273.2 + 373.3 - j246.2)$

$\quad = 248.8 - j119.4 = 275.97 \underline{/25.6°}$ A

$\mathbf{I}_{a0} = \frac{1}{3}(\mathbf{I}_a + \mathbf{I}_b + \mathbf{I}_c) = \frac{1}{3}(300 + j400 + 200 + j200 - 400 - j200) = 33.3 + j133.3 = 137.4 \underline{/76°}$ A

14.213 The line currents in a delta-connected load are $\mathbf{I}_a = 5 \underline{/0°}$, $\mathbf{I}_b = 7.07 \underline{/225°}$, and $\mathbf{I}_c = 5\underline{/90°}$. Calculate the positive-, negative-, and zero-sequence components of currents for phase a. Also determine the positive- and negative-sequence components of the current $\mathbf{I}_{ab}$ and hence calculate $\mathbf{I}_{ab}$.

$\blacksquare$ $\qquad \mathbf{I}_{a0} = \frac{1}{3}(\mathbf{I}_a + \mathbf{I}_b + \mathbf{I}_c) \qquad \mathbf{I}_{a1} = \sqrt{3}\mathbf{I}_{ab1} \underline{/-30°} \qquad \mathbf{I}_{a2} = \sqrt{3}\mathbf{I}_{ab2} \underline{/30°}$

From the given data,

$\qquad \mathbf{I}_{a0} = \frac{1}{3}(5 \underline{/0°} + 7.07 \underline{/225°} + 5 \underline{/90°}) = 0$

$\qquad \mathbf{I}_{a1} = \frac{1}{3}[5 \underline{/0°} + 1 \underline{/120°}(7.07 \underline{/225°}) + 1 \underline{/-120°}(5 \underline{/90°})]$

$\qquad \quad = \frac{1}{3}(5 \underline{/0°} + 7.07 \underline{/345°} + 5 \underline{/-30}) = 5.38 - j1.44 = 5.57 \underline{/-15°}$

$\qquad \mathbf{I}_{a2} = \frac{1}{3}[5 \underline{/0°} + 1 \underline{/-120°}(7.07 \underline{/225°}) + 1 \underline{/120°}(5 \underline{/90°})]$

$\qquad \quad = \frac{1}{3}(5 \underline{/0°} + 7.07 \underline{/105°} + 5 \underline{/210°}) = -0.387 + j1.44 = 1.49 \underline{/150°}$

$\qquad \mathbf{I}_{ab1} = \frac{1}{\sqrt{3}} \mathbf{I}_{a1} \underline{/30°} = \frac{1}{\sqrt{3}} \times 5.57 \underline{/-15° + 30°} = 3.1 + j0.83$

$\qquad \mathbf{I}_{ab2} = \frac{1}{\sqrt{3}} \mathbf{I}_{a2} \underline{/-30°} = \frac{1}{\sqrt{3}} \times 1.49 \underline{/-30° + 150°} = 0.223 + j0.831$

$\qquad \mathbf{I}_{ab} = \mathbf{I}_{ab1} + \mathbf{I}_{ab2} + \mathbf{I}_{b0} = 3.1 + j0.83 + 0.223 + j0.831 = 3.323 + j1.661 = 3.715\underline{/26.56°}$A

14.214 A three-phase unbalanced delta load draws 100 A of line current from a balanced three-phase supply. An open-circuit fault occurs on one of the lines. Determine the sequence components of the currents in the unfaulted lines.

▮ Let the fault occur in phase c. Then, for a delta-connected load, we have

$$\mathbf{I}_a = \mathbf{I}_{ab} - \mathbf{I}_{ca} \qquad \mathbf{I}_b = \mathbf{I}_{bc} - \mathbf{I}_{ab} \qquad \mathbf{I}_c = \mathbf{I}_{ca} - \mathbf{I}_{bc} = 0$$

or

$$\mathbf{I}_{ca} = \mathbf{I}_{bc} \qquad \text{and} \qquad \mathbf{I}_a = -\mathbf{I}_b$$

Hence,

$$\mathbf{I}_a = 100 \underline{/0°} \qquad \mathbf{I}_b = 100 \underline{/180°} \qquad \text{and} \qquad \mathbf{I}_c = 0$$

$$\mathbf{I}_{a0} = \tfrac{1}{3}(100 \underline{/0°} + 100 \underline{/180°} + 0) = 0$$

$$\mathbf{I}_{a1} = \tfrac{1}{3}[100 \underline{/0°} + 1 \underline{/120°}(100 \underline{/180°})] = 50 - j28.86$$

$$\mathbf{I}_{a2} = \tfrac{1}{3}[100 \underline{/0°} + 1 \underline{/-120°}(100 \underline{/180°})] = 50 + j28.86$$

14.215 Balanced three-phase system problems are often solved on a per-phase basis. A three-phase wye-connected load consists of equal resistances of 100 Ω/phase. The load is connected across a 220-V three-phase source. Determine the total power drawn by the load by calculating the per-phase power.

▮ On a per-phase basis we have

$$\mathbf{Z}_p = 100 + j0 \ \Omega \qquad \mathbf{V}_p = \frac{220}{\sqrt{3}} \underline{/0°} = 127 \underline{/0°} \ \text{V} \qquad \mathbf{I}_p = \frac{127 \underline{/0°}}{100 \underline{/0°}} = 1.27 \ \text{A}$$

$$P_p = (I_p)^2 R_p = (1.27)^2 100 = 161.33 \qquad P = 3P_p = 3(161.33) = 484 \ \text{W}$$

14.216 Repeat Prob. 14.215 if the resistors are connected in delta.

▮

$$\mathbf{Z}_p = 100 \underline{/0°} \ \Omega \qquad \mathbf{V}_p = 220 \underline{/0°} \ \text{V} \qquad \mathbf{I}_p = \frac{220}{100} \underline{/0°} = 2.2 \ \text{A}$$

$$P_p = (2.2)^2 100 = 484 \ \text{W} \qquad P = 3(484) = 1452 \ \text{W}$$

14.217 A balanced wye-connected load consisting of $\mathbf{Z}_Y = (3 + j4) \ \Omega$/phase and a balanced delta-connected load having $\mathbf{Z}_\Delta = (9 + j12) \ \Omega$/phase are connected to a 220-V three-phase source. On a per-phase basis, calculate the line current $\mathbf{I}_a$.

▮ First, we convert $\mathbf{Z}_\Delta$ into an equivalent $\mathbf{Z}_{Ye}$. Thus,

$$\mathbf{Z}_{Ye} = \tfrac{1}{3}\mathbf{Z}_\Delta = \tfrac{1}{3}(9 + j12) = 3 + j4 \ \Omega/\text{phase}$$

Thus,

$$\mathbf{Z}_p = \frac{(3 + j4)(3 + j4)}{3 + j4 + 3 + j4} = \frac{25 \underline{/106.26°}}{10 \underline{/53.13°}} = 2.5 \underline{/53.13°} \ \text{V}$$

$$\mathbf{I}_p = \mathbf{I}_a = \frac{\mathbf{V}_p}{\mathbf{Z}_p} \qquad \text{but} \qquad \mathbf{V}_p = \frac{220 \underline{/0°}}{\sqrt{3}} = 127 \underline{/0°} \ \text{V}$$

Hence, $\mathbf{I}_a = 127 \underline{/0°}/2.5 \underline{/53.13°} = 50.8 \underline{/-53.13°} \text{A}$.

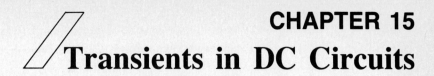

CHAPTER 15
Transients in DC Circuits

15.1 The voltage across a capacitor C in an electric circuit at $t = t_0$ is $v(t_0)$. What is the voltage at some instant t if the current through the capacitor is $i(t)$?

   ▐ The v-i relationship for a capacitor is

$$v_C = \frac{1}{C} \int i \, dt$$

which becomes, for the problem at hand,

$$v_C(t) = v(t_0) + \frac{1}{C} \int_{t_0}^{t} i(u) \, du \tag{1}$$

15.2 Obtain a relationship similar to Eq. (1) of Prob. 15.1 for an inductor L if the current through it is $i(t_0)$ at $t = t_0$.

   ▐ For the inductor, we have

$$i_L = \frac{1}{L} \int v \, dt$$

Thus, $$i_L(t) = i(t_0) + \frac{1}{L} \int_{t_0}^{t} v(u) \, du$$

15.3 A capacitor C initially charged to a voltage V_0 is suddenly connected across a resistor R. Find $v_C(t)$.

   ▐ The circuit is shown in Fig. 15-1. The voltage $v(t) = v_C$ satisfies

$$C \frac{dv_C}{dt} + \frac{v_C}{R} = 0$$

from which we obtain

$$v_C = V_0 \, e^{-t/RC} \tag{1}$$

since $v_C = V_0$ at $t = 0$.

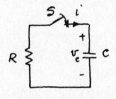

Fig. 15-1

15.4 The quantity RC in Eq. (1) of Prob. 15.3 has the dimension of second (s), and is known as the *time constant*. If $R = 10 \, k\Omega$ and $C = 50 \, \mu F$, what is the time constant τ?

   ▐ $$\tau = RC = (10 \times 10^3)(50 \times 10^{-6}) = 500 \, ms \text{ (or } 0.5 \, s)$$

15.5 Given $R = 2 \, M\Omega$ in an RC circuit of the form shown in Fig. 15-1, find C if we want a time constant of 10 s.

   ▐ $$\tau = 10 = RC = (2 \times 10^6)C \quad \text{or} \quad C = 5 \times 10^{-6} = 5 \, \mu F$$

15.6 To what value will the voltage V_0 of the capacitor of Prob. 15.3 decay over a period of one time constant?

   ▐ Substituting $t = \tau = RC$ in Eq. (1) of Prob. 15.3 we obtain

$$v_C(\tau) = V_0 e^{-1} = 0.368 V_0 \text{ V}$$

or 36.8 percent of its initial value.

15.7 Determine the time constant of the circuit shown in Fig. 15-2a.

∎ The given circuit may be reduced to that of Fig. 15-2b, from which

$$\tau = R_e C_e \quad \text{where} \quad R_e = R_1 + \frac{R_2 R_3}{R_2 + R_3} \quad \text{and} \quad C_e = C_1 + C_2$$

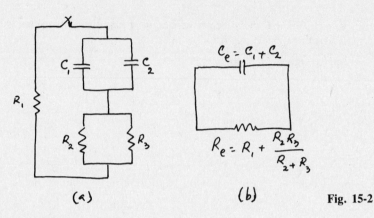

(a)   (b)   **Fig. 15-2**

15.8 Determine the energy stored in the capacitor of Prob. 15.3.

∎ $w_C(t) = \frac{1}{2}C(v_C)^2$. From Prob. 15.3, $v_C = V_0 e^{-t/RC}$. Hence,

$$w_C = \frac{1}{2}CV_0^2 e^{-2t/RC} = W_0 e^{-2t/RC} \text{ J} \tag{1}$$

where $W_0 = \frac{1}{2}CV_0^2$ is the initial stored energy.

15.9 Obtain an expression for the transfer of energy from the capacitor to the resistor of the circuit of Prob. 15.3.

∎
$$w_R(t) = W_0 - w_C$$
$$= W_0 - W_0 e^{-2t/RC} \quad \text{(from Prob. 15.8)}$$
$$= W_0(1 - e^{-2t/RC}) \text{ J}$$

15.10 A 50-μF capacitor is discharged through a 100-kΩ resistor. If the capacitor was initially charged to 400 V, determine its initial energy and the energy stored after 600 ms.

∎
$$W_0 = \frac{1}{2}CV_0^2 = \frac{1}{2}(50 \times 10^{-6})(400)^2 = 4 \text{ J} \qquad \tau = RC = (100 \times 10^3)(50 \times 10^{-6}) = 5 \text{ s}$$
$$W_C(600 \text{ ms}) = W_0 e^{-2t/RC} = 4e^{-2(600 \times 10^{-3})/5} = 3.14 \text{ J}$$

15.11 How long will it take the capacitor of Prob. 15.10 to discharge to 0.072-J stored energy?

∎ Substituting the numbers in Eq. (1) of Prob. 15.8 we obtain

$$0.072 = 4e^{-2t/5} \quad \text{or} \quad \frac{-2t}{5} = \ln \frac{0.072}{4} = -4.017$$

Hence, $t = 10$ s.

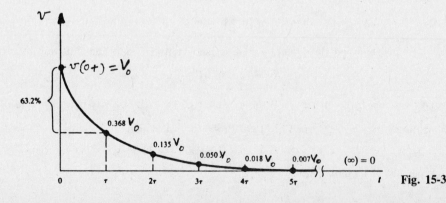

Fig. 15-3

15.12   Sketch the decay of voltage of a charged capacitor C being discharged through a resistor R as a function of time.

❙   The voltage is given by Eq. (1) of Prob. 15.3, which may be written as $v_C = V_0 e^{-t/\tau}$.   The plot is shown in Fig. 15-3.

15.13   A portion of the decay of voltage of the capacitor of Prob. 15.12 is shown in Fig. 15-4. If $v_C = v_1$ at $t = t_1$ and $v_C = v_2$ at $t = t_2$ are the readings from Fig. 15-4, determine the time constant of the circuit.

❙ $$v_C = V_0 e^{-t/\tau} \quad \text{or} \quad v_1 = V_0 e^{-t_1/\tau} \qquad v_2 = V_0 e^{-t_2/\tau}$$

Hence, $$\tau = \frac{t_2 - t_1}{\ln v_1 - \ln v_2}$$

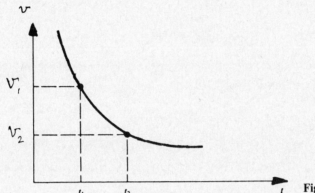

Fig. 15-4

15.14   In the circuit of Fig. 15-1 we have $v_1 = 600\ \text{V}$ at $t_1 = 1\ \text{s}$ and $v_2 = 300\ \text{V}$ at $t_2 = 4\ \text{s}$.   What is the time constant of the circuit?

❙   From Eq. (1) of Prob. 15.13,

$$\tau = \frac{4 - 1}{\ln 600 - \ln 300} = 4.328\ \text{s}$$

15.15   The voltage across a 20-μF capacitor varies with time and is given by $v_C = 10.75 - 1.5 e^{-1000t}$ V.   What is the current through the capacitor?

❙ $$i_C = C \frac{dv_C}{dt} = (20 \times 10^{-6})(-1.5)(-1000)e^{-1000t} = 0.03 e^{-1000t}\ \text{A}$$

15.16   In the circuit of Fig. 15-1, we have $C = 40\ \mu$F   and $R = 400\ \Omega$.   Obtain the current transient if $V_0 = 100\ \text{V}$.

❙ $$RC = (40 \times 10^{-6})(400) = 16\ \text{ms} \qquad \frac{1}{RC} = \tfrac{1000}{16} = 62.5\ \text{s}^{-1} \qquad V_0 = 100\ \text{V}$$

Thus, $$v_C = v_R = 100 e^{-62.5t} \qquad i = \frac{v_R}{R} = 0.25 e^{-62.5t}\ \text{A}$$

15.17   How does the charge vary as a function of time in the circuit of Prob. 15.16?

❙ $$q = C v_C = (40 \times 10^{-6})100 e^{-62.5t} = 4000 e^{-62.5t}\ \mu\text{C}$$

15.18   In the circuit of Fig. 15-5 the switch is closed at $t = 0$ when the 6-μF capacitor has charge $Q_0 = 300\ \mu$C. Obtain the expression for the transient voltage v_R.

❙   The two parallel capacitors have an equivalent capacitance of 3 μF.   Then this capacitance is in series with the 6 μF.   Thus, $\tau = RC_{eq} = 40\ \mu$s.   At $t = 0^+$,   KVL gives $v_R = 300/6 = 50\ \text{V}$;   and, as $t \to \infty$, $v_R \to 0$ (since $i \to 0$).   Therefore, $v_R = 50 e^{-t/\tau} = 50 e^{-t/40}$ V,   in which t is measured in μs.

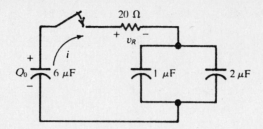

Fig. 15-5

15.19 An *RC* transient identical to that in Prob. 15.3 has a power transient $p_R = 360e^{-t/0.00001}$ W. Obtain the initial charge Q_0, if $R = 10\ \Omega$.

    ❙ $p_R = P_0 e^{-2t/RC}$ or $\dfrac{2}{RC} = 10^5$ or $C = 2\ \mu F$ $w_R = \displaystyle\int_0^t p_R\, dt = 3.6(1 - e^{-t/0.00001})$ mJ

Then, $w_R(\infty) = 3.6$ mJ $= Q_0^2/2C$,   from which $Q_0 = 120\ \mu C$.

15.20 A 100-μF capacitor, carrying an initial charge of 500 μC, is discharged through a 50-Ω resistor. Determine the time it takes the capacitor to discharge to 184-μC charge.

    ❙   Since $q = Cv_C$ or $Q_0 = CV_0$,   we may write Eq. (1) of Prob. 15.3 as $q = Q_0 e^{-t/RC}$.   Thus, $184 \times 10^{-6} = 500 \times 10^{-6} e^{-t/(50 \times 100 \times 10^{-6})}$.   Solving for t yields $t = 5.0$ ms.

15.21 From the graph of Fig. 15-3, find the time taken by the capacitor of Prob. 15.20 to discharge to a level of 25 μC.

    ❙ $\tau = RC = (50)(100 \times 10^{-6}) = 5$ ms.   25 μC corresponds to $0.05Q_0$ (since $Q_0 = 500\ \mu C$). From Fig. 15-3, at $0.05Q_0$, $t = 3\tau$.   Hence the required time is $t = 3(5 \times 10^{-3}) = 15$ ms.

15.22 For the circuit of Fig. 15-1 we have $C = 1$ mF, $R = 2$ kΩ,   and $V_0 = 120$ V.   Determine the current in the circuit 2 s after the switch is closed.

    ❙ $i_C = C\dfrac{dv_C}{dt} = -\dfrac{C}{RC}V_0 e^{-t/RC} = -\left(1 \times \dfrac{10^{-3}}{2}\right)120e^{-2/2} = -0.0221$ A

15.23 A 100-μF capacitor charged to 24 V is connected in series with a 200-μF uncharged capacitor, a 1-kΩ resistor, and a switch as shown in Fig. 15-6. Find the current 0.1 s after the switch is closed.

    ❙   By kVL we have

$$\frac{10^6}{200}\int i\, dt + \frac{10^6}{100}\int i\, dt + 1000i = 0$$

which upon differentiating with respect to t becomes $15i + (di/dt) = 0$ or

$$i = Ae^{-15t} \tag{1}$$

At $t = 0^+$,

$$v_{C1} + v_{C2} + v_R = 0 \qquad \text{or} \qquad 0 + 24 + 1000(i)_{t=0^+} = 0$$

Thus,

$$(i)_{t=0^+} = -0.024 \text{ A} \tag{2}$$

From Eqs. (1) and (2), $A = -0.024$ and $i = -0.024e^{-15t}$. Finally, at $t = 0.1$ s, $i = -0.024e^{-15(0.1)} = -0.00536$ A.

Fig. 15-6

15.24 What is the voltage across the 200-μF capacitor of the circuit of Prob. 15.23 at $t = 0.1$ s?

$$v_{C2} = \frac{10^6}{200} \int_0^{0.1} i \, dt = 0.5 \times 10^4 \int_0^{0.1} (-0.024 e^{-15t}) \, dt = -6.215 \text{ V}$$

15.25 In the circuit of Fig. 15-1, $R = 1$ kΩ and $C = 100$ μF. The capacitor is initially charged to 24 V. What is the initial current when the switch is closed?

By kVL, $v_C + v_R = 0$ or $24 + 1000i = 0$. Thus, $i(0^+) = -0.024$ A.

15.26 Determine the circuit current 0.02 s after the switch is closed, for the circuit of Prob. 15.25.

Since $RC = (1000)(100 \times 10^{-6}) = 0.1$ s, the solution to

$$Ri + \frac{1}{C} \int i \, dt = 0 \quad \text{or} \quad R \frac{di}{dt} + \frac{1}{C} i = 0$$

becomes $i = Ae^{-t/RC} = Ae^{-10t}$. From Prob. 15.25, $i(0^+) = -0.024$ A yields $A = -0.024$. Thus, $i = -0.024 e^{-10t}$. At $t = 0.02$ s we obtain $i = -0.024 e^{-10(0.02)} = -0.0196$ A.

15.27 What is the voltage across the capacitor of Prob. 15.25 at $t = 0.02$ s?

By KVL, $v_R + v_C = 0$ or $v_C = -1000i$. At $t = 0.02$ s, $i = -0.0196$ A (from Prob. 15.26). Thus, $v_C = (-1000)(-0.0196) = 19.6$ V.

15.28 Sketch i_C and v_C for the circuit of Prob. 15.25.

See Fig. 15-7.

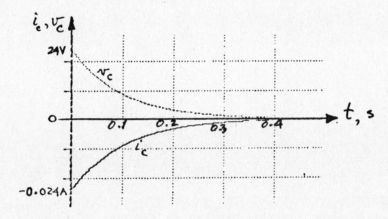

Fig. 15-7

15.29 The circuit of Fig. 15-8 was under steady state before the switch was opened. If $R_1 = 1.0\,\Omega$, $R_2 = 2.0\,\Omega$, $C = 0.167$ F, and the battery voltage is 24 V, determine $v_C(0^-)$ and $v_C(0^+)$. Also find $i(0^+)$.

Since the capacitor voltage cannot change instantaneously, we have $v_C(0^+) = v_C(0^-) = 24$ V. After the switch is opened, at $t = 0^+$, $v_C + v_{R1} + v_{R2} = 0$ or $24 + i(1+2) = 0$. Hence, $i(0^+) = -8$ A.

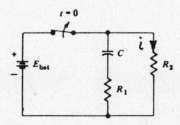

Fig. 15-8

15.30 Determine i in the circuit of Prob. 15.29 1 s after the switch is opened.

$RC = (1+2)(0.167) = 0.5$ s. Thus, the current is of the form $i = Ae^{-t/RC} = Ae^{-2t}$. Since $i = -8$ A at $t = 0^+$, we obtain $i = -8e^{-2t}$. At $t = 1$, $i = -8e^{-2(1)} = -1.08$ A.

15.31 The circuit parameters in Fig. 15-9 are $C = 2.4\,F$ and $R = 5.0\,\Omega$. The battery voltage is 100 V. Assuming the circuit is at steady state, determine the current in the resistor 10 s after the switch is opened.

■
$$v_C(0^+) = v_C(0^-) = 100\,V \qquad v_R + v_C = 0$$

or, at $t = 0^+$,

$$5i + 100 = 0 \quad \text{and} \quad i(0^+) = -\frac{100}{5} = -20\,A \qquad RC = 5(2.4) = 12\,s$$

Thus, $i = Ae^{-t/12}$. At $t = 0^+$, $i = -20\,A$ yields $A = -20$. Thus, $i = -20e^{-t/12}$. At $t = 10\,s$, $i = -20^{-10/12} = -8.69\,A$.

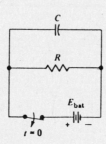

Fig. 15-9

15.32 What is the energy stored in the capacitor of Prob. 15.31 (10 s after the switch is opened)?

■ At $t = 10\,s$,

$$v_C + (-8.69)5 = 0 \quad \text{or} \quad v_C = 43.45\,V$$

Thus, $W = \frac{1}{2}C(v_C)^2 = \frac{1}{2}(2.4)(43.45)^2 = 2265.5\,J$.

15.33 Determine the current at $t = 0^+$ in the circuit of Fig. 15-10. Given: $C = 0.2\,F$, $R_1 = 3\,\Omega$, $R_2 = 7\,\Omega$, and the capacitor is charged to 100 V initially.

■
$$v_C(0^+) = v_C(0^-) = 100\,V \qquad v_C + v_{R1} + v_{R2} = 0$$

or
$$100 + (3 + 7)i = 0 \quad \text{or} \quad i(0^+) = -10A$$

15.34 What is the current at $t = 6\,s$ in the circuit of Fig. 15-10?

■ Since $RC = (3 + 7)(0.2) = 2$, $i = Ae^{-t/2}$. Since $i(0^+) = -10$, $A = -10$ and $i = -10e^{-0.5t}$, which yields $i = -0.5\,A$ at $t = 6\,s$.

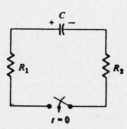

Fig. 15-10

15.35 The initial current in the inductor L of the circuit of Fig. 15-11 with S open is I_0. Determine the current after S is closed.

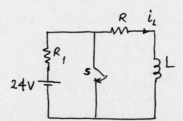

Fig. 15-11

▐ By KVL we have $L(di/dt) + Ri = 0$, from which we obtain

$$i_L = I_0 e^{-(R/L)t} \tag{1}$$

since $i = I_0$ at $t = 0$.

15.36 The quantity L/R in Eq. (1) of Prob. 15.35 has the dimension of second (s) and is known as the time constant. What is the time constant of a coil having $R = 10\,\Omega$ and $L = 100\,\text{mH}$?

▐ $$\tau = \frac{L}{R} = \frac{100 \times 10^{-3}}{10} = 10\,\text{ms}$$

15.37 It is desired to decrease the time constant of the coil of Prob. 15.36 to 2 ms by connecting a resistor in series with the coil. Determine the resistance of the resistor.

▐ $$\tau = \frac{L}{R} = 2\,\text{ms} = \frac{100 \times 10^{-3}}{10 + R_x} = 2 \times 10^{-3}$$

Hence, $R_x = 40\,\Omega$.

15.38 To what value will the current I_0 through the inductor of Prob. 15.35 decay over a period of one time constant.

▐ Substituting $t = \tau = L/R$ in Eq. (1) of Prob. 15.35 yields $i_L(\tau) = I_0 e^{-1} = 0.368 I_0$ A or 36.8 percent of its initial value.

15.39 Sketch the decay of current through the inductor of Prob. 15.35.

▐ The sketch is identical to that of Fig. 15-3, except that for V_0 we substitute I_0.

15.40 What is the time constant of the circuit shown in Fig. 15-12a?

▐ The given circuit may be reduced to that shown in Fig. 15-12b, for which we have

$$R_e = \frac{R_1 R_2}{R_1 + R_2} \quad \text{and} \quad L_e = L_1 + L_2$$

Hence, $\tau = L_e/R_e$ s.

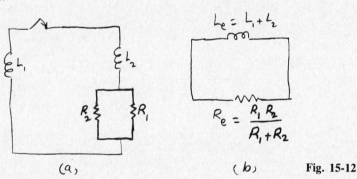

(a) (b) **Fig. 15-12**

15.41 The decay of current in a coil is recorded. It is found that $i_L = 10\,\text{mA}$ at $t = 2\,\text{ms}$ and $i_L = 3.68\,\text{mA}$ at $t = 6\,\text{ms}$. Determine the time constant of the coil.

▐ From Eq. (1) of Prob. 15.35 we obtain for the given data: at $t = 2\,\text{ms}$, $10 = I_0 e^{-2 \times 10^{-3}/\tau}$ mA. At $t = 6\,\text{ms}$, $3.68 = I_0 e^{-6 \times 10^{-3}/\tau}$ mA or

$$\tau = \frac{(6 - 2) \times 10^{-3}}{\ln 10 - \ln 3.68} = 4\,\text{ms}$$

15.42 The current through a 50-mH inductor is given by $i_L = 5 - 2e^{-10t}$ A. What is the voltage across the inductor?

▐ $$v_L = L \frac{di_L}{dt} = (50 \times 10^{-3})(-2 \times -10)e^{-10t} = e^{-10t}\,\text{V}$$

15.43 In the circuit of Fig. 15-11, we have $R_1 = R = 2\,\Omega$ and $L = 0.4\,\text{H}$. Determine the current transient.

▮ $$I_0 = \frac{24}{2+2} = 6\,\text{A} \qquad \frac{L}{R} = \frac{0.4}{2} = 0.2\,\text{s}$$

Hence, $i = 6e^{-t/0.2} = 6e^{-5t}\,\text{A}$.

15.44 Determine the energy stored in the inductor of the circuit of Fig. 15-11.

▮ $i_L = I_0 e^{-(R/L)t}$ and

$$w_L(t) = \tfrac{1}{2}L(i_L)^2 = (\tfrac{1}{2}LI_0^2)e^{-(2R/L)t} = W_0 e^{-(2R/L)t}$$

where $W_0 = \tfrac{1}{2}LI_0^2$ is the initial stored energy.

15.45 Obtain an expression for the transfer of energy from the inductor to the resistor of the circuit of Fig. 15-11.

▮ $$w_R(t) = W_0 - w_L = W_0 - W_0 e^{-(2R/L)t} \quad \text{(from Prob. 15.44)}$$
$$= W_0(1 - e^{-(2R/L)t})\,\text{J}$$

15.46 In the circuit of Fig. 15-11, $L = 2\,\text{H}$ and $R = 4\,\Omega$. If the initial current is 4 A through the inductor, what is the energy stored at $t = 0.25\,\text{s}$?

▮ $$\tau = L/R = 2/4 = 0.5\,\text{s} \qquad W_0 = \tfrac{1}{2}LI_0^2 = \tfrac{1}{2}(2)(4)^2 = 16\,\text{J}$$
$$W_L(0.25\,\text{s}) = W_0 e^{-(2R/L)t} = 16e^{-[(2\times 4)/2]0.25} = 5.89\,\text{J}$$

15.47 How long will it take the inductor of Prob. 15.46 to discharge to 0.8-J stored energy?

▮ From Prob. 15.46, $0.8 = 16e^{-4t}$. Thus $t = 0.75\,\text{s}$.

15.48 How does the flux linkage with the inductor of the coil of Prob. 15.43 vary with time?

▮ Flux linkage $\lambda \equiv Li$ or

$$\lambda = LI_0 e^{-t/\tau} = (0.4)6e^{-5t} = 2.4e^{-5t}\,\text{A}$$

15.49 In the circuit of Fig. 15-13, the switch is closed at $t = 0$ when the 2-H inductor has a current $I_0 = 10\,\text{A}$. Find the voltage across the resistor.

▮ $$L_e = 2 + \frac{(3)(6)}{3+6} = 4\,\text{H} \qquad \tau = \frac{L_e}{R} = \frac{4}{4} = 1\,\text{s}$$
$$i = I_0 e^{-t/\tau} = 10e^{-t} \qquad v_R(t) = Ri = (4)10e^{-t} = 40e^{-t}\,\text{V}$$

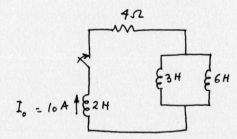

Fig. 15-13

15.50 The power transient in an RL circuit of the type shown in Fig. 15-11 is given by $p_R = 72e^{-10t}\,\text{W}$. Determine the initial current if $R = 2\,\Omega$.

▮ Since $p_R = P_0 e^{-(2R/L)t}$, $$\tau = \frac{L}{R} = \frac{2}{10} = \frac{L}{2} \qquad \text{or} \qquad L = 0.4\,\text{H}$$

$$w_R = \int_0^t p_R\,dt = 72\int_0^t e^{-10t}\,dt = 7.2(1 - e^{-10t})\,\text{J}$$

Maximum energy stored is $7.2 = \tfrac{1}{2}LI_0^2 = \tfrac{1}{2}(0.4)I_0^2$. Thus $I_0 = 6\,\text{A}$.

15.51 In the circuit of Fig. 15-11 we have $R = 1\,\Omega$ and $L = 1\,\Omega$. If the initial current through the inductor is 10 A, determine the current after 3 s.

$\blacksquare$ $$i = I_0 e^{-(R/L)t} = 10e^{-t} \qquad \text{or} \qquad i(3) = 10e^{-3} = 0.4978\,\text{A}$$

15.52 The 3-H inductor in the circuit of Fig. 15-14 carries a 10-A initial current. The switch is closed at $t = 0$. Solve for i.

$\blacksquare$ At $t = 0^+$, we have, by KVL,

$$L_e \frac{di}{dt} + Ri = 0 \qquad \text{where} \qquad L_e = \frac{(3)(6)}{3+6} = 2\,\text{H} \qquad \text{and} \qquad R = 4\,\Omega$$

Thus, $i = Ae^{-(4/2)t} = Ae^{-2t} = 10e^{-2t}$ since $i = 10\,\text{A}$ at $t = 0$.

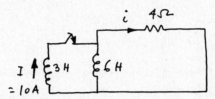

Fig. 15-14

15.53 A 240-V dc generator supplies current to a parallel circuit consisting of a resistor and a coil as shown in Fig. 15-15a. The system is at steady state. Determine the current in the coil one second after the breaker is tripped.

$\blacksquare$ The new circuit is shown in Fig. 15-15b, from which we have $i_L(0^+) = i_L(0^-) = \frac{240}{300} = 0.8\,\text{A}$. By KVL $(600 + 300)i + 200\,di/dt = 0$. Thus, $i = Ae^{-4.5t}$. Since $i(0^+) = 0.8$, $A = 0.8$ and $i = 0.8e^{-4.5t}\,\text{A}$. Hence, at $t = 1\,\text{s}$, $i = 0.8e^{-4.5(1)} = 0.0089\,\text{A}$.

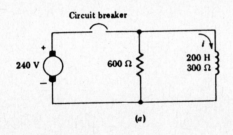

(a)

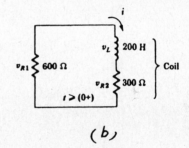

(b)   Fig. 15-15

15.54 What is the voltage induced in the coil and the voltage across the coil 1 s after the breaker is tripped in the circuit of Fig. 15-15a?

$\blacksquare$ By KVL, from Fig. 15-15b,

$$v_{R1} + v_{R2} + v_L = 0 \qquad \text{or} \qquad (R_1 + R_2)i + v_L = 0$$

At $t = 1\,\text{s}$, $i = 0.0089\,\text{A}$ from Prob. 15.53. Thus,

$$v_L(1\,\text{s}) = -0.0089(600 + 300) = -8.01\,\text{V}$$

$$v_{\text{coil}} + v_{R1} = 0 \qquad \text{or} \qquad v_{\text{coil}} = -v_{R1} = -0.0089(600) = -5.34\,\text{V}$$

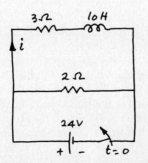

Fig. 15-16

15.55   The circuit in Fig. 15-16 is at steady state.   At $t = 0$ the switch is opened.   Determine $i(0^+)$ and $i(0^-)$.

$$i(0^+) = i(0^-) = \tfrac{24}{3} = 8\,\text{A}$$

15.56   Find the current in the 2-Ω resistor at $t = 0^-$ and at $t = 0^+$ in the circuit of Fig. 15-16.

$$i_{2\Omega}(0^-) = \tfrac{24}{2} = 12\,\text{A} \qquad i_{2\Omega}(0^+) = i(0^+) = 8\,\text{A}$$

15.57   What is the current through the inductor of the circuit of Fig. 15-16 at $t = 1.5\,\text{s}$?

By KVL,

$$10\frac{di}{dt} + (3 + 2)i = 0 \qquad \text{or} \qquad i = Ae^{-0.5t}$$

Since $i = 8\,\text{A}$ at $t = 0$, $A = 8$ and $i = 8e^{-0.5t}$.   At $t = 1.5\,\text{s}$, $i = 8e^{-0.5(1.5)} = 3.78\,\text{A}$.

15.58   Sketch $i(t)$ for the circuit of Fig. 15-16 after the switch has been opened.

See Fig. 15-17.

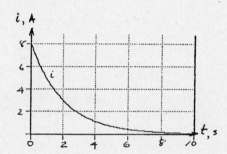

Fig. 15-17

15.59   In Fig. 15-18a, $V = 100\,\text{V}$, $R_1 = 50\,\Omega$,   and the coil parameters are 100 H and 200 Ω. At $t = 0$ the switch is opened.   What is the coil current at $t = 1.5\,\text{s}$?

$i(0^-) = i(0^+) = \frac{100}{200} = 0.5\,\text{A}$.   With the switch open, by KVL,

$$100\frac{di}{dt} + (200 + 50)i = 0 \qquad \text{or} \qquad i = Ae^{-2.5t}\,\text{A}$$

Since $i = 0.5$ at $t = 0$, $A = 0.5$.   Thus, $i = 0.5e^{-2.5t}\,\text{A}$.   At $t = 1.5\,\text{s}$, $i = 0.5e^{-(2.5)(1.5)} = 0.012\,\text{A}$.

15.60   Determine the time constant of the circuit of Fig. 15-18a and sketch $i(t)$.

$\tau = L/R = 100/(200 + 50) = 0.4\,\text{s}$.   For $i(t)$ see Fig. 15-18b.

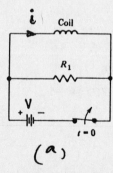

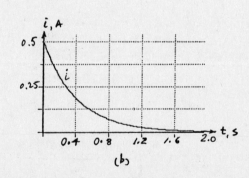

(a)   (b)   **Fig. 15-18**

15.61   In Fig. 15-19a a field discharge resistor is connected in parallel with the motor field winding to discharge the energy in the magnetic field when the switch is opened.   This allows for a gradual discharge of the energy and thus avoids damage to the switch and to the coil when the switch is opened.   The energy stored in the magnetic field is dissipated as heat energy in R_D and in the resistance of the field windings.   Assuming R_D is 1000 Ω, the generator is operating at 120 V, the parameters of the field winding are 100 H and 94 Ω, and the circuit current is at steady state, determine   (a) the current in the discharge resistor at $t = (0^-)$,   and   (b) the current in the discharge resistor at $t = (0^+)$.

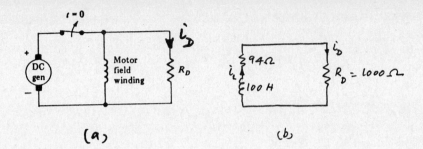

(a)   (b)

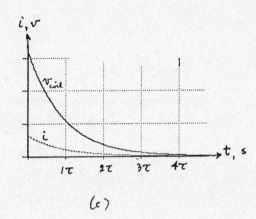

(c)   **Fig. 15-19**

▌ The circuit at $t = (0^+)$ is shown in Fig. 15-19b. (a) $i_D(0^-) = \frac{120}{1000} = 0.12$ A   (b) $i_D(0^+) = i_L(0^+) = i_L(0^-) = \frac{120}{94} = 1.28$ A.

15.62   In the circuit of Prob. 15.61, determine the field current 0.5 s after the switch is opened.

▌ From Fig. 15-19b,

$$100 \frac{di}{dt} + (94 + 1000)i = 0 \quad \text{or} \quad i = Ae^{-10.94t}$$

At $t = 0$, $i = 1.28$ A. Thus, $A = 1.28$ and $i = 1.28e^{-10.94t}$ A. At $t = 0.5$ s, $i = 1.28e^{(-10.94)(0.5)} = 5.39$ mA.

15.63   What is the voltage across the field winding in the circuit of Prob. 15.61 at $t = 0^+$?

▌ $$V_{\text{field}}(0^+) = V_{RD}(0^+) = iR_D(0^+) = (1.28)(1000) = 1280 \text{ V}$$

15.64   In the circuit of Prob. 15.61, determine the time elapsed for the voltage across the field winding to decay to 40 V.

▌ At the instant the voltage across the field winding is 40 V, the voltage across R_D is 40 V, and

$$i_D = \frac{V}{R} = \frac{40}{1000} = 0.04 \text{ A}$$

But $i_D = 1.28e^{-10.94t}$, so that $0.04 = 1.28e^{-10.94t}$. Hence, $t = 0.317$ s.

15.65   Sketch $i(t)$ and $v_{\text{field}}(t)$ for the circuit of Fig. 15-19.

▌ See Fig. 15-19c.

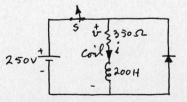

Fig. 15-20

15.66 In the circuit of Fig. 15-20 a charged coil is discharged through a diode of negligible resistance by opening the switch at $t = 0$. Determine the coil current 0.2 s after the switch is opened.

▮ $i(0^+) = i(0^-) = \frac{250}{350} = 0.714$ A. By KVL,

$$200 \frac{di}{dt} + 350i = 0 \quad \text{or} \quad i = Ae^{-1.75t} \text{ A}$$

Since $i = 0.714$ A at $t = 0$, $A = 0.714$. Thus, $i = 0.714e^{-1.75t}$ A. At $t = 0.2$ s, $i = 0.714e^{(-1.75)(0.2)} = 0.503$ A.

15.67 What is voltage across the coil at (a) $t = (0^-)$ and (b) $t = (0^+)$ in the circuit of Fig. 15-20?

▮ (a) $v(0^-) = 250 \text{ V} = v_{\text{battery}}$ (b) $v(0^+) = v_{\text{diode}} = 0.714(0) = 0$ V

15.68 What is the instantaneous power in the circuit of Prob. 15.66?

▮ $$p = i^2 R = (350)(0.714)^2 (e^{2(-1.75)t}) = 178.43e^{-3.5t} \text{ W}$$

15.69 How much energy is dissipated in the resistor of the circuit of Fig. 15-20 in 0.2 s?

▮ $$W = \int_0^{0.2} (i^2 R) \, dt = 178.43 \int_0^{0.2} e^{-3.5t} \, dt \quad \text{(from Prob. 15.68)}$$
$$= 25.66 \text{ J}$$

15.70 In Fig. 15-21 the two paralleled field windings are protected by a common discharge resistor. The parameters of winding 1 are 300 H and 200 Ω, the parameters of winding 2 are 100 H and 200 Ω, R_D is 600 Ω, and the generator voltage is 240 V. Determine (a) the steady-state current in each winding and in the resistor before the switch is opened and (b) the voltage across each winding at $t = (0^-)$.

▮ (a) $i_{W1}(0^-) = \frac{240}{200} = 1.2$ A $\quad i_{W2}(0^-) = \frac{240}{200} = 1.2$ A $\quad i_{RD}(0^-) = \frac{240}{600} = 0.4$ A

(b) $V_{W1}(0^-) = V_{W2}(0^-) = V_{RD}(0^-) = 240$ V

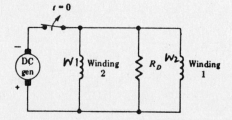

Fig. 15-21

15.71 What are the voltages across the circuit elements in the circuit of Fig. 15-21 at $t = 0^+$?

▮ Because of the inductances the currents cannot change instantaneously. Thus,

$$i_{RD}(0^+) = 1.2 + 1.2 = 2.4 \text{ A} \quad V_{RD}(0^+) = (2.4)(600) = 1440 \text{ V} = V_{W1}(0^+) = V_{W2}(0^+)$$

(the windings being in parallel).

15.72 Determine the value R_D in the circuit of Prob. 15.70 to limit the voltage across the windings to 240 V when the switch is opened.

▮ $$V_{RD} = iR_D' \quad \text{or} \quad 240 = 2.4R_D'$$

Thus $R_D' = 240/2.4 = 100$ Ω.

15.73 When the switch is closed, a current i flows in the circuit of Fig. 15-22 because of an initial charge on the capacitor. Write the equation governing i and the form of the solution to the equation.

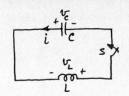

Fig. 15-22

▮ By KVL,

$$L \frac{di}{dt} + \frac{1}{C} \int i\, dt = 0 \qquad \text{or} \qquad L \frac{d^2 i}{dt^2} + \frac{1}{C} i = 0$$

which has the characteristic roots given by

$$p_1, p_2 = \pm \frac{j}{\sqrt{LC}} \equiv \pm j\omega$$

where $\omega \equiv 1/\sqrt{LC}$. Hence the solution is of the form

$$i = A_1 e^{j\omega t} + A_2 e^{-j\omega t} \; \text{A} \tag{1}$$

15.74 Using Euler's identity, express Eq. (1) of Prob. 15.73 as a sum of sine and cosine functions.

▮ Since, $e^{j\omega t} = \cos \omega t + j \sin \omega t$ and $e^{-j\omega t} = \cos \omega t - j \sin \omega t$, Eq. (1) of Prob. 15.73 may be written as

$$i = A_1(\cos \omega t + j \sin \omega t) + A_2(\cos \omega t - j \sin \omega t) = (A_1 + A_2) \cos \omega t + j(A_1 - A_2) \sin \omega t$$

$$= B_1 \cos \omega t + B_2 \sin \omega t \tag{1}$$

15.75 Show that B_1 and B_2 in Eq. (1) of Prob. 15.73 are real numbers and A_1 and A_2 are complex conjugates.

▮ Since i is real, the quantity on the right-hand side must be real. Thus $B_1 = A_1 + A_2$ and $B_2 = j(A_1 - A_2)$ must be real. Consequently, $A_1 = a + jb$ and $A_2 = a - jb$ must be complex conjugates.

15.76 If the initial voltage on the capacitor of the circuit of Fig. 15-22 is V_0, determine the constants B_1 and B_2 in Eq. (1) of Prob. 15.73.

▮ At $t = 0$, $i = 0$. Thus, $0 = B_1 + B_2(0)$ or $B_1 = 0$. At $t = 0^+$,

$$L \frac{di}{dt} + V_0 = 0 \qquad \text{or} \qquad \frac{di}{dt}(0^+) = -\frac{V_0}{L}$$

Since $B_1 = 0$, $di/dt = B_2 \omega \cos \omega t$. At $t = 0^+$, we have $-(V_0/L) = B_2 \omega$. Hence, $B_1 = 0$ and $B_2 = -(V_0/\omega L)$.

15.77 Sketch the current for the circuit of Prob. 15.76.

▮ From Prob. 15.76, $i = (V_0/\omega L) \cos \omega t$. Hence, the sketch is as shown in Fig. 15-23.

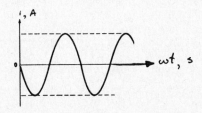

Fig. 15-23

15.78 In the circuit of Fig. 15-24, $L = 1.0\,\text{H}$, $R = 6.0\,\Omega$, and $C = 0.2\,\text{F}$. The capacitor is initially charged to 24 V and the switch is closed at $t = 0$. Determine i one second after the switch is closed.

▮ By KVL (and after differentiation),

$$\frac{d^2 i}{dt^2} + 6 \frac{di}{dt} + \frac{1}{0.2} i = 0$$

The characteristic roots of this equation are -5 and -1. Thus, the solution is of the form $i = A_1 e^{-5t} + A_2 e^{-t}$; $i(0^+) = 0$ yields $A_1 + A_2 = 0$ and $di/dt + 0 + 24 = 0$ yields $di/dt = -24 = -5A_1 - A_2$. Hence, $A_1 = 6$ and $A_2 = -6$; $i = 6(e^{-5t} - e^{-t})$. At $t = 1\,\text{s}$, $i = 6(e^{-5} - e^{-1}) = -2.17\,\text{A}$.

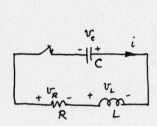

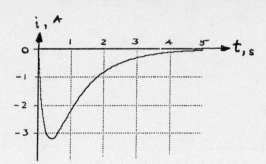

Fig. 15-24   Fig. 15-25

15.79 Sketch the current in the circuit of Fig. 15-24.

▮ See Fig. 15-25.

15.80 In the circuit of Fig. 15-22, $C = 2.55\ \mu\text{F}$ and $L = 200\ \text{mH}$. The capacitor is charged to 60 V. The switch is closed at $t = 0$. Calculate i at $t = 0.4\ \text{s}$.

▮ From Prob. 15.74, $i = B_1 \cos \omega t + B_2 \sin \omega t$.

$$\omega = \frac{1}{\sqrt{LC}} = \frac{1}{\sqrt{(200 \times 10^{-3})(2.55 \times 10^{-6})}} = 1400\ \text{rad/s}$$

$i(0^+) = i(0^-) = 0$ yields $B_1 = 0$.

$$\frac{di}{dt}(0^+) = -\frac{V_0}{L} = \frac{-60}{0.2} = -300 = \omega B_2 \cos \omega t = \omega B_2 = 1400 B_2$$

Thus, $B_2 = -0.214$, $i = -0.214 \sin 1400t$ A. At $t = 0.4$, $i = -0.214 \sin (1400 \times 0.4) = -0.153$ A.

15.81 Determine $v_C(t)$ from the data of Prob. 15.80.

▮
$$v_C + 0.2 \frac{d}{dt}(-0.214 \sin 1400t) = 0$$
or
$$v_C = -(0.2)(0.214)(1400) \cos 1400t = -59.92 \cos 1400t \text{ A}$$

15.82 From the data of Prob. 15.81 determine the first zero crossing of the voltage across the inductor.

▮ $v_L = 0$ when $\cos 1400t = 0$ or $1400t = \pi/2$. Hence, $t = 1.122$ ms.

15.83 In the circuit of Fig. 15-22, $C = 100\ \mu\text{F}$. Find L so that the first zero crossing of the voltage across the capacitor occurs at $t = 10$ ms.

▮ $v_C = 0$ when $\cos \omega t = 0$ or $\omega t = \pi/2$. For $t = 10$ ms, $\omega = (\pi/2) \times 10^2 = 1/\sqrt{LC}$, from which $L = 0.405$ H.

15.84 For the circuit of Fig. 15-24, write the equation governing the current i and obtain a general form of solution to the equation.

▮ By KVL,

$$L \frac{di}{dt} + Ri + \frac{1}{C} \int i\, dt = 0$$

or
$$L \frac{d^2i}{dt^2} + R \frac{di}{dt} + \frac{1}{C} i = 0 \qquad (1)$$

The characteristic roots are

$$p_1, p_2 = -\frac{R}{2L} \pm \sqrt{\left(\frac{R}{2L}\right)^2 - \frac{1}{LC}}$$

and the form of the solution is $i = A_1 e^{p_1 t} + A_2 e^{p_2 t}$ A.

15.85 Write the form of solution to Eq. (1) of Prob. 15.84 when it has two distinct real roots. Obtain the relationship between R, L, and C for this case.

▌ For distinct real roots, we must have $(R/2L)^2 > 1/LC$. Let $-a$ and $-b$ be the two real roots. Then the form of the solution becomes $i = A_1 e^{-at} + A_2 e^{-bt}$ A.

15.86 What is the form of solution to Eq. (1) of Prob. 15.84 when it has two real but coincidental roots? What is the relationship between R, L, and C for this particular case?

▌ For the roots to be coincident we must have $(R/2L)^2 = 1/LC$. The roots are $p_1 = p_2 = -(R/2L) = -\alpha$. If we write the solution as

$$i = A_1 e^{-\alpha t} + A_2 e^{-\alpha t} = (A_1 + A_2)e^{-\alpha t} = Ae^{-\alpha t}$$

we have only one unknown constant. For a second-order differential equation we must have two arbitrary constants. Therefore, the correct form of solution is

$$i = A_1 e^{-\alpha t} + A_2 t e^{-\alpha t}$$

15.87 Obtain the form of solution to Eq. (1) of Prob. 15.84 when it has a pair of complex conjugate roots. Find the relationship between R, L, and C for this case.

▌ For a pair of complex conjugate roots we must have $(R/2L)^2 < 1/LC$. Let the roots be $-\alpha \pm j\omega$, where $\alpha = R/2L$ and $\omega = \sqrt{(R/2L)^2 - 1/LC}$. Then, the solution becomes

$$i = A_1 e^{-(\alpha + j\omega t)} + A_2 e^{-(\alpha - j\omega t)} \qquad (1)$$

15.88 Simplify Eq. (1) of Prob. 15.87 to obtain the solution in terms of $\sin \omega t$ and $\cos \omega t$.

▌ Proceeding as in Prob. 15.74, using Euler's identity, we may write Eq. (1) of Prob. 15.87 as

$$i = e^{-\alpha t}(B_1 \cos \omega t + B_2 \sin \omega t) \qquad (1)$$

15.89 Sketch the form of Eq. (1) of Prob. 15.88 for $B_1 = 2$, $B_3 = 3$, $\omega = 1$, and $\alpha = 0.0796$.

▌ See Fig. 15-26.

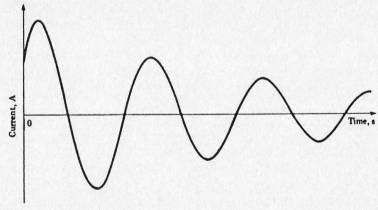

Fig. 15-26

In Eq. (1) of Prob. 15.88, α is known as the *damping coefficient* and ω is called the *damped frequency of oscillation*.

15.90 In the circuit of Fig. 15-24, $C = 14.28$ mF, $R = 45\,\Omega$, and $L = 5$ H. The capacitor is charged to 50 V. The switch is closed at $t = 0$. List all conditions on voltages and currents at $t = 0^-$ and at $t = 0^+$.

▌ Because of inductance,

$$i(0^+) = i(0^-) = 0 \qquad (1)$$

Because of capacitance, $v_C(0^+) = v_C(0^-) = 50$ V. KVL at $t = 0^+$ implies that $v_L(0^+) + v_C(0^+) + v_R(0^+) = 0$. But

$$v_L = L\frac{di}{dt} \quad \text{and} \quad v_R = Ri$$

We have
$$v_L(0^+) = L\frac{di}{dt}(0^+) \qquad v_R(0^+) = 0$$

since $i(0^+) = 0$. Consequently,

$$\frac{di}{dt}(0^+) = -\frac{v_C(0^+)}{L} = -\frac{50}{5} = -10 \tag{2}$$

15.91 For the circuit of Prob. 15.90, obtain the general solution for the current i.

∎ Since the characteristic roots are -7, -2,
$$i = A_1 e^{-7t} + A_2 e^{-2t} \tag{1}$$

15.92 Apply the initial conditions obtained in Prob. 15.90 to Eq. (1) of Prob. 15.91. Hence evaluate A_1 and A_2.

∎ From Eq. (1) of Prob. 15.90 we have
$$0 = A_1 + A_2 \quad \text{or} \quad A_1 = -A_2$$
From Eq. (2) of Prob. 15.90 and Eq. (1) of Prob. 15.91 we obtain
$$\frac{di}{dt}(0^+) = -10 = -7A_1 - 2A_2$$
Solving for A_1 and A_2 yields $A_1 = 2$ and $A_2 = -2$.

15.93 What is the current in the circuit of Prob. 15.90 at $t = 0.5$ s?

∎ From Probs. 15.91 and 15.92 we have $i = 2(e^{-7t} - e^{-2t})$ A. At $t = 0.5$ s, $i = 2(e^{(-7)(0.5)} - e^{(-2)(0.5)}) = -0.675$ A.

15.94 What is the voltage across the inductor of the circuit of Prob. 15.90 at $t = 0.5$ s?

∎
$$v_L = L\frac{di}{dt} = (5)(2)(-7e^{-7t} + 2e^{-2t}) \text{ V}$$
At $t = 0.5$ s, $v_L(0.5) = 10(-7e^{-3.5} + 2e^{-1}) = 5.24$ V.

15.95 In the circuit of Fig. 15-24, $C = 0.04$ F, $R = 10\,\Omega$, and $L = 1$ H. The capacitor is charged to 20 V and the switch is closed at $t = 0$. Find $i(t)$.

∎ The characteristic roots are, from Prob. 15.84, $p_1 = p_2 = p = -5$. The solution takes the form $i = A_1 e^{-5t} + A_2 te^{-5t}$. $i(0^+) = 0$ requires that $A_1 = 0$. Thus, $i = A_2 te^{-5t}$,
$$\frac{di}{dt} = A_2(e^{-5t} - 5te^{-5t}) \qquad \frac{di}{dt}(0^+) = -20 = A_2 \qquad \text{and} \qquad i = -20te^{-5t} \text{ A}$$

15.96 Determine the voltage across the inductor of the circuit of Prob. 15.95 at $t = 1$ s.
$$v_L = L\frac{di}{dt} = -20(e^{-5t} - 5te^{-5t})$$
At $t = 1$ s, $v_L = -20(e^{-5} - 5e^{-5}) = 0.54$ V.

15.97 In the circuit of Fig. 15-24, $C = 76.92$ mF, $R = 4\,\Omega$, and $L = 1$ H. The capacitor is charged to 100 V and the switch is closed at $t = 0$. Determine i for 0.1 s after the switch is closed.

∎ In this case the roots are $-2 \pm j3$ and the solution takes the form of $i = e^{-2t}(B_1 \cos 3t + B_2 \sin 3t)$. Since $i(0^+) = 0$, $B_1 = 0$ and $i = B_2 e^{-2t} \sin 3t$. $(di/dt)(0^+) = -100$ requires that $-100 = B_2(3)$ or $B_2 = -33.33$. Thus, $i = -33.33e^{-2t} \sin 3t$ A. At $t = 0.1$ s, $i = (-33.33)e^{-2(0.1)} \sin[3(0.1)] = -8.06$ A.

15.98 Determine the damping ratio and the damped frequency of oscillation of the current in the circuit of Prob. 15.97.

∎
$$\text{Damping ratio } \alpha = -2 \qquad \omega = 2\pi f = 3 \text{ rad/s}$$
Thus, $f = 3/2\pi = 0.48$ Hz.

15.99 Sketch $i(t)$ as obtained in Prob. 15.97.

▌ See Fig. 15-27.

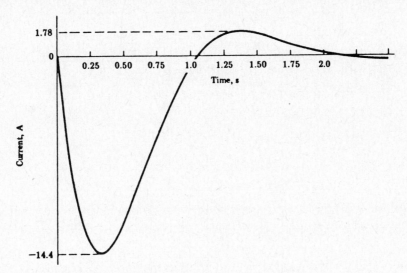

Fig. 15-27

15.100 In this problem we present a technique of plotting $i(t)$ for the circuit of Fig. 15-24. The procedure is as follows: (*a*) Determine the period of the sinusoidal function (or portion) of the solution, mark off time scale corresponding to time constants, and plot the sine wave. (*b*) Plot the exponential and its mirror image. (*c*) circle all points on the curves of (*b*) that correspond to the positive and negative peak values, respectively, of the sine wave. (*d*) Draw a smooth curve joining all the circled points. Using steps (*a*) through (*d*) plot $i = 6e^{-0.5t} \sin 4.186t$ A.

▌ The procedure is illustrated in Fig. 15-28*a* from which we obtain Fig. 15-28*b*.

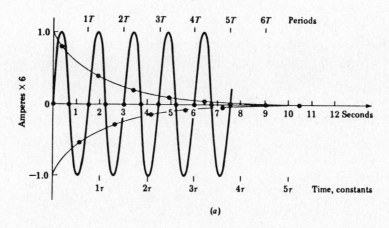

(*a*)

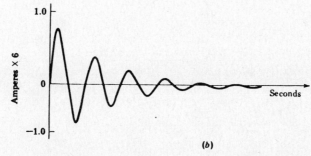

(*b*)

Fig. 15-28

15.101 Sketch the curve $i = 6e^{-0.5} \sin 3.142t$ A.

▌ See Fig. 15-29, where $\omega = 3.14$ or $f = 0.5$ Hz and $\tau = 2$ s.

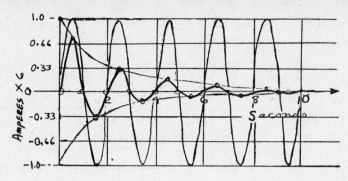

Fig. 15-29

15.102 Sketch $i = 10e^{-2.5t} \sin (12.56t + 30°)$ A.

▮ See Fig. 15-30, where $f = 12.56/2\pi = 2$ Hz, $T = 0.5$ s, and $\tau = 12.5 = 0.4$ s.

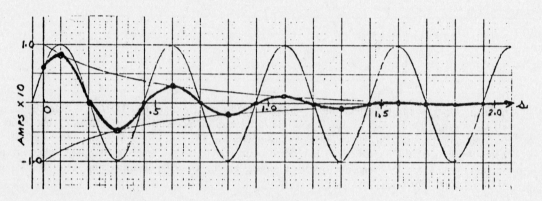

Fig. 15-30

15.103 Sketch $i = e^{-0.5t}(6 \cos 11.06t - 1.63 \sin 11.06t)$ A.

▮ First we express the quantity in parantheses as a pure sine function. Let $A \sin (11.06t + \theta°) = 6 \cos 11.06t - 1.63 \sin 11.06t$. Expanding and equating coefficients, we obtain

$$A = 6.22 \quad \text{and} \quad \theta = 105.2°$$

Thus, $i = (6.22)e^{-0.5t} \sin (11.06t + 105.2°)$ A, for which $\omega = 11.06$ rad/s, $f = 1.76$ Hz, and $\tau = 2$ s. The plot is shown in Fig. 15-31.

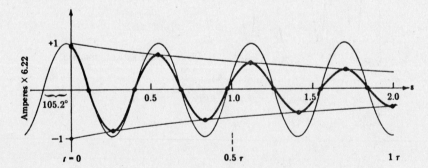

Fig. 15-31

15.104 In the circuit of Fig. 15-24, $C = 62.5$ mF, $L = 2$ H, and $R = 12 \Omega$. The capacitor is charged to 100 V and the switch is closed at $t = 0$. Solve for the transient current.

▮ By KVL we have (after differentiating),

$$2 \frac{d^2i}{dt^2} + 12 \frac{di}{dt} + \frac{1}{0.0625} i = 0$$

which has the characteristic roots $p_1 = -4$ and $p_2 = -2$. The current is of the form $i = A_1 e^{-4t} + A_2 e^{-2t}$ A. $i(0^+) = 0$ yields $A_1 + A_2 = 0$. Proceeding as in Probs. 15.90 and 15.91, we obtain

$$\frac{di}{dt}(0^+) = -50 = -4A_1 - 2A_2$$

Solving for A_1 and A_2 yields $A_1 = 25$ and $A_2 = -25$. Thus, $i = 25(e^{-4t} - e^{-2t})$ A.

15.105 What is the current in the circuit of Prob. 15.104 at $t = 0.5$ s?

▮ At $t = 0.5$ s, $i = 25(e^{-4(0.5)} - e^{-2(0.5)}) = -5.81$ A.

15.106 Determine the voltage across the capacitor of Prob. 15.104 at $t = 1$ s.

▮ $$v_C = \frac{1}{C} \int i \, dt = \frac{25}{0.0625} \int (e^{-4t} - e^{-2t}) \, dt = \frac{25}{0.25} (2e^{-2t} - e^{-4t})$$

At $t = 1$ sec., we have

$$v_C(1 \text{ s}) = 100(2e^{-2(1)} - e^{-4(1)}) = 25.23 \text{ V}$$

15.107 In the circuit of Fig. 15-24, let $L = 4$ H, $R = 40 \, \Omega$, and $C = 0.01$ F, which is initially charged to 600 V. The switch is closed at $t = 0$. What is the current 0.01 s after the switch is closed?

▮ Proceeding as in Prob. 15.106, the characteristic equation is $4p^2 + 40p + 1/0.01 = 0$, which has a pair of coincident roots, $p = -5$. The current has the form (see Prob. 15.86): $i = A_1 e^{-5t} + A_2 t e^{-5t}$. Since $i(0^+) = 0$, $A_1 = 0$ and $i = A_2 t e^{-5t}$.

$$\frac{di}{dt}(0^+) = -\frac{V_0}{4} = -150 = A_2$$

Thus, $i = -150 t e^{-5t}$ A. At $t = 0.01$ s, $i = (-150)(0.01)e^{-5(0.01)} = -1.43$ A.

15.108 Determine the steady-state current and the steady-state charge on the capacitor in the circuit of Prob. 15.107.

▮ Since $i = -150 t e^{-5t}$, $i \to 0$ A as $t \to \infty$. Also, $Q = CV = 0.01(0) = 0$ C. Physically, these conclusions imply that the capacitor is completely discharged through the resistor as $t \to \infty$.

15.109 In the circuit of Fig. 15-32 the parameters of coil 1 and coil 2 are, respectively, 1.5 H and 8 Ω and 0.5 H and 4 Ω. If $C = \frac{1}{18}$ F and it is charged to 100 V, determine the current 0.2 s after the switch is closed.

▮ The characteristic equation is $2p^2 + 12p + 18 = 0$, which has two coincident roots at $p = -3$. The solution takes the form of $i = A_1 e^{-3t} + A_2 t e^{-3t}$. Since $i(0^+) = 0$, $A_1 = 0$ and $i = A_2 t e^{-3t}$.

$$\frac{di}{dt}(0^+) = -\frac{100}{2} = -50 = A_2 \quad \text{(as in Prob. 15.107)}$$

Thus, $i = -50 t e^{-3t}$ A. At $t = 0.2$ s, $i = -50(0.2)e^{(-3)(0.2)} = -5.49$ A.

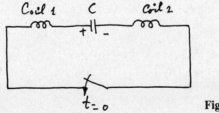

Fig. 15-32

15.110 What is the voltage across coil 2 in the circuit of Prob. 15.109 at $t = 0.2$ s?

▮ $$v_{coil2} = L_2 \frac{di}{dt} + R_2 i = (0.5)(-50)\frac{d}{dt}(te^{-3t}) - (4)(50)te^{-3t}$$

$$= -25(1 - 3t)e^{-3t} - 200te^{-3t} = -e^{-3t}(25 + 125t) \text{ V}$$

At $t = 0.2$ s, $v_{coil2} = -e^{(-3)(0.2)}(25 + 125 \times 0.2) = -27.44$ V.

15.111 Sketch the current in the circuit of Prob. 15.109.

▮ See Fig. 15-33.

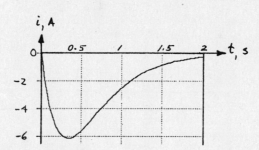

Fig. 15-33

15.112 Determine the time constant of the circuit shown in Fig. 15-24 for which $R = 16\,\Omega$, $L = 2\,H$, and $C = 0.0122\,F$. *Note:* It will be incorrect to take L/R or RC as the time constant of this circuit.

▮ We determine the time constant from the damping coefficient α as follows. By KVL, after differentiation, we have

$$2\frac{d^2i}{dt^2} + 16\frac{di}{dt} + \frac{1}{0.0122} = 0$$

The corresponding characteristic roots are $p = -4 \pm j5$. Thus, the form of solution is similar to that of Prob. 15.87, and $\alpha = 4$ and $\tau = \frac{1}{4} = 0.25\,s$.

15.113 Obtain an expression for the current in the circuit of Prob. 15.112, with $v_C(0^-) = 480\,V$.

▮ Since we have a pair of complex conjugate roots of the characteristic equation, the current is given by (as in Prob. 15.88) $i = e^{-4t}(A_1 \cos 5t + A_2 \sin 5t)$. $i(0^+) = 0$ requires $A_1 = 0$ and $i = A_2 e^{-4t} \sin 5t$.

$$\frac{di}{dt}(0^+) = -240 = A_2[(1)(5)(1) + 0]$$

or $$A_2 = -48 \quad \text{and} \quad i = -48e^{-4t} \sin 5t\,\text{A}$$

15.114 What is the voltage across the inductor of the circuit of Prob. 15.112 at $t = 0.5\,s$?

▮ $$v_L = L\frac{di}{dt} = 2\frac{d}{dt}(-48e^{-4t} \sin 5t) = -96e^{-4t}(-4 \sin 5t + 5 \cos 5t)$$

At $t = 0.5\,s$,

$$v_L = -96e^{(-4)(0.5)}[-4 \sin (5)(0.5) + 5 \cos (5)(0.5)] = 84.86\,\text{V}$$

15.115 Determine the voltage across the capacitor of the circuit of Prob. 15.112 at $t = 0.5\,s$.

▮ $$v_C = -(v_R + v_L) \qquad v_R = 16i = 16(-48e^{-4t} \sin 5t)$$

or at $t = 0.5\,s$,

$$v_R = (16)(-3.89) = -62.24\,\text{V} \qquad v_L = 84.86\,\text{V} \quad \text{(from Prob. 15.114)}$$

Thus, $v_C = -(-62.24 + 84.86) = -22.62\,\text{V}$.

15.116 What is the period of oscillation of the current in the circuit of Prob. 15.112?

▮ From Prob. 15.112,

$$\omega = 5 = 2\pi f \quad \text{or} \quad f = \frac{5}{2\pi} = \frac{1}{T}$$

Thus, $T = 2\pi/5 = 1.25\,s$.

15.117 Sketch the current in the circuit of Prob. 15.112.

▮ See Fig. 15-34 where $\tau = 0.25\,s$ and $T = 1.25\,s$.

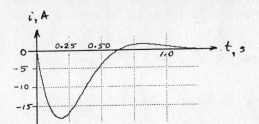

Fig. 15-34

15.118 In the circuit of Fig. 15-24, $R = 12\,\Omega$, $L = 1.0\,H$, and $C = 0.01\,F$. Determine its time constant and the damped frequency of oscillation.

▌ The characteristic equation is $p^2 + 12p + 1/0.01 = 0$, from which the roots are $p = -6 \pm j8$. Thus $\alpha = 6$ and $\tau = \frac{1}{6} = 0.167\,s$.

$$\omega = 8 = 2\pi f \quad \text{or} \quad f = \frac{8}{2\pi} = 1.273\,Hz$$

15.119 Obtain an expression for the current in the circuit of Prob. 15.118 if the capacitor is initially charged to 60 V.

▌ Proceeding as in Prob. 15.113, $i = A_2 e^{-6t} \sin 8t$,

$$\frac{di}{dt}(0^+) = -60 = A_2(8) \quad \text{or} \quad A_2 = -\frac{60}{8} = -7.5$$

Hence, $i = -7.5 e^{-6t} \sin 8t\,A$.

15.120 What is the voltage across the capacitor of the circuit of Prob. 15.118 at $t = 0.2\,s$?

▌ $$v_C = \frac{1}{C}\int i\,dt = \frac{-7.5}{0.01}\int (e^{-6t}\sin 8t)\,dt = -\frac{750}{100}\left[e^{-6t}(-6\sin 8t - 8\cos 8t)\right]\big|_{t=0.2\,s} = 13.02\,V$$

15.121 Verify that the result of Prob. 15.120 may also be obtained from $v_c = -(v_L + v_R)$ at $t = 0.2\,s$.

▌ $$v_L = L\frac{di}{dt} = \frac{d}{dt}(-7.5 e^{-6t}\sin 8t) = -7.5(-6e^{-6t}\sin 8t + e^{-6t}8\cos 8t)$$

$$= 14.0\,V \quad \text{at} \quad t = 0.2\,s$$

$$v_R = Ri = 12(-7.5 e^{-6t}\sin 8t) = -27.12 \quad \text{at} \quad t = 0.2\,s$$

Thus, $v_L + v_R = 14.04 - 27.12 = -13.08\,V$ or $v_C = -(v_L + v_R) = 13.08\,V$, which agrees with the result of Prob. 15.120.

15.122 Sketch the current for the circuit of Prob. 15.119.

▌ See Fig. 15-35.

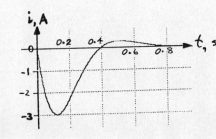

Fig. 15-35

15.123 Given: $R = 1\,\Omega$, $L = 2\,H$, and $C = 1\,F$, which is charged to 100 V in the circuit of Fig. 15-24. Determine the time constant and the frequency of damped oscillations.

▌ The characteristic equation is $2p^2 + p + 1 = 0$, which has the roots $p = -0.25 \pm j0.66$. Thus,

$$\tau = \frac{1}{0.25} = 4\,s \qquad \omega = 2\pi f = 0.66 \qquad \text{or} \qquad f = \frac{0.66}{2\pi} = 0.105\,Hz$$

15.124 What is the current in the circuit of Prob. 15.123 after one time constant?

▌ Proceeding as in Prob. 15.119,

$$i = A_2 e^{-0.25t} \sin 0.66t \qquad \frac{di}{dt}(0^+) = 0.66 A_2 = -50 \qquad \text{or} \qquad A_2 = -75.7$$

Thus, $i = -75.7 e^{-0.25t} \sin 0.66t$ A. At $t = 4\,\text{s} = \tau$,

$$i = -75.7 e^{-(0.25)(4)} \sin (4)(0.66) = -13.24 \text{ A}$$

15.125 Sketch the current for the circuit of Prob. 15.123.

▌ See Fig. 15-36.

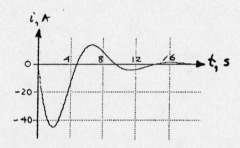

Fig. 15-36

15.126 A circuit consisting of a voltage (or current) source has a source-free response and a forced response. The sum of these components is the circuit response. Using this procedure, find the current in the circuit of Fig. 15-37 if the switch is closed at $t = 0$.

▌ Forced response,

$$i_f = I_0 = \frac{V}{R}$$

Natural or source-free response (from Prob. 15.35),

$$i_n = -I_0 e^{-(R/L)t}$$

Complete response,

$$i = i_f + i_n = I_0(1 - e^{-(R/L)t}) = \frac{V}{R}(1 - e^{-(R/L)t}) \text{ A} \qquad (1)$$

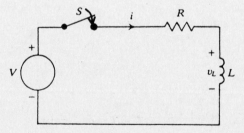

Fig. 15-37

15.127 Obtain the solution given by Eq. (1) of Prob. 15.126 by solving the equation that governs the current in the circuit of Fig. 15-37.

▌ The governing equation is

$$L \frac{di}{dt} + Ri = V$$

which may be solved by separating the variables as

$$\frac{L}{V - Ri} di = dt$$

By integration we obtain

$$-\frac{L}{R}\ln(V-Ri) = t + A \tag{1}$$

Using the initial condition to evaluate the constant of integration,

$$A = -\frac{L}{R}\ln V \tag{2}$$

Substituting Eq. (2) into Eq. (1) and simplifying the resulting expression yields

$$i = \frac{V}{R}(1 - e^{-Rt/L})$$

15.128 Sketch the current through and the voltage across the inductor of the circuit of Prob. 15.126.

▮ $$i_L = i = \frac{V}{R}(1 - e^{-Rt/L})\,\text{A} \qquad v_L = L\frac{di}{dt} = Ve^{-Rt/L}\,\text{V}$$

These are plotted in Fig. 15-38.

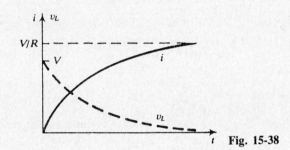

Fig. 15-38

15.129 Repeat Prob. 15.126 for v_C, the voltage across the circuit of Fig. 15-39.

▮ Forced response,

$$v_f = V$$

Natural or source-free response,

$$v_n = -Ve^{-t/RC} \quad \text{(from Prob. 15.3)}$$

Complete response, $$\qquad v_C = v_f + v_n = V(1 - e^{-t/RC}) \tag{1}$$

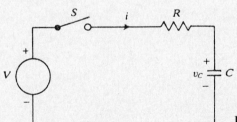

Fig. 15-39

15.130 Obtain Eq. (1) of Prob. 15.129 by using KVL.

▮ For $t > 0$, KVL gives

$$Ri + \frac{1}{C}\int_0^t i\,dt = V$$

which (since $i = dq/dt$) may also be written as

$$R\frac{dq}{dt} + \frac{1}{C}q = V$$

The solution becomes $q = q_n + q_f = Q_0 e^{-t/RC} + CV$, where, from the initial condition, $Q_0 = -CV$. Thus $q = CV(1 - e^{-t/RC})$ and $v_C = q/C = V(1 - e^{-t/RC})$.

15.131 Sketch the current through and the voltage across the capacitor of Prob. 15.130.

$$i_C = \frac{dq}{dt} = \frac{d}{dt}[CV(1 - e^{-t/RC})] = \frac{V}{R}e^{-t/RC}\text{ A}$$

$$v_C = V(1 - e^{-t/RC})\text{ V}$$

These are shown in Fig. 15-40.

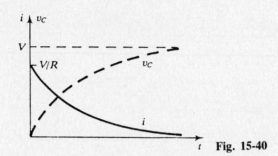

Fig. 15-40

15.132 In the circuit of Fig. 15-37, $R = 0.041\,\Omega$, $L = 0.17\,\text{H}$, and $V = 250\,\text{V}$. Determine the time for the current to reach 2000 A if the switch is closed at $t = 0$.

From Eq. (1) of Prob. 15.126,

$$i = 6098(1 - e^{-0.2412t})\text{ A} \qquad\text{or}\qquad 2000 = 6098(1 - e^{-0.2412t})$$

Solving for t yields $t = 1.65\,\text{s}$.

15.133 In the circuit of Fig. 15-37 we have $R = 8\,\Omega$, $L = 10\,\text{H}$, and $V = 12\,\text{V}$. Find i at $t = 0.1\,\text{s}$.

From Prob. 15.126, with the given values,

$$i = \tfrac{12}{8}(1 - e^{-8t/10}) = 1.5(1 - e^{-0.8t})\text{ A}$$

At $t = 0.1\,\text{s}$, $i = 1.5(1 - e^{(-0.8)(0.1)}) = 0.115\,\text{A}$.

15.134 Determine the time in the circuit of Prob. 15.133 when the voltage across the inductor is 5 V.

From Prob. 15.128,

$$v_L = L\frac{di}{dt} = Ve^{-Rt/L} \qquad\text{or}\qquad 5 = 12e^{-8t/10} \qquad\text{or}\qquad -\frac{8t}{10} = \ln\frac{5}{12}$$

Thus, $t = 1.094\,\text{s}$.

15.135 What is the voltage across the inductor of the circuit of Prob. 15.133 at $t = 0.1\,\text{s}$?

$v_L = 12e^{-0.8t}$. At $t = 0.1\,\text{s}$, $v_L = 12e^{(-0.8)(0.1)} = 11.08\,\text{V}$.

15.136 A coil having $L = 150\,\text{H}$ and $R = 200\,\Omega$ is connected in series with a 100-Ω resistor. A 240-V dc source is connected to the circuit at $t = 0$. Determine the voltage across the coil at $t = 0.5\,\text{s}$.

Proceeding as in Prob. 15.126,

$$i = \frac{240}{100 + 200}(1 - e^{-300t/150}) = 0.8(1 - e^{-2t})\text{ A}$$

At $t = 0.5\,\text{s}$, $i = 0.8(1 - e^{(-2)(0.5)}) = 0.506\,\text{A}$. Thus,

$$Ri = 100(0.506) = 50.6\,\text{V} \qquad v_{\text{coil}} = 240 - Ri = 240 - 50.6 = 189.4\,\text{V}$$

15.137 In the circuit of Fig. 15-41, the coil has a 10-Ω resistance and a 6-H inductance. If $R = 14\,\Omega$, $V = 24\,\text{V}$, and the switch is opened at $t = 0$, determine i.

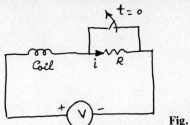

Fig. 15-41

▌ Forced response,

$$i_f = \frac{24}{10 + 14} = 1 \text{ A}$$

Natural or source-free response,

$$i_n = Ae^{-Rt/L} = Ae^{-4t} \quad \text{or} \quad i = 1 + Ae^{-4t}$$

$i(0^+) = \frac{24}{10} = 2.4 \text{ A}$ yields $A = 2.4 - 1 = 1.4$. Thus, $i = 1 + 1.4e^{-4t}$ A.

15.138 Determine the voltage across the coil of the circuit of Prob. 15.137 at $t = 0.1$ s.

▌ From Prob. 15.137, $i = 1 + 1.4e^{-4t}$ A. At $t = 0.1$ s, $i = 1 + 1.4e^{(-4)(0.1)} = 1.94$ A. Thus,

$$v_R = 14(1.94) = 27.16 \text{ V} \quad \text{and} \quad v_L = 24 - v_R = -3.16 \text{ V}$$

15.139 Calculate the current i_2 in the circuit of Fig. 15-42 at $t = 0.3$ s.

▌ Notice that the 12-Ω resistor has no effect on the current i_2. Therefore, by inspection (or from Prob. 15.126), $i_2 = \frac{24}{4}(1 - e^{-4t/8}) = 6(1 - e^{-0.5t})$ A. At $t = 0.3$ s, $i_2 = 6(1 - e^{(-0.5)(0.3)}) = 0.836$ A.

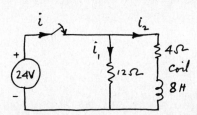

Fig. 15-42

15.140 Determine the steady-state power supplied by the source of the circuit of Fig. 15-42.

▌ $$P = VI = 24(I_1 + I_2) = 24(\tfrac{24}{12} + \tfrac{24}{4}) = 24(2 + 6) = 192 \text{ W}$$

15.141 In the circuit of Fig. 15-42, when the system reaches steady state, the switch is opened. Solve for the current through the inductor.

▌ Under steady state,

$$i_{\text{coil}} = I_0 = \tfrac{24}{4} = 6 \text{ A} \qquad \tau = \frac{L}{R} = \frac{8}{4 + 12} = 0.5 \text{ s}$$

Thus, $i_L = I_0 e^{-t/\tau} = 6e^{-2t}$ A.

15.142 How much energy is stored in the coil of the circuit of Problem 15.141 at $t = 0.3$ s?

▌ At $t = 0.3$ s, $i_L = 6e^{(-2)(0.3)} = 3.29$ A and $W_L = \tfrac{1}{2}L(i_L)^2 = \tfrac{1}{2}(8)(3.29)^2 = 43.3$ J.

15.143 The circuit of Fig. 15-43 is under steady state with the switch at position 1. At $t = 0$, the switch is moved to position 2. Find i.

▌ The current is of the form $i = A + Be^{-Rt/L}$. Since

$$i(\infty) = \tfrac{10}{40} = 0.25 \text{ A} \qquad A = 0.25$$

$$i(0^-) = i(0^+) = \tfrac{50}{40} = 1.25 \qquad B = i(0^+) - A = 1$$

Thus $i = 0.25 + e^{-2000t}$ A.

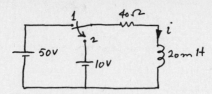

Fig. 15-43

15.144 The switch in the circuit of Fig. 15-44 is moved from 1 to 2 at $t = 0$. Find v_C.

∎
$$v_C(0^-) = v_C(0^+) = 100 \text{ V} \qquad v_C(\infty) = -50 \text{ V}$$

and
$$v_C = A + Be^{-t/RC} \qquad \frac{1}{RC} = 200$$

Applying the above conditions to v_C yields

$$A = v_C(\infty) = -50 \qquad B = v_C(0^+) - A = 100 + 50 = 150$$

Thus, $v_C = -50 + 150e^{-200t}$ V.

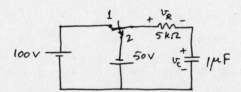

Fig. 15-44

15.145 Determine the current in the circuit of Fig. 15-44 for $t > 0$ from the results of Prob. 15.144.

∎
$$i = \frac{v_R}{R} = C \frac{dv_C}{dt}$$

By KVL, $v_R + v_C + 50 = 0$. Thus,

$$v_R = -150e^{-200t} \text{ V} \qquad \text{and} \qquad i = -\frac{150}{5000}e^{-200t} = -0.03e^{-200t} \text{ A}$$

Otherwise,
$$C \frac{dv_C}{dt} = (10^{-6})(150)(-200)e^{-200t} = -0.03e^{-200t} \text{ A}$$

as expected.

15.146 Obtain the energy w_C and w_R in the circuit of Prob. 15.144.

∎
$$w_C = \tfrac{1}{2}C(v_C)^2 = 1.25(3e^{-200t} - 1)^2 \text{ mJ} \qquad w_R = \int_0^t \frac{(v_R)^2}{R}\, dt = 11.25(1 - e^{-400t}) \text{ mJ}$$

15.147 In the circuit of Fig. 15-39, $R = 600\,\Omega$, $C = 400\,\mu\text{F}$, and $V = 12\,\text{V}$. Find v_C at $t = 0.1\,\text{s}$.

∎ From Eq. (1) of Prob. 15.129,

$$v_C = V(1 - e^{-t/RC}) = 12(1 - e^{-t/(600)(400)(10^{-6})}) \text{ V}$$

At $t = 0.1\,\text{s}$, $v_C = 12(1 - e^{-0.1/0.24}) = 4.09\,\text{V}$.

15.148 Determine the current in the circuit of Prob. 15.147 at $t = 0.1\,\text{s}$.

∎
$$i_C = C \frac{dv_C}{dt} = \frac{V}{R}e^{-t/RC} = \frac{12}{600}e^{-t/0.24} \text{ A}$$

At $t = 0.1\,\text{s}$, $i_C = 0.02e^{-0.1/0.24} = 0.0132\,\text{A} = 13.2\,\text{mA}$.

15.149 For the circuit of Fig. 14-45 determine the current through and the voltage across the capacitor at $t = 0^+$ and at $t = 0^-$.

∎
$$v_C(0^-) = v_C(0^+) = 0 \text{ V} \qquad i_C(0^-) = 0 \text{ A}$$

At $t = 0^+$, $v_R + v_C = 24$. Since $v_R(0^+) = Ri(0^+)$ and $v_C(0^+) = 0$, we obtain $i(0^+) = i_C(0^+) = 24/(2)(10^6) = 12\,\mu\text{A}$.

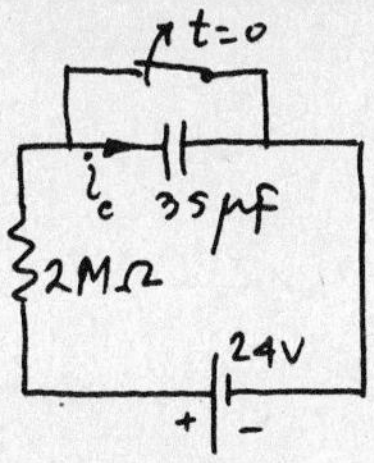

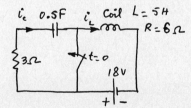

Fig. 15-45

15.150 Obtain the current in the circuit of Prob. 15.149 at $t = 70$ s.

┃ In general (see Prob. 15.148), $i_C = (V/R)e^{-t/RC}$. Since $RC = 2 \times 10^6 \times 35 \times 10^{-6} = 70$,

$$V = 24 \qquad R = 2\,\text{M}\Omega \qquad i_C = 12 \times 10^{-6} e^{-t/70}\,\text{A}$$

or at $t = 70$ s, $i_C = 12 \times 10^{-6} e^{-1} = 4.415\,\mu\text{A}$.

15.151 In the circuit of Fig. 15-39, $R = 1\,\text{M}\Omega$, $C = 20\,\mu\text{F}$, and $V = 50$ V. The capacitor is initially charged to -20 V, with the polarities as shown. Determine i_C and v_C at $t = 0^-$ and at $t = 0^+$.

┃
$$v_C(0^-) = v_C(0^+) = 20\,\text{V} \qquad i_C(0^-) = 0\,\text{A}$$

since the switch is open. At $t = 0^+$,

$$i_C(0^+)R + v_C = V \qquad \text{or} \qquad i_C(0^+)10^6 - 20 = 50$$

Thus, $i_C(0^+) = 70\,\mu\text{A}$.

15.152 Calculate the current in the circuit of Fig. 15-39 at $t = 0.5$ s.

┃
$$i = i_f + i_n = 0 + Ae^{-t/\tau} \qquad \tau = RC = 20\,\text{s}$$

Thus, $i = Ae^{-t/20}$. At $t = 0$ s, $i = i_C(0^+) = 70\,\mu\text{A}$ so that $A = 70 \times 10^{-6}$ and $i = 70e^{-t/20}\,\mu\text{A}$. At $t = 0.5$ s, $i = 70e^{-0.5/20} = 68.27\,\mu\text{A}$.

15.153 How much charge is accumulated on the capacitor of the circuit of Fig. 15-39 when the circuit has reached steady state.

┃
$$Q = CV_C \qquad V_C = 50\,\text{V}$$

Thus, $Q = 20 \times 10^{-6} \times 50 = 1\,\text{mC}$.

15.154 In the circuit of Fig. 15-46 determine the current through the inductor and the voltage across the capacitor at $t = 0^-$ and at $t = 0^+$.

┃
$$i_L(0^-) = i_L(0^+) = 0 \qquad v_C(0^-) = v_C(0^+) = 18\,\text{V}$$

Fig. 15-46

15.155 Find i_C when the switch has been closed in the circuit of Fig. 15-46, at $t = 0.5$ s.

┃ In this case, we have a source-free RC circuit for which $i_C = Ae^{-t/RC} = Ae^{-t/1.5}$. At $t = 0^+$,

$$i_C(0^+)(R) + v_C(0^+) = 0 \qquad \text{or} \qquad i_C(0^+) = -\tfrac{18}{3} = -6\,\text{A}$$

Thus $A = -6$ and $i_C = -6e^{-t/1.5}$. At $t = 0.5$ s, $i_C = -6e^{-0.5/1.5} = -4.3\,\text{A}$.

15.156 Find i_L when the switch has been closed in the circuit of Fig. 15-46, at $t = 0.5$ s.

▮ In this case we have an *RL* circuit excited by an 18-V source. Thus,

$$i_L = i_f + i_n = \tfrac{18}{6} + Ae^{-6t/5} \text{ A}$$

At $t = 0$, $i_L = 0$ so that $A = -\tfrac{18}{6} = -3$ or $i = 3 - 3e^{-6t/5}$ A. At $t = 0.5$ s, $i = 3(1 - e^{-(6)(0.5)/5}) = 1.35$ A.

15.157 At $t = 0$ the switch in Fig. 15-47 is moving from position 1 to 2. Solve for i.

▮ With switch at position 1, the capacitor is charged to the battery voltage, 20 V. Since $RC = (500 \times 10^3)(500 \times 10^{-6}) = 250$ s,

$$v_C = V_0 e^{-t/RC} = 20e^{-t/250}$$

$$i_C = C \frac{dv_C}{dt} = (500 \times 10^{-6})[20(-\tfrac{1}{250})e^{-t/250}] = -40e^{-t/250} \ \mu\text{A}$$

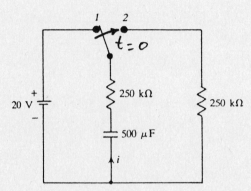

Fig. 15-47

15.158 Determine the voltage across each resistor of the circuit of Fig. 15-47, at $t = 1$ s.

▮ The two voltages are equal and $v_R = Ri = Ri_C = -250 \times 10^{+3} \times 40 \times 10^{-6}e^{-t/250}$. At $t = 1$ s, $v_R = -250 \times 10^3 \times 40 \times 10^{-6}e^{-1/250} = -9.96$ V.

15.159 In the circuit of Fig. 15-48, the switch is moved from 1 to 2 at $t = 0$. Determine i.

▮
$$i = i_f + i_n = \frac{V}{R} + I_0 e^{-Rt/L} = \tfrac{40}{2} + (\tfrac{20}{5} - \tfrac{40}{2})e^{-2t/0.5} = 20 - 16e^{-4t} \text{ A}$$

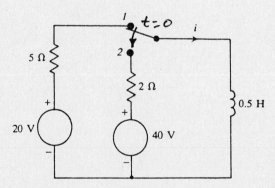

Fig. 15-48

15.160 How much energy is dissipated in the 2-Ω resistor of Prob. 15.159 in 0.25 s?

▮
$$w_R = \int_0^t (i^2 R)\, dt = 2\int_0^{0.25} (20 + 4e^{-4t})^2\, dt = 254 \text{ Ws}$$

15.161 The switch in the *RL* circuit shown in Fig. 15-49 is moved from position 1 to position 2 at $t = 0$. Obtain v_R and v_L with polarities as indicated.

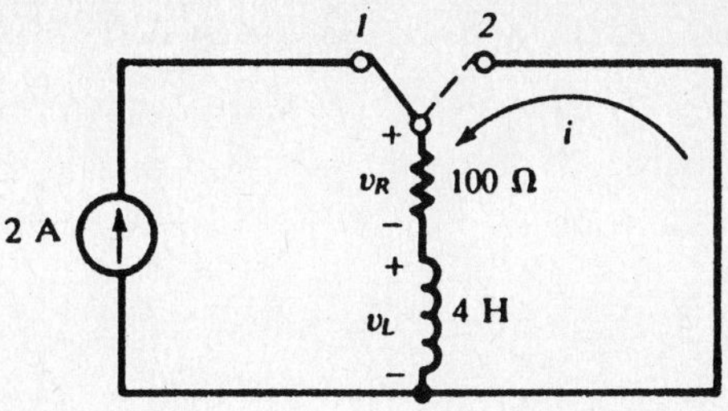

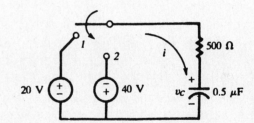

Fig. 15-49

▮ The constant-current source drives a current through the inductance in the same direction as that of the transient current i. Then, for $t > 0$,

$$i = I_0 e^{-Rt/L} = 2e^{-25t}\,\text{A} \qquad v_R = Ri = 200e^{-25t}\,\text{V} \qquad v_L = -v_R = -200e^{-25t}\,\text{V}$$

15.162 For the transient of Prob. 15.161 obtain p_R and p_L.

▮
$$p_R = v_R i = 400e^{-50t}\,\text{W} \qquad p_L = v_L i = -400e^{-50t}\,\text{W}$$

Negative power for the inductance is consistent with the fact that energy is leaving the element, and, since this energy is being transferred to the resistance, p_R is positive.

15.163 The switch in the circuit shown in Fig. 15-50 is closed at $t = 0$, at which moment the capacitor has charge $Q_0 = 500\,\mu\text{C}$, with the polarity indicated. Obtain i and q, for $t > 0$, and sketch the graph of q.

▮ The initial charge has a corresponding voltage $V_0 = Q_0/C = 25\,\text{V}$, whence $v_C(0^+) = -25\,\text{V}$. The sign is negative because the capacitor voltage, in agreement with the positive direction of the current, would be + on the top plate. Also $v_C(\infty) = +50\,\text{V}$ and $\tau = 0.02\,\text{s}$. Thus, $v_C = -75e^{-50t} + 50\,\text{V}$ from which

$$q = Cv_C = -1500e^{-50t} + 1000\,\mu\text{C} \qquad i = \frac{dq}{dt} = 75e^{-50t}\,\text{mA}$$

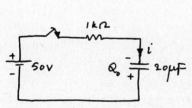

Fig. 15-50

Fig. 15-51

15.164 The switch in the circuit of Fig. 15-51 is closed on position 1 at $t = 0$ and then moved to 2 after one time constant, at $t = \tau = 250\,\mu\text{s}$. Obtain the current for $t > 0$.

▮ It is simplest first to find the charge on the capacitor, since it is known to be continuous (at $t = 0$ and at $t = \tau$), and then to differentiate it to obtain the current. For $0 \le t \le \tau$, q must have the form $q = Ae^{-t/\tau} + B$. From the assumption $q(0) = 0$ and the condition

$$i(0^+) = \frac{dq}{dt}\bigg|_{0^+} = \frac{20\,\text{V}}{500\,\Omega} = 40\,\text{mA}$$

we find that $A = -B = -10\,\mu\text{C}$, or

$$q = 10(1 - e^{-4000t})\,\mu\text{C} \qquad (0 \le t \le \tau) \tag{1}$$

From Eq. (1), $q(\tau) = 10(1 - e^{-1})\,\mu\text{C}$; and we know that $q(\infty) = (0.5\,\mu\text{F})(-40\,\text{V}) = -20\,\mu\text{C}$. Hence, q is determined for $t \ge \tau$ as

$$q = [q(\tau) - q(\infty)]e^{-(t-\tau)/\tau} + q(\infty) = 71.55e^{-4000t} - 20\,\mu\text{C} \tag{2}$$

Differentiating Eqs. (1) and (2),

$$i = \frac{dq}{dt} = \begin{cases} 40e^{-4000t}\,\text{mA} & (0 < t < \tau) \\ -286.2e^{-4000t}\,\text{mA} & (t > \tau) \end{cases}$$

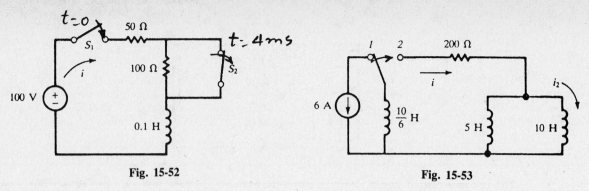

Fig. 15-52   **Fig. 15-53**

15.165 A series RL circuit has a constant voltage V applied at $t = 0$. At what time does $v_R = v_L$?

▌ The current in an RL circuit is a continuous function, starting at zero in this case, and reaching the final value V/R. Thus, for $t > 0$,

$$i = \frac{V}{R}(1 - e^{-t/\tau}) \quad \text{and} \quad v_R = Ri = V(1 - e^{-t/\tau})$$

where $\tau = L/R$ is the time constant of the circuit. Since $v_R + v_L = V$, the two voltages will be equal when

$$v_R = \tfrac{1}{2}V \qquad V(1 - e^{-t/\tau}) = \tfrac{1}{2}V \qquad e^{-t/\tau} = \tfrac{1}{2} \qquad \frac{t}{\tau} = \ln 2$$

that is, when $t = 0.693\tau$. Note that this time is independent of V.

15.166 A constant voltage is applied to a series RL circuit at $t = 0$. The voltage across the inductance is 20 V at 3.46 ms and 5 V at 25 ms. Obtain R if $L = 2$ H.

▌ Using the result of Prob. 15.128, we have

$$\tau = \frac{t_2 - t_1}{\ln v_1 - \ln v_2} = \frac{25 - 3.46}{\ln 20 - \ln 5} = 15.54 \text{ ms} \qquad R = \frac{L}{\tau} = \frac{2}{15.54 \times 10^{-3}} = 128.7\ \Omega$$

15.167 In Fig. 15-52 switch S_1 is closed at $t = 0$. Switch S_2 is opened at $t = 4$ ms. Obtain i for $t > 0$.

▌ As there is always inductance in the circuit, the current is a continuous function at all times. In the interval $0 \le t \le 4$ ms, with the 100 Ω shorted out and a time constant $\tau = (0.1 \text{ H})/(50\ \Omega) = 2$ ms, i starts at zero and builds toward $100 \text{ V}/50\ \Omega = 2$ A, even though it never gets close to that value. Hence,

$$i = 2(1 - e^{-t/2})\ \text{A} \qquad (0 \le t \le 4) \tag{1}$$

wherein t is measured in ms. In particular, $i(4) = 2(1 - e^{-2}) = 1.729$ A. In the interval $t \ge 4$ ms, i starts at 1.729 A and decays toward $100/150 = 0.667$ A, with a time constant $0.1/150 = \tfrac{2}{3}$ ms. Therefore, with t again in ms,

$$i = (1.729 - 0.667)e^{-(t-4)/(2/3)} + 0.667 = 428.4e^{-3t/2} + 0.667\ \text{A} \qquad (t \ge 4) \tag{2}$$

15.168 In the circuit shown in Fig. 15-53, the switch is moved to position 2 at $t = 0$. Obtain the current i_2 at $t = 34.7$ ms.

▌ After the switching, the three inductances have the equivalent

$$L_{\text{eq}} = \frac{10}{6} + \frac{5(10)}{15} = 5 \text{ H}$$

Then $\tau = 5/200 = 25$ ms, and so, with t in ms,

$$i = 6e^{-t/25}\ \text{A} \qquad i_2 = \tfrac{5}{15}i = 2e^{-t/25}\ \text{A} \qquad \text{and} \qquad i_2(34.7) = 2e^{-34.7/25} = 0.50 \text{ A}$$

15.169 In the circuit of Fig. 15-54, with i_1 and i_2 as shown, obtain a differential equation for i_1.

▌ By KVL,

$$R_1 i_1 + L_1 \frac{di_1}{dt} + R_1 i_2 = V \tag{1}$$

$$R_1 i_1 + (R_1 + R_2)i_2 + L_2 \frac{di_2}{dt} = V \tag{2}$$

Differentiating Eq. (1) with respect to t,

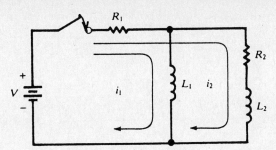

Fig. 15-54

$$R_1 \frac{di_1}{dt} + L_1 \frac{d^2i_1}{dt^2} + R_1 \frac{di_2}{dt} = 0 \tag{3}$$

and then eliminate i_2 and di_2/dt between Eqs. (1), (2), and (3). The result is a second-order equation for i_1:

$$\frac{d^2i_1}{dt^2} + \frac{R_1L_1 + R_2L_1 + R_1L_2}{L_1L_2} \frac{di_1}{dt} + \frac{R_1R_2}{L_1L_2} i_1 = \frac{R_2V}{L_1L_2} \tag{4}$$

15.170 Obtain the characteristic equation for Eq. (4) of Prob. 15.169 and write the initial conditions.

❚ The characteristic equation is

$$p^2 + \frac{(R_1 + R_2)L_1 + R_1L_2}{L_1L_2} p + \frac{R_1R_2}{L_1L_2} = 0$$

The initial conditions are

$$i_1(0^+) = i_1(0^-) = 0 \qquad i_2(0^+) = i_2(0^-) = 0 \qquad \frac{di_1}{dt}(0^+) = \frac{V}{L_1}$$

15.171 In the circuit of Fig. 15-55, determine v_C.

❚ As far as the natural response of the circuit is concerned, the two resistors are in parallel; hence, $\tau = R_{\text{eq}}C = (5\,\Omega)(2\,\mu\text{F}) = 10\,\mu\text{s}$. By continuity, $v_C(0^+) = v_C(0^-) = 0$. Furthermore, as $t \to \infty$, the capacitor becomes an open circuit, leaving $20\,\Omega$ in series with the $50\,\text{V}$. That is,

$$i(\infty) = \tfrac{50}{20} = 2.5\,\text{A} \qquad v_C(\infty) = (2.5\,\text{A})(10\,\Omega) = 25\,\text{V}$$

Knowing the end conditions on v_C, we can write $v_C = [v_C(0^+) - v_C(\infty)]e^{-t/\tau} + v_C(\infty) = 25(1 - e^{-t/10})\,\text{V}$, wherein t is measured in μs.

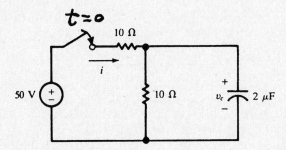

Fig. 15-55

15.172 Solve for i in the circuit of Prob. 15.171.

❚ The current in the capacitor is given by

$$i_C = C \frac{dv_C}{dt} = 5e^{-t/10}\,\text{A}$$

and the current in the parallel $10\text{-}\Omega$ resistor is $i_{10\Omega} = v_C/10\,\Omega = 2.5(1 - e^{-t/10})\,\text{A}$. Hence, $i = i_C + i_{10\Omega} = 2.5(1 + e^{-t/20})\,\text{A}$.

15.173 The switch in the two-mesh circuit shown in Fig. 15-56 is closed at $t = 0$. Obtain the currents i_1 and i_2, for $t > 0$.

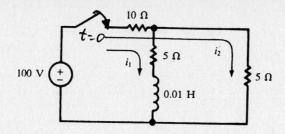

Fig. 15-56

I
$$10(i_1 + i_2) + 5i_1 + 0.01 \frac{di_1}{dt} = 100 \tag{1}$$

$$10(i_1 + i_2) + 5i_2 = 100 \tag{2}$$

From Eq. (2), $i_2 = (100 - 10i_1)/15$. Substituting in Eq. (1),

$$\frac{di_1}{dt} + 833i_1 = 3333 \tag{3}$$

The steady-state solution (particular solution) of Eq. (3) is $i_1(\infty) = 3333/833 = 4.0 \text{ A}$; hence $i_1 = Ae^{-833t} + 4.0 \text{ A}$. The initial condition $i_1(0^+) = 0$ now gives $A = -4.0 \text{ A}$, so that $i_1 = 4.0(1 - e^{-833t}) \text{ A}$ and $i_2 = 4.0 + 2.67e^{-833t} \text{ A}$.

15.174 Set up a differential equation with initial conditions for i in the circuit shown in Fig. 15-57, where the sources V and I are simultaneously turned on at $t = 0$. At $t = 0^-$, the capacitor is uncharged and the inductor is unenergized.

I For $t > 0$, KCL at node a yields

$$i - C \frac{dv_C}{dt} + I = 0 \tag{1}$$

and KVL around the left mesh yields

$$L \frac{di}{dt} + Ri + v_C - V = 0 \tag{2}$$

Now eliminate dv_C/dt between Eqs. (1) and the derivative of (2) to obtain

$$L \frac{d^2i}{dt^2} + R \frac{di}{dt} + \frac{1}{C} i = -\frac{I}{C} \tag{3}$$

The capacitor voltage and inductor current must be continuous at $t = 0$. Therefore, the initial conditions to be imposed on Eq. (3) read

$$i(0) = 0 \qquad L \frac{di}{dt}\Big|_0 = V \tag{4}$$

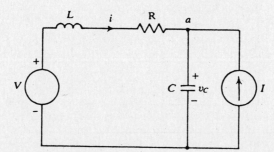

Fig. 15-57

15.175 In the circuit of Fig. 15-58, switch S represents a current-operated relay, the contacts of which close when $i_L = 0.9 \text{ A}$ and open when $i_L = 0.25 \text{ A}$. Determine the time period for one cycle of the relay operation.

I Let us measure time from a moment at which the switch opens. Then the inductor current builds up from 0.25 A, with time constant

$$\frac{L}{R} = \frac{1/11}{70 + 30} = \frac{1}{1100} \text{ s}$$

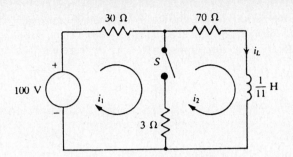

Fig. 15-58

toward a final value of $100/(70+30) = 1$ A. That is, $i_L(t) = 1 - 0.75e^{-1100t}$ A. This current reaches 0.9 A when $1100t_1 = \ln 7.5$, or $t_1 = 1.83$ ms. At this instant, S closes, producing a two-mesh circuit with mesh currents i_1 and $i_2 = i_L$. KVL gives

$$33i_1 - 3i_2 = 100 \qquad 73i_2 - 3i_1 + \frac{1}{11}\frac{di_2}{dt} = 0$$

or, eliminating i_1,

$$\frac{di_2}{dt} + 800i_2 = 100 \tag{1}$$

The solution of Eq. (1) that satisfies the initial condition $i_2(t_1) = 0.9$ A is $i_2(t) = i_L(t) = 0.125 + 0.775e^{-800(t-t_1)}$. This current decays to 0.25 A when $800(t_2 - t_1) = \ln 6.2$ or $t_2 - t_1 = 2.28$ ms. Hence the relay period is $t_2 = t_1 + 2.28 = 1.83 + 2.28 = 4.11$ ms.

15.176 Assuming that Thévenin's and Norton's theorems are applicable to circuits containing inductances and/or capacitances, represent (*a*) a capacitance C, with an initial charge Q_0, by a Thévenin equivalent circuit and (*b*) an inductance L, with an initial current I_0, by a Norton equivalent circuit.

❚ (*a*) The open-circuit voltage across the capacitor of Fig. 15-59*a* is $V_0 = Q_0/C$. Hence we obtain the Thévenin equivalent circuit of Fig. 15-59*b*, where the capacitor is uncharged. (*b*) The required circuit is shown in Fig. 15-60*b*, where the initial current through L is zero.

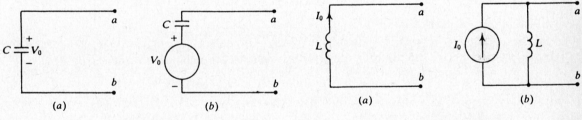

Fig. 15-59   **Fig. 15-60**

15.177 The switch of the circuit of Fig. 15-61*a* has been closed for a long time. It is opened at $t = 0$. Determine the voltage across the 200-Ω resistor.

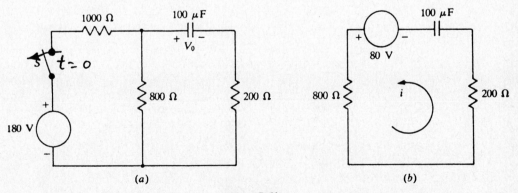

Fig. 15-61

❚ Before S was opened, the network was under steady state and the capacitance was charged to a voltage V_0. This voltage is the same as the voltage across the 800-Ω resistance; thus, by voltage division, $V_0 = \frac{800}{1800}(180) = 80$ V. In view of Prob. 15.176a the circuit for $t > 0$ may be represented as in Fig. 15-59b. We have

$$800i + 200i + \frac{1}{100 \times 10^{-6}} \int_0^t i \, dt = 80$$

The solution is $i = \frac{80}{1000} e^{-t/(1000)(100 \times 10^{-6})}$ A, and the voltage across the 200-Ω resistor becomes $v = 200i = 16e^{-10t}$ V.

15.178 The switch in the circuit of Fig. 15-62a is opened at $t = 0$; prior to this the network was under steady state. Find the voltage across the 6-Ω resistor.

❚
$$i_L(0^-) = \frac{36\,(6/9)}{10 + (3)(6)/(3+6)} = 2 \text{ A}$$

Applying Prob. 15.176b, we obtain the circuit of Fig. 15-62b, for which

$$2 = \frac{v}{9} + \frac{1}{0.1} \int_0^t v \, dt \tag{1}$$

The solution to Eq. (1) is $v = 18e^{-90t}$ V. Hence the voltage across the 6-Ω resistance becomes $v_{6\Omega} = \frac{6}{9}(18e^{-90t}) = 12e^{-90t}$ V.

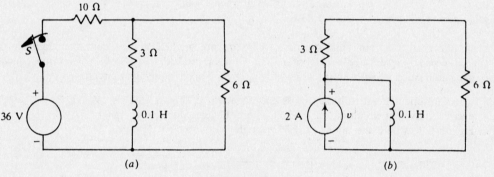

(a)   (b)

Fig. 15-62

15.179 In the circuit of Fig. 15-63, the switch is moved from position 1 to position 2 at $t = 0$. Find v_R.

❚
$$i = I_0 e^{-Rt/L} \qquad I_0 = 2 \text{ A} \qquad R = 100 \,\Omega \qquad L = 4 \text{ H}$$

Thus $i = 2e^{-25t}$ A and $v_R = Ri = 200e^{-25t}$ V.

15.180 Determine the initial energy stored in the inductor of the circuit of Fig. 15-63. Next, calculate the energy stored at $t = 0.1$ s and, hence, find the energy dissipated in the resistor in 0.1 s.

❚
$$W_{L0} = \tfrac{1}{2} L I_0^2 = \tfrac{1}{2}(4)(2)^2 = 8 \text{ J}$$

At $t = 0.1$ s,

$$i = 2e^{-25t} = 2e^{-25 \times 0.1} = 0.164 \text{ A} \qquad w_L(0.1) = \tfrac{1}{2}(4)(0.164)^2 = 0.054 \text{ J}$$

$$w_R = 8 - 0.054 = 7.946 \text{ J}$$

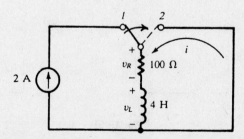

Fig. 15-63

15.181 Verify that the result of Prob. 15.180 is correct by solving the problem by direct integration.

▌
$$w_R = \int_0^{0.1} i^2 R \, dt = 100 \int_0^{0.1} (2e^{-25t})^2 \, dt$$

$$= \frac{200}{-25} (e^{-50t})_0^{0.1} = 7.946 \text{ J}$$

which agrees with the result of Prob. 15.180.

15.182 In the circuit of Prob. 15.164 determine (*a*) the charge at $t = 0.1$ ms; (*b*) the instantaneous energy stored in the capacitor; (*c*) the power dissipated in the resistor; (*d*) the power in the resistor; and (*e*) the voltage across the resistor at $t = 0.1$ ms.

▌ (*a*) Since $\tau = RC = (500)(0.5 \times 10^{-6}) = 0.25$ ms, Eq. (1) of Prob. 15.164 holds. Thus,
$$q = 10 (1 - e^{-4000t}) \, \mu \text{ C}$$

At $t = 0.1$ ms
$$q = 10 (1 - e^{-4000 \times 0.1 \times 10^{-3}}) = 3.3 \, \mu \text{ C}$$

(*b*)
$$w_C = \frac{q^2}{2C} = \begin{cases} (1 - e^{-4000t})^2 \times 10^{-4} \text{ J} & 0 \le t \le \tau \\ (71.55 e^{-4000t} - 20)^2 \times 10^{-6} \text{ J} & \tau \le t \end{cases}$$

(*c*)
$$p_R = i^2 (500) = \begin{cases} 0.8 e^{-8000t} \text{ W} & 0 \le t \le \tau \\ 40.95 e^{-8000t} \text{ W} & \tau \le t \end{cases}$$

(*d*) At $t = 0.1$ ms we use the first expression of part (*c*), since $\tau = 0.25$ ms. Thus, p_R at $t = 0.1$ ms becomes
$$p_R = 0.8 e^{-8000(0.1 \times 10^{-3})} = 0.36 \text{ W}$$

(*e*)
$$v_R(0.1) = (40 e^{-4000 \times 0.1 \times 10^{-3}})(500) \times 10^{-3} = 13.4 \text{ V}$$

15.183 Sketch the current for the circuit of Prob. 15.164.

▌ See Fig. 15-64.

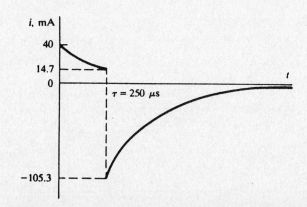

Fig. 15-64

15.184 Determine the voltage across the capacitor of the circuit of Prob. 15.164 for $0 < t < \infty$.

▌ Since $v_C = q/C$, from Eq. (1) of Prob. 15.164 we have
$$v_C = 20(1 - e^{-4000t}) \text{ V} \qquad (0 \le t \le \tau)$$

Similarly, from Eq. (2) of Prob. 15.164 we obtain,
$$v_C = 143.1 e^{-4000t} - 40 \text{ V} \qquad (\tau \le t < \infty)$$

15.185 In the circuit of Prob. 15.163, determine the instant when the charge on the capacitor changes its polarity. Sketch $q(t)$.

▌ From Prob. 15.163, $q(t) = 1000 - 1500e^{-50t} \mu C$. For polarity reversal $q(t)$ must go through zero; that is, t is given by $0 = 1000 - 1500e^{-50t}$ or $t = 8.11$ ms. The sketch $q(t)$ is shown in Fig. 15-65.

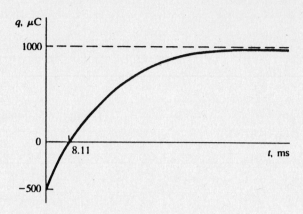

Fig. 15-65

15.186 In the RLC circuit of Fig. 15-66, V is a dc source. Write a formal expression for the current i if the initial charge on the capacitor is zero.

▌ The voltage equation is

$$L \frac{di}{dt} + Ri + \frac{1}{C} \int_0^t i \, dt = V$$

or, differentiating with respect to time,

$$L \frac{d^2i}{dt^2} + R \frac{di}{dt} + \frac{1}{C} i = 0 \tag{1}$$

Since Eq. (1) is homogeneous, $i_f = 0$ and

$$i = i_n = A_1 e^{p_1 t} + A_2 e^{p_2 t} \tag{2}$$

where p_1 and p_2 are the *characteristic roots* of Eq. (1):

$$p_1 = -\frac{R}{2L} + \sqrt{\left(\frac{R}{2L}\right)^2 - \frac{1}{LC}} \equiv -\alpha + \beta$$

$$p_2 = -\frac{R}{2L} - \sqrt{\left(\frac{R}{2L}\right)^2 - \frac{1}{LC}} \equiv -\alpha - \beta \tag{3}$$

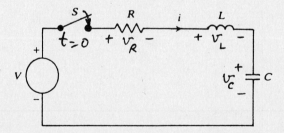

Fig. 15-66

15.187 State the initial conditions to evaluate the constants of integration in Eq. (2) of Prob. 15.186. Define $\omega_0 \equiv 1/\sqrt{LC}$, the resonance frequency, and express the characteristic roots of Eq. (3) of Prob. 15.186 in terms of α and ω_0. Comment on the significance of α.

▌ The initial conditions are

$$i(0^+) = 0 \quad \text{and} \quad L \frac{di}{dt} (0^+) = V$$

Since $\alpha = R/2L$ and $\omega_0 = 1\sqrt{LC}$,

$$\beta = \sqrt{\left(\frac{R}{2L}\right)^2 - \frac{1}{LC}} = \sqrt{\alpha^2 - \omega_0^2}$$

$$p_1, p_2 = -\alpha \pm \sqrt{\alpha^2 - \omega_0^2} \tag{1}$$

Because α in Eq. (1) is a positive real number, the transient current decays in magnitude like an exponential function, and α is called the *damping coefficient* (see also Prob. 15.89).

15.188   Notice from Eq. (1) of Prob. 15.187 that p_1, p_2 may be real and distinct, real and coincident, or a pair of complex conjugate roots.   Write the forms of solutions for these three cases.

▌ *Case 1*: $\alpha > \omega_0$.   Here, β is real and positive, and $\beta < \alpha$.   The solution takes the form

$$i = A_1 e^{-(\alpha - \beta)t} + A_2 e^{-(\alpha + \beta)t} \tag{1}$$

i.e., the sum of two decaying exponentials.   In this case the circuit is said to be *overdamped*.

Case 2: $\alpha = \omega_0$.   It can be shown that as $\beta \to 0$,   Eq. (1) goes over into

$$i = (A_1 + A_2 t)e^{-\alpha t} \tag{2}$$

Case 3: $\alpha < \omega_0$. Now β is a pure imaginary, $\beta = j|\beta|$,   and Eq. (2) becomes $i = e^{-\alpha t}(A_1 e^{j|\beta|t} + A_2 e^{-j|\beta|t})$ or, equivalently,

$$i = A e^{-\alpha t} \sin(|\beta|t + \psi) \tag{3}$$

As given by Eq. (3) the response is a damped sine wave of frequency $|\beta|$ (rad/s); the circuit is *underdamped*.

15.189   Sketch the forms of solutions given by Eqs. (1) through (3) of Prob. 15.188.

▌ See Fig. 15-67.

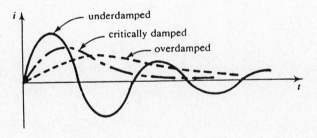

Fig. 15-67

15.190   In the circuit of Fig. 15-66, $V = 0$, $R = 200\,\Omega$, $L = 0.1\,H$, $C = 13.33\,\mu F$,   and $v_C(0^-) = 200\,V$.   Determine the resonance frequency, damping coefficient, and the damped frequency of oscillation, β, in rad/s.

▌

$$\omega_0 = \frac{1}{\sqrt{LC}} = \frac{1}{\sqrt{0.1 \times 13.33 \times 10^{-6}}} = \sqrt{75 \times 10^4} = 2\pi f_0$$

Thus, $$f_0 = \frac{100\sqrt{75}}{2\pi} = 137.85\,Hz \qquad \alpha = \frac{R}{2L} = \frac{200}{2 \times 0.1} = 1000\,s^{-1}$$

$$\beta = \sqrt{\alpha^2 - \omega_0^2} = \sqrt{(10^3)^2 - (7.5 \times 10^5)} = 500\,s^{-1}$$

15.191   For the circuit of Prob. 15.190, solve for i if the switch is closed at $t = 0$.

▌ Noting that $\alpha^2 > \omega_0^2$, we have, for $t > 0$ (with numerical values taken from Prob. 15.190),

$$i = e^{-1000t}(A_1 e^{500t} + A_2 e^{-500t}) \tag{1}$$

With inductance in the circuit, $i(0^+) = i(0^-) = 0$, which is one condition for establishing the values of the constants A_1 and A_2.   The other condition is provided by the continuity of the capacitor charge, and hence of the capacitor voltage, at $t = 0$.   Thus, at $t = 0^+$,   KVL reads:

$$(0)R + L \frac{di}{dt}\Big|_{0^+} + v_C(0^-) = 0 \quad \text{or} \quad \frac{di}{dt}\Big|_{0^+} = -2000 \text{ A/s}$$

Applying these two conditions to Eq. (1) and its time derivative, $0 = A_1 + A_2$ and $-2000 = -500A_1 - 1500A_2$, from which $A_1 = -2 \text{ A}$, $A_2 = 2 \text{ A}$, and $i = -2e^{-500t} + 2e^{-1500t} \text{ A}$.

15.192 Repeat Prob. 15.191 for $C = 10 \ \mu\text{F}$, other data remaining unchanged.

    ⫽ In this case $\omega_0 = \alpha$, and the initial conditions are

$$i(0^+) = 0 \qquad \frac{di}{dt}\Big|_{0^+} = -2000 \text{ A/s} \qquad \alpha = 1000 \text{ s}^{-1}$$

These determine the unknown constants as $A_1 = 0$, $A_2 = -2000 \text{ A}$; hence, $i = -2000te^{-1000t} \text{ A}$.

15.193 Repeat Prob. 15.191 for $C = 1 \ \mu\text{F}$, other data remaining unchanged.

    ⫽ In this case $\alpha < \omega_0$. As before,

$$i(0^+) = 0 \qquad \frac{di}{dt}\Big|_{0^+} = -2000 \text{ A/s} \qquad \alpha = 1000 \text{ s}^{-1}$$

but now $\beta = \sqrt{10^6 - 10^7} = j3000 \text{ rad/s}$. Then $i = e^{-1000t}A_3 \sin(3000t + \phi)$. The constants are obtained from the initial conditions as $\phi = 0$, $A_3 = -0.667 \text{ A}$; hence, $i = -0.667e^{-1000t} \sin 3000t \text{ A}$.

15.194 An inductance L, a capacitance C, and a resistance R are all connected in parallel. If the initial current through the inductance is I_0 and the initial charge on the capacitance is Q_0, determine the natural behavior of the circuit in terms of the common voltage $v(t)$ across the elements.

    ⫽ For $t > 0$, KCL gives

$$\frac{v}{R} + \left[\frac{1}{L}\int_0^t v(u)\,du + I_0\right] + C\frac{dv}{dt} = 0$$

or, taking the time derivative,

$$C\frac{d^2v}{dt^2} + \frac{1}{R}\frac{dv}{dt} + \frac{1}{L}v = 0 \tag{1}$$

with initial conditions

$$v(0) = \frac{Q_0}{C} \qquad C\frac{dv}{dt}\Big|_0 = -\left(\frac{Q_0}{RC} + I_0\right) \tag{2}$$

Equation (1) has the same form as Eq. (1) of Prob. 15.186. Thus, we have the solution from Eq. (2) of Prob. 15.186, $v(t) = A_1 e^{p_1 t} + A_2 e^{p_2 t}$, where

$$p_1 = -\alpha + \sqrt{\alpha^2 - \omega_0^2} \qquad p_2 = -\alpha - \sqrt{\alpha^2 - \omega_0^2}$$

$$\alpha = \frac{1}{2RC} \equiv \text{damping coefficient} \qquad \omega_0 = \frac{1}{\sqrt{LC}} \equiv \text{resonant frequency}$$

15.195 Consider the natural behavior of a critically damped series RLC circuit (see Fig. 15-66) in which the initial current is zero. Determine the time at which the current reaches its maximum value in $R = 5 \ \Omega$ and $L = 10 \text{ mH}$.

    ⫽ For a critically damped circuit the natural current is given by Eq. (2) of Prob. 15.188, $i = (A_1 + A_2 t)e^{-\alpha t}$. Since $i = 0$ at $t = 0$, we have $A_1 = 0$, and $i = A_2 te^{-\alpha t}$. For a maximum i,

$$\frac{di}{dt} = A_2 e^{-\alpha t}(1 - \alpha t) = 0$$

from which

$$t = \frac{1}{\alpha} = \frac{2L}{R} = \frac{2(10 \times 10^{-3})}{5} = 4 \text{ ms}$$

15.196 The circuit of Fig. 15-66 is critically damped. If $R = 200\,\Omega$ and $L = 100\,\text{mH}$, determine the value of C.

▌ The condition for critical damping is $\alpha^2 = \omega_0^2$, or

$$\left(\frac{R}{2L}\right)^2 = \frac{1}{LC}$$

Thus

$$C = \frac{4L}{R^2} = \frac{4(100 \times 10^{-3})}{(200)^2} = 10\,\mu\text{F}$$

15.197 With the C determined in Prob. 15.196 and with zero initial conditions, the switch is closed at $t = 0$ (see Fig. 15-66). If $V = 100\,\text{V}$, find v_C.

▌ By Eq. (2) of Prob. 15.188, the current in the circuit is

$$i(t) = (A_1 + A_2 t)e^{-\alpha t} \quad \text{with} \quad \alpha = \frac{R}{2L} = 1000\,\text{s}^{-1}$$

At $t = 0$, $i = 0$, and $di/dt = V/L = 1000\,\text{A/s}$; thus, $A_1 = 0$, $A_2 = 1000\,\text{A/s}$, and $i(t) = 1000te^{-1000t}\,\text{A}$. Then,

$$v_C(t) = \frac{1}{C}\int_0^t i(u)\,du = \frac{1}{10 \times 10^{-6}}\int_0^t 1000ue^{-1000u}\,du = 100[1 - e^{-1000t}(1 + 1000t)]\,\text{V}$$

15.198 The parameters of the circuit of Fig. 15-66 are such that the circuit is underdamped. With zero initial conditions, the switch is closed at $t = 0$. Obtain an expression for the voltage across the capacitor.

▌ Applying the initial conditions

$$i(0) = 0 = A\sin\psi \qquad \left.\frac{di}{dt}\right|_0 = \frac{V}{L} = A(-\alpha\sin\psi + |\beta|\cos\psi)$$

which imply that $\sin\psi = 0$ and $A\cos\psi = V/L|\beta|$. Thus, Eq. (3) of Prob. 15.188 becomes

$$i(t) = \frac{V}{L|\beta|}e^{-\alpha t}\sin|\beta|t$$

From this, using $\alpha^2 + |\beta\tau|^2 = \omega_0^2 \equiv 1/LC$, we obtain

$$v_C(t) = \frac{1}{C}\int_0^t i(u)\,du = V\left[1 - \frac{e^{-\alpha t}}{|\beta|}(\alpha\sin|\beta|t + |\beta|\cos|\beta|t)\right] = V\left[1 - \frac{e^{-\alpha t}}{\sin\phi}\sin(|\beta|t + \phi)\right]$$

in which the new phase angle ϕ is defined by $\cos\phi \equiv \alpha/\omega_0$.

15.199 Because the circuit in Prob. 15.198 is underdamped, the voltage across C will undergo (damped) oscillations. Determine the time at which the first maximum of the capacitor voltage occurs. What is the value of the voltage at this instant?

▌ From the expression for $i = C(dv_C/dt)$ obtained in Prob. 15.198 the first maximum of $v_C(t)$ occurs at $t = \pi/|\beta|$. We have

$$v_C(\pi|\beta|) = V\left[1 - \frac{e^{-\alpha\pi/|\beta|}}{\sin\phi}\sin(\pi + \phi)\right] = V(1 + e^{-\pi\cot\phi})$$

15.200 Sketch $v_C(t)$ determined in Prob. 15.198 and indicate the time when the first maximum of $v_C(t)$ occurs. This maximum is known as the *peak overshoot*.

▌ See Fig. 15-68.

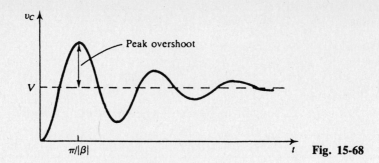

Fig. 15-68

15.201 Calculate the *percent overshoot* of the capacitor voltage in Prob. 15.198.

▌ The function $v_C(t)$ is graphed in Fig. 15-68. It is seen that the greatest deviation of the voltage from its steady-state value occurs at $t = \pi/|\beta|$. Expressing this peak overshoot as a fraction,

$$\text{Percent overshoot} \equiv \frac{v_C(\pi/|\beta|) - V}{V} \times 100\% \equiv 100e^{-\pi \cot \phi}$$

15.202 For the circuit of Prob. 15.198, $V = 100$ V, $R = 200 \,\Omega$, and $L = 100$ mH. Calculate C such that the peak overshoot is 5 percent.

▌ By Prob. 15.201,

$$100e^{-\pi \cot \phi} = 5 \quad \text{or} \quad \cot \phi = \frac{\ln 20}{\pi} = 0.954$$

whence $\cos \phi = \alpha/\omega_0 = 0.690$. For this circuit,

$$\alpha = \frac{R}{2L} = \frac{200}{2(100 \times 10^{-3})} = 1000 \text{ s}^{-1} \quad \text{and} \quad \frac{1}{\omega_0^2} = \left(\frac{0.690}{1000}\right)^2 = 4.76 \times 10^{-7} = LC$$

from which

$$C = \frac{4.76 \times 10^{-7}}{100 \times 10^{-3}} = 4.76 \,\mu\text{F}$$

15.203 In an RC series circuit, $C = 40 \,\mu\text{F}$, $R = 400 \,\Omega$, and the charge on the capacitor varies as $q = 4000e^{-62.5t} \,\mu\text{C}$. Determine the energy dissipated in the resistor for 1 ms.

▌
$$i = \frac{dq}{dt} = \frac{d}{dt}(4000e^{-62.5t} \times 10^{-6}) = -0.25e^{-62.5t} \text{ A}$$

$$p_R = i^2 R = (0.25e^{-62.5t})^2 400 = 25e^{-125t} \text{ W}$$

$$w_R = \int_0^{10^{-3}} (25e^{-125t} \, dt) = 0.2(1 - e^{-125 \times 10^{-3}}) = 23.5 \text{ mJ} \tag{1}$$

15.204 To what voltage was the capacitor of Prob. 15.203 initially charged? Obtain the result from the definition of capacitance as well as from energy storage.

▌ Since $C = q/V$, we have:

$$V_0 = \frac{Q_0}{C} = \frac{4000 \times 10^{-6}}{40 \times 10^{-6}} = 100 \text{ V}$$

At $t = \infty$, the energy dissipated in the resistor is the initial energy stored in the capacitor. Thus, from Eq. (1) of Prob. 15.203,

$$w_R(\infty) = 0.2 = \tfrac{1}{2}CV_0^2 \quad \text{or} \quad V_0 = \sqrt{\frac{(0.2)(2)}{40 \times 10^{-6}}} = 100 \text{ V}$$

15.205 In the circuit of Fig. 15-66, $R = 3 \text{ k}\Omega$, $L = 10$ H, $C = 200 \,\mu\text{F}$, and $V = 50$ V at $t = 0$. Find $i(t)$ if all initial conditions are zero.

▌
$$\alpha = \frac{R}{2L} = 150 \text{ s}^{-1} \quad \omega_0^2 = \frac{1}{LC} = 500 \text{ s}^{-2} \quad \beta = \sqrt{\alpha^2 - \omega_0^2} = 148.3 \text{ s}^{-1}$$

The circuit is overdamped $(\alpha > \omega_0)$.

$$s_1 = -\alpha + \beta = -1.70 \text{ s}^{-1} \quad s_2 = -\alpha - \beta = -298.3 \text{ s}^{-1} \quad \text{and} \quad i = A_1 e^{-1.70t} + A_2 e^{-298.3t}$$

Since the circuit contains an inductance, $i(0^+) = i(0^-) = 0$; also, $q(0^+) = q(0^-) = 0$. Thus, at $t = 0^+$, KVL gives

$$0 + 0 + L \left.\frac{di}{dt}\right|_{0^+} = V \qquad \text{or} \qquad \left.\frac{di}{dt}\right|_{0^+} = 5 \, \text{A/s}$$

Applying these initial conditions to the expression for i,

$$0 = A_1(1) + A_2(1) \qquad 5 = -1.70 A_1(1) - 298.3 A_2(1)$$

from which $\quad A_1 = -A_2 = 16.9 \, \text{mA} \quad$ and $\quad i = 16.9(e^{-1.70t} - e^{-298.3t}) \, \text{mA}$.

15.206 Sketch the transient current in the circuit of Prob. 15.205.

$\blacksquare$ See Fig. 15-69.

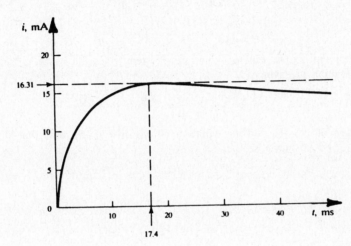

Fig. 15-69

15.207 At what instant does the current in the circuit of Prob. 15.205 reach its maximum?

$\blacksquare$ For the time of maximum current, $di/dt = 0 = -28.73 e^{-1.70t} + 5041.3 e^{-298.3t}$. Solving by logarithms, $t = 17.4 \, \text{ms}$. See also Fig. 15-69.

15.208 A series RLC circuit, with $R = 50 \, \Omega$, $L = 0.1 \, \text{H}$, and $C = 50 \, \mu\text{F}$, has a constant voltage $V = 100 \, \text{V}$ applied at $t = 0$. Obtain the current transient, assuming zero initial charge on the capacitor.

$\blacksquare \qquad \alpha = \frac{R}{2L} = 250 \, \text{s}^{-1} \qquad \omega_0^2 = \frac{1}{LC} = 2.0 \times 10^5 \, \text{s}^{-2} \qquad \beta = \sqrt{\alpha^2 - \omega_0^2} = j370.8 \, \text{rad/s}$

This is an oscillatory case $(\alpha < \omega_0)$, and the general current expression is $i = e^{-250t}(A_1 \cos 370.8t + A_2 \sin 370.8t)$. The initial conditions, obtained as in Prob. 15.205, are

$$i(0^+) = 0 \qquad \left.\frac{di}{dt}\right|_{0^+} = 1000 \, \text{A/s}$$

and these determine the values: $A_1 = 0$, $A_2 = 2.70 \, \text{A}$. Then $i = e^{-250t}(2.70 \sin 370.8t) \, \text{A}$.

15.209 Repeat Prob. 15.208 for $Q_0 = 2500 \, \mu\text{C}$.

$\blacksquare$ In this case the second initial condition in Prob. 15.208 changes to

$$0 + L \left.\frac{di}{dt}\right|_{0^+} + \frac{Q_0}{C} = V \qquad \text{or} \qquad \left.\frac{di}{dt}\right|_{0^+} = \frac{100 - (2500/50)}{0.1} = 500 \, \text{A/s}$$

Thus $A_2 = 1.35$ and $i = e^{-250t}(1.35 \sin 370.8t) \, \text{A}$.

15.210 At $t = 0$, the switch is opened in the circuit of Fig. 15-70. All initial conditions are zero. Set up a differential equation for the node voltage v and state the initial conditions to evaluate the arbitrary constants in the corresponding solution.

▮ For $t > 0$, we have

$$i_1 + i_2 = I \tag{1}$$

$$v = R_1 i_1 + L \frac{di_1}{dt} \tag{2}$$

$$v = R_2 i_2 + \frac{1}{C} \int_0^t i_2 \, dt \tag{3}$$

and their first and second derivatives

$$\frac{di_1}{dt} + \frac{di_2}{dt} = 0 \qquad \frac{d^2 i_1}{dt^2} + \frac{d^2 i_2}{dt^2} = 0$$

$$\frac{dv}{dt} = R_1 \frac{di_1}{dt} + L \frac{d^2 i_1}{dt^2} \tag{4}$$

$$\frac{dv}{dt} = R_2 \frac{di_2}{dt} + \frac{1}{C} i_2 \qquad \frac{d^2 v}{dt^2} = R_2 \frac{d^2 i_2}{dt^2} + \frac{1}{C} \frac{di_2}{dt}$$

Equations (1) and (2) and the five Eqs. (4) compose a system from which i_1 and i_2 and their first and second derivatives may be eliminated, giving

$$L \frac{d^2 v}{dt^2} + (R_1 + R_2) \frac{dv}{dt} + \frac{1}{C} v = \frac{R_1 I}{C} \tag{5}$$

which is the sought equation. To find the initial conditions on Eq. (5), note that at $t = 0^+$, the capacitor voltage is zero, and $i_2 = I$; hence,

$$v(0^+) = R_2 I \tag{6}$$

Moreover, Eq. (2) becomes

$$R_2 I = L \frac{di_1}{dt} \bigg|_{0^+}$$

and Eq. (1) and the fourth Eq. (4) give

$$\frac{dv}{dt} \bigg|_{0^+} = -R_2 \frac{di_1}{dt} \bigg|_{0^+} + \frac{I}{C}$$

These two relations imply

$$\frac{dv}{dt} \bigg|_{0^+} = \left(\frac{1}{C} - \frac{R_2^2}{L} \right) I$$

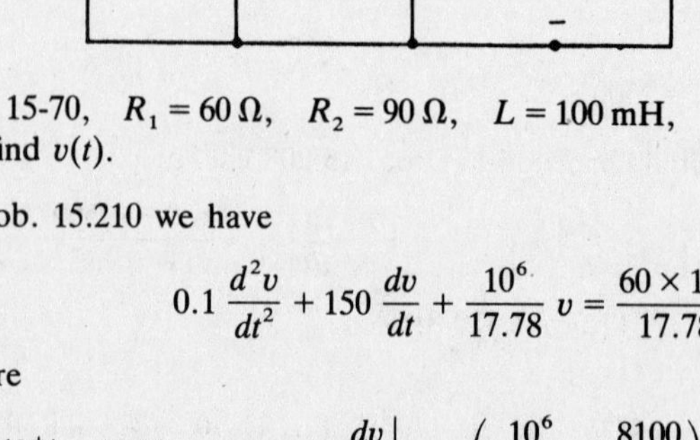

Fig. 15-70

15.211 In the circuit of Fig. 15-70, $R_1 = 60 \, \Omega$, $R_2 = 90 \, \Omega$, $L = 100 \, \text{mH}$, $C = 17.78 \, \mu\text{F}$, and $I = 1.0 \, \text{A}$. For zero initial conditions find $v(t)$.

▮ From Eq. (5) of Prob. 15.210 we have

$$0.1 \frac{d^2 v}{dt^2} + 150 \frac{dv}{dt} + \frac{10^6}{17.78} v = \frac{60 \times 10^6}{17.78}$$

The initial conditions are

$$v(0^+) = 90 \, \text{V} \qquad \text{and} \qquad \frac{dv}{dt} \bigg|_{0^+} = \left(\frac{10^6}{17.78} - \frac{8100}{0.1} \right) = -24.75 \times 10^3$$

The solution then becomes $v = 30[2 + (1 - 75t)e^{-750t}] \, \text{V}$.

15.212 In the circuit of Fig. 15-66, $R = 1.0\,\Omega$, $L = 2\,\text{H}$, $C = 200\,\mu\text{F}$, and $V = 50\,\text{V}$. Find i at $t = 0.5\,\text{s}$.

❚ By KVL,

$$2\frac{di}{dt} + i + \frac{10^6}{200}\int i\,dt = 50$$

which has the characteristic equation $2p^2 + p + 5000 = 0$, and the roots are $p = -0.25 \pm j50$. With $i = 0$ at $t = 0$, the solution takes the form

$$i = Ae^{-0.25t}\sin 50t \qquad \frac{di}{dt}(0^+) = \frac{V}{L} = \frac{50}{2} = 25\,\text{A} \qquad \text{or} \qquad A = 0.5$$

Thus, $i = 0.5e^{-0.25t}\sin 50t\,\text{A}$. At $t = 0.5\,\text{s}$, $i = 0.5e^{-0.25 \times 0.5}\sin(50)(0.5) = -0.058\,\text{A}$.

15.213 Determine the voltage across the inductor of the circuit of Prob. 15.212 at $t = 0.5\,\text{s}$.

❚ $$v_L = L\frac{di}{dt} = 2\frac{d}{dt}(0.5e^{-0.25t}\sin 50t) = e^{-0.25t}(50\cos 50t - 0.25\sin 50t)\,\text{V}$$

At $\qquad t = 0.5\,\text{s}$, $v_L = e^{-0.25 \times 0.5}[50\cos(50)(0.5) - 0.25\sin(50)(0.5)] = 43.59\,\text{V}$

15.214 How much energy is stored in the capacitor of the circuit of Prob. 15.212 at $t = 0.5\,\text{s}$?

❚ At $t = 0.5\,\text{s}$, from Probs. 15.212 and 15.213 we have

$$v_R = 1i = 1(-0.058) = -0.058\,\text{V} \qquad v_L = 43.59\,\text{V}$$

By KVL,

$$v_C + v_R + v_L = 50 \qquad \text{or} \qquad v_C = 50 - (43.59 - 0.058) = 6.47\,\text{V}$$

$$w_C = \tfrac{1}{2}C(v_C)^2 = \tfrac{1}{2}(200 \times 10^{-6})(6.47)^2 = 4.186\,\text{mJ}$$

15.215 Figure 15-71 represents the primary circuit of a gasoline-engine ignition system. The contacts called "points" are closed and opened by a rotating cam. Assume the cam closes the points for a "dwell" period of 0.004 s, after which the contacts open. Determine the coil current 0.004 s after the contacts close.

❚ When the contacts close, the capacitor is short-circuited and only an RL circuit remains for which $0.005\,di/dt + i = 6$. The solution becomes $i = 6 + Ae^{-200t}\,\text{A}$. $i = 0$ at $t = 0$ requires $A = -6$. Thus, $i = 6(1 - e^{-200t})\,\text{A}$. At $t = 0.004\,\text{s}$, $i = 6(1 - e^{-200 \times 0.004}) = 3.304\,\text{A}$.

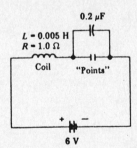

Fig. 15-71

15.216 Calculate the current in the circuit of Prob. 15.215 0.001 s after the contacts open.

❚ When the contacts open, we have an RLC series circuit for which the initial conditions are

$$i(0^+) = i(0^-) = 3.30\,\text{A} \qquad v_C(0^+) = v_C(0^-) = 0\,\text{V}$$

By KVL we obtain the circuit integrodifferential equation having the characteristic equation $0.005p^2 + p + 10^6/0.2 = 0$. The characteristic roots are $p = -100 \pm j3.2 \times 10^4$. Thus,

$$i = e^{-100t}(A_1\cos 32{,}000t + A_2\sin 32{,}000t)\,\text{A}$$

Since $i = 3.304\,\text{A}$ at $t = 0$, $A_1 = 3.304$. At $t = 0$, KVL gives $v_R + v_L = 6$, since

$$v_C(0^+) = v_C(0^-) = 0 \qquad \text{or} \qquad 3.304(1) + 0.005\frac{di}{dt}(0^+) = 6$$

Thus,
$$\frac{di}{dt}(0^+) = 539.2 = 32{,}000A_2 - 100A_1$$

Thus, $A_2 = 0.027$ and $i = e^{-100t}(3.304\cos 32{,}000t + 0.027\sin 32{,}000t)$ A
which, at $t = 0.001$ s, becomes $i = 2.51$ A.

15.217 Find the frequency of oscillation of the current wave in the circuit of Prob. 15.216.

▮ From Prob. 15.216,

$$\omega = 32{,}000 = 2\pi f \quad \text{or} \quad f = \frac{32{,}000}{2\pi} = 5093 \text{ Hz}$$

15.218 State all the initial conditions for the circuit of Fig. 15-72, which is under steady state for $t < 0$, and the switch is opened at $t = 0$.

▮
$$v_C(0^-) = v_C(0^+) = 0 \qquad i_L(0^-) = i_L(0^+) = \tfrac{120}{30} = 4 \text{ A}$$

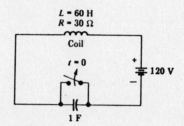

Fig. 15-72

15.219 Determine the current in the circuit of Prob. 15.218 0.4 s after the switch is opened.

▮ The KVL equation is

$$60\frac{di}{dt} + 30i + \int i\, dt = 120$$

from which the characteristic equation is $60p^2 + 30p + 1 = 0$.   The characteristic roots are $p = -0.46, -0.04$.

$$i = i_f + i_n = 0 + A_1 e^{-0.46t} + A_2 e^{-0.04t}$$

$i(0^+) = 4$ implies that $A_1 + A_2 = 4$. At $t = 0$,

$$60\frac{di}{dt}(0^+) + 30i(0^+) + v_C(0^+) = 120$$

Thus,
$$\frac{di}{dt}(0^+) = 0 = 0.46\,A_1 + 0.04\,A_2$$

Solving for A_1 and A_2 yields $A_1 = -0.38$ and $A_2 = 4.38$. Thus, $i = -0.38e^{-0.46t} + 4.38e^{-0.04+}$ A +
$i = 3.89$ A.

15.220 What is the induced voltage in the coil of the circuit of Fig. 15-72 at $t = 0.4$ s?

▮ From Prob. 15.219,

$$i = -0.38e^{-0.46t} + 4.38e^{-0.04t}$$

$$v_L = L\frac{di}{dt} = 60[(-0.38)(-0.46)e^{-0.46t} + (4.38)(-0.04)e^{-0.04t}]$$

or, at $t = 0.4$ s, $v_L = 60(0.145 - 0.172) = -1.62$ V.

15.221 Determine the total energy stored in the circuit of Fig. 15-72 at $t = 0.4$ s.

▮ $v_C + v_L + v_R = 120$. At $t = 0.4$ s, $v_C = 120 + 1.62 - (3.89)(30) = 4.92$ V.

$$w = w_L + w_C = \tfrac{1}{2}L(i)^2 + \tfrac{1}{2}C(V_C)^2 = \tfrac{1}{2}(60)(3.89)^2 + \tfrac{1}{2}(1)(4.92)^2 = 466.07 \text{ J}$$

15.222 A voltmeter is connected across the coil of the circuit of Fig. 15-72 to read the instantaneous voltage across the coil. What is the voltmeter reading at $t = 0.4$ s?

$\blacksquare$ $v_{\text{coil}} + v_C = 120$. At $t = 0.4$ s, $v_C = 4.92$ V. Thus, $v_{\text{coil}} = 120 - 4.92 = 115.08$ V = voltmeter reading.

15.223 An RL series circuit has $R = 3 \, \Omega$ and $L = 6$ H, and is excited by a decaying voltage source $v = 30e^{-0.5t}$ V at $t = 0$. Determine the current in the circuit at $t = 5$ s.

$\blacksquare$ The KVL equation is

$$6 \frac{di}{dt} + 3i = 30e^{-0.5t} \tag{1}$$

Thus,

$$i_n = A_1 e^{-0.5t} \text{ A} \tag{2}$$

which is the source-free response. Let

$$i_f = A_2 t e^{-0.5t} \text{ A} \tag{3}$$

Then

$$i = i_f + i_n \tag{4}$$

Combining Eqs. (1) through (4) yields

$$i = A_1 e^{-0.5t} + 5t e^{-0.5t} \tag{5}$$

At $t = 0$, $i = 0$ implies $A_1 = 0$. Thus $i = 5t e^{-0.5t}$ A. At $t = 5$, $i = 5(5)e^{-0.5 \times 5} = 2.05$ A.

15.224 A turbine-driven dc generator driven at 30 V feeds power to an electromagnet whose inductance and resistance are 6.0 H and 3.0 Ω, respectively. The resistance and inductance of the generator are negligible. Sketch the circuit and (**a**) determine the circuit current. (**b**) Tripping the turbine causes an exponential decay in turbine speed and voltage. Assuming the decay of generator voltage may be expressed by $e_{\text{gen}} = 30e^{-0.5t}$, determine the current 5 s after the turbine tripped.

$\blacksquare$ The problem is similar to that of Prob. 15.223 except for the initial condition, which is $i(0^+) = \frac{30}{3} = 10$ A (see Fig. 15-73). Using Eq. (5) of Prob. 15.223, we have $10 = A_1$. Thus, $i = 10e^{-0.5t} + 5t e^{-0.5t}$ A. At $t = 5$, $i = 2.87$ A.

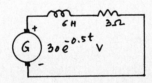

Fig. 15-73

15.225 A series circuit consisting of a 250-μF capacitor and a 1000-Ω resistor is connected to a generator whose voltage is represented by $e_{\text{gen}} = 60e^{-7t}$ V. The capacitor is initially discharged, and the generator voltage is applied at $t = 0$. Determine the current at $t = 0.2$ s.

$\blacksquare$ The initial conditions are

$$v_C(0^-) = v_C(0^+) = 0 \qquad i(0^+) = \frac{v(0^+)}{R} = \frac{60}{1000} = 0.06 \text{ A} \qquad i = i_f + i_n$$

The KVL equation is

$$\frac{10^6}{250} \int i \, dt + 1000i = 60e^{-7t}$$

Let $i_f = A_1 e^{-7t}$. For forced response,

$$\int i_f \, dt = \int A_1 e^{-7t} \, dt = -\frac{A_1}{7} e^{-7t} + k = q_f C$$

At $t = 0$, $q_f = 0$. Thus $k = 0$, and

$$\frac{10^6}{250} \left(-\frac{A_1}{7} \right) + 1000 A_1 = 60 \qquad \text{or} \qquad A_1 = 0.14$$

and

$$i_f = 0.14e^{-7t} \text{ A} \qquad i_n = A_2 e^{-4t} \text{ A} \qquad i = A_2 e^{-4t} + 0.14e^{-7t}$$

$$i(0^+) = 0.06 = A_2 + 0.14 \qquad \text{or} \qquad A_2 = -0.08 \qquad i = -0.08e^{-4t} + 0.14e^{-7t}$$

Finally, at $t = 0.2$ s, $i = -1.42$ mA.

15.226 In the circuit of Fig. 15-66, $R = 100\,\Omega$, $L = 5\,\text{H}$, $C = 184\,\mu\text{F}$, and $V = 470\,\text{V}$. Solve for i and evaluate i at $t = 0.01\,\text{s}$.

▎ By KVL,

$$5\frac{di}{dt} + 100i + \frac{10^6}{184}\int i\,dt = 470$$

The auxiliary equation is $p^2 + 20p + 1086.96 = 0$. The roots are $p = -10 \pm j31.42$, and the solution takes the form

$$i = e^{-10t}(A_1 \cos 31.42t + A_2 \sin 31.42t)$$

Since $i = 0$ at $t = 0$, $A_1 = 0$. Thus, $i = A_2 e^{-10t} \sin 31.42t$ A.
   Since $v_C(0^-) = v_C(0^+) = 0$,

$$\frac{di}{dt}(0^+) = \frac{V}{L} = \frac{470}{5} = 94$$

$$\frac{di}{dt} = A_2 e^{-10t}(31.42 \cos 31.42t - 10 \sin 31.42t) \quad \text{or} \quad \frac{di}{dt}(0^+) = 31.42\,A_2 = 94$$

Thus, $A_2 = 2.99$ and $i = 2.99e^{-10t} \sin 31.42t$ A. At $t = 0.01\,\text{s}$, $i = 2.99e^{-10\times0.01} \sin(31.42)(0.01) = 0.836$ A.

15.227 Sketch the current wave in the circuit of Prob. 12.226 and find the frequency of the wave.

▎ See Fig. 15-74.

$$\omega = 2\pi f = 31.42 \quad \text{(from Prob. 12.226)} \quad \text{or} \quad f = \frac{31.42}{2\pi} = 5\,\text{Hz}$$

or, from Fig. 15-74, $T = 1/f = 0.2\,\text{s}$. Thus, $f = 5\,\text{Hz}$.

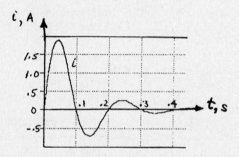

Fig. 15-74

15.228 What are the instantaneous powers in the R, L, and C of the circuit of Prob. 12.226?

▎ Since $i = 2.99e^{-10t} \sin 31.42t$ A,

$$p_R = i^2 R = 100(2.99e^{-10t} \sin 31.42t)^2 = 895e^{-20t} \sin^2 31.42t\,\text{W}$$

$$p_L = L\frac{di}{dt}i = (v_L)i = 5[e^{-10t}(94 \cos 31.42t - 29.9 \sin 31.42t)](2.99e^{-10t} \sin 31.42t)$$

$$= 1405e^{-20t}(\sin 31.42t)(\cos 31.42t) - 447e^{-20t} \sin^2 31.42t\,\text{W}$$

$$p_C = (v_C)i = \left(\frac{1}{C}\int i\,dt\right)i = \frac{10^6}{184}\left(\int 2.99e^{-10t} \sin 31.42\,dt\right)(2.99e^{-10t} \sin 31.42t)$$

$$= (-149.5e^{-10t} \sin 31.42t - 469.73e^{-10t} \cos 31.42t)(2.99e^{-10t} \sin 31.42t)$$

$$= -447e^{-20t} \sin^2 31.42t - 1404.8e^{-20t}(\sin 31.42t)(\cos 31.42t)\,\text{W}$$

15.229 A transistor pulse amplifier is shown in Fig. 15-75a. If a 0.5-V pulse is applied to the transistor input, how long does it take for the base-to-emitter voltage to reach 90 percent of the pulse amplitude?

▎ We first draw the equivalent circuit in Fig. 15-75b. The base-to-emitter voltage V_{BE} is across the capacitor, for which

$$V_{BE} = v_C = V(1 - e^{-t/RC}) = 0.5(1 - e^{-t/5\times10^{-9}})$$

Solving for t for 0.9 V, we obtain $t \simeq 2.3\tau = 11.5$ ns.

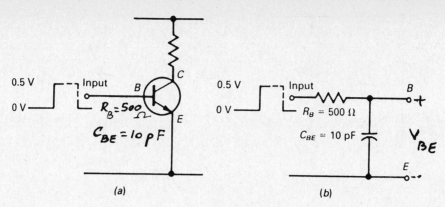

Fig. 15-75

15.230 The variable resistance and fixed-value capacitance given in Fig. 15-75 are used to determine the time during which voltage is applied to the electrodes of a welding machine. If this time is that taken for the capacitance to charge from 0 to 10 V, what is the time range covered by the extremes of the resistance values?

▮ The voltage required to determine the end of the welding time is $v_C = 10\,\text{V} = 25(1 - e^{-t/RC})\,\text{V}$. When $R = 50\,\text{k}\Omega$, $RC = 250\,\text{ms}$. Thus $t = 127.7\,\text{ms}$. When $R = 1.5\,\text{M}\Omega$, $RC = 7.5\,\text{s}$ and $t = 3.83\,\text{s}$. Therefore, the welding arc time range may be varied from 0.125 s to 3.83 s by varying R.

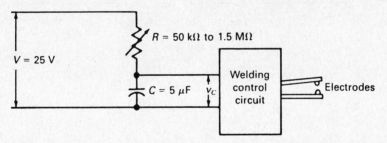

Fig. 15-76

15.231 Figure 15-77a is the circuit of a relaxation oscillator used for generating a pulse waveform. As the capacitor C charges through R_1, the voltage v_e rises. When v_e becomes 6 V, the unijunction transistor internal resistance R_e drops suddenly from a very high value to 400 Ω, discharging the capacitor. At this time an output voltage pulse v_o is produced. When v_e drops to 2 V, R_e again becomes very high, allowing the capacitor to recharge. The action automatically repeats itself, so that a series of output pulses occurs at regular time intervals. The resulting waveforms of v_e and v_o are shown in Fig. 15-77b. What is the time t between consecutive pulses?

▮ The complexity of Fig. 15-77a can be eliminated for this problem by considering the timing circuit equivalent in Fig. 15-77c. The switch simulates the transistor action. When the capacitor C is charging to 6 V, the switch is open; for discharging from 6 to 2 V, the switch is closed, connecting resistance R_3 across the capacitor. R_3 is the series equivalent of R_e (400 Ω during capacitor discharge), and $R_2 = 560\,\Omega$. While the capacitor C is charging between 2 and 6 V from the 20-V supply (switch open in Fig. 15-77c), the charging resistor is R_1. The charging time constant is

$$\tau_C = R_1 C = 1\,\text{M}\Omega \times 500\,\text{pF} = 500\,\mu\text{s}$$

The charging time is the difference between the times for charging to 6 and 2 V,

$$t_C = t_6 - t_2 = \tau \ln \frac{V}{V - 6\,\text{V}} - \tau \ln \frac{V}{V - 2\,\text{V}}$$

As subtracting logarithms corresponds to dividing their original numbers,

$$t_C = \tau \ln \frac{V - 2V}{V - 6V} = 500\,\mu\text{s} \times \ln \frac{(20 - 2)\,\text{V}}{(20 - 6)\,\text{V}} = 125.7\,\mu\text{s}$$

While the capacitor is discharging between 6 and 2 V (switch closed in Fig. 15-77c), the equivalent circuit is that of Fig. 15-77a. The series-parallel circuit in Fig. 15-77d must be converted into a series circuit for direct evaluation of discharge time. The Thévenin principle used with the capacitor as the load can be applied to perform the conversion. Figure 15.77e shows the resulting Thévenin equivalent circuit.

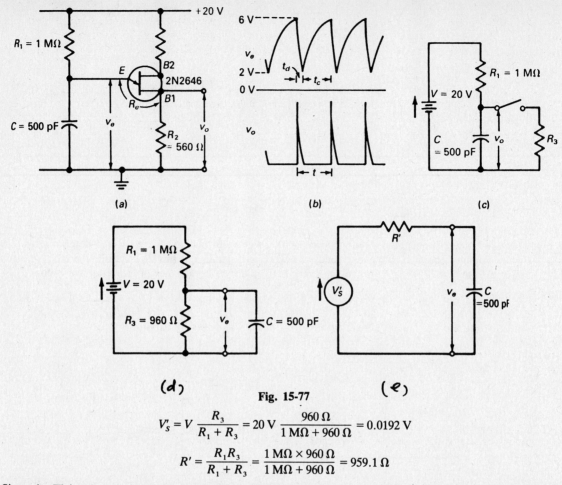

(a)

(b)

(c)

(d)

Fig. 15-77

(e)

$$V'_S = V \frac{R_3}{R_1 + R_3} = 20 \text{ V} \frac{960 \,\Omega}{1 \,\text{M}\Omega + 960 \,\Omega} = 0.0192 \text{ V}$$

$$R' = \frac{R_1 R_3}{R_1 + R_3} = \frac{1 \,\text{M}\Omega \times 960 \,\Omega}{1 \,\text{M}\Omega + 960 \,\Omega} = 959.1 \,\Omega$$

Since the Thévenin voltage $V'_S \simeq 0$ V and the Thévenin resistance $R' \simeq R_3$, for practical purposes it may be considered that C discharged directly into the 960 Ω of R_3. The discharge extends from $v_e = 6$ V to $v_e = 2$ V.

$$\tau_d \simeq R_3 C \simeq 960 \,\Omega \times 500 \,\text{pF} \simeq 480 \text{ ns} \simeq 0.48 \,\mu\text{s}$$

Now,
$$t_d = \tau \ln \frac{v_o}{v_e} = 0.48 \,\mu\text{s} \times \ln \frac{6 \text{ V}}{2 \text{ V}} = 0.5273 \,\mu\text{s}$$

The time between pulses is the sum of the charge and discharge times: $t = t_C + t_d = 125.7 \,\mu\text{s} + 0.5273 \,\mu\text{s} = 126.22 \,\mu\text{s}$.

15.232 Apply Thévenin's theorem to the circuit of Fig. 15-78a to reduce it to a series RC circuit. Then determine i_C at $t = 10$ ms.

∥ The Thévenin circuit is shown in Fig. 15-78b, from which we have

$$i_C = \frac{V_{\text{Th}}}{R_{\text{Th}}} e^{-t/\tau} = \frac{2.326}{76.74 \,\text{k}\Omega} e^{-t/7.674 \,\text{ms}} \text{ A} \qquad \tau = R_{\text{Th}} C$$

At $t = 10$ ms, $i_C = 8.3 \,\mu\text{A}$.

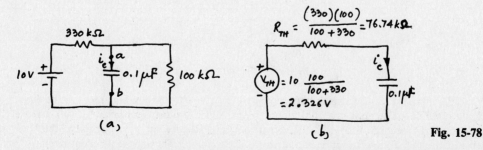

(a)

(b)

Fig. 15-78

15.233 In the box of the circuit of Fig. 15-79a we have a square-wave generator. The switch is operated so that it stays in each position (1 or 2) for about 1 ms and rapidly switches between the positions. If the time constant of the circuit, $\tau = RC$, is about 0.1 ms so that the resistive and capacitive voltages stabilize between operations, sketch v_C, v_R, and v_{in}.

❚ See Fig. 15-79b. When the switch is at position 1, $v_{in} = 0$ V and the RC network is short-circuited so that any charge on the capacitor will be dissipated in the resistor. When the switch is at position 2, $v_{in} = 10$ V is supplied to the RC network as a charging voltage. The resulting network supply voltage is shown as the square waveform at the bottom of Fig. 15-79b.

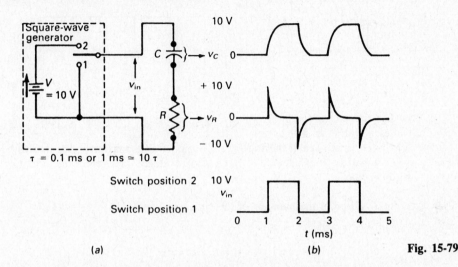

(a)   (b)   Fig. 15-79

15.234 The circuit of Fig. 15-80a performs differentiation. Thus, for the input voltage v_{in} of Fig. 15-80b we obtain the output voltage v_{out} also shown in Fig. 15-80b. What is the reason for this shape of the waveform?

❚ The rectangular wave v_{in} has unequal times for the pulse duration and the period between the pulses. Since the 23.5-μs time constant of the differentiator circuit (47 k$\Omega \times$ 500 pF) is short compared with the 200-μs pulse duration and with the 800-μs interval between pulses, the capacitor always has time to charge before the input pulse changes level. Thus the output voltage v_{out} is always close to zero prior to an input level change. When the input level changes from 0 to 10 V, a positive swing, the output rises suddenly from 0 to +10 V. When the input level drops from 10 to 0 V, a negative swing, the output *rises* from 0 to −10 V. The output voltage v_{out} consists of spikes which rise almost instantaneously in either a positive or negative direction on an input level change, dropping virtually to zero before another input level change occurs.

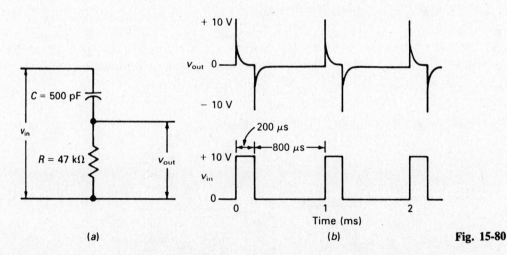

(a)   (b)   Fig. 15-80

15.235 Figure 15-81a shows an integrator. Explain why the output voltage has the waveform shown in Fig. 15-81b for the given input voltage consisting of a train of pulses.

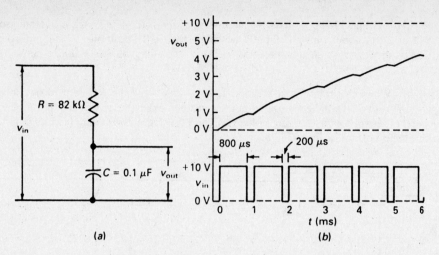

Fig. 15-81

The 8.2-ms time constant of the integrator is long compared with the 800-μs pulse duration and the 200 μs between the pulses. During an 800-μs period, the capacitor voltage increases by approximately 10 percent of the difference between its voltage at the start of the period and its maximum possible voltage 10 V. During a 200-μs period, the capacitor loses about 2.4 percent of its voltage. Therefore the output voltage v_{out} gradually builds up toward the maximum of 10 V.

15.236 How much energy is stored in the inductor of the circuit of Fig. 15-82 at $t = 0.1$ s?

At $t = 0^+$, $i = 6/1 = 6$ A $= I_0$.

Thus,
$$i(t) = I_0 e^{-t/\tau} = 6e^{-2t} \text{ A}$$
$$w_L = \tfrac{1}{2} L i^2 = \tfrac{1}{2}(1)(6e^{-2t})^2 = 18e^{-4t} \text{ J}$$

At $t = 0.1$ s, $w_L = 18e^{-4 \times 0.1} = 12.07$ J.

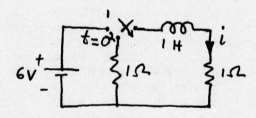

Fig. 15-82

15.237 Find the voltage v_0 in the circuit of Fig. 15-83.

$$i(0^+) = \tfrac{6}{2} = 3 \text{ A}$$

KVL gives (for $t > 0$): $\tfrac{1}{2} \int i \, dt + 2i + \int i \, dt = 6$ (since the 2-F capacitor has $v_{2\,F}(0^+) = 6$)

or
$$\frac{di}{dt} + \frac{3}{4} i = 0 \qquad \text{or} \qquad i = Ae^{-0.75t}$$

since $i(0^+) = 3$, $A = 3$, and $i = 3e^{-0.75t}$ A. Finally,

$$v_0 = 1 \int_0^t 3e^{-0.75t} \, dt = 4(1 - e^{-0.75t}) \text{ V}$$

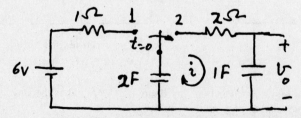

Fig. 15-83

15.238 In the circuit of Fig. 15-84, the initial voltages on the capacitors are 12 V and 6 V with polarities as shown. Determine $i(t)$.

$$i(0_+) = \frac{12-6}{1 \times 10^6} = 6 \ \mu A = I_0 \qquad \tau = RC = \frac{10^6 \times 10^{-6} \times 2 \times 10^{-6}}{(2+1)10^{-6}} = \frac{2}{3} \ s$$

Thus,
$$i = I_0 e^{-t/\tau} = 6 e^{-1.5t} \ \mu A$$

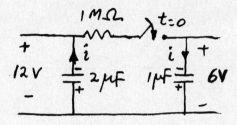

Fig. 15-84

15.239 Obtain the form of solution for $v_0(t)$ in the circuit of Fig. 15-85 when the switch is moved from position 1 to 2 at $t = 0$.

By KCL:
$$\frac{1}{L_1} \int_0^t v_0 \, dt + i_1(0_+) + \frac{v_0}{R_2} + \frac{1}{L_2} \int_0^t v_0 \, dt = 0$$

or
$$\frac{dv_0}{dt} + \frac{R_2(L_1 + L_2)}{L_1 L_2} \, v_0 = 0$$

which has the form of solution:
$$v_0 = V_0 e^{-[R_2(L_1+L_2)/L_1 L_2]t} \ V$$

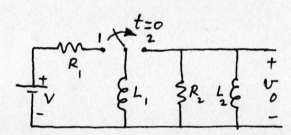

Fig. 15-85

15.240 In the circuit of Fig. 15-86, solve for i.

By KVL:
$$40 + 20 = 20i + 2 \frac{di}{dt} \qquad \text{or} \qquad \frac{di}{dt} + 10i = 30$$

$$i = i_f + i_n \qquad i_f = \tfrac{60}{20} = 3 \ A \qquad i_n = A e^{-10t} \qquad i(0_+) = \tfrac{20}{10} = 2 \ A$$

Thus, $i = 3 + A e^{-10t}$. Since $i(0_+) = 2$, $A = -1$ and $i = 3 - e^{-10t}$ A.

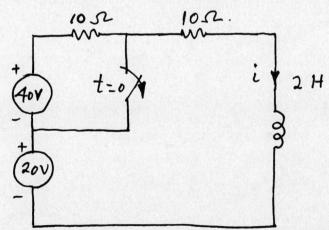

Fig. 15-86

15.241 Find the voltage across the uncharged capacitor of the circuit of Fig. 15-87 if $v = 2e^{-t}$ V.

▎ By KCL:

$$\frac{v_C}{2} + \frac{1}{2}\frac{dv_C}{dt} = \frac{2e^{t} - v_c}{1} \qquad \text{or} \qquad \frac{dv_C}{dt} + 3v_C = 4e^{-t}$$

Solution is of the form:

$$v_C = Ae^{-3t} + 2e^{-t}$$

$$v_C(0_+) = 0 = A + 2 \qquad \text{or} \qquad A = -2$$

Hence

$$v_C = 2(e^{-t} - e^{-3t})\ \text{V}$$

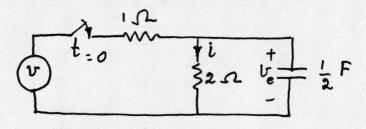

Fig. 15-87

15.242 Determine the current through the 2-Ω resistor of the circuit of Prob. 15.241 and sketch the current.

▎
$$i = \frac{v_C}{R} = \frac{2(e^{-t} - e^{-3t})}{2} = e^{-t} - e^{-3t}\ \text{A}$$

which is sketched in Fig. 15-87.

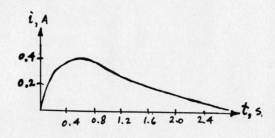

Fig. 15-88

15.243 Differential equations of the form:

$$\frac{dy}{dt} + P(t)y = Q(t) \tag{1}$$

are commonly encountered in circuit equations having one energy-storage element. Such equations have forms of solution as:

$$ye^{\int P\,dt} = \int Qe^{\int P\,dt}\,dt + A \tag{2}$$

Apply this result to solve for the current in the circuit of Fig. 15-37, if $V = 2e^{-t}$ V, $R = 4\,\Omega$, and $L = 2$ H.

▎ By KVL we have:

$$2\frac{di}{dt} + 4i = 2e^{-t} \qquad \text{or} \qquad \frac{di}{dt} + 2i = e^{-t}$$

which is similar to (1) above. Thus, from (2)

$$ie^{\int 2\,dt} = \int e^{-t}e^{\int 2\,dt}\,dt + A \qquad \text{or} \qquad ie^{2t} = \int (e^{-t})(e^{2t})\,dt + A \qquad \text{or} \qquad ie^{2t} = e^{t} + A$$

Thus $i = e^{-t} + Ae^{-2t}$. Since $i(0_+) = 0$, $A = -1$, and, finally, $i = e^{-t} - e^{-2t}$ A.

15.244 Solve for i in the circuit of Fig. 15-89.

▎
$$i(0_-) = i(0_+) = 6\left/\frac{3(3+3)}{3+3+3}\right. = 3\ \text{A} \tag{1}$$

By nodal analysis, at node 1:

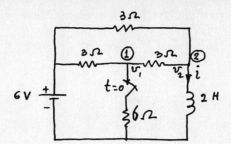

Fig. 15-89

$$\frac{6-v_1}{3} = \frac{v_1}{6} + \frac{v_1 - v_2}{3} \qquad \text{or} \qquad 5v_1 - 2v_2 = 12 \qquad (2)$$

Thus, $v_1 = 2.4 + 0.4v_2$. At node 2, including $i(0_+)$, we have:

$$\frac{6-v_2}{3} + \frac{v_1 - v_2}{3} = i(0_+) + \frac{1}{2}\int v_2\, dt \qquad (3)$$

Substituting (1) and (2) into (3) and simplifying yields:

$$3\int v_2\, dt + 3.2v_2 = -1.2 \qquad (4)$$

Since $\frac{1}{2}\int v_2\, dt = i$ we have

$$3\int v_2\, dt = 6i \qquad \text{and} \qquad v_2 = 2\frac{di}{dt}$$

Thus (4) becomes:

$$6.4\frac{di}{dt} + 6i - 1.2$$

Solution is of the form:

$$i = \frac{-1.2}{6} + Ae^{-(6/6.4)t} = -0.2 + Ae^{-0.9375t}$$

At $t=0$, $i=3$ requires that $A = 3.2$

Hence, $$i = -0.2 + 3.2e^{-0.9375t}\ \text{A}$$

15.245 What is the time constant of the circuit of Fig. 15-89?

❙ From Prob. 15.244 we have:

$$\frac{1}{\tau} = 0.9375 \qquad \text{or} \qquad \tau = 1.067\,\text{s}$$

15.246 How much energy is stored in the inductor of the circuit of Fig. 15-89 at $t=1$ s?

❙ From Prob. 15.244:

$$w_L = \tfrac{1}{2}Li^2 = \tfrac{1}{2}(2)(-0.2 + 3.2e^{-0.9375t})^2\ \text{J}$$

which becomes, at $t=1$, $w_L = 1.109$ J.

15.247 Determine the voltage across the 6-Ω resistor of the circuit of Fig. 15-89 for $t>0$.

❙ From Prob. 15.244:

$$v_{6\,\Omega} = v_1 = 2.4 + 0.4v_2$$

And $$v_2 = 2\frac{di}{dt} = 2\frac{d}{dt}\,(-0.2 + 3.2e^{-0.9375t}) = 2(-3.2 \times 0.9375e^{-0.9375t}) = -6e^{-0.9375t}\ \text{V}$$

Thus, $$v_1 = 2.4\,(1 - e^{-0.9375t})\ \text{V}$$

15.248 In the circuit of Fig. 15-39, V is a constant voltage V_0. Show that under steady-state, the energy supplied by the source is equally divided as that dissipated in the resistor and stored in the capacitor.

▮ Since $q = CV_0(1 - e^{-t/RC})$, from Prob. 15.130, the energy stored in the capacitor,

$$w_C = \frac{1}{2}\frac{q^2}{C} = \frac{1}{2}CV_0^2(1 - e^{-t/RC})^2 \text{ J}$$

Total energy supplied by the source

$$w_T = qV_0 = CV_0^2(1 - e^{-t/RC}) \text{ J}$$

As $t \to \infty$, $\qquad\qquad\qquad w_C = \frac{1}{2}CV_0^2 = \frac{1}{2}w_T$

Thus, $\frac{1}{2}w_T$ goes as dissipated energy in the resistor.

15.249 Evaluate the dissipated energy in the resistor of the circuit of Fig. 15-39 over the period that the capacitor is fully charged. Thus, show that the energy dissipated is the same as the energy stored in the capacitor.

▮ From Prob. 15.131:

$$i = \frac{V_0}{R}e^{-t/RC}$$

Thus, since the capacitor is fully charged as $t \to \infty$, energy dissipated in R

$$w_R = \int_0^\infty i^2R\,dt = R\left(\frac{V_0}{R}\right)^2\int_0^\infty e^{-2t/RC}\,dt = \frac{1}{2}CV_0^2 = w_C \qquad \text{from Prob. 15.248}$$

15.250 Determine the initial conditions on i_1, i_2, and i_3 of the circuit of Fig. 15-90.

▮ Before the switch is closed, $t < 0$

$$i_{4\,\Omega}(0_-) = i_{1\,H}(0_-) = \frac{6}{2+4} = 1\,\text{A}$$

$$v_{0.5\,F} + v_{1.0\,F} = \frac{(4)(6)}{4+2} = 4\,\text{V} \tag{1}$$

When the switch is closed, $t > 0$

$$2i_1 = 6 - (v_{0.5\,F} + v_{1.0\,F}) = 6 - 4 = 2 \qquad \text{or} \qquad i_1(0_+) = 1\,\text{A}$$

$$i_1(0_+) - i_3(0_+) = i_{1\,H}(0_+) = i_{1\,H}(0_-) = 1\,\text{A}$$

$$i_3(0_+) = i_1(0_+) - 1 = 1 - 1 = 0\,\text{A}$$

Since $v_{0.5\,F}(0_-) = v_{0.5\,F}(0_+)$ and $v_{1.0\,F}(0_-) = v_{1.0\,F}(0_+)$

$$i_1(0_+) - i_2(0_+) = \frac{v_{0.5F}(0_+)}{4} \tag{2}$$

Because the capacitors are connected in series

$$\frac{v_{0.5\,F}}{v_{1.0\,F}} = \frac{1}{0.5} = 2 \qquad \text{or} \qquad v_{0.5\,F} = 2v_{1.0\,F} \tag{3}$$

From (1) to (3) we finally obtain:

$$i_2(0_+) = \frac{1}{3} = 0.333\,\text{A}$$

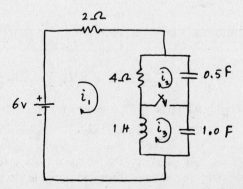

Fig. 15-90

15.251 In the circuit of Fig. 15-91, the switch is moved from position 1 to 2 at $t = 0$. Determine $d^2i/dt^2(0_+)$.

▮ By KVL:

$$0.1 \frac{di}{dt} + (100 \times 10^3)i + \frac{10^6}{100} \int i \, dt = 0 \qquad (1)$$

or

$$\frac{d^2i}{dt^2} + 10^6 \frac{di}{dt} + 10^5 i = 0 \qquad (2)$$

Since $i(0_+) = 10/10^5 = 10^{-4}$ A, Eq. (1) yields

$$\frac{di}{dt}(0_+) = -\frac{10^5}{0.1} i(0_+) = -100 \text{ A/s}$$

From Eq. (2), therefore,

$$\frac{d^2i}{dt^2}(0_+) = -\left[10^6 \frac{di}{dt}(0_+) + 10^5 i(0_+)\right] = -[10^6(-100) + 10^5(10^{-4})] \simeq 10^8 \text{ A/s}^2$$

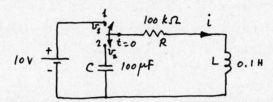

Fig. 15-91

15.252 In the circuit of Prob. 15.251, find $dv_1/dt(0_+)$ and $dv_2/dt(0_+)$, assuming $v_1(0_+) = 10$ V and $v_2(0_+) = 0$ V.

▮ Since $i = (v_1 - v_2)/R$

$$i(0_+) = \frac{v_1(0_+) - v_2(0)}{10^5} = \frac{10 - 0}{10^5} = 10^{-4} \text{ A}$$

$$\frac{dv_1}{dt} = -\frac{i}{C} \quad \text{or} \quad \frac{dv_1}{dt}(0_+) = -\frac{10^{-4}}{100 \times 10^{-6}} = -1 \text{ V/s}$$

$$v_2 = L \frac{di}{dt} = 0.5 \frac{di}{dt} \quad \text{and} \quad \frac{dv_2}{dt} = 0.5 \frac{d^2i}{dt^2}$$

or

$$\frac{dv_2}{dt}(0_+) = 0.5 \frac{d^2i}{dt^2}(0_+) = 0.5(-10^8) \text{ (from Prob. 15.251)} = -5 \times 10^{-7} \text{ V/s}$$

15.253 In the circuit of Fig. 15-92 determine the voltage $v_C(0_+)$ and its derivative $dv_C/dt(0_+)$.

▮ Since $v_C(0_-) = v_C(0_+)$ and $v_C(0_-) = 0$, $v_C(0_+) = 0$.

Now

$$i_L = C \frac{dv_C}{dt} \quad \text{and} \quad i_L(0_+) = i_L(0_-) = \frac{12}{2} = 6 \text{ A}$$

Thus,

$$\frac{dv_C}{dt}(0_+) = \frac{6}{0.5} = 12 \text{ V/s}$$

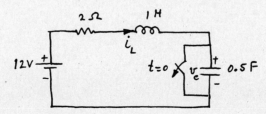

Fig. 15-92

15.254 Determine $d^2v/dt^2(0_+)$ in the circuit of Fig. 15-93.

▮

$$v(0_+) = 0 \qquad C \frac{dv}{dt} + \frac{v}{R} = I \quad \text{or} \quad \frac{dv}{dt}(0_+) = \frac{I}{C} \text{ V/s}$$

$$C \frac{d^2v}{dt^2} + \frac{1}{R} \frac{dv}{dt} = 0 \quad \text{or} \quad \frac{d^2v}{dt^2}(0_+) = -\frac{1}{RC} \frac{dv}{dt}(0_+) = -\frac{I}{RC^2} \text{ V/s}^2$$

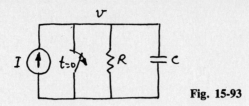

Fig. 15-93

15.255 Repeat Prob. 15.254 for the circuit of Fig. 15-94.

▮
$$\frac{v}{R} + \frac{1}{L}\int v\,dt = I \quad \text{or} \quad v(0_+) = RI$$

$$\frac{1}{R}\frac{dv}{dt} + \frac{v}{L} = 0 \quad \text{or} \quad \frac{dv}{dt}(0_+) = \frac{R}{L}[v(0_+)] = -\frac{R^2 I}{L}\text{ V/s}$$

$$\frac{1}{R}\frac{d^2v}{dt^2} + \frac{1}{L}\frac{dv}{dt} = 0 \quad \text{or} \quad \frac{d^2v}{dt^2}(0_+) = -\frac{R}{L}\frac{dv}{dt}(0_+) = \frac{IR^3}{L^2}\text{V/s}^2$$

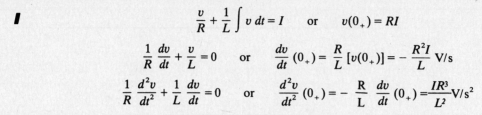

Fig. 15-94

15.256 In the circuit of Fig. 15-95 determine the initial and final conditions on v_L and v_R.

▮
$$v_C(0_-) = v_C(0_+) = 0 = v_L(0_+) + v_R(0_+) \qquad i_L(0_-) = i_L(0_+) = 0$$

Thus,
$$v_R(0_+) = 0 \quad \text{and} \quad v_L(0_+) = 0$$

$$v_L(\infty) = 0 \quad \text{and} \quad v_R(\infty) = \frac{VR}{R + R_1}$$

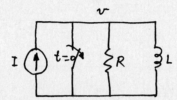

Fig. 15-95

15.257 Find $dv_L/dt(0_+)$ and $dv_R/dt(0_+)$ in the circuit of Prob. 15.256.

▮
$$\frac{dv_c}{dt} = \frac{i_C}{C} = \frac{dv_L}{dt} + \frac{dv_R}{dt} \qquad \frac{di_L}{dt} = \frac{v_L}{L} \quad \text{and} \quad \frac{dv_R}{dt} = r\frac{di_L}{dt}$$

Thus,
$$\frac{di_L}{dt}(0_+) = 0 \quad \text{and} \quad \frac{dv_R}{dt}(0_+) = 0$$

$$\frac{dv_L}{dt}(0_+) = \frac{1}{C}i_C(0_+) = \frac{V}{R_1 C}\text{ V/s}$$

15.258 In the circuit of Prob. 15.257 let the switch be closed for $t < 0$ and the circuit be under steady state. Then at $t = 0$ the switch is opened. Solve for the initial and final conditions on v_L and v_R.

$$i_L(0_+) = \frac{V}{R + R_1} \qquad v_C(0_+) = \frac{VR}{R_1 + R}$$

$$v_R(0_+) = i(0_+)R = \frac{VR}{R + R_1} \qquad v_L(0_+) = 0$$

$$v_L(\infty) = 0 \quad \text{and} \quad v_R(\infty) = 0$$

15.259 Determine $dv_C/dt(0_+)$ for the circuit conditions stated in Prob. 15.258.

▌ When the switch is open and C is charged $-i_L = i_C = i$. Then

$$\frac{dv_C}{dt} = -\frac{i}{C} \quad \text{or} \quad \frac{dv_C}{dt}(0_+) = -\frac{V}{(R+R_1)C} \text{ V/s}$$

15.260 The switch in the circuit of Fig. 15-96 is opened at $t = 0$. Determine the initial current i and its derivative (at $t = 0_+$).

▌
$$i(0_+) = \frac{V}{R_2} \text{ A}$$

Since the capacitor is charged to a voltage V, we have, by KVL,

$$V = L\frac{di}{dt} + (R_1 + R_2)i + \frac{1}{C}\int i\,dt \tag{1}$$

$$\frac{di}{dt}(0_+) = \frac{V - (R_1 + R_2)[i(0_+)]}{L} = -\frac{VR_1}{R_2 L} \text{ A/s}$$

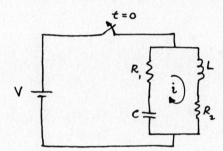

Fig. 15-96

15.261 If $V = R_1 = R_2 = L = C = 1$ in the circuit of Prob. 15.260, find $d^2i/dt^2(0_+)$.

▌ From Prob. 12.260 we have:

$$L\frac{d^2i}{dt^2} + (R_1 + R_2)\frac{di}{dt} + \frac{1}{C}i = 0 \quad \text{or} \quad \frac{d^2i}{dt^2} + 2\frac{di}{dt} + i = 0$$

$$\frac{d^2i}{dt^2}(0_+) = -2\frac{di}{dt}(0_+) - i(0_+) = -2(-1) - (1) = 1 \text{ A/s}^2$$

15.262 The switch in the circuit of Fig. 15-97 is moved from position 1 to 2 at $t = 0$. Determine the initial conditions on the three mesh currents.

▌
$$i_{2H}(0_-) = i_{2H}(0_+) = 0 = i_3(0_+)$$

Since $\quad i_{1H}(0_-) = i_{1H}(0_+) = 0 \quad i_1(0_+) = i_2(0_+) \quad -12 = i_1(0^+)(1+2)$

Thus, $\quad i_1(0_+) = -\frac{12}{3} = -4 \text{ A} \quad i_2(0_+) = -4 \text{ A} \quad \text{and} \quad i_3(0_+) = 0$

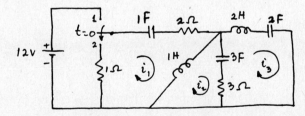

Fig. 15-97

15.263 In the circuit of Fig. 15-98, the 4-Ω resistor is shorted out at $t = 0$. Obtain the initial conditions on the currents i_C and i_L. Write the general equations governing these currents for $t > 0$.

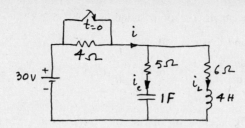

Fig. 15-98

∎ $$i_L(0_+) = \frac{30}{4+6} = 3\,A \qquad v_C(0_+) = \frac{(30)(6)}{4+6} = 18\,V \qquad i_C(0_+) = \frac{30-18}{5} = 2.4\,A$$

$$4\frac{di_L}{dt} + 6i_L = 30 \tag{1}$$

$$5i_C + \int i_C\,dt + v_C(0_+) = 30 \tag{2}$$

15.264 For the circuit of Prob. 15.263 determine $di_L/dt(0_+)$, $di_L/dt(\infty)$, and $di_C/dt(0_+)$.

∎ From Eq. (1) of Prob. 12.263

$$\frac{di_L}{dt}(0_+) = \frac{30 - 6i_L(0_+)}{4} = \frac{30 - 6\times 3}{4} = 3\,A/s \qquad \frac{di_L}{dt}(\infty) = 0$$

From Eq. (2) of Prob. 12.263

$$\frac{di_C}{dt}(0_+) = -\frac{i_C(0_+)}{(5)(1)} = -\frac{2.4}{5} = -0.48\,A/s$$

15.265 Write the equations governing v_1 and v_2 in the circuit of Fig. 15-99 and determine the initial conditions on these voltages.

∎ By KCL at nodes 1 and 2:

$$10 = \frac{v_1}{5} + \int v_1\,dt - \int v_2\,dt \qquad 0 = -\int v_1\,dt + 0.5\frac{dv_2}{dt} + \frac{v_2}{2} + \int v_2\,dt$$

Initial conditions: $\qquad v_1(0_+) = 10\times 5 = 50\,V \qquad v_2(0_+) = 0\,V$

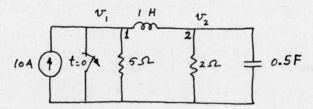

Fig. 15-99

15.266 What are the initial conditions on the first derivatives of the voltages v_1 and v_2 in the circuit of Prob. 15.265?

∎ $$\frac{dv_2}{dt}(0_+) = 0\,V/s \qquad \frac{dv_1}{dt}(0_+) = -5\,v_1(0_.) = -250\,V/s$$

15.267 Repeat Prob. 15.265 if the 10-A current source in the circuit is replaced by a current source $i = e^{-t}\,A$.

∎ The voltage equations are:

$$e^{-t} = \frac{v_1}{5} + \int v_1\,dt - \int v_2\,dt \tag{1}$$

$$0 = -\int v_1\,dt + 0.5\frac{dv_2}{dt} + \frac{v_2}{2} + \int v_2\,dt \tag{2}$$

and $\qquad v_1(0_+) = 5i(0_+) = 5(1) = 5\,V \qquad v_2(0_+) = 0$

15.268   Repeat Prob. 15.266 for the data of Prob. 15.267.

  $\blacksquare$ From Eq. (1) of Prob. 15.267:

$$-e^{-t}(0_+) = \frac{1}{5}\frac{dv_1}{dt}(0_+) + v_1(0_+) - v_2(0_+) \qquad \text{or} \qquad -1 = \frac{1}{5}\frac{dv_1}{dt}(0_+) + 5 - 0$$

Thus,
$$\frac{dv_1}{dt}(0_+) = -30 \text{ V/s} \qquad \frac{dv_2}{dt}(0_+) = 0$$

15.269   In the circuit of Fig. 15-100, find $v_L(0_+)$, $v_L(\infty)$, and $v_C(0^+)$.

  $\blacksquare$ Since $v_C(0_-) = v_C(0_+)$,

$$v_L(0_+) = 12 \text{ V} \qquad v_L(\infty) = 0 \qquad v_C(0_-) = 0 \text{ V} = v_C(0_+)$$

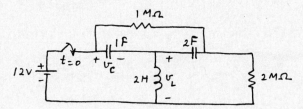

Fig. 15-100

15.270   For the circuit of Fig. 15-101, write a set of integrodifferential equations to solve for v.

  $\blacksquare$ By KVL:
$$100 = 4\frac{di}{dt} + (2+1)i + \frac{1}{2}\int_0^t i\,dt \qquad v = i + \frac{1}{2}\int_0^t i\,dt$$

with the initial conditions:

$$i(0_+) = \tfrac{100}{2} = 50 \text{ A} \qquad v(0_+) = \tfrac{1}{2}(100) = 50 \text{ V}$$

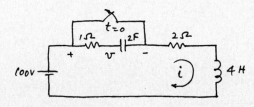

Fig. 15-101

15.271   The natural response of a circuit is given by:

$$\frac{d^2i}{dt^2} + 4\frac{di}{dt} + 4i = 0$$

for which the initial conditions are: $i(0_+) = 2 \text{ A}$ and $di/dt(0_+) = 4 \text{ A/s}$.   Solve for i.

  $\blacksquare$ The auxiliary equation is

$$p^2 + 4p + 4 = (p+2)^2 = 0$$

And the roots are $p = -2$.   The solution is of the form:

$$i = Ae^{-2t} + Bte^{-2t} \qquad \frac{di}{dt} = -2Ae^{-2t} + Be^{-2t} - 2Bte^{-2t}$$

$$i(0_+) = 2 \qquad \text{yields} \qquad 2 = A$$

$$\frac{di}{dt}(0_+) = 4 \qquad \text{gives} \qquad 4 = -2A + B \qquad \text{or} \qquad B = 8$$

and
$$i = e^{-2t}(2 + 8t) \text{ A}$$

15.272   A critically damped circuit has the natural response $i = 4te^{-10t} \text{ A}$.   When does i reach its maximum value?

  $\blacksquare$ For i_{max},
$$di/dt = 0 = 4(e^{-10t} - 10te^{-10t}) = 4e^{-10t}(1 - 10t)$$

Thus,
$$t = 0.1 \text{ s}$$

15.273 The current in a circuit is given by:

$$\frac{d^2i}{dt^2} + 3\frac{di}{dt} + 2i = 0$$

The initial conditions are: $i(0_+) = 2$ A and $di/dt(0_+) = 1$ A/s. Determine the time when the current reaches its maximum value.

▌ The characteristic roots are:

$$p = -2, -1$$

Thus,

$$i = Ae^{-2t} + Be^{-t} \qquad \frac{di}{dt} = -2Ae^{-2t} - Be^{-t}$$

$$i(0_+) = 2 \qquad \text{yields} \qquad 2 = A + B$$

$$\frac{di}{dt}(0_+) = 1 \qquad \text{yields} \qquad 1 = -2A - B$$

Thus, $A = -3$ and $B = 5$ and $i = 5e^{-t} - 3e^{-2t}$ A.

For i_{max}, $\qquad \frac{di}{dt}(t_1) = 0 \qquad$ or $\qquad 6e^{-2t_1} - 5e^{-t_1} = 0 \qquad$ or $\qquad e^{-t_1} = \frac{5}{6}$

Thus, $\qquad\qquad\qquad\qquad\qquad t_1 = \ln\left(\frac{6}{5}\right) = 0.182$ s

15.274 The current response of a damped *RLC*-series circuit is shown in Fig. 15-102, and is given by $i = Ae^{-\alpha t}\sin(\omega t + \theta)$. Find: A, α, ω, and θ from the graph.

▌ From Fig. 15-102, $i = 0$ at $t = 0$. Thus, $\theta = 0$. We construct an envelope to the curve for i, as shown by the dotted line from which $A = 4$, which is the amplitude of the envelope at $t = 0$.

From the graph, $\qquad\qquad\qquad\qquad T = 0.8$ s

Thus, $\qquad\qquad\qquad\qquad \omega = \frac{2\pi}{T} = \frac{2\pi}{0.8} = 7.85$ rad/s

Finally, from the envelope:

$$1 = 4e^{-0.8\alpha} \qquad \text{or} \qquad \alpha = 1.733$$

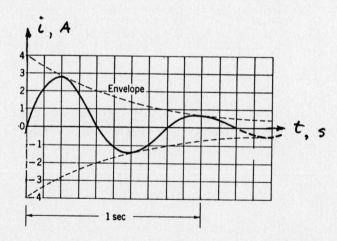

Fig. 15-102

15.275 In the response shown in Fig. 15-103, the construction of the envelope does not yield an exact result. If $i = Ae^{-\alpha t}\sin(\omega t + \theta)$ A, find (without any geometrical construction) A, α, ω, and θ.

▌ Since $i = 0$ at $t = 0$, $\theta = 0$.

Thus, $\qquad\qquad\qquad\qquad i = Ae^{-\alpha t}\sin\omega t$

From Fig. 15-103, $T \simeq 4$ ms. Thus, $\omega = 2\pi/T = 1570$ r/s, $\quad 0.85 = Ae^{-\alpha \times 10^{-3}}$, and $0.5 = Ae^{-\alpha(5 \times 10^{-3})}$.

Thus, $\qquad\qquad\qquad\qquad A = 0.97 \qquad$ and $\qquad \alpha = 133$

Finally, $\qquad\qquad\qquad\qquad i = 0.97e^{-133t}\sin 1570t$ A

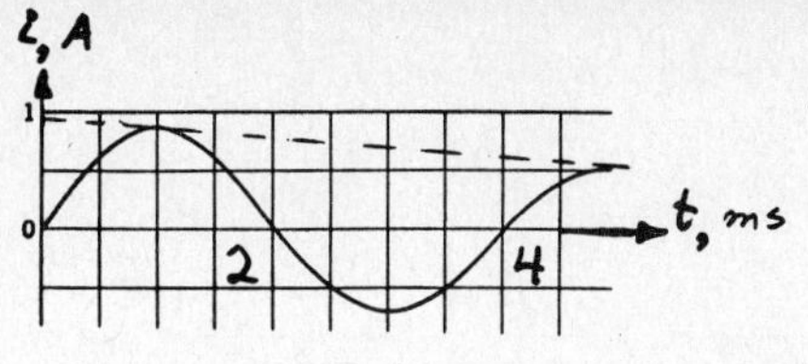

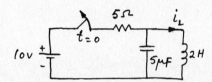

Fig. 15-103

15.276 The circuit of Fig. 15-104 is under steady state and the switch is opened at $t = 0$. Find the frequency of the current i_L. Also, determine its magnitude.

▮ $$i_L(0_+) = \tfrac{10}{5} = 2\,\text{A} \qquad \frac{di}{dt}(0_+) = 0\,\text{A/s} \qquad 2\frac{di_L}{dt} + \frac{10^6}{5}\int i_L\,dt = 0$$

The roots are: $$p = \pm j316.22$$

Thus, $$i_L = A\cos 316.22t + B\sin 316.22t$$

$$\omega = 2\pi f = 316.22 \qquad \text{or} \qquad f = 50.3\,\text{Hz}$$

$i_L(0_+) = 2$ requires $A = 2$ and $B = 0$. The amplitude is $i_L = 2\,\text{A}$.

Fig. 15-104

15.277 A 1-μF capacitor is charged to 2 V. It is then discharged across an RL-parallel circuit having $R = \frac{1}{3}\,\text{M}\Omega$ and $L = 0.5 \times 10^6\,\text{H}$. Determine the voltage across the RLC-parallel combination.

▮ Let v be the required voltage. Then:

$$1 \times 10^{-6}\frac{dv}{dt} + (3 \times 10^{-6})v + (2 \times 10^{-6})\int v\,dt = 0$$

The characteristic roots are: $p = -2, -1$.

Thus, $$v = Ae^{-2t} + Be^{-t} \qquad v(0_+) = 2 = A + B$$

$$\frac{dv}{dt}(0_+) = \frac{2 \times 3 \times 10^{-6}}{1 \times 10^{-6}} = 6 = -2A + B$$

Thus, $$A = -8 \qquad \text{and} \qquad B = 10 \qquad \text{and} \qquad v = 10e^{-t} - 8e^{-2t}\,\text{V}$$

15.278 The response of a circuit excited by a dc source is given by:

$$\frac{d^2i}{dt^2} + 2\frac{di}{dt} + i = 10$$

The initial conditions are $i(0_+) = 0$ and $di/dt(0_+) = -5\,\text{A/s}$. Solve for i.

▮ The characteristic roots are: $p = -1, -1$. The solution becomes:

$$i = 10 + Ae^{-t} + Bte^{-t}$$

Since $i(0_+) = 0$,

$$A = -10 \qquad \frac{di}{dt} = -Ae^{-t} + Be^{-t} - Bte^{-t} \qquad \frac{di}{dt}(0_+) = -5 = -A + B$$

Thus, $$B = A - 5 = -15 \qquad \text{and} \qquad i = 10 - 10e^{-t} - 15te^{-t}\,\text{A}$$

15.279 Figure 15-105 shows a basic circuit for producing a voltage of sawtooth waveform. When the switch is closed, the gas tube is nonconducting and the voltage across C rises. When it reaches V_1, the tube fires, allowing the capacitor to discharge to a voltage V_2. Thereafter the cycle repeats. Neglecting the discharge time (with respect to the charging time), find the voltage v_C and determine its period.

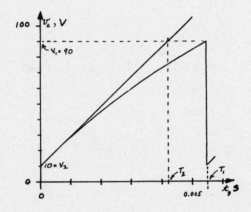

Fig. 15-105

I
$$v_C(0_+) = V_2$$

Since v_C in an RC circuit is given by

$$v_C = V(1 - e^{-t/RC}) \quad \text{(see Prob. 15.131)}$$

for the given circuit we have

$$v_C = V + (V_2 - V)e^{-t/RC} \tag{1}$$

When $v_C = V_1$, let $t = T$. Then:

$$T = RC \ln \frac{(V_2 - V)}{(V_1 - V)} = RC \ln \frac{(V - V_2)}{(V - V_1)} \text{ s}$$

15.280 In the circuit of Fig. 15-105, $RC = 0.01$ s, $V = 200$ V, $V_1 = 90$ V, and $V_2 = 10$ V. Sketch 1 cycle of v_C.

I See Fig. 15-106.

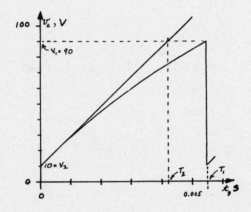

Fig. 15-106

15.281 From (1) of Prob. 15.279, find $dv_C/dt(0_+)$ and approximate the sawtooth curve of Fig. 15-106 by a straight line. Draw this line.

I The straight line is drawn in Fig. 15-106. From (1) of Prob. 15.280

$$\frac{dv_C}{dt}(0_+) = \frac{V - V_2}{RC}$$

The equation to the straight line is

$$v_C = V_2 + \frac{V - V_2}{RC} t$$

15.282 Compare the periods obtained in the exact analysis of Prob. 15.279 and the approximate analysis of Prob. 15.281.

I Let these periods be T_e and T_a. From Prob. 15.279:

$$T_e = RC \ln \left(\frac{V - V_2}{V - V_1} \right)$$

For the straight line, $v_C = V_1$ at $t = T_a$ or

$$T_a = RC \left(\frac{V_1 - V_2}{V - V_2} \right)$$

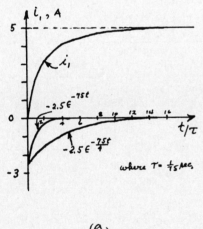

Fig. 15-107

Thus,

$$\frac{T_e}{T_a} = \frac{\ln\left[(V-V_2)/(V-V_1)\right]}{(V_1-V_2)/(V-V_2)}$$

For the given numerical values:

$$\frac{T_e}{T_a} = \frac{\ln\left[(200-10)/(200-90)\right]}{(90-10)/(200-10)} = 1.3$$

15.283 In the circuit of Fig. 15-107 we have: $V = 240\,\text{V}$, $R_1 = 48\,\Omega$, $R_2 = 27\,\Omega$, $L_1 = 1.6\,\text{H}$, $L_2 = 0.9\,\text{H}$, and $M = 0.72$. All initial conditions are zero. The switch is closed at $t=0$. Solve for i_1 and i_2.

❚ By mesh analysis:

$$1.6\frac{di_1}{dt} + 48i_1 - 0.72\frac{di_2}{dt} = 240 \qquad -0.72\frac{di_1}{dt} + 27i_2 + 0.9\frac{di_2}{dt} = 0$$

Solving simultaneously for i_1 and i_2 yields

$$i_1 = 5 - 2.5e^{-75t} - 2.5e^{-(75/4)t}\,\text{A} \qquad i_2 = -3.33e^{-75t} + 3.33e^{-(75/4)t}\,\text{A}$$

15.284 Sketch i_1 and i_2 obtained in Prob. 15.283. Also show the components of these currents.

❚ See Fig. 15-108.

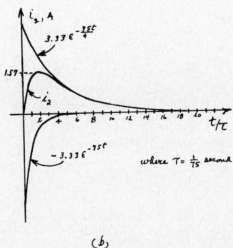

Fig. 15-108

15.285 In the circuit of Prob. 15.283, all circuit parameters are unchanged, except M. Recall from Chap. 11 that the coefficient of coupling k is defined by $k = M/\sqrt{L_1 L_2}$. If k is a variable, solve for the currents i_1 and i_2.

❚ Writing the KVL equations in terms of symbols, we have

$$L_1\frac{di_1}{dt} + R_1 i_1 - M\frac{di_2}{dt} = V \qquad -M\frac{di_1}{dt} + R_2 i_2 + L_2\frac{di_2}{dt} = 0$$

Combining these equations for i_1 yields

$$\left(1 - \frac{M^2}{L_1 L_2}\right)\frac{d^2 i_1}{dt^2} + \left(\frac{R_1}{L_1} + \frac{R_2}{L_2}\right)\frac{di_1}{dt} + \frac{R_1 R_2}{L_1 L_2}i_1 = \frac{R_2 V}{L_2}$$

Or, in terms of k and numerical values, Eq. (1) becomes

$$(1 - k^2) \frac{d^2 i_1}{dt^2} + 60 \frac{di_1}{dt} + 900 i_1 = 30 \text{ V}$$

A similar equation may be obtained for i_2. The solutions become

$$i_1 = 5 - 2.5 e^{-[30/(1+k)]t} - 2.5 e^{-[30/(1-k)]t} \text{ A} \qquad i_2 = 3.33 [e^{-30t/(1+k)} - e^{-30t/(1-k)}] \text{ A}$$

15.286 Discuss the effect upon the transient terms of variation in values of k in the circuit of Prob. 15.285.

❚ As $k \to 1$, one transient term predominates while the other decays to zero rapidly. As $k \to 0$, the time constants of the transients merge to form one exponential term.

15.287 Solve for i_1 and i_2 of the circuit of Prob. 15.285 for the specific values of $k = 0$ and $k = 1$.

❚ For $k = 0$ $\qquad\qquad\qquad i_1 = 5 - 5 e^{-30t} \text{ A} \qquad i_2 = 0 \text{ A}$

For $k = 1$ $\qquad\qquad\qquad i_1 = 5 - 2.5 e^{-15t} \text{ A} \qquad i_2 = 3.33 e^{-15t} \text{ A}$

15.288 In the circuit of Fig. 15-109a, S_2 has been open and S_1 closed. At $t = 0$, S_1 is opened and S_2 remains open. Draw an equivalent circuit to represent the initial conditions. Write the loop equation for i_1.

❚ $$i_1(0_+) = I_0 = \frac{V}{R_1} \qquad \text{(See Fig. 15-109}b\text{)}$$

$$L_1 \frac{di_1}{dt} + R_1 i_1 + \frac{1}{C} \int i_1 \, dt = V + L I_0 = V + \frac{L}{R_1} V$$

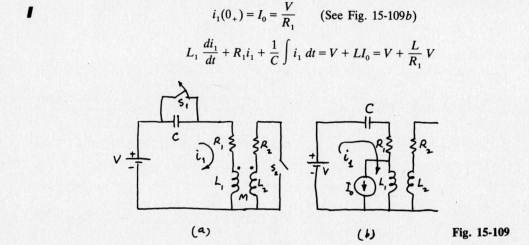

(a) $\qquad\qquad\qquad\qquad\qquad$ (b) $\qquad\qquad$ **Fig. 15-109**

15.289 In the circuit of Fig. 15-110, ignoring the effect of the rectifier, solve for i_C and v_C, assuming that the circuit is underdamped.

❚ From (3) of Prob. 15.188:

$$i_C = \frac{V}{\beta} (\beta^2 + \alpha^2) e^{-\alpha t} \sin \beta t$$

where $\qquad\qquad\qquad \alpha = \frac{R}{2L} \qquad \beta = \sqrt{\alpha^2 - \omega_0^2} \qquad \text{and} \qquad \omega_0 = \frac{1}{\sqrt{LC}}$

$$v_C = \frac{1}{C} \int i_C \, dt = V \left[1 - \frac{\sqrt{\alpha^2 + \beta^2}}{\beta} e^{-\alpha t} \sin (\beta t + \theta) \right]$$

where $\qquad\qquad\qquad\qquad \theta = \tan^{-1}(\beta/\alpha)$

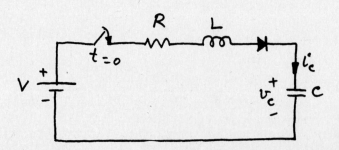

Fig. 15-110

15.290 Sketch i_C and v_C obtained in Prob. 15.289.

▌ See Fig. 15-111.

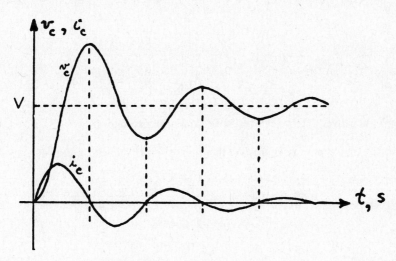

Fig. 15-111

15.291 From Fig. 15-111 show when the rectifier comes into action.   What is the constant value of v_C after the rectifier comes into play?

▌ The rectifier comes into action when v_C is going through its first maximum.   At that time $\beta t = \pi$ and $i_C = 0$.

$$(v_C)_{\beta t = \pi} = V(1 + e^{-\alpha \pi/\beta})\ \text{V}$$

15.292 Show that the response of the circuit of Fig. 15-112 can never be oscillatory, regardless of the values of the circuit parameters.

▌ The mesh equations may be written as

$$R_1 i_1 + \frac{1}{C_1} \int i_1\, dt - \frac{1}{C_1} \int i_2\, dt = V \qquad -\frac{1}{C_1} \int i_1\, dt + R_2 i_2 + \left(\frac{1}{C_1} + \frac{1}{C_2}\right) \int i_2\, dt = 0$$

Eliminating i_1 from these equations, we obtain the characteristic equation

$$p^2 + \left(\frac{1}{R_1 C_1} + \frac{1}{R_2 C_1} + \frac{1}{R_2 C_2}\right) p + \frac{1}{R_1 R_2 C_1 C_2} = 0$$

Let its roots be $p = \frac{1}{2}(-A \pm \sqrt{B})$,   where

$$B = \left(\frac{1}{R_1 C_1} - \frac{1}{R_2 C_2}\right)^2 + \frac{2}{R_2 C_1}\left(\frac{1}{R_1 C_1} + \frac{1}{R_2 C_2}\right) + \left(\frac{1}{R_2 C_1}\right)^2$$

Because B cannot be negative, the roots of the auxiliary equation can never be complex.   Hence, the response of the circuit can never be oscillatory.

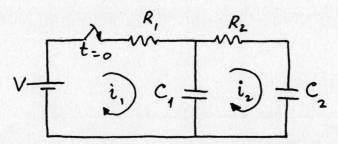

Fig. 15-112

15.293 Repeat Prob. 15.292 if the capacitors C_1 and C_2 are replaced by inductors L_1 and L_2, respectively.

▮ In this case we have:

$$R_1 i_1 + L_1 \frac{di_1}{dt} - L_1 \frac{di_2}{dt} = V \qquad -L_1 \frac{di_1}{dt} + R_2 i_2 + (L_1 + L_2) \frac{di_2}{dt} = 0$$

The characteristic equation for i_2 becomes

$$p^2 + \left(\frac{R_L}{L_2} + \frac{R_1}{L_2} + \frac{R_1}{L_1} \right) p + \frac{R_1 R_L}{L_1 L_2} = 0$$

$$B = \left(\frac{R_1}{L_1} - \frac{R_2}{L_2} \right)^2 + \frac{2 R_1 R_L}{(L_2)^2} + \frac{2(R_1)^2}{L_1 L_2} + \left(\frac{R_1}{L_2} \right)^2$$

which can never be negative. Hence the response cannot be oscillatory.

15.294 Determine the instantaneous power supplied by the current source in the circuit of Fig. 15-113 when the switch is opened at $t = 0$.

▮

$$v_C(0_-) = v_C(0_+) = I_s \left(\frac{R_1 R_2}{R_1 + R_2} \right) = 5 \left(\frac{2 \times 2}{2 + 2} \right) = 5 \text{ V}$$

$$\tau = R_1 C = 6 \text{ s}$$

$$v_C(t) = v_{Cf} + v_{Cn} = 10 + (5 - 10)e^{-t/6} = v_s$$

Thus, $$p_s = I_s v_s = 50 - 25e^{-t/6} \text{ W}$$

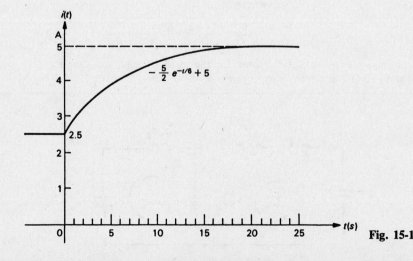

Fig. 15-113

15.295 Obtain the current i in the circuit of Prob. 15.294. Sketch the current. Verify that the total power supplied by the source, as obtained in Prob. 15.294, is the same as that absorbed by the resistor under steady state.

▮ Since $v_s = v_C$

$$i = \frac{v_C}{R_1} = \frac{10 - 5e^{-t/6}}{2} = 5 - 2.5e^{-t/6} \text{ A}$$

The sketch for i is shown in Fig. 15-114.

$$I_s = 5 \qquad P_s = (5)^2 2 = 50 \text{ W}$$

From Prob. 15.294, $P_s = 50 \text{ W}$.

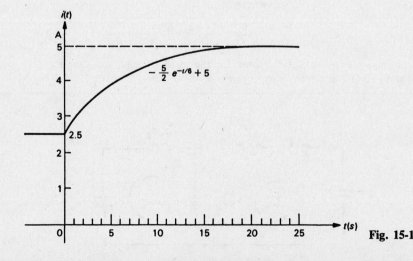

Fig. 15-114

15.296 find $i_L(t)$ in the circuit of Fig. 15-115.

▮ The initial conditions are

$$v_C(0_-) = v_C(0_+) = 2\,\text{V} \qquad i_L(0_-) = i_L(0_+) = 0\,\text{A}$$

The characteristic equation for the circuit under transient condition is

$$p^2 + 4p + 2 = 0$$

having the roots $p_1, p_2 = -3.414, -0.586$.

Thus, $$i_L = A_1 e^{-3.414t} + A_2 e^{-0.586t}\,\text{A}$$

$i_L(0_+) = 0$ requires that $A_1 + A_2 = 0$. Now, $v_L(0_+) = -2i_L(0_+) - v_C(0_+) = -2\,\text{V} = L\,di_L/dt(0_+)$

or $$\frac{di_L}{dt}(0_+) = -\frac{v_L(0_+)}{L} = -\frac{2}{0.5} = -4\,\text{A/s}$$

Thus, $$-3.414A_1 - 0.586A_2 = -4$$

Solving for A_1 and A_2 yields

$$A_1 = 1.414 \qquad \text{and} \qquad A_2 = -1.414$$

Finally, $$i_L = 1.414(e^{-3.414t} - e^{-0.586t})\,\text{A}$$

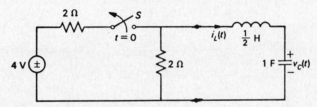

Fig. 15-115

15.297 Repeat Prob. 15.296 for $L = 1\,\text{H}$ and $C = 1\,\text{F}$.

▮ In this case the characteristic equation becomes

$$p^2 + 2p + 1 = 0$$

which has the roots $p_1, p_2 = -1$. The solution is

$$i_L = A_1 e^{-t} + A_2 t e^{-t}$$

Proceeding as in Prob. 15.296: $i_L(0_+) = 0$ requires that $A_1 = 0$ and $di_L/dt(0_+) = -2 = A_2$. Hence $i_L = -2te^{-t}\,\text{A}$.

15.298 Repeat Prob. 15.296 for $L = 5\,\text{H}$ and $C = 1\,\text{F}$.

▮ The characteristic equation is

$$p^2 + \tfrac{2}{5}p + \tfrac{1}{5} = 0$$

The roots are

$$p_1, p_2 = -\tfrac{1}{5} \pm j\tfrac{2}{5}$$

The solution is of the form

$$i_L = e^{-t/5}(A_1 \cos \tfrac{2}{5}t + A_2 \sin \tfrac{2}{5}t)$$

Applying the initial conditions

$$i_L(0_+) = 0 \qquad \text{and} \qquad \frac{di_L}{dt}(0_+) = -\tfrac{2}{5}$$

yields $$A_1 = 0 \qquad \text{and} \qquad A_2 = -1$$

Consequently, $$i_L = -e^{-t/5} \sin \tfrac{2}{5}t\,\text{A}$$

15.299 Sketch the currents obtained in Probs. 15.296 through 15.298. Verify that these represent, respectively, the overdamped, the critically damped, and the underdamped responses.

▮ See Fig. 15-116.

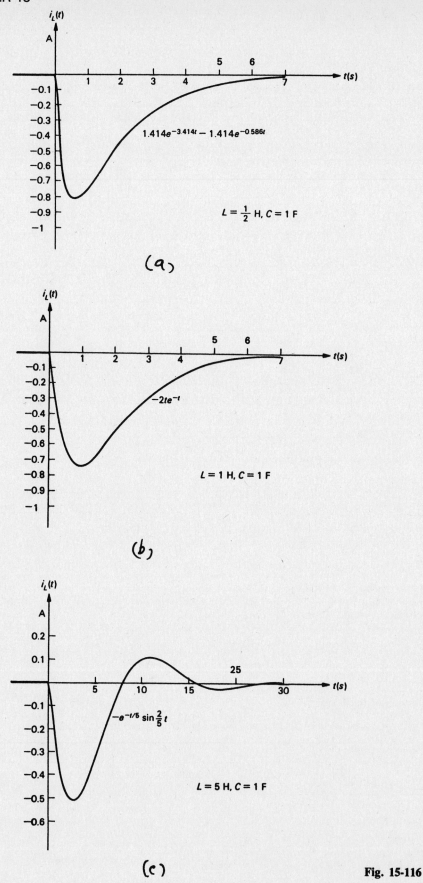

Fig. 15-116

15.300 Determine the current i_x in the circuit of Fig. 15-117. First state the initial conditions and then obtain the solution.

▮ The initial conditions are

$$i_L(0_-) = i_L(0_+) = -\tfrac{3}{4} \text{ A} \qquad v_C(0_-) = v_C(0_+) = 0 \text{ V}$$

$$\frac{dv_C}{dt}(0_+) = \frac{i_C(0_+)}{C} \qquad \left(\text{since} \quad i_C = C\frac{dv_C}{dt}\right)$$

The characteristic equation is

$$p^2 + \tfrac{4}{15}p + \tfrac{4}{45} = 0$$

The roots are

$$p_1, p_2 = -\tfrac{2}{15} \pm j\tfrac{4}{15}$$

Thus,

$$v_C = e^{-2t/15}(A_1 \cos \tfrac{4}{15}t + A_2 \sin \tfrac{4}{15}t)$$

Applying the above-stated initial conditions yields

$$A_1 = 0 \qquad \text{and} \qquad A_2 = -\tfrac{3}{4} \qquad [\text{since} \quad i_x(0_+) = i_2(0_+) + i_C(0_+)]$$

Therefore,

$$v_C = -\tfrac{3}{4}e^{-2t/15}\sin \tfrac{4}{15}t \text{ V}$$

and

$$i_x = \frac{-3 - v_C}{3} = -1 + \tfrac{1}{4}e^{-2t/15}\sin \tfrac{4}{15}t \text{ A}$$

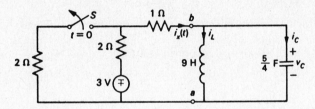

Fig. 15-117

15.301 Sketch $i_x(t)$ of Prob. 15.300 and verify that the circuit is underdamped.

▮ Because the roots of the characteristic equation are a pair of complex conjugate numbers, the circuit is underdamped. The sketch shown in Fig. 15-118 also validates this fact.

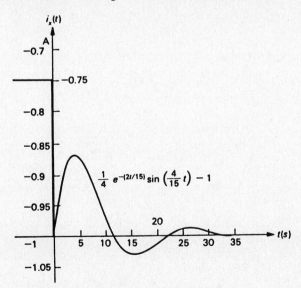

Fig. 15-118

15.302 Determine $i(t)$ in the circuit of Fig. 15-119.

▮
$$i(0_+) = 2 \text{ A} \qquad \tau = L/R = 10 \text{ ms} \qquad i_f = 2 + 1 = 3 \text{ A} \qquad i_n = (2 - 3)e^{-100t} \text{ A}$$

Thus,
$$i = 3 - e^{-100t} \text{ A}$$

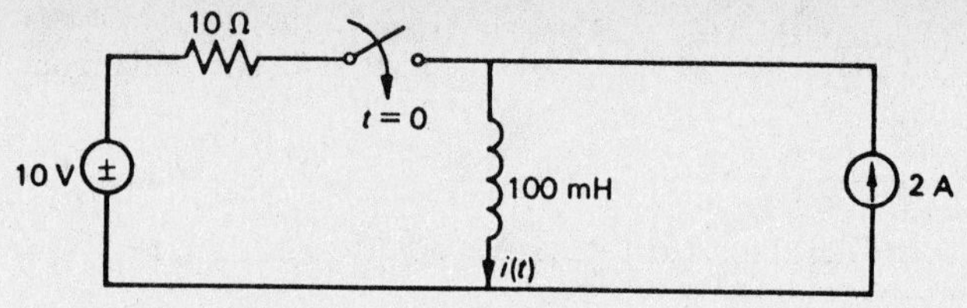

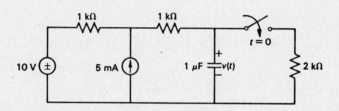

Fig. 15-119

15.303 Solve for $v(t)$ in the circuit of Fig. 15-120.

▮

$$v(0_+) = 10 + 5 = 15 \text{ V} \qquad v(\infty) = 5 + \tfrac{1}{4}(10) = 7.5 \text{ V}$$

Hence, by inspection,

$$v(t) = (15 - 7.5)e^{-1000t} + 7.5 = 7.5(1 + e^{-1000t}) \text{ V}$$

Fig. 15-120

15.304 In the circuit of Fig. 15-121a, the switch is initially closed at $t = 0$, opens and remains open for $0 < t < 10$ ms. At $t = 10$ ms it closes once again and remains closed for $10 \text{ ms} < t < 20 \text{ ms}$. At $t = 20$ ms it opens again and closes at $t = 30$ ms. Sketch $v(t)$ for $0 < t < 30$ ms.

▮

$$v(\infty) = 0 \qquad \tau = RC = 5 \text{ ms}$$

$$v(t) = 10e^{-200t} \qquad 0 \le t \le 10 \text{ ms}$$

$$v(10 \text{ ms}) = 10e^{-2} = 1.35 \text{ V}$$

$$v(t) = 10 + (1.35 - 10)e^{-(t-10)/5 \text{ ms}} = -8.65e^{-(t-10 \text{ ms})/5 \text{ ms}} + 10 \qquad 10 \le t \le 20 \text{ ms}$$

$$v(20 \text{ ms}) = -8.65e^{-2} + 10 = 8.83 \text{ V}$$

$$v(t) = 8.83e^{-(t-20 \text{ ms})/5 \text{ ms}} \qquad 20 \le t \le 30 \text{ ms}$$

$$v(30 \text{ ms}) = 1.2 \text{ V}$$

Hence the sketch of Fig. 15-121b.

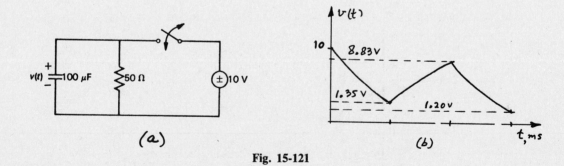

Fig. 15-121

15.305 In the circuit of Fig. 15-122, determine $v(t)$.

▮

$$i_L(0^-) = 0 \qquad i_L(\infty) = \tfrac{5}{4} + 2 = \tfrac{13}{4} \text{ A} \qquad i_L(t) = -\tfrac{13}{4}e^{-t/2} + \tfrac{13}{4}$$

$$v_L(t) = v(t) = L\,\frac{di_L}{dt} = \tfrac{13}{4}e^{-t/2} \text{ V}$$

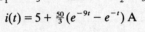

Fig. 15-122

15.306 Solve for $i(t)$ in the circuit of Fig. 15-123. State all initial and final conditions.

$$v_C(0_-) = v_C(0_+) = 0\,\text{V} \qquad i_L(0_-) = i_L(0_+) = i(0_+) = 5\,\text{A}$$

$$v_C(\infty) = 30 \times 5 = 150\,\text{V} \qquad i_L(\infty) = 5\,\text{A} \qquad \text{and} \qquad v_L(0_+) = -150\,\text{V}$$

The roots of the characteristic equation are found to be $(-1, -9)$.

Thus,
$$i(t) = i_L(t) = A_1 e^{-t} + A_2 e^{-9t} + 5\,\text{A}$$

Applying the initial conditions gives

$$A_1 = -\tfrac{50}{3} \qquad \text{and} \qquad A_2 = \tfrac{50}{3}$$

Thus,
$$i(t) = 5 + \tfrac{50}{3}(e^{-9t} - e^{-t})\,\text{A}$$

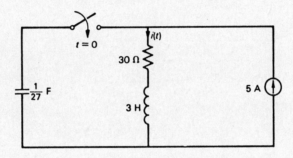

Fig. 15-123

15.307 Write a set of differential equations to solve for the node voltage v in the circuit of Fig. 15-124.

The required equations are

$$\frac{v}{R_1} + C\frac{dv}{dt} + i_1 = i \qquad L_1\frac{di_1}{dt} + M\frac{di_2}{dt} = v$$

$$M\frac{di_1}{dt} + L_2\frac{di_2}{dt} + R_2 i_2 = 0$$

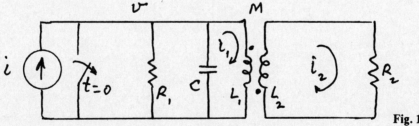

Fig. 15-124

15.308 In the circuit of Fig. 15-124, we have $L_1 = L_2 = 1\,\text{H}$, $R_1 = 0.5\,\Omega$, $R_2 = 2\,\Omega$, $C = 1\,\text{F}$, $M = 0.5\,\text{H}$, and $i = 2\,\text{A}$. Obtain a differential equation to solve for the node voltage v.

Substituting the numerical values yields

$$2v + \frac{dv}{dt} + i_1 = 2 \tag{1}$$

$$\frac{di_1}{dt} + 0.5\frac{di_2}{dt} = v \tag{2}$$

$$0.5 \frac{di_1}{dt} + \frac{di_2}{dt} + 2i_2 = 0 \qquad (3)$$

Multiplying Eq. (3) by 2 and differentiating with respect to t gives

$$\frac{d^2i_1}{dt^2} + 2 \frac{d^2i_2}{dt^2} + 4 \frac{di_2}{dt} = 0 \qquad (4)$$

Substituting $\qquad \dfrac{di_2}{dt} = 2v - 2 \dfrac{di_1}{dt} \qquad$ and $\qquad \dfrac{d^2i_2}{dt^2} = 2 \dfrac{dv}{dt} - 2 \dfrac{d^2i_1}{dt^2}$

from Eq. (2) in Eq. (4) results in

$$-3 \frac{d^2i_1}{dt^2} - 8 \frac{di_1}{dt} + 4 \frac{dv}{dt} + 8v = 0 \qquad (5)$$

Substituting $\qquad \dfrac{di_1}{dt} = -2 \dfrac{dv}{dt} - \dfrac{d^2v}{dt^2} \qquad$ and $\qquad \dfrac{d^2i_1}{dt^2} = -2 \dfrac{d^2v}{dt^2} - \dfrac{d^3v}{dt^3}$

from Eq. (1) in Eq. (5) finally yields

$$3 \frac{d^3v}{dt^3} + 14 \frac{d^2v}{dt^2} + 20 \frac{dv}{dt} + 8v = 0$$

CHAPTER 16
Step, Ramp, and Impulse Functions

16.1 In Chap. 15, we considered the responses of circuits to suddenly applied sources by opening and/or closing of switches. Thus, a suddenly applied 1-V dc source may be represented by the graph of Fig. 16-1a. We term this a *unit-step function*, and denote it by $u(t)$. Sketch the function $v = u(t) - u(t-4)$.

▍ The steps are shown in Fig. 16-1b, which also shows the final result. Notice that v is a square wave of 4 s duration.

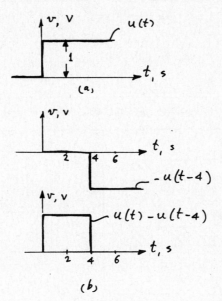

Fig. 16-1

16.2 From Prob. 16.1, we now have a technique to represent sources having finite durations. Sketch the following functions: (*a*) $v_1(t) = 10u(t)$ V; (*b*) $v_2(t) = (115\sqrt{2}\cos 377t)u(t)$ V; (*c*) $v_3(t) = 20e^{-t}u(t)$ V.

▍ See Fig. 16-2a to c. Notice that the functions are of the form $v(t) = f(t)u(t)$.

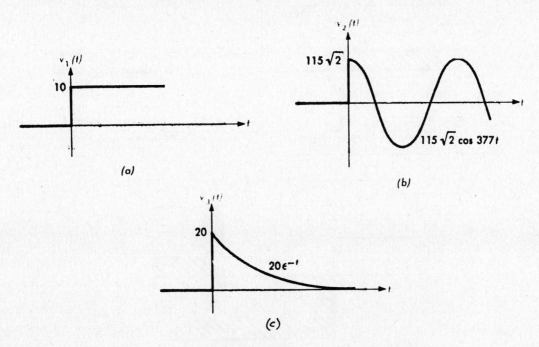

Fig. 16-2

16.3 Sketch a unit-step function which begins at $t = T$.

▌ This is a delayed unit step and is shown in Fig. 16-3.

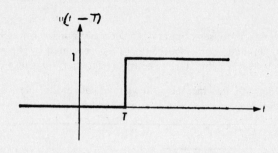

Fig. 16-3

16.4 Make a table showing the sketches of the following unit-step functions: $u(t)$, $-u(t)$, $u(t + t')$, $-u(t + t')$, $u(t - t')$, $-u(t - t')$, $u(-t)$, $-u(-t)$, $u(-t + t')$, $-u(-t + t')$, $u(-t - t')$, and $-u(-t - t')$.

▌ The sketches are shown in Fig. 16-4.

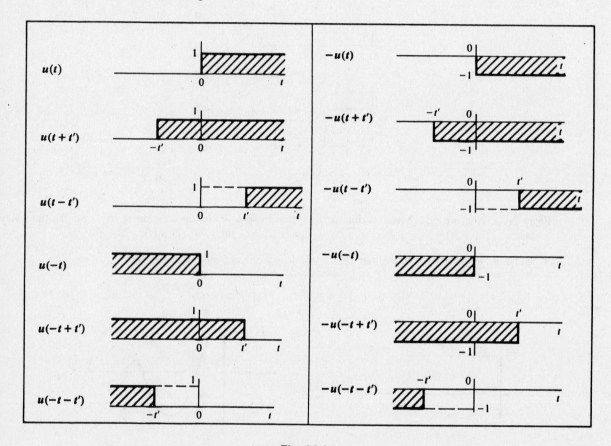

Fig. 16-4

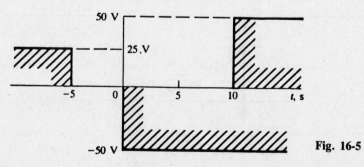

Fig. 16-5

16.5 Evaluate $v = 25u(-t-5) - 50u(t) + 50u(t-10)$ at (a) $t = -6$ s, (b) -3 s, (c) 3 s, and (d) 11 s.

▌ See Fig. 16-5. First, each term is sketched separately, and then combined to obtain the following results: (a) 25 V, (b) 0, (c) -50 V, (d) 0.

16.6 Obtain the current i, for all values of t, in the circuit of Fig. 16-6.

▌ For $t < 0$, the voltage source is a short circuit and the current source shares 2 A equally between the two 10-Ω resistors:

$$i(t) = i(0_-) = i(0_+) = 1 \text{ A}$$

For $t > 0$, the current source is replaced by an open circuit and the 50-V source acts in the RL series circuit ($R = 20\,\Omega$). Consequently, as $t \to \infty$, $i \to -50/20 = -2.5$ A. Then,

$$i(t) = [i(0_+) - i(\infty)]e^{-Rt/L} + i(\infty) = 3.5e^{-100t} - 2.5 \quad \text{A}$$

By means of unit-step functions, the two formulas may be combined into a single formula valid for all t:

$$i(t) = 1u(-t) + (3.5e^{-100t} - 2.5)u(t) \quad \text{A}$$

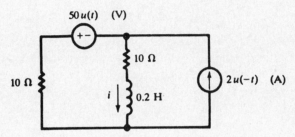

50 $u(t)$ (V)

10 Ω

10 Ω

i 0.2 H

$2u(-t)$ (A)

Fig. 16-6

16.7 Determine $v_0(t)$ in the circuit of Fig. 16-7 when $v(t) = 0.25u(t)$.

▌ By nodal analysis:

$$-6v_1 + \frac{v_0}{10} + \frac{1}{20}\frac{dv_0}{dt} = 0 \qquad (1)$$

The constraints are $v = 6i_1$ and $v_1 = 4i_1$. Thus (1) becomes

$$\frac{v_0}{10} + \frac{1}{20}\frac{dv_0}{dt} = 4v \qquad (2)$$

For $t < 0$, $v = 0$. For $t > 0$, $v = 0.25$, and (2) becomes

$$\frac{dv_0}{dt} + 2v_0 = 20$$

The solution for all t becomes

$$v_0 = 10(1 - e^{-2t})u(t)$$

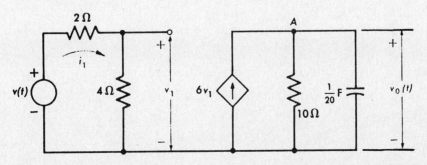

2 Ω

i_1

$v(t)$

4 Ω v_1 $6v_1$

A

10 Ω $\frac{1}{20}$ F $v_0(t)$

Fig. 16-7

16.8   Repeat Prob. 16.7 if $v(t) = 0.25u(t-1)$.

▮ In this case $v = 0$ for $t < 1$.   Other conditions remain the same.   Hence the solution becomes

$$v_0 = 10[1 - e^{-2(t-1)}]u(t-1)$$

16.9   Sketch, and compare, the responses obtained in Probs. 16.7 and 16.8.

▮ See Fig. 16-8.

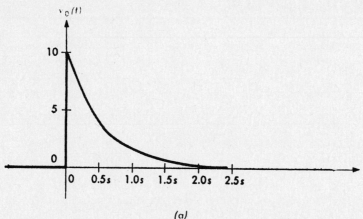

(a)

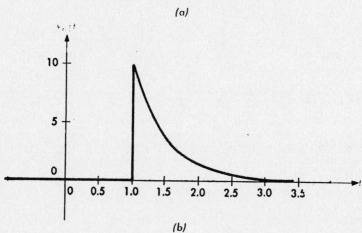

(b)

Fig. 16-8

16.10   A series RC circuit, with $R = 5\,\text{k}\Omega$ and $C = 20\,\mu\text{F}$,   has two voltage sources in series,

$$v_1 = 25u(-t)\ \text{V} \qquad v_2 = 25u(t - t')\qquad \text{V}$$

Obtain the complete expression for the voltage across the capacitor and make a sketch, if t' is positive.

▮ The capacitor voltage is continuous.   For $t \le 0$, v_1 results in a capacitor voltage of 25 V.   For $0 \le t \le t'$, both sources are zero, so that v_C decays exponentially from 25 V toward zero:

$$v_C = 25e^{-t/RC} = 25e^{-10t}\qquad \text{V}\qquad (0 \le t \le t')$$

In particular, $v_C(t') = 25e^{-10t'}$ V.

For $t \ge t'$, v_C builds from $v_C(t')$ toward the final value 25 V established by v_2:

$$v_C = [v_C(t') - v_C(\infty)]e^{-(t-t')/RC} + v_C(\infty) = 25[1 - (e^{10t'} - 1)e^{-10t}]\qquad \text{V}\qquad (t \ge t')$$

Thus, for all t,

$$v_C = 25u(-t) + 25e^{-10t}[u(t) - u(t - t')] + 25[1 - (e^{10t'} - 1)e^{-10t}]u(t - t')\qquad \text{V}$$

16.11   Sketch the voltage obtained across the capacitor of Prob. 16.10.

▮ See Fig. 16-9.

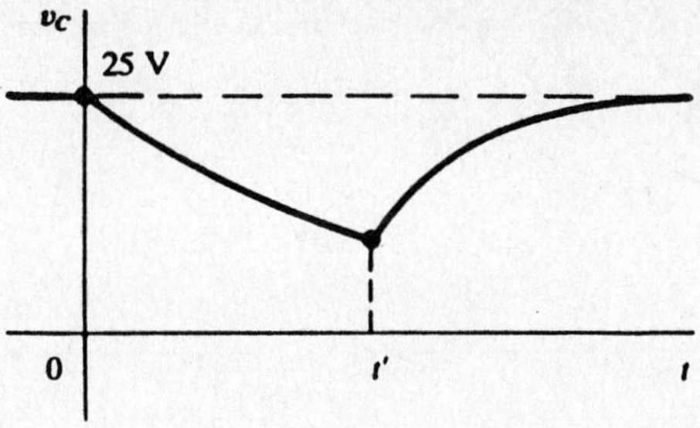

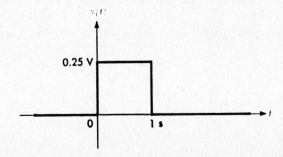

Fig. 16-9

16.12 The circuit of Fig. 16-7 is excited by the pulse shown in Fig. 16-10. Determine $v_0(t)$.

▮ As determined in Prob. 16.7, for v_0 we have

$$\frac{v_0}{10} + \frac{1}{20}\frac{dv_0}{dt} = v$$

And
$$v = 0.25[u(t) - u(t-1)]$$

The net response may be considered to consist of two parts:

$$v_{01}(t) = 10(1 - e^{-2t})u(t)$$

and
$$v_{02}(t) = -10[1 - e^{-2(t-1)}]u(t-1)$$

Thus,
$$v_0 = 10(1 - e^{-2t})u(t) - 10[1 - e^{-2(t-1)}]u(t-1)$$

0.25 V

0   1 s

Fig. 16-10

16.13 Sketch the response of the circuit of Fig. 16-7 to the signal of Fig. 16-10.

▮ The response is given by v_0 of Prob. 16.12, which is sketched in Fig. 16-11.

16.14 Represent the train of pulses shown in Fig. 16-12 in terms of V_0 and unit steps.

▮ In this case, each pulse may be expressed by a step and a delayed step. Hence,

$$v(t) = V_0 u(t) - V_0 u(t-T) + V_0 u(t-3T) - V_0 u(t-4T) + V_0 u(t-5T) - V_0 u(t-6T)$$

16.15 If we integrate the unit-step function, we obtain a *unit-ramp function*. Express this statement mathematically and sketch a unit ramp, $r(t)$.

▮
$$r(t) = \int_0^t u(t)\, dt$$

and
$$\frac{d}{dt}[r(t)] = u(t) = \begin{cases} 0 & -\infty < t < 0 \\ 1 & 0 \le t < \infty \end{cases}$$

The unit ramp is sketched in Fig. 16-13. Notice that

$$r(t) = \begin{cases} 0 & -\infty < t < 0 \\ t & 0 \le t < \infty \end{cases}$$

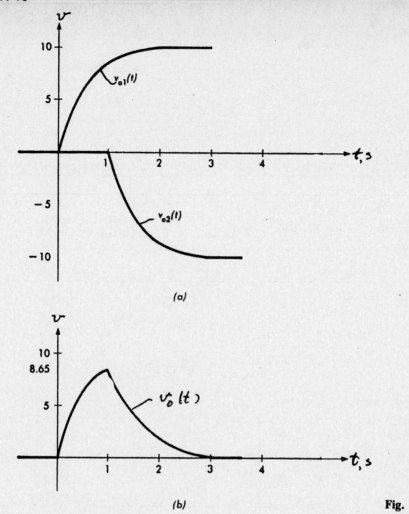

(a)

(b)

Fig. 16-11

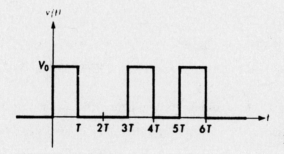

Fig. 16-12

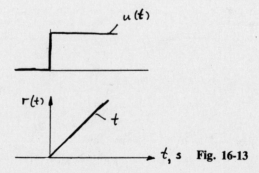

Fig. 16-13

16.16 Sketch the following ramp functions: $kr(t-1)$ and $kr(t+1)$.

▌ The sketches are shown in Fig. 16-14.

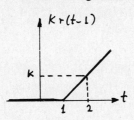
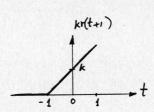

Fig. 16-14

16.17 Represent the voltage waveform of Fig. 16-15 in terms of ramp functions.

▌ We obtain the desired result by adding and subtracting ramps (see also Probs. 16.1 and 16.5). Thus,

$$v(t) = r(t) - r(t-1) - r(t-1) = r(t) - 2r(t-1)$$

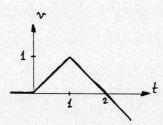

Fig. 16-15

16.18 A current of the waveform shown in Fig. 16-16 flows through a 2-mH inductor. Determine the corresponding voltage across the inductor.

$$v_L = L\,\frac{di}{dt}$$

In terms of unit ramps, i may be written as

$$i(t) = r(t) - 2r(t-1) + r(t-2)$$

Thus,

$$v_L(t) = (2 \times 10^{-3})\,\frac{d}{dt}\,[r(t) - 2r(t-1) + r(t-2)]$$

$$= 2u(t) - 4u(t-1) + 2u(t-2) \qquad \text{mV}$$

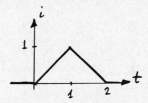

Fig. 16-16

16.19 Sketch the voltage across the inductor of Prob. 16.18.

▌ See Fig. 16-17.

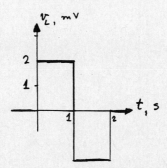

Fig. 16-17

16.20 Figure 16-18 shows a voltage waveform. Express in terms of unit steps and unit ramps.

▌ The given voltage may be expressed as

$$v_C(t) = u(t) - \tfrac{1}{2}r(t) + \tfrac{1}{2}r(t-4) + u(t-4)$$

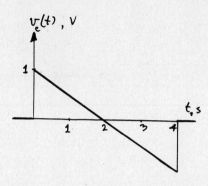

Fig. 16-18

16.21 The voltage of Fig. 16-18 is applied across a 2-μF capacitor. What is the current through the capacitor?

▌
$$i_C = C\frac{dv_C}{dt} = C\frac{d}{dt}\left[u(t) - \tfrac{1}{2}r(t) + \tfrac{1}{2}r(t-4) + u(t-4)\right]$$
$$= 2[\delta(t) - \tfrac{1}{2}u(t) + \tfrac{1}{2}u(t-4) + \delta(t-4)] \tag{1}$$

16.22 In (1) of Prob. 16.21, we have symbolically denoted the derivative $d[u(t)]/dt$ by $\delta(t)$, which is known as the *unit-impulse* or *unit-delta function*. Sketch the two terms involving these functions in (1) of Prob. 16.21.

▌ See Fig. 16-19.

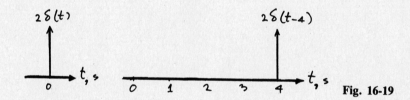

Fig. 16-19

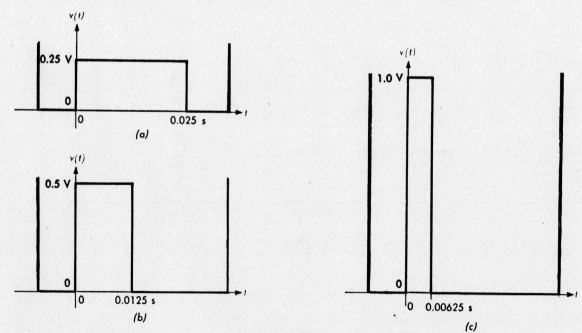

Fig. 16-20

16.23 Sketch the following pulses of voltages: $v(t) = 0.25u(t) - 0.25u(t - 0.025)$; $v(t) = 0.50u(t) - 0.50u(t - 0.0125)$; $v(t) = 1.00u(t) - 1.00u(t - 0.00625)$. Observe that as the period gets shorter, the pulse tends to the impulse function.

❙ See Fig. 16-20. From Fig. 16-20c it follows that the pulse tends to the impulse.

16.24 Determine the current through a 2-mH inductor across which the voltage has the waveform shown in Fig. 16-21.

❙
$$v = 20u(t) - 30u(t - 1) + 10u(t - 2)$$

Thus,
$$i = \frac{1}{L} \int_{-\infty}^{t} v\, dt = \frac{10^3}{2} \int_{-\infty}^{t} [20u(t) - 30u(t - 1) + 10u(t - 2)]\, dt$$

$$= \frac{10^3}{2} [20r(t) - 30r(t - 1) + 10r(t - 2)]$$

$$= [10r(t) - 15r(t - 1) + 5r(t - 2)] \times 10^3 \quad \text{A}$$

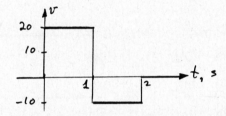

Fig. 16-21

16.25 Sketch the current i of Prob. 16.24.

❙ See Fig. 16-22, which shows all the steps of adding (and subtracting) the ramps.

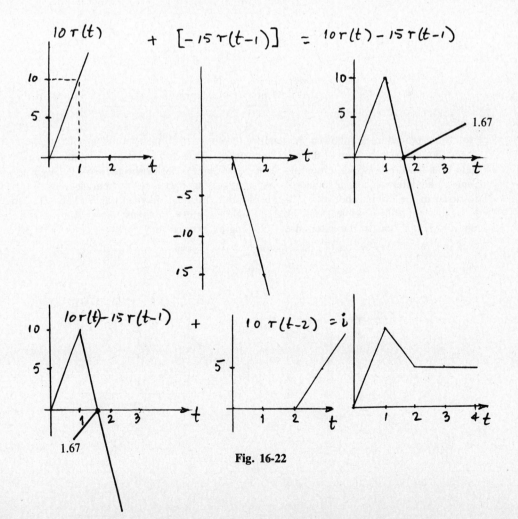

Fig. 16-22

CHAPTER 17
Duals and Analogs

17.1 Write the loop equation for the circuit of Fig. 17-1a, and the node equation for the circuit of Fig. 17-1b. Verify that the two equations are identical, and thus their solutions have the same form. The networks are *duals* of each other.

▮ For the circuit of Fig. 17-1a:

$$L_1 \frac{di_1}{dt} + R_1 i_1 + \frac{1}{C_1} \int i_1 \, dt = v_1 \tag{1}$$

$$C_2 \frac{dv_2}{dt} + G_2 v_2 + \frac{1}{L_2} \int v_2 \, dt = i_2 \tag{2}$$

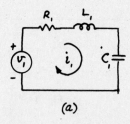
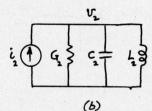

(a)   (b)   **Fig. 17-1**

17.2 From (1) and (2) of Prob. 17.1, it follows that the roles of voltage and current have been interchanged. Make a table to show the pairs of dual quantities.

▮

TABLE 17.1 Pairs of duals

Resistance, R	Conductance, G
Inductance, L	Capacitance, C
$\int i \, dt$	$\int v \, dt$
Loop	Node
Short circuit	Open circuit

17.3 The following procedure is followed, in general, to obtain the dual of a network.
1. Place a dot within each loop of the given network. These dots correspond to independent nodes. Number these dots (and the respective nodes). Place a node external to the network. This is the datum node.
2. Connect all internal dots in adjacent loops, traversing only one element at a time. For each element traversed in the original network, connect the dual element on the dual network. Continue this process until the number of possible paths through single elements is exhausted.
3. Join all internal dots to the external dot crossing all external branches.

   Using this procedure, obtain the dual of the network shown in Fig. 17-2a.

▮ The procedure is shown in Fig. 17-2a, and the dual in Fig. 17-2b.

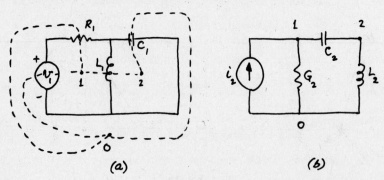

(a)   (b)   **Fig. 17-2**

17.4 Repeat Prob. 17.3 for the circuit of Fig. 17-3a.

❙ See Fig. 17-3b.

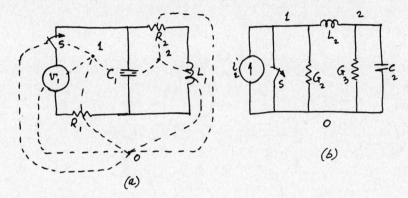

(a) (b) **Fig. 17-3**

17.5 Draw the dual of the network shown in Fig. 17-4a.

❙ The dual is shown in Fig. 17-4b.

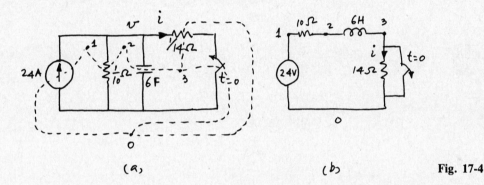

(a) (b) **Fig. 17-4**

17.6 Using the dual shown in Fig. 17-4b, solve for the current in the $1/14$-Ω resistor of the circuit of Fig. 17-4a.

$$i = i_f + i_n = \frac{24}{10 + 14} + Ae^{-(14+10)t/6} = 1 + Ae^{-4t}$$

$i(0_+) = \frac{24}{10} = 2.4$ A. Thus, $A = 2.4 - 1 = 1.4$.

Finally, $\qquad\qquad\qquad\qquad i = 1 + 1.4e^{-4t}$ A

17.7 Verify that the result of Prob. 17.6 can be obtained by using the original circuit of Fig. 17-4a.

❙ In the dual the current corresponds to the voltage. Thus, the problem reduces to the determination of v_{6F} or v. Thus, by nodal analysis:

$$6\frac{dv}{dt} + 24v = 24$$

With the initial condition $v(0_+) = v(0_-) = 2.4$ V the solution becomes $v = 1 + 1.4e^{-4t}$ V.

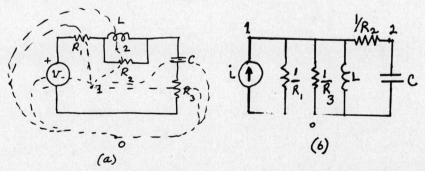

(a) (b) **Fig. 17-5**

17.8 Find the dual of the network shown in Fig. 17-5a.

❚ See Fig. 17-5b.

17.9 Repeat Prob. 17.8 for the network of Fig. 17-6a.

❚ See Fig. 17-6b.

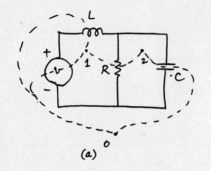 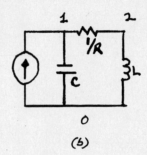

(a)   (b)   **Fig. 17-6**

17.10 Repeat Prob. 17.8 for the network of Fig. 17-7a.

❚ See Fig. 17-7b.

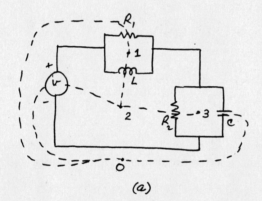 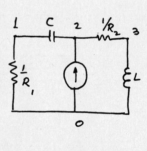

(a)   (b)   **Fig. 17-7**

17.11 Figure 17-8 shows a purely mechanical system. Assuming that all forces are linear, apply Newton's law to write the equation of motion of the system, where F is an externally applied force.

❚ By Newton's law

$$F = F_{\text{mass}} + F_{\text{friction}} + F_{\text{spring}}$$

or

$$F = M \frac{d^2x}{dt^2} + b \frac{dx}{dt} + kx \qquad (1)$$

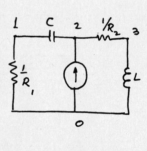

Fig. 17-8

17.12 Compare (1) of Prob. 17.11 with (1) of Prob. 17.1 and make a table of *force-voltage analogy*.

❚ In terms of electric charge q and dropping the subscripts, we may rewrite (1) of Prob. 17.1 as

$$L \frac{d^2q}{dt^2} + R \frac{dq}{dt} + \frac{1}{C} q = v \qquad (1)$$

Hence, we obtain the Table 17.2.

TABLE 17.2 Force-voltage analogy

Force, F	Voltage, v
Velocity, x	Current, i
Damping, b	Resistance, R
Mass, M	Inductance, L
Spring constant, k	Elastance = reciprocal of capacitance, $1/C$

17.13 Compare (1) of Prob. 17.11 with (2) of Prob. 17.1 and make a table of *force-current analogy*.

▮ On the basis of duality, if force is taken to be analogous to current, the Table 17.3 is obtained.

TABLE 17.3 Force-current analogy

Force, F	Current, i
Velocity, $\dot{x}$	Voltage, v
Damping, b	Conductance, G
Mass, M	Capacitance, C
Spring constant, k	Reciprocal of inductance, $1/L$

17.14 Draw the circuits for the analogs obtained in Probs. 17.12 and 17.13.

▮ These circuits are, respectively, shown in Figs. 17-9a and b.

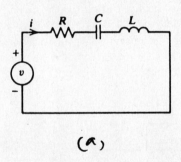

(a)

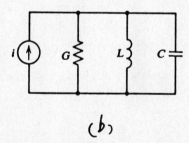

(b)   Fig. 17-9

17.15 A construction procedure for drawing electrical analogs for mechanical systems is as follows:

1. Denote all masses by capacitors to ground.
2. Node voltages on capacitors correspond to velocities.
3. Draw current sources to denote forces.
4. Connect all other components between the nodes in an arrangement which parallels the connections between the masses in the mechanical system.

Using the above procedure, draw an electrical analog for the system shown in Fig. 17-10a.

▮ By inspection, using the above procedure, we obtain the circuit of Fig. 17-10b.

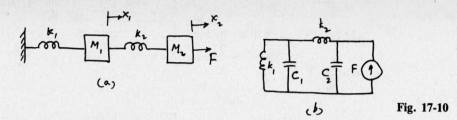

Fig. 17-10

17.16 Obtain a circuit on the basis of force-voltage analogy for the system of Fig. 17-10a.

❚ The circuit of Fig. 17-11a shows the force-current analogy (just obtained in Prob. 17.15). We draw the dual network in Fig. 17-11b to obtain the force-voltage analog.

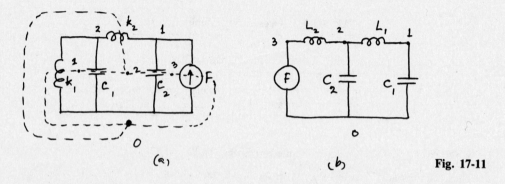

Fig. 17-11

17.17 Draw an electrical analog for the mechanical system shown in Fig. 17-12a.

❚ See Fig. 17-12b.

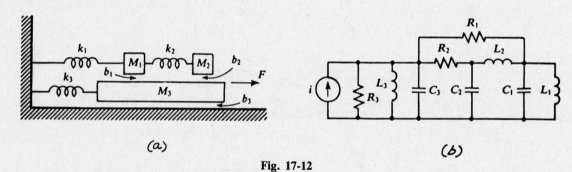

Fig. 17-12

17.18 Repeat Prob. 17.17 for the system shown in Fig. 17-13a.

❚ See Fig. 17-13b.

17.19 Repeat Prob. 17.17 for the system shown in Fig. 17-14a.

❚ See Fig. 17-14b.

17.20 A wheel mounted on bearings has a 10-kg · m² inertia and a bearing friction of 0.05 N · m/rad/s. At $t = 0$, a 10-N · m torque is applied to the wheel, starting from rest. Write its equation of motion and solve for its speed.

❚ The equation of motion is

$$10 \frac{d\omega}{dt} + 0.05\omega = 10$$

Thus,

$$\omega = 200(1 - e^{-0.005t}) \quad \text{rad/s}$$

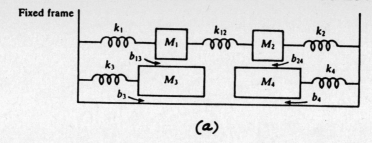

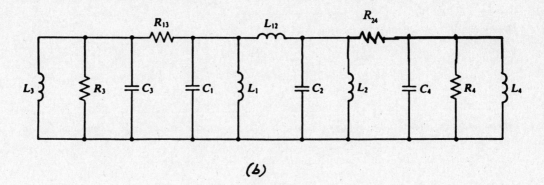

(b)

Fig. 17-13

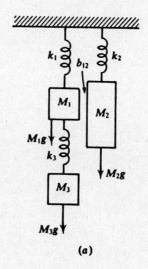

(a)

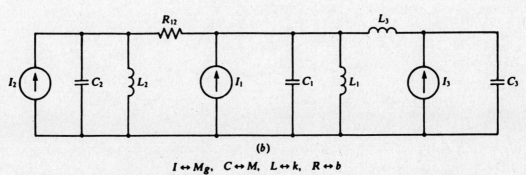

(b)

$$I \leftrightarrow Mg, \quad C \leftrightarrow M, \quad L \leftrightarrow k, \quad R \leftrightarrow b$$

Fig. 17-14

17.21 Draw an electrical analog for the wheel of Prob. 17.20.

▮ See Fig. 17-15.

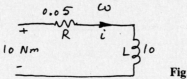

Fig. 17-15

17.22 How much energy is stored in the wheel of Prob. 17.20 under steady state?

▮ From Fig. 17-15:

$$W_{\text{stored}} = \tfrac{1}{2}Li^2 = \tfrac{1}{2}(10)(\omega_{\text{steady state}})^2 = \tfrac{1}{2}(10)(200)^2 = 0.2\,\text{MJ}$$

17.23 After the wheel of Prob. 17.20 has a steady speed, the torque is removed. How many revolutions will the wheel make before it comes to rest?

▮ The speed corresponds to the discharge of the stored energy and is given by

$$\omega = 200e^{-0.005t} \qquad \text{rad/s}$$

or

$$\theta = \int \omega\,dt = (4 \times 10^4)(1 - e^{-0.005t}) \qquad \text{rad}$$

or

$$\theta_{\text{steady state}} = (4 \times 10^4)\,\text{rad} = 6360\,\text{revolutions}$$

17.24 Draw a torque-current analog for the wheel of Prob. 17.20. Label all parameters numerically, and write the nodal equation.

▮ See Fig. 17-16.

$$10\,\frac{dv}{dt} + \frac{v}{20} = 10$$

where v corresponds to ω.

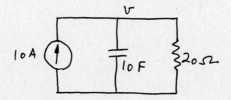

Fig. 17-16

17.25 The equation of motion of a mechanical system is (Fig. 17-17a)

$$M\,\frac{d^2x_2}{dt^2} = k(x_1 - x_2) - b\,\frac{dx_2}{dt} \tag{1}$$

Obtain an electrical analog for the system if $M = 1\,\text{kg}$, $k = 4.01\,\text{N/m}$, $b = 0.2\,\text{N/m/s}$. At $t = 0$, point 1 on the spring is moved to the right at a speed $2\,\text{m/s}$.

▮ Let

$$i_2 = \frac{dx_2}{dt} \qquad \text{or} \qquad \int i_2\,dt = x_2$$

Thus, (1) becomes

$$\frac{di_2}{dt} + 0.2i_2 + 4.01\int (i_2 - 2)\,dt = 0$$

which is represented by the circuit of Fig. 17-17b.

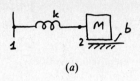

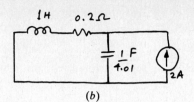

(a)

(b)   **Fig. 17-17**

17.26   Draw a voltage analog for the system of Prob. 17.25.

▮ See Fig. 17-18, obtained from duality.

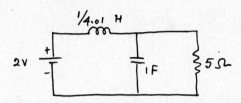

Fig. 17-18

17.27   Determine the instantaneous compression of the spring of the system of Prob. 17.25.

▮ The instantaneous compression is x_2.   Substituting the numerical values and rewriting (1) of Prob. 17.25 we obtain

$$\frac{d^2x_2}{dt^2} + 0.2\frac{dx_2}{dt} + 4.01(x_2 - 2) = 0$$

The solution is

$$x_2 = 2t - 0.09975e^{-0.1t}\sin(2t + 174.3°)\qquad\text{m}$$

which is the required compression.

17.28   After the system of Prob. 17.25 has reached steady state, the spring is detached at point 2.   Obtain and solve the equation of subsequent motion.

▮ The equation is

$$\frac{di_2}{dt} + 0.2i_2 = 0$$

At $t = 0$, $i_2 = 2\,\text{m/s}$.   Thus,

$$i_2 = 2e^{-0.2t}\qquad\text{m/s}$$

17.29   How far does the mass in Prob. 17.28 travel before it comes to rest?

▮ $x_2 = \int i_2\,dt = 10(1 - e^{-0.2t})$ m   or $(x_2)_{\text{steady state}} = 10\,\text{m}$

17.30   The equation of motion of a mechanical system is

$$10\frac{dx}{dt} + 120x + 360\int x\,dt = 98.1$$

Represent the system by an electrical analog.

▮ See Fig. 17-19.

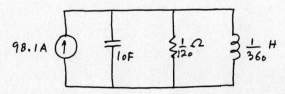

Fig. 17-19

17.31 The dynamics of an electromechanical system is given by

$$J\ddot{\theta}_1 + b\dot{\theta}_1 + k\theta_1 = \beta i_1 \qquad L_1\frac{di_1}{dt} + R_1 i_1 + \beta\dot{\theta}_1 = v_1$$

Obtain a corresponding set of analog equations involving only electrical quantities.

▋ Let $\beta\dot{\theta}_1 = v_2$. Then we have

$$C_2\frac{dv_2}{dt} + G_2 v_2 + \frac{1}{L_2}\int v_2\,dt = i_1 \qquad \text{and} \qquad L_1\frac{di_1}{dt} + R_1 i_1 = v_1 - v_2$$

where

$$L_2 = \frac{k}{\beta^2} \qquad C_2 = \frac{J}{\beta^2} \qquad G_2 = \frac{b}{\beta^2}$$

17.32 Draw an electrical analog for the system of Prob. 17.31.

▋ See Fig. 17-20.

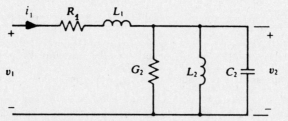

Fig. 17-20

17.33 The electromechanical dynamics of a system is given by

$$v_1 = R\dot{q}_1 + S_0 q_1 + \beta x_1 \qquad 0 = M\ddot{x}_1 + b\dot{x}_1 + kx_1 + \beta q_1$$

Express these equations in terms of purely electrical quantities.

▋ Let $\dot{x}_1 = i_2$ and $\dot{q}_1 = i_1$. Thus:

$$v_1 = Ri_1 + S_0\int i_1\,dt + \beta\int i_2\,dt \qquad 0 = M\frac{di_2}{dt} + bi_2 + k\int i_2\,dt + \beta\int i_1\,dt$$

17.34 Represent the system of Prob. 17.33 by an electrical analog.

▋ See Fig. 17-21, where $C_0 = 1/S_0$ and $C_m = 1/\beta$.

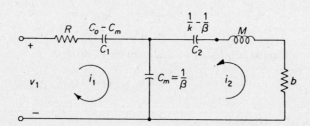

Fig. 17-21

17.35 Under what conditions is the circuit of Fig. 17-21 physically realizable.

▋ Since the capacitors cannot assume negative values, we must have

$$C_0 \geq C_m \qquad \text{and} \qquad \beta \geq k$$

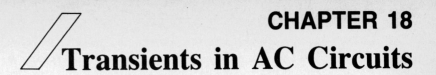

CHAPTER 18
Transients in AC Circuits

18.1 A 60-Hz 2400-V (rms) generator is connected in series with a switch and a load whose resistance and inductance are 0.24 Ω and 0.030 H, respectively. Assume the impedance of the generator is negligible. If the switch is closed at the instant the voltage wave passes through 0 V rising in the positive direction, determine the current.

▌ By KVL:

$$0.03 \frac{di}{dt} + 0.24i = 2400\sqrt{2} \sin 377t \qquad i = i_f + i_n$$

$$\bar{I}_f = \frac{\bar{V}}{\bar{Z}} = \frac{2400 \underline{/0°}}{0.24 + j(377)(0.03)} = 212.14 \underline{/-88.8°} \quad \text{A}$$

$$i_f = 212.14\sqrt{2} \sin(377t - 88.8°) \qquad i_n = Ae^{-(0.24/0.03)t} = Ae^{-8t} \quad \text{A}$$

Thus, $i = Ae^{-8t} + 300 \sin(377t - 88.8°)$. The initial condition requires that $0 = A + 300 \sin(-88.8°)$, or $A = 299.93$. Thus,

$$i = 299.93e^{-8t} + 300 \sin(377t - 88.8°) \quad \text{A}$$

[*Note*: In problems of this chapter, phasors are indicated by overbars rather than by boldface type.]

18.2 Determine the current 0.1 s after the switch is closed in the circuit of Prob. 18.1. Also calculate the steady-state current.

▌ From Prob. 18.1, at $t = 0.1$ s

$$i(0.1 \text{ s}) = 299.93e^{-(8)(0.1)} + 300 \sin\left(377 \times 0.1 - \frac{88.78}{57.3}\right) = -165.17 \quad \text{A}$$

$$i(\infty) = \frac{300}{\sqrt{2}} = 212.14 \quad \text{A}$$

18.3 Repeat Prob. 18.1, assuming that the switch is closed at the instant the voltage wave is at its positive maximum.

▌ From Prob. 18.1

$$\bar{Z} = 0.24 + j11.31 = 11.313 \underline{/88.8°} \quad \Omega \qquad \bar{I}_f = \frac{2400 \underline{/90°}}{11.313 \underline{/88.8°}} = 212.4 \underline{/1.22°} \quad \text{A} \qquad i_n = Ae^{-8t} \quad \text{A}$$

Thus,

$$i = Ae^{-8t} + 300 \sin(377t + 1.22°) \quad \text{A}$$

$$i = 0 \quad \text{at} \quad t = 0 \quad \text{yields} \quad A = -6.39$$

or

$$i = -6.39e^{-8t} + 300 \sin(377t + 1.22°) \quad \text{A}$$

18.4 Repeat Prob. 18.2 for the data of Prob. 18.3.

▌ From Prob. 18.3 at $t = 0.1$ s

$$i(0.1 \text{ s}) = -6.39e^{-(8)(0.1)} + \left[\sin\left(377 \times 0.1 + \frac{1.22}{57.3}\right)\right]300 = 3.78 \text{ A}$$

$$i(\infty) = 212.14 \text{ A} \qquad \text{(same as in Prob. 18.2)}$$

18.5 Set up the differential equation and the initial conditions for the circuit of Fig. 18-1a excited by the voltage wave of Fig. 18-1b.

▌ From Fig. 18-1b, $T = 2 \times 0.05 = 0.1$ s, $f = 1/T = 1/0.1 = 10$ Hz, and $\omega = 2\pi(10) = 62.83$ rad/s.

$$e_{\text{gen}} = 500 \sin(62.83t + 150°) \quad \text{V}$$

Thus

$$2 \frac{di}{dt} + 180i = 500 \sin(62.83t + 150°) \qquad \text{with} \qquad i(0_-) = i(0_+) = 0$$

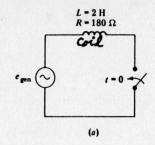

(a)

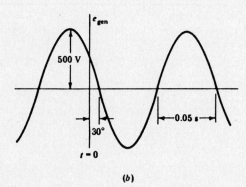

(b) Fig. 18-1

18.6 Solve for i in the circuit of Fig. 18-1a.

$$i = i_f + i_n \qquad \bar{I}_f = \frac{\bar{V}}{\bar{Z}} = \frac{(500/\sqrt{2})\,\underline{/150°}}{180 + j2(62.83)} = 1.61\,\underline{/115°} \qquad A$$

$$i_f = 1.61\sqrt{2} \sin{(62.83t + 115°)} = 2.28 \sin{(62.83t + 115°)} \qquad A$$

$$i_n = Ae^{-90t} \qquad \text{or} \qquad i = Ae^{-90t} + 2.28 \sin{(62.83t + 115°)}$$

Since $i(0_+) = 0$, $A = -2.28 \sin 115° = -2.07$. Hence,

$$i = -2.07e^{-90t} + 2.28 \sin{(62.83t + 115°)} \qquad A$$

18.7 How much energy is stored in the coil of the circuit of Fig. 18-1a at $t = 0.01$ s?

At $t = 0.01$ s, $\quad i = -2.07e^{-90 \times 0.01} + 2.28 \sin\left(62.83 \times 0.01 + \dfrac{115°}{57.3°}\right) = 0.26$ A

$$W_{\text{coil}} = \tfrac{1}{2}L(i)^2 = \tfrac{1}{2}(2)(0.26)^2 = 67.6 \text{ mJ}$$

18.8 A 450-V 60-Hz generator supplies a series circuit consisting of a switch, a 40-Ω capacitive reactance, and a coil whose inductive reactance and resistance are 50 Ω and 2.0 Ω, respectively. The switch is closed 20° after the voltage wave passes through zero rising in the positive direction. (a) Sketch the circuit; (b) sketch the voltage wave and indicate time-zero; (c) determine the steady-state current.

(a) See Fig. 18-2a. (b) See Fig. 18-2b.

(c) $\bar{Z} = 2 + j(50 - 40) = 10.2\,\underline{/78.7°}\ \Omega \qquad \bar{V} = 450\,\underline{/20°}\ V \qquad \bar{I}_f = \dfrac{\bar{V}}{\bar{Z}} = \dfrac{450\,\underline{/20°}}{10.2\,\underline{/78.7°}} = 44.12\,\underline{/-58.7°}\ A$

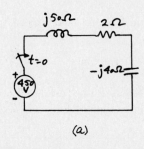

(a)

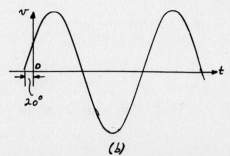

(b) Fig. 18-2

18.9 Determine the instantaneous current in the circuit of Prob. 18.8.

▮ $$L = \frac{50}{377} = 0.133\ \text{H} \qquad C = \frac{1}{377 \times 40} = 66.31\ \mu\text{F}$$

The current is governed by

$$0.133\frac{di}{dt} + 2i + \frac{10^6}{66.31}\int i\,dt = 450\sqrt{2}\sin(377t + 20°)$$

The solution is $i = i_f + i_n$. Since $\bar{I}_f = 44.12\ \underline{/-58.7°}$ A

$$i_f = 44.12\sqrt{2}\sin(377t - 58.7°) \qquad \text{A} \tag{1}$$

The characteristic equation of the circuit is

$$0.133p^2 + 2p + \frac{10^6}{66.31} = 0$$

and the roots are $p_1, p_2 = -7.5 \pm j336.8$.

Thus, $$i_n = e^{-7.5t}(A_1\cos 336.8t + A_2\sin 336.8t) \tag{2}$$

Combining (1) and (2) to obtain i, and applying the initial condition $i(0_-) = i(0_+) = 0$, yields $A_1 = 53.3$. To determine A_2 we use $v_C(0_-) = v_C(0_+) = 0$ and $di(0_+)/dt = 450\sqrt{2}\sin 20°/0.133 = 1636.55$. After considerable manipulation we obtain $A_2 = -30.25$.

Hence, $$i = 62.4\sin(377t - 58.7°)$$
$$+ e^{-7.5t}(53.3\cos 336.8t - 30.25\sin 336.8t) \qquad \text{A} \tag{3}$$

18.10 How much average power is absorbed by the circuit of Prob. 18.9?

▮ To determine the average power, we consider only the steady-state terms in the current and voltage at the terminals of the given circuit. Thus,

$$P = |\bar{V}|\,|\bar{I}|\cos\phi = (450)(44.12)\cos[20 - (-58.7)] = 3890.3\ \text{W}$$

Otherwise, $$P = I^2 R = (44.12)^2(2) = 3893.1\ \text{W}$$

18.11 How much energy is stored in the inductor of the circuit of Prob. 18.9 at $t = 0.01$ s?

▮ At $t = 0.01$ s from (3) of Prob. 18.9, we obtain $i = -17.85$ A.

Thus, $$W_L = \tfrac{1}{2}L(i)^2 = \tfrac{1}{2}(0.133)(-17.85)^2 = 21.19\ \text{J}$$

18.12 Determine the value of the capacitance that should be connected in parallel with the original capacitor, or in series with the original capacitor, so that the circuit of Prob. 18.9 is under resonance.

▮ $$f_r = \frac{1}{2\pi\sqrt{LC}} = 60 = \frac{1}{2\pi\sqrt{0.133C}} \qquad \text{or} \qquad C = 52.9\ \mu\text{F}$$

Therefore, a series-connected capacitor is required to bring the equivalent capacitance down to the required value. For a series connection we have

$$C_e = \frac{C_1 C_2}{C_1 + C_2} = 52.9 = \frac{(66.31)C_2}{66.31 + C_2} \qquad \text{or} \qquad C_2 = 261.6\ \mu\text{F}$$

18.13 Calculate the power dissipated in the circuit of Prob. 18.9 under resonance.

▮ At resonance, $\bar{Z} = R$.

Thus, $$I = \frac{V}{R} = \frac{450}{2} = 225\ \text{A} \qquad P = I^2 R = (225)^2(2) = 101.25\ \text{kW}$$

18.14 The voltage across a series RL circuit is $v = 150\sin(500t + 0.785)$ V. Given: $R = 50\ \Omega$ and $L = 0.2$ H. Find the voltage across the resistor at $t = 0.002$ s. Use the method of undetermined coefficients.

▮ The circuit equation for $t > 0$ is

$$\frac{di}{dt} + 250i = 750\sin(500t + 0.785) \tag{1}$$

The solution is in two parts, the complementary function (i_c) and the particular solution (i_p), so that $i = i_c + i_p$. The complementary function is the general solution of (1) when the right-hand side is replaced by zero: $i_c = ke^{-250t}$. The *method of undetermined coefficients* for obtaining i_p consists in assuming that

$$i_p = A\cos 500t + B\sin 500t$$

since the right-hand side of (1) can also be expressed as a linear combination of these two functions.

Then
$$\frac{di_p}{dt} = -500A\sin 500t + 500B\cos 500t$$

Substituting these expressions for i_p and di_p/dt into (1) and expanding the right-hand side,

$$-500A\sin 500t + 500B\cos 500t + 250A\cos 500t + 250B\sin 500t = 530.3\cos 500t + 530.3\sin 500t$$

Now equating the coefficients of like terms,

$$-500A + 250B = 530.3 \quad\text{and}\quad 500B + 250A = 530.3$$

Solving these simultaneous equations, $A = -0.4243$ A, $B = 1.273$ A.

$$i_p = -0.4243\cos 500t + 1.273\sin 500t = 1.342\sin(500t - 0.322) \quad\text{A}$$

and
$$i = i_c + i_p = ke^{-250t} + 1.342\sin(500t - 0.322) \quad\text{A}$$

At $t = 0$, $i = 0$. Applying this condition, $k = 0.425$ A, and, finally,

$$i = 0.425e^{-250t} + 1.342\sin(500t - 0.322) \quad\text{A}$$

At $t = 0.002$ s, $i = 1.1$ A.

Thus,
$$v_R = (50)(1.1) = 55\text{V}$$

18.15 In the circuit of Fig. 18-3, $i(0_+) = i(0_-) = 0.5$ A. Determine i for $t > 0$.

❚ The voltage equation is

$$0.1\frac{di}{dt} + 100i = 100\sin 10^3 t$$

$$\bar{Z} = 100 + j100 = 100\sqrt{2}\,\underline{/45^\circ}\ \Omega \qquad \bar{I}_f = \frac{(100/\sqrt{2})\,\underline{/0^\circ}}{(100\sqrt{2})\,\underline{/45^\circ}} = \frac{1}{2}\,\underline{/-45^\circ}\ \text{A}$$

$$i_f = \frac{1}{\sqrt{2}}\sin(10^3 t - 45^\circ) \qquad i_n = Ae^{-1000t}$$

$$i = i_f + i_n = \frac{1}{\sqrt{2}}\sin(10^3 t - 45^\circ) + Ae^{-1000t}$$

$i(0_+) = 0.5$ implies that $0.5 = -0.5 + A$. Thus, $A = 1$

and
$$i = \frac{1}{\sqrt{2}}\sin(10^3 t - 45^\circ) + e^{-1000t} \quad\text{A}$$

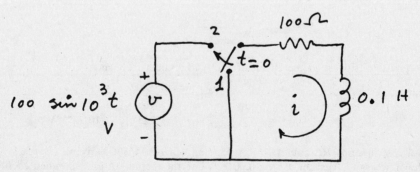

Fig. 18-3

18.16 Sketch the current obtained in Prob. 18.15.

❚ See Fig. 18-4.

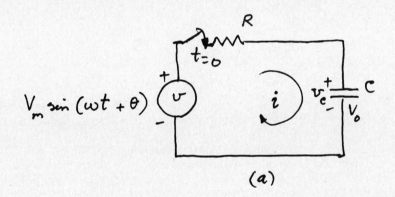

Fig. 18-4

18.17 It may be shown that the current i in the circuit of Fig. 18-5a is given by:

$$i = \frac{V_m}{\sqrt{R^2 + (1/\omega C)^2}} \sin(\omega t + \theta + \beta) - \frac{[V_0 + V_m \cos(\theta + \beta) \sin \beta]}{R} e^{-t/RC} \qquad (1)$$

where $\beta = \tan^{-1}(1/\omega CR)$ and V_0 is the initial voltage on the capacitor. For the following numerical values, sketch the current: $V_m = 10$ V, $V_0 = -5\sqrt{3}$ V, $R = 5\,\Omega$, $C = 30.63\,\mu$F, $\theta = 60°$, and $\omega = 377$ rad/s.

$$\beta = \tan^{-1}\left(\frac{10^3}{377 \times 30.63 \times 5}\right) = 60°$$

❚ The current is sketched in Fig. 18-5b.

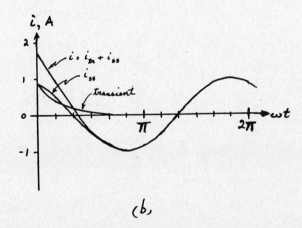

(a)

(b)   **Fig. 18-5**

18.18 In the circuit of Prob. 18.17, it is feasible to close the switch at an instant so that no transient occurs. Determine the condition for which there will be no transient in the circuit.

For no transient to occur, the coefficient of the transient term in (1) of Prob. 18.17 must be zero. Hence, the required condition is

$$\theta + \beta - \frac{\pi}{2} = \sin^{-1}\left(\frac{V_0}{V_m \sin \beta}\right)$$

18.19 Repeat Prob. 18.18 by determining the voltage across the capacitor of the circuit of Fig. 18-5a.

Considering only the transient term in (1):

$$v_{\text{ctr}} = \frac{1}{C} \int i_{tr} \, dt = (V_m \sin \beta) \sin\left(\omega t + \beta + \theta - \frac{\pi}{2}\right) + k e^{-t/RC}$$

At $t = 0$, $\qquad\qquad V_0 = (V_m \sin \beta) \sin\left(\theta + \beta - \frac{\pi}{2}\right) + k$

The value of k will be zero if

$$V_0 = (V_m \sin \beta) \sin\left(\theta + \beta - \frac{\pi}{2}\right)$$

which is the same condition as derived in Prob. 18.18.

18.20 Sketch the voltages v and v_C of the circuit of Fig. 18-5a. From the sketch, find the condition on V_0 to avoid transients.

The voltages are sketched in Fig. 18-6 from which it may be seen that the transient can be avoided only if $|V_0| < V_m \sin \beta$.

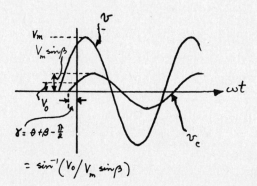

Fig. 18-6

18.21 The circuit of Fig. 18-3 is under steady state with the switch in position 2. The switch is thrown to position 1 at the instant when the current is going through a positive maximum. Sketch the current for $t < 0$ and for $t > 0$.

See Fig. 18-7.

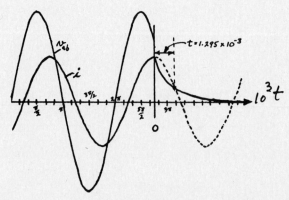

Fig. 18-7

18.22 Refer to Prob. 18.21. If the voltage of the source continues independent of the switch position, are there any subsequent instants of time when the switch could be thrown back to position 2 without causing any transients?

▮ Yes. The switch could be thrown back to position 1 without causing a transient at any instant when the actual current has the same value as the continuation of the original function. The first such moment [determined graphically (see Fig. 18-7) or by trial-and-error] is $t = 1.295$ ms.

18.23 In the circuit of Fig. 18-5a, $R = 10 \, \Omega$, $C = 10 \, \mu$F, $V_0 = 0$, and $v = 10e^{-t} \sin t$ V. Solve for i.

▮ The voltage equation is

$$10i + 10^5 \int i \, dt = 10e^{-t} \sin t \tag{1}$$

with $i(0_+) = 0$, $v_C(0_-) = v_C(0_+) = 0$. Let the forced solution be

$$i_f = e^{-t}(C_1 \sin t + C_2 \cos t) \tag{2}$$

Substituting (2) in (1) yields

$$10^4 C_1 - C_2 = -1 \qquad C_1 + 10^4 C_2 = 1$$

Thus
$$C_1 = -C_2 = -10^{-4}$$

and
$$i_f = 10^{-4} e^{-t}(\cos t - \sin t) \qquad i_n = Ae^{-10^4 t}$$

Thus
$$i = 10^{-4} e^{-t}(\cos t - \sin t) + Ae^{-10^4 t}$$

$i(0_+) = 0$ requires that $A = -10^{-4}$. Hence,

$$i = 10^{-4}[e^{-t}(\cos t - \sin t) - e^{-10^4 t}] \qquad \text{A}$$

18.24 Determine the voltage across the resistor of the circuit of Prob. 18.23 at $t = 0.1$ ms.

▮ From Prob. 18.23

$$i(0.1 \, \text{ms}) = 63.2 \, \mu\text{A} \qquad \text{or} \qquad v_R = Ri = (10)(63.2 \times 10^{-6}) = 0.632 \, \text{mV}$$

18.25 What is the energy stored in the capacitor of the circuit of Prob. 18.23 at $t = 0.1$ ms.

▮ $$v_C = v - v_R = 0.9999 - 0.632 = 0.3679 \, \text{mV} \qquad \text{or} \qquad w = \tfrac{1}{2} C(v_C)^2 = 0.677 \times 10^{-12} \, \text{J}$$

18.26 The circuit of Fig. 18-8 is under steady state with $v = 100 \sin 377t$ V. The switch is closed at $t = 0$, and the circuit is allowed to come to steady state again. What is the initial condition on the current and what is the steady-state current?

▮ For $t < 0$, $\bar{Z} = 10^3 + j(377 - 5300) = 5023 \, \underline{/-78.5°} \, \Omega$

$$\bar{I}_m = \frac{100 \, \underline{/0°}}{5023 \, \underline{/-78.5°}} = 19.9 \, \underline{/78.5°} \quad \text{mA} = 3.97 + j19.5 \quad \text{mA}$$

The reactive component of the current cannot change instantaneously. Thus,

$$i(0_-) = i(0_+) = 19.5 \, \text{mA}$$

For $t > 0$, $R = 0$. Thus,

$$(\bar{I}_m)_{\text{steady state}} = \frac{100}{-j4923} = 20.3 \, \underline{/90°} \quad \text{mA} \qquad \text{or} \qquad i_{ss} = 20.3 \cos 377t \quad \text{mA}$$

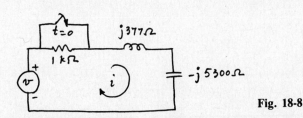

Fig. 18-8

18.27 Solve for i for the circuit of Prob. 18.26 for $t > 0$.

▮
$$i = i_f + i_n$$

where i_f is the same as i_{ss} of Prob. 18.26.
The characteristic roots are

$$p_1, p_2 = \pm j10^3\sqrt{2}$$

Thus,
$$i_n = C_1 \cos 10^3\sqrt{2}t + C_2 \sin 10^3\sqrt{2}t$$

and
$$i = 20.3 \cos 377t + C_1 \cos 10^3\sqrt{2}t + C_2 \sin 10^3\sqrt{2}t$$

From Prob. 18.26,

$$\bar{V}_{cm} = 19.9 \times 10^{-3} \times 5300 \, \underline{/(78.5° - 90°)} = 105.5 \, \underline{/-11.5°} = 103.5 - j21$$

Thus,
$$v_C(0_-) = v_C(0_+) = -21\,\text{V} = -\frac{di}{dt}(0_+) \qquad i(0_+) = 19.5\,\text{mA}$$

These initial conditions yield

$$C_1 = -0.8 \times 10^{-3} \qquad \text{and} \qquad C_2 = 14.85 \times 10^{-3}$$

Finally, therefore,

$$i = 20.3 \cos 377t - 0.8 \cos 10^3\sqrt{2}t + 14.85 \sin 10^3\sqrt{2}t \qquad \text{mA}$$

18.28 Obtain a differential equation to solve for the current through the 1-Ω resistor in the circuit of Fig. 18-9.

▮ For the two mesh currents i_1 and i_2, we have

$$2i_1 + \frac{di_1}{dt} + 3\int (i_1 - i_2)\, dt = v_s \tag{1}$$

$$3\int (i_2 - i_1)\, dt + i_2 = 0 \tag{2}$$

From (2):
$$3\int (i_1 - i_2)\, dt = i_2 \tag{3}$$

and
$$3i_1 = 3i_2 + \frac{di_2}{dt} \tag{4}$$

$$\frac{di_1}{dt} = \frac{di_2}{dt} + \frac{1}{3}\frac{d^2i_2}{dt^2} \tag{5}$$

Substituting (3) to (5) in (1) yields

$$\frac{d^2i_2}{dt^2} + 5\frac{di_2}{dt} + 9i_2 = 6t + 9\sin 4t$$

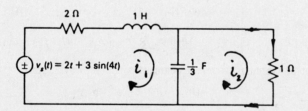

Fig. 18-9

18.29 List the initial conditions required to solve for i_x in the circuit of Fig. 18-10.

▮
$$v_C(0_-) = v_C(0_+) = 0 \qquad i_L(0_-) = i_L(0_+) = 5\,\text{A}$$

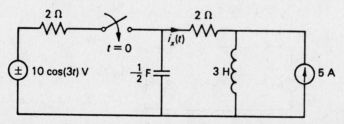

Fig. 18-10

18.30 Solve for i_x in the circuit of Fig. 18-10.

■
$$i_x = i_f + i_n$$

By steady-state circuit analysis

$$i_f = 0.36 \cos (3t - 146.9°) \qquad A$$

The characteristic equation is

$$p^2 + \tfrac{5}{3} p + \tfrac{4}{3} = 0$$

The roots are
$$p_1, p_2 = -\frac{5}{6} \pm j \frac{\sqrt{23}}{6}$$

Thus,
$$i_n = e^{-5/6t} \left(C_1 \cos \frac{\sqrt{23}}{6} t + C_2 \sin \frac{\sqrt{23}}{6} t \right)$$

The initial conditions on i_x are

$$i_x(0_+) = i_L(0_+) - 5 = 0 \text{ A} \qquad \frac{di_x}{dt}(0_+) = \frac{di_L}{dt}(0_+) = \frac{1}{L} v_L(0_+) = 0$$

Consequently,
$$C_1 = 0.3 \quad \text{and} \quad C_2 = -0.43$$

Hence,
$$i_x = 0.36 \cos (3t - 146.9°) + e^{-5/6t} \left(0.3 \cos \frac{\sqrt{23}}{6} t - 0.43 \sin \frac{\sqrt{23}}{6} t \right) \qquad A$$

CHAPTER 19
Circuits with Multifrequency Inputs

19.1 Linear circuits, excited by multifrequency sources, may be solved by superposition. On this basis, solve for the current in the circuit of Fig. 19-1a under steady state. Given: $e_{10\sim} = 30 \sin 2\pi 10t$ V and $e_{20\sim} = 50 \sin 2\pi 20t$. Obtain an expression for the instantaneous current.

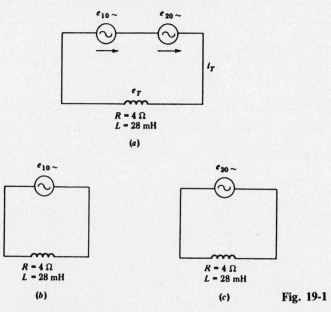

$e_{10\sim}$ $e_{20\sim}$

i_T

e_T

$R = 4\,\Omega$
$L = 28$ mH

(a)

$e_{10\sim}$

$R = 4\,\Omega$
$L = 28$ mH

(b)

$e_{20\sim}$

$R = 4\,\Omega$
$L = 28$ mH

(c)   **Fig. 19-1**

■ First, we decompose the circuit of Fig. 19-1a into two components, each with its own single-frequency input, as shown in Fig. 19-1b and c. We now have:

For Fig. 19-1b	For Fig. 19-1c
$\mathbf{Z}_{10\sim} = R + jX_{L,10\sim}$ $= 4 + j2\pi(10)(0.028)$ $= 4 + j1.76$ $= 4.37\ \underline{/23.75°}\ \Omega$	$\mathbf{Z}_{20\sim} = R + jX_{L,20\sim}$ $= 4 + j2\pi(20)(0.028)$ $= 4 + j3.52$ $= 5.33\ \underline{/41.34°}\ \Omega$
$\mathbf{I}_{10\sim} = \dfrac{\mathbf{E}_{10\sim}}{\mathbf{Z}_{10\sim}}$	$\mathbf{I}_{20\sim} = \dfrac{\mathbf{E}_{20\sim}}{\mathbf{Z}_{20\sim}}$
$\mathbf{E}_{10\sim} = \dfrac{30\ \underline{/0°}}{\sqrt{2}} = 21.21$ V	$\mathbf{E}_{20\sim} = \dfrac{50\ \underline{/0°}}{\sqrt{2}} = 35.36$ V
$\mathbf{I}_{10\sim} = \dfrac{21.21\ \underline{/0°}}{4.37\ \underline{/23.75°}}$	$\mathbf{I}_{20\sim} = \dfrac{35.36\ \underline{/0°}}{5.33\ \underline{/41.34°}}$
$= 4.85\ \underline{/-23.75°}$ A	$= 6.63\ \underline{/-41.34°}$ A

The phasor components $(\mathbf{I}_{10\sim}, \mathbf{I}_{20\sim})$ of the circuit current rotate at different angular velocities. Hence phasor addition cannot be used to obtain the resultant rms current.

The resultant instantaneous value can be determined by expressing the component currents in the time domain, and adding. Thus,

$$i_{10\sim} = 4.85\sqrt{2} \sin (2\pi 10t - 23.75°) \qquad i_{20\sim} = 6.63\sqrt{2} \sin (2\pi 20t - 41.34°)$$

From the superposition theorem,

$$i_T = i_{10\sim} + i_{20\sim} = 6.86 \sin (2\pi 10t - 23.75°) + 9.38 \sin (2\pi 20t - 41.34°) \tag{1}$$

19.2 Plot (1) of Prob. 19.1 and verify that a nonsinusoidal is produced by sinusoidal inputs of different frequencies.

❚ See Fig. 19-2.

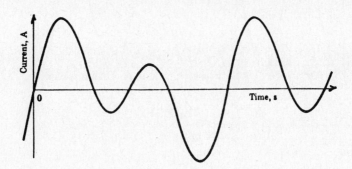

Fig. 19-2

19.3 Determine the instantaneous power drawn by the circuit of Fig. 19-1a.

$$p = e_T i_T = (e_{10\sim} + e_{20\sim})(i_{10\sim} + i_{20\sim}) = e_{10\sim}i_{10\sim} + e_{20\sim}i_{20\sim} + e_{10\sim}i_{20\sim} + e_{20\sim}i_{10\sim} \tag{1}$$

where all the instantaneous voltages and currents may be substituted from Prob. 19.1.

19.4 Sketch the four components of instantaneous power obtained in (1) of Prob. 19.3.

❚ See Fig. 19-3.

19.5 From Fig. 19-3a through d infer if the corresponding average power will be zero or nonzero.

❚ In Fig. 19-3c and d, the voltage and current waves have different frequencies, and the average power calculated over one or more periods of the lower-frequency wave is zero.

In Fig. 19-3a and b, the current and voltage waves have the same frequency, and the average power calculated over one or more periods is not zero. A comparison of Fig. 19-3a, b, c, and d indicates that *only current and voltage waves of the same frequency provide a nonzero value for the average power.*

19.6 Calculate the average power associated with each instantaneous power wave of Fig. 19-3, using the relationship $P = EI \cos \phi$. Hence determine the total average power supplied to the load.

$$P_{10\sim} = E_{10\sim} I_{10\sim} \cos \sphericalangle \begin{smallmatrix} \mathbf{E}_{10\sim} \\ \mathbf{I}_{10\sim} \end{smallmatrix} \qquad P_{20\sim} = E_{20\sim} I_{20\sim} \cos \sphericalangle \begin{smallmatrix} \mathbf{E}_{20\sim} \\ \mathbf{I}_{20\sim} \end{smallmatrix}$$

$$= (21.21)(4.85) \cos 23.75° \qquad = (35.36)(6.63) \cos 41.34°$$

$$= 94 \text{ W} \qquad = 176 \text{ W}$$

The total power supplied to the load is

$$P_T = P_{10\sim} + P_{20\sim} = 94 + 176 = 270 \text{ W}$$

19.7 Repeat Prob. 19.6 by using the I^2R relationship.

$$P_{10\sim} = I_{10\sim}^2 R = (4.85)^2 4 = 94 \text{ W} \qquad P_{20\sim} = I_{20\sim}^2 R = (6.63)^2 4 = 176 \text{ W} \qquad P_T = P_{10\sim} + P_{20\sim} = 270 \text{ W}$$

19.8 Multifrequency (MF) currents flow through a resistor R. Obtain an expression for the rms value of an equivalent single-frequency current producing the same loss in R.

❚ The power dissipated in R due to the MF currents is

$$P_{\mathrm{MF}} = I_{f1}^2 R + I_{f2}^2 R + \cdots + I_{fg}^2 R + \cdots + I_{fn}^2 R \tag{1}$$

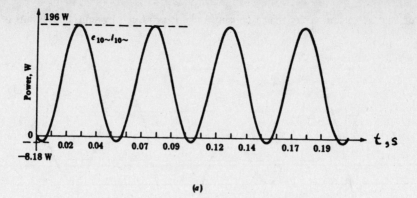

(a)

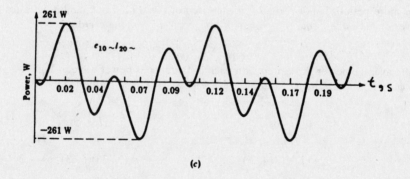

(b)

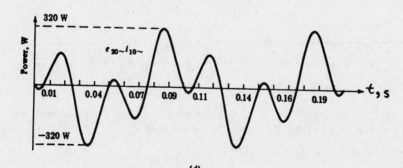

(c)

(d)

Fig. 19-3

Define I_{eq} as the rms value of an equivalent single-frequency current that would cause the same power dissipation in R as do the multifrequency components:

$$P_{MF} = I_{eq}^2 R \tag{2}$$

Equating (1) and (2) and solving for I_{eq} yields

$$I_{eq} = \sqrt{I_{f1}^2 + I_{f2}^2 + \cdots + I_{fg}^2 + \cdots + I_{fn}^2} \tag{3}$$

Since I_{eq} is the square root of the sum of the squares of the component currents, it is defined as the *root-sum-square current or rss current*. Thus (2) and (3) may be written as

$$I_{rss} = \sqrt{I_{f1}^2 + I_{f2}^2 + \cdots + I_{fg}^2 + \cdots + I_{fn}^2} \qquad P_{MF} = I_{rss}^2 R$$

where I_{f1}, I_{f2}, etc., are rms values.

19.9 Following the procedure of Prob. 19.8, obtain a general expression for the root-sum-square voltage E_{rss}.

▮ The power drawn by a resistor R may be calculated from the E^2/R relationship, *provided that the multifrequency voltage drops across the resistance component are known.* Thus,

$$P_{MF} = \frac{E_{f1}^2}{R} + \frac{E_{f2}^2}{R} + \cdots + \frac{E_{fg}^2}{R} + \cdots + \frac{E_{fn}^2}{R} \tag{1}$$

Defining E_{eq} as the rms value of an *equivalent single-frequency voltage drop across the resistance component* that would cause the same power dissipation in R as does the multifrequency components, then

$$P_{MF} = \frac{E_{eq}^2}{R} \tag{2}$$

Equating (1) and (2) and solving for E_{eq},

$$\frac{E_{eq}^2}{R} = \frac{E_{f1}^2}{R} + \frac{E_{f2}^2}{R} + \cdots + \frac{E_{fg}^2}{R} + \cdots + \frac{E_{fn}^2}{R}$$

$$E_{eq} = \sqrt{E_{f1}^2 + E_{f2}^2 + \cdots + E_{fg}^2 + \cdots + E_{fn}^2} = E_{rss} \tag{3}$$

19.10 Generalize the result (3) of Prob. 19.9 for rss voltage drops across L, C, and Z in a circuit excited by MF sources.

▮ $E_{rss,L} = \sqrt{E_{L1}^2 + E_{L2}^2 + \cdots + E_{Lg}^2 + \cdots + E_{Ln}^2}$ $E_{rss,C} = \sqrt{E_{C1}^2 + E_{C2}^2 + \cdots + E_{Cg}^2 + \cdots + E_{Cn}^2}$

$$E_{rss,Z} = \sqrt{E_{Z1}^2 + E_{Z2}^2 + \cdots + E_{Zg}^2 + \cdots + E_{Zn}^2}$$

where $\qquad E_{Lg} = I_{fg}(2\pi f_g L) \qquad E_{Cg} = I_{fg}\frac{1}{2\pi f_g C} \qquad E_{Zg} = I_{fg}(Z_{fg})$

19.11 The voltage impressed across a 10-Ω resistor is $e = (6 \sin 188.50t + 4 \sin 18,850t)$ V. Determine the frequency of each voltage component.

▮
$$2\pi f_1 = 188.5 \qquad \text{or} \qquad f_1 = \frac{188.5}{2\pi} = 30 \text{ Hz}$$

$$2\pi f_2 = 18850 \qquad \text{or} \qquad f_2 = 3 \text{ kHz}$$

19.12 Calculate E_{rss} for the circuit of Prob. 19.11.

▮
$$E_{f1} = \frac{6}{\sqrt{2}} = 4.24 \text{ V} \qquad E_{f2} = \frac{4}{\sqrt{2}} = 2.83 \text{ V} \qquad E_{rss} = \sqrt{(4.24)^2 + (2.83)^2} = 5.1 \text{ V}$$

19.13 Determine I_{rss} for the circuit of Prob. 19.11.

▮
$$I_{f1} = \frac{E_{f1}}{R} = \frac{4.24}{10} = 0.424 \text{ A} \qquad I_{f2} = \frac{2.83}{10} = 0.283 \text{ A} \qquad I_{rss} = \sqrt{(0.424)^2 + (0.283)^2} = 0.51 \text{ A}$$

19.14 How much average power is dissipated in the resistor of Prob. 19.11?

▮
$$P_{MF} = (I_{rss})^2 R = (0.51)^2 10 = 2.6 \text{ W} = (E_{rss})^2/R = (E_{rss})(I_{rss})$$

19.15 Two sinusoidal generators, an rms-reading ammeter, and a coil are connected in series. The inductance and resistance of the coil are 0.010 H and 6.0 Ω, respectively. The generator voltages are expressed by $e_1 = 10 \sin 377t$ and $e_2 = 25 \sin 754t$, respectively. Sketch the circuit and determine the ammeter reading.

▮ The circuit is shown in Fig. 19-4.

e_1	e_2
$f_1 = 60$ Hz	$f_2 = 120$ Hz
$\mathbf{Z}_{60\sim} = 6 + j3.77$	$\mathbf{Z}_{120\sim} = 6 + j7.54$
$= 7.09 \,\underline{/32.1°}\, \Omega$	$= 9.64 \,\underline{/51.5°}\, \Omega$
$E_1 = \dfrac{10}{\sqrt{2}} = 7.07$ V	$E_2 = \dfrac{25}{\sqrt{2}} = 17.68$ V
$I_1 = \dfrac{7.07}{7.09} = 0.997$	$I_2 = \dfrac{17.68}{9.64} = 1.83$ A

$$I_{rss} = \text{ammeter reading} = \sqrt{(1)^2 + (1.83)^2} = 2.09 \text{ A}$$

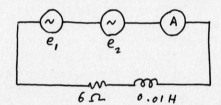

Fig. 19-4

19.16 What is the average power dissipated in the resistor of Prob. 19.15?

▮ $$P = (I_{rss})^2 R = (2.09)^2 6 = 26.21 \text{ W}$$

19.17 A $100 \,\underline{/0°}$-V 120-Hz generator and an $80 \,\underline{/0°}$-V 60-Hz generator are connected in series with a 60-V battery and a coil. The resistance and inductance of the coil are 3.0 Ω and 2.65 mH, respectively. Sketch the circuit and determine the impedance at each frequency.

▮ The circuit is sketched in Fig. 19-5.

$$\mathbf{Z}_{120\sim} = 3 + j2\pi(120)(0.00265) = 3.6 \,\underline{/33.66°}\, \Omega$$

$$\mathbf{Z}_{60\sim} = 3 + j2\pi(60)(0.00265) = 3.16 \,\underline{/18.43°}\, \Omega \qquad \mathbf{Z}_{0\sim} = 3 + j0 = 3 \,\underline{/0°}\, \Omega$$

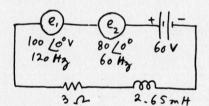

Fig. 19-5

19.18 Calculate I_{rss} for the circuit of Prob. 19.17.

▮ $$I_{120\sim} = \frac{100}{3.6} = 27.78 \text{ A} \qquad I_{60\sim} = \frac{80}{3.16} = 25.32 \text{ A} \qquad I_{0\sim} = \frac{60}{3} = 20.0 \text{ A}$$

$$I_{rss} = \sqrt{(27.78)^2 + (25.32)^2 + (20.0)^2} = 42.58 \text{ A}$$

19.19 Determine the voltmeter reading in the circuit of Fig. 19-6.

▮ The voltmeter reads E_{rss} which is given by

$$E_{rss} = \sqrt{(120)^2 + (40)^2 + (300)^2} = 326 \text{ V}$$

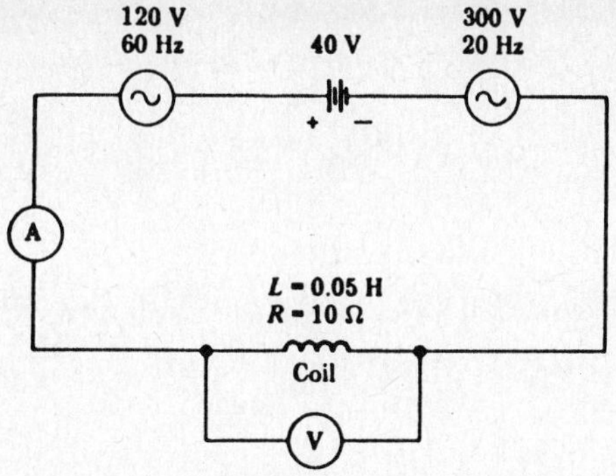

Fig. 19-6

19.20 Find the ammeter reading in the circuit of Fig. 19-6.

$\mathbf{Z}_{60\sim} = 10 + j[2\pi 60(0.05)] = 10 + j18.85 = 21.34 \underline{/62.05°}\ \Omega$

$\mathbf{Z}_{20\sim} = 10 + j[2\pi(20)(0.05)] = 10 + j6.28 = 11.81 \underline{/32.14°}\ \Omega$

$\mathbf{Z}_{0\sim} = 10 + j[2\pi(0)(0.05)] = 10 + j0 = 10 \underline{/0°}\ \Omega$

$\mathbf{I}_{60\sim} = \dfrac{120 \underline{/0°}}{21.34 \underline{/62.05°}} = 5.62 \underline{/-62.05°}\ \text{A}$

$\mathbf{I}_{20\sim} = \dfrac{300 \underline{/0°}}{11.81 \underline{/32.14°}} = 25.40 \underline{/-32.14°}\ \text{A}$

$\mathbf{I}_{0\sim} = \dfrac{40 \underline{/0°}}{10 \underline{/0°}} = 4.0 \underline{/0°}\ \text{A}$

$I_{rss} = \sqrt{(5.62)^2 + (25.40)^2 + (4)^2} = 26.32\ \text{A} = \text{ammeter reading}$

19.21 How much total power is drawn from the sources of the circuit of Fig. 19-6?

$$P_{\text{supplied}} = P_{\text{absorbed}} = (I_{rss})^2 R = (26.32)^2 10 = 6927.4\ \text{W}$$

19.22 The current and voltage to a load are expressed by

$$e_T = 20 + 30 \sin(377t) + 50 \sin(1130t + 20°) \qquad i_T = 15 \sin(377t) + 14 \sin(1130t - 36°)$$

Determine (*a*) the frequency of each component of the driving voltage; (*b*) the rss current; (*c*) the rss voltage.

(*a*) The three component frequencies are

1. 0 Hz (dc)
2. $2\pi f = 377 \qquad f = 60\ \text{Hz}$
3. $2\pi f = 1130 \qquad f = 180\ \text{Hz}$

(*b*) $I_{rss} = \sqrt{\left(\dfrac{15}{\sqrt{2}}\right)^2 + \left(\dfrac{14}{\sqrt{2}}\right)^2} = 14.5\ \text{A}$

(*c*) $E_{rss} = \sqrt{(20)^2 + \left(\dfrac{30}{\sqrt{2}}\right)^2 + \left(\dfrac{50}{\sqrt{2}}\right)^2} = 45.8\ \text{V}$

19.23 We define the apparent power S_{MF} and the power factor pf_{MF} relating to a multifrequency circuit by

$$S_{\text{MF}} = E_{rss} I_{rss} \qquad \text{and} \qquad \text{pf}_{\text{MF}} = P_{\text{MF}}/S_{\text{MF}}$$

Using this definition, find the apparent power drawn by the circuit of Prob. 19.22.

$$S_{\text{MF}} = E_{rss} I_{rss} = (45.8)(14.5) = 665\ \text{V}\cdot\text{A}$$

19.24 Determine the total active power and the power factor of the circuit of Prob. 19.22.

$$P_{MF} = P_{0\sim} + P_{60\sim} + P_{180\sim} \qquad P_{0\sim} = V_{0\sim}I_{0\sim} = 20(0) = 0$$

$$P_{60\sim} = V_{60\sim}I_{60\sim} \cos \not{\!\!<} \frac{\mathbf{V}_{60\sim}}{\mathbf{I}_{60\sim}} = \frac{30}{\sqrt{2}} \frac{15}{\sqrt{2}} \cos 0° = 225 \text{ W}$$

$$P_{180\sim} = V_{180\sim}I_{180\sim} \cos \not{\!\!<} \frac{\mathbf{V}_{180\sim}}{\mathbf{I}_{180\sim}} = \frac{50}{\sqrt{2}} \frac{14}{\sqrt{2}} \cos 56° = 196 \text{ W}$$

$$P_{MF} = 0 + 225 + 196 = 421 \text{ W} \qquad \text{and} \qquad \text{pf}_{MF} = \frac{P_{MF}}{S_{MF}} = \frac{421}{665} = 0.63$$

19.25 Obtain the impedances corresponding to the different frequencies in the circuit of Prob. 19.22.

$$Z_{0\sim} = \frac{V_{0\sim}}{I_{0\sim}} = \frac{20}{0} = \infty \; \Omega \quad Z_{60\sim} = \frac{V_{60\sim}}{I_{60\sim}} = \frac{30/\sqrt{2}}{15/\sqrt{2}} = 2 \; \Omega \quad Z_{180\sim} = \frac{V_{180\sim}}{I_{180\sim}} = \frac{50/\sqrt{2}}{14/\sqrt{2}} = 3.57 \; \Omega$$

19.26 Three sinusoidal generators and a battery are connected in series with a coil whose resistance and inductance are 8.0 Ω and 26.53 mH, respectively. The frequency and rms voltage of the respective generators are 20 Hz, 15 V; 60 Hz, 30 V; and 80 Hz, 50 V. The battery voltage is 6 V. Sketch the circuit and determine the rss voltage.

The circuit is shown in Fig. 19-7.

$$E_{rss} = \sqrt{(15)^2 + (30)^2 + (50)^2 + (6)^2} = 60.51 \text{ V}$$

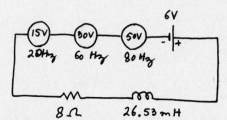

Fig. 19-7

19.27 Determine the complex impedances at the different frequencies of the circuit of Fig. 19-7.

$$\mathbf{Z}_{20\sim} = 8 + j2\pi(20)(0.02653) = 8.67 \;\underline{/22.62°} \; \Omega \qquad \mathbf{Z}_{60\sim} = 8 + j2\pi(60)(0.02653) = 12.81 \;\underline{/51.34°} \; \Omega$$

$$\mathbf{Z}_{80\sim} = 8 + j2\pi(80)(0.02653) = 15.55 \;\underline{/59.04°} \; \Omega \qquad \mathbf{Z}_{0\sim} = 8 + j0 = 8 \;\underline{/0°} \; \Omega$$

19.28 Calculate the I_{rss} in the circuit of Fig. 19-7.

$$I_{20\sim} = \frac{15}{8.67} = 1.73 \text{ A} \qquad I_{60\sim} = \frac{30}{12.81} = 2.34 \text{ A}$$

$$I_{80\sim} = \frac{50}{15.55} = 3.22 \text{ A} \qquad I_{0\sim} = \frac{6}{8} = 0.75 \text{ A}$$

Thus, $$I_{rss} = \sqrt{(1.73)^2 + (2.34)^2 + (3.22)^2 + (0.75)^2} = 4.40 \text{ A}$$

19.29 Find the average power, apparent power, and the power factor of the circuit of Fig. 19-7.

$$P_{MF} = (I_{rss})^2 R = (4.4)^2 8 = 154.88 \text{ W}$$

$$S_{MF} = E_{rss}I_{rss} = (60.51)(4.4) = 266.2 \text{ V} \cdot \text{A}$$

$$\text{pf}_{MF} = \frac{P_{MF}}{S_{MF}} = \frac{154.88}{266.2} = 0.58$$

19.30 In the circuit of Fig. 19-8

$$e_T = 141.42 \sin 2\pi 30t + 141.42 \sin 2\pi 90t \qquad i_T = 9.80 \sin(2\pi 30t - 30°) + 5.66 \sin(2\pi 90t - 60°)$$

Determine I_{rss}.

$$I_{30\sim} = \frac{9.80}{\sqrt{2}} = 6.93 \text{ A} \qquad I_{90\sim} = \frac{5.66}{\sqrt{2}} = 4.00 \text{ A} \qquad I_{rss} = \sqrt{(6.93)^2 + (4.00)^2} = 8.00 \text{ A}$$

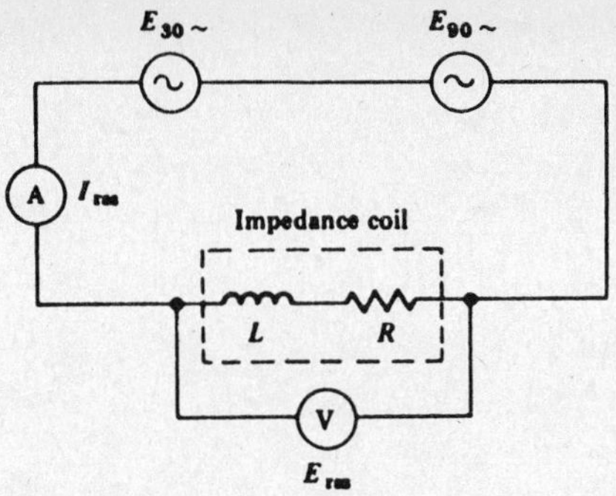

Fig. 19-8

19.31 Find E_{rss} in the circuit of Fig. 19-8.

$$E_{30\sim} = \frac{141.42}{\sqrt{2}} = 100 \text{ V} \qquad E_{90\sim} = \frac{141.42}{\sqrt{2}} = 100 \text{ V} \qquad E_{rss,Z} = \sqrt{(100)^2 + (100)^2} = 141.42 \text{ V}$$

19.32 Determine $\bar{Z}_{30\sim}$ and $\bar{Z}_{90\sim}$ for the circuit of Fig. 19-8.

$$\mathbf{Z}_{30\sim} = \frac{\mathbf{E}_{30\sim}}{\mathbf{I}_{30\sim}} = \frac{100 \underline{/0°}}{6.93 \underline{/-30°}} = 14.44 \underline{/30°} = (12.5 + j7.22) \ \Omega$$

$$\mathbf{Z}_{90\sim} = \frac{\mathbf{E}_{90\sim}}{\mathbf{I}_{90\sim}} = \frac{100 \underline{/0°}}{4 \underline{/-60°}} = 25 \underline{/60°} = (12.5 + j21.65) \ \Omega$$

19.33 Determine the resistance and the inductance of the coil of the circuit shown in Fig. 19-8.

From Prob. 19.32:

$$\mathbf{Z}_{30\sim} = (12.5 + j7.22) \qquad \Omega$$

Thus, $\quad R = 12.5 \ \Omega \quad X_{L30\sim} = 7.22 \ \Omega \quad 2\pi(30)L = 7.22 \quad L = 0.0383 \text{ H} \quad$ or $\quad 38.3 \text{ mH}$

19.34 How much active power is drawn by the coil of the circuit of Fig. 19-8?

$$P_{30\sim} = E_{30\sim} I_{30\sim} \cos \sphericalangle \begin{matrix} \mathbf{E}_{30\sim} \\ \mathbf{I}_{30\sim} \end{matrix} \qquad P_{90\sim} = E_{90\sim} I_{90\sim} \cos \sphericalangle \begin{matrix} \mathbf{E}_{90\sim} \\ \mathbf{I}_{90\sim} \end{matrix}$$

$$= (100)(6.93) \cos 30° \qquad = (100)(4.00) \cos 60°$$

$$= 600 \text{ W} \qquad\qquad = 200 \text{ W}$$

$$P_{MF} = 600 + 200 = 800 \text{ W}$$

19.35 Verify that the result of Prob. 19.34 will be obtained by the $I^2 R$ method.

$$P_{30\sim} = I_{30\sim}^2 R \qquad\qquad P_{90\sim} = I_{90\sim}^2 R$$

$$= (6.93)^2 (12.5) \qquad\qquad = (4.00)^2 (12.5)$$

$$= 600 \text{ W} \qquad\qquad = 200 \text{ W}$$

$$P_{MF} = 600 + 200 = 800 \text{ W}$$

19.36 Repeat Prob. 19.34 using the definition of I_{rss}.

From Prob. 19.30, $I_{rss} = 8$ A.

Thus, $$P_{MF} = (I_{rss,R})^2 R = (8)^2 (12.5) = 800 \text{ W}$$

19.37 Repeat Prob. 19.34 using the relationship $P_{MF} = (E_{rss,R})^2/R$, where $E_{rss,R}$ is the root-sum-square of the multifrequency voltage drop across the resistance component.

$$E_{30\sim,R} = I_{30\sim} R = 6.93(12.5) = 86.63 \text{ V} \qquad E_{90\sim,R} = I_{90\sim} R = 4.00(12.5) = 50.00 \text{ V}$$

$$E_{rss,R} = \sqrt{(86.63)^2 + (50.00)^2} = 100 \text{ V} \qquad \text{thus} \qquad P_{MF} = \frac{(100)^2}{12.5} = 800 \text{ W}$$

19.38 Obtain the results of Probs. 19.34 through 19.37 from $P_{MF} = (E_{rss,R})(I_{rss,R})$.

❚
$$P_{MF} = (100)(8) = 800 \text{ W}$$

19.39 Determine the apparent power and the power factor of the circuit of Fig. 19-8.

❚
$$S_{MF} = E_{rss}I_{rss} = (141.42)(8.00) = 1131 \text{ V} \cdot \text{A}$$

$$pf_{MF} = \frac{P_{MF}}{S_{MF}} = \frac{800}{1131} = 0.71$$

19.40 A 10-Ω resistor is connected in series with the following series-connected generators:

$$e_1 = 50 \sin (377t + 40°) \qquad e_2 = 40 \sin (377t + 20°) \qquad e_3 = 80 \sin 150t$$

Determine the frequency of the individual generators.

❚
$$f_1 = \frac{377}{2\pi} = 60 \text{ Hz} \qquad f_2 = \frac{377}{2\pi} = 60 \text{ Hz} \qquad f_3 = \frac{150}{2\pi} = 23.87 \text{ Hz}$$

19.41 Obtain the rss voltage across the resistor of the circuit of Prob. 19.40.

❚ Since voltages e_1 and e_2 have the same frequency, it is necessary to calculate the resultant voltage at that frequency before calculating the rss value. Thus,

$$\mathbf{E_1} + \mathbf{E_2} = \frac{50 \underline{/40°}}{\sqrt{2}} + \frac{40 \underline{/20°}}{\sqrt{2}} = (27.08 + j22.73) + (26.58 + j9.67) = (53.66 + j32.40) = 62.7 \underline{/31.12°} \text{ V}$$

The rms value of the 23.87-Hz wave is $E_3 = 80/\sqrt{2} = 56.6$ V.

$$E_{rss,R} = \sqrt{E_{60\sim}^2 + E_{23.87\sim}^2} = \sqrt{(62.7)^2 + (56.6)^2} = 84.5 \text{ V}$$

19.42 What is the rss current through the resistor of the circuit of Prob. 19.40?

❚
$$I_{60\sim} = \frac{V_{60\sim}}{Z_{60\sim}} = \frac{62.68}{10} = 6.268 \text{ A} \qquad I_{23.87\sim} = \frac{56.57}{10} = 5.657 \text{ A} \qquad I_{rss} = \sqrt{(6.268)^2 + (5.657)^2} = 8.44 \text{ A}$$

19.43 Determine the power delivered to the resistor of the circuit of Prob. 19.40.

❚
$$P_{MF} = (I_{rss,R})^2 R = (8.44)^2 10 = 712.3 \text{ W}$$

19.44 A coil whose resistance and inductance are 50 Ω and 88 mH, respectively, is connected in series with three sinusoidal generators. The generator voltages are $e_1 = 400 \sin 377t$, $e_2 = 100 \sin 754t$, $e_3 = 50 \sin 1131t$. Determine the frequency of each generator.

❚
$$2\pi f_1 = 377 \qquad f_1 = 60 \text{ Hz}$$
$$2\pi f_2 = 754 \qquad f_2 = 120 \text{ Hz}$$
$$2\pi f_3 = 1131 \qquad f_3 = 180 \text{ Hz}$$

19.45 Determine the rss voltage across the coil of the circuit of Prob. 19.44.

❚
$$E_1 = \frac{400}{\sqrt{2}} = 282.84 \text{ V} \qquad E_2 = \frac{100}{\sqrt{2}} = 70.71 \text{ V} \qquad E_2 = \frac{50}{\sqrt{2}} = 35.36 \text{ V}$$

$$E_{rss} = \sqrt{(282.84)^2 + (70.71)^2 + (35.36)^2} = 293.68 \text{ V}$$

19.46 Determine the rss current in the circuit of Prob. 19.44.

❚
$$\mathbf{Z}_{60\sim} = 50 + j377(0.088) = 60 \underline{/33.57°} \Omega \qquad \mathbf{Z}_{120\sim} = 50 + j754(0.088) = 83 \underline{/53.0°} \Omega$$

$$\mathbf{Z}_{180\sim} = 50 + j1131(0.088) = 111.38 \underline{/63.33°} \Omega$$

$$I_1 = \frac{282.84}{60} = 4.71 \text{ A} \qquad I_2 = \frac{70.71}{83} = 0.85 \text{ A} \qquad I_3 = \frac{35.36}{111.38} = 0.32 \text{ A}$$

$$I_{rss} = \sqrt{(4.71)^2 + (0.85)^2 + (0.32)^2} = 4.8 \text{ A}$$

19.47 A series circuit containing a 295-μF capacitor and a coil whose resistance and inductance are 3 Ω and 4.42 mH, respectively, are supplied by the following series-connected generators: 35 V at 60 Hz, 10 V at 180 Hz, and 8 V at 300 Hz. Determine the rss driving voltage.

$$E_{rss} = \sqrt{(35)^2 + (10)^2 + (8)^2} = 37.3 \text{ V}$$

19.48 What is the rss current in the circuit of Prob. 19.47?

At 60 Hz: $\quad X_L = 2\pi(60)(4.42 \times 10^{-3}) = 1.67 \,\Omega \quad X_C = \dfrac{1}{2\pi 60(295 \times 10^{-6})} = 8.99 \,\Omega$

$$\mathbf{Z}_{60} = 3 + j(1.67 - 8.99) = 7.91 \underline{/-67.72°} \,\Omega$$

$$\mathbf{I}_{60} = \frac{35 \underline{/0°}}{7.91 \underline{/-67.72°}} = 4.42 \underline{/67.72°} = 4.42 \text{ A}$$

At 180 Hz: $\quad X_L = 2\pi(180)(4.42 \times 10^{-3}) = 5 \,\Omega \quad X_C = \dfrac{1}{2\pi(180)(295 \times 10^{-6})} = 3 \,\Omega$

$$\mathbf{Z}_{180} = 3 + j(5 - 3) = (3 + j2) = 3.61 \underline{/33.69°} \,\Omega$$

$$\mathbf{I}_{180} = \frac{10 \underline{/0°}}{3.61 \underline{/33.69°}} = 2.77 \underline{/-33.69°} = 2.77 \text{ A}$$

At 300 Hz: $\quad X_L = 2\pi(300)(4.42 \times 10^{-3}) = 8.33 \,\Omega \quad X_C = \dfrac{1}{2\pi(300)(295 \times 10^{-6})} = 1.80 \,\Omega$

$$\mathbf{Z}_{300} = R + j(X_L - X_C) = 3 + j(8.33 - 1.80) = 7.19 \underline{/65.33°} \quad \Omega$$

$$\mathbf{I}_{300} = \frac{8 \underline{/0°}}{7.19 \underline{/65.33°}} = 1.11 \underline{/-65.33°} = 1.11 \text{ A}$$

$$I_{rss} = \sqrt{(4.42)^2 + (2.77)^2 + (1.11)^2} = 5.33 \text{ A}$$

19.49 Obtain the reading of an rms voltmeter connected across the coil of Prob. 19.44.

$$\mathbf{V}_{coil\ 60} = \mathbf{I}_{60}\mathbf{Z}_{coil\ 60} = 4.42 \underline{/67.72°}(3 + j1.67) = (4.42 \underline{/67.72°})(3.43 \underline{/29.10°}) = 15.16 \underline{/96.82°} \text{ V}$$

Similarly, $\quad \mathbf{V}_{coil\ 180} = (2.77 \underline{/-33.69°})(3 + j5) = (2.77 \underline{/-33.69°})(5.83 \underline{/59.04°}) = 16.15 \underline{/25.35°} \text{ V}$

$$\mathbf{V}_{coil\ 300} = (1.11 \underline{/-65.33°})(3 + j8.33) = (1.11 \underline{/-65.33°})(8.85 \underline{/70.19°}) = 9.82 \underline{/4.86°} \text{ V}$$

$$V_{rss\ coil} = \sqrt{(15.16)^2 + (16.15)^2 + (9.82)^2} = 24.2 \text{ V} = \text{voltmeter reading}$$

19.50 Determine the rss voltage across the capacitor of the circuit of Prob. 19.44.

$$V_{C60} = I_{C60}X_{C60} = 4.42(8.99) = 39.74 \text{ V}$$

$$V_{C180} = I_{C180}X_{C180} = 2.77(3) = 8.31 \text{ V}$$

$$V_{C300} = I_{C300}X_{C300} = (1.11)(1.80) = 2.00 \text{ V}$$

$$V_{rss,C} = \sqrt{(39.74)^2 + (8.31)^2 + (2.00)^2} = 40.65 \text{ V}$$

19.51 Obtain the active power, apparent power, and the power factor for the circuit of Prob. 19.44.

$$P_{MF} = RI_{rss,R}^2 = 3(5.33)^2 = 85.23 \text{ W} \qquad S_{MF} = E_{rss}I_{rss} = (37.27)(5.33) = 198.65 \text{ V·A}$$

$$\text{pf}_{MF} = \frac{P_{MF}}{S_{MF}} = \frac{85.23}{198.65} = 0.43$$

19.52 Determine the instantaneous current in the circuit of Prob. 19.44.

$$i = i_{60} + i_{180} + i_{300}$$

$$= 4.42\sqrt{2} \sin(2\pi 60t + 67.72°) + 2.77\sqrt{2} \sin(2\pi 180t - 33.69°) + 1.11\sqrt{2} \sin(2\pi 300t - 65.33°)$$

$$= 6.25 \sin(377t + 67.72°) + 3.92 \sin(1131t - 33.69°) + 1.57 \sin(1885t - 65.33°)$$

19.53 A 30-Ω resistor is connected in series with a 500-μF capacitor, a 120-V battery, an ammeter, and three sinusoidal generators. The generator voltages are 100 sin 30t, 50 sin 80t, and 70 sin 100t V. Sketch the circuit and include a voltmeter across the capacitor-resistor combination. Determine the voltmeter reading.

▌ See Fig. 19-9.

$$E_1 = \frac{100}{\sqrt{2}} = 70.71 \text{ V} \qquad E_2 = \frac{50}{\sqrt{2}} = 35.36 \text{ V} \qquad E_3 = \frac{70}{\sqrt{2}} = 49.50 \text{ V} \qquad E_4 = 120 \text{ V}$$

$$E_{rss} = \sqrt{(70.71)^2 + (35.36)^2 + (49.50)^2 + (120)^2} = 152 \text{ V} = \text{voltmeter reading}$$

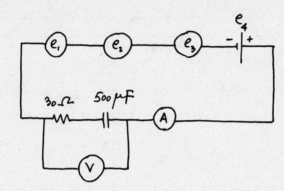

Fig. 19-9

19.54 Determine the ammeter reading in the circuit of Fig. 19-9.

▌ $\qquad Z_1 = 73.11 \,\Omega \qquad Z_2 = 39.05 \,\Omega \qquad Z_3 = 36.06 \,\Omega \qquad Z_4 = \infty$

$$I_1 = \frac{70.71}{73.11} = 0.97 \text{ A} \qquad I_2 = \frac{35.36}{39.05} = 0.91 \text{ A} \qquad I_3 = \frac{49.50}{36.06} = 1.37 \text{ A} \qquad I_4 = 0 \text{ A}$$

$$I_{rss} = \sqrt{(0.97)^2 + (0.91)^2 + (1.37)^2 + 0} = 1.91 \text{ A} = \text{ammeter reading}$$

19.55 Calculate the power dissipated in the resistor of the circuit of Fig. 19-9.

▌ From Prob. 19.54, $I_{rss} = 1.91$ A.

Thus, $\qquad\qquad\qquad\qquad P_{MF} = (1.91)^2(30) = 109.44 \text{ W}$

19.56 A load consisting of an 8.842-μF capacitor and a coil whose inductance and resistance are 88.4 mH and 5 Ω, respectively, is connected in series with three sinusoidal generators. The generator voltages are 100 sin 377t, 100 sin (377t + 50°), and 100 sin 1131t V. Sketch the circuit and determine the frequency of each generator.

▌ The circuit is shown in Fig. 19-10.

$$f_1 = \frac{377}{2\pi} = 60 \text{ Hz} \qquad f_2 = \frac{377}{2\pi} = 60 \text{ Hz} \qquad f_3 = \frac{1131}{2\pi} = 180 \text{ Hz}$$

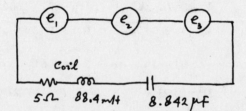

Fig. 19-10

19.57 Determine the rss voltage across the load of the circuit of Fig. 19-10.

▌ First, we combine the 60-Hz voltages to obtain

$$\mathbf{E}_{60\sim \text{ max}} = 100 \underline{/0°} + 100 \underline{/50°} = 181.26 \underline{/25°} \text{ V} \qquad E_{60\sim} = \frac{181.26}{\sqrt{2}} = 128.17 \text{ V} \qquad E_{180\sim} = \frac{100}{\sqrt{2}} = 70.71 \text{ V}$$

$$E_{rss} = \sqrt{(128.17)^2 + (70.71)^2} = 146.38 \text{ V}$$

19.58 Calculate the rss current in the circuit of Fig. 19-10.

$$Z_{60\sim} = 266.71 \,\Omega \qquad Z_{180\sim} = 5 \,\Omega \qquad I_{60\sim} = \frac{128.17}{266.71} = 0.48 \text{ A} \qquad I_{180\sim} = \frac{70.71}{5} = 14.14 \text{ A}$$

$$I_{\text{rss}} = \sqrt{(0.48)^2 + (14.14)^2} = 14.15 \text{ A}$$

19.59 How much active power is delivered by all the sources of the circuit of Fig. 19-10?

$$P_{\text{delivered}} = P_{\text{MF}} = (I_{\text{rss}})^2 R = (14.15)^2 5 = 1001 \text{ W}$$

19.60 A series *RLC* circuit excited by several multifrequency sources is shown in Fig. 19-11. Write the general expressions for I_{rss}, $E_{\text{rss},R}$, P_{MF}, S_{MF}, and pf_{MF}.

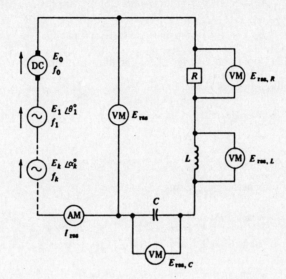

Fig. 19-11

$$\mathbf{I}_g = \frac{\mathbf{E}_g}{\mathbf{Z}_g} \qquad \mathbf{Z}_g = R + j\left(2\pi f_g L - \frac{1}{2\pi f_g C}\right)$$

$$\mathbf{E}_{Rg} = \mathbf{I}_g R \qquad \mathbf{E}_{Lg} = \mathbf{I}_g(jX_{Lg}) \qquad \mathbf{E}_{Cg} = \mathbf{I}_g(-jX_{Cg})$$

$$P_g = E_g I_g \cos\sphericalangle\begin{cases}\mathbf{E}_g \\ \mathbf{I}_g\end{cases} = I_{R,g}^2 R = \frac{E_{R,g}^2}{R} = E_{R,g} I_{R,g}$$

$$I_{\text{rss}} = \sqrt{I_0^2 + I_1^2 + I_2^2 + \cdots + I_g^2} \qquad E_{\text{rss},R} = \sqrt{E_{R1}^2 + E_{R2}^2 + E_{R3}^2 + \cdots + E_{R,g}^2}$$

$E_{\text{rss},L}$, $E_{\text{rss},C}$, $E_{\text{rss},Z}$ are similar to the preceding formula.

$$P_{\text{MF}} = P_0 + P_1 + P_2 + \cdots + P_k = E_{\text{rss},R} I_{\text{rss},R} = R I_{\text{rss},R}^2 = \frac{E_{\text{rss},R}^2}{R}$$

$$S_{\text{MF}} = E_{\text{rss}} I_{\text{rss}} \qquad \text{pf}_{\text{MF}} = \frac{P_{\text{MF}}}{S_{\text{MF}}}$$

CHAPTER 20
Circuits with Nonsinusoidal Sources

20.1 Nonsinusoidal periodic waves may be expressed as (when certain conditions are satisfied):

$$f(t) = \tfrac{1}{2}A_0 + A_1 \cos \omega t + A_2 \cos 2\omega t + A_3 \cos 3\omega t + \cdots + B_1 \sin \omega t + B_2 \sin 2\omega t + B_3 \sin 3\omega t + \cdots \quad (1)$$

This series is known as *Fourier series*. The coefficients As and Bs in (1) are given by

$$A_n = \frac{\omega}{\pi} \int_0^{2\pi/\omega} f(t) \cos n\omega t \, dt = \frac{2}{T} \int_0^T f(t) \cos \frac{2\pi nt}{T} \, dt \quad (2)$$

and
$$B_n = \frac{\omega}{\pi} \int_0^{2\pi/\omega} f(t) \sin n\omega t \, dt = \frac{2}{T} \int_0^T f(t) \sin \frac{2\pi nt}{T} \, dt \quad (3)$$

On the basis of (1) to (3) obtain the Fourier series for the waveform shown in Fig. 20-1.

❙ The waveform is periodic, of period $2\pi/\omega$ in t or 2π in ωt. It is continuous for $0 < \omega t < 2\pi$ and given therein by $f(t) = (10/2\pi)\omega t$, with discontinuities at $\omega t = n2\pi$ where $n = 0, 1, 2, \ldots$. The Dirichlet conditions are satisfied. The average value of the function is 5, by inspection, and thus $\tfrac{1}{2}a_0 = 5$. For $n > 0$, (2) gives

$$A_n = \frac{1}{\pi} \int_0^{2\pi} \left(\frac{10}{2\pi}\right) \omega t \cos n\omega t \, d(\omega t) = \frac{10}{2\pi^2} \left[\frac{\omega t}{n} \sin n\omega t + \frac{1}{n^2} \cos n\omega t \right]_0^{2\pi} = \frac{10}{2\pi^2 n^2} (\cos n2\pi - \cos 0) = 0$$

Thus the series contains no cosine terms. Using (3), we obtain

$$B_n = \frac{1}{\pi} \int_0^{2\pi} \left(\frac{10}{2\pi}\right) \omega t \sin n\omega t \, d(\omega t) = \frac{10}{2\pi^2} \left[-\frac{\omega t}{n} \cos n\omega t + \frac{1}{n^2} \sin n\omega t \right]_0^{2\pi} = -\frac{10}{\pi n}$$

Using these sine-term coefficients and the average term, the series is

$$f(t) = 5 - \frac{10}{\pi} \sin \omega t - \frac{10}{2\pi} \sin 2\omega t - \frac{10}{3\pi} \sin 3\omega t - \cdots = 5 - \frac{10}{\pi} \sum_{n=1}^{\infty} \frac{\sin n\omega t}{n} \quad (4)$$

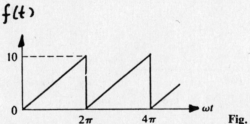

Fig. 20-1

20.2 Based on the concept of Prob. 20.1, and on the contents of Chap. 19, draw an equivalent circuit for the circuit of Fig. 20-2a, excited by the generator voltage of the waveform of Fig. 20-2b.

❙ The equivalent circuit is shown in Fig. 20-2c, which has sinusoidal sources whose algebraic sum produces the same nonsinusoidal output voltage as shown in Fig. 20-2b, where

$$e_{\text{gen}} = e_{f1} + e_{f2} + e_{f3} + \cdots + e_{fn}$$

Once the sinusoidal components that make up the nonsinusoidal wave are known, the respective current and power components may be determined using the techniques developed in Chap. 19.

20.3 For the waveform shown in Fig. 20-3, find A_0, A_3, and B_4.

❙ The constant term can be easily determined from the net area of the wave for one cycle. Thus,

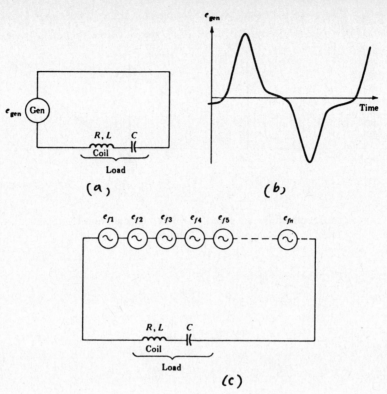

Fig. 20-2

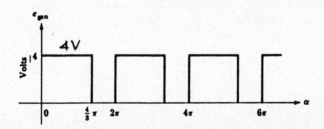

Fig. 20-3

$$A_0 = \frac{1}{2\pi} \text{ (net area)}_0^{2\pi} = \frac{1}{2\pi} \left(4 \times \frac{4\pi}{3} \right) = 2.67$$

$$A_3 = \frac{1}{\pi} \int_0^{4\pi/3} 4 \cos (3\alpha) \, d\alpha = \frac{4}{\pi} \left(\frac{\sin 3\alpha}{3} \right)_0^{4\pi/3} = \frac{4}{3\pi} (\sin 4\pi) = 0$$

$$B_4 = \frac{1}{\pi} \int_0^{4\pi/3} 4 \sin (4\alpha) \, d\alpha = \frac{4}{\pi} \left(-\frac{\cos 4\alpha}{4} \right)_0^{4\pi/3} = -\frac{1}{\pi} \left(\cos \frac{16\pi}{3} - \cos 0 \right) = -\frac{1}{\pi} (-0.5 - 1) = 0.48$$

20.4 What is the frequency of the fourth harmonic of the waveform of Fig. 20-3, if the period of the wave is 0.04 s?

▮ The frequency of the nonsinusoidal wave is

$$f = \frac{1}{T} = \frac{1}{0.04} = 25 \text{ Hz}$$

The fourth harmonic is four times the frequency of the nonsinusoidal wave. Hence,

$$f_4 = 4(25) = 100 \text{ Hz}$$

20.5 Determine the Fourier-series coefficients A_0 and B_2 for the periodic voltage wave in Fig. 20-4.

▮ $$A_0 = \frac{1}{2\pi} \text{ (net area)}_0^{2\pi} = \frac{1}{2\pi} \text{ (area of large triangle - area of small triangle)}$$

$$A_0 = \frac{1}{2\pi} \left[\frac{1}{2} \left(\frac{7\pi}{4} \times 140 \right) - \frac{1}{2} \left(\frac{\pi}{4} \times 20 \right) \right] = 60$$

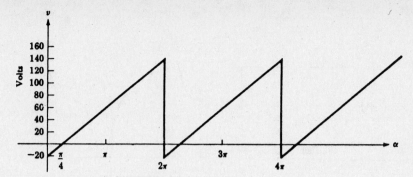

Fig. 20-4

If the dc term is to be calculated by the use of calculus, the equation for the straight-line function between $\alpha = 0$ and $\alpha = 2\pi$ must be determined. The equation for the straight line is

$$v = m\alpha + b = \frac{80}{\pi}\alpha - 20 \qquad \text{from Fig. 20-4}$$

Hence:
$$A_0 = \frac{1}{2\pi}\int_0^{2\pi}\left(\frac{80}{\pi}\alpha - 20\right)d\alpha = \frac{1}{2\pi}\left(\frac{80}{\pi}\frac{\alpha^2}{2} - 20\alpha\right)_0^{2\pi} = 60$$

$$B_2 = \frac{1}{\pi}\int_0^{2\pi} f(\alpha)\sin 2\alpha \, d\alpha = \frac{1}{\pi}\int_0^{2\pi}\left(\frac{80}{\pi}\alpha - 20\right)\sin 2\alpha \, d\alpha$$

$$= \frac{20}{\pi}\left\{\frac{4}{\pi}\left[\left(\frac{1}{2^2}\sin 2\alpha\right)_0^{2\pi} - \left(\frac{1}{2}\alpha\cos 2\alpha\right)_0^{2\pi}\right] - \left(-\frac{1}{2}\cos 2\alpha\right)_0^{2\pi}\right\} = -25.46$$

20.6 Determine the Fourier coefficients A_0, A_k, and B_k for the periodic voltage wave shown in Fig. 20-5.

▌ $$A_0 = \frac{1}{2\pi}(\text{net area})_0^{2\pi} = \frac{1}{2\pi}\left(2\pi - 3\frac{\pi}{4}\right) = 0.63 \qquad A_k = \frac{1}{\pi}\int_0^{2\pi} f(\alpha)\cos(k\alpha)\,d\alpha$$

where $f(\alpha) = 2$ for $\alpha = 0$ to $\alpha = \pi$; $f(\alpha) = 0$ for $\alpha = \pi$ to $\alpha = \frac{7}{4}\pi$; $f(\alpha) = -3$ for $\alpha = \frac{7}{4}\pi$ to $\alpha = 2\pi$.

$$A_k = \frac{1}{\pi}\int_0^{\pi} 2\cos(k\alpha)\,d\alpha + \frac{1}{\pi}\int_\pi^{7\pi/4} 0\cos(k\alpha)\,d\alpha + \frac{1}{\pi}\int_{7\pi/4}^{2\pi}(-3)\cos(k\alpha)\,d\alpha$$

$$= \frac{1}{\pi}\left[\frac{2\sin k\alpha}{k}\bigg|_0^\pi + 0 + \frac{(-3)\sin k\alpha}{k}\bigg|_{7\pi/4}^{2\pi}\right] = \frac{3}{k\pi}\left(\sin\frac{7k\pi}{4}\right)$$

Similarly,

$$B_k = \frac{1}{\pi}\int_0^{2\pi} f(\alpha)\sin(k\alpha)\,d\alpha = \frac{1}{\pi}\int_0^\pi 2\sin(k\alpha)\,d\alpha + \frac{1}{\pi}\int_\pi^{7\pi/4} 0\sin(k\alpha)\,d\alpha + \frac{1}{\pi}\int_{7\pi/4}^{2\pi} -3\sin(k\alpha)\,d\alpha$$

$$= \frac{1}{\pi}\left[\frac{2(-\cos k\alpha)}{k}\bigg|_0^\pi + 0 - 3\frac{-\cos k\alpha}{k}\bigg|_{7\pi/4}^{2\pi}\right] = \frac{1}{k\pi}\left[-2(\cos k\pi - 1) + 3\left(1 - \cos\frac{7k\pi}{4}\right)\right]$$

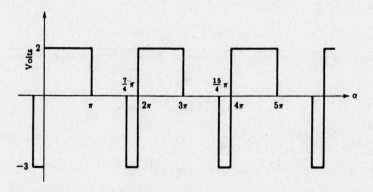

Fig. 20-5

20.7 Evaluate the first three harmonics in the waveform of Prob. 20.6.

∎ $B_1 = \dfrac{1}{\pi}\left(-2\cos\pi + 2 + 3 - 3\cos\dfrac{7\pi}{4}\right) = 1.55$ $\quad B_2 = \dfrac{1}{2\pi}\left(-2\cos 2\pi + 2 + 3 - 3\cos\dfrac{14\pi}{4}\right) = 0.48$

$$B_3 = \dfrac{1}{3\pi}\left(-2\cos 3\pi + 2 + 3 - 3\cos\dfrac{21\pi}{4}\right) = 0.97$$

Thus the dc term and the first three harmonics of the driving voltage in Fig. 20-5 are

$$v = 0.63 - 0.68\cos\alpha + 1.55\sin\alpha - 0.48\cos 2\alpha + 0.48\sin 2\alpha - 0.23\cos 3\alpha + 0.97\sin 3\alpha$$

20.8 One cycle of a nonsinusoidal periodic voltage wave has a value of 1 V from 0 to $\pi/2$, 0 V from $\pi/2$ to π, and -0.5 V from π to 2π. Sketch the wave and determine (*a*) the dc term; (*b*) the coefficients of the third harmonic.

∎ The waveform is shown in Fig. 20-6.

(*a*) $$A_0 = \dfrac{1}{2\pi}\,[\text{net area}]_0^{2\pi} = \dfrac{1}{2\pi}\left[\left(\dfrac{\pi}{2}\right)(1) - \pi(0.5)\right] = 0$$

(*b*) $$A_3 = \dfrac{1}{\pi}\int_0^{\pi/2}(1)\cos 3\alpha\,d\alpha + \dfrac{1}{\pi}\int_\pi^{2\pi}(-0.5)\cos 3\alpha\,d\alpha = -0.106$$

$$B_3 = \dfrac{1}{\pi}\int_0^{\pi/3}(1)\sin 3\alpha\,d\alpha + \dfrac{1}{\pi}\int_\pi^{2\pi}(-0.5)\sin 3\alpha\,d\alpha = 0.212$$

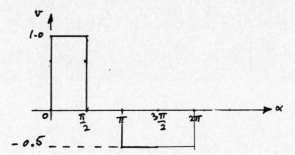

Fig. 20-6

20.9 Determine the rms value of the third harmonic of the voltage wave from the results of Prob. 20.8.

∎ $$e_3 = -0.106\cos 3\alpha + 0.212\sin 3\alpha = -0.106\sin(3\alpha + 90°) + 0.212\sin 3\alpha$$

or $$E_{3,\text{max}} = -0.106\,\underline{/90°} + 0.212\,\underline{/0°} = 0.237\,\underline{/-26.6°}$$

or $$E = \dfrac{0.237}{\sqrt{2}} = 0.1676\text{ V}$$

20.10 For the voltage wave shown in Fig. 20-7, determine the constant term and the coefficients of the fifth harmonic.

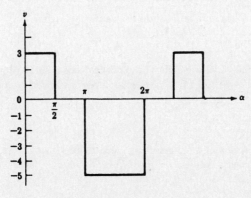

Fig. 20-7

$$A_0 = \frac{1}{2\pi}\left[3\left(\frac{\pi}{2}\right) - 5\pi\right] = -1.75$$

$$A_5 = \frac{1}{\pi}\int_0^{\pi/2} 3\cos 5\alpha \, d\alpha + \frac{1}{\pi}\int_\pi^{2\pi} -5\cos 5\alpha \, d\alpha = 0.191$$

$$B_5 = \frac{1}{\pi}\int_0^{\pi/2} 3\sin 5\alpha \, d\alpha + \frac{1}{\pi}\int_\pi^{2\pi} -5\sin 5\alpha \, d\alpha = 0.828$$

20.11 Let $\alpha = \omega t$. Express the fifth harmonic component of the voltage in Fig. 20-7 in the time domain.

$$e_5 = 0.191\sin(5\alpha + 90°) + 0.828\sin 5\alpha$$

or $\qquad E_{5,\text{max}} = 0.191\,\underline{/90°} + 0.828\,\underline{/0°} = j0.191 + 0.828 \qquad$ or $\qquad E_{5,\text{max}} = 0.849\,\underline{/77°}\,\text{V}$

Hence, $\qquad\qquad\qquad\qquad\qquad e_5 = 0.849\sin(5\omega t + 77°)\,\text{V}$

20.12 Determine the amplitude of the voltage wave shown in Fig. 20-8.

$$A_1 = \frac{1}{\pi}\int_0^{\pi/10} 6\cos \alpha \, d\alpha + \frac{1}{\pi}\int_{2/5\pi}^{\pi/2} -6\cos \alpha \, d\alpha = \frac{6}{\pi}[\sin \alpha]_0^{\pi/10} - \frac{6}{\pi}[\sin \alpha]_{2/5\pi}^{\pi/2} = 0.497$$

$$B_1 = \frac{1}{\pi}\int_0^{\pi/10} 6\sin \alpha \, d\alpha + \frac{1}{\pi}\int_{2/5\pi}^{\pi/2} -6\sin \alpha \, d\alpha = \frac{6}{\pi}[-\cos \alpha]_0^{\pi/10} - \frac{6}{\pi}[-\cos \alpha]_{2/5\pi}^{\pi/2} = -0.497$$

$$C_1 = \sqrt{(0.497)^2 + (-0.497)^2} = 0.703$$

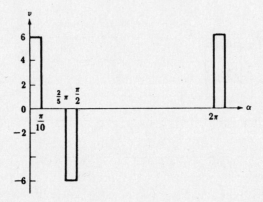

Fig. 20-8

20.13 The following symmetry checks determine the absence of even-numbered terms, cosine terms, or sine terms in the Fourier series, and thus reduce the number of calculations.

Half-Wave Symmetry

If the bottom half of a nonsinusoidal wave is the mirror image of the top half but displaced from it by π rad as shown in Fig. 20.9a, the wave is said to have *half-wave symmetry*. A wave possessing half-wave symmetry will have no dc term and no even harmonics. That is, if $f(\alpha) = -f(\alpha + \pi)$,

$$A_0 = 0 \qquad A_2, A_4, A_6, \ldots, A_n = 0 \qquad B_2, B_4, B_6, \ldots, B_n = 0$$

Half-wave symmetry is unaffected by the location of the vertical axis.

Even Symmetry

If the symmetry of the nonsinusoidal wave about the vertical axis is similar to that shown in Fig. 20.9b, the wave is said to have *even symmetry*. *A wave possessing even symmetry will have no sine terms.* That is, if $f(\alpha) = f(-\alpha)$, $B_1, B_2, B_3, \ldots, B_n = 0$.

Odd Symmetry

If the symmetry of the nonsinusoidal wave about the vertical axis is similar to that shown in Fig. 20.9c, the wave is said to have *odd symmetry*. *A wave possessing odd symmetry will have no cosine terms.* That is, if $f(\alpha) = -f(-\alpha)$, $A_1, A_2, A_3, \ldots, A_n = 0$.

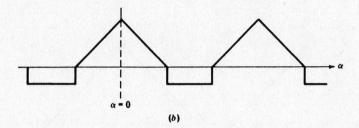

(a)

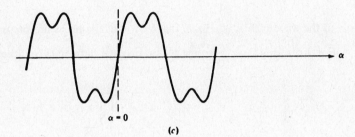

α = 0

(b)

α = 0

(c)

Fig. 20-9

On the basis of the above, determine the type of symmetry present in the voltage waveform shown in Fig. 20-10.   State which coefficients are zero in the Fourier series.

I   The waveform has an even symmetry.   Hence the coefficients $B_1 = B_2 = \cdots = B_n = 0$,   and only cosine terms will be present in the Fourier series.

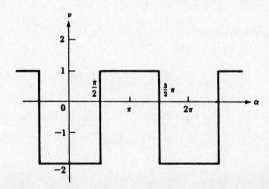

Fig. 20-10

20.14   Shifting the vertical axis of the graph of a periodic wave can reduce the number of terms in Fourier series.   In Fig. 20-11a the wave has half-wave symmetry.   Thus, only odd harmonics are present.   Shift the vertical axis so that sine terms may also be absent from the Fourier series.

I   The result of shifting the vertical axis is shown in Fig. 20-11b.   For this choice of the vertical axis, only odd cosine terms are present in the Fourier series.

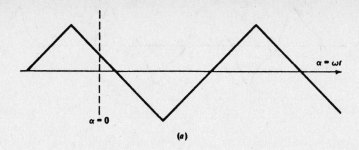

(a)

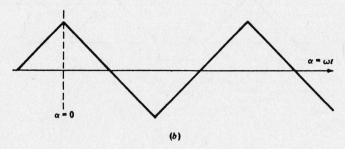

(b)

Fig. 20-11

20.15 Shift the vertical axis of the wave of Fig. 20-11a so that only odd sine terms are present in the Fourier serie.

$\blacksquare$ See Fig. 20-12. In this case we have no cosine terms, no even harmonics, and no constant term.

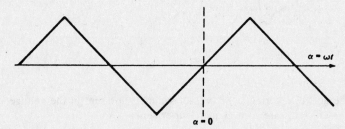

Fig. 20-12

20.16 Determine the coefficients A_0, A_3, and B_3, for the 300-Hz voltage wave shown in Fig. 20-10.

$$\blacksquare \qquad A_0 = \frac{1}{2\pi} \text{ [net area]}_0^{2\pi} = \frac{1}{2\pi} \left[-2\left(\frac{\pi}{2}\right) + 1(\pi) - 2\left(\frac{\pi}{2}\right) \right] = -0.5$$

The periodic wave exhibits even symmetry. Hence, only cosine terms are present. Therefore,

$$B_3 = 0$$

$$A_3 = \frac{1}{\pi} \int_0^{\pi/2} -2 \cos 3\alpha \, d\alpha + \frac{1}{\pi} \int_{\pi/2}^{3/2\pi} 1 \cos 3\alpha \, d\alpha + \frac{1}{\pi} \int_{3/2\pi}^{2\pi} -2 \cos 3\alpha \, d\alpha = 0.637$$

20.17 Write the third harmonic voltage of the wave of Prob. 20.16 in the time domain.

$$\blacksquare \qquad e_3 = 0.637 \cos 3\alpha$$

But $\alpha = \omega t = 2\pi 300 t$. Thus,

$$e_3 = 0.637 \cos 3(2\pi 300)t = 0.637 \cos 5654.87t = 0.637 \sin (5654.87t + 90°) \qquad \text{V}$$

20.18 What is the rms value of the third harmonic voltage of the waveform shown in Fig. 20-10?

$\blacksquare$ From Prob. 20.17

$$E_{3,\text{max}} = 0.637 \qquad \text{or} \qquad E = \frac{0.637}{\sqrt{2}} = 0.45 \text{ V}$$

20.19 For the wave shown in Fig. 20-13, obtain A_0, A_5, and B_5.

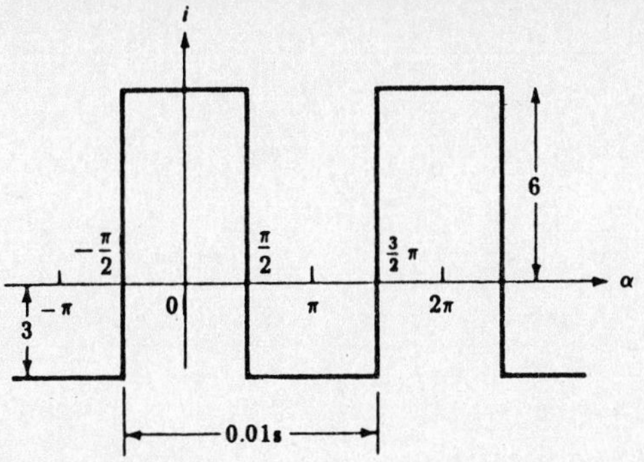

Fig. 20-13

▮ Because of even symmetry, $B_5 = 0$.

$$A_0 = \frac{1}{2\pi}\,[\text{net area}]_{-\pi}^{\pi} = \frac{1}{2\pi}\,[6(\pi) - 3(\pi)] = 1.5$$

$$A_5 = \frac{1}{\pi}\int_0^{\pi/2} 6\cos 5\alpha\,dx + \frac{1}{\pi}\int_{\pi/2}^{3/2\pi} -3\cos 5\alpha\,d\alpha + \frac{1}{\pi}\int_{3/2\pi}^{2\pi} 6\cos 5\alpha\,d\alpha = 1.15$$

20.20 Determine the frequency of the fifth harmonic of the voltage wave shown in Fig. 20-13.

▮ From Fig. 20-13

$$T = 0.01\,\text{s} \qquad f = \frac{1}{T} = 100\,\text{Hz} \qquad \text{or} \qquad f_s = 5(100) = 500\,\text{Hz}$$

20.21 Express the fifth harmonic of the voltage wave of Fig. 20-13 in the time domain.

▮ From Prob. 20.19

$$E_{5,\text{max}} = 1.15\text{V}$$

From Prob. 20.20

$$\omega = 2\pi(500) = 3140\,\text{rad/s}$$

Thus, $\qquad\qquad\qquad\qquad e_5 = 1.15\cos 3140t \qquad \text{V}$

20.22 The amplitude and phase angle of any harmonic may be obtained by combining the respective sine and cosine components for that frequency. For example, the addition of the two components of the k harmonic is

$$A_k\cos k\omega t + B_k\sin k\omega t = C_k\sin(k\omega t + \phi_k^\circ) \tag{1}$$

where C_k = amplitude of harmonic k and ϕ_k = phase angle of harmonic k.
Express C_k and ϕ_k in terms of A_k and B_k.

▮ Converting the cosine term to an equivalent sine term,

$$A_k\sin(k\omega t + 90°) + B_k\sin k\omega t = C_k\sin(k\omega t + \phi_k^\circ)$$

Expressing Eq. (1) in phasor form,

$$A_k\,\underline{/90°} + B_k\,\underline{/0°} = C_k\,\underline{/\phi_k^\circ} \qquad jA_k + B_k = C_k\,\underline{/\phi_k^\circ}$$

Hence, $\qquad\qquad\qquad\qquad C_k = \sqrt{A_k^2 + B_k^2} \tag{2}$

$$\phi_k = \tan^{-1}\frac{A_k}{B_k} \tag{3}$$

20.23 Write the Fourier-series equation represented by the following Fourier coefficients of a certain 20-Hz nonsinusoidal periodic voltage wave.

$A_0 = 8.00$	$A_1 = -6.63$	$A_2 = 0.26$	$A_3 = -0.97$	$A_4 = 0.26$	$A_5 = -0.52$	$A_6 = 0.26$
	$B_1 = 10.00$	$B_2 = -4.99$	$B_3 = 3.33$	$B_4 = -2.49$	$B_5 = 1.99$	$B_6 = -1.65$

▮ Using (2) and (3) of Prob. 20.22, the calculated values for C_k and ϕ_k are

k	f, Hz	C_k, V	ϕ_k, degrees
0	0	8.00	
1	20	12.00	−33.54
2	40	5.00	+177.02
3	60	3.47	−16.24
4	80	2.50	+174.04
5	100	2.06	−14.64
6	120	1.67	+171.05

Using the calculated data, the Fourier-series representation of the nonsinusoidal voltage wave is

$$e = 8 + 12 \sin(2\pi 20t - 33.54°) + 5.0 \sin(2\pi 40t + 177.02°) + 3.47 \sin(2\pi 60t - 16.24°)$$

$$+ 2.5 \sin(2\pi 80t + 174.04°) + 2.06 \sin(2\pi 100t - 14.64°) + 1.67 \sin(2\pi 120t + 171.05°)$$

20.24 The frequency spectrum of a nonsinusoidal periodic wave is a plot of harmonic amplitude versus harmonic frequency. The plot is in the form of a bar graph or line graph as shown in Fig. 20-14. No frequencies exist between the plotted lines. Plot the frequency spectrum of the wave expressed by the coefficients given in Prob. 20.23.

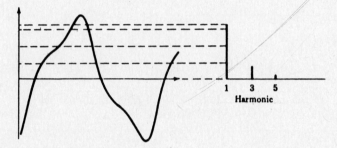

Fig. 20-14

❚ The frequency spectrum is plotted in Fig. 20-15.

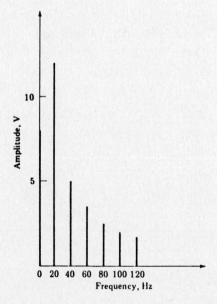

Fig. 20-15

20.25 Determine the rss voltage (see Chap. 19) of the wave given in Prob. 20.23.

❚ $$E_{\text{rss}} = \sqrt{(8)^2 + \left(\frac{12}{\sqrt{2}}\right)^2 + \left(\frac{5}{\sqrt{2}}\right)^2 + \left(\frac{3.47}{\sqrt{2}}\right)^2 + \left(\frac{2.5}{\sqrt{2}}\right)^2 + \left(\frac{2.06}{\sqrt{2}}\right)^2 + \left(\frac{1.67}{\sqrt{2}}\right)^2} = 12.69 \text{ V}$$

20.26 The following Fourier coefficients represent the components of a certain 20-Hz periodic current wave in a 6-Ω resistor:

$$A_0 = -8.70 \quad A_1 = -4.64 \quad A_2 = 4.14 \quad A_3 = -0.59 \quad A_4 = 0.57 \quad A_5 = 0.22$$
$$B_1 = -6.06 \quad B_2 = 0.47 \quad B_3 = -0.24 \quad B_4 = -0.38 \quad B_5 = 0.26$$

Plot the frequency spectrum.

❚ The Fourier coefficients are

$$A_0 = -8.70 \qquad C_k = B_k + jA_k$$
$$C_1 = (-6.06 - j4.64) = 7.63\ \underline{/-142.56°} \qquad C_2 = (0.47 + j4.14) = 4.17\ \underline{/83.52°}$$
$$C_3 = (-0.24 - j0.59) = 0.64\ \underline{/-112.14°} \qquad C_4 = (-0.38 + j0.57) = 0.69\ \underline{/123.69°}$$
$$C_5 = (0.26 + j0.22) = 0.34\ \underline{/40.24°}$$

The frequency spectrum is plotted in Fig. 20-16.

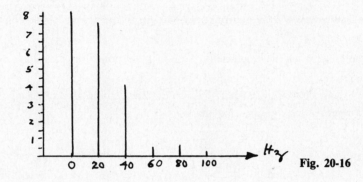

Fig. 20-16

20.27 Determine the rss current in the resistor of Prob. 20.26.

❚
$$I_{\text{rss}} = \sqrt{(-8.7)^2 + \left(\frac{7.63}{\sqrt{2}}\right)^2 + \left(\frac{4.17}{\sqrt{2}}\right)^2 + \left(\frac{0.64}{\sqrt{2}}\right)^2 + \left(\frac{0.69}{\sqrt{2}}\right)^2 + \left(\frac{0.34}{\sqrt{2}}\right)^2} = 10.68 \text{ A}$$

20.28 How much average power is drawn from the resistor of Prob. 20.27?

❚
$$P_{\text{MF}} = (I_{\text{rss}})^2 R = (10.68)^2 6 = 684.3 \text{ W}$$

20.29 Determine the dc term and the coefficients of the first and second harmonics of the periodic wave shown in Fig. 20-17.

❚
$$A_0 = \frac{1}{2\pi} [\text{net area}] = \frac{1}{2\pi}\left[\frac{\frac{1}{2}(6)}{(2\pi)}\right] = 3$$

The equation of the ramp is determined by

$$y = mx + b \qquad v = \left(\frac{6}{2\pi}\right)\alpha + 0 = \left(\frac{3}{\pi}\right)\alpha$$

$$A_1 = \frac{1}{\pi}\int_0^{2\pi}\left(\frac{3}{\pi}\alpha\right)\cos\alpha\,d\alpha = \frac{3}{\pi^2}\left[\frac{1}{1^2}\cos\alpha + \frac{\alpha}{1}\sin\alpha\right]_0^{2\pi} = 0.304$$

$$B_1 = \frac{1}{\pi}\int_0^{2\pi}\left(\frac{3\alpha}{\pi}\right)\sin\alpha\,d\alpha = \frac{3}{\pi^2}\left[\frac{1}{1^2}\sin\alpha - \frac{\alpha}{1}\cos\alpha\right]_0^{2\pi} = -1.910$$

$$\bar{C}_1 = (-1.910 + j0.304) = 1.93\ \underline{/170.96°}$$

$$A_2 = \frac{1}{\pi}\int_0^{2\pi}\left(\frac{3}{\pi}\alpha\right)\cos 2\alpha\,d\alpha = \frac{3}{\pi^2}\left[\frac{1}{2^2}\cos 2\alpha + \frac{\alpha}{2}\sin 2\alpha\right]_0^{2\pi} = 0$$

$$B_2 = \frac{1}{\pi}\int_0^{2\pi}\left(\frac{3}{4}\alpha\right)\sin 2\alpha\,d\alpha = \frac{3}{\pi^2}\left[\frac{1}{2^2}\sin 2\alpha - \frac{\alpha}{2}\cos 2\alpha\right]_0^{2\pi} = -0.955$$

$$\bar{C}_2 = B_2 + jA_2 = (-0.955 + j0) = 0.955\ \underline{/180°}$$

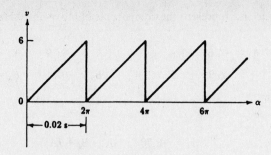

Fig. 20-17

20.30 Write the time-domain equation represented by the coefficients of Prob. 20.29.

▮ The frequency of the nonsinusoidal wave is

$$f = \frac{1}{T} = \frac{1}{0.02} = 50 \text{ Hz}$$

$$v = 3 + 1.93 \sin (2\pi 50 t + 170.96°) + 0.955 \sin (2\pi 100 t + 180°)$$

$$= 3 + 1.93 \sin (314.16 t + 170.96°) + 0.955 \sin (628.32 t + 180°)$$

20.31 Determine the dc term and the coefficient of the fifth harmonic for the voltage wave of Fig. 20-18.

▮
$$A_0 = \frac{1}{2\pi} [\text{net area}]_0^{2\pi} = \frac{1}{2\pi} \left[\frac{1}{2} ((6) \frac{\pi}{2}) - 3(\frac{\pi}{2}) \right] = 0$$

The equation representing the ramp function is

$$v = \left(\frac{6}{\pi/2} \right) \alpha + 0 = \frac{12}{\pi} \alpha$$

$$A_5 = \frac{1}{\pi} \int_0^{\pi/2} \left(\frac{12}{\pi} \alpha \right) \cos 5\alpha \, d\alpha + \frac{1}{\pi} \int_{3/2\pi}^{2\pi} -3 \cos 5\alpha \, d\alpha = 0.142$$

$$B_5 = \frac{1}{\pi} \int_0^{\pi/2} \left(\frac{12}{\pi} \right) \alpha \sin 5\alpha \, dx + \frac{1}{\pi} \int_{3/2\pi}^{2\pi} -3 \sin 5\alpha \, d\alpha = 0.255$$

$$\mathbf{C}_5 = B_5 + jA_5 = 0.255 + j0.142 = 0.292 \underline{/29.11°}$$

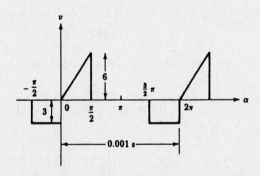

Fig. 20-18

20.32 Write the time-domain equation represented by the coefficients in Prob. 20.31.

▮
$$f = \frac{1}{T} = \frac{1}{0.001} = 1000 \text{ Hz}$$

$$v = 0 + 0.292 \sin [2\pi 1000(5t) + 29.11°] = 0.292 \sin (31,415.95 t + 29.11°)$$

20.33 Show that the Fourier series containing sine and cosine terms may be written as

$$f(t) = \cdots + \mathbf{A}_{-2} e^{-j2\omega t} + \mathbf{A}_{-1} e^{-j\omega t} + \mathbf{A}_0 + \mathbf{A}_1 e^{j\omega t} + \mathbf{A}_2 e^{j2\omega t} + \cdots \qquad (1)$$

where
$$\mathbf{A}_n = \tfrac{1}{2}(A_n - jB_n) \quad \text{and} \quad \mathbf{A}_{-n} = \tfrac{1}{2}(A_n + jB_n) \qquad (2)$$

▮ Expressing each of the sine and cosine terms in the trigonometric Fourier series by its exponential equivalent, the result is a series of exponential terms:

$$f(t) = \frac{A_0}{2} + A_1\left(\frac{e^{j\omega t} + e^{-j\omega t}}{2}\right) + A_2\left(\frac{e^{j2\omega t} + e^{-j2\omega t}}{2}\right) + \cdots + B_1\left(\frac{e^{j\omega t} - e^{-j\omega t}}{2j}\right) + B_2\left(\frac{e^{j2\omega t} - e^{-j2\omega t}}{2j}\right) + \cdots$$

Rearranging,

$$f(t) = \cdots + \left(\frac{A_2}{2} - \frac{B_2}{2j}\right)e^{-j2wt} + \left(\frac{A_1}{2} - \frac{B_1}{2j}\right)e^{-j\omega t} + \frac{A_0}{2} + \left(\frac{A_1}{2} + \frac{B_1}{2j}\right)e^{j\omega t} + \left(\frac{A_2}{2} + \frac{B_2}{2j}\right)e^{j2\omega t} + \cdots \qquad (3)$$

Now defining $\mathbf{A}_n$ and $\mathbf{A}_{-n}$ as given by (2), (3) may be rewritten as (1).

20.34   Evaluate the coefficients $\mathbf{A}_n$ given by (2) of Prob. 20.33.

❚   To obtain the evaluation integral for the $\mathbf{A}_n$ coefficients, we multiply (1) of Prob. 20.33 on both sides by $e^{-jn\omega t}$ and integrate over the full period:

$$\int_0^{2\pi} f(t)e^{-jn\omega t}\, d(\omega t) = \cdots + \int_0^{2\pi} \mathbf{A}_{-2}e^{-j2\omega t}\, e^{-jn\omega t}\, d(\omega t) + \int_0^{2\pi} \mathbf{A}_{-1}e^{-j\omega t}\, e^{-jn\omega t}\, d(\omega t)$$

$$+ \int_0^{2\pi} A_0 e^{-jn\omega t}\, d(\omega t) + \int_0^{2\pi} \mathbf{A}_1 e^{j\omega t}\, e^{-jn\omega t}\, d(\omega t) + \cdots$$

$$+ \int_0^{2\pi} \mathbf{A}_n e^{jn\omega t}\, e^{-jn\omega t}\, d(\omega t) + \cdots \qquad (1)$$

The definite integrals on the right side of (1) are all zero except $\int_0^{2\pi} \mathbf{A}_n\, d(\omega t)$, which has the value $2\pi\mathbf{A}_n$. Then

$$\mathbf{A}_n = \frac{1}{2\pi}\int_0^{2\pi} f(t)e^{-jn\omega t}\, d(\omega t) \qquad \text{or} \qquad \mathbf{A}_n = \frac{1}{T}\int_0^T f(t)e^{-j2\pi nt/T}\, dt \qquad (2)$$

20.35   Express the real Fourier coefficients A_n and B_n in terms of complex coefficients $\mathbf{A}_n$, defined by (2) of Prob. 20.33.

❚   Since $f(t)$ is real, $\mathbf{A}_{-n} = \mathbf{A}_n^*$ and only positive n need be considered.   Hence from (2) of Prob. 20.33, we obtain:

$$A_n = 2\,\text{Re}\,(\mathbf{A}_n) \qquad (1)$$

and

$$B_n = -2\,\text{Im}\,(\bar{\mathbf{A}}_n) \qquad (2)$$

20.36   Equation (1) of Prob. 20.33 is known as the *exponential Fourier series*.   Find the exponential Fourier series for the waveform shown in Fig. 20-1.

❚   In the interval $0 < \omega t < 2\pi$ the function is given by $f(t) = (10/2\pi)\omega t$.   By inspection, the average value of the function is $A_0 = 5$.   Substituting $f(t)$ in (2) of Prob. 20.34, we obtain the coefficients $\mathbf{A}_n$.

$$\mathbf{A}_n = \frac{1}{2\pi}\int_0^{2\pi} \left(\frac{10}{2\pi}\right)\omega t e^{-jn\omega t}\, d(\omega t) = \frac{10}{(2\pi)^2}\left[\frac{e^{-jn\omega t}}{(-jn)^2}(-jn\omega t - 1)\right]_0^{2\pi} = j\frac{10}{2\pi n}$$

Inserting the coefficients $\mathbf{A}_n$ in (2) of Prob. 20.33, the exponential form of the Fourier series for the given waveform is

$$f(t) = \cdots - j\frac{10}{4\pi}e^{-j2\omega t} - j\frac{10}{2\pi}e^{-j\omega t} + 5 + j\frac{10}{2\pi}e^{j\omega t} + j\frac{10}{4\pi}e^{j2\omega t} + \cdots \qquad (1)$$

20.37   Verify that (1) of Prob. 20.36 is consistent with (1) of Prob. 20.1.

❚ $A_0 = 0$ by inspection.   From (1) of Prob. 20.35:

$$B_n = -2\,\text{Im}\left(j\frac{10}{2\pi n}\right) = -\frac{10}{\pi n}$$

Hence,

$$f(t) = 5 - \frac{10}{\pi}\sin\omega t - \frac{10}{2\pi}\sin 2\omega t - \frac{10}{3\pi}\sin 3\omega t - \cdots$$

20.38   Obtain the frequency spectrum of the waveform of Fig. 20-1.

❚   The series has only sine terms, as obtained in (1) of Probs. 20.1 and 20.37.   Hence the desired frequency spectrum is shown in Fig. 20-19.

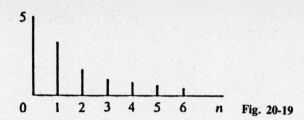

Fig. 20-19

20.39 Plot the first four terms of the series:

$$f(t) = 5 - \frac{10}{\pi} \sin \omega t - \frac{10}{2\pi} \sin 2\omega t - \frac{10}{3\pi} \sin 3\omega t - \cdots$$

Verify how closely the resultant of these four terms approximates a sawtooth.

❚ See Fig. 20-20.

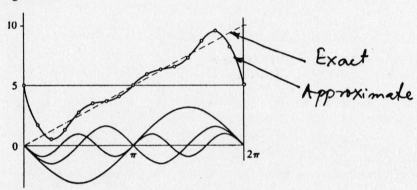

Fig. 20-20

20.40 The voltage v and the current i in a circuit are given by

$$v = V_0 + \sum V_n \sin(n\omega t + \phi_n) \qquad \text{and} \qquad i = I_0 + \sum I_n \sin(n\omega t + \psi_n)$$

Obtain expressions for instantaneous and average powers.

❚ Instantaneous power is given by

$$p = vi = \left[V_0 + \sum V_n \sin(n\omega t + \phi_n) \right]\left[I_0 + \sum I_n \sin(n\omega t + \psi_n) \right]$$

Since v and i both have period T, their product must have an integral number of its periods in T. (Recall that for a single sine wave of applied voltage, the product vi has a period half that of the voltage wave.) The average may therefore be calculated over one period of the voltage wave:

$$P = \frac{1}{T} \int_0^T \left[V_0 + \sum V_n \sin(n\omega t + \phi_n) \right]\left[I_0 + \sum I_n \sin(n\omega t + \psi_n) \right] dt$$

Examination of the possible terms in the product of the two infinite series shows them to be of the following types: the product of two constants, the product of a constant and a sine function, the product of two sine functions of different frequencies, and sine functions squared. After integration, the product of the two constants is still $V_0 I_0$ and the sine functions squared with the limits applied appear as $(V_n I_n/2) \cos(\phi_n - \psi_n)$; all other products upon integration over the period T are zero. Then the average power is

$$P = V_0 I_0 + \tfrac{1}{2} V_1 I_1 \cos \theta_1 + \tfrac{1}{2} V_2 I_2 \cos \theta_2 + \tfrac{1}{2} V_3 I_3 \cos \theta_3 + \cdots \tag{1}$$

where $\theta_n = \phi_n - \psi_n$ is the angle on the equivalent impedance of the network at the angular frequency $n\omega$, and V_n and I_n are the maximum values of the respective sine functions.

20.41 Obtain the expression for the average power in a circuit excited by a single-frequency source, from (1) of Prob. 20.40.

❚ In the special case of a single-frequency sinusoidal voltage, $V_0 = V_2 = V_3 = \cdots = 0$, and (1) of Prob. 20.40 reduces to the familiar

$$P = \tfrac{1}{2} V_1 I_1 \cos \theta_1 = V_{\text{eff}} I_{\text{eff}} \cos \theta$$

20.42 A series RL circuit in which $R = 5\,\Omega$ and $L = 20\,\text{mH}$ has an applied voltage $v = 100 + 50 \sin \omega t + 25 \sin 3\omega t$ V, with $\omega = 500\,\text{rads/s}$. Find the instantaneous current.

   ▮ Compute the equivalent impedance of the circuit at each frequency found in the voltage function. Then obtain the respective currents.

At $\omega = 0$, $Z_0 = R = 5\,\Omega$ and

$$I_0 = \frac{V_0}{R} = \frac{100}{5} = 20\,\text{A}$$

At $\omega = 500\,\text{rad/s}$, $\mathbf{Z}_1 = 5 + j(500)(20 \times 10^{-3}) = 5 + j10 = 11.15\ \underline{/63.4°}\ \Omega$ and

$$i_1 = \frac{V_{1,\text{max}}}{Z_1} \sin(\omega t - \theta_1) = \frac{50}{11.15} \sin(\omega t - 63.4°) = 4.48 \sin(\omega t - 63.4°) \quad \text{A}$$

At $3\omega = 1500\,\text{rad/s}$, $\mathbf{Z}_3 = 5 + j30 = 30.4\ \underline{/80.54°}\ \Omega$ and

$$i_3 = \frac{V_{3,\text{max}}}{Z_3} \sin(3\omega t - \theta_3) = \frac{25}{30.4} \sin(3\omega t - 80.54°) = 0.823 \sin(3\omega t - 80.54°) \quad \text{A}$$

The sum of the harmonic currents is the required total response:

$$i = 20 + 4.48 \sin(\omega t - 63.4°) + 0.823 \sin(3\omega t - 80.54°) \quad \text{A}$$

20.43 Determine the power dissipated in the resistor of the circuit of Prob. 20.42.

   ▮ This current has the effective value

$$I_{\text{eff}} = \sqrt{20^2 + (4.48^2/2) + (0.823^2/2)} = \sqrt{410.6} = 20.25\,\text{A}$$

which results in a power in the 5-Ω resistor of

$$P = I_{\text{eff}}^2 R = (410.6)5 = 2053\,\text{W}$$

20.44 Calculate the power contributed by each harmonic in the circuit of Prob. 20.42. Verify that the sum of these powers is the same as the power obtained in Prob. 20.43.

   ▮ At $\omega = 0$: $P_0 = V_0 I_0 = 100(20) = 2000\,\text{W}$

At $\omega = 500\,\text{rad/s}$: $P_1 = \frac{1}{2} V_1 I_1 \cos \theta_1 = \frac{1}{2}(50)(4.48) \cos 63.4° = 50.1\,\text{W}$

At $3\omega = 1500\,\text{rad/s}$: $P_3 = \frac{1}{2} V_3 I_3 \cos \theta_3 = \frac{1}{2}(25)(0.823) \cos 80.54° = 1.69\,\text{W}$

Then $P = 2000 + 50.1 + 1.69 = 2052\,\text{W}$

20.45 Determine the instantaneous and effective voltages across the resistor of Prob. 20.42. Hence obtain the power dissipated in the resistor.

   ▮ The Fourier-series expression for the voltage across the resistor is

$$v_R = Ri = 100 + 22.4 \sin(\omega t - 63.4°) + 4.11 \sin[3\omega t - 80.54°] \quad \text{V}$$

and $V_{R,\text{eff}} = \sqrt{100^2 + \frac{1}{2}(22.4)^2 + \frac{1}{2}(4.11)^2} = \sqrt{10{,}259} = 101.3\,\text{V}$

Then the power dissipated in R is $P = V_{R,\text{eff}}^2 / R = (10{,}259)/5 = 2052\,\text{W}$.

20.46 A voltage of the waveform shown in Fig. 20-21 is applied to a capacitor C. Find the current.

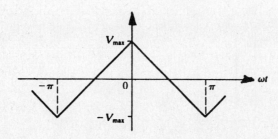

Fig. 20-21

❚ In the interval $-\pi < \omega t < 0$ the voltage function is $v = V_{max} + (2V_{max}/\pi)\omega t$; and for $0 < \omega t < \pi$, $v = V_{max} - (2V_{max}/\pi)\omega t$. Then the coefficients of the exponential series are determined by the evaluation integral

$$\mathbf{V}_n = \frac{1}{2\pi} \int_{-\pi}^{0} [V_{max} + (2V_{max}/\pi)\omega t]e^{-jn\omega t}\, d(\omega t) + \frac{1}{2\pi} \int_{0}^{\pi} [V_{max} - (2V_{max}/\pi)\omega t]e^{-jn\omega t}\, d(\omega t)$$

from which $\mathbf{V}_n = 4V_{max}/\pi^2 n^2$ for odd n, and $\mathbf{V}_n = 0$ for even n.

The phasor current produced by $\mathbf{V}_n$ (n odd) is

$$\mathbf{I}_n = \frac{\mathbf{V}_n}{\mathbf{Z}_n} = \frac{4V_{max}/\pi^2 n^2}{1/jn\omega C} = j\,\frac{4V_{max}\omega C}{\pi^2 n}$$

with an implicit time factor $e^{jn\omega t}$. The resultant current is therefore

$$i(t) = \sum_{-\infty}^{+\infty} \mathbf{I}_n e^{jn\omega t} = j\,\frac{4V_{max}\omega C}{\pi^2} \sum_{-\infty}^{+\infty} \frac{e^{jn\omega t}}{n}$$

where the summation is over odd n only.

20.47 Obtain the Fourier series for the square wave shown in Fig. 20-22.

❚ In the interval $0 < \omega t < \pi$, $f(t) = V$; and for $\pi < \omega t < 2\pi$, $f(t) = -V$. The average value of the wave is zero; hence $A_0/2 = 0$. The cosine coefficients are obtained by writing the evaluation integral with the functions inserted as follows.

$$A_n = \frac{1}{\pi}\left\{\int_{0}^{\pi} V\cos n\omega t\, d(\omega t) + \int_{\pi}^{2\pi}(-V)\cos n\omega t\, d(\omega t)\right\} = \frac{V}{\pi}\left\{\left[\frac{1}{n}\sin n\omega t\right]_0^\pi - \left[\frac{1}{n}\sin n\omega t\right]_\pi^{2\pi}\right\}$$

$$= 0 \quad \text{for all } n$$

Thus the series contains no cosine terms. Proceeding with the evaluation integral for the sine terms,

$$B_n = \frac{1}{\pi}\left\{\int_{0}^{\pi} V\sin n\omega t\, d(\omega t) + \int_{\pi}^{2\pi}(-V)\sin n\omega t\, d(\omega t)\right\} = \frac{V}{\pi}\left\{\left[-\frac{1}{n}\cos n\omega t\right]_0^\pi + \left[\frac{1}{n}\cos n\omega t\right]_\pi^{2\pi}\right\}$$

$$= \frac{V}{\pi n}(-\cos n\pi + \cos 0 + \cos n2\pi - \cos n\pi) = \frac{2V}{\pi n}(1 - \cos n\pi)$$

Then $B_n = 4V/\pi n$ for $n = 1, 3, 5, \ldots$, and $b_n = 0$ for $n = 2, 4, 6, \ldots$. The series for the square wave is

$$f(t) = \frac{4V}{\pi}\sin \omega t + \frac{4V}{3\pi}\sin 3\omega t + \frac{4V}{5\pi}\sin 5\omega t + \cdots$$

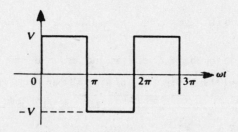

Fig. 20-22

20.48 Plot the frequency spectrum for the waveform shown in Fig. 20-22.

Fig. 20-23

❚ The line spectrum for this series is shown in Fig. 20-23. The series contains only odd-harmonic sine terms, as could have been anticipated by examination of the waveform for symmetry. Since the wave in Fig. 20-22 is odd, its series contains only sine terms; and since it also has half-wave symmetry, only odd harmonics are present.

20.49 Repeat Prob. 20.47 for the waveform shown in Fig. 20-24.

❚ The wave is an even function since $f(t) = f(-t)$, and if its average value $V/2$ is subtracted, it also has half-wave symmetry, i.e., $f(t) = -f(t + \pi)$. For $-\pi < \omega t < 0$, $f(t) = V + (V/\pi)\omega t$; and for $0 < \omega t < \pi$, $f(t) = V - (V/\pi)\omega t$. Since even waveforms have only cosine terms, all $b_n = 0$. For $n \geq 1$,

$$A_n = \frac{1}{\pi} \int_{-\pi}^{0} [V + (V/\pi)\omega t] \cos n\omega t\, d(\omega t) + \frac{1}{\pi} \int_{0}^{\pi} [V - (V/\pi)\omega t] \cos m\omega t\, d(\omega t)$$

$$= \frac{V}{\pi} \left\{ \int_{-\pi}^{\pi} \cos n\omega t\, d(\omega t) + \int_{-\pi}^{0} \frac{\omega t}{\pi} \cos n\omega t\, d(\omega t) - \int_{0}^{\pi} \frac{\omega t}{\pi} \cos n\omega t\, d(\omega t) \right\}$$

$$= \frac{V}{\pi^2} \left\{ \left[\frac{1}{n^2} \cos n\omega t + \frac{\omega t}{\pi} \sin n\omega t \right]_{-\pi}^{0} - \left[\frac{1}{n^2} \cos n\omega t + \frac{\omega t}{n} \sin n\omega t \right]_{0}^{\pi} \right\}$$

$$= \frac{V}{\pi^2 n^2} \left\{ \cos 0 - \cos(-n\pi) - \cos n\pi + \cos 0 \right\} = \frac{2V}{\pi^2 n^2} (1 - \cos n\pi)$$

As predicted from half-wave symmetry, the series contains only odd terms, since $A_n = 0$ for $n = 2, 4, 6, \ldots$. For $n = 1, 3, 5, \ldots$, $A_n = 4V/\pi^2 n^2$. Then the required Fourier series is

$$f(t) = \frac{V}{2} + \frac{4V}{\pi^2} \cos \omega t + \frac{4V}{(3\pi)^2} \cos 3\omega t + \frac{4V}{(5\pi)^2} \cos 5\omega t + \cdots$$

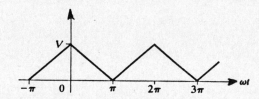

Fig. 20-24

20.50 Obtain the frequency spectrum of the waveform of Fig. 20-24.

❚ The coefficients decrease as $1/n^2$, and thus the series converges more rapidly than that of Prob. 20.47. This fact is evident from the line spectrum shown in Fig. 20-25.

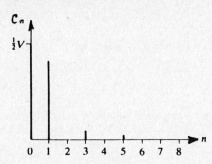

Fig. 20-25

20.51 Repeat Prob. 20.47 for the waveform of Fig. 20-26.

❚ By inspection, the waveform is odd (and therefore has average value zero). Consequently the series will contain only sine terms. A single expression, $f(t) = (V/\pi)\omega t$, describes the wave over the period from $-\pi$ to $+\pi$, and we will use these limits on our evaluation integral for b_n.

$$B_n = \frac{1}{\pi} \int_{-\pi}^{\pi} (V/\pi)\omega t \sin n\omega t\, d(\omega t) = \frac{V}{\pi^2} \left[\frac{1}{n^2} \sin n\omega t - \frac{\omega t}{n} \cos n\omega t \right]_{-\pi}^{\pi} = -\frac{2V}{n\pi} (\cos n\pi)$$

As $\cos n\pi$ is $+1$ for even n and -1 for odd n, the signs of the coefficients alternate. The required series is

$$f(t) = \frac{2V}{\pi} \left\{ \sin \omega t - \tfrac{1}{2} \sin 2\omega t + \tfrac{1}{3} \sin 3\omega t - \tfrac{1}{4} \sin 4\omega t + \cdots \right\}$$

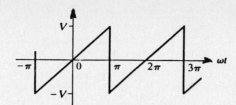

Fig. 20-26

20.52 Obtain the frequency spectrum of the waveform of Fig. 20-26.

❙ The coefficients decrease as $1/n$, and thus the series converges slowly, as shown by the spectrum in Fig. 20-27. Except for the shift in the origin and the average term, this waveform is the same as in Fig. 20-1; compare the two spectra.

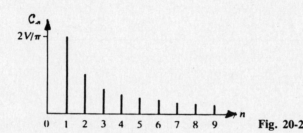

Fig. 20-27

20.53 Find the Fourier series for the waveform of Fig. 20-28.

❙ In the interval $0 < \omega t < \pi$, $f(t) = (V/\pi)\omega t$; and for $\pi < \omega t < 2\pi$, $f(t) = 0$. By inspection, the average value of the wave is $V/4$. Since the wave is neither even nor odd, the series will contain both sine and cosine terms. For $n > 0$, we have

$$A_n = \frac{1}{\pi}\int_0^\pi (V/\pi)\omega t \cos n\omega t\, d(\omega t) = \frac{V}{\pi^2}\left[\frac{1}{n^2}\cos n\omega t + \frac{\omega t}{n}\sin n\omega t\right]_0^\pi = \frac{V}{\pi^2 n^2}(\cos n\pi - 1)$$

When n is even, $\cos n\pi - 1 = 0$ and $a_n = 0$. When n is odd, $a_n = -2V/(\pi^2 n^2)$. The B_n coefficients are

$$B_n = \frac{1}{\pi}\int_0^\pi (V/\pi)\omega t \sin n\omega t\, d(\omega t) = \frac{V}{\pi^2}\left[\frac{1}{n^2}\sin n\omega t - \frac{\omega t}{n}\cos n\omega t\right]_0^\pi = -\frac{V}{\pi n}(\cos n\pi) = (-1)^{n+1}\frac{V}{\pi n}$$

Then the required Fourier series is

$$f(t) = \frac{V}{4} - \frac{2V}{\pi^2}\cos \omega t - \frac{2V}{(3\pi)^2}\cos 3\omega t - \frac{2V}{(5\pi)^2}\cos 5\omega t - \cdots + \frac{V}{\pi}\sin \omega t - \frac{V}{2\pi}\sin 2\omega t + \frac{V}{3\pi}\sin 3\omega t - \cdots$$

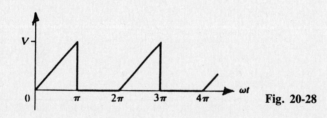

Fig. 20-28

20.54 Plot the frequency spectrum for the waveform shown in Fig. 20-28.

❙ The even-harmonic amplitudes are given directly by $|B_n|$ since there are no even-harmonic cosine terms. However, the odd-harmonic amplitudes must be computed using $C_n = \sqrt{A_n^2 + B_n^2}$. Thus

$$C_1 = \sqrt{(2V/\pi^2)^2 + (V/\pi)^2} = V(0.377) \qquad C_3 = V(0.109) \qquad C_5 = V(0.064)$$

The line spectrum is shown in Fig. 20-29.

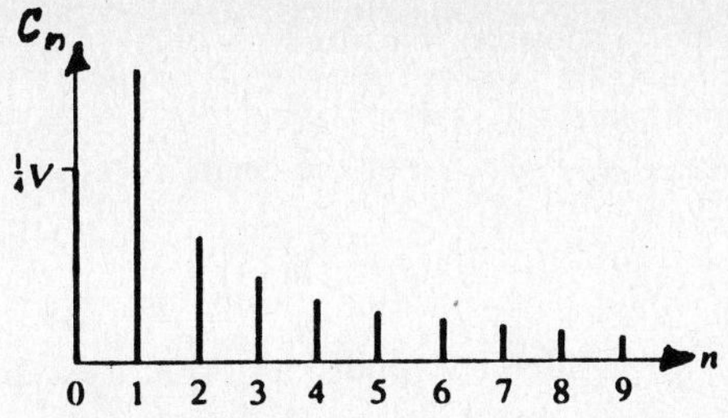

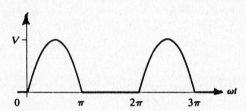

Fig. 20-29

20.55 Repeat Prob. 20.53 for the waveform shown in Fig. 20-30.

▌ The wave shows no symmetry, and we therefore expect the series to contain both sine and cosine terms. Since the average value is not obtainable by inspection, we evaluate a_0 for use in the term $a_0/2$.

$$A_0 = \frac{1}{\pi} \int_0^\pi V \sin \omega t \, d(\omega t) = \frac{V}{\pi} [-\cos \omega t]_0^\pi = \frac{2V}{\pi}$$

Next we determine a_n:

$$A_n = \frac{1}{\pi} \int_0^\pi V \sin \omega t \cos n\omega t \, d(\omega t)$$

$$= \frac{V}{\pi} \left[\frac{-n \sin \omega t \sin n\omega t - \cos n\omega t \cos \omega t}{-n^2 + 1} \right]_0^\pi = \frac{V}{\pi(1 - n^2)} (\cos n\pi + 1)$$

With n even, $A_n = 2V/\pi(1 - n^2)$; and with n odd, $A_n = 0$. However, this expression is indeterminate for $n = 1$, and therefore we must integrate separately for A_1.

$$A_1 = \frac{1}{\pi} \int_0^\pi V \sin \omega t \cos \omega t \, d(\omega t) = \frac{V}{\pi} \int_0^\pi \tfrac{1}{2} \sin 2\omega t \, d(\omega t) = 0$$

Now we evaluate B_n:

$$B_n = \frac{1}{\pi} \int_0^\pi V \sin \omega t \sin n\omega t \, d(\omega t) = \frac{V}{\pi} \left[\frac{n \sin \omega t \cos n\omega t - \sin n\omega t \cos \omega t}{-n^2 + 1} \right]_0^\pi = 0$$

Here again the expression is indeterminate for $n = 1$, and b_1 is evaluated separately.

$$B_1 = \frac{1}{\pi} \int_0^\pi V \sin^2 \omega t \, d(\omega t) = \frac{V}{\pi} \left[\frac{\omega t}{2} - \frac{\sin 2\omega t}{4} \right]_0^\pi = \frac{V}{2}$$

Then the required Fourier series is

$$f(t) = \frac{V}{\pi} \left\{ 1 + \frac{\pi}{2} \sin \omega t - \frac{2}{3} \cos 2\omega t - \frac{2}{15} \cos 4\omega t - \frac{2}{35} \cos 6\omega t - \cdots \right\} \qquad (1)$$

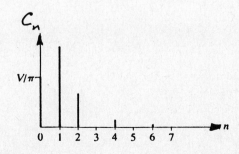

Fig. 20-30

20.56 Repeat Prob. 20.54 for the waveform shown in Fig. 20-30.

▌ See Fig. 20-31.

Fig. 20-31

20.57 Repeat Prob. 20.55 for the waveform shown in Fig. 20-32.

❚ The function is described in the interval $-\pi < \omega t < 0$ by $f(t) = -V \sin \omega t$. The average value is the same as that in Prob. 20.55, i.e., $\frac{1}{2}A_0 = V/\pi$. For the coefficients A_n, we have

$$A_n = \frac{1}{\pi} \int_{-\pi}^{0} (-V \sin \omega t) \cos n\omega t \, d(\omega t) = \frac{V}{\pi(1-n^2)} (1 + \cos n\pi)$$

For n even, $A_n = 2V/\pi(1-n^2)$; and for n odd, $A_n = 0$, except that $n = 1$ must be examined separately.

$$A_1 = \frac{1}{\pi} \int_{-\pi}^{0} (-V \sin \omega t) \cos \omega t \, d(\omega t) = 0$$

For the coefficients B_n, we obtain

$$B_n = \frac{1}{\pi} \int_{-\pi}^{0} (-V \sin \omega t) \sin n\omega t \, d(\omega t) = 0$$

except for $n = 1$.

$$B_1 = \frac{1}{\pi} \int_{-\pi}^{0} (-V) \sin^2 \omega t \, d(\omega t) = -\frac{V}{2}$$

Thus the series is

$$f(t) = \frac{V}{\pi} \left\{ 1 - \frac{\pi}{2} \sin \omega t - \frac{2}{3} \cos 2\omega t - \frac{2}{15} \cos 4\omega t - \frac{2}{35} \cos 6\omega t - \cdots \right\} \tag{1}$$

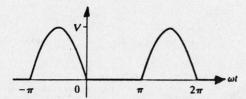

Fig. 20-32

20.58 Compare (1) of Prob. 20.57 with (1) of Prob. 20.55. Verify that the graph of Fig. 20-30 can be obtained from that of Fig. 20-32. Thus, the two waveforms have the same frequency spectrum.

❚ If $V \sin \omega t$ is subtracted from (1) of Prob. 20.55, or from Fig. 20-30, (1) of Prob. 20.57, or Fig. 20-32, is obtained. Hence, the two waveforms have the same frequency spectrum.

20.59 Obtain the Fourier series for the waveform shown in Fig. 20-33.

❚ With the vertical axis positioned as shown, the wave is even and the series will contain only cosine terms and a constant term. In the period from $-\pi$ to $+\pi$ used for the evaluation integrals, the function is zero except from $-\pi/6$ to $+\pi/6$.

$$A_0 = \frac{1}{\pi} \int_{-\pi/6}^{\pi/6} V \, d(\omega t) = \frac{V}{3} \qquad A_n = \frac{1}{\pi} \int_{-\pi/6}^{\pi/6} V \cos n\omega t \, d(\omega t) = \frac{2V}{n\pi} \sin \frac{n\pi}{6}$$

Since $\sin n\pi/6 = 1/2, \sqrt{3}/2, 1, \sqrt{3}/2, 1/2, 0, -1/2, \ldots$ for $n = 1, 2, 3, 4, 5, 6, 7, \ldots$, respectively, the series is

$$f(t) = \frac{V}{6} + \frac{2V}{\pi} \left\{ \frac{1}{2} \cos \omega t + \frac{\sqrt{3}}{2} \left(\frac{1}{2}\right) \cos 2\omega t + 1\left(\frac{1}{3}\right) \cos 3\omega t + \frac{\sqrt{3}}{2} \left(\frac{1}{4}\right) \cos 4\omega t \right.$$

$$\left. + \frac{1}{2} \left(\frac{1}{5}\right) \cos 5\omega t - \frac{1}{2} \left(\frac{1}{7}\right) \cos 7\omega t - \cdots \right\}$$

or

$$f(t) = \frac{V}{6} + \frac{2V}{\pi} \sum_{n=1}^{\infty} \frac{1}{n} \sin \frac{n\pi}{6} \cos n\omega t$$

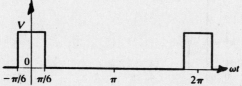

Fig. 20-33

20.60 Plot the frequency spectrum of the waveform shown in Fig. 20-33.

❚ The line spectrum, shown in Fig. 20-34, decreases very slowly for this wave, since the series converges very slowly to the function. Of particular interest is the fact that the 8th, 9th, and 10th harmonic amplitudes exceed the 7th. With the simple waves considered previously, the higher-harmonic amplitudes were progressively lower.

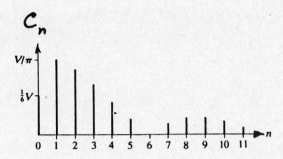

Fig. 20-34

20.61 Find the exponential Fourier series of the waveform shown in Fig. 20-22.

❚ In the interval $-\pi < \omega t < 0$, $f(t) = -V$; and for $0 < \omega t < \pi$, $f(t) = V$. The wave is odd; therefore, $A_0 = 0$ and the A_n will be pure imaginaries.

$$\mathbf{A}_n = \frac{1}{2\pi} \left\{ \int_{-\pi}^{0} (-V) e^{-jn\omega t} \, d(\omega t) + \int_{0}^{\pi} V e^{-jn\omega t} \, d(\omega t) \right\} = \frac{V}{2\pi} \left\{ -\left[\frac{1}{(-jn)} e^{-jn\omega t} \right]_{-\pi}^{0} + \left[\frac{1}{(-jn)} e^{-jn\omega t} \right]_{0}^{\pi} \right\}$$

$$= \frac{V}{(-j2\pi n)} (-e^0 + e^{jn\pi} + e^{-jn\pi} - e^0) = j \frac{V}{n\pi} (e^{jn\pi} - 1)$$

For n even, $e^{jn\pi} = +1$ and $\mathbf{A}_n = 0$; for n odd, $e^{jn\pi} = -1$ and $\mathbf{A}_n = -j(2V/n\pi)$ (half-wave symmetry). The required Fourier series is

$$f(t) = \cdots + j \frac{2V}{3\pi} e^{-j3\omega t} + j \frac{2V}{\pi} e^{-j\omega t} - j \frac{2V}{\pi} e^{j\omega t} - j \frac{2V}{3\pi} e^{j3\omega t} - \cdots$$

20.62 Sketch the frequency spectrum from the results of Prob. 20.61.

❚ The graph in Fig. 20-35 shows amplitudes for both positive and negative frequencies. Combining the values at $+n$ and $-n$ yields the same line spectrum as plotted in Fig. 20-23.

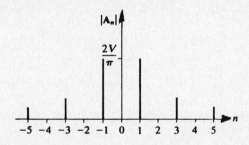

Fig. 20-35

20.63 Obtain the trigonometric Fourier series coefficients from those of the exponential series of Prob. 20.61, and compare the results with those of Prob. 20.47.

❚ The trigonometric-series cosine coefficients are

$$A_n = 2 \operatorname{Re} \mathbf{A}_n = 0 \quad \text{and} \quad B_n = -2 \operatorname{Im} \mathbf{A}_n = \frac{4V}{n\pi} \quad \text{for odd } n \text{ only}$$

These coefficients agree with those obtained in Prob. 20.47.

20.64 Find the exponential Fourier series for the waveform shown in Fig. 20-24.

❚ In the interval $-\pi < \omega t < 0$, $f(t) = V + (V/\pi)\omega t$; and for $0 < \omega t < \pi$, $f(t) = V - (V/\pi)\omega t$. The wave is even and therefore the A_n coefficients will be pure real. By inspection the average value is $V/2$.

$$A_n = \frac{1}{2\pi} \left\{ \int_{-\pi}^{0} [V + (V/\pi)\omega t] e^{-jn\omega t} \, d(\omega t) + \int_{0}^{\pi} [V - (V/\pi)\omega t] e^{-jn\omega t} \, d(\omega t) \right\}$$

$$= \frac{V}{2\pi^2} \left\{ \int_{-\pi}^{0} \omega t e^{-jn\omega t} \, d(\omega t) + \int_{0}^{\pi} (-\omega t) e^{-jn\omega t} \, d(\omega t) + \int_{-\pi}^{\pi} \pi e^{-jn\omega t} \, d(\omega t) \right\}$$

$$= \frac{V}{2\pi^2} \left\{ \left[\frac{e^{-jn\omega t}}{(-jn)^2} (-jn\omega t - 1) \right]_{-\pi}^{0} - \left[\frac{e^{-jn\omega t}}{(-jn)^2} (-jn\omega t - 1) \right]_{0}^{\pi} \right\} = \frac{V}{\pi^2 n^2} [1 - e^{jn\pi}]$$

For even n, $e^{jn\pi} = +1$ and $A_n = 0$; for odd n, $A_n = 2V/\pi^2 n^2$. Thus the series is

$$f(t) = \cdots + \frac{2V}{(-3\pi)^2} e^{-j3\omega t} + \frac{2V}{(-\pi)^2} e^{-j\omega t} + \frac{V}{2} + \frac{2V}{(\pi)^2} e^{j\omega t} + \frac{2V}{(3\pi)^2} e^{j3\omega t} + \cdots$$

20.65 Find the amplitudes of harmonics in the waveform of Fig. 20-24.

❚ $$C_0 = \frac{V}{2} \qquad C_n = 2|A_n| = \begin{cases} 0 & n = 2, 4, 6, \ldots \\ 4V/\pi^2 n^2 & n = 1, 3, 5, \ldots \end{cases}$$

20.66 Obtain the exponential Fourier series for the waveform shown in Fig. 20-30.

❚ In the interval $0 < \omega t < \pi$, $f(t) = V \sin \omega t$; and from π to 2π, $f(t) = 0$. Then

$$A_n = \frac{1}{2\pi} \int_{0}^{\pi} V \sin \omega t e^{-jn\omega t} \, d(\omega t) = \frac{V}{2\pi} \left[\frac{e^{-jn\omega t}}{(1 - n^2)} (-jn \sin \omega t - \cos \omega t) \right]_{0}^{\pi} = \frac{V(e^{-jn\pi} + 1)}{2\pi(1 - n^2)}$$

For even n, $A_n = V/\pi(1 - n^2)$; for odd n, $A_n = 0$. However, for $n = 1$, the expression for A_n becomes indeterminate. L'Hôpital's rule may be applied; i.e., the numerator and denominator are separately differentiated with respect to n, after which n is allowed to approach 1, with the result that $A_1 = -j(V/4)$.
The average value is

$$A_0 = \frac{1}{2\pi} \int_{0}^{\pi} V \sin \omega t \, d(\omega t) = \frac{V}{2\pi} [-\cos \omega t]_{0}^{\pi} = \frac{V}{\pi}$$

Then the exponential Fourier series is

$$f(t) = \cdots - \frac{V}{15\pi} e^{-j4\omega t} - \frac{V}{3\pi} e^{-j2\omega t} + j\frac{V}{4} e^{-j\omega t} + \frac{V}{\pi} - j\frac{V}{4} e^{j\omega t} - \frac{V}{3\pi} e^{j2\omega t} - \frac{V}{15\pi} e^{j4\omega t} - \cdots$$

20.67 Determine the amplitudes of harmonics in the waveform of Fig. 20-30.

❚ The harmonic amplitudes are

$$C_0 = A_0 = \frac{V}{\pi} \qquad C_n = 2|A_n| = \begin{cases} 2V/\pi(n^2 - 1) & (n = 2, 4, 6, \ldots) \\ V/2 & (n = 1) \\ 0 & (n = 3, 5, 7, \ldots) \end{cases}$$

20.68 A voltage waveform is given by

$$v = \begin{cases} V & 0 < t < T/4 \\ -V & T/4 < t < 3T/4 \\ V & 3T/4 < t < T \end{cases}$$

Determine its Fourier coefficients.

❚ By inspection $A_0 = 0$. Also, the waveform has an even symmetry. Thus, $B_n = 0$. Finally, with the period $T = 2\pi/\omega$

$$A_1 = \frac{2V}{T} \int_{0}^{T/4} \cos \omega t \, dt - \frac{2V}{T} \int_{T/4}^{3T/4} \cos \omega t \, dt + \frac{2V}{T} \int_{3T/4}^{T} \cos \omega t \, dt$$

$$= \frac{2V}{\omega T} \left[\sin \frac{\omega T}{4} - \left(\sin \frac{3\omega T}{4} - \sin \frac{\omega T}{4} \right) + \left(\sin \omega T - \sin \frac{3\omega T}{4} \right) \right]$$

Since $\omega T = 2\pi$, we obtain

$$A_1 = \frac{V}{\pi}(1+2+1) = \frac{4V}{\pi}$$

and
$$A_n = \begin{cases} \dfrac{4V}{n\pi}, & n = 1, 5, 9, \dots \\ \dfrac{-4V}{n\pi} & n = 3, 7, 11, \dots \\ 0 & n = \text{even} \end{cases}$$

20.69 Obtain the frequency spectrum for the waveform of Prob. 20.68.

$\blacksquare$ See Fig. 20-36, and compare with Fig. 20-27.

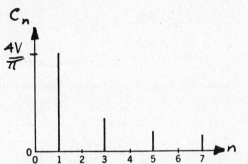

Fig. 20-36

20.70 Find the average power in a resistance $R = 10\,\Omega$, if the current in Fourier-series form is $i = 10 \sin \omega t + 5 \sin 3\omega t + 2 \sin 5\omega t$ A.

$\blacksquare$ The current has an effective value $I_{\text{eff}} = \sqrt{\frac{1}{2}(10)^2 + \frac{1}{2}(5)^2 + \frac{1}{2}(2)^2} = \sqrt{64.5} = 8.03$ A. Then the average power is $P = I_{\text{eff}}^2 R = (64.5)10 = 645$ W.

20.71 Obtain the result of Prob. 20.70 by adding the harmonic powers.

$\blacksquare$ The total power is the sum of the harmonic powers, which are given by $\frac{1}{2}V_{\max}I_{\max} \cos \theta$. But the voltage across the resistor and the current are in phase for all harmonics, and $\theta_n = 0$. Then

$$v_R = Ri = 100 \sin \omega t + 50 \sin 2\omega t + 20 \sin 5\omega t$$

and $P = \frac{1}{2}(100)(10) + \frac{1}{2}(50)(5) + \frac{1}{2}(20)(2) = 645$ W.

20.72 Find the average power supplied to a network if the applied voltage and resulting current are

$$v = 50 + 50 \sin 5 \times 10^3 t + 30 \sin 10^4 t + 20 \sin 2 \times 10^4 t \quad \text{V}$$

$$i = 11.2 \sin (5 \times 10^3 t + 63.4°) + 10.6 \sin (10^4 t + 45°) + 8.97 \sin (2 \times 10^4 t + 26.6°) \quad \text{A}$$

$\blacksquare$ The total average power is the sum of the harmonic powers:

$$P = (50)(0) + \tfrac{1}{2}(50)(11.2) \cos 63.4° + \tfrac{1}{2}(30)(10.6) \cos 45° + \tfrac{1}{2}(20)(8.97) \cos 26.6° = 317.7 \text{ W}$$

20.73 Obtain the constants of the two-element series circuit with the applied voltage and resultant current given in Prob. 20.72.

$\blacksquare$ The voltage series contains a constant term 50, but there is no corresponding term in the current series, thus indicating that one of the elements is a capacitor. Since power is delivered to the circuit, the other element must be a resistor.

$$I_{\text{eff}} = \sqrt{\tfrac{1}{2}(11.2)^2 + \tfrac{1}{2}(10.6)^2 + \tfrac{1}{2}(8.97)^2} = 12.6 \text{ A}$$

The average power is $P = I_{\text{eff}}^2 R$, from which $R = P/I_{\text{eff}}^2 = 317.7/159.2 = 2\,\Omega$.
At $\omega = 10^4$ rad/s, the current leads the voltage by 45°. Hence,

$$1 = \tan 45° = \frac{1}{\omega CR} \qquad \text{or} \qquad C = \frac{1}{(10^4)(2)} = 50\ \mu\text{F}$$

Therefore the two-element series circuit consists of a resistor of $2\,\Omega$ and a capacitor of $50\ \mu$F.

20.74 The voltage wave shown in Fig. 20-37 is applied to a series circuit of $R = 2\,\text{k}\Omega$ and $L = 10\,\text{H}$. Use the trigonometric Fourier series to obtain the voltage across the resistor.

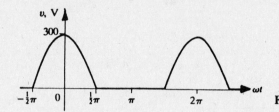

Fig. 20-37

▮ The applied voltage has an average value V_{max}/π. The wave function is even and hence the series contains only cosine terms, with coefficients obtained by the following evaluation integral:

$$A_n = \frac{1}{\pi} \int_{-\pi/2}^{\pi/2} 300 \cos \omega t \cos n\omega t \, d(\omega t) = \frac{600}{\pi(1-n^2)} \cos \frac{n\pi}{2} \quad \text{V}$$

Here, $\cos n\pi/2$ has the value -1 for $n = 2, 6, 10, \ldots$, and $+1$ for $n = 4, 8, 12, \ldots$. For n odd, $\cos n\pi/2 = 0$. However, for $n = 1$, the expression is indeterminate and must be evaluated separately.

TABLE 20.1

n	$n\omega$, rad/s	R, kΩ	$n\omega L$, kΩ	Z_n, kΩ	θ_n
0	0	2	0	2	0°
1	377	2	3.77	4.26	62⁰
2	754	2	7.54	7.78	75.1°
4	1508	2	15.08	15.2	82.45°
6	2262	2	22.62	22.6	84.92°

$$A_1 = \frac{1}{\pi} \int_{-\pi/2}^{\pi/2} 300 \cos^2 \omega t \, d(\omega t) = \frac{300}{\pi} \left[\frac{\omega t}{2} + \frac{\sin 2\omega t}{4} \right]_{-\pi/2}^{\pi/2} = \frac{300}{2} \quad \text{V}$$

Thus,
$$v = \frac{300}{\pi} \left\{ 1 + \frac{\pi}{2} \cos \omega t + \frac{2}{3} \cos 2\omega t - \frac{2}{15} \cos 4\omega t + \frac{2}{35} \cos 6\omega t - \cdots \right\} \quad \text{V}$$

In Table 20.1, the total impedance of the series circuit is computed for each harmonic in the voltage expression. The Fourier coefficients of the current series are the voltage series coefficients divided by the Z_n; the current terms lag the voltage terms by the phase angles θ_n.

$$I_0 = \frac{300/\pi}{2} \quad \text{mA}, \quad i_1 = \frac{300/2}{4.26} \cos(\omega t - 62°) \quad \text{mA}, \quad i_2 = \frac{600/3\pi}{7.78} \cos(2\omega t - 75.1°) \quad \text{mA}, \ldots$$

Then the current series is

$$i = \frac{300}{2\pi} + \frac{300}{(2)(4.26)} \cos(\omega t - 62°) + \frac{600}{3\pi(7.78)} \cos(2\omega t - 75.1°)$$

$$- \frac{600}{15\pi(15.2)} \cos(4\omega t - 82.45°) + \frac{600}{35\pi(22.6)} \cos(6\omega t - 84.92°) - \cdots \quad \text{mA}$$

and the voltage across the resistor is

$$v_R = Ri = 95.5 + 70.4 \cos(\omega t - 62°) + 16.4 \cos(2\omega t - 75.1°)$$

$$- 1.67 \cos(4\omega t - 82.45°) + 0.483 \cos(6\omega t - 84.92°) - \cdots \quad \text{V}$$

20.75 Sketch the spectra of the applied voltage and v_R to show the effect of the inductance on the harmonics. Assume $\omega = 377$ rad/s.

▮ Figure 20-38 shows clearly how the harmonic amplitudes of the applied voltage have been reduced by the 10-H series inductance.

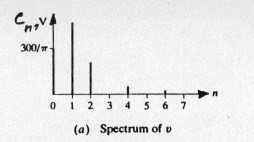

(a) Spectrum of v

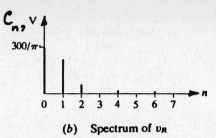

(b) Spectrum of v_R

Fig. 20-38

20.76 A current waveform is shown in Fig. 20-39a. Sketch its derivative.

▌ The derivative is shown in Fig. 20-39b.

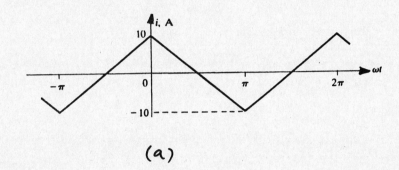

(a)

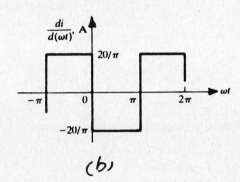

(b)

Fig. 20-39

20.77 The current in a 10-mH inductance has the waveform shown in Fig. 20-39a. Obtain the trigonometric series for the voltage across the inductance, given that $\omega = 500 \, \text{rad/s}$.

▌ The derivative of the waveform of Fig. 20-39a is graphed in Fig. 20-39b. This is just Fig. 20-22 with $V = -20/\pi$. Hence, from Prob. 20.47

$$\frac{di}{d(\omega t)} = -\frac{80}{\pi^2} \left[\sin \omega t + \tfrac{1}{3} \sin 3\omega t + \tfrac{1}{5} \sin 5\omega t + \cdots \right] \quad \text{A}$$

and so
$$v_L = L\omega \frac{di}{d(\omega t)} = -\frac{400}{\pi^2} \left[\sin \omega t + \tfrac{1}{3} \sin 3\omega t + \tfrac{1}{5} \sin 5\omega t + \cdots \right] \quad \text{V}$$

20.78 In Prob. 20.68, let $\omega = 1$. Obtain the trigonometric Fourier series for the waveform given in Prob. 20.68. Sketch the given waveform. Assume $V = \pi/4$.

▌ The sketch is shown in Fig. 20-40. Using the Fourier coefficients obtained in Prob. 20.68, with $\omega = 1$, the required Fourier series is

$$v(t) = \cos t - \tfrac{1}{3} \cos 3t + \tfrac{1}{5} \cos 5t - \cdots \tag{1}$$

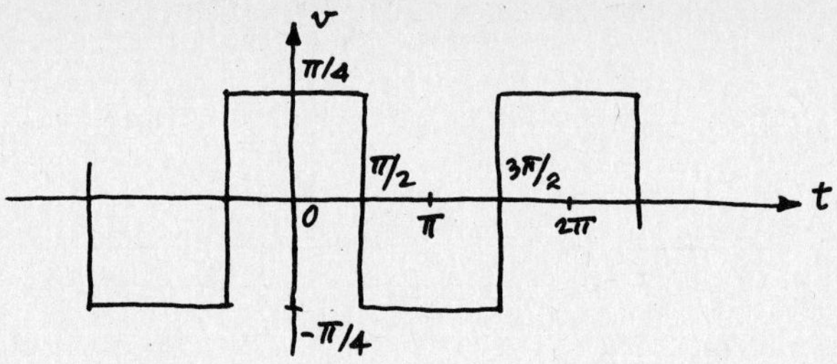

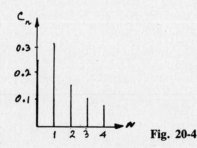

Fig. 20-40

20.79 If the voltage wave of Prob. 20.78 is applied to a series RL circuit, having $R = 1\,\Omega$ and $L = 1\,\text{H}$, determine the phasor currents for the first five harmonics of the input voltage wave.

▌ From (1) of Prob. 20.78, the phasor voltages are

$$\mathbf{V}_1 = 1e^{j0°} \qquad \mathbf{V}_3 = \tfrac{1}{3}e^{-j180°} \qquad \mathbf{V}_5 = \tfrac{1}{5}e^{j0°}$$

The admittances for the various harmonics are

$$\mathbf{Y}(jn) = \frac{1}{1+jn} \qquad \mathbf{Y}(j1) = \frac{1}{\sqrt{2}}\,e^{-j45°}$$

$$\mathbf{Y}(j3) = \frac{1}{\sqrt{10}}\,e^{-j71.6°} \quad \text{and} \quad \mathbf{Y}(j5) = \frac{1}{\sqrt{26}}\,e^{-j78.8°}$$

Hence,

$$\mathbf{I}_1 = 0.707e^{-j45°} \quad \text{A} \quad \mathbf{I}_3 = 0.105e^{-j251.6°} \quad \text{A} \quad \mathbf{I}_5 = 0.039e^{-j78.8°} \quad \text{A}$$

20.80 Obtain the current in the circuit of Prob. 20.79 in the time domain.

▌ The required current is given by

$$i(t) = 0.707\cos(t - 45°) + 0.105\cos(3t - 251.6°) + 0.039\cos(5t - 78.8°) + \cdots \quad \text{A}$$

20.81 What is the average power associated with the fifth harmonic current in the circuit of Prob. 20.79?

▌ $$p_5 = v_5 i_5 = (\tfrac{1}{5}\cos 5t)[0.039\cos(5t - 78.8°)] = 0.0078\cos 5t \cos(5t - 78.8°)$$

or $$P_5 = \tfrac{1}{2}(0.0078)\cos 78.8° = 0.7575\,\text{mW}$$

20.82 Sketch the frequency spectrum of the waveform given by

$$f(t) = \frac{1}{4} - \frac{1}{\pi}\left(\sin t + \frac{1}{2}\sin 2t + \frac{1}{3}\sin 3t + \cdots\right)$$

▌ See Fig. 20-41.

Fig. 20-41

20.83 Repeat Prob. 20.82 for

$$f(t) = \frac{1}{\pi}\left(1 + \frac{\pi}{2}\cos t + \frac{2}{3}\cos 2t - \frac{2}{15}\cos 4t + \cdots\right)$$

▌ See Fig. 20-42.

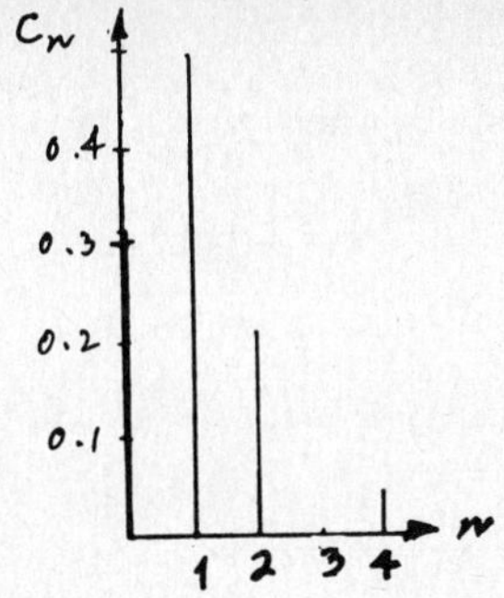

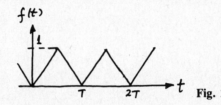

Fig. 20-42

20.84 Find the amplitude of the third harmonic in the waveform shown in Fig. 20-43.

▌ Because the function is an even function, only cosine terms are nonzero. Thus,

$$A_3 = \frac{4}{T}\int_0^{T/2}\frac{2t}{T}\cos\frac{2\pi}{T}(3t)\,dt = \frac{2}{9\pi^2}(\cos 3\pi - 1) = -\frac{4}{9\pi^2}$$

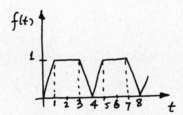

Fig. 20-43

20.85 Determine the amplitude of the fifth harmonic of the waveform shown in Fig. 20-44.

▌ Because of even symmetry, $B_n = 0$. Thus,

$$A_5 = \frac{4}{4}\left[\int_0^1 t\cos\frac{2\pi}{4}(5t)\,dt + \int_1^2 \cos\frac{2\pi}{4}(5t)\,dt\right] = \frac{4}{25\pi^2}\left(\cos\frac{5\pi}{2} - 1\right) = -\frac{4}{25\pi^2}$$

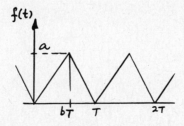

Fig. 20-44

20.86 Obtain the amplitude of the fundamental of the waveform shown in Fig. 20-45.

▌
$$A_1 = \frac{2}{T}\left[\int_0^{bT}\frac{at}{bT}\cos\frac{2\pi}{T}t\,dt + \int_{bT}^T -\frac{a(t-T)}{(1-b)T}\cos\frac{2\pi}{T}t\,dt\right] = \frac{a(\cos 2\pi b - 1)}{2\pi^2 b(1-b)}$$

$$B_1 = \frac{2}{T}\left[\int_0^{bT}\frac{at}{bT}\sin\frac{2\pi}{T}\,dt + \int_{bT}^T -\frac{a(t-T)}{(1-b)T}\cos\frac{2\pi}{T}t\,dt\right] = \frac{a\sin 2\pi b}{2\pi^2 b(1-b)}$$

Thus,
$$C_1 = \sqrt{A_1^2 + B_1^2} = \frac{a\sqrt{1-\cos 2\pi b}}{\sqrt{2}\pi^2 b(1-b)} \tag{1}$$

Fig. 20-45

20.87 From the result of Prob. 20.86, obtain the amplitude of the waveform of Fig. 20-43.

▌ Figure 20-43 is a special case of Fig. 20-45, when $a = 1$ and $b = 0.5$. Substituting these values in (1) of Prob. 20.86 yields

$$C_1 = \frac{\sqrt{1 - \cos 2\pi(0.5)}}{\sqrt{2}\pi^2(0.5)(1 - 0.5)} = \pm \frac{4}{\pi^2}$$

20.88 Verify the result of Prob. 20.87 by a direct evaluation of the Fourier coefficients for the fundamental of the waveform shown in Fig. 20-43.

▌

$$A_1 = \frac{4}{T}\int_0^{T/2} \frac{2t}{T} \cos \frac{2\pi}{T} t \, dt = \frac{2}{\pi^2}(-1 + \cos \pi) = -\frac{4}{\pi^2}$$

which is the same solution as in Prob. 20.87.

20.89 In a special case, $a = 1$ and $b = 0.75$ in the waveform of Fig. 20-45. If this waveform represents the voltage across a 1-Ω resistor, determine power corresponding to the fundamental component of power.

▌ From (1) of Prob. 20.86,

$$C_1 = \frac{1\sqrt{1 - \cos 2\pi(0.75)}}{\sqrt{2}(\pi^2)(0.75)(1 - 0.75)} = 0.382$$

or $$v_1 = 0.382 \sin \omega t \quad \text{V} \qquad p_1 = \frac{(v_1)^2}{R} = 0.146 \sin^2 \omega t \quad \text{W}$$

and $$P_1 = \tfrac{1}{2}(0.146) = 73 \text{ mW}$$

20.90 Compare the power obtained in Prob. 20.89 to the case when the applied voltage has the waveform shown in Fig. 20-43.

▌ From Prob. 20.87,

$$C_1 = A_1 = \frac{4}{\pi^2}$$

Thus, $$v_1 = \frac{4}{\pi^2} \sin \omega t \quad \text{V} \qquad p_1 = \frac{(4)^2}{(\pi^2)^2} \sin^2 \omega t \quad \text{W}$$

$$P_1 = \frac{1}{2}\left(\frac{4}{\pi^2}\right)^2 = 82.13 \text{ mW}$$

which is (obviously) greater than the power (73.0 mW) calculated in Prob. 20.89.

20.91 Determine the Fourier series for the waveform shown in Fig. 20-46.

▌ $$f(t) = 10 \cos \frac{\pi t}{T} \qquad -\frac{T}{2} \le t \le \frac{T}{2}$$

Thus, $$A_0 = \frac{2}{T}\int_0^{T/2} 10 \cos \frac{\pi t}{T} \, dt = \frac{20}{\pi}$$

$$A_n = \frac{4}{T}\int_0^{T/2} 10 \cos \frac{\pi t}{T} \cos \frac{2\pi n t}{T} \, dt \qquad \text{and} \qquad B_n = 0$$

Hence, $$f(t) = \frac{40}{\pi}\left(\frac{1}{2} + \frac{1}{3}\cos \frac{2\pi t}{T} - \frac{1}{15}\cos \frac{4\pi t}{T} + \frac{1}{35}\cos \frac{6\pi t}{T} - \cdots\right)$$

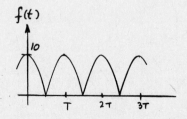

Fig. 20-46

20.92 Determine if the functions shown in Fig. 20-47 are odd or even.

▌ (*a*) Even, (*b*) odd.

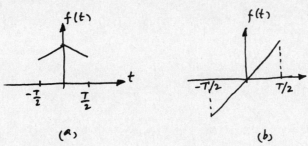

(*a*)   (*b*)   **Fig. 20-47**

20.93 Repeat Prob. 20.92 for the functions shown in Fig. 20-48.

▌ (*a*) Odd, (*b*) odd.

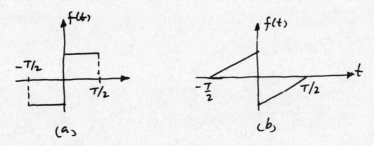

(*a*)   (*b*)   **Fig. 20-48**

20.94 Repeat Prob. 20.92 for the functions of Fig. 20-49.

▌ (*a*) Even, (*b*) odd.

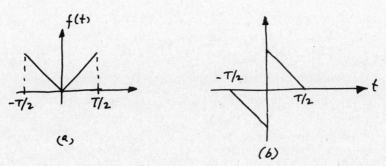

(*a*)   (*b*)   **Fig. 20-49**

20.95 Determine the coefficients of the exponential Fourier series for the waveform shown in Fig. 20-3.

▌
$$\mathbf{C}_n = \frac{1}{2\pi} \int_0^{4\pi/3} 4 e^{-j2\pi nt/2\pi}\, dt = \frac{j4}{2\pi n}\left[e^{-j(4\pi n/3)} - 1\right] \tag{1}$$

20.96 Evaluate $\mathbf{C}_2$ and $\mathbf{C}_3$ for the waveform of Prob. 20.95.

▌ From (1) of Prob. 20.95:

$$\mathbf{C}_2 = \frac{j4}{4\pi}\left(e^{-j8\pi/3} - 1\right) = -j0.753 \qquad \mathbf{C}_3 = \frac{j4}{6\pi}\left(e^{-j4\pi} - 1\right) = 0$$

20.97 Find the coefficients of the exponential Fourier series for the waveform shown in Fig. 20-43.

▌
$$C_0 = \tfrac{1}{2}$$
$$\mathbf{C}_n = \frac{2}{T} \int_0^{T/2} \frac{2}{T}\left(t - \frac{T}{4}\right) e^{-j2\pi nt/T}\, dt = -\frac{2}{\pi^2 n^2} \qquad n \text{ odd}$$

20.98 Repeat Prob. 20.97 for the waveform of Fig. 20-44.

▐ $\quad C_0 = \frac{3}{4}$

$$C_n = \frac{1}{4}\left[\int_0^1 te^{-j2\pi nt/4}\,dt + \int_1^3 e^{-j2\pi nt/4}\,dt + \int_3^4 -(t-4)e^{-j2\pi nt/4}\,dt\right] = \frac{2}{\pi^2 n^2}\left(\cos\frac{\pi n}{2} - 1\right)$$

20.99 Repeat Prob. 20.97 for the waveform of Fig. 20-45.

▐ $$\mathbf{C}_n = \frac{1}{T}\left[\int_0^{bT}\frac{at}{bT}e^{-j2\pi nt/T}\,dt + \int_{bT}^T\frac{-a(t-T)}{(1-b)T}e^{-j2\pi nt/T}\,dt\right]$$

or $$\qquad |\mathbf{C}_n| = \frac{a\sqrt{2(1-\cos 2\pi nb)}}{4\pi^2 n^2 b(1-b)}$$

20.100 Repeat Prob. 20.97 for the waveform of Fig. 20-46.

▐ $$\mathbf{C}_n = \frac{1}{T}\int_{-T/2}^{T/2} 10\cos\frac{\pi t}{T}e^{-j2\pi nt/T}\,dt = \frac{10}{2T}\int_{-T/2}^{T/2}\left[e^{j(\pi/T)(1-2n)t} + e^{-j(\pi/T)(1+2n)t}\,dt\right] = \frac{20\cos\pi n}{\pi(1-4n^2)}$$

20.101 A series RC circuit, having $R = 1\,\Omega$ and $C = 1\,\text{F}$, is excited by a voltage source of the waveform of Fig. 20-40. Assuming $\omega = 1\,\text{rad/s}$, determine the phasor current for the nth harmonic.

▐ In terms of exponential Fourier series we have

$$\mathbf{C}_n = \frac{1}{n}e^{-j(\pi/2)(n-1)}$$

Consequently, $$\qquad \mathbf{Y}_n = \frac{1}{1-(j/n)}$$

Hence, $$\qquad \mathbf{I}_n = \frac{e^{-j(\pi/2)(n-1)}}{n-j}$$

20.102 Repeat Prob. 20.101 if the input voltage has the waveform of Fig. 20-1.

▐ In this case:

$$\mathbf{C}_n = \frac{2}{T}\int_0^T\frac{10t}{T}e^{-j2\pi nt/T}\,dt = \frac{j10}{\pi n} \qquad \mathbf{Y}_n = \frac{1}{1-(j/n)} \qquad \mathbf{I}_n = \frac{j10}{\pi(n-j)}$$

20.103 Determine the average power for a network having

$$v = 2\cos(t+45°) + \cos(2t+45°) + \cos(3t-60°) \qquad \text{V}$$

and $$\qquad i = 10\cos t + 5\cos(2t-45°)$$

▐ $$\qquad P = \frac{1}{2}(2\times 10)\cos 45° + \frac{1}{2}(1\times 5)\cos 90° = 7.07\,\text{W}$$

20.104 In a three-phase network we have

$$i_a = 15\sin(\omega t - 30°) \qquad \text{A} \qquad i_b = 0.5\sin(3\omega t - 45°) \qquad \text{A}$$

Determine i_c.

▐ Since $$\qquad i_a + i_b + i_c = 0$$

$$i_c = -i_a - i_b = 15\sin(\omega t + 150°) + 0.5\sin(3\omega t + 135°) \qquad \text{A}$$

20.105 In a network $v = 2\sin t + \sin 3t$ and $i = \sin 2t + 0.5\sin 4t$. What is the average power?

▐ $$\qquad p = vi = (2\sin t + \sin 3t)(\sin 2t + 0.5\sin 4t)$$

Thus, $\quad P = 0$.

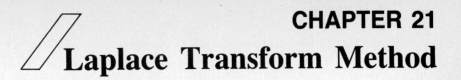

21.1 The Laplace transform method is a powerful technique for solving circuit problems. We define a Laplace transform as follows:

Let $f(t)$ be a time function which is zero for $t \le 0$ and which is (subject to some mild conditions) arbitrarily defined for $t > 0$. Then the *direct Laplace transform of* $f(t)$, denoted $\mathcal{L}[f(t)]$, is defined by

$$\mathcal{L}[f(t)] = F(s) = \int_{0+}^{\infty} f(t)e^{-st}\, dt \tag{1}$$

Thus, the operation $\mathcal{L}[\ ]$ transforms $f(t)$, which is in the *time domain*, into $F(s)$, which is in the *complex frequency domain*, or simply the *s domain*, where s is the complex variable $\sigma + j\omega$.

Using this definition find the Laplace transform of (**a**) the unit-step function and (**b**) the exponential decay function Ae^{-at}.

▌ (a)
$$\mathcal{L}[u(t)] = \int_0^{\infty} (1)e^{-st}\, dt = -\frac{1}{s}\,[e^{-st}]_0^{\infty} = \frac{1}{s}$$

(b)
$$\mathcal{L}[Ae^{-at}] = \int_0^{\infty} Ae^{-at}e^{-st}\, dt = \frac{-A}{a+s}\,[e^{-(a+s)t}]_0^{\infty} = \frac{A}{s+a}$$

21.2 Find the Laplace transform of $\sin \omega t$.

▌
$$\mathcal{L}[\sin \omega t] = \int_0^{\infty} (\sin \omega t)e^{-st}\, dt = \left[\frac{-s(\sin \omega t)e^{-st} - e^{-st}\omega \cos \omega t}{s^2 + \omega^2}\right]_0^{\infty} = \frac{\omega}{s^2 + \omega^2}$$

21.3 Find the Laplace transform of a derivative $df(t)/dt$.

▌
$$\mathcal{L}\left[\frac{df(t)}{dt}\right] = \int_0^{\infty} \frac{df(t)}{dt}\, e^{-st}\, dt$$

Integrating by parts,

1.5
$$\mathcal{L}\left[\frac{df(t)}{dt}\right] = [e^{-st}f(t)]_{0+}^{\infty} - \int_0^{\infty} f(t)(-se^{-st})\, dt = -f(0_+) + s\int_0^{\infty} f(t)e^{-st}\, dt = -f(0_+) + sF(s)$$

21.4 Prepare a table of Laplace transforms of some commonly encountered functions.

▌ See Table 21.1.

The *initial-value theorem* states that

$$f(0_+) = \lim_{s \to \infty} sF(s) \tag{1}$$

21.5 Apply this theorem to find the current $i(0_+)$ in a circuit, if the transform of the current is

$$I(s) = \frac{2s + 10}{s(s + 1)}$$

▌
$$i(0_+) = \lim_{s \to \infty} sI(s) = \lim_{s \to \infty} s\left[\frac{2s + 10}{s(s + 1)}\right] = 2\text{ A}$$

21.6 The voltage across a circuit is given by $v = 4e^{-t}$ V. What is the initial voltage?

▌
$$v(0_+) = 4e^{-0} = 4\text{ V}$$

21.7 Express v of Prob. 21.6 in the transform domain. Then apply the initial-value theorem to verify the result of Prob. 21.6.

▌ From Table 21.1:
$$\mathcal{L}[4e^{-t}] = \frac{4}{s + 1} = V(s)$$

$$v(0_+) = \lim_{s \to \infty} sV(s) = \lim_{s \to \infty} s\left(\frac{4}{s + 1}\right) = 4\text{ V}$$

TABLE 21.1 Table of Transform Pairs

$f(t)$	$F(s)$
1 $df(t)/dt$	$sF(s) - f(0_+)$
2 $\dfrac{d^2f(t)}{dt^2}$	$s^2F(s) - sf(0_+) - \dfrac{df}{dt}(0_+)$
3 $\dfrac{d^nf(t)}{dt^n}$	$s^nF(s) - s^{n-1}\dfrac{df}{dt}(0_+) - s^{n-2}\dfrac{d^2f}{dt^2} - \cdots - \dfrac{df^{n-1}}{dt^{n-1}}(0_+)$
4 $g(t) = \displaystyle\int_0^\infty f(t)\,dt$	$\dfrac{F(s)}{s} + \dfrac{g(0_+)}{s}$
5 $u(t)$ the unit-step function	$1/s$
6 $\delta(t)$ the unit impulse function	1
7 t	$1/s^2$
8 $t^{n-1}/(n-1)!$ n is an integer	$1/s^n$
9 ϵ^{-at}	$1/(s+a)$
10 $t\epsilon^{-at}$	$1/(s+a)^2$
11 $t^{n-1}\epsilon^{-at}$	$(n-1)!/(s+a)^n$
12 $\sin \omega t$	$\omega/(s^2+\omega^2)$
13 $\cos \omega t$	$s/(s^2+\omega^2)$
14 $\sin(\omega t + \theta)$	$[s\sin\theta + \omega\cos\theta]/(s^2+\omega^2)$
15 $\cos(\omega t + \theta)$	$[s\cos\theta - \omega\sin\theta]/(s^2+\omega^2)$
16 $\epsilon^{-at}\sin\omega t$	$\omega/[(s+a)^2+\omega^2]$
17 $\epsilon^{-at}\cos\omega t$	$(s+a)/[(s+a)^2+\omega^2]$
18 $t\epsilon^{-at}\sin\omega t$	$2\omega(s+a)/[(s+a)^2+\omega^2]^2$
19 $t\epsilon^{-at}\cos\omega t$	$[(s+a)^2-\omega^2]/[(s+a)^2+\omega^2]^2$

It is assumed that all $f(t)$ exist for $t \geq 0$ and $f(t) = 0$ for $t < 0$. Each of the functions from 7 to 19 can be considered as being multiplied by $u(t)$.

21.8 The transform of the voltage across a circuit is $V(s) = 1/s(s+1)$. Determine the initial voltage.

$$v(0_+) = \lim_{s\to\infty} sV(s) = \lim_{s\to\infty}\left[\frac{s}{s(s+1)}\right] = 0 \text{ V}$$

21.9 The circuit of Fig. 21-1a is labeled in the time domain. Draw a corresponding circuit in the transform domain.

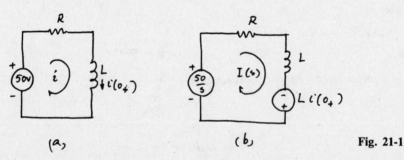

(a)   (b)   **Fig. 21-1**

Denoting the initial current in the inductor $i(0_+)$ by a voltage source $Li(0_+)$, we obtain the circuit of Fig. 21-1b.

21.10 The current in an RL series circuit is given by

$$2\frac{di}{dt} + 4i = 0$$

Express the current in the s domain.

$$\mathcal{L}\left[2\frac{di}{dt} + 4i\right] = 2[sI(s) - i(0_+)] + 4I(s) = 0$$

or

$$I(s) = \frac{2i(0_+)}{2s+4} \tag{1}$$

21.11 If the initial current in the inductor of the circuit of Prob. 21.10 is 5 A, determine $i(t)$.

▮ From (1) of Prob. 21.10 we have:

$$I(s) = \frac{10}{2s + 4} = \frac{5}{s + 2}$$

Thus

$$i(t) = \mathcal{L}^{-1}[I(s)] = \mathcal{L}^{-1}\left(\frac{5}{s + 2}\right) = 5e^{-2t} \quad A$$

21.12 Determine the inverse Laplace transform of

$$F(s) = \frac{3s + 15}{(s + 1)^2 + (3)^2}$$

▮ In order to use Table 21.1 of Laplace transform pairs, we rewrite $F(s)$ as

$$F(s) = \frac{3(s + 1) + 12}{(s + 1)^2 + (3)^2} = \frac{3(s + 1)}{(s + 1)^2 + (3)^2} + \frac{12}{(s + 1)^2 + (3)^2} = F_1(s) + F_2(s)$$

Now using results 9 and 10 of Table 21.1, we obtain

$$\mathcal{L}^{-1}[F(s)] = f(t) = \mathcal{L}^{-1}[F_1(s)] + \mathcal{L}^{-1}[F_2(s)] = 3e^{-t} \cos 3t + 4e^{-t} \sin 3t \tag{1}$$

21.13 Combine the trigonometric functions in (1) of Prob. 21.12 to express the result in terms of e^{-t} and a sine function.

▮ It may be shown that

$$A \cos x + B \sin x = \sqrt{A^2 + B^2} \sin [x + \tan^{-1}(A/B)] = \sqrt{A^2 + B^2} \cos [x - \tan^{-1}(B/A)]$$

From (1) of Prob. 21.12, we let $A = 3$ and $B = 4$. Hence, $\tan^{-1}(A/B) = \tan^{-1}(3/4) = 36.9°$ and $f(t) = e^{-t}(3 \cos 3t + 4 \sin 3t) = 5e^{-t} \sin (3t + 36.9°)$.

21.14 Express the voltage of the circuit of Fig. 21-2 in the s domain, if $v(0_+) = 0$.

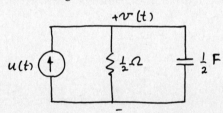

Fig. 21-2

▮ By KCL we have

$$2v + \frac{1}{2}\frac{dv}{dt} - u(t) = 0$$

Taking the Laplace transform of both sides

$$2V(s) + \frac{1}{2}[sV(s) - v(0_+)] - \frac{1}{s} = 0$$

or

$$V(s) = \frac{2}{s(s + 4)} \tag{1}$$

21.15 Solve for $v(t)$ in the circuit of Fig. 21-2, using the result of Prob. 21.14.

▮ In order to use Table 21.1, we rewrite (1) as

$$V(s) = \frac{2}{s(s + 4)} = \frac{k_1}{s} + \frac{k_2}{s + 4} = \frac{(k_1 + k_2)s + 4k_1}{s(s + 4)}$$

Equating the coefficients in the numerator yields $k_1 + k_2 = 0$ and $4k_1 = 2$.

Thus,

$$k_1 = 0.5 \quad \text{and} \quad k_2 = -0.5$$

and

$$V(s) = \frac{0.5}{s} + \frac{-0.5}{s + 4}$$

Finally,

$$v(t) = \mathcal{L}^{-1}\left(\frac{0.5}{s} - \frac{0.5}{s + 4}\right) = 0.5(1 - e^{-4t}) \quad V \quad t \geq 0$$

$$= 0.5(1 - e^{-4t})u(t) \quad V$$

21.16 According to the *final-value theorem* we have

$$f(\infty) = \lim_{s \to 0} sF(s)$$

Apply the final-value theorem to (1) of Prob. 21.14 to obtain the steady-state value of $v(t)$.

I
$$v_{\text{steady state}} = \lim_{s \to 0} sV(s) = \lim_{s \to 0} s\left[\frac{2}{s(s+4)}\right] = 0.5 \text{ V}$$

which agrees with the result of Prob. 21.15.

21.17 The current (in the s domain) through a circuit is given by

$$I(s) = \frac{6}{s(s+2)(s+3)}$$

What is $i(\infty)$?

I By the final-value theorem we have

$$i(\infty) = \lim_{s \to 0} sI(s) = \lim_{s \to 0} \frac{6s}{s(s+2)(s+3)} = 1 \text{ A}$$

21.18 The splitting of $V(s)$ into two functions in Prob. 21.15 is done on the basis of partial-fraction expansion. In general, the $F(s)$ whose inverse transform is required can be expressed as the ratio of two polynomials,

$$F(s) = \frac{A(s)}{B(s)} = \frac{a_m s^m + a_{m-1} s^{m-1} + \cdots + a_1 s + a_0}{s^n + b_{n-1} s^{n-1} + \cdots + b_1 s + b_0}$$

Furthermore, the denominator of $F(s)$ can be factored as

$$B(s) = (s + \alpha_1)(s + \alpha_2) \cdots (s + \alpha_n) = \prod_{i=1}^{n} (s + \alpha_i)$$

where each value $s = -\alpha_1$ is a root of $B(s)$.

To develop the general method, first consider $F(s)$ for which $A(s)$ is of lower degree than $B(s)$; that is, $m < n$. In addition, it is assumed that $B(s)$ has distinct roots (each of the α_i is different). For this situation, $F(s)$ can be expanded as

$$F(s) = \frac{A(s)}{B(s)} = \frac{K_1}{s + \alpha_1} + \frac{K_2}{s + \alpha_2} + \cdots + \frac{K_n}{s + \alpha_n} = \sum_{i=1}^{n} \frac{K_i}{s + \alpha_i} \tag{1}$$

A method to evaluate K_1 is to multiply both sides of Eq. (1) by $(s + \alpha_1)$ which gives

$$\frac{(s + \alpha_1)A(s)}{B(s)} = K_1 + (s + \alpha_1)\left[\frac{K_2}{s + \alpha_2} + \cdots + \frac{K_n}{s + \alpha_n}\right] \tag{2}$$

By setting $s = -\alpha_1$, the right-hand side of Eq. (2) is zero except for K_1 so that

$$K_1 = \frac{(s + \alpha_1)A(s)}{B(s)}\bigg|_{s = -\alpha_1}$$

Repetition of the process for each root yields the value of K_i for each term in Eq. (1). The general result can then be expressed as

$$K_i = \frac{(s + \alpha_i)A(s)}{B(s)}\bigg|_{s = -\alpha_i} \tag{3}$$

Apply this procedure to obtain the partial-fraction expansion of

$$F(s) = \frac{8(s + 2)}{(s + 1)(s + 3)(s + 5)}$$

I
$$F(s) = \frac{K_1}{s + 1} + \frac{K_2}{s + 3} + \frac{K_3}{s + 5}$$

From Eq. (3)

$$K_1 = (s + 1)F(s)\bigg|_{s = -1} = \frac{8(s + 2)}{(s + 3)(s + 5)}\bigg|_{s = -1} = \frac{8(-1 + 2)}{(-1 + 3)(-1 + 5)} = 1$$

$$K_2 = (s + 3)F(s)\bigg|_{s = -3} = \frac{8(s + 2)}{(s + 1)(s + 5)}\bigg|_{s = -3} = \frac{8(-3 + 2)}{(-3 + 1)(-3 + 5)} = 2$$

$$K_3 = (s+5)F(s)\Big|_{s=-5} = \frac{8(s+2)}{(s+1)(s+3)}\Big|_{s=-5} = \frac{8(-5+2)}{(-5+1)(-5+3)} = -3$$

These values give

$$F(s) = \frac{1}{s+1} + \frac{2}{s+3} - \frac{3}{s+5}$$

21.19 Obtain $f(t)$ for the $F(s)$ of Prob. 21.18.

❚ $$f(t) = \mathscr{L}^{-1}[F(s)] = \mathscr{L}^{-1}\left(\frac{1}{s+1} + \frac{2}{s+3} - \frac{3}{s+5}\right) = e^{-t} + 2e^{-3t} - 3e^{-5t}$$

21.20 Obtain the partial-fraction expansion of

$$F(s) = \frac{4(s+1)}{s(s^2 + 2s + 2)}$$

❚ The roots of the denominator of $F(s)$ are $s = 0, -1 \pm j1$. The partial-fraction expansion of $F(s)$ is

$$F(s) = \frac{K_1}{s} + \frac{K_2}{s+1-j1} + \frac{K_3}{s+1+j1}$$

The values of K_1, K_2, and K_3 are found by use of Eq. (3) of Prob. 21.18:

$$K_1 = sF(s)\Big|_{s=0} = \frac{4(s+1)}{s^2 + 2s + 2}\Big|_{s=0} = 2$$

$$K_2 = (s+1-j1)F_2(s)\Big|_{s=-1+j1} = \frac{4(s+1)}{s(s+1+j1)}\Big|_{s=-1+j1} = \frac{2}{-1+j1} = \sqrt{2}\epsilon^{-j135°}$$

$$K_3 = (s+1+j1)F(s)\Big|_{s=-1-j1} = \frac{4(s+1)}{s(s+1-j1)}\Big|_{s=-1-j1} = \frac{2}{-1+j1} = \sqrt{2}\epsilon^{+j135°}$$

The resulting $F(s)$ becomes

$$F(s) = \frac{2}{s} + \frac{\sqrt{2}\epsilon^{-j135°}}{s+1-j1} + \frac{\sqrt{2}\epsilon^{+j135°}}{s+1+j1}$$

21.21 Determine $f(t)$ for the function $F(s)$ of Prob. 21.20.

❚ From Table 21.1

$$f(t) = 2 + \sqrt{2}\epsilon^{-j135°} \cdot \epsilon^{(-1+j1)t} + \sqrt{2}\epsilon^{+j135°} \cdot \epsilon^{(-1-j1)t}$$

Rearrangement of the terms gives

$$f(t) = 2 + \sqrt{2}\epsilon^{-t}[\epsilon^{+j(t-135°)} + \epsilon^{-j(t-135°)}]$$

The use of Euler's identity, $\cos x = \frac{1}{2}(\epsilon^{jx} + \epsilon^{-jx})$, permits $f(t)$ to be expressed as

$$f(t) = 2 + 2\sqrt{2}\epsilon^{-t}\cos(t - 135°)$$

21.22 In Prob. 21.18, we assumed that $A(s)$ is of lower degree than $B(s)$; that is, $m < n$.
For the case where $A(s)$ is of the same degree as or higher degree than $B(s)$, that is, $m \geq n$, $F(s)$ can be rewritten as

$$F(s) = \frac{A(s)}{B(s)} = [A_m s^m + A_{m-1}s^{m-1} + \cdots + A_1 s + A_0] + \frac{A_1(s)}{B(s)} \tag{1}$$

where (1) is obtained by long division. Then the rules developed in Prob. 21.18 may be applied to the remainder $A_1(s)/B(s)$. Hence obtain

$$f(t) = \mathscr{L}^{-1}\left[\frac{s^2 + 7s + 14}{s^2 + 3s + 2}\right] = \mathscr{L}^{-1}[F(s)]$$

❚ Performing the required long division and factoring the denominator yields

$$F(s) = 1 + \frac{4s + 12}{(s+1)(s+2)} = 1 + \frac{A_1(s)}{B(s)}$$

The partial-fraction expansion of $A_1(s)/B(s)$ is

$$\frac{A_1(s)}{B(s)} = \frac{4s + 12}{(s + 1)(s + 2)} = \frac{K_1}{s + 1} + \frac{K_2}{s + 2}$$

Evaluation of K_1 and K_2 gives

$$K_1 = \frac{4s + 12}{s + 2}\bigg|_{s = -1} = 8 \quad \text{and} \quad K_2 = \frac{4s + 12}{s + 1}\bigg|_{s = -2} = -4$$

which result in

$$F(s) = 1 + \frac{8}{s + 1} - \frac{4}{s + 2}$$

The inverse transform is obtained

$$f(t) = \mathcal{L}^{-1}[F(s)] = \delta(t) + 8\epsilon^{-t} - 4\epsilon^{-2t}$$

The term $\delta(t)$ is the unit-impulse function.

21.23 Consider $F(s)$ with repeated roots:

$$F(s) = \frac{A(s)}{(s + a)^3} = \frac{K_1}{(s + a)^3} + \frac{K_2}{(s + a)^2} + \frac{K_3}{(s + a)} \tag{1}$$

in which the degree of $A(s)$ is no greater than 2. Multiplication of both sides of Eq. (1) by $(s + a)^3$ gives

$$(s + a)^3 F(s) = K_1 + K_2(s + a) + K_3(s + a)^2 \tag{2}$$

Setting $s = -a$ in Eq. (2) yields

$$K_1 = (s + a)^3 F(s)\bigg|_{s = -a} \tag{3}$$

K_2 is obtained by differentiating both sides of Eq. (2) with respect to s and setting $s = -a$. The result is

$$\frac{d}{ds}[(s + a)^3 F(s)] = K_2 + 2K_3(s + a) \tag{4}$$

and for $s = -a$

$$K_2 = \frac{d}{ds}[(s + a)^3 F(s)]\bigg|_{s = -a} \tag{5}$$

Differentiating both sides of Eq. (4) and setting $s = -a$ determines the value of K_3 as

$$K_3 = \frac{1}{2}\frac{d^2}{ds^2}[(s + a)^3 F(s)]\bigg|_{s = -a} \tag{6}$$

For the general case of repeated roots $F(s)$ is expanded as

$$F(s) = \frac{A(s)}{(s + \alpha)^k} = \frac{K_1}{(s + \alpha)^k} + \frac{K_2}{(s + \alpha)^{k-1}} + \cdots + \frac{K_k}{s + \alpha} \tag{7}$$

The constants K_1 to K_k are evaluated in a fashion similar to the development in Eqs. (1) to (6). The general term has the form

$$K_\nu = \frac{1}{(\nu - 1)!}\frac{d^{\nu-1}}{ds^{\nu-1}}[(s + \alpha)^k F(s)]\bigg|_{s = -\alpha} \tag{8}$$

Apply (8) to obtain the partial-fraction expansion of

$$F(s) = \frac{s + 2}{s(s + 1)^3} \tag{9}$$

▌ The expansion for $F(s)$ is

$$F(s) = \frac{K_0}{s} + \frac{K_1}{(s + 1)^3} + \frac{K_2}{(s + 1)^2} + \frac{K_3}{s + 1}$$

By use of Eq. (2) of Prob. 21.18.

$$K_0 = sF(s)\bigg|_{s = 0} = \frac{s + 2}{(s + 1)^3}\bigg|_{s = 0} = 2$$

The coefficients K_1, K_2, and K_3 are determined from Eqs. (3), (5), and (6), respectively, as

$$K_1 = (s+1)^3 F(s)\Big|_{s=-1} = \frac{s+2}{s}\Big|_{s=-1} = -1$$

$$K_2 = \frac{d}{ds}\left[(s+1)^3 F(s)\right]\Big|_{s=-1} = \frac{d}{ds}\left[\frac{s+2}{s}\right]\Big|_{s=-1} = \frac{-2}{s^2}\Big|_{s=-1} = -2$$

$$K_3 = \frac{1}{2}\frac{d^2}{ds^2}\left[(s+1)^3 F(s)\right]\Big|_{s=-1} = \frac{1}{2}\frac{d^2}{ds^2}\left[\frac{s+2}{s}\right]\Big|_{s=-1} = \frac{1}{2}\left[\frac{4}{s^3}\right]\Big|_{s=-1} = -2$$

These values of the K terms yield

$$F(s) = \frac{2}{s} - \frac{1}{(s+1)^3} - \frac{2}{(s+1)^2} - \frac{2}{(s+1)} \tag{10}$$

21.24 Find the inverse transform of (9) of Prob. 21.23.

▮ To obtain the inverse transform we use the partial expansion of (9) as given by (10). Hence,

$$f(t) = 2 - \frac{t^2}{2}\,\epsilon^{-t} - 2t\epsilon^{-t} - 2\epsilon^{-t} = 2 - \epsilon^{-t}\left(\frac{t^2}{2} + 2t + 2\right)$$

21.25 Certain useful properties of Laplace transforms are summarized in Table 21.2. Apply Laplace transform to a delayed unit step function to illustrate entry 1 in Table 21.2.

TABLE 21.2 Properties of the Laplace Transform

Property	Time domain	Frequency domain
1 Time delay	$f(t-T)u(t-T)$	$\epsilon^{-sT}F(s)$
2 Periodic function $f(t) = f(t+uT)$	$f(t) \quad 0 \le t \le t$	$F(s)/[1 - \epsilon^{Ts}]$ where $$F(s) = \int_0^T f(t)\epsilon^{-st}\,dt$$
3 Time scaling	$f(at)$	$\frac{1}{a}F(s/a)$
4 Frequency differentiation (multiplication by t)	$tf(t)$	$-\dfrac{dF(s)}{ds}$
5 Frequency integration (division by t)	$\dfrac{f(t)}{t}$	
6 Frequency shifting	$f(t)\epsilon^{-at}$	$F(s+a)$
7 Initial-value theorem	$\lim\limits_{t\to 0} f(t) = f(0^+)$	$\lim\limits_{s\to\infty} sF(s)$
8 Final-value theorem	$\lim\limits_{t\to\infty}$ where limit exists	$\lim\limits_{s\to 0} sF(s)$

▮
$$\mathscr{L}[u(t-T)] = \int_0^\infty u(t-T)\epsilon^{-st}\,dt = \int_T^\infty (1)\epsilon^{-st}\,dt = -\frac{1}{s}\epsilon^{-st}\Big|_T^\infty$$

Evaluation at the indicated limits gives

$$\mathscr{L}[u(t-T)] = \left(\frac{1}{s}\right)\epsilon^{-sT} = \mathscr{L}[u(t)]\epsilon^{-sT}$$

The effect of the delay in the application of the step function by T seconds is reflected in the ϵ^{-sT} term which multiplies the Laplace transform of the unit-step function. In the general case, delay in the time domain is indicated by the ϵ^{-sT} factor in the frequency domain.

21.26 Determine $\mathscr{L}[te^{-t}]$.

▮
$$\mathscr{L}[t\epsilon^{-t}] = \mathscr{L}[tf(t)]$$

where $f(t) = \epsilon^{-t}$. By use of entry 4 in Table 21.2

$$\mathscr{L}[tf(t)] = -\frac{dF(s)}{ds} \quad\text{and}\quad F(s) = [\epsilon^{-t}] = \frac{1}{s+1}$$

Performing the requisite differentiation,

$$-\frac{dF(s)}{ds} = \frac{1}{(s+1)^2}$$

so that

$$\mathscr{L}[t\epsilon^{-t}] = \frac{1}{(s+1)^2}$$

which is entry 10 in Table 21.2.

21.27 Apply the frequency-shifting property to evaluate $\mathscr{L}[t\epsilon^{-t}]$.

❚

$$\mathscr{L}[t\epsilon^{-t}] = \mathscr{L}[\epsilon^{-t}f(t)] = F(s+1)$$

and where $f(t) = t$.

By use of entry 7 in Table 21.2

$$\mathscr{L}[t] = \frac{1}{s^2} = F(s)$$

which causes

$$\mathscr{L}[t\epsilon^{-t}] = F(s+1) = \frac{1}{(s+1)^2}$$

21.28 The function

$$I(s) = \frac{5}{s+2}$$

is the frequency-domain response of an *RL* circuit. Determine $f(0_+)$ and $\lim_{t \to \infty} f(t)$.

❚ From the initial-value theorem

$$i(0_+) = \lim_{s \to \infty} sI(s) = \lim_{s \to \infty} \frac{5s}{s+2} = 5 \text{ A}$$

and from the final-value theorem

$$\lim_{t \to \infty} i(t) = \lim_{s \to 0} sI(s) = \lim_{s \to 0} \frac{5s}{s+2} = 0$$

21.29 Find the time-domain current $i(t)$ if its Laplace transform is

$$I(s) = \frac{s-10}{s^4 + s^2}$$

❚ Factoring the denominator,

$$I(s) = \frac{s-10}{s^2(s-j)(s+j)}$$

we see that the poles of $I(s)$ are $s = 0$ (double pole) and $s = \pm j$ (simple poles).

The partial-fraction expansion of $I(s)$ is therefore

$$I(s) = \frac{1}{s} - 10\frac{1}{s^2} - (0.5+j5)\frac{1}{s-j} - (0.5-j5)\frac{1}{s+j}$$

and term-by-term inversion using Table 21.2 gives

$$i(t) = 1 - 10t - (0.5+j5)e^{jt} - (0.5-j5)e^{-jt} = 1 - 10t - (\cos t - 10 \sin t)$$

21.30 Obtain the transformed equivalent circuits for *R*, *L*, and *C*, including initial conditions.

❚ The transformed network equivalents for the three elements *R*, *L*, and *C* are based on the Laplace transforms of their respective volt-ampere characteristics. These relations are

$$\mathscr{L}[v(t) = Ri(t)] \to V(s) = RI(s) \tag{1}$$

$$\mathscr{L}\left[v(t) = L\frac{di(t)}{dt}\right] \to V(s) = sLI(s) - Li(0_+) \tag{2}$$

$$\mathscr{L}\left[v(t) = \frac{1}{C}\int_{-\infty}^{t} v(t)\,dt\right] \to V(s) = \frac{1}{Cs}I(s) + \frac{v(0_+)}{s} \tag{3}$$

since

$$\int_{-\infty}^{0} i(t)\,dt = q(0_-)$$

and $q(0_-)/C$ is $v(0_-)$. By continuity of capacitance voltage, $v(0_-) = v(0_+)$, which is the term appearing in Eq. (3).

Equivalent circuit representations for the relations in Eqs. (1) to (3) are shown in Fig. 21-3.

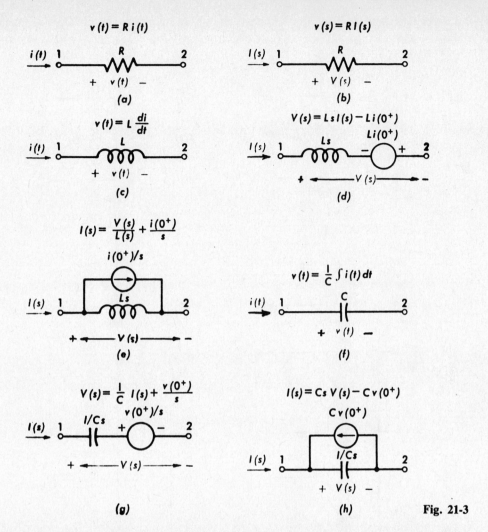

Fig. 21-3

21.31 Find the transformed network representations of independent voltage and current sources.

▮ The transformed network representations of current and voltage sources are simply the Laplace transforms of the time functions which define the source current and voltage as illustrated in Fig. 21-4.

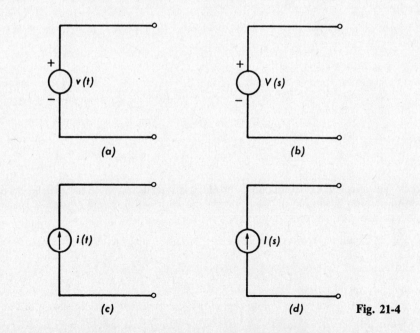

Fig. 21-4

21.32   Draw circuits showing dependent sources in the transformed domain.

▮ See Fig. 21-5.

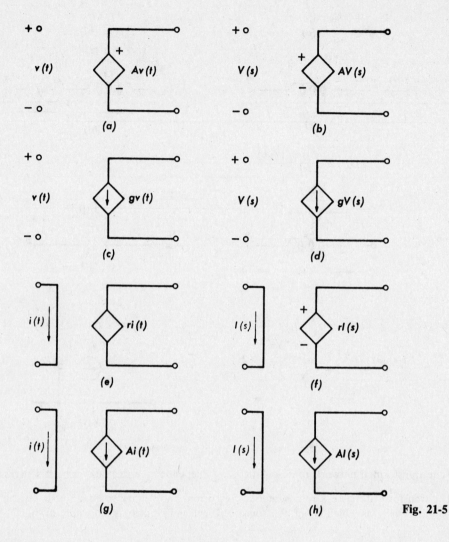

Fig. 21-5

21.33   In an RL series circuit $R = 5\,\Omega$, $L = 2.5\,\text{mH}$,   and $i(0_+) = 2\,\text{A}$.   If a source of 50 V is applied at $t = 0$, find $i(t)$ for $t > 0$.

▮ In the s domain we have

$$sLI(s) + RI(s) - Li(0_+) = V(s)$$

or

$$I(s) = \frac{10}{s} + \frac{(-8)}{s + 2000}$$

Thus,

$$i(t) = \mathscr{L}^{-1}\left(\frac{10}{s} - \frac{8}{s + 2000}\right) = 10 - 8e^{-2000t} \quad \text{A}$$

21.34   In the circuit shown in Fig. 21-6a, an initial current i_1 is established while the switch is in position 1.   At $t = 0$ it is moved to position 2, introducing both a capacitor with initial charge Q_0 and a constant-voltage source V_2. Obtain the s-domain circuit.

▮ The s-domain circuit is shown in Fig. 21.6b.   The s-domain equation is

$$RI(s) + sLI(s) - Li(0_+) + \frac{I(s)}{sC} + \frac{V_0}{sC} = \frac{V_2}{s}$$

in which $V_0 = Q_0/C$ and $i(0_+) = i_1 = V_1/R$.

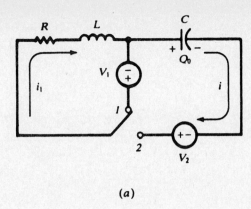 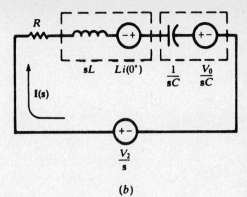

(a) (b)

Fig. 21-6

21.35   Find the Laplace transform of $e^{-at}\cos \omega t$, where a is a constant.

▮   Applying the defining equation $\mathscr{L}[f(t)] = \int_0^\infty f(t)e^{-st}\,dt$ to the given function, we obtain

$$\mathscr{L}[e^{-at}\cos \omega t] = \int_0^\infty \cos \omega t\, e^{-(s+a)t}\,dt = \left[\frac{-(s+a)\cos \omega t\, e^{-(s+a)t} + e^{-(s+a)t}\omega \sin \omega t}{(s+a)^2 + \omega^2}\right]_0^\infty = \frac{s+a}{(s+a)^2 + \omega^2}$$

21.36   If $\mathscr{L}[f(t)] = F(s)$ show that $\mathscr{L}[e^{-at}f(t)] = F(s+a)$. Apply this result to Prob. 21.35.

▮   By definition, $\mathscr{L}[f(t)] = \int_0^\infty f(t)e^{-st}\,dt = F(s)$. Then

$$\mathscr{L}[e^{-at}f(t)] = \int_0^\infty [e^{-at}f(t)]e^{-st}\,dt = \int_0^\infty f(t)e^{-(s+a)t}\,dt = F(s+a) \qquad (1)$$

Applying (1) to line 17 of Table 21.1 gives

$$\mathscr{L}[e^{-at}\cos \omega t] = \frac{s+a}{(s+a)^2 + \omega^2}$$

as determined in Prob. 21.35.

21.37   Find the Laplace transform of $f(t) = 1 - e^{-at}$, where a is a constant.

▮

$$\mathscr{L}[1 - e^{-at}] = \int_0^\infty (1 - e^{-at})e^{-st}\,dt = \int_0^\infty e^{-st}\,dt - \int_0^\infty e^{-(s+a)t}\,dt$$

$$= \left[-\frac{1}{s}e^{-st} + \frac{1}{s+a}e^{-(s+a)t}\right]_0^\infty = \frac{1}{s} - \frac{1}{s+a} = \frac{a}{s(s+a)}$$

21.38   Determine $\mathscr{L}^{-1}\left[\dfrac{1}{s(s^2 - a^2)}\right]$

▮   Using the method of partial fractions,

$$\frac{1}{s(s^2 - a^2)} = \frac{A}{s} + \frac{B}{s+a} + \frac{C}{s-a}$$

and the coefficients are

$$A = \frac{1}{s^2 - a^2}\bigg|_{s=0} = -\frac{1}{a^2} \qquad B = \frac{1}{s(s-a)}\bigg|_{s=-a} = \frac{1}{2a^2} \qquad C = \frac{1}{s(s+a)}\bigg|_{s=a} = \frac{1}{2a^2}$$

Hence $\quad \mathscr{L}^{-1}\left[\dfrac{1}{s(s^2 - a^2)}\right] = \mathscr{L}^{-1}\left[\dfrac{-1/a^2}{s}\right] + \mathscr{L}^{-1}\left[\dfrac{1/2a^2}{s+a}\right] + \mathscr{L}^{-1}\left[\dfrac{1/2a^2}{s-a}\right]$

The corresponding time functions are

$$\mathscr{L}^{-1}\left[\frac{1}{s(s^2 - a^2)}\right] = -\frac{1}{a^2} + \frac{1}{2a^2}e^{-at} + \frac{1}{2a^2}e^{at} = -\frac{1}{a^2} + \frac{1}{a^2}\left(\frac{e^{at} + e^{-at}}{2}\right) = \frac{1}{a^2}(\cosh at - 1)$$

21.39 Find
$$\mathscr{L}^{-1}\left[\frac{s+1}{s(s^2+4s+4)}\right]$$

▐ Using the method of partial fractions, we have

$$\frac{s+1}{s(s+2)^2}=\frac{A}{s}+\frac{B_1}{s+2}+\frac{B_2}{(s+2)^2}$$

Then
$$A=\frac{s+1}{(s+2)^2}\bigg|_{s=0}=\frac{1}{4}\qquad B_2=\frac{s+1}{s}\bigg|_{s=-2}=\frac{1}{2}\qquad\text{and}\qquad B_1=\frac{d}{ds}\left[\frac{s+1}{s}\right]_{s=-2}=-\frac{1}{4}$$

Hence
$$\mathscr{L}^{-1}\left[\frac{s+1}{s(s^2+4s+4)}\right]=\mathscr{L}^{-1}\left[\frac{\frac{1}{4}}{s}\right]+\mathscr{L}^{-1}\left[\frac{-\frac{1}{4}}{s+2}\right]+\mathscr{L}^{-1}\left[\frac{\frac{1}{2}}{(s+2)^2}\right]$$

The corresponding time functions are found in Table 21.1:

$$\mathscr{L}^{-1}\left[\frac{s+1}{s(s^2+4s+4)}\right]=\frac{1}{4}-\frac{1}{4}e^{-2t}+\frac{1}{2}te^{-2t}$$

21.40 In the series RC circuit of Fig. 21-7, the capacitor has initial charge 2.5 mC. At $t=0$, the switch is closed and a constant-voltage source $V=100\text{ V}$ is applied. Use the Laplace transform method to find the current.

Fig. 21-7

▐ The time-domain equation for the given circuit after the switch is closed is

$$Ri(t)+\frac{1}{C}\left[Q_0+\int_0^t i(\tau)\,d\tau\right]=V$$

or
$$10i(t)+\frac{1}{50\times10^{-6}}\left[(-2.5\times10^{-3})+\int_0^t i(\tau)\,d\tau\right]=V\tag{1}$$

Q_0 is opposite in polarity to the charge which the source will deposit on the capacitor. Taking the Laplace transform of the terms in (1), we obtain the s-domain equation

$$10I(s)-\frac{2.5\times10^{-3}}{50\times10^{-6}s}+\frac{I(s)}{50\times10^{-6}s}=\frac{100}{s}$$

or
$$I(s)=\frac{15}{s+(2\times10^3)}\tag{2}$$

The time function is now obtained by taking the inverse Laplace transform of

$$i(t)=\mathscr{L}^{-1}\left[\frac{15}{s+(2\times10^3)}\right]=15e^{-2\times10^3 t}\qquad\text{A}$$

21.41 In the RL circuit shown in Fig. 21-8, the switch is in position 1 long enough to establish steady-state conditions, and at $t=0$ it is switched to position 2. Find the resulting current.

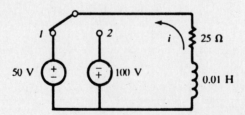

Fig. 21-8

❚ Assume that the direction of the current is as shown in the diagram. The initial current is therefore $i_0 = -50/25 = -2$ A.

The time-domain equation is

$$25i + 0.01 \frac{di}{dt} = 100 \tag{1}$$

Taking the Laplace transform of (1),

$$25I(s) + 0.01sI(s) - 0.01i(0_+) = 100/s$$

Substituting for $i(0_+)$,

$$25I(s) + 0.01sI(s) + 0.01(2) = 100/s$$

and

$$I(s) = \frac{100}{s(0.01s + 25)} - \frac{0.02}{0.01s + 25} = \frac{10^4}{s(s + 2500)} - \frac{2}{s + 2500}$$

Applying the method of partial fractions,

$$\frac{10^4}{s(s + 2500)} = \frac{A}{s} + \frac{B}{s + 2500}$$

with

$$A = \frac{10^4}{s + 2500}\bigg|_{s=0} = 4 \qquad B = \frac{10^4}{s}\bigg|_{s=-2500} = -4$$

Then

$$I(s) = \frac{4}{s} - \frac{4}{s + 2500} - \frac{2}{s + 2500} = \frac{4}{s} - \frac{6}{s + 2500} \tag{2}$$

Taking the inverse Laplace transform of (2), we obtain $i = 4 - 6e^{-2500t}$ A.

21.42 According to the *Heaviside expansion formula*, if all poles of $R(s)$ are simple, the partial-fraction expansion and termwise inversion can be accomplished in a single step:

$$\mathscr{L}^{-1}[R(s)] = \mathscr{L}^{-1}\left[\frac{P(s)}{Q(s)}\right] = \sum_{k=1}^{n} \frac{P(a_k)}{Q'(a_k)} e^{a_k t} \tag{1}$$

where $a_1, a_2, \ldots, a_n$ are the poles and $Q'(a_k)$ is $dQ(s)/ds$ evaluated at $s = a_k$.

Apply (1) to determine

$$\mathscr{L}^{-1}\left[\frac{250}{(s + 100)(s + 50)}\right] = f(t)$$

❚ Here

$$P(s) = 250 \qquad Q(s) = s^2 + 150s + 5000 \qquad Q'(s) = 2s + 150$$

$$a_1 = -100 \qquad \text{and} \qquad a_2 = -50$$

Hence,

$$f(t) = \frac{250}{-50} e^{-100t} + \frac{250}{50} e^{-50t} = -5e^{-100t} + 5e^{-50t}$$

21.43 Apply (1) of Prob. 21.42 to obtain

$$f(t) = \mathscr{L}^{-1}\left[\frac{4.5s^2}{(s^2 + 4 \times 10^6)(s + 10^3)} - \frac{1.25}{s + 10^3}\right] \tag{1}$$

❚ In this case we have: $P(s) = 4.5s^2$, $Q(s) = s^3 + 10^3 s^2 + 4 \times 10^6 s + 4 \times 10^9$, $Q'(s) = 3s^2 + 2 \times 10^3 s + 4 \times 10^6$, $a_1 = -j2 \times 10^3$, $a_2 = j2 \times 10^3$, and $a_3 = -10^3$. Then

$$f(t) = \frac{P(-j2 \times 10^3)}{Q'(-j2 \times 10^3)} e^{-j2 \times 10^3 t} + \frac{P(j2 \times 10^3)}{Q'(j2 \times 10^3)} e^{j2 \times 10^3 t} + \frac{P(-10^3)}{Q'(-10^3)} e^{-10^3 t} - 1.25e^{-10^3 t}$$

$$= (1.8 - j0.9)e^{-j2 \times 10^3 t} + (1.8 + j0.9)e^{j2 \times 10^3 t} - 0.35e^{-10^3 t}$$

$$= -1.8 \sin 2000t + 3.6 \cos 2000t - 0.35e^{-10^3 t}$$

$$= 4.02 \sin(2000t + 116.6°) - 0.35e^{-10^3 t} \tag{2}$$

21.44 In the series RL circuit of Fig. 21-9 an exponential voltage $v = 50e^{-100t}$ V   is applied by closing the switch at $t = 0$. Find the resulting current.

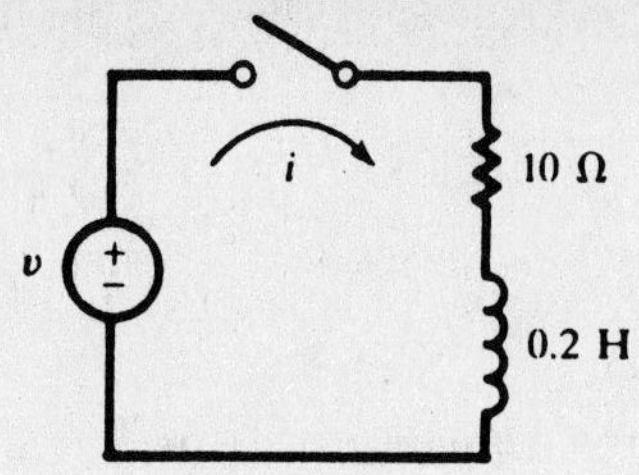

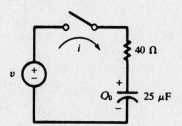

Fig. 21-9

▮ The time-domain equation for the given circuit is

$$Ri + L\frac{di}{dt} = v \tag{1}$$

In the s domain, (1) has the form

$$RI(s) + sLI(s) - Li(0_+) = V(s) \tag{2}$$

Substituting the circuit constants and the transform of the source, $V(s) = 50/(s + 100)$ in (2),

$$10I(s) + s(0.2)I(s) = \frac{50}{s + 100} \quad \text{or} \quad I(s) = \frac{250}{(s + 100)(s + 50)}$$

Now, using the result of Prob. 21.42,

$$i = \mathcal{L}^{-1}[I(s)] = \frac{250}{-50}e^{-100t} + \frac{250}{50}e^{-50t} = -5e^{-100t} + 5e^{-50t} \quad \text{A}$$

21.45 The series RC circuit of Fig. 21-10 has a sinusoidal voltage source $v = 180\sin(2000t + \phi)$ V and an initial charge on the capacitor $Q_0 = 1.25$ mC with polarity as shown. Determine the current if the switch is closed at a time corresponding to $\phi = 90°$.

Fig. 21-10

▮ The time-domain equation of the circuit is

$$40i(t) + \frac{1}{25 \times 10^{-6}}\left(1.25 \times 10^{-3} + \int_0^t i(\tau)\,d\tau\right) = 180\cos 2000t \tag{1}$$

The Laplace transform of (1) gives the s-domain equation

$$40I(s) + \frac{1.25 \times 10^{-3}}{25 \times 10^{-6}s} + \frac{4 \times 10^4}{s}I(s) = \frac{180s}{s^2 + 4 \times 10^6}$$

or

$$I(s) = \frac{4.5s^2}{(s^2 + 4 \times 10^6)(s + 10^3)} - \frac{1.25}{s + 10^3} \tag{2}$$

which is the same as (1) of Prob. 21.43. Hence, from (2) of Prob. 21.43 we have

$$i(t) = 4.02\sin(2000t + 116.6°) - 0.35e^{-10^3 t} \quad \text{A} \tag{3}$$

21.46 Find the initial current in the circuit of Prob. 21.45.

▮ Applying the initial-value theorem to (2) of Prob. 21.45, we obtain

$$i(0_+) = \lim_{s \to \infty}[sI(s)] = 4.5 - 1.25 = 3.25 \text{ A}$$

21.47 Verify the result of Prob. 21.46 from circuit considerations and from (3) of Prob. 21.45.

▮ At $t = 0$ the current is given by the instantaneous voltage, consisting of the source voltage and the charged capacitor voltage, divided by the resistance. Thus

$$i_0 = \left(180 \sin 90° - \frac{1.25 \times 10^{-3}}{25 \times 10^{-6}}\right)\bigg/40 = 3.25 \text{ A}$$

The same result is obtained if we set $t = 0$ in (3) of Prob. 21.45.

21.48 In the series RL circuit of Fig. 21-11, the source is $v = 100 \sin (500t + \phi)$ V. Determine the resulting current if the switch is closed at a time corresponding to $\phi = 0$.

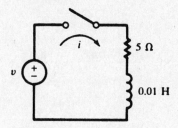

Fig. 21-11

▮ The s-domain equation of a series RL circuit is

$$RI(s) + sLI(s) - Li(0_+) = V(s) \tag{1}$$

The transform of the source with $\phi = 0$ is

$$V(s) = \frac{(100)(500)}{s^2 + (500)^2}$$

Since there is no initial current in the inductance $Li(0_+) = 0$. Substituting the circuit constants into (1),

$$5I(s) + 0.01sI(s) = \frac{5 \times 10^4}{s^2 + 25 \times 10^4} \quad \text{or} \quad I(s) = \frac{5 \times 10^6}{(s^2 + 25 \times 10^4)(s + 500)} \tag{2}$$

Expanding (2) by partial fractions,

$$I(s) = 5\left(\frac{-1+j}{s+j500}\right) + 5\left(\frac{-1-j}{s-j500}\right) + \frac{10}{s+500} \tag{3}$$

The inverse Laplace transform of (3) is

$$i = 10 \sin 500t - 10 \cos 500t + 10e^{-500t} = 10e^{-500t} + 14.14 \sin (500t - 45°) \quad \text{A}$$

21.49 Rework Prob. 21.48 by writing the voltage function as

$$v = 100e^{j500t} \quad \text{V} \tag{1}$$

Now $V(s) = 100/(s - j500)$, and the s-domain equation is

$$5I(s) + 0.01sI(s) = \frac{100}{s - j500} \quad \text{or} \quad I(s) = \frac{10^4}{(s - j500)(s + 500)}$$

Using partial fractions,

$$I(s) = \frac{10 - j10}{s - j500} + \frac{-10 + j10}{s + 500}$$

and, inverting, $\quad i = (10 - j10)e^{j500t} + (-10 + j10)e^{-500t} = 14.14e^{j(500t - \pi/4)} + (-10 + j10)e^{-500t} \quad$ A $\quad$ (2)

The actual voltage is the imaginary part of (1); hence the actual current is the imaginary part of (2).

$$i = 14.14 \sin (500t - \pi/4) + 10e^{-500t} \quad \text{A}$$

21.50 In the series RLC circuit shown in Fig. 21-12, there is no initial charge on the capacitor. If the switch is closed at $t = 0$, determine the resulting current.

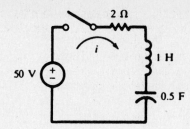

Fig. 21-12

I The time-domain equation of the given circuit is

$$Ri + L\frac{di}{dt} + \frac{1}{C}\int_0^t i(\tau)\,d\tau = V \tag{1}$$

Because $i(0_+) = 0$, the Laplace transform of (1) is

$$RI(s) + sLI(s) + \frac{1}{sC}\,I(s) = \frac{V}{s} \tag{2}$$

or

$$2I(s) + 1sI(s) + \frac{1}{0.5s}\,I(s) = \frac{50}{s} \tag{3}$$

Hence

$$I(s) = \frac{50}{s^2 + 2s + 2} = \frac{50}{(s + 1 + j)(s + 1 - j)} \tag{4}$$

Expanding (4) by partial fractions,

$$I(s) = \frac{j25}{(s + 1 + j)} - \frac{j25}{(s + 1 - j)} \tag{5}$$

and the inverse Laplace transform of (5) gives

$$i = j25\{e^{(-1-j)t} - e^{(-1+j)t}\} = 50e^{-t}\sin t \qquad A$$

21.51 In the two-mesh network of Fig. 21-13, the two loop currents are selected as shown. Write the s-domain equations in matrix form.

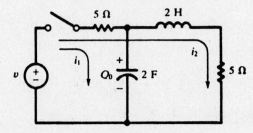

Fig. 21-13

I Writing the set of equations in the time domain,

$$5i_1 + \frac{1}{2}\left[Q_0 + \int_0^t i_1(\tau)\,d\tau\right] + 5i_2 = v \qquad \text{and} \qquad 10i_2 + 2\frac{di_2}{dt} + 5i_1 = v \tag{1}$$

Taking the Laplace transform of (1) to obtain the corresponding s-domain equations,

$$5I_1(s) + \frac{Q_0}{2s} + \frac{1}{2s}\,I_1(s) + 5I_2(s) = V(s) \qquad 10I_2(s) + 2sI_2(s) - 2i_2(0_+) + 5I_1(s) = V(s) \tag{2}$$

When this set of s-domain equations is written in matrix form,

$$\begin{bmatrix} 5 + (1/2s) & 5 \\ 5 & 10 + 2s \end{bmatrix}\begin{bmatrix} I_1(s) \\ I_2(s) \end{bmatrix} = \begin{bmatrix} V(s) - (Q_0/2s) \\ V(s) + 2i_2(0_+) \end{bmatrix}$$

21.52 Obtain a circuit in the s domain corresponding to the circuit of Fig. 21-13.

I See Fig. 21-14.

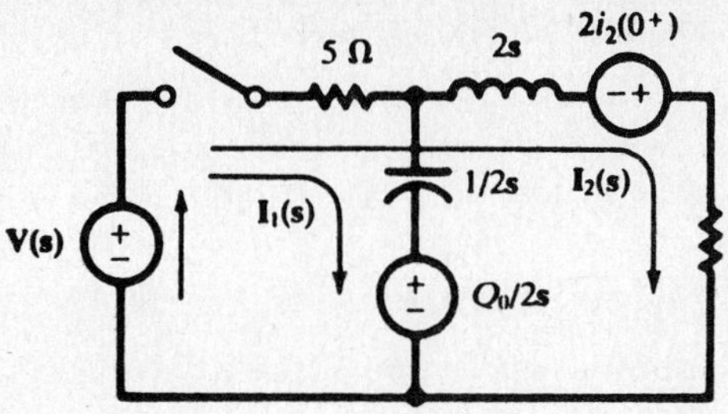

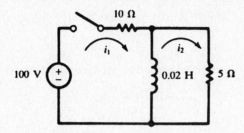

Fig. 21-14

21.53 In the two-mesh network of Fig. 21-15, find the currents which result when the switch is closed.

Fig. 21-15

❙ The time-domain equations for the network are

$$10i_1 + 0.02\frac{di_1}{dt} - 0.02\frac{di_2}{dt} = 100 \qquad 0.02\frac{di_2}{dt} + 5i_2 - 0.02\frac{di_1}{dt} = 0 \qquad (1)$$

Taking the Laplace transform of set (1),

$$(10 + 0.02s)I_1(s) - 0.02sI_2(s) = 100/s \qquad (5 + 0.02s)I_2(s) - 0.02sI_1(s) = 0 \qquad (2)$$

From the second equation in set (2) we find

$$I_2(s) = I_1(s)\left(\frac{s}{s + 250}\right) \qquad (3)$$

which when substituted into the first equation gives

$$I_1(s) = 6.67\left[\frac{s + 250}{s(s + 166.7)}\right] = \frac{10}{s} - \frac{3.33}{s + 166.7} \qquad (4)$$

Inverting (4), $\qquad i_1 = 10 - 3.33e^{-166.7t} \qquad$ A

Finally, substitute (4) into (3) and obtain

$$I_2(s) = 6.67\left(\frac{1}{s + 166.7}\right) \qquad \text{whence} \qquad i_2 = 6.67e^{-166.7t} \qquad \text{A}$$

21.54 Apply the initial- and final-value theorems in Prob. 21.53.

❙ The initial value of i_1 is given by

$$i_1(0_+) = \lim_{s\to\infty}[sI_1(s)] = \lim_{s\to\infty}\left[6.67\left(\frac{s + 250}{s + 166.7}\right)\right] = 6.67 \text{ A}$$

and the final value is

$$i_1(\infty) = \lim_{s\to0}[sI_1(s)] = \lim_{s\to0}\left[6.67\left(\frac{s + 250}{s + 166.7}\right)\right] = 10 \text{ A}$$

The initial value of i_2 is given by

$$i_2(0_+) = \lim_{s\to\infty}[sI_2(s)] = \lim_{s\to\infty}\left[6.67\left(\frac{s}{s + 166.7}\right)\right] = 6.67 \text{ A}$$

and the final value is

$$i_2(\infty) = \lim_{s\to0}[sI_2(s)] = \lim_{s\to0}\left[6.67\left(\frac{s}{s + 166.7}\right)\right] = 0$$

21.55 Verify the results of Prob. 21.54 from Fig. 21-15.

▎ Examination of Fig. 21-15 verifies each of the above initial and final values. At the instant of closing, the inductance presents an infinite impedance and the currents are $i_1 = i_2 = 100/(10+5) = 6.67$ A. Then, in the steady state, the inductance appears as a short circuit; hence $i_1 = 10$ A, $i_2 = 0$.

21.56 Solve for i_1 in Prob. 21.53 by determining an equivalent circuit in the s domain.

▎ In the s domain the 0.02-H inductor has impedance $Z(s) = 0.02s$. Therefore, the equivalent impedance of the network as seen from the source is

$$Z(s) = 10 + \frac{(0.02s)(5)}{0.02s + 5} = 15\left(\frac{s + 166.7}{s + 250}\right)$$

and the s-domain equivalent circuit is as shown in Fig. 21-16. The current is then

$$I_1(s) = \frac{V(s)}{Z(s)} = \frac{100}{s}\left[\frac{s + 250}{15(s + 166.7)}\right] = 6.67\left[\frac{s + 250}{s(s + 166.7)}\right]$$

This expression is identical with (4) of Prob. 21.53, and so the same time function i_1 is obtained.

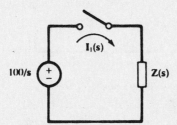

Fig. 21-16

21.57 In the two-mesh network shown in Fig. 21-17 there is no initial charge on the capacitor. Find the loop currents i_1 and i_2 which result when the switch is closed at $t = 0$.

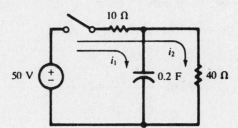

Fig. 21-17

▎ The time-domain equations for the circuit are

$$10i_1 + \frac{1}{0.2}\int_0^t i_1\,d\tau + 10i_2 = 50 \qquad 50i_2 + 10i_1 = 50$$

The corresponding s-domain equations are

$$10I_1(s) + \frac{1}{0.2s}I_1(s) + 10I_2(s) = \frac{50}{s} \qquad 50I_2(s) + 10I_1(s) = \frac{50}{s}$$

Solving,
$$I_1(s) = \frac{5}{s + 0.625} \qquad I_2(s) = \frac{1}{s} - \frac{1}{s + 0.625}$$

which invert to
$$i_1 = 5e^{-0.625t} \quad \text{A} \qquad i_2 = 1 - e^{-0.625t} \quad \text{A}$$

21.58 Referring to Prob. 21.57, obtain the equivalent impedance of the s-domain network and determine the total current and the branch currents using the current-division rule.

▎ The s-domain impedance as seen by the voltage source is

$$Z(s) = 10 + \frac{40(1/0.2s)}{40 + 1/0.2s} = \frac{80s + 50}{8s + 1} = 10\left(\frac{s + 5/8}{s + 1/8}\right)$$

The equivalent circuit is shown in Fig. 21-18; the resulting current is

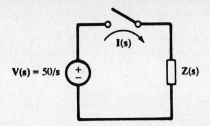

Fig. 21-18

$$I(s) = \frac{V(s)}{Z(s)} = 5\,\frac{s + 1/8}{s(s + 5/8)}$$

Expanding $I(s)$ in partial fractions,

$$I(s) = \frac{1}{s} + \frac{4}{s + 5/8} \qquad \text{from which} \qquad i = 1 + 4e^{-5t/8} \qquad \text{A}$$

Now the branch currents $I_1(s)$ and $I_2(s)$ can be obtained by the current-division rule. Referring to Fig. 21-19, we have

$$I_1(s) = I(s)\left(\frac{40}{40 + 1/0.2s}\right) = \frac{5}{s + 5/8} \qquad \text{and} \qquad i_1 = 5e^{-0.625t} \qquad \text{A}$$

$$I_2(s) = I(s)\left(\frac{1/0.2s}{40 + 1/0.2s}\right) = \frac{1}{s} - \frac{1}{s + 5/8} \qquad \text{and} \qquad i_2 = 1 - e^{-0.625t} \qquad \text{A}$$

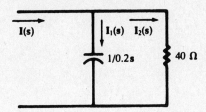

Fig. 21-19

21.59 Find i in the circuit of Fig. 21-20, if the initial conditions are all zero and the switch is closed at $t = 0$.

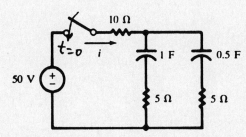

Fig. 21-20

I The network has an equivalent impedance in the s domain

$$Z(s) = 10 + \frac{(5 + 1/s)(5 + 1/0.5s)}{10 + 1/s + 1/0.5s} = \frac{125s^2 + 45s + 2}{s(10s + 3)}$$

Hence the current is

$$I(s) = \frac{V(s)}{Z(s)} = \frac{50}{s}\,\frac{s(10s + 3)}{(125s^2 + 45s + 2)} = \frac{4(s + 0.3)}{(s + 0.308)(s + 0.052)}$$

Expanding $I(s)$ in partial fractions,

$$I(s) = \frac{1/8}{s + 0.308} + \frac{31/8}{s + 0.052} \qquad \text{and} \qquad i = \frac{1}{8}\,e^{-0.308t} + \frac{31}{8}\,e^{-0.052t} \qquad \text{A}$$

21.60 Apply the initial- and final-value theorems to the s-domain current of Prob. 21.59.

I
$$i(0_+) = \lim_{s \to \infty} [sI(s)] = \lim_{s \to \infty}\left[\frac{1}{8}\left(\frac{s}{s + 0.308}\right) + \frac{31}{8}\left(\frac{s}{s + 0.052}\right)\right] = 4\,\text{A}$$

$$i(\infty) = \lim_{s \to 0} [sI(s)] = \lim_{s \to 0}\left[\frac{1}{8}\left(\frac{s}{s + 0.308}\right) + \frac{31}{8}\left(\frac{s}{s + 0.052}\right)\right] = 0$$

21.61 Verify the results of Prob. 21.60 from the circuit of Fig. 21-20.

▌ Examination of Fig. 21-20 shows that initially the total circuit resistance is $R = 10 + 5(5)/10 = 12.5\,\Omega$ and thus $i(0_+) = 50/12.5 = 4\,\text{A}$. Then, in the steady state, both capacitors are charged to 50 V and the current is zero.

21.62 Find the Laplace transform of $t^2 e^{3t}$ by applying the shifting property, item 6 in Table 21.2.

▌ $\mathscr{L}(t^2) = 2/s^3$. Then $\mathscr{L}(t^2 e^{3t}) = 2/(s-3)^3$.

21.63 Find $\mathscr{L}(e^{-2t}\sin 4t)$.

▌ $\mathscr{L}(\sin 4t) = 4/(s^2 + 16)$. Then, by the shifting property,

$$\mathscr{L}(e^{-2t}\sin 4t) = \frac{4}{(s+2)^2 + 16} = \frac{4}{s^2 + 4s + 20}$$

21.64 Find $\mathscr{L}[F(t)]$ if $F(t) = \begin{cases} \cos(t - 2\pi/3) & t > 2\pi/3 \\ 0 & t < 2\pi/3 \end{cases}$

▌
$$\mathscr{L}(\cos t) = \frac{s}{s^2 + 1}$$

Then using line 1 of Table 21.2,

$$\mathscr{L}[F(t)] = \frac{s e^{-2\pi s/3}}{s^2 + 1}$$

21.65 Verify the result of Prob. 21.64 by applying (1) of Prob. 21.1.

▌
$$\mathscr{L}[F(t)] = \int_0^{2\pi/3} e^{-st}(0)\,dt + \int_{2\pi/3}^{\infty} e^{-st}\cos[t - (2\pi/3)]\,dt = \int_0^{\infty} e^{-s(u + 2\pi/3)}\cos u\,du$$

$$= e^{-2\pi s/3}\int_0^{\infty} e^{-su}\cos u\,du = \frac{s e^{-2\pi s/3}}{s^2 + 1}$$

21.66 If $\mathscr{L}[f(t)] = F(s)$, show that $\mathscr{L}[F(at)] = (1/a)F(s/a)$.

▌
$$\mathscr{L}[F(at)] = \int_0^{\infty} e^{-st}F(at)\,dt = \int_0^{\infty} e^{-s(u/a)}F(u)\,d(u/a) = \frac{1}{a}\int_0^{\infty} e^{-su/a}F(u)\,du = \frac{1}{a}F\left(\frac{s}{a}\right)$$

21.67 Given $\mathscr{L}(\sin t/t) = \tan^{-1}(1/s)$. Apply the result of Prob. 21.66 to find $\mathscr{L}(\sin at/t)$.

▌
$$\mathscr{L}\left(\frac{\sin at}{at}\right) = \frac{1}{a}\mathscr{L}\left(\frac{\sin at}{t}\right) = \frac{1}{a}\tan^{-1}\left(\frac{1}{s/a}\right) = \frac{1}{a}\tan^{-1}\left(\frac{a}{s}\right)$$

Thus,
$$\mathscr{L}\left(\frac{\sin at}{t}\right) = \tan^{-1}\left(\frac{a}{s}\right)$$

21.68 If $F(t)$ has period $T > 0$ then show that

$$\mathscr{L}\{F(t)\} = \int_0^T e^{-st}F(t)\,dt \Big/ (1 - e^{-sT}) \tag{1}$$

▌ We have $\mathscr{L}\{F(t)\} = \int_0^{\infty} e^{-st}F(t)\,dt = \int_0^T e^{-st}F(t)\,dt + \int_T^{2T} e^{-st}F(t)\,dt + \int_{2T}^{3T} e^{-st}F(t)\,dt + \cdots$

In the second integral let $t = u + T$, in the third integral let $t = u + 2T$, etc. Then

$$\mathscr{L}\{F(t)\} = \int_0^T e^{-su}F(u)\,du + \int_0^T e^{-s(u+T)}F(u+T)\,du + \int_0^T e^{-s(u+2T)}F(u+2T)\,du + \cdots$$

$$= \int_0^T e^{-su}F(u)\,du + e^{-sT}\int_0^T e^{-su}F(u)\,du + e^{-2sT}\int_0^T e^{-su}F(u)\,du + \cdots$$

$$= (1 + e^{-sT} + e^{-2sT} + \cdots)\int_0^T e^{-su}F(u)\,du = \int_0^T e^{-su}F(u)\,du \Big/ (1 - e^{-sT})$$

where we have used the periodicity to write $F(u + T) = F(u)$, $F(u + 2T) = F(u), \ldots$, and the fact that

$$1 + r + r^2 + r^3 + \cdots = \frac{1}{1 - r} \qquad |r| < 1$$

21.69 (*a*) Graph the function

$$F(t) = \begin{cases} \sin t & 0 < t < \pi \\ 0 & \pi < t < 2\pi \end{cases}$$

extended periodically with period 2π.

(*b*) Find $\mathcal{L}\{F(t)\}$.

▌ (*a*) The graph appears in Fig. 21-21.

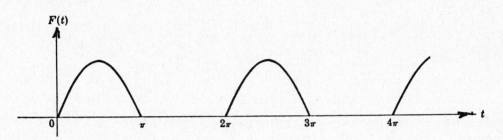

Fig. 21-21

(*b*) From (1) of Prob. 21.68 since $T = 2\pi$, we have

$$\mathcal{L}\{F(t)\} = \frac{1}{1 - e^{-2\pi s}} \int_0^{2\pi} e^{-st} F(t) \, dt = \frac{1}{1 - e^{-2\pi s}} \int_0^{\pi} e^{-st} \sin t \, dt$$

$$= \frac{1}{1 - e^{-2\pi s}} \left\{ \frac{e^{-st}(-s \sin t - \cos t)}{s^2 + 1} \right\} \bigg|_0^{\pi}$$

$$= \frac{1}{1 - e^{-2\pi s}} \left\{ \frac{1 + e^{-\pi s}}{s^2 + 1} \right\} = \frac{1}{(1 - e^{-\pi s})(s^2 + 1)}$$

21.70 The current, in the s domain, in a circuit is $I(s) = 3/(s + 2)$. Determine the initial and final currents.

▌ By the initial-value theorem:

$$i(0_+) = \lim_{s \to \infty} sI(s) = \frac{3s}{s + 2} = 3 \text{ A}$$

By the final-value theorem:

$$i(\infty) = \lim_{s \to 0} sI(s) = \frac{3s}{s + 2} = 0 \text{ A}$$

21.71 Verify the results of Prob. 21.70 by expressing the current in the time domain.

▌

$$i(t) = \mathcal{L}^{-1}[I(s)] = \mathcal{L}^{-1}\left(\frac{3}{s + 2}\right) = 3e^{-2t} \quad \text{A}$$

Thus,

$$i(0_+) = 3 \text{ A} \qquad i(\infty) = 0 \text{ A}$$

21.72 Find

$$\mathcal{L}^{-1}\left\{ \frac{2s^2 - 4}{(s + 1)(s - 2)(s - 3)} \right\}$$

▌ We have $P(s) = 2s^2 - 4$, $Q(s) = (s + 1)(s - 2)(s - 3) = s^3 - 4s^2 + s + 6$, $Q'(s) = 3s^2 - 8s + 1$, $\alpha_1 = -1$, $\alpha_2 = 2$, $\alpha_3 = 3$. Then the required inverse is, by the Heaviside expansion theorem,

$$\frac{P(-1)}{Q'(-1)} e^{-t} + \frac{P(2)}{Q'(2)} e^{2t} + \frac{P(3)}{Q'(3)} e^{3t} = \frac{-2}{12} e^{-t} + \frac{4}{-3} e^{2t} + \frac{14}{4} e^{3t} = -\frac{1}{6} e^{-t} - \frac{4}{3} e^{2t} + \frac{7}{2} e^{3t}$$

21.73 Find

$$\mathcal{L}^{-1}\left\{ \frac{3s + 1}{(s - 1)(s^2 + 1)} \right\}$$

We have $P(s) = 3s + 1$, $Q(s) = (s-1)(s^2+1) = s^3 - s^2 + s - 1$, $Q'(s) = 3s^2 - 2s + 1$, $\alpha_1 = 1$, $\alpha_2 = j$, $\alpha_3 = -j$ since $s^2 + 1 = (s-j)(s+j)$.   Then, by the Heaviside expansion formula, the required inverse is

$$\frac{P(1)}{Q'(1)}e^t + \frac{P(j)}{Q'(j)}e^{jt} + \frac{P(-j)}{Q'(-j)}e^{-jt} = \frac{4}{2}e^t + \frac{3j+1}{-2-2j}e^{jt} + \frac{-3j+1}{-2+2j}e^{-jt}$$

$$= 2e^t + (-1 - \tfrac{1}{2}j)(\cos t + j\sin t) + (-1 + \tfrac{1}{2}j)(\cos t - j\sin t)$$

$$= 2e^t - \cos t + \tfrac{1}{2}\sin t - \cos t + \tfrac{1}{2}\sin t = 2e^t - 2\cos t + \sin t$$

21.74 The voltage across a circuit is given by

$$\frac{d^2v}{dt^2} + v = t$$

The initial conditions are $v(0_+) = 1$ and $dv/dt(0_+) = -2$. Find $v(t)$.

Taking the Laplace transform of both sides:

$$s^2V(s) - sv(0_+) - \dot{v}(0_+) + V(s) = 1/s^2$$

or
$$V(s)(s^2+1) - s + 2 = 1/s^2$$

Thus,
$$V(s) = \frac{1}{s^2(s^2+1)} + \frac{s}{s^2+1} - \frac{2}{s^2+1} = \frac{1}{s^2} + \frac{s}{s^2+1} - \frac{3}{s^2+1}$$

Hence,
$$v(t) = \mathcal{L}^{-1}V(s) = t + \cos t - 3\sin t$$

21.75 The current in a circuit is given by

$$\frac{d^2i}{dt^2} - 3\frac{di}{dt} + 2i = 4e^{2t} \qquad (1)$$

Find $i(t)$ if the initial conditions are $i(0_+) = -3\,\text{A}$ and $di/dt(0_+) = 5\,\text{A/s}$.

From (1) and the initial conditions:

$$I(s)(s^2 - 3s + 2) + 3s - 14 = 4/(s-2)$$

or
$$I(s) = \frac{-3s^2 + 20s - 24}{(s-1)(s-2)^2} = \frac{-7}{s-1} + \frac{4}{s-2} + \frac{4}{(s-2)^2}$$

Thus,
$$i(t) = -7e^t + 4e^{2t} + 4te^{2t}$$

21.76 Solve for $i(t)$ if $i(0_+) = 0$, $di/dt(0_+) = 1$ and

$$\frac{d^2i}{dt^2} + 2\frac{di}{dt} + 5i = e^{-t}\sin t$$

Taking Laplace transforms and substituting initial conditions yields

$$s^2I(s) - 1 + 2sI(s) + 5I(s) = \frac{1}{s^2 + 2s + 2}$$

or
$$I(s) = \frac{s^2 + 2s + 3}{(s^2 + 2s + 2)(s^2 + 2s + 5)} = \frac{1}{3}\left[\frac{1}{(s+1)^2 + 1}\right] + \frac{2}{3}\left[\frac{1}{(s+1)^2 + 4}\right]$$

Hence,
$$i(t) = \tfrac{1}{3}e^{-t}(\sin t + \sin 2t) \qquad \text{A}$$

21.77 The current in a circuit is periodic. Two values of the current are $i(0_+) = 1$, $i(\pi/2) = -1$. Find $i(t)$ if it is governed by

$$\frac{d^2i}{dt^2} + 9i = \cos 2t$$

In the transform domain:

$$s^2I(s) - si(0_+) - \frac{di}{dt}(0_+) + 9I(s) = \frac{s}{s^2+4}$$

or
$$I(s)(s^2+9) - s - A = \frac{s}{s^2+4} \qquad \text{where} \qquad A = \frac{di}{dt}(0_+)$$

Solving for $I(s)$ and breaking into partial fractions yields

$$I(s) = \frac{4}{5}\left(\frac{s}{s^2 + 9}\right) + \frac{A}{s^2 + 9} + \frac{s}{5(s^2 + 4)}$$

or

$$i(t) = \frac{4}{5}\cos 3t + \frac{A}{3}\sin 3t + \frac{1}{5}\cos 2t$$

$$i\left(\frac{\pi}{2}\right) = -1 = -\frac{A}{3} - \frac{1}{5} \quad \text{or} \quad A = \frac{12}{5}$$

Hence,

$$i(t) = \tfrac{4}{5}(\cos 3t + \sin 3t) + \tfrac{1}{5}\cos 2t$$

21.78 The currents in a coupled circuit are given by

$$\frac{di_1}{dt} = 2i_1 - 3i_2 \quad \text{and} \quad \frac{di_2}{dt} = -2i_1 + i_2$$

The initial conditions are $i_1(0_+) = 8\,\text{A}$ and $i_2(0_+) = 3\,\text{A}$. Determine $i_1(t)$.

❚ In the transform domain, the equations become

$$sI_1(s) - 8 = 2I_1(s) - 3I_2(s) \quad \text{and} \quad sI_2(s) - 3 = -2I_1(s) + I_2(s)$$

Solving for $I_1(s)$ yields

$$I_1(s) = \frac{8s - 17}{(s+1)(s-4)} = \frac{5}{s+1} + \frac{3}{s-4} \quad \text{or} \quad i_1(t) = 5e^{-t} + 3e^{4t} \quad \text{A}$$

21.79 The charge q in an electric circuit is given by

$$\frac{d^2q}{dt^2} + 8\frac{dq}{dt} + 25q = 150 = E$$

If all initial conditions are zero, determine the current through the circuit.

❚ In the s domain we have

$$s^2Q(s) - sQ(0_+) - \frac{dQ}{dt}(0_+) + 8sQ(s) - 8Q(0_+) + 25Q(s) = \frac{150}{s}$$

or

$$Q(s) = \frac{150}{s(s^2 + 8s + 25)} = \frac{6}{s} - \frac{6(s+4)}{(s+4)^2 + 9} - \frac{24}{(s+4)^2 + 9}$$

or

$$Q = 6 - 6e^{-4t}\cos 3t - 8e^{-4t}\sin 3t$$

and

$$i(t) = \frac{dq}{dt} = 50e^{-4t}\sin 3t \quad \text{A}$$

21.80 Repeat Prob. 21.79 if $E = 50\sin 3t$.

❚ Proceeding as in Prob. 21.79, we have

$$Q(s)(s^2 + 8s + 25) = \frac{150}{s^2 + 9}$$

or

$$Q(s) = \frac{150}{(s^2 + 9)(s^2 + 8s + 25)}$$

$$= \frac{75}{26}\frac{1}{s^2 + 9} - \frac{75}{52}\frac{s}{s^2 + 9} + \frac{75}{26}\frac{1}{(s+4)^2 + 9} + \frac{75}{52}\frac{s+4}{(s+4)^2 + 9}$$

Thus,

$$q(t) = \tfrac{25}{52}(2\sin 3t - 3\cos 3t) + \tfrac{25}{52}e^{-4t}(3\cos 3t + 2\sin 3t)$$

and

$$i(t) = \frac{dq}{dt} = \frac{75}{52}(2\cos 3t + 3\sin 3t) - \frac{25}{52}e^{-4t}(17\sin 3t + 6\cos 3t)$$

21.81 The mesh currents in an electric circuit are given by

$$-5i_1 - \frac{di_1}{dt} + 2\frac{di_2}{dt} + 10i_2 = 0 \qquad \frac{di_1}{dt} + 20i_1 + 15i_2 = 55$$

The initial conditions are $i_1(0_+) = i_2(0_+) = 0$. Determine i_2.

❚ Transforming and applying the initial conditions yields

$$I_1(s)(s+5) - I_2(s)(2s+10) = 0 \qquad I_1(s)(s+20) + 15I_2(s) = \frac{55}{s}$$

Solving for $I_2(s)$:

$$I_2(s) = \frac{55}{s(2s+55)} = \frac{1}{s} - \frac{2}{2s+55} \qquad \text{or} \qquad i_2(t) = 1 - e^{-55t/2} \qquad \text{A}$$

21.82 The current in a circuit is given by

$$2\frac{d^2i}{dt^2} + 8i = 4\cos\omega t = v(t)$$

Determine $i(t)$ if the initial conditions are $i(0_+) = 10\,\text{A}$ and $di/dt(0_+) = 0$.

❚ In the transform domain, with the given initial conditions, we have

$$2[s^2I(s) - 10s - 0] + 8I(s) = \frac{4s}{s^2+\omega^2} \qquad (1)$$

or

$$I(s) = \frac{10s}{s^2+4} + \frac{2}{\omega^2-4}\left(\frac{s}{s^2+4} - \frac{s}{s^2+\omega^2}\right) \qquad \omega^2 \neq 4$$

Thus,

$$i(t) = 10\cos 2t + \frac{2}{(\omega^2-4)}(\cos 2t - \cos\omega t)$$

21.83 Repeat Prob. 21.82 for $\omega^2 = 4$, and explain its significance.

❚ From (1) of Prob. 21.82 we have

$$I(s) = \frac{10s}{s^2+4} + \frac{2s}{(s^2+4)^2} \qquad \text{and} \qquad i(t) = 10\cos 2t + \tfrac{1}{4}t\sin 2t$$

$\omega = 2$ is the resonance frequency.

21.84 Repeat Prob. 21.82 if $v(t) = u(t-a)$.

❚ In the transformed domain:

$$2[s^2I(s) - 10s] + 8I(s) = \frac{e^{-as}}{s} \qquad \text{or} \qquad I(s) = \frac{10s}{s^2+4} + \frac{e^{-as}}{8}\left(\frac{1}{s} - \frac{s}{s^2+4}\right)$$

Thus,

$$i(t) = \begin{cases} 10\cos 2t + \tfrac{1}{8}[1 - \cos 2(t-a)] & t > a \\ 10\cos 2t & t < a \end{cases}$$

21.85 Repeat Prob. 21.82 if $v(t) = \delta(t)$.

❚ In this case we have

$$2[s^2I(s) - 10s] + 8i(s) = 1 \qquad \text{or} \qquad I(s) = \frac{10s}{s^2+4} + \frac{1}{2(s^2+4)}$$

Thus,

$$i(t) = 10\cos 2t + \tfrac{1}{4}\sin 2t$$

21.86 Find the Laplace transform of the rectangular pulse shown in Fig. 21-22a.

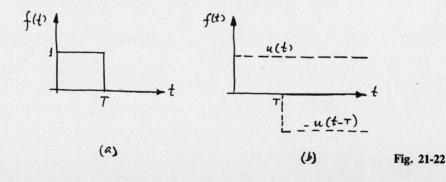

(a)   (b)   **Fig. 21-22**

❚ The given pulse may be synthesized as $f(t) = u(t) - u(t - T)$, as shown in Fig. 21-22b. Then

$$F(s) = \mathcal{L}[u(t) - u(t - T)] = \frac{1}{s} - \frac{1}{s} e^{-Ts} = \frac{1 - e^{-Ts}}{s}$$

21.87   Solve Prob. 21.86 by applying differentiation and shifting theorems.

❚ Differentiating the pulse with respect to t gives the two impulses shown in Fig. 21-23, whose Laplace transform is $1 - e^{-Ts}$.   Hence,

$$\mathcal{L}\left[\frac{d}{dt} f(t)\right] = sF(s) - f(0_+) = 1 - e^{-Ts} \quad \text{or} \quad F(s) = \frac{1 - e^{-Ts}}{s} \quad \text{since} \quad f(0_+) = 0$$

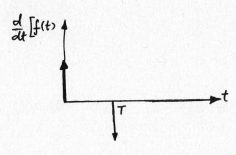

Fig. 21-23

21.88   Find and compare the Laplace transforms of the following two functions:

$$g_1(t) = e^{-a(t-T)}u(t - T) \qquad g_2(t) = e^{-at}u(t - T)$$

where T is positive.

The two signals are depicted in Fig. 21-24.   It is important to note that although $g_1(t)$ is the exponential function e^{-at} delayed at T, $g_2(t)$ does not involve any shifting; it is simply the signal e^{-at} multiplied by the delayed unit step $u(t - T)$.   Thus $g_2(t) = 0$ for $t < T$.   The Laplace transform of $g_1(t)$ is obtained by direct application of the shifting theorem.   Since the Laplace transform of e^{-at} is $1/(s + a)$, the Laplace transform of the shifted e^{-at} is

$$G_1(s) = \frac{1}{s + a} e^{-Ts}$$

The signal $g_2(t)$ may be formed by first shifting $e^{-at}u(t)$ to the left by T, multiplying it by $u(t)$, and then shifting it back by T.   This process is illustrated in Fig. 21-24c to e.   The Laplace transform of $e^{-a(t+T)}u(t)$ is

$$\mathcal{L}[e^{-a(t+T)}u(t)] = e^{-aT}\mathcal{L}[e^{-at}u(t)] = e^{-aT}\frac{1}{s + a}$$

Now shifting the function $e^{-a(t+T)}u(t)$ to the right by T gives

$$G_2(s) = \mathcal{L}[g_2(t)] = \mathcal{L}[e^{-at}u(t - T)] = \frac{e^{-aT}}{s + a} e^{-Ts} \tag{1}$$

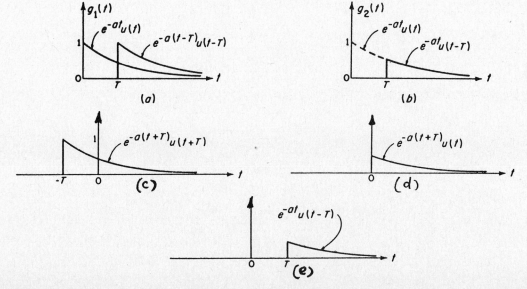

Fig. 21-24

21.89 Verify (1) of Prob. 21.88 by using (1) of Prob. 21.1.

▮ The result can be verified by substituting $g_2(t)$ directly in the Laplace transform integral.

$$G_2(s) = \mathscr{L}[g_2(t)] = \int_{0^-}^{\infty} e^{-at} u(t-T) e^{-st}\, dt = \int_{T^-}^{\infty} e^{-at} e^{-st}\, dt = \left[-\frac{1}{s+a} e^{-(s+a)t} \right]_{T^-}^{\infty} = \frac{e^{-aT}}{s+a} e^{-Ts}$$

21.90 Determine the Laplace transform of the triangular pulse shown in Fig. 21-25a.

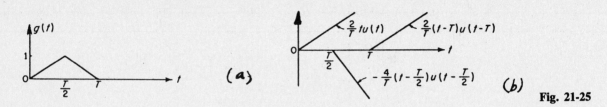

Fig. 21-25

▮ The triangular pulse is considered to be the sum of three ramp functions as shown in Fig. 21-25b. The expression for the pulse signal is given by

$$g(t) = \frac{2}{T} t u(t) - \frac{4}{T} \left(t - \frac{T}{2} \right) u\left(t - \frac{T}{2} \right) + \frac{2}{T} (t - T) u(t - T)$$

Taking the Laplace transform on both sides of the last equation, we get

$$G(s) = \frac{2}{Ts^2} - \frac{4}{Ts^2} e^{-Ts/2} + \frac{2}{Ts^2} e^{-Ts} = \frac{2}{Ts^2} (1 - 2e^{-Ts/2} + e^{-Ts}) \tag{1}$$

21.91 Obtain the Laplace transform of the pulse of Fig. 21-25a by differentiation.

▮ We take the derivative of the original pulse signal with respect to t successively until impulses occur. The first and the second derivatives of $g(t)$ are shown in Fig. 21-26b and c.

The Laplace transform of $d^2 g(t)/dt^2$, as obtained by inspection, is

$$\mathscr{L}\left[\frac{d^2 g(t)}{dt^2} \right] = \frac{2}{T} (1 - 2e^{-Ts/2} + e^{-Ts})$$

Using the derivative theorem, we write

$$\mathscr{L}\left[\frac{d^2 g(t)}{dt^2} \right] = s^2 G(s) - s g(0_-) - g^{(1)}(0_-) = \frac{2}{T} (1 - 2e^{-Ts/2} + e^{-Ts})$$

Solving for $G(s)$ from this equation gives the same result as in (1) of Prob. 21.90, since $g(0_-)$ and $g^{(1)}(0_-)$ are zero in this case.

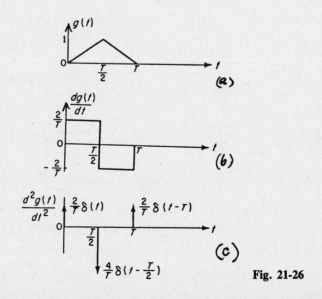

Fig. 21-26

21.92 Find the Laplace transform of the periodic signal shown in Fig. 21-27.

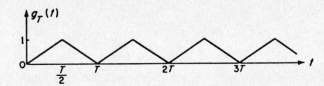

Fig. 21-27

▌ We notice that the waveform of this periodic signal during one period is described by the triangular pulse in Fig. 21-25, whose Laplace transform is given by (1) of Prob. 21.90. Therefore from line 2 of Table 21.2 of Prob. 21.25 we have

$$G_T(s) = \frac{1}{1 - e^{-Ts}} \left[\frac{2}{Ts^2} (1 - 2e^{-Ts/2} + e^{-Ts}) \right] = \frac{2}{Ts^2} \frac{1 - e^{-Ts/2}}{1 + e^{-Ts/2}}$$

21.93 Determine the Laplace transform of the unit impulse train shown in Fig. 21-28.

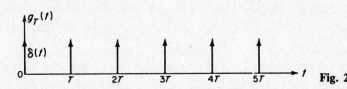

Fig. 21-28

▌ The Laplace transform of $g(t)$ for $0 \le t < T$ is $\mathcal{L}[\delta(t)] = 1$. Thus from Table 21.2 we obtain

$$G_T(s) = \frac{1}{1 - e^{-Ts}}$$

21.94 Find the Laplace transform of the train of pulses shown in Fig. 21-29.

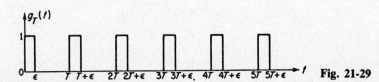

Fig. 21-29

▌ Proceeding as in the last two problems,

$$G(s) = \frac{1 - e^{-\epsilon s}}{s} \quad \text{and} \quad G_T(s) = \frac{1 - e^{-\epsilon s}}{s(1 - e^{-Ts})}$$

21.95 Given: $\ddot{x} + 3\dot{x} + 2x = 3$, $\dot{x}(0_+) = 0$, and $x(0_+) = -1$. Solve for $x(t)$.

▌ In the transformed domain:

$$s^2 X(s) - sx(0_+) - \dot{x}(0_+) + 3sX(s) - 3x(0_+) + 2X(s) = 3/s$$

or
$$X(t) = (\tfrac{3}{2} - 5e^{-t} + \tfrac{5}{2}e^{-2t})u(t)$$

21.96 For the network shown in Fig. 21-30, write the general mesh equations (in terms of symbols) including all initial conditions.

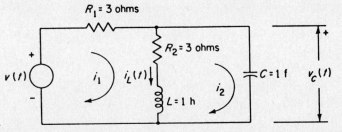

Fig. 21-30

❙ The required equations are

$$v(t) = (R_1 + R_2)i_1(t) + L\frac{di_1(t)}{dt} - R_2 i_2(t) - L\frac{di_2(t)}{dt}$$

$$0 = -R_2 i_1(t) - L\frac{di_1(t)}{dt} + R_2 i_2(t) + L\frac{di_2(t)}{dt} + \frac{1}{C}\int_{0^+}^{t} i_2(\tau)\,d\tau + v_c(0_+)$$

21.97 Write the transformed equations corresponding to the general equations of Prob. 21.96.

❙ Taking the Laplace transform of both sides of the loop equations, we get

$$V(s) = (R_1 + R_2)I_1(s) + LsI_1(s) - Li_1(0_+) - R_2 I_2(s) - LsI_2(s) + Li_2(0_+)$$

$$0 = -R_2 I_1(s) - LsI_1(s) + Li_1(0_+) + R_2 I_2(s) + LsI_2(s) - Li_2(0_+) + \frac{1}{Cs}I_2(s) + \frac{v_c(0_+)}{s}$$

Rearranging terms, these equations become

$$V(s) + L[i_1(0_+) - i_2(0_+)] = (R_1 + R_2 + Ls)I_1(s) - (R_2 + Ls)I_2(s)$$

$$- L[i_1(0_+) - i_2(0_+)] - \frac{v_c(0_+)}{s} = -(R_2 + Ls)I_1(s) + \left(R_2 + Ls + \frac{1}{Cs}\right)I_2(s)$$

21.98 Substitute the numerical values from the circuit of Fig. 21-30 in the transformed equations of Prob. 21.97. Solve for $i_1(t)$ in terms of $v = Vu(t)$ and the unknown initial conditions.

❙ Substituting the values of the network parameters in the transformed equations, we get

$$V(s) + i_L(0_+) = (s + 6)I_1(s) - (s + 3)I_2(s) \tag{1}$$

$$-i_L(0_+) - \frac{v_c(0_+)}{s} = -(s + 3)I_1(s) + \left(s + 3 + \frac{1}{s}\right)I_2(s) \tag{2}$$

where $i_1(0_+) - i_2(0_+)$ has been replaced by $i_L(0_+)$, which is the initial current in the inductor L. Solving for $I_1(s)$ from (1) and (2) yields

$$I_1(s) = \frac{[V(s) + i_L(0_+)](s + 3 + 1/s) + (s + 3)[-i_L(0_+) - v_C(0_+)/s]}{(s + 6)(s + 3 + 1/s) - (s + 3)^2}$$

$$= \frac{[V(s) + i_L(0_+)](s^2 + 3s + 1) + (s + 3)[-i_L(0_+)s - v_C(0_+)]}{3s^2 + 10s + 6}$$

Taking the inverse transform of $I_1(s)$ finally gives

$$i_1(t) = \frac{V}{6}u(t) + [0.178V + 0.19i_L(0_+) - 0.42v_C(0_+)]e^{-0.788t}u(t)$$

$$+ [-0.012V - 0.19i_L(0_+) + 0.087v_C(0_+)e^{-2.54t}]u(t)$$

21.99 Find the voltage across the capacitor of the circuit of Fig. 21-30.

❙ From (1) and (2) of Prob. 21.98 we have

$$I_2(s) = \frac{(s + 6)[-i_L(0_+)s - v_C(0_+)] + s(s + 3)[V(s) + i_L(0_+)]}{3s^2 + 10s + 6}$$

Taking the inverse transform yields

$$i_2(t) = [0.42V + 0.45i_L(0_+) - 0.99v_C(0_+)e^{-0.788t}]u(t)$$

$$+ [-0.087V - 1.45i_L(0_+) + 0.657v_C(0_+)e^{-2.54t}]u(t) \tag{1}$$

The voltage across the capacitor for $t \geq 0$ can be obtained from

$$v_C(t) = \frac{1}{C}\int_{0^+}^{t} i_2(\tau)\,d\tau + v_C(0_+) \tag{2}$$

Substituting $i_2(t)$ from (1) in (2):

$$v_C(t) = 0.5Vu(t) + [-0.534V - 0.57i_L(0_+) + 1.25v_C(0_+)]e^{-0.788t}u(t)$$

$$+ [0.034V + 0.57i_L(0_+) - 0.25v_C(0_+)]e^{-2.54t}u(t)$$

21.100 Write the loop equations for the transformer shown in Fig. 21-31a. Obtain the transformed equations and the corresponding equivalent circuit.

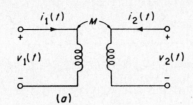

(a)

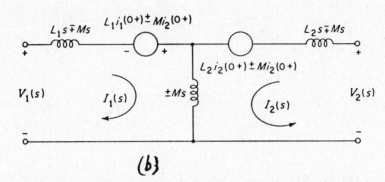

(b)

Fig. 21-31

▌ For the transformer circuit shown, the loop equations in the time domain are

$$v_1(t) = L_1 \frac{di_1(t)}{dt} \pm M \frac{di_2(t)}{dt} \qquad v_2(t) = \pm M \frac{di_1(t)}{dt} + L_2 \frac{di_2(t)}{dt}$$

Taking the Laplace transforms of this set of equations, we get

$$V_1(s) = L_1 s I_1(s) \pm M s I_2(s) - L_1 i_1(0_+) \mp M i_2(0_+)$$
$$V_2(s) = \pm M s I_1(s) + L_2 s I_2(s) - L_2 i_2(0_+) \mp M i_1(0_+)$$

where plus and minus signs are used in front of M to indicate variations in winding orientations of the transformer. The two transform equations are represented by the circuit of Fig. 21-31b.

21.101 Let $\Gamma \equiv 1/L$. Write the node equations for the transformer of Fig. 21-31a, in the time domain and in the s domain. Obtain an equivalent circuit in the s domain.

▌ The node equations are

$$i_1(t) = \Gamma_1 \int_{0_+}^{t} v_1(\tau)\, d\tau \mp \Gamma_M \int_{0_+}^{t} v_2(\tau)\, d\tau + i_1(0_+)$$

$$i_2(t) = \mp \Gamma_M \int_{0_+}^{t} v_1(\tau)\, d\tau + \Gamma_2 \int_{0_+}^{t} v_2(\tau)\, d\tau + i_2(0_+)$$

Taking the Laplace transforms on both sides of these equations, we get

$$I_1(s) = \frac{\Gamma_1 V_1(s)}{s} \mp \frac{\Gamma_M V_2(s)}{s} + \frac{i_1(0^+)}{s} \qquad I_2(s) = \mp \frac{\Gamma_M V_1(s)}{s} + \frac{\Gamma_2 V_2(s)}{s} + \frac{i_2(0_+)}{s}$$

The corresponding transform network is shown in Fig. 21-32.

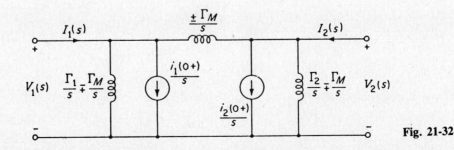

Fig. 21-32

21.102 Find the transform network in loop form for the network shown in Fig. 21-33a.

❙ See Fig. 21-33b.

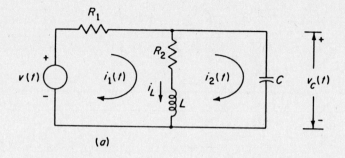

(a)

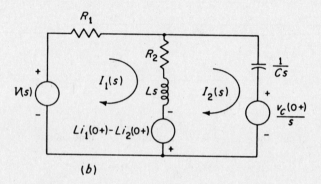

(b)

Fig. 21-33

21.103 Repeat Problem 21.102 to obtain the transform network in node form.

❙ See Fig. 21-34.

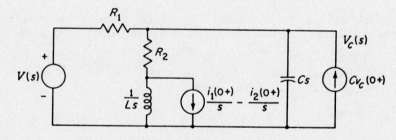

Fig. 21-34

21.104 In the network of Fig. 21-35a, S is switched from a neutral position to position a at $t = 0$. At $t = T$, S is moved from a to b. Obtain transform networks corresponding to these switching operations.

❙ See Fig. 21-35b and c.

21.105 Find $i_L(t)$ in the circuit of Fig. 21-35a.

❙ From Fig. 21-35b:

$$LsI_L(s) = \frac{V}{s} - R_1 I_L(s) + Li_L(0_+)$$

Solving for $I_L(s)$, and since $i_L(0_+)$ is zero, we get

$$I_L(s) = \frac{V}{R_1 s(1 + Ls/R_1)}$$

The inverse Laplace transform of $I_L(s)$ is

$$i_L(t) = \frac{V}{R_1}(1 - e^{-R_1 t/L}) \qquad 0 \le t < T \tag{1}$$

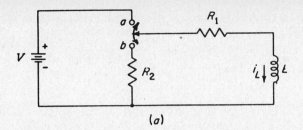

(a)

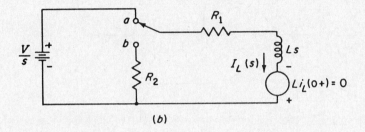

(b)

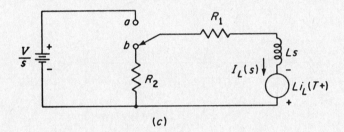

(c)

Fig. 21-35

At $t = T^+$, the switch is moved from position a to position b. Substituting $t = T^+$ in (1) yields

$$i_L(T^+) = \frac{V}{R_1} (1 - e^{-R_1 T^+/L})$$

which is the initial inductor current at $t = T^+$. Now the transform equivalent network for $t > T$ is shown in Fig. 21-35c. Notice that the equivalent-voltage source has a voltage strength of $Li_L(T^+)$, which corresponds to an impulse in the time domain. The state-transition equation of the network for $t > T$ is written from Fig. 21-35c.

$$LsI_L(s) = Li_L(T^+) - (R_1 + R_2)I_L(s) = \frac{VL}{R_1} (1 - e^{-R_1 T^+/L}) - (R_1 + R_2)I_L(s)$$

Solving for $I_L(s)$,

$$I_L(s) = \frac{V}{R_1} (1 - e^{-R_1 T^+/L}) \frac{1}{s + (R_1 + R_2)/L}$$

The inverse Laplace transform of $I_L(s)$ is

$$i_L(t) = \frac{V}{R_1} (1 - e^{-R_1 T^+/L}) e^{-(R_1 + R_2)(t-T)/L} \qquad t > T$$

21.106 Sketch the complete waveform for $i_L(t)$ for $t > 0$.

❙ See Fig. 21-36.

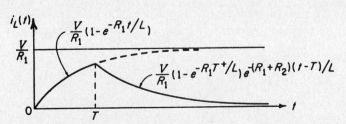

Fig. 21-36

21.107 In the network of Fig. 21-37a, S_1 is closed at $t = 0$, with $v_C(0_+) = 0$. After S_1 is closed for T seconds, S_2 is closed. Corresponding to this switching, obtain the transformed equivalent circuit.

∎ See Fig. 21-37b and c.

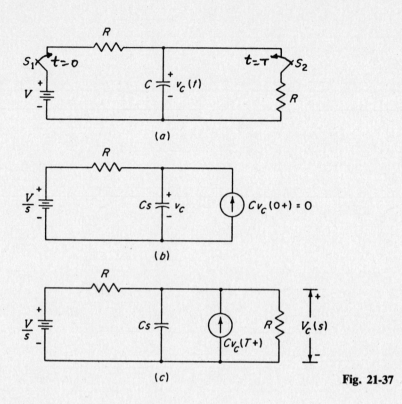

(a)

(b)

(c)

Fig. 21-37

21.108 Find $v_C(t)$ in the circuit of Fig. 21-37a.

∎ From Fig. 21-37b we have

$$CsV_C(s) = \frac{V}{Rs} - \frac{V_C(s)}{R} + Cv_C(0_+)$$

Solving for $V_C(s)$ from this expression, and since $v_C(0_+)$ is zero, we have

$$V_C(s) = \frac{V}{s(1 + RCs)}$$

The inverse transform of $V_C(s)$ is, simply,

$$v_C(t) = V(1 - e^{-t/RC}) \qquad 0 < t < T \tag{1}$$

Thus the capacitor voltage rises exponentially toward V volts with a time constant of RC. At $t = T$ seconds, the switch S_2 is closed, and S_1 remains closed. The transform network for $t > T$ is shown in Fig. 21-37c. The initial voltage on the capacitor at $t = T^+$ is obtained by substituting $t = T^+$ in (1); then we have

$$v_C(T^+) = V(1 - e^{-T^+/RC}) \tag{2}$$

For $t > T$, from Fig. 21-37c, we obtain

$$CsV_C(s) = \frac{V}{Rs} - \frac{V_C(s)}{R} - \frac{V_C(s)}{R} + Cv_C(T^+)$$

Solving for $V_C(s)$ from this expression, we get

$$V_C(s) = \frac{V}{2s(1 + RCs/2)} + \frac{v_C(T^+)}{(s + 2/RC)} \tag{3}$$

The inverse transform of $V_C(s)$ is

$$v_C(t) = \left[\frac{V}{2} \left(1 - e^{-2(t-T)/RC}\right) + v_C(T^+)e^{-2(t-T)/RC} \right] u(t - T) \qquad (4)$$

where $v_C(T^+)$ is defined in (2). When t approaches infinity, $v_C(t)$ approaches $V/2$. This result may be obtained by letting t approach infinity in (4) or by applying the final-value theorem to (3). Substituting $v_C(T^+)$ from (2) in (4) and simplifying, we have

$$v_C(t) = \left[\frac{V}{2} + V\left(\frac{1}{2} - e^{-T/RC}\right)e^{-2(t-T)/RC} \right] u(t - T)$$

21.109 Sketch $v_C(t)$ for $e^{-T/RC} > \frac{1}{2}$ and for $e^{-T/RC} < \frac{1}{2}$.

▮ See Fig. 21-38.

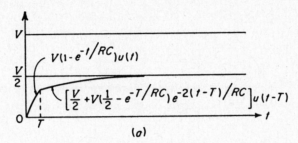

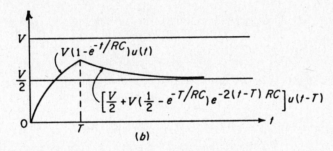

Fig. 21-38

21.110 For the network shown in Fig. 21-39a, obtain the transform network.

▮ See Fig. 21-39b.

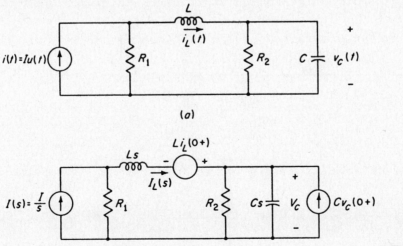

Fig. 21-39

21.111 For a step input I, determine the voltage across the capacitor of the circuit of Fig. 21-39b.

▮ The circuit is in the s domain. Thus,

$$LsI_L(s) = [I(s) - I_L(s)] R_1 + Li_L(0_-) - V_C(s) \qquad (1)$$

Next, the current in the capacitor is equated with the difference between $I_L(s) + Cv_C(0_+)$ and the current through R_2. Thus

$$CsV_C(s) = I_L(s) + Cv_C(0_+) - \frac{V_C(s)}{R_2} \tag{2}$$

Solving for $V_C(s)$ in (1) and (2), we get

$$V_C(s) = \frac{R_1 I(s) + (R_1 + Ls)Cv_C(0_+) + Li_L(0_+)}{1 + (R_1 + Ls)(Cs + 1/R_2)} \tag{3}$$

For a step-function input, $I(s) = I/s$; (3) becomes

$$V_C(s) = \frac{IR_1 + s(R_1 + Ls)Cv_C(0_+) + Lsi_L(0_+)}{s[LCs^2 + (R_1C + L/R_2)s + 1 + R_1/R_2]}$$

21.112 Obtain the steady-state voltage across the capacitor of the circuit of Prob. 21.111, and show that the result is independent of initial conditions.

❚ By the final-value theorem:

$$\lim_{t \to \infty} v_C(t) = \lim_{s \to 0} sV_C(s) = \lim_{s \to 0} \frac{IR_1 + s(R_1 + Ls)Cv_C(0_+) + sLi_L(0_+)}{LCs^2 + (R_1C + L/R_2)s + 1 + R_1/R_2} = \frac{R_1R_2}{R_1 + R_2} I$$

which is independent of $v_C(0_+)$ and $i_L(0_+)$.

21.113 Verify that the result of Prob. 21.112 can be directly obtained from the circuit of Fig. 21-39a.

❚ In the steady state, the inductor acts as a short circuit and the capacitor acts as an open circuit; thus the current $i(t)$ is divided between R_1 and R_2. We easily observe that

$$\lim_{t \to \infty} v_C(t) = \frac{R_1R_2}{R_1 + R_2} I$$

21.114 Obtain the s-domain circuit corresponding to the circuit of Fig. 21-40a.

❚ See Fig. 21-40b.

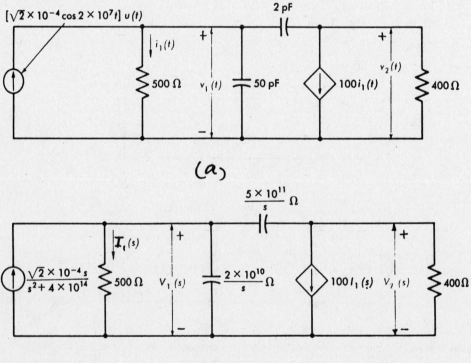

(a)

(b)

Fig. 21-40

21.115 Determine $V_2(s)$ in the circuit of Fig. 21-40b.

▮ From Fig. 21-40b, with zero initial conditions,

$$\frac{V_1(s)}{500} + 50 \times 10^{-12}sV_1(s) + 2 \times 10^{-12}s[V_1(s) - V_2(s)] - \frac{\sqrt{2} \times 10^{-4}s}{s^2 + 4 \times 10^{14}} = 0$$

$$2 \times 10^{-12}s[V_2(s) - V_1(s)] + \frac{V_2(s)}{400} + 100I_1(s) = 0$$

The constraint equation for the dependent source is

$$I_1(s) = V_1(s)/500$$

Combination of the three equations yields

$$V_1(s)(2 \times 10^{-3} + 52 \times 10^{-12}s) - V_2(s)(2 \times 10^{-12}s) = \frac{\sqrt{2} \times 10^{-4}s}{s^2 + 4 \times 10^{14}}$$

$$-V_1(s)(2 \times 10^{-12}s - 0.2) + V_2(s)(2.5 \times 10^{-3} + 2 \times 10^{-12}s) = 0$$

The third step is to obtain the simultaneous solution for $V_2(s)$, which, after rearrangement of terms, is

$$V_2(s) = \frac{2\sqrt{2} \times 10^6(s - 10^{11})}{(s^2 + 4 \times 10^{14})(s^2 + 53.4 \times 10^8 s + 5 \times 10^{16})} \tag{1}$$

21.116 Obtain the partial fraction of $V_2(s)$ in (1) of Prob. 21.115. Hence determine $v_2(t)$.

▮ From (1) of Prob. 21.115 we have

$$V_2(s) = \frac{2\sqrt{2} \times 10^6 s(s - 10^{11})}{(s - j2 \times 10^7)(s + j2 \times 10^7)(s + 0.94 \times 10^7)(s + 53.3 \times 10^8)}$$

$$= \frac{K_1}{s - j2 \times 10^7} + \frac{K_1^*}{s + j2 \times 10^7} + \frac{K_2}{s + 0.94 \times 10^7} + \frac{K_3}{s + 53.3 \times 10^8}$$

Solving for K_1, K_2, and K_3 yields,

$$K_1 = 1.20 \underline{/-245°} \qquad K_2 = 1.022 \qquad K_3 = -0.0105$$

or

$$v_2(t) = [2.40 \cos(2 \times 10^7 t - 245°) + 1.022\epsilon^{-0.94 \times 10^7 t} - 0.0105\epsilon^{-53.3 \times 10^8 t}]u(t)$$

21.117 Obtain the transformed network for the circuit shown in Fig. 21-41a.

▮ See Fig. 21-41b.

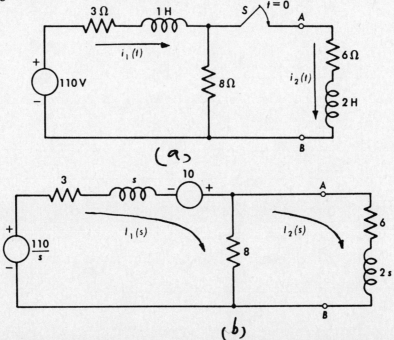

Fig. 21-41

21.118 Determine the current $i_1(t)$ in the circuit of Fig. 21-41a.

▌ With the initial condition $i_1(0_+) = 110 (3 + 8) = 10$ A, the mesh equations are

$$-\frac{110}{s} + (3 + s)I_1(s) - 10 + 8[I_1(s) - I_2(s)] = 0 \qquad -8[I_1(s) - I_2(s)] + (6 + 2s)I_2(s) = 0$$

Rearrangement of terms gives

$$I_1(s)(11 + s) - 8I_2(s) = \frac{110}{s} + 10 \qquad -8I_1(s) + I_2(s)(14 + 2s) = 0$$

After simultaneous solution and factoring,

$$I_1(s) = \frac{10(s + 11)(s + 7)}{s(s + 3)(s + 15)} = \frac{154}{9}\frac{1}{s} - \frac{80}{9}\frac{1}{s + 3} + \frac{16}{9}\frac{1}{s + 15}$$

or

$$i_1(t) = \frac{154}{9} - \frac{80}{9}e^{-3t} + \frac{16}{9}e^{-15t} \qquad \text{A}$$

21.119 Determine $i_2(t)$ at $t = 0.1$ s in the circuit of Fig. 21-41a.

▌ From the mesh equations of Prob. 21.118 we have

$$I_2(s) = \frac{40(s + 11)}{s(s + 3)(s + 15)} = \frac{88}{9}\frac{1}{s} - \frac{80}{9}\frac{1}{s + 3} - \frac{8}{9}\frac{1}{s + 15}$$

Consequently, $\qquad\qquad i_2(t) = \frac{88}{9} - \frac{80}{9}e^{-3t} - \frac{8}{9}e^{-15t}$

or at $t = 0.1$ s $\qquad\qquad i_2(0.1) = 2.994$ A

21.120 Replace the circuit to the left of AB (Fig. 21-41) by its Thévenin equivalent and solve for $i_2(t)$.

▌ $V_{\text{Th}}(s)$ and $Z_{\text{Th}}(s)$ are found from Fig. 21-42a and b, respectively. Thus we obtain the Thévenin equivalent of the given circuit, as shown in Fig. 21-42c.

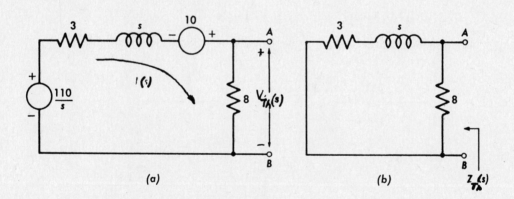

(a)   (b)

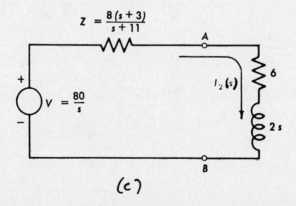

(c)

Fig. 21-42

❚ From Fig. 21-42*a* $V_{Th}(s) = I(s) \times 8$ and $-(110/s) + (3 + s)I(s) - 10 + 8I(s) = 0$

from which

$$I(s) = \frac{(110/s) + 10}{11 + s}$$

and, after rearrangement,

$$V_{Th}(s) = \frac{80(s + 11)}{s(s + 11)} = \frac{80}{s}$$

The Thévenin impedance is computed from the circuit of Fig. 21-42*b* as the parallel combination of the 8-Ω resistance and the $(3 + s)$-Ω impedance.

$$Z_{Th}(s) = \frac{8(3 + s)}{8 + 3 + s} = \frac{8(3 + s)}{11 + s}$$

Finally, from Fig. 21-42*c*:

$$I_2(s) = \frac{80/s}{[8(3 + s)/(11 + s)] + (6 + 2s)} = \frac{40(s + 11)}{s(s^2 + 18s + 45)}$$

Upon factoring,

$$I_2(s) = \frac{40(s + 11)}{s(s + 3)(s + 15)}$$

which is the same result as obtained in Prob. 21.119.   Thus,

$$i_2(t) = \tfrac{88}{9} - \tfrac{80}{9}\epsilon^{-3t} - \tfrac{8}{9}\epsilon^{-15t}$$

21.121   The current in a transformed circuit is given by

$$I(s) = \frac{s^2 + 6s + 5}{s(s^2 + 4s + 5)})$$

Find $i(t)$.

❚ $$I(s) = \frac{s^2 + 6s + 5}{s(s + 2 + j1)(s + 2 - j1)} = \frac{1}{s} + \frac{-j}{s + 2 - j1} + \frac{j}{s + 2 + j1}$$

or

$$i(t) = 1 + 2e^{-2t} \sin t$$

21.122   A $\frac{1}{2}$-F capacitor initially charged to 1 V is discharged at $t = 0$ across a coil having $R = 2 \Omega$ and $L = 1$ H. Determine $i(t)$ for $t > 0$.

❚   By KVL:

$$\frac{di}{dt} + 2i + 2 \int_{-\infty}^{t} i \, dt = 0$$

or

$$[sI(s) - i(0_+)] + 2I(s) + \frac{2}{s} [I(s) + q(0_+)] = 0$$

Since the capacitor was initially charged to 1 V,

$$\frac{2q(0_+)}{s} = -\frac{1}{s}$$

Thus,

$$I(s) = \frac{1}{s^2 + 2s + 2} = \frac{1}{(s + 1)^2 + 1} \quad \text{or} \quad i(t) = e^{-t} \sin t \, u(t)$$

21.123   For a transformed network we have

$$(s + 20)I_1(s) - 10I_2(s) = \frac{100}{s} \qquad -10I_1(s) + (s + 20)I_2(s) = 0$$

Determine $i_2(t)$ at $t = 0.1$ s.

❚   Solving for $I_2(s)$ yields

$$I_2(s) = \frac{1000}{s(s^2 + 40s + 300)} = \frac{1000}{s(s + 10)(s + 30)} = \frac{3.33}{s} - \frac{5}{s + 10} + \frac{1.67}{s + 30}$$

or

$$i_2(t) = 3.33 - 5e^{-10t} + 1.67e^{-30t} \quad \text{A}$$

At $t = 0.1$ s

$$i_2(0.1) = 1.574 \text{ A}$$

21.124   The capacitor in the circuit of Fig. 21-43*a* is charged to 10 V.   Obtain the transformed network.

❚   See Fig. 21-43*b*.

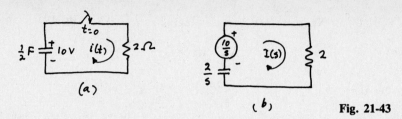

Fig. 21-43

21.125 Determine the current $i(t)$ in the circuit of Fig. 21-43a.

▌ From Fig. 21-43b:

$$I(s) = \frac{10}{s[2 + (2/s)]} = \frac{10}{2(s + 1)} \qquad \text{or} \qquad i(t) = 5e^{-t} \qquad \text{A}$$

21.126 In the circuit of Fig. 21-44a, the switch is moved from a to b at $t = 0$. Obtain the transformed network.

▌ See Fig. 21-44b.

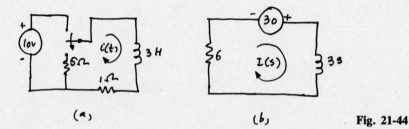

Fig. 21-44

21.127 Determine $i(t)$ in the circuit of Fig. 21-44a.

▌ From Fig. 21-44b: $\qquad I(s) = \dfrac{30}{3s + 6} = \dfrac{10}{s + 2} \qquad \text{or} \qquad i(t) = 10e^{-2t} \qquad$ A

21.128 Obtain the transformed circuit for the circuit of Fig. 21-45a.

▌ See Fig. 21-45b.

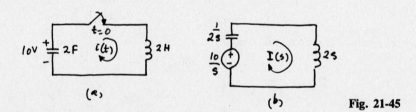

Fig. 21-45

21.129 Find $i(t)$ in the circuit of Fig. 21-45a.

▌ From Fig. 21-45b: $\qquad I(s) = \dfrac{10/s}{2s + (1/2s)} = \dfrac{10}{2(s^2 + \frac{1}{4})} \qquad \text{or} \qquad i(t) = 10 \sin t/2$

21.130 Find the transformed circuit for the circuit of Fig. 21-46a, where S is moved from a to b at $t = 0$.

▌ See Fig. 21-46b.

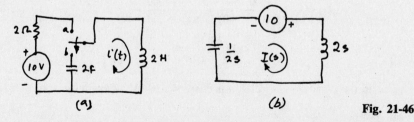

Fig. 21-46

21.131 Solve for $i(t)$ in the circuit of Fig. 21-46a.

$\blacksquare$ From Fig. 21-46b:
$$I(s) = \frac{10s}{2(s^2 + \frac{1}{4})} = \frac{5s}{s^2 + \frac{1}{4}} = \frac{5s}{s^2 + \frac{1}{4}}$$

Thus,
$$i(t) = 5 \cos{(t/2)} \quad \text{A}$$

21.132 Determine the transformed circuit corresponding to that shown in Fig. 21-47a.

$\blacksquare$ See Fig. 21-47b.

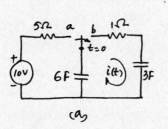 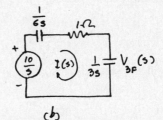

(a)   (b)   **Fig. 21-47**

21.133 Solve for $i(t)$ in the circuit of Fig. 21-47a in which the switch is moved from a to b at $t = 0$.

$\blacksquare$ From Fig. 21-47b:
$$I(s) = \frac{10}{s[1 + (1/6s) + (1/3s)]} = \frac{60}{6s + 3} = \frac{20}{2s + 1} = \frac{10}{s + \frac{1}{2}}$$
or
$$i(t) = 10e^{-t/2} \quad \text{A}$$

21.134 What is the voltage across the 3-F capacitor in the circuit of Prob. 21.133 at $t = 1$ s. Formulate the problem in the s domain.

$\blacksquare$
$$V_{3\,F}(s) = V(s) = \frac{I(s)}{3s} = \frac{20}{3s(2s + 1)} = \frac{20}{3}\left(\frac{1}{s} - \frac{2}{2s + 1}\right) \quad \text{or} \quad v(t) = \frac{20}{3}(1 - e^{-t/2})$$

At $t = 1$,
$$v(1) = 2.62 \text{ V}$$

21.135 Obtain the transformed circuit for that shown in Fig. 21-48a in which the 3-F capacitor is initially charged to 20 V, the 6-F capacitor to 10 V, and the switch is closed at $t = 0$.

$\blacksquare$ See Fig. 21-48b.

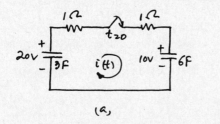 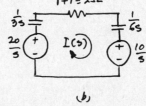

(a)   (b)   **Fig. 21-48**

21.136 Solve for $i(t)$ in the circuit of Prob. 21.135.

$\blacksquare$ From Fig. 21-48b
$$I(s) = \frac{20 - 10}{s[2 + (1/3s) + (1/6s)]} = \frac{20}{4s + 1} = \frac{5}{s + \frac{1}{4}}$$

Hence,
$$i(t) = 5e^{-t/4} \quad \text{A}$$

21.137 Determine the voltages on the capacitors at $t = 1s$.

$\blacksquare$
$$V_{3\,F}(s) = \frac{20}{s} - \frac{I(s)}{3s} = \frac{20}{s} - \frac{20}{3s(4s + 1)} = \frac{20}{s} - \frac{20}{3}\left(\frac{1}{s} - \frac{1}{s + \frac{1}{4}}\right) = \frac{40}{3s} + \frac{20}{3}\frac{1}{s + \frac{1}{4}}$$

or
$$v_{3\,F}(t) = \tfrac{40}{3} + \tfrac{20}{3}e^{-t/4}$$

At $t = 1s$, $\qquad\qquad\qquad\qquad v_{3F}(1) = 18.525 \text{ V}$

$$V_{6F}(s) = \frac{10}{s} + \frac{I(s)}{6s} = \frac{10}{s} + \frac{20}{6s(4s+1)} = \frac{10}{s} + \frac{10}{3}\left(\frac{1}{s} - \frac{4}{4s+1}\right) = \frac{40}{3s} - \frac{10}{3}\frac{1}{s + \frac{1}{4}}$$

or $\qquad\qquad\qquad\qquad v_{6F}(t) = \frac{40}{3} - \frac{10}{3}e^{-t/4}$

At $t = 1s$, $\qquad\qquad\qquad\qquad v_{6F}(1) = 10.737 \text{ V}$

21.138 At what instant will the voltages across the capacitors of the circuit of Fig. 21-48a be equal?

❙ Let T be the required time. Then, from Prob. 21.137, we must have

$$\tfrac{40}{3} + \tfrac{20}{3}e^{-T/4} = \tfrac{40}{3} - \tfrac{10}{3}e^{-T/4}$$

Obviously, this can happen at $T = \infty$.

21.139 At what instant will the voltage across the 3-F capacitor be one-and-a-half times the voltage across the 6-F capacitor?

❙ Let T be the required time. Then:

$$\tfrac{40}{3} + \tfrac{20}{3}e^{-T/4} = \tfrac{3}{2}\left(\tfrac{40}{3} - \tfrac{10}{3}e^{-T/4}\right) \qquad \text{or} \qquad \tfrac{35}{3}e^{-T/4} = \tfrac{20}{3}$$

Thus, $\qquad\qquad\qquad\qquad T = 2.24 \ s$

21.140 Obtain the transformed circuit corresponding to that shown in Fig. 21-49a, where S is moved from a to b at $t = 0$.

❙ See Fig. 21-49a.

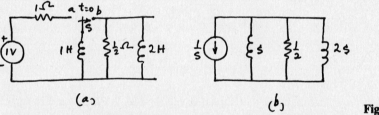

(a)

(b)

Fig. 21-49

21.141 Determine the voltage across the 2-H inductor in the circuit of Prob. 21.140.

❙ $\qquad V_{2H}(s) = -\dfrac{1}{s[(1.5/s) + 2]} = -\dfrac{1}{2(s + 0.75)} \qquad \text{or} \qquad v_{2H}(t) = -0.5e^{-0.75t} \qquad \text{V}$

21.142 The switch S is closed at $t = 0$ in the circuit of Fig. 21-50a. Obtain the transformed circuit.

❙ See Fig. 21-50b.

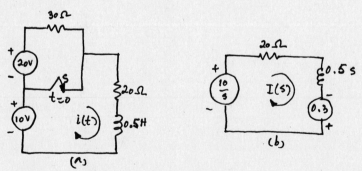

(a)

(b)

Fig. 21-50

21.143 Determine $i(t)$ in the circuit of Fig. 21-50a.

❙ $\qquad I(s) = \dfrac{0.3 + (10/s)}{0.5s + 20} = \dfrac{1}{2s} + \dfrac{1}{10(s + 40)} \qquad \text{or} \qquad i(t) = 0.5 + 0.1e^{-40t} \qquad \text{A}$

21.144 The current through a circuit is given by

$$I(s) = \frac{7s + 2}{s^3 + 3s^2 + 2s}$$

Find $i(t)$.

$\blacksquare$ $\quad I(s) = \frac{7s+2}{s(s+2)(s+1)} = \frac{1}{s} - \frac{6}{s+2} + \frac{5}{s+1}$ $\quad$ or $\quad i(t) = 1 - 6e^{-2t} + 5e^{-t}$ $\quad$ A

21.145 The current in a circuit is given by

$$I(s) = \frac{5s + 13}{s^2 + 5s + 6} \tag{1}$$

Find its value at $t = 0.5$ s.

$\blacksquare$ $\quad I(s) = \frac{5s+13}{(s+2)(s+3)} = \frac{3}{s+2} + \frac{2}{s+3}$

or $\quad i(t) = 3e^{-2t} + 2e^{-3t} \tag{2}$

At $t = 0.5$ s we have $i(0.5) = 1.55$ A.

21.146 What is the initial current in the circuit of Prob. 21.145? Solve the problem in the s domain as well as in the time domain.

$\blacksquare$ From (1) of Prob. 21.145, by the initial-value theorem:

$$i(0_+) = \lim_{s \to \infty} sI(s) = \lim_{s \to \infty} \frac{s(5s+13)}{s^2 + 5s + 6} = 5 \text{ A}$$

From (2) of Prob. 21.145:

$$i(0_+) = \lim_{t \to 0} 3e^{-2t} + 2e^{-3t} = 3 + 2 = 5 \text{ A}$$

21.147 The current in a circuit is given by

$$I(s) = \frac{2(s+1)}{s^2 + 1}$$

Find the instant when the current is (*a*) zero and (*b*) a maximum.

$\blacksquare$ $\quad I(s) = \frac{2(s+1)}{s^2+1} = \frac{2(s+1)}{(s+j)(s-j)} = \frac{1+j}{s+j} + \frac{1-j}{s-j}$

or $\quad i(t) = (1+j)e^{-jt} + (1-j)e^{jt} = 2\cos t + 2\sin t = 2\sqrt{2}\sin\left(t + \frac{\pi}{4}\right)$

(*a*) For $i = 0$ we must have $t = -\pi/4$ s or $3\pi/4$ s, etc.
(*b*) For $i = 2\sqrt{2}$ (or maximum) $t = \pi/4$ s.

21.148 The voltage across a circuit is given by

$$V(s) = \frac{(s+1)(s+3)}{s(s+2)(s+4)}$$

What is the voltage at $t = 0.1$ s?

$\blacksquare$ $\quad V(s) = \frac{(s+1)(s+3)}{s(s+2)(s+4)} = \frac{3}{8}\frac{1}{s} + \frac{1}{4}\frac{1}{s+2} + \frac{3}{8}\frac{1}{s+4}$ $\quad$ or $\quad v(t) = \frac{3}{8} + \frac{1}{4}e^{-2t} + \frac{3}{8}e^{-4t}$

At $t = 0.1$, $\quad v(0.1) = \frac{3}{8} + \frac{1}{4}e^{-0.2} + \frac{3}{8}e^{-0.4} = 0.831$ V

21.149 Determine the initial and final voltages across the circuit of Prob. 21.148.

$\blacksquare$ By the initial-value theorem:

$$v(0_+) = \lim_{s \to \infty} sV(s) = \lim_{s \to \infty} \frac{s(s+1)(s+3)}{s(s+2)(s+4)} = 1.0 \text{ V}$$

By the final-value theorem:

$$v(\infty) = \lim_{s \to 0} sV(s) = \lim_{s \to 0} \frac{s(s+1)(s+3)}{s(s+2)(s+4)} = \frac{3}{8} \text{ V}$$

21.150 Find $v(t)$ from $V(s) = [(s^2+1)(s^2+3)]/s[(s^2+2)(s^2+4)]$.

$$V(s) = \frac{3}{8}\frac{1}{s} + \frac{1}{8}\frac{1}{s+j\sqrt{2}} + \frac{1}{8}\frac{1}{s-j\sqrt{2}} + \frac{3}{16}\frac{1}{s+j2} + \frac{3}{16}\frac{1}{s-j2}$$

$$v(t) = \tfrac{3}{8} + \tfrac{1}{8}(e^{j\sqrt{2}t} + e^{-j\sqrt{2}t}) + \tfrac{3}{16}(e^{j2t} + e^{-j2t}) = \tfrac{3}{8} + \tfrac{1}{4}\cos\sqrt{2}t + \tfrac{3}{8}\cos 2t \quad \text{V}$$

21.151 Find $i(t)$ if $I(s) = 1/[s(s+1)^2(s+2)]$.

$$I(s) = \frac{1}{s(s+1)^2(s+2)} = \frac{1}{2}\frac{1}{s} - \frac{1}{(s+1)^2} - \frac{1}{2(s+2)}$$

or

$$i(t) = \tfrac{1}{2} - te^{-t} - \tfrac{1}{2}e^{-2t} \quad \text{A}$$

21.152 Find $v(t)$ if $V(s) = 3s/[(s^2+1)(s^2+4)]$.

$$V(s) = \frac{3s}{(s^2+1)(s^2+4)} = \frac{3s}{(s+j)(s-j)(s+j2)(s-j2)} = \frac{1}{2}\frac{1}{s+j} + \frac{1}{2}\frac{1}{s-j} - \frac{1}{2}\frac{1}{s+j2} - \frac{1}{2}\frac{1}{s-j2}$$

$$v(t) = \tfrac{1}{2}(e^{jt} + e^{-jt}) - \tfrac{1}{2}(e^{j2t} + e^{-j2t}) = \cos t - \cos 2t \quad \text{V}$$

21.153 The current in a circuit is given by

$$I(s) = \frac{1}{(s+1)(s+2)^2}$$

What is its value at $t = 0.25\,\text{s}$?

$$I(s) = \frac{1}{(s+1)(s+2)^2} = \frac{1}{s+1} - \frac{1}{(s+2)^2} - \frac{1}{s+2}$$

or

$$i(t) = e^{-t} - te^{-2t} - e^{-2t} = e^{-t} - e^{-2t}(1+t)$$

At $t = 0.25\,\text{s}$, $\qquad\qquad i(0.25) = 20\,\text{mA}$

21.154 The current in a circuit is given by

$$I(s) = \frac{s^2}{(s^2+1)^2}$$

At what instant does the current reach its maximum value?

$$I(s) = \frac{s^2}{(s^2+1)^2} = \frac{s^2}{(s+j)^2(s-j)^2} = \frac{1}{4}\frac{1}{(s+j)^2} + \frac{j}{4}\frac{1}{s+j} + \frac{1}{4}\frac{1}{(s-j)^2} - \frac{j}{4}\frac{1}{s-j}$$

$$i(t) = \frac{1}{4}(te^{-jt} + te^{jt}) + \frac{j}{4}(e^{-jt} - e^{jt}) = \frac{1}{2}t\cos t + \frac{1}{2}\sin t$$

For i_{max}, $di/dt = 0$ requires that

$$0 = \cos t - t\sin t + \cos t \qquad \text{or} \qquad \tan t = 2/t$$

Solving for t yields $t = 1.07\,\text{s}$.

21.155 In a circuit, the current is given by

$$I(s) = \frac{s^2 + 2s + 1}{(s+2)(s^2+4)}$$

What is the value of the current at $t = 0.5\,\text{s}$?

$$I(s) = \frac{s^2 + 2s + 1}{(s+2)(s^2+4)} = \frac{s^2 + 2s + 1}{(s+2)(s+j2)(s-j2)} = \frac{1}{8}\frac{1}{s+2} + \frac{7}{8}\frac{s}{s^2+4} + \frac{1}{4}\frac{1}{s^2+4}$$

or

$$i(t) = \tfrac{1}{8}e^{-2t} + \tfrac{7}{8}\cos 2t + \tfrac{1}{8}\sin 2t$$

At $t = 0.5\,\text{s}$, $\qquad i(0.5) = \tfrac{1}{8}e^{-1} + \tfrac{7}{8}\cos 1 + \tfrac{1}{8}\sin 1 = 0.624\,\text{A}$

21.156 The natural response of a circuit is given by

$$\frac{d^2i}{dt^2} + 3\frac{di}{dt} + 2i = 0$$

Determine $i(t)$ if the initial conditions are $i(0_+) = 1$ and $di/dt(0_+) = 0$.

▮ Taking the Laplace transform and using the initial conditions yields

$$(s^2 + 3s + 2)I(s) = s + 3 \qquad \text{or} \qquad I(s) = \frac{s+3}{(s+1)(s+2)} = \frac{2}{s+1} - \frac{1}{s+2}$$

Thus,
$$i(t) = 2e^{-t} - e^{-2t} \qquad \text{A}$$

21.157 Repeat Prob. 21.156 if the initial conditions are $i(0_+) = 2$ and $di/dt(0_+) = 1$.

▮ Proceeding as in Prob. 21.156 yields

$$(s^2 + 3s + 2)I(s) = 2s + 7 \qquad \text{or} \qquad I(s) = \frac{2s+7}{(s+1)(s+2)} = \frac{5}{s+1} - \frac{3}{s+2}$$

Thus,
$$i(t) = 5e^{-t} - 3e^{-2t} \qquad \text{A}$$

21.158 The current in a circuit is given by

$$\frac{d^2i}{dt^2} + 2\frac{di}{dt} + i = 0$$

The initial conditions are $i(0_+) = 1$ and $di/dt(0_+) = 0$. Find $i(t)$.

▮ In this case $I(s)$ is given by

$$I(s) = \frac{s+2}{s^2 + 2s + 1} = \frac{s+2}{(s+1)^2} = \frac{1}{s+1} + \frac{1}{(s+1)^2}$$

Thus,
$$i(t) = e^{-t}(1 + t) \qquad \text{A}$$

21.159 Repeat Prob. 21.158 for the initial conditions $i(0_+) = 2$ and $di/dt(0_+) = 1$.

▮
$$I(s) = \frac{2s+5}{(s+1)^2} = \frac{2}{s+1} + \frac{3}{(s+1)^2}$$

or
$$i(t) = e^{-t}(2 + 3t) \qquad \text{A}$$

21.160 The current in a circuit is given by

$$\frac{d^2i}{dt^2} + 4i = \sin t - \cos 2t$$

The initial conditions are $i(0_+) = 4\,\text{A}$ and $di/dt(0_+) = -2\,\text{A/s}$. Determine $i(t)$.

▮ Taking the Laplace transform of both sides yields

$$(s^2 + 4)I(s) - si(0_+) - \frac{di}{dt}(0_+) \; 4i = \frac{1}{s^2 + 1} - \frac{s}{s^2 + 4}$$

or $I(s) = \dfrac{4s-2}{s^2+4} + \dfrac{1}{(s^2+4)(s^2+1)} - \dfrac{s}{(s^2+4)^2} = \dfrac{4s}{s^2+4} + \dfrac{-2}{s^2+4} + \dfrac{1}{3(s^2+4)} + \dfrac{1}{3(s^2+1)} - \dfrac{s}{(s^2+4)^2}$

Thus,
$$i(t) = 4\cos 2t + 0.833 \sin 2t + 0.33 \sin t - 0.25\, t \sin 2t \qquad \text{A}$$

21.161 Determine $I(s)$ from

$$\frac{d^2i}{dt^2} + \frac{di}{dt} = t^2 + 2t$$

with $i(0_+) = 4\,\text{A}$ and $di/dt(0_+) = -2\,\text{A/s}$.

▌ Taking the Laplace transform and substituting the initial conditions yields

$$s(s+1)I(s) = 4s + 2 + \frac{2}{s^3} + \frac{2}{s^2} \quad \text{or} \quad I(s) = \frac{4s+2}{s(s+1)} + \frac{2(s+1)}{s^4(s+1)} = \frac{2}{s} + \frac{2}{s+1} + \frac{2}{s^4}$$

21.162 A coil having $R = 3\,\Omega$ and $L = 10.61\,\text{mH}$ is suddenly connected across a 110-V 60-Hz source. Determine $i(t)$.

▌
$$L\frac{di}{dt} + Ri = V_m \sin \omega t \quad \text{or} \quad 10.61 \times 10^{-3} sI(s) + 3I(s) = \frac{110\sqrt{2}(377)}{s^2 + (377)^2}$$

or
$$I(s) = \frac{110\sqrt{2}(377)}{[s^2 + (377)^2](10.61 \times 10^{-3}s + 3)} = \frac{110\sqrt{2}(377)}{10.61 \times 10^{-3}(s+j377)(s-j377)[s+(3 \times 10^3/10.61)]}$$

$$= \frac{j110\sqrt{2}}{2(3-j4)}\frac{1}{s+j377} - \frac{j110\sqrt{2}}{2(3+j4)}\frac{1}{s-j377} + \frac{4(110\sqrt{2})}{5^2}\frac{1}{s+(3\times 10^3/10.61)}$$

Hence, after some manipulation:

$$i(t) = \frac{110\sqrt{2}}{5}\sin(377t - 53.13°) + \frac{4(110\sqrt{2})}{5^2} e^{-282.75t} = 31.108 \sin(377t - 53.13°) + 24.886 e^{-282.75t} \quad \text{A}$$

21.163 The 2-F capacitor in the circuit of Fig. 21-51a is charged to 10 V and S is closed at $t = 0$. Obtain the transformed network.

▌ See Fig. 21-51b.

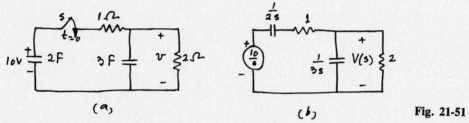

(a)   (b)   **Fig. 21-51**

21.164 Determine $V(s)$ in the circuit of Fig. 21-51b.

▌
$$V(s) = \frac{10}{s[1+(1/2s)]} \bigg/ \left\{ \frac{1}{1+(1/2s)} + 3s + \frac{1}{2} \right\} = \frac{40}{12s^2 + 12s + 1}$$

21.165 Find $v(t)$ in the circuit of Fig. 21-51a.

▌
$$V(s) = \frac{40}{12s^2 + 12s + 1} = \frac{40}{(s+0.09175)(s+0.90825)} = \frac{40}{0.8165}\left(\frac{1}{s+0.09175} - \frac{1}{s+0.90825}\right)$$

or
$$v(t) = 49(e^{-0.09175t} - e^{-0.90825t}) \quad \text{V}$$

21.166 At what time does $v(t)$ reach its maximum value?

▌ For v_{max}, we must have $dv/dt = 0$

or
$$-0.09175 e^{-0.09175T} + 0.90825 e^{-0.90825T} = 0$$

Thus, $e^{0.8125T} = 0.90825/0.09175$. Hence $T = 2.82\,\text{s}$.

21.167 What is the maximum value of v in the circuit of Prob. 21.165?

▌ v_{max} occurs at $T = 2.82\,\text{s}$, from Prob. 21.166. Therefore,

$$v_m = 49(e^{(-0.09175)(2.82)} - e^{(-0.90825)(2.82)}) = 34\,\text{V}$$

21.168 Find the current through the 1-H inductor in the circuit of Fig. 21-52.

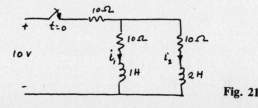

Fig. 21-52

▮ In the transform domain, by KVL, we have

$$(s + 20)I_1(s) + 10I_2(s) = \frac{10}{s} \qquad 10I_1(s) + (2s + 20)I_2(s) = \frac{10}{s}$$

Solving for $I_1(s)$ yields

$$I_1(s) = \frac{5(s + 10)}{s(s^2 + 30s + 150)} = \frac{5(s + 10)}{s(s + 6.34)(s + 23.66)}$$

$$= \frac{3.33}{s} + \frac{18.3}{6.34 \times 17.32(s + 6.34)} - \frac{68.3}{23.66 \times 17.32(s + 23.66)}$$

or $\qquad i_1(t) = 3.33 + 0.167e^{-6.34t} - 0.167e^{-23.66t}$ A

21.169 In the circuit of Fig. 21-53a, S is moved from a to b at $t = 0$. Obtain the corresponding circuit in the s domain.

▮ See Fig. 21-53b.

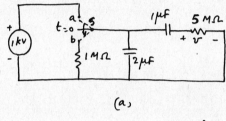

(a)

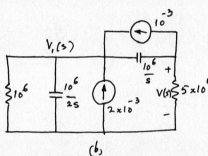

(b)   **Fig. 21-53**

21.170 Find the voltage across the 5-MΩ resistor in the circuit of Fig. 21-53a.

▮ From Fig. 21-53b:

$$(3 \times 10^{-6}s + 10^{-6})V_1(s) - 10^{-6}sV(s) = 3 \times 10^{-3} \qquad -10^6sV_1(s) + (10^{-6}s + 0.2 \times 10^{-6})V(s) = -10^{-3}$$

Solving for $V(s)$ gives

$$V(s) = -\frac{500}{s^2 + 0.8s + 0.1} = -\frac{500}{(s + 0.155)(s + 0.645)} = \frac{-1020}{s + 0.155} + \frac{1020}{s + 0.645}$$

or $\qquad v(t) = 1020(e^{-0.645t} - e^{-0.155t})$ V

21.171 What is the current through the 1-μF capacitor in the circuit of Fig. 21-53a at $t = 1$ s?

▮ $$i_{1\,\mu\text{F}} = i_{5\,\text{M}\Omega} = \frac{v(t)}{5 \times 10^6} = \frac{1020}{5 \times 10^6}(e^{-0.645t} - e^{-0.155t})$$

At $t = 1$ $\qquad i(1) = 204(e^{-0.645} - e^{-0.155}) \, 10^{-6} = -67.68 \, \mu\text{A}$

21.172 Determine the instantaneous voltage across the 1-μF capacitor in the circuit of Fig. 21-53b.

▮ $$v_{1\,\mu\text{F}}(t) = 10^6 \int_0^t i_{1\,\mu\text{F}}(t) \, dt$$

From Prob. 21.171:

$$v_{1\,\mu\text{F}}(t) = 204 \int_0^t (e^{-0.645t} - e^{-0.155t}) \, dt = 204 \, (-4.9 + 6.45e^{-0.155t} - 1.55e^{-0.645t}) \qquad \text{V}$$

21.173 Find $i_1(t)$ in the circuit of Fig. 21-54.

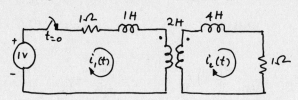

Fig. 21-54

▮ The mesh equations in the transform domain are

$$(s + 1)I_1(s) - 2sI_2(s) = \frac{1}{s} \qquad -2sI_1(s) + (4s + 1)I_2(s) = 0$$

Solving for $I_1(s)$:

$$I_1(s) = \frac{4s + 1}{s(5s + 1)} = \frac{1}{s} - \frac{0.2}{s + 0.2} \qquad \text{or} \qquad i_1(t) = 1 - 0.2e^{-0.2t} \quad \text{A}$$

21.174 Determine the voltage across the 4-H inductor in the circuit of Fig. 21-54.

▮
$$v_{4\,\text{H}}(t) = 4\frac{di_2}{dt}$$

From Prob. 21.173: $\qquad I_2(s) = \dfrac{2}{5s + 1} = \dfrac{0.4}{s + 0.2} \qquad \text{or} \qquad i_2(t) = 0.4e^{-0.2t} \quad \text{A}$

Thus, $\qquad v_{4\,\text{H}}(t) = 4(0.4)(-0.2)e^{-0.2t} = -0.32e^{-0.2t} \quad \text{V}$

21.175 How much energy is stored in the two inductors of the circuit of Fig. 21-54 under steady state?

▮ Since $\qquad i_1(\infty) = 1\,\text{A} \qquad W_{1\,\text{H}} = \frac{1}{2}(1)^2(1) = 0.5\,\text{J}$

Since $\qquad i_2(\infty) = 0\,\text{A} \qquad W_{4\,\text{H}} = 0\,\text{J}$

21.176 How much energy is stored in the 4-H inductor at $t = 0.1\,\text{s}$?

▮
$$W_{4\,\text{H}}(0.1) = \tfrac{1}{2}(4)[(-0.32e^{-0.2t})^2]_{t=0.1} = 0.197\,\text{J}$$

21.177 Determine $v_0(t)$ in the circuit of Fig. 21-55.

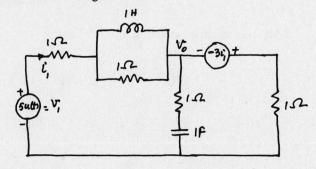

Fig. 21-55

▮
$$I_1(s) = \frac{V_1(s) - V_0(s)}{1 + \{1/[1 + (1/s)]\}}$$

$$\frac{V_1(s)}{1 + [s/(1 + s)]} - \frac{[V_1(s) - V_0(s)][-3(s + 1)]}{2s + 1} = \left(\frac{s + 1}{2s + 1} + \frac{s}{s + 1} + 1\right)V_0(s)$$

Substituting $V_1(s) = 5/s$ and solving for $V_0(s)$ gives

$$V_0(s) = \frac{20(s + 1)^2}{s(8s^2 + 12s + 5)} = \frac{4}{s} + \frac{-0.75 + j0.25}{s + 0.75 + j0.25} + \frac{-0.75 - j0.25}{s + 0.75 - j0.25}$$

Hence, $\qquad v_0(t) = 4u(t) + e^{-0.75t}(0.5\sin 0.25t - 1.5\cos 0.25t) \quad \text{V}$

21.178 A square pulse of 1 V and of 1-s duration is applied across a coil having $R = 1\,\Omega$ and $L = 1\,\text{H}$ at $t = 0$. Find the current.

$$\frac{di}{dt} + i = v \quad\text{or}\quad I(s)(s+1) = V(s) = \frac{1}{s}(1 - e^{-s})$$

Thus,
$$I(s) = \frac{1 - e^{-s}}{s(s+1)} = \frac{1}{s(s+1)} - \frac{e^{-s}}{s(s+1)} = \frac{1}{s} - \frac{1}{s+1} - \frac{e^{-s}}{s} + \frac{e^{-s}}{s+1}$$

Hence,
$$i(t) = (1 - e^{-t})u(t) - [1 - e^{-(t-1)}]u(t-1) \quad \text{A}$$

21.179 Obtain the Laplace transform of a train of pulses of period b and width a.

$\blacksquare$ The Laplace transform of a single pulse is $(1/s)(1 - e^{-as})$. From line 2 of Table 21.2 we obtain

$$F(s) = \frac{1 - e^{-as}}{s(1 - e^{-bs})}$$

21.180 If $\mathcal{L}[f_1(t)] = F_1(s)$ and $\mathcal{L}[f_2(t)] = F_2(s)$, the product of $F_1(s)$ and $F_2(s)$ is $\mathcal{L}[f(t)]$ obtained from the convolution of $f_1(t)$ and $f_2(t)$ as given by

$$f(t) = \mathcal{L}^{-1}[F_1(s)F_2(s)] \equiv f_1(t) * f_2(t) = \int_0^t f_1(\tau)f_2(t - \tau)\, d\tau = \int_0^t f_1(t - \tau)f_2(\tau)\, d\tau \qquad (1)$$

Using (1), evaluate

$$f(t) \equiv f_1(t) * f_2(t) = \int_0^t u(t - \tau)e^{-\tau}\, d\tau \qquad (2)$$

and verify that $f(t) = \mathcal{L}^{-1}[F_1(s)F_2(s)]$, where $F_1(s) = 1/s$ and $F_2(s) = 1/(s+1)$.

$\blacksquare$ Integrating (2) we obtain

$$f(t) = \int_0^t e^{-\tau}\, d\tau = 1 - e^{-t}$$

Otherwise

$$f(t) = \mathcal{L}^{-1}\left[\frac{1}{s(s+1)}\right] = \mathcal{L}^{-1}\left[\frac{1}{s} - \frac{1}{1+s}\right] = 1 - e^{-t}$$

21.181 A 3-V rectangular pulse of 0.1-s duration is applied to an RL series circuit, with $R = 2\,\Omega$ and $L = 0.5\,\text{H}$, at $t = 0$. Determine $i(t)$.

$\blacksquare$
$$I(s) = \frac{3(1 - e^{-0.1s})}{s(0.5s + 2)} = \frac{6(1 - e^{-0.1s})}{s(s+4)} = \frac{6}{4}(1 - e^{-0.1s})\left(\frac{1}{s} - \frac{1}{s+4}\right)$$

Thus,
$$i(t) = 1.5(1 - e^{-4t})u(t) - 1.5[1 - e^{-4(t-0.1)}]u(t - 0.1) \quad \text{A}$$

21.182 Qualitatively sketch $i(t)$ of Prob. 21.181.

$\blacksquare$ See Fig. 21-56.

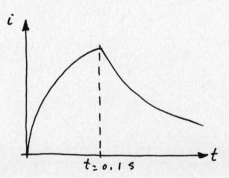

Fig. 21-56

21.183 Repeat Prob. 21.181 for an RC series circuit having $C = 0.5\,\text{F}$. Other data remain the same as in Prob. 21.181.

$\blacksquare$
$$I(s) = \frac{3(1 - e^{-0.1s})}{s[2 + (1/0.5s)]} = \frac{3(1 - e^{-0.1s})}{2(s+1)} = \frac{1.5}{s+1} - 1.5\left(\frac{e^{-0.1s}}{s+1}\right)$$

or
$$i(t) = 1.5e^{-t} - 1.5e^{-(t-0.1)}u(t - 0.1) \quad \text{A}$$

21.184 Sketch $i(t)$ of Prob. 21.183.

▮ See Fig. 21-57.

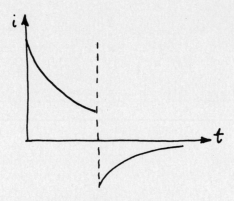

Fig. 21-57

21.185 Determine the voltage across the capacitor of Prob. 21.183.

▮
$$V_C(s) = \frac{I(s)}{Cs} = \frac{3(1 - e^{-0.1s})}{2(s + 1)(0.5s)} = 3(1 - e^{-0.1s})\left(\frac{1}{s} - \frac{1}{s + 1}\right)$$

Thus,
$$v_C(t) = 3(1 - e^{-t}) - 3[1 - e^{-(t-0.1)}]u(t - 0.1) \quad V$$

21.186 A voltage of waveform of Fig. 21-58 is applied to the circuit of Prob. 21.181.   Determine $i(t)$.

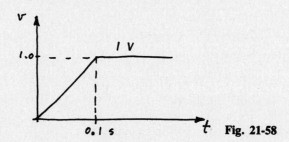

Fig. 21-58

▮
$$I(s) = \frac{1}{0.1}\left[\frac{(1 - e^{-0.1s})}{s^2(0.5s + 2)}\right] = 20\frac{(1 - e^{-0.1s})}{s^2(s + 4)} = 20(1 - e^{-0.1s})\left[\frac{1}{2s^2} - \frac{1}{8s} + \frac{1}{8(s + 4)}\right]$$

Thus,
$$i(t) = (10t - 2.5 + 2.5e^{-4t})u(t) - [10(t - 0.1) - 2.5 + 2.5e^{-4(t-0.1)}]u(t - 0.1) \quad A$$

21.187 Sketch $i(t)$ of Prob. 21.186.

▮ See Fig. 21-59.

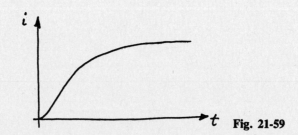

Fig. 21-59

21.188 Repeat Prob. 21.183 for the waveform of Fig. 21-58.

▮
$$I(s) = \frac{1}{0.1}\left[\frac{(1 - e^{-0.1s})}{s^2[2 + (1/0.5s)]}\right] = \frac{5(1 - e^{-0.1s})}{s(s + 1)} = 5(1 - e^{-0.5s})\left(\frac{1}{s} - \frac{1}{s + 1}\right)$$

Hence,
$$i(t) = 5(1 - e^{-t}) - 5[1 - e^{-(t-0.1)}]u(t - 0.1) \quad A$$

21.189 Repeat Prob. 21.185 for the waveform of Fig. 21-58.

$$V_C(s) = \frac{I(s)}{Cs} = \frac{5(1 - e^{-0.1s})}{(0.5s)(s)(s + 1)} = \frac{10(1 - e^{-0.1s})}{s^2(s + 1)} = 10(1 - e^{-0.1s})\left(\frac{1}{s^2} - \frac{1}{s} + \frac{1}{s + 1}\right)$$

Thus,

$$v_c(t) = 10\{[(t - 1 + e^{-t})\,u(t) - [(t - 0.1) - 1 + e^{-(t - 0.1)}]u(t - 0.1)\}$$

21.190 Sketch the current obtained in Prob. 21.188.

See Fig. 21-60.

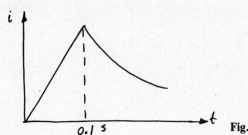

Fig. 21-60

21.191 Sketch the voltage determined in Prob. 21.189.

See Fig. 21-61.

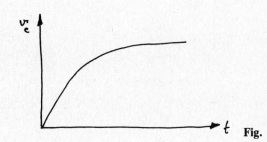

Fig. 21-61

21.192 A voltage of waveform of Fig. 21-62 is applied to a series RL circuit, having $R = 1\,\Omega$ and $L = 1\,H$, at $t = 0$. Determine $i(t)$.

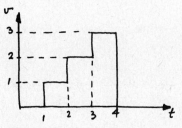

Fig. 21-62

The waveform may be synthesized by using unit steps. Thus,

$$v(t) = u(t - 1) + u(t - 2) + u(t - 3) - 3u(t - 4)$$

Hence, by inspection:

$$i(t) = [1 - e^{-(t-1)}]u(t - 1) + [1 - e^{-(t-2)}]u(t - 2) + [1 - e^{-(t-3)}]u(t - 3) - 3[1 - e^{-(t-4)}]u(t - 4)$$

21.193 Sketch the current of Prob. 21.192.

See Fig. 21-63.

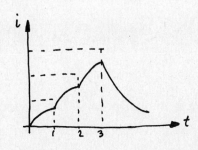

Fig. 21-63

21.194 Given: $F_1(s) = 1/(s-2) = F_2(s)$. Find $f(t)$ by convolution.

▮ $$f(t) = \int_0^t e^{2(t-\tau)} e^{2\tau} d\tau = \tau e^{2t} \Big|_0^t = t e^{2t} \quad \text{and} \quad \mathcal{L}^{-1}[F_1(s)F_2(s)] = \mathcal{L}^{-1}\left[\frac{1}{(s-2)^2}\right] = t e^{2t}$$

21.195 Find $\mathcal{L}^{-1}[F_1(s)F_2(s)]$ by convolution for $F_1(s) = F_2(s) = 1/(s^2 + 1)$.

▮ $$f(t) = \int_0^t \sin t \sin (t - \tau)\, d\tau = -\frac{t}{2} \cos t + \frac{1}{4} \sin t + \frac{1}{4} \sin t = -\frac{t}{2} \cos t + \frac{1}{2} \sin t$$

21.196 A capacitor C initially charged to a voltage V_0 is connected to a voltage source V having an internal resistance R. Write an expression for v_C, the voltage across the capacitor, in the time domain.

▮ The required equation is (see Fig. 21-64)

$$C \frac{dv_C}{dt} + \frac{v_C}{R} = \frac{V}{R} \tag{1}$$

with

$$v_C(0_+) = V_0 \tag{2}$$

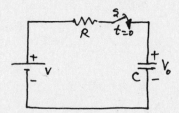

Fig. 21-64

21.197 Obtain an expression for v_C in the transformed domain.

▮ From (1) and (2) we have

$$C[sV_C(s) - v_C(0_+)] + \frac{V_C(s)}{R} = \frac{V}{Rs}$$

or

$$V_C(s) = \frac{V_0 s + (V/RC)}{s[s + (1/RC)]} \tag{1}$$

21.198 Solve for $v_C(t)$ for the circuit of Fig. 21-64, if S is closed at $t = 0$.

▮ From (1) of Prob. 21.197

$$v_C(t) = V + (V_0 - V)e^{-t/RC}$$

21.199 In the circuit of Fig. 21-65, the switch is moved from 1 to 2 at $t = 0$, with $i_L(0_+) = 0.5\,\text{A}$. Solve for $i(t)$.

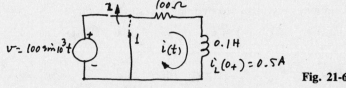

Fig. 21-65

▮ By KVL:

$$0.1 \frac{di}{dt} + 100i = 100 \sin 10^3 t$$

or

$$100 I(s) + 0.1[sI(s) - 0.5] = \frac{10^5}{s^2 + 10^6} \quad \text{or} \quad I(s) = \frac{0.5s^2 + 1.5 \times 10^6}{(s^2 + 10^6)(s + 1000)}$$

Hence,

$$i(t) = \frac{1}{\sqrt{2}} \sin \left(10^3 t - \frac{\pi}{4}\right) + e^{-1000t} \quad \text{A}$$

21.200 Sketch $i(t)$ of Prob. 21.199 showing the two components of the current.

▮ See Fig. 21-66.

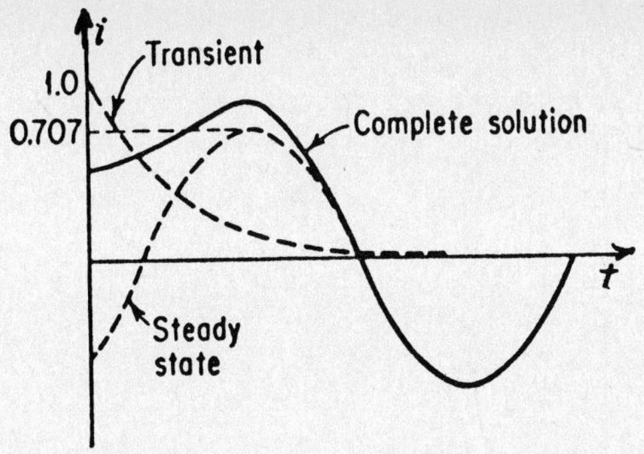

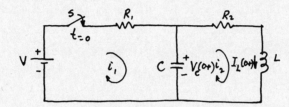

Fig. 21-66

21.201 In the circuit of Fig. 21-67, S is closed at $t = 0$. Write the loop equations in the s domain to solve for i_1 and i_2.

Fig. 21-67

▮ The required equations are

$$-\frac{V}{s} + R_1 I_1(s) + \frac{V_C(0_+)}{s} + \frac{1}{Cs}\left[I_1(s) - I_2(s)\right] = 0$$

$$-\frac{V_C(0_+)}{s} + \frac{1}{Cs}\left[I_2(s) - I_1(s)\right] + R_2 I_2(s) + sLI_2(s) - LI_L(0_+) = 0$$

which simplify to

$$\left(R_1 + \frac{1}{Cs}\right)I_1(s) - \frac{1}{Cs}I_2(s) = \frac{1}{s}\left[V - V_C(0_+)\right] \tag{1}$$

$$-\frac{1}{Cs}I_1(s) + \left(\frac{1}{Cs} + R_2 + Ls\right)I_2(s) = LI_L(0_+) + \frac{V_C(0_+)}{s} \tag{2}$$

21.202 Solve for $I_2(s)$ in the circuit of Fig. 21-67 using Cramer's rule.

▮ From (1) and (2) of Problem 21.201

$$I_2(s) = \frac{\begin{vmatrix} R_1 + \dfrac{1}{Cs} & \dfrac{V - V_C(0_+)}{s} \\[2ex] -\dfrac{1}{Cs} & LI_L(0_+) + \dfrac{V_C(0_+)}{s} \end{vmatrix}}{\begin{vmatrix} R_1 + \dfrac{1}{Cs} & -\dfrac{1}{Cs} \\[2ex] -\dfrac{1}{Cs} & R_2 + Ls + \dfrac{1}{Cs} \end{vmatrix}}$$

21.203 If $I_2(s)$ of Prob. 21.202 takes the form

$$I_2(s) = \frac{a_2 s^2 + a_1 s + a_0}{s(s + \alpha)(s + \gamma)}$$

write the form of the solution and sketch $i_2(t)$ showing all its components.

▮

$$I_2(s) = \frac{a_2 s^2 + a_1 s + a_0}{s(s + \alpha)(s + \gamma)} = \frac{k_1}{s + \alpha} + \frac{k_2}{s + \gamma} + \frac{k_3}{s}$$

Thus,

$$i_2(t) = k_1 e^{-\alpha t} + k_2 e^{-\gamma t} + k_3$$

Hence we obtain the sketch shown in Fig. 21-68.

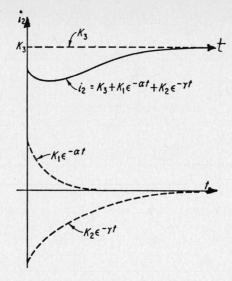

Fig. 21-68

21.204 If $I_2(s)$ of Prob. 21.202 is of the form

$$I_2(s) = \frac{a_2 s^2 + a_1 s + a_0}{s[(s + \alpha)^2 + \beta^2]}$$

write the form of solution and sketch $i_2(t)$.

▌ The given $I_2(s)$ may be written as

$$I_2(s) = \frac{k_1}{(s + \alpha)^2 + \beta^2} + \frac{k_2}{s}$$

Thus,
$$i_2(t) = k_1 e^{-\alpha t} \sin(\beta t + \theta) + k_2$$

which is sketched in Fig. 21-69.

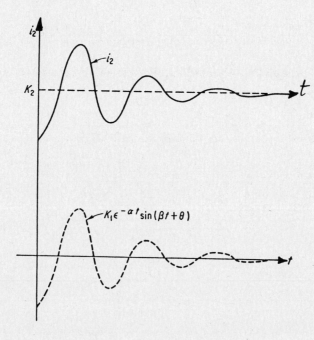

Fig. 21-69

21.205 If $I_2(s)$ of Prob. 21.202 is of the form

$$I_2(s) = \frac{a_2 s^2 + a_1 s + a_0}{s(s + \alpha)^2}$$

write the form of solution and sketch $i_2(t)$.

❙ Proceeding as in the previous two problems, we may write

$$i_2(t) = K_1 + (K_2 t + K_3)e^{-\alpha t}$$

which is sketched in Fig. 21-70.

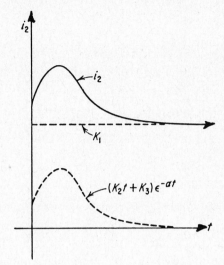

Fig. 21-70

21.206 Draw the circuit of Fig. 21-67 in the s domain.

❙ See Fig. 21-71.

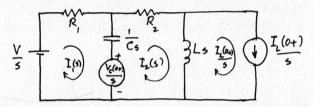

Fig. 21-71

21.207 In the circuit of Fig. 21-72, choose node 1 as the reference node. Write a set of integrodifferential equations to solve for $v_2(t)$.

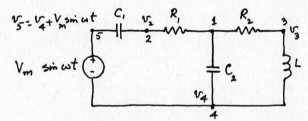

Fig. 21-72

❙ The required equations are

$$C_1 \frac{d}{dt}[v_2 - (v_4 + V_m \sin \omega t)] + \frac{1}{R_1}v_2 = 0 \qquad \frac{1}{L}\int (v_3 - v_4)\, dt + \frac{1}{R_2}v_3 = 0$$

$$\frac{1}{L}\int (v_4 - v_3)\, dt + C_2 \frac{dv_4}{dt} + C_1 \frac{d}{dt}[(v_4 + V_m \sin \omega t) - v_2] = 0$$

21.208 Obtain $V_2(s)$ from the equations of Prob. 21.207.

❙ The equations in the s domain are

$$\left(sC_1 + \frac{1}{R_1}\right)V_2 - (sC_1)V_4 = \frac{V_m \omega s C_1}{s^2 + \omega^2} \qquad \left(\frac{1}{sL} + \frac{1}{R_2}\right)V_3 - \left(\frac{1}{sL}\right)V_4 = 0$$

$$-(sC_1)V_2 - \left(\frac{1}{sL}\right)V_3 + \left(sC_1 + sC_2 + \frac{1}{sL}\right)V_4 = -\frac{V_m \omega s C_1}{s^2 + \omega^2}$$

Solving for V_2 by determinants, we obtain

$$V_2 = \frac{\begin{vmatrix} \dfrac{V_m \omega s C_1}{s^2 + \omega^2} & 0 & -sC_1 \\[2mm] 0 & \left(\dfrac{1}{sL} + \dfrac{1}{R_2}\right) & -\dfrac{1}{sL} \\[2mm] -\dfrac{V_m \omega s C_1}{s^2 + \omega^2} & -\dfrac{1}{sL} & \left(sC_1 + sC_2 + \dfrac{1}{sL}\right) \end{vmatrix}}{\begin{vmatrix} \left(sC_1 + \dfrac{1}{R_1}\right) & 0 & -sC_1 \\[2mm] 0 & \left(\dfrac{1}{sL} + \dfrac{1}{R_2}\right) & -\dfrac{1}{sL} \\[2mm] -sC_1 & -\dfrac{1}{sL} & \left(sC_1 + sC_2 + \dfrac{1}{sL}\right) \end{vmatrix}}$$

$$= \frac{(\omega V_m)s^3 + \left(\dfrac{\omega V_m R_2}{L}\right)s^2 + \left(\dfrac{\omega V_m}{LC_2}\right)s}{(s^2 + \omega^2)\left[s^3 + \left(\dfrac{R_2}{L} + \dfrac{1}{R_1 C_2} + \dfrac{1}{R_1 C_1}\right)s^2 + \left(\dfrac{1}{LC_2} + \dfrac{1}{LC_1} + \dfrac{R_2}{R_1 LC_2}\right)s + \left(\dfrac{1}{LC_1 C_2 R_1}\right)\right]}$$

In the above equations V_2, V_3, and V_4 stand for $V_2(s)$, $V_3(s)$, and $V_4(s)$, respectively.

21.209 The voltage $V_2(s)$ obtained in Prob. 21.208 may be written in the general form

$$V_2(s) = \frac{a_3 s^3 + a_2 s^2 + a_1 s + a_0}{(s^2 + \omega^2)(s^3 + b_2 s^2 + b_1 s + b_0)}$$

Depending on the circuit parameters, $V_2(s)$ may have one of four forms. Write these forms of $V_2(s)$ and the corresponding forms of solutions, v_2.

❚ The required forms of $V_2(s)$ are

$$V_2(s) = \frac{a_3 s^3 + a_2 s^2 + a_1 s + a_0}{(s^2 + \omega^2)(s + \delta)(s + \alpha)(s + \gamma)}$$

$$V_2(s) = \frac{a_3 s^3 + a_2 s^2 + a_1 s + a_0}{(s^2 + \omega^2)(s + \delta)[(s + \alpha)^2 + \beta^2]}$$

$$V_2(s) = \frac{a_3 s^3 + a_2 s^2 + a_1 s + a_0}{(s^2 + \omega^2)(s + \delta)(s + \alpha)^2}$$

$$V_2(s) = \frac{a_3 s^3 + a_2 s^2 + a_1 s + a_0}{(s^2 + \omega^2)(s + \alpha)^3}$$

The corresponding forms of solutions are:

$$v_2 = K_1 \sin(\omega t + \theta_1) + K_2 \epsilon^{-\delta t} + K_3 \epsilon^{-\alpha t} + K_4 \epsilon^{-\gamma t}$$

$$v_2 = K_1 \sin(\omega t + \theta_1) + K_2 \epsilon^{-\delta t} + K_3 \epsilon^{-\alpha t} \sin(\beta t + \theta_3)$$

$$v_2 = K_1 \sin(\omega t + \theta_1) + K_2 \epsilon^{-\delta t} + (K_3 t + K_4)\epsilon^{-\alpha t}$$

$$v_2 = K_1 \sin(\omega t + \theta_1) + (K_2 t^2 + K_3 t + K_4)\epsilon^{-\alpha t}$$

21.210 The node equations for a circuit are

$$0.002v_1 + 5\int v_1\,dt - 0.002v_2 = 0 \qquad -0.002v_1 + 0.003v_2 + 10^4\frac{dv_2}{dt} = 0.01$$

$v_2(0_+) = 100\text{ V}$ and all other initial conditions are zero. Determine $V_1(s)$.

I $\qquad 0.002V_1(s) + \dfrac{5V_1(s)}{s} - 0.002V_2(s) = 0 \qquad -0.002V_1(s) + 0.003V_2(s) + 10^4[sV(s) - 100] = \dfrac{0.01}{s}$

Solving for $V_1(s)$ yields

$$V_1(s) = \frac{100(s + 1)}{s^2 + 2510s + 75,000}$$

21.211 Obtain a circuit which will satisfy the equations of Prob. 21.210.

I See Fig. 21-73.

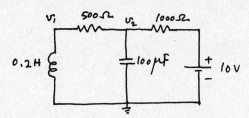

Fig. 21-73

21.212 The voltage across a 2-H inductor is given by

$$V_L(s) = \frac{80s + 5000}{s^2 + 80s + 2500}$$

If $I_L(0_+) = 1\,\text{A}$, find $i_L(t)$.

I $\qquad\qquad V_L(s) = sLI_L(s) - I_L(0_+) \qquad \text{or} \qquad 2sI_L(s) - (2)(1) = \dfrac{80s + 5000}{s^2 + 80s + 2500}$

Thus, $\qquad\qquad\qquad\qquad I_L(s) = \dfrac{s^2 + 120s + 5000}{s[(s + 40)^2 + (30)^2]}$

and $\qquad\qquad\qquad\qquad i_L(t) = 2 - e^{-40t}\cos 30t \qquad \text{A}$

21.213 The current through a 0.1-H inductor is given by

$$I_L(s) = \frac{-s + 100}{s(s + 100)}$$

If $I_L(0_+) = -1\,\text{A}$, find $v_L(t)$.

I $v_L = L(di_L/dt)$ yields

$$V_L(s) = L[sI_L(s) - I_L(0_+)] = 0.1\left[\frac{s(-s + 100)}{s(s + 100)} + 1\right] = \frac{20}{s + 100}$$

Thus, $\qquad\qquad\qquad\qquad v_L(t) = 20e^{-100t} \qquad \text{V}$

21.214 Find $i_L(t)$ in the circuit of Prob. 21.213, and explain how $v_L(t)$ can be obtained without specifying $I_L(0_+)$.

I From Prob. 21.213: $\qquad\qquad I_L(s) = \dfrac{-s + 100}{s(s + 100)} = \dfrac{1}{s} - \dfrac{2}{s + 100}$

Thus, $\qquad\qquad\qquad\qquad i_L(t) = 1 - 2e^{-100t} \qquad \text{A} \qquad\qquad\qquad\qquad\qquad\qquad (1)$

$v_L(t)$ can be obtained directly from (1) and $v_L = L\,d[i_L(t)]/dt$. The initial value $I_L(0_+)$ is implicit in (1).

21.215 The current in a 20-μF capacitor is given by

$$I_C(s) = \frac{30}{s^2 + 3000s + 2 \times 10^6}$$

If $V_C(0_+) = 10\,\text{V}$, find $V_C(s)$.

I Since $\qquad\qquad\qquad\qquad v_C = \dfrac{1}{c}\displaystyle\int_0^t i_C\,dt$

$$V_C(s) = \frac{1}{Cs}I_C(s) + \frac{V_C(0_+)}{s} = \frac{30}{(20 \times 10^{-6})s(s^2 + 3000s + 2 \times 10^6)} + \frac{10}{s}$$

$$= \frac{10(s^2 + 3 \times 10^3 s + 2.15 \times 10^6)}{s(s^2 + 3000s + 2 \times 10^6)}$$

21.216 Determine $v_C(t)$ of Prob. 21.215 at $t = 1$ ms.

▮

$$V_C(s) = \frac{10.75}{s} - \frac{1.5}{s + 1000} + \frac{0.75}{s + 2000}$$

Thus,

$$v_C(t) = 10.75 - 1.5e^{-1000t} + 0.75e^{-2000t}$$

At $t = 1$ ms, $v_C(10^{-3}) = 10.3$ V.

21.217 The voltage across a 2-μF capacitor is given by $V_C(s) = (60s + 8 \times 10^4)/(s^2 + 10^6)$. Find $i_C(t)$.

▮

$$I_C(s) = CsV_C(s) = 2 \times 10^{-6} s(60s + 8 \times 10^4)/(s^2 + 10^6)$$

Taking the inverse transform yields

$$i_C(t) = 2 \times 10^{-6} [60s(t) + 10^4 (8 \cos 10^3 t - 6 \sin 10^3 t)] \quad A$$

21.218 In an RL series circuit the initial current through the inductor L is $I(0_+) = I_0$. If the circuit is connected across a battery of voltage V at $t = 0$, find $i(t)$.

▮

$$L\frac{di}{dt} + Ri = V$$

or

$$L[sI(s) - I(0_+)] + RI(s) = \frac{V}{s} \tag{1}$$

or

$$I(s)(Ls + R) = \frac{V}{s} + LI(0_+)$$

Thus,

$$I(s) = \frac{V}{s(sL + R)} + \frac{LI_0}{sL + R} \tag{2}$$

and

$$i(t) = \frac{V}{R} + \left(I_0 - \frac{V}{R}\right)e^{-Rt/L}$$

21.219 In the circuit of Prob. 21.218, let $R \to 0$. Solve for $i(t)$.

▮ From (2) of Prob. 21.218, with $R = 0$, we obtain

$$I(s) = \frac{V}{s^2 L} + \frac{I_0}{s} \qquad i(t) = I_0 + \frac{V}{L}t \quad A$$

21.220 At $t = 0$, S is closed in the circuit of Fig. 21-74. Find $v_C(t)$ and $i_C(t)$. All initial conditions are zero.

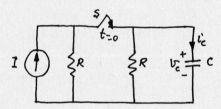

Fig. 21-74

▮ In the s domain we have

$$\frac{I}{s} = \frac{V_C(s)}{R} + \frac{V_C(s)}{R} + CsV_C(s) \qquad \text{or} \qquad V_C(s) = \frac{I}{Cs}\left[\frac{1}{s + (2/RC)}\right]$$

Thus,

$$v_C(t) = \tfrac{1}{2}RI(1 - e^{-2t/RC}) \qquad \text{and} \qquad i_C(t) = C\frac{d}{dt}[v_C(t)] = Ie^{-2t/RC}$$

21.221 Sketch $v_C(t)$ and $i_C(t)$ of Prob. 21.220.

▮ See Fig. 21-75.

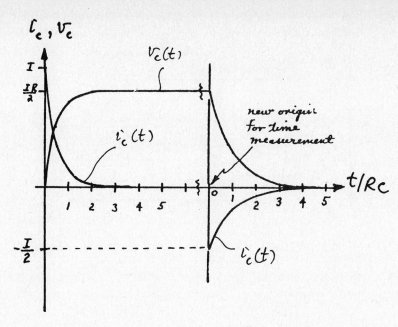

Fig. 21-75

21.222 Assume that the switch in the circuit of Fig. 21-74 is closed a long enough time for the transients to die out. Next, S is opened. Find $v_C(t)$ and $i_C(t)$.

▌ In this case, we have C initially charged to a voltage $RI/2$ and discharging through R for $t > 0$. Thus,

$$v_C(t) = \frac{RI}{2} e^{-t/RC} \quad \text{and} \quad i_C(t) = -\frac{I}{2} e^{-t/RC}$$

21.223 Plot $v_C(t)$ and $i_C(t)$ of Prob. 21.222 on the graph of Fig. 21-75. Note any significant changes in the shape and magnitude of the curves.

▌ See Fig. 21-75. The second current function differs from the first by being negative and having twice the time constant. The second voltage likewise has double the time constant of the first, but it is an exponential decay rather than a rise.

21.224 Obtain the areas under the two current curves of Fig. 21-75; compare and explain the results.

▌ The first area is $IRC/2$, the second is $-IRC/2$. They should be equal and opposite because they are charged dimensionally, the one being the charge stored during voltage buildup and the other being the charge delivered during voltage decay.

21.225 With zero initial conditions, S is closed at $t = 0$ in the circuit of Fig. 21-76. Determine $i(t)$ and $v(t)$.

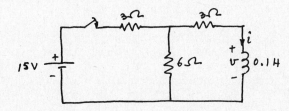

Fig. 21-76

▌ The circuit has a time constant

$$T = \frac{0.1}{3 + [(3 \times 6)/(3 + 6)]} = 0.02 \text{ s} \qquad I_{\text{steady state}} = \frac{15}{5}\left(\frac{2}{3}\right) = 2 \text{ A}$$

Thus, $\qquad i = 2(1 - e^{-t/0.02}) = 2(1 - e^{-50t}) \quad$ A $\quad$ and $\quad v = L\dfrac{di}{dt} = 10e^{-50t} \quad$ V

21.226 Sketch $v(t)$ and $i(t)$ of Prob. 21.225.

▌ See Fig. 21-77.

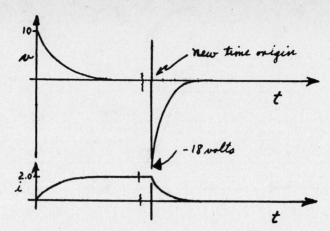

Fig. 21-77

21.227 In the circuit of Prob. 21.225, after the circuit has reached steady state, the switch is opened. Determine the voltage across and the current through the inductance. Plot $v(t)$ and $i(t)$.

▮ In this case $I_L(0_+) = 2.0$ A and $T = (0.1/9)$ s.

Thus, $$i = 2e^{-90t} \quad \text{A} \quad \text{and} \quad v = L\frac{di}{dt} = -18e^{-90t} \quad \text{V}$$

The plot is shown in Fig. 21-77 as a continuation of $v(t)$ and $i(t)$ of Prob. 21.225.

21.228 Compute and compare the areas under the voltage curves of Fig. 21-77. Dimensionally, what do these areas represent? Explain.

▮ The areas, which are flux linkages dimensionally, are plus and minus 0.2, respectively. The result simply shows that the total flux built up during the first transient collapses during the second transient.

21.229 The circuit of Fig. 21-78 is under steady state with the switch at position 1. At $t = 0$ the switch is moved to position 2. Solve for the circuit current for $t > 0$.

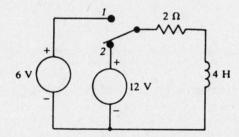

Fig. 21-78

▮ For $t > 0$, $$4\frac{di}{dt} + 2i = 12$$

which transforms to $$4sI(s) - 4i(0_+) + 2I(s) = \frac{12}{s} \tag{1}$$

As $i(0_+) = i(0_-)$ is the steady-state current with the switch in position 1,

$$i(0_+) = 6/2 = 3 \text{ A} \tag{2}$$

From (1) and (2), $$I(s) = \frac{6(s+1)}{s(2s+1)} = 6\left(\frac{1}{s} - \frac{1}{2s+1}\right) = 6\left(\frac{1}{s} - \frac{0.5}{s+0.5}\right) \tag{3}$$

Hence $$i(t) = 6(1 - 0.5e^{-0.5t}) \quad \text{A}$$

21.230 Without solving for $i(t)$, find the steady-state current in the circuit of Fig. 21-78.

▮ Applying the final-value theorem to (3) of Prob. 21.229, we have

$$\lim_{t\to\infty} i(t) = \lim_{s\to 0} s\left[\frac{6(s+1)}{s(2s+1)}\right] = 6 \text{ A}$$

21.231 For the circuit shown in Fig. 21-79, solve for i_1 and i_2 if the switch is closed at $t = 0$. The mutual inductance is of additive polarity.

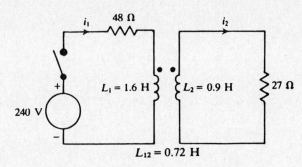

Fig. 21-79

▮ The circuit equations are, for $t > 0$,

$$1.6\frac{di_1}{dt} + 48i_1 - 0.72\frac{di_2}{dt} = 240 \qquad -0.72\frac{di_1}{dt} + 0.9\frac{di_2}{dt} + 27i_2 = 0$$

These equations in the transform domain become (zero initial values)

$$(1.6s + 48)I_1(s) - 0.72sI_2(s) = 240/s \qquad -0.72sI_1(s) + (0.9s + 27)I_2(s) = 0$$

Solving for $I_1(s)$ and $I_2(s)$ and taking their inverse transforms,

$$i_1(t) = 5 - 2.5e^{-75t} - 2.5e^{-75t/4} \quad \text{A} \qquad i_2(t) = -3.33e^{-75t} + 3.33e^{-75t/4} \quad \text{A}$$

21.232 Sketch $i_1(t)$ and $i_2(t)$ of Prob. 21.231. Show their components also.

▮ See Fig. 21-80.

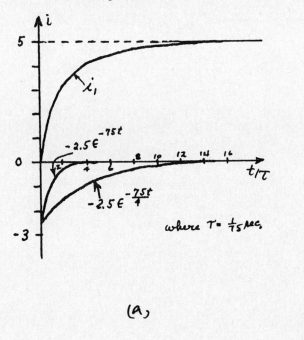

(a)

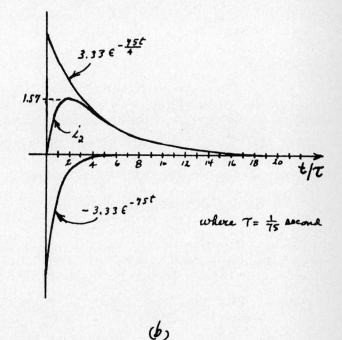

(b)

Fig. 21-80

21.233 Find $i(t)$ in the circuit of Fig. 21-81, where S is closed at $t = 0$ and the circuit is initially unenergized.

▮ Writing the node equation:

$$\left(\frac{1}{48} + \frac{1}{1.6s} + \frac{1}{48}\right)V(s) = \frac{240}{(48)(s)} \qquad \text{or} \qquad V(s) = \frac{120}{s + 15}$$

Thus, $v(t) = 120e^{-15t}$ V and $i(t) = \frac{1}{48}(240 - 120e^{-15t}) = 5 - 2.5e^{-15t}$ A.

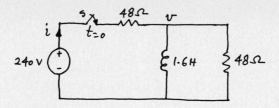

Fig. 21-81

21.234 Draw the circuit of Fig. 21-81 in the s domain.

▌ See Fig. 21-82.

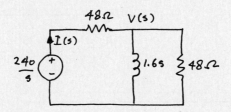

Fig. 21-82

21.235 Find the current in a series RC circuit, if the capacitor is initially uncharged and the applied voltage has the waveform of Fig. 21-83.

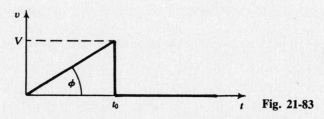

Fig. 21-83

▌ By KVL:

$$R\frac{dq}{dt} + \frac{1}{C}q = v = \begin{cases} Vt/t_0 & 0 < t < t_0 \\ 0 & t > t_0 \end{cases} \tag{1}$$

Taking the Laplace transform of (1) and applying the initial condition,

$$RsQ(s) + \frac{1}{C}Q(s) = \frac{V}{t_0}\int_0^{t_0} te^{-st}\,dt = \frac{V}{t_0}\left(\frac{1}{s^2} - \frac{1}{s^2}e^{-t_0 s} - \frac{t_0}{s}e^{-t_0 s}\right) \tag{2}$$

Now, because $i = dq/dt$ and $q(0_+) = 0$, $I(s) = sQ(s)$. Solving (2), with $\alpha \equiv 1/RC$, then gives

$$I(s) = sQ(s) = \frac{V}{Rt_0}\frac{1}{s(s+\alpha)} - \frac{V}{Rt_0}\frac{e^{-t_0 s}}{s(s+\alpha)} - \frac{V}{R}\frac{e^{-t_0 s}}{s+\alpha} \equiv I_1(s) + I_2(s) + I_3(s) \tag{3}$$

Inverting (3) termwise, we have

$$i_1(t) = \frac{V}{Rt_0\alpha}(1 - e^{-\alpha t})$$

Then, by the shifting theorem,

$$i_2(t) = -\frac{V}{Rt_0\alpha}[1 - e^{-\alpha(t-t_0)}]u(t - t_0)$$

Similarly,

$$i_3(t) = -\frac{V}{R}e^{-\alpha(t-t0)}u(t - t_0)$$

Finally,

$$i(t) = i_1(t) + i_2(t) + i_3(t) \quad \text{with} \quad \alpha = 1/RC$$

$$= \frac{CV}{t_0}(1 - e^{-t/RC}) - \frac{CV}{t_0}\left[1 - \left(1 - \frac{t_0}{RC}\right)e^{-(t-t_0)/RC}\right]u(t - t_0)$$

21.236 Apply the final-value theorem to find the steady-state current in the circuit of Prob. 21.235.

▌ $i_{ss} = \lim_{s\to 0} sI(s) = (CV/t_0) - (CV/t_0) = 0$, from (3) of Prob. 21.235.

21.237 A series RLC circuit has $R = 250\,\Omega$, $L = 10\,\text{mH}$, and $C = 100\,\mu\text{F}$. Assuming zero initial conditions, use Laplace transforms to determine the (natural) current for a unit impulse voltage input.

❚ The circuit voltage equation is, for an initially uncharged capacitor,

$$\frac{1}{C}\int_0^t i(\tau)\,d\tau + Ri + L\frac{di}{dt} = v(t) \qquad (1)$$

With the given numerical values, (1) becomes

$$10^4 \int_0^t i(\tau)\,d\tau + 250i + 10^{-2}\frac{di}{dt} = \delta(t) \qquad (2)$$

Taking the Laplace transform of (2) yields

$$\frac{10^4}{s}I(s) + 250I(s) + 10^{-2}sI(s) = 1 \qquad (3)$$

whence, using partial fractions,

$$I(s) = \frac{100s}{s^2 + 25{,}000s + 10^6} = \frac{100s}{(s + 24{,}960)(s + 40)} = \frac{100.16}{s + 24{,}960} - \frac{0.16}{s + 40}$$

Inverting, $\qquad\qquad i(t) = 100.16e^{-24960t} - 0.16e^{-40t} \qquad$ A $\qquad\qquad (4)$

21.238 Solve for $i_2(t)$ in the circuit of Fig. 21-84, where S is closed at $t = 0$ with zero initial conditions.

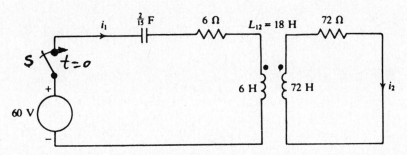

Fig. 21-84

❚ The circuit equations in the transform domain become

$$\left(6s + 6 + \frac{15}{2s}\right)I_1(s) - 18sI_2(s) = \frac{60}{s} \qquad -18sI_1(s) + (72s + 72)I_2(s) = 0$$

Solving for $I_2(s)$ gives

$$I_2(s) = \frac{10s}{s^3 + 8s^2 + 9s + 5} = \frac{10s}{(s + s_0)(s + s_1)(s + s_2)}$$

where $s_0 = 6.782$, $s_1 = s_2^* = 0.609 + j0.607$. The method of partial fractions then gives

$$I_2(s) = \left[\frac{-10s_0}{(s_1 - s_0)(s_2 - s_0)}\right]\frac{1}{s + s_0} + \left[\frac{-10s_1}{(s_0 - s_1)(s_2 - s_1)}\right]\frac{1}{s + s_1} + \left[\frac{-10s_2}{(s_0 - s_2)(s_1 - s_2)}\right]\frac{1}{s + s_2}$$

$$= \frac{-1.763}{s + 6.782} + \left\{\frac{0.882 - j0.726}{s + s_1} + \text{(complex conjugate)}\right\}$$

Inverting, $\quad i_2(t) = -1.763e^{-6.782t} + \{(0.882 - j0.726)e^{-(0.609 + j0.607)t} + \text{(complex conjugate)}\}$

$$= -1.763e^{-6.782t} + \{1.142e^{-0.609t}e^{-j(0.607t + 39.5°)} + \text{(complex conjugate)}\}$$

$$= -1.763e^{-6.782t} + 2.284e^{-0.609t}\cos(0.607t + 39.5°) \qquad \text{A}$$

21.239 In the circuit of Fig. 21-85, when $\sqrt{L/C} = R_1 = R_2 = R$, the circuit becomes purely resistive and experiences no transients. Verify this phenomenon of *universal* resonance by a Laplace transform solution of $v(t)$.

❚ In view of the initial conditions $i_1(0_+) = 0$ and $i_2(0_+) = I$, we obtain the transformed equations

$$I_1(s) + I_2(s) = \frac{I}{s} \qquad V(s) = RI_1(s) + LsI_1(s) \qquad V(s) = RI_2(s) + \frac{I_2(s)}{Cs}$$

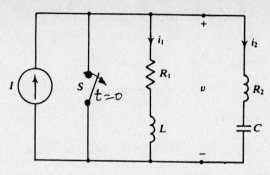

Fig. 21-85

Solve the second and third equations, respectively, for $I_1(s)$ and $I_2(s)$, substitute in the first equation, and use $R^2 = L/C$ to obtain

$$V(s) = \frac{RI}{s} \qquad \text{whence} \qquad v(t) = RI \qquad (t > 0)$$

and the circuit does not undergo any transients.

21.240 For the general circuit of Fig. 21-85, write all the initial conditions in the transformed domain.

❙ $$v(0_+) = R_2 I \qquad \text{or} \qquad v(0_+)/s = R_2 I(s)$$

Since $$R_2 I = L \frac{di_1}{dt}(0_+) \qquad \text{and} \qquad \frac{dv}{dt}(0_+) = -R_2 \frac{di_1}{dt}(0_+) + \frac{I}{C}$$

we obtain $$\frac{dv}{dt}(0_+) = \left(\frac{1}{C} - \frac{R_2^2}{L}\right)I \qquad \text{or} \qquad \left[\frac{dv}{dt}(0_+)\right]\bigg/s = \left(\frac{1}{C} - \frac{R_2^2}{L}\right)I(s)$$

21.241 In an RLC series circuit we have $R = 200\,\Omega$ and $L = 0.1\,\text{H}$. Find C for the circuit to be critically damped.

❙ In the transformed domain, the denominator of the polynomial is $[s^2 + 2000s + (10/C)]$. For critical damping, the roots must be real and coincident. This occurs when $C = 10\,\mu\text{F}$.

21.242 For the value of C determined in Prob. 21.241, find the voltage across the capacitor if 100 V is applied to the circuit at $t = 0$.

❙ In the s domain we have

$$(s^2 + 2000s + 10^6)\,I(s) = \frac{100}{s}\,(10s) \quad \text{or} \quad I(s) = \frac{1000}{(s^2 + 2000s + 10^6)} = \frac{1000}{(s + 1000)^2}$$

$$V_C(s) = \frac{I(s)}{Cs} = \frac{10^8}{s\,(s + 1000)^2}$$

Thus $$v_C(t) = 100[1 - (1 + 1000t)e^{-1000t}] \qquad \text{V}$$

21.243 Sketch the voltage across the capacitor of the circuit of Prob. 21.242.

❙ See Fig. 21-86.

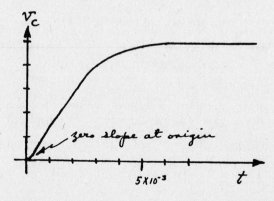

Fig. 21-86

21.244 How long does it take the capacitor of Prob. 21.242 to get within 5 percent of its final value.

$$v_C(\infty) = 100 \quad \text{or} \quad 0.95 = 1 - (1 + 1000t)e^{-1000t}$$

which yields $t = 5$ ms.

21.245 The dc sources V and I are simultaneously turned on in the circuit of Fig. 21-87. Write the equation governing the voltage across the capacitor in the s domain, with zero initial conditions.

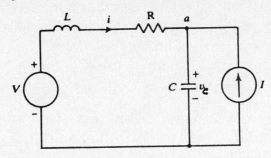

Fig. 21-87

▮ The required equations are

$$I(s) - CsV_C(s) + \frac{I}{s} = 0 \qquad sLI(s) + RI(s) + V_C(s) - \frac{V}{s} = 0$$

Eliminating $I(s)$ yields

$$(sL + R)\left[CsV_C(s) - \frac{I}{s}\right] + V_C(s) = \frac{V}{s} \quad \text{or} \quad V_C(s) = \frac{V + I(sL + R)}{s[1 + Cs(Ls + R)]}$$

21.246 Determine the voltage across the capacitor of the circuit of Fig. 21-87 under steady state.

▮ $$v_C(\infty) = \lim_{s \to 0} sV_C(s) = \lim_{s \to 0} \frac{[V + I(sL + R)]}{1 + Cs(Ls + R)} = V + IR$$

21.247 In the circuit of Fig. 21-88, S_1 is opened and S_2 is closed at $t = 0$. Write the mesh equations in the transformed domain. Also write an expression for the voltage across the switch S_2.

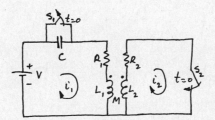

Fig. 21-88

▮ Let the initial current through L_1 be I_0. Then, the required equations are

$$\left(L_1 s + R_1 + \frac{1}{Cs}\right)I_1(s) = \frac{V}{s} + LI_0 \qquad I_2(s) = 0$$

$$V_{S2}(s) = \frac{M}{L}\left[(V - I_0 R)s - \frac{I_0}{C}\right]\bigg/\left(s^2 + \frac{R}{L}s + \frac{1}{LC}\right)$$

21.248 Obtain a circuit in the s domain corresponding to the circuit of Fig. 21-88.

▮ See Fig. 21-89.

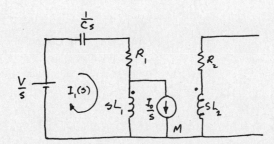

Fig. 21-89

21.249 In the circuit of Fig. 21-67, $L = 0.1$ H, $C = 10$ μF, $R_1 = 25$ Ω, and $R_2 = 200$ Ω. If $V = 90$ V, determine $i_2(t)$.

▮ From Prob. 21.202 we have (with zero initial conditions):

$$I_2(s) = \frac{V}{R_1 LC} \bigg/ \left\{ s \left[s^2 + \left(\frac{R_2}{L} + \frac{1}{R_1 C} \right) s + \frac{1}{LC} \left(1 + \frac{R_2}{R_1} \right) \right] \right\} \tag{1}$$

For the given numerical values, (1) becomes

$$I_2(s) = \frac{36 \times 10^5}{s(s^2 + 6000s + 9 \times 10^6)} = \frac{36 \times 10^5}{s(s + 3000)^2}$$

Thus,

$$i_2(t) = 0.4[1 - (1 + 3000t)e^{-3000t}] \quad \text{A}$$

21.250 Repeat Prob. 21.249 for $R_2 = 600$ Ω and $V = 250$ V.

▮ In this case we have

$$I_2(s) = \frac{10 \times 10^6}{s(s^2 + 10,000s + 25 \times 10^6)} = \frac{10 \times 10^6}{s(s + 5000)^2}$$

Thus,

$$i_2(t) = 0.4[1 - (1 + 5000t)e^{-5000t}] \quad \text{A}$$

21.251 Plot the results of Probs. 21.249 and 21.250 on one graph.

▮ See Fig. 21-90.

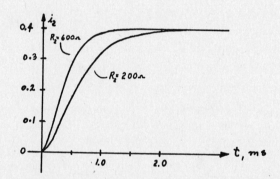

Fig. 21-90

21.252 Determine the current in the transformed domain in the circuit of Fig. 21-91, in which S is opened at $t = 0$ and the initial conditions are zero.

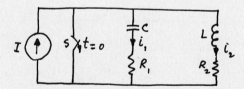

Fig. 21-91

▮ Designating the currents as I_1 and I_2 as shown in Fig. 21-91, we have

$$\frac{I}{s} = I_1(s) + I_2(s) \quad \text{and} \quad (sL + R_2)I_2(s) = \left(\frac{1}{sC} + R_1 \right) I_1(s)$$

Solving for $I_2(s)$ yields

$$I_2(s) = \frac{IR_1}{L} \left(s + \frac{1}{R_1 C} \right) \bigg/ \left\{ s \left[s^2 + \frac{1}{L}(R_1 + R_2)s + \frac{1}{LC} \right] \right\} \tag{1}$$

21.253 Find the voltage across the current source in the circuit of Fig. 21-91 in the transformed domain.

▮

$$V_I(s) = (R_2 + sL)I_2(s) = IR_1 \left[s^2 + \left(\frac{R_2}{L} + \frac{1}{R_1 C} \right) s + \frac{R_2}{R_1 LC} \right] \bigg/ \left\{ s \left[s^2 + \frac{1}{L}(R_1 + R_2)s + \frac{1}{LC} \right] \right\} \tag{1}$$

21.254 Determine the current in the inductor of the circuit of Fig. 21-91 if $I = 1$ A, $L = 0.1$ H, $C = \frac{160}{9} \mu$F, $R_1 = 0$, and $R_2 = 90 \Omega$.

▌ Substituting the numerical values in (1) of Prob. 21.252 gives

$$I_2(s) = \frac{\frac{9}{16} \times 10^6}{s(s^2 + 900s + \frac{9}{16} \times 10^6)}$$

Taking the inverse transform yields

$$i_2(t) = 1 + 1.25e^{-450t} \sin(600t - 127°) \quad A$$

21.255 Sketch the current obtained in Prob. 21.254 and verify that the circuit is slightly underdamped.

▌ See Fig. 21-92.

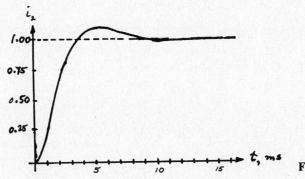

Fig. 21-92

21.256 Find the voltage across the current source in the circuit of Fig. 21-91 if $I = 1$ A, $L = 0.1$ H, $C = \frac{160}{9} \mu$F, $R_1 = 160 \Omega$, and $R_2 = 90 \Omega$.

▌ Substituting the numerical values in (1) of Prob. 21.253 yields

$$V_1(s) = 160\left[s^2 + \left(900 + \frac{9 \times 10^6}{160^2}\right)s + \left(\frac{90}{160}\right)^2 10^6\right] \bigg/ s[s^2 + 2500s + \frac{9}{16} \times 10^6]$$

and

$$v_1(t) = 90 - 21.125e^{-250t} + 91.125e^{-2250t} \quad V$$

21.257 Sketch $v_1(t)$ obtained in Prob. 21.256.

▌ See Fig. 21-93.

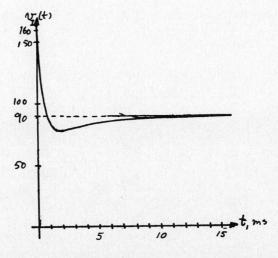

Fig. 21-93

21.258 In the circuit of Fig. 21-91, $I = 1$ A, $L = 0.1$ H, and $C = \frac{160}{9} \mu$F. Find the condition for universal resonance. Determine the current through the inductor for this condition.

For universal resonance we must have

$$R_1 = R_2 = \sqrt{\frac{L}{C}} = \sqrt{\frac{0.1}{(160/9) \times 10^{-6}}} = 75 \ \Omega$$

Thus, from (1) of Prob. 21.252 we have

$$I_2(s) = \frac{750}{s(s + 750)} \quad \text{and} \quad i_2(t) = 1 - e^{-750t} \quad \text{A}$$

21.259 How much power is delivered by the current source in the circuit of Fig. 21-91 under the condition of universal resonance.

Since $R_1 = R_2 = \sqrt{L/C} = 75 \ \Omega$ for universal resonance, (1) of Prob. 21.253 yields

$$V_I(s) = 75/s \quad \text{or} \quad V_I = 75 \text{ V}$$

Thus, $\qquad\qquad\qquad$ Power $= V_I(I) = 75(1) = 75$ W

21.260 Draw the s-domain circuit corresponding to that shown in Fig. 21-94a.

See Fig. 21-94b.

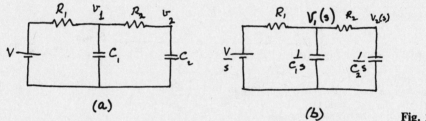

(a) $\qquad\qquad\qquad\qquad\qquad$ (b) $\qquad\qquad$ **Fig. 21-94**

21.261 Write the node equations for the circuit of Fig. 21-94b and obtain the voltage $V_2(s)$.

The required equations are

$$\left(\frac{1}{R_1} + C_1 s + \frac{1}{R_2}\right)V_1(s) - \left(\frac{1}{R_2}\right)V_2(s) = \frac{V}{sR_1} \qquad -\left(\frac{1}{R_2}\right)V_1(s) + \left(\frac{1}{R_2} + C_2 s\right)V_2(s) = 0$$

Solving for $V_2(s)$ yields

$$V_2(s) = \frac{V}{R_1 R_2 C_1 C_2} \bigg/ \left\{s\left[s^2 + \left(\frac{1}{R_2 C_2} + \frac{1}{R_1 C_1} + \frac{1}{R_2 C_1}\right)s + \frac{1}{R_1 R_2 C_1 C_2}\right]\right\}$$

21.262 Obtain an s-domain circuit for that shown in Fig. 10-128, where $C_1 = C_2 = C$, R_1 and R_2 are replaced by L, V_2 by R, and V_1 by V.

See Fig. 21-95.

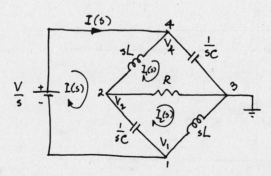

Fig. 21-95

21.263 The capacitor C_2 of Fig. 21-94 is replaced by an inductor L. Determine the voltage across the inductor (in the s domain).

▮ By nodal analysis:

$$\left(\frac{1}{R_1} + \frac{1}{R_2} + Cs\right)V_1(s) + \left(-\frac{1}{R_2}\right)V_2(s) = \frac{V}{sR_1} \qquad \left(-\frac{1}{R_2}\right)V_1(s) + \left(\frac{1}{R_2} + \frac{1}{sL}\right)V_2(s) = 0$$

Hence

$$V_2(s) = V_C(s) = \frac{V}{R_1C}\left(s + \frac{R_2}{L}\right) \Big/ \left\{s\left[s^2 + \left(\frac{R_2}{L} + \frac{1}{R_1C}\right)s + \frac{1}{LC}\left(1 + \frac{R_2}{R_1}\right)\right]\right\}$$

21.264 In the circuit of Fig. 21-88, let $V = 60\text{ V}$, $R_1 = 6\,\Omega$, $R_2 = 72\,\Omega$, $L_1 = 6\text{ H}$, $L_2 = 72\text{ H}$, $M = 18\text{ H}$, and $C = \frac{2}{15}\text{ F}$. Let S_1 be always open, and S_2 always closed. If the 60-V battery is connected at $t = 0$, solve for $i_2(t)$.

▮ The loop equations in the s domain are

$$\left(6s + 6 + \frac{15}{2s}\right)I_1(s) - 18sI_2(s) = \frac{60}{s} \qquad -18sI_1(s) + (72s + 72)I_2(s) = 0$$

or

$$I_2(s) = \frac{10s}{s^3 + 8s^2 + 9s + 5} = \frac{10s}{(s + 6.782)[(s + 0.609)^2 + (0.607)^2]}$$

Hence,

$$i_2(t) = 2.28e^{-0.609t}\sin(0.609t + 129.4°) - 1.76e^{-6.782t}$$

21.265 A bridge circuit in the s domain is shown in Fig. 21-95. Choosing node 3 as the reference node, obtain an expression for $V_2(s)$.

▮ By nodal analysis

$$\left(\frac{1}{sL} + \frac{1}{R} + sC\right)V_2(s) + \left(-sC - \frac{1}{sL}\right)V_4(s) = -sC\frac{V}{s} \qquad \left(-sC - \frac{1}{sL}\right)V_2(s) + \left(\frac{2}{sL} + 2\,sC\right)V_4(s) = \frac{V}{s}\left(\frac{1}{sL} + sC\right)$$

Solving for $V_2(s)$ yields

$$V_2(s) = -\left(s^4 - \frac{1}{C^2L^2}\right)s \Big/ \left\{s\left(s^4 + \frac{2}{RC}s^3 + \frac{2}{LC}s^2 + \frac{2}{C^2LR}s + \frac{1}{C^2L^2}\right)\right\} \tag{1}$$

21.266 Determine $I(s)$ in the circuit of Fig. 21-95.

▮ By mesh analysis we have

$$\left(sL + \frac{1}{sC}\right)I(s) - (sL)I_1(s) - \left(\frac{1}{sC}\right)I_2(s) = \frac{V}{s} \qquad -(sL)I(s) + \left(sL + R + \frac{1}{sC}\right)I_1(s) - RI_2(s) = 0$$

$$-\left(\frac{1}{sC}\right)I(s) - RI_1(s) + \left(sL + R + \frac{1}{sC}\right)I_2(s) = 0$$

Hence, $\quad I(s) = \frac{V}{R}\left(s^4 + \frac{2R}{L}s^3 + \frac{2}{LC}s^2 + \frac{2R}{CL^2}s + \frac{1}{L^2C^2}\right) \Big/ \left\{s\left(s^4 + \frac{2}{RC}s^3 + \frac{2}{LC}s^2 + \frac{2}{RLC^2}s + \frac{1}{L^2C^2}\right)\right\} \tag{1}$

21.267 For the special case $R = \sqrt{L/C}$ in the circuit of Prob. 21.265, show that the circuit is purely resistive and find $I(s)$.

▮ From (1) of Prob. 21.266, we obtain, for $R^2 = L/C$,

$$I(s) = V/sR \qquad \text{or} \qquad i(t) = V/R$$

21.268 Determine the voltage across R of the circuit of Fig. 21-95 if the battery is suddenly connected to the circuit at $t = 0$ for the special case when $R = \sqrt{L/C}$.

▮ Substituting $R^2 = L/C$ in (1), by Prob. 21.265, yields

$$V_2(s) = -\frac{V(s - R/L)}{s(s + R/L)}$$

Thus,

$$v_2(t) = V(1 - 2e^{-Rt/L})$$

21.269 The equation of motion of a flywheel is

$$10\frac{d\omega}{dt} + 0.05\omega = T$$

At $t = 0$, with zero initial conditions, the torque $T = 10\,\text{N}\cdot\text{m}$. Determine the energy stored in the flywheel at $t = 20\,\text{s}$.

▮ In the s domain we have:

$$\Omega(s)(10s + 0.05) = \frac{10}{s} \quad \text{or} \quad \Omega(s) = \frac{1}{s(s + 0.005)}$$

Thus,
$$\omega(t) = 200(1 - e^{-0.005t})$$

At $t = 20\,\text{s}$,
$$\omega(20) = 200(1 - e^{-0.005 \times 20}) = 19.03\,\text{rad/s}$$

$$\text{Energy stored} = \tfrac{1}{2}J\omega^2 = \tfrac{1}{2}(10)(19.03)^2 = 1811.2\,\text{J}$$

21.270 What is the steady-state energy stored in the flywheel of Prob. 21.269?

▮ $\quad$ Steady-state stored energy $= \tfrac{1}{2}J(\omega_s)^2 = \tfrac{1}{2}(10)[\lim\limits_{s \to 0} s\,\Omega(s)]^2 = \tfrac{1}{2}(10)\left[\lim\limits_{s \to 0} \dfrac{s}{s(s + 0.005)}\right]^2 = 200\,\text{kJ}$

21.271 After the flywheel of Prob. 21-269 has reached its steady speed, the torque is removed. How many revolutions does the flywheel make after 20 s?

▮ The equation for ω becomes

$$10\frac{d\omega}{dt} + 0.05\omega = 0 \quad \text{or} \quad \Omega(s)(10s + 0.05) - \omega(0_+) = 0$$

Since $\omega(0_+) = 200\,\text{rad/s}$, from Prob. 21-270,

$$\Omega(s) = 200/[10(s + 0.005)]$$

Since $\dot{\theta} = \omega$, we have $s\Theta(s) = \Omega(s)$

and $\qquad \Theta(s) = 20/[s(s + 0.005)] \quad \text{or} \quad \theta = 4 \times 10^3(1 - e^{-0.005t}) \quad \text{rad}$

Finally, at $t = 20\,\text{s}$,

$$\theta(20) = 380.65\,\text{rad} \quad \text{or} \quad 60.58\ \text{revolutions}$$

21.272 Figure 21-96a shows a circuit in the s domain. Obtain the corresponding circuit in the time domain.

▮ See Fig. 21-96b.

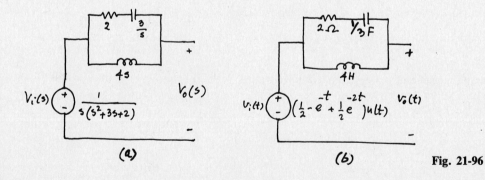

$$(a) \qquad\qquad\qquad (b) \qquad\qquad \textbf{Fig. 21-96}$$

21.273 Obtain the s-domain circuit corresponding to the circuit of Fig. 21-97a.

▮ See Fig. 21-97b.

21.274 Determine $V_0(s)$ in the circuit of Fig. 21-97b.

▮ By KCL we have

$$I_1(s) - 3I_1(s) + I_0(s) = 0 \quad \text{or} \quad I_1(s) = 0 \quad \text{since} \quad I_0(s) = 0$$

Thus, $\qquad\qquad V_0(s) = I_2(s)5 = (10/s)5 = 50/s$

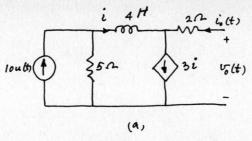

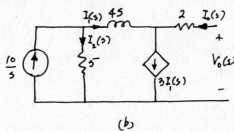

Fig. 21-97

21.275 Obtain the Thévenin equivalent circuit for the circuit of Fig. 21-97b.

▮ To find $Z_0(s)$ we apply a voltage $V_0(s)$ as shown in Fig. 21-98a. Then by KCL we have

$$I_1(s) + I_0(s) = 3I_1(s) \qquad \text{or} \qquad I_0(s) = 2I_1(s)$$

and
$$V_0(s) = I_0(s)(2) - (5 + 4s)I_1(s) = I_0(s)[2 - (5 + 4s)\tfrac{1}{2}] = I_0(s)[(-1 - 4s)/2)]$$

or
$$V_0(s)/I_0(s) = Z_0(s) = -\tfrac{1}{2} - 2s$$

Thus we obtain the Thévenin equivalent of Fig. 21-98b.

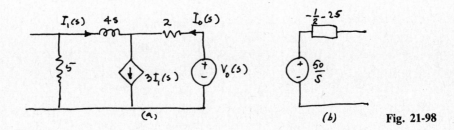

Fig. 21-98

21.276 Obtain the Norton equivalent of the circuit of Fig. 21-97b.

▮ In this case

$$I_N(s) = \frac{V_0}{Z_0} = -\frac{50}{s(\tfrac{1}{2} + 2s)}$$

Hence we obtain the circuit of Fig. 21-99.

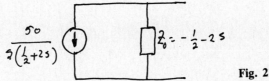

Fig. 21-99

21.277 Draw the circuit of Fig. 21-100a in the s domain.

▮ See Fig. 21-100b.

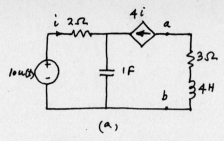

(a)

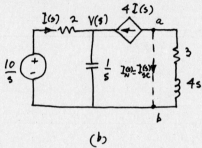

(b)

Fig. 21-100

21.278 Obtain the Norton equivalent circuit for the circuit for Fig. 21-100, at the terminals ab.

▌ To find $I_N(s)$, we apply a short-circuit ab as shown by the dashed line in the circuit of Fig. 21-100b and notice that $I_N(s) = I_{sC}(s)$. Then, by nodal analysis,

$$4I(s) + I(s) = \frac{V(s)}{1/s} \quad \text{or} \quad 5I(s) = sV(s) \quad \text{or} \quad V(s) = \frac{5}{s} I(s)$$

and

$$(10/s) - V(s) = 2I(s)$$

Hence

$$I(s) = \frac{10}{2s + 5}$$

Thus,

$$I_N(s) = I_{sC}(s) = -4I(s) = \frac{-40}{2s + 5}$$

To obtain $Z_0(s)$ we use the circuit of Fig. 21-101a, from which,

$$5I(s) = sV(s) = -5V(s)/2$$

So,

$$V(s) = 0 \qquad I(s) = 0$$

And $I_0(s) = 0$. Thus, $Z_0(s) = \infty$.
Thus, we obtain the circuit of Fig. 21-101b.

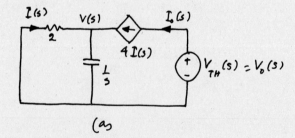

(a)

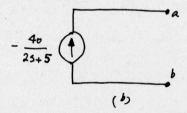

(b)

Fig. 21-101

21.279 Obtain the Norton equivalent of the circuit of Fig. 21-101a in the time domain.

▮ We obtain the required circuit directly from the circuit of Fig. 21-101b. Hence we obtain the circuit of Fig. 21-102, since

$$\mathscr{L}^{-1}\left(\frac{-40}{2s+3}\right) = -20e^{-(5/2)t}\,u(t)$$

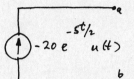

Fig. 21-102

21.280 Draw the s-domain circuit for the circuit of Fig. 21-103a, in which S is moved from 1 to 2 at $t = 0$.

▮ $$v_C(0_-) = 6[2/(4+2)] = 2\,\text{V} = v_C(0_+) \qquad I(s) = Cv(0_+) = (1)(2) = 2\,\text{A}$$

Hence we obtain the circuit of Fig. 21-103b.

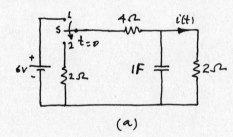
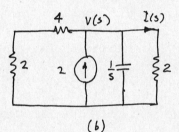

(a) $\qquad\qquad\qquad\qquad\qquad$ (b) $\qquad$ **Fig. 21-103**

21.281 Find $i(t)$ in the circuit of Fig. 21-103a for $t > 0$.

▮ By nodal analysis, from Fig. 21-103b,

$$V(s)(\tfrac{1}{6} + s + \tfrac{1}{2}) = 2 \qquad \text{or} \qquad V(s) = 6/(3s+2)$$

$$I(s) = 2V(s) = 12/(3s+2) \qquad \text{or} \qquad i(t) = 4e^{-2t/3}u(t) \qquad \text{A}$$

21.282 The current through a 1F capacitor in a network is given by

$$I(s) = \frac{12(s+1)(s+3)}{(s+2)(s+4)(s+5)}$$

Find the voltage $v(t)$ across the capacitor.

▮ $$V(s) = \frac{I(s)}{Cs} = \frac{12(s+1)(s+3)}{s(s+2)(s+4)(s+5)} = \frac{9}{10}\frac{1}{s} + \frac{1}{s+2} + \frac{9}{2}\frac{1}{s+4} - \frac{32}{5}\frac{1}{s+5}$$

Thus, $$v(t) = \left(\tfrac{9}{10} + e^{-2t} + \tfrac{9}{2}e^{-4t} - \tfrac{32}{5}e^{-5t}\right)u(t)$$

21.283 The voltage across a 0.1-H inductor in a certain circuit is given by $V(s) = (s+1)/(s^2 + 2s + 2)$. Find the current $i(t)$ through the inductor.

▮ $$I(s) = \frac{V(s)}{Ls} = \frac{10(s+1)}{s(s^2+2s+2)} = \frac{5}{s} + \frac{7.07\,\underline{/-135°}}{s+(1-j1)} + \frac{7.07\,\underline{/135°}}{s+(1+j1)}$$

or $$i(t) = [5 + 7.07e^{-t}\cos(t - 135°)]u(t) \qquad \text{A}$$

21.284 The current in a circuit is given by $I(s) = (4s+12)/(s^2 + 8s + 16)$. If this current flows through a 4-Ω resistor, which is an element of the circuit, determine the power dissipated in the resistor at $t = 0$.

▮ $$i(0_+) = \lim_{s\to\infty} sI(s) = \frac{s(4s+12)}{s^2+8s+16} = 4\,\text{A}$$

Thus, $$P = [i(0_+)]^2 4 = (4)^2 4 = 64\,W$$

21.285 Find $i(t)$ for the circuit of Prob. 21.284.

$$i(t) = \mathcal{L}^{-1}\left(\frac{4s+12}{s^2+8s+16}\right) = \mathcal{L}^{-1}\left[\frac{4s+12}{(s+4)^2}\right]$$

$$= 4\mathcal{L}^{-1}\left(\frac{1}{s+4}\right) - 4\mathcal{L}^{-1}\left[\frac{1}{(s+4)^2}\right] = 4e^{-4t}(1-t) \quad \text{A}$$

21.286 The transient current in an ac circuit is given by $I(s) = (s+1)/(s^2+s+1)$. Find the initial current.

$$i(0_+) = \lim_{s\to\infty} sI(s) = \lim_{s\to\infty} \frac{s(s+1)}{s^2+s+1} = 1\,\text{A}$$

21.287 Obtain $i(t)$ in the circuit of Prob. 21-286, and verify its result.

$$i(t) = \mathcal{L}^{-1}\left(\frac{s+1}{s^2+s+1}\right) = \mathcal{L}^{-1}\left[\frac{s+\frac12+\frac12}{(s+\frac12)^2+\frac34}\right] = \mathcal{L}^{-1}\left[\frac{s+\frac12}{(s+\frac12)^2+\frac34}\right] + \frac{1}{\sqrt3}\mathcal{L}^{-1}\left[\frac{\sqrt3/2}{(s+\frac12)^2+\frac34}\right]$$

$$= e^{-t/2}\cos\frac{\sqrt3}{2}t + \frac{1}{\sqrt3}e^{-t/2}\sin\frac{\sqrt3}{2}t = e^{-t/2}\left(\cos\frac{\sqrt3}{2}t + \frac{1}{\sqrt3}\sin\frac{\sqrt3}{2}t\right) \quad \text{A}$$

At $t=0$ we have $i(0_+) = 1\,\text{A}$.

21.288 The charge on a capacitor connected in series with an inductor, with the combination connected across a voltage source, is given by $(d^2q/dt^2) + 9q = \cos 2t$, with the initial conditions $q(0_+) = 1$ and $q(\pi/2) = -1$. Find $q(t)$.

In the s domain we have

$$s^2 Q(s) - sq(0_+) - \dot q(0_+) + 9Q(s) = s/(s^2+4)$$

or

$$Q(s) = \frac{s+\dot q(0_+)}{s^2+9} + \frac{s}{(s^2+9)(s^2+4)} = \frac{s}{s^2+9} + \frac{\dot q(0_+)}{s^2+9} + \frac{s}{5(s^2+4)} - \frac{s}{5(s^2+9)}$$

$$= \frac45\left(\frac{s}{s^2+9}\right) + \frac{\dot q(0_+)}{s^2+9} + \frac{s}{5(s^2+4)}$$

or

$$q(t) = \frac45\cos 3t + \frac{\dot q(0_+)}{3}\sin 3t + \frac15\cos 2t$$

At $t=\pi/2$, $q=-1$ yields $\dot q(0_+) = \frac{12}{5}$. Hence,

$$q(t) = \tfrac45\cos 3t + \tfrac45\sin 3t + \tfrac15\cos 2t \quad \text{C}$$

21.289 The voltage at the node of a circuit is given by $V(s) = 1/[s(s+a)]$. If $v(\infty) = 2\,\text{V}$, find $v(1)$.

$$v(\infty) = \lim_{s\to0} sV(s) = \lim_{s\to0}\frac{s}{s(s+a)} = \frac1a = 2 \quad \text{or} \quad a = 0.5$$

Thus,

$$V(s) = \frac{1}{s(s+0.5)} = 2\left(\frac1s - \frac{1}{s+0.5}\right)$$

and

$$v(t) = 2(1-e^{-0.5t}) \quad \text{or} \quad v(1) = 2(1-e^{-0.5}) = 0.787\,\text{V}$$

21.290 Two node voltages v_1 and v_2 are related by

$$\frac{dv_1}{dt} - 2v_1 + 3v_2 = 0 \tag{1}$$

$$\frac{dv_2}{dt} - v_2 + 2v_1 = 0 \tag{2}$$

Determine $v_1(t)$, if $v_1(0_+) = 8\,\text{V}$ and $v_2(0_+) = 3\,\text{V}$.

From (1) and (2) with the given initial conditions, we obtain

$$(s-2)V_1(s) + 3V_2(s) = 8 \qquad 2V_1(s) + (s-1)V_2(s) = 3$$

Thus,

$$V_1(s) = \frac{8s-17}{s^2-3s-4} = \frac{8s-17}{(s+1)(s-4)} = \frac{5}{s+1} + \frac{3}{s-4}$$

or

$$v_1(t) = 5e^{-t} + 3e^{4t} \quad \text{V}$$

21.291 Do (1) and (2) of Prob. 21.290 represent a physically realizable circuit? Explain.

▮ No, the circuit is not physically realizable since $v_1(t) \to \infty$ as $t \to \infty$. The same is true for $v_2(t)$.

21.292 A network is governed by the equation

$$t\frac{d^2x}{dt^2} + 2\frac{dx}{dt} + tx = 0$$

with $x(0_+) = 1$ and $x(\pi) = 0$. Determine $x(t)$.

▮ In the s domain we have

$$-\frac{d}{ds}[s^2X(s) - sx(0_+) - \dot{x}(0_+)] + 2[sX(s) - x(0_+)] - \frac{d}{ds}X(s) = 0$$

or $$-s^2X'(s) - 2sX(s) + 1 + 2sX(s) - 2 - X'(s) = 0$$

or $$X'(s) = \frac{-1}{s^2+1} \quad \text{and} \quad X(s) = -\tan^{-1}s + A$$

Since $X(s) \to 0$ as $s \to \infty$, $A = \pi/2$.

Thus, $$X(s) = \frac{\pi}{2} - \tan^{-1}s = \tan^{-1}\left(\frac{1}{s}\right) \quad \text{and} \quad x(t) = (\sin t)/t$$

21.293 Verify that the conditions $x(0_+) = 1$ and $x(\pi) = 0$ are satisfied by the solution obtained in Prob. 21.292.

▮ $$x(t) = \frac{1}{t}\left(t - \frac{t^3}{3!} + \cdots\right) = 1 - \frac{t^2}{3!} + \cdots$$

Thus, $$x(0_+) = 1 \quad \text{and} \quad x(\pi) = (\sin \pi)/\pi = 0$$

21.294 A voltage $v = 2e^{-4t}$ V is applied to an LC series circuit having $L = 1.0$ H and $C = 1.0$ F at $t = 0$. Determine $q(t)$, the charge on the capacitor, if $q(0_+) = \dot{q}(0_+) = 0$.

▮ The equation governing q is

$$\frac{d^2q}{dt^2} + q = 2e^{-4t}$$

or $$Q(s)(s^2+1) = \frac{2}{s+4} \quad \text{or} \quad Q(s) = \frac{2}{(s^2+1)(s+4)}$$

and $$q(t) = \tfrac{2}{17}(e^{-4t} - \cos t + 4\sin t) \quad \text{C}$$

21.295 Determine the current in the circuit of Prob. 21.294 at $t = \pi/4$ s.

▮ $$i = \frac{dq}{dt} = \tfrac{2}{17}(-4e^{-4t} + \sin t + 4\cos t)$$

or $$i\left(\frac{\pi}{4}\right) = \frac{2}{17}\left(-4e^{-4\pi/4} + \sin\frac{\pi}{4} + 4\cos\frac{\pi}{4}\right) = 0.396 \text{ A}$$

21.296 How much energy is stored in the capacitor of Prob. 21.294 at $t = \pi/4$ s?

▮ $$W_{\text{stored}} = \tfrac{1}{2}Cv^2 = \tfrac{1}{2}(q^2/C)$$

At $t = \pi/4$, $$q = \frac{2}{17}\left(e^{-\pi} - \cos\frac{\pi}{4} + 4\sin\frac{\pi}{4}\right) = 0.255 \text{ C}$$

Thus, $$W_{\text{stored}} = (0.255)^2/2 = 32.426 \text{ mJ}$$

21.297 The current in a circuit is related to the input voltage e^{-t} by

$$\frac{d^2i}{dt^2} + 5\frac{di}{dt} + 6i = e^{-t}$$

The initial conditions are $i(0_+) = di/dt(0_+) = 1$. Determine $i(t)$.

In the s domain,

$$s^2 I(s) - si(0_+) - \frac{di}{dt}(0_+) + 5[sI(s) - i(0_+)] + 6I(s) = \frac{1}{s+1}$$

or $\quad I(s)(s^2 + 5s + 6) = \frac{1}{s+1} + s + 1 + 5 \quad$ or $\quad I(s) = \frac{1}{(s+1)(s^2 + 5s + 6)} + \frac{s+6}{s^2 + 5s + 6}$

and $\qquad\qquad i(t) = (\frac{1}{2}e^{-t} + 3e^{-2t} - \frac{5}{2}e^{-3t})u(t) \qquad$ A

21.298 At $t = 0$, S_1 is opened and S_2 is closed in the circuit of Fig. 21-104a. Draw the corresponding circuit in the s domain.

▌ See Fig. 21-104b.

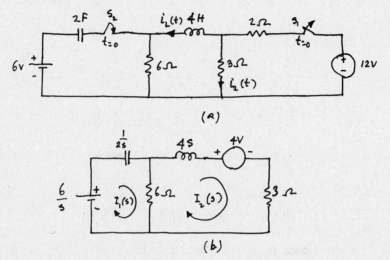

Fig. 21-104

21.299 Write a set of equations to solve for $I_1(s)$ and $I_2(s)$ in the circuit of Fig. 21-104.

▌ The required equations are

$$\frac{I_1(s)}{2s} + 6I_1(s) - 6I_2(s) = \frac{6}{s} \qquad -6I_1(s) + 9I_2(s) + 4sI_2(s) = -4$$

21.300 Draw the circuit of Fig. 21-105a in the s domain.

▌ See Fig. 21.105b.

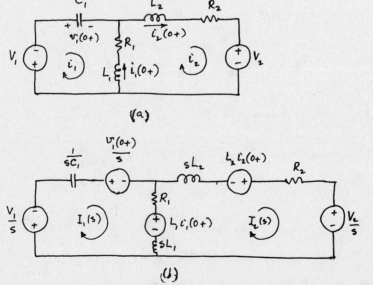

Fig. 21-105

21.301 In the circuit of Fig. 21.106a the capacitor C_2 has no initial charge. Other initial conditions are as shown. Draw a corresponding circuit in the s domain.

▌ See Fig. 21.106b.

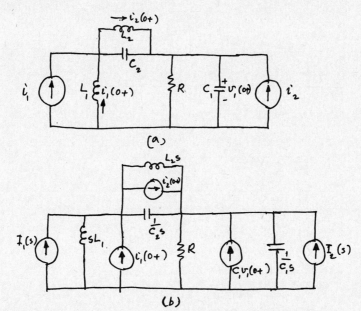

(a)

(b)   **Fig. 21-106**

21.302 Replace the current source by a voltage source in the circuit of Fig. 21.107a.

▌ See Fig. 21.107b.

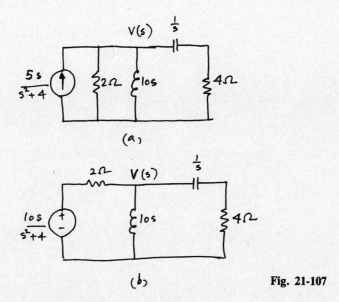

(a)

(b)   **Fig. 21-107**

21.303 Verify that $V(s)$ in the two circuits of Fig. 21-107 is the same.

▌ From Fig. 21.107a, by nodal analysis,

$$\frac{5s}{s^2+4} = \frac{V(s)}{2} + \frac{V(s)}{10s} + \frac{V(s)}{(1/s)+4} \qquad \text{or} \qquad V(s) = \frac{25s^2(1+4s)}{(3+7s)(s^2+4)}$$

Similarly, from Fig. 21-107b,

$$\frac{1}{2}\left(\frac{10s}{s^2+4} - V(s)\right) = \frac{V(s)}{10} + \frac{V(s)}{(1/s)+4} \qquad \text{or} \qquad V(s) = \frac{25s^2(1+4s)}{(3+7s)(s^2+4)}$$

21.304 Draw the circuit of Fig. 21-108a in the s domain.

▮ See Fig. 21-108b.

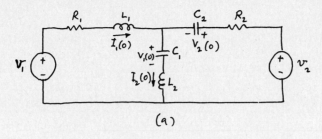

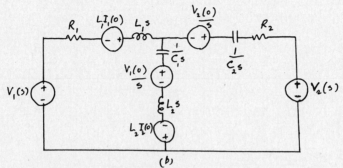

(b)   **Fig. 21-108**

21.305 Draw the circuit of Fig. 21-109a in the s domain.

▮ See Fig. 21-109b.

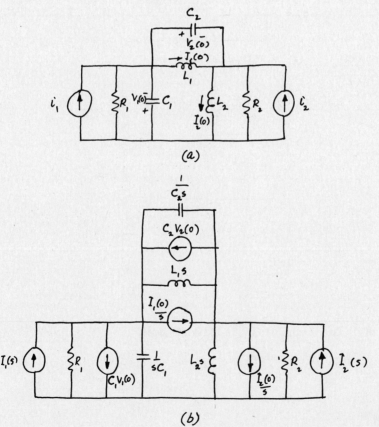

(b)   **Fig. 21-109**

21.306 Obtain the Thévenin equivalent of the circuit shown in Fig. 21-110a in the s domain, at the terminal *ab*.

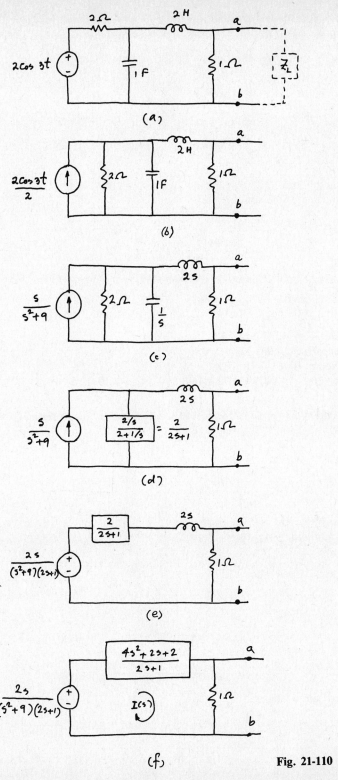

Fig. 21-110

▌ First we convert the voltage source to a current source to obtain the circuit of Fig. 21-110b and then proceed in the steps indicated in Fig. 21-110c to f. From Fig. 21-110f we obtain

$$I(s) = \frac{2s}{(s^2 + 9)(4s^2 + 4s + 3)} \qquad \text{and} \qquad V_{\text{Th}}(s) = I(s)(1) = \frac{2s}{(s^2 + 9)(4s^2 + 4s + 3)}$$

Finally,

$$Z_{\text{Th}}(s) = \left(\frac{4s^2 + 2s + 2}{2s + 1}\right)(1) \Big/ \left[1 + \frac{4s^2 + 2s + 2}{2s + 1}\right] = \frac{4s^2 + 2s + 2}{4s^2 + 4s + 3}$$

21.307 A capacitor C is discharged through a resistor R, with an initial voltage V_0 across the capacitor. Obtain an expression for the instantaneous stored energy in the capacitor.

▮ If v is the voltage across the capacitor at some time t, then

$$C\frac{dv}{dt} + \frac{v}{R} = 0 \quad \text{or} \quad C[sV(s) - V_0] + \frac{V(s)}{R} = 0 \quad \text{or} \quad V(s) = \frac{V_0}{s + (1/RC)}$$

Thus,
$$v(t) = V_0 e^{-t/RC}$$

and
$$w(t) = \tfrac{1}{2}Cv^2 = \tfrac{1}{2}CV_0^2 e^{-2t/RC} \tag{1}$$

21.308 If the capacitor of Prob. 21.307 is initially charged to 400 V with $C = 50\ \mu\text{F}$ and $R = 100\ \text{k}\Omega$, how much energy is dissipated in the resistor after 600 ms?

▮ From Prob. 21.307:

$$w(600\ \text{ms}) = 4e^{-2(0.6)/5} = 3.14\ \text{J} \quad \text{and} \quad W_0 = \tfrac{1}{2}(50 \times 10^{-6})(400)^2 = 4.0\ \text{J}$$

Thus,
$$w_{\text{dissipated}} = 4.0 - 3.14 = 0.86\ \text{J}$$

21.309 How long does it take the resistor of Prob. 21.308 to dissipate 98.2 percent of the energy stored in the capacitor?

▮ Initial stored energy, $W_0 = 4.0\ \text{J}$
Energy dissipated $= (0.982)(4) = 3.928\ \text{J}$
Energy stored at time $T = 4 - 3.928 = 0.072\ \text{J}$
From (1) of Prob. 21.307, $0.072 = 4e^{-2T/5}$ or $T = 10\ \text{s}$.

21.310 A 100-μF capacitor initially charged to 24 V is discharged across a series combination of a 1-kΩ resistor and a 200-μF capacitor. Find the current after 1 s.

▮ In the s domain we have

$$\frac{10^6}{100}\frac{I(s)}{s} + \frac{24}{s} + \frac{10^6}{200}\frac{I(s)}{s} + 10^3 I(s) = 0 \quad \text{or} \quad I(s)\left(\frac{10}{s} + 1 + \frac{5}{s}\right) = -\frac{0.024}{s} \quad \text{or} \quad I(s) = -\frac{0.024}{s + 15}$$

and
$$i(t) = -0.024e^{-15t} \quad \text{A}$$

(Compare this solution with that of Prob. 15.23.)

21.311 Solve Prob. 15.24 in the s domain.

▮
$$V_{C2} = \frac{I(s)}{C_2 s} = -\left(\frac{0.024}{s + 15}\right)\left(\frac{10^6}{200s}\right) = -\frac{120}{15}\left(\frac{1}{s} - \frac{1}{s + 15}\right)$$

Thus
$$v_{C2}(t) = -8(1 - e^{-15t}) \quad \text{and} \quad v_{C2}(0.1) = -6.215\ \text{V}$$

21.312 Solve Prob. 15.30 by using a Laplace transform.

▮ In the s domain we have

$$\left(3 + \frac{1}{0.167s}\right)I(s) = -\frac{24}{s} \quad \text{or} \quad I(s) = -\frac{4}{0.5s + 1} = -8\left(\frac{1}{s + 2}\right)$$

Thus,
$$i(t) = -8e^{-2t} \quad \text{and} \quad i(1) = -1.08\ \text{A}$$

21.313 Solve Prob. 15-34 by using a Laplace transform.

▮ For an RC circuit we have

$$RI(s) + \frac{1}{Cs}I(s) + \frac{V_0}{s} = 0 \quad \text{or} \quad \left(10 + \frac{5}{s}\right)I(s) = -\frac{100}{s}$$

or
$$I(s) = -\frac{10}{s + 0.5} \quad \text{and} \quad i(t) = -10e^{-0.5t} \quad \text{A}$$

21.314 An inductor L, initially storing an energy W_0, is discharged across a resistor R. Obtain an expression of $w(t)$.

$\blacksquare$
$$w(t) = \tfrac{1}{2} L[i(t)]^2$$

where $i(t)$ is governed by

$$(sL + R)I(s) = LI_0 \quad \text{or} \quad I(s) = \frac{I_0}{s + R/L}$$

Thus,
$$i(t) = I_0 e^{-(R/L)t}$$

where $I_0 = \sqrt{2W_0/L}$.

Finally,
$$w(t) = (\tfrac{1}{2} LI_0^2) e^{(-2R/L)t} = W_0 e^{-(2R/L)t}$$

21.315 Solve Prob. 15.57 in the s domain.

$\blacksquare$ In the s domain we have

$$10[sI(s) - i(0_+)] + 5I(s) = 0 \quad \text{or} \quad I(s) = \frac{8}{s + 0.5} \quad \text{and} \quad i(t) = 8e^{-0.5t} \quad \text{A}$$

21.316 Solve Prob. 15.59 in the s domain.

$\blacksquare$
$$100[sI(s) - i(0_+)] + 250I(s) = 0 \quad \text{or} \quad I(s) = \frac{0.5}{s + 2.5} \quad \text{and} \quad i(t) = 0.5e^{-2.5t} \quad \text{A}$$

21.317 Solve Prob. 15.62 in the s domain.

$\blacksquare$
$$100[sI(s) - i(0_+)] + 1094I(s) = 0 \quad \text{or} \quad I(s) = \frac{1.28}{s + 10.94} \quad \text{and} \quad i(t) = 1.28e^{-10.94t} \quad \text{A}$$

21.318 Solve Prob. 15.66 in the s domain.

$\blacksquare$
$$200[sI(s) - i(0_+)] + 350I(s) = 0 \quad \text{or} \quad I(s) = \frac{0.714}{s + 1.75} \quad \text{and} \quad i(t) = 0.714e^{-1.75t} \quad \text{A}$$

21.319 Solve Prob. 15.78 in the s domain.

$\blacksquare$ In the s domain we have

$$\left[s^2 I(s) - si(0_+) - \frac{di}{dt}(0_+)\right] + 6[sI(s) - i(0_+)] + \frac{1}{0.2} I(s) = 0 \quad \text{or} \quad I(s) = -\frac{24}{s^2 + 6s + 5} = \frac{24}{4}\left(\frac{1}{s + 5} - \frac{1}{s + 1}\right)$$

or
$$i(t) = 6(e^{-5t} - e^{-t}) \quad \text{A}$$

21.320 In the circuit of Fig. 15-24, $C = 14.28\,\text{mF}$, $R = 45\,\Omega$, $L = 5\,\text{H}$, and the capacitor is charged to 50 V. The switch is closed at $t = 0$. Find $i(t)$.

$\blacksquare$ In the s domain we have

$$5[I(s)s - i(0_+)] + 45I(s) + \frac{10^3 I(s)}{14.28s} + \frac{50}{s} = 0 \quad \text{or} \quad I(s)\left(5s + 45 + \frac{70}{s}\right) = -\frac{50}{s}$$

$$I(s) = -\frac{10}{s^2 + 9s + 14} = \frac{2}{s + 7} - \frac{2}{s + 2} \quad \text{and} \quad i(t) = 2(e^{-7t} - e^{-2t}) \quad \text{A}$$

21.321 Determine the voltage across the 5-H inductor in the circuit of Prob. 21-320 in the s domain.

$\blacksquare$
$$V_L(s) = sLI(s) = 5s\left(\frac{-10}{s^2 + 9s + 14}\right) = -\frac{50s}{(s + 7)(s + 2)}$$

21.322 What is the voltage across the capacitor of Prob. 21-320 in the s domain?

$\blacksquare$
$$V_c(s) = \frac{I(s)}{Cs} = \frac{70}{s}\left(\frac{-10}{s^2 + 9s + 14}\right) = -\frac{700}{s(s + 7)(s + 2)}$$

21.323 In the circuit of Fig. 15.24, $C = 0.04\,\text{F}$, $R = 10\,\Omega$, and $L = 1\,\text{H}$. With the capacitor charged to 20 V, the switch is closed at $t = 0$. Find the voltage across the inductor in the s domain.

$\blacksquare$ Let $I(s)$ be the circuit current. Then

$$sI(s) + 10I(s) + \frac{I(s)}{0.04s} = -\frac{20}{s}$$

or
$$I(s) = -\frac{20}{s^2 + 10s + 25} = -\frac{20}{(s+5)^2} \tag{1}$$

and
$$V_L(s) = sLI(s) = -\frac{20s}{(s+5)^2} \tag{2}$$

21.324 What is the voltage across the inductor of Prob. 21.323 at $t = 1$ s?

▮ From (2) of Prob. 21.323: $v_L(t) = -20(e^{-5t} - 5te^{-5t}) = -20e^{-5t}(1 - 5t)$

At $t = 1$, $\qquad\qquad\qquad v_L(1) = -20e^{-5}(1 - 5) = 0.54$ V

21.325 How much energy is stored in the inductor of Prob. 21.323 at $t = 1$ s?

▮ From (1) of Prob. 21.323:

$$i_L(t) = -20te^{-5t} \quad i_L(1) = -20e^{-5} = -0.135 \text{ A} \quad \text{and} \quad W_L = \tfrac{1}{2}(1)(-0.135)^2 = 9.08 \text{ mJ}$$

21.326 In the circuit of Fig. 15.24, $C = 76.92$ mF, $R = 4\,\Omega$, and $L = 1$. The capacitor is charged to 100 V and the switch is closed at $t = 0$. Determine the voltage across the capacitor in the s domain.

▮ Proceeding as in Prob. 21.323:

$$I(s)\left(s + 4 + \frac{10^3}{76.92s}\right) = -\frac{100}{s}$$

or
$$I(s) = -\frac{100}{s^2 + 4s + 13} \tag{1}$$

and
$$V_C(s) = \frac{I(s)}{Cs} = -\frac{1300}{s(s^2 + 4s + 13)}$$

21.327 Determine the current in the circuit of Prob. 21.326 at $t = 0.1$ s.
From (1) of Prob. 21.326:

$$I(s) = -\frac{100}{(s + 2 + j3)(s + 2 - j3)}$$

Thus, from the Laplace transform tables:

$$i(t) = -33.33e^{-2t}\sin 3t \quad \text{or} \quad i(0.1) = -33.33e^{-2(0.1)}\sin 3(0.1) = -8.06 \text{ A}$$

21.328 Obtain an expression for the charge on the capacitor of Prob. 21.326 in the s domain.

▮ Since $i = dq/dt$, $\qquad\qquad I(s) = sQ(s) - q(0_+)$

Thus, $\qquad\qquad\qquad\qquad Q(s) = \frac{I(s)}{s} + \frac{q(0_+)}{s}$

From Prob. 21.326, finally,

$$Q(s) = -\frac{100}{s(s^2 + 4s + 13)} + \frac{(76.92 \times 10^{-3})(100)}{s} = -\frac{100}{s(s^2 + 4s + 13)} + \frac{7.692}{s}$$

21.329 In the circuit of Fig. 15.24, $C = 62.5$ mF, $L = 2$ H, and $R = 12\,\Omega$. The capacitor is charged to 100 V and the switch is closed at $t = 0$. Determine the voltage across the capacitor after 1 s.

▮ In the s domain: $\qquad\qquad I(s)\left(2s + 12 + \frac{1000}{62.5s}\right) = -\frac{100}{s}$

or
$$I(s) = -\frac{50}{s^2 + 6s + 8} \tag{1}$$

Thus, $\quad V_C(s) = \frac{I(s)}{Cs} + \frac{V_0}{s} = -\frac{800}{s(s+4)(s+2)} + \frac{100}{s} = -\frac{100}{s+4} + \frac{200}{s+2}$

and
$$v_C(t) = 100(2e^{-2t} - e^{-4t}) \quad \text{V} \tag{2}$$

or
$$v_C(1) = 25.23 \text{ V}$$

21.330 Find the energy stored in the inductor of the circuit of Prob. 21.329 at $t = 0.5$ s.

▮ From (1) of Prob. 21.329, we have

$$I(s) = -\frac{50}{(s+4)(s+2)}$$

and

$$i(t) = 25(e^{-4t} - e^{-2t}) \tag{1}$$

At $t = 0.5$ s,

$$i(0.5) = 25[e^{-4(0.5)} - e^{-2(0.5)}] = -5.81 \text{ A}$$

$$\text{Stored energy } W_L = \tfrac{1}{2}L(i)^2 = \tfrac{1}{2}(2)(-5.81)^2 = 33.8 \text{ J}$$

21.331 At what instant does the energy stored in the inductor of Prob. 21.329 equal the energy stored in the capacitor.

▮ For $W_C = W_L$ we must have

$$\tfrac{1}{2}C(v_C)^2 = \tfrac{1}{2}L(i_L)^2$$

From (1) of Prob. 21.330 and (2) of Prob. 21.329, we obtain

$$62.5 \times 10^{-3}[100(2e^{-2t} - e^{-4t})]^2 = 2[25(e^{-4t} - e^{-2t})]^2$$

Solving for t yields $t = 0.751$ s.

21.332 In the circuit of Fig. 15.24, we have $L = 4$ H, $R = 40 \, \Omega$, and $C = 0.01$ F, which is initially charged to 600 V. If the switch is closed at $t = 0$, find $i(t)$.

▮ Proceeding as in Prob. 21.329:

$$I(s)\left(4s + 40 + \frac{1}{0.01s}\right) = -\frac{600}{s} \quad \text{or} \quad I(s) = -\frac{150}{(s+5)^2}$$

Thus,

$$i(t) = -150te^{-5t} \quad \text{A}$$

21.333 In the circuit of Fig. 15-24, $L = 2$ H, $R = 12 \, \Omega$, and $C = 62.5$ mF. The initial conditions are $v_C(0_+) = 100$ V and $i_L(0_+) = 1.0$ A. The switch is closed at $t = 0$. Find $i(t)$.

▮ In the s domain:

$$2sI(s) - 2i_L(0_+) + 12I(s) + \frac{1000}{62.5s}I(s) + \frac{v_C(0_+)}{s} = 0$$

or

$$I(s)\left(\frac{2s^2 + 12s + 16}{s}\right) = -\frac{100}{s} + 2 \quad \text{or} \quad I(s) = -\frac{50}{(s+4)(s+2)} + \frac{s}{(s+4)(s+2)}$$

Hence,

$$i(t) = 25(e^{-4t} - e^{-2t}) + 2e^{-4t} - e^{-2t} = 27e^{-4t} - 26e^{-2t} \quad \text{A} \tag{1}$$

21.334 Find the voltage across the inductor of Prob. 21.333 at $t = 0.5$ s.

▮ $V_L(s) = sLI(s)$

or

$$v_L(t) = L\frac{di}{dt} = 2[27(-4e^{-4t}) - 26(-2e^{-2t})] = -216e^{-4t} + 104e^{-2t}$$

or

$$v_L(0.5) = 9.03 \text{ V} \tag{1}$$

21.335 What is the voltage across the capacitor of Prob. 21.333 at $t = 0.5$ s.

▮ We find $v_C(0.5)$ from the KVL equation.

$$v_L + v_C + v_R = 0 \quad \text{and} \quad v_R = Ri$$

From (1) of Prob. 21.333:

$$v_R(0.5) = 12[27e^{-4(0.5)} - 26e^{-2(0.5)}] = -70.93 \text{ V}$$

From (1) of Prob. 21.334: $v_L(0.5) = 9.03$ V

Hence,

$$v_C(0.5) = 70.93 - 9.03 = 61.90 \text{ V}$$

21.336 In the circuit of Fig. 15-24, $R = 16\,\Omega$, $L = 2\,\text{H}$, and $C = 0.0122\,\text{F}$. If the initial conditions are $i(0_+) = 0$ and $di/dt(0_+) = -240$, find $i(t)$.

∎ In the *s* domain:

$$2s^2 I(s) - 2si(0_+) - 2\frac{di}{dt}(0_+) + 16sI(s) - 16i(0_+) + \frac{1}{0.0122}\,I(s) = 0$$

or $\qquad I(s)(2s^2 + 16s + 81.96) = -480 \qquad$ or $\qquad I(s) = \dfrac{-240}{s^2 + 8s + 40.98} = \dfrac{-240}{(s + 4 + j5)(s + 4 - j5)}$

Hence, $\qquad\qquad\qquad\qquad\qquad i(t) = -48e^{-4t}\sin 5t \qquad$ **A**

21.337 In the circuit of Fig. 15-24, $R = 12\,\Omega$, $L = 1\,\text{H}$, and $C = 0.01\,\text{F}$, which is initially charged to 60 V. The switch is closed at $t = 0$. Find $i(t)$.

∎ In the *s* domain:

$$I(s)\left(s + 12 + \frac{1}{0.01s}\right) = -\frac{60}{s} \qquad \text{or} \qquad I(s) = \frac{-60}{s^2 + 12s + 100} = -\frac{60}{(s + 6 + j8)(s + 6 - j8)}$$

Hence, $\qquad\qquad\qquad\qquad\qquad i(t) = -7.5e^{-6t}\sin 8t \qquad$ **A**

21.338 Solve Prob. 15.137 by the Laplace transform method.

∎ In the *s* domain: $\qquad\qquad\qquad I(s)(6s + 24) - 6i(0_+) = \dfrac{24}{s}$

or $\qquad I(s)(s + 4) - \dfrac{24}{10} = \dfrac{4}{s} \qquad$ or $\qquad I(s) = \dfrac{4}{s(s+4)} + \dfrac{24}{10}\dfrac{1}{s+4} = \left(\dfrac{1}{s} - \dfrac{1}{s+4}\right) + 2.4\left(\dfrac{1}{s+4}\right)$

or $\qquad\qquad\qquad i(t) = 1.0 - e^{-4t} + 2.4e^{-4t} = 1 + 1.4e^{-4t} \qquad$ **A**

21.339 Find the voltage across the coil of Fig. 15-41.

∎ For the coil we have $\quad R_{co} = 10\,\Omega$, $\quad L_{co} = 6\,\text{H}$.

Thus, $\qquad V_{co}(s) = (sL_C + R_C)I(s) = \dfrac{(6s + 10)(4 + 2.4s)}{s(s+4)} = 14.4\left(1 - \dfrac{4}{s+4}\right) + \dfrac{48}{s+4} + \dfrac{10}{s} - \dfrac{10}{s+4}$

or $\qquad v_{co}(t) = 14.4\delta(t) - 57.6e^{-4t} + 48e^{-4t} + 10 - 10\,e^{-4t} = 14.4\delta(t) + 10 - 19.6e^{-4t} \qquad$ **V**

21.340 Solve Prob. 15.143 by the Laplace transform method.

∎ In the *s* domain:

$$20 \times 10^{-3}\left[sI(s) - \frac{50}{40}\right] + 40I(s) = \frac{10}{s} \qquad \text{or} \qquad I(s) = \frac{500}{s(s+2000)} + \frac{1.25}{s + 2000}$$

Thus, $\qquad\qquad\qquad\qquad\qquad i(t) = 0.25 + e^{-2000t} \qquad$ **A**

21.341 Find $i(t)$ in the circuit of Fig. 15-45.

∎ In the *s* domain: $\qquad 2 \times 10^6 I(s) + \dfrac{10^6}{35}\dfrac{I(s)}{s} = \dfrac{24}{s} \qquad$ or $\qquad I(s) = \dfrac{12 \times 10^{-6}}{s + \frac{1}{70}}$

Thus, $\qquad\qquad\qquad\qquad\qquad i(t) = 12e^{-t/70} \qquad$ μ**A**

21.342 Solve Prob. 15.155 by the Laplace transform method.

∎ In the *s* domain: $\qquad\qquad\qquad 3I_C(s) + \dfrac{2}{s}\,I_C(s) + \dfrac{18}{s} = 0$

or $\qquad I_C(s) = -\dfrac{18}{(3s + 2)} = \dfrac{6}{(s + 1/1.5)} \qquad$ or $\qquad i_C(t) = -6e^{-t/1.5} \qquad$ **A**

21.343 Solve Prob. 15.156 by the Laplace transform method.

▮ In the s domain:
$$6I(s) + 5sI(s) = \frac{18}{s} \quad \text{or} \quad I(s) = \frac{18}{s(5s + 6)} = 3\left(\frac{1}{s} - \frac{5}{5s + 6}\right) = 3\left(\frac{1}{s} - \frac{1}{s + \frac{6}{5}}\right)$$

Hence,
$$i(t) = 3(1 - e^{-1.2t}) \quad \text{A}$$

21.344 Solve Prob. 15.157 by the Laplace transform method.

▮ In the s domain:
$$0.5 \times 10^6\, I(s) + \frac{10^6}{500s}\, I(s) + \frac{20}{s} = 0$$

or
$$I(s) = -\frac{20 \times 10^{-6} \times 500}{250(s + \frac{1}{250})} = -\frac{40 \times 10^{-6}}{s + \frac{1}{250}} \quad \text{or} \quad i(t) = -40e^{-t/250} \quad \mu\text{A}$$

21.345 Solve Prob. 15.159 by the Laplace transform method.

▮ In the s domain:
$$(0.5s + 2)I(s) - 0.5(4) = \frac{40}{s}$$

or
$$I(s) = \frac{80}{s(s + 4)} + \frac{4}{s + 4} = \frac{20}{s} - \frac{20}{s + 4} + \frac{4}{s + 4} = \frac{20}{s} - \frac{16}{s + 4} \quad \text{or} \quad i(t) = 20 - 16e^{-4t} \quad \text{A}$$

21.346 In the circuit of Fig. 21-111, S_1 is closed at $t = 0$, and S_2 is opened at $t = 4$ ms. Determine $i(t)$ for $t > 0$.

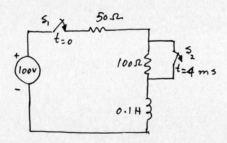

Fig. 21-111

▮ For $0 \le t \le 4$ ms:
$$50I(s) + 0.1sI(s) = \frac{100}{s} \quad \text{or} \quad I(s) = \frac{10^3}{s(s + 500)} \quad \text{or} \quad i(t) = 2(1 - e^{-t/2})$$

where t is measured in milliseconds. Thus $i(4) = 1.729$.

For $4 \le t < \infty$:
$$150I(s) + 0.1sI(s) - 0.1\,i(4 \times 10^{-3}) = \frac{100}{s} \quad \text{or} \quad I(s)(0.1s + 150) = \frac{100}{s} + 0.1729$$

Hence,
$$i(t) = 1.062e^{-1.5t} + 0.667 \quad \text{A}$$

t being in milliseconds.

21.347 Determine the voltage across the capacitor in the circuit of Fig. 21-112 if S is closed at $t = 0$.

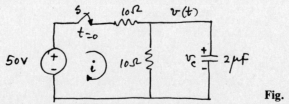

Fig. 21-112

❚ By nodal analysis:

$$\frac{50 - v_C}{10} = \frac{v_C}{10} + 2 \times 10^{-6} \frac{dv_C}{dt} \qquad \text{or} \qquad V_C(s) = \frac{25}{s[s + 10^5] \, 1 \times 10^{-5}}$$

or

$$v_C(t) = 25(1 - e^{-t/10})$$

where t is in microseconds.

21.348 In the s domain, the energy in a network is given by

$$W(s) = \frac{(s + 48)}{(s + 1)(s + 2)(s + 3)}$$

Express the energy in the time domain.

$$W(s) = \frac{s + 48}{(s + 1)(s + 2)(s + 3)} = \frac{47/2}{s + 1} - \frac{46}{s + 2} + \frac{45/2}{s + 3}$$

or

$$w(t) = \tfrac{47}{2}e^{-t} - 46e^{-2t} + \tfrac{45}{2}e^{-3t} \tag{1}$$

21.349 Determine the initial and final energies from $W(s)$, and verify that the result is consistent with that of (1) of Prob. 21.348.

❚

$$w(0) = \lim_{s \to \infty} sW(s) = \lim_{s \to \infty} \frac{s(s + 48)}{(s + 1)(s + 2)(s + 3)} = 0$$

From (1): $\quad w(0) = \dfrac{47}{2} - 46 + \dfrac{45}{2} = 0 \qquad w(\infty) = \lim_{s \to 0} sW(s) = \lim_{s \to 0} \dfrac{s(s + 48)}{(s + 1)(s + 2)(s + 3)} = 0$

21.350 Find the instantaneous power in the network of Prob. 21.348.

❚

$$p(t) = \frac{dw}{dt}$$

or

$$P(s) = sW(s) - w(0_+) = sW(s)$$

$$= \frac{s(s + 48)}{(s + 1)(s + 2)(s + 3)} = -\frac{47}{2} \frac{1}{s + 1} + \frac{92}{s + 2} - \frac{135}{2} \frac{1}{s + 3} \tag{1}$$

Thus,

$$p(t) = -\tfrac{47}{2}e^{-t} + 92e^{-2t} - \tfrac{135}{2}e^{-3t} \qquad \text{W}$$

21.351 Determine the initial and final powers from $P(s)$ of Prob. 21.350.

❚

$$p(0) = \lim_{s \to \infty} \frac{s^2(s + 48)}{(s + 1)(s + 2)(s + 3)} = 1 \text{ W} \qquad p(\infty) = \lim_{s \to 0} sP(s) = 0 \text{ W}$$

21.352 In the circuit of Fig. 21-113, S is closed at $t = 0$. Find the current in the 10-Ω resistor in the s domain.

❚

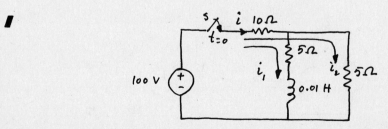

Fig. 21-113

▌ From Fig. 21-113: $\qquad\qquad\qquad\qquad I(s) = I_1(s) + I_2(s)$

$$0.01sI_1(s) + 5I_1(s) + 10I_1(s) + 10I_2(s) = \frac{100}{s} \qquad 10I_1(s) + 10I_2(s) + 5I_2(s) = \frac{100}{s}$$

Solving for $I_1(s)$ and $I_2(s)$ yields

$$I_1(s) = \frac{3333}{s(s + 833)} \qquad \text{and} \qquad I_2(s) = \frac{6.67s + 3333}{s(s + 833)}$$

Thus, $\qquad\qquad\qquad\qquad\qquad I(s) = \frac{6.67s + 6666}{s(s + 833)}$

21.353 Including initial conditions, write a set of equations in the s domain to determine the current through the inductor in the circuit of Fig. 21-114, where S is closed at $t = 0$.

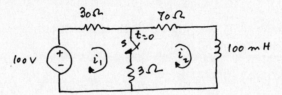

Fig. 21-114

▌ The mesh equations are

$$33I_1(s) - 3I_2(s) = \frac{100}{s} \qquad -3I_1(s) + (0.1s + 73)I_2(s) - 0.1i_2(0_+) = 0$$

where the initial current $i_2(0_+) = 100/(70 + 30) = 1\,\text{A}$.

21.354 In the circuit of Fig. 21-115, S is opened at $t = 0$. Determine the voltage across the 200-Ω resistor.

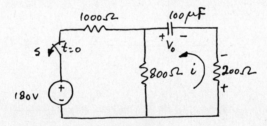

Fig. 21-115

▌ The initial condition is $v_C(0_+) = 180(800/1800) = 80\,\text{V}$. Now, for $t > 0$:

$$800I(s) + 200I(s) + \frac{10^6}{100}\frac{I(s)}{s} = \frac{80}{s} \qquad \text{or} \qquad I(s) = \frac{2}{25}\frac{1}{s + 10}$$

$$V_{200\,\Omega}(s) = 200I(s) = 200\left(\frac{2}{25}\right)\left(\frac{1}{s + 10}\right) = \frac{16}{s + 10}$$

Thus, $\qquad\qquad\qquad\qquad\qquad v_{200}(t) = 16e^{-10t} \qquad \text{V}$

21.355 Find i in the circuit of Fig. 21-116, where S is opened at $t = 0$.

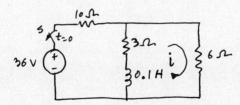

Fig. 21-116

▌ The initial condition is:

$$i(0_+) = \frac{36}{10 + 2} \times \frac{6}{9} = 2\,\text{A}$$

$$3I(s) + 6I(s) + 0.1sI(s) - 0.1(2) = 0$$

Thus, $\qquad\qquad\qquad\qquad I(s) = \frac{2}{s + 90} \qquad \text{or} \qquad i(t) = 2e^{-90t} \qquad \text{A}$

21.356 In the circuit of Fig. 21-117, S is moved from 1 to 2 at $t = 0$. Determine the voltage across the resistor.

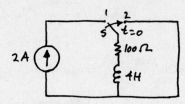

Fig. 21-117

▮

$$i(0_+) = 2 \text{ A} \qquad (100 + 4s)I(s) - 4(2) = 0 \qquad \text{or} \qquad I(s) = \frac{2}{s + 25}$$

$$V_R(s) = RI(s) = \frac{2(100)}{s + 25} \qquad \text{or} \qquad v_R(t) = 200e^{-25t} \quad \text{V}$$

21.357 The switch is moved from 1 to 2 at $t = 0$ in the circuit of Fig. 21-118. Solve for i.

▮

$$v_C(0_+) = 2 \text{ V}$$

For $t > 0$: $\qquad 4I(s) + \dfrac{I(s)}{0.5s} = -\dfrac{2}{s} + \dfrac{4}{s} = \dfrac{2}{s} \qquad \text{or} \qquad I(s) = \dfrac{1}{1 + 2s} = \dfrac{1}{2}\left(\dfrac{1}{s + 0.5}\right)$

Thus, $\qquad\qquad\qquad\qquad i(t) = 0.5e^{-0.5t} \quad \text{A}$

21.358 In the circuit of Fig. 21-118, let S be closed on position 1 at $t = 0$ and moved to position 2 after 2 s. Determine i.

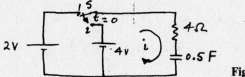

Fig. 21-118

▮ For $0 \le t \le 2s$ we have

$$4I(s) + \frac{I(s)}{0.5s} = \frac{2}{s} \qquad \text{or} \qquad I(s) = \frac{1}{2(s + \frac{1}{2})}$$

Thus, $\qquad\qquad V_C(s) = \dfrac{I(s)}{Cs} = \dfrac{1}{s(s + \frac{1}{2})} = 2\left(\dfrac{1}{s} - \dfrac{1}{s + \frac{1}{2}}\right)$

and $\qquad\qquad\qquad v_C(t) = 2(1 - e^{-t/2}) \quad \text{V}$

At $t = 2$, $\qquad\qquad v_C(2) = 2(1 - e^{-1}) = 1.264 \text{ V}$

Now proceeding as in Prob. 21.357,

$$4I(s) + \frac{I(s)}{0.5s} = -\frac{1.264}{s} + \frac{4}{s} \qquad \text{or} \qquad I(s) = \frac{0.684}{s(s + \frac{1}{2})} = 1.368\left(\frac{1}{s} - \frac{1}{s + \frac{1}{2}}\right)$$

Hence, $\qquad\qquad i(t) = 1.368(1 - e^{-t/2}) \quad \text{A}$

21.359 In the circuit of Fig. 21-119, obtain an equation for the node voltage v in the s domain and list all the initial conditions.

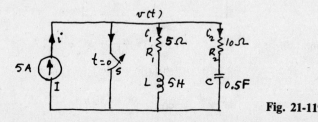

Fig. 21-119

❚ The governing equations are

$$I_1(s) + I_2(s) = I(s) = \frac{5}{s} \qquad V(s) = 5I_1(s) + 5sI_1(s) = 10I_2(s) + 2\frac{I_2(s)}{s}$$

Eliminating $I_1(s)$ and $I_2(s)$ yields

$$V(s)(5s^2 + 15s + 2) = \frac{50}{s} + 5sv(0_+) + 15v(0_+) + 5\frac{dv}{dt}(0_+)$$

The initial conditions are

$$v(0_+) = (10)(5) = 50 \text{ V} \qquad \text{and} \qquad \frac{dv}{dt}(0_+) = \left(2 - \frac{25}{5}\right)5 = -15 \text{ V/s}$$

21.360 In the circuit of Fig. 21-119, $R_1 = 60\,\Omega$, $R_2 = 90\,\Omega$, $L = 0.1\,\text{H}$, $C = 17.78\,\mu\text{F}$, and $I = 1.0\,\text{A}$. For zero energy stored in L and C, find $v(t)$.

❚ Proceeding as in Prob. 21.359, we have

Initial conditions: $\quad v(0_+) = 90 \text{ V} \qquad \frac{dV}{dt}(0_+) = \left(\frac{10^6}{17.78} - \frac{8100}{0.1}\right) = -24.75 \times 10^3 \text{ V/s}$

The equation for $V(s)$ is

$$\left(0.1s^2 + 150s + \frac{10^6}{17.78}\right)V(s) = \frac{60 \times 10^6}{17.78}\frac{1}{s} + 0.1s(90) + 15(90) + 5(-24.75 \times 10^3)$$

After combining terms and inverting:

$$v(t) = 30[2 + (1 - 75t)e^{-750t}] \qquad \text{V}$$

21.361 In the circuit of Fig. 21-120, S is opened at $t = 0$. Determine $I(s)$.

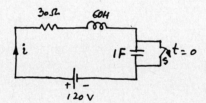

Fig. 21-120

❚ $\qquad\qquad v_C(0_+) = 0 \text{ V} \qquad i(0_+) = 120/30 = 4 \text{ A}$

and $\qquad\qquad 60[sI(s) - i(0_+)] + 30I(s) + \frac{I(s)}{s} = \frac{120}{s}$

or $\qquad\qquad I(s) = \frac{240s + 120}{60s^2 + 30s + 1} = \frac{240s + 120}{(s + 0.46)(s + 0.036)}$

21.362 Write a set of transformed equations to solve for i in the circuit of Fig. 21-121 where the switch is closed at $t = 0$. State all initial conditions.

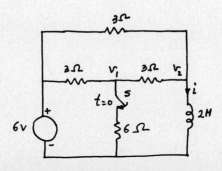

Fig. 21-121

■

$$i(0_+) = \frac{6}{[3(3+3)]/(3+3+3)} = 3\,\text{A}$$

At node 1:

$$\frac{(6/s) - V_1(s)}{3} = \frac{V_1(s)}{6} + \frac{V_1(s) - V_2(s)}{3}$$

or

$$5V_1(s) - 2V_2(s) = \frac{12}{s} \tag{1}$$

Similarly, at node 2, with $i(0_+) = 3$, we have

$$\frac{6/s - V_2(s)}{3} + \frac{V_1(s) - V_2(s)}{3} = 3 + \frac{1}{2}\frac{V_2(s)}{s}$$

or

$$V_1(s) - 2V_2(s) = 9 - \frac{6}{s} + \frac{3\,V_2(s)}{2s} \tag{2}$$

and

$$\frac{1}{2}\frac{V_2(s)}{s} = I(s) \tag{3}$$

Equations (1) to (3) are the required equations.

21.363 For the circuit of Fig. 21-122, write a set of equations to solve for $I(s)$. Include all initial conditions.

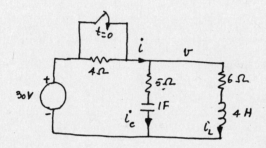

Fig. 21-122

■ The initial conditions are

$$i_L(0_+) = \frac{30}{4+6} = 3\,\text{A} \qquad v_C(0_+) = \frac{(30)\,(6)}{4+6} = 18\,\text{V} \qquad i_C(0_+) = \frac{30 - 18}{5} = 2.4\,\text{A}$$

The governing equations are

$$4[sI_L(s) - i_L(0_+)] + 6I_L(s) = \frac{30}{s} \qquad 5I_C(s) + \frac{I_C(s)}{s} + v_C(0_+) = \frac{30}{s}$$

and

$$I(s) = I_C(s) + I_L(s)$$

CHAPTER 22
State Variables Method

22.1   Express the following second-order differential equation as a set of two first-order differential equations:

$$\frac{d^2y}{dt^2} + 6\frac{dy}{dt} + 5y = u(t) \qquad (1)$$

$$\ddot{y} + 6\dot{y} + 5y = u(t)$$

▮ Let
$$x_1(t) = y(t) \qquad x_2(t) = \dot{x}_1(t) = \dot{y}(t) \qquad \dot{x}_2(t) = \ddot{y}(t)$$

Now (1) may be written as

$$\ddot{y} = -6\dot{y} - 5y + u(t)$$

or in terms of x_1 and x_2 the required equations are

$$\dot{x}_1 = x_2 \qquad \dot{x}_2 = -5x_1 - 6x_2 + u(t)$$

22.2   Express the result of Prob. 22.1 in a matrix form.

▮
$$\begin{bmatrix} \dot{x}_1 \\ \dot{x}_2 \end{bmatrix} = \begin{bmatrix} 0 & 1 \\ -5 & -6 \end{bmatrix} \begin{bmatrix} x_1 \\ x_2 \end{bmatrix} + \begin{bmatrix} 0 \\ 1 \end{bmatrix} u(t)$$

22.3   Write the result of Prob. 22.2 as a vector equation. Identify the components of the vector.

▮
$$[\dot{x}] = [A][x] + [B][u]$$

or
$$\bar{x} = \bar{A}\bar{x} + \bar{B}\bar{u} \qquad (1)$$

where
$$\bar{A} \text{ or } [A] = \begin{bmatrix} 0 & 1 \\ -5 & -6 \end{bmatrix} \qquad \bar{B} \text{ or } [B] = \begin{bmatrix} 0 \\ 1 \end{bmatrix} \qquad \bar{x} \text{ or } [x] = \begin{bmatrix} x_1 \\ x_2 \end{bmatrix}$$

and x_1 and x_2 are components of the vector $\bar{x}$, also known as *state variables* for a physical system represented by (1) of Prob. 22.1. Hence (1) is known as the *state equation* and $\bar{x}$ as the *state vector*.

22.4   Express $\dddot{y}(t) + 4\ddot{y}(t) + \dot{y}(t) - 6y(t) = u(t)$ as a state equation.

▮ Let
$$x_1 = y \qquad x_2 = \dot{x}_1 = \dot{y} \qquad x_3 = \dot{x}_2 = \ddot{y}$$

Then
$$\dot{x}_3 = \dddot{y} = -4\ddot{y} - \dot{y} + 6y + u \qquad \dot{x}_2 = x_3 \qquad \dot{x}_1 = x_2$$

Rewriting these equations in matrix form we obtain

$$\begin{bmatrix} \dot{x}_1 \\ \dot{x}_2 \\ \dot{x}_3 \end{bmatrix} = \begin{bmatrix} 0 & 1 & 0 \\ 0 & 0 & 1 \\ 6 & -1 & -4 \end{bmatrix} \begin{bmatrix} x_1 \\ x_2 \\ x_3 \end{bmatrix} + \begin{bmatrix} 0 \\ 0 \\ 1 \end{bmatrix} u(t)$$

or
$$\dot{\bar{x}} = \bar{A} \quad \bar{x} + \bar{B} \, u$$

22.5   As a general rule, the number of state variables in a system is the same as the number of energy storage elements in the system. Apply this rule to find the number of state variables in the system of Fig. 22-1.

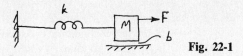

Fig. 22-1

▮ Since there are two energy storage elements—the mass and the spring—the system may be described in terms of two state variables.

22.6 The equations of motion related to the dynamics of a system are

$$\frac{di}{dt} + 3i + 2\dot{x} = v \qquad \ddot{x} + 3x + 2i = 0$$

Express these equations as a state equation.

∎ Let $i = y_1$, $x = y_2$, and $\dot{x} = \dot{y}_2 = y_3$ so that $\ddot{x} = \dot{y}_3$. The given equations then become

$$\frac{di}{dt} = -3i - 2\dot{x} + v \qquad \text{or} \qquad \dot{y}_1 = -3y_1 - 2y_3 + v$$

and

$$\ddot{x} = -3x - 2i \qquad \text{or} \qquad \dot{y}_3 = -2y_1 - 3y_2$$

The three first-order equations are

$$\dot{y}_1 = -3y_1 - 2y_3 + v \qquad \dot{y}_2 = y_3 \qquad \dot{y}_3 = -2y_1 - 3y_2$$

Hence, the state equation is

$$\dot{\bar{y}} = \bar{A}\bar{y} + \bar{B}\bar{u}$$

where

$$\bar{A} = \begin{bmatrix} -3 & 0 & -2 \\ 0 & 0 & 1 \\ -2 & -3 & 0 \end{bmatrix} \qquad \bar{B} = \begin{bmatrix} 1 \\ 0 \\ 0 \end{bmatrix} \qquad \text{and} \qquad \bar{y} = \begin{bmatrix} y_1 \\ y_2 \\ y_3 \end{bmatrix}$$

22.7 How many state variables may be associated with the circuit of Fig. 22-2? Specify a set of possible state variables.

∎ The energy storage elements are L and C, and hence there are two state variables $i_L(t)$ and $v_C(t)$.

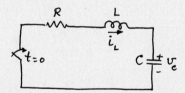

Fig. 22-2

22.8 Write the state equation for the circuit of Fig. 22-2 in matrix form.

∎ The equations governing the state variables i_L and v_C are

$$L\frac{di_L}{dt} + Ri_L + v_C = 0 \qquad \text{or} \qquad \frac{di_L}{dt} = -\frac{R}{L}i_L - \frac{1}{L}v_C$$

and

$$C\frac{dv_C}{dt} = i_L \qquad \text{or} \qquad \frac{dv_C}{dt} = \frac{1}{C}i_L$$

In matrix form, the state equation becomes

$$\begin{bmatrix} \dfrac{di_L}{dt} \\ \dfrac{dv_C}{dt} \end{bmatrix} = \begin{bmatrix} -\dfrac{R}{L} & -\dfrac{1}{L} \\ \dfrac{1}{C} & 0 \end{bmatrix} \begin{bmatrix} i_L \\ v_C \end{bmatrix}$$

or

$$\dot{\bar{y}} = \bar{A}\bar{y} \tag{1}$$

22.9 Notice that (1) of Prob. 22.8 is of the form $(dy/dt) - ay = 0$, which is a scalar equation, and has a solution of the form $x(t) = x(0)e^{at}$, where $x(0)$ is the initial condition. Assuming that this form of solution is applicable to the vector equation (1), write the form of the solution. Also express the exponential as a series.

∎ The form of solution is

$$\bar{y}(t) = e^{\bar{A}t}\bar{y}(0)$$

where $\bar{y}(0)$ is known as the *initial state*.

Since

$$e^{at} = 1 + at + \frac{a^2 t^2}{2!} + \frac{a^3 t^3}{3!} + \cdots$$

we may also write

$$e^{\bar{A}t} = \bar{I} + \bar{A}t + \frac{\bar{A}^2 t^2}{2!} + \frac{\bar{A}^3 t^3}{3!} + \cdots$$

where $\bar{I} \equiv$ identity matrix and $e^{\bar{A}t}$ is defined as the *state transition matrix*.

22.10 Obtain the state equation for the circuit of Fig. 22-3.

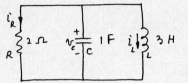

Fig. 22-3

▌ From the given data:

$$v_C = 3 \frac{di_L}{dt} \quad \text{or} \quad \frac{di_L}{dt} = \frac{1}{3} v_C \tag{1}$$

$$i_R = \frac{v_C}{2} \quad \text{and} \quad i_C = 1 \frac{dv_C}{dt}$$

Since $i_R + i_L + i_C = 0$, we have

$$i_C = \frac{dv_C}{dt} = -i_L - \frac{v_C}{2} \tag{2}$$

Expressing (1) and (2) in matrix form:

$$\begin{bmatrix} \dfrac{di_L}{dt} \\ \dfrac{dv_C}{dt} \end{bmatrix} = \begin{bmatrix} 0 & \dfrac{1}{3} \\ -1 & -\dfrac{1}{2} \end{bmatrix} \begin{bmatrix} i_L \\ v_C \end{bmatrix}$$

22.11 Write the general state equation in terms of R, L, and C for the circuit of Fig. 22-3.

▌ Proceeding as in Prob. 22.10, we have

$$\begin{bmatrix} \dfrac{di_L}{dt} \\ \dfrac{dv_C}{dt} \end{bmatrix} = \begin{bmatrix} 0 & \dfrac{1}{L} \\ -\dfrac{1}{C} & -\dfrac{1}{RC} \end{bmatrix} \begin{bmatrix} i_L \\ v_C \end{bmatrix}$$

22.12 Write the state equation for the circuit of Fig. 22-4.

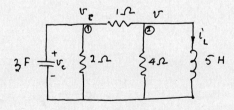

Fig. 22-4

▌ At node 1:

$$3 \frac{dv_C}{dt} + \frac{v_C}{2} + \frac{v_C - v}{1} = 0$$

or

$$\frac{dv_C}{dt} = -\frac{v_C}{2} + \frac{v}{3} \tag{1}$$

At node 2: $\qquad v_C - v = i_L + \dfrac{v}{4} \qquad$ and $\qquad 5\dfrac{di_L}{dt} = v = \dfrac{4}{5}v_C - \dfrac{4}{5}i_L$

or

$$\frac{di_L}{dt} = \frac{1}{5}v = \frac{4}{25}v_C - \frac{4}{25}i_L \tag{2}$$

Writing (1) and (2) in the form

$$\frac{d\bar{y}}{dt} = \bar{A}y$$

we have

$$\begin{bmatrix} \dfrac{dv_C}{dt} \\ \dfrac{di_L}{dt} \end{bmatrix} = \begin{bmatrix} -\dfrac{7}{30} & -\dfrac{4}{15} \\ \dfrac{4}{25} & -\dfrac{4}{25} \end{bmatrix} \begin{bmatrix} v_C \\ i_L \end{bmatrix}$$

22.13   The circuit of Fig. 22-4 is slightly modified by adding a capacitor across the inductor as shown in Fig. 22-5. Write the corresponding state equation.

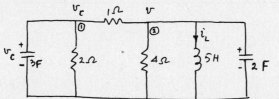

Fig. 22-5

▌ In this case (1) of Prob. 22.12 remains unchanged:

$$\frac{dv_C}{dt} = -\frac{v_C}{2} + \frac{v}{3} \tag{1}$$

Since there are three energy storage elements, we have three state variables—v_C, v, and i_L. Therefore, we must have three independent equations governing the state variables. Thus,

$$v = 5\frac{di_L}{dt} \qquad \text{or} \qquad \frac{di_L}{dt} = \frac{v}{5} \tag{2}$$

At node 2: $\qquad \dfrac{v_C - v}{1} = \dfrac{v}{4} + 2\dfrac{dv}{dt} + i_L$

or

$$\frac{dv}{dt} = \frac{v_C}{2} - \frac{5v}{8} - \frac{i_L}{2} \tag{3}$$

Hence,

$$\begin{bmatrix} \dfrac{dv_C}{dt} \\ \dfrac{di_L}{dt} \\ \dfrac{dv}{dt} \end{bmatrix} = \begin{bmatrix} -\dfrac{1}{2} & 0 & \dfrac{1}{3} \\ 0 & 0 & \dfrac{1}{5} \\ \dfrac{1}{2} & -\dfrac{1}{2} & -\dfrac{5}{8} \end{bmatrix} \begin{bmatrix} v_C \\ i_L \\ v \end{bmatrix}$$

22.14   Write the state equation for the circuit of Fig. 22-6.

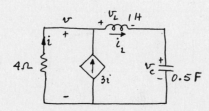

Fig. 22-6

▌ From Fig. 22-6: $\qquad i_L = i + 3i = 4i \qquad -i = \dfrac{v}{4} = \dfrac{v_L + v_C}{4} \qquad v_L = \dfrac{di_L}{dt}$

Thus,
$$\frac{di_L}{dt} = -i_L - v_C \quad \text{and} \quad 0.5 \frac{dv_C}{dt} = i_L \quad \text{or} \quad \frac{dv_C}{dt} = 2i_L$$

Thus,
$$\begin{bmatrix} \dfrac{di_L}{dt} \\ \dfrac{dv_C}{dt} \end{bmatrix} = \begin{bmatrix} -1 & -1 \\ 2 & 0 \end{bmatrix} \begin{bmatrix} i_L \\ v_C \end{bmatrix}$$

22.15 Write the state equation for the circuit of Fig. 22-7.

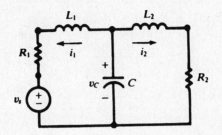

Fig. 22-7

▮ From Fig. 22-7

$$\frac{dv_C}{dt} = 0 - \frac{1}{C} i_1 - \frac{1}{C} i_2 \qquad \frac{di_1}{dt} = \frac{1}{L_1} v_C - \frac{R_1}{L_1} i_1 + 0 - \frac{v_s}{L_1} \qquad \frac{di_2}{dt} = \frac{1}{L_2} v_C + 0 - \frac{R_2}{L_2} i_2$$

or, in matrix form,
$$\frac{d}{dt} \begin{bmatrix} v_C \\ i_1 \\ i_2 \end{bmatrix} = \begin{bmatrix} 0 & -\dfrac{1}{C} & -\dfrac{1}{C} \\ \dfrac{1}{L_1} & -\dfrac{R_1}{L_1} & 0 \\ \dfrac{1}{L_2} & 0 & -\dfrac{R_2}{L_2} \end{bmatrix} \begin{bmatrix} v_C \\ i_1 \\ i_2 \end{bmatrix} + \begin{bmatrix} 0 \\ -\dfrac{v_s}{L_1} \\ 0 \end{bmatrix}$$

22.16 Write the state equation for the circuit of Fig. 22-8.

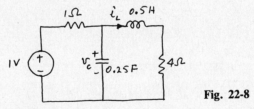

Fig. 22-8

▮ From Fig. 22-8:
$$0.5 \frac{di_L}{dt} = -4i_L + v_C \quad \text{or} \quad \frac{di_L}{dt} = -8i_L + 2v_C$$

$$0.25 \frac{dv_C}{dt} = -i_L + \frac{1 - v_C}{1} \quad \text{or} \quad \frac{dv_C}{dt} = -4i_1 - 4v_C + 4$$

Thus, the state equation becomes
$$\frac{d}{dt} \begin{bmatrix} i_L \\ v_C \end{bmatrix} = \begin{bmatrix} -8 & 2 \\ -4 & -4 \end{bmatrix} + \begin{bmatrix} 0 \\ 4 \end{bmatrix} 1$$

22.17 Write the state equation for the circuit of Fig. 22-9.

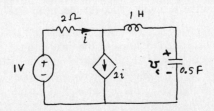

Fig. 22-9

▮ From Fig. 22-9: $\quad \dfrac{di_L}{dt} = 2i_L - v_C + 1 \qquad 0.5\dfrac{dv_C}{dt} = i_L \qquad \text{or} \qquad \dfrac{dv_C}{dt} = 2i_L$

Hence,

$$\frac{d}{dt}\begin{bmatrix} i_L \\ v_C \end{bmatrix} = \begin{bmatrix} 2 & -1 \\ 2 & 0 \end{bmatrix}\begin{bmatrix} i_L \\ v_C \end{bmatrix} + \begin{bmatrix} 1 \\ 0 \end{bmatrix}1$$

22.18 Obtain the state equation for the circuit of Fig. 22-10.

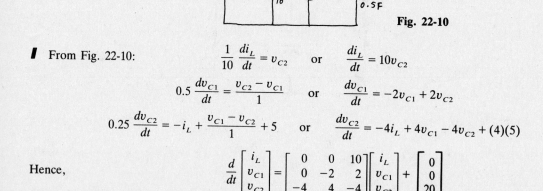

Fig. 22-10

▮ From Fig. 22-10: $\qquad \dfrac{1}{10}\dfrac{di_L}{dt} = v_{C2} \qquad \text{or} \qquad \dfrac{di_L}{dt} = 10v_{C2}$

$$0.5\frac{dv_{C1}}{dt} = \frac{v_{C2} - v_{C1}}{1} \qquad \text{or} \qquad \frac{dv_{C1}}{dt} = -2v_{C1} + 2v_{C2}$$

$$0.25\frac{dv_{C2}}{dt} = -i_L + \frac{v_{C1} - v_{C2}}{1} + 5 \qquad \text{or} \qquad \frac{dv_{C2}}{dt} = -4i_L + 4v_{C1} - 4v_{C2} + (4)(5)$$

Hence,

$$\frac{d}{dt}\begin{bmatrix} i_L \\ v_{C1} \\ v_{C2} \end{bmatrix} = \begin{bmatrix} 0 & 0 & 10 \\ 0 & -2 & 2 \\ -4 & 4 & -4 \end{bmatrix}\begin{bmatrix} i_L \\ v_{C1} \\ v_{C2} \end{bmatrix} + \begin{bmatrix} 0 \\ 0 \\ 20 \end{bmatrix}$$

22.19 Obtain the state equation for the circuit of Fig. 22-11.

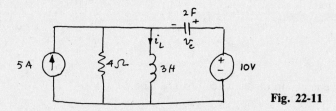

Fig. 22-11

▮ From Fig. 22-11: $\quad 3\dfrac{di_L}{dt} = -v_C + 10 \qquad \text{or} \qquad \dfrac{di_L}{dt} = -\dfrac{1}{3}v_C + \dfrac{10}{3}$

$$2\frac{dv_C}{dt} = i_L + \frac{-v_C + 10}{4} - 5 \qquad \text{or} \qquad \frac{dv_C}{dt} = \frac{1}{2}i_L - \frac{1}{8}v_C - \frac{5}{4}$$

Hence,

$$\frac{d}{dt}\begin{bmatrix} i_L \\ v_C \end{bmatrix} = \begin{bmatrix} 0 & -\frac{1}{3} \\ \frac{1}{2} & -\frac{1}{8} \end{bmatrix}\begin{bmatrix} i_L \\ v_C \end{bmatrix} + \begin{bmatrix} \frac{1}{3} & 0 \\ \frac{1}{8} & -\frac{1}{2} \end{bmatrix}\begin{bmatrix} 10 \\ 5 \end{bmatrix}$$

or

$$\dot{\bar{y}} = \bar{A} \quad \bar{y} + \bar{B} \quad \bar{u}$$

22.20 A general approach to obtaining the state equations is to use *planar graph theory*. To apply this technique, the following definitions are required.

Tree: A set of branches that connects all nodes of the network but contains no loop. (More precisely, this structure is called a *spanning subtree*.) The number of branches in a tree is one less than the number of nodes in the network. Any tree provides a unique path between any two nodes. A given network may have a number of distinct trees.

Cotree: The complement of a tree, that is, the set of all branches of the network that does not belong to the given tree. A branch of the cotree is called a *link* (of the given tree).

If a tree is augmented by any single link, the resulting structure has exactly one loop. From this fact, it can be proved that the set of loops generated by bringing the links into the tree one at a time constitutes a *basic set* of loops. The number of loops in a basic set equals the number of meshes in the network, and a basic set shares with the set of meshes the property that *any loop in the network can be constructed from loops belonging to the set*. On this basis draw the graph of the circuit of Fig. 22-12a.

▮ See Fig. 22-12b.

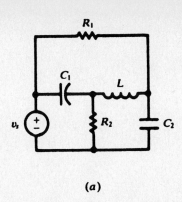

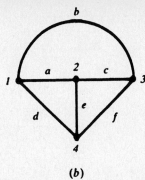

(a)   (b)   Fig. 22-12

22.21 Using the concepts of Prob. 22.20, the following procedure is used to write the state equation.

1. In the graph corresponding to the circuit, choose a *normal tree*, one that contains all voltage sources and the maximum possible number of capacitors. All current sources and inductors are left for the cotree. Resistors may be in either the tree or the cotree. As far as possible, control voltages should also be in the tree and control currents in the cotree.

2. To each capacitor assign a voltage and mark its polarity; to each inductor assign a current and specify its direction. These capacitor voltages and inductor currents are the state variables.

3. Using KCL, write a node equation at each capacitor. Using KVL, write a loop equation for each basic loop composed of an inductor link and a path in the normal tree.

4. If resistor voltages occur in the KVL equations of rule 3, use KCL to equate V_R/R to a sum of link currents. Similarly, if resistor currents occur in the KCL equations, use KVL to set $i_R R$ equal to a sum of basic loop voltages.

5. Substitute the expressions of rule 4 into the equations of rule 3, thereby obtaining the state equation.

Apply the above procedure to obtain the state equation of the circuit of Fig. 22-7.

❙ We proceed as follows:

1. Select a tree with all the capacitors and none of the inductors (Fig. 22-13a).

2. Use the tree-branch capacitor voltage v_C and the link inductor currents i_1 and i_2 as state variables. The reference direction for each state variable is shown in Fig. 22-13a.

3. Write KCL for the capacitor at the + end.

$$C \frac{dv_C}{dt} + i_1 + i_2 = 0 \tag{1}$$

Write KVL for the basic loops indicated in Fig. 22-13b.

$$L_1 \frac{di_1}{dt} + v_{R_1} + v_s - v_C = 0 \tag{2}$$

$$L_2 \frac{di_2}{dt} + v_{R_2} - v_C = 0 \tag{3}$$

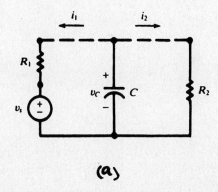

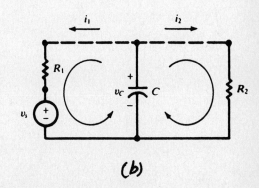

(a)   (b)

Fig. 22-13

4. In (1), only state variables occur, and no further simplification is needed.   In (2) and (3), express v_{R_1} and v_{R_2} in terms of the state variables:

$$v_{R_1} = R_1 i_1 \qquad v_{R_2} = R_2 i_2$$

5. Now (1), (2), and (3) become

$$\frac{dv_C}{dt} = 0 - \frac{1}{C} i_1 - \frac{1}{C} i_2$$

$$\frac{di_1}{dt} = \frac{1}{L_1} v_C - \frac{R_1}{L_1} i_1 + 0 - \frac{v_s}{L_1}$$

$$\frac{di_2}{dt} = \frac{1}{L_2} v_C + 0 - \frac{R_2}{L_2} i_2$$

or, in matrix form,

$$\frac{d}{dt} \begin{bmatrix} v_C \\ i_1 \\ i_2 \end{bmatrix} = \begin{bmatrix} 0 & -\dfrac{1}{C} & -\dfrac{1}{C} \\ \dfrac{1}{L_1} & -\dfrac{R_1}{L_1} & 0 \\ \dfrac{1}{L_2} & 0 & -\dfrac{R_2}{L_2} \end{bmatrix} \begin{bmatrix} v_C \\ i_1 \\ i_2 \end{bmatrix} + \begin{bmatrix} 0 \\ -\dfrac{v_s}{L_1} \\ 0 \end{bmatrix}$$

22.22 Similar to the classical solution of Prob. 22.9 and its solution by the Laplace transform method, we may also solve the vector state equation by the Laplace transform method.   Write the form of solution to

$$\dot{\bar{y}} = \bar{A}\bar{y} + \bar{B}\bar{u}$$

▮ In the transform domain we have

$$\bar{Y}(s) = [s\bar{I} - \bar{A}]^{-1} \bar{y}(0_+) + [s\bar{I} - \bar{A}]^{-1} \bar{B}u(s)$$

where $[s\bar{I} - \bar{A}]^{-1} = \bar{\phi}(s)$ is the *state-transition matrix*.   And $\bar{\phi}(t) \equiv e^{\bar{A}t}$ so that

$$\bar{y}(t) = e^{\bar{A}t} \bar{y}(0_+) + \int_0^t e_0^{\bar{A}(t-\tau)} \bar{B}u(\tau)\, d\tau$$

22.23 The equation $\det |s\bar{I} - \bar{A}|$ is called the characteristic equation, and its roots are known as the *eigenvalues* of $\bar{A}$. Find the eigenvalues of the circuit of Prob. 22.8.

▮

$$\det |s\bar{I} - \bar{A}| = \begin{vmatrix} s + \dfrac{R}{L} & \dfrac{1}{L} \\ -\dfrac{1}{C} & s \end{vmatrix} = 0 \qquad \text{or} \qquad s^2 + \frac{R}{L} s + \frac{1}{LC} = 0$$

or

$$s_1, s_2 = -\frac{R}{2L} \pm \sqrt{\left(\frac{R}{2L}\right)^2 - \frac{1}{LC}}$$

which are the natural frequencies of the circuit.

22.24 Find the eigenvalues for the circuit of Fig. 22-3.

▮ From Prob. 22.10,

$$\bar{A} = \begin{bmatrix} 0 & \frac{1}{3} \\ -1 & -\frac{1}{2} \end{bmatrix}$$

Thus,

$$\det |s\bar{I} - \bar{A}| = \begin{vmatrix} s & -\frac{1}{3} \\ 1 & s + \frac{1}{2} \end{vmatrix} = 0 \qquad \text{or} \qquad 6s^2 + 3s + 2 = 0$$

The eigenvalues are

$$s_1, s_2 = \frac{-3 \pm \sqrt{9 - 48}}{12} = -0.25 \pm j0.52$$

22.25 Determine the natural frequencies of the circuit of Prob. 22.11.

▮ The natural frequencies are the eigenvalues which are given by

$$\begin{vmatrix} s & -\dfrac{1}{L} \\ \dfrac{1}{C} & s+\dfrac{1}{RC} \end{vmatrix} = 0 \quad \text{or} \quad s^2 + \dfrac{1}{RC}s + \dfrac{1}{LC} = 0$$

Thus,

$$s_1, s_2 = -\dfrac{1}{2RC} \pm \sqrt{\left(\dfrac{1}{2RC}\right)^2 - \dfrac{1}{LC}}$$

22.26 Find the eigenvalues of the circuit of Prob. 22.14.

▮ The eigenvalues are given by

$$\begin{vmatrix} s+1 & 1 \\ -2 & s \end{vmatrix} = 0 \quad \text{or} \quad s^2 + s + 2 = 0$$

Thus,

$$s_1, s_2 = \dfrac{-1 \pm \sqrt{1-8}}{2} = -0.5 \pm j1.32$$

22.27 Write the state equation for the circuit of Fig. 22-14a.

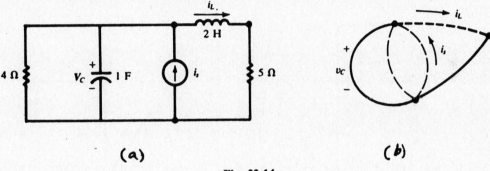

(a)   **(b)**

Fig. 22-14

▮ The normal tree is shown in Fig. 22-14b, with the capacitor in the tree and the inductor in the cotree. By KVL,

$$2\dfrac{di_L}{dt} + 5i_L - v_C = 0 \quad \text{or} \quad \dfrac{di_L}{dt} = -2.5i_L + 0.5v_C \tag{1}$$

By KCL at the plus end of the capacitor,

$$1\dfrac{dv_C}{dt} + i_L - i_s + \dfrac{v_C}{4} = 0 \quad \text{or} \quad \dfrac{dv_C}{dt} = -i_L - 0.25v_C + i_s \tag{2}$$

Rewriting (1) and (2) in matrix form,

$$\dfrac{d}{dt}\begin{bmatrix} i_L \\ v_C \end{bmatrix} = \begin{bmatrix} -2.5 & 0.5 \\ -1 & -0.25 \end{bmatrix}\begin{bmatrix} i_L \\ v_C \end{bmatrix} + \begin{bmatrix} 0 \\ i_s \end{bmatrix}$$

22.28 Write the state equation for the circuit of Fig. 22-15a.

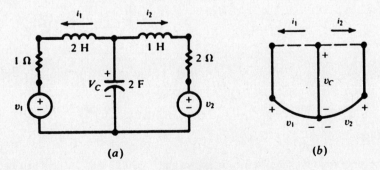

(a)   **(b)**

Fig. 22-15

▌ The normal tree is shown in Fig. 22-15b. By KVL in loop 1,

$$2\frac{di_1}{dt} + 1i_1 + v_1 - v_C = 0 \quad \text{or} \quad \frac{di_1}{dt} = -0.5i_1 + 0i_2 + 0.5v_C - 0.5v_1 \tag{1}$$

and in loop 2, $\qquad 1\frac{di_2}{dt} + 2i_2 + v_2 - v_C = 0 \quad \text{or} \quad \frac{di_2}{dt} = 0i_1 - 2i_2 + v_C - v_2 \tag{2}$

By KCL at the plus end of the capacitor,

$$2\frac{dv_C}{dt} + i_1 + i_2 = 0 \quad \text{or} \quad \frac{dv_C}{dt} = -0.5i_1 - 0.5i_2 + 0v_C \tag{3}$$

$$\frac{d}{dt}\begin{bmatrix} i_1 \\ i_2 \\ v_C \end{bmatrix} = \begin{bmatrix} -0.5 & 0 & 0.5 \\ 0 & -2 & 1 \\ -0.5 & -0.5 & 0 \end{bmatrix}\begin{bmatrix} i_1 \\ i_2 \\ v_C \end{bmatrix} + \begin{bmatrix} -0.5v_1 \\ -v_2 \\ 0 \end{bmatrix}$$

Observe that the components of the forcing vector are not the forcing functions v_1 and v_2, but linear combinations of these functions. Such will generally be the case.

22.29 Given $v_s(t) = 5e^{-2t}$ in the circuit of Fig. 22-16a, obtain the state equation.

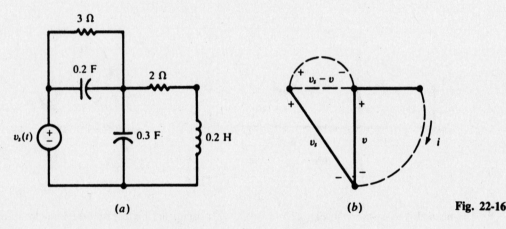

(a)   (b)   **Fig. 22-16**

▌ It is clear that the two capacitors and the voltage source cannot all be placed in a (normal) tree. Thus, in Fig. 22-16b, the 0.2-F capacitor is assigned to the cotree. By KVL,

$$0.2\frac{di}{dt} - v + 2i = 0 \quad \text{or} \quad \frac{di}{dt} = -10i + 5v \tag{1}$$

By KCL at the plus end of the 0.3-F capacitor,

$$0.3\frac{dv}{dt} + i - 0.2\frac{d(v_s - v)}{dt} - \frac{v_s - v}{3} = 0$$

or, since $\dot{v}_s = -2v_s$, $\qquad \frac{dv}{dt} = -2i - \frac{2}{3}v - \frac{2}{15}v_s \tag{2}$

In matrix form, the normal equations are

$$\frac{d}{dt}\begin{bmatrix} i \\ v \end{bmatrix} = \begin{bmatrix} -10 & 5 \\ -2 & -2/3 \end{bmatrix}\begin{bmatrix} i \\ v \end{bmatrix} + \begin{bmatrix} 0 \\ -2v_s/15 \end{bmatrix}$$

22.30 A linear system is described by the matrix

$$\bar{A} = \begin{bmatrix} 1 & 2 \\ -3 & 4 \end{bmatrix}$$

Use the power-series expansion to calculate the state transition matrix at $t = 0.1$ s.

▌ From Prob. 22.9: $\qquad \bar{\phi}(t) = e^{\bar{A}t} = \bar{I} + \bar{A}t + \bar{A}^2\frac{t^2}{2!} + \bar{A}^3\frac{t^3}{3!} + \cdots$

We will use only the first three terms to approximate $\bar{\phi}(0.1)$, because, as will become evident, higher-order terms become insignificant for the given values.

$$\bar{I} = \begin{bmatrix} 1 & 0 \\ 0 & 1 \end{bmatrix} \qquad \bar{A}t = \begin{bmatrix} 1 & 2 \\ -3 & 4 \end{bmatrix}(0.1) = \begin{bmatrix} 0.1 & 0.2 \\ -0.3 & 0.4 \end{bmatrix}$$

$$\bar{A}^2 = \bar{A}\bar{A} = \begin{bmatrix} 1 & 2 \\ -3 & 4 \end{bmatrix}\begin{bmatrix} 1 & 2 \\ -3 & 4 \end{bmatrix} = \begin{bmatrix} (1-6) & (2+8) \\ (-3-12) & (-6+16) \end{bmatrix} = \begin{bmatrix} -5 & 10 \\ -15 & 10 \end{bmatrix}$$

$$\bar{A}^2 \frac{t^2}{2!} = \begin{bmatrix} -5 & 10 \\ -15 & 10 \end{bmatrix}\left(\frac{0.01}{2}\right) = \begin{bmatrix} -0.025 & 0.05 \\ -0.075 & 0.05 \end{bmatrix}$$

Thus $$\bar{\phi}(0.1) \approx \begin{bmatrix} 1 & 0 \\ 0 & 1 \end{bmatrix} + \begin{bmatrix} 0.1 & 0.2 \\ -0.3 & 0.4 \end{bmatrix} + \begin{bmatrix} -0.025 & 0.05 \\ -0.075 & 0.05 \end{bmatrix} = \begin{bmatrix} 1.075 & 0.25 \\ -0.375 & 1.45 \end{bmatrix}$$

22.31 Refer to Prob. 22.30.   By means of the Laplace transform, find an exact expression for $\bar{\phi}(t)$, and use it to check the approximate calculation of $\bar{\phi}(0.1)$.

▮ We have $$\bar{\phi}(t) = \mathcal{L}^{-1}[(s\bar{I} - \bar{A})^{-1}]$$

For the given matrix $\bar{A}$, $$s\bar{I} - \bar{A} = \begin{bmatrix} s-1 & -2 \\ 3 & s-4 \end{bmatrix}$$

and so $$(s\bar{I} - \bar{A})^{-1} = \frac{\text{adj}(s\bar{I} - \bar{A})}{\det(s\bar{I} - \bar{A})} = \frac{\begin{bmatrix} s-4 & 2 \\ -3 & s-1 \end{bmatrix}}{s^2 - 5s + 10}$$

$$= \begin{bmatrix} \dfrac{s-4}{s^2-5s+10} & \dfrac{2}{s^2-5s+10} \\ \dfrac{-3}{s^2-5s+10} & \dfrac{s-1}{s^2-5s+10} \end{bmatrix} \qquad (1)$$

The inverse Laplace transform of the matrix (1) is obtained by taking the inverse Laplace transform of each element.   All elements have the same poles (the eigenvalues of $\bar{A}$),

$$s_1 = \frac{5}{2} + j\frac{\sqrt{15}}{2} \qquad s_2 = \frac{5}{2} - j\frac{\sqrt{15}}{2} = s_1^*$$

Now, $$\bar{\phi}(t) = \begin{bmatrix} \phi_{11} & \phi_{12} \\ \phi_{21} & \phi_{22} \end{bmatrix}$$

where

$$\phi_{11} = \mathcal{L}^{-1}\left[\frac{s-4}{s^2-5s+10}\right] = \left(\frac{s_1-4}{2s_1-5} e^{s_1 t}\right) + \text{(complex conjugate)} = \frac{e^{5t/2}}{\sqrt{15}}\left(\sqrt{15}\cos\frac{\sqrt{15}}{2}t - 3\sin\frac{\sqrt{15}}{2}t\right)$$

$$\phi_{12} = \mathcal{L}^{-1}\left[\frac{2}{s^2-5s+10}\right] = \frac{e^{5t/2}}{\sqrt{15}}\left(4\sin\frac{\sqrt{15}}{2}t\right)$$

$$\phi_{21} = \mathcal{L}^{-1}\left[\frac{-3}{s^2-5s+10}\right] = \frac{e^{5t/2}}{\sqrt{15}}\left(-6\sin\frac{\sqrt{15}}{2}t\right)$$

$$\phi_{22} = \mathcal{L}^{-1}\left[\frac{s-1}{s^2-5s+10}\right] = \frac{e^{5t/2}}{\sqrt{15}}\left(\sqrt{15}\cos\frac{\sqrt{15}}{2}t + 3\sin\frac{\sqrt{15}}{2}t\right)$$

Substitution of $t = 0.1$ gives

$$\phi(0.1) = \begin{bmatrix} 1.068 & 0.256 \\ -0.384 & 1.452 \end{bmatrix}$$

which shows that the approximation in Prob. 22.30 was quite good.

22.32 The differential equation of a certain electromechanical system is

$$\ddot{y} + 3\dot{y} + 2y = f(t)$$

Use the state-variable method to obtain the complete response of the system to the driving force $f(t) = u(t)$ (unit-step function), given the initial conditions

$$y(0_+) = 0 \qquad \dot{y}(0_+) = 1$$

▌ Choosing the state variables $x_1 = y$, $x_2 = \dot{y}$ and carrying out the reduction process, we obtain the matrix state equation

$$\begin{bmatrix} \dot{x}_1 \\ \dot{x}_2 \end{bmatrix} = \begin{bmatrix} 0 & 1 \\ -2 & -3 \end{bmatrix} \begin{bmatrix} x_1 \\ x_2 \end{bmatrix} + \begin{bmatrix} 0 \\ u(t) \end{bmatrix} \qquad \text{or} \qquad \dot{\bar{x}} = \bar{A}\bar{x} + \bar{f}$$

with the initial condition $\bar{x}(0_+) = [0, 1]^T$. Then,

$$(s\bar{I} - \bar{A})^{-1} = \begin{bmatrix} s & -1 \\ 2 & s+3 \end{bmatrix}^{-1} = \begin{bmatrix} \dfrac{s+3}{(s+2)(s+1)} & \dfrac{1}{(s+2)(s+1)} \\[2ex] \dfrac{-2}{(s+2)(s+1)} & \dfrac{s}{(s+2)(s+1)} \end{bmatrix}$$

and

$$\bar{\phi}(t) = \mathscr{L}^{-1}[(s\bar{I} - \bar{A})^{-1}] = \begin{bmatrix} 2e^{-t} - e^{-2t} & e^{-t} - e^{-2t} \\ 2e^{-2t} - 2e^{-t} & 2e^{-2t} - e^{-t} \end{bmatrix}$$

The solution to the matrix state equation is now given by

$$\bar{x}(t) = \bar{\phi}(t)\bar{x}(0_+) + \int_0^t \bar{\phi}(t - \tau)\bar{f}(\tau)\, d\tau$$

Only the first component of $\bar{x}(t)$ is of interest; thus,

$$x_1(t) = y(t) = [2e^{-t} - e^{-2t}, e^{-t} - e^{-2t}]\begin{bmatrix} 0 \\ 1 \end{bmatrix} + \int_0^t [2e^{-(t-\tau)} - e^{-2(t-\tau)}, e^{-(t-\tau)} - e^{-2(t-\tau)}]\begin{bmatrix} 0 \\ u(\tau) \end{bmatrix} d\tau$$

$$= e^{-t} - e^{-2t} + \int_0^t \{e^{-(t-\tau)} - e^{-2(t-\tau)}\}(1)\, d\tau = \frac{1}{2} - \frac{1}{2}e^{-2t}$$

22.33 Solve the state equations

$$\frac{di}{dt} = -4i + \frac{1}{2}e^{-t} \quad \text{A/s} \qquad \frac{dv}{dt} = -3v + e^{-t} \quad \text{V/s}$$

subject to the initial condition $i(0_+) = 1$ A and $v(0_+) = 2$ V.

▌ The equations in matrix form are

$$\frac{d}{dt}\begin{bmatrix} i \\ v \end{bmatrix} = \begin{bmatrix} -4 & 0 \\ 0 & -3 \end{bmatrix}\begin{bmatrix} i \\ v \end{bmatrix} + \begin{bmatrix} \frac{1}{2}e^{-t} \\ e^{-t} \end{bmatrix} \qquad \text{with} \qquad \begin{bmatrix} i(0_+) \\ v(0_+) \end{bmatrix} = \begin{bmatrix} 1 \\ 2 \end{bmatrix}$$

Here

$$\bar{A} = \begin{bmatrix} -4 & 0 \\ 0 & -3 \end{bmatrix} \quad (s\bar{I} - \bar{A})^{-1} = \begin{bmatrix} s+4 & 0 \\ 0 & s+3 \end{bmatrix}^{-1} = \begin{bmatrix} \dfrac{1}{s+4} & 0 \\[2ex] 0 & \dfrac{1}{s+3} \end{bmatrix}$$

and

$$\bar{\phi}(t) = \mathscr{L}^{-1}[(s\bar{I} - \bar{A})^{-1}] = \begin{bmatrix} e^{-4t} & 0 \\ 0 & e^{-3t} \end{bmatrix}$$

Consequently,

$$\begin{bmatrix} i(t) \\ v(t) \end{bmatrix} = \begin{bmatrix} e^{-4t} & 0 \\ 0 & e^{-3t} \end{bmatrix}\begin{bmatrix} 1 \\ 2 \end{bmatrix} + \int_0^t \begin{bmatrix} e^{-4(t-\tau)} & 0 \\ 0 & e^{-3(t-\tau)} \end{bmatrix}\begin{bmatrix} \frac{1}{2}e^{-\tau} \\ e^{-\tau} \end{bmatrix} d\tau = \begin{bmatrix} \frac{1}{6}e^{-t} + \frac{5}{6}e^{-4t} & \text{A} \\ \frac{1}{2}e^{-t} + \frac{3}{2}e^{-3t} & \text{V} \end{bmatrix}$$

22.34 The $\bar{A}$ matrix for the circuit of Fig. 22-17 is

$$\bar{A} = \begin{bmatrix} -0.5 & -2.5 \\ 0.5 & -3.5 \end{bmatrix}$$

Determine the eigenvalues.

▌

$$[s\bar{I} - \bar{A}] = \begin{bmatrix} s+0.5 & 2.5 \\ -0.5 & s+3.5 \end{bmatrix}$$

$$\det |s\bar{I} - \bar{A}| = (s + 0.5)(s + 3.5) + (2.5)(0.5) = s^2 + 4s + 3 = (s + 3)(s + 1) = 0$$

Thus, the eigenvalues are $s_1, s_2 = -3, -1$.

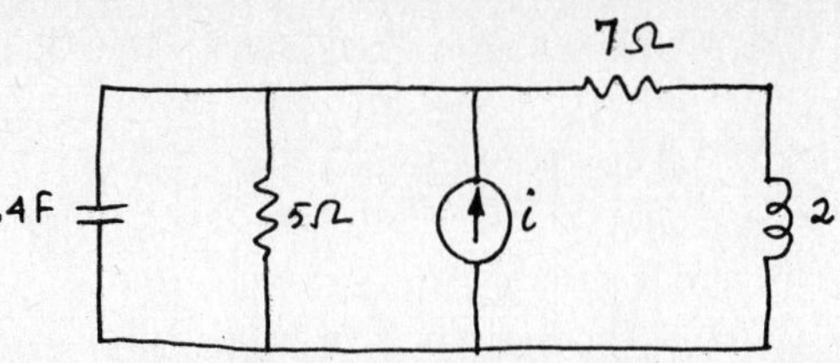

Fig. 22-17

22.35 The state equation of a second-order system is

$$\begin{bmatrix} \dot{y}_1 \\ \dot{y}_2 \end{bmatrix} = \begin{bmatrix} 0 & 1 \\ -5 & -2 \end{bmatrix} \begin{bmatrix} y_1 \\ y_2 \end{bmatrix} + \begin{bmatrix} 0 \\ 1 \end{bmatrix} u(t)$$

Obtain the state-transition matrix in the s domain.

▌ Since $\bar{A} = \begin{bmatrix} 0 & 1 \\ -5 & -2 \end{bmatrix}$

$$[s\bar{I} - \bar{A}] = \begin{bmatrix} s & 1 \\ -5 & s+2 \end{bmatrix} \quad \text{and} \quad [s\bar{I} - \bar{A}]^{-1} = \frac{1}{s^2 + 2s + 5} \begin{bmatrix} s+2 & 1 \\ -5 & s \end{bmatrix} = \bar{\phi}(s)$$

22.36 In the circuit of Fig. 22-2, $R = 3\,\Omega$, $L = 1\,H$, and $C = 0.5\,F$. Obtain the state transition matrix in the time domain.

▌ From Prob. 22.8:

$$\bar{A} = \begin{bmatrix} -3 & -1 \\ 2 & 0 \end{bmatrix} \qquad A^2 = \begin{bmatrix} 7 & 3 \\ -6 & -2 \end{bmatrix} \qquad A^3 = \begin{bmatrix} -15 & -7 \\ 14 & 6 \end{bmatrix} \cdots$$

The state transition matrix is now written

$$\bar{\phi}(t) = \bar{I} + \bar{A}t + \frac{1}{2!}\bar{A}^2 t^2 + \frac{1}{3!}\bar{A}^3 t^3 + \cdots$$

$$= \begin{bmatrix} 1 - 3t + \frac{7}{2}t^2 - \frac{5}{2}t^3 + \cdots & -t + \frac{3}{2}t^2 - \frac{7}{6}t^3 + \cdots \\ 2t - 3t^2 + \frac{7}{3}t^3 + \cdots & 1 - t^2 + t^3 + \cdots \end{bmatrix}$$

$$= \begin{bmatrix} -e^{-t} + 2e^{-2t} & -e^{-t} + e^{-2t} \\ 2e^{-t} - 2e^{-2t} & 2e^{-t} - e^{-2t} \end{bmatrix}$$

22.37 If the input to the circuit of Prob. 22.36 is a unit step and the initial state is zero, solve the state equation.

▌ For a unit-step function applied at $t = 0$, the complete solution of the state equation for $t > 0$ is

$$\bar{x}(t) = \bar{\Phi}(t)\bar{x}(0) + \int_0^t \bar{\Phi}(t-\tau)\bar{B}\bar{r}(\tau)\,d\tau = \bar{\Phi}(t)\bar{x}(0) + \int_0^t \begin{bmatrix} -e^{-(t-\tau)} + 2e^{-2(t-\tau)} \\ 2e^{-(t-\tau)} - 2e^{-2(t-\tau)} \end{bmatrix} d\tau$$

or
$$\bar{x}(t) = \begin{bmatrix} -e^{-t} + 2e^{-2t} & -e^{-t} + e^{-2t} \\ 2e^{-t} - 2e^{-2t} & 2e^{-t} - e^{-2t} \end{bmatrix} \begin{bmatrix} x_1(0) \\ x_2(0) \end{bmatrix} + \begin{bmatrix} e^{-t} - e^{-2t} \\ 1 - 2e^{-t} + e^{-2t} \end{bmatrix} \qquad (1)$$

where the state variables are $x_1 = i_L$ and $x_2 = v_C$. If the initial state of the network is zero, $\bar{x}(0) = \bar{0}$, (1) becomes

$$\bar{x}(t) = \begin{bmatrix} e^{-t} - e^{-2t} \\ 1 - 2e^{-t} + e^{-2t} \end{bmatrix} \qquad t > 0$$

22.38 The dynamic equations of a network may be written as

$$\frac{d\bar{x}(t)}{dt} = \bar{A}\bar{x}(t) + \bar{B}\bar{r}(t) \qquad (1)$$

$$\bar{y}(t) = \bar{C}\bar{x}(t) + \bar{D}\bar{r}(t) \qquad (2)$$

where $\bar{x}(t)$ are the state variables, $\bar{r}(t)$ are the input variables, $\bar{y}(t)$ are the output variables, and $\bar{A}$, $\bar{B}$, $\bar{C}$, and $\bar{D}$ are constant matrices. Write the corresponding equations for the circuit of Fig. 22-2 for a voltage input $v(t)$.

❚ The state equation is (see Prob. 22.8)

$$\begin{bmatrix} \dfrac{di_L}{dt} \\[2mm] \dfrac{dv_C}{dt} \end{bmatrix} = \begin{bmatrix} -\dfrac{R}{L} & -\dfrac{1}{L} \\[2mm] \dfrac{1}{C} & 0 \end{bmatrix} \begin{bmatrix} i_L \\ v_C \end{bmatrix} + \begin{bmatrix} \dfrac{1}{L} \\[2mm] 0 \end{bmatrix} v(t)$$

which corresponds to (1) above.

The output equation is

$$\bar{y}(t) = \begin{bmatrix} y_1(t) \\ y_2(t) \end{bmatrix} = \begin{bmatrix} 1 & 0 \\ 0 & 1 \end{bmatrix} \begin{bmatrix} i_L \\ v_C \end{bmatrix}$$

which corresponds to (2), $\bar{D} \equiv 0$ (or null matrix).

22.39 Obtain the $\bar{A}$, $\bar{B}$, $\bar{C}$, and $\bar{D}$ matrices for the circuit of Fig. 22-18.

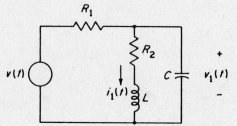

Fig. 22-18

❚ The state equations are

$$\begin{bmatrix} \dfrac{dv_1}{dt} \\[2mm] \dfrac{di_1}{dt} \end{bmatrix} = \begin{bmatrix} -\dfrac{1}{R_1 C} & -\dfrac{1}{C} \\[2mm] \dfrac{1}{L} & -\dfrac{R_2}{L} \end{bmatrix} \begin{bmatrix} v_1 \\ i_1 \end{bmatrix} + \begin{bmatrix} \dfrac{1}{CR_1} \\[2mm] 0 \end{bmatrix} v$$

Therefore $\qquad \bar{A} = \begin{bmatrix} -\dfrac{1}{R_1 C} & -\dfrac{1}{C} \\[2mm] \dfrac{1}{L} & -\dfrac{R_2}{L} \end{bmatrix}$ and $\qquad \bar{B} = \begin{bmatrix} \dfrac{1}{CR_1} \\[2mm] 0 \end{bmatrix}$

Since the output variable is also the state variable v_1, the output equation is simply

$$\bar{y} = v_1 = \begin{bmatrix} 1 & 0 \end{bmatrix} \begin{bmatrix} v_1 \\ i_1 \end{bmatrix} + [0]v \qquad \text{and} \qquad \bar{C} = \begin{bmatrix} 1 & 0 \end{bmatrix} \qquad \bar{D} = [0]$$

22.40 Write the state equation for the circuit of Fig. 22-19. If the voltage across C_2 is the output, find the $\bar{A}$, $\bar{B}$, $\bar{C}$, and $\bar{D}$ matrices.

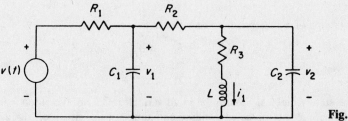

Fig. 22-19

▌ From Fig. 22-19,

$$C_1 \frac{dv_1}{dt} = \frac{v - v_1}{R_1} + \frac{v_2 - v_1}{R_2} \qquad \text{current through } C_1$$

$$C_2 \frac{dv_2}{dt} = \frac{v_1 - v_2}{R_2} - i_1 \qquad \text{current through } C_2$$

$$L \frac{di_1}{dt} = v_2 - R_3 i_1 \qquad \text{voltage across } L$$

Rearranging, these equations are written

$$\frac{dv_1}{dt} = -\frac{1}{C_1}\left(\frac{1}{R_1} + \frac{1}{R_2}\right)v_1 + \frac{1}{C_1 R_2}v_2 + \frac{1}{C_1 R_1}v$$

$$\frac{dv_2}{dt} = \frac{1}{C_2 R_2}v_1 - \frac{1}{C_2 R_2}v_2 - \frac{1}{C_2}i_1$$

$$\frac{di_1}{dt} = \frac{1}{L}v_2 - \frac{R_3}{L}i_1$$

The $\bar{A}$ matrix is now obtained from the coefficients associated with v_1, v_2, and i_1 in the state equations.

$$\bar{A} = \begin{bmatrix} -\dfrac{1}{C_1}\left(\dfrac{1}{R_1} + \dfrac{1}{R_2}\right) & \dfrac{1}{C_1 R_2} & 0 \\[4mm] \dfrac{1}{C_2 R_2} & -\dfrac{1}{C_2 R_2} & -\dfrac{1}{C_2} \\[4mm] 0 & \dfrac{1}{L} & -\dfrac{R_3}{L} \end{bmatrix}$$

The $\bar{B}$ matrix is determined from the coefficients of v; that is,

$$\bar{B} = \begin{bmatrix} \dfrac{1}{C_1 R_1} \\[3mm] 0 \\[2mm] 0 \end{bmatrix}$$

Since the output variable is also the state variable v_2, we have

$$\bar{C} = [0 \quad 1 \quad 0] \qquad \bar{D} = [0]$$

Therefore the output equation is

$$\bar{y} = [v_2] = [0 \quad 1 \quad 0]\begin{bmatrix} v_1 \\ v_2 \\ i_1 \end{bmatrix} + [0]v$$

CHAPTER 23
Two-Port Networks

23.1 A general two-port network is shown in Fig. 23-1a, for which we have

$$\bar{V}_1 = \bar{z}_{11}\bar{I}_1 + \bar{z}_{12}\bar{I}_2 \quad (1) \quad \text{and} \quad \bar{V}_2 = \bar{z}_{21}\bar{I}_1 + \bar{z}_{22}\bar{I}_2 \quad (2)$$

In (1) and (2) $(\bar{z}_{11}, \bar{z}_{12}, \bar{z}_{21}, \bar{z}_{22})$ are known as the *impedance* or *$\bar{z}$ parameters*. Using this definition, find the $\bar{z}$ parameters of the network of Fig. 23-1b.

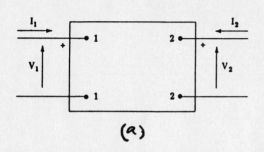 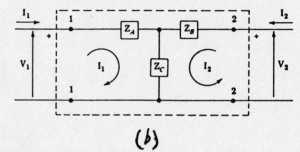

(a)   (b)

Fig. 23-1

▍ The loop equations for Fig. 23-1b are

$$\bar{V}_1 = (\bar{Z}_A + \bar{Z}_C)\bar{I}_1 + \bar{Z}_C\bar{I}_2 \qquad \bar{V}_2 = \bar{Z}_C\bar{I}_1 + (\bar{Z}_B + \bar{Z}_C)\bar{I}_2$$

Defining the coefficients of the currents in (1) and (2) above, the $\bar{z}$ parameters are

$$\bar{z}_{11} = \bar{Z}_A + \bar{Z}_C \qquad \bar{z}_{12} = \bar{Z}_C \qquad \bar{z}_{21} = \bar{Z}_C \qquad \bar{z}_{22} = \bar{Z}_B + \bar{Z}_C$$

23.2 Draw the $\bar{z}$-parameter circuit for the circuit of Fig. 23-1b.

▍ See Fig. 23-2. Note that the $\bar{z}$ parameters are expressed in ohms and the *$\bar{z}$ parameter model includes two controlled voltage sources*. The broken line joining the ports is included when a common connection is used.

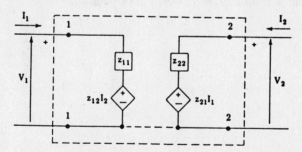

Fig. 23-2

23.3 Establish experimental procedures to determine the $\bar{z}$ parameters of a two-port network.

▍ Refer to Fig. 23-3. From Fig. 23-3a:

$$\bar{V}_1 = \bar{z}_{11}\bar{I}_1 \Big|_{\bar{I}_2=0}$$
$$\bar{V}_2 = \bar{z}_{21}\bar{I}_1 \Big|_{\bar{I}_2=0}$$

From Fig. 23-3b:

$$\bar{V}_1 = \bar{z}_{12}\bar{I}_2 \Big|_{\bar{I}_1=0}$$
$$\bar{V}_2 = \bar{z}_{22}\bar{I}_2 \Big|_{\bar{I}_1=0}$$

Consequently,

$$\bar{z}_{11} = \frac{\bar{V}_1}{\bar{I}_1} \Bigg| \qquad \bar{z}_{12} = \frac{\bar{V}_1}{\bar{I}_2} \Bigg|$$

$$\bar{z}_{21} = \frac{\bar{V}_2}{\bar{I}_1} \Bigg|_{\bar{I}_2=0} \qquad \bar{z}_{22} = \frac{\bar{V}_2}{\bar{I}_2} \Bigg|_{\bar{I}_1=0}$$

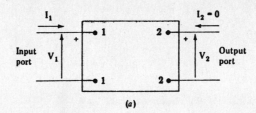

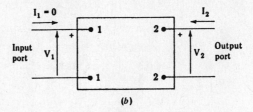

Fig. 23-3

23.4 Determine the $\bar{z}$ parameters for the circuit shown in Fig. 23-4. The output port includes a controlled voltage source.

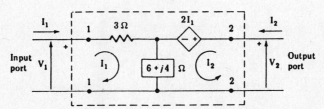

Fig. 23-4

❚ Since the actual parameters of the circuit are known, and the circuit is relatively simple, the $\bar{z}$ parameters may be determined by writing the two loop equations

$$\bar{V}_1 = [3 + (6 + j4)]\bar{I}_1 + [6 + j4]\bar{I}_2 \qquad \bar{V}_2 - 2\bar{I}_1 = [6 + j4]\bar{I}_1 + [6 + j4]\bar{I}_2$$

Simplifying, $\qquad \bar{V}_1 = [9 + j4]\bar{I}_1 + [6 + j4]\bar{I}_2 \qquad \bar{V}_2 = [8 + j4]\bar{I}_1 + [6 + j4]\bar{I}_2$

Thus the $\bar{z}$ parameters are

$$\bar{z}_{11} = (9 + j4)\,\Omega \qquad \bar{z}_{12} = (6 + j4)\,\Omega \qquad \bar{z}_{21} = (8 + j4)\,\Omega \qquad \bar{z}_{22} = (6 + j4)\,\Omega$$

23.5 Draw the $\bar{z}$-parameter model for the circuit of Fig. 23-4.

❚ See Fig. 23-5.

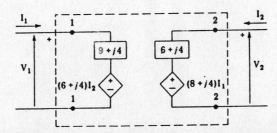

Fig. 23-5

23.6 The following open-circuit currents and voltages were determined experimentally for an unknown two-port:

$$\left. \begin{array}{l} \bar{V}_1 = 100 \underline{/0^\circ} \text{ V} \\ \bar{V}_2 = 75 \underline{/0^\circ} \quad \text{V} \\ \bar{I}_1 = 12.5 \underline{/0^\circ} \text{ A} \end{array} \right|_{\bar{I}_2 = 0} \qquad \left. \begin{array}{l} \bar{V}_1 = 30 \underline{/0^\circ} \text{ V} \\ \bar{V}_2 = 50 \underline{/0^\circ} \text{ V} \\ \bar{I}_2 = 5 \underline{/0^\circ} \quad \text{A} \end{array} \right|_{\bar{I}_1 = 0}$$

Determine the $\bar{z}$ parameters.

$$\bar{z}_{11} = \frac{\bar{V}_1}{\bar{I}_1}\bigg| = \frac{100}{12.5} = 8\,\Omega \qquad \bar{z}_{12} = \frac{\bar{V}_1}{\bar{I}_2}\bigg| = \frac{30}{5} = 6\,\Omega$$

$$\bar{z}_{21} = \frac{\bar{V}_2}{\bar{I}_1}\bigg|_{\bar{I}_2=0} = \frac{75}{12.5} = 6\,\Omega \qquad \bar{z}_{22} = \frac{\bar{V}_2}{\bar{I}_2}\bigg|_{\bar{I}_1=0} = \frac{50}{5} = 10\,\Omega$$

23.7 Draw a $\bar{z}$-parameter model for the circuit of Prob. 23.6.

▐ See Fig. 23-6.

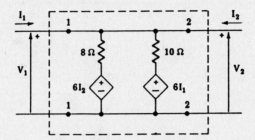

Fig. 23-6

23.8 Determine the $\bar{z}$ parameters for the network of Fig. 23-7.

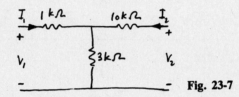

Fig. 23-7

▐ The loop equations become

$$\bar{V}_1 = 4000\bar{I}_1 + 3000\bar{I}_2 \qquad \bar{V}_2 = 3000\bar{I}_1 + 13{,}000\bar{I}_2$$

Thus, $\qquad \bar{z}_{11} = 4\,\text{k}\Omega \qquad \bar{z}_{12} = \bar{z}_{21} = 3\,\text{k}\Omega \qquad \bar{z}_{22} = 13\,\text{k}\Omega$

23.9 Determine the $\bar{z}$ parameters of the general T network shown in Fig. 23-8.

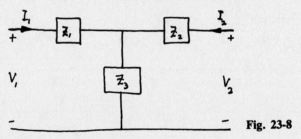

Fig. 23-8

▐ Using the experimental procedure of Prob. 23.3:

$$\bar{z}_{11} = \frac{\bar{V}_1}{\bar{I}_1}\bigg|_{\bar{I}_2=0} = \bar{Z}_1 + \bar{Z}_3 \qquad \text{since} \qquad \bar{I}_1 = \frac{\bar{V}_1}{\bar{Z}_1 + \bar{Z}_2}$$

$$\bar{z}_{12} = \frac{\bar{V}_1}{\bar{I}_2}\bigg|_{\bar{I}_1=0} = \frac{\bar{I}_2\bar{Z}_3}{\bar{I}_2} = \bar{Z}_3 = \bar{z}_{21}$$

$$\bar{z}_{22} = \frac{\bar{V}_2}{\bar{I}_2}\bigg|_{\bar{I}_1=0} = \frac{\bar{I}_2(\bar{Z}_2 + \bar{Z}_3)}{\bar{I}_2} = \bar{Z}_2 + \bar{Z}_3$$

23.10 In a T network $\bar{Z}_1 = 3\,\underline{/0°}\,\Omega$, $\bar{Z}_2 = 4\,\underline{/90°}\,\Omega$, $\bar{Z}_3 = 3\,\underline{/-90°}\,\Omega$. Find the $\bar{z}$ parameters.

▐ From the results of Prob. 23.9:

$$\bar{z}_{11} = 3\,\underline{/0°} + 3\,\underline{/-90°} = 4.242\,\underline{/-45°}\,\Omega$$

$$\bar{z}_{12} = \bar{z}_{21} = \bar{Z}_3 = 3\,\underline{/-90°}\,\Omega$$

$$\bar{z}_{22} = 4\,\underline{/90°} + 3\,\underline{/-90°} = 1\,\underline{/90°}\,\Omega$$

23.11 Determine the $\bar{z}$ parameters of a T network having $\bar{Z}_1 = (3 + j2) \, \Omega$, $\bar{Z}_2 = 1 \underline{/-90°}$, and $\bar{Z}_3 = (3 + j4) \, \Omega$.

▮ Proceeding as in Prob. 23.10:

$$\bar{z}_{11} = \bar{Z}_1 + \bar{Z}_3 = (3 + j2) + (3 + j4) = 6 + j6 = 8.484 \underline{/45°} \, \Omega$$

$$\bar{z}_{12} = \bar{z}_{21} = \bar{Z}_3 = 3 + j4 = 5 \underline{/53.13°} \, \Omega$$

$$\bar{z}_{22} = \bar{Z}_2 + \bar{Z}_3 = -j1 + 3 + j4 = 3 + j3 = 4.242 \underline{/45°} \, \Omega$$

23.12 Draw the $\bar{z}$-parameter model for the circuit of Prob. 23.10.

▮ See Fig. 23-9.

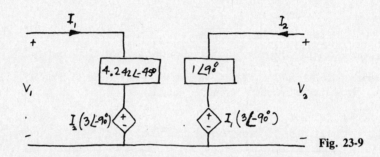

Fig. 23-9

23.13 Draw the $\bar{z}$-parameter model for the circuit of Prob. 23.11.

▮ See Fig. 23-10.

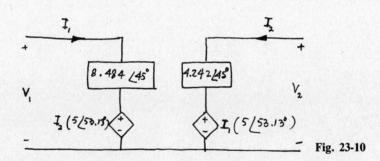

Fig. 23-10

23.14 Determine the $\bar{z}$ parameters of the network shown in Fig. 23-11.

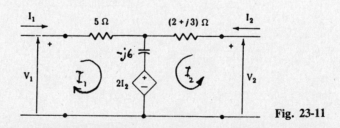

Fig. 23-11

▮ Writing the loop equations yields

$$\bar{V}_1 - 2\bar{I}_2 = (5 - j6)\bar{I}_1 - j6\bar{I}_2 \qquad \bar{V}_2 - 2\bar{I}_2 = -j6\bar{I}_1 + (2 + j3 - j6)\bar{I}_2$$

or $\qquad \bar{V}_1 = (5 - j6)\bar{I}_1 + (2 - j6)\bar{I}_2 \qquad \bar{V}_2 = (-j6)\bar{I}_1 + (4 - j3)\bar{I}_2$

Hence, $\qquad \bar{z}_{11} = (5 - j6) \, \Omega \qquad \bar{z}_{12} = (2 - j6) \, \Omega \qquad \bar{z}_{21} = (-j6) \, \Omega \qquad$ and $\qquad \bar{z}_{22} = (4 - j3) \, \Omega$

23.15 The following open-circuit currents and voltages were determined experimentally for an unknown two-port. Measurements were made at 300 Hz.

$$\bar{V}_1\Big| = 208.1\,\underline{/54.8°} \qquad \bar{V}_1\Big| = 53.24\,\underline{/-133°}$$
$$\bar{V}_2\Big| = 133.1\,\underline{/-133°} \qquad \bar{V}_2\Big| = 79.8\,\underline{/25.54°}$$
$$\bar{I}_1\Big|_{I_2=0} = 10\,\underline{/0°} \qquad \bar{I}_2\Big|_{I_1=0} = 4\,\underline{/0°}$$

Determine the equivalent $\bar{z}$ parameters.

❚

$$\bar{z}_{11} = \frac{208.1\,\underline{/54.8°}}{10\,\underline{/0°}} = 20.81\,\underline{/54.8°} = (12 + j17)\ \Omega$$

$$\bar{z}_{21} = \frac{133.1\,\underline{/-133°}}{10\,\underline{/0°}} = 13.31\,\underline{/-133°} = (-9.08 - j9.73)\ \Omega$$

$$\bar{z}_{12} = \frac{53.24\,\underline{/-133°}}{4\,\underline{/0°}} = 13.31\,\underline{/-133°} = (-9.08 - j9.73)\ \Omega$$

$$\bar{z}_{22} = \frac{79.8\,\underline{/25.54°}}{4\,\underline{/0°}} = 19.95\,\underline{/25.54°} = (18 + j8.6)\ \Omega$$

23.16 A 20-V 300-Hz source is connected to the input port of the circuit of Prob. 23.15 and a 10-Ω resistor to the output port. Draw the equivalent $\bar{z}$-parameter model.

❚ See Fig. 23-12.

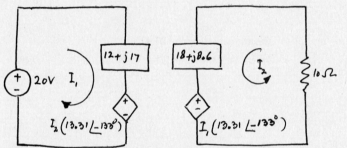

Fig. 23-12

23.17 Determine the output current in the circuit of Prob. 23.16.

❚ From Fig. 23-12 we obtain

$$20 + j0 = (12 + j17)\bar{I}_1 + (-9.08 - j9.73)\bar{I}_2 \qquad 0 = (-9.08 - j9.73)\bar{I}_1 + (28 + j8.6)\bar{I}_2$$

Solving for $\bar{I}_2$ yields

$$\bar{I}_2 = \frac{266.17\,\underline{/46.98°}}{450.17\,\underline{/63.35°}} = 0.59\,\underline{/-16.37°}\ \text{A}$$

23.18 Similar to the $\bar{z}$ parameters, we define the *admittance* or $\bar{y}$ *parameters* by

$$\bar{I}_1 = \bar{y}_{11}\bar{V}_1 + \bar{y}_{12}\bar{V}_2 \qquad \bar{I}_2 = \bar{y}_{21}\bar{V}_1 + \bar{y}_{22}\bar{V}_2 \tag{1}$$

Using this definition, find the $\bar{y}$ parameters of the circuit of Fig. 23-13.

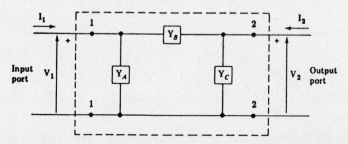

Fig. 23-13

▮ From Fig. 23-13 we obtain

$$\bar{I}_1 = (\bar{Y}_A + \bar{Y}_B)\bar{V}_1 - \bar{Y}_B\bar{V}_2 \qquad \bar{I}_2 = -\bar{Y}_B\bar{V}_1 + (\bar{Y}_C + \bar{Y}_B)\bar{V}_2 \tag{2}$$

Comparing (1) and (2) yields

$$\bar{y}_{11} = \bar{Y}_A + \bar{Y}_B \qquad \bar{y}_{12} = -\bar{Y}_B \qquad \bar{y}_{21} = -\bar{Y}_B \qquad \bar{y}_{22} = \bar{Y}_C + \bar{Y}_B$$

23.19 Draw a $\bar{y}$-parameter model for the circuit of Fig. 23-13.

▮ See Fig. 23-14.

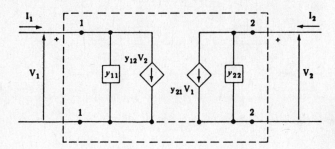

Fig. 23-14

23.20 Establish experimental procedures to determine the $\bar{y}$ parameters of a network.

▮ Refer to Fig. 23-15a, from which

$$\bar{I}_1 = \bar{y}_{11}\bar{V}_1 \\ \bar{I}_2 = \bar{y}_{21}\bar{V}_1 \Big|_{\bar{V}_2 = 0}$$

From Fig. 23-15b:

$$\bar{I}_1 = \bar{y}_{12}\bar{V}_2 \\ \bar{I}_2 = \bar{y}_{22}\bar{V}_2 \Big|_{\bar{V}_1 = 0}$$

Consequently:

$$\bar{y}_{11} = \frac{\bar{I}_1}{\bar{V}_1} \qquad \bar{y}_{12} = \frac{\bar{I}_1}{\bar{V}_2}$$

$$\bar{y}_{21} = \frac{\bar{I}_2}{\bar{V}_1}\Big|_{\bar{V}_2 = 0} \qquad \bar{y}_{22} = \frac{\bar{I}_2}{\bar{V}_2}\Big|_{\bar{V}_1 = 0}$$

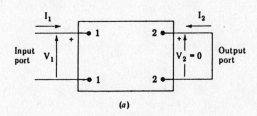

(a)

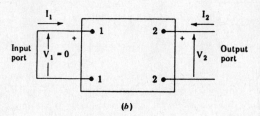

(b)

Fig. 23-15

23.21 Determine the $\bar{y}$ parameters for the circuit shown in Fig. 23-16a.

▮ The $\bar{y}$ parameters may be determined by writing the two node equations. Converting the impedances to admittances,

$$100\,\text{k}\Omega \Rightarrow 10\,\mu\text{S} \qquad 75\,\text{k}\Omega \Rightarrow 13.33\,\mu\text{S} \qquad 50\,\text{k}\Omega \Rightarrow 20\,\mu\text{S}$$

Figure 23-16b shows the circuit expressed in terms of admittance.

$$\bar{I}_1 = [13.33 + 10]10^{-6}\bar{V}_1 - [10]10^{-6}\bar{V}_2 \qquad \bar{I}_2 = -[10]10^{-6}\bar{V}_1 + [10 + 20]10^{-6}\bar{V}_2$$

Thus, the $\bar{y}$ parameters are

$$\bar{y}_{11} = 23.33\,\mu\text{S} \qquad \bar{y}_{12} = -10\,\mu\text{S} \qquad \bar{y}_{21} = -10\,\mu\text{S} \qquad \bar{y}_{22} = 30\,\mu\text{S}$$

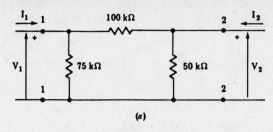

(a)

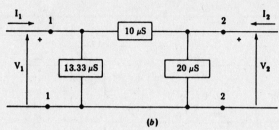

(b)   **Fig. 23-16**

23.22 Draw a $\bar{y}$-parameter model of the circuit of Prob. 23.21.

▮ See Fig. 23-17.

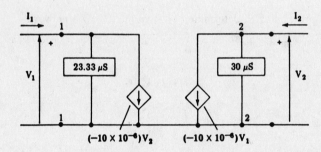

$(-10 \times 10^{-6})V_2$ $(-10 \times 10^{-6})V_1$ **Fig. 23-17**

23.23 The following short-circuit currents and voltages were determined experimentally for an unknown two-port:

$$\bar{I}_1 = 3\,\text{mA} \qquad\qquad \bar{I}_1 = -1\,\text{mA}$$
$$\bar{I}_2 = -0.6\,\text{mA} \qquad\quad \bar{I}_2 = 12\,\text{mA}$$
$$\bar{V}_1 = 24\,\text{V} \Big|_{\bar{V}_2=0} \qquad \bar{V}_2 = 40\,\text{V} \Big|_{\bar{V}_1=0}$$

Determine the $\bar{y}$ parameters.

▮

$$\bar{y}_{11} = \frac{\bar{I}_1}{\bar{V}_1}\bigg|_{\bar{V}_2=0} = \frac{0.003}{24} = 125\ \mu\text{S} \qquad \bar{y}_{12} = \frac{\bar{I}_1}{\bar{V}_2}\bigg|_{\bar{V}_1=0} = \frac{-0.001}{40} = -25\ \mu\text{S}$$

$$\bar{y}_{21} = \frac{\bar{I}_2}{\bar{V}_1}\bigg|_{\bar{V}_2=0} = \frac{-0.0006}{24} = -25\ \mu\text{S} \qquad \bar{y}_{22} = \frac{\bar{I}_2}{\bar{V}_2}\bigg|_{\bar{V}_1=0} = \frac{0.012}{40} = 300\ \mu\text{S}$$

23.24 Draw the equivalent $\bar{y}$-parameter model of the circuit of Prob. 23.23.

▮ See Fig. 23-18.

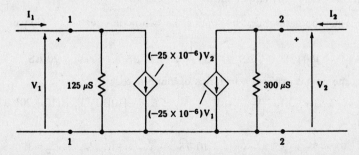

$(-25 \times 10^{-6})V_2$

$(-25 \times 10^{-6})V_1$ **Fig. 23-18**

23.25 If a 100-V dc source is connected to the input port and a 5-kΩ load to the output port of the circuit of Prob. 23.23, determine the current and power drawn by the load.

▮ With the circuit shown in Fig. 23-19 and load and admittance $= 1/5000 = 200 \ \mu S$, we have

$$-\bar{y}_{21}\bar{V}_1 = [\bar{y}_{22} + 200 \times 10^{-6}]\bar{V}_2 \qquad -(-25 \times 10^{-6})\bar{V}_1 = [300 \times 10^{-6} + 200 \times 10^{-6}]\bar{V}_2$$

Substituting 100 for $\bar{V}_1$, and solving for $\bar{V}_2$,

$$25(100) = 500\bar{V}_2 \qquad \bar{V}_2 = 5 \ V$$

Applying Ohm's law to the 5000-Ω load,

$$\bar{I}_{\text{load}} = \frac{5}{5000} = 1 \ mA$$

The power drawn by the load is

$$P_{\text{load}} = I_{\text{load}}^2 R_{\text{load}} = (0.001)^2(5000) = 5 \ mW$$

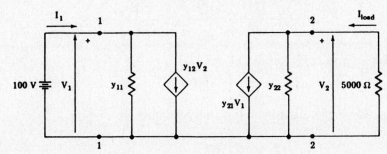

Fig. 23-19

23.26 Determine the current input from the 100-V source in the circuit of Fig. 23-19.

▮ The node equation for node 1 is

$$[\bar{I}_1 - \bar{y}_{12}\bar{V}_2] = [\bar{y}_{11}]\bar{V}_1 \qquad \bar{I}_1 - (-25 \times 10^{-6})\bar{V}_2 = (125 \times 10^{-6})\bar{V}_1$$

Substituting the known values of $\bar{V}_1$ and $\bar{V}_2$, and solving,

$$\bar{I}_1 - (-25 \times 10^{-6})5 = (125 \times 10^{-6})100 \qquad \bar{I}_1 = 12.4 \ mA$$

23.27 Obtain the equivalent $\bar{y}$ parameters for the two-port network of Fig. 23-20.

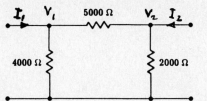

Fig. 23-20

▮ The node equations yield

$$\bar{I}_1 = (250 + 200)10^{-6}\bar{V}_1 - (200 \times 10^{-6})\bar{V}_2 = 450 \times 10^{-6}\bar{V}_1 - 200 \times 10^{-6}\bar{V}_2$$

$$\bar{I}_2 = -(200 \times 10^{-6})\bar{V}_1 + (200 + 500) \times 10^{-6}\bar{V}_2 = -200 \times 10^{-6}\bar{V}_1 + 700 \times 10^{-6}\bar{V}_2$$

Hence, $\qquad \bar{y}_{11} = 450 \ \mu S \qquad \bar{y}_{12} = \bar{y}_{21} = -200 \ \mu S \qquad$ and $\qquad \bar{y}_2 = 700 \ \mu S$

23.28 The $\bar{y}$ parameters of a network are $\bar{y}_{11} = 14 \ mS$, $\bar{y}_{12} = \bar{y}_{21} = -10 \ mS$, and $\bar{y}_{22} = 12 \ mS$. For a 50-V dc input and a 100-Ω resistive load at the output, draw the $\bar{y}$-parameter model.

▮ See Fig. 23-21.

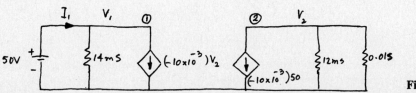

Fig. 23-21

23.29 Calculate the current drawn by the load in the circuit of Prob. 23.28.

$$\bar{Y}_{\text{load}} = \frac{1}{R_L} = \frac{1}{100} = 0.01 \text{ S}$$

The node equation at node 2 is

$$-(-10 \times 10^{-3})V_1 = (12 \times 10^{-3} + 0.01)V_2 \quad \text{and} \quad V_1 = 50 \text{ V} \quad \text{(given)}$$

Hence, $\qquad V_2 = 22.73 \text{ V} \quad \text{and} \quad I_{\text{load}} = \frac{V_2}{R_{\text{load}}} = \frac{22.73}{100} = 0.2273 \text{ A}$

23.30 Determine the input current to the circuit of Prob. 23.29.

For node 1 we have

$$\bar{I}_1 - (-10 \times 10^{-3})\bar{V}_2 = 14 \times 10^{-3}\bar{V}_1$$

Since $\bar{V}_1 = 50 \text{ V}$ (given) and $\bar{V}_2 = 22.73 \text{ V}$, from Prob. 23.29,

$$\bar{I}_1 = -(0.01)(22.73) + (0.014)(50) = 0.473 \text{ A}$$

23.31 What is the amount of losses in the circuit of Fig. 23-21?

$$\text{Losses} = \text{input} - \text{output} = (50)(0.473) - (22.73)(0.2273) = 18.48 \text{ W}$$

23.32 Determine the $\bar{y}$ parameters for the general Π network shown in Fig. 23-22.

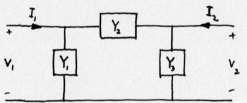

Fig. 23-22

Using the experimental procedure of Prob. 23.20, from Fig. 23-22 we have

$$\bar{y}_{11} = \frac{\bar{I}_1}{\bar{V}_1}\bigg|_{\bar{V}_2=0} = \bar{Y}_1 + \bar{Y}_2 \qquad \bar{y}_{12} = \frac{\bar{I}_1}{\bar{V}_2}\bigg|_{\bar{V}_1=0} = -\bar{Y}_2 = \bar{y}_{21} \qquad \bar{y}_{22} = \frac{\bar{I}_2}{\bar{V}_2}\bigg|_{\bar{V}_1=0} = \bar{Y}_2 + \bar{Y}_3$$

23.33 In a Π network we have $\bar{Y}_1 = 0.2 \times 10^{-3}\ \underline{/0°}\ \text{S}$, $\bar{Y}_2 = 0.02 \times 10^{-3}\ \underline{/-90°}\ \text{S}$, and $\bar{Y}_3 = 0.25 \times 10^{-3}\ \underline{/90°}\ \text{S}$. Find the $\bar{y}$ parameters.

$$\bar{y}_{11} = \bar{Y}_1 + \bar{Y}_2 = (0.2 - j0.02)10^{-3} \qquad \bar{y}_{12} = \bar{y}_{21} = -\bar{Y}_2 = -(-j0.02)10^{-3} = (j0.02)10^{-3}$$

$$\bar{y}_{22} = \bar{Y}_2 + \bar{Y}_3 = (-j0.02 + j0.25)10^{-3} = j0.23 \times 10^{-3}$$

23.34 Find the $\bar{z}$ parameters of the network of Fig. 23-23, and show that the network is not reciprocal, i.e., $\bar{z}_{12} \neq \bar{z}_{21}$.

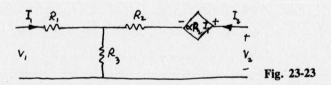

Fig. 23-23

By KVL we have

$$\bar{V}_1 = (R_1 + R_3)\bar{I}_1 + R_3\bar{I}_2 \qquad \bar{V}_2 = (\alpha R_2 + R_3)\bar{I}_1 + (R_2 + R_3)\bar{I}_2$$

Hence, $\qquad \bar{z}_{11} = R_1 + R_3 \qquad \bar{z}_{12} = R_3 \qquad \bar{z}_{21} = \alpha R_2 + R_3 \qquad \bar{z}_{22} = R_2 + R_3$

Clearly, $\qquad\qquad\qquad\qquad\qquad \bar{z}_{12} \neq \bar{z}_{21}$

23.35 In Fig. 23-2 we have obtained a two-generator equivalent two-port network. Obtain a one-generator equivalent network corresponding to that of Fig. 23-2.

$\blacksquare$ We add and subtract $\bar{z}_{12}\bar{I}_1$ from (2) of Prob. 23.1. Thus, (1) and (2) become

$$\bar{V}_1 = \bar{z}_{11}\bar{I}_1 + \bar{z}_{12}\bar{I}_2 \qquad \bar{V}_2 = \bar{z}_{12}\bar{I}_1 + \bar{z}_{22}\bar{I}_2 + (\bar{z}_{21} - \bar{z}_{12})\bar{I}_1$$

which are represented by the circuit of Fig. 23-24.

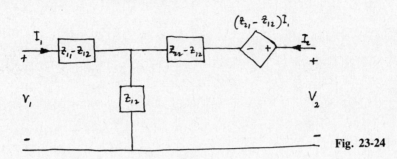

Fig. 23-24

23.36 The voltage-current relationships of a two-port network, of the type shown in Fig. 23-1a, are expressed as

$$\bar{V}_1 = \bar{A}\bar{V}_2 - \bar{B}\bar{I}_2 \tag{1}$$

$$\bar{I}_1 = \bar{C}\bar{V}_2 - \bar{D}\bar{I}_2 \tag{2}$$

The parameters $\bar{A}$, $\bar{B}$, $\bar{C}$, and $\bar{D}$ are known as *transmission parameters*. Notice that the negative signs associated with $\bar{B}\bar{I}_2$ and $\bar{D}\bar{I}_2$ arise from the assumed direction of $\bar{I}_2$. Develop experimental procedures to determine these constants.

$\blacksquare$ By open-circuit and short-circuit tests, as in Probs. 23.3 and 23.20, we have

$$\frac{1}{\bar{A}} = \frac{\bar{V}_2}{\bar{V}_1}\bigg|_{\bar{I}_2=0} \tag{3}$$

$$\frac{-1}{\bar{B}} = \frac{\bar{I}_2}{\bar{V}_1}\bigg|_{\bar{V}_2=0} \tag{4}$$

$$\frac{1}{\bar{C}} = \frac{\bar{V}_2}{\bar{I}_1}\bigg|_{\bar{I}_2=0} \tag{5}$$

$$\frac{-1}{\bar{D}} = \frac{\bar{I}_2}{\bar{I}_1}\bigg|_{\bar{V}_2=0} \tag{6}$$

23.37 Draw circuits to represent (3) and (4) of Prob. 23.36.

$\blacksquare$ See Fig. 23-25.

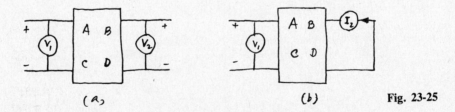

(a) (b) Fig. 23-25

23.38 Express the $\bar{z}$ parameters in terms of the $\bar{y}$ parameters of a two-port network.

$\blacksquare$ Solving for $\bar{V}_1$ and $\bar{V}_2$ in (1) of Prob. 23.18 we obtain

$$\bar{V}_1 = \frac{\bar{y}_{22}}{\bar{\Delta}_y}\bar{I}_1 - \frac{\bar{y}_{12}}{\bar{\Delta}_y}\bar{I}_2 = \bar{z}_{11}\bar{I}_1 + \bar{z}_{12}\bar{I}_2 \qquad \bar{V}_2 = -\frac{\bar{y}_{21}}{\bar{\Delta}_y} + \frac{\bar{y}_{11}}{\bar{\Delta}_y}\bar{I}_2 = \bar{z}_{21}\bar{I}_1 + \bar{z}_{22}\bar{I}_2$$

where $$\bar{\Delta}_y = \bar{y}_{11}\bar{y}_{22} - \bar{y}_{12}\bar{y}_{21}$$

Hence, $$\bar{z}_{11} = \frac{\bar{y}_{22}}{\bar{\Delta}_y} \qquad \bar{z}_{12} = -\frac{\bar{y}_{12}}{\bar{\Delta}_y} \qquad \bar{z}_{21} = -\frac{\bar{y}_{21}}{\bar{\Delta}_y} \qquad \bar{z}_{22} = \frac{\bar{y}_{11}}{\bar{\Delta}_y}$$

23.39 Express the $\bar{y}$ parameters in terms of the $\bar{z}$ parameters of a two-port network.

▮ Solving for $\bar{I}_1$ and $\bar{I}_2$ in (1) and (2) of Prob. 23.1, we obtain

$$\bar{I}_1 = \frac{\bar{z}_{22}}{\bar{\Delta}_z} \bar{V}_1 - \frac{\bar{z}_{12}}{\bar{\Delta}_z} \bar{V}_2 = \bar{y}_{11}\bar{V}_1 + \bar{y}_{12}\bar{V}_2$$

$$\bar{I}_2 = -\frac{\bar{z}_{21}}{\bar{\Delta}_z} \bar{V}_1 + \frac{\bar{z}_{11}}{\bar{\Delta}_z} \bar{V}_2 = \bar{y}_{21}\bar{V}_1 + \bar{y}_{22}\bar{V}_2$$

Hence,

$$\bar{y}_{11} = \frac{\bar{z}_{22}}{\bar{\Delta}_z} \qquad \bar{y}_{12} = -\frac{\bar{z}_{12}}{\bar{\Delta}_z} \qquad \bar{y}_{21} = -\frac{\bar{z}_{21}}{\bar{\Delta}_z} \qquad \bar{y}_{22} = \frac{\bar{z}_{11}}{\bar{\Delta}_z}$$

where

$$\bar{\Delta}_z = \bar{z}_{11}\bar{z}_{22} - \bar{z}_{12}\bar{z}_{21}$$

23.40 For a two-port network show that

$$\bar{z}_{11}\bar{y}_{11} = \bar{z}_{22}\bar{y}_{22}$$

▮ From Probs. 23.38 and 23.39 we obtain

$$\bar{z}_{11}\bar{y}_{11} = \left(\frac{\bar{y}_{22}}{\bar{\Delta}_y}\right)\left(\frac{\bar{z}_{22}}{\bar{\Delta}_z}\right) = \left(\frac{\bar{y}_{22}}{\bar{\Delta}_y}\right)\bar{y}_{11} \tag{1}$$

$$\bar{z}_{22}\bar{y}_{22} = \left(\frac{\bar{y}_{11}}{\bar{\Delta}_y}\right)\left(\frac{\bar{z}_{11}}{\bar{\Delta}_z}\right) = \left(\frac{\bar{y}_{11}}{\bar{\Delta}_y}\right)\bar{y}_{22} \tag{2}$$

Hence,

$$\bar{z}_{11}\bar{y}_{11} = \bar{z}_{22}\bar{y}_{22}$$

23.41 Express the $\bar{A}, \bar{B}, \bar{C}, \bar{D}$ parameters in terms of the $\bar{z}$ parameters for a two-port network.

▮ From (1) and (2) of Prob. 23.1 and from (1) and (2) of Prob. 23.36 we obtain

$$\bar{A} = \frac{\bar{z}_{11}}{\bar{z}_{21}} \qquad \bar{B} = \frac{\bar{z}_{11}\bar{z}_{22} - \bar{z}_{12}\bar{z}_{21}}{\bar{z}_{21}} \qquad \bar{C} = \frac{1}{\bar{z}_{21}} \quad \text{and} \quad \bar{D} = \frac{\bar{z}_{22}}{\bar{z}_{21}}$$

23.42 For a reciprocal two-port network show that $\bar{A}\bar{D} - \bar{B}\bar{C} = 1$.

▮ From the results of Prob. 23.41 we obtain

$$\bar{A}\bar{D} - \bar{B}\bar{C} = \frac{\bar{z}_{11}\bar{z}_{22}}{(\bar{z}_{21})^2} - \frac{\bar{z}_{11}\bar{z}_{22} - \bar{z}_{12}\bar{z}_{21}}{(\bar{z}_{21})^2} = \frac{\bar{z}_{12}}{\bar{z}_{21}} = 1$$

since $\bar{z}_{12} = \bar{z}_{21}$ for a reciprocal network.

23.43 *Hybrid* or $\bar{h}$-*parameter* models of two-port networks include admittance and impedance parameters such that we may write

$$\bar{V}_1 = \bar{h}_{11}\bar{I}_1 + \bar{h}_{12}\bar{V}_2 \tag{1}$$

$$\bar{I}_2 = \bar{h}_{21}\bar{I}_1 + \bar{h}_{22}\bar{V}_2 \tag{2}$$

Establish experimental procedures to determine the $\bar{h}$ parameters.

▮ The $\bar{h}$ parameters are given by

$$\bar{h}_{11} = \frac{\bar{V}_1}{\bar{I}_1}\bigg|_{\bar{V}_2=0} \qquad \bar{h}_{12} = \frac{\bar{V}_1}{\bar{V}_2}\bigg|_{\bar{I}_1=0} \qquad \bar{h}_{21} = \frac{\bar{I}_2}{\bar{I}_1}\bigg|_{\bar{V}_2=0} \qquad \bar{h}_{22} = \frac{\bar{I}_2}{\bar{V}_2}\bigg|_{\bar{I}_1=0}$$

23.44 Draw an $\bar{h}$-parameter model of a general two-port network.

▮ The general equations are (1) and (2) of Prob. 23.43, which are represented by the model shown in Fig. 23-26.

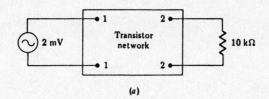

Fig. 23-26

23.45 A two-port network containing a common-emitter transistor amplifier is connected to a 2-mV signal source and a 10-kΩ resistor load as shown in Fig. 23-27a. The $\bar{h}$ parameters for the two-port are

$$\bar{h}_i = \bar{h}_{11} = 1.4\,k\Omega \qquad \bar{h}_r = \bar{h}_{12} = 3.4 \times 10^{-4} \qquad \bar{h}_f = \bar{h}_{21} = 44 \qquad \bar{h}_o = \bar{h}_{22} = 27\,\mu S$$

In the above we have used the following $\bar{h}$-parameter descriptive symbols and names

$$\bar{h}_{11} = \bar{h}_i = \text{short-circuit input impedance, } \Omega$$

$$\bar{h}_{21} = \bar{h}_f = \text{short-circuit forward current ratio}$$

$$\bar{h}_{12} = \bar{h}_r = \text{open-circuit reverse voltage ratio}$$

$$\bar{h}_{22} = \bar{h}_o = \text{open-circuit output admittance, S}$$

Draw the equivalent $\bar{h}$-parameter model.

❙ See Fig. 23-27b.

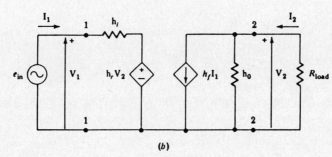

(a)

(b)

Fig. 23-27

23.46 In the circuit of Prob. 23.45, determine the voltage across the load.

❙ Using the circuit of Fig. 23-27b, the loop equation for the input port is

$$\bar{V}_1 - \bar{h}_r\bar{V}_2 = \bar{I}_1\bar{h}_i$$

The node equation for the output port is

$$-\bar{h}_f\bar{I}_1 = \left[\bar{h}_o + \frac{1}{R_{\text{load}}}\right]\bar{V}_2$$

Substituting the given parameters,

$$0.002 - 3.4 \times 10^{-4}\bar{V}_2 = 1400\bar{I}_1 \tag{1}$$

$$-44\bar{I}_1 = [27 \times 10^{-6} + 100 \times 10^{-6}]\bar{V}_2 \tag{2}$$

Solving Eq. (2) for $\bar{I}_1$, and then substituting into Eq. (1):

$$\bar{I}_1 = -2.886 \times 10^{-6}\bar{V}_2 \qquad 0.002 - 3.4 \times 10^{-4}\bar{V}_2 = 1400(-2.886 \times 10^{-6})\bar{V}_2 \qquad \bar{V}_2 = -0.54\,V$$

23.47 Calculate the load current in the circuit of Prob. 23.45.

$\blacksquare$
$$\bar{I}_L = \frac{\bar{V}_L}{R_L} = \frac{-0.54}{10,000} = -54\ \mu\text{A}$$

23.48 What is the voltage gain of the circuit of Prob. 23.45?

$\blacksquare$
$$A_v = \frac{\bar{V}_2}{\bar{V}_1} = -\frac{0.54}{0.002} = -270$$

23.49 A 0.020-V 100-kHz source and a 2000-Ω resistor load are connected to the respective input and output ports of a certain common-emitter transistor amplifier. The parameters of the equivalent two-port are $\bar{h}_{11} = 1.2\ \text{k}\Omega$, $\bar{h}_{12} = 0.001$, $\bar{h}_{21} = 45$, $\bar{h}_{22} = 100\ \mu\text{S}$. Determine the voltage across the load.

$\blacksquare$ The circuit is similar to those of Figs. 23-26 and 23-27. Thus, for the input port, we have the loop equation:

$$0.02 - 0.001V_2 = 1200I_1$$

For the output port the node equation is

$$-45I_1 = (100 \times 10^{-6} + 500 \times 10^{-6})V_2$$

Solving for V_2 yields
$$V_2 = -1.33\ \text{V}$$

23.50 What is the load current in the circuit of Prob. 23.49?

$\blacksquare$
$$I_L = \frac{-1.33}{2000} = -666\ \mu\text{A}$$

23.51 Determine the voltage gain of the circuit of Prob. 23.49.

$\blacksquare$
$$A_v = \frac{V_2}{V_1} = -\frac{1.33}{0.02} = -66.65$$

23.52 Obtain the current gain $A_i = \bar{I}_2/\bar{I}_1$ for the circuit of Fig. 23-27.

$\blacksquare$ By current division we have

$$\bar{I}_2 = \frac{(1/\bar{h}_o)\bar{h}_f\bar{I}_1}{(1/\bar{h}_o) + R_L} = \frac{\bar{h}_f\bar{I}_1}{1 + \bar{h}_o R_L}$$

or
$$A_i = \frac{\bar{I}_2}{\bar{I}_1} = \frac{\bar{h}_f}{1 + \bar{h}_o R_L} \tag{1}$$

23.53 Obtain an expression for the voltage gain for the circuit of Fig. 23-27.

$\blacksquare$ At the input port:

$$\bar{I}_1 = \frac{\bar{V}_1 - \bar{h}_r\bar{V}_2}{\bar{h}_i} \tag{1}$$

At the output port:

$$\bar{I}_2 = -\bar{V}_2/R_L = \bar{h}_f\bar{I}_1 + \bar{h}_o\bar{V}_2 \tag{2}$$

Eliminating I_1 from (1) and (2) yields

$$A_v = \frac{\bar{V}_2}{\bar{V}_1} = \frac{-\bar{h}_f R_L}{\bar{h}_i(1 + \bar{h}_o R_L) - \bar{h}_r\bar{h}_f R_L} \tag{3}$$

23.54 In the circuit of Fig. 23-27 we have $\bar{h}_i = 1000\ \Omega$, $\bar{h}_r = 4 \times 10^{-4}$, $\bar{h}_f = 50$, $\bar{h}_o = 25\ \mu\text{S}$, and $R_L = 2000\ \Omega$. Determine the current and voltage gains.

$\blacksquare$ From (1) of Prob. 23.52:

$$A_i = \frac{50}{1 + 25 \times 10^{-6} \times 2000} = 47.62$$

From (3) of Prob. 23.53:
$$A_v = \frac{-(50)(2 \times 10^3)}{(1 \times 10^3)(1.05) - (4 \times 10^{-4})(50)(2 \times 10^3)} = -99$$

23.55 The equivalent two-port network of a common-base transistor amplifier has the following parameters: $\bar{h}_i = 35\,\Omega$, $\bar{h}_f = -0.98$, $\bar{h}_r = 260 \times 10^{-6}$, $\bar{h}_o = 0.3\,\mu$S. Assuming a sinusoidal input voltage of 1 mV and a load resistance of 10.0 kΩ, determine the voltage across the load.

▌ Using the circuit of Fig. 23-27b, the loop equation at the input port is

$$0.001 - 260 \times 10^{-6} V_2 = 35 I_1$$

The node equation at the output port is

$$-(-0.98)I_1 = (0.3 \times 10^{-6} + 100 \times 10^{-6})V_2$$

Solving for V_2 yields $V_2 = 0.26$ V.

23.56 What is the voltage gain of the amplifier of Prob. 23.55?

▌
$$A_v = \frac{V_2}{V_1} = \frac{0.260}{0.001} = 260$$

23.57 In Prob. 23.43 we have defined the $\bar{h}$ parameters. The inverse of the $\bar{h}$ parameters is the $\bar{g}$ parameters defined by

$$\bar{I}_1 = \bar{g}_{11}\bar{V}_1 + \bar{g}_{12}\bar{I}_2 \tag{1}$$

$$\bar{V}_2 = \bar{g}_{21}\bar{V}_1 + \bar{g}_{22}\bar{I}_2 \tag{2}$$

Establish experimental procedures to determine the $\bar{g}$ parameters.

▌ The $\bar{g}$ parameters are obtained from open-circuit and short-circuit tests as given by

$$\bar{g}_{11} = \frac{\bar{I}_1}{\bar{V}_1}\bigg|_{\bar{I}_2=0} \qquad \bar{g}_{21} = \frac{\bar{V}_2}{\bar{V}_1}\bigg|_{\bar{I}_2=0} \qquad \bar{g}_{12} = \frac{\bar{I}_1}{\bar{I}_2}\bigg|_{\bar{V}_1=0} \qquad \bar{g}_{22} = \frac{\bar{V}_2}{\bar{I}_2}\bigg|_{\bar{V}_1=0}$$

23.58 Draw a $\bar{g}$-parameter model to represent (1) and (2) of Prob. 23.57.

▌ See Fig. 23-28.

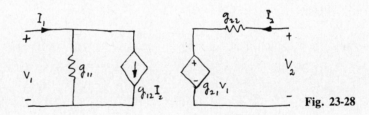

Fig. 23-28

23.59 Find the $\bar{h}$ parameters of the common-emitter connected transistor circuit of Fig. 23-29.

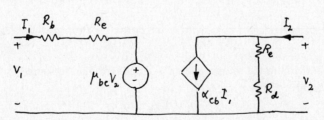

Fig. 23-29

▌ For the input loop:

$$V_1 = (R_b + R_e)I_1 + \mu_{bc}V_2$$

For the output node:
$$I_2 = \alpha_{cb}I_1 + \frac{V_2}{R_e + R_d}$$

Thus, $h_{11} = R_b + R_e$, $h_{12} = \mu_{bc}$, $h_{21} = \alpha_{cb}$, and $h_{22} = 1/(R_e + R_d)$.

23.60 The input impedance of a network is defined by $\bar{Z}_{in} = \bar{V}_1/\bar{I}_1$. According to this definition, find the input impedance of the network shown in Fig. 23-30.

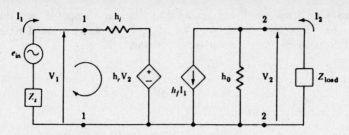

Fig. 23-30

▌ Referring to Fig. 23-30, the loop equation for the input port is

$$\bar{V}_1 - \bar{h}_r \bar{V}_2 = \bar{h}_i \bar{I}_1 \tag{1}$$

The node equation for the output port is

$$-\bar{h}_f \bar{I}_1 = \bar{V}_2 \left[\bar{h}_o + \frac{1}{\bar{Z}_{\text{load}}} \right]$$

Solving for $\bar{V}_2$ and substituting into (1):

$$V_2 = \frac{-\bar{h}_f \bar{I}_1 \bar{Z}_{\text{load}}}{\bar{h}_o \bar{Z}_{\text{load}} + 1} \qquad \bar{V}_1 - \bar{h}_r \frac{-\bar{h}_f \bar{I}_1 \bar{Z}_{\text{load}}}{\bar{h}_o \bar{Z}_{\text{load}} + 1} = \bar{h}_i \bar{I}_1$$

Solving for $\bar{V}_1$,

$$\bar{V}_1 = \bar{I}_1 \left[\bar{h}_i - \frac{\bar{h}_r \bar{h}_f \bar{Z}_{\text{load}}}{\bar{h}_o \bar{Z}_{\text{load}} + 1} \right]$$

Hence,

$$\bar{Z}_{\text{in}} = \frac{\bar{V}_1}{\bar{I}_1} = \bar{h}_i - \frac{\bar{h}_r \bar{h}_f \bar{Z}_{\text{load}}}{\bar{h}_o \bar{Z}_{\text{load}} + 1}$$

23.61 The output impedance of any two-port may be determined from the ratio of output voltage to output current, with the *source voltage set to zero*. That is,

$$Z_{\text{out}} = \frac{\bar{V}_2}{\bar{I}_2} \bigg|_{e_{\text{in}} = 0}$$

In accordance with this definition, find the output impedance of the network shown in Fig. 23-31.

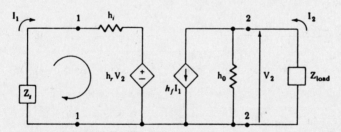

Fig. 23-31

▌ Referring to Fig. 23-31 where the source voltage is set to zero but the source impedance is maintained, the loop equation for the input port is

$$-\bar{h}_r \bar{V}_2 = (\bar{h}_i + \bar{Z}_s) \bar{I}_1 \tag{1}$$

The node equation for node 2 at the output port is

$$\bar{I}_2 - \bar{h}_f \bar{I}_1 = \bar{h}_o \bar{V}_2$$

Solving for I_1, substituting into Eq. (1), and then rearranging the terms,

$$\bar{I}_1 = \frac{-\bar{h}_r \bar{V}_2}{\bar{h}_i + \bar{Z}_s} \qquad -\bar{h}_f \frac{-\bar{h}_r \bar{V}_2}{\bar{h}_i + \bar{Z}_s} = \bar{h}_o \bar{V}_2 - \bar{I}_2$$

$$\bar{V}_2 \left[\bar{h}_o - \frac{\bar{h}_r \bar{h}_f}{\bar{h}_i + \bar{Z}_s} \right] = \bar{I}_2 \qquad \bar{Z}_{\text{out}} = \frac{\bar{V}_2}{\bar{I}_2} = 1 \bigg/ \left[\bar{h}_o - \frac{\bar{h}_r \bar{h}_f}{\bar{h}_i + \bar{Z}_s} \right]$$

23.62 Given the following two-port parameters:

$$\bar{h}_i = 1.4 \text{ k}\Omega \qquad \bar{h}_r = 3.0 \times 10^{-4}$$

$$\bar{h}_f = 40 \qquad \bar{h}_o = 25 \ \mu\text{S}$$

$$\bar{Z}_{\text{gen}} = 1.2 \text{ k}\Omega \qquad \bar{Z}_{\text{load}} = 15 \text{ k}\Omega$$

Determine the input impedance.

I $$\bar{Z}_{\text{in}} = \bar{h}_i - \frac{\bar{h}_r \bar{h}_f \bar{Z}_{\text{load}}}{\bar{h}_o \bar{Z}_{\text{load}} + 1} = 1400 - \frac{(3.0 \times 10^{-4})(40)(15{,}000)}{(25 \times 10^{-6})(15{,}000) + 1} = 1269 \ \Omega$$

23.63 Find the output impedance of the network of Prob. 23.62.

I $$\bar{Z}_{\text{out}} = 1 \Big/ \left[\bar{h}_o - \frac{\bar{h}_r \bar{h}_f}{\bar{h}_i + \bar{Z}_s} \right] = 1 \Big/ \left[25 \times 10^{-6} - \frac{(3.0 \times 10^{-4})40}{1400 + 1200} \right] = 49 \text{ k}\Omega$$

23.64 Determine the voltage gain of the network of Prob. 23.62.

I $$A_v = \frac{-\bar{h}_f \bar{Z}_{\text{load}}}{\bar{h}_i(\bar{h}_o \bar{Z}_{\text{load}} + 1) - \bar{h}_r \bar{h}_f \bar{Z}_{\text{load}}}$$

$$= \frac{-40(15{,}000)}{1400[(25 \times 10^{-6})(15{,}000) + 1] - (3.0 \times 10^{-4})(40)(15{,}000)} = -343.8$$

The minus sign indicates a 180° phase shift between $\bar{V}_2$ and $\bar{V}_1$.

23.65 What is the current gain for the network of Prob. 23.62?

I $$A_i = \frac{\bar{h}_f}{\bar{h}_o \bar{Z}_{\text{load}} + 1} = \frac{40}{(25 \times 10^{-6})(15{,}000) + 1} = 29$$

23.66 Using the $\bar{h}$ parameters of Prob. 23.49, determine the $\bar{Z}_{\text{in}}$ of the network if the source resistance is $1000 \ \Omega$.

I From the result of Prob. 23.60:

$$\bar{Z}_{\text{in}} = 1200 - \frac{(0.001)(45)(2000)}{(100 \times 10^{-6})(2000) + 1} = 1125 \ \Omega$$

23.67 What is output impedance of the circuit of Prob. 23.66?

I From Prob. 23.61:

$$\bar{Z}_{\text{out}} = 1 \Big/ \left[100 \times 10^{-6} - \frac{0.001(45)}{1200 + 1000} \right] = 11.63 \text{ k}\Omega$$

23.68 Determine the voltage gain of the network of Prob. 23.66.

I $$A_v = \frac{-45(2000)}{1200(100 \times 10^{-6} \times 2000 + 1) - 0.001(45)(2000)} = -66.7$$

23.69 Find the current gain of the network of Prob. 23.66.

I $$A_i = \frac{45}{(100 \times 10^{-6})(2000) + 1} = 37.5$$

23.70 Using the $\bar{h}$ parameters of Prob. 23.55 and assuming a source resistance of $800 \ \Omega$, determine the input impedance.

I $$\bar{Z}_{\text{in}} = 35 - \frac{(260 \times 10^{-6})(-0.98)(10{,}000)}{(0.3 \times 10^{-6})(10{,}000) + 1} = 37.54 \ \Omega$$

23.71 What is the output impedance of the network of Prob. 23.70?

I $$\bar{Z}_{\text{out}} = 1 \Big/ \left[(0.3 \times 10^{-6}) - \frac{(260 \times 10^{-6})(-0.98)}{35 + 800} \right] = 1.65 \text{ M}\Omega$$

23.72 Determine the voltage gain of the network of Prob. 23.70.

$$A_v = \frac{-(-0.98)(10,000)}{35[(0.3 \times 10^{-6})(10,000) + 1] - (260 \times 10^{-6})(-0.98)10,000} = 260.3$$

23.73 Calculate the current gain of the network of Prob. 23.70.

$$A_i = \frac{-0.98}{0.3 \times 10^{-6}(10,000) + 1} = -0.98$$

23.74 The input, or the *driving-point*, impedance of the ladder network shown in Fig. 23-32 is given by

$$\bar{Z}_{\text{in}} = \bar{Z}_1 + \cfrac{1}{\bar{Y}_2 + \cfrac{1}{\bar{Z}_3 + \cfrac{1}{\bar{Y}_4 + \cfrac{1}{\bar{Z}_5 + \cfrac{1}{\bar{Y}_6} \cdots}}}} = \bar{z}_{11} \qquad (1)$$

Apply this result to obtain the input impedance of the network of Fig. 23-33.

$$\bar{Z}_{\text{in}} = \bar{z}_{11} = s + \left\{ 1 \Big/ \left[s + \frac{1}{s + (1/s)} \right] \right\} = \frac{s^4 + 3s^2 + 1}{s^3 + 2s}$$

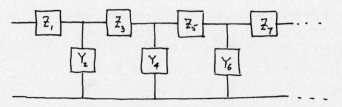

Fig. 23-32

23.75 Determine the open-circuit transfer impedance, $\bar{z}_{12}$, of the network of Fig. 23-33.

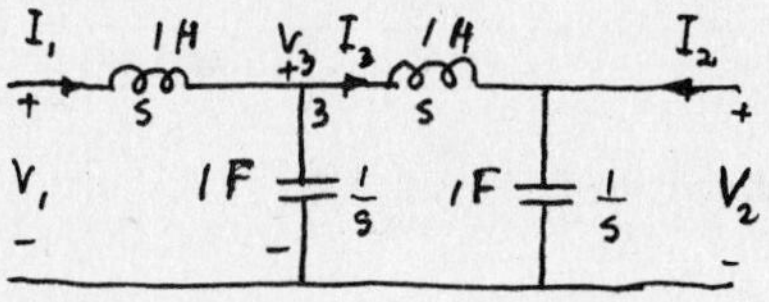

Fig. 23-33

At the output node: $\qquad\qquad\qquad \bar{I}_3 = s\bar{V}_2$

At node 3:

$$\bar{V}_3 = \bar{V}_2 + s(s\bar{V}_2) = (s^2 + 1)\bar{V}_2 \qquad \bar{I}_1 = s\bar{V}_2 + s\bar{V}_3 = [s(s^2 + 1) + s]\bar{V}_2$$

Hence,

$$\bar{z}_{12} = \frac{\bar{V}_2}{\bar{I}_1}\bigg|_{\bar{I}_2 = 0} = \frac{1}{s(s^2 + 1) + s} = \frac{1}{s^3 + 2s}$$

23.76 Find the $\bar{z}$ parameters of the network of Fig. 23-34.

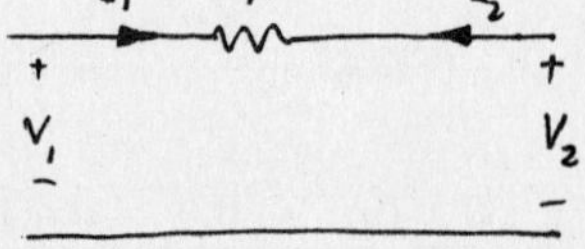

Fig. 23-34

Since $\bar{I}_1$ and $\bar{I}_2$ are *not* independent, the $\bar{z}$ parameters cannot be found.

23.77 Find the $\bar{y}$ parameters of the network of Fig. 23-34.

Since $\bar{I}_1 = -\bar{I}_2$, from (1) of Prob. 23.18, with $\bar{V}_2 = 0$, we obtain

$$\bar{y}_{11} = \frac{1}{R} \quad \text{and} \quad \bar{y}_{21} = -\frac{1}{R}$$

With $\bar{V}_1 = 0$, we have

$$\bar{y}_{21} = -\frac{1}{R} \quad \text{and} \quad \bar{y}_{22} = \frac{1}{R}$$

23.78 Determine the $\bar{z}$ parameters of the network of Fig. 23-35.

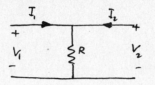

Fig. 23-35

▌ Since $\bar{V}_1 = \bar{V}_2$:

with $\bar{I}_2 = 0$ $\qquad\qquad \bar{z}_{11} = R \quad \text{and} \quad \bar{z}_{21} = R$

with $\bar{I}_1 = 0$ $\qquad\qquad \bar{z}_{12} = R \quad \text{and} \quad \bar{z}_{22} = R$

23.79 Obtain the $\bar{y}$ parameters of the network of Fig. 23-35.

▌ Since $\bar{V}_1$ and $\bar{V}_2$ are *not* independent, the $\bar{y}$ parameters cannot be found.

23.80 Find the $\bar{z}$ parameters of the network of Fig. 23-36.

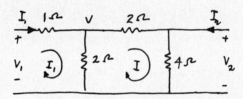

Fig. 23-36

▌ $\bar{I}_2 = 0$: $\qquad\qquad \bar{V}_2 = 4\bar{I} \quad \text{and} \quad 2\bar{I}_1 = (2 + 2 + 4)\bar{I} = 8\bar{I} = 2\bar{V}_2$

Thus, $$\bar{z}_{21} = \frac{\bar{V}_2}{\bar{I}_1} = \frac{2}{2} = 1\,\Omega = \bar{z}_{12}$$

$$\bar{V}_1 = (1)\bar{I}_1 + 2(\bar{I}_1 - \bar{I}) = (1)\bar{I}_1 + 2(\bar{I}_1 - \tfrac{1}{4}I_1) = \tfrac{5}{2}\bar{I}_1$$

Thus, $$\bar{z}_{11} = \bar{V}_1/\bar{I}_1 = \tfrac{5}{2}\,\Omega$$

$\bar{I}_1 = 0$: $\qquad\qquad \bar{V}_2 = 2\bar{I}_2 \quad \text{or} \quad \bar{z}_{22} = \frac{\bar{V}_2}{\bar{I}_2} = 2\,\Omega$

23.81 Find the $\bar{y}$ parameters of the network of Fig. 23-36.

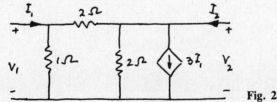

Fig. 23-37

▌ $\bar{V}_2 = 0$: $\qquad \bar{I}_1 = \frac{\bar{V}_1}{1 + 1} = \frac{\bar{V}_1}{2} \quad \text{and} \quad \frac{\bar{I}_1}{\bar{V}_1} = \bar{y}_{11} = \frac{1}{2}\,\text{S}$

$$\bar{I}_2 = -\frac{\bar{I}_1}{2} = -\frac{1}{2}\left(\frac{\bar{V}_1}{2}\right) = -\frac{1}{4}\bar{V}_1 \quad \text{and} \quad \frac{\bar{I}_2}{\bar{V}_1} = \bar{y}_{12} = -\frac{1}{4} = \bar{y}_{21}$$

$\bar{V}_1 = 0$:

$$\bar{I}_2 = \frac{\bar{V}_2}{\frac{8}{5}}$$

Hence

$$\frac{\bar{I}_2}{\bar{V}_2} = \bar{y}_{22} = \frac{1}{\frac{8}{5}} = \frac{5}{8} \text{ S}$$

23.82 Verify that the results of Probs. 23.80 and 23.81 are correct by applying the formulas obtained in Prob. 23.39.

⬛

$$\bar{\Delta}_z = \bar{z}_{11}\bar{z}_{22} - \bar{z}_{12}\bar{z}_{21} = (\tfrac{5}{2})(2) - (1)^2 = 4$$

$$\bar{y}_{11} = \frac{\bar{z}_{22}}{\bar{\Delta}_z} = \frac{2}{4} = \frac{1}{2} \text{ S} \qquad \bar{y}_{21} = \bar{y}_{12} = -\frac{\bar{z}_{12}}{\bar{\Delta}_z} = -\frac{1}{4} \text{ S}$$

$$\bar{y}_{22} = \frac{\bar{z}_{11}}{\bar{\Delta}_z} = \frac{\frac{5}{2}}{4} = \frac{5}{8} \text{ S}$$

23.83 Verify the result of Prob. 23.40 for the circuit of Fig. 23-36.

⬛ It is to be verified that

$$\bar{z}_{11}\bar{y}_{11} = \bar{z}_{22}\bar{y}_{22} \qquad (\tfrac{5}{2})(\tfrac{1}{2}) = (2)(\tfrac{5}{8}) = \tfrac{5}{4}$$

23.84 Find the $\bar{z}$ parameters of the network of Fig. 23-37.

⬛ $\bar{I}_2 = 0$: $\qquad\qquad \bar{I}_1 = 1.5\bar{V}_1 - 0.5\bar{V}_2 \qquad -3\bar{I}_1 = -0.5\bar{V}_1 + \bar{V}_2$

Eliminating $\bar{V}_1$ yields

$$-8\bar{I}_1 = 2.5\bar{V}_2 \qquad \text{or} \qquad \bar{z}_{21} = -3.2 \ \Omega$$

Eliminating $\bar{V}_2$ yields $\qquad\qquad -\bar{I}_1 = 2.5\bar{V}_1$

Thus, $\qquad\qquad\qquad\qquad \bar{z}_{11} = -\frac{1}{2.5} = -0.4 \ \Omega$

$\bar{I}_1 = 0$: $\qquad\qquad \bar{V}_1 = \tfrac{1}{3}\bar{V}_2 \qquad \bar{I}_2 = \bar{V}_2(\tfrac{1}{2} + \tfrac{1}{3}) = \tfrac{5}{6}\bar{V}_2$

or $\qquad\qquad\qquad\qquad \bar{z}_{22} = \tfrac{6}{5} \ \Omega \qquad \bar{z}_{12} = (\tfrac{1}{3})(\tfrac{6}{5}) = 0.4 \ \Omega$

23.85 Determine the $\bar{y}$ parameters of the network of Fig. 23-36.

⬛ $\bar{V}_2 = 0$: $\qquad\qquad \bar{I}_1 = \bar{V}_1(1.5) \qquad \bar{I}_2 = 3\bar{I}_1 - \tfrac{1}{2}\bar{V}_1 = 4\bar{V}_1$

Thus, $\qquad\qquad\qquad\qquad \bar{y}_{11} = 1.5 \qquad \text{and} \qquad \bar{y}_{21} = 4$

$\bar{V}_1 = 0$: $\qquad\qquad \bar{I}_1 = -0.5\bar{V}_2 \qquad \text{or} \qquad \bar{y}_{12} = -0.5$

$$\bar{I}_2 = \bar{V}_2 + 3\bar{I}_1 = -0.5\bar{V}_2 \qquad \text{or} \qquad \bar{y}_{22} = -0.5$$

23.86 Verify the results of Probs. 23.84 and 23.85 by applying the results of Prob. 23.39.

⬛

$$\bar{\Delta}_z = (-0.4)(\tfrac{6}{5}) - (-3.2)(0.4) = 0.8$$

$$\bar{y}_{11} = \frac{1.2}{0.8} = 1.5 \text{ S} \qquad \bar{y}_{12} = -\frac{0.4}{0.8} = -0.5 \text{ S} \qquad \bar{y}_{21} = \frac{3.2}{0.8} = 4 \text{ S} \qquad \text{and} \qquad \bar{y}_{22} = -\frac{0.4}{0.8} = -0.5 \text{ S}$$

23.87 Find the $\bar{z}$ parameters of the circuit of Fig. 23-38.

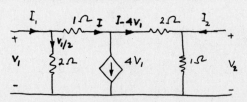

Fig. 23-38

▌ $I_2 = 0$: Referring to Fig. 23-38,

$$\bar{I} = \bar{I}_1 - \frac{\bar{V}_1}{2} = -\frac{(2+1)(I - 4\bar{V}_1) + \bar{V}_1}{1}$$

or $\qquad -3\left(\bar{I}_1 - \frac{\bar{V}_1}{2} - 4\bar{V}_1\right) + \bar{V}_1 = \bar{I}_1 - \frac{\bar{V}_1}{2}$ or $\quad 15\bar{V}_1 = 4\bar{I}_1$

Thus, $\qquad\qquad\qquad\qquad \bar{z}_{11} = \frac{\bar{V}_1}{\bar{I}_1} = \frac{4}{15}\ \Omega$

$$\bar{V}_2 = \left(\bar{I}_1 - \frac{9\bar{V}_1}{2}\right)(1) = \bar{I}_1(1 - \tfrac{9}{2} \times \tfrac{4}{15}) \qquad \bar{z}_{21} = \frac{\bar{V}_2}{\bar{I}_1} = -\frac{1}{5}\ \Omega$$

$\bar{I}_1 = 0$: $\qquad\qquad \bar{I}_2 - \frac{\bar{V}_2}{1} = \frac{\bar{V}_2 - 3(\bar{I}_2 - 5\bar{V}_2/1)}{2}$ or $\quad 18\bar{V}_2 = 5\bar{I}_2$

Thus, $\qquad\qquad\qquad\qquad \bar{z}_{22} = \bar{V}_2/\bar{I}_2 = \tfrac{5}{18}\ \Omega$

$$\bar{V}_1 = 2(\bar{I}_2 - 5\bar{V}_2) = 2(\bar{I}_2 - 5 \times \tfrac{5}{18}\bar{I}_2) = -\tfrac{7}{9}\bar{I}_2 \quad \text{or} \quad \bar{z}_{12} = \bar{V}_1/\bar{I}_2 = -\tfrac{7}{9}\ \Omega$$

23.88 A ladder network is shown in the s domain in Fig. 23-39. Find the $\bar{z}$ parameters.

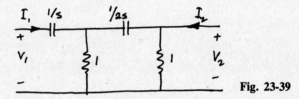

Fig. 23-39

▌ Proceeding as in Probs. 23.74 and 23.75, we obtain

$$\bar{z}_{11} = \frac{1}{s} + \frac{1[1 + (1/2s)]}{1 + 1 + (1/2s)} = \frac{2s^2 + 5s + 1}{s(4s + 1)}$$

Similarly, $\qquad \bar{z}_{12} = \frac{2s}{4s + 1} = \bar{z}_{21}$ and $\qquad \bar{z}_{22} = \frac{2s + 1}{4s + 1}$

23.89 Obtain the $\bar{y}$ parameters of the network of Fig. 23-39 from the results of Prob. 23.88.

▌ $\qquad \bar{\Delta}_z = \bar{z}_{11}\bar{z}_{22} - (\bar{z}_{12})^2 = \dfrac{(2s^2 + 5s + 1)(2s + 1)}{s(4s + 1)^2} - \dfrac{4s^2}{(4s + 1)^2} = \dfrac{12s^2 + 7s + 1}{s(4s + 1)^2}$

$$\bar{y}_{11} = \frac{\bar{z}_{22}}{\bar{\Delta}_z} = \left(\frac{2s + 1}{4s + 1}\right)\frac{s(4s + 1)^2}{12s^2 + 7s + 1} = \frac{s(2s + 1)(4s + 1)}{12s^2 + 7s + 1}$$

$$\bar{y}_{12} = \bar{y}_{21} = -\frac{\bar{z}_{12}}{\bar{\Delta}_z} = -\frac{2s}{(4s + 1)}\left[\frac{s(4s + 1)^2}{12s^2 + 7s + 1}\right] = -\frac{2s^2(4s + 1)}{12s^2 + 7s + 1}$$

and $\qquad\qquad \bar{y}_{22} = \frac{\bar{z}_{11}}{\bar{\Delta}_z} = \frac{(2s^2 + 5s + 1)s(4s + 1)^2}{s(4s + 1)\ 12s^2 + 7s + 1} = \frac{(4s + 1)(2s^2 + 5s + 1)}{12s^2 + 7s + 1}$

23.90 Determine the $\bar{A}, \bar{B}, \bar{C}$, and $\bar{D}$ constants of the network of Fig. 23-40.

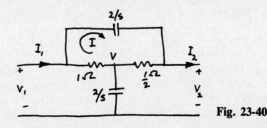

Fig. 23-40

∎ $\bar{I}_2 = 0$:
$$\bar{V}_1 = \left(1 + \frac{2}{s}\right)\bar{I}_1 - \bar{I} \qquad 0 = -\bar{I}_1 + \left(1.5 + \frac{2}{s}\right)\bar{I}$$

or
$$\bar{I}_1 = \frac{\bar{V}_1[1.5 + (2/s)]}{0.5 + (5/s) + (4/s^2)} = \frac{V_1 s(1.5s + 2)}{0.5s^2 + 5s + 4} \qquad \bar{V}_2 = \frac{\bar{V}_1(0.5s^2 + 3s + 4)}{0.5s^2 + 5s + 4}$$

Hence,
$$\bar{A} = \frac{\bar{V}_1}{\bar{V}_2} = \frac{0.5s^2 + 5s + 4}{0.5s^2 + 3s + 4} \qquad \bar{C} = \frac{\bar{I}_1}{\bar{V}_2} = \frac{s(1.5s + 2)}{0.5s^2 + 3s + 4}$$

$\bar{V}_2 = 0$:
$$\bar{V}_2 = \frac{\bar{V}_1}{(s/3) + 3} = \frac{2\bar{V}_1}{s + 6} \qquad \bar{I}_2 = \bar{V}_1\left(\frac{s}{2} + \frac{4}{s + 6}\right) = \frac{\bar{V}_1(s^2 + 6s + 8)}{2(s + 6)}$$

$$\bar{I}_1 = \bar{V}_1\left(\frac{s}{2} + 1 - \frac{2}{s + 6}\right) = \frac{\bar{V}_1(s^2 + 8s + 8)}{2(s + 6)}$$

$$\bar{B} = \frac{\bar{V}_1}{\bar{I}_2} = \frac{2(s + 6)}{s^2 + 6s + 8} \qquad \bar{D} = \frac{\bar{I}_1}{\bar{I}_2} = \frac{s^2 + 8s + 8}{s^2 + 6s + 8}$$

23.91 Verify that $\bar{A}\bar{D} - \bar{B}\bar{C} = 1$ for the circuit of Fig. 23-40.

∎ From Prob. 23.90 we have

$$\bar{A}\bar{D} - \bar{B}\bar{C} = \frac{(0.5s^2 + 5s + 4)}{(0.5s^2 + 3s + 4)}\frac{(s^2 + 8s + 8)}{(s^2 + 6s + 8)} - \frac{2(s + 6)}{(s^2 + 6s + 8)}\frac{s(1.5s + 2)}{(0.5s^2 + 3s + 4)} = 1$$

23.92 Find the hybrid parameters $\bar{h}_{11}$ and $\bar{h}_{21}$ for the circuit of Fig. 23-41 (which represents a transistor).

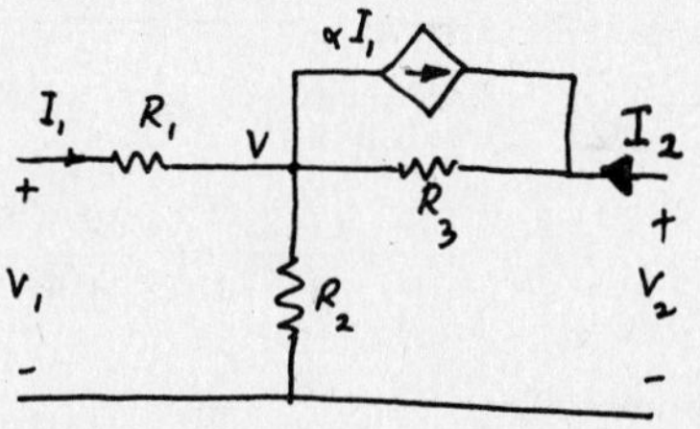

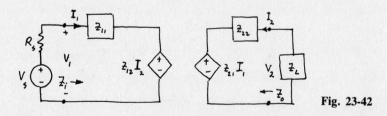

Fig. 23-41

∎ $\bar{V}_2 = 0$:
$$\bar{V} = \frac{(1 - \alpha)\bar{I}_1 R_2 R_3}{R_2 + R_3}$$

$$\bar{h}_{11} = \frac{\bar{V}_1}{\bar{I}_1} = R_1 + \frac{(1 - \alpha)R_2 R_3}{R_2 + R_3} = \frac{R_1(R_2 + R_3) + (1 - \alpha)R_2 R_3}{R_2 + R_3}$$

$$\bar{h}_{21} = -\alpha - \frac{(1 - \alpha)R_2}{R_2 + R_3} = -\frac{(\alpha R_3 + R_2)}{R_2 + R_3}$$

23.93 Find the $\bar{g}$ parameters $\bar{g}_{12}$ and $\bar{g}_{22}$ for the circuit of Fig. 23-41.

∎
$$\bar{g}_{12} = \frac{\bar{I}_1}{\bar{I}_2} = -\frac{R_1}{R_1 + R_2} \qquad \bar{V}_2 = (\alpha\bar{I}_1 + \bar{I}_2)R_3 + (\bar{I}_1 + I_2)R_2$$

$$\bar{g}_{22} = \frac{\bar{V}_2}{\bar{I}_2} = \left(1 - \frac{\alpha R_2}{R_1 + R_2}\right)R_3 + \left(1 - \frac{R_2}{R_1 + R_2}\right)R_2 = \frac{R_1(R_2 + R_3) + (1 - \alpha)R_2 R_3}{R_1 + R_2}$$

23.94 Determine the input impedance, in terms of the $\bar{z}$ parameters, for the circuit of Fig. 23-42.

Fig. 23-42

I

$$\bar{I}_1 = \frac{\bar{V}_1 - \bar{z}_{12}\bar{I}_2}{\bar{z}_{11}} \qquad \bar{I}_2 = \frac{-\bar{z}_{21}\bar{I}_1}{\bar{z}_{22} + \bar{Z}_L}$$

$$\bar{V}_1 = \bar{z}_{11}\bar{I}_1 + \bar{z}_{12}\bar{I}_2 = \bar{z}_{11}\bar{I}_1 + \bar{z}_{12}\left(\frac{-\bar{z}_{21}}{\bar{z}_{22} + \bar{Z}_L}\right)\bar{I}_1$$

Thus,

$$\bar{Z}_i = \frac{\bar{V}_1}{\bar{I}_1} = \bar{z}_{11} - \frac{\bar{z}_{12}\bar{z}_{21}}{\bar{z}_{22} + \bar{Z}_L}$$

23.95 Find the output impedance for the circuit of Fig. 23-42.

I First, we set $\bar{V}_s = 0$. Then,

$$\bar{I}_1 = \frac{-\bar{z}_{12}\bar{I}_2}{R_s + \bar{z}_{11}} \qquad \text{and} \qquad \bar{I}_2 = \frac{\bar{V}_2 - \bar{z}_{21}\bar{I}_1}{\bar{z}_{22}}$$

$$\bar{V}_2 = \bar{z}_{21}\bar{I}_1 + \bar{z}_{22}\bar{I}_2 = \bar{z}_{21}\left(\frac{-\bar{z}_{12}}{R_s + \bar{z}_{11}}\right)\bar{I}_1 + \bar{z}_{22}\bar{I}_2$$

Thus,

$$\bar{Z}_0 = \frac{\bar{V}_2}{\bar{I}_2} = \bar{z}_{22} - \frac{\bar{z}_{21}\bar{z}_{12}}{R_s + \bar{z}_{11}}$$

23.96 Calculate the input impedance of the circuit of Fig. 23-36. The source impedance is $2\,\Omega$, and $\bar{Z}_L = 2\,\Omega$.

I From Prob. 23.80, $\bar{z}_{11} = \frac{5}{2}\,\Omega$, $\bar{z}_{12} = 1 = \bar{z}_{21}$, and $\bar{z}_{22} = 2\,\Omega$. Thus,

$$\bar{Z}_i = \frac{5}{2} - \frac{(1)^2}{2+2} = 2.25\,\Omega$$

23.97 What is the output impedance of the circuit of Prob. 23.96?

I

$$\bar{Z}_0 = 2 - \frac{(1)^2}{2 + 2.5} = 1.78\,\Omega$$

23.98 Express the $\bar{z}$ parameters in terms of the $\bar{h}$ parameters of a two-port network.

I We rewrite (1) and (2) of Prob. 23.43:

$$\bar{V}_1 = \bar{h}_{11}\bar{I}_1 + \bar{h}_{12}\bar{V}_2 \qquad \bar{I}_2 = \bar{h}_{21}\bar{I}_1 + \bar{h}_{22}\bar{V}_2$$

Solving for $\bar{I}_1$:

$$\bar{I}_1 = \frac{\bar{h}_{22}}{\Delta_h}\bar{V}_1 - \frac{\bar{h}_{12}}{\Delta_h}\bar{I}_2$$

or

$$\bar{V}_1 = \frac{\Delta_h}{\bar{h}_{22}}\bar{I}_1 + \frac{\bar{h}_{12}}{\bar{h}_{22}}\bar{I}_2 \tag{1}$$

where

$$\bar{\Delta}_h = \bar{h}_{11}\bar{h}_{22} - \bar{h}_{12}\bar{h}_{21}$$

In terms of $\bar{z}$ parameters:

$$\bar{V}_1 = \bar{z}_{11}\bar{I}_1 + \bar{z}_{12}\bar{I}_2 \tag{2}$$

Comparing (1) and (2) yields

$$\bar{z}_{11} = \bar{\Delta}_h/\bar{h}_{22} \qquad \text{and} \qquad \bar{z}_{12} = \bar{h}_{12}/\bar{h}_{22}$$

Similarly,

$$\bar{z}_{21} = -\bar{h}_{21}/\bar{h}_{22} \qquad \text{and} \qquad \bar{z}_{22} = 1/\bar{h}_{22}$$

23.99 Find the $\bar{z}$ parameters of the circuit of Prob. 23.54.

I

$$\bar{h}_{11} = \bar{h}_i = 1000\,\Omega \qquad \bar{h}_{21} = \bar{h}_f = 50 \qquad \bar{h}_{12} = \bar{h}_r = 4 \times 10^{-4} \qquad \bar{h}_{22} = \bar{h}_o = 25\,\mu\text{S}$$

$$\bar{\Delta}_h = (1000)(25 \times 10^{-6}) - (50)(4 \times 10^{-4}) = 5 \times 10^{-3}$$

$$\bar{z}_{11} = \frac{5 \times 10^{-3}}{25 \times 10^{-6}} = 200\,\Omega \qquad \bar{z}_{12} = \frac{4 \times 10^{-4}}{25 \times 10^{-6}} = 16\,\Omega$$

$$\bar{z}_{21} = -\frac{50}{25 \times 10^{-6}} = -2\,\text{M}\Omega \qquad \text{and} \qquad \bar{z}_{22} = \frac{1}{25 \times 10^{-6}} = 4 \times 10^{4}\,\Omega$$

23.100 Determine the $\bar{z}$ parameters of the network of Prob. 23.62.

$$\bar{\Delta}_h = (1.4 \times 10^3)(25 \times 10^{-6}) - (3 \times 10^{-4})(40) = 23 \times 10^{-3}$$

$$\bar{z}_{11} = \frac{23 \times 10^{-3}}{25 \times 10^{-6}} = 920 \,\Omega \qquad \bar{z}_{12} = \frac{3 \times 10^{-4}}{25 \times 10^{-6}} = 12 \,\Omega$$

$$\bar{z}_{21} = -\frac{40}{25 \times 10^{-6}} = -1.6\,\text{M}\Omega \quad \text{and} \quad \bar{z}_{22} = \frac{1}{25 \times 10^{-6}} = 4 \times 10^4 \,\Omega$$

23.101 Verify the result of Prob. 23.62, using the $\bar{z}$ parameters obtained in Prob. 23.100.

$$\bar{Z}_{in} = \bar{z}_{11} - \frac{\bar{z}_{12}\bar{z}_{21}}{\bar{z}_{22} + \bar{Z}_L} = 920 + \frac{(12)(1.6 \times 10^6)}{4 \times 10^4 + 15 \times 10^3} = 1269 \,\Omega$$

23.102 Verify the result of Prob. 23.63, using the results of Prob. 23.100.

$$\bar{Z}_{out} = \bar{z}_{22} - \frac{\bar{z}_{12}\bar{z}_{21}}{R_s + \bar{z}_{11}} = 4 \times 10^4 + \frac{(12)(1.6 \times 10^6)}{1.2 \times 10^3 + 920} = 49\,\text{k}\Omega$$

23.103 Find the $\bar{h}$ parameters of the circuit of Fig. 23-43.

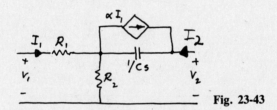

Fig. 23-43

▮ $\bar{V}_2 = 0$:
$$\bar{V}_1 = \bar{I}_1 R_1 + \bar{I}_1 \left[\frac{(1-\alpha)R_2}{1 + R_2 Cs} \right] = \bar{I}_1 \left[\frac{R_1 + R_1 R_2 Cs + (1-\alpha)R_2}{1 + R_2 Cs} \right]$$

Hence,
$$\frac{\bar{V}_1}{\bar{I}_1} = \bar{h}_{11} = \frac{R_1 + R_1 R_2 Cs + (1-\alpha)R_2}{1 + R_2 Cs}$$

Similarly,
$$\frac{\bar{I}_2}{\bar{I}_1} = \bar{h}_{21} = \frac{\alpha + R_2 Cs}{1 + R_2 Cs}$$

$\bar{I}_1 = 0$:
$$\bar{h}_{12} = \frac{\bar{V}_1}{\bar{V}_2} = \frac{R_2 Cs}{1 + R_2 Cs} \qquad \bar{h}_{22} = \frac{\bar{I}_2}{\bar{V}_2} = \frac{Cs}{1 + R_2 Cs}$$

23.104 Determine the parameters $\bar{g}_{11}$ and $\bar{g}_{12}$ for the circuit of Fig. 23-43.

▮ $\bar{g}_{11} = \frac{\bar{I}_1}{\bar{V}_1}\bigg|_{\bar{I}_2=0} = \frac{I_1}{I_1(R_1 + R_2)} = \frac{1}{R_1 + R_2} \qquad \bar{g}_{12} = \frac{\bar{I}_1}{\bar{I}_2}\bigg|_{\bar{V}_1=0} = \frac{-R_2}{R_1 + R_2}$ by current division

23.105 Find the $\bar{z}$ parameters of the network of Fig. 23-44a.

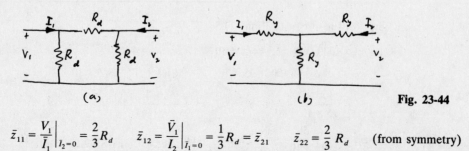

(a)   (b)   **Fig. 23-44**

▮ $\bar{z}_{11} = \frac{V_1}{I_1}\bigg|_{I_2=0} = \frac{2}{3}R_d \qquad \bar{z}_{12} = \frac{\bar{V}_1}{I_2}\bigg|_{I_1=0} = \frac{1}{3}R_d = \bar{z}_{21} \qquad \bar{z}_{22} = \frac{2}{3}R_d$ (from symmetry)

23.106 Find the $\bar{z}$ parameters of the network of Fig. 23-44b.

$\blacksquare$ From the results of Prob. 23.9 we have

$$\bar{z}_{11} = R_y + R_y = 2R_y \qquad \bar{z}_{12} = R_y = \bar{z}_{21} \qquad \bar{z}_{22} = R_y + R_y = 2R_y$$

23.107 Under what condition would the two networks of Fig. 23-44 be equivalent to each other?

$\blacksquare$ For equivalence the $\bar{z}$ parameters of the two networks must be the same. Hence, from the results of Probs. 23.105 and 23.106 we must have

$$R_y = \tfrac{1}{3}R_d$$

which is identical to the wye-delta equivalence condition.

23.108 Consider the circuits of Figs. 23-8 and 23-13. Find the conditions under which the Π network of Fig. 23-13 will be equivalent to the T network of Fig. 23-8.

$\blacksquare$ For Fig. 23-8: $\qquad \bar{V}_1 = \bar{I}_1(\bar{Z}_1 + \bar{Z}_3) + \bar{I}_2\bar{Z}_3 \qquad \bar{V}_2 = \bar{I}_1\bar{Z}_3 + \bar{I}_2(\bar{Z}_2 + \bar{Z}_3)$

Solving for $\bar{I}_1$ and $\bar{I}_2$ yields

$$\bar{I}_1 = \frac{(\bar{Z}_2 + \bar{Z}_3)}{\bar{\Delta}_z}\bar{V}_1 - \frac{\bar{Z}_3}{\bar{\Delta}_z}\bar{V}_2 \tag{1}$$

$$\bar{I}_2 = -\frac{\bar{Z}_3}{\bar{\Delta}_z}\bar{V}_1 + \frac{(\bar{Z}_1 + \bar{Z}_3)}{\bar{\Delta}_z}\bar{V}_2 \tag{2}$$

where $\bar{\Delta}_z = \bar{Z}_1\bar{Z}_2 + \bar{Z}_2\bar{Z}_3 + \bar{Z}_3\bar{Z}_1$.

For Fig. 23-13: $\qquad \bar{I}_1 = (\bar{Y}_A + \bar{Y}_B)\bar{V}_1 - \bar{Y}_B\bar{V}_2 \tag{3}$

$$\bar{I}_2 = -\bar{Y}_B\bar{V}_1 + (\bar{Y}_B + \bar{Y}_C)\bar{V}_2 \tag{4}$$

Comparing (1) and (3), and (2) and (4), yields

$$\bar{Y}_A = \frac{\bar{Z}_2}{\bar{\Delta}_z} \qquad \bar{Y}_B = \frac{\bar{Z}_3}{\bar{\Delta}_z} \quad \text{and} \quad \bar{Y}_C = \frac{\bar{Z}_1}{\bar{\Delta}_z}$$

23.109 Find the conditions under which the T network of Fig. 23-8 will be equivalent to the Π network of Fig. 23-13.

$\blacksquare$ For Fig. 23-13: $\qquad \bar{V}_1 = \frac{(\bar{Y}_B + \bar{Y}_C)}{\bar{\Delta}_y}\bar{I}_1 + \frac{\bar{Y}_B}{\bar{\Delta}_y}\bar{I}_2 \qquad \bar{V}_2 = \frac{\bar{Y}_B}{\bar{\Delta}_y}\bar{I}_1 + \frac{(\bar{Y}_A + \bar{Y}_B)}{\bar{\Delta}_y}\bar{I}_2$

where $\bar{\Delta}_y = \bar{Y}_A\bar{Y}_B + \bar{Y}_B\bar{Y}_C + \bar{Y}_C\bar{Y}_A$.

For Fig. 23-8: $\qquad \bar{V}_1 = (\bar{Z}_1 + \bar{Z}_3)\bar{I}_1 + \bar{Z}_3\bar{I}_2 \qquad \bar{V}_2 = \bar{Z}_3\bar{I}_2 + (\bar{Z}_2 + \bar{Z}_3)\bar{I}_2$

For equivalence, therefore,

$$\bar{Z}_1 = \frac{\bar{Y}_C}{\bar{\Delta}_y} \qquad \bar{Z}_2 = \frac{\bar{Y}_A}{\bar{\Delta}_y} \quad \text{and} \quad \bar{Z}_3 = \frac{\bar{Y}_B}{\bar{\Delta}_y}$$

23.110 Obtain the $\bar{z}$ parameters for the network of Fig. 23-45a.

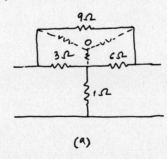
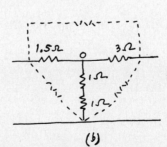

(a)   (b)   **Fig. 23-45**

$\blacksquare$ First, we obtain the equivalent T circuit of Fig. 23-45b. Then, we use the result of Prob. 23.1. Hence, $\bar{z}_{11} = 3.5\,\Omega$, $\bar{z}_{21} = \bar{z}_{12} = 2\,\Omega$, and $\bar{z}_{21} = 5\,\Omega$. (Note construction by dashed lines in Fig. 23-45b.)

23.111 Repeat Prob. 23.110 by converting the T network to an equivalent Π network.

Ø The construction is shown by the dashed lines in Fig. 23-45b, from which we obtain the circuit of Fig. 23-46, from which:

$$\bar{z}_{11} = \frac{\bar{V}_1}{\bar{I}_1}\bigg|_{\bar{I}_2=0} = \frac{(15.75)(4.5)}{15.75 + 4.5} = 3.5\ \Omega \qquad \bar{z}_{21} = \bar{z}_{12} = \frac{\bar{V}_2}{\bar{I}_1}\bigg|_{\bar{I}_2=0} = \frac{\bar{V}_1}{\bar{I}_2}\bigg|_{\bar{I}_1=0} = 2\ \Omega$$

and

$$\bar{z}_{22} = \frac{\bar{V}_2}{\bar{I}_2}\bigg|_{\bar{I}_1=0} = \frac{(6.75 + 4.5)9}{9 + 6.75 + 4.5} = 5\ \Omega$$

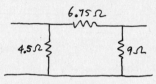

Fig. 23-46

23.112 For the lattice network of Fig. 23-47, find the $\bar{z}$ parameters.

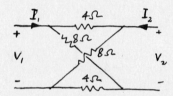

Fig. 23-47

Ø
$$\bar{V}_1 = \bar{z}_{11}\bar{I}_1 + \bar{z}_{12}\bar{I}_2 \qquad \bar{V}_2 = \bar{z}_{21}\bar{I}_1 + \bar{z}_{22}\bar{I}_2$$

$$\bar{z}_{11} = \bar{z}_{22} = \frac{4+8}{2} = 6\ \Omega \quad \text{with} \quad \bar{I}_2 = 0 \qquad \bar{V}_2 = \frac{\bar{V}_1(8-4)}{8+4} \qquad \bar{I}_1 = \frac{2\bar{V}_1}{8+4}$$

Hence,
$$\bar{z}_{21} = \frac{\bar{V}_2}{\bar{I}_1}\bigg|_{\bar{I}_2=0} = \frac{8-4}{2} = 2\ \Omega = \bar{z}_{12}$$

23.113 Find the $\bar{y}$ parameters of the network of Fig. 23-47.

Ø
$$\bar{\Delta}_z = \bar{z}_{11}\bar{z}_{22} - \bar{z}_{12}\bar{z}_{21} = (6)(6) - (2)(2) = 32 \qquad \text{from Prob. 23.112}$$

$$\bar{y}_{11} = \frac{\bar{z}_{22}}{\bar{\Delta}_z} = \frac{6}{32} = \frac{3}{16} = \bar{y}_{22} \qquad \bar{y}_{12} = -\frac{\bar{z}_{21}}{\bar{\Delta}_z} = -\frac{2}{32} = -\frac{1}{16} = \bar{y}_{21} \qquad \text{from symmetry}$$

23.114 Verify that $\bar{z}_{11}\bar{y}_{11} - \bar{z}_{22}\bar{y}_{22} = 0$ holds for the circuit of Fig. 23-47.

Ø From Probs. 23.112 and 23.113:

$$\bar{z}_{11}\bar{y}_{11} - \bar{z}_{22}\bar{y}_{22} = 6\left(\tfrac{3}{16}\right) - 6\left(\tfrac{3}{16}\right) = 0$$

23.115 Find the $\bar{A}$, $\bar{B}$, $\bar{C}$, and $\bar{D}$ parameters for the network of Fig. 23-47.

Ø
$$\bar{A} = \frac{\bar{z}_{22}}{\bar{z}_{12}} = \frac{6}{2} = 3 \qquad \bar{B} = \frac{\bar{\Delta}_z}{\bar{z}_{21}} = \frac{32}{2} = 16$$

$$\bar{C} = \frac{1}{\bar{z}_{21}} = \frac{1}{2} = 0.5 \quad \text{and} \quad \bar{D} = \frac{\bar{z}_{22}}{\bar{z}_{21}} = \frac{6}{2} = 3$$

Check:
$$\bar{A}\bar{D} - \bar{B}\bar{C} = (3)(3) - (16)(0.5) = 1$$

23.116 Obtain the $\bar{h}$ parameters of the network of Fig. 23-47.

Ø
$$\bar{h}_{11} = \frac{\bar{\Delta}_z}{\bar{z}_{22}} = \frac{32}{6} = \frac{16}{3} \qquad \bar{h}_{22} = \frac{1}{\bar{z}_{22}} = \frac{1}{6}$$

$$\bar{h}_{12} = \frac{\bar{z}_{12}}{\bar{z}_{22}} = \frac{2}{6} = \frac{1}{3} \qquad \bar{h}_{21} = -\frac{\bar{z}_{21}}{\bar{z}_{22}} = -\frac{2}{6} = -\frac{1}{3}$$

23.117 Determine the $\bar{g}$ parameters of the network of Fig. 23-47.

❚

$$\bar{g}_{11} = \frac{1}{\bar{z}_{11}} = \frac{1}{6} \qquad \bar{g}_{12} = -\frac{\bar{z}_{12}}{\bar{z}_{11}} = -\frac{2}{6} = -\frac{1}{3}$$

$$\bar{g}_{21} = \frac{\bar{z}_{21}}{\bar{z}_{11}} = \frac{2}{6} = \frac{1}{3} \qquad \text{and} \qquad \bar{g}_{22} = \frac{\bar{\Delta}_z}{\bar{z}_{22}} = \frac{32}{6} = \frac{16}{3}$$

23.118 The network of Fig. 23-47 is connected to a source having a 2-Ω internal resistance, and a 4-Ω load is connected across the output port. Determine the input impedance.

❚ From the results of Prob. 23.94,

$$\bar{Z}_i = \bar{z}_{11} - \frac{\bar{z}_{12}\bar{z}_{21}}{\bar{z}_{22} + \bar{Z}_L} = 6 - \frac{(2)^2}{6+4} = 5.6 \, \Omega$$

23.119 Determine the output impedance for the circuit of Prob. 23.118.

❚ From the result of Prob. 23.95:

$$\bar{Z}_o = \bar{z}_{22} - \frac{\bar{z}_{12}\bar{z}_{21}}{\bar{R}_s + \bar{z}_{11}} = 6 - \frac{(2)^2}{2+6} = 5.5 \, \Omega$$

CHAPTER 24
Review Problems

Note: In this chapter we review the topics presented in the preceding chapters. The problems are not arranged in any specific order.

24.1 A pair of conductors accumulate a 25-nC charge when they are connected across a 240-V source. Determine the capacitance.

I
$$C = \frac{q}{V} = \frac{25 \times 10^{-9}}{240} = 104 \ \mu\mu F$$

24.2 An *RC* series circuit, having $R = 10 \ k\Omega$ and $C = 150 \ \mu F$, is connected across a 13.2-V battery, at $t = 0$. Determine the voltage across and the current through the capacitor at $t = 0$, if the capacitor was initially uncharged.

I
$$v_C(0_-) = v_C(0_+) = 0$$

Since the capacitor acts as a short-circuit at $t = 0$,

$$i_C(0_+) = \frac{V}{R} = \frac{13.2}{10 \times 10^3} = 0.132 \ mA$$

24.3 Determine the steady-state charge in the capacitor, and the voltage across it, in the *RC* circuit of Prob. 24.2. Also, find the voltage across the resistor.

I
$$q_{ss} = CV_{ss} \qquad V_{ss} = V_{battery} = 13.2 \ V$$

$$q_{ss} = 150 \times 10^{-6} \times 13.2 = 1.98 \ mC \qquad V_R = 0 \ V$$

24.4 Three capacitors having capacitances 125 μF, 65 μF, and 425 μF are connected in series. What is the total capacitance?

I
$$\frac{1}{C_e} = 10^6 \left(\frac{1}{125} + \frac{1}{65} + \frac{1}{425} \right) \qquad C_e = 38.9 \ \mu F$$

24.5 If the capacitors of Prob. 24.4 are connected in parallel, what is the equivalent capacitance?

I
$$C_e = 10^{-6}(125 + 65 + 425) = 615 \ \mu F$$

24.6 Find the equivalent capacitance of the circuit of Fig. 24-1.

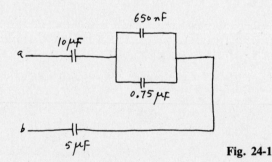

Fig. 24-1

I
$$C_{e,parallel} = 650 \times 10^{-9} + 0.75 \times 10^{-6} = 1.4 \times 10^{-6} \ F$$

$$\frac{1}{C_e} = 10^6 \left(\frac{1}{10} + \frac{1}{1.4} + \frac{1}{5} \right) = 1.014 \times 10^6 \qquad or \qquad C_e = \frac{10^{-6}}{1.014} = 986 \ nF$$

24.7   A 100-V battery is connected across the terminals *ab* of the circuit of Fig. 24-1. Obtain the voltage across the 10-μF capacitor.

   ▌   Charge, $q = CV = 986 \times 10^{-9}(100) = 98.6\ \mu\text{C}$.
     For capacitors in series, the charge must be the same. Thus,

$$V_{10\ \mu\text{F}} = \frac{q}{10 \times 10^{-6}} = \frac{98.6 \times 10^{-6}}{10 \times 10^{-6}} = 9.86\ \text{V}$$

24.8   What is the voltage across the parallel-connected capacitors in the circuit of Prob. 24-7?

   ▌ $C_{e,\text{parallel}} = 1.4 \times 10^{-6}$.

Thus, $V_{\text{parallel}} = \dfrac{98.6 \times 10^{-6}}{1.4 \times 10^{-6}} = 70.43\ \text{V}$

24.9   Determine the voltage across the 5-μF capacitor in the circuit of Prob. 24.7 by applying KVL. Verify that the same result is obtained from charge calculations.

   ▌   From Probs. 24.7 and 24.8, by KVL

$$V_{5\ \mu\text{F}} = 100 - (9.86 + 70.43) = 19.71\ \text{V}$$

Otherwise: $V_{5\ \mu\text{F}} = \dfrac{98.6 \times 10^{-6}}{5 \times 10^{-6}} = 19.72\ \text{V}$

24.10   Express $0.0025\ \text{m}^2$ in mm^2.

   ▌

$$0.0025\ \text{m}^2 \left(\frac{\text{mm}^2 \times 10^6}{1\ \text{m}^2} \right) = 2500\ \text{mm}^2$$

24.11   Express the following voltages in engineering notation: 4000 V; 58,000 V; 735,000 V; 6,875,000 V; 0.000 000 056 2 V; 0.000 001 7 V; 0.084 V.

   ▌   *Engineering notation*

$$
\begin{aligned}
4000\ \text{V} &= 4 \times 10^3\ \text{V} & &= 4\ \text{kV}\\
58,000\ \text{V} &= 58 \times 10^3\ \text{V} & &= 58\ \text{kV}\\
735,000\ \text{V} &= 735 \times 10^3\ \text{V} & &= 735\ \text{kV}\\
6,875,000\ \text{V} &= 6.875 \times 10^6\ \text{V} & &= 6.875\ \text{MV}\\
0.000\,000\,056\,2\ \text{V} &= 56.2 \times 10^{-9}\ \text{V} & &= 56.2\ \text{nV}\\
0.000\,001\,7\ \text{V} &= 1.7 \times 10^{-6}\ \text{V} & &= 1.7\ \mu\text{V}\\
0.084\ \text{V} &= 84 \times 10^{-3}\ \text{V} & &= 84\ \text{mV}
\end{aligned}
$$

24.12   Determine the current I in a 400-MΩ resistor when 24 kV is applied. Use $I = V/R$ (Ohm's law).

   ▌ $R = 400\ \text{M}\Omega = 400 \times 10^6\ \Omega$ $V = 24\ \text{kV} = 24 \times 10^3\ \text{V}$ $I = \dfrac{V}{R} = \dfrac{24 \times 10^3}{400 \times 10^6} = 60 \times 10^{-6} = 60\ \mu\text{A}$

24.13   The resistance of a certain annealed copper cable is $10.0\ \text{m}\Omega$ at $20\,°\text{C}$. During normal current-carrying operations the cable temperature rises to $80\,°\text{C}$. Determine its resistance at the operating temperature. The temperature coefficient for annealed copper is 0.00393.

   ▌ $R_H = R_L[1 + \alpha(T_H - T_L)]$ $R_H = 0.0100[1 + 0.00393(80 - 20)]$ $R_H = 12.4 \times 10^{-3}\ \Omega = 12.4\ \text{m}\Omega$

24.14   Determine the resistance of the cable in Prob. 24.13 if it is cooled to $-50°\text{C}$.

   ▌ $R_H = R_L[1 + \alpha(T_H - T_L)]$ $0.0100 = R_L\{1 + 0.00393[20 - (-50)]\}$ $R_L = 7.84 \times 10^{-3} = 7.84\ \text{m}\Omega$

24.15   Express the following voltages in engineering notation: 10,000 V; 0.000 005 V; 500 V; 0.000 12 V; and 50 V.

   ▌

$$
\begin{aligned}
10,000\ \text{V} &= 10 \times 10^3 & &= 10\ \text{kV}\\
0.000\,005\ \text{V} &= 5 \times 10^{-6} & &= 5\ \mu\text{V}\\
500\ \text{V} & & &= 500\ \text{V}\\
0.00012\ \text{V} &= 120 \times 10^{-6} & &= 120\ \mu\text{V}\\
50\ \text{V} & & &= 50\ \text{V}
\end{aligned}
$$

24.16 What is the resistance of a 2-m-long aluminum wire having a diameter of 10 mm. The resistivity of aluminum is $2.826 \times 10^{-8}\ \Omega \cdot m$.

▮ $\qquad A = \dfrac{\pi D^2}{4} = \dfrac{\pi (0.01)^2}{4} = 78.54 \times 10^{-6}\ m^2 \qquad R = \dfrac{\rho \ell}{A} = \dfrac{2.826 \times 10^{-8}(2)}{78.54 \times 10^{-6}} = 719 \times 10^{-6} = 719\ \mu\Omega$

24.17 Calculate the resistance of an annealed copper bus of length 10 ft and cross section $\frac{1}{2}$ in by 6 in, if the resistivity of the material is $10.371\ \Omega \cdot cmil/ft$.

▮ $\qquad \text{cmil} = 1.273\,A(10^6) = 1.273(\tfrac{1}{2} \times 6)10^6 = 3.819 \times 10^6 \qquad R = \dfrac{\rho \ell}{A} = \dfrac{10.371(10)}{3.819 \times 10^6} = 27\ \mu\Omega$

24.18 A piece of wire has a resistance of $11\ \Omega$ at $20\,°C$. What is its resistance at $40\,°C$ if the temperature coefficient $\alpha = 0.00393$.

▮ $\qquad\qquad R_{40} = R_{20}[1 + \alpha(40 - 20)] = 11[1 + 0.00393(40 - 20)] = 11.8\ \Omega$

24.19 Determine the conductance of each of the following resistors: $25\ \Omega$, $60\ k\Omega$, $1.2\ M\Omega$.

▮ $$G = \frac{1}{25} = 0.040\ S$$

$$G = \frac{1}{60,000} = 16.667 \times 10^{-6}\ S = 16.7\ \mu S$$

$$G = \frac{1}{1.20 \times 10^6} = 833 \times 10^{-9}\ S = 833\ nS$$

24.20 The resistance of a conductor is $80\ \Omega$ at $40\,°C$. What is its resistance at $20\,°C$ if $\alpha = 0.0039$?

▮ Proceeding as in Prob. 24.18,

$$R_{40} = 80 = R_{20}[1 + 0.0039(40 - 20)]$$

Thus, $\qquad\qquad\qquad\qquad\qquad R_{20} = 74.2\ \Omega$

24.21 A copper coil has a resistance of $162\ \Omega$ at $60\,°C$. What is the percent decrease in resistance at $20\,°C$ if $\alpha = 0.00393$?

▮ $\qquad\qquad R_{60} = 162 = R_{20}[1 + 0.00393(60 - 20)] \qquad$ or $\qquad R_{20} = 140\ \Omega$

$$\text{Percent decrease} = \frac{162 - 140}{162} \times 100 = 13.58\%$$

24.22 Determine the resistance of a 564-m-long aluminum conductor of cross section 40 mm by 20 mm. Given: $\rho_{Al} = 2.826 \times 10^{-8}\ \Omega \cdot m$.

▮ $$R = \frac{2.826 \times 10^{-8}}{0.04 \times 0.02} \times 564 = 0.02\ \Omega$$

24.23 A copper bus has a cross section of 0.5 in by 6.0 in. Calculate the area in circular mils (cmil).

▮ $\qquad\qquad \text{cmil} = 1.273\,A(10^6) = 1.273(\tfrac{1}{2} \times 6)\ 10^6 = 3.82 \times 10^6$

24.24 If the bus of Prob. 24.23 is 200 ft long, what is the resistance? Given: $\rho = 10.371\ \Omega \cdot cmil/ft$.

▮ $$R = \frac{10.371(200)}{3.82 \times 10^6} = 543\ \mu\Omega$$

24.25 A 30-m-long conductor, of cross section 20 mm by 200 mm, has a resistance of $212\ \mu\Omega$. What is the conductivity of the material?

▮ $\qquad R = \dfrac{\ell}{\sigma A} \quad$ or $\quad \sigma = \dfrac{\ell}{RA} = \dfrac{30}{212 \times 10^{-6}(20 \times 200)10^{-6}} = 35.38 \times 10^6\ S/m$

24.26 What is the area in circular mils of a 4.0-in-diameter round wire?

▮ $\qquad\qquad \text{cmil} = D^2(10^6) = 4^2(10^6) = 16 \times 10^6$

24.27   A 4-in-diameter wire is 1000 ft long.   Determine its resistance if the resistivity of the material is $17\,\Omega \cdot \text{cmil/ft}$.

$$R = \frac{17(1000)}{16 \times 10^6} = 1.06\,\text{m}\Omega$$

24.28   Determine the area of cross section of a 30-m-long conductor having a $212\text{-}\mu\Omega$ resistance if the resistivity of the material is $2.826 \times 10^{-8}\,\Omega \cdot \text{m}$.

$$A = \frac{\rho\ell}{R} = \frac{2.826 \times 10^{-8}(30)}{212 \times 10^{-6}} = 0.004\,\text{m}^2$$

24.29   Calculate the conductance of the following resistors: $50\,\text{k}\Omega$; $465\,\Omega$; $0.018\,\Omega$; and $0.0004\,\Omega$.

$$G_1 = \frac{1}{50,000} = 20\,\mu\text{S} \qquad G_2 = \frac{1}{465} = 2.15\,\text{mS} \qquad G_3 = \frac{1}{0.018} = 55.6\,\text{S} \qquad G_4 = \frac{1}{0.0004} = 2500\,\text{S}$$

24.30   Determine the resistance of the following conductances: $0.0041\,\text{S}$; $3.25\,\text{S}$; $180.55\,\text{S}$; and $1000\,\text{S}$.

$$R_1 = \frac{1}{0.0041} = 244\,\Omega \qquad R_2 = \frac{1}{3.25} = 0.308\,\Omega \qquad R_3 = \frac{1}{180.55} = 5.5386\,\text{m}\Omega \qquad R_4 = \frac{1}{1000} = 0.001\,\Omega$$

24.31   Connect twelve 6-V batteries to obtain a 12-V output.   If each battery can deliver 5 A of current, what is the current rating of the connection?

❚   The connection is shown in Fig. 24-2.   Since each parallel path can deliver 5 A, and we have 6 paths, the total current rating is $6 \times 5 = 30\,\text{A}$.

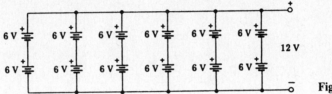

Fig. 24-2

24.32   Repeat Prob. 24.31 for an 18-V output connection.

❚   See Fig. 24-3.   Current rating $= 4 \times 5 = 20\,\text{A}$.

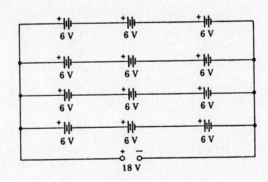

Fig. 24-3

24.33   Repeat Prob. 24.31 for a 36-V output connection.

❚   See Fig. 24-4.   Current rating $= 2 \times 5 = 10\,\text{A}$.

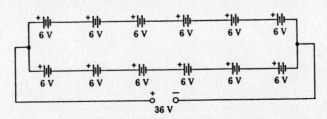

Fig. 24-4

24.34 Verify that the power rating of the battery connections in Probs. 24.31 through 24.33 does not change with the type of connection.

▌ Power for the three connections $= 12 \times 30 = 18 \times 20 = 36 \times 10 = 360$ W.

24.35 Design a series-parallel arrangement of forty 6-V batteries to obtain an output of 24 V.

▌ Since each battery is rated at 6 V, the number of series-connected batteries per branch required to obtain 24 V is

$$\frac{24}{6} = 4 \text{ batteries per branch}$$

The number of parallel branches is

$$\frac{40}{4} = 10 \text{ branches}$$

Thus, the required arrangement is 10 parallel branches, each containing 4 batteries in series.

24.36 How much current will be supplied by each battery of Prob. 24.35 if the "arrangement" is connected across a 4-Ω resistor?

▌

$$I_{\text{total}} = \frac{24}{4} = 6 \text{ A}$$

Since the "arrangement" has 10 parallel paths,

$$I_{\text{battery}} = \frac{6}{10} = 0.6 \text{ A}$$

24.37 Find the resistance of each resistor from the data of Fig. 24-5.

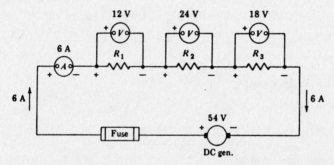

Fig. 24-5

▌ As indicated in the diagram, a current of 6 A is passing through each of the resistors, and the voltages measured across R_1, R_2, and R_3 are 12 V, 24 V, and 18 V, respectively. From Ohm's law,

$$R_1 = \frac{V_1}{I} = \frac{12}{6} = 2 \, \Omega \qquad R_2 = \frac{24}{6} = 4 \, \Omega \qquad R_3 = \frac{18}{6} = 3 \, \Omega$$

24.38 A 240-V dc source is connected to an 8-Ω resistor. Determine the heat power expended in the resistor, using three different power formulas.

▌

$$P = \frac{V^2}{R} = \frac{(240)^2}{8} = 7200 \text{ W} \qquad I = \frac{V}{R} = \frac{240}{8} = 30 \text{ A}$$

$$P = I^2 R = (30)^2(8) = 7200 \text{ W} \qquad P = VI = (240)(30) = 7200 \text{ W}$$

24.39 Which of the following combinations of current and time will result in the greater expenditure of heat energy in a 0.50-Ω resistor: 150 A for 1 s, 60 A for 3 s, or 25 A for 40 s?

▌

Combination	$W_R = I_R^2 R t$
150 A, 1 s	$W_R = (150)^2(0.5)(1) = 11{,}250 \text{ J} = 3.13 \text{ W} \cdot \text{h}$
60 A, 3 s	$W_R = (60)^2(0.5)(3) = 5400 \text{ J} = 1.50 \text{ W} \cdot \text{h}$
25 A, 40 s	$W_R = (25)^2(0.5)(40) = 12{,}500 \text{ J} = 3.47 \text{ W} \cdot \text{h}$

The 25-A 40-s combination will result in the greater expenditure of heat energy.

24.40 Figure 24-6 shows a plot of the voltage impressed across a 10-Ω resistor. Determine the total heat energy expended by the resistor in 8 s.

$$W_R = Pt = \frac{V_R^2}{R}\,t \qquad W_R = \frac{(30)^2(2)}{10} + \frac{(40)^2(4)}{10} + \frac{(10)^2(2)}{10} \qquad W_R = 180 + 640 + 20 = 840\ \text{J}$$

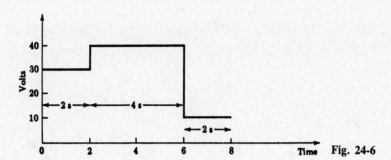

Fig. 24-6

24.41 Obtain a series-parallel arrangement of fifty 12-V batteries to provide a 120-V output.

$$\frac{120}{12} = 10 \text{ batteries in series.}$$

$$\frac{50}{10} = 5 \text{ parallel branches each containing 10 series-connected batteries.}$$

24.42 Repeat Prob. 24.41 for thirty-six 6-V batteries to provide an output voltage of 18 V.

$$\frac{18}{6} = 3 \text{ batteries in series.}$$

$$\frac{36}{3} = 12 \text{ parallel branches each containing 3 batteries in series.}$$

24.43 A 6-V battery, a 12-V battery, and a 360-Ω resistor are connected in series. Determine the current through the circuit if the battery voltages are additive.

$$I = \frac{12 + 6}{360} = 50\ \text{mA}$$

24.44 Repeat Prob. 24.43 if the battery voltages are subtractive.

$$I = \frac{12 - 6}{360} = 17\ \text{mA}$$

24.45 Determine the voltage required to pass a 150-μA current through a 10-MΩ resistor.

$$V = RI = 10 \times 10^6 \times 150 \times 10^{-6} = 1500\ \text{V}$$

24.46 How much current must flow through a 16-MΩ resistor to obtain 420 V across it?

$$I = \frac{V}{R} = \frac{420}{16 \times 10^6} = 26.3\ \mu\text{A}$$

24.47 An electric heater draws 2000 W at 100 V. Determine its resistance.

$$P = I^2 R = \frac{V^2}{R} \qquad \text{or} \qquad R = \frac{V^2}{P} = \frac{(100)^2}{2000} = 5\ \Omega$$

24.48 A soldering iron consumes 6 kW·h energy in 12 h at 120 V. What is the power rating of the soldering iron?

$$6000 = P(12) \qquad \text{or} \qquad P = \frac{6000}{12} = 500\ \text{W}$$

24.49 How much current is drawn by the soldering iron of Prob. 24.48?

$$P = VI \qquad \text{or} \qquad I = \frac{P}{V} = \frac{500}{120} = 4.17\ \text{A}$$

24.50 Determine the resistance of the heating element of the soldering iron of Prob. 24.49.

❚
$$R = \frac{V}{I} = \frac{120}{4.17} = 28.75\,\Omega$$

24.51 Which of the following combinations of current and time will result in the greatest expenditure of energy in a 10-Ω resistor: 50 A for 1 s; 80 A for 0.5 s; 10 A for 10 s; or 1 A for 1000 s?

❚ I^2Rt:
$$(50)^2(10)(1) = 25\text{ kJ}$$
$$(80)^2(10)(0.5) = 32\text{ kJ}$$
$$(10)^2(10)(10) = 10\text{ kJ}$$
$$(1)^2(10)(1000) = 10\text{ kJ}$$

Thus 80 A for 0.5 s results in maximum energy.

24.52 A motor field circuit, consisting of four coils of wire connected in series, is connected to a 240-V dc driver. Each coil has a resistance of 26 Ω.   Sketch the circuit and determine   (a) the resistance of the field circuit;   (b) the circuit current;   (c) the total heat-power loss;   (d) the voltage drop across each coil;   (e) the total heat energy expended in 8 h of operation.

❚ The circuit is shown in Fig. 24-7.

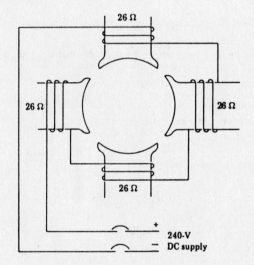

**240-V
DC supply**

Fig. 24-7

(a)
$$R_{eq,S} = 26 \times 4 = 104\,\Omega$$

(b)
$$I = \frac{E}{R} = \frac{240}{104} = 2.308\text{ A}$$

(c)
$$P = I^2R = (2.308)^2(104) = 553.9 = 554\text{ W}$$

(d)
$$V = IR = (2.308)(26) = 60\text{ V}$$

(e)
$$W = Pt = 554(8) = 4432 = 4.43\text{ kW}\cdot\text{h}$$

24.53 Assume the voltage sources in Fig. 24-8 are 100 V, 200 V, and 125 V for E_1, E_2, and E_3, respectively, and resistors R_1, R_2, R_3, and R_4 are, respectively, 5 Ω, 10 Ω, 20 Ω, and 15 Ω.   Determine the current.

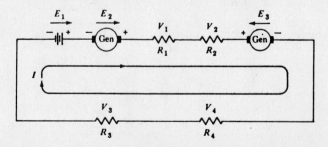

Fig. 24-8

$\blacksquare$ Applying Kirchhoff's voltage law,

$$100 + 200 - 125 = 5I + 10I + 20I + 15I \qquad 175 = 50I \qquad I = 3.5 \text{ A}$$

24.54 What is the voltage across each resistor of the circuit of Fig. 24-8.

$\blacksquare$
$$V_1 = IR_1 = 3.5(5) = 17.5 \text{ V} \qquad V_2 = IR_2 = 3.5(10) = 35 \text{ V}$$
$$V_3 = IR_3 = 3.5(20) = 70 \text{ V} \qquad V_4 = IR_4 = 3.5(15) = 52.5 \text{ V}$$

24.55 It is desired to obtain 48 V from a 240-V system using a 1000-Ω rheostat. Determine the required slide setting.

$\blacksquare$ See Fig. 24-9.

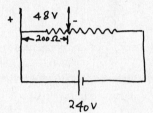

Fig. 24-9

$$\frac{48}{240} = 0.20 \qquad \text{or} \qquad 20 \text{ percent of the input voltage}$$

Thus, the resistance embraced by the output terminals must be

$$0.20(1000) = 200 \ \Omega$$

24.56 Derive a general voltage divider equation for the circuit of Fig. 24-10.

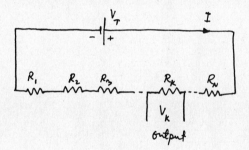

Fig. 24-10

$\blacksquare$
$$I = \frac{V_T}{R_T} = \frac{V_T}{\sum_k R_k} \qquad V_k = IR_k = V_T \left(\frac{R_k}{R_T} \right) \tag{1}$$

24.57 (*a*) Using the voltage-divider equation, determine the voltage between terminals 3 and 4 in Fig. 24-11; (*b*) determine the voltage between terminals 5 and 7.

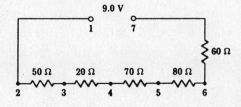

Fig. 24-11

$\blacksquare$ (*a*)
$$R_T = 50 + 20 + 70 + 80 + 60 = 280 \ \Omega \qquad V_{3,4} = V_T \frac{R_{3,4}}{R_T} = 9.0 \frac{20}{280} = 0.64 \text{ V}$$

(*b*)
$$V_{5,7} = V_T \frac{R_{5,7}}{R_T} = 9.0 \frac{140}{280} = 4.5 \text{ V}$$

24.58 Determine the equivalent resistance of a group of paralleled resistors whose values are $5\,k\Omega$, $10\,k\Omega$, $2\,k\Omega$, and $50\,k\Omega$.

▮
$$\frac{1}{R_{eq}} = \frac{1}{5000} + \frac{1}{10,000} + \frac{1}{2000} + \frac{1}{50,000}$$
$$= 200 \times 10^{-6} + 100 \times 10^{-6} + 500 \times 10^{-6} + 20 \times 10^{-6} = 820 \times 10^{-6}$$

or
$$R_{eq} = 1219.5\,\Omega$$

24.59 Determine the equivalent resistance if the resistors of Prob. 24.58 are connected in series.

▮
$$R_{eq} = 5\,k\Omega + 10\,k\Omega + 2\,k\Omega + 50\,k\Omega = 67\,k\Omega$$

24.60 A $2400\text{-}\Omega$ resistor is connected in parallel with a $9100\text{-}\Omega$ resistor. What is the equivalent resistance?

▮
$$R_e = \frac{R_A R_B}{R_A + R_B} = \frac{2400(9100)}{2400 + 9100} = 1899\,\Omega$$

24.61 Solve Prob. 24.60 by using conductances.

▮
$$G_P = G_1 + G_2 = \frac{1}{2400} + \frac{1}{9100} = 416.67 \times 10^{-6} + 109.89 \times 10^{-6} = 526.55 \times 10^{-6}\,S$$
$$R_{eq,P} = \frac{1}{G_P} = \frac{1}{526.55 \times 10^{-6}} = 1899\,\Omega$$

24.62 Derive the general current-divider equation of N conductances connected in parallel.

▮ Let I_P be the total current supplied to the circuit. Then,
$$I_P = V_P G_P$$
where
$$G_P = G_1 + G_2 + \cdots + G_N \qquad I_k = V_P G_k$$
Thus,
$$I_k = I_P\left(\frac{G_k}{G_P}\right) \tag{1}$$

24.63 Determine the current in the $6200\text{-}\Omega$ resistor of the circuit of Fig. 24-12 by the current-divider equation.

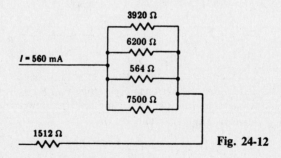

Fig. 24-12

▮ The total conductance of the parallel section is
$$G_P = \frac{1}{3920} + \frac{1}{6200} + \frac{1}{564} + \frac{1}{7500} = 255.1 \times 10^{-6} + 161.3 \times 10^{-6} + 1773.0 \times 10^{-6} + 133.3 \times 10^{-6}$$
$$= 2322.7 \times 10^{-6}\,S$$
$$I_k = I_P \frac{G_k}{G_P} = 0.560\,\frac{161.3 \times 10^{-6}}{2322.7 \times 10^{-6}} = 38.9 \times 10^{-3}\,A = 38.9\,mA$$

24.64 What is the voltage across the parallel-connected resistors in the circuit of Fig. 24-12?

▮
$$I_P = V_P G_P \qquad 0.560 = V_P(2322.7 \times 10^{-6}) \qquad V_P = 241\,V$$

24.65 How much current is drawn by the 564-Ω resistor of the circuit of Fig. 24-12?

▌ Since the voltage across the parallel section is 241 from Prob. 24.64, the current through the 564-Ω resistor may be determined by Ohm's law:

$$I = \frac{V}{R} = \frac{241}{564} = 0.427 \text{ A} = 427 \text{ mA}$$

24.66 Calculate the power drawn by the 6200-Ω resistor of the circuit of Fig. 24-12.

▌ From Prob. 24-63, $I = 38.9$ mA.

Hence, $$P = I^2R = (0.0389)^2(6200) = 9.38 \text{ W}$$

24.67 A 240-V dc generator supplies power through a 300-m cable to a heating load whose resistance is 5.76 Ω. The two conductors that make up the cable are each size AWG 8 copper wire. Determine the current in the cable if the resistance of AWG 8 wire is 2.061 Ω/km.

▌ $$R_{\text{cable}} = 2(0.3)(2.061) = 1.237 \,\Omega \quad \text{see Fig. 24-13}a$$

Then from the equivalent circuit of Fig. 24-13b:

$$R_e = 1.237 + 5.76 = 6.997 \,\Omega$$

$$I = \frac{V}{R} = \frac{240}{6.997} = 34.3 \text{ A}$$

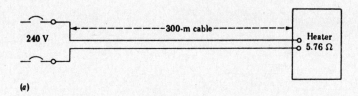

(a)

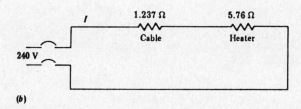

(b)   **Fig. 24-13**

24.68 In the circuit of Prob. 24-67 determine (a) the voltage drop in the cable; (b) the power loss in the cable; (c) the power drawn by the load; (d) the current in the cable if an accidental solid short occurs across the heater terminals.

▌ (a) $V_{\text{cable}} = IR_{\text{cable}} = 34.3(1.237) = 42.4$ V

(b) $P_{\text{cable}} = I^2R_{\text{cable}} = (34.3)^2(1.237) = 1455$ W

(c) $P_{\text{load}} = I^2R_{\text{load}} = (34.3)^2(5.76) = 6777$ W

(d) A solid short across the heater terminals bypasses the heater, leaving only the cable resistance to limit the current.

$$I = \frac{V}{R} = \frac{240}{1.237} = 194 \text{ A}$$

24.69 A 12-V dc source with an internal resistance of 2 Ω is connected through a switch to an 18-Ω load as shown in Fig. 24-14. The voltmeter connected across terminals T_1, T_2 is a digital voltmeter (DVM) whose internal resistance of 2 MΩ draws negligible current from the source. With the switch closed, determine the current to the load, the voltmeter reading, and the voltage drop within the source.

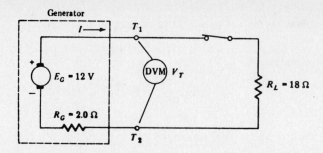

Fig. 24-14

▮ Since the DVM draws insignificant current, it can be neglected when making circuit calculations. Applying Ohm's law to the series circuit,

$$I = \frac{V}{R} = \frac{12}{2+18} = 0.60 \text{ A}$$

Or, using Kirchhoff's voltage law,

$$\sum \text{voltage rises} = \sum \text{voltage drops} \qquad 12 = 18I + 2I \qquad I = 0.60 \text{ A}$$

The voltmeter reads the voltage drop across the T_1, T_2 terminals, which is equal to the IR drop across the 18-Ω resistor. Thus

$$V_T = (0.60)(18) = 10.8 \text{ V}$$

The voltage drop within the source is

$$V_{\text{drop,source}} = (0.60)(2) = 1.2 \text{ V}$$

24.70 Determine the voltmeter reading in the circuit of Prob. 24.69 with the switch open as shown in Fig. 24-15.

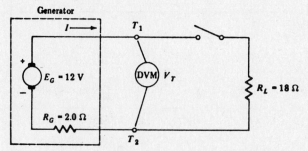

Fig. 24-15

▮ By KVL: $$\sum \text{voltage rises} = \sum \text{voltage drops}$$

The only voltage rise is that of the 12-V source; the voltage drops are the IR drop in the 2-Ω source resistance and the voltage drop across the 2 MΩ of the voltmeter.

$$12 = 2I + 2 \times 10^6 I \qquad I = 6 \times 10^{-6} \text{ A} = 6 \text{ μA}$$

The voltage drop across the DVM is

$$V = IR = 6 \times 10^{-6}(2 \times 10^6) = 12 \text{ V}$$

24.71 Repeat Prob. 24.71, neglecting the current drawn by the DVM.

▮ $$12 = 2I + V_T$$

where V_T = voltage drop across the DVM. With $I \approx 0$,

$$12 = 2(0) + V_T \qquad V_T = 12 \text{ V}$$

24.72 Plot the voltage-current characteristic of a source that has an open-circuit voltage of 24 V, a source resistance of 0.20 Ω, and a current rating of 30 A.

▮ $V_T = 24 - 0.2I_T$, which is plotted in Fig. 24-16.

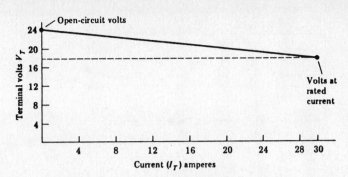

Fig. 24-16

24.73 A certain dc generator, shown in Fig. 24-17, has a terminal voltage of 240 V when delivering its rated 200 kW to a load. The internal resistance of the generator is 8.00 mΩ. Determine (*a*) the rated current (full-load current); (*b*) the open-circuit voltage.

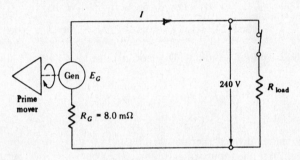

Fig. 24-17

▌ (*a*) $$P = VI \qquad 200{,}000 = 240I \qquad I = 833.3 \text{ A}$$

(*b*) The open-circuit voltage is E_G. Applying Kirchoff's voltage law,
$$E_G = 240 + 0.008(833.3) = 246.7 \text{ V}$$

24.74 Obtain the percent voltage regulation for the generator of Prob. 24.73.

▌ $$\text{Percent reg.} = \frac{V_{NL} - V_{FL}}{V_{FL}} \times 100 = \frac{246.7 - 240}{240} \times 100 = 2.79 \text{ percent}$$

24.75 Determine the equivalent resistance of the following series-connected resistors: 6 Ω, 10 Ω, 5 Ω, 30 Ω.

▌ $$R_e = 6 + 10 + 5 + 30 = 51 \text{ Ω}$$

24.76 The equivalent resistance of six series-connected resistors is 10 kΩ. If the values of five of the resistors are 1000 Ω, 2400 Ω, 1800 Ω, and 500 Ω, respectively, determine the resistance of the sixth resistor.

▌ $$10{,}000 = 1000 + 2400 + 1800 + 4000 + 500 + R_X \qquad \text{or} \qquad R_X = 300 \text{ Ω}$$

24.77 A 120-V source of negligible resistance is connected in series with the following resistors: 20 Ω, 200 Ω, 2000 Ω, and 20 kΩ. Determine (*a*) the current; (*b*) the voltage drop across each resistor; (*c*) the power supplied by the source.

▌ (*a*) $$I = \frac{E}{R} = \frac{120}{20 + 200 + 2000 + 20{,}000} = 5.4 \text{ mA}$$

(*b*) $$V = IR$$

$$V_{20} = 20(0.0054) = 0.108 \text{ V} \qquad V_{200} = 200(0.0054) = 1.08 \text{ V}$$

$$V_{2000} = 2000(0.0054) = 10.8 \text{ V} \qquad V_{20{,}000} = 20{,}000(0.0054) = 108 \text{ V}$$

(*c*) $$P = VI = 120(0.0054) = 0.648 \text{ W}$$

24.78 Referring to the circuit in Fig. 24-18, determine (*a*) the current; (*b*) the voltage drop across the 6-Ω resistor; (*c*) the power drawn by the 6-Ω resistor; (*d*) the energy expended in the 6-Ω resistor if the circuit is energized for 20 h; (*e*) the current if the 24-V generator is reversed.

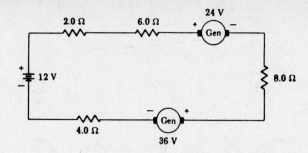

Fig. 24-18

$\blacksquare$ (a) By KVL: $\qquad 36 + 24 - 12 = (2 + 6 + 8 + 4)I \qquad I = 2.4 \text{ A}$

(b) $\qquad\qquad V = IR = 2.4 \times 6 = 14.4 \text{ V}$

(c) $\qquad\qquad P = I^2 R = (2.4)^2 6 = 34.6 \text{ W}$

(d) $\qquad\qquad W = Pt = 34.56 \times 20 = 691 \text{ W} \cdot \text{h}$

(e) $\qquad 36 - 24 - 12 = (2 + 6 + 8 + 4)I \qquad \text{or} \qquad I = 0$

24.79 Determine the slide setting required on a 4000-Ω rheostat in order to get a 9-V output from a 12-V battery. Sketch the circuit.

$\blacksquare$ $\qquad\qquad V_k = V_T\left(\dfrac{R_k}{R_T}\right) \qquad 9 = 12\left(\dfrac{R_k}{4000}\right) \qquad R_k = 3000\ \Omega$

24.80 A 10,000-Ω slide-wire potential divider rheostat is adjusted so that the output terminals embrace 8000 Ω. Sketch the circuit and determine the input voltage required to obtain a 50-V output.

$\blacksquare$ $\qquad\qquad V_k = V_T\left(\dfrac{R_k}{R_T}\right) \qquad 50 = V_T\left(\dfrac{8000}{10,000}\right) \qquad V_T = 62.5 \text{ V}$

24.81 Using the voltage-divider equation, determine the voltage between points c and d in Fig. 24-19.

$\blacksquare$ $\qquad\qquad V_{cd} = 24\left(\dfrac{20}{10 + 40 + 20 + 60}\right) = 3.69 \text{ V}$

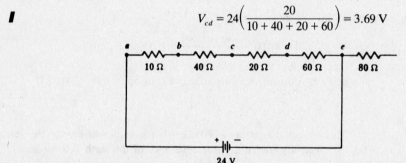

Fig. 24-19

24.82 Determine the equivalent resistance of the following parallel-connected resistors: $6\ \Omega$, $10\ \Omega$, $5\ \Omega$, $30\ \Omega$.

$\blacksquare$ $\qquad\qquad \dfrac{1}{R_{\text{eq}(P)}} = \dfrac{1}{6} + \dfrac{1}{10} + \dfrac{1}{5} + \dfrac{1}{30} \qquad R_{\text{eq}(P)} = 2\ \Omega$

24.83 The equivalent resistance of six paralleled resistors is 0.45 Ω. If five of the resistors are 3 Ω, 4 Ω, 2 Ω, 8 Ω, and 6 Ω, respectively, determine the resistance of the sixth resistor.

$\blacksquare$ $\qquad\qquad \dfrac{1}{0.45} = \dfrac{1}{3} + \dfrac{1}{4} + \dfrac{1}{2} + \dfrac{1}{8} + \dfrac{1}{6} + \dfrac{1}{R_X} \qquad R_X = 1.18\ \Omega$

24.84 (a) Using the conductance method, determine the battery current in Fig. 24-20; (b) determine the power drawn by the 150-Ω resistor.

$\blacksquare$ (a) $\qquad G_P = \dfrac{1}{200} + \dfrac{1}{150} + \dfrac{1}{120} + \dfrac{1}{100} = 0.030 \text{ S} \qquad I = EG = (48)(0.03) = 1.44 \text{ A}$

(b) $\qquad\qquad P = V^2/R = (48)^2/150 = 15.4 \text{ W}$

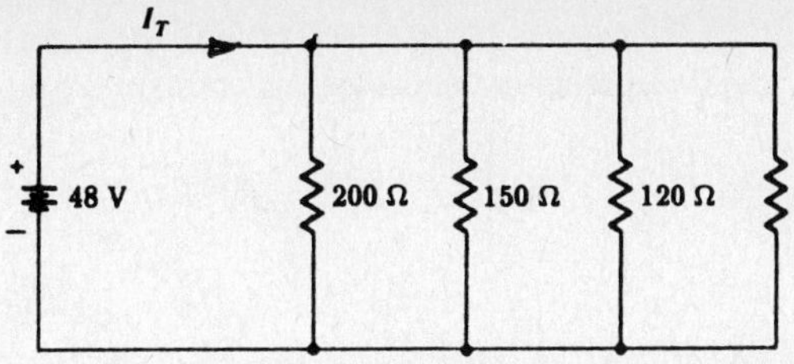

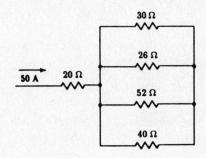

Fig. 24-20

24.85 Determine the equivalent resistance of each of the following sets of paralleled resistors: (a) $100\,\Omega$, $80\,\Omega$;   (b) $5\,\Omega$, $500\,\Omega$;   (c) $2\,k\Omega$, $2\,k\Omega$;   (d) $0.01\,\Omega$, $100\,\Omega$.

    ■   (a) $R_{eq} = \dfrac{100(80)}{100 + 80} = 44.4\,\Omega$ (b) $R_{eq} = \dfrac{5(500)}{5 + 500} = 4.95\,\Omega$

                (c) $R_{eq} = \dfrac{(2000)(2000)}{2000 + 2000} = 1000\,\Omega$ (d) $R_{eq} = \dfrac{0.01(100)}{0.01 + 100} = 0.00999\,\Omega$

24.86 Referring to Fig. 24-21, determine   (a) the current in the 40-Ω resistor;   (b) the heat power expended in the 40-Ω resistor;   (c) the voltage drop across the 20-Ω resistor;   (d) the voltage drop across the parallel section.

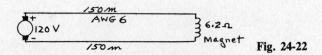

Fig. 24-21

    ■ (a) $G_T = \dfrac{1}{30} + \dfrac{1}{26} + \dfrac{1}{52} + \dfrac{1}{40} = 0.116\,\text{S}$ $G_{40} = 0.025\,\text{S}$ $I_k = 50\left(\dfrac{0.025}{0.116}\right) = 10.8\,\text{A} = I_{40\,\Omega}$

      (b) $I^2 R = (10.8)^2 40 = 4665.6\,\text{W}$

      (c) $V_{20\,\Omega} = (50)(20) = 1000\,\text{V}$

      (d) $V_P = (I_{40\,\Omega})40 = (10.8)(40) = 432\,\text{V}$

24.87 Twenty 12-Ω resistors are connected in parallel, and the combination is connected to a 40-V source. Determine   (a) the equivalent parallel resistance;   (b) the total current supplied by the driver.

    (a) $R_{eq(P)} = \dfrac{12}{20} = 0.60\,\Omega$

    (b) $I = \dfrac{E}{R_{eq}} = \dfrac{40}{0.60} = 66.7\,\text{A}$

24.88 A 120-V dc generator supplies power to an electromagnet through a 150-m cable. The two conductors that make up the cable are each size AWG 6 copper wire.   The resistance of the electromagnet is $6.2\,\Omega$. Sketch the circuit and determine the current in the magnet. The resistance of 6 AWG is $1.297\,\Omega/\text{km}$.

    ■ See Fig. 24-22.

$$R_{cable} = \left(\frac{150 \times 2}{1000}\right)(1.297) = 0.389\,\Omega \qquad I = \frac{E}{R} = \frac{120}{6.2 + 0.389} = 18.2\,\text{A}$$

Fig. 24-22

24.89   From the data of Prob. 24.88, calculate   (*a*) the voltage drop in the cable;   (*b*) the voltage across the magnet; (*c*) the power loss in the cable;   (*d*) the current in the cable if an accidental solid short occurs across the magnet terminals.

∎   (*a*) $V = IR = 18.2(0.389) = 7.08 \text{ V}$ (*c*) $P = I^2R = (18.2)^2(0.389) = 128.9 \text{ W}$

    (*b*) $V = 120 - 7.08 = 112.9 \text{ V}$ (*d*) $I = \dfrac{E}{R} = \dfrac{120}{0.389} = 308.5 \text{ A}$

24.90   A 50-V dc generator with an internal resistance of 0.26 Ω is connected to a 12-Ω resistor through a switch. Sketch the circuit and determine the voltage at the generator terminals with the switch closed.

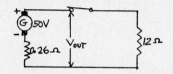

Fig. 24-23

∎   See Fig. 24-23.   With the switch closed, the output voltage equals the voltage drop across the 12-Ω resistor.

$$V_{\text{out}} = 50\left(\frac{12}{12 + 0.26}\right) = 48.9 \text{ V}$$

24.91   Repeat Prob. 24.90 with the switch open.

∎   See Fig. 24-24.   With the switch open, by applying Kirchhoff's voltage law to loop *abcda*,

$$50 = 0.26I + V_{\text{out}}$$

However, with the switch open $I = 0$;   hence, $V_{\text{out}} = 50 \text{ V}$.

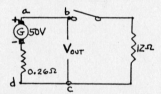

Fig. 24-24

24.92   Calculate the percent voltage regulation from the results of Probs. 24.90 and 24.91.

∎ $$\text{Percent reg.} = \frac{50 - 48.9}{48.9} \times 100 = 2.25\%$$

24.93   A certain dc generator is delivering rated 100 A at 200 V to a load.   The resistance of the generator is 0.2 Ω. Sketch the circuit, showing a switch between the generator and the load, and determine   (*a*) the voltage drop in the generator;   (*b*) the open-circuit voltage;   (*c*) the voltage regulation.

∎   See Fig. 24-25.

    (*a*) $IR = 100 \times 0.2 = 20 \text{ V}$ (*b*) $200 + 20 = 220 \text{ V}$

    (*c*) $\text{Percent reg.} = \left(\dfrac{V_{\text{NL}} - V_{\text{FL}}}{V_{\text{FL}}}\right)100 = \left(\dfrac{220 - 200}{200}\right)100 = 10.0\%$

24.94   An audio amplifier acts as a source when it supplies power to a speaker.   If the resistance of the amplifier is 8 Ω, what should be the resistance of the speaker in order that maximum power may be delivered?

∎   For maximum power transfer,   load resistance = source resistance

or   Resistance of speaker = resistance of amplifier = 8 Ω

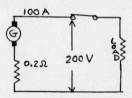

Fig. 24-25

24.95   For the circuit of Fig. 24-26a, find the input resistance.

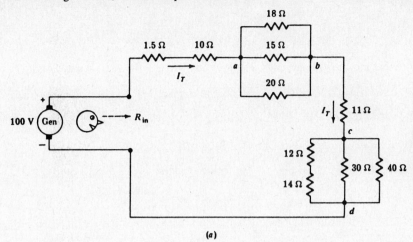

(a)

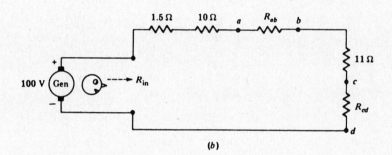

(b)

Fig. 24-26

▌ From Fig. 24-26b, for parallel section ab,

$$G_{ab} = \frac{1}{18} + \frac{1}{15} + \frac{1}{20} = 0.0556 + 0.0667 + 0.0500 = 0.1723 \text{ S}$$

$$R_{ab} = \frac{1}{G_{ab}} = \frac{1}{0.1723} = 5.8 \, \Omega$$

For parallel section cd, the 12-Ω and 14-Ω resistors in series total $12 + 14 = 26 \, \Omega$. The conductance of the parallel combination of 26 Ω, 30 Ω, and 40 Ω is

$$G_{cd} = \frac{1}{26} + \frac{1}{30} + \frac{1}{40} = 0.0385 + 0.0333 + 0.0250 = 0.0968 \text{ S}$$

$$R_{cd} = \frac{1}{G_{cd}} = \frac{1}{0.0968} = 10.3 \, \Omega$$

Substituting R_{ab} and R_{cd} for the respective parallel sections results in the equivalent series circuit shown in Fig. 24-26b. Thus the overall resistance of the circuit, called the *input resistance* or *driving-point resistance*, is

$$R_{in} = 1.5 + 10 + 5.8 + 11 + 10.3 = 38.6 \, \Omega$$

24.96   Find the input current to the circuit of Fig. 24-26a.

▌

$$I_T = \frac{100}{38.6} = 2.59 \text{ A}$$

24.97   Determine the current in the 15-Ω resistor of the circuit of Fig. 24-26a.

▌ Using the current-divider equation,

$$I_{15} = I_T \frac{G_{15}}{G_{ab}} = 2.59 \frac{0.0667}{0.1723} = 1.00 \text{ A}$$

24.98 What is the voltage across the 11-Ω resistor of the circuit of Fig. 24-26a?

❚
$$V_{11\,\Omega} = I_{11\,\Omega}(11) = (2.59)(11) = 28.5\ \text{V}$$

24.99 Using three different methods, determine the power absorbed by the 11-Ω resistor of the circuit of Fig. 24-26a.

❚ $P_{11} = V_{11}I_{11} = 28.5(2.59) = 73.8\ \text{W}$ $P_{11} = I_{11}^2 R_{11} = (2.59)^2 11 = 73.8\ \text{W}$ $P_{11} = \dfrac{V_{11}^2}{R_{11}} = \dfrac{(28.5)^2}{11} = 73.8\ \text{W}$

24.100 Calculate the input resistance of the circuit of Fig. 24-27a.

❚ By network reduction shown in Fig. 24-27b to d we obtain

❚
$$R_{ce} = \frac{(10+50)(60)}{(10+50)+60} = 30\ \Omega \qquad R_{bf} = \frac{(40+30)(15)}{40+30+15} = 12.4\ \Omega$$

$$R_{ag} = \frac{(18+12.4)(12)}{18+12.4+12} = 8.6\ \Omega \qquad R_{\text{in}} = 45 + 8.6 = 53.6\ \Omega$$

24.101 What is the input current in the circuit of Prob. 24.100?

❚
$$I_T = \frac{12}{53.6} = 0.224\ \text{A}$$

24.102 Determine the voltage drop in the 60-Ω resistor of the circuit of Fig. 24-27a.

❚ From Fig. 24-27c: $\qquad\qquad\qquad\qquad I_T = I_{ag} + I_{ab}$

where I_{ag} = current in branch ag and I_{ab} = current in branch abf. Using the current-divider equation,

$$I_{ab} = I_T \frac{G_{abf}}{G_P} \qquad G_P = G_{ag} + G_{abf} = \frac{1}{12} + \frac{1}{18+12.4} = 0.0833 + 0.0329 = 0.1162\ \text{S}$$

$$G_{abf} = 0.0329\ \text{S} \qquad I_{ab} = 0.224\,\frac{0.0329}{0.1162} = 0.0634\ \text{A}$$

Applying Kirchhoff's current law to node b in Fig. 24-27b

$$I_{ab} = I_{bf} + I_{bc}$$

where I_{bf} = current in branch bf and I_{bc} = current in branch bce. Using the current-divider equation,

$$I_{bc} = I_{ab} \frac{G_{bce}}{G_P} \qquad G_P = G_{bf} + G_{bce} = \frac{1}{15} + \frac{1}{40+30} = 0.0667 + 0.0143 = 0.0810\ \text{S}$$

$$I_{bc} = 0.0634\,\frac{0.0143}{0.0810} = 0.0112\ \text{A}$$

Applying Kirchhoff's current law to node c in Fig. 24-27a

$$I_{bc} = I_{ce} + I_{cd}$$

where I_{ce} = current in branch ce and I_{cd} = current in branch cde. Using the current-divider equation,

$$I_{ce} = I_{bc} \frac{G_{ce}}{G_P} \qquad G_P = G_{ce} + G_{cde} = \frac{1}{60} + \frac{1}{10+50} = 0.0167 + 0.0167 = 0.0334$$

$$G_{ce} = 0.0167\ \text{S} \qquad I_{ce} = 0.0112\,\frac{0.0167}{0.0334} = 0.00560\ \text{A}$$

Hence the voltage drop across the 60-Ω resistor is

$$V_{60\,\Omega} = I_{60\,\Omega} R_{60\,\Omega} = 0.00560 \times 60 = 0.336\ \text{V}$$

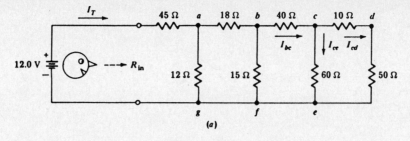

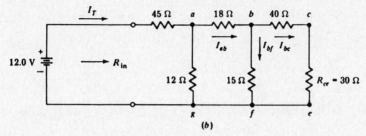

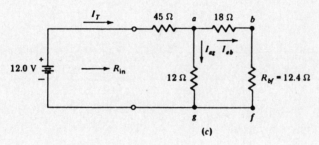

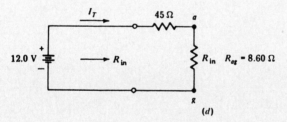

Fig. 24-27

24.103 Simplify the circuit of Fig. 24-28a to a series circuit. Hence determine the input resistance.

❙ See Fig. 24-28b and c, which are obtained as follows:

$$G_P = \frac{1}{30} + \frac{1}{20} + \frac{1}{10} = 0.1833 \text{ S} \quad \text{or} \quad R_{ep} = \frac{1}{0.1833} = 5.46 \ \Omega$$

$$G_{adc} + G_{abc} = \frac{1}{5.46 + 15} + \frac{1}{40 + 60} = 0.0589 \text{ S}$$

$$R_{ac} = \frac{1}{0.0589} = 17 \ \Omega \qquad R_{in} = 17 + 6.5 = 23.5 \ \Omega$$

$$I_T = \frac{V}{R_{in}} = \frac{120}{23.5} = 5.11 \text{ A}$$

24.104 Find the voltage across the 10-Ω resistor in the circuit of Fig. 24-28a.

❙ Applying the current-divider equation to the three paralleled resistors,

$$I_{10} = I_{ac} \frac{G_{10}}{G_P} \tag{1}$$

Conductances G_P and G_{10} for the *three* paralleled branches were determined in Prob. 24.103 to be 0.1833 S and 0.1000 S, respectively. Substituting these values into Eq. (1),

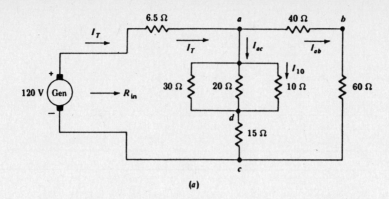

(a)

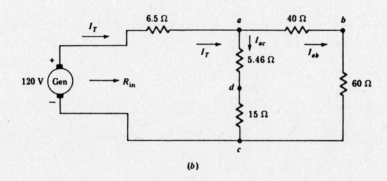

(b)

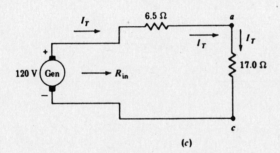

(c)

Fig. 24-28

$$I_{10} = I_{ac} \frac{0.1000}{0.1833} \qquad I_{10} = I_{ac}(0.5455) \tag{2}$$

Current I_{ac} may be calculated by applying the current-divider equation to the two paralleled branches in Fig. 24-28.

$$I_{ac} = I_T \frac{G_{adc}}{G_P} \tag{3}$$

Conductances G_P and G_{adc} for the *two* paralleled branches were determined in part *a* to be 0.0589 S and 0.0489 S, respectively.

Substituting the known values into Eq. (3), and evaluating,

$$I_{ac} = 5.11 \frac{0.0489}{0.0589} = 4.24 \text{ A}$$

Substituting 4.24 for I_{ac} in Eq. (2),

$$I_{10} = 4.24(0.5455) = 2.31 \text{ A} \qquad V_{10} = I_{10}R_{10} = 2.31(10) = 23.1 \text{ V}$$

24.105 Neglecting the voltmeter current, determine the voltmeter reading in the circuit of Fig. 24-29.

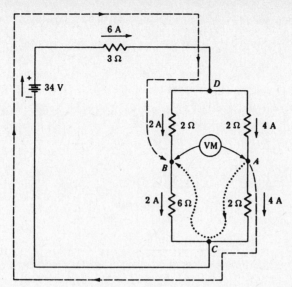

Fig. 24-29

▮ Following the path shown by the dotted line in Fig. 24-29 we obtain

$$V_{AB} = \left(\sum \text{driving voltages}\right) - \left(\sum \text{voltage drops}\right) = 0 - [4 \times 2 + (-2) \times 6] = 4 \text{ V}$$

24.106 Solve Prob. 24.105 following the path indicated by the dashed line in Fig. 24-29.

▮ This path includes the driving voltage.

$$V_{AB} = \left(\sum \text{driving voltages}\right) - \left(\sum \text{voltage drops}\right) = 34 - (4 \times 2 + 6 \times 3 + 2 \times 2) = 4 \text{ V}$$

24.107 For the circuit of Fig. 24-30, calculate the input voltage.

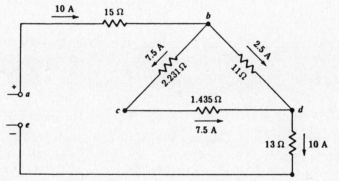

Fig. 24-30

▮ Taking path *abde*,

$$V_{ae} = \left(\sum \text{driving voltages}\right) - \left(\sum \text{voltage drops}\right) = 0 - (10 \times 15 + 2.5 \times 11 + 10 \times 13) = -307.5 \text{ V}$$

The sign of the answer (+ or −) depends on the direction of travel. If the direction of travel was from *e* to *a* along path *edba*,

$$V_{ea} = 0 - [(-10) \times 13 + (-2.5)(11) + (-10) \times 15] = 307.5 \text{ V}$$

24.108 Obtain the voltage between nodes *a* and *c* in the circuit of Fig. 24-30.

▮ Taking path *abc*

$$V_{ac} = \left(\sum \text{driving voltages}\right) - \left(\sum \text{voltage drops}\right) = 0 - [10 \times 15 + 7.5 \times 2.231] = -166.73 \text{ V}$$

If we take path *abdc*

$$V_{ac} = 0 - [10 \times 15 + 2.5 \times 11 + (-7.5) \times 1.435] = -166.73 \text{ V}$$

24.109   What is the voltage between nodes e and b of the circuit of Fig. 24-30?

 ▮   Taking path edb, $V_{eb} = 0 - [(-10) \times 13 + (-2.5) \times 11] = 157.5$ V

24.110   In the bridge circuit of Fig. 24-31, assuming R_2 and R_1 have resistance values of 1000 Ω and 10,000 Ω, respectively, and the rheostat setting that balances the bridge is 1242 Ω, calculate the resistance of the unknown.

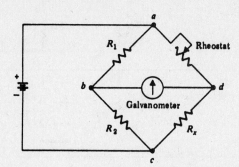

Fig. 24-31

 ▮ $$R_X = R_{\text{rheo}} \frac{R_2}{R_1} = 1242 \frac{1000}{10,000} = 124.2 \ \Omega$$

24.111   In the circuit of Fig. 24-32, determine   (a) the input resistance;   (b) the feeder current;   (c) the voltage drop across each resistor;   (d) the current through the 21-Ω resistor.

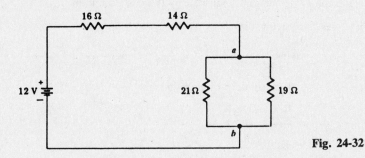

Fig. 24-32

(a) $$R_{eq(P)} = \frac{21 \times 19}{21 + 19} = 9.98 \ \Omega \qquad R_{in} = 16 + 14 + 9.98 = 40 \ \Omega$$

(b) $$I = \frac{E}{R} = \frac{12}{40} = 0.30 \text{ A}$$

(c) $$V_{16} = 16(0.30) = 4.8 \text{ V} \qquad V_{14} = 14(0.30) = 4.2 \text{ V}$$

$$V_{ba} = \sum \text{ driving volts} - \sum \text{ voltage drops} = 12 - [4.8 + 4.2] = 3 \text{ V}$$

Thus $$V_{21} = 3 \text{ V} \qquad V_{19} = 3 \text{ V}$$

(d) $$V = IR \qquad 3 = I(21) \qquad I = 0.14 \text{ A}$$

24.112   Calculate the current through the 12-Ω resistor in the circuit of Fig. 24-33.

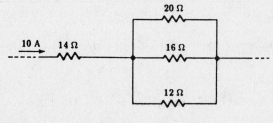

Fig. 24-33

 ▮ $$G_P = \frac{1}{20} + \frac{1}{16} + \frac{1}{12} = 0.1958 \text{ S} \qquad G_{12} = 0.0833 \text{ S} \qquad I_{12} = 10\left[\frac{0.0833}{0.1958}\right] = 4.25 \text{ A}$$

24.113 For the circuit of Fig. 24-34 determine (a) the input resistance, (b) the input current, (c) the current through the 500-Ω resistor, (d) the power supplied by the generator, and (e) the energy expended over a 36-h period.

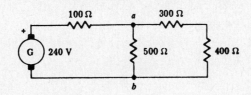

Fig. 24-34

▮ (a)
$$R_{eq} = \frac{(500)(400 + 300)}{500 + 400 + 300} = 291.67\,\Omega \qquad R_{in} = 100 + 291.67 = 391.7\,\Omega$$

(b)
$$I = \frac{E}{R} = \frac{240}{391.7} = 0.613\,\text{A}$$

(c)
$$I_{500\Omega} = 0.613\left[\frac{G_{500}}{G_T}\right] = 0.613\left[\frac{0.0020}{0.0034}\right] = 0.361\,\text{A}$$

(d)
$$P = EI = 240(0.613) = 147.1\,\text{W}$$

(e)
$$W = Pt = 147.1 \times 36 = 5296 = 5.30\,\text{kW·h}$$

24.114 Determine the (a) input resistance and (b) input current for the circuit of Fig. 24-35.

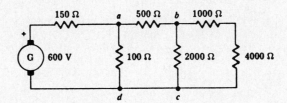

Fig. 24-35

▮ By network reduction we obtain

(a)
$$R_{eq(bc)} = \frac{2000(1000 + 4000)}{2000 + 1000 + 4000} = 1428.6\,\Omega$$

$$R_{eq(ad)} = \frac{100(500 + 1428.6)}{100 + 500 + 1428.6} = 95.0\,\Omega$$

$$R_{in} = 150 + 95.0 = 245\,\Omega$$

(b)
$$I = \frac{E}{R_{in}} = \frac{600}{245} = 2.45\,\text{A}$$

24.115 What is the current in the 2000-Ω resistor of the circuit of Fig. 24-35?

▮
$$I_{2\,k\Omega} = I_{ab}\left[\frac{G_{2\,k\Omega}}{G_P}\right] \qquad G_{2\,k\Omega} = \frac{1}{2000} = 500\,\mu\text{S} \qquad G_P = \frac{1}{2000} + \frac{1}{5000} = 700\,\mu\text{S}$$

$$I_{2\,k\Omega} = I_{ab}\left[\frac{500\,\mu\text{S}}{700\,\mu\text{S}}\right] = I_{ab}(0.714) \tag{1}$$

$$I_{ab} = 2.45\left[\frac{G_{abc}}{G_{abc} + G_{ad}}\right] = 2.45\left[\frac{5.19 \times 10^{-4}}{10.52 \times 10^{-3}}\right] = 0.1209\,\text{A}$$

Substituting into Eq. (1) yields

$$I_{2\,k\Omega} = 86.3\,\text{mA}$$

24.116 Obtain the input resistance for the circuit of Fig. 24-36a.

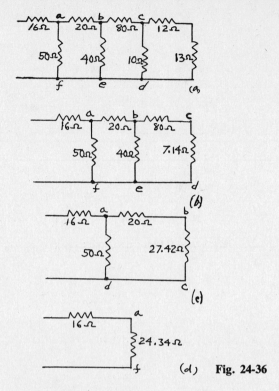

(d) **Fig. 24-36**

▌ By network reduction shown in Fig. 24-36 we obtain

$$R_{cd} = \frac{10(12 + 13)}{10 + 12 + 13} = 7.14\,\Omega \qquad R_{be} = \frac{40(80 + 7.14)}{40 + 80 + 7.14} = 27.42\,\Omega$$

$$R_{af} = \frac{50(20 + 27.42)}{50 + 20 + 27.42} = 24.34\,\Omega \qquad R_{in} = 16 + 24.34 = 40.3\,\Omega$$

24.117 Find (*a*) the input resistance and (*b*) the input current for the network of Fig. 24-37.

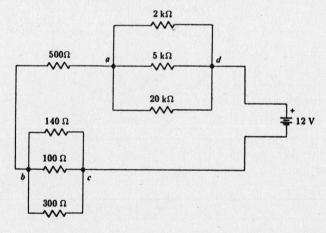

Fig. 24-37

▌ (*a*)

$$G_{ad} = \frac{1}{2000} + \frac{1}{5000} + \frac{1}{20,000} = 750\,\mu S \qquad R_{ad} = 1/G_{ad} = 1333.33\,\Omega$$

$$G_{bc} = \frac{1}{140} + \frac{1}{100} + \frac{1}{300} = 20.48\,\text{mS} \qquad R_{bc} = 1/G_{bc} = 48.83\,\Omega$$

$$R_{in} = 48.83 + 500 + 1333.33 = 1882.2\,\Omega$$

(*b*)

$$I = \frac{E}{R} = \frac{12}{1882.2} = 6.375\,\text{mA}$$

24.118 Find (*a*) the current through the 2-kΩ resistor and (*b*) the voltage across the 500-Ω resistor in the circuit of Fig. 24-37.

$$I_k = I_P\left[\frac{G_k}{G_P}\right] \qquad G_k = \frac{1}{2000} = 500\ \mu S \qquad G_P = G_{ad} = 750\ \mu S$$

$$I_k = 6.375 \times 10^{-3}\left[\frac{500\ \mu S}{750\ \mu S}\right] = 4.25\ mA$$

$$V = IR = 6.375 \times 10^{-3}(500) = 3.1875 = 3.19\ V$$

24.119 What is the voltage between nodes *a* and *c* in the circuit of Fig. 24-37?

Taking path *cda*,

$$V_{ca} = \sum \text{driving volts} - \sum \text{voltage drops} = 12 - [IR_{ad}]$$
$$= 12 - [6.375 \times 10^{-3} \times 1333.33] = 3.5\ V$$

24.120 Determine (*a*) the current through and (*b*) the voltage across each circuit element in the circuit of Fig. 24-38 under steady state.

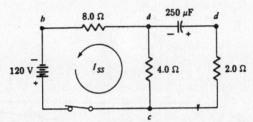

Fig. 24-38

(*a*) At steady state, the capacitor is fully charged, and its charging current is reduced to zero. Hence, there can be no current in the 2-Ω resistor; the charged capacitor acts as an open circuit. The only steady-state current in the circuit is through the loop formed by the battery, the 8-Ω resistor, and the 4-Ω resistor. Applying Ohm's law,

$$I_{ss} = \frac{E_{bat}}{R} = \frac{120}{8+4} = 10\ A$$

(*b*) The voltage drops across the resistors, as determined from Ohm's law, are

$$V_8 = I_8R_8 = 10(8) = 80\ V \qquad V_4 = I_4R_4 = 10(4) = 40\ V \qquad V_2 = I_2R_2 = 0(2) = 0\ V$$

The voltage drop across the capacitor may be determined by applying the voltage balance to nodes *a* and *d*. Thus,

$$V_{ad} = \left(\sum \text{driving voltages}\right) - \left(\sum \text{voltage drops}\right)$$

Traveling counterclockwise along path *acd*,

$$V_{ad} = 0 - [(-10) \times 4 + (0) \times 2] = 40\ V$$

24.121 Obtain the voltage across the capacitor of the circuit of Prob. 24.120 if the switch is opened at $t = 0_+$. Also determine the discharge current.

Since the capacitance property of a capacitor delays a change in the voltage across it,

$$v_C|_{t=(0_+)} = v_C|_{t=(0_-)} = 40\ V$$

The current in the discharge loop, at the instant the switch is opened, may be determined by applying Kirchhoff's voltage law to that loop. Thus,

$$\sum \text{driving voltages} = \sum \text{voltage drops}$$

With the switch open, the driving voltage is zero. Hence,

$$0 = 2i_D + 4i_D + v_C$$

At $t = (0_+)$, $\qquad\qquad 0 = (2+4)i_D + 40 \qquad i_D|_{t=(0_+)} = -6.7\ A$

24.122 Sketch the voltage across and the current through the capacitor of the circuits of Fig. 24-39a and b. Draw the graphs in a normalized form.

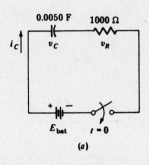

(a)

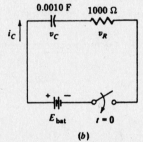

(b)

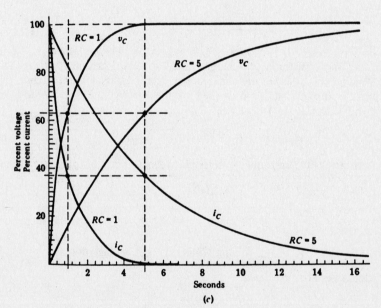

Fig. 24-39

(c)

▌ The current and the voltage in an RC series are given by

$$i_C = \frac{E_{bat}}{R}(e^{-t/RC}) = I_0 e^{-t/RC} \tag{1}$$

and

$$v_C = E_{bat}(1 - e^{-t/RC}) \tag{2}$$

In normalized forms these become

$$\frac{i_C}{I_0} = e^{-t/\tau} \quad \text{and} \quad \frac{v_C}{E_{bat}} = 1 - e^{-t/\tau}$$

where $\tau = RC$ = time constant.

For the two circuits the normalized graphs are shown in Fig. 24-39c.

24.123 Sketch v_C and i_C in a series RC circuit as a function of the time constant, τ.

▌ See Fig. 24-40.

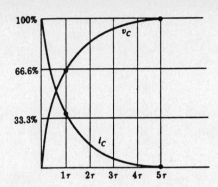

Fig. 24-40

24.124 In a circuit similar to that of Fig. 24-39a, $R = 2\,M\Omega$, $C = 5\,\mu F$, and $E_{bat} = 120\,V$. The switch is closed at $t = 0$. Obtain (a) the time constant, (b) the current at $t = \tau$, and (c) the voltage drop across the capacitor at $t = \tau$.

▌ Refer to Eqs. (1) and (2) of Prob. 24.122. Then:

(a) $$\tau = RC = 2 \times 10^6 \times 5 \times 10^{-6} = 10\,s$$

(b) $$i_C|_{t=1\tau} = 0.368\,\frac{E}{R} = 0.368\,\frac{120}{2 \times 10^6} = 22.1 \times 10^{-6}\,A = 22.1\,\mu A$$

(c) $$v_C|_{t=1\tau} = 0.632E = 0.632(120) = 75.8\,V$$

24.125 Determine graphically the time constant of a series RC circuit.

▌ Since $v_C = E_{bat}(1 - e^{-t/RC})$,

$$\frac{dv_C}{dt} = E_{bat}\left[0 - \left(-\frac{1}{RC}\,e^{-t/RC}\right)\right] = \frac{E_{bat}}{RC}\,e^{-t/RC}$$

$$\frac{dv_C}{dt}\bigg|_{t=(0_+)} = \frac{E_{bat}}{RC} \tag{1}$$

The slope of the voltage obtained graphically from Fig. 24-41 at $t = (0_+)$ is

$$Slope|_{t=(0_+)} = \frac{E_{bat}}{\Delta T} \tag{2}$$

Thus, equating (1) and (2), we obtain

$$\frac{E_{bat}}{RC} = \frac{E_{bat}}{\Delta T} \qquad or \qquad \Delta T = RC = \tau$$

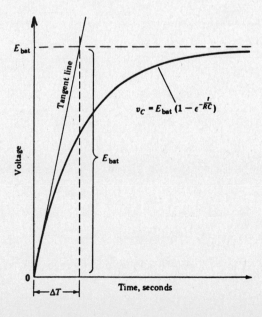

Fig. 24-41

24.126 A 6.0-Ω resistor is connected in series with a 2000-μF capacitor, a 48-V battery, and a switch. Assume the capacitor has zero initial charge. Determine (*a*) the voltage across the capacitor at the instant the switch is closed ($t = 0_+$); (*b*) the current to the capacitor at the instant the switch is closed ($t = 0_+$); (*c*) the voltage across the capacitor at $t = 1$ time constant; (*d*) the current at $t = 1$ time constant.

■ (*a*) Since a capacitor delays a change in the voltage across it, and the capacitor has zero initial charge,

$$v_C|_{t=(0_+)} = v_C|_{t=(0_-)} = 0 \text{ V}$$

(*b*) Applying Kirchhoff's voltage law,

$$E_{\text{bat}} = v_C + v_R \qquad 48 = 0 + 6i \qquad i|_{t=(0_+)} = 8 \text{ A}$$

(*c*) $$v_C|_{t=1\tau} = 0.632E_{\text{bat}} = 0.632(48) = 30.3 \text{ V}$$

(*d*) $$i_C|_{t=1\tau} = 0.368 \frac{E_{\text{bat}}}{R} = \frac{0.368(48)}{6.0} = 2.94 \text{ A}$$

24.127 For the circuit of Prob. 24.126, determine (*a*) the rate of transfer of energy at $t = 1$ time constant; (*b*) the energy stored in the capacitor at steady state; (*c*) the voltage across the resistor at $t = 0.02$ s.

■ (*a*) $$P_C|_{t=1\tau} = (v_C|_{t=1\tau})(i_C|_{t=1\tau}) = (30.3)(2.94) = 89.1 \text{ W}$$

(*b*) $$W_C = \tfrac{1}{2}Cv_C^2 \qquad W_{C,\text{ss}} = \tfrac{1}{2}(2000 \times 10^{-6})(48)^2 = 2.30 \text{ J}$$

(*c*) $$E_{\text{bat}} = v_C + v_R$$

$$v_R = E_{\text{bat}} - v_C = E_{\text{bat}} - E_{\text{bat}}(1 - e^{-t/RC}) = 48 - 48\left(1 - \exp\frac{-0.02}{6(2000 \times 10^{-6})}\right)$$

$$= 48 - 38.93 = 9.07 \text{ V}$$

24.128 Assuming a certain driving voltage causes the current to an initially discharged 1000-μF capacitor to increase at a constant rate of 0.06 A/s ($i_C = 0.06t$), determine the voltage across the capacitor at $t = 10$ s.

■ $$v_C = \frac{1}{C}\int_0^T i \, dt = \frac{1}{1000(10^{-6})}\int_0^{10} 0.06t \, dt = 1000(0.06)\left(\frac{t^2}{2}\right)_0^{10} = 60\left(\frac{10^2}{2}\right) \qquad V_C = 3000 \text{ V}$$

24.129 (*a*) Assuming the resistance and capacitance in Fig. 24-42*a* are 4 Ω and 1000 μF, respectively, determine the current at $t = (0_+)$. (*b*) Repeat part *a* for the discharge conditions in Fig. 24-42*b*.

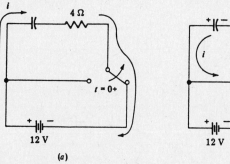 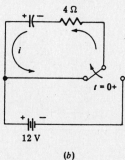

(*a*)   (*b*)   **Fig. 24-42**

(*a*) Applying Kirchhoff's voltage law,

$$E_{\text{bat}} = v_C + v_R \qquad v_C|_{t=(0_+)} = v_C|_{t=(0_-)} = 0 \qquad 12 = 0 + 4i \qquad i|_{t=(0_+)} = 3 \text{ A}$$

(*b*) Assuming the capacitor is fully charged before the switch is thrown to the discharge position,

$$v_C|_{t=(0_+)} = v_C|_{t=(0_-)} = 12 \text{ V}$$

Applying Kirchhoff's voltage law, and recognizing that there is no voltage source in the loop,

$$0 = v_C + v_R \qquad 0 = 12 + 4i \qquad i = -3 \text{ A}$$

24.130 A 400-μF capacitor charged to 2500 V is to be discharged through a 50-kΩ resistor. Determine (*a*) the recommended minimum discharge time; (*b*) the capacitor voltage for the conditions in part *a*.

∎ (a) $5\tau = 5RC = 5(50,000)(400 \times 10^{-6}) = 100\,\text{s}.$

(b) The discharge loop is similar to that shown in Fig. 24-42b. Applying Kirchhoff's voltage law,

$$v_{C,\text{dis}} + v_R = 0 \qquad v_{C,\text{dis}} + (-iR) = 0$$

The negative sign indicates a discharge current. Thus,

$$v_{C,\text{dis}} = iR$$

Substituting, $\qquad\qquad i = I_0 e^{-t/RC} \qquad v_{C,\text{dis}} = I_0 R e^{-t/RC}$

Defining, $\qquad\qquad V_0 = I_0 R \qquad v_{C,\text{dis}} = V_0 e^{-t/RC}$

where $\qquad\qquad I_0 = i_C \;\text{ at }\; t = (0_+) \qquad V_0 = v_C \;\text{ at }\; t = (0_+)$

In five time constants,

$$v_{C,\text{dis}} = 2500 e^{-5RC/RC} = 2500 e^{-5} = 2500(0.0067) = 16.8\,\text{V}$$

24.131 Determine the equivalent capacitance of the following series-connected capacitors: $2\,\mu\text{F}$, $18\,\mu\text{F}$, $60\,\mu\text{F}$, and $140\,\mu\text{F}$.

∎
$$\frac{1}{C_{\text{eq}(s)}} = \frac{1}{2 \times 10^{-6}} + \frac{1}{18 \times 10^{-6}} + \frac{1}{60 \times 10^{-6}} + \frac{1}{140 \times 10^{-6}} \qquad \text{or} \qquad C_{\text{eq}(s)} = 1.73\,\mu\text{F}$$

24.132 If the capacitances of Prob. 24.131 are connected in parallel, what is the equivalent capacitance?

∎
$$C_{\text{eq}(P)} = 10^{-6}(2 + 18 + 60 + 140) = 220\,\mu\text{F}$$

24.133 A set of parallel capacitors are connected in series with $300\text{-}\mu\text{F}$ and $100\text{-}\mu\text{F}$ capacitors. The paralleled capacitors are $200\,\mu\text{F}$, $50\,\mu\text{F}$, and $150\,\mu\text{F}$. Sketch the circuit and determine the equivalent capacitance of the series-parallel combination.

∎ See Fig. 24-43.

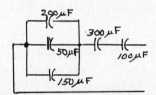

Fig. 24-43

$$C_{\text{eq}(P)} = (200 + 50 + 150)10^{-6} = 400\,\mu\text{F}$$

$$\frac{1}{C_{\text{eq}(s)}} = \frac{10^6}{400} + \frac{10^6}{300} + \frac{10^6}{100} \qquad C_{\text{eq}(s)} = 63.2\,\mu\text{F}$$

24.134 Determine the equivalent capacitance for the circuit of Fig. 24-44.

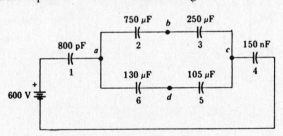

Fig. 24-44

∎
$$\frac{1}{C_{abc}} = \frac{10^6}{750} + \frac{10^6}{250} \qquad C_{abc} = 187.5\,\mu\text{F}$$

$$\frac{1}{C_{adc}} = \frac{10^6}{130} + \frac{10^6}{105} \qquad C_{adc} = 58.1\,\mu\text{F}$$

$$C_{\text{eq}(P)ac} = 187.5 \times 10^{-6} + 58.1 \times 10^{-6} = 245.6\,\mu\text{F}$$

$$\frac{1}{C_e} = \frac{10^{12}}{800} + \frac{10^6}{245.6} + \frac{10^9}{150} \qquad C_e = 795.75 \times 10^{-12} = 796\,\text{pF}$$

24.135 Calculate the voltage across each capacitor in the circuit of Fig. 24-44.

▮
$$q = CV = 796 \times 10^{-12}(600) = 477 \text{ nC}$$

For capacitor 1	For capacitor 4
$q = CV$	$q = CV$
$477 \times 10^{-9} = (800 \times 10^{-12})V_1$	$477 \times 10^{-9} = (150 \times 10^{-9})V_4$
$V_1 = 596.3 \text{ V}$	$V_4 = 3.18 \text{ V}$

$$V_{ca} = \sum \text{ driving voltages} - \sum \text{ voltage drops} = 600 - [3.18 + 596.25] = 0.570 \text{ V}$$

The charge in each capacitor of the series branch *abc* is

$$q = CV = (187.5 \times 10^{-6})(0.570) = 106.9 \times 10^{-6} \text{ C}$$

Hence the drop in voltages across capacitors 2 and 3 is

For capacitor 2	For capacitor 3
$q = CV$	$V_{ca} = V_2 + V_3$
$106.9 \times 10^{-6} = (750 \times 10^{-6})V_2$	$0.570 = 0.143 + V_3$
$V_2 = 0.143 \text{ V}$	$V_3 = 0.427 \text{ V}$

The charge in each capacitor of series branch *adc* is

$$q = CV = (58.1 \times 10^{-6})(0.570) = 33.12 \times 10^{-6} \text{ C}$$

Hence, the voltage drops across capacitors 5 and 6 are

For capacitor 5	For capacitor 6
$q = CV$	$V_{ca} = V_5 + V_6$
$33.12 \times 10^{-6} = (105 \times 10^{-6})V_5$	$0.570 = 0.315 + V_6$
$V_5 = 0.315 \text{ V}$	$V_6 = 0.255 \text{ V}$

24.136 In the circuit of Fig. 24-45 under steady state determine (*a*) the voltage across the capacitor and (*b*) the accumulated charge.

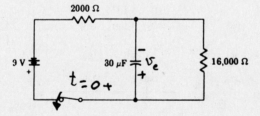

Fig. 24-45

▮ Under steady state $I_C = 0$.

(*a*)
$$I = \frac{E}{R} = \frac{9}{2000 + 16{,}000} = 500 \ \mu A$$

$$V_C = \text{voltage across the 1600-}\Omega \text{ resistor} = IR = (500 \times 10^{-6})(16{,}000) = 8 \text{ V}$$

(*b*)
$$q = CV_C = (30 \times 10^{-6})8 = 240 \ \mu C$$

24.137 In the circuit of Fig. 24-45, the switch is opened after the circuit has reached steady state. Determine (*a*) $v_C(0_+)$ and (*b*) the initial discharge current.

▮ (*a*)
$$V_C(0_+) = v_C(0_-) = 8 \text{ V}$$

(*b*)
$$I_d = \frac{V_C}{R} = \frac{8}{16{,}000} = 500 \ \mu A$$

24.138 The circuit of Fig. 24-46 is under steady state. Determine *(a)* the voltage across the capacitor and *(b)* the accumulated charge.

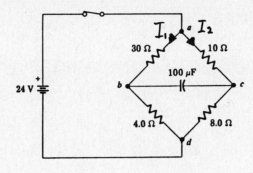

Fig. 24-46

▌ *(a)* Under steady state, the circuit reduces to parallel paths.

$$I_1 = \frac{24}{30 + 4} = 0.706 \text{ A} \qquad I_2 = \frac{24}{10 + 8} = 1.333 \text{ A}$$

$$V_{bc} = \sum \text{driving voltages} - \sum \text{voltage drops}$$

Taking path *bdc*:

$$V_{bc} = 0 - [4I_1 + 8(-I_2)] = -[4(0.706) + 8(-1.333)] = 7.82 \text{ V}$$

(b)
$$q = CV_{bc} = (100 \times 10^{-6})(7.82) = 782 \ \mu\text{C}$$

24.139 Repeat Prob. 24.137 for the circuit of Fig. 24-46.

$$R_{eq(P)} = \frac{40(12)}{40 + 12} = 9.23 \ \Omega \qquad i|_{t=0_+} = \frac{v_C}{R} = \frac{7.82}{9.23} = 0.85 \text{ A}$$

24.140 A 3000-μF capacitor is connected in series with a 10-MΩ resistor, a 60-V battery, and a switch. Determine *(a)* the time constant; *(b)* i_C, v_C, and v_R at $t = (0_+)$; *(c)* i_C, v_C, and v_R at $t = 1\,\tau$.

▌ *(a)*
$$\tau = RC = 3000 \times 10^{-6} \times 10 \times 10^6 = 30,000 \text{ S}$$

(b)
$$i|_{t=0_+} = \frac{E_{bat}}{R} = \frac{60}{10 \times 10^6} = 6 \ \mu\text{A} \qquad v_C|_{t=0_+} = 0 \qquad v_R|_{t=0_+} = iR = (6 \times 10^{-6})(10 \times 10^6) = 60 \text{ V}$$

(c)
$$i|_{t=1\tau} = 0.368(6 \ \mu\text{A}) = 2.21 \ \mu\text{A}$$

$$v_R|_{t=\tau} = iR = (2.21 \times 10^{-6})(10 \times 10^6) = 22.08 \text{ V}$$

$$v_C|_{t=\tau} = 0.632(60) = 37.92 \text{ V}$$

24.141 In the circuit of Prob. 24-140, determine *(a)* the charge at $t = \tau$ and *(b)* the steady-state stored energy in the capacitor.

▌ *(a)*
$$q = CV \qquad \text{or} \qquad q|_{t=\tau} = (3000 \times 10^{-6})(37.92) = 0.114 \text{ C}$$

(b)
$$W = \tfrac{1}{2}CV^2 = \tfrac{1}{2}(3000 \times 10^{-6})(60)^2 = 5.4 \text{ J}$$

24.142 A 20-kΩ resistor is connected in series with a 1000-μF capacitor, a 20-V battery, and a switch. Determine *(a)* the time constant; *(b)* i_C, v_C, and v_R at $t = 1\tau$; *(c)* i_C, v_C, and v_R at steady state.

▌ *(a)*
$$\tau = RC = 20,000 \times 1000 \times 10^{-6} = 20 \text{ s}$$

(b)
$$i|_{t=0_+} = \frac{E_{bat}}{R} = \frac{20}{20,000} = 1 \text{ mA} \qquad i|_{t=\tau} = 0.368(0.001) = 368 \ \mu\text{A}$$

$$v_C|_{t=\tau} = 0.632(20) = 12.64 \text{ V} \qquad v_R|_{t=\tau} = iR = (368 \times 10^{-6})(20,000) = 7.36 \text{ V}$$

(c)
$$i_{ss} = 0 \qquad v_{R(ss)} = i_{ss}R = 0(20,000) = 0 \qquad v_C = 20 \text{ V}$$

24.143 In the circuit of Prob. 24.142, obtain the rate of transfer of energy to the capacitor and its energy stored under steady state.

❚ Rate of energy transfer = power. Thus:

$$P_C = v_C i_C = (20)(0) = 0 \qquad W = \tfrac{1}{2}CV^2 \qquad W_{ss} = \tfrac{1}{2}(1000 \times 10^{-6})(20)^2 = 0.20 \text{ J}$$

24.144 In a series RC circuit, $R = 16\,\Omega$ and $C = 2.5\,\text{mF}$. A 240-V battery is connected in series with the circuit at $t = 0$. Evaluate $i(0_+)$, $v_C(0_+)$, and $v_R(0_+)$.

❚
$$i(0_+) = \frac{E}{R} = \frac{240}{16} = 15 \text{ A} \qquad v_C(0_+) = 0 \qquad v_R(0_+) = i(0_+)R = 15 \times 16 = 240 \text{ V}$$

24.145 Determine i and v_R in the circuit of Prob. 24.144, at $t = \tau$.

❚
$$\tau = RC = (2.5 \times 10^{-3})(16) = 40 \text{ ms}$$
$$i|_{t=\tau} = (0.368)(15) = 5.52 \text{ A}$$
$$v_R|_{t=\tau} = iR = (5.52)(16) = 88.32 \text{ V}$$

24.146 In the circuit of Prob. 24.144, determine: (*a*) the rate of energy transfer to the capacitor at $t = \tau$, (*b*) the steady-state stored energy, and (*c*) the voltage across the capacitor at $t = 0.06\,\text{s}$.

❚ (*a*)
$$P_C = v_C i_C|_{t=\tau} = (151.68)(5.52) = 837.27 \text{ W}$$

(*b*)
$$W = \tfrac{1}{2}CV^2 = \tfrac{1}{2}(2500 \times 10^{-6})(240)^2 = 72 \text{ J}$$

(*c*)
$$v_C = E_{\text{bat}}(1 - e^{-t/\tau}) = 240(1 - e^{-t/0.04})$$
$$v_C(0.06) = 240(1 - e^{-0.06/0.04}) = 186.45 \text{ V}$$

24.147 A 24-V battery is connected to a series RC circuit having $R = 1\,\text{k}\Omega$ and $C = 150\,\mu\text{F}$ at $t = 0$. Evaluate (*a*) $i_C(0_+)$ and $v_C(0_+)$; (*b*) steady-state current; (*c*) $i(\tau)$ and (*d*) $v_R(\tau)$.

❚ (*a*)
$$i_C(0_+) = 24/1000 = 24 \text{ mA} \qquad v_C(0_+) = 0$$

(*b*)
$$i_C(\infty) = 0$$

(*c*)
$$i(\tau) = 0.368(24 \times 10^{-3}) = 8.8 \text{ mA}$$

(*d*)
$$v_R(\tau) = (8.8 \times 1000) \times 10^{-3} = 8.8 \text{ V}$$

24.148 For the circuit of Prob. 24.147, determine under steady state (*a*) v_C, v_R; (*b*) stored energy; and (*c*) charge.

❚ (*a*)
$$v_C(\infty) = 24 \text{ V} \qquad v_R(\infty) = 0$$

(*b*)
$$W = \tfrac{1}{2}(150 \times 10^{-6})(24)^2 = 43 \text{ mJ}$$

(*c*)
$$q = CV = 150 \times 10^{-6} \times 24 = 3.6 \text{ mC}$$

24.149 In the circuit of Prob. 24.147, calculate (*a*) the rate of energy transfer to the capacitor at $t = \tau$ and (*b*) the power dissipated at $t = \tau$.

❚
$$P_C(\tau) = v_C(\tau)i_C(\tau) = [24(0.632)]0.0088 = 0.1335 \text{ W}$$
$$P_R(\tau) = [i(\tau)]^2 R = (0.0088)^2(1000) = 77.4 \text{ mW}$$

24.150 A 100-V battery is connected in series with a 10-Ω resistor and a capacitor. If the total energy accumulated in the capacitor at steady state is 200 J, determine (*a*) the capacitance of the capacitor; (*b*) the accumulated charge in coulombs.

❚ (*a*)
$$W_{ss} = \tfrac{1}{2}CV^2 \qquad 200 = \tfrac{1}{2}C(100)^2 \qquad C = 0.04 \text{ F}$$

(*b*)
$$q = CV \qquad q = (0.04)(100) = 4 \text{ C}$$

24.151 A 600-μF capacitor is charged to 400 V. It is then discharged through a 2-kΩ resistor. Calculate: (*a*) $i(0_+)$ and (*b*) $v_C(3\,\text{s})$.

❚ (*a*)
$$i(0_+) = 400/2000 = 0.2 \text{ A}$$

(*b*)
$$v_C(t) = V_0 e^{-t/RC} = 400 e^{-t/1.2} \qquad \text{or} \qquad v_C(3) = 400 e^{-3/1.2} = 32.83 \text{ V}$$

24.152 Given the following ideal inductors (zero resistance): 2.5 H, 6.3 H, and 5.2 H. Determine (a) the equivalent inductance if connected in series; (b) the equivalent inductance if connected in parallel.

▌ (a)
$$L_{eq,S} = L_1 + L_2 + L_3 = 2.5 + 6.3 + 5.2 = 14\,H$$

(b)
$$\frac{1}{L_{eq,P}} = \frac{1}{2.5} + \frac{1}{6.3} + \frac{1}{5.2} \qquad L_{eq,P} = 1.33\,H$$

24.153 Sketch the current in a series $\overset{\cdot}{RL}$ circuit connected across a battery at $t = 0$. Plot the normalized current as a function of the time constant.

▌ See Fig. 24-47, where $i_{norm} = i/(V/R)$.

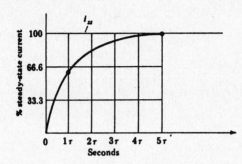

Fig. 24-47

24.154 Develop a graphical method for the determination of the time constant of an RL series circuit.

▌ Since
$$i = \frac{V}{R}(1 - e^{-t/\tau}) = \frac{V}{R}[1 - e^{-(R/L)t}]$$

$$\frac{di}{dt} = \frac{V}{L} e^{-(R/L)t} \qquad \text{and} \qquad \frac{di}{dt}(0_+) = \frac{V}{L} \tag{1}$$

Now, from Fig. 24-48:

$$\frac{\Delta I}{\Delta T}(0_+) = \frac{i_{ss}}{\Delta T} = \frac{V/R}{\Delta T} = \frac{V}{R\,\Delta T} \tag{2}$$

For (1) and (2) to be equivalent

$$\frac{V}{L} = \frac{V}{R\,\Delta T}$$

Hence,
$$\frac{L}{R} = \tau = \Delta T$$

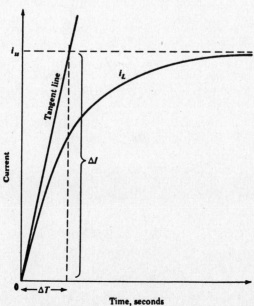

Fig. 24-48

24.155 The time constant of an *LR* circuit was determined to be 2.4 ms from an oscilloscope recording. An ohmmeter measurement of the circuit indicates the circuit resistance to be 2000 Ω. Determine the circuit inductance.

∎
$$\tau = \frac{L}{R} \qquad 0.0024 = \frac{L}{2000} \qquad L = 4.8 \text{ H}$$

24.156 A coil whose resistance and inductance are 2.0 Ω and 8.0 Ω, respectively, is connected to a 12-V battery and a switch. Determine *(a)* the steady-state current; *(b)* the time constant; *(c)* the current after one time constant has elapsed; *(d)* the current after 20 time constants have elapsed.

∎ *(a)*
$$i_{ss} = \frac{E_{bat}}{R} = \frac{12}{2} = 6 \text{ A}$$

(b)
$$\tau = \frac{L}{R} = \frac{8}{2} = 4 \text{ s}$$

(c)
$$i|_{t=1\tau} = 0.632(6) = 3.9 \text{ A}$$

(d) After 20τ, which is $20 \times 4 = 80$ s, the circuit is at essentially steady state: $i_{ss} \approx 6$ A.

24.157 The shunt-field circuit of a certain 30-hp dc motor has a resistance of 55.0 Ω and an inductance of 120 H. Calculate the accumulated energy stored in the magnetic field when the switch is closed and the current attains its steady-state value. Assume the driving voltage is 240 V dc.

∎
$$I_{ss} = \frac{E}{R} = \frac{240}{55} = 4.363 \text{ A} \qquad W_{\phi,ss} = \tfrac{1}{2} L I_{ss}^2 = \tfrac{1}{2}(120)(4.363)^2 = 1142 \text{ J}$$

24.158 A coil is connected in series with a 24-V battery and a switch as shown in Fig. 24-49*a*. The inductance and resistance of the coil are 6.0 H and 2.0 Ω, respectively. Determine *(a)* the time constant; *(b)* the steady-state current; *(c)* the current at one time constant; *(d)* the voltage drop caused by the inductance at one time constant; *(e)* the energy stored in the magnetic field when the current reaches steady state.

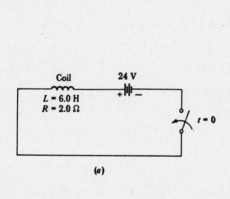

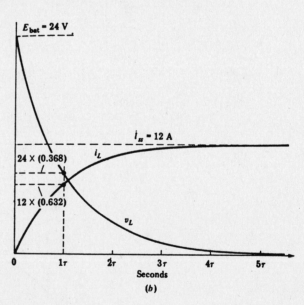

Fig. 24-49

∎ Figure 24-49*b* illustrates the v_L and i_L curves for the circuit.

(a)
$$\tau = \frac{L}{R} = \frac{6}{2} = 3.0 \text{ s}$$

(b)
$$i_{ss} = \frac{E_{bat}}{R} = \frac{24}{2.0} = 12 \text{ A}$$

(c)
$$i_{L,1\tau} = 12(0.632) = 7.58 \text{ A}$$

(d)
$$v_{L,1\tau} = 0.368(24) = 8.83 \text{ V}$$

(e)
$$W_{\phi,ss} = \tfrac{1}{2} L i_{ss}^2 = \tfrac{1}{2}(6)(12)^2 = 432 \text{ J}$$

24.159 In the circuit of Prob. 24.158 obtain (*a*) *the rate of expenditure* of heat energy at t = one time constant; (*b*) the *rate of accumulation* of magnetic energy at t = one time constant; (*c*) the magnetic energy accumulated 80 s after the switch has been closed; (*d*) the *rate of expenditure* of heat energy at steady state; (*e*) the *rate of accumulation* of magnetic energy at steady state.

(*a*)
$$P_{\text{heat},1\tau} = i^2 R = (7.584)^2(2) = 115.0 \text{ W}$$

(*b*)
$$P_{\phi,1\tau} = v_L i_L = 8.832(7.584) = 66.98 \text{ W}$$

(*c*)
$$80 \text{ s} = \frac{80}{3.0} = 26.7 \text{ time constants}$$

Hence, current is at steady state.

$$W_{\phi,\text{ss}} = \tfrac{1}{2} L i_{\text{ss}}^2 = 432 \text{ J}$$

(*d*)
$$P_{\text{heat,ss}} = i_{\text{ss}}^2 R = (12)^2(2) = 288 \text{ W}$$

(*e*)
$$P_{\phi,\text{ss}} = v_L i_L = 0(2) = 0 \text{ W}$$

24.160 An inductor whose resistance and inductance are $2.0\,\Omega$ and $6.0\,\text{H}$, respectively, is connected in series with a $10\text{-}\Omega$ resistor, a switch, and a 12-V battery as shown in Fig. 24-50. Another switch is connected across the $10\text{-}\Omega$ resistor. If both switches are closed, the steady-state circuit current is

$$I_{\text{ss}} = \frac{E_{\text{bat}}}{R} = \frac{12}{2.0} = 6.0 \text{ A}$$

The energy accumulated in the magnetic field of the inductor at steady state is

$$W_{\phi,\text{ss}} = \tfrac{1}{2} L i_{\text{ss}}^2 = \tfrac{1}{2}(6)(6)^2 = 108 \text{ J}$$

Opening switch 2 introduces an additional $10\,\Omega$ in series with the inductor. This causes the current to change to a lower value, resulting in the release of some stored energy.

The new steady-state current is

$$I_{\text{ss}} = \frac{E_{\text{bat}}}{R} = \frac{12}{2 + 10} = 1 \text{ A}$$

The energy remaining in the magnetic field of the inductor, at the new steady-state current, is

$$W_{\phi,\text{ss}} = \tfrac{1}{2} L i_{\text{ss}}^2 = \tfrac{1}{2}(6)(1)^2 = 3 \text{ J}$$

Thus the total energy released from the magnetic field after switch 2 was opened is

$$W_{\text{released}} = 108 - 3 = 105 \text{ J}$$

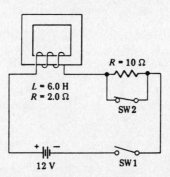

Fig. 24-50

24.161 Sketch the behavior of the current for the two conditions stated in Prob. 24.160.

See Fig. 24-51. Note that the time constant of the circuit with switch 2 closed was

$$\tau = \frac{L}{R} = \frac{6}{2} = 3 \text{ s}$$

but the time constant for the circuit with switch 2 open is

$$\tau = \frac{L}{R} = \frac{6}{2 + 10} = 0.5 \text{ s}$$

The difference in time constants accounts for the slow buildup of current to 6 A and the rapid decrease to 1 A as shown.

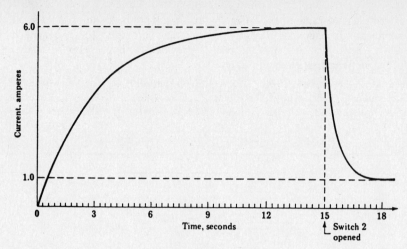

Fig. 24-51

24.162 A purely inductive circuit carries a current $i = I_m \sin t$. Sketch the current and energy stored in the inductor as functions of time.

▌ See Fig. 24-52.

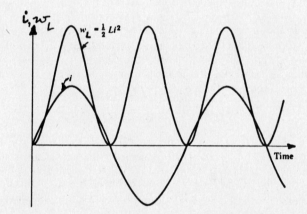

Fig. 24-52

24.163 What is the equivalent inductance of the following series-connected inductors: 5 H, 1 H, 100 H, and 12 H?

▌ $$L_{es} = 5 + 1 + 100 + 12 = 118 \text{ H}$$

24.164 The inductors of Prob. 24.163 are connected in parallel. Find the equivalent inductance.

▌ $$\frac{1}{L_{ep}} = \frac{1}{5} + \frac{1}{1} + \frac{1}{100} + \frac{1}{12} = 0.773 \text{ H}$$

24.165 A 10-H 16-Ω coil is connected in series with a 4.0-Ω resistor, a 120-V battery, and a switch. Determine (a) the time constant of the coil; (b) the time constant of the circuit; (c) the steady-state current; (d) the current at $t =$ one time constant after the switch is closed.

▌ (a) $$\tau_{coil} = \frac{L_{coil}}{R_{coil}} = \frac{10}{16} = 0.63 \text{ s}$$

(b) $$\tau_{circ} = \frac{L_{circ}}{R_{circ}} = \frac{10}{16 + 4} = 0.5 \text{ s}$$

(c) $$I = \frac{E_{bat}}{R} = \frac{120}{16 + 4} = 6 \text{ A}$$

(d) $$i|_{t=\tau} = 0.632 \times 6 = 3.79 \text{ A}$$

24.166 In the circuit of Prob. 24.165, determine (a) the voltage across the coil at $t = \tau$ and (b) the steady-state voltage across the coil.

▮ (a) $\qquad E_{\text{bat}} = v_{\text{coil}} + v_R \qquad 120 = v_{\text{coil}} + iR = v_{\text{coil}} + 3.79(4) \qquad v_{\text{coil}} = 104.84 \text{ V}$

(b) $\qquad E_{\text{bat}} = v_{\text{coil}} + iR \qquad 120 = v_{\text{coil}} + 6(4) \qquad v_{\text{coil}} = 96 \text{ V}$

24.167 An 8.0-H 4.0-Ω coil is connected in series with a 2.0-Ω resistor, a 6.0-V battery, and a switch. Sketch the circuit and determine (a) the initial current when the switch is closed; (b) the final current; (c) the voltage drop across the coil at $t = (0_+)$; (d) the current in the 2.0-Ω resistor at $t =$ one time constant; (e) the voltage across the 2.0-Ω resistor at $t =$ one time constant.

▮ (a) $i(0_+) = 0$. See Fig. 24-53.

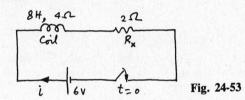

Fig. 24-53

(b) $\qquad i_{ss} = \dfrac{E_{\text{bat}}}{R_{\text{coil}} + R_R} = \dfrac{6}{4 + 2} = 1 \text{ A}$

(c) $\qquad E_{\text{bat}} = v_{\text{coil}} + iR \qquad 6 = v_{\text{coil}} + 0(2) \qquad v_{\text{coil}}(0_+) = 6 \text{ V}$

(d) $\qquad i|_{t=\tau} = 0.632(1) = 0.632 \text{ A}$

(e) $\qquad v_{2\,\Omega} = 0.632 \times 2 = 1.264 \text{ V}$

24.168 In the circuit of Prob. 24.167, if the 2.0-Ω resistor is to be replaced by another that would cause the time constant of the circuit to be $\frac{1}{3}$ s, determine the resistance value of the new resistor.

▮ $\qquad \tau_{\text{ckt}} = \dfrac{L_{\text{ckt}}}{R_{\text{ckt}}} \qquad \text{or} \qquad \dfrac{1}{3} = \dfrac{8}{R_{\text{ckt}}}$

Thus, $\qquad R_{\text{ckt}} = 24 \ \Omega = R_{\text{coil}} + R_X = 4 + R_X$

and $\qquad R_X = 20 \ \Omega$

24.169 A 10-Ω resistor, a 24-V battery, and a switch are connected in series with a coil whose resistance and inductance are 20 Ω and 6.0 H, respectively. Determine (a) the current at the instant the switch is closed $(t = 0_+)$; (b) the steady-state current; (c) the circuit time constant; (d) the current in the circuit and the voltage across the 10-Ω resistor at $t = 1\tau$; (e) the energy stored in the magnetic field at steady state.

▮ (a) $\qquad\qquad\qquad i(0_+) = 0$

(b) $\qquad\qquad\qquad i_{ss} = \dfrac{24}{10 + 20} = 0.8 \text{ A}$

(c) $\qquad\qquad\qquad \tau_{\text{cir}} = \dfrac{L_{\text{cir}}}{R_{\text{cir}}} = \dfrac{6}{30} = 0.2 \text{ s}$

(d) $\qquad i|_{t=\tau} = 0.632 \times 0.8 = 0.51 \text{ A} \qquad v_R|_{t=\tau} = iR = 0.51(10) = 5.1 \text{ V}$

(e) $\qquad\quad W = \frac{1}{2}LI^2 \qquad W_{ss} = \frac{1}{2}(6)(0.8)^2 = 1.92 \text{ J}$

24.170 A 6.0-H coil whose resistance is 12 Ω is connected in series with a 24-Ω resistor, a 144-V battery, and a switch. The switch is closed at $t = 0$. Determine (a) the time constant of the coil; (b) the time constant of the circuit; (c) the current at $t = (0_+)$; (d) the steady-state current; (e) the energy stored in the magnetic field at steady state.

▮ (a) $\qquad\qquad\qquad \tau_{\text{coil}} = \frac{6}{12} = 0.5 \text{ s}$

(b) $\qquad\qquad\qquad \tau_{\text{circ}} = \dfrac{6}{12 + 24} = 0.17 \text{ s}$

(c) $\qquad\qquad\qquad i|_{t=0_+} = 0$

(d) $\qquad\qquad\qquad i_{ss} = \dfrac{E_{\text{bat}}}{R_{\text{circ}}} = \dfrac{144}{12 + 24} = 4 \text{ A}$

(e) $\qquad W_{ss} = \frac{1}{2}Li_{ss}^2 = \frac{1}{2}(6)(4)^2 = 48 \text{ J}$

24.171 In the circuit of Prob. 24.170, determine: (*a*) the heat power dissipated by the coil at $t = \tau_{\text{circ}}$; (*b*) the heat power dissipated by the circuit at $t = \tau_{\text{circ}}$; (*c*) the rate of storage of energy in the magnetic field at $t = \tau_{\text{circ}}$.

▌ (*a*) $$P_{H(\text{coil})} = i^2 R_{\text{coil}} \qquad P_{H(\text{coil})}|_{t=\tau} = [(0.632)(4)]^2 12 = 76.69 \text{ W}$$

(*b*) $$P_{H(\text{circ})}|_{t=\tau} = [(0.632)(4)]^2 (12 + 24) = 230.1 \text{ W}$$

(*c*) $$E_{\text{bat}} = v_L + i R_{\text{coil}} + iR$$

At $t = \tau$, $$i_L = (0.632)(4) = 2.53 \text{ A}$$

$$144 = v_L + 2.53[12 + 24] \qquad v_L = 52.99 \text{ V}$$

$$P_\phi|_{t=\tau} = v_L i_L = (52.99)(2.53) = 133.96 \text{ W}$$

24.172 A coil whose resistance and inductance are $3.0\,\Omega$ and $10\,\text{H}$, respectively, is connected in series with a $2.0\text{-}\Omega$ resistor, a 60-V battery, and a switch. Determine (*a*) the time constant of the circuit; (*b*) the current at $t = (0_+)$; (*c*) the steady-state current; (*d*) the energy stored in the magnetic field at steady state.

▌ (*a*) $$\tau_{\text{circ}} = \frac{10}{3 + 2} = 2 \text{ s}$$

(*b*) $$i(0_+) = 0$$

(*c*) $$i_{\text{ss}} = \frac{E_{\text{bat}}}{R_{\text{circ}}} = \frac{60}{3 + 2} = 12 \text{ A}$$

(*d*) $$W_{\text{ss}} = \tfrac{1}{2} L i_{\text{ss}}^2 = \tfrac{1}{2}(10)(12)^2 = 720 \text{ J}$$

24.173 In the circuit of Prob. 24.172, determine (*a*) the heat power dissipated by the coil at an elapsed time equal to one time constant; (*b*) the rate of storage of energy at $t = $ one time constant.

▌ (*a*) $$P_{\text{heat(coil)}} = i^2 R_{\text{coil}} \qquad P_{H(\text{coil})}|_{t=\tau} = (0.632 \times 12)^2 3 = 172.55 \text{ W}$$

(*b*) $$P_\phi = v_L i_L \qquad i_L|_{t=\tau} = (0.632)12 = 7.58 \text{ A} \qquad E_{\text{bat}} = v_L + i R_{\text{coil}} + iR$$

At $t = \tau$, $$60 = v_L + 7.58(3 + 2)$$

$$v_L|_{t=\tau} = 22.10 \text{ V} \qquad P_\phi|_{t=\tau} = 22.1 \times 7.58 = 167.5 \text{ J}$$

24.174 A $6.0\text{-}\Omega$ 4.0-H coil is connected in series with a $2.0\text{-}\Omega$ resistor, a switch, and a 48-V 0-Hz generator. Determine (*a*) the circuit time constant; (*b*) the current at $t = (0_+)$; (*c*) the steady-state current; (*d*) the current at $t = 1\tau$.

▌ (*a*) $$\tau_{\text{circ}} = \frac{4}{6 + 2} = 0.5 \text{ s}$$

(*b*) $$i|_{t=0_+} = 0$$

(*c*) $$i_{\text{ss}} = \frac{E_{\text{bat}}}{R_{\text{circ}}} = \frac{48}{6 + 2} = 6 \text{ A}$$

(*d*) $$i|_{t=\tau} = (0.632)6 = 3.79 \text{ A}$$

24.175 In the circuit of Prob. 24.174, determine, under steady state, (*a*) v_R; (*b*) v_{coil}; (*c*) the energy stored in the magnetic field.

▌ (*a*) $$v_{R(\text{ss})} = i_{\text{ss}} R = 6 \times 2 = 12 \text{ V}$$

(*b*) $$E_{\text{bat}} = v_{\text{coil}} + v_R$$

At steady state, $$48 = v_{\text{coil(ss)}} + 12 \qquad v_{\text{coil(ss)}} = 36 \text{ V}$$

(*c*) $$W_{\phi(\text{ss})} = \tfrac{1}{2} L i_{\text{ss}}^2 = \tfrac{1}{2}(4)(6)^2 = 72 \text{ J}$$

24.176 In the circuit of Prob. 24.174 determine (*a*) the voltage induced in the coil at $t = 1\tau$; (*b*) the rate of storage of energy in the magnetic field at $t = 1\tau$; (*c*) the rate of expenditure of heat energy in the coil at $t = 1\tau$.

▌ (*a*) $$E_{\text{bat}} = v_{\text{coil}} + v_R = \underbrace{[v_{L(\text{coil})} + v_{R(\text{coil})}]}_{\text{coil}} + v_R = v_{L(\text{coil})} + i R_{\text{coil}} + iR$$

At $t = \tau$, $$48 = v_{L(\text{coil})} + 3.79(6 + 2) \qquad v_{L(\text{coil})}|_{t=\tau} = 17.68 \text{ V}$$

(b) $$P_\phi = v_L i_L$$

At $t = \tau$, $$P_\phi = (17.68)(3.79) = 67.01 \text{ W}$$

(c) $$P_{H(\text{coil})} = i^2 R_{\text{coil}}$$

At $t = \tau$, $$P_{H(\text{coil})} = (3.79)^2 6 = 86.18 \text{ W}$$

24.177 A certain sinusoidal voltage is expressed mathematically by $e = 0.40 \sin 377t$ V. Determine (*a*) the frequency of the wave; (*b*) the period; (*c*) the value of the voltage when the elapsed time is 0.01 s.

▌ **(a)** $$\omega = 2\pi f \qquad 377 = 2\pi f \qquad f = 60 \text{ Hz}$$

(b) $$T = \frac{1}{f} = \frac{1}{60} = 0.0167 \text{ s}$$

(c) $$e = 0.4 \sin (377 \times 0.01) = 0.4 \sin (3.77) = 0.4(-0.588) = -0.235 \text{ V}$$

24.178 (*a*) What is the equation of a sinusoidal voltage wave that has a maximum value of 200 V and a frequency of 50 Hz? (*b*) What is the value of voltage 0.0025 s after the wave crosses the ωt axis going in the positive direction?

▌ **(a)** $$e = E_m \sin 2\pi f t = 200 \sin 2\pi 50 t = 200 \sin 314.16 t$$

(b) $$e = 200 \sin (314.16 \times 0.0025) = 200 \sin (0.7854) = 200(0.707) = 141 \text{ V}$$

24.179 For the voltage wave and time-zero corresponding to Fig. 24-54, angle $\beta = 30°$, $f = 60$ Hz, and $E_m = 100$ V. Determine the voltage 0.0080 s after the switch is closed.

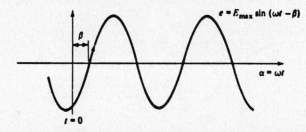

t = 0   **Fig. 24-54**

▌ $$e = E_{\text{max}} \sin (\omega t - \beta) = 100 \sin (2\pi 60 t - 30°) = 100 \sin [2\pi 60 (0.008)(57.3) - 30]° = 100 \sin (142.81)° = 60 \text{ V}$$

24.180 The equation for a sinusoidal current wave is
$$i = 25 \sin \left(208 t + \frac{\pi}{3} \right)$$

Determine (*a*) the frequency; (*b*) the period; (*c*) the current at $t = 0.012$ s.

▌ **(a)** $$\omega = 208 \text{ rad/s} \qquad 2\pi f = 208 \qquad f = \frac{208}{2\pi} = 33.10 \text{ Hz}$$

(b) $$T = \frac{1}{f} = \frac{1}{33.1} = 0.030 \text{ s}$$

(c) $$i = 25 \sin [208(0.012) + \pi/3] = 25 \sin [3.543] = 25(-0.3909) = -9.77 \text{ A}$$

24.181 The equation of a certain sinusoidal voltage wave is given by $e = 120 \sin 230t$. Determine (*a*) the maximum value of the wave; (*b*) the rms value; (*c*) the frequency; (*d*) the instantaneous voltage 0.01 s after the wave passes the zero-voltage value going in the positive direction; (*e*) the period of the wave.

▌ **(a)** $$E_m = 120 \text{ V}$$

(b) $$E = 120(0.707) = 84.84 \text{ V}$$

(c) $$\omega = 230 = 2\pi f \qquad \text{rad/s} \qquad f = \frac{230}{2\pi} = 36.62 \text{ Hz}$$

(d) $$e = 120 \sin [230(0.01)]^R = 120 \sin (2.3)^R = 120(0.7457) = 89.5 \text{ V}$$

(e) $$T = \frac{1}{f} = \frac{1}{36.6} = 0.027 \text{ s}$$

24.182 A 240-V 25-Hz sinusoidal generator is connected to a 20-Ω resistor through a circuit breaker and an ammeter as shown in Fig. 24-55a. Determine (a) the ammeter reading; (b) the period of the wave; (c) the average power; (d) the equation for the current wave if the circuit breaker is closed 30° after the wave crosses the time axis going in the positive direction; (e) the instantaneous current when the elapsed time is 0.01 s; (f) the ammeter reading if the generator is replaced by a 240-V battery.

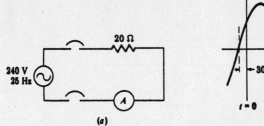 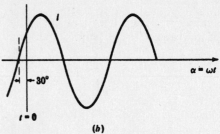

(a) (b)

Fig. 24-55

(a)
$$I_R = \frac{V_R}{R} = \frac{240}{20} = 12 \text{ A}$$

(b)
$$T = \frac{1}{f} = \frac{1}{25} = 0.040 \text{ s}$$

(c)
$$P_{av} = I_R^2 R = (12)^2(20) = 2880 \text{ W}$$
$$= V_R I_R = (240)(12) = 2880 \text{ W}$$
$$= \frac{V_R^2}{R} = \frac{(240)^2}{20} = 2880 \text{ W}$$

(d) The current wave is sketched in Fig. 24-55b.

$$I_m = 12\sqrt{2} = 16.97 \text{ A} \qquad \omega = 2\pi f = 2\pi(25) = 157 \text{ rad/s} \qquad \beta = 30° \qquad i = 16.97 \sin(157t + 30°)$$

(e)
$$i = 16.97 \sin[(157 \times 0.01)^R + 30°]$$

Changing radians to degrees,
$$i = 16.97 \sin[(1.57 \times 57.3) + 30]° = 16.97 \sin(119.96)° = 14.7 \text{ A}$$

Or, using radians, $\quad i = 16.97 \sin\left(1.57 + \frac{30}{57.3}\right)^R = 16.97 \sin(2.09)^R = 14.7 \text{ A}$

(f)
$$I_R = \frac{E_{bat}}{R} = \frac{240}{20} = 12 \text{ A}$$

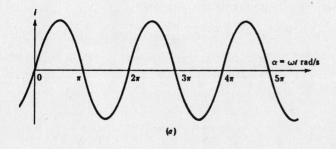

(a)

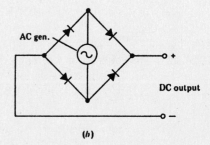

(b)

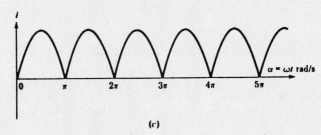

(c)

Fig. 24-56

24.183 A sinusoidal current, shown in Fig. 24-56a, is rectified by the circuit of Fig. 24-56b, to obtain the rectified wave of Fig. 24-56c. Determine the average value of the rectified wave.

❚ $I_{av} = \dfrac{1}{2\pi}\left[\int_{\alpha=0}^{\pi} I_m \sin \alpha\, d\alpha + \int_{\pi}^{2\pi} - I_m \sin \alpha\, d\alpha\right] = \dfrac{I_m}{2\pi}\left(-\cos \alpha\,\big|_0^{\pi} + \cos \alpha\,\big|_{\pi}^{2\pi}\right) = \dfrac{I_m}{2\pi}\,(2+2) = \dfrac{2I_m}{\pi}$

24.184 Figure 24-57 shows two sinusoidal generators of the same frequency connected in series with a 20-Ω resistor and a switch. The voltage equations indicate the values of the respective generator voltages for the instant the switch is closed $(t = 0)$, and for all elapsed time thereafter. Calculate the current at $t = 0$.

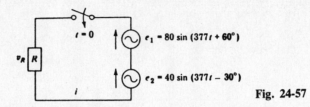

$e_1 = 80 \sin (377t + 60°)$

$e_2 = 40 \sin (377t - 30°)$

Fig. 24-57

❚ When the switch is closed, the voltage impressed across the resistor will be $(e_1 + e_2)$, and the current to the resistor will be

$$i = \frac{v_R}{R} = \frac{e_1 + e_2}{R}$$

where $\qquad e_1 = 80 \sin (377t + 60°) \qquad$ and $\qquad e_2 = 40 \sin (377t - 30°)$

Thus, $\qquad\qquad i = \dfrac{80 \sin (377t + 60°) + 40(\sin 377t - 30°)}{20}$

The current at the instant the switch is closed $(t = 0)$ is

$$i\big|_{t=0} = \frac{80 \sin 60° + 40 \sin (-30°)}{20} = \frac{69.28 - 20}{20} = 2.46 \text{ A}$$

24.185 Repeat Prob. 24.184 for $t = 0.02$ s.

❚ The current, after an elapsed time of 0.02 s, is

$$i\big|_{t=0.02} = \frac{80 \sin [377(0.02)(57.3) + 60]° + 40 \sin [377(0.02)(57.3) - 30]°}{20} = \frac{59.41 + 26.79}{20} = 4.31 \text{ A}$$

24.186 (a) Write the equation of a voltage wave that has a maximum value of 300 V and a frequency of 25 Hz; (b) what is the instantaneous value of voltage 10 s after the wave passes the zero position going in the positive direction?

(a) $\qquad\qquad e = E_{max} \sin (2\pi ft + \phi) = 300 \sin (2\pi 25t)$

(b) $\qquad\qquad e\big|_{t=10} = 300 \sin (157.08 \times 10)^R = 0 \text{ V}$

24.187 The equation of a certain current wave is $i = 32 \sin 375t$. Determine (a) the maximum value of the wave; (b) the frequency; (c) the period; (d) the instantaneous value of current 0.060 s after the wave passes the zero position going in the positive direction.

❚ (a) $\qquad\qquad\qquad I_{max} = 32 \text{ A}$

(b) $\qquad\qquad\qquad 2\pi f = 375 \qquad f = 59.68 \text{ Hz}$

(c) $\qquad\qquad\qquad T = \dfrac{1}{f} = \dfrac{1}{59.68} = 0.017 \text{ s}$

(d) $\qquad\qquad\qquad i = 32 \sin (375 \times 0.06)^R = -15.64 \text{ A}$

24.188 The equation of the generated emf of an alternator is $e = 100 \sin 157t$. Determine (a) the maximum instantaneous voltage; (b) the rms value of voltage; (c) the average value of voltage; (d) the frequency; (e) the period of the wave; (f) the instantaneous value of voltage when $t = 0.020$ s.

❚ (a) $\qquad\qquad\qquad E_{max} = 100 \text{ V}$

(b) $\qquad\qquad\qquad E = 100/\sqrt{2} = 70.71 \text{ V}$

(c) $$E_{avg} = 0$$

(d) $$2\pi f = 157 \qquad f = 24.99 \text{ Hz}$$

(e) $$T = \frac{1}{f} = \frac{1}{24.99} = 0.04 \text{ s}$$

(f) $$e = 100 \sin [157(0.02)(57.3)]° \qquad e|_{t=0.02} = 0.136 \text{ V}$$

24.189 The equation of a voltage wave is $e = 100 \sin 188t$ and that of its corresponding current wave is $i = 20 \sin [188t + (\pi/2)]$. Determine (a) the frequency of the voltage wave; (b) the frequency of the current wave; (c) the maximum value of the voltage; (d) the equivalent dc value of the current wave.

▌ (a) $$2\pi f = 188 \qquad f = 29.92 \text{ Hz}$$

(b) $$2\pi f = 188 \qquad f = 29.92 \text{ Hz}$$

(c) $$E_{max} = 100 \text{ V}$$

(d) $$I = 20/\sqrt{2} = 14.14 \text{ A}$$

24.190 From the data of Prob. 24.189, determine (a) the magnitude of the current when the voltage is zero and (b) the phase angle between the two waves. (c) Sketch the two waves on one set of coordinate axes.

▌ (a) The voltage is zero at $t = 0$. Hence

$$i = 20 \sin [188 \times 0 + (\pi/2)] = 20 \text{ A}$$

(b) $\pi/2$ rad or 90°.

(c) See Fig. 24-58.

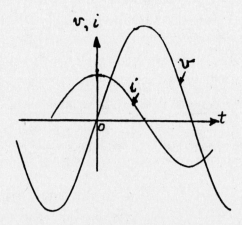

Fig. 24-58

24.191 The equation of a current wave passing through a 10-Ω resistor is $i = 2.08 \sin 1000t$. Calculate (a) the average power; (b) the maximum instantaneous power; (c) the power at an elapsed time of 0.001 s.

▌ (a) $$P = I^2R \qquad I = 2.08/\sqrt{2} = 1.471 \text{ A} \qquad P = (1.471)^2(10) = 21.63 \text{ W}$$

(b) $$P_{max} = I_{max}^2 R = (2.08)^2(10) = 43.26 \text{ W}$$

(c) $$i|_{t=0.001} = 2.08 \sin (1000 \times 0.001)^R = 1.75 \text{ A} \qquad P = i^2R = (1.75)^2R = 30.64 \text{ W}$$

24.192 If the current of Prob. 24.191 is rectified by a full-wave rectifier, determine the rms and average values of the output current.

▌ $$I_{rms} = 2.08/\sqrt{2} = 1.471 \text{ A} \qquad I_{av} = 2.08(2/\pi) = 1.324 \text{ A}$$

24.193 A 2000-Ω resistor is connected across a 240-V 60-Hz generator. (a) Calculate the current; (b) calculate the power.

▌ (a) $$I = V/R = 240/2000 = 0.12 \text{ A}$$

(b) $$P = I^2R = (0.12)^2 2000 = 28.8 \text{ W}$$

24.194 A certain incandescent lamp draws 100 W when connected to a 120-V 60-Hz generator. (*a*) Calculate the resistance of the lamp; (*b*) calculate the current; (*c*) write the equation of the current wave.

❚ (*a*) $$P = V^2/R \qquad 100 = (120)^2/R \qquad R = 144\ \Omega$$

(*b*) $$P = VI \qquad 100 = 120I \qquad I = 0.833\ \text{A}$$

(*c*) $$i = 0.833\sqrt{2}\sin(2\pi 60t) = 1.18\sin 377t$$

24.195 A 440-V 60-Hz voltage wave, when impressed across a certain resistor, dissipates energy at the rate of 10.0 kW. Determine (*a*) the rms value of current; (*b*) the maximum value of current.

❚ (*a*) $$P = VI \qquad 10,000 = 440I \qquad I = 22.73\ \text{A}$$

(*b*) $$I_{\max} = 22.73\sqrt{2} = 32.15\ \text{A}$$

24.196 From the data of Prob. 24.195, obtain (*a*) the maximum instantaneous value of power; (*b*) the average value of power; (*c*) the resistance of the load.

❚ (*a*) $$P_{\max} = V_{\max}I_{\max} = (440\sqrt{2})(32.15) = 20\ \text{kW}$$

(*b*) $$P_{\text{av}} = 10\ \text{kW}$$

(*c*) $$P = V^2/R \qquad 10,000 = (440)^2/R \qquad R = 19.36\ \Omega$$

24.197 Repeat Probs. 24.195 and 24.196 if the input to the resistor is 440 V dc.

❚ From the data of Prob. 24.195,

(*a*) $$P = VI \qquad 10,000 = 440I \qquad I = 22.73\ \text{A}$$

(*b*) $$I = 22.73\ \text{A}$$

For parts *a* to *c* of Prob. 24.196, we have

(*a*) $$P_{\max} = 10\ \text{kW}$$

(*b*) $$P_{\text{av}} = 10\ \text{kW}$$

(*c*) $$P = V^2/R \qquad 10,000 = (440)^2/R \qquad R = 19.36\ \Omega$$

24.198 (*a*) Write the equations for the current and voltage waves in Fig. 24-59. Determine (*b*) the current at $t = 0.1$ s; (*c*) the rms value of the current wave; (*d*) the average value of the current wave; (*e*) the average value if the current wave is rectified.

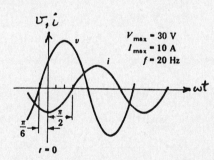

Fig. 24-59

❚ (*a*) $$v = 30\sin[2\pi 20t + (\pi/6)] \qquad i = 10\sin[2\pi 20t - (\pi/2)]$$

(*b*) $$i = 10\sin[125.66 \times 0.1 - (\pi/2)]^R \qquad i|_{t=0.1} = -10\ \text{A}$$

(*c*) $$I = 10/\sqrt{2} = 7.07\ \text{A}$$

(*d*) $$I_{\text{av}} = 0$$

(*e*) $$I_{\text{av}} = 10(2/\pi) = 6.37\ \text{A}$$

24.199 (*a*) Write the time-domain equations corresponding to the sinusoidal waves in Fig. 24-60. Determine (*b*) the current and voltage at $t = 0$ s; (*c*) the rms voltage; (*d*) the average value of the voltage wave; (*e*) the average value of the rectified voltage wave.

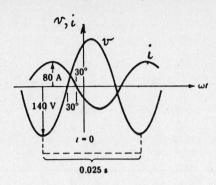

Fig. 24-60

(a)
$$T = 0.025 \text{ s} \qquad f = \frac{1}{T} = \frac{1}{0.025} = 40 \text{ Hz}$$

$$v = 140 \sin [2\pi 40t + 60°] = 140 \sin [251.3t + 60°] \qquad i = 80 \sin [251.3t - 150°]$$

(b) $\qquad v|_{t=0} = 140 \sin [0 + 60°] = 121.24 \text{ V} \qquad i|_{t=0} = 80 \sin [0 - 150°] = -40 \text{ A}$

(c) $\qquad V = 140/\sqrt{2} = 98.99 \text{ V}$

(d) $\qquad V_{av} = 0$

(e) $\qquad V_{av} = V_{max}(2/\pi) = 140(2/\pi) = 89.13 \text{ V}$

24.200 Two 60-Hz generators are connected in series and the voltage wave of one is displaced 25° away from that of the other. The amplitude of each voltage wave is 339.5 V. (*a*) Draw the phasor diagram; (*b*) calculate the magnitude of the resultant voltage; (*c*) find what angle the resultant makes with respect to the others.

(a) See Fig. 24-61.

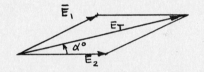

Fig. 24-61

(b)

	Σ vertical	Σ horizontal
E_1	0	339.5
E_2	339.5 sin 25°	339.5 cos 25°

$$\Sigma \text{ vertical} = 143.48 \qquad \Sigma \text{ horizontal} = 647.19 \qquad E_T = \sqrt{(143.48)^2 + (647.19)^2} = 662.9 \text{ V}$$

(c) $\qquad \alpha = \tan^{-1}\frac{\Sigma V}{\Sigma H} = \tan^{-1}\left(\frac{143.48}{647.19}\right) = 12.5° \qquad \text{from } \bar{E}_2$

24.201 Sketch the three voltage waves of Prob. 24.200, and write the equations for these waves.

See Fig. 24-62.

$$e_1 = 399.5 \sin (2\pi 60t + 25°) \qquad e_2 = 339.5 \sin (2\pi 60t + 0°) \qquad e_T = 662.9 \sin (2\pi 60t + 12.5°)$$

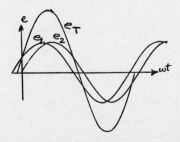

Fig. 24-62

24.202 Two 240-V dc generators, connected in series, have their voltages in phase opposition. Sketch the circuit, draw the phasor diagram, and find the resultant voltage.

▌ See Fig. 24-63a and b, from which

$$E_T = E_1 + E_2 = 240 + (-240) = 0 \text{ V}$$

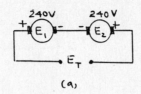

(a)

(b)   **Fig. 24-63**

24.203 Repeat Prob. 24.202 for two 60-Hz generators.

▌ See Fig. 24-64a and b, from which

$$\bar{E}_T = \bar{E}_1 + \bar{E}_2 = 240 \underline{/0°} + 240 \underline{/180°} = 0$$

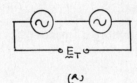

(a)

(b)   **Fig. 24-64**

24.204 The resultant magnitude of two 10-kHz voltage waves connected in series is 325 V. One of the component waves has a magnitude of 120 V and is displaced from the resultant by 25°. Draw the phasor diagram and calculate the magnitude and phase displacement of the other component.

▌ $$\bar{E}_T = 325 \underline{/25°} \qquad \bar{E}_1 = 120 \underline{/0°} \qquad \bar{E}_2 = \bar{E}_T - \bar{E}_1$$

	vertical	horizontal
$\bar{E}_T$	325 sin 25°	325 cos 25°
$\bar{E}_1$	0	120
$\bar{E}_T - \bar{E}_1$	137.35	174.55

$$E_2 = \sqrt{(137.35)^2 + (174.55)^2} = 222.11 \text{ V} \qquad \alpha = \tan^{-1}\left(\frac{\text{vertical}}{\text{horizontal}}\right) = \tan^{-1}\left(\frac{137.35}{174.55}\right) = 38.20°$$

See Fig. 24-65 for the phasor diagram.

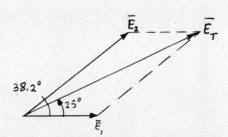

Fig. 24-65

24.205 Repeat Prob. 24.204 if the angle between $\bar{E}_1$ and $\bar{E}_T$ is 160°.

	vertical	horizontal
$\bar{E}_T$	325 sin 160°	325 cos 160°
$\bar{E}_1$	0	120
$\bar{E}_T - \bar{E}_1$	111.16	−425.4

$$E_2 = \sqrt{(111.16)^2 + (-425.4)^2} = 439.7 \text{ V}$$

$$\beta = \tan^{-1}\left[\frac{111.16}{425.4}\right] = 14.64° \qquad \alpha = 180 - 14.64 = 165.36°$$

See Fig. 24-66 for the phasor diagram.

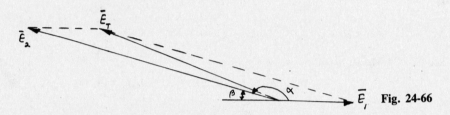

Fig. 24-66

24.206 Three 90-Hz voltage waves are displaced from each other by 120°. The respective maximum voltages are 100, 115, and 130 V. Assuming that the three generators are connected in series, draw the phasor diagram and calculate the resultant voltage.

▌ See Fig. 24-67.

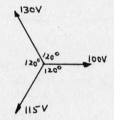

Fig. 24-67

phasor	vertical	horizontal
100 $\underline{/0°}$	0	100
130 $\underline{/120°}$	112.58	−65
115 $\underline{/240°}$	−99.59	−57.5
$\bar{E}_T$	12.99	−22.5

$$E_T = \sqrt{(12.99)^2 + (-22.5)^2} = 25.98$$

$$\beta = \tan^{-1}\left(\frac{12.99}{22.5}\right) = 30° \qquad \alpha = 180° - 30° = 150°$$

Thus,

$$\bar{E}_T = 25.98 \ \underline{/150°} \text{ V}$$

24.207 Determine the resultant of the following voltage phasors. The voltages are in series and the indicated angle is measured from the 0° reference line: 120 V at 30°; 85 V at −45°; 200 V at 0°; 191 V at 90°; 74 V at 120°. All operate at 400 Hz.

phasor	vertical	horizontal
120 /30°	60.0	103.9
85 /−45°	−60.1	60.1
200 /0°	0	200.0
191 /90°	191.0	0
74 /120°	64.1	−37.0
$\bar{E}_T$	255.1	327.0

$$E_T = \sqrt{(255.1)^2 + (327.0)^2} = 414.7 \text{ V} \quad \alpha = \tan^{-1}\left[\frac{255.1}{327}\right] = 37.9°$$

Thus, $$\bar{E}_T = 414.7 \ \underline{/37.9°}$$

24.208 Figure 24-68a shows two generators in series supplying current to a 12-Ω resistor. (a) Determine the frequency; (b) write the equations of e_1 and e_2 for the given time-zero; (c) determine the rms value of e_1; (d) sketch the corresponding phasor diagram.

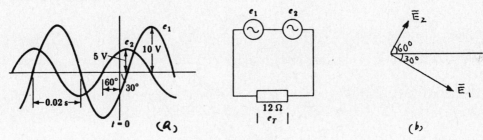

Fig. 24-68

(a) $$T = (0.02)2 = 0.04 \text{ s} \qquad f = \frac{1}{T} = \frac{1}{0.04} = 25 \text{ Hz}$$

(b) $$e_1 = 10 \sin (2\pi 25t - 30°) \qquad e_2 = 5 \sin (2\pi 25t + 60°)$$

(c) $$E_1 = 10/\sqrt{2} = 7.07 \text{ V}$$

(d) The phasor diagram is shown in Fig. 24-68b.

24.209 In the circuit of Prob. 24.208, determine the resultant E_{max} across the 12-Ω resistor and the power drawn by it at $t = 0$.

phasor	vertical	horizontal
10 /−30°	−5.00	8.66
5 /60°	4.33	2.50
$\bar{E}_T$	−0.67	11.16

$$E_T = \sqrt{(-0.67)^2 + (11.16)^2} = 11.18 \text{ V}$$

$$\alpha = \tan^{-1}\left[\frac{-0.67}{11.16}\right] = -3.44° \qquad \bar{E}_T = 11.18 \ \underline{/-3.44°} \text{ V}$$

$$P = \frac{v_T^2}{R} = \frac{[10 \sin (157 \times 0 - 30°) + 5 \sin (157 \times 0 + 60°)]^2}{12} = \frac{[-5 + 4.33]^2}{12} = 37 \text{ mW}$$

24.210 The voltage equations for three generators connected in series are

$$e_1 = 25 \sin [600t + (\pi/6)] \qquad e_2 = 60 \sin (600t + 54°) \qquad e_3 = 20 \sin (600t - 20°)$$

Determine (a) the rms value of the e_1 wave; (b) the frequency of the e_1 wave; (c) the period of the e_1 wave.

❚ $\qquad \bar{E}_1 = 25 \,\underline{/30°} \qquad \bar{E}_2 = 60 \,\underline{/54°} \qquad \bar{E}_3 = 20 \,\underline{/-20°}$

(*a*) $\qquad\qquad\qquad\qquad E_1 = 25/\sqrt{2} = 17.68 \text{ V}$

(*b*) $\qquad\qquad\qquad\qquad 2\pi f = 600 \qquad f = 95.49 \text{ Hz}$

(*c*) $\qquad\qquad\qquad\qquad T = \dfrac{1}{f} = \dfrac{1}{95.49} = 0.010 \text{ s}$

24.211 From the data of Prob. 24.210 (*a*) sketch the three waves on a common time axis using the same time-zero; (*b*) sketch the corresponding phasor diagram to scale, and determine the magnitude and phase angle of the resultant voltage by tip-to-tail addition.

❚ See Figs. 24-69*a* and *b*, respectively, for parts (*a*) and (*b*) above.   From Fig. 24-69*b* we have

$$\bar{E}_T = 93.11 \,\underline{/35.9°} \text{ V}$$

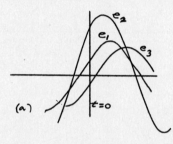

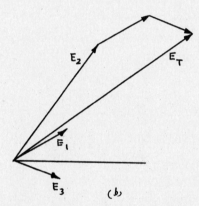

Fig. 24-69

24.212 Verify the result of part (*b*) of Prob. 24.211 using trigonometry.

❚

phasor	vertical	horizontal
25 $\underline{/30°}$	12.50	21.65
60 $\underline{/54°}$	48.54	35.26
20 $\underline{/-20°}$	−6.84	18.79
E_T	54.2	75.71

$$E_T = \sqrt{(54.2)^2 + (75.71)^2} = 93.11 \text{ V} \qquad \alpha = \tan^{-1}\left[\frac{54.2}{75.71}\right] = 35.6°$$

24.213 Two generators e_1 and e_2 are connected in series and supply current to a 10-Ω resistor.   The generator voltages are

$$e_1 = 12 \sin 125.6t \qquad e_2 = 6 \sin [125.6t + (\pi/3)]$$

(*a*) Sketch the two voltage waves on a common time axis and enter the time-zero line; (*b*) draw the corresponding phasor diagram; (*c*) calculate the maximum instantaneous voltage across the resistor.

▌ (*a*)   See Fig. 24-70*a*.

    (*b*)   See Fig. 24-70*b*.

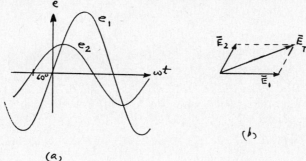

(*a*)

(*b*)

Fig. 24-70

(*c*)

phasor	vertical	horizontal
12 $\underline{/0°}$	0	12
6 $\underline{/60°}$	5.2	3
$\bar{E}_T$	5.2	15

Thus, $E_T = 15.88$ V.

24.214   In the circuit of Prob. 24.213, find   (*a*) the rms resistor current;   (*b*) its frequency;   (*c*) its value at $t = 0.01$ s.

▌ (*a*)
$$I_{rms} = \frac{E_{rms}}{R} = \frac{15.88/\sqrt{2}}{10} = 1.12 \text{ A}$$

    (*b*)
$$2\pi f = 125.6 \quad \text{or} \quad f = 19.99 \text{ Hz}$$

    (*c*)
$$i|_{t=0.01} = \frac{e_1 + e_2}{R}\bigg|_{t=0.01} = \frac{12 \sin [125.6(0.01)57.3]° + 6 \sin [125.6(0.01)57.3 + 60]°}{10}$$

$$= \frac{11.41 + 4.46}{10} = 1.59 \text{ A}$$

24.215   A series connection of three 20-Hz sinusoidal generators supplies power to a 40-Ω resistor load. The phasor voltages are

$$\bar{E}_1 = 100 \underline{/45°} \qquad \bar{E}_2 = 100 \underline{/-135°} \qquad \bar{E}_3 = 100 \underline{/90°}$$

(*a*) Sketch the three voltage waves on a common time axis and indicate time-zero;   (*b*) sketch the corresponding phasor diagram and construct the resultant voltage phasor; determine   (*c*) the phasor expression and the time-domain equation for the voltage across the resistor.

▌ (*a*)   See Fig. 24-71*a*.

    (*b*)   See Fig. 24-71*b*.

    (*c*)   From the phasor diagram, or the sketch of the voltage waves, it may be determined that $\bar{E}_1$ and $\bar{E}_2$ add to zero.   Hence the resultant voltage is

$$\bar{E}_T = \bar{E}_3 = 100 \underline{/90°} \qquad e_T = 100 \sin (2\pi 20t + 90°)$$

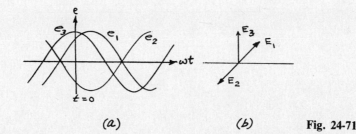

(*a*)

(*b*)

Fig. 24-71

24.216 In the circuit of Prob. 24.215, determine   (a) the rms voltage across the resistor;   (b) the rms current;   (c) the average heat power drawn by the resistor;   (d) the current at an elapsed time of 0.006 s from time-zero.

❚ (a) $$E_{T(\text{rms})} = 100/\sqrt{2} = 70.71 \text{ V}$$

(b) $$I_{\text{rms}} = 70.71/40 = 1.77 \text{ A}$$

(c) $$P = I_{\text{rms}}^2 R = (1.77)^2(40) = 125 \text{ W}$$

(d) $$i\big|_{t=0.006} = \frac{e_T}{R}\bigg|_{t=0.006} = \frac{100 \sin\left[2\pi20(0.006)57.3 + 90\right]^{\circ}}{40} = 1.82 \text{ A}$$

24.217 Three series-connected generators supply power to a 100-Ω resistor load. The time-domain equations representing the three generators are

$$e_1 = 36 \sin(377t + 56^{\circ}) \qquad e_2 = 41 \sin(377t + 76^{\circ}) \qquad e_3 = 86 \sin(377t - 54^{\circ})$$

(a) Sketch the phasor diagram;   (b) determine the resultant rms voltage across the resistor;   (c) determine the average power drawn by the resistor.

❚ (a) See Fig. 24-72.

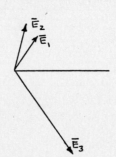

Fig. 24-72

(b)

phasor	vertical	horizontal
$36 \underline{/56^{\circ}}$	29.85	20.13
$41 \underline{/76^{\circ}}$	39.78	9.92
$86 \underline{/-54^{\circ}}$	−69.58	50.55
$\bar{E}_T$	0.05	80.60

$$E_T = \sqrt{(0.05)^2 + (80.60)^2} = 80.6 \text{ V} \qquad E_{T(\text{rms})} = 80.60/\sqrt{2} = 56.99 \text{ V}$$

(c) $$P_{\text{av}} = \frac{E_{T(\text{rms})}^2}{R} = \frac{(56.99)^2}{100} = 32.48 \text{ W}$$

24.218 Two 60-Hz sinusoidal generators are connected in series and the resultant voltage is connected across a 10-Ω resistor.   Generator 1 has an rms value of 100 V and a phase angle of 30°.   Generator 2 has an rms value of 200 V and a phase angle of −60°.   Determine   (a) the rms voltage across the resistor;   (b) the rms current through the resistor;   (c) the equations for each generator voltage as functions of time;   (d) the phasor diagram showing $\bar{E}_1$, $\bar{E}_2$, $\bar{V}_R$, and $\bar{I}_R$.

❚ (a)

phasor	vertical	horizontal
$100 \underline{/30^{\circ}}$	50.00	86.60
$200 \underline{/-60^{\circ}}$	−173.21	100.00
$\bar{E}_T$	−123.21	186.00

$$E_T = \sqrt{(-123.21)^2 + (186.0)^2} = 223.61 \text{ V} \qquad \alpha = \tan^{-1}\left(-\frac{123.21}{186.0}\right) = -33.44^{\circ}$$

(b) $$I_{\text{rms}} = \frac{223.61}{10} = 22.36 \text{ A}$$

(c) $$e_1 = 100\sqrt{2} \sin\left[2\pi60t + 30^{\circ}\right] \qquad e_2 = 200\sqrt{2} \sin\left[2\pi60t - 60^{\circ}\right]$$

(d) See Fig. 24-73.

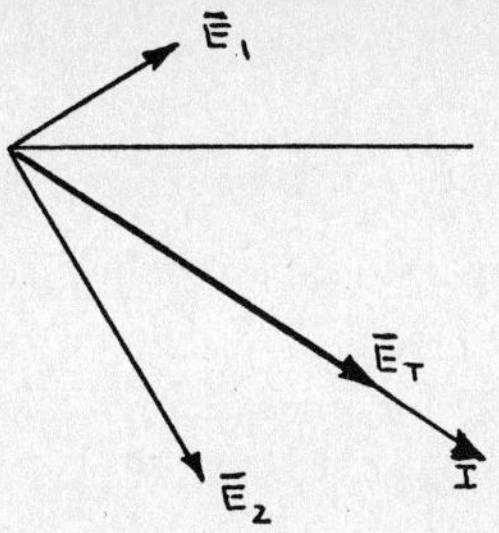

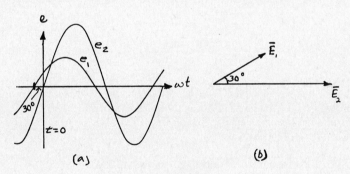

Fig. 24-73

24.219 In the circuit of Prob. 24.218, obtain the current at $t = 0.004\,s$ and the heat dissipated over a period of two cycles.

∎ $\quad i = 22.36\sqrt{2}\sin[377t - 33.4°] \qquad i|_{t=0.004} = 22.36\sqrt{2}\sin[377(0.004)57.3 - 33.4]° = 25.26\,A$

$$T = 1/60 = 0.01667 \qquad t = 2T = 2(0.01667) = 0.0333\,s$$

$$W_H = I_{rms}^2 Rt = (22.36)^2(10)(0.0333) = 166.49\,J$$

24.220 Two 50-Hz generators are connected in series and supply energy to a 10-Ω resistor. The phasors representing the generator voltages are

$$\bar{E}_1 = 50\ \underline{/30°} \qquad \bar{E}_2 = 100\ \underline{/0°}$$

(*a*) Sketch the corresponding sine waves and indicate time-zero; (*b*) sketch the corresponding phasor diagram and indicate the resultant phasor; (*c*) calculate the amplitude and phase angle of the resultant voltage.

∎ (*a*) See Fig. 24-74*a*.

(*b*) See Fig. 24-74*b*.

Fig. 24-74

(*c*)

phasor	vertical	horizontal
50 /30°	25	43.3
100 /0°	0	100
$\bar{E}_T$	25	143.3

$$E_T = \sqrt{(25)^2 + (143.3)^2} = 145.46\,V \qquad \alpha = \tan^{-1}\left[\frac{25}{143.3}\right] = 9.9°$$

24.221 In the circuit of Prob. 24.220 (*a*) determine the rms current and the average heat power dissipated; (*b*) find how much *heat energy* is expended during three cycles of the current wave.

∎ (*a*) $\qquad I_{rms} = (145.46/\sqrt{2})/10 = 10.29\,A \qquad P_H = I^2R = (10.29)^2(10) = 1058\,W$

(*b*) $\qquad T = 1/50 = 0.02\,s \qquad W_H = I^2Rt = (1058)(0.02 \times 3) = 63.5\,J$

24.222 Figure 24-75a shows a sinusoidal generator connected in series with a switch and a 20-Ω resistor. The voltage v_R across the resistor is equal to the generator voltage:

$$v_R = 100 \sin (2\pi ft + 30°)$$

Sketch the voltage v_R and i_R. Also, draw the corresponding phasor diagram.

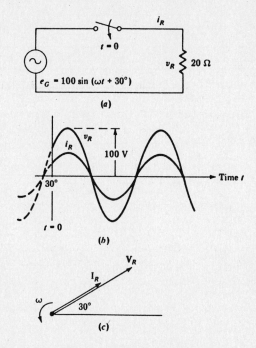

Fig. 24-75

▌ The current through the resistor, as determined by Ohm's law, is

$$i_R = \frac{v_R}{R} = \frac{100 \sin (2\pi ft + 30°)}{20} = 5 \sin (2\pi ft + 30°)$$

Note that both i_R and v_R have the same frequency and are in phase. *There is no angular difference between the current in a resistor and the voltage across it.* Expressed as phasors,

$$\bar{V}_R = 100 \underline{/30°}\ \text{V} \qquad \bar{I}_R = 5\ \underline{/30°}\ \text{A}$$

Hence, we obtain Fig. 24-75b and c.

24.223 A 258-Ω resistor is connected to a sinusoidal generator whose voltage is expressed by $e_G = 126 \sin 1131t$. Determine (a) the rms voltage; (b) the rms current; (c) the time-domain equation for the current wave; (d) the instantaneous power delivered to the resistor at $t = 0.04$ s; (e) the average heat power expended by the resistor; (f) the heat energy expended in 10 s of operation.

▌ (a) $$E_G = 126 /\sqrt{2} = 89.1 \text{ V}$$

(b) $$I_R = \frac{V_R}{R} = \frac{89.1}{258} = 0.345 \text{ A}$$

(c) $$i = 0.345\sqrt{2} \sin 1131t = 0.4879 \sin 1121t$$

(d) $$P_{\text{inst}} = vi = 126 \sin 1131t \times 0.4879 \sin 1131t$$

$$P|_{t=0.004 \text{ s}} = 126 \sin (1131 \times 0.04)^R \times 0.4879 \sin (1131 \times 0.04)^R = 119.90 \times 0.4642 = 55.6 \text{ W}$$

(e) $$P_{\text{av}} = VI = (89.1)(0.345) = 30.74 \text{ W}$$

(f) $$W = P_{\text{av}} \times t = 30.74 \times 10 = 307.4 \text{ J}$$

24.224 A 10-H inductor of negligible resistance is connected to a 60-Hz sinusoidal driver whose voltage is 120 V rms. Calculate (a) the inductive reactance; (b) the rms current; (c) the current if the rms voltage remains the same but the frequency is changed to 10 Hz; (d) the polar form for the current and voltage in part (b); (e) the equations for the voltage drop across the inductance, and the current to the inductance, as functions of time in part (b).

❚ (a) $$X_L = 2\pi fL = 2\pi(60)(10) = 3768 \; \Omega$$

(b) $$I_{rms} = \frac{V_{rms}}{X_L} = \frac{120}{3768} = 0.0318 \; A$$

(c) $$X_L = 2\pi(10)(10) = 628 \; \Omega \qquad I_{rms} = \frac{120}{628} = 0.191 \; A$$

(d) Assigning the driving voltage as the reference phasor at $0°$,

$$\bar{E} = 120 \; \underline{/0°}$$

Since the current lags the voltage across the inductor by $90°$,

$$\bar{I} = 0.0318 \; \underline{/-90°}$$

(e) $\quad v_L = 120\sqrt{2} \sin 2\pi 60t = 169.7 \sin 377t \qquad i_L = 0.0318\sqrt{2} \sin (2\pi 60t - 90°) = 0.045 \sin (377t - 90°)$

Note that the frequency of the current wave is the frequency of the driver, and the current wave lags the voltage wave by $90°$.

24.225 Repeat parts (a) and (b) of Prob. 24.224 for a frequency of 0 Hz.

❚ $$X_L = 2\pi fL = 2\pi(0)10 = 0 \qquad I = \frac{V}{X_L} = \frac{120}{0} = \infty$$

If the frequency of the driving voltage is zero (direct current), the inductance will not limit the current. Hence, when used in dc systems, a coil must be designed with adequate internal resistance, by choice of conductor size, or connected in series with an external resistor of such magnitude as to prevent excessive current drain from the generator or battery.

24.226 An ideal 12-V dc source is connected in series with an ideal 4.0-H inductor and a switch. Determine (a) the current 8.0 s after the switch is closed; (b) the steady-state current.

❚ (a) $$i_L|_{f=0} = \frac{V_L}{L} t = \frac{12}{4} \times 8 = 24 \; A$$

(b) $$i_{ss} = \frac{E_{bat}}{X_L} = \frac{12}{2\pi(0)4} = \infty$$

24.227 A 250-μF capacitor is connected across a 120-V 60-Hz system. Determine (a) the capacitive reactance; (b) the steady-state current; (c) the maximum instantaneous value of energy stored in the capacitor.

❚ (a) $$X_C = \frac{1}{2\pi fC} = \frac{1}{2\pi(60)250 \times 10^{-6}} = 10.61 \; \Omega$$

(b) $$I = \frac{V}{X_C} = \frac{120}{10.61} = 11.31 \; A$$

(c) $$W = \tfrac{1}{2}CV^2 = \tfrac{1}{2}(250 \times 10^{-6})(120\sqrt{2})^2 = 3.6 \; J$$

24.228 Repeat Prob. 24.227 for a frequency of 6 Hz.

❚ (a) $$X_C = \frac{1}{2\pi fC} = \frac{1}{2\pi(6)(250 \times 10^{-6})} = 106.1 \; \Omega$$

(b) $$I = \frac{V}{X_C} = \frac{120}{106.1} = 1.131 \; A$$

(c) $$W = \tfrac{1}{2}CV^2 = \tfrac{1}{2}(250 \times 10^{-6})(120\sqrt{2})^2 = 3.6 \; J$$

24.229 Repeat Prob. 24.227 for a dc input.

❚ (a) $$X_C = \frac{1}{2\pi fC} = \frac{1}{2\pi(0)(250)10^{-6}} = \infty \; \Omega$$

(b) $$I = \frac{V}{X_C} = \frac{120}{\infty} = 0 \; A$$

(c) $$W = \tfrac{1}{2}CV^2 = \tfrac{1}{2}(250 \times 10^{-6})(120 \sqrt{2})^2 = 3.6$$

24.230 A 25-Hz 120-V generator is connected to a 1568-Ω resistor. Determine (a) the rms current; (b) the average heat power expended; (c) the time-domain equations for the current and voltage waves.

(a) $$I = \frac{E}{R} = \frac{120}{1568} = 76.5 \text{ mA}$$

(b) $$P = I^2 R = (0.0765)^2 (1568) = 9.18 \text{ W}$$

(c) $$v = 120\sqrt{2} \sin(2\pi 25t) \qquad i = 0.0765\sqrt{2} \sin(2\pi 25t)$$

24.231 A 154-Ω resistor is connected to a sinusoidal generator whose voltage is expressed by $e = 75 \sin 1000t$. Determine (a) the frequency; (b) the rms current; (c) the instantaneous power at $t = 0.01$ s.

(a) $$e = 75 \sin 1000t \qquad 2\pi f = 1000 \qquad f = 159 \text{ Hz}$$

(b) $$I = \frac{E}{R} = \frac{75/\sqrt{2}}{154} = 344 \text{ mA}$$

(c) $$P = \frac{v^2}{R} = \frac{(75 \sin 1000t)^2}{R} \qquad P|_{t=0.01} = \frac{[75 \sin(1000 \times 0.01)^R]^2}{154} = 10.81 \text{ W}$$

24.232 How much power is dissipated in the circuit of Prob. 24.231? Also, calculate the heat energy expended over 56 h.

$$P = I^2 R = (0.344)^2 (154) = 18.22 \text{ W} \qquad W = Pt = 18.22 \times 56 = 1020 \text{ W} \cdot \text{h} = 1.02 \text{ kW} \cdot \text{h}$$

24.233 A 12-H ideal inductor is connected across a 240-V 25-Hz generator. Determine (a) the inductive reactance; (b) the rms current.

(a) $$X_L = 2\pi f L = 2\pi(25)12 = 1884.96 \ \Omega$$

(b) $$I = \frac{V}{X_L} = \frac{240}{1884.96} = 0.127 \text{ A}$$

24.234 A 1.2-H ideal inductor is connected across a 208-V 60-Hz driver. Determine (a) the inductive reactance; (b) the rms current; (c) the peak instantaneous energy stored in the magnetic field.

(a) $$X_L = 2\pi(60)(1.2) = 452.4 \ \Omega$$

(b) $$I = \frac{V}{X_L} = \frac{208}{452.4} = 0.46 \text{ A}$$

(c) $$W_{\phi(\text{max})} = \tfrac{1}{2} L i_{\text{max}}^2 = \tfrac{1}{2}(1.2)(0.46\sqrt{2})^2 = 254 \text{ mJ}$$

24.235 An ideal 3-H inductor is connected to a sinusoidal generator whose voltage is expressed by $e = 100 \sin 400t$. Determine (a) the inductive reactance of the inductor; (b) the rms current; (c) the equation for the current wave; (d) the energy stored in the magnetic field at the instant the voltage wave goes through zero; (e) the rate of storage of energy in the field at the instant the voltage across the coil is zero.

(a) $$X_L = 2\pi f L = 400 \times 3 = 1200 \ \Omega$$

(b) $$I = \frac{V}{X_L} = \frac{100/\sqrt{2}}{1200} = 58.9 \text{ mA}$$

(c) $$I_{\text{max}} = 0.0589\sqrt{2} = 83.3 \text{ mA} \qquad i = 0.0833 \sin(400t - 90°)$$

(d) When the voltage wave goes through zero, the current wave has its maximum value.

$$W_\phi = \tfrac{1}{2} L i^2 = \tfrac{1}{2}(3)(0.0833)^2 = 10.4 \text{ mJ}$$

(e) $$P_\phi = e_L i_L = (0)(0.0833) = 0$$

24.236 If the ac source in Prob. 24.235 is replaced by a 100-V dc source, what is the current at $t = 12$ s?

$$i = \left(\frac{V}{L}\right)t = \frac{100}{3} \times 12 = 400 \text{ A}$$

24.237 A 240-V 60-Hz 1200-rpm generator is connected across an inductive reactance of 2.0 Ω. Determine (a) the rms current; (b) the peak value of the sinusoidal current; (c) the inductance.

▮ **(a)** $$I = \frac{E}{X_L} = \frac{240}{2} = 120 \text{ A}$$

(b) $$I_{\text{max}} = 120\sqrt{2} = 169.71 \text{ A}$$

(c) $$X_L = 2\pi fL \qquad 2 = 2\pi(60)L \qquad L = 5.3 \text{ mH}$$

24.238 For the circuit of Prob. 24.237 **(a)** write the equations for the voltage and current waves and **(b)** determine the energy stored in the inductor when the voltage across it is zero.

▮ **(b)** $$v_L = 240\sqrt{2} \sin(2\pi 60t) \qquad i_L = 169.71 \sin(2\pi 60t - 90°)$$

(b) $$W = \tfrac{1}{2}Li^2 = \tfrac{1}{2}(0.0053)(169.71)^2 = 76.32 \text{ J}$$

24.239 A 0.010-H ideal inductor is connected to a sinusoidal generator whose voltage is expressed by $v_{\text{gen}} = 50 \sin 10{,}584t$. **(a)** Determine the inductive reactance; **(b)** determine the rms current; **(c)** sketch the phasor diagram and the associated waves for the current and driving voltage; **(d)** write the equation for the current wave.

▮ **(a)** $$X_L = 2\pi fL = 10{,}584(0.01) = 105.84 \ \Omega$$

(b) $$I = \frac{50/\sqrt{2}}{105.84} = 334 \text{ mA}$$

(c) See Fig. 24-76.

(d) $$i = 0.334 \ \sqrt{2} \sin(10{,}584t - 90°) \qquad \text{A}$$

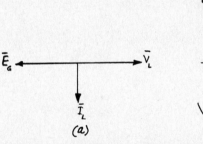 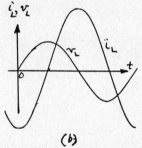

(a)   (b)   **Fig. 24-76**

24.240 Determine the steady-state current in the circuit of Prob. 24.239, if the ac generator is replaced by a 200-V battery.

▮ $$X_L = 2\pi fL = 2\pi(0)(0.01) = 0 \qquad I = \frac{E_{\text{bat}}}{X_L} = \frac{200}{0} = \infty$$

24.241 A 1000-μF capacitor is connected in series with a 120-V 60-Hz generator. **(a)** Determine the capacitive reactance; **(b)** determine the rms current; **(c)** sketch the phasor diagram, and the corresponding current and voltage waves on a common time axis.

▮ **(a)** $$X_C = \frac{1}{2\pi fC} = \frac{1}{2\pi(60)(1000 \times 10^{-6})} = 2.65 \ \Omega$$

(b) $$I = \frac{E}{X_C} = \frac{120}{2.65} = 45.2 \text{ A}$$

(c) See Fig. 24-77.

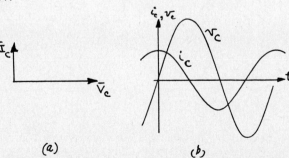

(a)   (b)   **Fig. 24-77**

24.242 A 400-μF capacitor is connected to a 208-V 25-Hz driver. Determine (*a*) the capacitive reactance; (*b*) the steady-state current; (*c*) the maximum instantaneous energy stored in the capacitor.

▮ (*a*)
$$X_C = \frac{1}{2\pi fC} = \frac{1}{2\pi(25)400 \times 10^{-6}} = 15.915 \,\Omega$$

(*b*)
$$I_C = \frac{E}{X_C} = \frac{208}{15.915} = 13.07 \text{ A}$$

(*c*)
$$W = \tfrac{1}{2}CV^2 \qquad W_{\text{max}} = \tfrac{1}{2}(400 \times 10^{-6})(208\sqrt{2})^2 = 17.31 \text{ J}$$

24.243 In the circuit of Prob. 24.242, calculate the capacitive reactance and the steady current if the 25-Hz driver is replaced by a 208-V battery.

▮
$$X_C = \frac{1}{2\pi fC} = \frac{1}{2\pi(0)(400 \times 10^{-6})} = \infty \qquad I = V/X_C = \frac{208}{\infty} = 0$$

24.244 A 240-V 60-Hz sinusoidal driver is connected to a 500-μF capacitor. Determine (*a*) the capacitive reactance; (*b*) the steady-state current; (*c*) the maximum instantaneous voltage across the capacitor; (*d*) the maximum instantaneous charge in the capacitor; (*e*) the maximum instantaneous energy stored in the capacitor.

▮ (*a*)
$$X_C = \frac{1}{2\pi fC} = \frac{1}{2\pi 60(500 \times 10^{-6})} = 5.305 \,\Omega$$

(*b*)
$$I_C = \frac{V_C}{X_C} = \frac{240}{5.3} = 45.28 \text{ A}$$

(*c*)
$$V_{C(\text{max})} = 240\sqrt{2} = 339.41 \text{ V}$$

(*d*)
$$q_1 = CV = 500 \times 10^{-6}(339.41) = 170 \text{ mC}$$

(*e*)
$$W = \tfrac{1}{2}CV^2 = \tfrac{1}{2}(500 \times 10^{-6})(339.41)^2 = 28.80 \text{ J}$$

24.245 A 100-μF capacitor is connected to a generator whose voltage is expressed by $e_{\text{gen}} = 4.6 \sin 40{,}678t$. Determine (*a*) the capacitive reactance; (*b*) the rms current.

▮ (*a*)
$$X_C = \frac{1}{2\pi fC} = \frac{1}{40{,}678(100 \times 10^{-6})} = 0.246 \,\Omega$$

(*b*)
$$I_C = \frac{V_C}{X_C} = \frac{4.6/\sqrt{2}}{0.246} = 13.22 \text{ A}$$

24.246 A 650-nF capacitor is connected to a 180-V 55-kHz generator. Determine (*a*) X_C; (*b*) the rms current; (*c*) the maximum instantaneous charge in the capacitor; (*d*) the maximum instantaneous energy stored in the capacitor.

▮ (*a*)
$$X_C = \frac{1}{2\pi 55{,}000(650 \times 10^{-9})} = 4.452 \,\Omega$$

(*b*)
$$I = \frac{V}{X_C} = \frac{180}{4.452} = 40.43 \text{ A}$$

(*c*)
$$q = CV = 650 \times 10^{-9}(180\sqrt{2}) = 165.5 \,\mu\text{C}$$

(*d*)
$$W = \tfrac{1}{2}CV^2 = \tfrac{1}{2}(650 \times 10^{-9})(180\sqrt{2})^2 = 21.1 \text{ mJ}$$

24.247 A 0.020-F capacitor is connected to a sinusoidal generator. If the current to the capacitor is $i = 10 \sin 30t$. determine (*a*) the rms voltage across the capacitor; (*b*) the time-domain equation for the voltage in part *a*.

▮ (*a*)
$$X_C = \frac{1}{30(0.02)} = 1.667 \,\Omega \qquad V_C = IX_C = (10/\sqrt{2})(1.667) = 11.79 \text{ V}$$

(*b*)
$$v_C = 11.79\sqrt{2} \sin (30t - 90°)$$

24.248 In the circuit of Prob. 24.247 determine (*a*) the charge at $t = 0.08$ s and (*b*) the maximum instantaneous stored energy.

▮ (*a*)
$$q = CV \qquad q|_{t=0.08} = (0.02)11.79\sqrt{2} \sin [30(0.08)57.3 - 90]° = 0.25 \text{ C}$$

(*b*)
$$W = \tfrac{1}{2}CV^2 = \tfrac{1}{2}(0.02)(11.79\sqrt{2})^2 = 2.78 \text{ J}$$

24.249 What is the steady-state current in the circuit of Prob. 24.248 if the ac source is replaced by a 200-V battery?

$$X_C = \frac{1}{2\pi 0(0.02)} = \infty \qquad I_{C(dc)} = \frac{V_C}{X_C} = \frac{200}{\infty} = 0$$

24.250 Express $\bar{V} = 50 \,\underline{/36.87°}$ in rectangular form.

$$u = 50 \cos 36.87° = 40 \qquad v = 50 \sin 36.87° = 30 \qquad \bar{V} = u + jv = (40 + j30)$$

24.251 Depict $\bar{V}$ of Prob. 24.250 graphically.

See Fig. 24-78.

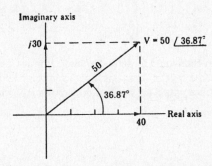

Fig. 24-78

24.252 Determine the resultant voltage of three sinusoidal generators connected in series, whose voltages are $\bar{E}_1 = 100 \,\underline{/42°}$, $\bar{E}_2 = 60 \,\underline{/-36°}$, $\bar{E}_3 = 50 \,\underline{/140°}$.

The resultant voltage $\bar{E}_T$ is

$$\bar{E}_T = \bar{E}_1 + \bar{E}_2 + \bar{E}_3$$

Converting the polar form to rectangular form,

$$\bar{E}_1 = 100 \cos 42° + j100 \sin 42° = 74.31 + j66.91 \qquad \bar{E}_2 = 60 \cos - 36° + j60 \sin - 36° = 48.54 - j35.27$$

$$\bar{E}_3 = 50 \cos 140° + j50 \sin 140° = -38.30 + j32.14 \qquad \bar{E}_T = \bar{E}_1 + \bar{E}_2 + \bar{E}_3 = 84.55 + j63.79$$

Returning to polar form, $\qquad \bar{E}_T = 106 \,\underline{/37.0°}$ V

24.253 Show graphically the operations performed in Prob. 24.252.

See Fig. 24-79.

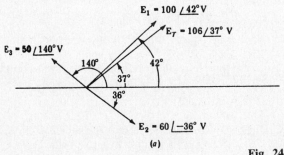 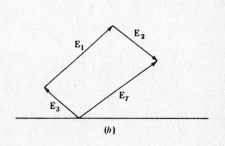

Fig. 24-79

24.254 Obtain the product $\bar{A} \cdot \bar{B}$, where

$$\bar{A} = 4 + j3 \qquad \bar{B} = 5 + j6$$

$$\bar{A} \cdot \bar{B} = (4 + j3)(5 + j6)$$

Multiplying through, $\qquad \bar{A} \cdot \bar{B} = 20 + j24 + j15 + j^2 18$

Collecting real and imaginary terms (note $j^2 = -1$),

$$\bar{A} \cdot \bar{B} = (20 - 18) + j(24 + 15) = 2 + j39 = 39.05 \,\underline{/87.06°}$$

24.255 Given $\bar{A} = 35 \,\underline{/40°}$, determine $\bar{A} + \bar{A}^*$.

▮ $\bar{A} = 35 \,\underline{/40°} = 26.81 + j22.50$ $\bar{A}^* = 35 \,\underline{/-40°} = 26.81 - j22.50$ $\bar{A} + \bar{A}^* = 53.62 + j0 = 53.62$

24.256 Evaluate $\bar{A}/\bar{B}$ where

$$\bar{A} = 4 + j3 \qquad \bar{B} = 5 + j6$$

▮ $\dfrac{\bar{A}}{\bar{B}} = \dfrac{4 + j3}{5 + j6} = \dfrac{(4 + j3)(5 - j6)}{(5 + j6)(5 - j6)} = \dfrac{20 - j24 + j15 - j^2 18}{25 - j30 + j30 - j^2 36} = \dfrac{38 - j9}{61} = \dfrac{39.05 \,\underline{/-13.32°}}{61} = 0.64 \,\underline{/-13.32°}$

24.257 Use the exponential form to evaluate the product $(4 + j3)(5 + j6)$.

▮ $$\bar{A} = 4 + j3 = 5e^{j36.87°} \qquad \bar{B} = 5 + j6 = 7.81e^{j50.19°}$$

$$\bar{A} \cdot \bar{B} = (5e^{j38.87°})(7.81e^{j50.19°}) = (5)(7.81)e^{j(36.87° + 50.19°)} = 39.05e^{j87.06°} = 39.05 \,\underline{/87.06°}$$

24.258 Use the exponential form to evaluate $(5 \,\underline{/36.87°})/(7.81 \,\underline{/50.19°})$.

▮ $$\frac{\bar{A}}{\bar{B}} = \frac{5e^{j36.87°}}{7.81e^{j50.19°}} = 0.640e^{j(36.87° - 50.19°)} = 0.64e^{-j13.32°}$$

Converting to polar form, $\qquad \dfrac{\bar{A}}{\bar{B}} = 0.64 \,\underline{/-13.32°}$

24.259 Using the polar form, evaluate $\bar{A} \cdot \bar{B}$ and $\bar{A}/\bar{B}$, where

$$\bar{A} = 4 + j3 = 5 \,\underline{/36.87°} \qquad \bar{B} = 5 + j6 = 7.81 \,\underline{/50.19°}$$

▮ $$\bar{A} \cdot \bar{B} = (5 \,\underline{/36.87°})(7.81 \,\underline{/50.19°}) = (5)(7.81) \,\underline{/36.87° + 50.19°} = 39.05 \,\underline{/87.06°}$$

Similarly, $\qquad \dfrac{\bar{A}}{\bar{B}} = \dfrac{5 \,\underline{/36.87°}}{7.81 \,\underline{/50.19°}} = \dfrac{5}{7.81} \,\underline{/36.87° - 50.19°} = 0.64 \,\underline{/-13.32°}$

24.260 Simplify the following using polar form:

$$\bar{X} = \frac{(40 \,\underline{/30°})(60 \,\underline{/20°})}{(70 \,\underline{/-40°})(35 \,\underline{/70°})}$$

▮ $$\bar{X} = \frac{(40)(60)}{(70)(35)} \,\underline{/30° + 20° + 40° - 70°} = 0.98 \,\underline{/20°}$$

$$\bar{X} = (0.92 + j0.34)$$

24.261 Rework Prob. 24.260 in rectangular form.

▮ $$40 \,\underline{/30°} = (34.64 + j20) \qquad 60 \,\underline{/20°} = (56.38 + j20.52)$$
$$70 \,\underline{/-40°} = (53.62 - j45) \qquad 35 \,\underline{/70°} = (11.97 + j32.89)$$

$$\bar{X} = \frac{(34.64 + j20)(56.38 + j20.52)}{(53.62 - j45)(11.97 + j32.89)} = \frac{1953.06 + j710.81 + j1127.60 + j^2 410.40}{641.83 + j1763.56 - j538.65 - j^2 1480.05} = \frac{1542.66 + j1838.41}{2121.88 + j1224.91}$$

Rationalizing the denominator,

$$\bar{X} = \frac{(1542.66 + j1838.41)(2121.88 - j1224.91)}{(2121.88 + j1224.91)(2121.88 - j1224.91)} = \frac{3,273,339.40 - j1,889,619.66 + j3,900,885.41 - j^2 2,251,886.79}{4,502,374.73 + 1,500,404.51}$$

$$= \frac{5,525,226.19 + j2,011,265.75}{6,002,779.24} = (0.92 + j0.34) = 0.98 \,\underline{/20°}$$

24.262 Express the following complex numbers in rectangular form: (**a**) $50 \,\underline{/80°}$; (**b**) $30 \,\underline{/20°}$; (**c**) $120 \,\underline{/180°}$; (**d**) $70 \,\underline{/-90°}$; (**e**) $150 \,\underline{/45°}$.

▮ (**a**) $50 \,\underline{/80°} = 8.68 + j49.24$ $\qquad$ (**d**) $70 \,\underline{/-90°} = 0 - j70$

(**b**) $30 \,\underline{/20°} = 28.19 + j10.26$ $\qquad$ (**e**) $150 \,\underline{/45°} = 106.07 + j106.07$

(**c**) $120 \,\underline{/180°} = -120 + j0$

24.263 Express the following complex numbers in polar form: (*a*) $(3 + j7)$; (*b*) $(6 - j8)$; (*c*) $(0 + j4)$; (*d*) $(3 - j5)$; (*e*) $(-2 - j6)$.

▮ (*a*) $(3 + j7) = 7.62 \underline{/66.80°}$ (*d*) $(3 - j5) = 5.83 \underline{/-59.04°}$

(*b*) $(6 - j8) = 10 \underline{/-53.13°}$ (*e*) $(-2 - j6) = 6.32 \underline{/-108.43°}$

(*c*) $(0 + j4) = 4 \underline{/90°}$

24.264 Determine the conjugate of the following complex numbers: (*a*) $3 \underline{/70°}$; (*b*) $5 \underline{/-40°}$; (*c*) $(2 + j5)$; (*d*) $(-5 - j6)$; (*e*) $(4 + j0)$.

▮ (*a*) $(3 \underline{/70°})^* = 3 \underline{/-70°}$ (*d*) $(-5 - j6)^* = (-5 + j6)$

(*b*) $(5 \underline{/-40°})^* = 5 \underline{/40°}$ (*e*) $(4 + j0)^* = (4 + j0)$

(*c*) $(2 + j5)^* = (2 - j5)$

24.265 Perform the indicated operations and express the results in polar form:

(*a*) $(3 + j4) + (5 - j7) + (3 - j6) - (10 - j8)$ (*b*) $(5 + j9) - (6 + j15) + (4 - j3) + (6 - j5)$

(*c*) $3 \underline{/30°} + 5 \underline{/-50°} - 7 \underline{/20°} + (6 + j5)$

▮ (*a*) $(3 + j4) + (5 - j7) + (3 - j6) - (10 - j8) \doteq (1 - j1) = 1.41 \underline{/-45°}$

(*b*) $(5 + j9) - (6 + j15) + (4 - j3) + (6 - j5) = (9 - j14) = 16.64 \underline{/-57.26°}$

(*c*) $3 \underline{/30°} + 5 \underline{/-50°} - 7 \underline{/20°} + (6 + j5) = (2.6 + j1.5) + (3.21 - j3.83) - (6.58 + j2.39) + (6 + j5)$

$$= (5.23 + j0.28) = 5.24 \underline{/3.06°}$$

24.266 Perform the indicated operations and express the results in polar form:

(*a*) $\dfrac{(3 + j9)(5 + j10)(9 - j7)}{5(3 + j6)}$ (*b*) $\dfrac{(17 + j9)(5 - j8)}{(4 + j7)(8 - j4)}$

▮ (*a*) $\dfrac{(3 + j9)(5 + j10)(9 - j7)}{5(3 + j6)} = \dfrac{(9.49 \underline{/71.57°})(11.18 \underline{/63.43°})(11.4 \underline{/-37.87°})}{5(6.71 \underline{/63.43°})} = 36.05 \underline{/33.70°}$

(*b*) $\dfrac{(17 + j9)(5 - j8)}{(4 + j7)(8 - j4)} = \dfrac{(19.24 \underline{/27.90°})(9.43 \underline{/-57.99°})}{(8.06 \underline{/60.26°})(8.94 \underline{/-26.57°})} = 2.52 \underline{/-63.78°}$

24.267 Perform the indicated operations and express the results in polar form:

(*a*) $\dfrac{(13 + j19)(5 - j10)^* 52e^{-j13.4°}}{(14 \underline{/30°})(17 \underline{/50°})^*}$ (*b*) $\left[\dfrac{(15 - j7)(3 + j2)^*}{(4 + j6)^*(3 \underline{/70°})} \right]^*$

▮ (*a*) $\dfrac{(13 + j19)(5 - j10)^*(52e^{-j13.4°})}{(14 \underline{/30°})(17 \underline{/50°})^*} = \dfrac{(23.02 \underline{/55.62°})(11.18 \underline{/63.43°})(52 \underline{/-13.4°})}{(14 \underline{/30°})(17 \underline{/-50°})} = 56.23 \underline{/125.65°}$

(*b*) $\left[\dfrac{(15 - j7)(3 + j2)^*}{(4 + j6)^*(3 \underline{/70°})} \right]^* = \left[\dfrac{(16.55 \underline{/-25.02°})(3.61 \underline{/-33.69°})}{(7.21 \underline{/-56.31°})(3 \underline{/70°})} \right]^* = 2.76 \underline{/72.40°}$

24.268 A coil whose resistance and inductive reactance are 10.0 Ω and 8.0 Ω, respectively, is connected in series with a 3.0-Ω capacitive reactance. If the circuit current is $30 \underline{/20°}$ A, as shown in Fig. 24-80*a*, determine the magnitude and phase angle of the driving voltage.

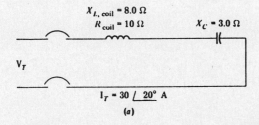 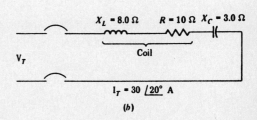

Fig. 24-80

The equivalent series circuit is shown in Fig. 24-80b. Applying Kirchhoff's voltage law,

$$\bar{V}_T = \bar{V}_R + \bar{V}_L + \bar{V}_C = \bar{I}_T R + \bar{I}_T(jX_L) + \bar{I}_T(-jX_C) = (30\ \underline{/20°})(10) + (30\ \underline{/20°})(j8) + (30\ \underline{/20°})(-j3)$$

$$= 30\ \underline{/20°}(10 + j8 - j3) = (30\ \underline{/20°})(11.18\ \underline{/26.57°}) = 335.4\ \underline{/46.57°}\ V$$

24.269 For the circuit of Fig. 24-81 determine   (a) the driving voltage in polar form;   (b) the input impedance;   (c) the circuit current;   (d) the voltage drop across each component in the circuit;   (e) the equation for the current as a function of time.

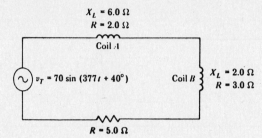

Fig. 24-81

(a)
$$\bar{V}_T = \frac{70}{\sqrt{2}}\ \underline{/40°} = 49.50\ \underline{/40°}\ V$$

(b)
$$\bar{Z}_s = (2 + j6) + (3 + j2) + 5 = 10 + j8 = 12.81\ \underline{/38.66°}\ \Omega$$

(c)
$$\bar{I}_T = \frac{\bar{V}_T}{\bar{Z}_S} = \frac{49.50\ \underline{/40°}}{12.81\ \underline{/38.66°}} = 3.86\ \underline{/1.34°}\ A$$

(d)
$$\bar{V}_{\text{coil}A} = \bar{I}_T\bar{Z}_{\text{coil}A} = (3.86\ \underline{/1.34°})(2 + j6) = (3.86\ \underline{/1.34°})(6.32\ \underline{/71.57°}) = 24.40\ \underline{/72.91°}\ V$$

$$\bar{V}_{\text{coil}B} = \bar{I}_T\bar{Z}_{\text{coil}B} = (3.86\ \underline{/1.34°})(3 + j2) = (3.86\ \underline{/1.34°})(3.61\ \underline{/33.69°}) = 13.93\ \underline{/35.03°}\ V$$

$$\bar{V}_R = \bar{I}_T R = (3.86\ \underline{/1.34°})(5) = 19.3\ \underline{/1.34°}\ V$$

(e)
$$i = 3.86\sqrt{2}\ \sin(377t + 1.34°)$$

24.270 For the circuit shown in Fig. 24-82a,   (a) determine the current, and then   (b) sketch the phasor diagram showing the net driving voltage phasor and the current phasor.

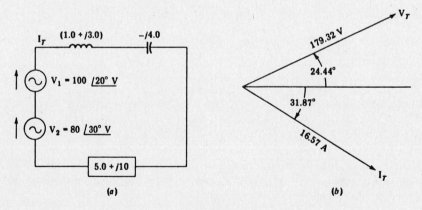

Fig. 24-82

(a) Applying Kirchhoff's voltage law,

$$80\ \underline{/30°} + 100\ \underline{/20°} = \bar{I}_T(1 + j3) + \bar{I}_T(-j4) + \bar{I}_T(5 + j10) \qquad (69.28 + j40) + (93.97 + j34.20) = \bar{I}_T(6 + j9)$$

$$(163.25 + j74.20) = \bar{I}_T(6 + j9) \qquad (179.32\ \underline{/24.44°}) = \bar{I}_T(10.82\ \underline{/56.31°})$$

$$\bar{I}_T = \frac{179.32\ \underline{/24.44°}}{10.82\ \underline{/56.31°}} = 16.57\ \underline{/-31.87°}\ A$$

(b) The phasor diagram is shown in Fig. 24-82b. The net driving voltage is the phasor sum of the two series-connected driving voltages.

24.271 A coil whose resistance and inductance are $60.0\,\Omega$ and $0.20\,H$, respectively, is connected to a 120-V 60-Hz generator. Determine (a) the inductive reactance; (b) the input impedance; (c) the steady-state current; (d) the steady-state current if the 60-Hz generator is replaced by a 120-V battery.

▌ (a)
$$X_L = 2\pi f L = 2\pi(60)(0.2) = 75.4\,\Omega$$

(b)
$$\bar{Z}_S = (60 + j75.4) = 96.36\,\underline{/51.49°}\,\Omega$$

(c)
$$\bar{I}_T = \frac{\bar{V}_T}{\bar{Z}_S} = \frac{120\,\underline{/0°}}{96.36\,\underline{/51.49°}} = 1.25\,\underline{/-51.49°}\,A$$

(d) With a battery applied, $f = 0$.

$$X_L = 2\pi(0)(0.2) = 0\,\Omega \qquad \bar{Z}_S = R + jX_L = 60 + j0 = 60\,\Omega \qquad I_{dc} = \frac{V_{dc}}{Z_S} = \frac{120}{60} = 2\,A$$

24.272 For the circuit of Fig. 24-83, find $\bar{V}_k$ in terms of $\bar{V}_T$. Hence obtain the voltage divider rule.

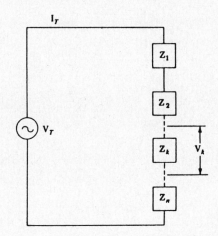

Fig. 24-83

▌ The current in the series circuit is

$$\bar{I}_T = \frac{\bar{V}_T}{\bar{Z}_T} \tag{1}$$

where $\bar{Z}_T = \bar{Z}_1 + \bar{Z}_2 + \cdots + \bar{Z}_k + \cdots + \bar{Z}_n.$
The voltage drop across impedance $\bar{Z}_k$ is

$$\bar{V}_k = \bar{I}_T \bar{Z}_k \tag{2}$$

Substituting Eq. (1) into Eq. (2), we obtain the *voltage divider equation*

$$\bar{V}_k = \bar{V}_T \frac{\bar{Z}_k}{\bar{Z}_T}$$

24.273 Using the voltage divider rule, determine the rms voltage across the 5.0-Ω resistor in Fig. 24-81.

▌
$$\bar{Z}_T = (2 + j6) + (3 + j2) + 5 = (10 + j8) = 12.81\,\underline{/38.66°}\,\Omega$$

$$\bar{V}_T = \frac{70}{\sqrt{2}}\,\underline{/40°} = 49.50\,\underline{/40°}\,V \qquad \bar{V}_{5\,\Omega} = (49.50\,\underline{/40°})\frac{5\,\underline{/0°}}{12.81\,\underline{/38.66°}} = 19.3\,\underline{/1.34°}\,V$$

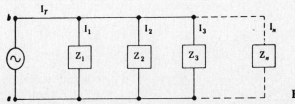

Fig. 24-84

24.274 In the circuit of Fig. 24-84, assume $\bar{Z}_1 = 2.8\,\underline{/-56°}$, $\bar{Z}_2 = 1.9\,\underline{/79°}$, $\bar{Z}_3 = 1.5\,\underline{/-63°}$, and $\bar{V}_T = 100\,\underline{/0°}$. Determine (a) the input admittance of the circuit; (b) the steady-state current supplied by the generator.

▮ (a)
$$\bar{Y}_1 = \frac{1}{2.8\,\underline{/-56°}} = 0.3571\,\underline{/56°} = (0.1997 + j0.2961)\,\text{S}$$

$$\bar{Y}_2 = \frac{1}{1.9\,\underline{/79°}} = 0.5263\,\underline{/-79°} = (0.1004 - j0.5166)\,\text{S}$$

$$\bar{Y}_3 = \frac{1}{1.5\,\underline{/-63°}} = 0.6667\,\underline{/63°} = (0.3027 + j0.5940)\,\text{S}$$

$$\bar{Y}_T = \bar{Y}_1 + \bar{Y}_2 + \bar{Y}_3 = (0.1997 + j0.2961) + (0.1004 - j0.5166) + (0.3027 + j0.5940)$$
$$= 0.6028 + j0.3735 = 0.7091\,\underline{/31.78°}\,\text{S}$$

(b)
$$\bar{I}_T = \bar{V}_T\bar{Y}_T = (100\,\underline{/0°})(0.709\,\underline{/31.78°}) = 70.9\,\underline{/31.78°}\,\text{A}$$

24.275 What is the input impedance of the circuit of Prob. 24.274?

▮
$$\bar{Z}_T = \frac{1}{\bar{Y}_T} = \frac{1}{0.7091\,\underline{/31.78°}} = 1.41\,\underline{/-31.78°}\,\Omega$$

The input impedance may also be determined from Ohm's law:

$$\bar{Z}_T = \frac{\bar{V}_T}{\bar{I}_T} = \frac{100\,\underline{/0°}}{70.91\,\underline{/31.78°}} = 1.41\,\underline{/-31.78°}\,\Omega$$

24.276 Assume R_S, X_S, and E_G in Fig. 24-85a are 3.0 Ω, 4.0 Ω, and 100 V, respectively. Determine (a) the circuit current; (b) the equivalent parallel circuit parameters; (c) the feeder current to the equivalent parallel circuit.

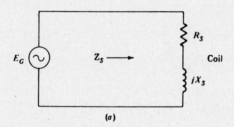

(a)

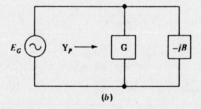

(b)

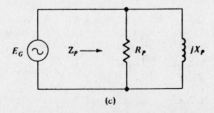

(c)

Fig. 24-85

▌ (a)
$$\bar{I}_T = \frac{\bar{V}_T}{\bar{Z}_T} = \frac{100 \,\underline{/0^\circ}}{3.0 + j4.0} = 20 \,\underline{/-53.1^\circ}\,\text{A}$$

(b) $R_P = \dfrac{R_S^2 + X_S^2}{R_S} = \dfrac{(3)^2 + (4)^2}{3} = 8.33\,\Omega$ $X_P = \dfrac{R_S^2 + X_S^2}{X_S} = \dfrac{(3)^2 + (4)^2}{4} = 6.25\,\Omega$ See Fig. 24-85b

(c) Using Fig. 24-85c as a guide,

$$\bar{I}_T = \bar{I}_{R_P} + \bar{I}_{X_P} = \frac{\bar{E}_G}{\bar{R}_P} + \frac{\bar{E}_G}{jX_P} = \frac{100 \,\underline{/0^\circ}}{8.33} + \frac{100 \,\underline{/0^\circ}}{6.25 \,\underline{/90^\circ}} = (12.0 - j16.0) = 20 \,\underline{/-53.1^\circ}\,\text{A}$$

24.277 From the circuit of Fig. 24-86, obtain the current divider equation; that is, express $\bar{I}_k$ in terms of $\bar{I}_T$.

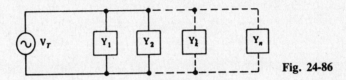

Fig. 24-86

▌ The total current supplied to the parallel circuit is

$$\bar{I}_T = \bar{V}_T \bar{Y}_T \tag{1}$$

where
$$\bar{Y}_T = \bar{Y}_1 + \bar{Y}_2 + \cdots + \bar{Y}_k + \cdots + \bar{Y}_n$$

The current to admittance $\bar{Y}_k$ is

$$\bar{I}_k = \bar{V}_T \bar{Y}_k \tag{2}$$

Solving Eq. (1) for $\bar{V}_T$ and substituting it into Eq. (2) results in the current divider equation

$$\bar{I}_k = \bar{I}_T \frac{\bar{Y}_k}{\bar{Y}_T}$$

24.278 Using the current divider equation, determine the current in impedance $\bar{Z}_2$ of Prob. 24.274.

▌
$$\bar{I}_2 = \bar{I}_T \frac{\bar{Y}_2}{\bar{Y}_T} = (70.91 \,\underline{/31.78^\circ}) \frac{0.5263 \,\underline{/-79^\circ}}{0.7091 \,\underline{/31.78^\circ}} = (52.63 \,\underline{/-79.00^\circ})\,\text{A}$$

24.279 A 350-μF capacitor, a 10.0-Ω resistor, and a coil whose inductance and resistance are 0.030 H and 5 Ω, respectively, are connected in parallel and supplied by a 120-V 60-Hz generator. Sketch the circuit and determine **(a)** the steady-state current through each branch; **(b)** the steady-state line current; **(c)** the input impedance; **(d)** the input admittance.

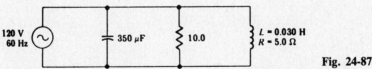

Fig. 24-87

▌ The circuit diagram is shown in Fig. 24-87.

(a)
$$X_C = \frac{1}{2\pi(60)(350 \times 10^{-6})} = 7.58\,\Omega \qquad X_L = 2\pi(60)(0.03) = 11.31\,\Omega$$

$$\bar{Z}_{\text{coil}} = (5 + j11.31) = 12.37 \,\underline{/66.15^\circ}\,\Omega \qquad \bar{I}_C = \frac{\bar{V}_T}{-jX_C} = \frac{120 \,\underline{/0^\circ}}{7.58 \,\underline{/-90^\circ}} = 15.83 \,\underline{/90^\circ}\,\text{A}$$

$$\bar{I}_{\text{coil}} = \frac{\bar{V}_T}{\bar{Z}_{\text{coil}}} = \frac{120 \,\underline{/0^\circ}}{12.37 \,\underline{/66.15^\circ}} = 9.70 \,\underline{/-66.15^\circ}\,\text{A} \qquad \bar{I}_R = \frac{\bar{V}_T}{R} = \frac{120 \,\underline{/0^\circ}}{10 \,\underline{/0^\circ}} = 12 \,\underline{/0^\circ}\,\text{A}$$

(**b**)
$$\bar{I}_T = \bar{I}_C + \bar{I}_{coil} + \bar{I}_R = 15.83\ \underline{/90°} + 9.70\ \underline{/-66.15°} + 12\ \underline{/0°}$$
$$= (0 + j15.83) + (3.92 - j8.87) + (12 + j0) = 15.92 + j6.96 = 17.38\ \underline{/23.60°}\ \text{A}$$

(**c**) From Ohm's law,
$$\bar{Z}_{in} = \frac{\bar{V}_T}{\bar{I}_T} = \frac{120\ \underline{/0°}}{17.38\ \underline{/23.60°}} = 6.90\underline{/-23.60°}\ \Omega$$

(**d**)
$$\bar{Y}_{in} = \frac{1}{\bar{Z}_{in}} = \frac{1}{6.90\ \underline{/-23.60°}} = 0.1448\ \underline{/23.60°}\ \text{S}$$

24.280 In the circuit of Prob. 24.279, calculate the steady-state current if the ac source is replaced by a 120-V battery.

$$X_L = 2\pi(0)L = 0\ \Omega \qquad \bar{Z}_{coil} = R + jX_L = 5 + j0 = 5\ \Omega \qquad X_C = \frac{1}{2\pi(0)C} = \infty\ \Omega$$

$$I_C = \frac{120}{\infty} = 0\ \text{A} \qquad I_{coil} = \frac{120}{5} = 24\ \text{A} \qquad I_R = \frac{120}{10} = 12\ \text{A} \qquad I_T|_{f=0} = 24 + 12 = 36\ \text{A}$$

24.281 For the series-parallel circuit in Fig. 24-88a determine (**a**) the input impedance;   (**b**) the circuit current;   (**c**) the voltage drop across $\bar{Z}_1$;   (**d**) the voltage drop across $\bar{Z}_2$.

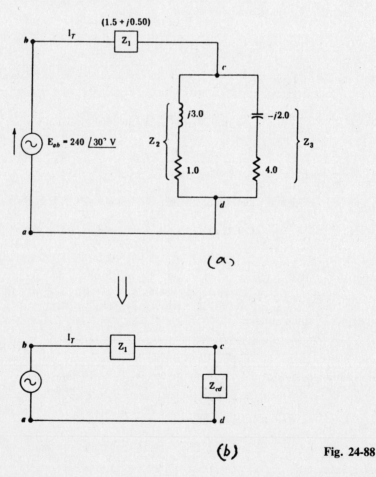

(**a**) From Fig. 24-88b:

$$\bar{Z}_{cd} = \frac{\bar{Z}_2\bar{Z}_3}{\bar{Z}_2 + \bar{Z}_3} = \frac{(1+j3)(4-j2)}{(1+j3)+(4-j2)} = \frac{4 - j2 + j12 - j^2 6}{5 + j1} = \frac{10 + j10}{5 + j1} = \frac{14.14\ \underline{/45°}}{5.10\ \underline{/11.31°}} = 2.77\ \underline{/33.69°}$$
$$= 2.31 + j1.54\ \Omega$$

$$\bar{Z}_{in} = (1.5 + j0.5) + (2.31 + j1.54) = (3.81 + j2.04) = 4.32\ \underline{/28.17°}\ \Omega$$

(b)
$$\bar{I} = \frac{\bar{V}}{\bar{Z}_{in}} = \frac{240\,\underline{/30°}}{4.32\,\underline{/28.17°}} = 55.56\,\underline{/1.83°}\,\text{A}$$

(c)
$$\bar{V}_{Z1} = \bar{I}\bar{Z}_1 = (55.56\,\underline{/1.83°})(1.5 + j0.5) = (55.56\,\underline{/1.83°})(1.58\,\underline{/18.44°}) = 87.79\,\underline{/20.27°}\,\text{V}$$

(d)
$$\bar{V}_{Z2} = \bar{I}\bar{Z}_{cd} = (55.56\,\underline{/1.83°})(2.77\,\underline{/33.69°}) = 153.9\,\underline{/35.52°}\,\text{V}$$

24.282 For the circuit shown in Fig. 24-89, determine (a) the input impedance of the series-parallel combination; (b) the ammeter reading; (c) the equation for the current wave as a function of time.

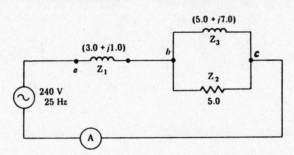

Fig. 24-89

❚ From Fig. 24-89:

(a) $\bar{Z}_{bc} = \dfrac{(5 + j7)5}{(5 + j7) + 5} = 3.52\,\underline{/19.47°} = (3.32 + j1.17)\,\Omega$ $\qquad \bar{Z}_{in} = (3.32 + j1.17) + (3 + j1) = 6.68\,\underline{/18.95°}\,\Omega$

(b) $\bar{I} = \dfrac{\bar{V}}{\bar{Z}_{in}} = \dfrac{240\,\underline{/0°}}{6.68\,\underline{/18.95°}} = 35.92\,\underline{/-18.95°}\,\text{A}$ $\qquad$ Ammeter indicates 35.92 A

(c) $\qquad\qquad i = 35.92\sqrt{2}\sin{(2\pi 25t - 18.95°)}$

24.283 What is the input current to the circuit of Fig. 24-89 if the ac source is replaced by a 240-V battery?

❚ In this case, the circuit becomes as shown in Fig. 24-90. Hence:

$$R_{in} = 3 + 2.5 = 5.5\,\Omega \qquad I_{in} = \frac{240}{5.5} = 43.64\,\text{A}$$

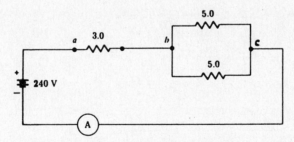

Fig. 24-90

24.284 Determine the input impedance of the circuit shown in Fig. 24-91a. The circuit impedances are

$$\bar{Z}_1 = (0.054 + j0)\,\Omega \qquad \bar{Z}_2 = (1 + j2)\,\Omega$$
$$\bar{Z}_3 = (0 - j4)\,\Omega \qquad \bar{Z}_4 = (3 - j3)\,\Omega$$
$$\bar{Z}_5 = (1 + j3)\,\Omega \qquad \bar{Z}_6 = 0.278\,\underline{/-56.3°}\,\Omega$$

❚ By network reduction shown in Fig. 24-91b through d we obtain

$$\bar{Z}_2 = 1 + j2 = 2.24\,\underline{/63.43°}\,\Omega \qquad \bar{Z}_3 = 0 - j4 = 4\,\underline{/-90°}\,\Omega \qquad \bar{Z}_4 = 3 - j3 = 4.24\,\underline{/-45°}\,\Omega$$

$$\bar{Y}_2 = \frac{1}{\bar{Z}_2} = \frac{1}{2.24\,\underline{/63.43°}} = 0.4464\,\underline{/-63.43°} = (0.1997 - j0.3993)\,\text{S}$$

$$\bar{Y}_3 = \frac{1}{\bar{Z}_3} = \frac{1}{4\,\underline{/-90°}} = 0.2500\,\underline{/90°} = (0 + j0.2500)\,\text{S}$$

$$\bar{Y}_4 = \frac{1}{\bar{Z}_4} = \frac{1}{4.24\ \underline{/-45°}} = 0.2357\ \underline{/45°} = (0.1667 + j0.1667)\ \text{S}$$

$$\bar{Y}_A = \bar{Y}_2 + \bar{Y}_3 + \bar{Y}_4 = (0.3664 + j0.0174) = 0.3668\ \underline{/2.72°}\ \text{S}$$

$$\bar{Z}_A = \frac{1}{\bar{Y}_A} = \frac{1}{0.3668\ \underline{/2.72°}} = 2.726\ \underline{/-2.72°} = (2.723 - j0.1294)\ \Omega$$

$$\bar{Z}_B = \bar{Z}_A + \bar{Z}_5 = (2.723 - j0.1294) + (1 + j3) = 4.701\ \underline{/37.64°}\ \Omega$$

$$\bar{Z}_C = \frac{\bar{Z}_B \bar{Z}_6}{\bar{Z}_B + \bar{Z}_6} = \frac{(4.701\ \underline{/37.64°})(0.278\ \underline{/-56.3°})}{(4.701\ \underline{/37.64°}) + (0.278\ \underline{/-56.3°})} = \frac{1.307\ \underline{/-18.66°}}{4.69\ \underline{/34.25°}} = 0.2787\ \underline{/-52.91°}$$

$$= (0.1680 - j0.2223)\ \Omega$$

$$\bar{Z}_{\text{input}} = \bar{Z}_C + \bar{Z}_1 = (0.1680 - j0.2223) + (0.054 + j0) = 0.3142\ \underline{/-45.04°}\ \Omega$$

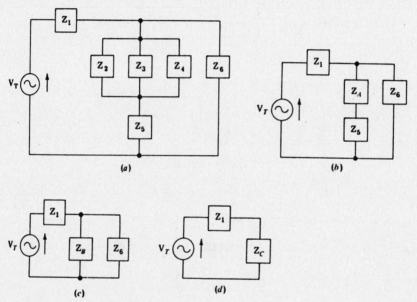

Fig. 24-91

24.285 Determine the potential difference between points B and D and hence the voltmeter reading in the circuit of Fig. 24-92.

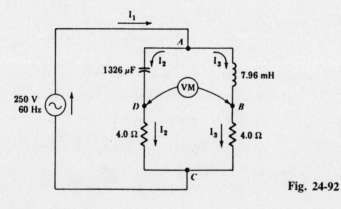

Fig. 24-92

▌ Traveling the path DCB:

$$\bar{V}_{DB} = \left(\sum \text{driving voltages}\right) - \left(\sum \text{voltage drops}\right) = 0 - \left(4\bar{I}_2 + (-4)(\bar{I}_3)\right) \tag{1}$$

The current in each of the two branches may be determined by calculating the impedance of each branch and then applying Ohm's law.   Thus,

$$X_L = 2\pi fL = 2\pi(60)(7.96 \times 10^{-3}) = 3.00\,\Omega \qquad X_C = \frac{1}{2\pi 60(1326 \times 10^{-6})} = 2.00\,\Omega$$

The current in branch ADC is

$$\bar{I}_2 = \frac{250\,/0°}{(4-j2)} = \frac{250\,/0°}{4.47\,/-26.47°} = 55.90\,/26.57°\ \text{A}$$

The current in branch ABC is

$$\bar{I}_3 = \frac{250\,/0°}{(4+j3)} = \frac{250\,/0°}{5\,/36.87°} = 50.0\,/-36.87°\ \text{A}$$

Substituting the values for $\bar{I}_2$ and $\bar{I}_3$ into Eq. (1)

$$\bar{V}_{DB} = -[4(55.90\,/26.57°) - 4(50\,/-36.87°)] = -223.6\,/26.57° + 200\,/-36.87°$$

$$= (-199.99 - j100.01) + (160.00 - j120) = (-39.99 - j220.01) = 223.6\,/-100.3°\ \text{V}$$

The voltmeter will indicate 223.6 V.

24.286   If the ac generator is replaced by a 250-V battery in the circuit of Fig. 24-92, determine the voltmeter reading.

❚   In this case the circuit becomes as shown in Fig. 24-93 for which:

$$X_L = 2\pi fL = 2\pi(0)(7.96 \times 10^{-3}) = 0 \qquad X_C = \frac{1}{2\pi fC} = \frac{1}{2\pi 0(1326 \times 10^{-6})} = \infty$$

The current in branch ADC is $\qquad \bar{I}_2 = \dfrac{250\,/0°}{4+j\infty} = \dfrac{250}{\infty\,/90°} = 0\ \text{A}$

The current in branch ABC is $\qquad \bar{I}_3 = \dfrac{250\,/0°}{4+j0} = \dfrac{250}{4} = 62.5\ \text{A}$

Traveling path DCB,

$$\bar{V}_{DB} = \left(\sum \text{driving voltages}\right) - \left(\sum \text{voltage drops}\right) = 0 - [4\bar{I}_2 + (-1)(4\bar{I}_3)] = -(4 \times 0 - 4 \times 62.5) = 250\ \text{V}$$

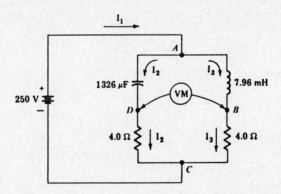

Fig. 24-93

24.287   A 6.0-Ω resistor and a 4.0-Ω inductive reactance are connected in series with a sinusoidal generator.   If the generator voltage is given as $e = 20\sin 157t$ V,   determine   (**a**) the complex impedance;   (**b**) the circuit current in polar form;   (**c**) the frequency of the alternating current.

❚   (**a**) $\qquad\qquad\qquad\qquad \bar{Z} = R + jX_L = (6 + j4) = 7.21\,/33.69°\ \Omega$

(**b**) $\qquad\qquad \bar{E} = 20/\sqrt{2}\,/0° \qquad \bar{I} = \dfrac{\bar{E}}{\bar{Z}} = \dfrac{20/\sqrt{2}\,/0°}{7.21\,/33.69°} = 1.96\,/-33.69°\ \text{A}$

(**c**) $\qquad\qquad\qquad\qquad\qquad 2\pi f = 157 \qquad f = 25\ \text{Hz}$

24.288 A coil, a capacitor, and a resistor are connected in series and supplied by a 1.5-kHz generator. The capacitive reactance is $4.0\,\Omega$, the resistor is $4.0\,\Omega$, and the coil has a resistance of $3.0\,\Omega$ and an inductive reactance of $4.0\,\Omega$. If the current in the circuit is $10\underline{/20°}$ A, determine **(a)** the complex impedance and **(b)** the phasor voltage drop across the coil.

▮ **(a)** $$\bar{Z} = R + jX_L - jX_C = 4 + (3 + j4) - j4 = 7 + j0 = 7\underline{/0°}\,\Omega$$

   (b) $$\bar{V}_{coil} = \bar{I}\bar{Z}_{coil} = (10\underline{/20°})(3 + j4) = (10\underline{/20°})(5\underline{/53.13°}) = 50\underline{/73.13°}\,V$$

24.289 Determine the resistance and inductance or capacitance values of series-connected elements that will draw a current of $20\underline{/-30°}$ A from a 60-Hz sinusoidal generator whose voltage is $100\underline{/0°}$ V.

▮ $$\bar{I} = \frac{\bar{E}}{\bar{Z}} \qquad 20\underline{/-30°} = \frac{100\underline{/0°}}{\bar{Z}}$$
$$\bar{Z} = 5\underline{/30°} = (4.33 + j2.5)\,\Omega$$

Thus, the impedance has a resistance of $4.33\,\Omega$, and an inductive reactance of $2.5\,\Omega$. Now,
$$X_L = 2\pi fL \qquad 2.5 = 2\pi 60L \qquad L = 6.63\,mH$$

24.290 A current of $(2.0 + j3.0)$ A is determined to be in a series circuit consisting of a sinusoidal generator and the following impedances: $\bar{Z}_1 = 4.0\underline{/0°}$, $\bar{Z}_2 = (6.0 + j5.0)$, $\bar{Z}_3 = -j2.0$. Calculate **(a)** the circuit impedance; **(b)** the voltage drop (in polar form) across each component; **(c)** the generator voltage.

▮ **(a)** $$\bar{Z}_T = \bar{Z}_1 + \bar{Z}_2 + \bar{Z}_3 = 4\underline{/0°} + (6 + j5) + (-j2) = (10 + j3) = 10.44\underline{/16.70}\,\Omega$$

   (b) $$\bar{I}\bar{Z}_1 = (2 + j3)(4\underline{/0°}) = (3.61\underline{/56.31°})(4\underline{/0°}) = 14.42\underline{/56.31°}\,V$$
   $$\bar{I}\bar{Z}_2 = (3.61\underline{/56.31°})(6 + j5) = 28.20\underline{/96.12°}\,V$$
   $$\bar{I}\bar{Z}_3 = (3.61\underline{/56.31°})(2\underline{/-90°}) = 7.22\underline{/-33.7°}\,V$$

   (c) $$\bar{V}_{gen} = \bar{I}_T\bar{Z}_T = (3.61\underline{/56.31°})(10.44\underline{/16.70°}) = 37.69\underline{/73.01°}\,V$$

24.291 A certain series circuit is composed of two generators, a 4.0-Ω resistor, a 10.0-Ω inductive reactance, and a 3.0-Ω capacitive reactance. If the generator voltages are $60\sin(1000t + 50°)$ and $100\sin(1000t + 30°)$, determine **(a)** the complex impedance; **(b)** the total driving voltage in polar form; **(c)** the magnitude and phase angle of the circuit current.

▮ **(a)** $$\bar{Z}_T = j10 + 4 - j3 = (4 + j7) = 8.06\underline{/60.26°}\,\Omega$$

   (b) $\bar{E}_T = 42.43\underline{/50°} + 70.71\underline{/30°} = (27.27 + j32.5) + (61.24 + j35.36) = (88.51 + j67.86) = 111.52\underline{/37.48°}\,V$

   (c) $$\bar{I} = \frac{\bar{E}_T}{\bar{Z}_T} = \frac{111.52\underline{/37.48°}}{8.06\underline{/60.26°}} = 13.84\underline{/-22.78°}\,A$$

24.292 A 100-V ac generator is connected in series with a $3.61\underline{/33.69°}\,\Omega$ impedance, a 5.0-Ω capacitive reactance, and a 2.0-Ω resistor. Sketch the circuit and determine the reading of a clip-on ammeter hooked over one of the connecting wires.

▮ See Fig. 24-94.
$$\bar{Z} = 2 - j5 + 3.61\underline{/33.69°} = 2 - j5 + (3.00 + j2.00) = 5.83\underline{/-30.96°}$$
$$\bar{I} = \frac{100\underline{/0°}}{5.83\underline{/-30.96°}} = 17.15\underline{/30.96°}\,A \qquad \text{Ammeter reads } 17.15\,A$$

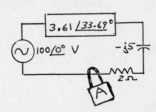

Fig. 24-94

24.293 A 240-V 400-Hz generator supplies a series connection of three ideal circuit elements. The elements are a 2.0-Ω resistor, a 3.0-Ω inductive reactance, and a 4.0-Ω capacitive reactance. Determine (a) the complex impedance; (b) the rms current; (c) the voltage drop across the inductance; (d) the steady-state current if the driver is replaced by a 240-V battery; (e) the steady-state voltage across the capacitor for the conditions in part (d).

▌ (a) $$\bar{Z} = 2 + j3 - j4 = 2 - j1 = 2.24 \underline{/-26.57°} \ \Omega$$

(b) $$\bar{I} = \frac{\bar{V}}{\bar{Z}} = \frac{240 \underline{/0°}}{2.24 \underline{/-26.57°}} = 107.33 \underline{/26.57°} \ \text{A} \qquad I = 107.33 \ \text{A}$$

(c) $$\bar{V}_L = \bar{I}jX_L = (107.33 \underline{/26.57°})(3 \underline{/90°}) = 321.99 \underline{/116.57°} \qquad V_L = 321.99 \ \text{V}$$

(d) The impedance of the capacitor at 0 Hz equals ∞. Hence, the steady-state current is *zero*.

(e) At steady state, the capacitor will have attained full charge, and $V_C = 240 \ \text{V}$.

24.294 A high-impedance rms voltmeter is used to measure the voltage drop across each of three series-connected ideal circuit elements. If the rms readings are 40 V, 25 V, and 60 V for V_L, V_R, and V_C, respectively, determine the equation for the voltage wave representing the driving voltage whose frequency is 20 Hz.

$$\bar{V}_T = \bar{V}_R + jV_L - jV_C = 25 + j40 - j60 = 25 - j20 = 32.02 \underline{/-38.66°}$$

$$v_T = 32.02\sqrt{2} \sin [2\pi 20t - 38.66°] = 45.28 \sin [125.66t - 38.66°]$$

24.295 A 6000-Hz 200-V generator is connected in series with a capacitive reactance of 6.0 Ω and a coil whose resistance and inductive reactance are 4.0 Ω and 2.0 Ω, respectively. Determine (a) the circuit impedance; (b) the circuit current; (c) the phasor diagram; (d) the rms voltage across the capacitor; (e) the rms voltage across the coil.

▌ (a) $$\bar{Z}_T = 4 + j2 - j6 = 5.66 \underline{/-45°} \ \Omega$$

(b) $$\bar{I} = \frac{\bar{V}_T}{\bar{Z}_T} = \frac{200 \underline{/0°}}{5.66 \underline{/-45°}} = 35.36 \underline{/45°} \ \text{A} \qquad I_{rms} = 35.36 \ \text{A}$$

(c) See Fig. 24-95.

(d) $$V_C = IX_C = 35.36(6) = 212.16 \ \text{V}$$

(e) $$\bar{Z}_{coil} = (4 + j2) = 4.47 \underline{/26.57°} \ \Omega \qquad V_{coil} = IZ_{coil} = (35.36)(4.47) = 158.06 \ \text{V}$$

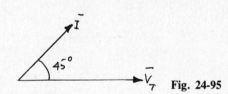

Fig. 24-95

24.296 In the circuit of Prob. 24-295 obtain (a) the maximum instantaneous stored energy in the capacitor and (b) the maximum instantaneous charge stored.

▌ $$X_C = \frac{1}{2\pi fC} \qquad 6 = \frac{1}{2\pi 6000C} \qquad C = 4.42 \ \mu\text{F}$$

$$W = \tfrac{1}{2}(4.42 \times 10^{-6})(212.13\sqrt{2})^2 = 198.9 \ \text{mJ}$$

$$q_{max} = CV_{max} = 4.42 \times 10^{-6}(212.13\sqrt{2}) = 1.33 \ \text{mC}$$

24.297 A coil of 30 mH, a resistor of 10 Ω, and a capacitance of 350 μF are connected in parallel and supplied by a 120-V 60-Hz generator. Determine (a) the current through each element; (b) the total line current; (c) the circuit impedance; (d) the phase angle between the feeder current and the driving voltage.

▌ (a) $$X_L = 2\pi fL = 2\pi 60(0.03) = 11.31 \ \Omega \qquad \bar{I}_L = \frac{\bar{V}_L}{jX_L} = \frac{120 \underline{/0°}}{11.31 \underline{/90°}} = 10.61 \underline{/-90°} \ \text{A}$$

$$\bar{I}_R = \frac{V_R}{R} = \frac{120\,\underline{/0°}}{10\,\underline{/0°}} = 12\,\underline{/0°}\,A \qquad X_C = \frac{1}{2\pi fC} = \frac{1}{2\pi 60(350 \times 10^{-6})} = 7.58\,\Omega$$

$$\bar{I}_C = \frac{\bar{V}_C}{-jX_C} = \frac{120\,\underline{/0°}}{7.58\,\underline{/-90°}} = 15.83\,\underline{/90°}$$

(b) $$\bar{I}_T = \bar{I}_R + \bar{I}_C + \bar{I}_L = 12 + j15.83 - j10.61 = (12 + j5.22) = 13.09\,\underline{/23.51°}\,A$$

(c) $$\bar{I}_T = \frac{\bar{V}_T}{\bar{Z}_T} \qquad 13.09\,\underline{/23.51°} = \frac{120\,\underline{/0°}}{\bar{Z}_T} \qquad \bar{Z}_T = 9.17\,\underline{/-23.51°}\,\Omega$$

(d) 23.51°.

24.298 A parallel circuit consisting of a 4.0-Ω resistor, a 2.0-Ω capacitive reactance, and a 6.0-Ω inductive reactance is fed from a 30-Hz 240-V generator. Determine (a) the circuit admittance; (b) the circuit impedance; (c) the feeder current; (d) the time-domain equations for the driving voltage and the feeder current; (e) the phasor diagram (drawn to scale) showing branch currents, feeder current, and driving voltage.

▌(a) $$\bar{Y}_T = \bar{Y}_1 + \bar{Y}_2 + \bar{Y}_3 = \frac{1}{4} + \frac{1}{j6} + \frac{1}{-j2} = (0.25 + j0.333) = 0.417\,\underline{/53.13°}\,S$$

(b) $$\bar{Z}_T = \frac{1}{\bar{Y}_T} = \frac{1}{0.417\,\underline{/53.13°}} = 2.40\,\underline{/-53.13°}\,\Omega$$

(c) $$\bar{I}_T = \frac{\bar{V}_T}{\bar{Z}_T} = \frac{240\,\underline{/0°}}{2.40\,\underline{/-53.13°}} = 100\,\underline{/53.13°}$$

(d) $$v_T = 240\sqrt{2}\sin(2\pi 30t) = 339.41\sin(188.5t)$$

$$i_T = 100\sqrt{2}\sin(2\pi 30t + 53.13°) = 141.42\sin(188.5t + 53°)$$

(e) $$\bar{I}_R = \frac{240\,\underline{/0°}}{4} = 60\,\underline{/0°}\,A \qquad \bar{I}_L = \frac{240\,\underline{/0°}}{6\,\underline{/90°}} = 40\,\underline{/-90°}\,A \qquad \bar{I}_C = \frac{240\,\underline{/0°}}{2\,\underline{/-90°}} = 120\,\underline{/90°}\,A$$

See Fig. 24-96 for the phasor diagram.

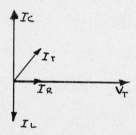

Fig. 24-96

24.299 A 400-V 50-Hz generator supplies current to a parallel circuit consisting of a 4.0-Ω resistor, a 5.0-Ω inductive reactance, and a 3.0-Ω capacitive reactance. Determine (a) the input admittance; (b) the input impedance; (c) the feeder current; (d) the time-domain equation for the feeder current.

▌(a) $$\bar{Y}_T = \frac{1}{4} + \frac{1}{-j3} + \frac{1}{j5} = 0.25 + j0.3333 - j0.2 = 0.283\,\underline{/28.01°}\,S$$

(b) $$\bar{Z}_T = \frac{1}{\bar{Y}_T} = \frac{1}{0.283\,\underline{/28.01°}} = 3.53\,\underline{/-28.01°}\,\Omega$$

(c) $$\bar{I}_T = \frac{\bar{V}_T}{\bar{Z}_T} = \frac{400\,\underline{/0°}}{3.53\,\underline{/-28.01°}} = 113.27\,\underline{/28.01°}\,A$$

(d) $$i = 113.27\sqrt{2}\sin[2\pi 50t + \underline{/28.01°}]\,A$$

24.300 In the circuit of Prob. 24.299, find the steady-state current if the ac source is replaced by a 400-V dc source.

❚ For dc input $f = 0$, $R = 4\,\Omega$, $X_L = 0$, and $X_C = \infty$.

And
$$\bar{Y}_T = \frac{1}{4} + \frac{1}{j0} + \frac{1}{j\infty} = -j\infty = \infty \,\underline{/-90°}\,\text{S}$$

or
$$\bar{I}_T = \bar{V}\bar{Y}_T = (400)(\infty\,\underline{/-90°}) = \infty\,\text{A}$$

24.301 A parallel circuit consisting of a 2.0-Ω resistor, a 4.0-H inductor, and a 0.0070-F capacitor is connected to a sinusoidal driver. The equation for the driving voltage is $v = 100 \sin(30t + 40°)$. Determine (*a*) the frequency of the supply voltage; (*b*) the inductive reactance; (*c*) the rms current drawn by the inductor; (*d*) the equation for the current wave to the inductor; (*e*) the instantaneous energy stored in the capacitor at $t = 0.1\,\text{s}$; (*f*) the rate of expenditure of heat energy at $t = 0.1\,\text{s}$.

❚ (*a*)
$$2\pi f = 30 \qquad f = 4.77\,\text{Hz}$$

(*b*)
$$X_L = 2\pi fL = 30(4) = 120\,\Omega$$

(*c*)
$$\bar{I}_L = \frac{\bar{V}_L}{jX_L} = \frac{100/\sqrt{2}\,\underline{/40°}}{120\,\underline{/90°}} = 0.59\,\underline{/-50°}\,\text{A}$$

(*d*)
$$i_L = 0.59\sqrt{2} \sin(30t - 50°)$$

(*e*)
$$W_C = \tfrac{1}{2}CV^2 = \tfrac{1}{2}(0.007)\{100\sin[30(0.1)(57.3) + 40°]\}^2 = 9.8\,\text{J}$$

(*f*)
$$P_H = \frac{v_R^2}{R} = \frac{\{100\sin[30(0.1)(57.3) + 40°]\}^2}{2} = 1396\,\text{W}$$

24.302 A parallel circuit consisting of a 5.0-Ω capacitive reactance, a 4.0-Ω resistor, and a 2.0-Ω inductive reactance is connected to a 240-V 60-Hz generator. Determine (*a*) the circuit admittance; (*b*) the current to each component; (*c*) the feeder current.

❚ (*a*)
$$\bar{Y}_T = \frac{1}{4} + \frac{1}{-j5} + \frac{1}{j2} = 0.25 + j0.20 - j0.50 = 0.25 - j0.3 = 0.391\,\underline{/-50.19°}\,\text{S}$$

(*b*)
$$\bar{I}_C = \frac{240\,\underline{/0°}}{5\,\underline{/-90°}} = 48\,\underline{/90°}\,\text{A} \qquad \bar{I}_R = \frac{240\,\underline{/0°}}{4\,\underline{/0°}} = 60\,\underline{/0°}\,\text{A} \qquad \bar{I}_L = \frac{240\,\underline{/0°}}{2\,\underline{/90°}} = 120\,\underline{/-90°}\,\text{A}$$

(*c*)
$$\bar{I}_T = \bar{I}_R + \bar{I}_L + \bar{I}_C = j48 + 60 + (-j120) = 60 - j72 = 93.72\,\underline{/-50.19°}\,\text{A}$$

24.303 In the circuit of Prob. 24.302, find (*a*) the values of inductance and capacitance; (*b*) the maximum instantaneous energy stored in the magnetic field.

❚
$$X_L = 2\pi fL \qquad 2 = 2\pi 60L \qquad L = 5.3\,\text{mH}$$
$$X_C = \frac{1}{2\pi fC} \qquad 5 = \frac{1}{2\pi 60C} \qquad C = 530.5\,\mu\text{F}$$
$$W_\phi = \tfrac{1}{2}Li_L^2 = \tfrac{1}{2}(0.0053)(120\sqrt{2})^2 = 76.32\,\text{J}$$

24.304 Two parallel-connected impedances are fed by a sinusoidal voltage wave expressed by $v_t = 170\sin(377t + 60°)$. The impedances are $2.9\,\underline{/-16°}\,\Omega$ and $8.5\,\underline{/10.5°}\,\Omega$. Determine the rms current in each impedance and the rms feeder current.

❚
$$\bar{V}_T = (170/\sqrt{2})\,\underline{/60°} = 120.2\,\underline{/60°}\,\text{V} \qquad \bar{I}_A = \frac{120.2\,\underline{/60°}}{2.9\,\underline{/-16°}} = 41.45\,\underline{/76°}\,\text{A}$$

$$\bar{I}_B = \frac{120.2\,\underline{/60°}}{8.5\,\underline{/10.5°}} = 14.14\,\underline{/49.5°}\,\text{A} \qquad I_A = 41.45\,\text{A} \qquad I_B = 14.14\,\text{A}$$

$$\bar{I}_T = \bar{I}_A + \bar{I}_B = 41.45\,\underline{/76°} + 14.14\,\underline{/49.5°} = (10.03 + j40.22) + (9.18 + j10.75)$$

$$= (19.21 + j50.97) = 54.47\,\underline{/69.35°}\,\text{A}$$

$$I_T = 54.47\,\text{A}$$

24.305 A branch consisting of a 200-μF capacitor in series with a 5.0-Ω resistor is connected in parallel with a $(10 + j4.0)$-Ω impedance. The generator voltage is $100\sin377t$. Determine (*a*) the current in the series branch; (*b*) the current in the $(10 + j4.0)$-Ω branch; (*c*) the feeder current.

▌ (a) $\quad X_C = \dfrac{1}{2\pi fC} = \dfrac{1}{377(200 \times 10^{-6})} = 13.26\,\Omega \quad \bar{Z} = R - jX_C = (5 - j13.26) = 14.17\,\underline{/-69.34°}\,\Omega$

$$\bar{I} = \dfrac{\bar{V}_T}{\bar{Z}} = \dfrac{100/\sqrt{2}\,\underline{/0°}}{14.17\,\underline{/-69.34°}} = 4.99\,\underline{/69.34°}\,A$$

(b) $\qquad\qquad \bar{Z} = (10 + j4) = 10.77\,\underline{/21.8°}\,\Omega \quad \bar{I} = \dfrac{\bar{V}}{\bar{Z}} = \dfrac{100/\sqrt{2}\,\underline{/0°}}{10.77\,\underline{/21.8°}} = 6.57\,\underline{/-21.8°}\,A$

(c) $\quad \bar{I}_T = 4.99\,\underline{/69.34°} + 6.57\,\underline{/-21.8°} = (1.76 + j4.67) + (6.10 - j2.44) = (7.86 + j2.23) = 8.17\,\underline{/15.83°}$

24.306 Determine the input impedance of a parallel circuit consisting of a 2.0-Ω resistor branch, a $(3.0 + j8.0)$-Ω branch, and a branch containing a 4.0-Ω capacitive reactance.

▌ $\qquad \bar{Y}_T = \dfrac{1}{2} + \dfrac{1}{3 + j\,8} + \dfrac{1}{-j4} = 0.5 + 0.1171\,\underline{/-69.44°} + 0.25\,\underline{/90°} = 0.5 + (0.041 - j0.110) + j0.25$

$\qquad\quad = (0.541 + j0.14) = 0.56\,\underline{/14.51°}\,S$

$$\bar{Z}_T = \dfrac{1}{\bar{Y}_T} = \dfrac{1}{0.56\,\underline{/14.51°}} = 1.79\,\underline{/-14.51°}\,\Omega$$

24.307 A 240-V 60-Hz generator supplies energy to a parallel circuit consisting of a 5.0-Ω capacitive reactance, a 2.0-Ω resistor, and a $(0.10 + j0.40)$-S admittance. Determine the feeder current.

▌ $\qquad \bar{Y}_T = \dfrac{1}{5\,\underline{/-90°}} + \dfrac{1}{2} + (0.1 + j0.4) = j0.2 + 0.5 + 0.1 + j0.4 = (0.6 + j0.6) = 0.85\,\underline{/45°}\,S$

$$\bar{I}_T = \bar{V}_T\bar{Y}_T = (240\,\underline{/0°})(0.85\,\underline{/45°}) = 203.65\,\underline{/45°}\,A$$

24.308 A 400-V 50-Hz generator supplies current to a parallel circuit consisting of a $(2.0 + j3.0)$-Ω impedance and a $(3.0 + j4.0)$-Ω impedance. Determine (a) the input admittance; (b) the feeder current; (c) the time-domain equation for the current in the $(3.0 + j4.0)$-Ω impedance.

▌ (a) $\quad \bar{Y}_T = \dfrac{1}{2 + j3} + \dfrac{1}{3 + j4} = 0.2770\,\underline{/-56.31°} + 0.200\,\underline{/-53.13°} = (0.1537 - j0.2305) + (0.120 - j0.160)$

$\qquad\quad = 0.4769\,\underline{/-55.0°}\,S$

(b) $\qquad\qquad\qquad \bar{I}_T = \bar{V}_T\bar{Y}_T = (400\,\underline{/0°})(0.4769\,\underline{/-55.0°}) = 190.8\,\underline{/-55°}\,A$

(c) $\qquad\qquad \bar{I} = \dfrac{\bar{V}}{\bar{Z}} = \dfrac{400\,\underline{/0°}}{(3 + j4)} = 80\,\underline{/-53.13°}\,A \qquad i = 80\sqrt{2}\sin\,(2\pi 50t - 53.13°)$

24.309 A branch consisting of a 200-μF capacitor in series with a 5.0-Ω resistor is connected in parallel with a coil whose resistance and inductance are 10 Ω and 0.0106 H, respectively. The generator voltage is 100 sin 377t V. Sketch the circuit and determine (a) the current to the capacitor; (b) the current in the coil; (c) the feeder current.

▌ See Fig. 24-97.

(a) $\qquad\qquad\qquad\qquad V_T = (100/\sqrt{2})\,\underline{/0°} = 70.71\,\underline{/0°}\,V$

$$X_C = \dfrac{1}{377(200 \times 10^{-6})} = 13.26\,\Omega$$

$$\bar{Z}_{\text{ser}} = (5 - j13.26) = 14.17\,\underline{/-69.34°}\,\Omega$$

$$I_{\text{ser}} = \dfrac{V_T}{\bar{Z}_{\text{ser}}} = \dfrac{70.7\,\underline{/0°}}{14.17\,\underline{/-69.34°}} = 4.99\,\underline{/69.34°}\,A$$

(b) $\qquad \bar{Z}_{\text{coil}} = (10 + j4) = 10.77\,\underline{/21.78°}\,\Omega \quad X_L = 2\pi fL = 377(0.0106) = 4\,\Omega$

$$\bar{I}_{\text{coil}} = \dfrac{\bar{V}_T}{\bar{Z}_{\text{coil}}} = \dfrac{70.71\,\underline{/0°}}{10.77\,\underline{/21.78°}} = 6.57\,\underline{/-21.78°}\,A$$

(c) $\qquad\qquad\qquad \bar{I}_T = \bar{I}_{\text{ser}} + \bar{I}_{\text{coil}} = 4.99\,\underline{/69.34°} + 6.57\,\underline{/-21.78°}$

$$= (1.76 + j4.67) + (6.10 - j2.44) = 8.17\,\underline{/15.84°}\,A$$

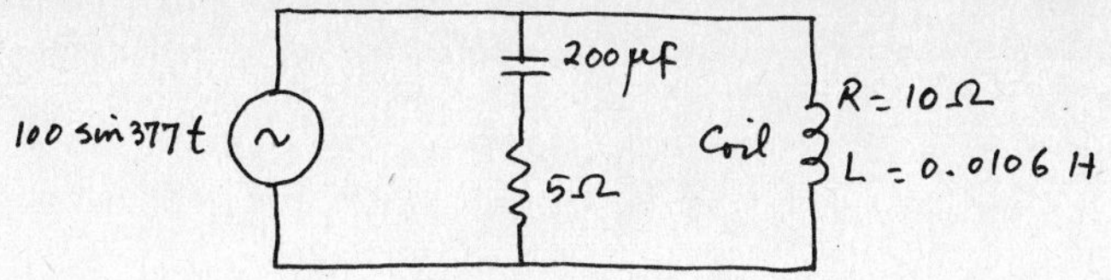

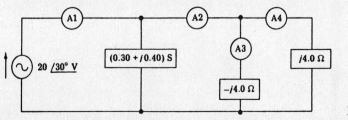

Fig. 24-97

24.310 In the circuit of Fig. 24-97, the ac source is replaced by a 12-V battery. What is the steady-state current input to the circuit?

▮ In this case, since the capacitor acts as an open circuit, the current is determined by the resistance of the coil. Hence,

$$I_T = 12/10 = 1.2 \text{ A}$$

24.311 A 450-V 60-Hz source supplies a phasor current of $5.0\ \underline{/-60°}$ A to an impedance. Determine (a) the impedance in ohms; (b) a set of series-connected circuit elements that can be used to construct the impedance (express the elements in henrys, ohms, and/or farads as applicable); (c) a set of parallel-connected circuit elements that can be used to make an equivalent impedance.

▮ (a) $\qquad \bar{I}_T = \dfrac{\bar{V}_T}{\bar{Z}_T} \qquad 5\ \underline{/-60°} = \dfrac{450\ \underline{/0°}}{\bar{Z}_T} \qquad \bar{Z}_T = 90\ \underline{/60°}\ \Omega$

(b) $\qquad \bar{Z}_T = (45 + j77.94) \qquad$ or $\qquad R = 45\ \Omega \qquad X_L = 77.94\ \Omega = 2\pi(60)L \qquad L = 0.207 \text{ H}$

(c) $\qquad \bar{Y}_T = \dfrac{1}{\bar{Z}_T} = \dfrac{1}{90\ \underline{/60°}} = 0.0111\ \underline{/-60°} = (0.0056 - j0.0096) = \bar{Y}_1 + \bar{Y}_2$

$$\bar{Z}_1 = \dfrac{1}{\bar{Y}_1} = \dfrac{1}{0.0056} = 180\ \Omega \qquad \bar{Z}_2 = \dfrac{1}{\bar{Y}_2} = \dfrac{1}{0.0096\ \underline{/-90°}} = 103.92\ \underline{/90°}\ \Omega$$

Thus, $\qquad \bar{Z}_1 = 180\text{-}\Omega$ resistor $\qquad \bar{Z}_2 = 103.92\text{-}\Omega$ inductive reactance

$$X_L = 2\pi fL \qquad 103.92 = 2\pi 60 L \qquad L = 275.7 \text{ mH}$$

24.312 Determine the resistance, inductance, and/or capacitive values of parallel-connected circuit elements that draw a total of $20\ \underline{/-30°}$ A from a 60-Hz sinusoidal generator whose driving voltage is $100\ \underline{/0°}$ V.

▮ $\qquad \bar{I}_T = \bar{V}_T \bar{Y}_T \qquad 20\ \underline{/-30°} = 100\ \underline{/0°} \bar{Y}_T \qquad \bar{Y}_T = 0.20\ \underline{/-30°} = (0.1732 - j0.1000) \text{ S}$

$\qquad \bar{Y}_1 = 0.1732 \text{ S} \qquad \bar{Y}_2 = -j0.1000 \qquad \bar{Z}_1 = 1/\bar{Y}_1 = 5.77\ \Omega \qquad \bar{Z}_2 = 1/\bar{Y}_2 = j10\ \Omega$

Thus, Z_1 is a resistor of $5.77\ \Omega$ and Z_2 is an inductive reactance of $10\ \Omega$, and

$$X_L = 2\pi fL \qquad 10 = 2\pi 60 L \qquad L = 26.5 \text{ mH}$$

24.313 Repeat Prob. 24.312 for series-connected elements.

▮ $\qquad \bar{I}_T = \dfrac{\bar{V}_T}{\bar{Z}_T} \qquad 20\ \underline{/-30°} = \dfrac{100\ \underline{/0°}}{\bar{Z}_T} \qquad \bar{Z}_T = 5\ \underline{/30°} = (4.33 + j2.50)$

Thus, $\qquad R = 4.33\ \Omega \qquad X_L = 2\pi fL \qquad 2.5 = 2\pi 60 L \qquad L = 6.63 \text{ mH}$

24.314 Determine the ammeter readings in the circuit shown in Fig. 24-98.

Fig. 24-98

$$\bar{I}_4 = \frac{\bar{V}_4}{j4} = \frac{20\ \underline{/30°}}{4\ \underline{/90°}} = 5\ \underline{/60°} \qquad A_4 = 5\ \text{A}$$

$$\bar{I}_3 = \frac{\bar{V}_3}{-j4} = \frac{20\ \underline{/30°}}{4\ \underline{/-90°}} = 5\ \underline{/120°} \qquad A_3 = 5\ \text{A}$$

$$\bar{I}_2 = \bar{I}_3 + \bar{I}_4 = 5\ \underline{/-60°} + 5\ \underline{/120°} = 0 \qquad A_2 = 0\ \text{A}$$

$$\bar{I}_1 = \bar{V}_T \bar{Y}_1 = (20\ \underline{/30°})(0.3 + j0.4) = (20\ \underline{/30°})(0.5\underline{/53.13°}) \qquad I_1 = 10\ \underline{/83.13°} \qquad A_1 = 10\ \text{A}$$

24.315 A feeder current of 250 A is supplied to the following paralleled impedances:

$$\bar{Z}_1 = 5\ \underline{/20°}\ \Omega \qquad \bar{Z}_2 = 6\ \underline{/0°}\ \Omega \qquad \bar{Z}_3 = 10\ \underline{/15°}\ \Omega \qquad \bar{Z}_4 = 8\ \underline{/-60°}\ \Omega$$

Determine the current drawn by $\bar{Z}_3$.

$$\bar{Y}_T = \frac{1}{5\ \underline{/20°}} + \frac{1}{6\ \underline{/0°}} + \frac{1}{10\ \underline{/15°}} + \frac{1}{8\ \underline{/-60°}} = 0.1879 - j0.0684 + 0.1667 + j0.0$$

$$+\ 0.0966 - j0.0259 + 0.0625 + j0.1083$$

$$= (0.5137 + j0.0140) = 0.5139\ \underline{/1.5574°}\ \text{S}$$

$$\bar{I}_3 = \bar{I}_T\left[\frac{\bar{Y}_3}{\bar{Y}_T}\right] = 250\left[\frac{0.1\ \underline{/-15°}}{0.5139\ \underline{/1.56°}}\right] = 48.65\ \underline{/-16.56°}\ \text{A}$$

24.316 A dc generator supplies a total of 100 A to the following paralleled resistors:

$$R_1 = 2\ \Omega \qquad R_2 = 3\ \Omega \qquad R_3 = 5\ \Omega \qquad R_4 = 7\ \Omega \qquad R_5 = 4\ \Omega \qquad R_6 = 9\ \Omega$$

Determine the current in R_1 and R_6.

$$Y_T = \tfrac{1}{2} + \tfrac{1}{3} + \tfrac{1}{5} + \tfrac{1}{7} + \tfrac{1}{4} + \tfrac{1}{9} = 1.5373\ \text{S}$$

$$I_1 = \bar{I}_T\left[\frac{Y_1}{Y_T}\right] = 100\left[\frac{0.5}{1.5373}\right] = 32.52\ \text{A} \qquad I_6 = 100\left[\frac{0.1111}{1.5373}\right] = 7.23\ \text{A}$$

24.317 A $40\ \underline{/30°}$-Ω impedance is connected in series with the following paralleled group of impedances:

$$\bar{Z}_1 = 3\ \underline{/60°}\ \Omega \qquad \bar{Z}_2 = 5\ \underline{/40°}\ \Omega \qquad \bar{Z}_3 = 8\ \underline{/60°}\ \Omega \qquad \bar{Z}_4 = 4\ \underline{/-25°}\ \Omega$$

If the voltage drop across the $40\ \underline{/30°}$-Ω impedance is $200\ \underline{/0°}$ V, determine   (*a*) the current in $\bar{Z}_3$,   (*b*) the voltage drop across the paralleled section.

(*a*) By Ohm's law:

$$\bar{I}_Z = \frac{\bar{V}_Z}{\bar{Z}} = \frac{200\ \underline{/0°}}{40\ \underline{/30°}} = 5\ \underline{/-30°}\ \text{A} \qquad \bar{Y}_T = \frac{1}{3\ \underline{/60°}} + \frac{1}{5\ \underline{/40°}} + \frac{1}{8\ \underline{/60°}} + \frac{1}{4\ \underline{/-25°}}$$

$$\bar{Y}_T = 0.1667 - j0.2886 + 0.1532 - j0.1286 + 0.0625 - j0.1083 + 0.2266 + j0.1057$$

$$= (0.6089 - j0.4198) = 0.7396\ \underline{/-34.58°}\ \text{S}$$

The current in $\bar{Z}_3$ is

$$\bar{I}_3 = \bar{I}_T\left[\frac{\bar{Y}_3}{\bar{Y}_T}\right] = 5\ \underline{/-30°}\left[\frac{0.1250\ \underline{/-60°}}{0.7396\ \underline{/-34.58°}}\right] = 0.845\ \underline{/-55.42°}\ \text{A}$$

(*b*) $$\bar{V}_{\text{parallel sec}} = \bar{V}_3 = \bar{I}_3\bar{Z}_3 = (0.845\ \underline{/-55.42°})(8\ \underline{/60°}) = 6.76\ \underline{/4.58°}\ \text{V}$$

24.318 Determine the input impedance for the circuit shown in Fig. 24-99.   The circuit parameters are $\bar{Z}_1 = (3 + j4)$, $\bar{Z}_2 = 9.8\ \underline{/-78°}$, $\bar{Z}_3 = 18.5\ \underline{/21.8°}$.   The 400-Hz sinusoidal generator has an rms voltage of 100 V.

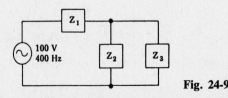

Fig. 24-99

$$\bar{Y}_{par} = \bar{Y}_2 + \bar{Y}_3 = \frac{1}{9.8 \underline{/-78°}} + \frac{1}{18.5 \underline{/21.8°}} = (0.0212 + j0.0998) + (0.0502 - j0.0201)$$

$$= 0.1070 \underline{/48.14°} \text{ S}$$

$$\bar{Z}_{par} = \frac{1}{0.1070 \underline{/48.14°}} = 9.345 \underline{/-48.14°} = (6.236 - j6.961)$$

$$\bar{Z}_{in} = \bar{Z}_1 + \bar{Z}_{par} = (3 + j4) + (6.236 - j6.961)$$

$$= (9.236 - j2.961) = 9.699 \underline{/-17.78°} \text{ } \Omega$$

24.319 For the circuit section shown in Fig. 24-100, $\bar{Z}_1 = 4 \underline{/50°}$, $\bar{Z}_2 = 6 \underline{/40°}$, $\bar{Z}_3 = 5 \underline{/30°}$, $\bar{Z}_4 = 2 \underline{/20°}$, $\bar{Z}_5 = 6 \underline{/60°}$. Determine (*a*) the voltmeter reading; (*b*) the ammeter reading, (*c*) the time-domain equation for the current in $\bar{Z}_1$ (assume a 60-Hz driver).

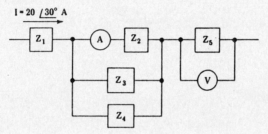

Fig. 24-100

(*a*) $\qquad \bar{V}_5 = \bar{I}_5\bar{Z}_5 = (20 \underline{/30°})(6 \underline{/60°}) = 120 \underline{/90°} \text{ V} \qquad$ Voltmeter reads 120 V

(*b*) For the parallel branch,

$$\bar{Y}_T = \frac{1}{6 \underline{/40°}} + \frac{1}{5 \underline{/30°}} + \frac{1}{2 \underline{/20°}} = (0.7708 - j0.3782) = 0.8585 \underline{/-26.135°} \text{ S}$$

$$\bar{I}_2 = \bar{I}_T \left[\frac{\bar{Y}}{\bar{Y}_T} \right] = 20 \underline{/30°} \left[\frac{0.1667 \underline{/-40°}}{0.8585 \underline{/-26.14°}} \right] = 3.88 \underline{/16.14°} \text{ A} \qquad \text{Ammeter reads 3.88 A}$$

(*c*) $\qquad\qquad\qquad i = 20\sqrt{2} \sin (2\pi 60t + 30°)$

24.320 A certain series-parallel circuit contains an impedance $\bar{Z}_1$ in series with a parallel combination of $\bar{Z}_2$ and $\bar{Z}_3$. The sinusoidal driving voltage is $240 \underline{/30°}$ V. The impedances are $\bar{Z}_1 = (1 - j1)$, $\bar{Z}_2 = (1 + j1)$, $\bar{Z}_3 = (1 - j1)$. Determine (*a*) the driving-point impedance; (*b*) the driving-point admittance; (*c*) the current supplied by the generator; (*d*) the voltage drop across $\bar{Z}_1$.

(*a*) $\qquad \bar{Z}_P = \frac{\bar{Z}_2\bar{Z}_3}{\bar{Z}_2 + \bar{Z}_3} = \frac{(1 + j1)(1 - j1)}{(1 + j1) + (1 - j1)} = 1.0 \text{ } \Omega$

$$\bar{Z}_{in} = \bar{Z}_1 + \bar{Z}_P = (1 - j1) + 1.0 = 2 - j1 = 2.2359 \underline{/-26.57°} \text{ } \Omega$$

(*b*) $\qquad\qquad \bar{Y}_{in} = \frac{1}{\bar{Z}_{in}} = \frac{1}{2.236 \underline{/-26.57°}} = 0.4472 \underline{/26.57°} \text{ S}$

(*c*) $\qquad\qquad \bar{I}_T = \bar{V}_T\bar{Y}_{in} = (240 \underline{/30°})(0.4472 \underline{/26.57°}) = 107.34 \underline{/56.57°} \text{ A}$

(*d*) $\qquad\qquad \bar{V}_1 = \bar{I}\bar{Z}_1 = (107.34 \underline{/56.57°})(1 - j1) = 151.78 \underline{/11.57°} \text{ V}$

24.321 Determine the ammeter and voltmeter readings for the circuit shown in Fig. 24-101. The 60-Hz generator supplies 240 V to the circuit, and the impedances are $\bar{Z}_1 = 3 + j2$, $\bar{Z}_2 = 4 + j1$, $\bar{Z}_3 = 2 - j5$, $\bar{Z}_4 = 3 + j6$, $\bar{Z}_5 = 4 + j7$, $\bar{Z}_6 = 2 + j3$.

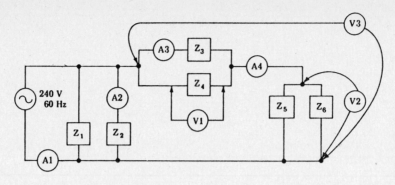

Fig. 24-101

$\blacksquare$ $\bar{Z}_1 = (3 + j2) = 3.606\ \underline{/33.69°}\ \Omega$ $\bar{Z}_2 = (4 + j1) = 4.123\ \underline{/14.036°}\ \Omega$ $\bar{Z}_3 = (2 - j5) = 5.385\ \underline{/-68.199°}\ \Omega$

$\bar{Z}_4 = (3 + j6) = 6.708\ \underline{/63.435°}\ \Omega$ $\bar{Z}_5 = (4 + j7) = 8.062\ \underline{/60.255°}\ \Omega$ $\bar{Z}_6 = (2 + j3) = 3.606\ \underline{/56.310}\ \Omega$

$$\bar{I}_2 = \frac{240\ \underline{/0°}}{4.123\ \underline{/14.036°}} = 58.21\ \underline{/-14.036°}\quad\text{Ammeter A2 reads 58.21 A}$$

$$\bar{Z}_{P(1,2)} = \frac{(3.606\ \underline{/33.69°})(4.123\ \underline{/14.036°})}{(3 + j2) + (4 + j1)} = 1.952\ \underline{/24.53°}\ \Omega$$

$$\bar{Z}_{P(3,4)} = \frac{(5.385\ \underline{/-68.199°})(6.708\ \underline{/63.435°})}{(2 - j5) + (3 + j6)} = 7.0827\ \underline{/-16.06°}\ \Omega$$

$$\bar{Z}_{P(5,6)} = \frac{(8.062\ \underline{/60.255°})(3.606\ \underline{/56.310°})}{(4 + j7) + (2 + j3)} = 2.4932\ \underline{/57.53°}\ \Omega$$

$$\underbrace{\bar{Z}_{P(3,4)} + \bar{Z}_{P(5,6)}}\ = 7.0827\ \underline{/-16.06°} + 2.4932\ \underline{/57.53°}$$

$$\bar{Z}_A = (6.8063 - j1.9594) + (1.3385 + j2.1034)$$

$$= (8.1448 + j0.1441) = 8.1460\ \underline{/1.0133°}\ \Omega$$

$$\bar{Z}_{in} = \frac{\bar{Z}_{(1,2)}\bar{Z}_A}{\bar{Z}_{(1,2)} + \bar{Z}_A} = \frac{(1.952\ \underline{/24.53°})(8.1460\ \underline{/1.0133°})}{(1.7758 + j0.81041) + (8.1448 + j0.1441)} = 1.5957\ \underline{/20.04°}\ \Omega$$

$$\bar{I}_1 = \frac{\bar{V}_T}{\bar{Z}_{in}} = \frac{240\ \underline{/0°}}{1.5957\ \underline{/20.040°}} = 150.41\ \underline{/-20.04°}\ \text{A}\quad\text{Ammeter A1 reads 150.4 A}$$

$$\bar{I}_4 = \frac{\bar{V}_T}{\bar{Z}} = \frac{240\ \underline{/0°}}{8.1460\ \underline{/1.0133°}} = 29.4623\ \underline{/-1.0133°}\ \text{A}\quad\text{Ammeter A4 reads 29.46 A}$$

$$\bar{I}_3 = \bar{I}_4\left[\frac{\bar{Y}_3}{\bar{Y}_{3,4}}\right] = [29.46\ \underline{/-1.01}]\left[\frac{0.1857\ \underline{/68.199°}}{0.1412\ \underline{/16.06°}}\right] = 38.74\ \underline{/51.13°}\ \text{A}\quad\text{Ammeter A3 reads 38.74 A}$$

$$V_1 = I_3 Z_3 = (38.74)(5.385) = 208.64\ \text{V}\quad\text{Voltmeter V1 reads 208.64 V}$$

$$V_2 = I_4 Z_{(5,6)} = (29.46)(2.4932) = 73.45\ \text{V}\quad\text{Voltmeter V2 reads 73.45 V}$$

24.322 The voltage across a certain parallel section of a series-parallel circuit is $120\ \underline{/60°}$ V. The parallel section consists of a $(2.0 + j3.0)$-Ω branch in parallel with a $(4.0 - j8.0)$-Ω branch. Determine *(a)* the current in each branch; *(b)* the total current to the parallel section.

$\blacksquare$ $\bar{Z}_A = 2 + j3 = 3.61\ \underline{/56.31°}\ \Omega$ $\bar{Z}_B = 4 - j8 = 8.94\ \underline{/-63.43°}\ \Omega$

(a) $\bar{I}_A = \dfrac{120\ \underline{/60°}}{3.61\ \underline{/56.31°}} = 33.24\ \underline{/3.69°}\ \text{A}$ $\bar{I}_B = \dfrac{120\ \underline{/60°}}{8.94\ \underline{/-63.43°}} = 13.42\ \underline{/123.43°}\ \text{A}$

(b) $\bar{I}_T = \bar{I}_A + \bar{I}_B = (33.17 + j2.14) + (-7.39 + j11.2) = 29.02\ \underline{/27.36°}\ \text{A}$

24.323 An inductive reactance of $1.0\ \Omega$ is connected in series with two parallel-connected branches whose respective impedances are $(4.0 + j3.0)$ and $(2.0 - j3.0)\ \Omega$. The circuit is supplied by a 450-V 25-Hz generator. Sketch the circuit and determine *(a)* the input impedance; *(b)* the current supplied by the generator; *(c)* the current in the $(2.0 - j3.0)$-Ω impedance; *(d)* the voltage drop across the $(4.0 + j3.0)$-Ω impedance; *(e)* the voltage drop across the 1.0-Ω inductive reactance.

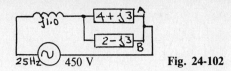

Fig. 24-102

I See Fig. 24-102.

(a)
$$\bar{Z}_A = 5\ \underline{/36.87°}\ \Omega \qquad \bar{Z}_B = 3.61\ \underline{/-56.31°}\ \Omega$$

$$\bar{Y}_A = 0.200\ \underline{/-36.87°}\ S \qquad \bar{Y}_B = 0.2774\ \underline{/56.31°}\ S$$

$$\bar{Z}_P = \frac{\bar{Z}_A \bar{Z}_B}{\bar{Z}_A + \bar{Z}_B} = \frac{(5\ \underline{/36.87°})(3.61\ \underline{/-56.31°})}{(4+j3)+(2-j3)} = 3.00\ \underline{/-19.44°}$$

$$Z_{\text{in}} = \overbrace{(2.83 - j1.00)} + j1.0 = 2.83\ \underline{/0°}\ \Omega$$

(b)
$$\bar{I}_T = \frac{\bar{V}_T}{\bar{Z}_{\text{in}}} = \frac{450\ \underline{/0°}}{2.83\ \underline{/0°}} = 159.01\ A$$

(c)
$$\bar{I}_B = \bar{I}_T\left(\frac{\bar{Y}_B}{\bar{Y}_P}\right) = 159.01\left(\frac{0.2774\ \underline{/56.31°}}{0.333\ \underline{/19.44°}}\right) = 132.5\ \underline{/36.87°}\ A$$

(d)
$$\bar{V}_A = \bar{I}_T \bar{Z}_P = 159.01(3.00\ \underline{/-19.44°}) = 477\ \underline{/-19.44°}\ V$$

(e)
$$\bar{V} = (159.01)(1\ \underline{/90°}) = 159.01\ \underline{/90°}\ V$$

24.324 Draw the phasor diagram for the circuit of Prob. 24.323.

I See Fig. 24-103.

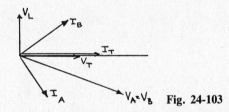

Fig. 24-103

24.325 In the circuit of Prob. 24.323 (a) write the time-domain equation for the current through the $(4.0 + j3.0)$-Ω impedance; (b) assuming the sinusoidal generator is replaced by a 450-battery, solve for the steady-state current supplied by the battery.

I (a)
$$\bar{I}_A = \bar{I}_T\left[\frac{\bar{Y}_A}{\bar{Y}_P}\right] = 159.01\left[\frac{0.2000\ \underline{/-36.87°}}{0.333\ \underline{/19.44°}}\right] = 95.53\ \underline{/-56.31°}\ A$$

$$i_A = 95.53\sqrt{2}\sin{[2\pi 25t - 56.31°]}$$

(b) At 0 Hz and steady state, the capacitor acts as an open circuit and the inductance has no effect. Thus,

$$\bar{I}_{\text{ss}} = \tfrac{450}{4} = 112.5\ A$$

24.326 Determine the voltmeter and ammeter readings in the circuit of Fig. 24-104.

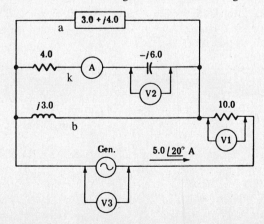

Fig. 24-104

∎ $V_1 = (10 \underline{/0°})(5 \underline{/20°}) = 50 \underline{/20°}$ Voltmeter V1 reads 50 V

The admittance of parallel branches a, k, b is

$$\bar{Y}_P = \frac{1}{3+j4} + \frac{1}{4-j6} + \frac{1}{j3} = 0.1200 - j0.1600 + 0.0769 + j0.1154 + 0 - j0.3333$$

$$= (0.1969 - j0.3779) = 0.4262 \underline{/-62.48°} \text{ S}$$

$$\bar{I}_k = I_T\left(\frac{y_k}{Y_T}\right) = 5 \underline{/20°}\left(\frac{0.0769 + j0.1154}{0.4262 \underline{/-62.48}}\right) = 1.63 \underline{/138.79°}$$ Ammeter reads 1.63 A

$$\bar{V}_2 = (1.63 \underline{/138.79°})(6 \underline{/-90°}) = 9.78 \underline{/48.79°}$$ Voltmeter V2 reads 9.78 V

$$\bar{Z}_{in} = 10 + \bar{Z}_P = 10 + \frac{1}{0.4262 \underline{/-62.48°}} = 10 + (1.08 + j2.08) = 11.08 + j2.08 = 11.27 \underline{/10.64°} \Omega$$

$$\bar{V}_3 = \bar{I}\bar{Z}_{in} = (5 \underline{/20°})(11.27 \underline{/10.64°}) = 56.37 \underline{/30.64°}$$ Voltmeter V3 reads 56.37 V

24.327 Repeat Prob. 24.326 if the ac source is replaced by a battery delivering 5 A current to the circuit.

∎ For a dc input, the circuit becomes as shown in Fig. 24-105, since $X_L = 0$ and $X_C = \infty$. Hence, we have

V_1 reads $10 \times 5 = 50$ V V_2 reads 0 V V_3 reads 50 V A reads 0 A

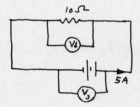

Fig. 24-105

24.328 A 20-Ω resistor, a 50-μF capacitor, and a coil whose inductance and resistance are 50 mH and 8.0 Ω, respectively, are connected in parallel and supplied by a 400-V 60-Hz system as shown in Fig. 24-106a. (a) Calculate the current to each branch; (b) calculate the feeder current; (c) draw the corresponding phasor diagram.

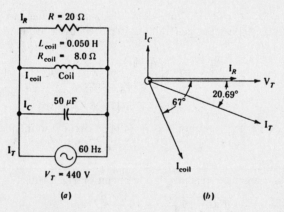

(a)   (b)   **Fig. 24-106**

∎ (a) $\bar{I}_R = \dfrac{\bar{V}_T}{R} = \dfrac{440 \underline{/0°}}{20 \underline{/0°}} = 22 \underline{/0°}$ A $\bar{Z}_{coil} = R + jX_L = 8 + j(2\pi)(60)(0.05) = 8 + j18.85 = 20.48 \underline{/67.0°} \Omega$

$$\bar{I}_{coil} = \frac{\bar{V}_T}{\bar{Z}_{coil}} = \frac{440 \underline{/0°}}{20.48 \underline{/67.0°}} = 21.48 \underline{/-67°} \text{ A} \qquad X_C = \frac{1}{2\pi fC} = \frac{1}{2\pi 60(50 \times 10^{-6})} = 53.05 \Omega$$

$$\bar{I}_C = \frac{\bar{V}_C}{-jX_C} = \frac{440 \underline{/0°}}{53.05 \underline{/-90°}} = 8.29 \underline{/90°} \text{ A}$$

(b) $$\bar{I}_T = \bar{I}_R + \bar{I}_{coil} + \bar{I}_C = 22 \underline{/0°} + 21.48 \underline{/-67.0°} + 8.29 \underline{/90°}$$

$$= (22 + j0) + (8.39 - j19.77) + (0 + j8.29) = 32.49 \underline{/-20.69°} \text{ A}$$

(c)   The phasor diagram is shown in Fig. 24-106b.

24.329 In the circuit of Fig. 24-106a, determine: (*a*) the system active power; (*b*) the system reactive power; (*c*) the system apparent power; (*d*) the system power factor and power-factor angle.

❚ (*a*) From Fig. 24-106a

$$P_T = V_T i_T \cos \angle \frac{\bar{V}_T}{\bar{I}_T} = 440(32.49) \cos(+20.69°) = 13,373.62 \text{ W}$$

(*b*)

$$Q_T = V_T I_T \sin \angle \frac{\bar{V}_T}{\bar{I}_T} = 440(32.49) \sin(+20.69°) = 5050.80 \text{ var}$$

(*c*)

$$S_T = \sqrt{P_T^2 + Q_T^2} = \sqrt{(13,373.62)^2 + (5050.80)^2} = 14,295.60 \text{ VA}$$

(*d*)

$$\text{pf} = \frac{P_T}{S_T} = \frac{13,373.62}{14,295.60} = 0.9355 \qquad \theta_T = \cos^{-1} 0.9355 = 20.7°$$

24.330 A coil whose resistance and inductance are 40 Ω and 0.20 H, respectively, is supplied by a 120-V dc generator. Calculate (*a*) the circuit impedance; (*b*) the circuit current.

❚ Direct current is considered the special case of alternating current with the frequency approaching 0 Hz. Thus,

(*a*) $$X_L = 2\pi f L = 2\pi(0)(0.2) = 0 \text{ Ω} \qquad Z_T = \sqrt{R^2 + X_L^2} = \sqrt{(40)^2 + 0^2} = 40 \text{ Ω}$$

(*b*) $$I_T = \frac{V_T}{Z_T} = \frac{120}{40} = 3 \text{ A}$$

24.331 In the circuit of Prob. 24.330, determine: (*a*) the total active power; (*b*) the circuit power factor and the power-factor angle; (*e*) the circuit var; (*d*) the phasor diagram.

❚ (*a*) $$P_T = I_R^2 R = (3)^2 40 = 360 \text{ W}$$

(*b*) $$S_T = V_T I_T = 120 \times 3 = 360 \text{ VA} \qquad \text{pf}_T = \frac{P_T}{S_T} = \frac{360}{360} = 1 \qquad \theta_T = \cos^{-1}(\text{pf}) = \cos^{-1}(1) = 0°$$

(*c*) $$Q_T = V_T I_T \sin \theta_T = 120 \times 3 \times \sin 0° = 0 \text{ var}$$

(*d*) The phasor diagram is shown in Fig. 24-107.

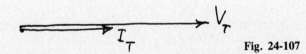

Fig. 24-107

24.332 A 220-V $1\frac{1}{2}$-hp single-phase 60-Hz induction motor draws 7.6 A when operating at rated conditions. The efficiency at rated conditions is 85 percent. Calculate (*a*) the kVA input; (*b*) the kW input; (*c*) the power factor.

❚ (*a*) $$S_T = V_T I_T = 220(7.6) = 1672 \text{ VA} = 1.672 \text{ kVA}$$

(*b*) $$\text{Eff.} = \frac{P_\text{out}}{P_\text{in}} \qquad 1 \text{ hp} = 746 \text{ W} \qquad 0.85 = \frac{1.5(746)}{P_\text{in}} \qquad P_\text{in} = 1316.5 \text{ W}$$

(*c*) $$\text{pf}_T = \frac{P_T}{S_T} = \frac{1316.5}{1672} = 0.787$$

24.333 In the system of Prob. 24.332, determine the capacitance of a parallel-connected capacitor that will cause the system to operate at unity power factor.

❚ $$\theta_T = \cos^{-1} \text{pf} = \cos^{-1} 0.787 = 38.1° \qquad Q_T = V_T I_T \sin \theta_T = 220(7.6) \sin 38.1° = 1030.8 \text{ var}$$

To restore the power factor to unity, the capacitor must supply all the vars. Therefore, $Q_C = 1030.8$ var.

$$Q_C = \frac{V_C^2}{X_C} \qquad 1030.8 = \frac{(220)^2}{X_C} \qquad X_C = 46.95 \text{ Ω} = \frac{1}{2\pi f C} \qquad 46.95 = \frac{1}{2\pi(60)C} \qquad C = 0.0000565 \text{ F} = 56.5 \text{ μF}$$

24.334 In the circuit of Prob. 24.333, determine (*a*) the generator current, (*b*) the motor current, and (*c*) the capacitor current.

▌ (a) At unity power factor,

$$S_T = P_T = V_T I_T \qquad 1316.5 = 220 I_T \qquad I_T = 5.98 \text{ A}$$

(b) $$I_{\text{motor}} = 7.6 \text{ A}$$

(c) $$\bar{I}_C = \frac{\bar{V}_T}{-jX_C} = \frac{220\ \underline{/0°}}{46.95\ \underline{/-90°}} = 4.69\ \underline{/90°} \text{ A}$$

24.335 Draw the circuit and phasor diagrams for the conditions of Probs. 24.332 through 24.334.

▌ See Fig. 24-108, where Fig. 24-108a and b represent Prob. 24.332 and Fig. 24-108c and d correspond to the conditions in Probs. 24.333 and 24.334.

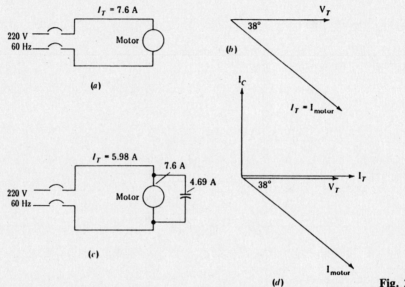

Fig. 24-108

24.336 A 12-kVA load A operating at 0.70 pf lagging and a 10-kVA load B operating at 0.80 pf lagging are connected in parallel and supplied by a 440-V 60-Hz generator. Determine (a) the total active power; (b) the total reactive power; (c) the total apparent power; (d) the system power factor.

▌ (a) $$P_T = P_A + P_B = 12 \times 0.7 + 10 \times 0.8 = 16.4 \text{ kW}$$

(b) $$\theta_A = \cos^{-1} 0.7 = 45.57° \qquad \theta_B = \cos^{-1} 0.8 = 36.87°$$

$$Q_A = S_A \sin \theta_A = 12 \sin 45.57° = 8.57 \text{ kvar} \qquad Q_B = S_B \sin \theta_B = 10 \sin 36.87° = 6.00 \text{ kvar}$$

$$Q_T = Q_A + Q_B = 8.57 + 6.00 = 14.57 \text{ var}$$

(c) $$S_T = \sqrt{P_T^2 + Q_T^2} = \sqrt{(16.4)^2 + (14.57)^2} = 21.94 \text{ kVA}$$

(d) $$\text{pf}_T = \frac{P_T}{S_T} = \frac{16.4}{21.94} = 0.747 \qquad \theta_T = \cos^{-1} \text{pf}_T = 41.62°$$

24.337 Determine the kvar rating of a parallel-connected capacitor to make the power factor of the circuit of Prob. 24.336 unity.

▌ To obtain unity pf, a capacitor must have a kvar rating equal to the lagging kilovars of the system. Thus,

$$Q_C = Q_T = 14.57 \text{ kvar}$$

24.338 Draw a phasor diagram and the circuit for Prob. 24.336. Show the reactive powers corresponding to power factors of 0.747 and 0.9 lagging.

▌ See Fig. 24-109.

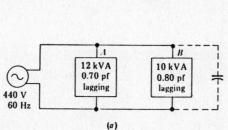

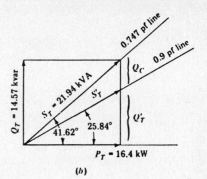

Fig. 24-109

24.339 Determine the reactive kVA of a capacitor to obtain a 0.9 lagging power factor in the circuit of Prob. 24.336.

▎ Figure 24-109b shows the system power diagram. For a system power factor of 0.9 lagging, the new power-factor angle will be

$$\theta_T' = \cos^{-1} 0.9 = 25.84°$$

Regardless of the value to which the power factor has been corrected, the active power component for a given load will always remain the same. This must be so, because the capacitor draws little or no active power. Hence the total circuit power for all possible power-factor corrections will be

$$P_T = 16.4 \text{ kW}$$

The value of Q_T' can be obtained from the power diagram in Fig. 24-109b by using the system active power and the new power-factor angle. Thus,

$$\tan 25.84° = \frac{Q_T'}{16.4} \qquad Q_T' = 7.94 \text{ kvar}$$

As indicated in the power diagram, the kvar rating of the capacitor required to obtain a pf of 0.90 lagging is

$$Q_C = Q_T - Q_T' = 14.57 - 7.94 = 6.63 \text{ kvar}$$

24.340 Show that in an ac circuit, operating under steady state, the complex power is correctly given by $\bar{S}_T = \bar{V}_T \bar{I}_T^*$ (and *not* by $\bar{S}_T = \bar{V}_T \bar{I}_T$).

▎ Let $$\bar{V}_T = V_T \underline{/\alpha°} \qquad \bar{I}_T = I_T \underline{/\beta°} \qquad \bar{I}_T^* = I_T \underline{/-\beta°}$$

$$\bar{S}_T = \bar{V}_T \bar{I}_T^* = (V_T \underline{/\alpha°})(I_T \underline{/-\beta°}) = V_T I_T \underline{/(\alpha° - \beta°)} = V_T I_T \cos(\alpha° - \beta°) + jV_T I_T \sin(\alpha° - \beta°)$$

If we *erroneously* use $\bar{S}_T = \bar{V}_T \bar{I}_T$ instead of $\bar{V}_T \bar{I}_T^*$,

$$\bar{S}_T = (V_T \underline{/\alpha°})(I_T \underline{/\beta°}) = V_T I_T \underline{/\alpha° + \beta°} = V_T I_T \cos(\alpha° + \beta°) + jV_T I_T \sin(\alpha° + \beta°) \qquad \text{Wrong}$$

24.341 The voltage across a circuit and the current to it are given by

$$\bar{V}_T = 140 \underline{/30°} \text{ V} \qquad \bar{I}_T = 7.0 \underline{/80°} \text{ A}$$

(*a*) Using the phasor-power equation, determine the active power, reactive power, apparent power, and power factor; (*b*) determine the equivalent input impedance.

▎ (*a*) $\bar{S}_T = \bar{V}_T \bar{I}_T^* = (140 \underline{/30°})(7 \underline{/-80°}) = 980 \underline{/-50°} = 980 \cos(-50°) + j980 \sin(-50°) = 629.93 - j750.72$

Thus, $S_T = 980 \text{ VA}$ $P_T = 629.93 \text{ W}$ $Q_T = -750.72 \text{ var}$ pf $= \cos(-50°) = 0.64$

The negative sign for the reactive power indicates a leading power factor (net capacitive effect).

(*b*) $$\bar{Z}_{\text{in}} = \frac{\bar{V}_T}{\bar{I}_T} = \frac{140 \underline{/30°}}{7.0 \underline{/80°}} = 20 \underline{/-50°} \ \Omega = 12.86 - j15.32 \ \Omega$$

24.342 Repeat Prob. 24.341 for a circuit that draws 10 A from a 120-V dc supply.

$$\bar{V}_T = 120 \,\underline{/0°}\,\text{V} \qquad \bar{I}_T = 10 \,\underline{/0°}\,\text{A}$$

$$\bar{S}_T = \bar{V}_T \bar{I}_T^* = (120 \,\underline{/0°})(10 \,\underline{/0°})^* = 1200 \,\underline{/0°}\,\text{VA} = 1200 + j0 = 1200\,\text{VA}$$

$$P_T = 1200\,\text{W} \qquad Q_T = 0\,\text{var} \qquad \text{pf} = \frac{P_T}{S_T} = 1$$

$$\bar{Z}_{\text{in}} = \frac{\bar{V}_T}{\bar{I}_T} = \frac{120 \,\underline{/0°}}{10 \,\underline{/0°}} = 12 \,\underline{/0°} = (12 + j0)\,\Omega$$

24.343 A $160 \,\underline{/30°}\,$V ac generator, having an internal impedance of $(4 + j6)\,\Omega$, supplies maximum power to a certain circuit. Calculate the generator current.

❚ $\quad \bar{Z}_{\text{load}} = \bar{Z}_G^* = 4 - j6 = 7.21 \,\underline{/-56.31°}\,\Omega \qquad \bar{I}_T = \dfrac{\bar{V}_T}{\bar{Z}_T} = \dfrac{\bar{V}_T}{\bar{Z}_G + \bar{Z}_{\text{load}}} = \dfrac{160 \,\underline{/30°}}{(4 + j6) + (4 - j6)} = 20 \,\underline{/30°}\,\text{A}$

24.344 Determine the apparent power, active power, and reactive power drawn by the load of Prob. 24.343.

❚ $\qquad\qquad \bar{V}_{\text{load}} = \bar{I}_T \bar{Z}_{\text{load}} = (20 \,\underline{/30°})(7.21 \,\underline{/-56.31°}) = 144.20 \,\underline{/-26.31°}\,\text{V}$

$$\bar{S}_{\text{load}} = \bar{V}_{\text{load}} \bar{I}_T^* = (144.20 \,\underline{/-26.31°})(20 \,\underline{/-30°}) = 2884 \,\underline{/-56.31°} = (1599.75 - j2399.63)\,\text{VA}$$

Thus,   Apparent power = 2884 VA   Active power = 1600 W   Reactive power = 2400 var (leading)

24.345 Determine the reactive power and the power factor of a load drawing 79.1 kVA apparent power and 20 kW active power.

❚ $\quad S = \sqrt{P^2 + Q^2} \qquad 79,100 = \sqrt{(20,000)^2 + Q^2} \qquad Q = 76,529.8\,\text{var} = 76.5\,\text{kvar} \qquad \text{pf} = \dfrac{P}{S} = \dfrac{20,000}{79,100} = 0.253$

24.346 A 100-V dc source with an internal resistance of $2.0\,\Omega$ is connected through a switch to an 18-Ω load as shown in Fig. 24-110. Determine the voltage at terminals T_1T_2 with the switch closed and with the switch open.

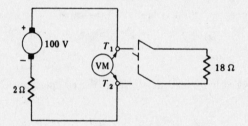

Fig. 24-110

❚   With the switch closed, the current in the circuit is

$$I = \frac{V}{R} = \frac{100}{2 + 18} = 5\,\text{A}$$

The voltmeter reads the IR drop across the 18-Ω resistor:

$$V_{T_1 T_2} = IR = 5 \times 18 = 90\,\text{V}$$

The internal voltage drop due to the resistance of the generator is

$$V_{\text{drop}} = IR_G = 5 \times 2 = 10\,\text{V}$$

With the switch open, there can be no current. Hence there can be no voltage drop across the internal resistance of the generator, and the voltmeter will read 100 V.

24.347 Determine the voltage at the source terminals T_1T_2 in Fig. 24-111, with the switch closed and with the switch open. Assume a high-impedance voltmeter that draws insignificant current.

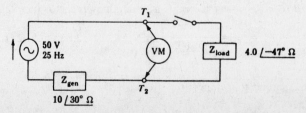

Fig. 24-111

▮ With the switch closed,

$$\bar{Z}_T = 10\ \underline{/30°} + 4\ \underline{/-47°} = (8.66 + j5.00) + (2.73 - j2.93) = (11.39 + j2.07) = 11.58\ \underline{/10.32°}\ \Omega$$

$$\bar{I} = \frac{\bar{V}}{\bar{Z}_T} = \frac{50\ \underline{/0°}}{11.58\ \underline{/10.32°}} = 4.32\ \underline{/-10.32°}\ A$$

The voltmeter will read the magnitude of the IZ drop across the load.

$$V = IZ = 4.32 \times 4 = 17.28\ V$$

With the switch open, there can be no current. Hence there can be no voltage drop across the internal impedance of the generator, and the voltmeter will read 50 V.

24.348 A 120-V voltage source with an internal resistance of 3.0 Ω is shown in Fig. 24-112a. Determine the parameters for an equivalent current source.

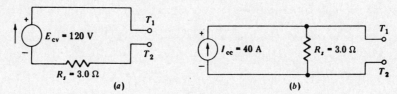

Fig. 24-112

▮ Using the source-conversion formula,

$$\bar{I}_{ce} = \frac{\bar{E}_{cv}}{\bar{Z}_S} = \frac{120}{3} = 40\ A$$

$\bar{Z}_S = 3.0\text{-}\Omega$ resistance in parallel with the constant-current generator. Figure 24-112b shows the equivalent current source.

24.349 Write the loop equations for the circuit of Fig. 24-113.

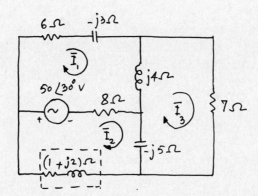

Fig. 24-113

▮ By KVL, we have

$$50\ \underline{/30°} = 6\bar{I}_1 - j3\bar{I}_1 + (\bar{I}_1 - \bar{I}_3)(j4) + (\bar{I}_1 - \bar{I}_2)8$$

$$-50\ \underline{/30°} = (\bar{I}_2 - \bar{I}_1)8 + (\bar{I}_2 - \bar{I}_3)(-j5) + \bar{I}_2(1 + j2)$$

$$0 = 7\bar{I}_3 + (\bar{I}_3 - \bar{I}_2)(-j5) + (\bar{I}_3 - \bar{I}_1)(j4)$$

Or, combining and rearranging terms, we obtain

$$50\ \underline{/30°} = \bar{I}_1(14 + j1) + \bar{I}_2(-8) + \bar{I}_3(-j4) \qquad -50\ \underline{/30°} = \bar{I}_1(-8) + \bar{I}_2(9 - j3) + \bar{I}_3(j5)$$

$$0 = \bar{I}_1(-j4) + \bar{I}_2(j5) + \bar{I}_3(7 - j1)$$

24.350 The loop equations of a network are

$$3\bar{I}_1 + j4\bar{I}_2 = 10\ \underline{/0°} \qquad j7\bar{I}_1 + (3 + j4\bar{I}_2) = 8\ \underline{/90°}$$

Determine the complex power supplied by the 10-V source.

Solving for $\bar{I}_1$ yields

$$\bar{I}_1 = \frac{73.78 \underline{/32.83°}}{38.90 \underline{/17.97°}} = 1.9 \underline{/14.9°} \text{ A}$$

Hence,
$$\bar{S}_1 = \bar{V}_1 \bar{I}_1^* = (10 \underline{/0°})(1.9 \underline{/-14.9°}) = 19 \underline{/-14.9°} \text{ VA}$$

24.351 Determine the voltage across the $(1 + j2)$-Ω impedance of the circuit of Fig. 24-113.

From Prob. 24.349,
$$\bar{I}_2 = \frac{1950 \underline{/-148.53°}}{676 \underline{/-28.16°}} = 2.885 \underline{/-120.37°} \text{ A}$$

$$\bar{V}_2 = \bar{I}_2 \bar{Z}_2 = (2.885 \underline{/-120.37°})(1 + j2) = 6.453 \underline{/-56.95°} \text{ V}$$

24.352 How much active and reactive power is absorbed by the $(1 + j2)$-Ω impedance of the circuit of Fig. 24-113.

$$P_2 = I_2^2 R_2 = (2.885)^2 (1) = 8.32 \text{ W} \qquad Q_2 = I_2^2 X_2 = (2.885)^2 (2) = 16.64 \text{ var}$$

24.353 Verify the result of Prob. 24.352 by determining the complex power.

$$\bar{S}_2 = \bar{V}_2 \bar{I}_2^* = (6.453 \underline{/-56.95°})(2.885 \underline{/120.37}) = 18.623 \underline{/63.43} = 8.33 + j16.65 = P_2 + jQ_2$$

which agrees with the result of Prob. 24.352.

24.354 Determine the ammeter reading in the circuit of Fig. 24-114.

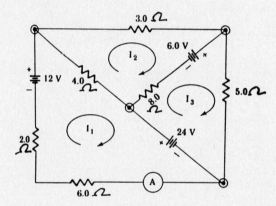

Fig. 24-114

The loop equations for the circuit may be written as

$$-12 = (12)\bar{I}_1 + (-4)\bar{I}_2 + (0)\bar{I}_3 \qquad -6 = (-4)\bar{I}_1 + (15)\bar{I}_2 + (-8)\bar{I}_3 \qquad 30 = (0)\bar{I}_1 + (-8)\bar{I}_2 + (13)\bar{I}_3$$

from which
$$\bar{I}_1 = \frac{\Delta_{Z1}}{\Delta_Z} = \frac{-924}{1364} = -0.68 \text{ A} \qquad \text{Ammeter reads 0.68 A}$$

24.355 What is the ammeter reading in the circuit of Fig. 24-115?

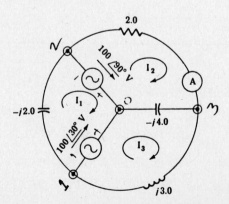

Fig. 24-115

▎ The loop equations are

$$100 \underline{/90°} - 100 \underline{/30°} = -j2\bar{I}_1 \qquad -100 \underline{/90°} = (2-j4)\bar{I}_2 - (-j4)\bar{I}_3 \qquad 100 \underline{/30°} = -(-j4)\bar{I}_2 + (3-j4)\bar{I}_3$$

Solving for $\bar{I}_2$ yields $\qquad \bar{I}_2 = 32.41 \underline{/-33.9°}$ A $\qquad$ Ammeter reads 32.4 A

24.356 A parallel circuit consisting of a 3.0-Ω resistor, a 10-Ω capacitive reactance, and an ideal inductor whose inductive reactance is 6.0 Ω is connected to a 120-V 60-Hz source. Determine (a) the circuit impedance; (b) the current through each branch; (c) the feeder current.

▎ (a) $\qquad \bar{Y}_T = \dfrac{1}{3} + \dfrac{1}{-j10} + \dfrac{1}{j6} = 0.34 \underline{/-11.32°}$ S $\qquad \bar{Z}_T = \dfrac{1}{\bar{Y}_T} = 2.94 \underline{/11.32°}$ Ω

(b) $\qquad \bar{I}_R = \dfrac{120 \underline{/0°}}{3 \underline{/0°}} = 40 \underline{/0°}$ A $\qquad \bar{I}_L = \dfrac{120 \underline{/0°}}{6 \underline{/90°}} = 20 \underline{/-90°}$ A $\qquad \bar{I}_C = \dfrac{120 \underline{/0°}}{10 \underline{/-90°}} = 12 \underline{/90°}$ A

(c) $\qquad \bar{I}_T = \bar{I}_R + \bar{I}_L + \bar{I}_C = 40 - j20 + j12 = (40 - j8) = 40.79 \underline{/-11.31°}$ A

24.357 In the circuit of Prob. 24.356, calculate (a) the total active power input; (b) the total reactive power input; (c) the apparent power input; (d) the power factor.

▎ (a) $\qquad P_T = V_T I_T \cos \measuredangle \dfrac{\bar{V}_T}{\bar{I}_T} = 120(40.79) \cos 11.31° = 4799.75$ W

(b) $\qquad Q_T = V_T I_T \sin \measuredangle \dfrac{\bar{V}_T}{\bar{I}_T} = 120(40.79) \sin 11.31° = 959.95$ var

(c) $\qquad S_T = \sqrt{P_T^2 + Q_T^2} = \sqrt{(4799.75)^2 + (959.95)^2} = 4894.8$ VA

(d) $\qquad \text{pf}_T = \dfrac{P_T}{S_T} = \dfrac{4799.75}{4894.8} = 0.9806$

24.358 A 120-V 60-Hz source supplies energy to a circuit consisting of a 6.0-μF capacitor in series with an inductor whose resistance and inductance are 500 Ω and 2.0 H, respectively. Determine (a) the circuit impedance; (b) the circuit current; (c) the active power; (d) the apparent power; (e) the reactive power; (f) the power factor.

▎ (a) $\qquad X_L = 2\pi(60)(2) = 753.98$ Ω $\qquad X_C = \dfrac{10^6}{2\pi(60)6} = 442.09$ Ω

$$\bar{Z} = 500 + j753.98 - j442.09 = 589.3 \underline{/31.96°}$ Ω$$

(b) $\qquad \bar{I} = \dfrac{\bar{E}}{\bar{Z}} = \dfrac{120 \underline{/0°}}{589.3 \underline{/31.96°}} = 0.20 \underline{/-31.96°}$ A

(c) $\qquad P_T = V_T I_T \cos \measuredangle \dfrac{\bar{V}_T}{\bar{I}_T} = 120(0.20) \cos 31.96° = 20.36$ W

(d) $\qquad Q_T = V_T I_T \sin \measuredangle \dfrac{\bar{V}_T}{\bar{I}_T} = 120(0.20) \sin 31.96° = 12.7$ var

(e) $\qquad S_T = V_T I_T = 120(0.20) = 24$ VA

(f) $\qquad \text{pf}_T = \dfrac{P_T}{S_T} = \dfrac{20.36}{24} = 0.85$

24.359 A 440-V 60-Hz source supplies 20 kVA to a load whose power factor is 70 percent. Determine (a) kW; (b) kvar.

(a) $\qquad$ Power $= S$ (power factor) $= 20(0.7) = 14$ kW

(b) $\qquad 20 = \sqrt{(14)^2 + Q^2} \qquad$ or $\qquad Q = 14.28$ kvar

24.360 A 120-V 60-Hz generator supplies power to two parallel loads. One load draws 10 kVA at unity power factor, and the other draws 40 kVA at 0.60 pf lagging. Sketch the circuit and determine (a) the total active power; (b) the total reactive power; (c) the total apparent power; (d) the system power factor.

I The circuit is shown in Fig. 24-116.

$$S_A = 10 \underline{/0°} \qquad S_B = 40 \underline{/53.13°} \qquad \cos^{-1}\theta = 0.6 \qquad \theta = 53.13°$$

(a)
$$P_T = 10 \times 1 + 40 \times 0.6 = 34 \text{ kW}$$

(b)
$$Q_T = 10 \sin 0° + 40 \sin 53.13° = 32 \text{ kvar}$$

(c)
$$S_T = \sqrt{(34)^2 + (32)^2} = 46.69 \text{ kVA}$$

(d)
$$\text{pf}_T = \frac{P_T}{S_T} = \frac{34}{46.69} = 0.73$$

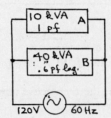

Fig. 24-116

24.361 A capacitor, an electric resistance heater, and an impedance are connected in parallel to a 120-V 60-Hz system. The capacitor draws 50 var, the heater draws 100 W, and the impedance draws 269 VA at a power factor of 0.74 lagging. Sketch the circuit and determine (a) the system active power; (b) the system reactive power; (c) the system apparent power; (d) the system power factor.

I See Fig. 24-117.

(a)
$$P_T = 0 + 100 + 269 \times 0.74 = 299.61 \text{ W}$$

(b)
$$Q_T = -50 + 269 \sin 42.27° = 130.93 \text{ var}$$

(c)
$$S_T = \sqrt{(299.61)^2 + (130.93)^2} = 326.97 \text{ VA}$$

(d)
$$\text{pf} = \frac{P}{S} = \frac{299.61}{326.97} = 0.92$$

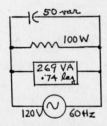

Fig. 24-117

24.362 A 250-V 30-Hz generator supplies power to a parallel circuit consisting of a 20-hp motor whose efficiency and power factor are 0.8 and 0.9 respectively an electric resistance heater which draws 100 kW, and an impedance Z. The generator current is 648 $\underline{/23°}$ A. Sketch the circuit and determine the currents drawn by each element.

I See Fig. 24-118.

$$P_H = V_H I_H \qquad 100,000 = 250 I_H \qquad I_H = 400 \text{ A}$$

$$P_M = \frac{20 \times 746}{0.80} = 18,650 \text{ W} = V_M I_M \text{ pf} \qquad \text{or} \qquad 18,650 = 250 I_M (0.9) \qquad \text{or} \qquad I_M = 82.89 \text{ A}$$

$$\bar{I}_T = \bar{I}_R + \bar{I}_M + \bar{I}_Z \qquad 648 \underline{/23°} = 400 \underline{/0°} + 82.89 \underline{/-25.84°} + \bar{I}_Z$$

$$(596.49 + j253.19) = 400 + (74.60 - j36.13) + \bar{I}_Z \qquad \bar{I}_Z = 313.95 \underline{/67.15°} \text{ A}$$

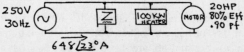

Fig. 24-118

24.363 In the system of Prob. 24.362, calculate the complex power and then determine the active and reactive powers.

$$\bar{S}_T = \bar{V}_T \bar{I}_T^* = (250\,\underline{/0°})(648\,\underline{/-23°}) = 162,000\,\underline{/-23°} = 149,121.79 - j63,298.44$$

$$P_T = 149,121.8\,\text{W} \qquad Q = -63,298.4\,\text{var (leading)}$$

24.364 What is the power factor of the system of Prob. 24.362?

▌ From Prob. 24.363,

$$\text{Power factor angle} = 23° \qquad \text{or} \qquad \text{Power factor} = \cos 23° = 0.92\,\text{leading}$$

24.365 Two parallel-connected loads A and B are supplied by a 440-V 60-Hz generator. Load A draws an apparent power of 100 kVA at 0.80 pf lagging, and load B draws an apparent power of 70 kVA at unity pf. Determine (*a*) the system active power; (*b*) the system reactive power; (*c*) the system apparent power; (*d*) the system power factor; (*e*) the feeder current; (*f*) the kW·h of energy supplied by the generator in 20 min; (*g*) the kvar·h supplied by the generator in 20 min.

$$\bar{S}_A = 100\,\underline{/36.87°} = 80 + j60 \qquad \bar{S}_B = 70\,\underline{/0°} = 70 + j0$$

$$\bar{S}_T = \bar{S}_A + \bar{S}_B = 150 + j60 = 161.555\,\underline{/21.80°}$$

(*a*) $$P_T = 150\,\text{kW}$$

(*b*) $$Q_T = 60\,\text{kvar}$$

(*c*) $$S_T = 161.555\,\text{kVA}$$

(*d*) $$\text{pf}_T = \cos^{-1} 21.80 = 0.93$$

(*e*) $$S_T = V_T I_T \qquad 161,555 = 440 I_T \qquad I_T = 367.17\,\text{A}$$

(*f*) $$\text{kW·h} = 150 \times \tfrac{20}{60} = 50$$

(*g*) $$60 \times \tfrac{20}{60} = 20\,\text{kvar·h}$$

24.366 An electric circuit draws an active power of 100 kW at 0.8 pf lagging from a 240-V 60-Hz source. Determine (*a*) the apparent power input; (*b*) the kvar input; (*c*) the capacitance of a parallel-connected capacitor required to adjust the system power factor to 95 percent.

(*a*) $$\text{pf} = \frac{P}{S} \qquad 0.8 = \frac{100}{S} \qquad S = 125\,\text{kVA}$$

(*b*) $$S = \sqrt{P^2 + Q^2} \qquad 125 = \sqrt{(100)^2 + Q^2} \qquad Q = 75\,\text{kvar}$$

(*c*) $$\theta' = \cos^{-1} 0.95 = 18.19° \qquad \tan 18.19° = Q'/100 \qquad Q' = 32.87\,\text{kvar}$$

$$Q_C = Q - Q_2' = 75 - 32.87 = 42.13\,\text{kvar} = V_C^2 / X_C$$

$$42,130 = \frac{(240)^2}{X_C} \qquad X_C = 1.367\,\Omega = \frac{1}{2\pi(60)C} \qquad \text{or} \qquad C = 1940.2\,\mu\text{F}$$

24.367 A 240-V 60-Hz single-phase system supplies energy to a fully loaded 20-hp induction motor. The full-load efficiency and power factor of the motor are 85.5 percent and 74 percent respectively. Determine (*a*) the kW drawn by the motor; (*b*) the apparent power; (*c*) the reactive power; (*d*) the kilovar rating of a capacitor required to adjust the power factor to 0.90 lagging.

▌ See Fig. 24-119 for the circuit and the phasor diagram.

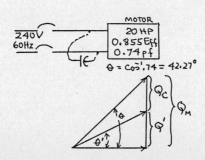

Fig. 24-119

(a)
$$P_{in} = \frac{20 \times 746}{0.855} = 17.450 \text{ kW}$$

(b)
$$pf = \frac{P}{S} \qquad 0.74 = \frac{17.450}{S} \qquad S = 23.58 \text{ kVA}$$

(c)
$$Q_M = S \sin \theta = 23.58 \sin 42.27° = 15.86 \text{ kvar}$$

(d)
$$\theta' = \cos^{-1} 0.9 = 25.84° \qquad \tan \theta' = Q'/P \qquad \tan 25.84 = Q'/17.45 \qquad Q' = 8.451 \text{ kvar}$$

Thus,
$$Q_C = Q_M - Q' = 15.86 - 8.451 = 7.409 \text{ kvar}$$

24.368 A 4.0-kW resistor is in parallel with a 10-hp 0.82-pf 76 percent efficient motor. The driving voltage is 230 V at 60 Hz, and the motor is operating at rated load. Determine (*a*) the circuit active power; (*b*) the circuit reactive power; (*c*) the circuit apparent power; (*d*) the power factor; (*e*) the kvar of capacitance required to eliminate the reactive component of current supplied by the generator.

❚ (a)
$$P_{in} = P_{res} + P_{motor} \qquad P_T = 4.0 + \frac{10 \times 746}{0.76 \times 1000} = 4 + 9.816 = 13.816 \text{ kW}$$

(b)
$$Q_T = Q_{res} + Q_{motor} = 0 + 6.852 = 6.852 \text{ kvar}$$

$$Q_{motor} = 9.816 \tan 34.9 = 6.852 \text{ kvar}$$

(c)
$$S_T = \sqrt{P_T^2 + Q_T^2} = \sqrt{(13.816)^2 + (6.852)^2} = 15.422 \text{ kVA}$$

(d)
$$pf_T = \frac{P_T}{S_T} = \frac{13.816}{15.422} = 0.896$$

(e)
$$6.852 \text{ kvar}$$

24.369 A 2.0-kW heater is in parallel with a 5.0-hp 240-V 60-Hz induction motor whose efficiency and power factor are 0.85 and 0.72, respectively. The parallel combination is supplied by a 240-V 60-Hz system. Determine (*a*) the system active power; (*b*) the system reactive power; (*c*) the system apparent power.

❚ (a)
$$P_T = P_H + P_M$$

$$P_T = 2.0 + \frac{5 \times 746}{0.85(1000)} = 2.0 + 4.388 = 6.388 \text{ kW}$$

(b)
$$\tan \theta_M = \frac{Q_M}{P_M} \qquad \theta_M = \cos^{-1} 0.72 = 43.95° \qquad 0.964 = \frac{Q_M}{4.388} \qquad Q_M = 4.229 \text{ kvar}$$

$$Q_T = Q_H + Q_M = 0 + 4.229 \text{ kvar}$$

$$S_T = \sqrt{P_T^2 + Q_T^2} = \sqrt{(6.388)^2 + (4.229)^2} = 7.661 \text{ kVA}$$

24.370 In the circuit of Prob. 24.369 obtain (*a*) the kVA rating of a capacitor required to adjust the system power factor to 0.80 leading; (*b*) the capacitance of the capacitor. Also draw the phasor diagram.

❚ See Fig. 24-120 for the phasor diagram.

(a)
$$\theta' = \cos^{-1} 0.8 = 36.87° \qquad Q_C = Q' + Q_T = 4.791 + 4.229 = 9.020 \text{ kvar} = V_C^2/X_C$$

(b)
$$9020 = (240)^2/X_C \qquad X_C = 6.386 \text{ Ω} \qquad 6.386 = 1/(2\pi fC) \qquad C = 415.4 \text{ μF}$$

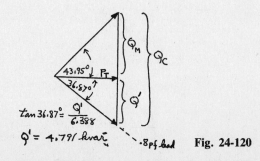

$$\tan 36.87° = \frac{Q'}{6.388}$$

$$Q' = 4.791 \text{ kvar} \qquad .8 \text{ pf lead} \qquad \textbf{Fig. 24-120}$$

24.371 A 450-V 60-Hz generator supplies power to a 150 kVA 0.80-pf lagging load and a 100-kVA 0.75-pf lagging load. Determine (*a*) the total active power; (*b*) the total reactive power; (*c*) the total apparent power; (*d*) the overall system power factor; (*e*) the kilovar rating of a capacitor required to adjust the system power factor to 0.90 lagging.

▌ (*a*) $$P_T = 100(0.75) + (150)(0.8) = 195 \text{ kW}$$

(*b*) $$Q_T = 100 \sin 41.41° + 150 \sin 36.87° = 66.14 + 90.0 = 156.14 \text{ kvar}$$

(*c*) $$\bar{S}_T = P_T + jQ_T = 195 + j156.14 = 249.81 \;\underline{/38.69°} = 249.81 \text{ kVA}$$

(*d*) $$\text{pf} = \cos 38.69° = 0.78$$

(*e*) $$\tan 25.84° = Q'/195 \qquad Q' = 94.44 \text{ kvar}$$

$$Q_C = Q_T - Q' = 156.14 - 94.44 = 61.70 \text{ kvar}$$

24.372 A 20-hp 450-V motor operating at rated load has an efficiency of 85 percent and a power factor of 0.76 lagging. The motor is in parallel with a 30-kVA load whose power factor angle is 35° lagging. The two loads are supplied from a 450-V 60-Hz source. Determine (*a*) the active power and reactive power drawn by the motor; (*b*) the active power and reactive power drawn by the 30-kVA load; (*c*) the total active power supplied by the system; (*d*) the total reactive power supplied by the system; (*e*) the total apparent power supplied by the system.

▌ (*a*) $$P_M = \frac{20 \times 746}{0.85(1000)} = 17.553 \text{ kW} \qquad S_M = \frac{P_M}{\text{pf}_M} = \frac{17.553}{0.76} = 23.096 \text{ kVA}$$

$$\theta_M = \cos^{-1} 0.76 = 40.54° \qquad Q_M = 23.096 \sin 40.54° = 15.012 \text{ kvar}$$

(*b*) $$\bar{S} = 30 \;\underline{/35°} = 24.575 + j17.207 \qquad P = 24.575 \text{ kW} \qquad Q = 17.207 \text{ kvar}$$

(*c*) $$P_T = 17.553 + 24.575 = 42.128 \text{ kW}$$

(*d*) $$Q_T = 15.012 + 17.207 = 32.219 \text{ kvar}$$

(*e*) $$\bar{S}_T = P_T + jQ_T = 42.128 + j32.219 = 53.036 \;\underline{/37.408°} \text{ kVA}$$

24.373 The current and driving voltage to a single-phase motor are $50 \;\underline{/-30°}$ A and $100 \;\underline{/0°}$ V, respectively. Determine (*a*) the apparent power; (*b*) the active power; (*c*) the reactive power; (*d*) the power factor.

▌ $$\bar{S} = \bar{V}\bar{I}^* = (100 \;\underline{/0°})(50 \;\underline{/+30°}) = 5000 \;\underline{/30°} \text{ VA}$$

(*a*) $$\bar{S} = 4330 + j2500 = 5000 \text{ VA}$$

(*b*) $$P = 4330 \text{ W}$$

(*c*) $$Q = 2500 \text{ var}$$

(*d*) $$\text{pf} = \cos 30° = 0.87$$

24.374 A 220-V 60-Hz generator supplies power to an $11 \;\underline{/20°}$ Ω impedance. Determine (*a*) the current; (*b*) the apparent power; (*c*) the active power; (*d*) the reactive power.

▌ (*a*) $$\bar{I} = \frac{\bar{V}}{\bar{Z}} = \frac{220 \;\underline{/0°}}{11 \;\underline{/20°}} = 20 \;\underline{/-20°} \text{ A}$$

$$\bar{S} = \bar{V}\bar{I}^* = (220 \;\underline{/0°})(20 \;\underline{/+20°}) = 4400 \;\underline{/20°} = 4134.7 + j1504.9 = 4400 \text{ VA}$$

(*b*) $$P = 4134.7 \text{ W}$$

(*c*) $$Q = 1504.9 \text{ var}$$

24.375 A voltage of $100 \;\underline{/40°}$ V appears across an impedance when it passes a current of $30 \;\underline{/-50°}$ A. Determine (*a*) the apparent power drawn by the impedance; (*b*) the active power; (*c*) the reactive power; (*d*) the power factor.

▌ (*a*) $$S = \bar{V}\bar{I}^* = (100 \;\underline{/40°})(30 \;\underline{/+50°}) = 3000 \;\underline{/90°} = 0 + j3000 = 3000 \text{ VA}$$

(*b*) $$P = 0$$

(*c*) $$Q = 3000 \text{ var}$$

(*d*) $$\text{pf} = \cos 90° = 0 \text{ lagging}$$

24.376 Oscilloscope recordings indicate that the 60-Hz voltage across an impedance and the current through it are $100 \underline{/20°}$ V and $10 \underline{/60°}$ A, respectively. Determine (*a*) the apparent power; (*b*) the active power; (*c*) the reactive power; (*d*) the power factor.

$$\bar{S} = \bar{V}\bar{I}^* = (100 \underline{/20°})(10 \underline{/-60°}) = 1000 \underline{/-40°} = 766.04 - j642.79$$

(*a*) $\qquad\qquad S = 1000 \text{ VA}$

(*b*) $\qquad\qquad P = 766.04 \text{ W}$

(*c*) $\qquad\qquad Q = -642.79 \text{ var}$

(*d*) $\qquad\qquad \text{pf} = \cos(-40°) = 0.77 \text{ leading}$

24.377 Obtain the circuit parameters of the circuit of Prob. 24.376.

From Prob. 24.376 $\qquad \bar{Z} = \dfrac{\bar{V}}{\bar{I}} = \dfrac{100 \underline{/20°}}{10 \underline{/60°}} = 10 \underline{/-40°} \ \Omega = 7.66 - j6.43$

$$R = 7.66 \ \Omega \qquad X_C = \dfrac{1}{2\pi f C} \qquad 6.43 = \dfrac{1}{2\pi 60 C} \qquad C = 412.7 \ \mu\text{F}$$

24.378 The voltage and current to a certain induction motor are 100 V and 30 A, respectively, and the phase angle between the current and the voltage is 40°. Determine (*a*) the apparent power; (*b*) the active power; (*c*) the reactive power; (*d*) the power factor; (*e*) the equivalent impedance of the load.

$$\bar{S} = \bar{V}\bar{I}^* = (100 \underline{/0°})(30 \underline{/+40°}) = 3000 \underline{/+40°} = 2298.1 + j1928.4$$

(*a*) $\qquad\qquad S = 3000 \text{ VA}$

(*b*) $\qquad\qquad P = 2298.1 \text{ W}$

(*c*) $\qquad\qquad Q = 1928.4 \text{ var}$

(*d*) $\qquad\qquad \text{pf} = \cos 40° = 0.77 \text{ lagging}$

(*e*) $\qquad\qquad \bar{Z} = \dfrac{\bar{V}}{\bar{I}} = \dfrac{100 \underline{/0°}}{30 \underline{/-40°}} = 3.33 \underline{/40°} \ \Omega$

24.379 Oscilloscope measurements of the voltage across an impedance and the current to it are $208 \underline{/30°}$ V and $40 \underline{/10°}$ A, respectively. Determine (*a*) the active and reactive power drawn by the impedance; (*b*) the power factor.

$$\bar{S} = \bar{V}\bar{I}^* = (208 \underline{/30°})(40 \underline{/-10°}) = 8320 \underline{/20°} = 7818.24 + j2845.61$$

(*a*) $\qquad\qquad P = 7818.2 \text{ W} \qquad Q = 2845.61 \text{ var}$

(*b*) $\qquad\qquad \text{pf} = \cos 20° = 0.94 \text{ lagging}$

24.380 A certain impedance draws 300 W and 600 lagging var from a 100-V 25-Hz supply. Determine (*a*) the current; (*b*) the equivalent values of R and L that make up the impedance.

$$\bar{S} = \bar{P} + j\bar{Q} = 300 + j600 = 670.82 \underline{/63.43°} \text{ VA}$$

(*a*) $\qquad\qquad \bar{S} = \bar{V}\bar{I}^* \qquad 670.82 \underline{/63.43°} = (100 \underline{/0°})(\bar{I}^*)$

$$\bar{I}^* = 6.71 \underline{/63.43°} \qquad \bar{I} = 6.71 \underline{/-63.43°} \text{ A}$$

(*b*) $\qquad\qquad \bar{Z} = \dfrac{\bar{V}}{\bar{I}} = \dfrac{100 \underline{/0°}}{6.71 \underline{/-63.43°}} = 14.90 \underline{/63.43°} \ \Omega = 6.67 + j13.33$

$$R = 6.67 \ \Omega \qquad X_L = 13.33 = 2\pi 25 L \qquad L = 85 \text{ mH}$$

24.381 A 25-Hz generator supplies a total of 60 kW and 20 kvar to a circuit containing two impedances (*A* and *B*) in parallel. The driving voltage is $120 \underline{/0°}$ V and the current to *A* is $60 \underline{/30°}$ A. Determine (*a*) the apparent power drawn by *A*; (*b*) the apparent power drawn by *B*.

(*a*) $\qquad \bar{S}_A = \bar{V}_A \bar{I}_A^* = (120 \underline{/0°})(60 \underline{/-30°}) = 7200 \underline{/-30°} = 6235.38 - j3600 = 7200 \text{ VA}$

(*b*) $\qquad \bar{S}_T = \bar{S}_A + \bar{S}_B = 60,000 + j20,000 = 6235.38 - j3600 + \bar{S}_B$

$$\bar{S}_B = (53,764.62 + j23,600) = 58,716.22 \underline{/23.7°} = 58,716.22 \text{ VA}$$

24.382 The phasor power supplied by a 240-V 25-Hz generator to a series connection of ideal circuit elements is $300 \underline{/20°}$ V·A. Determine (*a*) the complex impedance of the series circuit; (*b*) the equivalent values of the circuit elements that comprise the series circuit.

▌ (*a*)
$$\bar{S} = \bar{V}\bar{I}^* \qquad 300 \underline{/20°} = 240 \underline{/0°}\bar{I}^* \qquad \bar{I}^* = 1.25 \underline{/20°} \qquad \bar{I} = 1.25 \underline{/-20°}$$

$$\bar{Z} = \frac{\bar{V}}{\bar{I}} = \frac{240 \underline{/0°}}{1.25 \underline{/-20°}} = 192 \underline{/20°} = 180.42 + j65.67 \ \Omega$$

(*b*)
$$R = 180.42 \ \Omega \qquad X_L = 65.67 \ \Omega \qquad 65.67 = 2\pi 25 L \qquad L = 418 \text{ mH}$$

24.383 Determine the required components (R, L, C) for a load that will maximize the transfer of power from a 120-V 60-Hz source. The source impedance is $5.0 \underline{/30°} \ \Omega$.

▌
$$\bar{Z}_{\text{load}} = \bar{Z}^*_{\text{gen}} = 5 \underline{/-30°} \ \Omega = 4.33 - j2.5$$

$$R = 4.33 \ \Omega \qquad X_C = 2.5 \ \Omega \qquad 2.5 = \frac{1}{2\pi 60 C} \qquad \text{or} \qquad C = 1061 \ \mu\text{F}$$

24.384 A generator whose voltage and internal impedance are $300 \underline{/60°}$ V and $(5.0 + j10) \ \Omega$, respectively, is connected to a load whose components are such as to provide maximum power transfer. Determine (*a*) the impedance of the load in polar form; (*b*) the active power drawn by the load.

▌ (*a*)
$$\bar{Z}_{\text{load}} = \bar{Z}^*_{\text{gen}} \qquad \bar{Z}_{\text{load}} = (5 - j10) = 11.18 \underline{/-63.43°} \ \Omega$$

(*b*)
$$\bar{I}_{\text{load}} = \frac{\bar{V}_I}{\bar{Z}_T} = \frac{300 \underline{/60°}}{(5 + j10) + (5 - j10)} = 30 \underline{/60°} \text{ A}$$

$$P_{\text{load}} = I^2 R_{\text{load}} = (30)^2 \times 5 = 4500 \text{ W}$$

24.385 The input current, voltage, and power to an ac motor are 7.3 A, 450 V, and 2797 W, respectively. What is the motor power factor and how much reactive power is drawn by the motor?

▌
$$S_M = V_M I_M = 450(7.3) = 3285 \text{ VA} \qquad P_M = 2797 \text{ W}$$

$$\text{pf}_M = \frac{P_M}{S_M} = \frac{2797}{3285} = 0.85 \qquad \theta_M = \cos^{-1} 0.85 = 31.63° \qquad Q_M = S_M \sin\theta = 3285 \sin 31.63° = 1722.79 \text{ var}$$

24.386 A 60-A current source is in parallel with a 0.5-S conductance. Obtain an equivalent voltage source. Sketch the circuits.

▌
$$V_S = \frac{60}{0.5} = 120 \text{ V} \qquad R_S = \frac{1}{0.5} = 2 \ \Omega$$

See Fig. 24-121.

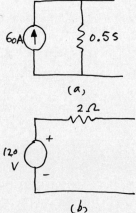

(*a*)

(*b*) **Fig. 24-121**

24.387 A 50-V voltage source is in series with a 2.5-Ω resistance. Obtain an equivalent current source. Sketch the circuits.

▌
$$I_S = 50/2.5 = 20 \text{ A} \qquad G = 1/2.5 = 0.4 \text{ S}$$

See Fig. 24.122 for sketches of the circuits.

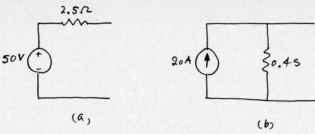

Fig. 24-122

24.388 A 10-Ω resistor is connected to the terminals of a current source. The source consists of a 90-A constant-current generator and a 5.0-Ω paralleled resistor. (a) Sketch the circuit and determine the current to the 10-Ω resistor and the voltage across it; (b) replace the current source by an equivalent voltage source and determine the current to the 10-Ω resistor and the voltage across it. Sketch the circuits.

$\blacksquare$ (a) See Fig. 24-123a.

$$Y_T = \tfrac{1}{5} + \tfrac{1}{10} = 0.3\ \text{S} \qquad I_k = I_T\,\frac{Y_k}{Y_T} = 90\left[\frac{0.1}{0.3}\right] = 30\ \text{A}$$

$$V_{10\,\Omega} = IR = 30 \times 10 = 300\ \text{V}$$

(b) See Fig. 24-123b.
$$I_{CC} = \frac{V_{CV}}{Z_s} = 90\ \text{A} \quad V_{CV} = 450\ \text{V}$$

$$I_{10\,\Omega} = \frac{450}{10+5} = 30\ \text{A} \qquad V_{10\,\Omega} = IR = 30 \times 10 = 300\ \text{V}$$

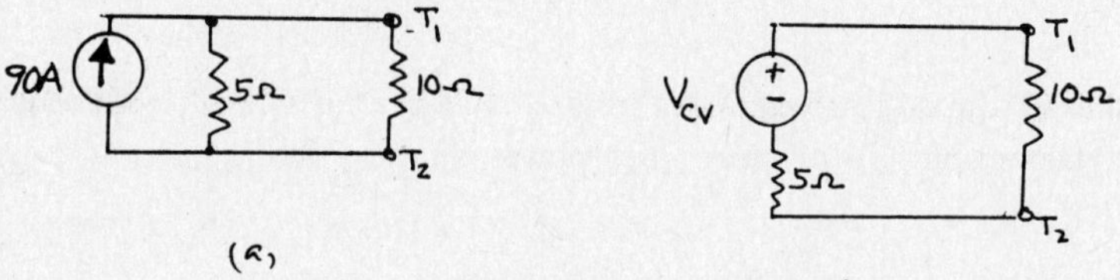

Fig. 24-123

24.389 A 60-Hz 200-V sinusoidal voltage source, whose internal impedance is $4\ \underline{/60°}\ \Omega$, is connected to a $10\ \underline{/20°}$-Ω load. (a) Determine the current to the load and the voltage across the load; (b) replace the voltage source by an equivalent current source and determine the current to the load and the voltage across the load. Sketch the circuits.

$\blacksquare$ (a)
$$\bar{I} = \frac{\bar{V}}{\bar{Z}} = \frac{200\ \underline{/0°}}{4\ \underline{/60°} + 10\ \underline{/20°}}$$

$$\bar{I} = \frac{200\ \underline{/0°}}{13.31\ \underline{/31.13°}} = 15.02\ \underline{/-31.13°}\ \text{A} \qquad \bar{V}_{T_1 T_2} = \bar{I}\,\bar{Z}_{\text{load}} = (15.02\ \underline{/-31.13°})(10\ \underline{/20°}) = 150.2\ \underline{/-11.13°}\ \text{V}$$

See Fig. 24-124a.

(b)
$$\bar{I}_k = \bar{I}_T\left[\frac{\bar{Y}_k}{\bar{Y}_T}\right] = 50\ \underline{/-60°}\left[\frac{0.1\ \underline{/-20°}}{0.3329\ \underline{/-48.87°}}\right] = 15.02\ \underline{/-31.13°}\ \text{A}$$

$$\bar{I}_T = \bar{V}_T\,\bar{Y}_T \qquad 56\ \underline{/-60°} = \bar{V}_T(0.333\ \underline{/-48.87°}) \qquad \bar{V}_T = 150.2\ \underline{/-11.13°}\ \text{V}$$

$$\bar{I}_{CC} = \frac{\bar{E}_{CV}}{\bar{Z}_s} = \frac{200\ \underline{/0°}}{4\ \underline{/60°}} = 50\ \underline{/-60°}\ \text{A} \qquad \bar{Y}_T = \frac{1}{4\ \underline{/60°}} + \frac{1}{10\ \underline{/20°}} = 0.25\ \underline{/-60°} + 0.1\ \underline{/-20°} = 0.3329\ \underline{/-48.87°}\ \text{S}$$

See Fig. 24-124b.

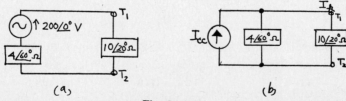

Fig. 24-124

24.390 The loop currents and two impedances for the 60-Hz network shown in Fig. 24-125 are

$$\bar{I}_1 = 20\;\underline{/60°}\;\text{A} \qquad \bar{I}_2 = 50\;\underline{/30°}\;\text{A} \qquad \bar{I}_3 = 10\;\underline{/210°}\;\text{A}$$
$$\bar{I}_4 = 70\;\underline{/100°}\;\text{A} \qquad \bar{Z}_5 = 6.0\;\underline{/25°}\;\Omega \qquad \bar{Z}_6 = 15\;\underline{/40°}\;\Omega$$

Determine (*a*) the ammeter reading; (*b*) the voltmeter reading.

▌ (*a*) $\quad \bar{I}_3 - \bar{I}_2 = 10\;\underline{/210°} - 50\;\underline{/30°} = (-8.66 - j5) - (43.30 + j25) = (-51.96 - j30) = 60\;\underline{/-150°}\;\text{A}$

Ammeter reads 60 A.

(*b*) $\qquad \bar{I}_2\bar{Z}_5 = (50\;\underline{/30°})(6\;\underline{/25°}) = 300\;\underline{/55°}\;\text{V} \qquad$ Voltmeter reads 300 V

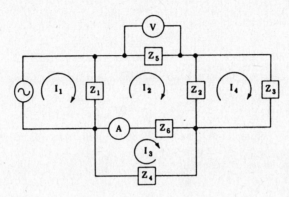

Fig. 24-125

24.391 How much active, reactive, and apparent powers are drawn by $\bar{Z}_5$ of the circuit of Fig. 24-125?

▌ $\qquad \bar{S}_5 = \bar{V}_5\bar{I}_5^* = (300\;\underline{/55°})(50\;\underline{/+30°})^*$

$\qquad\qquad = 300\;\underline{/55}(50\;\underline{/-30°}) = 15{,}000\;\underline{/25°} = (13{,}594.62 + j6339.27)$

$\qquad P = 13{,}594.6\;\text{W} \qquad Q = 6339.3\;\text{var} \qquad S = 15{,}000\;\text{VA}$

24.392 Determine the circuit elements which make up $\bar{Z}_5$ in the circuit of Fig. 24-125.

▌ $\qquad\qquad \bar{I}_5 = \bar{V}_5/\bar{Z}_5 \quad\text{or}\quad 50\;\underline{/30°} = (300\;\underline{/55°})/\bar{Z}_5$

Thus, $\qquad\qquad\qquad \bar{Z}_5 = 6\;\underline{/25°} = (5.44 + j2.54)$

$\qquad R = 5.44\;\Omega \qquad X_L = 2.54\;\Omega \qquad 2.54 = 2\pi60L \qquad L = 6.74\;\text{mH}$

24.393 (*a*) Write the loop equations for the network shown in Fig. 24-126; (*b*) determine the ammeter readings.

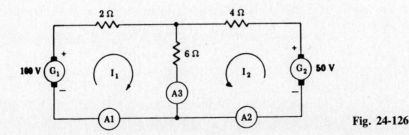

Fig. 24-126

▌ (*a*) $\qquad\qquad 100 = (2 + 6)I_1 + 6I_2 = 8I_1 + 6I_2 \qquad 50 = 6I_1 + (4 + 6)I_2 = 6I_1 + 10I_2$

Thus, $\qquad\qquad\qquad\qquad I_1 = 15.91\;\text{A} \qquad I_2 = -4.55\;\text{A}$

(*b*) Ammeter 1 reads 15.91 A; ammeter 2 reads 4.55 A; ammeter 3 reads 15.91 + (−4.55) = 11.36 A.

24.394 Determine the ammeter readings in the circuit of Fig. 24-127.

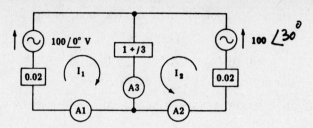

Fig. 24-127

▮ The loop equations are

$$100 \,\underline{/0°} = [0.02 + (1 + j3)]\bar{I}_1 + [1 + j3]\bar{I}_2 \qquad 100 \,\underline{/30°} = [1 + j3]\bar{I}_1 + [0.02 + (1 + j3)]\bar{I}_2$$

or

$$100 \,\underline{/0°} = [1.02 + j3]\bar{I}_1 + [1 + j3]\bar{I}_2 \qquad 100 \,\underline{/30°} = [1 + j3]\bar{I}_1 + [1.02 + j3]\bar{I}_2$$

Hence,

$$\bar{I}_1 = \frac{\Delta_{Z1}}{\Delta_Z} = \frac{165.69 \,\underline{/-3.39°}}{0.1266 \,\underline{/71.40°}} = 1308.77 \,\underline{/-74.79°} \text{ A}$$

$$\bar{I}_2 = \frac{\Delta_{Z2}}{\Delta_Z} = \frac{162.03 \,\underline{/176.18°}}{0.1266 \,\underline{/71.40°}} = 1279.86 \,\underline{/104.78°} \text{ A}$$

$$\bar{I}_1 + \bar{I}_2 = 1308.77 \,\underline{/-74.79} + 1279.86 \,\underline{/104.78°} \text{ A} = (16.86 - j25.41) = 30.5 \,\underline{/-56.4°} \text{ A}$$

Ammeter A1 reads 1308.77, ammeter A2 reads 1279.86, and ammeter A3 reads 30.5.

24.395 Determine the ammeter readings in the circuit of Fig. 24-128.

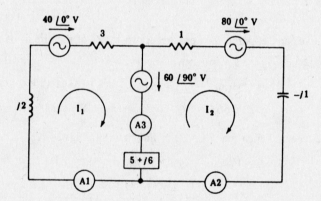

Fig. 24-128

▮ By KVL:

$$[40 \,\underline{/0°} + 60 \,\underline{/90°}] = [3 + (5 + j6) + j2]\bar{I}_1 + [-(5 + j6)]\bar{I}_2$$

$$[80 \,\underline{/0°} - 60 \,\underline{/90°}] = [-(5 + j6)]\bar{I}_1 + [1 - j1 + (5 + j6)]\bar{I}_2$$

or

$$(40 + j60) = [8 + j8]\bar{I}_1 + [-5 - j6]\bar{I}_2 \qquad (80 - j60) = [-5 - j6]\bar{I}_1 + [6 + j5]\bar{I}_2$$

Hence,

$$\bar{I}_1 = \frac{\Delta_{Z1}}{\Delta_Z} = \frac{1018.627 \,\underline{/46.595°}}{33.838 \,\underline{/55.84°}} = 30.10 \,\underline{/-9.245°} \text{ A}$$

$$\bar{I}_2 = \frac{\Delta_{Z2}}{\Delta_Z} = \frac{1188.108 \,\underline{/36.101°}}{33.838 \,\underline{/55.84°}} = 35.11 \,\underline{/-19.74°} \text{ A}$$

$$\bar{I}_1 - \bar{I}_2 = (29.71 - j4.84) - (33.05 - j11.86) = (-3.34 + j7.02) = 7.77 \,\underline{/115.44°} \text{ A}$$

Ammeter A1 reads 30.10 A, A2 reads 35.11 A, and A3 reads 7.77 A.

24.396 In the circuit of Prob. 24.395, obtain the voltage across the $(5 + j6)$-Ω impedance.

▮

$$\bar{V} = \bar{I}_3(5 + j6) = (7.77 \,\underline{/115.44°})(7.81 \,\underline{/50.19°}) = 60.69 \,\underline{/165.63°} \text{ V}$$

24.397 Determine the complex power drawn by the $(5 + j6)$-Ω impedance of the circuit of Prob. 24.395.

▮

$$\bar{S} = \bar{V}\bar{I}^* = (60.69 \,\underline{/165.63°})(7.77 \,\underline{/-115.44°}) = 471.56 \,\underline{/50.19°} = (301.91 + j362.24) \text{ VA}$$

24.398 Solve for $\bar{I}_1$ in the circuit of Fig. 24-129.

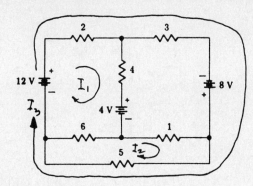

Fig. 24-129

▮ The loop equations may be written as

$$8 = 12I_1 - 6I_2 + 2I_3 \qquad 0 = -6I_1 + 12I_2 + 5I_3 \qquad 20 = 2I_1 + 5I_2 + 10I_3$$

from which

$$I_1 = \frac{\Delta_{Z1}}{\Delta_Z} = \frac{-320}{612} = -0.52 \text{ A}$$

24.399 Convert the voltage source to a current source in the circuit of Fig. 24-130a.

▮
$$I_C = 12/9 = 1.33 \text{ A}$$

Thus, we obtain Fig. 24-130b.

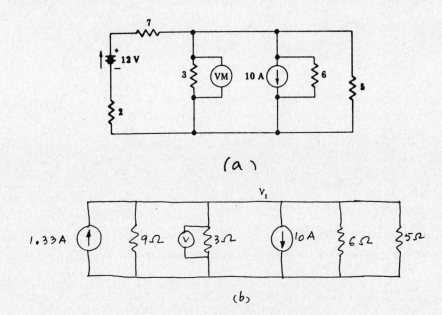

(a)

(b)

Fig. 24-130

24.400 Determine the voltmeter reading in the circuit of Fig. 24-130a by nodal analysis.

▮ By nodal analysis $\qquad [1.33 - 10] = [\frac{1}{9} + \frac{1}{3} + \frac{1}{6} + \frac{1}{5}]V_1 \qquad V_1 = -10.69 \text{ V}$

The voltmeter reads 10.69 V.

24.401 Obtain a current-source excited circuit corresponding to that shown in Fig. 24-131a.

▮
$$\bar{I}_C = \frac{40\,\underline{/30°}}{5\,\underline{/20°}} = 8\,\underline{/10°} \text{ A}$$

Hence we obtain the circuit of Fig. 24-131b.

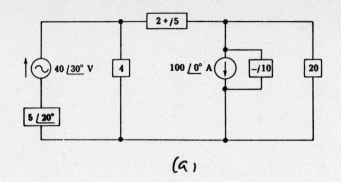

(a)

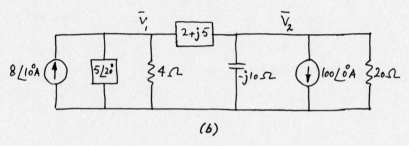

(b)

Fig. 24-131

24.402 Determine the voltage across the 20-Ω resistor of the circuit of Fig. 24-131a.

▮ By nodal analysis we obtain

$$[7.88 + j1.39] = [0.5069 - j0.2408]\bar{V}_1 - [0.0690 - j0.1724]\bar{V}_2$$

$$[-100 + j0] = -[0.0690 - j0.1724]\bar{V}_1 + [0.1190 - j0.0724]\bar{V}_2$$

Solving for $\bar{V}_2$ yields

$$\bar{V}_2 = \bar{V}_{20\,\Omega} = 689.5 \,\underline{/186.9°}\,\text{V}$$

24.403 Find the voltage across the $(1 + j3)$-Ω impedance of the circuit shown in Fig. 24-127.

▮ First we convert the given circuit to one with current sources only, as shown in Fig. 24-132, from which:

$$[5000\,\underline{/0°} + 5000\,\underline{/30°}] = \left[\frac{1}{0.02} + \frac{1}{(1+j3)} + \frac{1}{0.02}\right]\bar{V} \qquad 9659.26\,\underline{/15°} = 100.10\,\underline{/-0.17°}\,\bar{V} \qquad \bar{V} = 96.50\,\underline{/15.17°}$$

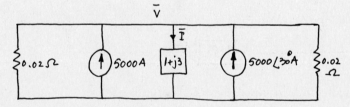

Fig. 24-132

24.404 Determine the complex power drawn by the $(1 + j3)$-Ω impedance of the circuit of Fig. 24-132.

▮ From Prob. 24-403, the current $\bar{I}$ is given by

$$\bar{I} = \frac{\bar{V}}{\bar{Z}} = \frac{96.50\,\underline{/15.17°}}{3.16\,\underline{/71.57°}} = 30.52\,\underline{/-56.40°}\,\text{A}$$

Thus, $\qquad \bar{S} = \bar{V}\bar{I}^* = (96.5\,\underline{/15.17°})(30.52\,\underline{/56.40°}) = 2945.18\,\underline{/71.57°} = 931.11 + j2794.45\,\text{VA}$

24.405 Convert the circuit of Fig. 10.81 (Chap. 10) to one having only current sources and impedances.

▮ See Fig. 24-133.

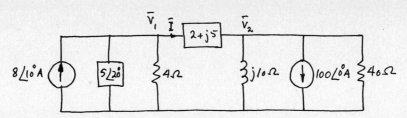

Fig. 24-133

24.406 Solve for the voltages $\bar{V}_1$ and $\bar{V}_2$ in the circuit of Fig. 24-133.

▮ By nodal analysis we have

$$[8\,\underline{/10°}] = \left[\frac{1}{5\,\underline{/20°}} + \frac{1}{4} + \frac{1}{(2+j5)}\right]\bar{V}_1 - \left[\frac{1}{(2+j5)}\right]\bar{V}_2$$

$$[-100\,\underline{/0°}] = -\left[\frac{1}{(2+j5)}\right]\bar{V}_1 + \left[\frac{1}{(2+j5)} + \frac{1}{j10} + \frac{1}{40}\right]\bar{V}_2$$

or

$$[7.88 + j1.39] = [0.5069 - j0.2408]\bar{V}_1 + [-0.0690 + j0.1724]\bar{V}_2$$

$$[-100 + j0] = [-0.0690 + j0.1724]\bar{V}_1 + [0.0940 - j0.2724]\bar{V}_2$$

Hence,

$$\bar{V}_1 = \frac{\bar{\Delta}_{Y1}}{\bar{\Delta}_Y} = \frac{16.285\,\underline{/110.79°}}{0.1371\,\underline{/-87.07°}} = 118.78\,\underline{/197.86°}\ \text{V}$$

$$\bar{V}_2 = \frac{\bar{\Delta}_{Y2}}{\bar{\Delta}_Y} = \frac{54.875\,\underline{/155.43°}}{0.1371\,\underline{/-87.07°}} = 400.26\,\underline{/242.50°}\ \text{V}$$

24.407 Determine the complex power drawn by the $(2+j5)$-Ω impedance of the circuit of Fig. 24-133.

▮ The voltage across the $(2+j5)$-Ω impedance is

$$\bar{V}_1 - \bar{V}_2 = 118.78\,\underline{/197.86} - 400.26\,\underline{/242.50} = (-113.05 - j36.43) - (-184.83 - j355.02) = 326.85\,\underline{/77.28°}$$

$$\bar{I} = \frac{\bar{V}}{\bar{Z}} = \frac{326.85\,\underline{/77.28°}}{(2+j5)} = 60.69\,\underline{/9.08°}\ \text{A}$$

and

$$\bar{S} = \bar{V}\bar{I}^* = (326.85\,\underline{/77.28°})(60.69\,\underline{/-9.08°}) = 19.836\,\underline{/68.2°} = (7.37 + j18.42)\ \text{kVA}$$

24.408 Convert the voltage sources of the circuit of Fig. 10-82 to equivalent current sources and draw the resulting circuit.

▮ See Fig. 24-134.

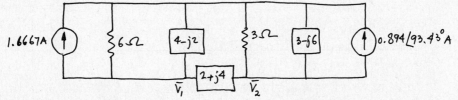

Fig. 24-134

24.409 Write the node equation for the circuit of Fig. 24-134 and solve for $\bar{V}_1$.

▮ The node equations are

$$[-1.6667] = \left[\frac{1}{6} + \frac{1}{(4-j2)} + \frac{1}{(2+j4)}\right]\bar{V}_1 - \left[\frac{1}{(2+j4)}\right]\bar{V}_2$$

$$[-0.894\,\underline{/93.43°}] = -\left[\frac{1}{(2+j4)}\right]\bar{V}_1 + \left[\frac{1}{(2+j4)} + \frac{1}{3} + \frac{1}{(3-j6)}\right]\bar{V}_2$$

or

$$[-1.6667 + j0] = [0.4667 - j0.1000]\bar{V}_1 + [-0.1000 + j0.2000]\bar{V}_2$$

$$[0.0535 - j0.8924] = [-0.1000 + j0.2000]\bar{V}_1 + [0.5000 - j0.0667]\bar{V}_2$$

Hence,

$$\bar{V}_1 = \frac{\Delta_{Y1}}{\Delta_Y} = \frac{1.0067\,\underline{/179.36°}}{0.260\,\underline{/-9.104°}} = 3.87\,\underline{/188.46°}\ \text{V}$$

24.410 What is the voltage across the $(2 + j4)$-Ω impedance of the circuit of Fig. 24-134?

 ▮ From Prob. 24.409:

$$\bar{V}_2 = \frac{\Delta_{Y2}}{\Delta_Y} = \frac{0.2473\,\underline{/-159.05°}}{0.260\,\underline{/-9.104°}} = 0.95\,\underline{/-149.95°}\ \text{V}$$

The voltage drop across $(2 + j4)$ is

$$\bar{V}_1 - \bar{V}_2 = (-3.83 - j0.57) - (-0.82 - j0.48) = 3.01\,\underline{/-178.22°}$$

Thus, the voltage drop across $(2 + j4)$ is 3.01 V.

24.411 For the circuit of Fig. 10-84, obtain one having a current source.

 ▮ See Fig. 24-135.

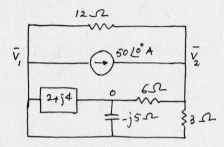

Fig. 24-135

24.412 Solve for the voltage $\bar{V}_2$ in the circuit of Fig. 24-135.

 ▮ By nodal analysis, after some simplification, we obtain

$$-50 = 0.5166\bar{V}_1 - 0.4166\bar{V}_2 \qquad 50 = -0.4166\bar{V}_1 + 0.5833\bar{V}_2$$

Thus, $$\bar{V}_2 = 39.13\,\underline{/0°}\ \text{V}$$

24.413 How much power is absorbed by the 6-Ω resistor of the circuit of Fig. 11-84?

 ▮ We use the equivalent circuit of Fig. 24-135. From Prob. 24-412 we have $V_2 = 39.13$ V.

Hence, $$P_{6\,\Omega} = (39.13)^2/6 = 255.2\ \text{W}$$

24.414 Determine the Thévenin equivalent of the circuit section to the left of terminals $T_1 T_2$ in Fig. 24-136a.

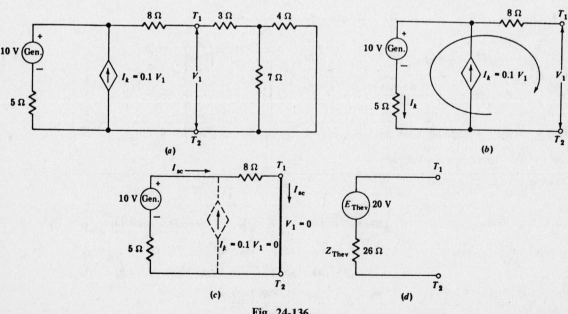

Fig. 24-136

❚ Using the circuits of Fig. 24-136b and c we obtain

$$V_1 = 10 - [(-I_k)5] \qquad I_k = 0.1V_1$$

Thus, $$V_1 = 20 \text{ V} = E_{\text{Th}}$$

and $$10 = 8I_{\text{SC}} + 5I_{\text{SC}} \quad \text{or} \quad I_{\text{SC}} = 0.769 \text{ A}$$

$$Z_{\text{Th}} = 20/0.769 = 26 \text{ }\Omega$$

Hence we obtain the circuit of Fig. 24-136d.

24.415 Obtain the Thévenin equivalent of the network of Fig. 24-137a, at the terminals T_1T_2.

❚ The sequence of networks for the calculations are shown in Fig. 24-137b to e, from which

$$E_{\text{Th}} = V_{\text{OC}} = 40 \text{ V} \qquad I_{\text{SC}} = 1.67 \text{ A} \qquad Z_{\text{Th}} = 40/1.67 = 24 \text{ }\Omega$$

Hence we obtain the circuit of Fig. 24-137f.

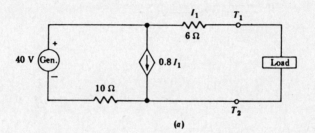

(a)

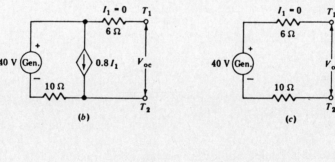

(b)   (c)

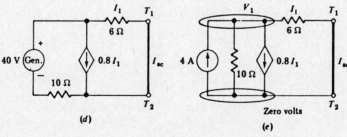

(d)   (e)

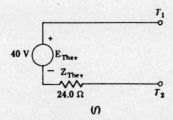

(f)

Fig. 24-137

24.416 A 12-V battery and a sinusoidal generator are connected in series with a coil, as shown in Fig. 24-138a. The inductance and resistance of the coil are 1.0 H and 6.0 Ω, respectively. The equation for the generator voltage wave is $e_{gen} = 30 \sin 10t$. Assume the resistance of the battery is negligible, and the inductance and resistance of the generator are 0.20 H and 0.10 Ω, respectively. Determine the steady-state circuit current.

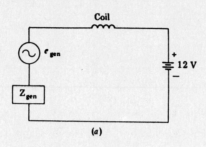

(a)

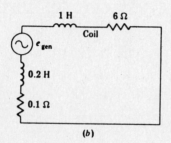

(b)

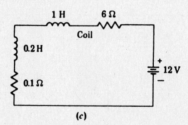

(c)   Fig. 24-138

❚ To calculate the sinusoidal component of the current, replace the battery by its internal resistance (which is assumed to be zero in this problem). This is shown in Fig. 24-138b.

$$X_{L,coil} = \omega L_{coil} = 10(1) = 10 \ \Omega \qquad X_{L,gen} = \omega L_{gen} = 10(0.2) = 2 \ \Omega$$

$$\bar{Z}_T = \bar{Z}_{gen} + \bar{Z}_{coil} = (0.1 + j2) + (6 + j10) = 6.1 + j12 = 13.46 \ \underline{/63.05°} \ \Omega$$

$$\bar{I} = \frac{\bar{E}_{gen}}{\bar{Z}_T} = \frac{30/\sqrt{2}\underline{/0°}}{13.46 \ \underline{/63.05°}} = 1.58 \ \underline{/-63.05°} \ A \qquad i_\sim = 1.58\sqrt{2} \sin(10t - 63.05°) = 2.23 \sin(10t - 63.05°)$$

To calculate the dc component of current, replace the sinusoidal generator by its internal impedance, as shown in Fig. 24-138c. The inductance of the circuit has no effect on direct current at steady state. Hence,

$$I_{dc} = \frac{E_{bat}}{R_T} = \frac{12}{6 + 0.1} = 1.97 \ A$$

or using phasors, $\qquad \bar{Z} = R + j2\pi fL = 6.1 + j2\pi 0(1.2) = 6.1 \ \Omega$

The total current in the circuit is

$$i_T = i_\sim + I_{dc} = 2.23 \sin(10t - 63.05°) + 1.97$$

24.417 Sketch the current i_T obtained in Prob. 24-416.

❚ See Fig. 24-139.

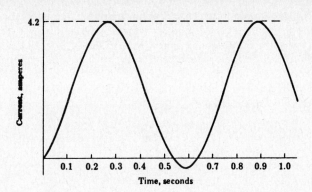

Fig. 24-139

24.418 By superposition, find the current in the inductor of the circuit of Fig. 24-140.

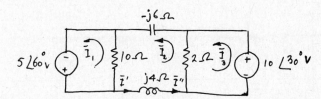

Fig. 24-140

❚ With the $5 \underline{/60°}$-V source removed,

$$\bar{I}' = 10 \underline{/30°}/(j4 - j6) = 5 \underline{/120°} \text{ A}$$

With the $10 \underline{/30°}$-V source removed,

$$\bar{I}'' = 5 \underline{/60°}/(j4 - j6) = 2.5 \underline{/150°} \text{ A}$$

Thus, $\qquad \bar{I} = \bar{I}' + \bar{I}'' = 5 \underline{/120°} + 2.5 \underline{/150°} = 7.27 \underline{/129.9°} \text{ A}$

24.419 Verify the result of Prob. 24.418 by loop analysis.

❚ Defining the loop currents as shown, by KVL we obtain

$$5 \underline{/60°} = 10\bar{I}_1 - 10\bar{I}_2 \qquad 0 = -10\bar{I}_1 + (10 + j4 - j6 + 2)\bar{I}_2 - 2\bar{I}_3 \qquad 10 \underline{/30°} = -2\bar{I}_2 + 2\bar{I}_3$$

Solving for $\bar{I}_2$ yields

$$\bar{I}_2 = 7.27 \underline{/129.9°} \text{ A}$$

24.420 Express the sinusoidal pulse of Fig. 24-141 in terms of unit-step functions.

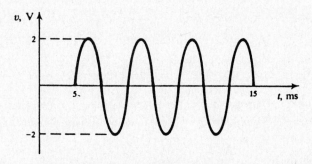

Fig. 24-141

❚ The sinusoid has 7 half-periods in 10 ms; i.e.,

$$7T/2 = 10^{-2} \qquad \text{or} \qquad \omega = 2\pi/T = 700\pi \text{ rad/s}$$

and the amplitude is 2 V. Therefore, it is the function

$$2 \sin 700\pi(t - 5 \times 10^{-3})$$

that must be cut off to zero for $t < 5 \times 10^{-3}$ s and for $t > 15 \times 10^{-3}$ s. Thus,

$$v(t) = [2 \sin 700\pi(t - 5 \times 10^{-3})][u(t - 5 \times 10^{-3}) - u(t - 15 \times 10^{-3})] \qquad \text{V}$$

24.421 A series *RL* circuit experiences a pulse of voltage *V* occurring during the interval $t_0 < t < t_1$. Determine the circuit current, $i(t)$.

▌ The pulse is indicated in Fig. 24-142a, and the electric circuit, with step voltage sources simulating the pulse, is shown in Fig. 24-142b. Let $i_0(t)$ and $i_1(t)$ be the currents due to sources $Vu(t - t_0)$ and $-Vu(t - t_1)$, respectively, each acting alone. Thus,

$$i_0(t) = \frac{V}{R}[1 - e^{-R(t-t_0)/L}]u(t - t_0) \qquad i_1(t) = -\frac{V}{R}[1 - e^{-R(t-t_1)/L}]u(t - t_1)$$

and, by superposition, $i(t) = i_0(t) + i_1(t)$. The current is plotted in Fig. 24-142a.

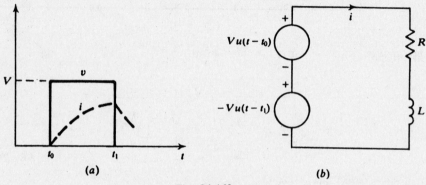

Fig. 24-142

24.422 A single sawtooth voltage waveform is shown in Fig. 24-143a. Synthesize this waveform by a superposition of step and ramp functions.

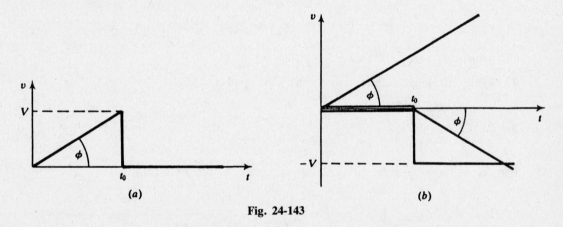

Fig. 24-143

▌ The three components needed in the synthesis are shown in Fig. 24-143b. Analytically,

$$v(t) = \frac{V}{t_0} r(t) - Vu(t - t_0) - \frac{V}{t_0} r(t - t_0)$$

24.423 Find the current in a series *RC* circuit if the capacitor is initially uncharged and the applied voltage is of the form shown in Fig. 24-143a.

▌ The differential equation for the current is

$$R \frac{di}{dt} + \frac{1}{C} i = \frac{dv}{dt} = \frac{V}{t_0} u(t) - \frac{V}{t_0} u(t - t_0) \tag{1}$$

The two steps composing the forcing function give rise to currents with steady-state values CV/t_0 and $-CV/t_0$, respectively. Thus, for $t > 0$,

$$i(t) = \left[Ae^{-t/RC} + \frac{CV}{t_0} \right] + \left[Be^{-(t-t_0)/RC} - \frac{CV}{t_0} \right]u(t - t_0) \tag{2}$$

The initial condition, $i(0_+) = 0$ [because $v(0) = 0$], determines

$$A = -CV/t_0$$

The continuity of the capacitor voltage at $t = t_0$ requires that

$$\Delta v|_{t=t_0} = R \, \Delta i|_{t=t_0} \qquad -V = R\left[B - \frac{CV}{t_0}\right] \qquad B = \frac{CV}{t_0} - \frac{V}{R}$$

With these values for the constants, (2) becomes

$$i(t) = \frac{CV}{t_0}(1 - e^{-t/RC}) - \frac{CV}{t_0}\left[1 - \left(1 - \frac{t_0}{RC}\right)e^{-(t-t_0)/RC}\right]u(t - t_0)$$

24.424 Solve Prob. 24.423 by the Laplace transform method.

❚ The Laplace transform method is useful only if all conditions on the time function are applied at $t = 0_+$. Therefore, we first consider $q(t)$, the capacitor charge, which is subject to the sole condition $q(0_+) = 0$. The circuit equation is

$$R\frac{dq}{dt} + \frac{1}{C}q = v = \begin{cases} Vt/t_0 & 0 < t < t_0 \\ 0 & t > t_0 \end{cases} \tag{1}$$

Taking the Laplace transform of (1) and applying the initial condition,

$$RsQ(s) + \frac{1}{C}Q(s) = \frac{V}{t_0}\int_0^{t_0} te^{-st}\,dt = \frac{V}{t_0}\left(\frac{1}{s^2} - \frac{1}{s^2}e^{-t_0 s} - \frac{t_0}{s}e^{-t_0 s}\right) \tag{2}$$

Now, because $i = dq/dt$ and $q(0_+) = 0$, $I(s) = sQ(s)$. Solving (2), with $\alpha \equiv 1/RC$, then gives

$$I(s) = sQ(s) = \frac{V}{Rt_0}\frac{1}{s(s+\alpha)} - \frac{V}{Rt_0}\frac{e^{-t_0 s}}{s(s+\alpha)} - \frac{V}{R}\frac{e^{-t_0 s}}{s+\alpha} \equiv I_1(s) + I_2(s) + I_3(s) \tag{3}$$

Inverting (3) termwise, we have

$$i_1(t) = \frac{V}{Rt_0\alpha}(1 - e^{-\alpha t})$$

Then, by the shifting theorem,

$$i_2(t) = \frac{V}{Rt_0\alpha}[1 - e^{-\alpha(t-t_0)}]u(t - t_0)$$

Finally,

$$i_3(t) = -\frac{V}{R}e^{-\alpha(t-t_0)}u(t - t_0)$$

The reader should verify that the solution just found,

$$i(t) = i_1(t) + i_2(t) + i_3(t)$$

24.425 A series RLC circuit has $R = 250\,\Omega$, $L = 10\,\text{mH}$, and $C = 100\,\mu\text{F}$. Assuming zero initial conditions, use Laplace transforms to determine the (natural) current for a unit impulse voltage input.

❚ The circuit voltage equation is, for an initially uncharged capacitor,

$$\frac{1}{C}\int_0^t i(\tau)\,d\tau + Ri + L\frac{di}{dt} = v(t) \tag{1}$$

With the given numerical values, (1) becomes

$$10^4 \int_0^t i(\tau) + 250i + 10^{-2}\frac{di}{dt} = \delta(t) \tag{2}$$

Taking the Laplace transform of (2) yields

$$\frac{10^4}{s}I(s) + 250I(s) + 10^{-2}sI(s) = 1 \tag{3}$$

whence, using partial fractions,

$$I(s) = \frac{100s}{s^2 + 25,000s + 10^6} = \frac{100s}{(s + 24,960)(s + 40)} = \frac{100.16}{s + 24,960} - \frac{0.16}{s + 40}$$

Inverting,

$$i(t) = 100.16e^{-24,960t} - 0.16e^{-40t} \qquad \text{A}$$

24.426 Show graphically that *any* waveform may be approximated, as closely as desired, by a superposition of (shifted) step functions.

▌ Figure 24-144 shows an arbitrary waveform approximated to the desired precision by square pulses. Each square pulse may, in turn, be expressed as the difference of two step functions.

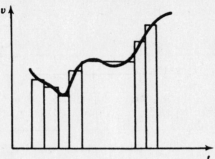

Fig. 24-144

24.427 For the circuit in Fig. 24-145, the transfer impedance between branches $(1-4)$ and $(3-5)$ is determined to be $28.4 \underline{/39.59°}$ Ω at 1000 Hz. Calculate the current in the 7-Ω resistor if the generator voltage is 40 V at 1000 Hz.

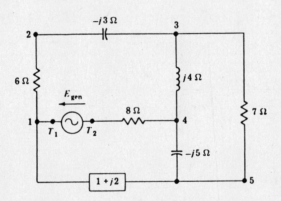

Fig. 24-145

▌ $$\bar{Z}_1 = \frac{\bar{V}_{in}}{\bar{I}_{out}} \qquad 28.4 \underline{/39.59°} = \frac{40 \underline{/10°}}{\bar{I}_{out}} \qquad \bar{I}_{out} = 1.41 \underline{/-29.59°} \text{ A}$$

24.428 Repeat Prob. 24.427 if the generator terminals T_1 and T_2 are interchanged.

▌ Reversal of the generator terminals reverses the generator polarity. Hence,

$$28.4 \underline{/39.59°} = \frac{-40 \underline{/10°}}{\bar{I}_{out}} \qquad \bar{I}_{out} = -1.41 \underline{/-29.59°} \text{ A}$$

24.429 For the circuit in Fig. 24-146a, assume

$$\bar{Z}_A = 5.0 \underline{/20°} \text{ Ω} \qquad \bar{Z}_B = 10 \underline{/90°} \text{ Ω} \qquad \bar{Z}_C = 8.0 \underline{/0°} \text{ Ω} \qquad \bar{Z}_D = 6.0 \underline{/-45°} \text{ Ω} \qquad \bar{Z}_E = 2.0 \underline{/0°} \text{ Ω}$$

Convert the lower delta into an equivalent wye.

▌ $$\bar{Z}_1 = \frac{\bar{Z}_A \bar{Z}_B}{\bar{Z}_A + \bar{Z}_B + \bar{Z}_C} = \frac{(5 \underline{/20°})(10 \underline{/90°})}{5 \underline{/20°} + 10 \underline{/90°} + 8 \underline{/0°}} = \frac{50 \underline{/110°}}{4.70 + j1.71 + j10 + 8} = \frac{50 \underline{/110°}}{12.7 + j11.71}$$

$$\bar{Z}_1 = \frac{50 \underline{/110°}}{17.27 \underline{/42.68°}} = 2.90 \underline{/67.32°} = (1.12 + j2.67) \text{ Ω}$$

$$\bar{Z}_2 = \frac{\bar{Z}_B \bar{Z}_C}{\bar{Z}_A + \bar{Z}_B + \bar{Z}_C} = \frac{(10 \underline{/90°})(8 \underline{/0°})}{17.27 \underline{/42.68°}} = 4.63 \underline{/47.32°} = (3.14 + j3.40) \text{ Ω}$$

$$\bar{Z}_3 = \frac{\bar{Z}_C \bar{Z}_A}{\bar{Z}_A + \bar{Z}_B + \bar{Z}_C} = \frac{(8 \underline{/0°})(5 \underline{/20°})}{17.27 \underline{/42.68°}} = 2.32 \underline{/-22.68°} = (2.14 - j0.89) \text{ Ω}$$

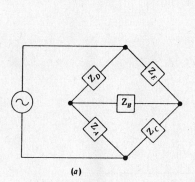

Fig. 24-146

24.430 Find the input impedance of the circuit of Fig. 24-146a.

$\blacksquare$ Proceeding with Fig. 24-146b we obtain the circuit of Fig. 24-147, from which

$$\bar{Z}_1 + \bar{Z}_D = (1.12 + j2.67) + 6 \underline{/-45°} = (1.12 + j2.67) + (4.24 - j4.24) = 5.59 \underline{/-16.34°} \ \Omega$$

$$\bar{Z}_2 + \bar{Z}_E = (3.14 + j3.40) + 2 \underline{/0°} = 5.14 + j3.40 = 6.16 \underline{/33.48°} \ \Omega$$

Using the special-case formula for two impedances in parallel,

$$\bar{Z}_{P,2} = \frac{(5.59 \underline{/-16.34°})(6.16 \underline{/33.48°})}{5.59 \underline{/-16.34°} + 6.16 \underline{/33.48°}} = \frac{34.43 \underline{/17.14°}}{10.66 \underline{/9.86°}} = 3.23 \underline{/7.28°} = (3.20 + j0.41) \ \Omega$$

Hence, $\qquad \bar{Z}_{in} = \bar{Z}_{P,2} + \bar{Z}_3 = (3.20 + j0.41) + (2.14 - j0.89) = (5.34 - j0.48) = 5.36 \underline{/-5.14°} \ \Omega$

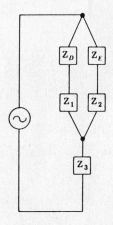

Fig. 24-147

24.431 Determine the input impedance of the circuit shown in Fig. 24-148a.

$\blacksquare$ Assume: $\quad \bar{Z}_1 = 2.0 \underline{/30°} \ \Omega \qquad \bar{Z}_2 = 3.0 \underline{/40°} \ \Omega \qquad \bar{Z}_3 = 6.0 \underline{/90°} \ \Omega \qquad \bar{Z}_4 = 7.0 \underline{/50°} \ \Omega \qquad \bar{Z}_5 = 10 \underline{/-60°} \ \Omega$

First convert the wye into an equivalent delta, as shown in Fig. 24-148b, and then determine the input impedance.

$$\bar{Z}_A = \frac{\bar{Z}_1\bar{Z}_2 + \bar{Z}_2\bar{Z}_3 + \bar{Z}_3\bar{Z}_1}{\bar{Z}_2} = \frac{(2\underline{/30°})(3\underline{/40°}) + (3\underline{/40°})(6\underline{/90°}) + (6\underline{/90°})(2\underline{/30°})}{3\underline{/40°}} = 11.21 \underline{/77.49°} \ \Omega$$

$$\bar{Z}_B = \frac{\bar{Z}_1\bar{Z}_2 + \bar{Z}_2\bar{Z}_3 + \bar{Z}_3\bar{Z}_1}{\bar{Z}_3} = \frac{33.62 \underline{/117.49°}}{6 \underline{/90°}} = 5.60 \underline{/27.49°} \ \Omega$$

$$\bar{Z}_C = \frac{\bar{Z}_1\bar{Z}_2 + \bar{Z}_2\bar{Z}_3 + \bar{Z}_3\bar{Z}_1}{\bar{Z}_1} = \frac{33.62 \underline{/117.49°}}{2 \underline{/30°}} = 16.81 \underline{/87.49°} \ \Omega$$

Combining parallel branches, using the special-case formula,

$$\bar{Z}_{kl} = \frac{\bar{Z}_C \bar{Z}_5}{\bar{Z}_C + \bar{Z}_5} = \frac{(16.81\ \underline{/87.49°})(10\ \underline{/-60°})}{16.81\ \underline{/87.49°} + 10\ \underline{/-60°}} = \frac{168.1\ \underline{/27.49°}}{(5.74 + j8.13)} = \frac{168.1\ \underline{/27.49°}}{9.95\ \underline{/54.81°}} = 16.89\ \underline{/-27.32°}\ \Omega$$

$$\bar{Z}_{ml} = \frac{\bar{Z}_A \bar{Z}_4}{\bar{Z}_A + \bar{Z}_4} = \frac{(11.21\ \underline{/77.49°})(7\ \underline{/50°})}{11.21\ \underline{/77.49°} + 7\ \underline{/50°}} = \frac{78.47\ \underline{/127.49°}}{(6.93 + j16.31)} = 4.43\ \underline{/60.51°}\ \Omega$$

The reduced circuit is shown in Fig. 24-148c.

$$\bar{Z}_{kl} + \bar{Z}_{ml} = 16.89\ \underline{/-27.32°} + 4.43\ \underline{/60.51°} = (15.01 - j7.75) + (2.18 + j3.86) = (17.19 - j3.90)$$

$$= 17.62\ \underline{/-12.77°}\ \Omega$$

Combining the two parallel branches in Fig. 24-148c,

$$\bar{Z}_{\text{in}} = \frac{\bar{Z}_B(\bar{Z}_{kl} + \bar{Z}_{ml})}{\bar{Z}_B + (\bar{Z}_{kl} + \bar{Z}_{ml})} = \frac{(5.60\ \underline{/27.49°})(17.62\ \underline{/-12.77°})}{(5.60\ \underline{/27.49°} + 17.62\ \underline{/-12.77°})} = \frac{98.67\ \underline{/14.72°}}{22.19\ \underline{/-3.38°}} = 4.45\ \underline{/18.1°}\ \Omega$$

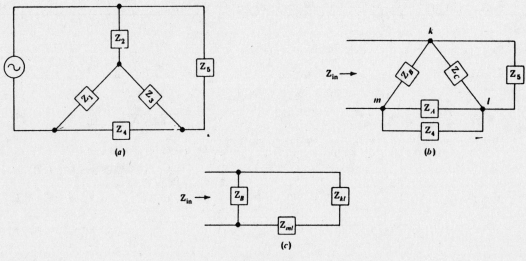

Fig. 24-148

24.432 Find the Thévenin equivalent of the circuit of Fig. 24-149 at the terminals $T_1 T_2$.

$$V_{\text{Th}} = 120\left(\frac{6}{2 + 4 + 6}\right) = 60\ \text{V} \qquad R_{\text{Th}} = \frac{6(2 + 4)}{6 + 2 + 4} + 5 = 8\ \Omega$$

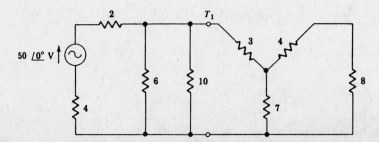

Fig. 24-149

24.433 Determine E_{Th} and Z_{Th} at $T_1 T_2$ of the circuit of Fig. 24-150.

$$Z_P = \frac{6 \times 10}{6 + 10} = 3.75\ \Omega \qquad E_{\text{Th}} = 50\ \underline{/0°}\left(\frac{3.75}{3.75 + 2 + 4}\right) = 19.23\ \text{V} \qquad Z_{\text{Th}} = \frac{3.75(2 + 4)}{3.75 + 2 + 4} = 2.308\ \Omega$$

Fig. 24-150

24.434 Repeat Prob. 24.433 for the circuit of Fig. 24-151.

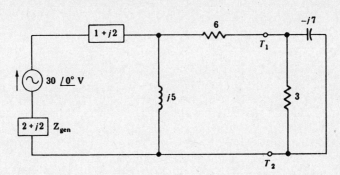

Fig. 24-151

$E_{\text{Th}} = 30 \underline{/0^\circ}\left[\dfrac{j5}{(2+j2)+(1+j2)+j5} \right] = 15.81 \underline{/18.43^\circ} \text{ V}$ $\bar{Z}_P = \dfrac{j5[(2+j2)+(1+j2)]}{j5+(2+j2)+(1+j2)} = 2.64 \underline{/71.57^\circ} \Omega$

$\bar{Z}_{\text{Th}} = 2.64 \underline{/71.57^\circ} + 6 = (6.835+j2.505) = 7.28 \underline{/20.12^\circ} \Omega$

24.435 Repeat Prob. 24-433 for the circuit of Fig. 24-152.

$\bar{Z}_P = \dfrac{j5(-j4)}{j5+(-j4)} = -20j \ \Omega$ $E_{\text{Th}} = 100 \underline{/0^\circ}\left[\dfrac{10}{(10+j20)-j20+10} \right] = 50 \underline{/0^\circ} \text{ V}$

$\bar{Z}_P = \dfrac{(10+j20-j20)10}{10+j20-j20+10} = 5 \ \Omega$ $Z_{\text{Th}} = 5+7 = 12 \ \Omega$

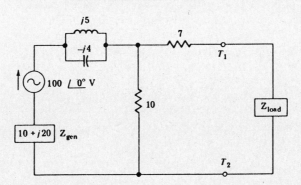

Fig. 24-152

24.436 In the circuit of Fig. 24-152, determine the maximum power that can be absorbed by the load.

For maximum power:

$\bar{Z}_{\text{load}} = \bar{Z}_{\text{Th}}^* = 12 \ \Omega$ $\bar{I}_{\text{load}} = \dfrac{50 \underline{/0^\circ}}{12+12} = 2.08 \underline{/0^\circ} \text{ A}$ $P_{\max} = (2.08)^2(12) = 51.92 \text{ W}$

24.437 Replace the 100-V sinusoidal generator in Fig. 24-152 with a 100-V battery, and determine   (*a*) the steady-state Thévenin equivalent section to the left of terminals $T_1 T_2$;   (*b*) $\bar{Z}_{\text{load}}$ that will result in maximum power transfer;   (*c*) the power drawn by $\bar{Z}_{\text{load}}$ in part (*b*).

(*a*) $E_{\text{Th}} = 100\left(\dfrac{10}{10+10} \right) = 50 \text{ V}$ $\bar{Z}_{\text{Th}} = 5+7 = 12 \ \Omega$

(*b*) $Z_{\text{load}} = Z_{\text{Th}} = 12 \ \Omega$

(*c*) $P_{\max} = \left(\dfrac{50}{12+12} \right)^2 12 = 51.92 \text{ W}$

24.438 Repeat Prob. 24.433 for the circuit of Fig. 24-153.

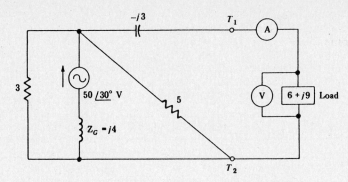

Fig. 24-153

$$\bar{Z}_P = \frac{5 \times 3}{5 + 3} = 1.875 \; \underline{/0°} \; \Omega \qquad \bar{E}_{\text{Th}} = 50 \; \underline{/30°} \left[\frac{1.875}{1.875 + j4} \right] = 21.22 \; \underline{/-34.88°} \; \text{V}$$

$$\bar{Y}_P = \frac{1}{3} + \frac{1}{5} + \frac{1}{j4} = 0.5890 \; \underline{/-25.12°} \qquad \bar{Z}_P = \frac{1}{\bar{Y}_P} = 1.698 \; \underline{/25.12°} \; \Omega$$

$$\bar{Z}_{\text{Th}} = 1.698 \; \underline{/25.12°} + (-j3) = 2.7493 \; \underline{/-56.0°} \; \Omega$$

24.439 Determine the ammeter and voltmeter readings in the circuit of Fig. 24-153.

▮ Using the Thévenin equivalent of Prob. 24.438, we have

$$\bar{I} = \frac{21.22 \; \underline{/-34.88°}}{2.7493 \; \underline{/-56°} + (6 + j9)} = 2.10 \; \underline{/-76.6°}$$

The ammeter reads 2.10 A.

$$\bar{V} = \bar{I} \bar{Z}_{\text{load}} = (2.10 \; \underline{/-76.6°})(6 + j9) = 22.71 \; \underline{/-20.29°} \; \text{V}$$

The voltmeter reads 22.71 V.

24.440 How much complex, active, and reactive powers are drawn by the load of the circuit of Fig. 24-153?

▮ $$\bar{S} = \bar{V}\bar{I}^* = (22.71 \; \underline{/-20.29°})(2.10 \; \underline{/+76.6°}) = 47.69 \; \underline{/56.31°} = 26.45 + j39.68$$

$$P = 26.45 \; \text{W} \qquad Q = 39.68 \; \text{var (lagging)} \qquad S = 47.69 \; \text{VA}$$

24.441 Repeat Prob. 24-433 for the circuit of Fig. 24-154.

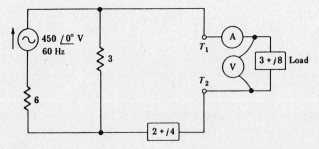

Fig. 24-154

▮ $$\bar{E}_{\text{Th}} = 450 \; \underline{/0°} \left[\frac{3}{3 + 6} \right] = 150 \; \underline{/0°} \; \text{V} \qquad \bar{Z}_P = \frac{6 \times 3}{6 + 3} = 2 \; \underline{/0°} \; \Omega \qquad \bar{Z}_{\text{Th}} = 2 + (2 + j4) = 5.657 \; \underline{/45°} \; \Omega$$

24.442 Determine the voltmeter and ammeter readings in the circuit of Prob. 24-441.

▮ $$\bar{I} = \frac{150 \; \underline{/0°}}{(4 + j4) + (3 + j8)} = 10.80 \; \underline{/-59.74°} \; \text{A} \qquad \text{Ammeter reads 10.8 A}$$

$$\bar{V}_{\text{load}} = \bar{I} \bar{Z}_{\text{load}} = (10.8 \; \underline{/-59.74°})(3 + j8) = 92.28 \; \underline{/9.70°} \; \text{V} \qquad \text{Voltmeter reads 92.28 V}$$

24.443 Calculate the active and reactive powers drawn by the load of the circuit of Fig. 24-154.

▮ $$\bar{S}_{\text{load}} = \bar{V}_{\text{load}} \bar{I}_{\text{load}}^* = (92.28 \; \underline{/9.70°})(10.80 \; \underline{/+59.74°}) = 996.57 \; \underline{/69.44°} = (349.92 + j933.12) \; \text{VA}$$

$$P_{\text{load}} = 349.92 \; \text{W} \qquad Q_{\text{load}} = 933.12 \; \text{var}$$

24.444 (*a*) Replace the 450-V sinusoidal generator in Fig. 24-154 with a 450-V dc generator, and determine the Thévenin equivalent section to the left of terminals $T_1 T_2$;   (*b*) sketch the new equivalent circuit and determine the ammeter and voltmeter readings;   (*c*) determine the energy *stored* in the load at steady state.

▮ (*a*)
$$E_{\text{Th}} = 450\left(\frac{3}{3+6}\right) = 150 \text{ V} \qquad Z_P = \frac{3 \times 6}{3+6} = 2 \,\Omega \qquad Z_{\text{Th}} = 2 + 2 = 4 \,\Omega$$

(*b*)
$$I_{\text{load}} = \frac{V}{R} = \frac{150}{4+3} = 21.43 \text{ A} \qquad \text{Ammeter reads } 21.43 \text{ A}$$

$$V_{\text{load}} = I_{\text{load}} Z_{\text{load}} = 21.43 \times 3 = 64.29 \text{ V} \qquad \text{Voltmeter reads } 64.29 \text{ V}$$

(*c*)
$$X_L = 2\pi f L \qquad 8 = 2\pi 60 L \qquad L = 21.2 \text{ mH}$$

$$W = \tfrac{1}{2} L I^2 = \tfrac{1}{2}(0.0212)(21.43)^2 = 4.87 \text{ J}$$

24.445 Repeat Prob. 24.433 for the circuit of Fig. 24-155.

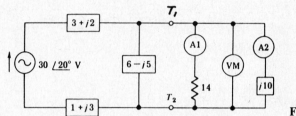

Fig. 24-155

▮
$$\bar{E}_{\text{Th}} = 30 \,\underline{/20^\circ}\left[\frac{(6-j5)}{(1+j3)+(3+j2)+(6-j5)}\right] = 23.43 \,\underline{/-19.81^\circ} \text{ V}$$

$$\bar{Z}_{\text{Th}} = \bar{Z}_P = \frac{[(3+j2)+(1+j3)](6-j5)}{(3+j2)+(1+j3)+(6-j5)} = 5.0 \,\underline{/11.55^\circ} \,\Omega = 4.899 + j1.001$$

24.446 Determine the voltmeter and ammeter readings in the circuit of Fig. 24-155.

▮ $\bar{Z}_{\text{load}} = \dfrac{(14)(j10)}{14+j10} = 8.137 \,\underline{/54.46^\circ} = (4.7296 + j6.6209) \,\Omega \quad \bar{Z}_{\text{in}} = 5 \,\underline{/11.55^\circ} + 8.137 \,\underline{/54.46^\circ} = 12.28 \,\underline{/38.36^\circ} \,\Omega$

$$\bar{I}_{\text{Th}} = \frac{\bar{V}_{\text{Th}}}{\bar{Z}_{\text{in}}} = \frac{23.43 \,\underline{/-19.81^\circ}}{12.28 \,\underline{/38.36^\circ}} = 1.91 \,\underline{/-58.17^\circ} \text{ A}$$

$$\bar{V}_{\text{load}} = \bar{I}_{\text{Th}} \bar{Z}_{\text{load}} = (1.91 \,\underline{/-58.17^\circ})(8.137 \,\underline{/54.46^\circ}) = 15.54 \,\underline{/-3.71^\circ} \text{ V}$$

$$\bar{I}_{\text{A1}} = \frac{\bar{V}}{\bar{Z}} = \frac{15.54 \,\underline{/-3.71^\circ}}{14} = 1.11 \,\underline{/-3.71^\circ} \text{ A} \qquad \bar{I}_{\text{A2}} = \frac{\bar{V}}{\bar{Z}} = \frac{15.54 \,\underline{/-3.71^\circ}}{10 \,\underline{/90^\circ}} = 1.55 \,\underline{/-93.71^\circ} \text{ A}$$

The voltmeter reads 15.54 V; ammeter A1 reads 1.11 A; ammeter A2 reads 1.55 A.

24.447 The Thévenin equivalent voltage and Thévenin equivalent impedance of a circuit section are $60 \,\underline{/30^\circ}$ V and $20 \,\underline{/30^\circ} \,\Omega$, respectively.   Determine the Norton equivalent section.

▮
$$\bar{E}_{\text{Th}} = 60 \,\underline{/30^\circ} \text{ V} \qquad \bar{Z}_{\text{Th}} = 20 \,\underline{/30^\circ} \,\Omega$$

$$\bar{I}_{\text{Nort}} = \frac{\bar{E}_{\text{Th}}}{\bar{Z}_{\text{Th}}} = \frac{60 \,\underline{/30^\circ}}{20 \,\underline{/30^\circ}} = 3 \,\underline{/0^\circ} \text{ A} \qquad \bar{Z}_{\text{Nort}} = \bar{Z}_{\text{Th}} = 20 \,\underline{/30^\circ} \,\Omega$$

24.448 Repeat Prob. 24.447, if $\bar{Z}_{\text{Th}} = 5 \,\underline{/20^\circ} \,\Omega$ and $\bar{E}_{\text{Th}} = 100 \,\underline{/60^\circ}$ V.

▮
$$\bar{E}_{\text{Th}} = 100 \,\underline{/60^\circ} \text{ V} \qquad \bar{Z}_{\text{Th}} = 5 \,\underline{/20^\circ} \,\Omega$$

$$\bar{I}_{\text{Nort}} = \frac{\bar{E}_{\text{Th}}}{\bar{Z}_{\text{Th}}} = \frac{100 \,\underline{/60^\circ}}{5 \,\underline{/20^\circ}} = 20 \,\underline{/40^\circ} \text{ A} \qquad \bar{Z}_{\text{Nort}} = \bar{Z}_{\text{Th}} = 5 \,\underline{/20^\circ} \,\Omega$$

24.449 Repeat Prob. 24.433 for the circuit of Fig. 24-156.

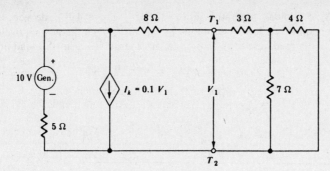

Fig. 24-156

▮ The open-circuit voltage is given by

$$10 = V_0 + 5(0.1)V_0 \quad \text{or} \quad V_0 = 6.67 \text{ V}$$

The short-circuit current is

$$I_s = \frac{10}{5 + 8} = 0.77 \text{ A}$$

Thus,

$$Z_{\text{Th}} = 6.67/0.77 = 8.66 \, \Omega \qquad V_{\text{Th}} = V_0 = 6.67 \text{ V}$$

24.450 Repeat Prob. 24.433 for the circuit of Fig. 24-157.

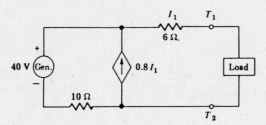

Fig. 24-157

▮ Proceeding as in Prob. 24.449, since $I_1 = 0$ under open circuit, $E_{\text{Th}} = 40$ V. The short-circuit current is given by $I_s = 5$ A. Thus,

$$Z_{\text{Th}} = 40/5 = 8 \, \Omega$$

24.451 Repeat Prob. 24.433 for the circuit of Fig. 24-158.

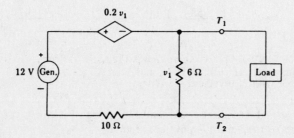

Fig. 24-158

▮ Open-circuit:
Writing the loop equation,

$$12 - 0.2 V_1 = 6i_1 + 10i_1$$

However, from Ohm's law,

$$i_1 = V_1/6$$

Thus,

$$12 - 0.2V_1 = (6 + 10)(V_1/6) \qquad V_1 = 4.19V = V_0 = E_{\text{Th}}$$

Short-circuit:
$V_1 = 0$; hence, $0.2V_1 = 0$.

$$I_{\text{SC}} = 12/10 = 1.2 \text{ A} \qquad Z_{\text{Th}} = \frac{V_{\text{OC}}}{I_{\text{SC}}} = 4.19/1.2 = 3.49 \, \Omega$$

24.452 Repeat Prob. 25.451, if the polarity of the controlled source is reversed.

❙ Open-circuit:

$$12 + 0.2V_1 = 6i_1 + 10i_1 \qquad i_1 = V_1/6$$

$$12 + 0.2V_1 = [6 + 10](V_1/6) \qquad V_1 = 4.86\text{ V} = V_0 = E_{\text{Th}}$$

Short-circuit:
$V_1 = 0$; hence, $0.2V_1 = 0$.

$$I_{\text{SC}} = \frac{12}{10} = 1.2\text{ A} \qquad Z_{\text{Th}} = \frac{V_{\text{OC}}}{I_{\text{SC}}} = \frac{4.86}{1.2} = 4.05\ \Omega$$

24.453 Repeat Prob. 24.433 for the circuit of Fig. 24-159.

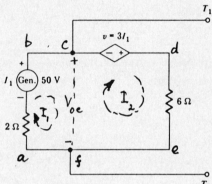

T_2 **Fig. 24-159**

❙ Writing the loop equation for loop *abdea*,

$$50 + 3I_1 = 6I_1 + 2I_1 \qquad I_1 = 10\text{ A}$$

Writing the loop equation for loop *abcfa*,

$$50 = V_{\text{OC}} + 2I_1 = V_{\text{OC}} + 2(10) \qquad V_{\text{OC}} = V_{\text{Th}} = 30\text{ V}$$

With the short circuit, shown by dashed lines in Fig. 24-159, the currents I_1 and I_2 are

$$I_1 = \frac{50}{2} = 25\text{ A} \qquad I_2 = \frac{3I_1}{6} = \frac{3(25)}{6} = 12.5\text{ A}$$

$$I_{\text{SC}} = I_1 - I_2 = 25 - 12.5 = 12.5\text{ A}$$

$$Z_{\text{Th}} = \frac{V_{\text{OC}}}{I_{\text{SC}}} = \frac{30}{12.5} = 2.4\ \Omega$$

24.454 Repeat Prob. 24.453 if the polarity of the controlled source is reversed.

❙ Proceeding as in Prob. 24.453, with I_2 reversed, we obtain

$$50 - 3I_1 = 6I_1 + 2I_1 \qquad I_1 = 4.55\text{ A}$$

$$50 = V_{\text{OC}} + 2(4.55) \qquad V_{\text{OC}} = 40.90\text{ V} = E_{\text{Th}}$$

$$I_1 = \frac{50}{2} = 25\text{ A} \qquad I_2 = \frac{3I_1}{6} = \frac{3(25)}{6} = 12.5\text{ A} \qquad I_{\text{SC}} = I_1 + I_2 = 25 + 12.5 = 37.5\text{ A}$$

Thus, $$Z_{\text{Th}} = 40.9/37.5 = 1.09\ \Omega$$

24.455 Given: $\bar{E}_A = 100\ \underline{/0°}\text{ V}$, $\bar{E}_B = 25\ \underline{/30°}\text{ V}$. Find the current I by superposition in the circuit of Fig. 24-160.

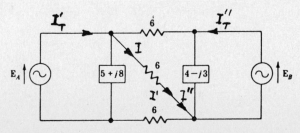

Fig. 24-160

▌ With $\bar{E}_B$ shorted: $\bar{I}' = 100\ \underline{/0°}/\ 2\,(6+3)\ = (11.11\ \underline{/0°})/2$ A

With $\bar{E}_A$ shorted: $\bar{I}'' = 25\ \underline{/30°}/\ 2\,(6+3) = (2.78\ \underline{/30°})/2$ A

or $\bar{I} = \bar{I}' + \bar{I}'' = 5.56 + 1.2 + j0.7 = 6.8\ \underline{/5.87°}$ A

24.456 What are the ammeter readings in the circuit of Fig. 24-161, where $\bar{E}_A = 100\ \underline{/0°}$ V and $\bar{E}_B = 25\ \underline{/0°}$ V.

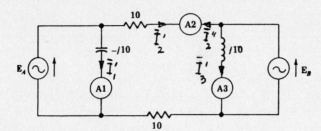

Fig. 24-161

▌ With one source at a time, we have

$$\bar{I}_1' = \frac{100\ \underline{/0°}}{-j10} = 10\ \underline{/90°} \qquad \bar{I}_2' = \frac{100\ \underline{/0°}}{20} = 5\ \underline{/0°} \qquad \bar{I}_2'' = \frac{25\ \underline{/0°}}{20} = 1.25\ \underline{/0°} \qquad \bar{I}_3'' = \frac{25\ \underline{/0°}}{j10} = 2.5\ \underline{/-90°}$$

Ammeter 1 reads the magnitude of $\bar{I}_1' = 10$ A; ammeter 3 reads the magnitude of $\bar{I}_3'' = 2.5$ A; ammeter 2 reads the magnitude of $\bar{I}_2' - \bar{I}_2''$.

$$\bar{I}_2' - \bar{I}_2'' = 5\ \underline{/0°} - 1.25\ \underline{/0°} = 3.75\ \text{A}$$

24.457 How much reactive power is supplied by the two sources of the circuit of Fig. 24-161?

▌ $$Q_T = (I_1)^2(-10) + (I_3)^2(10) = (10)^2(-10) + (2.5)^2(10) = 937.5\ \text{var (leading)}$$

24.458 Replace the 100-V and 25-V sinusoidal generators in Prob. 24.456 with 100-V and 25-V batteries, respectively, and determine the ammeter readings. Assume the internal resistance of the 25-V battery is 0.20 Ω and that of the 100-V battery is 0.80 Ω.

▌ Since the capacitor acts as an open circuit, A1 reads zero. The circuits, with one source at a time, become as shown in Fig. 24-162, from which (with ammeters acting as short circuits)

$$I_T' = \frac{100}{10 + 10 + 0.8} = 4.81\ \text{A} \qquad I_T'' = \frac{25}{0.2} = 125\ \text{A}$$

Ammeter 2 reads $I_T' = 4.81$ A; ammeter 3 reads $I_T' + I_T'' = 4.81 + 125 = 129.81$ A.

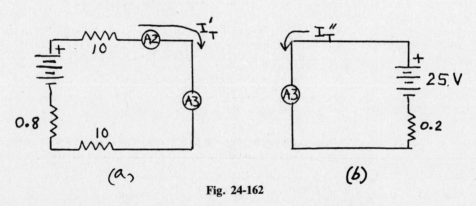

Fig. 24-162

24.459 Determine the ammeter reading in the circuit of Fig. 24-163 by superposition.

▌ With one source at a time, we have:

$$\bar{I}' = \frac{45\ \underline{/60°}}{-j6 + j5} = 45\ \underline{/150°}\ \text{A} \qquad I'' = \frac{100\ \underline{/80°}}{-j6 + j5} = 100\ \underline{/170°}\ \text{A}$$

$$\bar{I}' - \bar{I}'' = 45\ \underline{/150°} - 100\ \underline{/170°} = (59.51 + j5.14) = 59.73\ \underline{/4.93°}\ \text{A}$$

The ammeter reads 59.73 A.

24.460 Solve for the currents in each element of the circuit of Fig. 24-163.

▮ $\bar{I}_1 = 45\underline{/60°}/10 = 4.5\underline{/60°}$ A $\qquad \bar{I}_2 = 100\underline{/80°}/8 = 12.5\underline{/80°}$ A $\qquad \bar{I}_3 = \dfrac{45\underline{/60°} - 100\underline{/80°}}{6\underline{/-90°} - 5\underline{/90°}} = 59.73\underline{/4.93°}$ A

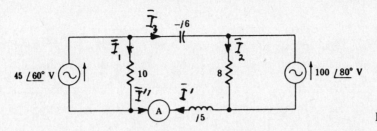

Fig. 24-163

24.461 Determine i_1, i_2, i_3 in the circuit of Fig. 24-164 (under steady state, in the time domain).

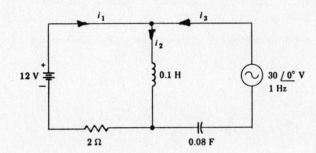

Fig. 24-164

▮ With one source at a time, for the dc source we have

$$i'_i = i'_2 = 12/2 = 6 \text{ A} \qquad i'_3 = 0$$

Similarly, for the ac source we obtain

$$X_L = 2\pi fL = 2\pi(1)(0.1) = 0.63 \ \Omega \qquad X_C = \frac{1}{2\pi fC} = \frac{1}{2\pi(1)(0.08)} = 1.99 \ \Omega$$

$$\bar{Z}_P = \frac{(2)(j0.63)}{2 + j0.63} = 0.60\underline{/72.51°} \qquad \bar{I}''_3 = \frac{30\underline{/0°}}{0.60\underline{/72.51°} - j1.99} = 20.96\underline{/82.78°}$$

$$\bar{I}''_2 = 20.96\underline{/82.78°}\left[\frac{2\underline{/0°}}{2.097\underline{/17.48°}}\right] = 19.99\underline{/65.29°} \text{ A}$$

$$\bar{I}''_1 = 20.96\underline{/82.78°}\left[\frac{j\,0.63}{2.097\underline{/17.48°}}\right] = 6.30\underline{/-114.71°} \text{ A}$$

Hence,
$$i_1 = i'_1 - i''_1 = 6 - 6.30\sqrt{2}\sin[2\pi(1)t - 114.71°]$$
$$i_2 = i'_2 + i''_2 = 6 + 19.99\sqrt{2}\sin[2\pi(1)t + 65.29°]$$
$$i_3 = i''_3 = 20.96\sqrt{2}\sin(6.28t + 82.78°)$$

24.462 What is the ammeter reading in the circuit of Fig. 24-165?

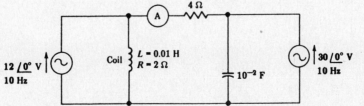

Fig. 24-165

▮ By superposition, with one source at a time, we have

$$\bar{I}' = 12\underline{/0°}/4 = 3\underline{/0°} \text{ A} \qquad I'' = 30\underline{/0°}/4 = 7.5\underline{/0°} \text{ A} \qquad I' - I'' = 3\underline{/0°} - 7.5\underline{/0°} = 4.5\underline{/180°}$$

The ammeter reads 4.5 A.

24.463 What is the current through the coil of the circuit of Fig. 24-165?

▮ The voltage drop across the coil is $12 \underline{/0°}$ V.

$$X_L = 2\pi f L = 2\pi(10)(0.01) = 0.628 \ \Omega$$

$$\bar{Z}_{coil} = R + jX_L = (2 + j0.628) = 2.096 \underline{/17.44°} \ \Omega \qquad \bar{I}_{coil} = \frac{\bar{V}_{coil}}{\bar{Z}_{coil}} = \frac{12 \underline{/0°}}{2.096 \underline{/17.44°}} = 5.72 \underline{/-17.44°} \ A$$

24.464 Determine the active and reactive powers drawn by the coil of the circuit of Fig. 24-165.

▮ $$\bar{S}_{coil} = \bar{V}\bar{I}^* = (12 \underline{/0°})(5.72 \underline{/+17.44°}) = 68.69 \underline{/17.44°} \ VA = [65.53 + j20.59]$$
$$P = 65.53 \ W \qquad Q = 20.59 \ var \ (lag) \qquad S = 68.69 \ V \cdot A$$

24.465 Repeat Prob. 24.462 if the ac sources are replaced by 12-V and 30-V batteries.

▮ By superposition, with one source acting at a time (as in Prob. 24.462)

$$I' = 12/4 = 3 \ A \qquad I'' = 30/4 = 7.5 \ A \qquad I' - I'' = 3 - 7.5 = -4.5 \ A \qquad \text{Ammeter reads 4.5 A}$$

24.466 How much current is drawn by the coil of the circuit of Prob. 24.465?

▮ $$V_{coil} = 12 \ V \qquad R_{coil} = 2 \ \Omega \qquad I_{coil} = 12/2 = 6 \ A$$

24.467 Evaluate the complex power for the coil of the circuit of Prob. 24.465.

▮ $$\bar{S} = \bar{V}\bar{I}^* = (12)(6) + j0 = 72 + j0 \ VA$$

24.468 Determine the input impedance for the circuit of Fig. 24-166.

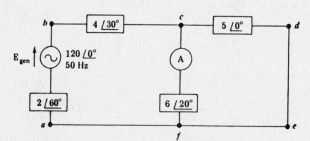

Fig. 24-166

▮ $$Z_P = \frac{(5 \underline{/0°})(6 \underline{/20°})}{5 \underline{/0°} + 6 \underline{/20°}} = 2.77 \underline{/9.08°} \ \Omega \qquad \bar{Z}_{in} = 2 \underline{/60°} + 4 \underline{/30°} + 2.77 \underline{/9.08°} = 8.32 \underline{/30.08°}$$

24.469 What is the ammeter reading in the circuit of Prob. 24.468?

▮ $$\bar{I}_T = \frac{\bar{E}}{\bar{Z}_{in}} = \frac{120 \underline{/0°}}{8.32 \underline{/30.08°}} = 14.42 \underline{/-30.08°} \ A$$

$$\bar{V}_P = \bar{Z}_P \bar{I}_T = (2.77 \underline{/9.08°})(14.42 \underline{/-30.08°}) \ A = 39.943 \underline{/-21.0°} \ V$$

$$\bar{I}_{cf} = \frac{\bar{V}_P}{\bar{Z}_{cf}} = \frac{39.943 \underline{/-21.0°}}{6 \underline{/20°}} = 6.66 \underline{/-41°} \ A$$

The ammeter reads 6.67 A.

24.470 Determine the transfer impedance between branch *abc* and branch *cf* of the circuit of Fig. 24-166.

▮ $$\bar{Z}_{tr} = \frac{\bar{V}_{in(abc)}}{\bar{I}_{out(cf)}} = \frac{120 \underline{/0°}}{6.67 \underline{/-41°}} = 17.9 \underline{/41°} \ \Omega$$

24.471 In the circuit of Fig. 24-166 in branch *abc* if the generator is replaced with an ammeter and the ammeter in branch *cf* is replaced with an 80 $\underline{/20°}$-V 50-Hz generator, as shown in Fig. 24-167, determine the ammeter reading.

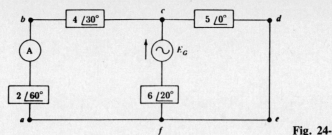

Fig. 24-167

I $$\bar{Z}_{tr} = \frac{\bar{V}_{in(cf)}}{\bar{I}_{out(abc)}} \qquad 17.9\,\underline{/41°} = \frac{80\,\underline{/20°}}{\bar{I}_{out(abc)}} \qquad \bar{I}_{out(abc)} = 4.47\,\underline{/-21°}\ \text{A}$$

The ammeter reads 4.47 A.

24.472 Correct a balanced delta section of $8\,\underline{/25°}\ \Omega$ per branch to an equivalent wye.

I $$\bar{Z}_\Delta = 3\bar{Z}_Y \qquad 8\,\underline{/25°} = 3\bar{Z}_Y \qquad \bar{Z}_Y = 2.67\,\underline{/25°}\ \Omega$$

24.473 Convert a balanced wye section of $12\,\underline{/40°}\ \Omega$ per branch to an equivalent delta.

I $$\bar{Z}_\Delta = 3Z_Y \qquad \bar{Z}_\Delta = 3[12\,\underline{/40°}] \qquad \bar{Z}_\Delta = 36\,\underline{/40°}\ \Omega$$

24.474 Determine the battery current in the circuit of Fig. 24-168a.

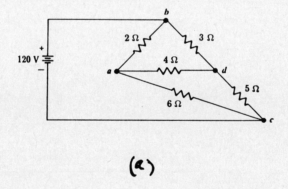

(a)

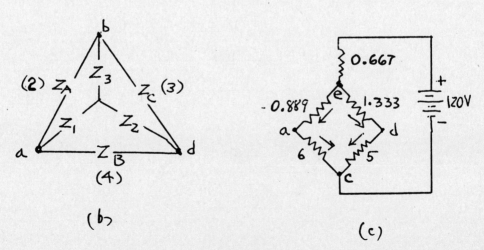

(b)

(c)

Fig. 24-168

▮ Referring to the network reductions of Fig. 24-168b and c we obtain

$$Z_1 = \frac{Z_A Z_B}{Z_A + Z_B + Z_C} = \frac{(2)(4)}{2 + 4 + 3} = 0.889 \ \Omega$$

$$Z_2 = \frac{Z_B Z_C}{Z_A Z_B Z_C} = \frac{(4)(3)}{9} = 1.333 \ \Omega \qquad Z_3 = \frac{Z_C Z_A}{Z_A Z_B Z_C} = \frac{(3)(2)}{9} = 0.667 \ \Omega$$

The impedance of the paralleled section is

$$Z_P = \frac{(6 + 0.889)(5 + 1.333)}{(6 + 0.889) + (5 + 1.333)} = 3.3 \ \Omega \qquad Z_{\text{in}} = 0.667 + 3.30 = 3.967 \ \Omega \qquad I_T = \frac{E_{\text{bat}}}{Z_{\text{in}}} = \frac{120}{3.967} = 30.25 \ \text{A}$$

24.475 Calculate the currents in the 6-Ω and 5-Ω resistors of the circuit of Fig. 24-168a.

▮ From Fig. 24-168c:

$$V_P = I_T Z_P = 30.25(3.3) = 99.83 \ \text{V}$$

$$I_{6 \ \Omega} = I_{eac} = \frac{V_P}{Z_{eac}} = \frac{99.83}{6.889} = 14.49 \ \text{A}$$

$$I_{5 \ \Omega} = I_{edc} = \frac{V_P}{Z_{edc}} = \frac{99.83}{6.333} = 15.763 \ \text{A}$$

24.476 What is the voltage across the 4-Ω resistor of the circuit of Fig. 24-168a?

▮ $$V_{4 \ \Omega} = V_{da} = 0 - [-6(14.49) + 5(15.763)] = 8.15 \ \text{V}$$

24.477 How much power is dissipated in the 4-Ω resistor of the circuit of Fig. 24-168a?

▮ $$P_{4 \ \Omega} = \frac{(V_{4\Omega})^2}{4} = \frac{(8.15)^2}{4} = 16.61 \ \text{W}$$

24.478 How much total power is absorbed by the 2-Ω, 3-Ω, 5-Ω, and 6-Ω resistors of the circuit of Fig. 24-168a?

▮ $$P_T = P_{\text{batt}} - P_{4 \ \Omega} = (120)(30.25) - 16.61 = 3613.39 \ \text{W}$$

from Probs. 24.474 and 24.477.

24.479 A balanced wye section of $6.0 \ \underline{/20°} \ \Omega$ per branch is paralleled with a balanced delta section of $3.0 \ \underline{/40°} \ \Omega$ per branch. Sketch the circuit and determine a single equivalent delta section that can replace the two paralleled sections.

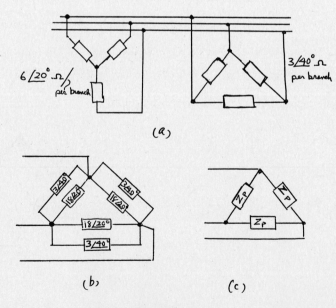

(a)

(b)   (c)

Fig. 24-169

I See Fig. 24-169a. The network reduction is shown in Fig. 24-169b and c. Converting the wye to an equivalent Δ,

$$Z_{\Delta br} = 3Z_{Ybr} = 3(6\ \underline{/20°}) = 18\ \underline{/20°}\ \Omega$$

$$\bar{Z}_P = \frac{(18\ \underline{/20°})(3\ \underline{/40°})}{18\ \underline{/20°} + 3\ \underline{/40°}} = 2.59\ \underline{/37.18°}$$

24.480 Express the following differential equation in terms of Laplace transforms and general initial conditions:

$$2\frac{d^2r}{dt^2} + 5\frac{dr}{dt} + 3r = 10 \sin (t + 0.6)$$

I Taking the Laplace transform of both sides yields

$$2[s^2R(s) - sr(0_+) - r'(0_+)] + 5[sR(s) - r(0_+)] + 3R(s) = \frac{10}{s^2+1}(s \sin 0.6 + \cos 0.6) = 5.646\left(\frac{s+1.462}{s^2+1}\right)$$

or

$$R(s)[2s^2 + 5s + 3] = 5.646\left(\frac{s+1.462}{s^2+1}\right) + r(0_+)(2s+5) + 2r'(0_+)$$

24.481 A 10-V battery is suddenly connected across a series RLC circuit having $R = 2\,\Omega$, $L = 2\,\text{mH}$, and $C = 10^{-3}\,\text{F}$. The initial voltage on C is 20 V, and the initial current through L is -10 A. Write the differential equation for the charge on the capacitor.

I The required equation is

$$10u(t) = 2 \times 10^{-3}\ddot{q}(t) + 2\dot{q}(t) + 10^3 q(t) + 20u(t)$$

24.482 At $t = 0$, a unit pulse voltage of unit width is applied to a series RL circuit, with $R = 1\,\Omega$ and $L = 1\,\text{H}$ and zero initial conditions. Obtain an expression for $I(s)$, the current in the transform domain.

I Since

$$v(t) = u(t) - u(t-1) \qquad V(s) = (1 - e^{-s})/s$$

and

$$sI(s) - i(0_+) + I(s) = \frac{1 - e^{-s}}{s} \qquad \text{or} \qquad I(s) = \frac{1}{(s+1)s} - \frac{e^{-s}}{(s+1)s} \tag{1}$$

24.483 What is the current in the time domain in the circuit of Prob. 24.482?

I From (1) of Prob. 24.482 we have

$$I(s) = \frac{1}{s} - \frac{1}{s+1} - \frac{e^{-s}}{s} + \frac{e^{-s}}{s+1}$$

or

$$i(t) = (1 - e^{-t})u(t) - [1 - e^{-(t-1)}]u(t-1)$$

24.484 If the circuit of Prob. 24.482 is excited by a unit impulse at $t = 0$, determine $i(t)$.

I Since $\mathcal{L}[\delta(t)] = 1$, in the transform domain we have

$$sI(s) + I(s) = 1 \qquad \text{or} \qquad I(s) = 1/(s+1) \qquad \text{and} \qquad i(t) = e^{-t}$$

24.485 Synthesize the pulse of Fig. 24-170a by step functions.

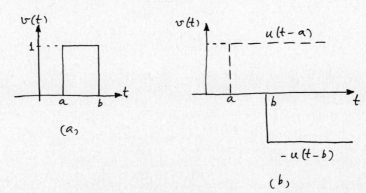

Fig. 24-170

▮ From Fig. 24-170*b* we obtain

$$v(t) = u(t - a) - u(t - b)$$

24.486 Obtain an expression for the shifted sine wave of Fig. 24-171 in terms of unit-step function, and obtain its Laplace transform.

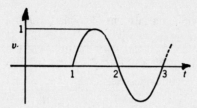

Fig. 24-171

▮ The required expression is

$$v(t) = [\sin \pi(t - 1)]u(t - 1)$$

$$V(s) = \pi e^{-s}/(s^2 + \pi^2) \quad \text{by shifting theorem}$$

24.487 Express the waveform of Fig. 24-172 in terms of unit-step functions.

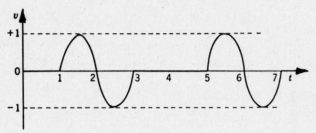

Fig. 24-172

▮ The waveform may be expressed as the "sum" of four sinusoids occurring at $t = 1, 3, 5,$ and 7.

Hence, $v(t) = u(t - 1)\sin \pi(t - 1) - u(t - 3)\sin \pi(t - 3) + u(t - 5)\sin \pi(t - 5) - u(t - 7)\sin \pi(t - 7)$

24.488 Synthesize the waveform of Fig. 24-173 by sine waves and step functions.

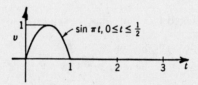

Fig. 24-173

▮ We may obtain the given waveform from the "sum" of a sine wave starting at $t = 0$, and that is shown in Fig. 24-171. Hence,

$$v(t) = (\sin \pi t)u(t) + [\sin \pi(t - 1)]u(t - 1) \tag{1}$$

24.489 Determine the Laplace transform of the wave shown in Fig. 24-173.

▮ From (1) of Prob. 24.485 we get

$$V(s) = \frac{\pi}{s^2 + \pi^2} + \frac{\pi e^{-s}}{s^2 + \pi^2} = \frac{\pi(1 - e^{-s})}{s^2 + \pi^2}$$

24.490 Express the waveform of Fig. 24-174 in terms of unit-step functions.

▮ The required expression is

$$v(t) = u(t) - 2u(t - a) + 2u(t - 2a) - 2u(t - 3a) + \cdots \tag{1}$$

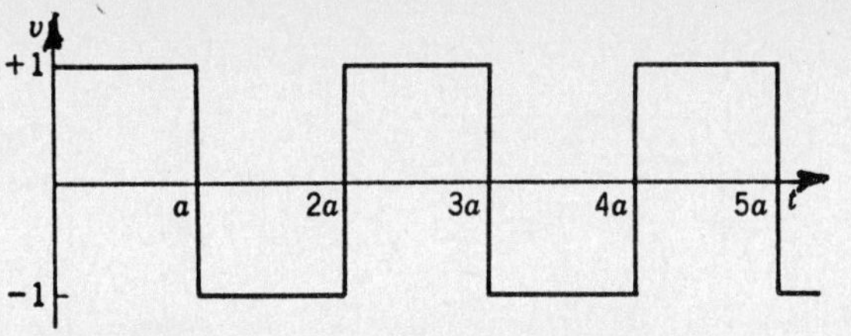

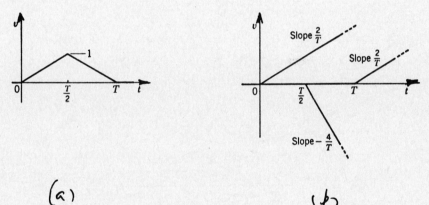

Fig. 24-174

24.491 Obtain the Laplace transform of the function shown in Fig. 24-174.

▌ Taking the Laplace transform of (1) of Prob. 24.490 term by term, we obtain

$$V(s) = \frac{1}{s} - 2\frac{e^{-as}}{s} + 2\frac{e^{-2as}}{s} - 2\frac{e^{-3as}}{s} + \cdots$$

By factoring out common terms, the equation becomes

$$V(s) = \frac{1}{s}[1 - 2e^{-as}(1 - e^{-as} + e^{-2as} - e^{-3as} + \cdots)]$$

The infinite series appearing in this equation may be identified by the following expansion from the binomial theorem,

$$\frac{1}{1 + e^{-as}} = 1 - e^{-as} + e^{-2as} - e^{-3as} + \cdots$$

such that $V(s)$ becomes

$$V(s) = \frac{1}{s}\left(1 - \frac{2e^{-as}}{1 + e^{-as}}\right) = \frac{1}{s}\left(\frac{1 - e^{-as}}{1 + e^{-as}}\right)$$

or, finally,
$$V(s) = \frac{1}{s}\tanh\frac{as}{2}$$

24.492 Express the waveform of Fig. 24-175a in terms of ramp functions.

Fig. 24-175

▌ The desired ramp functions are shown in Fig. 24-175b, from which

$$v(t) = \frac{2}{T}r(t) - \frac{4}{T}r\left(t - \frac{T}{2}\right) + \frac{2}{T}r(t - T) \tag{1}$$

24.493 Obtain the Laplace transform of the waveform of Fig. 24-175a.

▌ Taking the Laplace transform of (1) term by term we obtain

$$V(s) = \frac{2}{Ts^2} - \frac{4}{Ts^2}e^{-Ts/2} + \frac{2}{Ts^2}e^{-Ts} = \frac{2}{T}\frac{(1 - e^{-Ts/2})^2}{s^2}$$

24.494 Express the two pulses of Fig. 24-176 as a function of unit-step voltages.

▌
$$v(t) = u(t - 2) - u(t - 3) + u(t - 7) - u(t - 8)$$

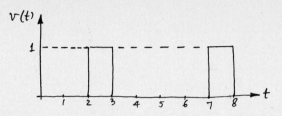

Fig. 24-176

24.495 Express the waveform of Fig. 24-177 in terms of step functions.

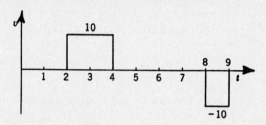

Fig. 24-177

▮ $$v(t) = 10u(t-2) - 10u(t-4) - 10u(t-8) + 10u(t-9)$$

24.496 Using step, ramp, and sine functions obtain an expression for the waveform of Fig. 24-178.

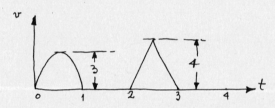

Fig. 24-178

$$v(t) = 3[\sin \pi t u(t) + \sin \pi(t-1)u(t-1)] + 8(t-2)u(t-2) - 16(t-2.5)u(t-2.5) + 8(t-3)u(t-3)$$

24.497 Write an expression for the waveform of Fig. 24-179 in terms of step functions.

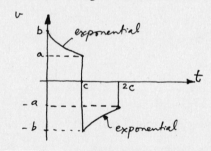

Fig. 24-179

▮ Let $$a = be^{-mc} \qquad m = (1/c)\ln b/a$$

then $$v = be^{-(t/c)\, \mathrm{ub}\, b/a}u(t) - (a+b)e^{-[(t-c)/c]\ln b/a}u(t-c) + ae^{-[(t-2c)/c]\ln b/a}u(t-2c)$$

24.498 A 10-V pulse of 5-μs duration is applied to a series RL circuit with $R = 2\,\Omega$ and $L = 2\,\mu$H. Determine $i(t)$.

▮ Proceeding as in Prob. 24.482, we obtain

$$I(s) = \frac{10(1 - e^{-5 \times 10^{-6}s})}{s(2 \times 10^{-6}s + 2)} = \frac{10}{2}(1 - e^{-5 \times 10^{-6}s})\left(\frac{1}{s} - \frac{1}{s + 10^6}\right)$$

or $$i(t) = 5\left[1 - e^{-10^6 t}\right]u(t) - 5\left[1 - e^{-10^6(t - 5 \times 10^{-6})}\right]u(t - 5 \times 10^{-6})$$

24.499 Sketch the input voltage and the output current for the circuit of Prob. 24.498.

▮ See Fig. 24-180.

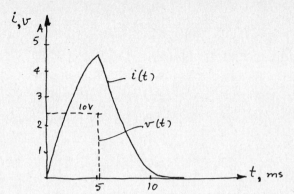

Fig. 24-180

24.500 If the voltage pulse of Prob. 24.498 is applied to a series RC circuit with $R = 100\,\Omega$ and $C = 0.05\,\mu F$, find $i(t)$.

❙ In this case:

$$I(s) = \frac{10(1 - e^{-5 \times 10^{-6}s})}{s[100 + (10^6/0.05s)]} = \frac{10(1 - e^{-5 \times 10^{-6}s})}{100[s + (10^6/5)]}$$

or

$$i(t) = 0.1e^{-t/5 \times 10^{-6}}u\,(t) - 0.1e^{-(t - 5 \times 10^{-6})/5 \times 10^{-6}}u(t - 5 \times 10^{-6})$$

24.501 Sketch $i(t)$ obtained in Prob. 24.500.

❙ See Fig. 24-181.

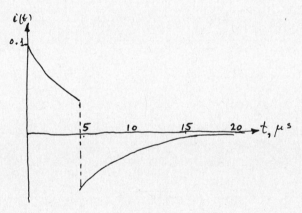

Fig. 24-181

24.502 A 10-V 5-μs pulse is applied across a series RC circuit. Determine the voltage across the capacitor in the s domain.

$$V_C(s) = \frac{10(1 - e^{-5 \times 10^{-6}s})}{sR(sC + (1/R))} = \frac{10}{RCs} \frac{(1 - e^{-5 \times 10^{-6}s})}{[s + (1/RC)]} = 10(1 - e^{-5 \times 10^{-6}s})\left[\frac{1}{s} - \frac{1}{s + (1/RC)}\right] \qquad (1)$$

24.503 Find $v_C(t)$ in the circuit of Prob. 24.502 if $R = 100\,\Omega$ and $C = 0.04\,\mu F$.

❙ Substituting $1/RC = 10^6/4$ in (1) of Prob. 24.502 and taking the inverse transform yields

$$v_C(t) = 10(1 - e^{-2 \times 10^5 t}) - 10[1 - e^{-2 \times 10^5(t - 5 \times 10^{-6})}]u(t - 5 \times 10^{-6})$$

24.504 A voltage of the waveform of Fig. 24-182 is applied to a series RL circuit. Find $I(s)$.

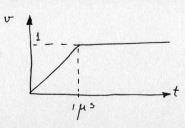

Fig. 24-182

$$I(s) = \frac{10^6[1 - e^{-10^{-6}s}]}{s^2[sL + R]} = \frac{10^6[1 - e^{-10^{-6}s}]}{Ls^2[s + (R/L)]} \qquad (1)$$

24.505 In the circuit of Prob. 24.504, let $R = 2\,\Omega$ and $L = 2\,\text{mH}$. Find $i(t)$.

▌ Equation (1) of Prob. 24.504 may be written as

$$I(s) = 10^6[1 - e^{-10^{-6}s}]\left[\frac{1}{Rs^2} - \frac{L}{R^2s} + \frac{L}{R^2(s + R/L)}\right] = 10^6(1 - e^{-10^{-6}s})\left[\frac{1}{2s^2} - \frac{10^{-3}}{2s} + \frac{10^{-3}}{2(s + 10^3)}\right]$$

or $\quad i(t) = [5 \times 10^5 t \; - 500 + 500e^{-10^3 t}]u(t) - [5 \times 10^5(t - 10^{-6}) \; - 500 + 500e^{-10^3\,(t - 10^{-6})}]u(t - 10^{-6})$

24.506 Sketch the current of Prob. 24.505.

▌ See Fig. 24-183.

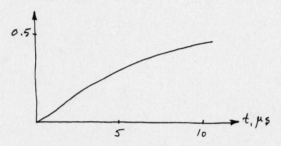

Fig. 24-183

24.507 If the waveform of Fig. 24-182 is applied to a series RC circuit, find $I(s)$.

▌ $$I(s) = \frac{10^6[1 - e^{-10^{-6}s}]}{s^2[R + (1/sC)]} = \frac{10^6[1 - e^{-10^{-6}s}]}{Rs[s + (1/RC)]} = 10^6(1 - e^{-10^{-6}s})\left[\frac{C}{s} - \frac{C}{s + (1/RC)}\right]$$

24.508 What is the voltage $V_C(s)$ in the circuit of Prob. 24.507?

▌ $$V(s) = \frac{10^6[1 - e^{-10^{-6}s}]}{s^2R[sC + (1/R)]} = \frac{10^6[1 - e^{-10^{-6}s}]}{RCs^2[s + (1/CR)]} = 10^6[1 - e^{-10^{-6}s}]\left[\frac{1}{s^2} - \frac{RC}{s} + \frac{RC}{s + (1/CR)}\right]$$

24.509 Express the waveform of Fig. 24-184 in terms of step functions.

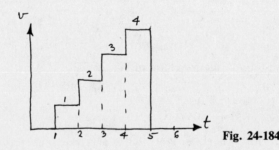

Fig. 24-184

▌ $$v(t) = u(t - 1) + u(t - 2) + u(t - 3) + u(t - 4) - 4u(t - 5)$$

24.510 Find the Laplace transform of the waveform of Fig. 24-176.

▌ Using the result of Prob. 24-494 we obtain

$$V(s) = \frac{e^{-2s} - e^{-3s} + e^{-7s} - e^{-8s}}{s}$$

24.511 Express the ramp of Fig. 24-185 in terms of a step function.

▌ $$f(t) = 2(t + 3)u(t)$$

24.512 Find the Laplace transform of the ramp of Fig. 24-185.

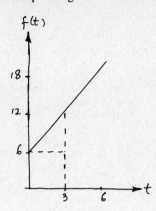

Fig. 24-185

▮ $$F(s) = \frac{2}{s^2} + \frac{6}{s}$$

24.513 Find the Laplace transform of the waveform of Fig. 24-178.

▮ From the result of Prob. 24.496 we obtain

$$V(s) = \frac{3\pi}{s^2 + \pi^2}(1 + e^{-s}) + \frac{8}{s^2}(e^{-2s} - 2e^{-2.5s} + e^{-3s})$$

24.514 Determine the Laplace transform of the waveform shown in Fig. 24-184.

▮ From the result of Prob. 24.509 we obtain

$$V(s) = (e^{-s} + e^{-2s} + e^{-3s} + e^{-4s} - 4e^{-5s})/s$$

24.515 Find the Laplace transform of the waveform of Fig. 24-186.

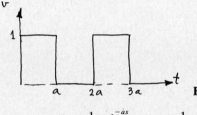

Fig. 24-186

▮ $$V(s) = \frac{1 - e^{-as}}{s(1 - e^{-2as})} = \frac{1}{s(1 + e^{-as})}$$

24.516 Find the Laplace transform of the waveform of Fig. 24-187.

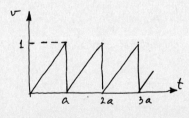

Fig. 24-187

▮ $$V(s) = \left[\frac{1 - e^{-as}}{as^2} - \frac{e^{-as}}{s}\right]\left[\frac{1}{1 - e^{-as}}\right]$$

24.517 A "staircase" waveform extends to infinity. At $t = nt_0$, it jumps to the value $n + 1$, being a superposition of step functions. Find its Laplace transform.

▮ $$V(s) = \frac{1 + e^{-t_0 s} + e^{-2t_0 s} + e^{-3t_0 s}}{s} = \frac{1}{s(1 - e^{-t_0 s})}$$

24.518 Find the Laplace transform of the waveform of Fig. 24-188.

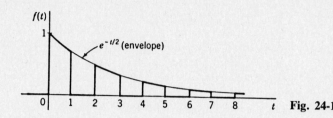

Fig. 24-188

$$F(s) = \frac{[1 - e^{-(0.5+s)} + e^{-(1+2s)} - e^{-(1.5+3s)} + \cdots}{s + \frac{1}{2}}$$

Let

$$F_1(s) = 1 - e^{-(0.5+s)} + e^{-(1+2s)} - \cdots$$

$$F_1(s) = \frac{1}{1 + e^{-(0.5+s)}}$$

Thus,

$$F(s) = \frac{1}{(s + \frac{1}{2})(1 + e^{-(0.5+s)})}$$

24.519 Find $\mathscr{L}^{-1}[F_1(s)F_2(s)]$ by convolution if $F_1(s) = 1/(s^2 + 1)$ and $F_2(s) = 1/(s^2 + 1)$.

$$f(t) = \int_0^t \sin \tau \sin (t - \tau) \, d\tau = \int_0^t \frac{e^{j\tau} - e^{-j\tau}}{2j} \times \frac{e^{j(t-\tau)} - e^{-j(t-\tau)}}{2j} \, d\tau$$

$$= -\frac{1}{4} \int_0^t e^{jt} - e^{-jt+j2\tau} - e^{jt-j2\tau} + e^{-jt} \, d\tau = -\frac{1}{4} \left[(e^{jt} + e^{-jt})\tau - \frac{e^{-jt+j2\tau}}{j2} + \frac{e^{jt-j2\tau}}{j2} \right]_0^t$$

$$= -\frac{t}{2} \cos t + \frac{1}{4} \sin t + \frac{1}{4} \sin t = -\frac{t}{2} \cos t + \frac{1}{2} \sin t$$

24.520 Repeat Prob. 24.519 if $F_1(s) = s/(s + 1)$ and $F_2(s) = 1/(s^2 + 1)$.

$$f(t) = \int_0^t [\delta(t - \tau) - e^{-(t-\tau)}] \sin \tau \, d\tau = \sin t - e^{-t} \int_0^t \frac{e^{(1+j)\tau} - e^{(1-j)\tau}}{2j} \, d\tau$$

$$= \sin t - \frac{e^{-t}}{2j} \left[\frac{e^{(1+j)\tau}}{1+j} - \frac{e^{(1-j)\tau}}{1+j} \right]_0^t = \sin t - \frac{e^{-t}}{j4} \left[(1-j)e^{(1+j)\tau} - (1+j)e^{(1-j)\tau} \right]_0^t$$

$$= \sin t - \frac{1}{j4} [(1-j)e^{jt} - (1+j)e^{-jt} + e^{-t}(+j2)] = \sin t - \frac{1}{2} \sin t + \frac{1}{2} \cos t - \frac{1}{2} e^{-t} = \tfrac{1}{2}[\sin t + \cos t - e^{-t}]$$

24.521 Find the ratio $Y_{11}(s) = I(s)/V_1(s)$ for the circuit of Fig. 24-189.

$$RI(s) + \frac{1}{Cs} I(s) = V_1(s) \qquad \frac{1}{Cs} I(s) = V_2(s)$$

$$Y_{11}(s) = \frac{I(s)}{V_1(s)} = \frac{1}{R} \frac{s}{s + 1/RC}$$

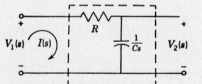

Fig. 24-189

24.522 Determine $Z(s)$ for the circuit of Fig. 24-190.

$$Z(s) = \frac{1}{Cs + 1/(R + Ls)} = \frac{1}{C} \frac{s + R/L}{s^2 + Rs/L + 1/LC}$$

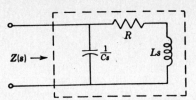

Fig. 24-190

24.523 Find the ratio $G_{12}(s) = V_2(s)/V_1(s)$ for the circuit of Fig. 24-191.

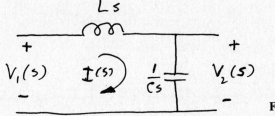

Fig. 24-191

$$G_{12}(s) = \frac{V_2(s)}{V_1(s)} = \frac{1/Cs}{Ls + 1/Cs} = \frac{1}{LCs^2 + 1} = \frac{1/LC}{s^2 + (1/LC)}$$

24.524 Find $G_{12}(s)$ for the circuit of Fig. 24-192.

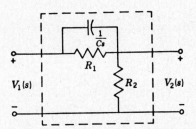

Fig. 24-192

❚ The transform impedances R_1 and $1/Cs$ can be combined into an equivalent impedance having the value

$$Z_{eq}(s) = \frac{1}{Cs + 1/R_1} = \frac{R_1}{R_1Cs + 1}$$

Then the transfer function becomes

$$G_{12}(s) = \frac{V_2(s)}{V_1(s)} = \frac{R_2}{R_2 + Z_{eq}(s)} = \frac{R_2R_1Cs + R_2}{R_2R_1Cs + R_1 + R_2}$$

which may be reduced to

$$G_{12}(s) = \frac{s + 1/R_1C}{s + (R_1 + R_2)/R_1R_2C}$$

24.525 Determine the ratio $\alpha_{12}(s) = I_2(s)/I_1(s)$ for the circuit of Fig. 24-193.

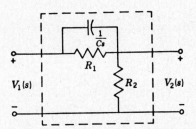

Fig. 24-193

$$I_1(s) = I_a(s) + I_2(s) = V_1(s)[Y_a(s) + Y_2(s)]$$

and since $I_2(s) = Y_2(s)V_1(s)$, we have

$$I_2(s) = \frac{Y_2(s)}{Y_a(s) + Y_2(s)} I_1(s)$$

so that
$$\alpha_{12}(s) = \frac{I_2(s)}{I_1(s)} = \frac{Y_2(s)}{Y_a(s) + Y_2(s)}$$

Since $Y_2(s) = (s/R_1)/(s + 1/R_1C_2)$, and $Y_a(s) = C_1s$, we have

$$\alpha_{12}(s) = \frac{1}{R_1C_1} \frac{1}{s + (C_1 + C_2)/R_1C_1C_2}$$

24.526 Obtain $Z_{12}(s) = V_2(s)/I_1(s)$ for the network of Fig. 24-193.

▮ Now, $V_2(s) = (1/C_2s)I_2(s)$ in the network

$$Z_{12}(s) = \frac{V_2(s)}{I_1(s)} = \frac{1}{R_1C_1C_2} \frac{1}{s[s + (C_1 + C_2)/R_1C_1C_2]}$$

24.527 Determine $\alpha_{12}(s)$ and $Z_{12}(s)$ for the network of Fig. 24-193 if $C_2 = 2C_1 = 2\,\text{F}$ and $R = 1\,\Omega$.

▮ Substituting these values yields

$$\alpha_{12}(s) = \frac{1}{s + 1.5} \quad \text{and} \quad Z_{12}(s) = \frac{0.5}{s(s + 1.5)}$$

24.528 For the network of Fig. 24-194 determine (*a*) G_{12} and (*b*) Z_{12}.

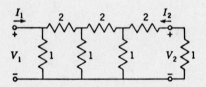

Fig. 24-194

▮
$$I_1 = 1.5V_1 - 0.5V_a \qquad 0 = -0.5V_1 + 2V_a - 0.5V_b$$
$$0 = -0.5V_a + 2V_b - 0.5V_2 \qquad 0 = -0.5V_b + 1.5V_2$$
$$V_b = 3V_2 \qquad V_a = 11V_2 \qquad V_1 = 41V_2 \qquad I_1 = 56V_2$$

(*a*) $$V_2/V_1 = G_{12} = \tfrac{1}{41}$$
(*b*) $$V_2/I_1 = z_{12} = \tfrac{1}{56}$$

24.529 Find Y_{12} and α_{12} for the circuit of Fig. 24-194.

▮ From the results of Prob. 24.528 we have

$$I_2/V_1 = Y_{12} = -\tfrac{1}{41} \qquad I_2/I_1 = \alpha_{12} = -\tfrac{1}{56}$$

24.530 Determine Z_{12} for the circuit of Fig. 24-195.

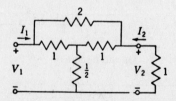

Fig. 24-195

▮
$$I_1 = 1.5V_1 - V_0 - 0.5V_2 \qquad 0 = -V_1 + 4V_0 - V_2 \qquad 0 = -0.5V_1 - V_0 + 2.5V_2$$

Hence, $$V_2/I_1 = Z_{12} = \tfrac{1}{3}$$

24.531 What is α_{12} for the circuit of Fig. 24-195?

▮ From Prob. 24.530

$$V_2 = -I_2 \qquad I_2/I_1 = \alpha_{12} = -\tfrac{1}{3}$$

24.532 Find G_{12} for the circuit of Fig. 24-195.

∎ $V_1 = 4V_0 - V_2$ $0.5V_1 = -V_0 + 2.5V_2$ $3V_1 = 9V_2$ $V_2/V_1 = G_{12} = \frac{1}{3}$

24.533 Determine Y_{12} for the circuit of Fig. 24-195.

∎ $$Y_{12} = I_2/V_1 = -\frac{1}{3}$$

24.534 Find G_{12} for the circuit of Fig. 24-196.

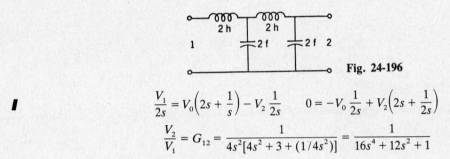

Fig. 24-196

∎ $$\frac{V_1}{2s} = V_0\left(2s + \frac{1}{s}\right) - V_2\frac{1}{2s} \qquad 0 = -V_0\frac{1}{2s} + V_2\left(2s + \frac{1}{2s}\right)$$

$$\frac{V_2}{V_1} = G_{12} = \frac{1}{4s^2[4s^2 + 3 + (1/4s^2)]} = \frac{1}{16s^4 + 12s^2 + 1}$$

24.535 Find $G_{12}(s)$ for the network of Fig. 24-197.

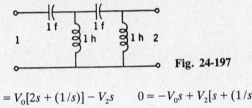

Fig. 24-197

∎ $$sV_1 = V_0[2s + (1/s)] - V_2s \qquad 0 = -V_0s + V_2[s + (1/s)]$$

$$\frac{V_2}{V_1} = G_{12} = \frac{s^2}{s^2 + 3 + (1/s^2)} = \frac{s^4}{s^4 + 3s^2 + 1}$$

24.536 Find $Z_{12}(s)$ for the network of Fig. 24-198.

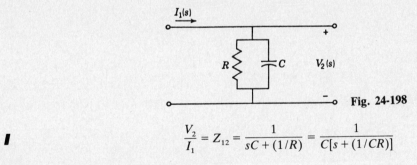

Fig. 24-198

∎ $$\frac{V_2}{I_1} = Z_{12} = \frac{1}{sC + (1/R)} = \frac{1}{C[s + (1/CR)]}$$

24.537 Find $G_{12}(s)$ for the network of Fig. 24-199.

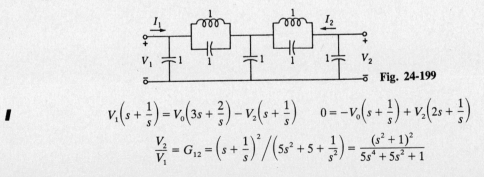

Fig. 24-199

∎ $$V_1\left(s + \frac{1}{s}\right) = V_0\left(3s + \frac{2}{s}\right) - V_2\left(s + \frac{1}{s}\right) \qquad 0 = -V_0\left(s + \frac{1}{s}\right) + V_2\left(2s + \frac{1}{s}\right)$$

$$\frac{V_2}{V_1} = G_{12} = \left(s + \frac{1}{s}\right)^2 \bigg/ \left(5s^2 + 5 + \frac{1}{s^2}\right) = \frac{(s^2 + 1)^2}{5s^4 + 5s^2 + 1}$$

24.538 Determine $Y_{12}(s)$ for the network of Fig. 24-200.

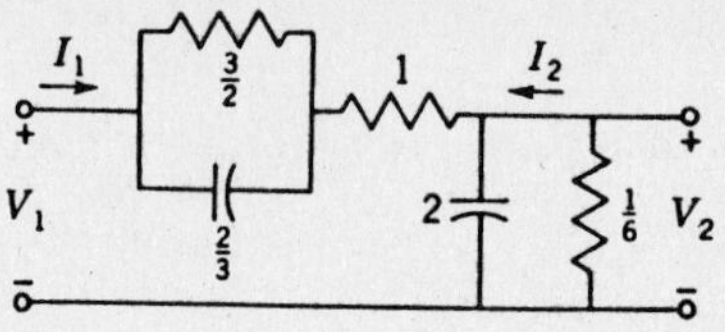

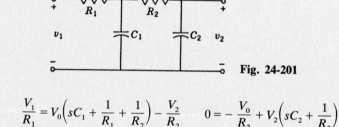

Fig. 24-200

$$\frac{V_1}{1 + \left[1 \middle/ \left(\frac{2s}{3} + \frac{2}{3}\right)\right]} = V_2\left\{2s + 6 + \frac{1}{1 + [3/2(s+1)]}\right\} \qquad I_2 = -V_2 6$$

$$\frac{2(s+1)V_1}{2s+5} = -\frac{I_2}{6}\left[2s + 6 + \frac{2(s+1)}{2s+5}\right] \qquad 2(s+1)V_1 = -\frac{I_2}{6}[4s^2 + 24s + 32]$$

$$\frac{I_2}{V_1} = Y_{12} = \frac{-12(s+1)}{4s^2 + 24s + 32} = \frac{-3(s+1)}{s^2 + 6s + 8} = \frac{-3(s+1)}{(s+2)(s+4)}$$

24.539 Find $G_{12}(s)$ for the network of Fig. 24-201.

Fig. 24-201

$$\frac{V_1}{R_1} = V_0\left(sC_1 + \frac{1}{R_1} + \frac{1}{R_2}\right) - \frac{V_2}{R_2} \qquad 0 = -\frac{V_0}{R_2} + V_2\left(sC_2 + \frac{1}{R_2}\right)$$

$$\frac{V_2}{V_1} = G_{12} = 1\left\{R_1 R_2\left[s^2 C_1 C_2 + s\left(\frac{C_1}{R_2} + \frac{C_2}{R_1} + \frac{C_2}{R_2}\right) + \frac{1}{R_1 R_2}\right]\right\}$$

$$G_{12} = \frac{1}{R_1 R_2 C_1 C_2\left[s^2 + \dfrac{s(R_1 C_1 + R_1 C_2 + R_2 C_2)}{R_1 R_2 C_1 C_2} + \dfrac{1}{R_1 R_2 C_1 C_2}\right]}$$

SCHAUM'S SOLVED PROBLEMS SERIES

■ **Learn the best strategies for solving tough problems in step-by-step detail**
■ **Prepare effectively for exams and save time in doing homework problems**
■ **Use the indexes to quickly locate the types of problems you need the most help solving**
■ **Save these books for reference in other courses and even for your professional library**

To order, please check the appropriate box(es) and complete the following coupon.

❑ **3000 SOLVED PROBLEMS IN BIOLOGY**
ORDER CODE 005022-8/**$16.95** 406 pp.

❑ **3000 SOLVED PROBLEMS IN CALCULUS**
ORDER CODE 041523-4/**$19.95** 442 pp.

❑ **3000 SOLVED PROBLEMS IN CHEMISTRY**
ORDER CODE 023684-4/**$20.95** 624 pp.

❑ **2500 SOLVED PROBLEMS IN COLLEGE ALGEBRA & TRIGONOMETRY**
ORDER CODE 055373-4/**$14.95** 608 pp.

❑ **2500 SOLVED PROBLEMS IN DIFFERENTIAL EQUATIONS**
ORDER CODE 007979-x/**$19.95** 448 pp.

❑ **2000 SOLVED PROBLEMS IN DISCRETE MATHEMATICS**
ORDER CODE 038031-7/**$16.95** 412 pp.

❑ **3000 SOLVED PROBLEMS IN ELECTRIC CIRCUITS**
ORDER CODE 045936-3/**$21.95** 746 pp.

❑ **2000 SOLVED PROBLEMS IN ELECTROMAGNETICS**
ORDER CODE 045902-9/**$18.95** 480 pp.

❑ **2000 SOLVED PROBLEMS IN ELECTRONICS**
ORDER CODE 010284-8/**$19.95** 640 pp.

❑ **2500 SOLVED PROBLEMS IN FLUID MECHANICS & HYDRAULICS**
ORDER CODE 019784-9/**$21.95** 800 pp.

❑ **1000 SOLVED PROBLEMS IN HEAT TRANSFER**
ORDER CODE 050204-8/**$19.95** 750 pp.

❑ **3000 SOLVED PROBLEMS IN LINEAR ALGEBRA**
ORDER CODE 038023-6/**$19.95** 750 pp.

❑ **2000 SOLVED PROBLEMS IN Mechanical Engineering THERMODYNAMICS**
ORDER CODE 037863-0/**$19.95** 406 pp.

❑ **2000 SOLVED PROBLEMS IN NUMERICAL ANALYSIS**
ORDER CODE 055233-9/**$20.95** 704 pp.

❑ **3000 SOLVED PROBLEMS IN ORGANIC CHEMISTRY**
ORDER CODE 056424-8/**$22.95** 688 pp.

❑ **2000 SOLVED PROBLEMS IN PHYSICAL CHEMISTRY**
ORDER CODE 041716-4/**$21.95** 448 pp.

❑ **3000 SOLVED PROBLEMS IN PHYSICS**
ORDER CODE 025734-5/**$20.95** 752 pp.

❑ **3000 SOLVED PROBLEMS IN PRECALCULUS**
ORDER CODE 055365-3/**$16.95** 385 pp.

❑ **800 SOLVED PROBLEMS IN VECTOR MECHANICS FOR ENGINEERS**
Vol I: STATICS
ORDER CODE 056835-9/**$20.95** 800 pp.

❑ **700 SOLVED PROBLEMS IN VECTOR MECHANICS FOR ENGINEERS**
Vol II: DYNAMICS
ORDER CODE 056687-9/**$20.95** 672 pp.

**ASK FOR THE SCHAUM'S SOLVED PROBLEMS SERIES AT YOUR LOCAL BOOKSTORE
OR CHECK THE APPROPRIATE BOX(ES) ON THE PRECEDING PAGE
AND MAIL WITH THIS COUPON TO:**

MCGRAW-HILL, INC.
ORDER PROCESSING S-1
PRINCETON ROAD
HIGHTSTOWN, NJ 08520

OR CALL
1-800-338-3987

_____

NAME (PLEASE PRINT LEGIBLY OR TYPE)

_____

ADDRESS (NO P.O. BOXES)

_____   _____   _____

CITY   **STATE**   **ZIP**

ENCLOSED IS   ❒ **A CHECK**   ❒ **MASTERCARD**   ❒ **VISA**   ❒ **AMEX**   (✓ ONE)

ACCOUNT # _____   **EXP. DATE** _____

SIGNATURE _____

MAKE CHECKS PAYABLE TO MCGRAW-HILL, INC. **PLEASE INCLUDE LOCAL SALES TAX AND $1.25** SHIPPING/HANDLING. PRICES SUBJECT TO CHANGE WITHOUT NOTICE AND MAY VARY OUTSIDE THE U.S. FOR THIS INFORMATION, WRITE TO THE ADDRESS ABOVE OR CALL THE **800** NUMBER.